MW00803999

Praise for *La Bonne Cuisine de Madame E. Saint-Ange*

"Finally, this great book has been translated. My French edition has lost its cover from thirty years of almost constant use. *La Bonne Cuisine de Madame E. Saint-Ange* is filled with good sense, logic, and boundless information about the world's best home cooking, and it is deeply grounded in the traditions and techniques that define a great cuisine. It's not just a book of recipes; it helps us master a subtle and immensely satisfying art."

—James Peterson, author of *Sauces*

"Among its many treasures, this marvelous book offers as clear a picture as we can ever hope to get of the workings of the French home kitchen at a time when the meals that came from it were justly the pride of France. The supernaturally knowledgeable Madame Saint-Ange was to her country what Fannie Farmer was to America, but she had the better tools and the better cuisine to work with, and she possessed a forthright Gallic charm entirely her own. For decades, the absence of this book in English translation has been a culinary embarrassment. Paul Aratow has now decisively changed all that, for which he has my endless thanks."

—John Thorne, author of *Outlaw Cook* and *Pot on the Fire*

"As we work toward simplifying our lives and our food, the timing for the return of this classic is perfect."

—Bonnie Stern, author of *Bonnie Stern's Essentials of Home Cooking*

"With his masterful translation of *La Bonne Cuisine de Madame E. Saint-Ange,* Paul Aratow has done a great service to lovers of food, food lorists, and curious cooks everywhere. It's a *Joy of Cooking* and a *Mastering the Art of French Cooking* stitched together with dishes from the French family home—all wrapped into one comprehensive volume that will entice and intrigue anyone interested in one of the major foundations of our new American cooking."

—Victoria Wise, author of *The Armenian Table* and the first chef of Chez Panisse

"The classic cooking of Madame Saint-Ange—so fresh and so French—lives on as testament to a true passion for *bonne cuisine* and a wonderful lesson in technique."

—Daniel Boulud, author of *Café Boulud Cookbook*

"This book will fascinate students of French gastronomy and those with a particular interest in the mores of middle-class French households in the early part of the twentieth century. As a window into French cookery, it is an extraordinary work. When read alongside Escoffier, whilst the scope is very similar, Madame Saint-Ange includes far more explanatory information, and although the tone is formal, it is also meticulous and often illuminating."

—Stephanie Alexander, author of *The Cook's Companion*

"Styles of cuisine may change, but the fundamentals are forever. There is more commonsense basic cooking instruction in this book than in most libraries."

—Russ Parsons, *Los Angeles Times* food columnist and author of *How to Read a French Fry*

"This book is a treasure trove of food knowledge and wit. It belongs on every chef's bookshelf."

—Mark Peel, author of *The Food of Campanile*

"*La Bonne Cuisine de Madame E. Saint-Ange* is the first French blockbuster written by a woman cook, and it remains my favorite. Saint-Ange has a turn of phrase and a depth of culinary knowledge that have rarely been equaled. At first glance her book appears inordinately long, but she carries us without faltering. Some recipes may take a couple pages of dense print to explain, but at the end you know you will emerge triumphant, with perfection on the plate."

—Anne Willan, author of *La Varenne Pratique*

LA BONNE CUISINE DE MADAME E. SAINT-ANGE

LA BONNE CUISINE

THE ORIGINAL COMPANION FOR FRENCH HOME COOKING

de Madame E. Saint-Ange

TRANSLATED AND WITH AN INTRODUCTION BY PAUL ARATOW

FOREWORD BY MADELEINE KAMMAN

1,300 RECIPES

MORE THAN 100 ILLUSTRATIONS

TEN SPEED PRESS

Berkeley | Toronto

Some of the recipes in this book include raw eggs, meat, or fish. When these foods are consumed raw, there is always the risk that bacteria, which is killed by proper cooking, may be present. For this reason, when serving these foods raw, always buy certified salmonella-free eggs and the freshest meat and fish available from a reliable grocer, storing them in the refrigerator until they are served. Because of the health risks associated with the consumption of bacteria that can be present in raw eggs, meat, and fish, these foods should not be consumed by infants, small children, pregnant women, the elderly, or any persons who may be immunocompromised.

Ten Speed Press
P.O. Box 7123
Berkeley, California 94707
www.tenspeed.com

Distributed in Australia by Simon & Schuster Australia, in Canada by Ten Speed Press Canada, in New Zealand by Southern Publishers Group, in South Africa by Real Books, and in the United Kingdom and Europe by Airlift Book Company.

Cover and interior design by Nancy Austin

Library of Congress Cataloging-in-Publication Data
Saint-Ange, E., Mme.
[Livre de cuisine de Mme. E. Saint-Ange. English]
La bonne cuisine de Madame E. Saint-Ange : the original companion for French home cooking / translated and with an introduction by Paul Aratow.
p. cm.
Includes bibliographical references and index.
ISBN-13: 978-1-58008-605-9 (alk. paper)
ISBN-10: 1-58008-605-5 (alk. paper)
1. Cookery, French. I. Aratow, Paul. II. Title.
TX719.S29 2005
641.5944—dc22 2005018000

First printing, 2005
Printed in the United States of America
Printed on acid-free, 50 percent recycled, elemental chlorine–free paper

1 2 3 4 5 6 7 8 9 10 — 09 08 07 06 05

Translator's acknowledgments: Many good people were involved in the production of this book, and I am very grateful for their expert assistance. They are: Janice Hoffmann, for her constant help and support. At Ten Speed Press: Lorena Jones, Brie Mazurek, Meghan Keeffe, and Lisa Westmoreland in editorial; and Nancy Austin, Betsy Stromberg, and Jon Haug in production. Our liaisons with Larousse: Mireille Debenne and Jean-François Richez. Freelance help: Damon Larson and Gene Rhim for typesetting; Laura Washburn and Caroline Curtis for copyediting; Suzanne Sherman and Abigail Bok for proofreading; and Ken Della Penta for indexing. And of course Phil Wood, publisher at Ten Speed Press, who saw the light and knew it was good.

CONTENTS

FOREWORD

What a great pleasure it is for me to write the foreword for the first translation into English of possibly the best cookbook ever written in France by a French woman. *La Bonne Cuisine de Madame E. Saint-Ange* is to this day recognized by many French home and restaurant cooks, be they men or women, as the most articulate and popular home cookbook available in bookstores, from the time of its first publication by Larousse in the late 1920s to these first years of the twenty-first century.

I grew up in the 1930s, in a suburb of Paris that lay tight to the first bend of the Seine, across from one of the busiest western access bridges to the big city. Antique shops were just as plentiful in the western suburbs as they were all over the capital city as well as in the other major cities of France.

Troves of books on the most diverse subjects, written just one generation before, were offered for sale in those shops. Many had been the former valued kitchen companions of Paris citizens of the late 1800s and early 1900s. Once put on the shelves for sale, these often handsomely bound volumes disappeared rapidly, sought out as they were not only by the homemakers of the time, but also by the male and female owners or chefs of small restaurants and weekend inns from attractive country towns lying just beyond the boundaries of the city. This was the time when, on the weekend of Mayday, one left Paris to go feast and rest, close to one of the still existing royal forests of oaks and chestnut trees that each spring grew their new, high canopies over a fragrant rug of lily of the valley.

It was during one of those weekends that my mother discovered her first *Saint-Ange.* I still have this little book, dated 1929, the edges of its pages now almost worn away and browned with age. I still love what is left of this small volume of recipes written by the author of excellent books for passionate cooks with not so flush budgets—the one and unique, Madame Saint-Ange.

In 1960, I married my husband of now forty-five years, Alan Kamman, a Philadelphian, and for that momentous occasion, my mother gave me a more modern edition of Madame Saint-Ange's cookbook. It was thick with information, and I soon used it with such enthusiasm that, after only a year of mutual companionship, it started to fall apart without possible hope of rehabilitation. In my laycook opinion, Saint-Ange explained better than any great chef. I was, however, very taken by the books of chefs Escoffier and Pellaprat, whose works of the early 1900s had been given to me by my great-aunt Madame Claire Robert, chef and restaurateur in the pretty town of Chateau-la-Valliere in Touraine. (During school vacations, she mentored me in her professional kitchen and dining room.)

Upon my arrival in Philadelphia, my luggage included these treasures as well as two other older volumes, which I had bought in two of the many *brocante* (second-hand) shops that lined the streets of the better parts of old Paris as well as those of its bourgeois suburbs. A *brocanteur* is an antique dealer who deals in all kinds of housewares, as long as they are different, interesting, or pretty enough to give a happy allure to any middle- to upper-middle-class home. One could still find all kinds of lovely old things in those shops, from handmade lace collars to old copper pots and pans, personal journals that families had not thought to either destroy or save, a well-worn child's toy from a long-gone era that could make one's heart melt with recognition. But the best finds still remained the cookbooks and the glorious old faience plates, and I became a dedicated collector of both.

Madame Saint-Ange had been preceded in her gastronomic writing by at least two talented women cooks, who each wrote a pretty neat cookery book. A Mademoiselle Madeleine became the author of *La Parfaite Cuisinière Bourgeoise et Economique,* and a Mademoiselle Catherine, of *La Cuisinière Bourgeoise.* Neither books carries a copyright notice and both are undated. They were possibly inspired by the celebrated volume of the great Urbains Dubois's *L'Ecole des Cuisinières* (*The School for Women Cooks*). Chef Dubois's book, written in 1888, remains one of the major witnesses to the large beneficial influence on the French working classes of the most important French law to ever have been voted by the French parliament; namely, the Jules Ferry Law of 1882, which resulted in the establishment of the nonreligious, fully democratic, and mandatory national system of basic and tuition-free education for all French citizens. Applicable identically to male and female children of all layers of French society, it still exists today, modified only when needed to update the school programs in all subjects. Within a few years of the inception of that important law, illiteracy in the working classes had almost completely disappeared, and some bright young women started composing cookbooks destined to entertain the friends of their bourgeois employers—almost royally at that!

Among the many volumes to be found *chez le brocanteur* were also a number of cookbooks written by both women and men who had lived and been active in the food professions before the first great war of 1914 to 1918. There is no doubt that some of these books were also written by women of the upper middle class, who had developed a true passion for the art of cooking. Madame Saint-Ange gives her readers the distinct impression that she was among those, as were probably Marie-Claude Finebouche in *La Cuisine de Madame* (1932) and Suzanne Laboureur and X. M. Boulestin in *Les Grands et Petits Plats* (1928).

So it is my great pleasure to introduce *La Bonne Cuisine de Madame E. Saint-Ange* to English readers. This unique book was published and copyrighted in 1927 by the French book publisher Larousse, the very same who gave us the well known *Larousse Gastronomique* and its translation into English in the 1960s.

The translation of such a book represents a very demanding and true labor of love and a deep understanding of the way the author met the challenge of relating to her readers. For this, translator Paul Aratow and the editorial team at Ten Speed Press must be commended and thanked by all cooks. They paid particular attention to the way the properties of all the ingredients entering each composition had to be respected, so that the voice of the author could come through as it does in its original French version.

Madame Saint-Ange is the one cookbook author of the twentieth century who knew, way before we'd even heard about food chemistry, that what happens in the pan during the preparation of any dish is most important for the success of its final taste and its consequent successful and attractive presentation at the table. I owe my passion for well-balanced dishes, in which all ingredients are so well blended that each can be perceived without any particular one overwhelming the taste of another, in part to Madame Saint-Ange, in part to the women of my family who guided me at the stove in my formative years, and finally in part to the wonderful culinary artists of the twentieth century whose restaurants I visited all over Europe. May this wonderful book become a true companion to all future cooks as well.

MADELEINE KAMMAN
Barre, Vermont

TRANSLATOR'S INTRODUCTION

I lived in Paris in the 1960s, when the food market, Les Halles, "the stomach of Paris," was still the center of the city. Naturally, I wanted to dine frequently on excellent French cuisine. However, I was on an academic stipend and could only occasionally afford the finer restaurants. The solution was to cook the classic French dishes myself. I investigated the cooking schools, only to discover they were just as costly as dining out. I realized that I was going to have to learn on my own.

I had rented an authentic atelier, a greenhouse-like structure built in the courtyard of an old apartment building. Some kind of manufacturing took place there once, and the glass roof saved the factory owner the cost of electricity. The atelier had magnificent light. It had been converted to an artist's studio, and contained a tiny rudimentary kitchen consisting of a sink, a shower and an old gas stove.

I knew that good equipment was a necessity for a competent craftsman. I made a pilgrimage to Dehillerin in Les Halles (founded in 1820) and bought my cookware, just as Escoffier and countless others had done in the same shop many years before.

I discovered *La Bonne Cuisine de Madame E. Saint-Ange* in a little bookstore in the Latin Quarter. I was fascinated by the book. It was so precise, so assured. Every page contained another revelation. I felt that I had found culinary gold. Bridging the gap between her career as a professional chef and her life as a housewife, Madame Saint-Ange finds a sophisticated compromise between professional haute cuisine and the home hearth. It is not surprising that this cookbook has been in print in France, with barely any revision, since 1927. It is as current as the first day it was published.

This book is intended for the practical home cook who intends to produce fine meals while managing time and money efficiently, but you could also open a fine restaurant based on the knowledge contained herein. Madame's charming but authoritarian voice echoes in every recipe. She virtually stands over your shoulder, dictating how you must hold the spoon, pouring out a stream of expert advice that guides every move. The underlying principles of the recipes are stated so clearly that the reader obtains a true understanding of the culinary arts.

I devoured the introductory chapters, learning things about cooking that I never dreamed existed. The subtlety, the perfection, the exactitude, the skill of execution. A new world opened to me. And of course, in Paris, it was easy to find a restaurant that specialized in whichever dish I was trying to make. On special occasions I would dine in one of them and sample their version after I had carefully followed Madame's instructions and cooked my own. To my delight, they were generally remarkably similar. The owners and chefs were always happy to discuss the fine points of culinary art. If the French love anything more than eating, it's talking about it.

When I returned to my teaching position at the University of California at Berkeley, my companions enthusiastically shared in my pursuit of culinary excellence, particularly at the table.

Then some friends came to me with an idea. Let's open a restaurant! I would supervise the refurbishment of an old Berkeley apartment house in which we planned to build a simple commercial kitchen and serve the same kinds of meals we loved to eat ourselves. I was to plan the menus with my partner Alice Waters, hire the cooks, and function as *chef de cuisine.* Madame Saint-Ange would be my guide. Alice would run the dining room. A year later, after much agony and hard work, we opened Chez Panisse.

Our menus were unheard of in a California restaurant. They were drawn from our experiences eating abroad and advice from *La Bonne Cuisine de Madame E. Saint-Ange.* Fortunately, an extraordinary quantity of quality raw materials was available in our community. We knew where to look for them. Our challenge was to replicate those classic French dishes in Northern California, with a few concessions to what was eventually to become "California Cuisine."

There were many new things for me to learn, since I was the practical culinary expert, in charge of the kitchen. I had a few sources of information, but in general I handily solved my problems with one book, that which you now hold in your hands. It was not just the lists of ingredients and how to combine them that came from Madame Saint-Ange. It was also an appreciation of what fine dining was, and an understanding of how to get the best results from what was available in the marketplace. It was making sure that when the food was put on the table, it was correct in every way.

Some years later I had the opportunity to produce a Hollywood film. I sold my half of Chez Panisse and moved to Los Angeles. It has been my great pleasure to see Chez Panisse continue to flourish under the brilliant direction of Alice Waters.

Although I no longer cook professionally, I still love to cook for my friends and family. Dinner for six or eight is just right for me. Whenever I can press a willing helper into service to slice mushrooms or knead the dough, I do. But Madame Saint-Ange is still my valued kitchen companion. You would be well advised to make her yours too.

Several materials and appliances were not available or current when the French version of this book was first published in 1927. Madame has a section on cookware that I am sure she would have amended had she possessed a set of excellent stainless steel utensils, thickly constructed, with other metals sandwiched into the base to spread and retain the heat. I recommend these modern metallurgical miracles heartily, with a few exceptions. However, the only really good sauté pan is made of heavy copper. Only copper gives you the conductance necessary for the strong heat required to seize and seal the food. The most sophisticated sauté chefs prefer tin-lined copper, whose conductance is slightly better than a stainless steel lining, although much more maintenance is required. Choose one or the other, but you should invest in a good heavy copper sauté pan. And be certain your stove top burner generates a sufficient amount of heat.

Ovens are now all regulated by thermostat, but instructions for baking often require heat principally from the bottom or from the top. Convection ovens, which heat very evenly, can sometimes be switched to operate as conventional ovens, giving more control over the heat source.

I am sure that Madame would have used a food processor had it existed. Once the techniques of these machines are mastered, they are prime timesavers in the kitchen. But they won't do everything. Let your judgment be your guide. Microwave ovens are marvelous for reheating and defrosting, and occupy a narrow but useful spectrum in classic food preparation. Electric stand mixers are now commonplace for kneading doughs and mixing batters, and can even be fitted with unlined copper bowls for correctly whisking egg whites. Local supplies of food and equipment are variable. Now there is the Internet, where even the most obscure ingredients and equipment are available at the click of a mouse.

I have attempted to replicate Madame Saint-Ange's accurate, no-nonsense tone in the translation, making only the necessary emendations to ease the transition from French to English. Madame's colorful style of writing does not always fit easily into the English mold. Except for certain parts of the original text that deal with matters of French vocabulary and therefore have no relevance in the English translation, and certain Gallic circumlocutions and asides that have no comparable English equivalent, the text is reproduced accurately and in its entirety. I have expanded the index to make the book more useful as a culinary encyclopedia and added non-metric conversions for the North American reader (though I strongly recommend using the original metric measurements for greater precision). Adaptation and alteration is laudable once you have mastered the basic recipes.

Should the reader find a locution awkward, I hasten to point out that the fault is mine, the translator, and not that of Madame Saint-Ange. *Bon appétit!*

Paul Aratow
Los Angeles, California

NOTICE

This book is a careful compilation of the culinary knowledge acquired by a homemaker who, for a long time, actually "put her hands in the dough." Her experience was further enhanced by studying professional cuisine during a long collaboration with distinguished practitioners in exceptional circumstances. So this enables us to put the practice and principles of genuine fine French cuisine within the grasp of everyone, ranging from the simplest home-style dishes to the most sophisticated preparations of the French culinary repertoire. We will provide thorough explanations to aid even the most inexperienced reader.

The uninitiated will perhaps find these explanations tiresome. But, on closer examination, you will realize that they are indispensable because they embody the fundamental principles that underlie each and every recipe. They will be presented as generalizations, suggestions, methods, procedures, etc., that, provided the explanations have been understood, will allow you to achieve perfect success in any recipe you undertake. Furthermore, you will then be able to better assess recipes from other sources and, finally, be able to improvise recipes yourself using tried and true methods. To get the most benefit from this book, we recommend immersing yourself in these basic principles: spoken aloud, they will command your attention; if you merely read them you might be tempted to disregard them. We insist on this, without fear of going too far.

Finally, you must never attempt a new recipe without having studied it in advance. The most reputable professionals never do otherwise. Do not believe it makes no difference if you modify the quantities, the procedures, and the cooking time to suit yourself. Success, in such a case, will not be guaranteed. You should always remember that if the total quantity is not sufficient for the number of people at dinner, it can be increased, but you must scrupulously respect the relationship among the elements that compose the dish.

One last word, and it's personal. In this book, we have condensed the results of more than 30 years of practice and study applied to culinary education. This lengthy effort permits us to have a valid hope in the usefulness of our work.

—MME. E. SAINT-ANGE

Unless otherwise specified, all the recipes are calculated for 6 people.
The times indicated include preparation time and cooking time.

WHAT YOU NEED TO KNOW

PRELIMINARY CONCEPTS

Managing the Stove

Gas and electric stoves are being used more and more in both large and small kitchens. These appliances, if well made, both give excellent results. The way to use them, which varies with each brand, will be indicated by the maker.

The construction of all coal-fired cast iron stoves is fairly uniform. Here's how to use them.

The pieces of coal must always be broken into the proper size in advance, about the size of an egg, not larger. One never puts a large piece into the firebox in order to break it up later with a poker. You will deprive the fire of oxygen by pushing it down. Furthermore, you will ruin the grate and the floor of the firebox.

You should never dispose of old papers, trash, etc., in the firebox. If you have something to burn in the firebox, you must add it when the fire is already burning extremely well.

Every morning, before lighting the fire, thoroughly clean the firebox and the ash pan. In other words, begin by lifting the grate that is at the bottom of the firebox. Failure to carry out this task daily will cause carbon residue to build up between the bars and prohibit the flow of air needed for the draft.

When all the cinders and all the residue have fallen into the ash pan, empty it. Then, with a poker, scrape the ashes that have accumulated all the way to the back and in the angles of the ash pan, and remove those as well. When you replace the ash pan, you must be sure that it can slide easily all the way to the back of the rack; it should close exactly like the drawer in a dresser. The draft is regulated as much from underneath as from above.

The boiler: The most important point to note is that it must be full of water, which must be replaced as it evaporates. If you neglect this, repairs will be necessary because, if the boiler is dry while the stove is lit, it will become damaged.

Lighting the fire: Insofar as it is possible, you must avoid burning too much paper, particularly heavy paper, because the smoke deposits humidity in the flue. The best thing to use is a bundle of thin, wooden sticks (kindling) that form a bed solid enough to sustain the pieces of coal and also allow some openings where the air can pass, which helps the draft and facilitates the burning.

Begin by putting some crumpled paper on the bottom of the firebox. On top of the paper place a bundle of kindling, with equal proportions of sticks of different thicknesses. Arrange them, smallest sticks first, crisscrossed on top of the paper. In order to be able fit them in the firebox, break them in half over your knee; they should not be completely broken. This makes it easier to build up the pyramid of sticks.

Place only a small pile of coal on top of the kindling. Now light the paper. Close the door to the firebox and close the spin-wheel on the firebox door.

Keep the damper blade open and the door to the ash pan open. Let the fire get started, then only half-fill with coal to begin.

To control the fire: You must never load the firebox to its fullest, no matter what the circumstances and no matter how much you need a stronger heat. Overfilling it in this way will only choke the fire, restrict the draft, and make it completely impossible to control the draft from one moment to the next by the use of the damper blade.

Outside the hours of major activity, maintain the fire by putting a small shovelful of coal in from time to time. Include some coal dust in each shovelful. These pieces of coal—added from time to time so that the firebox is only ever filled to two-thirds of its capacity—must be dropped in lightly, without stirring and rummaging in the fire. If you disturb the lit coals, these will shift and block the flow of air. All the red-hot coals are necessary to keep the pyramid structure intact and to let the air pass through.

Throughout this time, the draft must be maintained at the correct level, so the fire does not go out, but stays moderate. The best way to do this is to keep the ash pan door tightly closed and the damper blade half open. It is only when you need more combustion that you open the damper blade. The system, which consists of putting wet sacks over the fire, is not recommended for kitchen stoves because it dampens the dried cinders. It is not necessary to cover a fire when you know how to control the draft with the damper blade.

Some Essential Accessories

This is what you must have in even the most modest kitchen:

A *scale* with all its weights or a spring-loaded scale.

A *clock* that gives you that the exact time.

A *deciliter measure,* a measuring cup that contains one-tenth of a liter.

Pots and pans: They were once the pride of preceding generations, but one rarely finds pots and pans in tin-lined copper nowadays. They are excellent for cooking because the thickness of the metal ensures even heat distribution. That is why some professional cooks use them still. They do, however, present several disadvantages. You can't leave food standing in them. And to their rather expensive purchase price you have to add the cost of regular re-tinning. Their maintenance, which is off-putting to many, is not as difficult as it might seem because copper pots in constant use must simply be scrubbed on the exterior with a little grit and not polished. This is how you always see them in the professional kitchens.

After copper, aluminum is the most widely used material. However, it is essential to choose carefully if you are to achieve a result equivalent to that of tin-lined copper. Choose very good quality aluminum, very well finished and not at all porous. The bottoms must be thick enough so that they are not distorted by the heat. These kinds of pots are also useful for electric ranges. Specialized kitchen stores stock a large variety of pots, roasting pans, and soufflé pans, as well as special glass baking dishes. The glass dishes are especially good for oven-baked preparations because their transparency makes it easy to see how the cooking is progressing. You can also use them on the stovetop, using a protective metal plate made especially for this purpose.

Also of note are strong frying pans made of steel, and pots made of enameled cast iron of all sizes and depths, which are thick and solid. They are easily cared for.

The wooden spoon: Called a "mouvette" in many regions of France, the wooden spoon is the only instrument you should use for mixing. You must never use a metal spoon as a substitute, for many reasons: Metal scratches the tin lining in the pots; the handle of the spoon is too short to stir properly; the metal of the spoon heats up too rapidly and burns your fingers. In short, the wooden spoon is an *indispensable* tool for the kitchen.

Weights and Measures

A *deciliter of liquid* equals 6 tablespoons.

A *level tablespoon of flour* weighs 10 grams (1/3 ounce).

Whisking Egg Whites

Imagine this scenario, which could occur in any number of houses possessing kitchen equipment that is otherwise quite respectable. Madame demands, in vain, that her oven produce soufflés as well risen as those at her favorite restaurant, or Mademoiselle wants to amuse herself making cookies and meringues but they are completely unsuccessful.

If, in these houses, anyone had seen egg whites whisked by a professional, they would have understood the significance of the term "firm snow peaks." It would have been obvious why egg whites, beaten carelessly, in a salad bowl, with a fork, could never have become firm enough to be capable of supporting the weight of an egg in its shell. They would also have understood why, even if they had succeeded in whisking the eggs properly, or nearly, the egg whites would have gone grainy. (That's the professional term.) The egg white that goes grainy divides, like a cream that curdles, into one part liquid, another part millions of little wet lumps, instead of retaining the firmness of a batter. When beaten to the consistency of "firm snow peaks," egg whites appear more like a batter than a mousse.

To achieve this result, otherwise known as success, three conditions must be fulfilled: The purity of the egg whites, the use of appropriate utensils, and the technique of the endeavor.

The egg whites: Their perfect purity is a prerequisite. The most experienced professional would never manage to whisk egg whites properly if they had retained *the least bit of yolk,* or if they had been put into a greasy receptacle. Thus it is essential to take great care and avoid any contact with a greasy substance or object. It should be noted that the yolk is particularly oily.

As for freshness, it is not very important. We could even say, for the benefit of those who might hesitate to use egg whites that are several days old, that they are whisked more easily and remain firmer than whites separated from their yolks just before being whipped. However, they must be kept cool and covered. These whites are less subject to going grainy—in other words, decomposing.

The utensils: A copper bowl, which is not lined with tin and which is made uniquely for whisking egg whites, is practically mandatory (*fig.* 1). Alternatively, you could use an aluminum bowl whose interior surface has been anodized so that the whites don't discolor. In any other receptacle—enameled, stoneware, porcelain—you run the risk of seeing the whites go grainy. In any case, if you have none of these utensils, you must at least have a bowl in the shape of a hemisphere and without an angle at the bottom, and one that is big enough to allow the whisk to work easily.

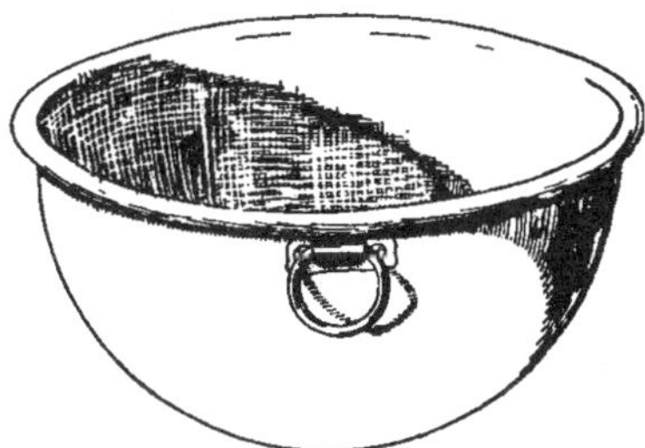

FIG. 1. EGG WHITE BASIN.

Moreover, cakes and biscuits made with a batter containing beaten egg whites, prepared in a copper bowl, yield one third more volume. They are not only more attractive prepared this way, but they are much lighter and fluffier. One egg white yields almost $1^1/_2$ deciliters (5 fluid ounces, $^2/_3$ cup), while in its natural state it consists of only $3^1/_2$ centiliters ($1^3/_{16}$ ounces). Of course, this assumes the use of the copper bowl.

Upkeep of a copper bowl is simple. Before using this preferred utensil—assuming it is not used daily—wipe the inside with a little vinegar and salt, or rub it with a lemon wedge, which will leave it perfectly clean. It is not necessary to buff it with anything else, even for major cleaning. Right after use, it will be enough to wipe off the bowl with a clean, dry kitchen towel. Be equally careful to keep the outside of the bowl clean, because if you don't, your hands will acquire an odor of copper when you handle the bowl, and this will be passed on to everything you touch afterwards.

Along with this copper bowl, you must have *a large whisk with very thin wires made of tinned steel (or stainless steel)* (*fig.* 2) that should only be used to whisk egg whites. Otherwise, you must wash the whisk in boiling water and rub it with vinegar or lemon before using it again. It's really better to restrict its use to whisking egg whites. Choose one with a wooden handle. This is much less tiring than a metal handle. It should be big enough and strong enough, about 40 centimeters (16 inches) from the end of the handle to the end of the wires. A small sauce whisk is much too weak for this job. Using mechanical beaters makes the work much less tiring.

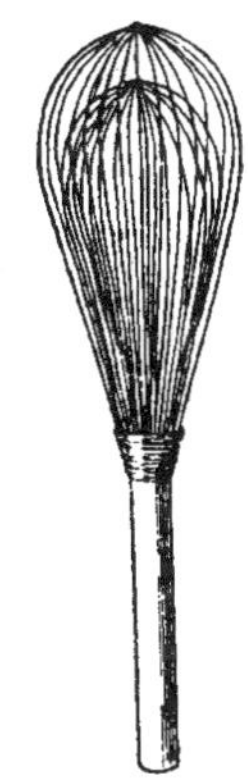

FIG. 2. EGG WHITE WHIP.

Technique: We will split the whisking of egg whites into two parts. The first covers the disintegration of the mucous mass up to the point when it becomes a grayish, roundish mass. This part requires mixing with an easy and rhythmic effort. The second part covers the conversion of the round, gray mass into a smooth, light, firm, stunningly white batter. This second part, unlike the first, requires a very vigorous and accelerated effort.

During both these periods, the whisking, even though different in strength and speed, must not be interrupted. *Under no circumstances should you stop once you have begun to whisk.* Stopping causes the whites to disintegreate. Instead of rising and firming up more and more, their mass will remain semi-solid and will take on a blotchy, grainy look.

Since this job is rather difficult during the second part, it's a good idea to take turns with another person. Or, if you have the necessary staying power, switch the whisk to the other hand (this is how professional pastry chefs do it) so you can rest your arm while the other one works.

The process: As already explained, wipe the inside of the bowl and the wires of the whisk with a lemon wedge, or with a little vinegar and salt. Dry them with a clean towel.

Take a dishtowel, twist it up from the corners, loosely, then arrange it on the table in a circle, like a turban or little crown. Place the bowl in the center of this crown, tilting it a little toward you. Rolled like this, the towel serves to steady the bowl and keep it on the table. Without this, the instability of the rounded bottom would make the work more difficult and slower.

Put the whites in the bowl. If you break the eggs directly into the bowl, be careful when you have separated the yolks to run your thumb, which should be scrupulously clean, around the inside of the shell to remove all of the white. Make sure that not even the slightest bit of yolk has fallen into the bowl. Should that happen, use a bit of eggshell to carefully remove it.

Begin to whisk, in any direction, but not too hard, and not too high. You must beat with very small strokes, quietly, barely lifting the whisk, which must stay in contact with the whites. Nothing but a little movement in place, without splashing, without noise, in a steady rhythm. Little by little, the mucous mass dissolves and liquefies. The globules shoot up, and everything condenses into a huge foam with an unattractive grayish color.

It is exactly at this moment that the movement of the whisk must, gradually, increase in breadth, in power, in speed. You will see, little by little, the foam will begin to swell more, become more homogenous, and whiten. *Do not stop for a second.* Continue to beat with larger and larger strokes, faster, more vigorously, until the foam, constantly increasing in volume, becomes absolutely smooth, like whipped cream, a stunning white in color with a *very firm* consistency. To gauge when it has reached the correct consistency, take the whisk out of the bowl and turn it over. The foam should stay attached in a solid block, forming a tassel, like that on a clown's wig (*fig.* 3).

FIG. 3.
WHIP LOADED WITH MOUSSE.

However, do not spend too long on these observations, given that the whites must always be used as soon as they are whisked, otherwise they might become grainy. Since they can be worked beyond the right point without spoiling, you can, should you want to, give them a couple of extra strokes, to be certain that they are completed adequately.

NOTE. When the preparation that the whites are intended for contains sugar, you can add a bit of powdered sugar to the whites, if you think they might go grainy, but only toward the end of the process. Be sure to continue whisking vigorously when you do this. Use about 20 grams (2/3 ounce) for 5–6 whites. This addition of powdered sugar gives cohesion and consistency to the whisked egg white.

Incorporating the whites: Once you have beaten the whites into a firm and robust state *(neige ferme)*, you are still far from done. In order for this result to be maintained in the final preparation, the whites must remain in this state *after* they are incorporated.

Cookbooks and recipes always recommend proceeding with this mixing "with caution, so you don't flatten the whites." Yet, it is rare that the method for doing this is explained, even though people who are uninitiated in the professional secrets of the kitchen would never discover it by themselves. In reality, it is quite simple.

FIG. 4. WOODEN SPATULA.

First of all, you should have a wooden spatula, thin and wide. Or, lacking that, a stiff card, like a large business card. If we are dealing with a substance *heavier* than the whites—for example, a mixture for a soufflé, rice or semolina for a pudding, or cake batter—proceed as follows:

With the spatula, spread the whites *on top* of the material to which they are to be incorporated. Cut into the whole mixture with the spatula, so that you pass under the mass, turning it and placing it over the whites. In other words: Put the spatula straight through the middle of the whites, right to the bottom of the bowl, just as you would to cut a slice of a *Saint-Honoré* pastry. Having reached the bottom, push the spatula underneath the mass and take up as much as you can carry on the spatula. Deposit all of this on top of the whites, to your right. With your left hand, turn the bowl from left to right, just as you would do with the plate that holds the *Saint-Honoré.* Once again, dive in with the spatula, just as you would to cut a slice of cake, to the left of the previous insertion. Once again, lift and place *on top* the mixture that was underneath. This movement of placing the mixture from below on top is the only technique that you should use. And you must do this with large, generous gestures, measured yet swift, going out from the middle to the edges, continually turning the bowl on the table. Any other kind of movement would flatten the whites by expelling the air they have absorbed. Furthermore, it would prevent them from rising properly when cooked.

When the whites are to be mixed with a substance *lighter* than them, for example, some flour or ground hazelnuts or almonds, powdered sugar, etc., you proceed with exactly the same motion, but reverse the positions. In other words, in this situation, you put the whites *underneath* and the lighter substance *above.* The whites should be left in the copper bowl for this. You sprinkle the flour or sugar on top of the whites, adding more flour or sugar gradually as you slice into the mass to put it on top of the added flour.

Larding Meats

[Translator's note: Modern-day meat is bred for tenderness, making surface larding virtually unnecessary, but at the time this book was written, tough cuts of meat were larded only on the top (with a tool called an aiguille à piquer*), usually in short strips across the grain, which differentiated from the long, interior larding strips (done with a tool called a* lardoire*) of more tender cuts.]*

The *raison d'être* for larding meats is different from what a goodly number of people think. When placed near the surface, it is not to infuse the interior of the meat with fat because the lard (bacon or salt pork) could never penetrate the interior. It is only the surface of the meat that is affected by this technique. Whether it is for roasting, or for braising, larding functions like barding, adding to the appearance as well as the taste.

In big cities, butchers offer cuts of ready-larded meat. But it's not the same in smaller towns, and you must lard the meat yourself at home. Therefore we offer detailed directions here, so they can be truly useful.

FIG. 5. NORMAL SIZE LARDON.

Larding fat: Use the fatback bacon or salt pork known as "half salted" (demi-sel)—in other words, not too salty, fresh, and with a nice white color. It will have to be cut into rectangular strips. The usual dimensions for beef filet, braised veal, etc., are 3 centimeters (1¼ inches) long and about 2 millimeters (1/16 inch) thick, the slices of fatback bacon being 3 centimeters (1¼ inches) wide. The length is not fixed. Sometimes they are as long as 12–15 centimeters (4½–6 inches). Thickness varies depending on the thickness of the fatback bacon.

Before cutting the strips (lardons), the fatback bacon should be chilled. In the summer, it should be kept on ice if possible. This is very important because it firms the bacon up and makes cutting much easier.

Using a good knife, with a long, thin blade that has previously been dipped in warm water, first cut a very thin slice from the top of the piece of fatback bacon, thus getting rid of the soiled and very salty part. Then, cut perpendicularly into the piece of fatback bacon in order to divide it into small slices the same size as the thickness of the lardons. In this case, 3 millimeters (1/8 inch) (*fig.* 6). Stop at the rind, which will keep the slices joined up. At one end of the fatback bacon, leave a 1-centimeter (3/8-inch) piece, on the left, to form a shield to protect your fingers from the crosswise cut of the knife.

Next, without moving the slices, hold them together, and, without moving the piece of fatback bacon, cut through to make slices of the same thickness, carefully controlling the knife so the blade stays quite flat. The last cut should graze the rind (*fig.* 7).

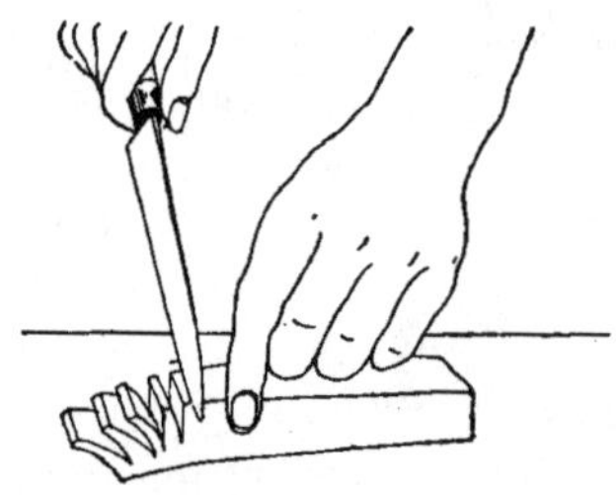

FIG. 6. DIVISION OF THE FATBACK BACON IN 3 MM SLICES HOLDING THE KNIFE PERPENDICULAR.

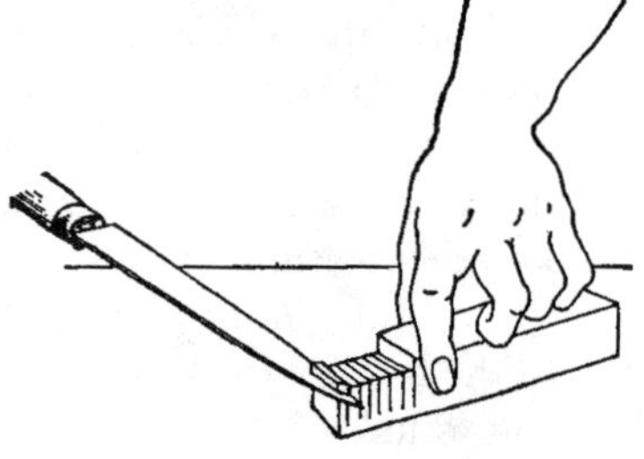

FIG. 7. CUTTING THE SLICES CROSSWISE, CUTTING WITH THE KNIFE COMPLETELY FLAT.

FIG. 8. HOW TO HOLD THE NEEDLE TO INSERT IT INTO THE MEAT.

FIG. 9. PIECE STUDDED HELD ON THE KNEE.

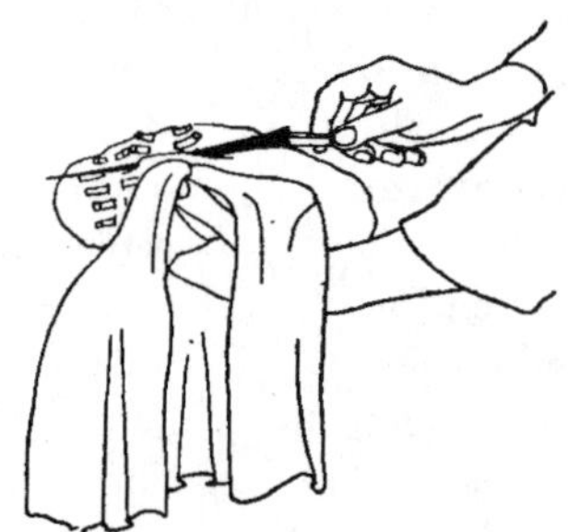

FIG. 10. INTRODUCTION OF THE LARDON INTO THE OPENINGS OF THE NEEDLE.

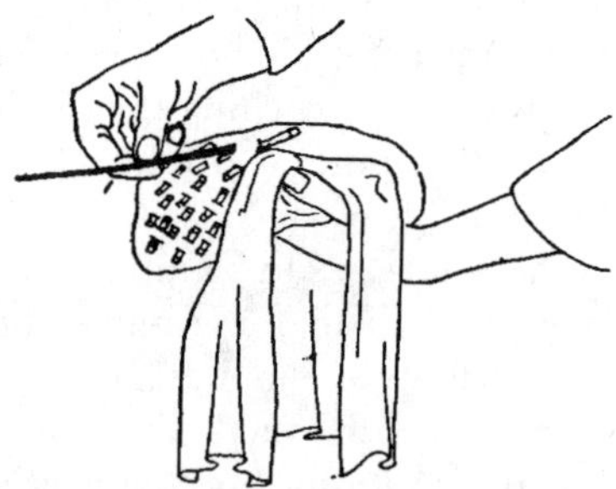

FIG. 11. PASSAGE OF THE LARDON THROUGH THE MEAT BY PULLING ON THE NEEDLE.

Short surface larding (studding): The incontestable rule of larding is to use only the right hand. The left hand serves only to hold the meat steady during the operation. This way you avoid handling it, which softens the fatback bacon and interferes with the precision of the technique.

Every professional will tell you that to lard well you must be comfortably seated. Depending upon the size of the piece to be larded, use the left hand to support it, as for a veal roast or medallions, or place it on the left knee, or on the table in front of you.

The direction of the needle in relation to the person threading can vary accordingly. In other words, work going forward, or from right to left. But what does not vary, no matter which way you work, is the method of inserting the fatback bacon into the flesh.

The movements break down thusly:

1. Hold the *empty* needle in your right hand. The position of the fingers remains the same, whatever the direction of the needle. Stick it in the meat beneath a very thin layer of flesh, and push it out at a point three-quarters of the needle's length. This is to ensure its stability.

2. Release the needle. Using only your right hand, thread a strip (lardon) into the channel of the needle. Only one third of the *lardon* need go through.

3. Grasp the needle and pull so it leaves the lardon in the meat, with the two ends of the lardon jutting out equally on either side. It would be fair to say that, without some practice, you will have difficulty in succeeding on the first try. Depending on the direction of the needle, the lardons form different rows. With the needle directed forward, the lardons are inserted next to one another in a horizontal line. With the needle directed sideways, from right to left, the lardons are inserted one underneath the other, in a vertical line. In any case, the rows should be very symmetrical and alternating, so that the ends of the lardons intertwine, making rows of little crests.

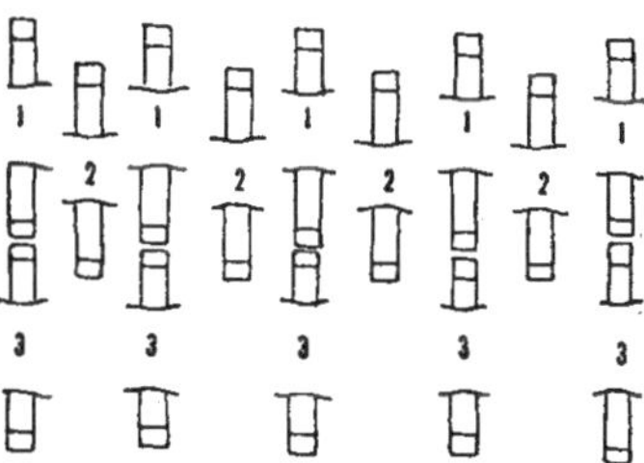

FIG. 12. SUCCESSIVE ALTERNATING ROWS OF LARDONS.

A general rule is that the grain of the meat guides the direction of the larding, making it easier for the needle to pierce the flesh without too much effort. But circumstances create frequent exceptions to this rule. What is always necessary, in the case of a cut of meat that is to be carved in rather thin slices after cooking, is to arrange the lardons in such a way that the knife cuts across them as it slices the meat. Otherwise, if the rows are too widely spaced, some slices will not have any larding.

Long interior larding of meats: Here we mean the process of inserting large lardons right inside meats, and not the *picquage,* or studding, which is done only at the surface.

For this, we use a large needle, like the smaller *aiguille à picquer*—that is to say, a needle where the end is split into four parts in order to hold the lardon. Insert the empty needle into the meat up to the channel in the needle. Place the lardon into the channel. Draw the needle by its point out of the meat, leaving the lardon inside; the ends should be sticking out. For large cuts of meat, a large *lardoire* (larding tool)—which resembles a tube cut in half and is horizontally equipped with a wooden handle—works best. Place the lardon in the larding needle channel and press it down with your finger so that it does not get stuck passing through the meat. Insert the instrument, little by little, in the direction of the grain of the meat. Push it through so that it comes out on the other side. Grab the end of the lardon with your left hand and hold it tight, while slowly retracting the instrument. This will leave the lardon in the meat as you pull back.

Straining Purées

A drum sieve *(tamis)* is essential. A fine metal sieve is most common, and for ultrafine purées, a very fine sieve made of horsehair (*fig.* 13). Use a medium sieve, rather large in size, even for small quantities. Movement is easier and you have a larger surface to work on.

In most households, this sieve is too often replaced by a strainer with relatively small openings. It is impossible to achieve the same result because its purpose is completely different. A strainer is for draining. In a pinch, you can use it to crush certain ingredients, but its use must not go beyond that. The utensil known as a "purée press" has undergone improvements and certainly has its place in a well-organized kitchen. However, only with a drum sieve can you work quickly, which is of the utmost importance for starchy ingredients so that the resulting purée will have perfect texture. The pestle used with a drum sieve is made of wood, in the shape of a mushroom.

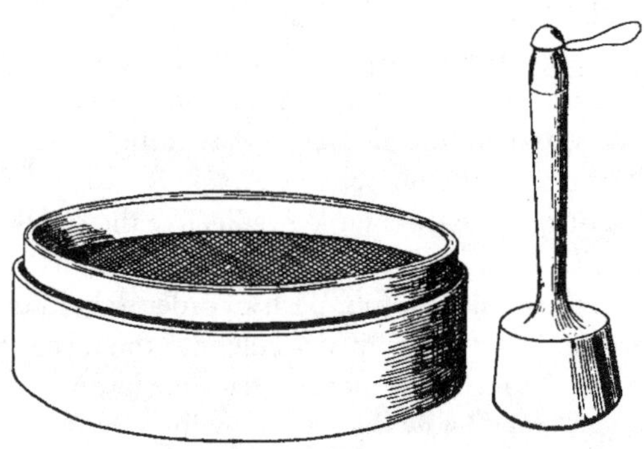

FIG. 13. *TAMIS* AND MUSHROOM-SHAPED PESTLE FOR PASSING PURÉES.

Position the drum sieve with the deepest part *down.* This facilitates arm movements during the operation. Furthermore, this way of positioning the drum sieve enables you, in cases where the substance is somewhat liquid, to place a receptacle under the sieve to catch the liquid. A shallow dish, with sides that are not too high, can easily be placed under the sieve, so that it will not touch the fabric of the sieve, which could be damaged if the pestle comes into contact with the dish. When you are dealing with a purée of vegetables that are solid, such as potatoes, chestnuts, or drained vegetables, you should replace the dish with a very clean cloth laid out under the drum sieve. You can then pick up the four corners to transfer the purée to the cooking vessel.

The pestle must not be tapped, used to grind, or rubbed in a circle in one spot. You must always move the pestle in a nearly straight line, *pulling it toward you* while pressing it down to crush along the path of the pestle. Then, take it back to the starting point, lifting it off the sieve each time. The action of rubbing and crushing on the metal fabric must only be carried out while pulling the pestle toward you. This method of handling the pestle is of paramount importance, especially when dealing with starchy vegetables. A badly handled pestle will damage the mesh of the sieve and impede the passage of ingredients. The purée that results will be heavy and glutinous, and there is no remedy.

Starchy ingredients—potatoes, chestnuts, legumes, beans, fresh peas, etc.—must be forced through the sieve when they are *boiling hot.* Therefore, put the pot that contains them on the table next to the drum sieve. Using a skimmer or slotted spoon, take small quantities of the ingredients each time, so that two or three strokes of the pestle forces the entire quantity through the sieve. If you are working with beans or lentils, scrape away the skins with a metal spoon each time so that they will not obstruct the following portion. Finally, do not forget to scrape off the material that sticks underneath the mesh.

Drying Purées

The aim of this operation is to evaporate all the moisture in the purée so that it can completely absorb what is added: butter, milk, broth, etc.

The operation takes place over high heat and in a pan with a rather large diameter—a sauté pan—because the large heating surface allows the purée to spread out, making it much easier to stir. Using a wooden spoon with a large, squared head, stir the purée continuously, stirring and scraping *on the bottom of the pan* so that there is no browning. As soon as the steam that rises from the purée diminishes and the purée has become rather thick and can be stirred into a lump, it is sufficiently dehydrated. This is when you should add the other ingredients.

Using a Pastry Bag

This is a pocket made of fabric in the form of a funnel, at the end of which is a metal nozzle, whose diameter varies. If necessary, use a large cone made of strong paper as a substitute. Snip the tip of the cone with scissors after the ingredients are inside. But the fabric bag is much easier to use.

To use the pasty bag, proceed as follows: Fill the pouch with batter, being careful to leave enough room so it can be closed. Fold over the end to close, then hold it in your right hand, supporting it with your left hand, in such a way that by pressing very lightly with the palm of your *right* hand, you push out the batter inside. Your left hand serves only to support and direct, without ever pressing. The nozzle must be resting on the surface when the batter comes out. If it is held above the surface, the batter will not come out smoothly. If you are making pastry for profiteroles, for example, the nozzle does not move and the batter forms a round ball as it emerges.

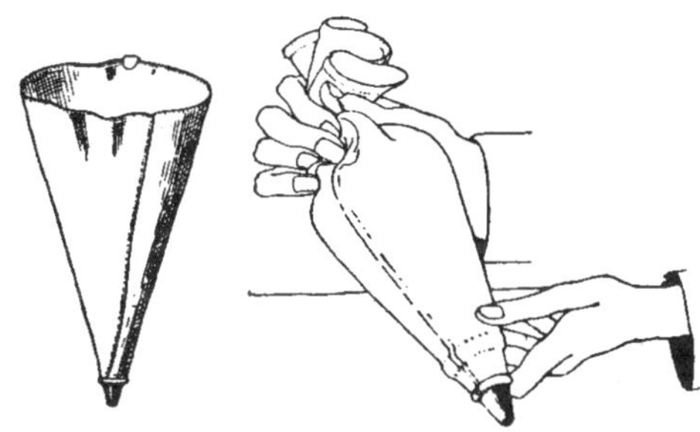

FIG. 14. PASTRY BAG.
FIG. 15. HOW TO HOLD THE PASTRY BAG.

For long pastries, like éclairs, you must always move the nozzle, while still touching the surface, as if it were a huge pencil and you wanted to write the number "1" on the baking sheet.

Glazing Sauced Dishes

Glazing a dish that is sauced involves forming a sort of glossy and colored skin on the surface of the sauce. You get this by using very high heat, which comes *from above.* The best method is under a broiler. Failing that, a very hot oven.

This glazing must take place in just a few minutes, so that the sauce does not have time to boil. Boiling thickens the sauce—breaks it down, in other words—makes it "separate" and become oily, given the proportion of butter that one has ended up adding. If the glazing cannot be accomplished rapidly and without boiling the sauce, it's better not to try it. Glazing does not add much flavor to the dish, it simply contributes to the look.

For all glazing, use a dish that is flat, not bowl-shaped—in other words, a dish that the sauce can cover. Glazing does not work well even in shallow bowls.

If you do the glazing in the oven, it must be very hot. And the plate should be placed so that the heat, hitting the top of the dish, immediately causes a skin to form. On average, this should take *3 minutes.* During that time, you must not take your eyes off the oven, as they say, so that you can both watch the glazing process and turn the plate if it becomes necessary.

When the oven is not hot enough to successfully glaze that fast, it is sensible to place the plate in another plate with some warm water in it, to make a double boiler (bain-marie), which will prevent the sauce from boiling.

Frying Parsley

In order to get parsley crisp and crunchy, a deep pot of smoking-hot oil is essential. It is not possible to get this result with a bit of butter or oil, heated up in the bottom of an omelet pan. Butter, even when it's clarified and used in large quantities, cannot, without burning, withstand the degree of heat necessary to "seize" the parsley as required. In addition, the fat or oil, which are the only appropriate ingredients here, must be available in a quantity sufficient to more or less submerge the parsley.

The technique is quite simple. The frying fat must be hot and smoking. Plunge in the parsley and remove it almost immediately. A few *seconds* suffice to then pull it out crisp and crunchy, a beautiful light green, the true color of fried parsley.

Blanching Fatback Bacon or Salt Pork

The purpose of this operation is twofold. It serves to cleanse the fatback bacon, frequently of doubtful cleanliness, and to rid it of excess salt, even when it's only lightly salted.

You must always put the fatback bacon you wish to blanch in *cold* water. Putting it into boiling water will not help it to give up its salt very well.

If the fatback bacon is to be cut into lardons, the rind must first be removed, then it is cut according to the appropriate dimensions. These pieces are then put into a small pan filled with enough cold water to cover.

Heat them up progressively, so that they do not boil too soon. This is to help remove the salt. Let them boil lightly 5–6 minutes or more, 8–10 minutes if the fatback bacon is very salty. Pour the *lardons* into a strainer. Plunge into a large quantity of cold water. Then drain them thoroughly. If they are to be sautéed later, they must first be dried thoroughly in a cloth, because the moisture that they retain prevents them from browning in the frying fat.

Softening Butter into a Pomade *(Pommade)*

The professional French term is *pommade* (meaning "ointment"), and it expresses the condition perfectly.

First warm up a thick earthenware bowl by running it under hot water. Dry it well. This method is the only one to use because it is the only way to obtain uniform heat. For this reason, never heat the bowl by putting it on the stove, where only the bottom heats up, usually overheating, which ultimately causes the butter to separate.

Break the butter into little pieces and place in the well-heated bowl. Using a large wooden spoon, work it into an ointment, a perfectly smooth cream, homogenous and without even the smallest trace of a lump.

Butter that is very hard is difficult to blend. In this case, it must first be softened. To do this, enclose it in the corner of a damp kitchen towel, and pummel it, crushing it with your hand against the table to break up the block that it forms. Take it out of the towel and leave it for a while in the kitchen, at moderate temperature, before turning it into a pomade.

Buttering

"Buttering" *(beurrer)* is a culinary term that means adding an appropriate quantity of good, fresh butter to a dish and, in particular, a sauce, at the very last moment. This butter must always be added *off the heat,* broken into equal parts so that it mixes easily and rapidly. You must stir continually with a sauce whisk.

The sauce must never return to the heat after the butter has been added. The heat would cause the butter to separate, leaving only oil instead of the creamy liaison that it should produce. Thus, the following is necessary. First, the sauce must be completed before the butter is added to finish. Next, the sauce must be boiling hot when it is removed from the heat to add the butter, since you will not have the opportunity to reheat it afterward. Finally, the last condition, the sauce must be safeguarded from all risk of heat surges, all the while being carefully kept warm.

Clarifying Butter

Butter is clarified to eliminate all traces of milk protein (casein) and other particles that ball up and attach themselves as little black spots on foods that are cooked in the butter.

In some homes, *beurre fondu* ("melted butter")—which is, actually, butter clarified in large quantities—is a staple. It is always on hand, thus eliminating the need to make it.

In order to clarify the small quantity generally necessary in our recipes, put the butter in a small pan. Heat it up over *very low* heat. It will foam. The foam produced condenses gradually, the butter appears clear as olive oil, while a whitish deposit forms in the bottom of the pan and solidifies. You must never go beyond the perfect color of light yellow. At this point, decant the butter into the utensil where it will be used.

Skimming

In culinary terms, skimming means purifying. Sauces and certain soups must be skimmed. Removing the foam, or scum, is done through a very special, gentle boiling, which brings impurities to the surface of the liquid.

TECHNIQUE. Strain the sauce into a deep, heavy saucepan large enough so that the liquid comes almost to the top, which makes the repeated skimming easier.

Put the saucepan on the heat. *Do not cover.* When it begins to boil, move the saucepan so that it sits only partway over the heat and lower the heat to maintain just a small, steady simmer, *always in the same spot.* To do this, which is of utmost importance, slightly raise the saucepan *by its handle* and slide some heatproof object under the corner of the saucepan—an iron plate, for example. In this way, the heat touches only the corner of the saucepan and it boils only at that one spot.

Boiling *slowly* in this manner causes the fat and impurities to rise and form a foam, or spots or skins of fat, which accumulate on the surface of the sauce that is not agitated by the boiling. They can then be easily skimmed with an ordinary metal cooking spoon. Do not use a pierced spoon or small strainer.

Removing these waste materials as they mount to the surface is "skimming." Add several small spoonfuls of *cold* liquid, occasionally, to encourage the materials to float to the surface, as one does when preparing a pot-au-feu.

When a Sauce Becomes Oily

It sometimes happens, when the moment to serve comes, that you find in your stew or ragout nothing but a layer of fat, clear as oil, at the bottom of which you can see a few drops of condensed sauce. Home cooks say that the sauce has "turned," without knowing either the cause or the remedy.

The cause, in this case, is that the cooking has been badly done, assuming that the right amount of liquid was added at the beginning. In other words, the boiling was too aggressive and the evaporation was excessive. The quantity of fat does not vary. It appears excessive only because the liquid has dried up.

The normal remedy is to reinstate the proportions of the necessary liquid. Thus, when you have established that the liquid is insufficient, without removing any of the oil, pour in the amount of liquid that should have remained after the cooking was complete. This could be stock, or other liquid, or failing that, water. Boil gently, covered, for 15 minutes, and be sure to degrease the sauce before serving.

Reheating Ragoûts, Purées, Vegetables, Etc.

It is an error to add butter to the food before reheating. While cooking, this butter turns to oil in the sauce of a ragoût. If you are reheating sautéed vegetables, the butter browns and dries out the dish. Liquid, but in very small quantities, must be the only thing added to compensate for the moisture lost to evaporation during cooking. This is also true for sauces and sautéed vegetables. One or two spoonfuls of water, stock, or even cooking water from the vegetables will generally be enough.

If you want to add butter to improve the flavor, it should always be added after reheating is complete and the food is off the heat.

Grating Fatback Bacon

Grating fatback bacon is the only way to get it into equal, tiny pieces. When you are working in small quantities, the machine used to grate fatback bacon does not work well. Or, you may not have the machine.

Cutting the fatback bacon with a knife in the usual manner will not allow you to reduce it to a *pomade* because there will always be little hard pieces that do not mix in properly.

With the tip of a strong, short knife, *scrape* the surface of a piece of fatback bacon, to obtain the necessary quantity. This means that you must use a piece of fatback bacon that is substantially larger than the amount of grated fatback bacon, so you are able to have something left to hold onto after you have grated what you require.

Slicing Vegetables

Even for the most simple dish, carrots, turnips, potatoes, onions, etc., that appear in slices must be cut evenly. This is impossible to achieve if you hold the vegetable in your hand over the pan or work surface to slice. Unless you have truly exceptional slicing talent, the slices will always be more or less beveled. They do not have the *finesse,* nor the same even thickness, as they have when cut by the professional method, which is just as fast. To

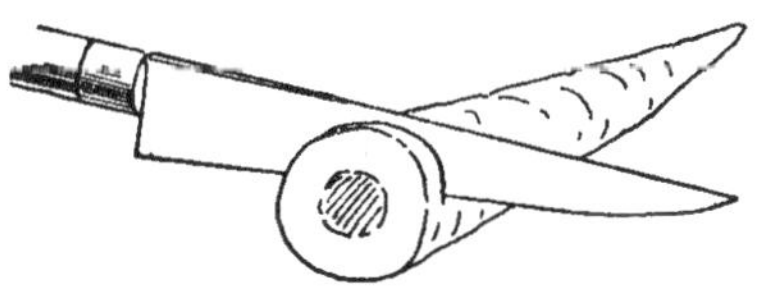

FIG. 16. HOW TO CUT A CARROT EVENLY.

do this, place the vegetable on the table and slice perpendicularly into the vegetable (see *fig.* 16).

Using Gelatin

Gelatin, also sold in France under the name of *grenetine,* is an industrial product extracted from gelatinous materials, replacing calves' feet used in olden times. Just like calves' feet, it is essential for giving certain preparations the solidity that they need and could not have without it. But its presence must remain undetected by the uninitiated. Good quality is the first prerequisite. Inferior quality gelatin leaves a taste of glue, which is one of the most unpleasant of tastes.

Good-quality gelatin comes in very thin, transparent sheets, which break neatly, like glass, and with no taste of glue. Each sheet weighs about 2 grams ($^{1}/_{14}$ ounce). They must be kept carefully, in a metal box. Stale gelatin acquires an unpleasant taste.

To use it, first rinse in cold water. Then soak it in a bowl of cold water so that it softens properly, ready for the moment of use. If you are using the gelatin in its sheet form, simply soaked to soften, dry it thoroughly and spread it out on a clean cloth. If it needs to be dissolved, leave it until nice and soft, then put it in a small pan with the necessary amount of water—a few spoonfuls, according to need—to melt it. Set the pan only partway over the heat, or, to be safer, set the pan over a pot of boiling water as for a bain-marie, because gelatin sticks and burns easily. When it is completely dissolved, strain it through a fine cloth.

Oiling a Mold

If you don't have sweet almond oil, which is preferable because it is the most fluid and tasteless, use an ordinary oil, but on condition that it *has absolutely no taste.* Using a small brush dipped in the oil, coat the inside of the mold, being very careful to get the brush everywhere, in the corners, crevasses, and grooves, if the mold is ornamented. Keep the mold upside down until needed, so the excess oil can drain.

This light coating of oil allows you to unmold with the greatest of ease. Also, the finished dish will look as if it has been varnished.

Preparing Marinades

The goal, depending upon the circumstances, is to conserve, to tenderize, or simply to flavor.

There are different types of marinades, which can be classified as follows: Fast marinades, raw marinades (that is, no cooking is involved), and cooked marinades.

Fast marinades: The sole aim is to flavor food, with lemon juice, oil, parsley, thyme, bay, and salt and pepper, to which, depending on the dish, white wine, cognac, or Madeira is added. Vinegar should not replace the lemon juice, because its effect is often corrosive. You can marinate cutlets, steaks for grilling, as well as meats for pâtés and terrines. The oil in these marinades serves as insulation against the heat of the grill.

Raw and cooked marinades: These contain the same elements and in the same proportions: carrots, onions, shallots, etc. What differs is the proportion of vinegar to white wine used in the marinade. Note that in certain instances—game, for example—special flavorings are added, such as rosemary or juniper.

Cooking the marinade develops the flavor of the vegetables and the scent of the other flavorings used, which are much stronger than in uncooked marinades. It is *only after complete chilling* that the cooked marinade is used. Exceptions are made only for very large and tough cuts of game, like a wild boar, or sometimes—only in special cases when time is of the essence—the marinade is poured, boiling, over the meat.

We recommend using very good wine vinegar. Certain vinegars are so acidic that, in addition to being corrosive, they denature the taste of the finished dish. If the vinegar is very strong, cut it with water proportional to the strength.

To marinate meat, when you want to keep the marinade in reserve, always use earthenware utensils, whether plates, terrines, or jars.

The length of time in the cooked marinade depends on room temperature. The meat is infused with the flavor a lot faster in summer than in winter. It's even faster in stormy weather and when the room is quite warm.

When a piece of meat is immersed in the marinade, it is not only turned over once or twice a day, but bathed with marinade with the help of a wooden spoon—a salad spoon, for example. As much as possible, do not introduce any metal utensil into the marinade.

If the meat has to marinate more than three days, and if there is stormy weather while it is marinating, the marinade must be boiled to avoid any risk of fermentation. Thus, transfer the meat to a plate, pour the liquid, vegetables, flavorings, etc., of the marinade into a saucepan, and add, for each liter ($4^1/_4$ cups) of marinade: 1 deciliter ($3^1/_3$ fluid ounces, scant $^1/_2$ cup) of white wine and 4 or 5 spoonfuls of vinegar. Boil for 5 minutes. Let the marinade *cool completely* before pouring it over the piece.

The receptacle—a terrine or similar utensil—should first have been rinsed with boiling water in order to destroy any bacteria.

Cooked marinades: We will not give the proportions of the different elements here. They will be found in each recipe where marinades are used.

PREPARATION. Finely mince carrot, onion, shallot, celery. When in season, celery is a highly recommended marinade ingredient. Break the parsley stalks into small pieces. On a plate, put the thyme, bay, peppercorns, and other flavorings to be used in the marinade.

Heat the oil in a deep saucepan—tin-lined copper if possible—of an appropriate size. Add the carrot, onion, shallot, celery, and parsley. Stir with a wooden spoon over high heat until these vegetables turn golden, only slightly browned, without turning a deep brown color. Then add the white wine and vinegar, garlic, thyme, bay, peppercorns, and the other aromatics. Bring to a boil, then immediately reduce the heat to low. From this point, simmer gently for a good half hour. Remove from the heat and allow to cool completely. The marinade is then poured over the meat, including all its vegetables and ingredients.

Breading or Coating with Bread Crumbs

Bread crumbs: Bread crumbs, or *panure,* are obtained from thinly sliced pieces of crustless bread and used to coat foods in a crust that can be more or less thick. Do not confuse this with *chapelure,* which are bread crumbs made with the crust of bread. "Panure" bread crumbs are completely white, fine grained, and homogenous, like semolina.

The bread used in making these bread crumbs is very white bread, allowed to get two or three days stale so that it can be easily made into crumbs, which will not happen with fresh bread.

Begin by eliminating all crust and hard parts with a knife. Next, break the bread into pieces, then place them in the corner of a new kitchen towel, lightly dusted with flour (a new towel will be easier to handle), and close the towel like a purse. Rub the bread pieces around to crush them. As soon as this is done, pour out the resulting crumbs into a fine strainer or a metal sieve with moderate openings set over a sheet of paper. Put everything back into the towel that does not pass. Crush it again and sieve it again. Keep doing this until the necessary amount has been obtained.

These bread crumbs must be fresh when you use them. Fresh bread crumbs are called fresh, even though the bread is somewhat stale, to distinguish them from bread crumbs dried in the oven, crushed, and sieved and then kept in a box. These dried bread crumbs are not recommended. It is true that they form a firm crust, but it's tough, without flavor, like cardboard.

Egg breading *(à l'anglaise):* *À l'anglaise* refers to egg beaten with salt, pepper, and oil, into which you dip ingredients before coating them with bread crumbs and frying them. The combination of egg and bread crumbs, when it comes into contact with the hot oil, forms a solid crust around the breaded object.

Although it is not necessary to have a rather substantial crust to contain runny or chopped substances, such as croquettes, one could, for reasons of economy, use only egg whites. But this is detrimental to the flavor, the tenderness, and even the beautiful golden tint that the yolk offers.

The *oil* makes the batter crustier. Add 1 teaspoon for every 2 eggs. A small pinch each of *salt and pepper* for every egg is, of course, not used in sweet dishes.

How to bread *à l'anglaise:* Break the eggs, both whites and yolks, into a shallow soup dish or small terrine, according to the type of food to be breaded.

Add oil, salt, and pepper. With a fork, beat them as if making an omelet. In other words, gently, until the white, mixed well with the yolk, no longer appears gelatinous, but make sure you do not overmix until foamy.

On a flat plate or large platter, or on the cutting board, depending on what you have to bread, spread out half the bread crumbs. (It's best to use the crumbs gradually. The crust will be lighter in the end since the gelatinous nature of the eggs causes the crumbs to form clumps.) On a third plate, spread out a little flour.

First, roll the object to be breaded in the flour, as lightly as possible, so that the surface is only dusted and the flour forms only a very thin coat. This preliminary dusting with flour is to absorb any moisture from the food, so that the egg adheres better. It also helps to shape some things, such as croquettes, so that the ingredients do not stick to your fingers. Next, dip the food in the beaten egg, making sure that it is *completely immersed, even in the crevices.*

Slide a fork under the object to transfer it to the bread crumbs, and roll it in them so that it is completely and equally covered all over. Use the flat side of the blade of a large knife to press against the bread crumbs so they stick well to the egg. They must be perfectly combined to produce the desired crust.

Keep the breaded objects cool until ready to cook. Don't bread them more than a half-hour in advance, because the bread crumbs tend to dry out and the resulting crust will not be as tender.

Croûtes and Croutons

Fried *croûtes* and croutons: Croutons to garnish soups or other dishes are made from slightly stale bread (with the crusts cut off) or from a good solid loaf of ordinary bread. The crusts are never used, and the croutons are generally little cubes with about 1-centimeter (3/8-inch) sides. *Croûtes* are thin slices. The size of the *croûtes* and the kind of bread will be indicated in individual recipes.

Croûtes and croutons are fried in just enough fat to cover. They should have enough space around them for the fat to circulate.

The utensil generally used is a very clean, ordinary frying pan. The usual frying oil is *clarified* butter. Sometimes, according to the dish, lard or oil are used.

Pour the butter, decanting it, into the frying pan. Put it over *very moderate* heat. When the butter begins to warm, put in the croutons. When the bread is light golden, toss them. If they are too large to toss, turn them over with a fork to color the other side.

Note that only the surface of the crouton must be firm and lightly crisped. The color must never go deeper than light gold, and so the butter must never be heated to the point of browning. Make sure you proceed carefully for the entire procedure, using, from beginning to end, only moderate heat. Keep the croutons warm in their frying pan until you use them, *without covering them,* so they don't soften.

Croutons for soup liaisons: Ordinary bread works very well for this. It is better to use the top crust, provided it is not burned or too dark, leaving underneath a good centimeter (3/8 inch) of bread. If the crust is not serviceable, use only the bread inside. Cut this bread into 1-centimeter (3/8-inch) cubes. Spread them out on a baking sheet or other ovenproof platter. Place in a rather hot oven to dry well without browning, stirring from time to time.

Potato croutons: To garnish soups, omelets, scrambled eggs, always use firm, thin-skinned potatoes. Choose rather large ones, so they are easier to cut into slices of the right size, without too much cutting or peeling. You can use all these bits and peelings elsewhere, in a soup or a purée. They must never be thrown away.

Peel the potato. Divide it into slices, 6–7 millimeters (about 1/4 inch) thick. Divide these slices into equal sticks, about 6–7 millimeters (1/4 inch) wide. Cut them perpendicularly to obtain small cubes of 6–7 millimeters (1/4 inch) on each side. Plunge them into a pot of cold water to rinse off the starch, which makes them stick to each other. Drain. Dry with a clean, dry dish cloth; they must not retain any moisture.

Heat some butter in a clean frying pan (about 25 grams/1 ounce/2 tablespoons for each potato used) about 15 minutes before needed. Add the cubes. Salt lightly. Cook over moderate heat, tossing them from time to time. They must slowly take on a golden color, but not dark brown, and should be crisp on the outside and tender on the inside.

Bread Paste for Stuffings *(Panade)*

This preparation, which has nothing in common with the soup of the same name *(panade)*, is used to give stuffings the necessary consistency. According to the type of stuffing, the "panade" can be prepared by two methods, which will be specified in individual recipes.

Bread *panade:* Crumble 125 grams (4 1/2 ounces) of slightly stale white bread into a small saucepan. Moisten it with a scant deciliter (3 1/3 fluid ounces, scant 1/2 cup) of boiling milk. Add a pinch of salt. Leave it to absorb completely. Then mash the bread into a paste. Next, dry it out over high heat—in other words, mix it with a wooden spoon, stirring constantly, until the paste no longer sticks to the spoon. Spread it out in a dish greased with butter. *Let it cool before use.*

Flour *panade:* Preparation is the same as for choux pastry, without the egg. In other words, in a saucepan, combine 2 deciliters (6 3/4 fluid ounces, 7/8 cup) of water, 30 grams (1 ounce, 2 tablespoons) of butter, and a pinch of salt. Bring to a boil. As soon as the boil causes the liquid to foam as if to overflow, like milk, remove from the heat and, without hesitating, add the flour (125 grams, 4 1/2 ounces) all at once, mixing it in with a wooden spoon. Return the pan to high heat, and stir with the spoon, without stopping, until the dough comes away from the sides of the pan and is only slightly moist. Spread it out on a dish greased with butter. Let it cool completely before use.

Mirepoix

This is the name of a combination of onions, carrots, parsley, thyme, bay leaf, and bacon, lightly browned in butter or other fat. It is used as an aromatic element for many dishes.

Vegetables and bacon, or cured ham, are cut into small cubes. This shape means that they will brown evenly and helps to extract from the vegetables everything they are capable of offering. It is therefore absolutely essential not to cut them in any other way. However, it is not necessary for the cubes to be cut absolutely evenly if the mirepoix will not subsequently be part of the final dish.

The bacon is cut in larger cubes than the rest, after the rind has been trimmed. If it is very salty, blanch for 5 minutes, once it has been cut into cubes. Sometimes a bit of celery is added to the mirepoix. Be careful about how much you use, so that it does not dominate.

The proportions for mirepoix are given in individual recipes.

To color the mirepoix, heat the butter or fat in a heavy-bottomed pan over medium heat. Add the mirepoix ingredients. Stir it with your wooden spoon, cooking until golden, or in other words, lightly sautéed. Don't cover the pan, and stir often because the browning must happen progressively. When finished, everything should be the same color, without dark brown pieces, certainly without burned pieces, which would impart a bitter flavor, and would have to be taken out.

Allow 7–8 minutes for the relatively modest quantities used in home cooking.

Duxelles

Used for gratin toppings, stuffings, etc., duxelles is composed of chopped mushrooms, onions, and shallots. If you have mushroom trimmings, this is the time to use them, because they will give you the same results as whole mushrooms. Calculate one-fifth, or a quarter of trimmings, from the stem end of the mushroom (the bit that is not used). Thus, about 100 grams (3 1/2 ounces) of trimmings equals 125 grams (4 1/2 ounces) of whole, untrimmed mushrooms, for which you need 100 grams (3 1/2 ounces) of onions, 2–3 shallots, 25 grams (1 ounce, 2 tablespoons) of butter, and 2 tablespoons of oil.

Trim the mushroom end. Peel the stem. Wash in two changes of water. Chop them. Put them in a dishtowel and squeeze to extract as much water as possible. This is much faster than waiting for it to evaporate.

Heat the butter and oil in a small pan. Add the finely chopped onion and shallot. Cook until light golden-brown, stirring constantly with the wooden spoon, so that no one part is more colored than the rest. Just as the onion turns golden, add the chopped mushrooms. Season with a pinch of salt, a pinch of pepper, and a hint of nutmeg. Stir over high heat for a few minutes to cook the mushrooms first, and also to reduce the rest of the liquid. Set aside or keep hot, depending on your needs.

Olives for Garnish

Use large, round green olives for this. With a small knife, peel them in a spiral, keeping the knife in contact with the pit as you work. Carefully remove the pit without breaking the olive, which will regain its former shape by rolling up upon itself.

Put them into a small pan of boiling water and boil for 5 minutes to remove all traces of salt. Drain well on a kitchen towel, taking care to ensure they do not retain any water on the inside.

Bouquet Garni

Unless otherwise specified, a bouquet garni contains parsley, thyme, and bay leaf. Any other ingredient, such as celery, garlic, scallion, clove, etc., required by some authors, must always be specified.

Thus, a bouquet garni is composed of 3–4 sprigs of parsley, depending on their size, leaving the entire length of the stems because this part contains the most flavor. Use one sprig of thyme, and only a half bay leaf, because of its very strong flavor. Surround the thyme and bay with the parsley, by folding over the stems of parsley. Tie it all together with kitchen twine.

Some Culinary Terms

We have attempted, in the present work, not to use terminology that is exclusively professional or incomprehensible for the general reader. Below we define the words commonly used in home cooking.

To arrange *(dresser):* Aesthetically place meat and garnish on the serving dish.

To bard: Wrap in a thin layer or sheet of bacon or fatback bacon.

To bind *(lier):* Enhance the consistency of a sauce, soup, or gravy, by the addition of egg yolks, cream, flour, starch, or blood.

To blanch *(blanchir):* Immerse certain foods in boiling water, either to part-cook them or to clean them. Either they are dropped into boiling water, or put into cold water that is then brought to a boil.

To braise: Slowly cook meats or vegetables in a small quantity of aromatic broth in a closed utensil.

To bread *(paner):* Roll in bread crumbs.

To brown in butter *(tomber à glace):* Cook in butter until lightly colored.

To brown on top *(gratiner):* Put a dish, sauced or not, but often sprinkled with grated cheese, into the oven or under the broiler to obtain a light coloring and sometimes a crispy surface (onion soup, pâtés, etc.).

To butter *(beurrer):* Grease a mold, a baking sheet, baking paper. Also, to finish a sauce by adding butter.

Chinois: A fine-meshed cone-shaped strainer (*fig.* 19).

To coat *(masquer, napper):* Cover with sauce. In confectionary, cover with icing or meringue.

To color *(revenir):* Color lightly in butter, fat, or oil that has been previously heated.

Cooking liquid *(cuisson):* Any liquid that has been rendered after cooking food. For example, the liquid resulting from cooking mushrooms.

To deglaze *(déglacer):* Dissolve, by moistening with a little liquid, the caramelized juice at the bottom of a saucepan.

To degrease *(dégraisser):* Remove all excess fat from stocks, cooking liquids, sauces, etc.

To dilute *(relâcher):* Add a liquid to thin out a sauce or a purée that is too thick; adjust consistency.

Double-boiler *(bain-marie):* A bain-marie can be any set-up of utensils where the lower part is filled with simmering water and the upper part, which can be a pan or a bowl, is placed on top. Allow 2 centimeters (3/4 inch) space between the two utensils.

Drum sieve *(tamis):* A sieve whose screen is stretched across a circular band of wood or metal, resembling a drum.

To glaze *(glacer, glaçage):* In addition to the literal meaning of the word, this term applies to: 1) Basting a cut of meat or other preparation with its own reduced juice and returning it to the oven to give it a glaze; 2) The formation on a sauced dish of a light, shining skin; 3) A layer of sugar spread over a pastry.

To lard *(larder):* Thread strips (lardons) of fatback bacon or bacon into a cut of meat with a larding needle.

To line *(foncer):* Arrange slices of bacon, onion, carrot on the bottom and sides of a utensil. Also, line a mold with dough.

To line with aspic *(chemiser):* Coat the insides of a mold with melted aspic and allow it to harden before filling with the required ingredients.

To marinate *(mariner):* Soak meat, game, or fish in a liquid either to flavor or to tenderize.

To melt *(fondre):* Cook thinly sliced, minced, julienned, or diced vegetables (or mirepoix) gently in butter until they begin to dissolve.

	Fahrenheit	Centigrade
Very low, gentle	225–275°F	107–135°C
Low	285–325°F	140–163°C
Medium	350–400°F	177–205°C
High	410–450°F	210–232°C
Very hot	475–550°F	246–288°C

To moisten *(mouiller):* Add the necessary cooking liquid.

Oven temperatures: Every oven has its own characteristics, and experimentation is the only way to truly comprehend your oven, but here is a general guide:

To poach *(pocher):* Simmer in a liquid kept just below boiling point.

Poaching liquid *(bouillon):* The liquid in which meat or poultry has been cooked.

Pre-cooking rice *(crever):* Put the rice you need in boiling salted water for a few seconds; then drain it thoroughly and moisten it with milk.

To purge *(dégorger):* Put certain foods, such as brains, sweetbreads, kidneys, etc., into cold water to flush out impurities and traces of blood. Snails, cucumbers, etc., are purged with a coating of sea salt.

To reduce *(réduire):* Boil a liquid or sauce, uncovered, to reduce the quantity and make it more concentrated.

To refresh *(rafraîchir):* Blanched food is immediately plunged into cool, running water to remove any foam and to cool completely.

Roux *(roux):* A mixture of flour and a fat, cooked more or less completely, according to requirements.

Salpicon *(salpicon):* A mixture of several ingredients, cut to the same shape, generally in cubes, to garnish savory pastry shells, interiors of croquettes, rissoles, etc.

To shrink *(pincer):* When cooking ingredients, having sweated off their moisture and juices, start to contract, they are said to shrink.

To simmer *(mijoter):* Boil very gently over low heat.

To skim *(dépouiller, écumer, épurer):* Skim (purify) a sauce or soup by removing the scum from the top.

To slice thinly *(émincer):* Cut into thin slices.

To soak *(mitonner):* Applied to bread that must be soaked in soup for an extended period of time and reheated before serving.

To stew *(étuver):* Cook almost without liquid, or without liquid in a closed container.

To strain *(passer):* Cook in butter, then strain through a chinois, sieve, cloth, or strainer stock, cooking liquid, sauces, or to force through a drum sieve *(tamis)* purées, stuffings, etc. Syrups and fruit juices are strained through cloth.

To stud ***(piquer):*** Inserting small pieces of fatback bacon or bacon near the surface of different cuts of meat, especially game.

To sweat ***(suer):*** To cook an ingredient, generally meat, covered and over low heat to make it give up its juices.

Tablespoon ***(cuillerée):*** In French cooking, a tablespoon (not level) is equal to a soup spoon that holds about 20 grams (2/3 ounce) of flour or sugar and about 25 percent more liquid than the American tablespoon measure.

To trim ***(parer):*** To make an ingredient more attractive by cutting away certain parts. For meat, removing excess fat. For a potato, the eyes, etc.

Trimmings ***(parures):*** The off-cuts resulting from trimming an ingredient.

To truss ***(brider, trousser):*** To retain the shape of poultry, game, and seafood by tying it up with a fine cord, sometimes using a needle.

To whisk or to whip ***(monter):*** Give volume to a substance, such as egg whites, a sauce, a hollandaise, etc.

COOKING TECHNIQUES

BRAISING

Almost everyone knows that braising requires time and careful attention. That is why braising is often replaced by a roast, served with a predictable sauce, and surrounded by an indifferent garnish. This ignorance no doubt reflects general confusion. Some think braising is simply slow cooking using a basic stock or even water for the liquid. In such a case, it is the meat that enriches the cooking liquid. But in braising, it is the cooking liquid that enriches the meat.

Braising is much more than a cooking method, it is also about what you put in the pot—such as slices of fatback bacon, poaching liquid, wine, eau-de-vie, etc. These additions are what give the meat greater succulence.

Succulence. This is the true goal of braising; it is the aim toward which one strives, from the very beginning, and it is the direction in which all the techniques and methods lead. To understand this, it is first necessary to know what was formerly meant by "braising." The grand culinary master Carême described it thus: "Place some slices of fatback bacon in the bottom of a pan, and, on top of these, some slices of meat. Then add either a goose, a turkey, a leg of lamb, a cut of beef, or a similar piece. Then, add sliced meat and fatback bacon, two carrots cut up, six medium onions, a bouquet garni, basil, mace, course ground pepper, a touch of garlic; then a half glass of old eau-de-vie and two generous tablespoons of consommé or stock. Cover with strong paper that has been greased, and cook it with heat from above and below."

The sum of all this was called braising. Since then, the great French chefs, beginning with Carême, have gradually simplified and perfected this primitive procedure. To braise, you must first prepare a flavorsome stock in which you will then cook the meat.

The methods vary according to the type of meat, either red or white, and they vary with different parts of the same animal and according to the availability of funds, the latter reason often taking precedence over the others. Whatever procedure you use, some conditions are essential for braising both red and white meats. You must know these before anything else.

General Principles

Any meat intended for braising must not only be of good quality, but also be *properly aged.* The longest cooking period will not produce the sought-after tenderness.

You will not be successful with a piece of meat that is too small. The amount of work and care is the same whether the size is small or large, so it is to your advantage to double the amount necessary for a meal. Braised meats reheat quite well, can be prepared in other ways, and are even excellent served cold.

You will need barding fat (fatback bacon), *and plenty of it,* when you braise. No other fat can be substituted. And you will need more when the meat is lean, or when it is dry by nature and not "marbled," or streaked with fat.

You can remedy this absence of inner fat by larding the cut from one end to the other with *large lardons,* a little less than 1 centimeter (3/8 inch) thick. These should be seasoned and inserted in the same direction as the grain. These lardons do not rule out the use of *fatback bacon slices* to wrap the cut, nor to line the bottom of the utensil. Pork fat imparts a distinctive velvety smoothness to a dish. It is an essential element in braising.

Increase the proportion of *pork rind* when you

have only a basic stock. It will give to the liquid, or the sauce, used for braising the gelatinous element that ordinary reduced stock lacks. Choose pieces of rind with a thick layer of fat. If there is not enough fat, the rind will burn, giving an acrid taste to the sauce without transmitting the necessary qualities. In addition, the sauce will not have a lustrous glaze.

In addition to pork fat or rind, you can use a lean piece of *cured ham,* known as *jambon de Bayonne.* This adds a very pleasant taste to the finished dish. You can also use *jambon de Bayonne* slices like lardons (chosen with lean and fatty parts), which are inserted through the cut to be braised, as mentioned above. This procedure was frequently employed in early classic cooking, and is worth mentioning here.

The *bones* should not be included when braising, for two reasons. First, it would require the use of a utensil too large for the correct proportions of meat and liquid. Second, it would not be able to release the gelatinous materials it contains, even though braising requires a long cooking time. The bone has to cook for at least 12 hours. For this reason, you should start cooking the bone well in advance, either in the liquid intended for braising, or simply in water. A paragraph in the chapter on pot-au-feu contains directions for cooking the bone.

The *cooking liquid* that keeps the meat moist, whether poaching liquid or stock, must be *only lightly salted or not salted at all.* The liquid will reduce by two-thirds, tripling its saltiness. If the poaching liquid or stock is properly salted to start with, you must dilute it by one-third or one-half with water. Otherwise, when the meat is cooked, the liquid will be too salty to use. *Poaching liquid made from veal,* although light, is always preferable to beef stock because it contains gelatinous elements that improve the reduction. The resulting sauce will have a smooth, velvety texture, which cannot be achieved with beef stock alone.

The *vegetables and other elements that remain after braising* the meat make excellent additions to other dishes, such as soups or stews. They have a wonderful, complex flavor, having been infused with the juice of the braising. Keep them after you have strained the juice.

Braising Techniques

Choice of utensil: You must use a special utensil for braising (*fig.* 17), made of thick aluminum, tin-lined copper, or cast iron. It must be *exactly the right size* to hold the correct amount of liquid needed for proper cooking.

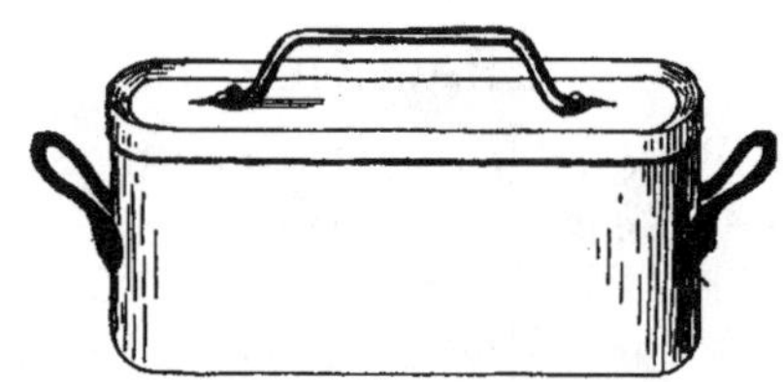

FIG. 17. BRAISING PAN.

FIG. 18. SAUCEPAN WITH HIGH SIDES AND ITS COVER.

Whatever the liquid used, it must cover a certain proportion of the cut to be braised. If the utensil is too large, you must increase the quantity of liquid. The result will no longer be a braised cut, but a disagreeably boiled and washed-out lump of meat, no matter how flavorsome the braising liquid. In addition, you must allow for shrinkage of the meat, as well as the gradual reduction of the liquid. In fact, toward the end of the cooking period, it is sometimes necessary to transfer the cooking juices and the meat to a smaller utensil, so the meat does not dry out and the evaporation is slowed.

The utensil should be appropriate to the size and shape of the cut of meat to be braised. If you are cooking a filet or a leg of lamb, you should choose a long utensil, because the space between the utensil and the meat should not exceed 1 1/2 centimeters (5/8 inch), 2 centimeters (3/4 inch) at the most.

Do not use a utensil that is too deep, leaving a considerable space between the meat and the cover, because the steam will accumulate in the lid and there will be too much evaporation.

The utensil must be *as thick as possible* in order to maintain even heat, which is essential for the cooking process. A utensil that is not thick enough will be subject to the slightest variations of heat. Tin-lined copper retains the heat best and is preferable to all other materials. Cast iron is excellent for this same reason, but the sauce frequently does not maintain the desired clarity. On contact with certain types of cast iron, the sauce becomes cloudy and off-color. Thick earthenware pots also work well and can be used in place of tin-lined copper or good cast iron. Aluminum is good, too, but it must be thick. Avoid enameled steel, because you need even heat regulation and clarity of the juice.

Basic braising ingredients: These are the elements used to line the braising vessel: fresh pork rind or fat, onion and carrot slices, and bouquet garni.

You should use *30 grams (1 ounce) of each of these ingredients for every 450 grams (1 pound) of meat* you want to braise. You can use a little less pork rind, however. Whatever you need to cover the bottom of the utensil will be enough.

Depending on which method you are following, raw onions and carrots are put in the braising utensil to "sweat" with the meat, as for *white braised meats,* or browned beforehand, as for *red braised meats.* In both cases, the manner of preparing the braiser remains absolutely the same.

Lining the braiser: Cut the pork rind or fatback bacon in strips the width of two or three fingers. Left whole, they buckle too much from the heat. If the pork rind is not very fresh, soak it in boiling water to soften it. Place the strips in the bottom of the pot, side by side, with the fatty side down. This is very important, because when this side comes into contact with the bottom of the pot, the fat melts and keeps the vegetables from sticking. If you put the rind side down, it would burn.

Arrange the slices of onion and carrot, cut about 1/2 centimeter (3/16 inch) thick, on top of the pork. First the onion, then the carrot. Put the bouquet garni in the center, then place the cut of meat on top.

Cooking the meat: True braising begins when the cooking vessel is put in the oven. Each recipe will give specific cooking times from this moment on.

A slow, even simmer is an essential condition for braising. If it boils too quickly at the start, not only will the meat dry out and the liquid diminish but, worst of all, the interior of the meat will heat too rapidly and will not undergo the gradual transformation which is the very reason for braising. A gentle simmer, uninterrupted and unvarying, must be maintained from the beginning to the end of the cooking process. It is only toward the end that the heat may be increased, rather than diminished. In sum, *careful control of heat is key when braising.*

The heat must come from *above and below* in order to braise properly. It used to be that the lid of the cooking vessel was heaped with glowing coals to supply the heat from above. Now is it much more convenient to use the oven. But even though it is easier to braise in the oven, it requires more care than the lid heaped with coals. You need experience to sense the degree of heat in the oven—a moderate heat that is even and stable—and not to exceed the limit. Raising the heat to cook faster will not save a minute. Quite the opposite, in fact.

If, for any reason, the simmering is interrupted, do not reheat rapidly and maintain a higher temperature to make up for lost time. A blast of violent boiling in mid-braise is the equivalent of torching a roast. It toughens the meat, and there's no remedy. Moreover, it clouds the sauce and alters its taste.

Do not use too much heat from above; you risk drying out and toughening the meat that is exposed, given that the surface is not covered by the cooking liquid.

Baste the meat with the cooking liquid; the frequency will vary depending on the size of the meat and the quantity of liquid. You must do this *more frequently toward the end* as the liquid will have reduced and more of the meat will be uncovered. If you notice a premature reduction of liquid during the course of the cooking, caused by boiling too rapidly and improper supervision, you should add a few tablespoons of *hot* stock to restore the balance.

For large cuts, the *degree of doneness* is determined by piercing the thickest part of the meat completely with a large kitchen needle. The needle must be easily withdrawn. If the meat is stuck, suspended on the needle when you try to withdraw it, it is not adequately cooked. Cook it until the needle withdraws easily.

NOTE. If absolutely necessary, you can braise a small cut *at home* heated from beneath only, on a well-regulated gas flame or on a charcoal burner that is well covered with ashes. But no matter how well you regulate the heat, you will still lack the all-over heat.

Glazing: The goal of glazing is to make the meat more appetizing by covering it with a light, shiny coat so that it looks almost varnished.

Glazing is only important for cuts served whole or in large slices. That said, it is essential for meat that has been larded on top. This final operation browns the lardons. For this, the broiler works better than the oven.

Meat that has been glazed does not take well to standing, so don't glaze until just before you serve. If the meat must wait, keep it warm near the oven, in its strained and degreased sauce.

To glaze, transfer the meat to any ovenproof platter. Remove all vegetable pieces. Strain the juice through a chinois and degrease it. Baste the meat with *just a little* of this liquid. Put the meat in a hot oven, on a high shelf so it gets the heat from above. Or put it under the broiler, if you have one. Baste it with the liquid a few more times, very lightly. The heat will cause the liquid to caramelize on the surface of the meat like a light, shiny coating. Hence, the term "glaze." Finally, baste no longer and let it set.

You will need *about 10 minutes* for this; longer if you are dealing with a large piece of meat.

The sauce: We use the term "sauce" here in order to be understood by everyone, but in culinary terms the liquid that results from braising is really a jus (juice).

The more concentrated the sauce, the greater its succulence will be. It should be a kind of liquid extract of all the ingredients, meat, vegetables, herbs, liquids, etc., that have gone into the dish. It must have the consistency and look of a light syrup, clinging to the spoon like a varnish. It must be crystal clear, with no trace of fat.

Classic cooking methods called for a great deal of meat to be used in the liquid that forms the base for braising and the resulting juice had the consistency of a syrup, without further additions. But modern bourgeois cooking has been obliged to find a more economical way to achieve a similar result. We do this now by binding the sauce.

A very little bit of *starch* will do if the liquid used for the braising is of good quality. But in a home kitchen where ordinary stock, or sometimes even water, has been used instead of a proper braising liquid *(jus),* a *roux* is preferable. Its light, nutty taste contributes to the general flavor of the dish—a small contribution not to be underrated—and, more important, it enhances the meager ingredients used in the liquid.

Beurre manié is also used. A final addition of the *finest quality unsalted French butter,* "beurre d'Isigny"—a method often used by the great old masters—is recommended. The butter is added to the reduced braising liquid, or sauce, after it has been removed from the heat, to be served separately, in a sauceboat. This butter contributes to the liaison of the sauce and gives it an incomparable smoothness. It is no wonder that the great chefs of contemporary cuisine have returned to this technique.

Braising White Meats

The braising technique used today for veal, lamb, poultry, etc., has not changed over the years. In other words, you first "sweat" the meat and other ingredients until they release their juices. The ingredients are lightly browned in this juice, and the liquid is reduced, almost to a syrup. Then the principal cooking liquid is added. The meat is cooked according to the recipe being used. Finally, you may choose to finish with a glaze before serving.

To line the braiser: Proceed with the vegetables as directed in "Lining the braiser" (PAGE 27)

The braiser can be prepared in advance and set aside until needed.

To sweat: The goal of this operation is to release the juices from the vegetables and meat by applying moderate and progressive heat. These juices will sink to the bottom of the utensil where they caramelize lightly, thus contributing to the flavor of the braising liquid. If the heat is excessive, the opposite will happen. Searing and browning due to high heat will seal the outside of these ingredients, thus sealing in juices and obstructing their release.

Sweating is accomplished directly over low heat, or with the braiser set off to one side on the coal stove, or in the oven, and always with a lid on the utensil. However it's done, the braiser must have a heavy bottom, smooth and without dents, and it must be heated equally over the entire surface.

This operation will take 15–20 minutes, depending on the size of the meat. Beginners will probably need a little more time. During this operation, nothing in the braiser should be disturbed. Everything must remain in the place where it was originally put.

When the *covered* braiser is heated, here's what happens: gradually, the meat releases its juices and blanches. It swells slightly because of the pressure of the juice that is trying to escape. If you carefully lift the meat and the slice of onion beneath, it will reveal an onion that has softened on the side in contact with the meat, while the part touching the pork rind will be slightly yellowed. From time to time, you should swiftly lift the lid to see and, above all, *smell* how the operation is proceeding. The pleasant aroma of cooking will rise from the braiser. You can smell that it's cooking, but it has not begun to brown. *You must never brown the vegetables when you braise white meats.* The juice should have a light golden hue and the flavor should not be too pronounced. (SEE BROWNING, THIS PAGE.)

To reduce to a glaze: *Moistening.* With the sweating process complete, the meat should not have taken on any color, but rather have become white. Don't move any of the ingredients. Add a deciliter (3 1/3 fluid ounces, scant 1/2 cup) of liquid, stock, or white wine. This amount hardly varies since the liquid is used to draw out more of the juices from the meat and vegetables so that nothing sticks. Raise the heat and boil, uncovered, until there is nothing left but a scant tablespoonful of pale golden syrup when you tilt the braiser. This process is called "reducing to a glaze." Add another deciliter (3 1/3 fluid ounces, scant 1/2 cup) of liquid and repeat the process. This reduction yields an extract of the juices from both the meat and vegetables and this, in turn, will add depth of flavor to the braising liquid.

Having completed this second phase of "sweating," add the remainder of liquid required for the definitive cooking process. This is the "moistening" phase. The liquid, or moistening agent, must reach the top, or partway to the top, of the meat. It must never be completely covered. Bring it to a boil over high heat. When it has begun to boil, place a piece of baking parchment directly on top of the meat, fitting it snugly in the braiser. Cover as tightly as possible. Put it into the oven.

Cooking: Follow the directions given (SEE COOKING THE MEAT, PAGE 27).

Browning: There is a single moment when the ingredients have released their moisture and juices and now begin to color. Professional French chefs call this *le pinçage.* These juices sink to the bottom of the pot, where they reduce and caramelize. This adds color and flavor to the cooking liquid. But if the precise point of browning is surpassed, everything will burn and the juice will become bitter beyond repair. It is therefore necessary to watch this process closely, because it happens very quickly.

From time to time, lift the lid so you can fan the fumes under your nose and smell the steam from the pot, just like the professionals. As long as only white steam escapes, there is nothing more to do. As soon as the steam transforms into a light blue smoky haze and, above all, when a faint aroma of browning vegetables rises from the braiser, it's ready. The process must be stopped immediately, for the reasons explained above.

Remove from the heat. Add a little liquid, making sure it circulates throughout the bottom of the braiser, then return to the heat, uncovered, to reduce completely. Then add the required liquid, as per the recipe directions.

Braising Red Meats

The following method, applied only to *red meats,* is the one currently used in fine restaurants as well as home kitchens. The meats are first browned over high heat, which has the effect of forming a sort of waterproof seal on the outside.

In addition, the vegetables for the braising are lightly browned in fat before they are used to line the braiser. In this way, they give to the cooking juices a flavor that would not be possible if they were added raw.

You can brown the meat and vegetables together if using a small cut of meat. If you have a larger cut, you must brown the meat and vegetables separately.

To brown the meat: There are two methods. In the *oven* or in the *braiser.*

In the oven: This procedure eliminates the inconvenience of splattering and splashing burning hot fat, which occurs when browning in a braiser, but you will need two ovens. The meat, greased all over, is put in a roasting pan in a *very hot* oven. It is turned on all sides during its time in the oven, which *must not exceed 20 minutes.* The meat must not begin its actual cooking here. Only the outside must be seared. This is why such intense heat is necessary.

An oven this hot is far too warm for the gentle cooking required by braising. Therefore, in ordinary home kitchens, the browning is done on the burner, in the braising utensil. This method cannot be used for meat that has been larded on the surface with small lardons, because it cannot be turned in the braiser. In such a case, the meat must be browned in the oven.

In the braiser: Add enough fat so the bottom of the braiser is completely covered, but not excessively, and so the fat can circulate under the meat. The meat should never be in direct contact with the metal.

In the utensil chosen for the braising, heat the fat over high heat until it just begins to smoke. Add the meat. Let the part that touches the bottom brown sufficiently before you turn the meat. Brown all the surfaces of the meat successively, lowering the heat as the process progresses. The utensil and the meat will warm up, requiring less heat from the stove. This will take about the same time as browning in the oven.

If the meat is very fatty and releases a lot of fat, you will have to remove some during the browning process. Too much fat will interfere with browning.

When you turn the meat, don't pierce it with a fork, because you will create an opening that allows the juice to escape.

The braising base: Cut the carrots and onions into thick rounds, about 1 centimeter ($^3/_8$ inch) thick. Heat enough cooking oil in a wide-bottomed frying pan to cover the surface. Add the onion and carrot. Sauté over a heat that is hot enough to brown them lightly. Do not brown too darkly, and never let them burn. Drain them in a strainer.

Braising: Remove all the fat from the utensil used to brown the meat. This fat has been overheated and now is only good for frying at a very high temperature.

Return the barding fat and browned vegetables to the braiser, as directed (SEE BASIC BRAISING INGREDIENTS, PAGE 27). Put the meat on top.

Depending on the individual recipe, add a small quantity of either wine or stock and reduce rapidly to a glaze (SEE PAGE 29). Add the cooking liquid. Or, add all the cooking liquid at once. In either case, the cooking is regulated exactly as directed (SEE COOKING THE MEAT, PAGE 27).

ROASTS

Roasting is appropriate only for choice cuts from young and tender animals. More than any other cooking procedure, it retains the integrity and the subtle flavorings inherent in the meat. Although this might seem a simple way of cooking, correct roasting is, on the contrary, one of the more difficult techniques.

For a good roast, it is essential to use choice meat, whatever the animal. And this meat must be roasted *à point* (to the correct point).

À point is the culinary term that summarizes the ideal roast. *À point* indicates a roast that is beautifully colored, the meat evenly cooked and juicy when carved. This juice will be pink, and not red, for red meats. It will be absolutely clear, and not pink, for white meats.

The precise goal of roasting is to preserve and concentrate all the juices of the meat inside the flesh.

In order to do this, the juices are sealed in at the beginning of cooking by the formation of a thin, browned coating on the outside of the meat. Think of it as a waterproof barrier that prevents juices inside from escaping.

To obtain and maintain this thin browned layer, which is the fundamental condition for all roasting, you must have dry heat from the beginning to the end of the cooking process. Any moisture will make the barrier deteriorate and the meat soggy. The pores will open and the juices will escape.

The only true roast is a roast cooked on a spit. Meat cooked in this way has no contact with any cooking vessel and is thus exposed to the heat in air. Whether it be an old-fashioned spit in front of the fireplace, or a rotisserie in front of a cage of burning coals, or any other system that keeps the meat suspended in front of an open fire, the principle of roasting does not change.

Meat roasted in an oven can be excellent, but not the same as roasting on a spit. The difference is so important that connoisseurs, like the English, who appreciate a good roast, refer to meat cooked in the oven as "baked."

Baking in the oven is more applicable to very large cuts that require a long cooking time, especially veal or pork. They will color more gradually in the oven than on the spit, where the large pieces get too browned unless they are wrapped in several layers of paper.

But the spit is the best—indeed, one could say, the only—method for roasting poultry and feathered game. It is even more important when smaller game birds are roasted.

Seasoning: Season roasts only after they have finished cooking, just a few moments before taking them off the spit or removing them from the oven. The reason is that putting salt on raw meat creates moisture that hinders proper browning, thus allowing juices from the inside to escape. In addition, pepper takes on a very unpleasant acrid taste when heated.

Barding the roast: The purpose of barding with fatback bacon is twofold. It provides fat for browning and it insulates the meat from exposure to heat that is too hot or too prolonged.

Fat facilitates the browning. Because it absorbs more heat than the meat, it helps the surface of the meat to support the extreme heat necessary for browning without burning. It is because of this quality that fat is used to baste a roast that has not been barded. Surface larding small roasts with small lardons serves the same purpose. It provides fat on the surface of the meat—not to the inside, where the lardons hardly penetrate, but on the surface, to provide a barrier and hinder the loss of juices.

In much the same way, barding protects the leaner parts of poultry from the high heat needed to roast certain fowl, such as partridge. It also protects poultry, such as turkey or chicken, from drying out when exposed to heat for a long time. Poultry wings and breasts are penetrated rapidly by the heat, while thighs take much longer to cook properly. For this reason, you must completely cover the breast sections with fatback bacon. Smaller birds should be wrapped completely. You will find all necessary directions on this subject in the appropriate chapters.

Large cuts of meat are often surrounded by very thin sheets of beef or pork fat, which serve the same purpose as barding. Some cuts contain more fat than others. Leg of lamb and fatty pork roasts do not require barding. Basting with fat will suffice.

Lean game birds are barded with greased baking or parchment paper.

There is no need to baste something that has been barded.

Basting: A roast must be basted frequently, whether on the spit or in the oven. *You must never use liquid for this basting.* You should use only oil, butter, or a good-quality fresh fat, which has the advantage of burning less easily than butter.

Do not baste with the fat that has fallen into the drip pan or the roasting pan, because it is very difficult to spoon this fat out of the pan without taking along some of the juice that has dripped from the meat. Let us repeat, *any form of liquid* must be excluded from basting at all stages of the roasting process.

Since basting with the pan juices is not possible, as stated directly above, baste the roast as needed with new fat. So, instead of dipping into the roasting pan with a spoon, use a kitchen brush dipped into a cup of fresh, melted fat, and brush the parts of the roast that are exposed to the heat. This procedure requires a relatively small amount of fat.

There is no need to baste or brush once the meat is browned. The fat cannot penetrate to the inside of the flesh. It can only brown the roast further, which would make it too dark.

Oven Roasting

To get a satisfactory result with the oven, it is essential to duplicate, as closely as possible, the conditions of roasting on a spit.

The essential condition is to isolate the meat completely from the fat and juices that fall into the roasting pan. There are special roasting pans that have a separate, raised metal grill, which is placed over the pan. For poultry, there is a very useful pan fitted with a spit. Use an appropriate-sized utensil for the piece you are roasting, making sure in particular that it is *not too large.* If the surface is too large, the juices and the fat will burn too easily. No matter what you do afterward, nothing will remedy the bitter taste of the juices. If you don't have a special roasting pan, use any grill set over a metal pan. The problem with such a grill is that many are too lightweight and deform easily, meaning that the roast is not stable.

Don't use earthenware pans, which will eventually become impregnated with the odor of burned meat or fat. You should only rarely add liquid to the roasting pan. All liquid produces steam, and even when the meat is not in contact with the pan, this steam will tend to soften the browned crust that seals in the flavorsome juices. However, in some cases, you may add one or two tablespoons of water to the pan to wet it down a little and avoid burning at the start of cooking. You can do this up to the time that the fat begins to melt and flow.

The heat of the oven: To be able to determine the necessary temperature requires experience and good judgment. With a visible fire, even a novice quickly learns to roast. In the oven, it's another thing. All ovens do not heat in the same way. It can depend on the draft, the construction of the oven and, above all, whether or not the oven has been preheated properly. Instead of searing in high, all-over heat, the roast will go limp and soften, soaked in its own juice. It's not until the cooking time has been completed that the oven reaches the temperature it should have achieved from the outset.

If, for any reason, the oven is not hot enough *at the moment when you are ready to put in the roast,* it would be better to forget about roasting and to cook the meat on top of the stove in a pot.

We must repeat again that, for any oven roasting, *the oven must be heated well in advance,* so that you need only adjust the heat, not increase it substantially.

The temperature of the oven should be lowered toward the end of cooking if you are roasting a large piece for a long time.

You must know your oven well in order to be able to control it. That is the prerequisite for oven roasting.

Roasting with Gas or Electricity

This kind of roasting gives excellent results when the equipment permits you to cook in the same way as roasting on a spit. In other words, the meat must be surrounded by air, and the heat must come from above or from the side, but never from below. Otherwise the juice that falls into the pan will overheat and burn. Some stoves permit this. However, on most home stoves, the space reserved for grilling is not large enough for a roast.

If you have a conventional oven, only the uppermost heat source should be used and the oven door should be left open during roasting. In this case, the time for roasting should be about the same as on a spit, perhaps a little longer. Generally speaking, it is difficult to estimate the correct time because each range is built differently, which influences its heating characteristics. It is absolutely essential to know your equipment well so you can accurately establish the roasting time of any cut.

Cooking Times

The cooking time is related to the weight of the meat, trimmed and ready for cooking.

Unusual as it may seem at first, relatively more time is needed for cooking a small roast than a large one. We say *relatively* because a small roast needs more time *per 450 grams (1 pound)* than a large one. A larger roast benefits from the heat that accumulates in the interior.

For example, a beef roast weighing just over 1 kilogram (2 pounds, 3 ounces), requires *15–16 minutes* per 450 grams (1 pound) for rare. For a roast weighing 1.8–2 kilograms (4 pounds–4 pounds, 6 ounces), you will need only *10–12 minutes* per 450 grams (1 pound) for rare.

The cooking time is a little longer on the spit than in the oven, since the meat is not completely surrounded by heat. Allow about *2 minutes more* per 450 grams (1 pound).

When you have a red-meat roast that won't be served immediately, you can take the meat out of the hot oven while it is still rare and keep it in a warm oven, or in the warming chamber of your stove. It will continue to cook because of the residual heat inside.

Note that the quality of the meat can influence the cooking time by several minutes overall, and that the times given are for a good-quality oven that produces a steady heat.

Cooking times for roasting different meats, poultry, and game are given in each individual recipe. The time can vary with different parts of the same animal and, in the case of red meat, according to individual preferences.

Correct doneness: A roast that is cooked correctly, will have a firmness to the touch that can only be recognized with a little experience. The roast that is not "done" sufficiently on the inside feels springy to the touch.

The most reliable method is to pierce the meat with a trussing needle. The juice that runs out must be pink, and not red, for red meats. It should be absolutely colorless for white meats.

Pierce poultry where the thigh joins the body. The juice that escapes from the rump when you tilt the bird over a plate must be absolutely colorless.

Pan Juices from the Roast

Since no liquid is added to the roasting pan or drip-pan during the cooking, there is not much left at the end. On a spit, where the drip-pan has heated less, there is a chance of finding some juice. In the oven, the juice that escapes from the meat caramelizes when it hits the pan and then forms a crust, so the only liquid element left is fat. Dissolving this crust with liquid that is added to the roasting pan or drip-pan, called "deglazing" in professional terms, provides gravy for the roast.

Many people use stock as the liquid for this operation, but it should always be water. Water does not interfere with the taste of the pan juices. In fine restaurants, veal stock *(jus)* is employed, because its neutral flavor is not as perceptible as other stocks. This is particularly true for roast game birds. If veal stock is unavailable, let me repeat that water is the only acceptable liquid.

This is only added, of course, after the roast has been taken off the spit or out of the roasting pan and kept in a warm place. First, remove some of the fat from the roasting pan or drip-pan. Add a few tablespoonfuls of warm water and scrape the bottom of the pan to loosen and dissolve the brown crust. Boil for a minute as you scrape. Pour it into a preheated sauce boat and through a strainer as well if the juice contains residues. If the fat left in the juice seems excessive, take out some more. But *do not de-fat completely,* because the fat from a roast retains much of the flavor, and many people greatly appreciate it.

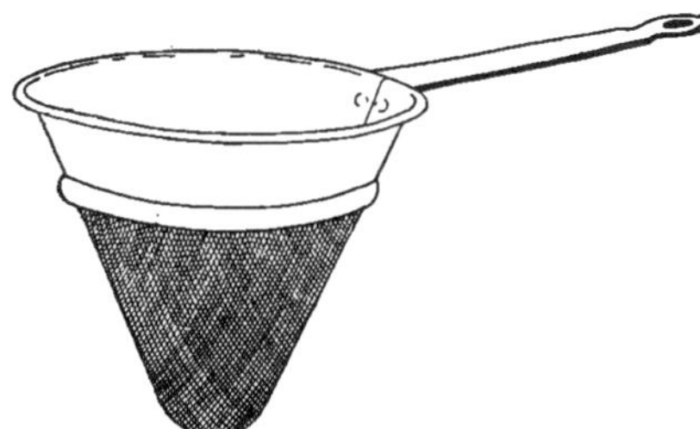

FIG. 19. CONICAL STRAINER CALLED A *CHINOIS.*

Allow about 1 tablespoon of juice per person. Thus for a roast to serve 12–15, you will need at least 2 1/2 deciliters (1 cup), bearing in mind that 1 deciliter (3 1/3 fluid ounces, scant 1/2 cup) measures about 6 tablespoons.

Deglazing: Deglazing, or dissolving, the browned crust in the pan can yield only a moderate quantity of gravy to serve with the roast. Only a small quantity of water can be added. Otherwise, the gravy will be weak and will be more like a broth or greasy water. When you need a larger quantity of gravy to accompany a roast, and you have no veal stock, you should prepare a stock from the bones and trimmings from the same kind of meat as the roast. Use this liquid for deglazing. To make this stock, brown the bones and trimmings with a little fat in a roasting pan, in the oven. Transfer them to a pot. Deglaze the roasting pan with a little warm water and add it to the saucepan with enough warm water to cover the contents. Salt lightly. Bring to a boil. Skim. Simmer for 2 or 3 hours. Strain and degrease.

For game birds, add a glass of cognac to the warm water used to deglaze the roasting pan.

SAUTÉING

Technically, the word *sauté* applies only to foods that are cooked rapidly from beginning to end in a very hot fat—butter, oil, or fat—without the addition of any liquid. That said, the meat does sometimes come into contact with liquid just a few moments before serving; just the time for the food to be infused, *but not cooked,* by the liquid. The principle rule of sautéing is never to allow the food to boil in the sauce. Many dishes of classic French cuisine are prime examples: tournedos, veal scallops, *poulet chasseur, veau Marengo,* and *Parmentier.* These all involve red meats cooked until just pink; white meat cooked but still juicy; and a *very concentrated sauce,* in which deglazing the caramelized juices of the meat on the bottom of the sauté pan plays an important role.

Actually, a sauté is a small roast done in a pan. High heat is used at first to sear the meat, to brown it and prevent the loss of juices, then the heat is immediately lowered for steady cooking. Never use a lid or you will trap the steam. All moisture during cooking will be harmful to the sauté. In short, you must observe all the principles that relate to cooking a roast.

However, there are a few preparations that are called sautés but which are more like stews, because the majority of their cooking time is spent in liquid. But the preliminary browning over high heat and the proper technique are common to both types of sautéing.

The Proper Pan

A utensil known as a "sauté pan" (*fig.* 20), with a wide, thick bottom and low sides, is absolutely essential. The bottom of the pan must be large, because the food that you wish to sauté must be *completely in contact with the bottom of the pan.* The food must be arranged *side by side,* and never stacked, never even one small piece on top of the others. The sides of the sauté pan are low so that the steam can escape rapidly from the food as it cooks. The food must not be swathed in its own steam, it must cook *dry.*

FIG. 20. SAUCEPAN CALLED A *SAUTÉ PAN.*

This is an absolute must. It is the very principle of sautéing. If you do not have a sauté pan, the only thing that could replace it is a frying pan with a very thick bottom. In an ordinary frying pan, the heat of the fire sears the food brutally, so the outside burns and the inside does not cook. That's why you get that violet-colored juice when you cut into a steak sautéed in a frying pan. The meat has not been cooked. If you must use a frying pan, because of circumstances beyond your control, use lower heat than you would for a tin-lined copper pan and keep a close eye on the cooking.

Always use a sauté pan proportional to the number of pieces to sauté. As we have said, they must be placed side by side, but not too close, so they can be moved when you shake the pan, and so their edges do not cook in the steam. Do not use a sauté pan that is too large, in which the objects are too spread out. The juice escaping from the food will caramelize too quickly and burn on the parts of the bottom that are too open. The juice from the deglazing will be too acrid or bitter to use. The juice obtained from the deglazing is an important ingredient in the concentrated sauce of a sauté, especially in home kitchens that do not keep a store of deglazed meat juice on hand.

The Cooking Fat

The fat must be able to withstand a high temperature without burning. According to the dish, and depending on what is available, you can use clarified butter, oil, butter mixed with oil, or good fresh pork fat, fat from a roast, or fat skimmed from the cooking pot.

Clarified butter, as it is called by professional chefs, is simply the *beurre fondu* ("melted butter") of home kitchens. Thoroughly purified by its preliminary cooking, it can reach a much higher temperature without burning than butter in its natural state. You must always use this *melted butter,* or clarified butter, in sautés where butter only is required. Butter in its natural state darkens, burns, and gives the entire dish an unpleasant taste. When clarified butter is not available, use ordinary butter and add enough oil to make it possible to heat the pan to the necessary temperature. Oil can be heated to a very high temperature without burning.

Even though the oil, when it is heated to the proper temperature, does not penetrate to the interior of the food, it is better to use only oils that do not have a distinctive taste. Make sure you use oil that has a neutral taste, and when you use fat that has been obtained by degreasing, never employ lamb fat.

The cooking fat that has been used for sautéing must be drained from the pan *before* adding the liquid needed for the sauce. This is a quick and easy method of degreasing. You may reuse this fat for frying and sautéing.

Whatever type it may be, the cooking fat must always be used in small quantities, because an excess will fry, rather than sauté, the food. You need just enough to cover the bottom of the sauté pan.

PAN GRILLING

The principles of pan grilling are the same as for roasts. One could say that grilling is roasting on a small scale. Just as for roasts, the temperature depends on the required cooking time. The longer it takes to cook, the lower the heat. The foods that need the longest time and the lowest temperatures are white meats and fish.

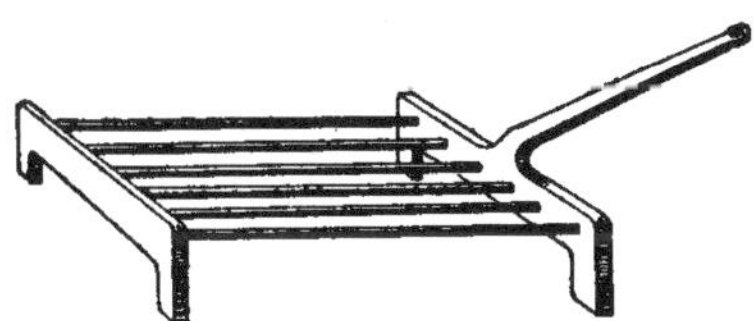

FIG. 21. IRON GRILL WITH ROUND BARS.

For all food to be grilled, cooking time is not measured *by weight,* as for roasts, but *by the thickness* of the piece to be grilled. The heat of the fire must diminish during the course of grilling; otherwise, flare-ups will inevitably occur.

The usual grilling implement—an iron grill with round bars—is now frequently replaced with a thick, heavy iron pan with ridges, resembling a kind of frying pan without sides. It can be used on coal, gas, or electric ranges if they do not have a built-in broiler.

Before you put anything on the grill, and whatever the nature of the fuel, the grill *must be heated for several minutes until it is very hot.* This will prevent the flesh from sticking to the grill, causing it to tear when you turn it. For meats, each tear will allow juices to escape. And for fish, the skin will shred.

Food to Be Grilled

It must always be *brushed with oil or clarified butter first.* Butter in its natural state—in other words, not melted and decanted—will burn. Oil *without a pronounced taste* is best, because it will withstand the highest temperatures without burning.

During cooking, and especially for cuts that must remain on the grill for a long time, basting with cooking oil is vital. Just as for roasts, it prevents the parts on the outside that have browned, or seared, from drying out while the inside continues cooking. For this purpose, keep a spoon for the oil or butter in a dish within easy reach. You may also use a kitchen brush or a large feather.

Do not season the meat before you put it on the grill. The salt melts when it comes in contact with the raw meat and creates moisture, which, in turn, prevents browning and causes the juices to run out just when they should be contained. Pepper burns when cooked, imparting a bitter and unpleasant taste. You should season on the grill just before the end of cooking, or right after turning off the heat, while the meat is still on the grill. When the food is smoking hot, it absorbs the seasoning better.

Red meats have even more specific requirements, explained further on, which do not apply to white meats. The cooking of white meats must be as complete as possible. Always follow the directions and recommendations given in the recipes that apply.

Fuel

The best is incontestably wood charcoal. Even though this is hardly used in modern kitchens, camping aficionados and American-style barbecue enthusiasts will find the following directions applicable to the various devices sold for open-air grilling.

Grilling over wood charcoal: Use medium-size pieces, about the size of a large egg. Break up the larger pieces.

Before forming the bed of glowing coals, you must light it well in advance so that the heat has time to spread out evenly, and to ensure that the flames have died down. Spread the coals out in an even layer 5–7$^1/_2$ centimeters (2–3 inches) thick, depending on your needs. Remember that the bed of coals must be wider than the food you are grilling. Heap the coals up at the edges. If you do not do this, the meat will remain uncooked around the edges even though both sides are perfectly browned.

The thickness of the bed of coals varies according to the size and type of meat being grilled. If you have a very hot fire, the meat should be large. Sometimes so much heat is required that more coals have to be added.

You can control the heat of the fire by sprinkling *hot* ashes on the bed of glowing coals. Do not use cold ashes, which might extinguish the fire.

In order to grill over *low heat* and avoid flare-ups, keep the fire covered with a thin layer of hot ashes.

Grilling on a coal-fired range: The round plates of the stove are removed when you grill. The iron grill is placed directly over the glowing coals.

Be sure the fire is not too hot. *The firebox should be only half full and the coals must be red-hot.* If there are some sections of the coals that are not completely red-hot, it will smoke or flame. Both are unfavorable for grilling, particularly because the odor of the coal will be communicated to the food. As with grilling on charcoal, the heat of the fire can be controlled by sprinkling it with *warm* coals. And don't forget that the heat from a coal fire is stronger than from charcoal.

Grilling with gas or electricity: You will get very good results if the appliance is well made and produces a sufficiently strong heat that can be easily regulated. Without that heat, especially for steaks and chops, the meat will not sear, so it will not be browned and it will taste as if it had been boiled.

Grilling Red Meat

Before putting meat on the grill, you should know how you want it done. Tastes differ substantially in this matter.

Some people will accept only meat that has been cooked very little, *extremely rare.* That is, bloody. Others want it *medium,* which is when the juices run pink. Another wants it *well done,* when no juices run. Most of the times, unless you know the preferences of your guests, cook it *medium.*

The *fire* must be hot enough to *sear* the piece of meat rapidly enough to obtain a rather resistant browned layer, which keeps the juices inside the meat. This juice, compressed inside the flesh, is gradually heated and, exactly as with a roast, the heat of the juice cooks the meat without drying it out—assuming that the cooking is stopped at the right time.

Once the meat is put on the grill, never turn it until the first side is perfectly browned. If you don't observe this primary rule, the meat will lose its juice rapidly, because the heat makes the juices flow. This is why a *rapid* browning is of primary importance when grilling red meats.

Grilling steaks or chops that are no thicker than 2–2$^1/_2$ centimeters ($^3/_4$–1 inch) should take 10–12 minutes, depending on how well-cooked you want them to be. When one side is cooked as desired, turn it and cook the other side for the same time, so that both sides will be equally done and the inside will be cooked evenly. Allow 5–6 minutes per side. You turn it only once.

The same is not true for a thicker steak, like a chateaubriand. Proceed as for a roast. In other words, when each side of the steak has been seared by the heat and is perfectly browned, you must turn it regularly until it is fully cooked. Make sure you coat the steak with melted butter so that it does not brown too much and turn black. As the cooking proceeds, the heat should be moderated accordingly.

Always avoid pricking the meat with a fork when you turn it. Every puncture opens a passage that allows the juices to escape. Turn the meat using 2 forks.

Doneness: You can tell by touching. When you poke the meat with your finger and the flesh seems elastic, it's because the inside is *undercooked.* The meat is very rare. Proper cooking can also be judged by looking. When the juice pearls in pink drops on the surface of the meat, it's *medium.*

Grilling Fish

Here we summarize the full directions that accompany each recipe for the different fish to be grilled.

Choose fish of medium size. Make a few crosswise incisions in the flesh. Flat fish should have an incision along the backbone. They should be dipped in milk, dusted with flour, and dipped in melted butter or a neutral-tasting oil. This forms a very light crust around the fish, which will prevent the flesh from drying out and will produce a golden hue that cannot be obtained without flour. An exception is made in the case of fish with oily flesh; salmon, mackerel, herring, mullet, etc. *Do not flour these fish.* Just dip them in melted butter or oil before you put them on the grill.

Whatever the thickness of the fish, they should be grilled on a moderate fire and brushed frequently with butter or oil as they cook. They are properly cooked when the backbone separates easily from the flesh.

DEEP-FRYING

A modern master of French cuisine, Philéas Gilbert, has justly remarked that only in the French language does one word, *friture,* designate: (1) the fat used; (2) the cooking technique; (3) the food that results. As for the last, we would like to stress that it absolutely must have a golden-blond color, and be dry and crisp.

But the technique itself is difficult to teach only theoretically, and it's not possible to offer a practical, physical demonstration. Frankly, observation and personal experience are the best guides in this case. But they must be rooted in an understanding of the rules and techniques that we are going to explain.

The Deep-Frying Utensil

To succeed in deep-frying, and to avoid potentially serious accidents, you must use a special frying utensil (*fig.* 22) This consists of a pan with slightly flared sides, made of cast iron or thick steel, with two solid handles. There is an oval-shaped pan for frying fish.

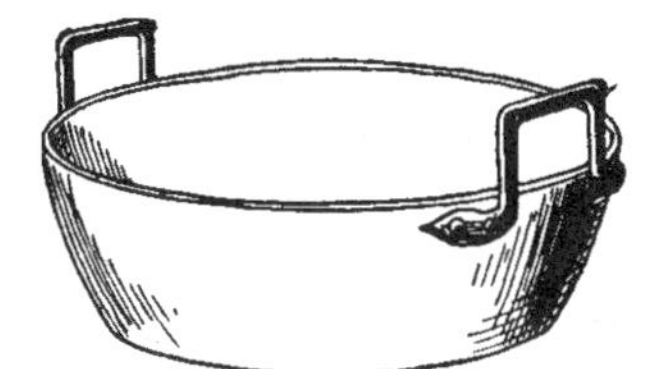

FIG. 22. DEEP-FAT FRYING PAN.

FIG. 23. DEEP-FAT FRYING BASKET.

This pan must be *deep,* for two reasons. First, because anything cooked by deep-frying must be plunged into a veritable bath of hot fat, and be completely submerged, without touching the bottom of the pan. Second, because the deep-frying pan must never be more than half full of hot fat. This is so that when the utensil is over the heat and the food is added and makes the level of fat rise, the hot fat does not overflow and catch fire. Only this special utensil will meet both conditions.

These two reasons also mean that an omelet pan is as useless as it is dangerous for deep-frying. Its long handle adds to the risk of accident, unsuitable as it is for handling a utensil full of burning hot fat. I want to make it clear that in every recipe requiring deep-fat frying, the use of this special utensil is required.

FIG. 24. DEEP-FRY SKIMMER.

Different Fats for Deep-Frying

The best is the kind that is used up least rapidly and can be heated often without losing its quality and going rancid. And, it must be capable of producing a coating with the qualities mentioned above.

Fat from beef kidneys: Without doubt, it is this fat that yields the best results in deep-frying. It can withstand a high temperature without burning better than any other animal fat, and the food that is fried in it remains crisp longer.

This is what we recommend, but we suggest adding some *veal fat,* which is finer but not stable enough to be used alone. Allow 1 kilogram (2 pounds, 3 ounces) of veal fat for each 2 kilograms (4 pounds, 6 ounces) of fat from around the beef kidneys. It is this *mixture* and these *quantities* that we expect to be used in most of the recipes. However, it is useful to consider other fats.

Clarified butter *(beurre fondu):* Reasons of economy aside, this must never be used for deep-fat frying. In most cases, it cannot sustain the elevated temperatures needed without burning. You should only use it for *small, low-temperature frying* for specific things, such as croutons, flat fish, etc. And it must be fresh and of very good quality. When it is not top quality, the resulting dish will be inedible. Butter gives a beautifully colored crust. It foams and runs over if it has not been well clarified.

Lard or melted pork fat: This produces a very fine color, but also a crust that is laden with fat and which dries with difficulty. It is used up rapidly, and tends to go bad very quickly. It should never be used alone. You can add it to the beef kidney fat and veal fat mixture recommended above. Use 1 kilogram (2 pounds, 3 ounces) of lard for each 2 kilograms (4 pounds, 6 ounces) of beef kidney fat and 450 grams (1 pound) of veal fat. It will foam and overflow if it has not been completely purified.

Fat leftover from cooking: Fat from stews and roasts can be used for reasons of economy. Their correct usage depends on where they come from and the care taken to purify them. The fat taken from a stew where one has boiled a large piece of beef can be used. In general, however, we do not recommend these fats for delicate frying. They always retain an aftertaste from the liquids where they were found if they are not meticulously purified by re-cooking. Fat from roasts, for the most part, is too darkened by cooking. It used to be that there were more opportunities for using it because the fat dripping from the spit was not overheated like the fat from today's oven roasts.

Lamb and mutton fat: Don't use it. The fat that comes from the older animal gives a taste of tallow to the frying, which gets stronger and stronger. The fat that comes from the younger animal foams and creates a risk of serious accidents because it spills onto the stove.

Olive oil: This is not reserved solely for frying fish. It is used for everything, especially in the South of France. It gives a glossy, lightly colored crust and can support much higher temperatures without burning than beef fat. If it has not been well purified, it foams and overflows.

Vegetable oils: There are many commercially available varieties. Their origins vary; they are derived from coconut, various grains, cotton, corn, etc. Their advantage is that they support very high temperatures, they have almost no taste, and they do not spoil easily. Unfortunately, they foam a great deal, even after repeated use, which should serve to purify them. This creates a risk of accident. These oils yield a dry, crisp crust that is colorless.

Preparation of Fat for Deep-Frying

Hot fat that has not been previously purified by adequate preparation will foam when the object to be fried is immersed. This happens with all fats, no matter what kind. Foaming and the risk of overflowing is not the only problem with insufficiently prepared frying fats. When they have not been sufficiently prepared by repeated heating, they will easily penetrate the objects that are immersed. These foods become laden with fat, taste unpleasant, and are difficult to digest.

Oil, for example, foams heavily, not having been previously heated, as is the case with animal fats. This serious inconvenience diminishes and disappears once the oil has been used two or three times, simply because the oil is purified by being heated. It should be an absolute rule that you never fry anything in any vegetable oil, until you have heated it *alone* for a half hour.

Rendering and cooking animal fat: From what has just been said, it should be clear that animal fat destined for deep-fat frying must not just be rendered. It must be completely and thoroughly cooked to ensure its purification.

Any animal fat intended for deep-fat frying must first be cut into very small, thin pieces about 1–2 centimeters (3/8–3/4 inches) long, practically chopped. Put the pieces in a large cast-iron pot or in the deep-fat frying utensil. Avoid, if possible, pots that have been lined with tin, since this process will darken the lining. Add a *scant deciliter (3 1/3 fluid ounces, scant 1/2 cup) of cold water per 450 grams (1 pound) of uncooked fat.* The steam coming from the water helps to melt the fat. Cover the utensil. Put it off to one side of the range or set it over low heat on a conventional stove.

As long as the water has not evaporated and there is still moisture in the fat, it will only liquefy. When all the moisture is gone, the real cooking that leads to the purification of the fat begins. While it is melting, use a skimmer or a large fork, and stir to separate all the little pieces that stick together as the fat melts.

You know the fat is cooked and thoroughly purified when only the rind remains unmelted and has turned into crisp little bits, thoroughly browned. When you skim these bits from the surface, the fat must be clear. The steam that rises will also give off a discernible odor.

Take the utensil off the stove so it loses some of its heat, but don't let it cool. The fat and bits of rind must remain very hot. If not, you will be unable to squeeze out the fat from them.

Spread out a *new* dish towel—so it can with stand tight twisting—over the bottom of a pot, making sure the towel extends over the sides of the pot. Pour in the melted fat and the residue. You will need the help of another person for this job. Each one takes a side of the towel and rolls it up, twisting toward the left in order to enclose the residues. As you continue to twist the towel firmly, you will see the fat drip from the towel. Don't let the bits of residue ball up in the middle. They should be spread out to make extracting the fat easier. You may need to do this more than once; in other words, unroll the towel, open it, divide and spread out the residues, then repeat the process. The bits of residue left after this process are not good for anything and should be discarded. Finally, when the fat has cooled some, pour it into its container.

Care of the cooking fat: The fat must not be left on the stove where it will be exhausted by constant heating. You can heat it gently, only to *melt it* in advance, if this helps with the preparation schedule; but it must be heated over high heat for frying, and only when necessary for its immediate use.

You should always take the pot from the heat before removing the food that has fried, so the fat does not burn. At that moment, when the food has completely cooked, it burns easily because the food no longer moderates the heat of the fat, as it did while cooking.

Each time you use the cooking fat, it should be strained through a cloth or a fine-meshed metallic sieve. This essential procedure will strain out the bits that have detached from the food you have fried. These residues, even if they are only bits of flour, will not only stick to the next food that you fry, and look terrible, but they will also encourage the fat to burn. It will then be useless. Keep the bottom of the utensil where you store the fat scrupulously clean. From time to time, when the fat is being used in the fryer, take advantage of this and clean and dry it well before refilling with fat.

Any fat is preserved by keeping out air and moisture. Nonporous containers are best. Do not use earthenware. The best container will be made from tin-lined steel with an airtight lid. These can be found in specialty shops and are called *pots de friture* (frying-fat pots).

Maintain the *supply of fat* by adding fresh fat as needed. This is called "refreshing" the fat. This new fat compensates for the gradually diminishing quantity of the fat, and it also slows down the gradual darkening. You can render a quantity of fat larger than your immediate needs and keep it on hand to "refresh" the frying fat as required.

When the fat has been used over a long time and has become too dark, it can be used to *fry fish,* until it is finally exhausted.

The utensil for deep-fat frying *must be kept scrupulously clean on the inside as well as the outside.* Residue on the outside could catch fire and cause the fat in the pot to catch fire.

Various Degrees of Deep-Frying

Deep-frying takes place at temperatures that are more, or less, hot, depending on the food to be fried. There are three different degrees of deep-frying, which can be recognized by the following indications:

1. *Moderately hot deep-frying:* A piece of bread the size of a hazelnut, thrown in the fat, is immediately surrounded by a light fluttering. If the fat does not sizzle around the bread, it is not hot enough to "sear" the food.

   This is the heat to use when beginning to cook certain raw foods, such as potatoes, medium-sized fish, certain pastries, etc. These must be completed at the "hot" temperature.

2. *Hot deep-frying:* The bread, put in as above, is surrounded by a well-defined bubbling. Furthermore, a very slight smoke rises off the fat. It's really more steam, because it can only be seen. It has no odor. This temperature is used for foods that have already been cooked and which require only a browned crust, such as croquettes, or for foods dipped in frying batter.

3. *Very hot deep-frying:* You don't need bread to recognize this temperature, because the fat gives off smoke with a distinct odor, indicating that the fat has reached the ultimate degree of heat. You must not increase the heat, because the fat will burn quickly and might even catch fire.

This temperature is used for small objects, for very small fish that are cooked and browned rapidly at the same time.

NOTE. When the volume of frying fat is less than required for what you wish to fry and you can't divide the food and fry in smaller quantities, as in the case of a whole fish, or if the food is very cold, remember to allow time, after adding the food, for the fat to return to the correct temperature. In this case, you should heat the fat to a higher temperature before submerging the food, so that it will immediately reach the proper temperature when cooking begins.

The quantity of frying fat: This must always be proportional to the quantity or volume of objects immersed, which, as previously discussed, must always be completely covered.

A greater quantity of fat in proportion to the objects immersed will diminish the loss of heat that occurs when the food is introduced. The food itself is cool and it gives off moisture, which lowers the temperature of the fat, like pouring cold water into a container of hot water. The more fat in the kettle, the better its ability to maintain the required temperature.

It is also wrong to overcrowd the kettle, because the cooling of the fat is even more severe, and the fat will not be hot enough to "sear" the food that has been immersed. The resulting food will be soggy and unattractive. This result is inevitable unless the heat is high enough to raise the temperature of the fat back up to the required point in just a *few seconds.*

When there are too many objects to be properly seared at once, fry them in two or more batches.

If the fat has lost heat from too many objects, it's best to take them out at once. Return the pot to a very high heat. Then, return the food *separately* for 2 minutes to color and crisp them.

Deep-Frying Fish

The first thing to say is that fat which has been used to fry fish must not be used for other foods because it retains the taste of the fish. You must store it in its own container.

The following summarizes the directions given in the different recipes for deep-fried fish.

If the fish are thick, make an incision on both sides. Whatever type of fish, before you immerse them in the hot fat, dip them in a plate of milk and roll them in flour that has been generously sprinkled on a towel or large sheet of paper towel. Shake them gently by the tail to get rid of the excess of flour that has built up in layers.

Generally speaking, you deep-fry only small or medium fish, or relatively thin slices. Cooking larger fish requires too long a time in the hot fat, where even a moderate temperature must be high enough so that the fat does not penetrate the immersed food. At any rate, the interior of large fish or thick slices will not cook sufficiently, while the exterior will be much too browned.

The heat of the frying fat depends on the size of the fish. *The thicker the fish, the lower the temperature of the fat.* Thicker fish must stay in the fat longer in order to cook through. If the fish browns too fast on the outside, the browning forms a shell, which prevents the heat from penetrating the inside of the flesh. The result will be a fish that is practically burned on the outside while the flesh around the bones remains bloody.

Medium-sized whiting, and fish of a similar size, must first cook in *fat of moderate heat,* and you then increase the temperature to *hot* to thoroughly color and dry the fish.

That's the theory. But practice depends on numerous things that you will have to learn on your own.

For example, if you need to fry a single whiting in a quantity of fat where you could easily fry three, heat the fat to *moderate.* Putting one lone fish into the pot will not cool the fat very much at all, so it will cook at *moderate heat* until you turn the heat up to finish. But, if you have three fish to fry in just enough fat for the job, heat the fat to *hot.* Putting in the three fish will immediately cool the fat and lower the temperature to *moderate,* the correct cooking temperature. Be sure to maintain this temperature until just before the end, then quickly bring the fat to *hot* to finish.

For *3 medium whitings,* deep-fried in about 2 kilograms (4 pounds, 6 ounces) of fat, allow *6–8 minutes of cooking* of which 3–4 minutes should be at a *moderate rather than hot* temperature.

Sole, flat fish, and other fish filets must be cooked at a *higher temperature* than thick fish. A sole weighing less than 350 grams (12 1/3 ounces), breaded filets, etc., must be cooked at *hot.* When the fat is at the proper temperature, moderate the heat source and put in the fish. Maintain the same temperature to the end. If the fat cools, the fish will be limp and greasy. If the fat is too hot, the outside of the fish will be too dark and the inside badly cooked. Cook for *8–10 minutes,* depending on the strength of the heat, without raising or lowering the temperature of the fat except for the change caused by putting in the fish. This assumes, of course, that you have a quantity of fat sufficient for the amount of fish.

The smaller the fish, the hotter the deep-frying fat. Very small fish are immersed in *very hot fat.* This elevated temperature must be restored immediately after the fish are added and maintained throughout the cooking; about *4–5 minutes* of deep-frying. The interior cooking and exterior browning will occur simultaneously.

Deep-Frying Croquettes, Fritters, Etc.

Let us finally examine deep-frying for croquettes, fruit and vegetable fritters, and all things covered with bread crumbs or frying batter.

The mixtures making up croquettes and fritters are already cooked and need only to be reheated. The formation of the crust and their reheating are accomplished at the same time. For fritters of raw fruit, apples, etc., the inside is quite quickly cooked and will be ready at the same time as the envelope of batter.

Here it's a matter of immediately *seizing* the layer of bread crumbs or batter in order to solidify it. The formation of the crust must be instantaneous. This crust must form a barrier to retain the substances within the croquette or fritter. Browning will be gradual.

If the items covered with *bread crumbs* are put into a deep-frying fat that is not hot enough, the coating of bread crumbs will soak up the fat and the crust will be soggy and difficult to digest. Furthermore, this greasy crust will be weak. It will crack open and allow what it should retain to escape into the frying fat, at the same time allowing the fat to flow in. The same is true for food covered with batter. If the fat is not hot enough at the moment when the food is introduced, the batter will disintegrate in the fat, leaving its contents unprotected.

Since the food to be fried must be immediately seared, it is better, in this case, to exceed the degree of heat indicated than to fall short. Heat the fat to *hot.* Lower the heat. As soon as the last piece of food has been immersed, return the heat to high to restore the same level of heat as before the immersion; *3–5 minutes* will be enough, depending on the particular case.

Avoid the use of the skimmer at the outset because it could damage the coating of batter or bread crumbs, which has not yet sufficiently solidified. You should use the skimmer only when the heat has caused the coating to transform into a stable crust. To shift fritters or croquettes in the frying fat, you need only gently slide the frying utensil around on the burner, keeping it flat, using the handle. The skimmer, in this case, is used only to remove the objects from the hot fat if you do not have a basket to remove them.

THE DOUBLE BOILER
Le Bain-Marie

This method of cooking is used for preparations that must not be exposed to direct heat. The utensil that contains them is placed in water kept just under the boiling point. The water must never boil rapidly. That's the theoretical definition.

For the practical execution, we will analyze cooking a dessert pudding or some kind of bread in a Charlotte mold. Having filled the mold with batter, put it in a deep saucepan just large enough to leave a space of 2 centimeters (3/4 inch) between the sides of the mold and the sides of the saucepan.

Keep your water boiling on the stove, preferably in a kettle with a spout. If not, you may use a funnel. Pour the boiling water into the saucepan so it reaches 2 centimeters (3/4 inch) below the top of the mold.

Put the saucepan in the oven. Cover immediately with a lid large enough to extend over everything. The mold should not be covered with its own lid, so that the steam from the boiling water will circulate under the larger cover, thereby preventing the formation of a crust on the surface of the preparation. If a crust is formed too early, it will impede the penetration of the heat coming from above.

From the moment the saucepan is in the oven to the instant when it is removed, the water must be maintained at the same temperature. As we have said, this should be as hot as possible without ever reaching a boil. This temperature will be indicated by an almost imperceptible rippling at some place in the liquid. Raise the lid from time to time to check the regularity of this light ripple in the water. If you perceive a tendency to boil, remove a few tablespoons of water from the pot and replace them with an equal quantity of cold water.

THE *BLANC*

This is a kind of court bouillon that is used for cooking meat and certain vegetables, and which includes flour and fat. These last ingredients serve only to preserve the whiteness of the food that is cooked in the *blanc*. They do not add any flavor. The fat, which spreads out over the surface of the liquid, acts as insulation. Should any ingredients rise to the surface during cooking, it keeps them from contact with the air. This skin of fat protects the cooking food most effectively when the boiling is maintained at a slow pace. The water boils beneath the fat without dislodging it. This is the best of lids.

The quantity of flour and aromatics is proportional to the amount of liquid. For meat, these aromatics often include bouquet garni, onion, and carrot. In this case, they will be listed in the recipe calling for a *blanc*. Below is a list of the most general formulae for all uses. Sometimes the vinegar is replaced by lemon juice. What does not change is the proportion of fat. Except in cases where you use a particularly large pot, the proportions remain the same whether you are using two quarts or three.

A *blanc* cannot be used more than once, like a court bouillon used for cooking fish. The flour will ferment. But you can reuse the fat, and you should recover it when it has congealed on the chilled liquid.

Quantities and preparation of the *blanc*: 30 grams (1 ounce) of flour; 2 liters (8 1/2 cups) of water; 15 grams (1/2 ounce) of salt; 3 tablespoons of vinegar; a bouquet garni; 3 good tablespoons of clarified fat, or 75–100 grams (2 2/3–3 1/2 ounces) of beef kidney fat, chopped fine.

In a deep, thick-bottomed pot, dissolve the flour gradually in a little cold water, avoiding lumps. Add the rest of the water, the salt, and the vinegar. Bring to a boil, *stirring constantly* with a whisk or wooden spoon to prevent the flour from settling on the bottom of the pot and sticking, which would require you to start over.

Cooking: Once the *blanc* is boiling, add the ingredients to be cooked. Add the bouquet garni and finally the fat. Lower the heat. Cover partially. *From this moment,* you must be sure that the boil is maintained gently and without stopping. This boiling is barely visible, because it takes place beneath the layer of fat that is spread out on top of the liquid.

Time the cooking, which varies according to the ingredients, from the moment when the gentle boiling is established.

JUS AND SAUCES

[Translator's note: The French word "jus" does not have an exact English equivalent. Jus is the extremely reduced liquid derived from cooking juices, a necessary ingredient in many dishes.]

JUS FOR SAUCES AND ASPICS
Jus pour Sauces et Gelées

Jus ranks very high among essential basic cooking ingredients and its importance must not be underestimated. In households, a major issue is the inherent cost and trouble in making jus, and many cooks finally end up substituting bouillon. They do not realize that the best bouillon cannot, in the majority of cases, equal the most simple jus, because it lacks the gelatinous elements inherent in the veal, veal bones, and pork rind.

Households often do not have any idea of the value that the great chefs put on butcher scraps, carcasses of fowl, trimmings, bones from roasts and braised meats (mutton excepted), ends of pork rind, etc. These things, if they are fresh, should all have a place in the stockpot and not take the road to the trash can.

FIG. 25. SMALL SAUCE WHISK.

In a small household, with a normal consumption of meat twice a day, a veal knuckle and a few pork rinds that you already have should be enough to obtain an acceptable jus. Even if you have nothing suitable on hand, and you purchase all the ingredients for the jus, remember that the meats and vegetables that are used in the preparation can be used again for stuffing or meatloaf mixtures.

The ingredients of a jus, like its preparation, vary according to its intended use, whether it is destined for brown or white sauce, braised beef or chicken, or the preparation of an aspic. In all cases, the meats used must be without fat. So, when you do not have peelings or scraps to use, buy meat specifically to make a jus, using the lean parts of the lesser cuts: shank from beef and veal knuckle.

The importance of bones in the jus is much greater than for a simple bouillon or pot-au-feu because of the gelatin they contain. The very first step when preparing a jus is to break the bones into small pieces the size of a walnut; that way, they most effectively render the necessary elements for the jus. These elements can only be extracted after long cooking, longer than the cooking time for the jus. (Allow 10–12 hours cooking for complete extraction.) If you are working in large quantities, it is best to use the technique employed in professional kitchens, which consists of preparing a bouillon with the bones only, to be later combined with the rest of the jus ingredients. We will explain that technique in the chapter on pot-au-feu.

When using pork rind, it must be absolutely fresh. Be sure there is no fat attached because it is required solely to render its gelatinous qualities.

As far as *aromatics* are concerned, use *thyme and bay,* but cautiously because bay especially has a very strong flavor that must never be obvious in the final dish.

In the following recipes, we are careful to specify the *quantity of salt.* This must always be kept minimal given that the jus is reduced, first during the initial cooking, and next during the cooking of the sauce or the dish in which it is used. For this reason, it is best not to salt at all in the beginning, but to add the salt at the last moment, in the right proportion.

Regarding *the utensil for cooking the jus,* good thick aluminum could be used if you don't have tin-lined copper, which is rarely used in home cooking now. Never use cast iron, which frequently gives the jus an unattractive tint. Choose a utensil that is deep rather than wide, so that there is not a large surface to encourage evaporation; it should be just large enough to hold its contents comfortably, so that the liquid almost comes up to the top. A depth of 1½ centimeters (⅝ inch) beneath the sides is good, *to make skimming easier,* which is of particular importance here, since it contributes to the clarity of the jus.

A gentle and steady boil, from the beginning to the end of cooking is essential, not only to assure the clarity of the jus, but also to facilitate the extraction of the various ingredients and to ensure the slow and gradual reduction of the liquid. If the boiling were to stop, it must be started again slowly, with the same precautions as for the pot-au-feu. A gas burner is the best way to maintain the desired steady boil without constant surveillance once you have accurately regulated the heat.

Generally speaking, you can expect *for the amount of liquid added* that it will reduce by one-third. If the cooking time is less than 3 hours, the reduction will obviously be less, and the quantity of liquid added must be slightly diminished.

It is always best to *prepare the jus the night before* the day that it must be used. This makes degreasing it easier and also gives you time for a more attentive preparation.

Do not cover a jus made in advance before it has cooled completely, because that could cause it to turn sour faster. *To keep the jus* for 2–3 days, in the summer, when it has not been refrigerated, you must boil it every day for at least 5 minutes, then strain it through a fine, clean cloth stretched out over a bowl. This bowl must also be washed and dried before pouring in the jus. The cloth retains the particles that sink to the bottom of the bowl, which are also the agents of fermentation.

Basic Jus *(Jus Ordinaire)*

This is made with an equal proportion of beef and veal, either scraps and trimmings, or, as mentioned above, beef shank cut into pieces and veal knuckle cut into short pieces. *Time: 5 hours. Makes 1 liter (4¼ cups) of jus ready for use—in other words, the amount after reduction.*

750 grams (1 pound, 10 ounces) total meat, weighed with bones; 500 grams (1 pound, 2 ounces) of bones; approximately 60 grams (2¼ ounces) of pork rind; 60–75 grams (2¼–2⅔ ounces of the orange part of the carrot, and the same amount of onion; a bouquet garni made from parsley sprigs (10 grams/⅓ ounce), the same of celery; a very small sprig of thyme; a fingernail size piece of bay leaf; 1½ liters (6⅓ cups) of water; 6 grams (about ⅕ ounce) of salt.

PROCEDURE. Line the bottom of the pot with the rind, fat side down. On top, arrange a layer of onions and carrots cut into rounds a good ½ centimeter (3/16 inch) thick. If the carrot has gone yellow down the middle, cut it out by trimming lengthwise with a good knife. Place the bones, the bouquet garni, and the meat on top of these vegetables. Cover.

"Sweat" the contents over low heat for about 20 minutes, without disturbing anything in the pot. As with braised dishes done in the classic style, it's a matter of coaxing out the juices from the meats and vegetables and letting them caramelize. It should brown only slightly (SEE BRAISING WHITE MEATS, PAGE 28). Add half a glass of warm water and let it reduce by this amount. By now, the meat should be cooked and appear to be "sweating."

Add the 1½ liters (6⅓ cups) *warm* water. Salt. If you have some carcasses or scraps of cooked poultry, add them now. Boil over high heat. Skim with a metal spoon. Cover the pot and leave a small opening for the steam. Reduce the heat to low, just enough to maintain a gentle and steady simmer, *for 4–5 hours.*

Strain the jus. Let cool at room temperature, uncovered.

Simplified procedure for home kitchens: Cut the meat into small pieces. Cut the carrots and onions into large cubes. In a pot, melt 30–40 grams (1–1⅜ ounces) of rendered lard or the same quantity of ordinary lard. Add the meat and vegetables. Brown lightly over high heat, mixing with a wooden spoon, so that they all color evenly, but do not allow them to brown.

Add the water, *hot,* only 1¼ liters (5⅓ cups), since the cooking time here is shortened. Add the bouquet garni and salt. Partly cover with the lid.

Adjust the boiling as directed above. Continue *for 3 hours.* Strain the jus as above.

Basic Uncolored Jus for White Preparations

The preparation is the same as for pot-au-feu, to which you should refer for details and cooking directions. In a deep pot, assemble all the elements as for the basic colored jus, above. Pour in the cold water, add salt, bring to a boil, skim, etc. Same cooking time.

Veal Jus *(Jus de Veau)*

Here you use, depending on availability, trimmings and scraps of lean bits of veal, or knuckle cut into rounds. You can also add trimmings of cooked or raw poultry. *Time: 5 hours. Makes 1 liter (4 1/4 cups) of jus ready to use.*

600 grams (1 pound, 5 ounces) of veal, boneless; 125 grams (4 1/2 ounces) of veal bones; a calf's foot, if possible; 100 grams (3 1/2 ounces) of carrot; 80 grams (2 3/4 ounces) of onion; a bouquet composed of the white part of a small leek, 2 stalks of parsley, a sprig of thyme, a bit of celery, a thumbnail-size piece of bay leaf; 1 1/2 liters (6 1/3 cups) of water; 6 grams (about 1/5 ounce) of salt.

PROCEDURE. It's the same as for basic jus (PAGE 44). If you want the jus to be slightly colored, let it brown lightly or let it "sweat" for 20 minutes or so, and add the liquid immediately thereafter.

The simplified procedure is the same as for standard jus.

White Veal Jus (Jus de Veau Blanc)

Same procedure as for standard uncolored jus.

CLARIFIED MEAT ASPIC
Gelée de Viande

Essentially, the ingredients and preparation of clarified aspic are those of a basic jus, to which one adds a veal foot to obtain the gelatin. The preparation is finished by the clarification of the jus, to obtain the characteristic sheen.

A jus intended for aspic must always be prepared well in advance, since it has to cook for a long time. Furthermore, the degreasing is much easier once it has cooled. It is of prime importance that the jus for aspic is completely degreased. And it is also vital to note the texture of the cooled jus, which will allow you to judge the final consistency and decide if it needs reinforcing with some *commercial gelatin,* depending on how you intend to use it. Normally, in this case, you would use 4–5 sheets gelatin for each liter (4 1/4 cups) of aspic. But it is always best to avoid this whenever possible. Natural gelatin is far more refined and has a better texture and a cleaner, more delicate flavor.

As for clarifying, it is also best to do this one day in advance because it takes a rather long time for the jelly to cool repeatedly and to then set. This is quite different from commercial gelatin, which melts completely when barely heated and rapidly regains its consistency, even without ice, just by being in a cool place.

Depending on the dish in which it will be used, and the amount of coloration desired, you "sweat" the meats and vegetables before adding the liquid. When you "sweat," you should always be careful not to brown, thus deepening the color. The indication of a well-made aspic is that it always completely reveals the food it covers. For this reason, it must not go beyond a light amber tint.

In recipes that call for aspic, we generally give the quantities of the required ingredients. These quantities can vary a little, depending on the occasion. The following recipe should be suitable for most uses.

We give quantities for 1 liter (4 1/4 cups) of aspic. But it's always better to work with larger quantities, since the trouble and effort are the same—2 liters (8 1/2 cups), for example.

For any aspic, allow for the liquid to reduce by one third, given the necessary cooking time.

A warning to more inexperienced cooks: An aspic that is cooled is not one that is necessarily set. Solidification happens only after a rather long period, or at very low temperatures. Without using ice, it takes a rather long time.

Some formulas for aspic, including those that may be in our recipes, call for the use of raw chopped beef to be added to the ingredients for clarification. The aim of this addition is to add depth of flavor, as well as to aid in the clarification, because the beef contains albumin. This meat must be chopped as fine as possible. It is added to the pot at the same time as the other ingredients, such as egg white, wine, herbs, etc.

Clarification of the aspic: *Degrease the jus extremely thoroughly.* If the jus has been completely cooled, this is quite easy. If you clarify the jus immediately after cooking, you must let it rest for a few moments so that the fat floats to the surface and can then be removed with a spoon as completely as possible. Lay a few sheets of paper towel on the surface of the jus, which will absorb the remaining fat.

In a deep, thick-bottomed pot, whisk the egg white. Add the broken eggshells, white wine, tarragon, chervil, and pepper. Pour in the jus. *Add it all at once, if it is cold,* taking care not to add the sediment that forms at the bottom of the bowl as it cools. *If it is still warm,* add it in several batches, whisking all the while, so that the egg white does not set. If the white cooks at this point, it will serve no further function, because clarification occurs gradually as the white hardens while cooking. *If extra gelatin seems necessary,* now is the moment to add it (SEE USING GELATIN, PAGE 18).

Put the pot over low heat, so that it comes slowly to a boil. *Whisk it continuously* until it achieves a full boil. This is essential for incorporating the egg white, launching the molecules into the mixture, as well as preventing the white from sticking to the bottom of the pot, where it could burn, thus spoiling the aspic irreparably with its odor.

Lower the heat so the liquid only simmers, and leave for *about 12–15 minutes.* Do not cover. At the end of this time, pull aside the white layer that has accumulated on the surface. The liquid underneath should appear quite clear. Now taste the aspic, in case you need to increase the salt.

Straining the aspic: Use a fine, tightly woven napkin that is completely clean and free of all odor. Wet it with cool water, and wring it out thoroughly. Now spread it out so that you can pour in the juice.

In professional kitchens, they use a tall stool that is turned upside down. They attach the four corners of the cloth to the four legs of the stool. Underneath, on the bottom of the seat, they put a bowl. If you don't have a tall stool, you can reverse a chair on the edge of a table, tie the napkin onto the four legs and slide the bowl underneath. Or, especially for relatively small quantities, like those here, proceed

FIG. 26. TO PASS THE JUICE.

as follows: Spread the napkin over any receptacle, salad bowl, soup bowl, mixing bowl, etc. Very gently pour in the entire contents of the pot. Gather the corners of the cloth and tie them with a string, so that you form a kind of loose purse. Suspend it over the edge of a table or work surface and secure it with a weight over a bowl placed on a chair in the normal position. Let it strain without pressure, without touching the cloth.

If the first batch is not very clear, remove the bowl containing the aspic and slide another in its place. Then open the napkin, leaving everything inside to act as a filter, and pour in the aspic and let it strain as before. If necessary, you can strain the aspic a third time.

Adding Madeira or other wine: If adding Madeira, this is the moment to add it, after the final straining. As for sauces, the wine must not be subjected to any boiling, which will spoil its aroma. The quantity of Madeira, port, or other wines of this kind is 1 deciliter (3 1/3 fluid ounces, scant 1/2 cup) for each liter (4 1/4 cups) of aspic. Increase this for wines that are less strong.

Allow in advance for a less firm texture because of this last addition of liquid. In order to maintain the desired solidity, you should increase somewhat the quantity of veal foot when making the jus.

Basic Aspic *(Gelée Simple)*

It is called basic because its preparation is as economical as possible. *Time: About 6 hours total. Makes 1 liter (4 1/4 cups) of aspic ready to use.*

500 grams (1 pound, 2 ounces) of veal knuckle cut into rounds, or very lean trimmings; 300–400 grams

(10½–14⅛ ounces) of beef shank; 125 grams (4½ ounces) of marrow bones broken into small pieces; a small calves' foot; 60 grams (2¼ ounces) of pork rind; 100 grams (3½ ounces) of carrots; 125 grams (4½ ounces) of onion; a bouquet garni composed of a small leek, 2–3 sprigs of parsley, a quarter of a stalk of celery, a small piece of thyme and bay; 1½ liters (6⅓ cups) of water; 6 grams (about ⅕ ounce) of salt.

***To clarify:* One egg white; 1 deciliter (3⅓ fluid ounces, scant ½ cup) of good white wine; 3–4 leaves of tarragon; pinch of chervil; 2–3 peppercorns.**

PROCEDURE. Refer to the section on "jus" for the choice of pots and the way of arranging the different ingredients inside the pot. There is no need to blanch the calves' foot. Bone it, tie it, and add its bones to the other bones.

If the aspic is to remain white: Immediately add cold water, then salt, and bring to a boil.

If the aspic is to be colored: "Sweat" the meat and vegetables for *about 20 minutes,* proceeding as directed for veal jus. Then add water and salt. Bring to a boil.

In both instances, carefully remove the foam. If necessary, slow the boil by adding a few spoonfuls of cold water from time to time. This ensures that the skimming, which is the first part of the clarification process, will be as complete as possible. Cook over low heat so that the liquid only simmers, at an uninterrupted and even pace. A forceful boil will not only reduce the liquid too much but will also cloud the jus. Let it cook thus for about *4½–5 hours.* Transfer the jus to a bowl.

THICKENING SAUCES
Liaisons

Thickening with Roux

The purpose of a roux and how to make it is little understood and poorly done in most home kitchens. Many a flaw has been attributed to them, even though the roux themselves are quite innocent. They should be better understood.

An indigestible roux is one that has been badly made. Undercooked flour or overheated fat are the usual suspects. And these heavy and greasy elements of the roux, all the more noxious because of their bad preparation, are often not remedied because the necessity of "skimming," or purifying, the sauce is unfamiliar to most people who are in charge of cooking. A very conscientious degreasing just before serving might, to some degree, tone down these annoying effects. Often, however, this does not work because the sauce will be too thick and cloudy, precisely because of the badly cooked roux.

What is a roux? Roux is flour cooked *very gently* in butter or fat until it has colored to a greater or lesser extent.

The deepest color must never go beyond a light hazelnut. That is the color of *brown roux.* This brown roux formerly was designated by Carême as a *"roux blond,"* which better describes this light tint, which is comparable to that of café au lait.

The color of *roux blond* is that of melted butter cooked with flour: a light straw yellow, no more. Formerly, this roux blond was known as *roux blanc* (white roux).

The term *roux blanc* now refers to a rapid mixture of butter and flour that is heated for 1–2 minutes just to take away the taste of raw flour.

It is not always necessary to use butter for *brown roux,* when the sauce featuring it has to exclude any fat. That would be a great waste of butter. For *white sauces,* only butter should be used, because both the cooking and skimming are more rapid, and the butter for the roux receives less heat.

The *flour* used must always be of an excellent quality and quite dry.

The *quantity* of butter and the flour, when it's a matter of minimal quantities such as ours, should be of equal weight. Sometimes, you slightly increase the proportion of the butter when using the roux for a light sauce. For sauces that have to be skimmed, and especially when making large quantities, as in a professional kitchen, the quantity of butter is a little less than the flour. The fat has to be removed by skimming, so the quantity is reduced as much as possible.

Roux can be prepared in advance and kept in reserve, as in professional kitchens. It is never diluted with liquid until it is ready to be used for the sauce. All roux, therefore, contain only flour and the fat used to cook them.

Cooking roux: To cook just a little bit of roux, which is all that you will need for home cooking, you must take many more precautions than when preparing a roux in large quantities. The minimal quantities of flour used for these small amounts of roux cannot provide a layer thick enough, in terms of the size of the pan, to cook without burning easily. This is why it is important not only to choose a pan that is very thick, but to use one of exactly the right size in proportion to the amount of liquid in the sauce for which the roux is made.

It is equally important to only ever use low heat, at a degree that was once expressed as "warm ashes." If the flour is seared by heat that is too strong at the outset, its starch will not be able to fulfill its thickening function in the sauce. For this reason, when making a roux in fat that is still hot from the meat that was just cooked in it, you must lower the heat and wait 1–2 minutes before putting in the flour.

PROCEDURE. Put only the butter in the pot over very *low heat.* Melt the butter evenly so that it covers the entire bottom of the pot, which you gently shake. This should take just a few seconds for such small quantities. As soon as it is melted, without giving it time to heat up, add the flour all at once. Mix it well with a wooden spoon, then let it cook very slowly, mixing the roux only from time to time. Do not cover the pot. Leave the spoon close by so it will always be available for stirring.

Carefully watch your roux. First, it will begin to swell, like a light dry crust on the bottom of the pot. If it swells more in one place, it is because the bottom of the pot is heating unevenly at that point. You must immediately stir the roux because it runs the risk of coloring too much and burning at that spot. When the swelling diminishes, the cooking of the roux begins. It forms a smooth batter spread out over the bottom of the pot in an even layer and gradually this batter becomes more liquid. Let it cook slowly, stirring from time to time, to shift the part of the roux that is in immediate contact with the bottom of the utensil.

For a small quantity of *blond roux,* allow about 10 minutes once the swelling goes down. Its color, we repeat, must be straw yellow.

For a *brown roux,* the procedure is exactly the same. It simply must cook longer in order to take on the desired color—café au lait—gradually. In addition, you can, toward the end of cooking, raise the heat to accelerate the coloration, but use extreme caution.

The roux is now ready for use. We should add here that *a roux is not thinned over the heat* because this will result in a lumpy sauce. The addition of liquid must thus be made off the heat and after waiting for a few moments, so that the roux will not be too warm. Once it is completely diluted and all the liquid has been added, return it to high heat and do not stop mixing with a small whisk or a wooden spoon until it has come to a full boil, as is always directed in our recipes. Otherwise, it will go lumpy.

Thickening with Beurre Manié

Beurre manié (literally, "handled butter") is a mixture of raw butter and flour, used for last-minute thickening and at the end of cooking. The proportions are 20 grams (2/3 ounce) of flour for 25 grams (1 ounce, 2 tablespoons) of butter.

Using a fork, blend the butter and flour on a plate, or in a bowl, until it forms a smooth paste. Then divide this paste into pieces the size of a bean, so that it will mix better with your liquid. Put this butter, divided this way, into the boiling liquid all at once. Shake the pot by moving it back and forth to help incorporate it, as you remove the pot from the heat. The sauce will have an unpleasant taste of flour if you let it boil vigorously after this addition. Subsequently, the sauce must be kept only at a barely perceptible boil.

The action of *shaking* the pot on the burner to mix it is necessary, because the use of a whisk or wooden spoon is hardly possible in the majority of cases where beurre manié is used. You will know when you can use a whisk or spoon.

Thickening with Starch

It used to be that potato starch was used to thicken sauces, but now arrowroot is preferred. Arrowroot gives a better result for smaller quantity and has a better sheen.

PROCEDURE. For each *teaspoon* of starch added to a glass, allow 2 tablespoons of cold water, added little by little, and dissolving the starch using a small wooden spoon.

Bring the liquid to be thickened to a rapid boil. When it's boiling, pour in the starch mixture with one hand while you stir rapidly with the other hand, using a wooden spoon or sauce whisk. *A few seconds* of rapid boiling should suffice.

Thickening with Egg Yolk

Many are unaware that a sauce thickened with egg yolk can boil without separating as long as the liquid contains some flour, even a small amount. In this case, if the sauce does separate, don't blame the boiling, but the lack of care.

A sauce thickened with egg yolk must boil. This is as much to avoid the taste of raw egg as to ensure a perfect blending. If it doesn't boil, the sauce runs the risk of separating and not thickening. If the addition of the thickener is handled properly, and the sauce is boiling rapidly, it can, if necessary, boil long and hard if this is required for reduction.

If the initial heat is too strong, the yolk will cook too quickly, and this causes the sauce to separate. Keeping the yolk from overheating is key to a successfully thickened sauce.

PROCEDURE. Completely dissolve the yolks with a little cold liquid in a bowl. The liquid can be milk, cream, liquid from cooking mushrooms, or any cooking liquid.

Take the sauce off the heat, pour 3–4 spoonfuls of warm sauce into the egg yolks, to gradually warm them. Then pour the yolks, little by little, into the sauce, which has been kept *off the heat,* mixing all the while with a small whisk. Return to the heat, mixing constantly until it has come back to *a full boil.*

Thickening with Blood

If the blood has been collected immediately after slaughter, add a little vinegar while the blood is still warm to prevent it from clotting. If some time has passed before collecting the blood, you may find some clots. You must mash them up with a fork, then strain the blood through a very fine sieve when you are ready to thicken the sauce.

Heat this blood gently, stirring in a few spoonfuls of sauce, one spoonful at a time. Then pour it into the sauce, *off the heat,* mixing with a whisk. Return to low heat and boil gently for *2–3 minutes.*

BASIC SAUCES

As numerous and diverse as French sauces are, they all originate from the same basic sauces: *espagnol* and demi-glace, which, in good home cooking, are replaced by what are known as "bourgeois sauces" and which we call "brown sauce" *(sauce brune);* or white sauces such as velouté (sometimes called *sauce blonde*); *parisienne;* and béchamel.

The primary function of these sauces is to provide—in strictly anonymous fashion, as it were—the fundamental elements of any sauce: concentrated flavors from extracts of meat, fish, or similar; liquid; and liaison. In other words, starting from a basic sauce, any number of ingredients can be added to give to each particular sauce its own distinctive flavor. For example, an infusion of vinegar and herbs in a brown sauce, or *espagnol,* turns it into a *sauce poivrade* (pepper sauce); a *sauce aurore* is made by adding tomato to a *sauce blonde,* or velouté. An unadorned *sauce béchamel* becomes a *sauce Mornay* when mixed with Gruyère and Parmesan.

The difference between the basic sauces of haute cuisine and those of the home cook is not necessarily in the ingredients used. For all intents and purposes, they are about the same. The difference is in the quantity of these ingredients, and, more important, in the time and care taken for the preparation, both of which are considerable in a professional kitchen.

It is impossible to overemphasize these last conditions: time and care. What particularly causes sauces to fail in home cooking, especially in the case of *sauce brune,* is the lack of preliminary preparation, gradual reduction, and a painstaking and interminable skimming—removing the foam and impurities. A well-skimmed sauce must not retain a single atom of fat. All the gluten from the flour in the roux must have disappeared. Nothing should remain but the starch, which makes the sauce transparent like a glaze and gives it the consistency of a light syrup. In this case, the sauce is not only pleasing to the eye, but it also has a refined taste and is easy to digest because the skimming will have eliminated all impurities.

We must mention here a recent development used for numerous dishes in modern-day haute cuisine. It involves replacing *sauce espagnol* with an extremely reduced veal coulis *(jus de veau)*, thickened with arrowroot. But this method works only when a considerable amount of meat is used for making the coulis, so it is not feasible for home cooking. For this reason, *sauce brune* remains useful for the contemporary home cook.

NOTE. The amount of flour used for a roux always depends on the amount of finished sauce required, no matter what the quantity of liquid used at the outset.

The juices that run from a beef or lamb roast when it is carved must never be added to a sauce. Far from intensifying or improving the sauce, this jus—which is actually raw—has the effect of diluting the sauce without adding any flavor, because flavor is only ever derived from cooking and caramelizing the juices.

Keeping sauces warm: When a sauce has to be made in advance, do not fail to add a few drops of liquid, pouring this *on top without mixing.* Or, dot around a few bits of butter *on the surface,* which will make a layer of oil when they melt. Used like this, the liquid or fat acts as an insulator. Failure to do this means that the sauce will form a skin or film on the surface while it waits, making it necessary to strain it again before serving. Just before serving, give it a quick mix with the whisk to mix everything together. The liquid, depending on the type of sauce, could be stock, broth, cooking water from mushrooms, Madeira, milk, etc.

Even if it is not buttered, a sauce is best kept warm in a double boiler as opposed to over a burner, where it runs all sorts of risks. If your kitchen equipment does not include a double boiler, put the pot containing the sauce in any cooking vessel that's a bit larger, then fill it with boiling water halfway up the sides of the pot. Keep this at a temperature that is quite warm, but not high enough to cause the water to boil.

FIG. 27. BAIN-MARIE.

Brown Sauce *(Sauce Brune)*

In the home kitchen, as we have already explained, this replaces *espagnole* sauce and also, in particular, demi-glace, which are favored in professional kitchens. It also serves as a base for other sauces, such as Madeira sauce, *périgueux* sauce, pepper sauce, etc. This speaks volumes about the importance of proper preparation.

The method outlined here seems to us to be the best for a home kitchen. It substitutes a very good bouillon for the jus—note that point well—while also simplifying the process to keep cooking time to a minimum and reducing the use of too many pans.

In keeping with this spirit of simplification, we suggest that the roux be cooked along with the mirepoix but, as a rule, a roux will be much more successful if the roux and the mirepoix are prepared separately. In other words, the mirepoix is browned in a separate utensil and subsequently added to the sauce.

The use of butter to brown the mirepoix and to make the roux is not absolutely essential. It can, in this case, be replaced by a high-quality, purified fat since it is removed during the course of the cooking and during the skimming process. This fat will not be present in the finished sauce.

The total time of this procedure has been, as we have said, considerably abridged here. We suggest that you do not try to shorten it any further. This would be most detrimental to the sauce, as much for its flavor as for its clarity. If it has been prepared and skimmed with all due care, it will be light, transparent like a glaze, and will not congeal on the plate.

We also recommend the use of a heavy-bottomed pan. If you do not have tin-lined copper, you can use a good thick aluminum utensil. Above all, do not use cast iron, which almost always imparts an unattractive color to the sauce.

Given that this sauce is very versatile, as well as easy to preserve over a period of time, we have given quantities for making 1 liter (4¼ cups) of sauce. It is always best to make this well in advance, in order to give its preparation the necessary time and care. This then offers the choice of whether to keep it warm over a double boiler or to prepare it the evening before, at your leisure, to be reheated directly when ready to use. *Time: At least 2 hours. Makes 1 liter (4¼ cups) of sauce, ready for use.*

For the mirepoix: **80–100 grams (2¾–3½ ounces, 6–7 tablespoons) of butter; 100 grams (3½ ounces) of carrot; 100 grams (3½ ounces) of onion; 100 grams (3½ ounces) of good-quality bacon; 4–5 sprigs of parsley, leaves stripped; 2 sprigs of thyme; 1 small bay leaf.**

50–60 grams (1¾ –2¼ ounces) of flour for the roux; 3 deciliters (1¼ cups) of good white wine; 1½ liters (6⅓ cups) of jus (or, failing that, very good bouillon completely degreased); 3 level tablespoonfuls of tomato concentrate; about 50 grams (1¾ ounces) of mushroom trimmings, if possible; 2 tablespoons of Madeira.

PROCEDURE. **First part:** Finely chop the carrots, onions, bacon, parsley, etc. (SEE MIREPOIX, PAGE 21). Choose a pan large enough to hold the liquid that will subsequently be added to the mirepoix, about 2–2½ liters (8½–10½ cups). The liquid must come almost to the top, which will help when skimming the sauce; it is also essential to anticipate the gradual reduction of the liquid. Melt the butter in the pan over low heat. Add all the mirepoix ingredients. Do not cover. Let it all brown gradually, without haste, mixing it from time to time with a wooden spoon.

Sprinkle the flour over the mirepoix, mixing it in with the wooden spoon. Lower the heat immediately. Do not cover. Let the flour cook, slowly, until it takes on a reddish but not too dark hue (SEE BROWN ROUX, PAGE 47). Be sure to stir the contents of the pan from time to time to ensure the flour cooks evenly; it will have more or less stuck to the fragments of the mirepoix. Allow *12–15 minutes* for the roux to color gradually.

Then, add the white wine and the jus or bouillon, gradually, mixing it with the spoon to completely dissolve everything that has attached to the mirepoix. Whether using jus or bouillon, *you must set aside about 2 deciliters* (6¾ fluid ounces, ⅞ cup) to use when clarifying the sauce. Add the tomato concentrate. Bring to a boil over high heat, stirring constantly with a wooden spoon or whisk. Add the mushroom trimmings.

Lower the heat, so that the boiling continues *very evenly and very gently,* and always in the same spot. Do not cover. *Let it simmer in this way for 1 hour.*

As it simmers, use a metal spoon to skim off the fat and foam that rise to the surface. The subsequent clarification will be much better if you do this carefully during this first stage of cooking the sauce.

Second part: At the end of the indicated time, strain the sauce through a *chinois* into another pan, stirring the mirepoix with the back of the spoon, to extract the flavorsome juices but not the solids. Return the strained sauce to the heat. When it boils, adjust the saucepan position for skimming (SEE SKIMMING, PAGE 16). Allow *a good half-hour* for this part of the cooking. It is during this stage that the real clarification of the sauce takes place, though some has already occurred during the first part of the cooking. You *must* proceed with great care and remove everything that the partial boiling brings to the surface. From time to time, add spoonfuls, as indicated previously, of the *cold* jus or bouillon that has been set aside for this purpose.

When the skimming is complete, the sauce must not show *one atom of fat.* And, since the heavy and sticky part of the flour has been eliminated, the remaining traces give the sauce a consistency of thin syrup.

If the quantity of sauce produced is more than 1 liter (4¼ cups), put the pan over high heat. Stir the sauce with a large wooden spoon, being sure to stir along the bottom of the pan, until the rapid boiling has reduced the sauce to the required quantity.

Remove the pan from the heat and add the Madeira. Strain once more through the *chinois,* either into a bowl, if preparing in advance, or into a clean pan so that it can be kept warm until needed (SEE ADVANCE PREPARATION OF SAUCES, PAGE 50).

OBSERVATION. If a sufficient supply of pots and pans is a problem, simply strain the sauce into a bowl, thoroughly wash the pan used for the skimming process, and return the strained sauce into it. The disadvantage is that, with rather small quantities, much is lost in the transfers. This is why we recommend the use of three pans for the same sauce.

Velouté

In professional kitchens, as well as in home cooking, the sauce known as velouté is the foundation of all white sauces, just as *espagnole* or *sauce brune* is for all the other brown sauces. Veal and poultry, with the usual vegetables, are the only meats to be used in the liquid. *Time: 1½ hours. Makes 1 liter (4¼ cups) of velouté.*

60 grams (2¼ ounces, 4½ tablespoons) of butter and 50–60 grams (1¾–2¼ ounces) of flour for the roux; 1½ liters (6⅓ cups) of white veal jus; 50–60 grams (1¾–2¼ ounces) of mushroom trimmings; bunch of parsley.

PROCEDURE. Use a deep, thick-bottomed pot, made of tin-lined copper or heavy aluminum, with a volume of about 1½ liters (6⅓ cups). In this, make a roux with a *light blond* color. Dilute it, using a whisk, by adding 1¼ liters (5⅓ cups) veal jus. Bring to a boil, stirring constantly. Then add the parsley and mushroom trimmings (if you have them at this time; if not, incorporate them when you are skimming). Skim (SEE SKIMMING, PAGE 16). During this time, add the *remaining veal jus,* 1 tablespoonful at a time. Allow *a full hour* of gentle cooking for the skimming. After this, strain the sauce through a *chinois,* and it is ready for use.

Sauce Allemande or "Parisienne" *(Sauce Allemande Dite "Parisienne"*

A classic sauce, this is now also known as "parisienne." It is used in a number of whimsical culinary creations as well as remaining a cornerstone for classic dishes such as vol-au-vent, puff pastries, etc. In the home kitchen, it is used for any dishes requiring a basic white sauce (for white foods, such as fowl and veal).

To sum up, this is a velouté, or white sauce, with a liaison of egg yolk added. We must stress, once again, the importance of boiling the sauce rapidly after adding the egg yolks. Many people, unaware of this essential point, do not understand the risks. A sauce that is taken off the heat too soon will separate, thin down, and not have the right consistency to coat the food it is supposed to cover. *Time: About 2 hours (including the preparation of the velouté). Makes 1 liter (4¼ cups) of sauce.*

1 liter (4¼ cups) of velouté; a good deciliter (3⅓ fluid ounces, ½ cup) of mushroom cooking juice; 5 nice egg yolks, or 6 small ones; a pinch of white pepper, a touch of ground nutmeg; 50 grams (1¾ ounces,3½ tablespoons) of butter, for the final buttering.

PROCEDURE. Prepare the velouté as directed. Having skimmed the sauce for the time required, strain it through a *chinois* into a sauté pan *with a thick bottom.* Keep it off the heat. (We suggest here straining the sauce into a sauté pan, which is much more appropriate for its rapid reduction after the liaison has been added. However, to reduce the amount of utensils, you could strain the sauce into a small bowl and return it to the original pot, which should be rinsed first.)

Dilute the egg yolks in a bowl with the mushroom water. Pour this liaison into the sauce, *off the heat,* gradually, stirring with a whisk. Add the pepper and nutmeg. Then return the pot to high heat. Stir constantly with a wooden spatula or a wooden spoon with a large square head, scraping all over the bottom of the pot to prevent the sauce from sticking. Do this until you have reduced the sauce to its original volume of *1 liter (4¼ cups).* Turn off the heat. Add the final butter (SEE BUTTERING, PAGE 16). Check the seasoning.

Immediately strain the sauce again through the *chinois.* Then, depending on whether you are using it right away, pour it over the food, or into a pot set over a double boiler, spreading a few drops of mushroom water over the surface (SEE KEEPING SAUCES WARM, PAGE 50).

Béchamel Sauce *(Sauce Béchamel)*

You must be familiar with culinary subtleties to know that béchamel is not always a sauce in which milk is the only liquid used. There is also "fat" béchamel, the most authentic, since it bears the name of the man "who thought of adding cream to velouté," as reported by the great chef Carême. *[Translator's note: Anton Carême (1783–1833) is considered one of the greatest of French chefs.]* In those days, béchamel was composed of velouté, enhanced with an addition of heavy cream, which was then reduced over high heat and stirred constantly to return to the original quantity of velouté.

No matter how inferior to the original concept of béchamel, *béchamel maigre* ("lean béchamel") has become better known and more representative of the name than classic béchamel. Without doubt, this is because it has become an important resource for meat-free cooking. In addition, its use in the home kitchen has resulted in a simplification of methods, reducing time and effort, thus making it more popular. But these simplifications are often detrimental to the sauce.

Lean béchamel must have an aromatic flavor base, furnished by lean elements that are also found in classic béchamel. That is, onion, carrot, parsley stems, and, if possible, mushroom trimmings, sometimes a hint of celery. Sometimes the white part of a leek, and a light note of thyme and bay.

When the béchamel is not destined for a meat-free dish, as well as the ingredients listed above, you can use a bit of purified lard or cured ham, which considerably enhances the flavor. Or, a nice mirepoix (SEE MIREPOIX, PAGE 21).

The proportion of flour for the roux is 6–7 grams (about 1/4 ounce) for each deciliter (3 1/3 fluid ounces, scant 1/2 cup) of sauce that is ready for use. The proportion of aromatics, as well as their use, often varies depending on how the sauce is to be used and will be established in the recipes employing béchamel.

Béchamel Maigre *(Lean Béchamel)*. The following recipe is a golden mean, suitable for most recipes calling for lean béchamel. *Time: About 1 hour, 15 minutes. Makes 1/2 liter (generous 2 cups) of sauce.*

For the mirepoix: **50 grams (1 3/4 ounces) of onion; 50 grams (1 3/4 ounces) of carrot; 50 grams (1 3/4 ounces) of cured ham (optional); 30 grams (1 ounce, 2 tablespoons) of butter.**

30–35 grams (1–1 1/4 ounces) of flour and the same of butter (2 tablespoons) for the roux blanc; 3/4 liter (generous 3 cups) of milk; a small bouquet garni; salt, pepper, and grated nutmeg.

PROCEDURE. Use a 1-liter (4-cup) pot—*above all, one that is thick*—aluminum or good-quality enameled iron. Make sure, above all, that you choose a pot in which the contents do not have a tendency to stick, which is why it must be very thick. This kind of sauce, with its thick consistency, sticks too easily to the bottom of a pot that is too thin.

Gently cook the mirepoix for 10 minutes or so *without letting it color at all,* first of all because the aromatic note would be too intense, but also because it might color the sauce.

The mirepoix thus cooked, transfer it to a plate. In the same pot, without rinsing, cook the butter and flour, without allowing it to take on any color (SEE ROUX BLANC, PAGE 47). Dilute with *boiling milk,* stirring rapidly with a sauce whisk, which is practically indispensable here. Immediately add the salt, pepper, and nutmeg. Stir the sauce continuously over the heat until it begins to boil. Add the reserved mirepoix and the bouquet garni.

Put the pot over low heat so that the boiling occurs in only one spot. Do this either by raising it slightly by propping the handle against something, or putting the pot off to one side of the heat. This is not to help you to *skim,* because you don't skim béchamel. With the pot set up this way, there is less chance of sticking. Don't cover the pot at all. Let it cook *gently for 45 minutes.* From time to time, stir it with a wooden spoon to make sure the sauce is not sticking to the bottom.

Once cooked, strain the sauce through a *chinois* into another, smaller pot, lightly pressing with the back of the spoon to help the flow, but without crushing the mirepoix. After straining, you should have nearly 5 deciliters (generous 2 cups) of sauce, as the cooking will have gradually reduced the quantity. The proportions of the roux are based on this quantity. If you have more than this, you must simply boil the sauce for a bit, stirring it constantly.

If the sauce will not be used immediately, dot a few bits of butter around the surface (SEE KEEPING SAUCES WARM, PAGE 50).

Alternative method: This is faster and easier for small quantities, and it makes the final steps easier because the sauce does not need to be strained at the last moment. However, the flavor of a sauce prepared in this way is inferior because the mirepoix is strained out sooner.

Prepare and cook the mirepoix in the butter. Add the boiling milk, salt, pepper, and nutmeg. The quantity of milk here must be reduced since the cooking time of the sauce is shorter. Cover and simmer gently over low heat *for 10 minutes.* The mirepoix has now infused the milk, so you can strain it through a fine sieve into a bowl. Rinse and dry the pot. Make the roux blanc. Dilute it with the infused milk. Bring to a boil. Cover and let the sauce cook gently for about another *10 minutes.*

SAUCES

Madeira Sauce *(Sauce Madère)*

In a first-class home kitchen, the preparation will be as follows: A *sauce brune* very carefully and patiently purified, such as we have previously outlined, and then enhanced with the addition of Madeira wine. This wine must be of excellent quality because it is added after cooking and it will therefore retain its bouquet. For this reason, when the sauce is made far in advance and must be reheated, the Madeira is added only at the instant when the sauce is poured into the sauceboat.

Also note that the bouillon is not sufficient to give the sauce its characteristic depth of flavor. In this case, jus is necessary. To obtain the necessary quantity of jus for this recipe, 7–8 deciliters ($3–3\frac{3}{8}$ cups), you will need at least 450 grams (1 pound) of veal shank from the meatiest part for this jus, which should be prepared the night before (SEE JUS, PAGE 44). *Serves about 10 people, or makes $\frac{1}{2}$ liter (generous 2 cups) of sauce.*

For the mirepoix: **50 grams ($1\frac{3}{4}$ ounces) of carrots; 50 grams ($1\frac{3}{4}$ ounces) of onion; 50 grams ($1\frac{3}{4}$ ounces) of streaky bacon; 2 small sprigs of parsley; 50 grams ($1\frac{3}{4}$ ounces, $3\frac{1}{2}$ tablespoons) of butter; sprig of thyme; a fingernail size piece of bay.**

25–30 grams (about 1 ounce) of flour for the roux; $1\frac{1}{2}$ deciliters (5 fluid ounces, $\frac{2}{3}$ cup) of good white wine; 8 deciliters ($3\frac{3}{8}$ cups) of jus or of excellent degreased bouillon; $1\frac{1}{2}$ tablespoons of tomato concentrate; 25 grams (1 ounce) of mushroom trimmings, if possible; 1 deciliter ($3\frac{1}{3}$ fluid ounces, scant $\frac{1}{2}$ cup) of Madeira wine.

PROCEDURE. Proceed exactly as for *sauce brune.* Apply the same cooking time and take the same care when skimming, for which you reserve jus or bouillon in the suggested quantities.

To compensate for the dilution that occurs when adding the Madeira, note that the sauce, once it has been skimmed, must measure 4 deciliters ($1\frac{2}{3}$ cups). If it is more than that, you must reduce it by boiling, *before* adding the Madeira that returns it to the right quantity.

If the sauce must be kept warm in a double boiler until serving, add the Madeira right away but do not allow it to boil or the aroma of the wine will evaporate. Strain it through a *chinois* into a double boiler (SEE KEEPING SAUCES WARM, PAGE 50).

Truffle Sauce *(Sauce Périgueux).* This is simply an excellent *sauce brune* with Madeira, to which the cooking essence of truffles and chopped truffles have been added. The proportion is 10–15 grams ($\frac{1}{3}–\frac{1}{2}$ ounce) of truffles for each deciliter ($3\frac{1}{3}$ fluid ounces, scant $\frac{1}{2}$ cup) of sauce.

The infusion of ham, which gives this sauce its distinctive flavor, is often wrongly suppressed. If you are preparing an essential "basic sauce," as is done in professional kitchens, skimping on any ingredient makes no sense. Even when this sauce is prepared with minimal resources, and our recipes here take into account the limits of the home kitchen, the infusion of ham is vital and must not be omitted. *Time: At least 2 hours. Serves 10, or makes 5 deciliters (generous 2 cups) of sauce ready to serve.*

For the basic sauce brune: **the same quantities as for Madeira sauce.**

To finish the sauce: **3 small raw truffles, or a $\frac{1}{4}$-liter (1-cup) can of preserved truffles.**

For the ham infusion: **60 grams ($2\frac{1}{4}$ ounces) of cured unsmoked ham, very lightly salted and absolutely lean; 15 grams ($\frac{1}{2}$ ounce) of shallot; a fragment of thyme and bay; 25 grams (1 ounce, 2 tablespoons) of butter; 1 deciliter ($3\frac{1}{3}$ fluid ounces, scant $\frac{1}{2}$ cup)**

of jus; 1 deciliter ($3^1/_3$ fluid ounces, scant $^1/_2$ cup) of Madeira; pinch of white pepper.

$^1/_2$ deciliter ($1^2/_3$ fluid ounces, scant $^1/_4$ cup) of Madeira to finish the sauce.

PROCEDURE. Prepare the basic *sauce brune* exactly as directed (SEE SAUCE BRUNE, PAGE 50). Follow the same procedure, the same cooking time. In addition, while the *sauce brune* is cooking, prepare the truffles and the ham infusion.

The truffles: Having cleaned and washed the truffles, peel them and save the trimmings on a plate. Chop the truffles, or cut them into small cubes. Put them in the top section of a double boiler. Cover and set aside. *If the truffles are the preserved kind,* peel and chop as above. Add them to the infusion without cooking, as they are already cooked. Keep the truffle juice from the can as a last-minute addition to the sauce.

The ham: Cut it into very small cubes. Heat the butter in a small pan. Add the ham and cook to color it lightly. Next, add the minced shallot, the thyme, a hint of bay, the Madeira, the jus, the truffle peels, the pepper.

Let it boil *very gently,* uncovered, until the liquid has reduced to *a scant deciliter ($3^1/_3$ fluid ounces, scant $^1/_2$ cup).*

Strain through a *chinois* directly onto the truffles, mixing the ham delicately with a wooden spoon. Put the lid on the top pot and place the double boiler over the heat. Cook *only a few minutes.* Keep the sauce warm, without letting it boil, until ready to finish.

Finishing the sauce: Once the sauce has been skimmed, put the pan over high heat. Stir with a wooden spoon until it has reduced to no more than *4 scant deciliters ($1^2/_3$ cups).*

Strain the sauce through a *chinois* into the pan containing the infusion and the chopped truffles. Let it simmer for 5–6 minutes over low heat. Turn off the heat. Add the rest of the Madeira (half a deciliter). Keep it warm without letting it boil (SEE KEEPING SAUCES WARM, PAGE 50).

Mushroom Sauce *(Sauce aux Champignons).* A popular companion for beef—roasted, grilled, or sautéed. For filets, tournedos, rib steaks, etc.

Preparation and quantities are the same as for Madeira sauce. One simply adds mushrooms, 250 grams ($8^7/_8$ ounces) for the stated quantities of Madeira sauce.

The Madeira can, according to preference, be partly or completely eliminated in mushroom sauce. You could simply confine yourself to adding only 1–2 tablespoons, always off the heat, to complement the overall flavor. Should you choose to omit the Madeira, bear in mind the quantities of liquid required and do not reduce the sauce after the skimming, as directed for Madeira sauce.

The mushrooms: Trim the gritty stalk ends and peel only the bits of stalk remaining. Rinse, drain, then repeat once more. After the final rinse, drain and dry them in a kitchen towel so they retain no moisture, which would prevent them from browning when cooked. Cut the caps into quarters or sixths, according to size. Cut the stalks in 2 or 3 pieces.

Heat 50 grams ($1^3/_4$ ounces, $3^1/_2$ tablespoons) of butter in a pan, throw in the mushrooms. Sauté over high heat until evenly and lightly colored. Transfer to a strainer to *drain all the butter.* (You can reuse this butter for similar tasks.) Put them in the sauce while it is being skimmed. They will finish cooking there and also impart their flavor. Continue skimming until ready to finish the sauce with the Madeira, *about 30 minutes.* It goes without saying that, in this case, the sauce is not strained further.

Venison Sauce *à la Française* *(Sauce Chevreuil)*

Not just for game, this sauce could also accompany a marinated roast—a leg of lamb, for example. When using with game, you include the mirepoix trimmings at the beginning. In professional kitchens, where *sauce brune* is always on hand, the work is made much faster and easier by adding the reduced marinade to the *sauce brune.* *Time: 2 hours. Serves 10, or makes 5–6 deciliters (generous 2–$2^1/_2$ cups).*

***For the mirepoix:* 30 grams (1 ounce) of carrots; 30 grams (1 ounce) of onions; 30 grams (1 ounce) of lean ham; 20 grams ($^2/_3$ ounce) of shallots; 5 grams ($^1/_6$ ounce) of parsley stalks; a sprig of thyme; a quarter leaf of bay; 40 grams ($1^3/_8$ ounces, 3 table-spoons) of butter.**

20–25 grams (2/3–1 ounce) of flour for the roux; 2 deciliters (6 3/4 fluid ounces) of light veal jus or bouillon; 3 tablespoons of vinegar; the marinade, about 1 1/4 liters (5 1/3 cups); 3 juniper berries and 6 peppercorns; 1 1/2 deciliters (5 fluid ounces, 2/3 cup) of good red wine for skimming the sauce; 60 grams (2 1/4 ounces, 4 1/2 tablespoons) of butter to finish the sauce.

PROCEDURE. In a heavy-bottomed pot with a 1 1/4-liter (5-cup) capacity, *lightly* color the mirepoix (SEE PAGE 21).

Mix in the flour. Cook it gently to obtain a lightly colored brown roux. Dilute with jus or bouillon the marinade that has been strained through the *chinois,* and the vinegar. Bring it to a boil. Lower the heat and boil gently for *40 minutes.* During the first part of cooking, degrease and remove the foam from the sauce to begin the skimming process.

After 25–30 minutes, while the sauce is still on the heat, add the peppercorns and juniper berries, previously crushed with a rolling pin or the flat part of a cleaver. About 10–15 minutes will be enough for them to impart their flavor to the sauce. The peppercorns, especially, should be removed after a short period, or they will make the sauce bitter.

After the first 40 minutes of cooking, strain the sauce through a *chinois* into another pot, vigorously whisking the mirepoix and the sauce to extract the quintessential flavor. Or, strain the sauce into a bowl and return it to the rinsed pot. Immediately bring it back to the boil and *adjust the pot for skimming for 30–45 minutes,* if possible. This is when you add the red wine, 1 or 2 tablespoons at a time (SEE SKIMMING, PAGE 16).

The progressive reduction during the second part of cooking should reduce the sauce to about 6 deciliters (2 1/2 cups), which is still a bit too much liquid for the necessary intensity of flavor. Return the pot to high heat to reduce the sauce to the point where it is no more than 5 1/2 deciliters (2 1/3 cups).

Off the heat, add the butter to *finish,* which should bring the sauce to the necessary 6 deciliters (2 1/2 cups). At this point, you can liven it up with a point of cayenne (the amount that will fit on the tip of a small knife). Strain the whole thing through a *chinois* into a double boiler (SEE KEEPING SAUCES WARM, PAGE 50).

Pepper Sauce *(Sauce Poivrade)*

This sauce is characterized by a very spicy infusion of aromatics and the flavor of good-quality vinegar. White wine is a popular addition and we have included it here.

Sauce poivrade can be served to accompany game, as well as marinated and unmarinated cuts of meats. If using marinated meat, add a bit of the marinade to the sauce, then proceed as indicated for large game (see below). *Time: 2 1/2 hours. Serves 10, or makes 1/2 liter (generous 2 cups) of sauce.*

***For the infusion:* 60 grams (2 1/4 ounces) of carrots; 60 grams (2 1/4 ounces) of onions; 25 grams (1 ounce) of shallots; 4 small sprigs of parsley; a sprig of thyme; one-third of a medium-size bay leaf; a scant deciliter (3 1/3 fluid ounces, scant 1/2 cup) of oil; 1 1/2 deciliters (5 fluid ounces, 2/3 cup) of good vinegar; 1 deciliter (3 1/3 fluid ounces, scant 1/2 cup) of white wine.**

30 grams (1 ounce, 2 tablespoons) of butter and 25–30 grams (about 1 ounce) of flour for the roux; 1 good liter (4 1/4 cups) of ordinary veal jus or bouillon; 6–8 peppercorns, coarsely crushed; 30 grams of butter (1 ounce, 2 tablespoons) to finish the sauce.

PROCEDURE. **The infusion:** Cut the onion, carrot, and parsley into a mirepoix (SEE PAGE 21). In a small sauté pan, heat the oil until it smokes. Add the carrot, onion, parsley, thyme, and bay. Cook over low heat until lightly colored. When the vegetables are lightly colored and golden, add the finely minced shallot. Heat it for a few minutes, without letting it brown or color, which would give it a bad flavor. Then, drain all the oil from the mirepoix. (This oil should be kept for other similar uses.) Once all the oil has been eliminated, add the vinegar and the white wine to the mirepoix. Let it boil gently until the liquid has reduced by half.

The sauce: Meanwhile, in a deep 1 1/4-liter (5-cup) pot, make a *roux brun* with the butter and the flour. Dilute it with *7 1/2 deciliters* (generous 3 cups) of jus or bouillon. The rest is used for skimming the sauce. Immediately add the mirepoix. Bring to a boil. Adjust the heat so that the sauce maintains an even boil *for 1 hour.* Skim the foam from time to time to start the purification process.

Peppercorns: These must not remain in the

sauce longer than the time necessary to impart their special flavor. So do not add them until, at the most, *8–10 minutes before straining the sauce* for the final skimming.

Skimming: Strain the sauce through a *chinois* into any receptacle, mixing the mirepoix with a wooden spoon to extract the maximum flavor from the aromatics. Rinse the pot with hot water. Return the sauce to the pot. Immediately add about 1 1/2 deciliters (5 fluid ounces, 2/3 cup) of the reserved jus. Adjust the heat and proceed as directed (SEE SKIMMING, PAGE 16). Allow *50 minutes* for this part of the cooking.

Finishing the sauce: After skimming, return the sauce to high heat. Reduce it, stirring constantly, until it is no more than *5 deciliters (generous 2 cups)*. Remove from the heat. Taste for salt. If you like, spice it up with a point of cayenne (as much as can be held on the tip of a knife). Add the butter. Strain through a *chinois* into a double boiler. Sauce kept warm in this manner, with due care, can easily be kept for a rather long time (SEE KEEPING SAUCES WARM, PAGE 50).

Pepper Sauce for Large Game. This is for furred game animals, such as haunch and saddle of venison, wild boar, etc.

Exactly the same ingredients and quantities as for the preceding *sauce poivrade,* but adding 100 grams (3 1/2 fluid ounces) of game trimmings and bones, and 3 deciliters (1 1/4 cups) of strained marinade. If the trimmings have not been marinated with the game, you can cook them with the vegetables of the mirepoix. If the trimmings have been marinated, add them directly to the sauce, after the roux is diluted, and at the same time as 2 deciliters (6 3/4 fluid ounces, 7/8 cup) of the marinade. The remaining deciliter is added during the skimming.

Pepper and Red Currant Sauce *(Sauce Venaison).* This is a *sauce poivrade* for game, which includes a last-minute addition of red currant jelly and cream. The addition of the red currant jelly is traditional, but the addition of cream is contemporary.

For the above quantities, allow 2 tablespoons of red currant jelly, melted and diluted with 1 deciliter (3 1/3 fluid ounces, scant 1/2 cup) of cream.

Huntsman's Sauce *(Sauce Grand Veneur).* The preparation is the same as for PEPPER SAUCE FOR LARGE GAME (PAGE 57), but is thickened with blood from game (preferably hare's blood).

Thus: 1/2 deciliter (1 2/3 fluid ounces, scant 1/4 cup) of blood is dissolved in the same quantity of marinade, added to the sauce at the end.

When *sauce grand veneur* is served with cuts of game, it is customary to offer the guests red currant jelly in small dishes, so they may help themselves to more.

Red Wine and Shallot Sauce *(Sauce Bordelaise)*

This is characterized by shallots infused in, of course, Bordeaux wine. The acclaimed French chef Gouffé and his contemporaries used white wine, Sauternes, or Graves. *[Translator's note: Jules Gouffé (1807–1877) was a renowned French chef, sometimes called the Carême of the Second Empire. He published two important books: one on French cuisine and one on pastry.]* These days, it's mostly red Bordeaux that is used to make the infusion. In home cooking, the infusion is added to the *sauce brune,* for which a good veal jus is absolutely essential. Ordinary bouillon does not have the intensity of flavor required to give the sauce the necessary degree of succulence. If using bouillon, you will need to supplement it with a meat glaze *(glace de viande).* In this case, make sure that the bouillon is not too salty since the sauce will be reduced almost by half for use.

When you need only a small quantity of sauce—to serve with steak, for example—you can replace the *sauce brune* with very good jus that has been reduced, to which you add an equally reduced infusion of shallot. Thicken with arrowroot. For the final buttering, you will need a larger quantity of butter, adding it off the heat.

Sauce bordelaise is most often accompanied by beef marrow, which is either cut into rounds and placed on top of the steak before it is sauced, or is cut into small cubes and mixed into the sauce just before serving.

In the following recipe, we repeat the preparation of the *sauce brune* (PAGE 50), slightly shortening the preparation time. But it is always preferable, when possible, to include the waiting times suggested. *Time: 2 hours. Makes 1/2 liter (generous 2 cups).*

4 deciliters (1 2/3 cups) of prepared *sauce brune,* or a mirepoix with 30 grams (1 ounce, 2 tablespoons) of butter; 40 grams (1 3/8 ounces, 3/8 stick) of carrots and the same of onion; parsley stems; a sprig of thyme; bit of bay; 20–25 grams (2/3–1 ounce) of flour for the roux; 6 deciliters (2 1/2 cups) of veal jus.

***For the infusion:* 40 grams (1 3/8 ounces) of finely chopped shallots; 3 deciliters (1 1/4 cups) of good white or red wine; a pinch of white pepper; a fragment of thyme and bay (*very little* of the latter); 75 grams (2 2/3 ounces, 1/3 cup) of butter to finish the sauce; if used, 80 grams (2 3/4 ounces) of beef marrow.**

PROCEDURE. **The sauce:** In a 1-liter (4-cup) pot, lightly color the mirepoix. Add the flour and cook it as for a *roux brun.* Dilute with the jus, proceeding just as directed for a *sauce brune* (PAGE 50). Allow *40 minutes of gentle boiling* for the first stage of cooking. Strain and skim the sauce.

The infusion: Meanwhile, put the ingredients for the infusion in a small sauté pan. Boil, uncovered, until the wine is reduced to a good deciliter (3 1/3 fluid ounces, 1/2 cup). Pour everything, just as it is, into the sauce. Continue with the skimming for *a good 15 minutes.* The final quantity of the sauce must be reduced to 4 good deciliters (1 2/3 cups). Strain again through the *chinois* and keep warm in a double boiler. Just before serving, add the butter, which will complete the sauce up to the right quantity, and depending on the dish, also add the poached marrow, as directed below.

The beef marrow: With a good knife dipped in warm water, cut the marrow into small cubes. Throw them into boiling water. Cover and keep the water barely simmering for *8–10 minutes.* Dry thoroughly on a cloth before adding the marrow cubes to the sauce.

Duck Liver Sauce *(Sauce Rouennaise).* Traditionally served to accompany Rouennaise roast duck, whether stuffed or not, *sauce rouennaise* is simply a bordelaise sauce made unique by the addition of duck liver.

Bear in mind the importance of purification for a truly successful sauce. Carefully follow the directions for handling the liver, so that it does not granulate and remains a smooth purée in the sauce. *Time: 2 hours. Makes sauce for 1 duck.*

4–5 deciliters (1 2/3–generous 2 cups) of bordelaise sauce; a duck liver; 30 grams (1 ounce, 2 tablespoons) of butter.

PROCEDURE. Prepare the sauce exactly as directed for *sauce bordelaise* until the moment when the infusion has been added and the sauce has been skimmed, and it is ready to be strained again through the *chinois.*

Meanwhile, thoroughly clean the liver. All the greenish parts contaminated by bile must be removed because they will make the sauce bitter. Cut the liver into small pieces. Force them through a fine sieve. Keep them cool until ready to use.

Strain the sauce through a *chinois* into a pot. Return to the heat and bring it just to the boiling point. First dilute the liver purée, gradually, with 3–4 tablespoons of the hot sauce, to prevent it from seizing. Next, put the pot on a double boiler. Here, it is a matter of keeping the sauce as warm as possible, but *never boiling,* because the slightest boil would make it go grainy.

Having taken these precautions, pour the diluted liver purée into the sauce. Cover. Let it poach for *5–6 minutes,* stirring from time to time.

Just before serving, finish the sauce with the butter. If you like, add a point of cayenne (as much as can be held on the tip of a knife).

Sauce Piquante *(Sauce Piquante)*

This is one of the most popular sauces for all beef and lamb dishes, whether boiled or roasted. It is equally good with roast or grilled pork, which always require a zesty sauce.

In home cooking, the vinegar is usually added to the sauce right from the bottle—in other words, without having previously cooked and reduced it with onion and shallot. This reduction, which does not require much time or trouble, has a dual purpose. First, to mitigate the vinegar's acidity, and also to saturate the onion and shallot, thereby enhancing the sauce with their combined flavors.

If your vinegar is very strong, cut it by half with white wine, or even water. This sauce can be prepared well in advance. But cornichons, herbs, and capers are added only at the last moment, as boiling will diminish their flavor. *Time: 30–35 minutes. Makes about 1/2 liter (generous 2 cups) of sauce.*

25 grams (1 ounce) of onion and the same of shallot, finely chopped; 2 scant deciliters (6 3/4 fluid ounces, 7/8 cup) of vinegar; 4 deciliters (1 2/3 cups) of standard jus or of degreased bouillon; 20 grams (2/3 ounce, 1 heaping tablespoon) of butter and 20 grams (2/3 ounce) of flour for the roux; 25 grams (1 ounce) of finely chopped cornichons; 25 grams (1 ounce) of capers; a teaspoon of chopped parsley, the same of chervil and tarragon; a pinch of ground pepper.

PROCEDURE. In a small saucepan, combine the chopped onion and shallot, and the vinegar. Boil rapidly, uncovered, until the liquid is reduced to 3 tablespoons. Then add the jus or bouillon. Boil for only *2–3 minutes.* Then, pour everything, *without straining,* into a small bowl.

Rinse and dry the saucepan. Make a small *roux brun* with the flour and butter. Dilute it with the unstrained liquid. Bring to a boil. Lower the heat and boil gently for *15 minutes,* skimming the fat and the foam with a metal spoon. This is not as complete a skimming as for a sauce prepared more thoroughly and for a longer time. However, this brief skimming produces a cleaner sauce.

Just before serving, check the seasoning of the sauce. Add the ground pepper, cornichons, capers, and herbs.

Onion, White Wine, and Mustard Sauce *(Sauce Robert)*

Classic, simple, and always excellent, this sauce is appropriate for numerous occasions, and is especially well suited to boiled beef, especially in a pot-au-feu. We provide the recipe suitable for home cooks. The other procedure consists of reducing the wine with onion that has been previously softened, then adding everything to the necessary quantity of *sauce brune.*

Of course, here, as elsewhere, a jus—even one made in the home kitchen—is preferable to bouillon. But given how this sauce is simplified, we expect that bouillon will be used. A bit of meat glaze will considerably improve the sauce in this case. Or, you might double the amount of bouillon suggested and reduce it to half by boiling before adding it to the onion.

We recommend using *large onions* so that you can cut them as required. There are no special requirements for the type of *mustard.* Use what you have. Ordinary Dijon mustard is what is generally implied. If the *white wine* is slightly sweet, like some Graves, do not add superfine sugar at the end. *Time: A little under an hour. Serves 6.*

2 large onions weighing a total of 200 grams (7 ounces); 60 grams (2 1/4 ounces, 4 1/2 tablespoons) of butter; 15 grams (1/2 ounce) of flour; 3 deciliters (1 1/4 cups) of excellent bouillon, perfectly degreased; 2 deciliters (6 3/4 fluid ounces, 7/8 cup) of white wine; a tablespoon of mustard; a pinch of pepper; a teaspoon of superfine sugar.

PROCEDURE. Cut the onions in slices 1/2 centimeter (3/16 inch) thick, which you will divide into cubes of the same size, i.e., 1/2 centimeter (3/16 inch) on each side.

In a deep, heavy-bottomed pot, with a capacity of 7–8 deciliters (3–3 3/8 cups) at the most, melt the butter. Add the onion cubes. Do not cover. Soften over low heat *without coloring,* stirring often with a wooden spoon. Allow about *30 minutes* until they are ready. They should be a bit yellowed and melting, like a compote.

Meanwhile, *reduce the wine by half* in a small pan. When the onions are ready, sprinkle them lightly with flour. Cook over *low heat,* stirring, for 5–6 minutes. It would be acceptable, even preferable, if this little roux colors, as long as the onion does not color at the same time, which you must avoid. Add the bouillon, hot or cool, and the wine. Bring to a boil while stirring, and arrange your pot for "skimming" *for 20–25 minutes.* At the end of this time, add the meat glaze, if you have some.

Only add the mustard just before serving; it must never boil. Dilute it first in a saucer with 2 tablespoons of the sauce before mixing it in with the rest. Add the pepper, and if necessary, the superfine sugar. Serve.

Hunter's Sauce *(Sauce Chasseur)*

Useful for tournedos, rib steaks, hash, beef roasts, etc. We give the fastest preparation for the home kitchen. *Time: 30 minutes. Serves 6.*

10 grams (1/3 ounce) of flour and 10 grams (1/3 ounce, 1 scant tablespoon) of butter for the roux; 2 1/2 deciliters (1 cup) of bouillon; 1 tablespoon of tomato paste; 4 medium mushrooms and 2 tablespoons of oil to sauté them; 2 shallots; 1 deciliter (3 1/3 fluid ounces, scant 1/2 cup) of white wine; 1 spoonful of chervil and tarragon, chopped; a good pinch of chopped parsley; 30 grams (1 ounce, 2 tablespoons) of butter to finish the sauce.

PROCEDURE. In a small pan, make a light brown roux. Dilute it with the bouillon. Add the tomato and pepper. Let it simmer slowly, *uncovered, 10–12 minutes.*

Rinse the mushrooms. Do not peel them. Cut them in thin slices. Heat the oil in a small sauté pan. Sauté the mushrooms over high heat, until lightly browned. Then add the chopped shallot. Sauté for *1 minute more.*

Put the cover on the sauté pan to extract all the oil and bring it to the surface. Add the mushrooms and white wine. Boil until reduced by *half.*

Skim the foam and the skin of oil that has formed on the sauce. Pour this sauce on the mushrooms. Stir. Simmer over *very low heat* for *6–7 minutes.*

Just before serving, remove from the heat and add the butter, chervil, and tarragon. Sprinkle the parsley over the sauce when it is poured on the meat.

Mushroom Sauce *(Sauce Duxelles)*

Mushrooms are the essential and characteristic element of this classic sauce. However, since they are chopped, you can use the stems and the trimmings, which give the same flavor as whole mushroom. *Time: 30 minutes. Serves 6.*

110–120 grams (about 3 7/8–4 1/4 ounces) of mushrooms; a good tablespoon of chopped onion; the same of chopped shallot; 10 grams (1/3 ounce, 1 scant tablespoon) of butter and 2 spoonfuls of oil to brown them; 1 deciliter (3 1/3 fluid ounces, scant 1/2 cup) of white wine; 2 1/2 deciliters (1 cup) of bouillon; a spoonful of tomato paste; 15 grams (1/2 ounce) of beurre manié (PAGE 48) with 15 grams 1/2 ounce) of flour; a spoonful of chopped parsley; a pea-sized piece of crushed garlic; 25 grams (1 ounce, 2 tablespoons) of butter to finish the sauce; a pinch of pepper and a soupçon (hint) of nutmeg.

PROCEDURE. Use a small, thick-bottomed sauté pan. Using this utensil is essential because mushrooms give off a great deal of liquid when cooked and the sauté pan will help both to evaporate the moisture from the mushrooms and reduce the liquid. Heat only 10 grams (1/3 ounce, 1 scant tablespoon) of butter until hot. Throw in the chopped onion and shallot. Lower the heat and sauté, uncovered, stirring often with a wooden spoon, until they turn a nice blond color; do not allow the mixture to brown. Then add the finely chopped mushrooms, pepper, and nutmeg.

Cook over high heat, stirring constantly, so that the mushroom juices evaporate. When the steam diminishes, add the white wine. Let it boil, uncovered, to reduce a little, by about one-third. Finish with tomato, bouillon, and finally the beurre manié (PAGE 48). Simmer gently for *8–10 minutes,* possibly even more.

Just before serving, add the garlic, crushed with the blade of a knife; the chopped parsley; and the butter, off the heat, of course.

Piquant Sauce *(Sauce à la Diable)*

This sauce is ideal for meat that has been breaded and grilled, such as breast of mutton, poultry, trotters, boiled beef, etc. To justify its name, the sauce should taste very zesty and peppery, though this should not be exaggerated. *Time: 15 minutes. Serves 6.*

25 grams (1 ounce) of finely minced shallot; 1 deciliter (3 1/3 fluid ounces, scant 1/2 cup) of white wine and 1 deciliter (3 1/3 fluid ounces, scant 1/2 cup) of tarragon vinegar; 2 1/2 deciliters (1 cup) of bouillon; a little brown roux made with 15 grams (1/2 ounce, 1 tablespoon) of butter and the same of flour; a spoonful of meat glaze, warmed; a teaspoon of minced chervil and tarragon; cayenne pepper or freshly ground black pepper.

PROCEDURE. In a small pan, combine the shallot, white wine, and vinegar. Bring to a boil over high heat, uncovered, until the quantity of liquid has reduced by three-quarters, leaving only about 1/2 deciliter (1 2/3 fluid ounces, scant 1/4 cup).

Meanwhile, prepare the roux in another small pan. When the wine and vinegar have reduced, add the bouillon. With this liquid, dilute the roux. Bring to a boil, then boil slowly for 5 minutes.

Just before serving, add the meat glaze and a point of cayenne (as much as can be held on the tip of a knife) or a pinch of pepper. Taste to check the salt note; finally, add minced chervil and tarragon. Do not let it boil any longer, *because boiling will absolutely spoil the fresh taste of the herbs.* If you prepare the sauce in advance, keep it warm in a double boiler.

Italian Sauce *(Sauce Italienne)*

There are numerous uses for this sauce. Lamb chops, veal escalope, various meat hashes, beef and veal tongue, etc., as well as fish and some vegetables—artichokes, to name just one. Essentially this is a duxelles combined with *sauce brune.* We offer the most simplified recipe, adapted to the resources of the home kitchen. *Time: 30–35 minutes. Serves 6.*

100 grams (3$^1/_2$ ounces) of mushrooms, which could be only trimmings and stems; 50 grams (1$^3/_4$ ounces) of onion; 2 shallots; 15 grams ($^1/_2$ ounce, 1 tablespoon) of butter and a spoonful of oil; 1 deciliter (3$^1/_3$ fluid ounces, scant $^1/_2$ cup) of white wine; 2 deciliters (6$^3/_4$ fluid ounces, $^7/_8$ cup) of veal jus; a spoonful of tomato paste; 50 grams (1$^3/_4$ ounces) of lean cooked ham; 15 grams ($^1/_2$ ounce) of beurre manié with 10 grams ($^1/_3$ ounce) of flour; a half spoonful of minced parsley; pepper; nutmeg.

PROCEDURE. In a small sauté pan, heat the butter and the oil. Lightly color the minced onion and shallot over low heat.

Chop the mushrooms *as fine as possible,* and add them to the vegetables that have already lightly browned. Season with pepper and nutmeg. Stir over high heat. Once all the steam from the mushrooms has disappeared, pour in the wine. Let it reduce almost completely. Add the tomato and the jus. Once it boils, let it simmer gently for *10 minutes.*

To finish: Bind the sauce with the beurre manié (SEE BINDING SAUCES, PAGE 28). Finish with the ham cut into little cubes, 3 millimeters ($^1/_8$ inch) per side, and the minced parsley. Keep it warm and don't let it boil.

NOTE. The ham is left out when the sauce is used for a fish dish.

Tomato and Butter Sauce *(Sauce Aurore)*

This sauce is based on a velouté, with tomato concentrate added. A pleasant rosy tint is the result, hence the name "aurore" (dawn). Allow about three-quarters of velouté to one-quarter tomato concentrate.

Sauce aurore is a particularly apt accompaniment for eggs, pork, veal, and poultry. The velouté should be made with either veal bouillon or chicken bouillon, depending on the dish with which it will be served. The chicken bouillon can be made with an old hen, or even with the carcass and bits and pieces of the bird that went into the main dish for which the sauce is the accompaniment. *Time: 45 minutes (if the bouillon has already been prepared). Makes 5 deciliters (generous 2 cups) of sauce.*

6 good deciliters (2$^1/_2$ cups) of clear bouillon, veal or fowl; 25 grams (1 ounce, 2 tablespoons) of butter and 20 grams ($^2/_3$ ounce) of flour for the roux; 30 grams (1 ounce) of mushroom trimmings; a small bouquet of 5–6 parsley stems; a good deciliter (3$^1/_3$ fluid ounces, scant $^1/_2$ cup) of tomato concentrate (this can be canned, or prepared with fresh tomatoes in season), see the recipe for TOMATO PURÉE (PAGE 534); 40 grams (1$^3/_8$ ounces, 3 tablespoons) of butter to finish the sauce.

PROCEDURE. Prepare the velouté in a small pan. That is, a *roux blond* diluted with bouillon. Add the parsley and mushroom trimmings. Skim the sauce for a good 30 minutes. Strain the velouté. Add the tomato concentrate. Reduce over high heat, stirring, until you have a little less than 5 deciliters (generous 2 cups).

Add the butter *off the heat.* Serve or keep warm in a double boiler.

Rich Mushroom Sauce *(Sauce Poulette)*

Classically served with lamb trotters, this is also served with other white meat dishes, some vegetables, mussels, and oysters. The sauce is always mixed directly with the ingredients and is never served on the side in a sauceboat.

Velouté sauce is the base, and the addition of egg yolk makes it similar to *sauce parisienne.*

Depending on the finished dish, you can enhance the basic elements with a mirepoix, some white wine, or some minced onion, as for mussels and shellfish. The mushrooms, in this case, can be left out. However, they are obligatory, so to speak, for any other dish, in the form of trimmings or cooking liquid. The characteristic acid note comes from lemon juice, which cannot be replaced by vinegar. *Time: 45 minutes. Makes 5 deciliters (generous 2 cups) of sauce.*

60 grams (2 1/4 ounces, 4 1/2 tablespoons) of butter; 30 grams (1 ounce) of flour; 5 deciliters (generous 2 cups) of jus or of *clear uncolored bouillon*; 1 deciliter (3 1/3 fluid ounces, scant 1/2 cup) of mushroom cooking water; 2 nice egg yolks; half a small lemon; salt, white pepper, nutmeg, a bunch of parsley tied with kitchen string; 15 grams (1/2 ounce) of mushroom trimmings; a pinch of minced parsley.

PROCEDURE. Use a thick-bottomed pot with a 1-liter (4-cup) capacity. Prepare a *roux blond* with 30 grams (1 ounce, 2 tablespoons) of butter and the flour. Dilute it with the jus or bouillon. Season. Bring to a boil. Add the bunch of parsley and the mushroom trimmings. Skim it carefully (SEE SKIMMING, PAGE 16) for 30 minutes.

For the thickener, put the egg yolks in a bowl, diluted with 2 tablespoons of the mushroom water. Squeeze the lemon into a small cup.

Remove the bunch of parsley from the sauce. Strain the sauce through a *chinois* into a sauté pan large enough to hold the food and sauce later on.

Pour the remainder of the mushroom water into the strained sauce. Mix. Stir the sauce over high heat with a wooden spoon, for *2–3 minutes.*

Thicken the sauce with the egg yolks, proceeding as directed (SEE THICKENING SAUCES, PAGE 47). Then remove from the heat and add: the remainder of the butter, the lemon juice, the minced parsley, and the mushrooms (if you are using them), previously cooked. Check the salt. Put the meat or the food you are serving into the sauce. Serve.

NOTE. Keep the sauce warm in a double boiler if you are not using it immediately. Do not add the butter or the lemon juice until the moment that you add in the food to be served.

Piquant White Sauce with Herbs *(Sauce Ravigote Chaud)*

Traditionally served to accompany veal head and white meats. The base is a white sauce, or velouté, which is enhanced with a reduction of white wine and vinegar flavored with herbs and shallots. It's a sort of piquant white sauce. *Time: 25 minutes. Serves 6.*

20 grams (2/3 ounce, 1 heaping tablespoon) of butter and 15 grams (1/2 ounce) of flour for the white roux; 3 deciliters (1 1/4 cups) of clear uncolored bouillon; 1 1/2 deciliters (5 fluid ounces, 2/3 cup) of vinegar (tarragon if possible) and white wine, which is 4 good tablespoons of each. If the vinegar is weak, use 1 deciliter (3 1/3 fluid ounces, scant 1/2 cup), with only 1/2 deciliter (about 1 2/3 fluid ounces, scant 1/4 cup) of white wine; 25 grams (1 ounce) of shallots minced very fine; 12 grams (3/8 ounce) of chives; 5 grams (1/6 ounce) of chervil; 5 grams (1/6 ounce) of minced tarragon; 30 grams (1 ounce, 2 tablespoons) of butter to finish the sauce.

PROCEDURE. In a small pan, prepare a white roux, cooked for 2 minutes over low heat. Dilute with the bouillon. Let it simmer slowly during the reduction.

The reduction: In another small pan, combine the vinegar, wine, and shallot. Being minced fine, it will not be noticed in the sauce. Reduce quickly to *1/2 deciliter (1 2/3 fluid ounces, scant 1/4 cup).* Pour this into the reduced sauce in the other pan. Simmer *5–6 minutes.*

Just before serving, remove from the heat. Add the chopped herbs, *which must not boil.* Finish with the butter. The sauce should be a bit tangy.

Onion Sauce *(Sauce Soubise)*

This is really more a *coulis* (a loose purée) than a sauce, given its consistency. It can be made with meat by using bouillon, or be meat-free by using milk. At any rate, it is served with white foods.

We offer here the simplest method, which, in our opinion, produces the best result. *Time: About 1 hour, 30 minutes. Makes about 1/2 liter (generous 2 cups) of sauce.*

250 grams (8 7/8 ounces) of onion; 60 grams (2 1/4 ounces, 4 1/2 tablespoons) of butter; 12 grams

($^3/_8$ ounce) of flour; $2^1/_2$ deciliters (1 cup) of clear uncolored bouillon, or the same quantity of milk; 2 tablespoons of *thick* crème fraîche; pinch of salt, pinch of pepper, touch of nutmeg, pinch of *superfine* sugar.

PROCEDURE. Peel the onions. Slice into rounds as thin as possible. *If the onions are old,* blanch them after they are sliced to remove the acidity. To do this, put them in a pan with cold water to cover. Bring to a boil. Let them boil for *7–8 minutes.* Cool. Drain thoroughly.

If the onions are fresh, blanching is not required. Put them immediately into a deep, heavy-bottomed pot, with 40 grams ($1^3/_8$ ounces, 3 tablespoons) of butter. Cover and stew gently for *a 15 minutes without coloring.* Sprinkle them with the flour. Mix well and let them cook for 1–2 minutes only to make a white roux. Add the bouillon or milk. Add the seasoning. Stir until it boils. Cover and put it in a moderate oven or over low heat for *a good 45 minutes,* stirring from time to time. Force through a fine metal sieve, rubbing it through with the pestle. Rinse the pan and put the purée back. Add 3–4 tablespoons of bouillon or milk to obtain a coulis, or a very light purée. Bring to a boil. Remove from the heat. Add the rest of the butter (20 grams, $^2/_3$ ounce, 1 heaping tablespoon) and the cream. Keep warm in a double boiler until ready to serve.

Cream Sauce *(Sauce Crème)*

This is a meat-free béchamel, very reduced, and with very fresh heavy cream added. You can prepare it as directed for lean béchamel sauce, with the onion stewed in butter. It will be tastier. Or, more simply, use a small bunch of parsley with a seasoning of salt, pepper, and grated nutmeg, which is the recipe that follows. If the sauce is served with boiled fish, add lemon juice. Cream sauce is also served with vegetables, eggs, and certain poultry dishes. *Time: 25–30 minutes. Serves 6–8.*

15 grams ($^1/_2$ ounce) of flour and 15 grams ($^1/_2$ ounce, 1 tablespoon) of butter; $3^1/_2$ deciliters ($1^1/_2$ cups) of milk; a small bunch of parsley tied with kitchen string; salt, pepper, and nutmeg; $1^1/_2$ deciliters (5 fluid ounces, $^2/_3$ cup) of crème fraîche.

PROCEDURE. In a small pan, make a *white* roux with the flour and butter. Dilute it next with the boiling milk. Season. Stir until boiling. Add the bunch of parsley. Let it cook gently for *10–12 minutes.*

Remove the parsley. Raise the heat. Boil, stirring constantly with a wooden spoon until the sauce is reduced to about *2 deciliters ($6^3/_4$ fluid ounces, $^7/_8$ cup).* It should be quite thick.

Lower the heat. Stir well, then add the heavy cream, which gives the sauce the right flavor and finesse, as well as the necessary consistency.

Strain through a *chinois* or fine sieve. Keep warm in a double boiler with a few bits of butter dotted over the surface.

Cheese Sauce *(Sauce Mornay)*

This has a lean béchamel as the base. When you add grated cheese, it becomes sauce Mornay.

This sauce is not served in a sauceboat. Unctuous and very much thicker than an ordinary sauce, it must completely coat the food over which it is spread.

It is used for fish in particular. But it is also appropriate for some white meats, as well as certain vegetables: cauliflower, Chinese artichokes (chirogi), endive, cardoons, celery, etc. Depending on how it is used, several modifications are made. *Time: About 1 hour, 15 minutes. Makes $^1/_2$ liter (generous 2 cups) of sauce Mornay.*

4 tablespoons of lean béchamel sauce; 60 grams ($2^1/_4$ ounces) of grated Gruyère and Parmesan, half of each (in other words, 3 medium tablespoons); 50 grams ($1^3/_4$ ounces, $3^1/_2$ tablespoons) of butter to finish the sauce.

PROCEDURE. The Gruyère must be a bit dry, because if it is too fresh it will make the sauce stringy. Make sure the Parmesan does not have too strong a flavor, which would overpower the sauce. It would be better, if that is the case, to replace it with the same quantity of Gruyère.

If the sauce is intended for fish, add the cooking liquid from the fish. A fish served with Mornay sauce should be cooked in only a small amount of liquid—in other words, poached, depending on the case, with a little fish bouillon, white wine, or water mixed with lemon juice. Using this cooking liquid in the sauce will give it a stronger fish flavor. If the sauce is intended for use with white meat, poultry, or sweetbreads, do the same with the cooking juices from these dishes.

When you add the cooking liquid from the fish or from the white meat, allow *1 deciliter (3 1/3 fluid ounces, scant 1/2 cup)* of liquid for the above proportions. Directions for the reduction are given below.

For vegetables, the sauce is simply finished with butter, added off the heat. For other dishes, you can add mushroom cooking liquid. And, no matter how the sauce is used, you can always refine it by adding *a bit of crème fraîche* and then continuing to reduce it until it reaches the correct consistency. In fact, the crème fraîche addition enhances the basic béchamel sauce.

Do not forget that the seasoning of *sauce Mornay,* whether it be for fish, meat, or vegetables, is most important. It must be verified very carefully, mainly due to the saltiness of the cheese itself. So, at the very last moment, when the butter has been added, taste the sauce to check if a little more salt is needed. You can spice it up with a point of cayenne (as much as can be held on the tip of a knife).

PROCEDURE. Prepare the necessary quantity of béchamel sauce, as directed (SEE BÉCHAMEL MAIGRE, PAGE 53). Strain it into a small pan. If using cream, or any cooking liquid, this is the moment to add it, as directed below, before any other ingredient. Otherwise, simply bring the sauce to a boil for a few seconds. Add the cheese. Cook, stirring, until it is completely melted. Remove from the heat; it will not be returned again in the course of this dish. Finish with the butter, mixed in as pieces about the size of a walnut. The sauce is now ready for use, and is equally good for vegetable dishes.

With Cream. For the quantities we give, use 3–4 tablespoons of excellent cream. Once the béchamel sauce has been brought to a boil, as above, stir it constantly over high heat and add the cream, spoonful by spoonful. Cook until you reduce the sauce to the original quantity of 4 deciliters (1 2/3 cups). Next, add the cooking liquid, then the cheese, the butter, etc., or, depending on the case, only the cheese and butter.

With Fish Cooking Liquid. You can use the liquid straight from the pan, but you must *subsequently* reduce the sauce over high heat for 2–3 minutes. Alternatively, put the cooking liquid in a small pan first and reduce to *2 spoonfuls,* then simply add it to the sauce. After this, add the cheese and butter, as directed.

With White Meat Cooking Liquid. Same procedures as above.

Anchovy Sauce *(Sauce Anchois)*

In professional kitchens, this sauce for fish dishes is prepared with "fumet," which is a very concentrated fish stock. Anchovy butter is added, as well as anchovy fillets cut into small cubes.

If you do not have fish stock or the amount of fish bones needed to prepare the right quantity, you can use the cooking liquid from mushrooms. But you may not have any of that, either, in your home kitchen. For this recipe, you will need almost 450 grams (1 pound) of mushrooms, or at least 325 grams (11 1/2 ounces), to obtain the 2 1/2 deciliters required to replace the fumet. However, these cooked mushrooms can be kept for 2–3 days and used for any kind of dishes that call for cooked mushrooms. *Serves 6.*

15 grams (1/2 ounce, 1 tablespoon) of butter and 15 grams (1/2 ounce) of flour for the white roux; 2 1/2 deciliters (1 cup) of mushroom cooking liquid; 1 deciliter (3 1/3 fluid ounces, scant 1/2 cup) of white wine; 5 small salted anchovies; 30 grams (1 ounce, 2 tablespoons) of butter for the anchovy butter.

PROCEDURE. Cook the mushrooms (SEE MUSHROOMS FOR GARNISH, PAGE 490) with 1 1/2 deciliters (5 fluid ounces) of water, a pinch of salt, 25 grams (1 ounce, 2 tablespoons) of butter, the juice of half a lemon.

In a small pan, cook the *white* roux. Bring to a boil and lower the heat. Let it simmer slowly while you prepare the anchovies.

The anchovies: Prepare as directed (SEE ANCHOVY BUTTER, PAGE 78), but be sure to first set aside 3 of the fillets, which you cut into small, 2-millimeter cubes.

To serve: Skim the foam that has formed on top of the sauce. *Remove from the heat,* add the anchovy butter to the sauce, divided into pieces the size of a hazelnut. Add the anchovy cubes.

Check the salt seasoning and finish with a dash of white pepper, or, if you like, a small point of cayenne (as much as can be held on the tip of a knife). Serve.

Shrimp Sauce *(Sauce Crevette)*

Depending on the times and the author, this recipe is interpreted in quite different ways: The classic master chefs preferred a *sauce allemande* finished with butter and lemon juice, and with shrimp tails added. Others make it like Nantua sauce, where shrimp are replaced by crayfish; another rendition is like a hollandaise enhanced with shrimp butter and shrimp tails. And, in modern professional kitchens, it is based on a velouté, or even a béchamel, prepared with fish bouillon to which cream, shrimp butter, and shrimp tails are added. It is this last recipe, adapted for the home cook, that we give here.

In professional kitchens, the rosy tint of the sauce comes from the addition of a very red butter, made with lobster carapaces. There is always a supply of this butter, and only a little bit is needed to give the sauce its color, which is supposed to be the same as the shrimp. The shrimp themselves can only provide the palest tint, even the more expensive "pink" shrimp, which would be an extravagance since gray shrimp are much finer. To replace the lobster butter, you can use food coloring, or *carmine,* sold in little bottles at the grocery store, which is what we call for here. *Time: 1 hour, 30 minutes, at least. Makes enough to fill a sauceboat.*

4 deciliters (1 2/3 cups) of lean béchamel sauce; 1 deciliter (3 1/3 fluid ounces, scant 1/2 cup) of crème fraîche; 125 grams (4 1/2 ounces) of nice grey shrimp, above all very fresh; 60 grams (2 1/4 ounces, 4 1/2 tablespoons) of excellent butter; 2–3 drops of red food coloring; a small point of cayenne (as much as can be held on the tip of a knife), optional.

PROCEDURE. Prepare the béchamel sauce as directed. (SEE BÉCHAMEL MAIGRE, PAGE 53).

Peel the shrimp. Leave the tails whole or cut them into little cubes, depending on their size. In a mortar, grind the heads and all debris into a fine paste. Add the butter, then the food coloring, the latter *very carefully,* since, if it is very concentrated, 1–2 drops will suffice. The rosy tint of the sauce must not be too strong. Force this paste through a very fine sieve. Set aside in a cup.

Strain the béchamel sauce into a small pan. Add the cream. Boil over high heat, mixing constantly with a wooden spoon, to reduce the sauce and restore it to its original consistency. *Remove from the heat,* and mix in the butter and shrimp, little by little, so they blend together as they should.

Check the seasoning. Add the cayenne and, finally, the shrimp tails. Keep warm in a double boiler until ready to serve (SEE HOLDING SAUCES, PAGE 50).

Rich White Sauce for Fish *(Sauce Genevoise)*

Appropriate only for fish, this sauce, such as it is made today, is simply the traditional *sauce génoise* called by a different name. The ingredients are still the same.

Geneva is not the place to find an authentic recipe for this sauce that coincides with those of modern French chefs. It is in households that respect regional traditions and which prepare this sauce using only the bouillon from the fish with which it is served. They absolutely do not use *sauce brune*—or even *espagnole*—as is generally the practice in contemporary professional kitchens.

So here, from the best source, is how to prepare a *sauce genevoise* in Switzerland, specifically as it is done in the territory of Vaud. The fish, primarily trout and char, is cooked in a court bouillon made with the local white wine—Yvorne, Villeneuve, etc. (in another region, the wine will naturally be different). Water is added to the wine, equal to one-third the volume of the wine.

The most common recipe is much like a *sauce blanche,* with the court bouillon replacing the water. It is finished with a liaison of egg yolks and cream. So: 25 grams (about 1 ounce) of flour blended with 30 grams (1 ounce, 2 tablespoons) of butter. Dilute with a glass and a half (3 deciliters, 1 1/4 cups) of court bouillon. Thicken with 2 egg yolks beaten with a spoonful of cream (the latter is optional). Add, as for a *sauce blanche,* 60 grams (2 1/4 ounces, 4 1/2 tablespoons) of butter to finish. Such is the authentic *sauce genevoise* made in fine home kitchens.

The method taught by our great modern chefs is very different. Briefly stated, it's like this: Add *sauce brune* to an excellent fish bouillon made with red wine and the head of a salmon, reduced but not strained. Cook gently for a good hour. Force everything through a fine sieve to make a sort of *coulis.* Add a little more red wine and fish bouillon. Skim the sauce for a long time, and reduce it if its consistency is not correct. Finish with a bit of good strong butter and a little anchovy butter, or a touch of anchovy essence from a bottle.

Note that the addition of anchovy butter is characteristic of the classic *sauce génoise.* Regarding its use in the sauce *genevoise* of today, all the modern authors, with one or two exceptions, are in agreement.

Finally, we offer this simplified recipe for a meat-free *sauce genevoise,* as prepared by Urbain Dubois: Use a mirepoix of onions and carrots, made with butter, sprinkled with flour; let it brown slightly and dilute with a court bouillon of fish. Cook for 15 minutes. Meanwhile, reduce some good red wine; 1/4 liter (1 cup) reduced by half for a sauce for 6. Strain the sauce into the wine. Reduce over high heat for a few minutes. Finish with anchovy butter. *[Translator's note: Urbain Dubois (1818–1901) trained in the kitchens of the Rothschild family before rising to fame as a chef, notably to the Russian Prince Orloff and then in Germany, where he presided over the kitchens of William I.]*

Oyster Sauce *(Sauce aux Huîtres)*

Although the price to which oysters have climbed encourages few to use them as an accompaniment, we shall nonetheless offer a recipe for the classic oyster sauce, which should never be left out of a culinary work.

This sauce accompanies turbot, brill, and salmon equally well and, in general, all large cuts of fish cooked in court bouillon. The liquid used here is bouillon, or fish fumet (very concentrated stock). This gives a characteristic savor to the sauce, which no other combination could obtain. Thus, you should not try to replace it with, for example, béchamel, counting on the cooking water from the oysters to give you the right result. This would just be a bad imitation of the real sauce. In any case, we have already said that the purchase of a few whitings for a sauce is not a useless expense, since the fillets can be used.

We will not specify the type of oysters (Marenne or similar). Above all, they must be very fresh. *Time: 1 hour, 30 minutes. Serves 10.*

For the fish bouillon: **The heads and bones of 3 small whitings; 4 thin rounds of carrot; 4 rounds of onion; a small bouquet garni; 3 deciliters (1 1/4 cups) of water; 2 1/2 deciliters (1 cup) of white wine; 3 grams (1/10 ounce) of salt; 4 peppercorns.**

24 small oysters; 25 grams (1 ounce, 2 tablespoons) of butter and 25 grams (1 ounce) of flour for the roux; 3 egg yolks; 4 spoonfuls of cream, very fresh; 150 grams (5 1/3 ounces, 10 1/2 tablespoons) of butter to finish the sauce; salt, pepper, nutmeg, a point of cayenne (as much as can be held on the tip of a knife).

PROCEDURE. The fish bouillon. Prepare as directed in fish bouillon (PAGE 165).

In a 1-liter (4-cup) capacity pot, make a *light blond roux.* Dilute with the strained fish bouillon. Season with: a half pinch of white pepper, a half pinch of grated nutmeg (about 1/2 gram). Once it boils, continue cooking over very low heat. Add the bouquet garni and a good pinch of mushroom trimmings, if you have them. From this time, simmer for *35 minutes.* Be sure to skim the sauce from time to time.

The oysters: Open them over a bowl so you don't lose any of their juice. As you open them, put them in a small pan placed near you. Afterward, spread a sheet of thin cheesecloth or a linen cloth over the pan and pour in the oyster juice. This way you will not add any pieces of shell with the juice.

Put the pan over high heat and do not leave, because *once it begins to boil you must turn off the heat.* It is simply a matter of cooking them a bit, without cooking them completely.

Leave them in their water until they have cooled somewhat. Then, drain them by transferring them to a plate with a slotted spoon. With a good knife, cut off the beard. *You serve only the heart* of the oyster. Put them back into their juice, and, as soon as you finish the sauce, reheat them completely, always without boiling, before you put them in the sauce.

To finish the sauce: In a bowl, prepare egg yolks diluted with cream for the liaison.

Strain the sauce through a fine *chinois* into a sauté pan. Add all the oyster juice. Reduce until there is no more than *4 deciliters* (1²/₃ cups). Turn off the heat to thicken. Turn the heat back on and, stirring constantly, cook for 30 seconds only. This is enough to cook the yolks and still retain the desired consistency, the cream having lightened and finished the sauce.

Add the butter *off the heat.* Check the salt. Add the point of cayenne. Strain the sauce again into a double boiler. Add the oysters. Keep the water in the double boiler almost boiling.

Mussel Sauce *(Sauce aux Moules)*

To accompany boiled fish. *Time: About 45 minutes. Serves 6.*

About 30 small mussels (about 3/4 liter, generous 3 cups) from the small species.

Cooking: 1 1/2 deciliters (5 fluid ounces, 2/3 cup) of white wine; 3 shallots; 3–4 parsley stems; some thyme sprigs; a quarter leaf of bay; pinch of pepper.

20 grams (2/3 ounce, 1 heaping tablespoon) of butter and 15 grams (1/2 ounce) of flour for the roux; the cooking liquid from the mussels and 1 1/2 deciliters (5 fluid ounces, 2/3 cup) of milk; 1 egg yolk, diluted in 3 tablespoons of cream, or, by default, milk; 30 grams (1 ounce, 2 table-spoons) of butter to finish; a teaspoon of minced parsley.

PROCEDURE. Clean the mussels (SEE MUSSELS, PAGE 241). Cook them with the above ingredients, as directed. As soon as they open, remove the shells; carefully reserve the cooking liquid; keep the mussels warm in a small pan, with a few drops of their cooking liquid to prevent them from drying out.

In a small pan, make a light blond roux. Dilute it with the cooking liquid from the mussels (about 2 deciliters, 6 3/4 fluid ounces), which should be free of sediment, and the milk, boiled beforehand. Add a pinch of pepper, but not yet salt. Bring to a boil. Simmer slowly for 5 minutes.

A few moments before serving, thicken the sauce (SEE THICKENING SAUCES WITH EGG YOLK, PAGE 49). Remove from the heat, then add the butter and taste for salt. Mix the mussels and minced parsley into the sauce. If preparing in advance, keep warm in a double boiler.

Crayfish Sauce *(Sauce Nantua)*

One of the best and most desired sauces, to serve as an accompaniment to turbot, brill, salmon, or trout, cooked in a court bouillon.

This preparation, a little more complicated than most sauces served with fish, can be described as follows: A béchamel sauce base, reduced with crème fraîche, and to which crayfish butter and crayfish tails are added at the last moment. *Time: A good hour. Serves 10.*

For the béchamel: 30 grams (1 ounce, 2 tablespoons) of butter and 35 grams (1 1/4 ounces) of flour for the roux blanc; 3/4 liter (generous 3 cups) of boiled milk; a half onion, finely minced; a bunch of parsley sprigs and a sprig of thyme tied together with kitchen string; 8 grams (1/3 ounce) of salt; pinch of pepper; a hint of grated nutmeg; 2 deciliters (6 3/4 fluid ounces, 7/8 cup) of very fresh thick cream.

8–10 medium crayfish or 15 smaller ones; 100 grams (3 1/2 ounces, 7 tablespoons) of butter; a few drops of red food coloring.

PROCEDURE. **The béchamel sauce:** Prepare it in a 1 1/4-liter (5-cup) capacity, heavy-bottomed pot. First, color the onion in the butter for 2 minutes, before adding the flour; follow the directions already given for preparing this sauce (SEE SAUCE BÉCHAMEL, PAGE 52).

The crayfish: For the quantity of crayfish suggested, put in a sauté pan: 30 grams (1 ounce, 2 tablespoons) of butter; 30 grams (1 ounce) of finely minced onion; 2 parsley stems, roughly chopped; a sprig of thyme; a portion of bay leaf almost the size of a fingernail; a deciliter (3 1/3 fluid ounces, scant 1/2 cup) of white wine; a pinch of salt and pepper. Heat without boiling, then add the crayfish, properly trimmed as directed in their section (SEE CRAYFISH, PAGE 228). Sauté over high heat; cover; cook over low heat for *a good 10 minutes.*

Next, remove the carapaces one by one. Put them on a plate. On another plate, gather all the debris, the shells, and heads. With a knife, remove the "string" in the tail. Cut them in half lengthwise. Put them in a small pan or other utensil that can withstand high heat, because the tails must be reheated before being added to the sauce, *although they must absolutely not boil.* Pour over the liquid from cooking through a fine linen cloth to strain; add a teaspoon of *fine champagne* (cognac) and a tablespoon of mushroom cooking liquid, if possible, or add some water. Cover. Set aside.

With the remaining 70 grams ($2^1/_2$ ounces, $^1/_3$ cup) of butter, prepare the *crayfish butter* (PAGE 79) as directed, straining through the sieve into a double boiler. Set aside at room temperature.

To finish the sauce: Strain the béchamel sauce through a *chinois* into a small sauté pan. Add some cream, *but reserve 4 good tablespoons.* Put the pan over high heat and reduce the sauce, stirring constantly, until it has thickened and is no more than about *$4^1/_2$ deciliters (scant 2 cups).*

Remove the sauce from the heat. Mix in the reserved cream, which thus retains its flavor. Again, strain through a *chinois* into a double boiler. Gradually, add the crayfish butter, in pieces about the size of a walnut, mixing with a whisk. Next, add the food coloring, *drop by drop,* until the sauce becomes a good pink color. Set the pan over the double boiler pan. Just before serving, add the crayfish tails.

Egg Sauce *(Sauce aux Oeufs)*

Very frequently used in English cuisine to accompany certain fish, notably haddock. This is simply a basic béchamel with the addition of hard-cooked egg. *Time: 30 minutes. For 500–600 grams (1 pound, 2 ounces to 1 pound, 5 ounces) of haddock or cod.*

30 grams (1 ounce) of flour and 40 grams ($1^3/_8$ ounces, 3 tablespoons) of butter for a roux blanc; 4 deciliters ($1^2/_3$ cups) of boiled milk; 2 *warm* hard-cooked eggs; a small bunch of parsley sprigs tied with kitchen string.

Mix the butter and flour over the heat, without letting it color. Dilute with the milk. Add the parsley, salt, pinch of pepper, and grated nutmeg. Stir until it boils, then simmer gently. Just before serving, remove the parsley and mix the hard-cooked eggs, cut into small cubes, into the sauce. Serve in a sauceboat.

White Sauce *(Sauce Blanche)*

This is the "butter sauce" of classical French cuisine. Indeed, the word "butter" emphasizes the importance of the role it plays here. Flour and water are the only other ingredients, along with a hint of lemon juice or a bit of very good vinegar. The sauce must not contain any egg yolk, which would turn it into a false hollandaise, or any cream.

We should make it clear here that this simple sauce, quite acceptable to accompany fish or some asparagus at home, would not be acceptable on a formal fine restaurant menu, where it would be a fault to fail to substitute a *proper* hollandaise sauce.

To prepare this white sauce *(sauce blanche),* two things must be noted.

1. *The flour must be of the highest quality,* so that it thickens immediately—in other words, the sauce must be sufficiently thick, since repair attempts using beurre manié never achieve a good result. It's quite simple to thin the sauce, if it is too thick, by adding a few spoonfuls of boiling water. However, it is extremely difficult to thicken it by adding flour.

2. *The sauce must not boil,* because it will then take on an unpleasant taste of glue, which will persist even after you have added the butter.

As for the butter, it must be, if not best quality, at least very good, and *very fresh. Time: 6–8 minutes. Makes 5 deciliters (generous 2 cups) of sauce.*

125 grams ($4^1/_2$ ounces, 9 tablespoons) of butter; 35 grams ($1^1/_4$ ounces) of flour; 4 deciliters ($1^2/_3$ cups) of boiling water; 5–6 grams (about $^1/_6$ ounce) of salt; a touch of grated nutmeg (optional); a dash of vinegar or the juice of a quarter lemon.

PROCEDURE. In a small pan, measure the 4 deciliters ($1^2/_3$ cups) of *boiling* water. Add the salt. Turn on the heat and bring to a boil so that you have *exactly the quantity of truly boiling salted water*—that is, still boiling—at the right moment.

You will have ready, on the other side, a pan that can contain *at least double the volume of your sauce.* Thus, for the quantities given above, you will need a pan with a capacity of 1–$1^1/_4$ liters (4–5 cups). This is essential so that you can work the sauce vigorously without it spilling out over the sides of the pan. Furthermore, as much as possible, this pan should have a rounded bottom. With completely straight sides, the flour collects in the angle formed by the bottom and sides of the utensil, so the whisk or wooden spoon has difficulty reaching it, and lumps result. This pan can be of any metal, or ceramic, or enameled steel. They will all do the job. If you are using a wooden spoon, have a sauce whisk ready as well.

Put the flour into the pan with only *one-third* of the butter. Here, about 40 grams (1³/₈ ounces, 3 tablespoons). Place over very low heat, just enough to melt the butter so that it can combine with the flour. *Do not cook.* This is not a roux and the flour must not cook in the butter. It is the boiling water that will do the cooking.

Remove from the heat. With a wooden spoon, stir the butter and the flour to obtain a smooth, easy-flowing batter. Keeping the pan still *off the heat,* pick up the sauce whisk in your *right* hand. With your left hand, grasp the pan containing the *rapidly boiling water.* Pour the entire contents, in one go, into the pan containing the batter of flour and butter. *Immediately stir in all directions* to completely blend the flour with the liquid. With just a few strokes of the whisk, you will achieve the right thickness, without lumps. If the water was at *full boil,* the flour should be sufficiently cooked. There is no reason whatsoever to replace the pan over the heat to further warm the sauce.

To finish the sauce, you just need to add the vinegar, 7–8 drops only, or the lemon juice. Still *off the heat,* add the rest of the butter, divided into small pieces to melt better and faster. Stir with a whisk until all the butter has been incorporated into the sauce. Pour it immediately into a heated sauceboat.

NOTE. If the sauce is made in advance, even by just a few minutes, do not leave it on the heat, where there is a risk of boiling. If this happens, it will not only take on a taste of glue, which nothing will remedy, but the butter will also turn to oil. Set the pan on top of a double boiler (SEE KEEPING SAUCES WARM, PAGE 50). When the sauce has to be made in advance, add the vinegar or lemon juice only at the very moment when you pour it into the sauceboat.

Caper Sauce *(Sauce au Câpres).* This is identical to *sauce blanche* (white sauce), or *sauce au beurre* (butter sauce), with the addition of capers just before serving. Allow 2 heaping tablespoonfuls for each ¹/₂ liter (generous 2 cups) of sauce.

Green Gooseberry Sauce *(Sauce aux Groseilles Vertes).* An extremely old French classic, this sauce accompanies poached or grilled fish, especially mackerel.

Instead of water, you can use the court bouillon used for a fish that has simply been boiled in salted water. *Time: 45 minutes. Makes about ¹/₂ liter (generous 2 cups) of sauce.*

250 grams (8⁷/₈ ounces) of gooseberries; 60 grams (2¹/₄ ounces, 4¹/₂ tablespoons) of butter; 20 grams (²/₃ ounce) of flour; 2 deciliters (6³/₄ fluid ounces, ⁷/₈ cup) of warm water; a pinch of minced fennel leaves; pepper, salt, nutmeg.

PROCEDURE. Choose rather large gooseberries, still very green and therefore not yet at complete maturity. Trim the stem and the little point at the end. Immerse them in a pot of boiling water. Put it over medium heat. As the gooseberries take on a yellowish color and rise to the surface, remove with a strainer. Avoid boiling, which will burst the fruits and cause them to lose their juice.

Force them through a sieve and collect the purée, about 1 deciliter (3¹/₃ fluid ounces, scant ¹/₂ cup), in order to add them to the prepared white sauce (SEE PAGE 68). At the same time, add the minced fennel, previously blanched in boiling water for 2 minutes and well drained.

Mustard Sauce *(Sauce Moutarde).* As an accompaniment for grilled or poached fish, particularly fresh herring, mustard sauce can be prepared in several different ways.

Some authors use hollandaise sauce as the base, then add the mustard. Others use a white sauce thickened with egg yolks.

More economically, but still remaining within the rules, you can stick with a classic white sauce—in other words, the true butter sauce that is not thickened with egg yolks—and add the mustard to this. But the most important point, whatever the sauce base, is that you must *never let the mustard boil.*

Allow, for 5 deciliters (generous 2 cups) of white sauce, 1 tablespoon of mustard, added with the butter, off the heat (SEE WHITE SAUCE, PAGE 68).

Parsley Sauce *(Sauce Persil)*. To be served with fish cooked in court bouillon; for brains, calf's head, calf's foot, etc. Basically, it's a butter sauce or a white sauce with an infusion of parsley.

Its preparation is the same whether serving with fish or meat, the only difference being that for fish you use a fish court bouillon—about one-third of the total liquid. In this case, the parsley infusion is made in the court bouillon. *Time: 30 minutes. Serves 6.*

100 grams (3 1/2 ounces, 7 tablespoons) of butter; 15 grams (1/2 ounce) of flour; 3 deciliters (1 1/4 cups) of boiling water (or 2 deciliters/6 3/4 fluid ounces /7/8 cups of water and 1 deciliter/3 1/3 fluid ounces/scant 1/2 cup of court bouillon); 12 grams (3/8 ounce) of parsley leaves; a tablespoon of minced parsley; 2 grams (1/14 ounce) of salt; a point of cayenne (as much as can be held on the tip of a knife); 7–8 drops of lemon juice.

PROCEDURE. In a small pan, boil the deciliter (3 1/3 fluid ounces, scant 1/2 cup) of court bouillon. Toss in the parsley leaves; cover; let it infuse *10 minutes.* Next, in another pan, make the sauce as directed (SEE WHITE SAUCE, PAGE 68), adding the boiling water to the strained deciliter (3 1/3 fluid ounces, scant 1/2 cup) of parsley infusion.

Put the minced parsley into a fine strainer, to dip it for only 3–4 seconds in boiling water. Dry it in a kitchen towel; twist it hard to extract all the water. Finish with lemon and cayenne. Check to see if the sauce has enough salt.

Tomato Sauce *(Sauce Tomate)*

The recipes for this are quite diverse, as much in terms of what is added to the sauce as of the actual cooking techniques.

Generally, in small home kitchens, cooks are content to add to the tomatoes cooking in the pan only a simple bouquet garni, sometimes a clove-studded onion, and a little bouillon if available, and binding the whole with *uncooked* flour. Adding this uncooked flour, and often in considerable quantity, produces a gluey sauce. To avoid this, many people believe that they must leave out the flour and instead reduce the tomato to a point where it is no longer a sauce, but a thick purée, which is not appropriate for the use made of it.

Depending on what it accompanies, a tomato sauce must have the consistency of a coulis that is more or less thick. For example, when it is meant to form a ribbon on a plate around certain foods, it should be a little more "stiff" than when it is served in a sauceboat. In one form or another, the flour is needed to bind the solid parts of the tomato with its purely liquid element. But, there is proportion and procedure. In professional kitchens, this is achieved by the addition of a demi-glace *(sauce demi-glace)*. In a good home kitchen, this is achieved with a light roux, or even with a bit of arrowroot added at the end. (SEE TOMATO SAUCE FOR CONNOISSEURS, PAGE 72.)

Many different ingredients can be included in a tomato sauce. The old masters of haute cuisine used, aside from the essential mirepoix and, of course, depending on the dish: garlic, shallot, chopped mushrooms, meat glaze, fresh butter, lemon. This is not exactly an *espagnole* sauce, which contains an extremely reduced amount of flour, jus, white wine, etc. The same goes for tomato sauces, in which fish stock replaces jus and meat glaze. All this should serve as an example of how to vary the sauce recipes according to need. So you can add a very small quantity of white wine, or a pinch of sugar when the sauce is completely reduced if the tomato used is not very sweet. Lean and *always uncured* ham is preferable to bacon in a mirepoix.

As well as these sauces, which tend to be both rich and complex, are the simple coulis that have minimal seasoning, to preserve only the true tomato flavor. We offer some of these recipes below. But you must be mindful that, even if these recipes are less trouble and less expensive than the others, they may require more time and a great deal of attention in their preparation.

RECOMMENDATIONS. The seeds, all the "mucusoid" parts, as well as the water from the tomato must be removed before cooking. A number of people leave the seeds and everything stuck to them in order to simplify the preliminary initial work, arguing that, since the tomato has to be strained, there is no need to remove anything beforehand. Further, they believe that the tomato water adds to the amount of sauce. This is a mistake. The seeds absorb the seasoning to no effect and then make straining the sauce more difficult. Done properly, only the pulp of the tomato should be forced through the sieve, without the elements that have flavored it, such as onion, carrot, ham, etc. (What's more, these leftovers are not wasted and should be used to prepare a soup or stock.) For this reason, in professional kitchens, the sauce is strained through a muslin cloth, which ensures that everything is extracted perfectly. In home cooking, where only a normal sieve is used, even if it is very fine, it is important to be particularly careful about what is allowed through. The seeds, in this case, can be very troublesome.

Tomato Sauce, Classic Procedure *(Sauce Tomate, Façon Classique).* Since tomato sauce is commonly used in even the most simple kitchens, and it keeps so well, we will give quantities for 1 liter (4¹/₄ cups) of sauce. *Time: 1 hour, 45 minutes.*

1¹/₄ kilograms (2 pounds, 12 ounces) of tomatoes, net weight.

***For the mirepoix:* 30 grams (1 ounce) of lean bacon; 40 grams (1³/₈ ounces) of carrot; 30 grams (1 ounce) of onion; 20 grams (²/₃ ounce, 1 heaping tablespoon) of butter; a quarter bay leaf; a fragment of thyme; 4–5 parsley sprigs.**

30 grams (1 ounce) of flour; 4 deciliters (1²/₃ cups) of completely degreased bouillon or light jus; a pea-size piece of garlic; a bit of ordinary sugar; salt and pepper.

PROCEDURE. In a heavy-bottomed saucepan, large enough to hold the tomatoes, lightly brown the mirepoix (SEE MIREPOIX, PAGE 21). Then sprinkle it with flour, mix it well, and cook gently as for a *roux blond.*

Cut the tomatoes in half. Press each half with your fingers to extract the water and seeds. Put them in the saucepan. Add the bouillon, the garlic smashed with the blade of a knife, the sugar, a pinch of pepper and salt, adjusting the latter according to the saltiness of the bouillon.

Bring to a boil over high heat, stirring with a wooden spoon. Then cover the saucepan. If possible, put it in the oven, where the heat of cooking is more even. If not, turn down the heat, taking care to stir frequently to bring the part on the bottom up to the top. Allow *1¹/₂ hours* of cooking.

Strain. The tomato must be completely cooked, with all the solid pulp now dissolved. There is no need to lean hard with the pestle. Simple stirring with a wooden spoon should suffice, because the sieve must only retain the skins and what is left of the mirepoix. Rinse the pan and pour in the sauce. Bring it to a boil, stirring. Then, remove from the heat and sprinkle the surface with a few bits of butter.

Tomato Sauce, Simple Procedure *(Sauce Tomate, Façon Simple).* *Time: 45 minutes. Makes enough to fill a sauceboat.*

500 grams (1 pound, 2 ounces) of tomatoes, net weight; 15 grams (¹/₂ ounce) of flour and 15 grams (¹/₂ ounce, 1 tablespoon) of butter for the roux; 1¹/₂ deciliters (5 fluid ounces, ²/₃ cup) of bouillon; a small bouquet garni; a pinch of superfine sugar; pinch of pepper; 30 grams (1 ounce, 2 tablespoons) of butter to finish the sauce.

PROCEDURE. In a thick-bottomed saucepan, make a small *roux blond.* Dissolve it with the bouillon. Add the tomatoes cut in half, their seeds and water removed; bouquet garni; sugar; pepper; and salt, according to the saltiness of the bouillon.

Cover. Cook slowly in the oven or over low heat. Strain. Reheat in the rinsed saucepan. *Remove from the heat* and add the final butter.

Tomato Sauce, Home-Style *(Sauce Tomate, Façon Ménagère).* This recipe calls for fat, which gives a special flavor to the sauce, as long as it is perfectly fresh and of high quality. The fat should come from roast pork, veal, or goose, or very good-quality lard. This quantity, relatively modest, cannot be replaced with the same quantity of butter because it will not give the sauce the same velvety rich texture as fat. *Time: 1 hour. Serves 6–8.*

750 grams (1 pound, 10 ounces) of tomatoes, net weight; 30 grams (1 ounce) of carrot; 30 grams (1 ounce) of onion; 5 grams (¹/₆ ounce) of parsley stems; 30 grams (1 ounce) of good fat; 15 grams (¹/₂ ounce) of flour; 1 good deciliter (3¹/₃ fluid ounces, scant ¹/₂ cup) of white wine; 5 grams (¹/₆ ounce) of salt; 5 grams (¹/₆ ounce) of sugar; a pinch of pepper.

PROCEDURE. Proceed as for the classic preparation. In the fat, lightly color the carrot and onion cut into mirepoix, then sprinkle with flour. Slowly, let it go golden. Add the tomatoes, wine, salt, sugar, pepper. Cook as directed, and strain as directed.

Tomato Sauce with Tomato Concentrate *(Sauce Tomate avec Purée de Conserve).* The dish is the same insofar as the elements added to the tomato remain the same. Only the time differs. The tomato concentrate is already cooked, so it is only a matter of letting the sauce cook long enough to become infused with the flavorings.

For example, *for the simple preparation:* Dissolve the small *roux blond* in the bouillon, add 3 good tablespoons of tomato concentrate; the sugar, pepper, salt. Bring to a boil. Simmer *7–8 minutes.* Add the final butter off the heat. Pour the sauce directly into the sauceboat.

Tomato Sauce for Connoisseurs *(Sauce Tomate des Amateurs).* A true culinary delight for the tomato lover. The preparation is very simple. But the most important thing is the length of cooking time, which must be *4 hours.*

PROCEDURE. Put the tomatoes, halved and with seeds and water extracted, into a deep, thick-bottomed saucepan. For 1 kilogram (2 pounds, 3 ounces) of tomatoes, add 2 tablespoons of good olive oil, 2 cubes of sugar, 3–4 parsley stalks, and 1 medium onion.

Cover the pot and put it over low heat. Keep the contents at a very slow and steady simmer. From time to time, stir the tomatoes with a wooden spoon. At the end of 4 hours, strain everything through a metal sieve *(tamis),* never through a strainer.

Return this purée to the heat. Add a teaspoon of arrowroot dissolved in a little of the cooled purée; 1–2 seconds of boiling will suffice. The starch is added to bind the little bit of liquid that remains with the most solid parts of the purée, and to thus give the sauce a smoother, more homogenous consistency. Now, add the slightest bit of salt and a pinch of pepper.

Hollandaise Sauce

This is the best sauce there is for poached fish and for certain vegetables, such as asparagus, etc. But this sauce also requires absolute precision when measuring the ingredients and great care during its preparation. Thus you should not be astonished by the abundance of explanations that follow, keeping in mind, above all, that some very inexperienced cooks have successfully made a hollandaise on the first try, and have never missed since, simply by applying the information given here.

A mixture of egg yolk and butter, with carefully adjusted seasoning—that's all there is to a *real* hollandaise sauce. The seasoning, apart from the salt and pepper, must come from lemon, and lemon only. Some people have taken to adding a reduction of vinegar. But this vinegar, which has no reason to be here as it does in a béarnaise, can be omitted. The flavor of the sauce will be superior and more characteristic. In this case, increase the amount of lemon juice at the end just a bit.

The quantity of butter, in relation to the amount of egg yolks, is a little more than 60 grams (2¼ ounces) for each yolk used. You should not exceed this quantity because this increases the risk that the sauce will separate. Here, we mean yolks from good-sized eggs. When you have only small eggs, you need 3 small yolks for 2 large ones.

The *butter* must be perfect, of the finest quality. However, some kinds of butter, even though quite good, leave a bitter aftertaste from the whey left behind after an incomplete churning. If this is the case, here's what you can do. Melt this butter (just warm it, don't heat it). Then let it rest for 7–8 minutes so the whey sinks to the bottom. Then carefully pour it into a bowl, leaving the white bits behind. Use it by tablespoonfuls, instead of putting little pieces of butter into the sauce; it will have absolutely the same effect while cooking.

To mount the sauce: Incorporating the butter into the yolks is called "mounting" the sauce, and there are two ways to proceed. But the most important point is to understand that if the sauce is not sufficiently heated, it will never arrive at its proper consistency. And, if the sauce is heated too much, it will curdle—in other words, it will separate. That said, the sauce will be capable of withstanding high heat as long as the heating is done gradually. *Any sudden burst of heat is liable to make the sauce separate.* In this case, the yolks will begin to solidify and the butter will become like oil. To mount the sauce, you can:

1. *Heat the pan directly on the burner,* provided that there is never more than a very gentle heat. This method requires a certain degree of experience, a great deal of care, and attention throughout, from beginning to end.
2. *Use a double boiler.* This involves putting the pan, from the outset, into another pan containing *almost* boiling water. With the double boiler, the risk of separation is gone since the degree of heat remains constant, though the heat source itself is much harder to control. And, you will be able to leave the sauce for a minute as it cooks to check on something else, and then find it as you left it when you return. The sauce can also be prepared well in advance, always a notable advantage, and left in its double boiler until needed.

Thus, we heartily recommend this second procedure, which is backed up by the opinion of professionals. But the double boiler must be used in a measured and comprehensive manner.

Choose any saucepan into which the saucepan containing the sauce can fit without tipping or floating. Two fingers (1 1/2 inches, or 4 centimeters) of space between the two saucepans, all around, is sufficient. Pour in the *rapidly boiling* water, or even better, boil the water in the saucepan, which is preferable.

Before putting in the pan with the sauce, make sure the flame under the water pan is turned down, so the water ceases to boil and retains *the same degree of heat.* This is very important throughout the process of making the sauce. Make sure your gas flame is spread out, not just in the middle of the pan. If you do not have a *very thick* pan, you will need to put either a saucer or a couple of pieces of wood at the bottom of *the water pan* so that the bottom of the saucepan is protected from too much heat. If the bottom of the saucepan rests directly on the bottom of the water pan, it would receive more heat than the rest. Once the pan bottom gets too much heat, the water cannot but boil, and so the sauce might get a burst of heat. This happens particularly when you are working with small quantities. *Time: 15 minutes. Makes enough to fill a sauceboat.*

200 grams (7 ounces, 14 tablespoons) of very fine butter; 3 large egg yolks; 3 tablespoons of good vinegar and 2 tablespoons of cold water; 6 grams (1/5 ounce) of fine salt; a pinch of white pepper; half a small lemon.

PROCEDURE. Whether heating directly or using a double boiler, you must first prepare the following:

For ease of operation, choose a *tall and narrow pot,* known as a *bain-marie,* or, failing that, an ordinary small saucepan made of tin-lined copper or thick aluminum, which is rather narrow, so that the sauce does not spread out over too large a surface and thus risk overheating.

Keep *a bowl with a little cool water and a teaspoon* in it always at the ready. A *small sauce whisk* is preferable to a wooden spoon but is nonetheless not essential.

Prepare the yolks in a second bowl. Be very careful not to allow any bit of white to remain, nor any specks of embryo, which would form white clots in the sauce, since, in the recipe we will use, the sauce does not need to be strained.

Divide the butter into pieces about the size of a walnut (about 30 grams, 1 ounce), that you put on a plate, somewhere cool enough to keep it from melting. (Or keep the melted and decanted butter ready, as directed above.)

PROCEDURE. **Summary:** Reduce the vinegar along with 2 tablespoons of water to a scant tablespoon. Let it cool almost completely. Add 1/2 teaspoon of cold water; mix in the egg yolks; add 30 grams (1 ounce, 2 tablespoons) of butter. Put the pan on the double boiler, whisk the mixture and, little by little, add the small bits of butter. Add a little cold water from time to time.

The details: Put the vinegar and the 2 tablespoons of water, the salt, and the pepper into the chosen pan. Boil, uncovered, until the liquid is reduced to *a scant tablespoon.* Remove from the heat. Let it cool a bit and add *1/2 tablespoon of cool water.*

Meanwhile, prepare your double boiler. When the reduced liquid and the pan are cool, first add the yolks to this liquid. Mix with a wooden spoon, then add about 30 grams (1 ounce, 2 tablespoons) of butter. *Then, put the pan in the bottom of the double boiler containing almost boiling water.*

Without stopping, even for an instant, mix with a wooden spoon or a sauce whisk, reaching into all areas of the pan. As soon as you perceive a slight thickening of the yolk and butter mixture, which indicates that the yolks have begun cooking, add another bit of butter. Do not add more butter until the preceding quantity is well incorporated.

The moment you see that the sauce appears too thick, add 1/2 teaspoon of cold water—in other words, only a few drops. This cold water slows down the cooking, which must happen only gradually and in relation to the overall quantity of butter. It is also the thing that makes the finished sauce lighter. The total quantity of cool water to be added is *1 1/2 tablespoons.*

We repeat that, in order to achieve the desired effect, the main principle to be respected during preparation is to never let the sauce overheat. The *gradual* cooking of the yolks is what is important here.

If, by chance, during preparation, you notice that the butter is beginning to separate or the yolks appear to solidify, you must, without losing a minute, remove the pan from the double boiler or from the heat. Rapidly add a healthy tablespoon of very cold water and whisk the sauce vigorously until it has regained its normal appearance—in other words, until it is smooth again. After this, you can continue to add the butter, after returning the pan to the double boiler and proceeding as directed.

When the butter is completely incorporated, remove the pan from the double boiler. Add 1 teaspoon of lemon juice and check the seasoning. You can add a little more salt or lemon juice if you feel that the sauce is not sufficiently tangy.

The sauce must be well bound, with a consistency thick enough to coat the back of a spoon, about 2–3 millimeters thick (about 1/8 inch). If it is thicker, simply add a very small quantity of water, about 1/2 teaspoon or even a full teaspoon.

If you are not serving the sauce immediately, you can keep it warm in the double boiler, taking care that the water is quite warm, but *not boiling.*

To serve, pour into a sauceboat, warmed first by rinsing with boiling water.

NOTE. If, despite using all the precautions indicated, the sauce curdles, or separates, you should transfer it to a bowl. Then, in the pan used for the sauce, removed from the heat and *cooled,* mix a new egg yolk and, *gradually,* pour in the curdled sauce, mixing all the while. Return the pan to the double boiler, which should not be too hot, to stir the sauce and remount it.

Hollandaise Sauce, Home-Style *(Sauce Hollandaise, Façon Ménagère).* This technique facilitates making the sauce so that it can be prepared over very low heat, without the protection of a double boiler.

It's simply a matter of adding a very small quantity of starch: rice flour or arrowroot.

What is important to understand is that the starch serves only to give the sauce the consistency that the yolks are able to supply. The starch is there only to support the egg yolks, to keep them from curdling—nothing else. When supported by starch, egg yolks can withstand high heat, even the boiling required to thicken a sauce. Thus, certain chefs mix a tablespoon of velouté sauce into the egg yolks of their hollandaise before they incorporate the butter to mount the sauce. The principle is the same. *Time: A scant 15 minutes.*

150 grams (5 1/3 ounces, 10 1/2 tablespoons) of good butter; 2 large egg yolks; 5 tablespoons of boiled and cooled milk; a small *teaspoonful* of starch; 3 grams (1/10 ounce) of salt; juice of half a lemon (a small one); pinch of white pepper.

PROCEDURE. Choose the correct small saucepan, as directed previously. Put in 25 grams (1 ounce, 2 tablespoons) of butter, the starch, 3 good tablespoons of milk, the yolks, the salt. With the whisk, *while still cool,* first mix these ingredients. Then put the pan over very moderate heat. Don't stop whisking for a second until the mixture has thickened and resembles creamy scrambled eggs. Remove the pan from the heat for just long enough to add a piece of butter. Lower the heat further, return the pan, mixing all the while to melt and incorporate this butter. Remove from the heat again to add another piece of butter. Return to the heat to whisk and incorporate. Repeat this until you have used up the last bit of butter.

To summarize, the technique consists of first *cooking* the egg yolks to the necessary stage, using the smallest possible amount of butter. Having done this, the sauce is "mounted" with the butter, which must not be heated beyond the point necessary to maintain the correct temperature.

Toward the end, add 2 tablespoons of warm, hot, or cold milk, depending on the temperature of the sauce at that moment, alternating with the last pieces of butter, to make it lighter, which is the desired consistency. To finish, mix in the lemon juice and the white pepper.

To keep the sauce hot until ready to serve, put the pan in the double boiler (SEE KEEPING SAUCES WARM, PAGE 50), leaving in the whisk to give it a final mix before pouring it into the preheated sauceboat.

Chantilly Hollandaise *(Sauce Mousseline).* This is a hollandaise sauce to which you add whipped cream just before serving. Its use is the same. The quantity of cream is 1 scant deciliter (3 1/3 fluid ounces, scant 1/2 cup) of thick, fresh cream, measured before whipping, for a hollandaise sauce that contains 4 egg yolks and 250 grams (9 ounces, 1 cup plus 2 tablespoons) of butter.

PROCEDURE. Whip the cream. See WHIPPED CREAM (PAGE 586).

Prepare the hollandaise sauce, following the first recipe, keeping in mind that the addition of cream will subtly soften the seasoning, which should thus initially be a bit stronger. At the very last moment, mix the whipped cream into the sauce by spinning the handle of the whisk between your hands, as you would to foam chocolate.

NOTE. *Sauce mousseline* has no additional ingredient other than cream. If it is of good quality and well whipped, this will be enough to obtain the desired result.

However, you may find that the cream you have does not whip well and that it is impossible to get it as firm as it should be. In this case, briskly beat an egg white, and add only *half* of it to the sauce. To make it frothy, incorporate it with the whisk, as explained directly above. This is a risky procedure, to be used only in dire need, because it strays from the basic rules. Furthermore, this addition of raw egg mars the flavor of the sauce.

Orange Hollandaise *(Sauce Maltaise).* Particularly recommended with asparagus, this is a hollandaise sauce that is flavored with the juice of a blood orange and some grated rind. Thus, for a hollandaise made with 3 egg yolks, use the juice of 1 orange and 1/3 teaspoon grated rind. Choose a quite ripe orange, with good healthy skin and a nice red color. Use a fine grater to grate the peel without getting the white part, which is very bitter. Cut the orange in half. Squeeze out the juice and strain it through a cloth. Just before serving, add the juice and zest to the hollandaise sauce, prepared exactly as in the basic recipe.

Béarnaise Sauce *(Sauce Béarnaise).* In sum, this is a hollandaise with a consistency thick enough to be picked up with a spoon, like a very firm mayonnaise, and in which the flavorings, much stronger than for hollandaise, include an infusion of shallot and tarragon. The shallot, as well as the thickness of the sauce, are the constants.

Sauce béarnaise best accompanies any kind of grilled food, including meat and fish.

For all the details of the techniques, see those for hollandaise sauce (PAGE 72), the skill and the risks being identical. *Time: 15 minutes. Serves 6.*

4 tablespoons of good tarragon vinegar; 4 tablespoons of white wine; 15 grams (1/2 ounce) of shallots; a sprig of tarragon; 2 sprigs of chervil; a pinch of coarse ground white pepper; 3 small egg yolks; 175 grams (6 ounces, 3/4 cup) of butter; a good teaspoonful of minced tarragon and chervil.

PROCEDURE. The *infusion* must be made without haste so that the ingredients have time to impart their flavor. It can be prepared well in advance and kept in a cup until you are ready to make the sauce.

In a small pan, combine: white wine, vinegar, coarse ground pepper, minced shallot, minced tarragon, and chervil. Slowly bring to a boil, uncovered, so that the liquid is thoroughly impregnated with the flavor of the aromatics, reducing it gradually, until there are only *2 full tablespoons.*

Strain through a fine strainer, pressing on the herbs to extract all their essence. If it is to be used immediately, let it cool.

The sauce: Same choice of pan and same technique as for the hollandaise. Use a double boiler if you are inexperienced, which will permit you to understand by instinct, so to speak, the degree of heat that is dangerous to exceed.

Put the infusion in the pan with the egg yolks. Mix it with a whisk. Add a pinch of salt and about 15 grams (1/2 ounce, 1 tablespoon) of butter divided into pieces. Set it on the double boiler. Stir continuously. When you notice it beginning to thicken, add some butter, *the size of a walnut,* and whisk, stirring vigorously. Do not add more butter until the preceding piece is completely mixed into the sauce.

With all the butter added, the sauce must have, as previously stated, the consistency of a very thick mayonnaise. The sauce need only be *warm* for serving and, in any case, it cannot be served too warm without separating. Just before serving, add the teaspoon of minced chervil and tarragon.

Mayonnaise Sauce *(Sauce Mayonnaise)*

True mayonnaise contains nothing more than egg yolk, oil, vinegar or lemon juice, salt, and pepper. Depending on preference, the lemon juice could completely replace the vinegar, or be used with it, in which case the quantity of vinegar is reduced. The addition of mustard is not part of a classic mayonnaise, this condiment being more or less reserved for tartar sauce. But, even so, this is something of a matter of individual taste.

A successful mayonnaise depends on three vital conditions of equal importance.

1. *The oil, the egg, the utensil, and the place where you work must all be at the same temperature, which should be lukewarm.* For many years it was claimed, erroneously, even by the great masters of classic cuisine, that cold facilitated the preparation of mayonnaise. Yet, just the opposite is true. Cold is its greatest enemy. And even though today there is no longer any professional who believes this to be true, it is still unknown in many a household, where the techniques of old recipes and family traditions are still followed. One might contest that mayonnaise is more difficult to make successfully in the summer because the heat is working against it. Bear in mind though, that people refrigerate more foods during the summer than they do during the winter. It is precisely this refrigeration, and nothing to do with the season, that is the cause of mayonnaise being more difficult to make in warm weather. Avoid ice, cold water, cool drafts, etc., and work with the oil at room temperature, about 35° Centigrade (53°F) in the shade, and your mayonnaise will mount as if by magic.

   The oil must always be used lukewarm. Thus, if it is kept in a cold or even a cool place, it is essential, *whatever the season,* to first let the bottle warm up near the stove or in warm water.

   The *eggs,* before being cracked, should be warmed up similarly, if necessary, by plunging them for the necessary time into warm water. The bowl to be used should have boiling water poured into it, *then be carefully dried.* Finally, *to make the mayonnaise,* find a warm place.

   All these directions apply in cold or cool weather. In warm weather they are unnecessary, so long as the elements of the sauce and the utensils are kept at room temperature.

2. *The precaution with which the oil must be added at the beginning:* Drop by drop, in the literal sense of the word.

   It is mostly at the beginning that this second condition is of utmost importance. Once the mayonnaise has taken well, you can pour in a thin stream and, further along, you can pour faster at the same time that you increase the movement of the whisk or spoon. To make it easier to control the flow of the oil, you can put the necessary amount into a small jug or pitcher. This is much easier than pouring directly from a large bottle or from a spoon that is refilled haphazardly when you do not have sufficient experience.

3. *The quantity of oil in relation to egg yolk.* If it is too high—that is, if there is too much oil relative to the quantity of egg—the sauce does not emulsify. On average, allow 1–1 1/2 deciliters (3 1/3–5 fluid ounces) for each yolk, depending

on how large the yolks are and how far in advance the mayonnaise is being made. If it is to be served immediately and the yolks are rather large, you can even go up to 2 deciliters (6 3/4 fluid ounces, 7/8 cup) per yolk.

On the other hand, an excess of egg in relation to the oil—in other words, too much yolk and not enough oil—could hinder emulsification, as will the opposite situation. It also has a distressing effect on the flavor of the mayonnaise, giving it a taste of *raw* egg. Now, this taste must never, ever be perceived. The egg acts as a binding element. It would be an error to believe that the more you use, the better it will be.

Time: 10–15 minutes. Makes enough to fill a sauceboat with mayonnaise.

2 large raw egg yolks; 3 deciliters (1 1/4 cups) of oil; 1 tablespoon of vinegar, or the juice of a small lemon; 8 grams (1/3 ounce) of fine salt; a good pinch of white pepper, ground fine (1 gram).

The quantity of vinegar suggested applies to good vinegar, not too strong. If not, you need less; dilute it with water.

Making the sauce: Professionals use only a sauce whisk, never any kind of beater. The latter is used only in households to replace the wooden spoon. But a simple whisk is preferable, because it allows you to moderate the pace and to control the action, which is not possible with a mechanical beater. If you don't have a whisk, a wooden spoon is better than a mechanical beater. Get one that is not too large and has a nice round end.

As previously stated, be sure all the ingredients and the utensils are absolutely lukewarm.

In a small or large bowl, place the egg yolks completely free of egg white and the germ. Add the salt, the pepper, and for our quantities, 1/2 teaspoon of vinegar to help dilute the yolks—professionals use the term *broyer* (to crush). This preliminary "breaking down" of the yolk before the addition of any oil is essential. Then, begin to pour the oil, drop by drop, stirring with the whisk or spoon, *in any direction*, frequently changing direction, provided that the movement is gentle, regular, and rather slow at this time.

Gradually, the mixture thickens, and when 2–3 tablespoons of oil, given the above quantities, have been thus incorporated into the yolks, you get a kind of thick batter that attaches to the wires of the whisk or to the spoon. To lighten the consistency of this batter, add a little vinegar.

From this point, you can pour the oil with less precaution, either adding it by small teaspoons at once, or by letting it flow in an uninterrupted stream. Now accelerate the movement of the whisk or the spoon until the end. Add the vinegar from time to time, when the consistency becomes so thick that it is difficult to incorporate the oil.

Finished mayonnaise must be just thick enough so that when you pick it up with the spoon and let it fall back into the bowl it does not spread out but holds together. It is an error to think that it must be so firm that it can be cut with a knife. If it is too firm when finished and the quantity of vinegar is sufficient, you can perfect the consistency with a bit of warm water, added little by little, a teaspoon at a time.

If, despite all due care, the sauce "turns"—that is, breaks down, with the yolk clumping into little clots in the clear oil—proceed as follows: In another small bowl, previously warmed to room temperature, put a raw egg yolk, crush it and pour in, little by little, the separated sauce, working exactly as you did for the initial batch.

Keep the sauce at moderate temperature until ready to serve. If kept cold, mayonnaise has a tendency to liquefy. If it must be prepared well in advance, it is better to diminish the quantity of oil in proportion to the yolk, the yolk being the element that supports the mixture. To keep the mayonnaise until the next day, simply place oiled parchment paper on the surface.

Tartar Sauce and Rémoulade Sauce *(Sauce Tartare and Sauce Rémoulade)*. The recipe for tartar sauce is rather difficult to pin down because, often, a single author will give two separate preparations. Generally, at least in contemporary cuisine, it's a mayonnaise enhanced with a considerable amount of mustard, as well as capers, cornichons, parsley, chervil, and tarragon, all minced fine.

Gouffé (SEE NOTE, PAGE 57) made it with mustard, shallots, and minced cornichons. Made thus, this tartar sauce hardly differs from rémoulade sauce, except for the anchovies added to the mayonnaise for rémoulade. These are in the form of fillets that are minced fine, or in a paste.

Real tartar sauce, it would seem, is made with hard-boiled yolks, reduced to a paste that is then blended just like mayonnaise. The inconvenience of a sauce made like this is that it separates rapidly. In other words, the oil returns to the liquid state, spilling over the yolks and the herbs.

The quantity of cooked egg surpasses that of the raw yolks in mayonnaise. For 2 deciliters (6 3/4 fluid ounces) of oil, you will need at least 3 large eggs, or 4 small ones.

PROCEDURE. For the eggs, SEE HARD-BOILED EGGS, PAGE 124. Force the yolks through a sieve into a small bowl and work them briefly with a wooden spoon. Add 1 teaspoon of good mustard, salt, and a good deal of pepper. Dilute with oil, poured drop by drop as with mayonnaise. Finally, mix in the parsley, chervil, tarragon, and capers, all minced. Use 1 heaped tablespoon of each for these proportions.

Green Sauce *(Sauce Verte)*

The term "green sauce" is used mainly to designate recipes for vinaigrettes, which include cornichons and capers minced with *fines herbes*, hard-boiled egg yolks, mustard, anchovies, etc.

The recipe given here, which is the one most commonly used, has become a kind of classic. It is, essentially, a mayonnaise to which a purée of herbs is added, giving it a particular flavor at the same time as giving it a pale green tint. If the herbs do not adequately color the sauce, add some spinach leaves. In certain preparations, these are often used as a coloring agent.

In haute cuisine, the herb purée is forced through a fine-mesh cloth *(étamine)*, instead of a fine sieve *(tamis)*, which allows some small specks of green to remain. With the *étamine*, you get a completely homogenous sauce resembling pistachio cream. However, it takes two people to force a mixture through an *étamine*, which is not always practical in a home kitchen. In this case, you must settle for a fine sieve and accept the small particles of herbs that might result. *Time: 30 minutes. Serves 12–15.*

40 grams (1 3/8 ounces) of spinach leaves; 40 grams (1 3/8 ounces) of watercress leaves; 20 grams (2/3 ounces) of parsley leaves; 20 grams (2/3 ounce) of chervil leaves; 20 grams (2/3 ounce) of tarragon leaves.

The weight of these herbs is *net*, completely trimmed, without stalks.

***For the mayonnaise:* 4 egg yolks; 6 deciliters (2 1/2 cups) of oil; 1 good tablespoon of vinegar; 8 grams (1/3 ounce) of salt; a generous pinch of pepper.**

PROCEDURE. Remove all the large and small stems of the herbs, because their weight must be based strictly on the leaves. Rinse them; dry them with a towel.

Prepare 1 liter (4 1/4 cups) of boiling water in a *copper pot that is not tin lined.* The copper preserves the fresh green tint of the herbs. If you do not have a copper pot, use an enameled one. But above all, nothing lined with tin. Plunge the herbs into the boiling water. Don't cover. Boil briskly *for 6 minutes.*

Drain the herbs in a strainer. Place under cold running water until completely cooled. Then put the herbs into a towel, twisting hard to extract all the water. Force them through the sieve *(tamis)*. Transfer the purée to a bowl, in which you will later mix them with the mayonnaise.

Make the mayonnaise as usual (SEE MAYONNAISE SAUCE, PAGE 76). Add it to the herb purée, spoonful by spoonful, mixing with a whisk. Taste to check the seasoning. Keep at a moderate temperature, and not refrigerated, as for any mayonnaise sauce, until ready to serve.

FLAVORED BUTTERS
Beurres pour Sauces et Garnitures

Anchovy Butter *(Beurre d'Anchois)*. You can prepare this with salted anchovies, or, more rapidly with anchovy paste, an excellent condiment, sold in bottles or tubes in all good grocery stores. Use only anchovies preserved *in salt,* and not in oil. These should not be used here. In France, salted anchovies can be found in fine gourmet stores, where they are kept in barrels and sold by weight. *Time: 15 minutes. Serves 8.*

125 grams (4½ ounces, 9 tablespoons) of butter; 6–7 salted anchovies (50–55 grams, 1¾–2 ounces).

PROCEDURE. Wash the anchovies in cold water to rid them of their salt. Dry them on a kitchen towel. With a small knife, scrape off the silver skin. Split them down the middle to remove the bones. Clean the fillets completely to remove all the little bones that remain. Crush them with a pestle. Having reduced them to a fine paste, add the butter and a pinch of pepper. Mix with the pestle until the anchovy paste is completely blended with the butter. Force it through a fine sieve. Nothing should remain on the surface. Gather this butter in a bowl. Mix briefly with a wooden spoon to smooth it out.

Without a mortar and pestle: Mince the anchovy fillets. With the blade of a strong knife, crush them into a paste as much as possible. Mix them with the butter, previously blended into a *pommade* in a bowl. Add pepper, salt. Sieve as above.

With anchovy paste. *Serves 8.*

150 grams (5⅓ ounces, 10½ tablespoons) of butter; 1½ tablespoons of anchovy paste; a small pinch of pepper.

PROCEDURE. Work the butter into a *pommade* (SEE BUTTER IN POMADE, PAGE 16). Mix in the anchovy paste and the pepper with the help of a small wooden spoon.

Shallot and White Wine Butter *(Beurre Bercy).* A very reduced infusion of shallots and white wine characterize the flavored butter known as "Bercy." In haute cuisine, when it accompanies grilled meats, small cubes of beef marrow are added. *Time: 15 minutes. Serves 6.*

150 grams (5⅓ ounces, 10½ tablespoons) of butter; ¾ tablespoon of finely minced shallots; 1½ deciliters (5 fluid ounces, ⅔ cup) of white wine; 80 grams (2¾ ounces) of beef marrow, very fresh; a teaspoon of minced parsley; a pinch of good salt and pepper; a quarter lemon.

PROCEDURE. Cut the marrow into ½ centimeter (3/16 inch) cubes. About 15 minutes before serving, put these cubes in a small pan of lightly salted boiling water. Poach them over low heat; the water should be barely simmering, not boiling.

Put the finely minced shallots and the white wine in another small pan. Boil rapidly, uncovered, until reduced by more than a good half. Let it come to room temperature. Add the butter that has been softened into a pomade (SEE BUTTER IN POMADE, PAGE 16), the warm and well-drained marrow, the minced parsley, salt, pepper, and lemon juice. If necessary, keep warm in a double boiler until ready to serve.

Crayfish Butter *(Beurre d'Ecrevisses).* Preparation is the same as for other butters made with shellfish—lobster, shrimp, etc.

Allow half the weight of the crayfish and debris in proportion to the weight of the butter. In other words, for about 250 grams (9 ounces) of carcasses and debris, use 125 grams (4½ ounces, 9 tablespoons) of good butter.

Generally, only the debris and carcasses are used for a butter. It is only when this debris has been used elsewhere, such as when making bisque, that the entire crayfish is used for the butter. It must then be prepared as for bisques: washed, cleaned, then cooked with a small mirepoix, white wine, and cognac only. SEE CRAYFISH, PAGE 228.

PROCEDURE. There are many ways to prepare the butter.

First method: Thoroughly pound the well-dried carcasses and all the debris in the mortar. Add the fresh butter. Mix well. Then add *red food coloring,* about 4–5 five drops for 250 grams (9 ounces) of carcasses and 100–125 grams (3½–4½ ounces, 7–9 tablespoons) of butter. Force through a fine sieve. Prepared thus, the butter has a very delicate and authentic flavor.

Second method: After the carcasses of the crayfish and the butter have been thoroughly pounded and mixed in the mortar, transfer the paste just as it is to a small pan over very low heat. Warm it and cook, mixing often, until the butter appears clear and colored like a red oil.

Pour everything through a kitchen towel stretched over a bowl of *very cold* water, and twist the cloth firmly to extract all the butter. This will solidify immediately when it falls into the water. You just need to take it out when ready to serve. If you need to make it in advance, *dry it* and press it down into a bowl that you keep chilled.

Parsley Butter *(Beurre à la Maître d'Hôtel).* If the butter is a normal consistency—in other words, malleable—put it in a bowl with salt, pepper, minced parsley, lemon juice, or vinegar. Mix well, either with the back of a fork or with a small wooden spoon. We say simply mix, not work the butter to a point where it becomes a *pommade.* It would be completely useless, and this overworking would also have the effect of altering the taste.

If the butter is very hard, knead it first in a damp towel until it has softened well, so that the seasoning and the parsley can be incorporated without having to work it too much.

When the butter is served beneath the item it accompanies, don't heat the plate to the point where it is very hot, because the butter will turn to oil and lose its creamy flavor.

Black Butter *(Beurre Noir).* Actually, the color of black butter is dark brown. If the butter were black, it would be burned, fit only to be thrown out.

Put the butter in a saucepan to melt and heat it until the indicated coloration. Pour it over the item it accompanies. In the still warm saucepan, add some vinegar and boil briskly until reduced by half. Allow 1 tablespoon of vinegar for 50 grams (1¾ ounces, 3½ tablespoons) of butter. Pour this over everything.

If you are using an omelet pan, after the vinegar, be sure to wipe clean and then grease the pan to avoid any risk of rust.

NOTE. You should not add the vinegar directly to the heated butter in the pan because it could overflow, which is dangerous. Always reduce the vinegar as directed. This cooking removes the acidity and adds to the flavor. When you are working with rather large quantities, the vinegar is reduced separately in a small saucepan while the butter is cooked in another saucepan. Remove the butter from the heat and wait a minute so it loses its initial heat before adding the vinegar, for the reason given above.

Hazelnut Butter *(Beurre Noisette).* This name does not imply the use of hazelnuts for the preparation of the butter. The term "hazelnut" refers to the method of cooking the butter, because when cooked in this manner it gives off a light aroma of hazelnut. It has many uses and is widely employed. In a small very clean pan, over low heat, cook the butter until it turns a blond color and gives off an aroma of hazelnut. Watch it carefully, without looking away even for an instant, so that you can remove it from the heat as soon as it has turned the right color. It takes only 1–2 seconds too many to end up with black butter, which will then not be correct for the kind of dish for which it is intended.

Shallot and Vinegar Butter *(Beurre Blanc).* The sauce known as "beurre blanc" traditionally accompanies freshwater fish, such as pike and shad from the Loire.

In a thick-bottomed pot, put 1 tablespoon of finely minced shallot, a good pinch of ground pepper, and 2 deciliters (6¾ fluid ounces) of very good wine vinegar. Bring to a boil, then lower the heat and reduce the vinegar until only 2 tablespoons remain. Add 4 deciliters (1⅔ cups) of court bouillon in which the fish has cooked—a court bouillon, made up of white wine, vegetables, and herbs, of course.

Melt 300–400 grams (10½–14 ounces, 1⅓–1¾ cups) of butter into this mixture (250 grams/9 ounces/1 cup plus 2 tablespoons will be enough for a 1.3 kilogram/2 pound, 14 ounce pike) previously divided into pieces the size of a walnut. Whisk constantly without letting it boil. The sauce will become frothy and acquire its characteristic whiteness. Check the seasoning and add salt if the court bouillon was not salty enough. Pour the sauce over the fish just before serving.

Since *beurre blanc* is a regional specialty, the recipes vary. Some authors add minced garlic to the shallot. Others thicken the sauce with egg yolks, but this compromises the whiteness of the sauce.

The addition of minced parsley just before serving is sometimes mentioned.

POTAGES AND SOUPS

POT-AU-FEU
Pot-au-Feu

A bowl of soup and a bit of beef is how many describe the uniquely French dish known as pot-au-feu. It should not be forgotten that there are a few vegetables in the pot as well, for pot-au-feu is a dish where nothing goes unused, and where the boiled food is not sacrificed to the bouillon, or vice versa. In a single dish, with the simplest of ingredients and for the same cost and care, pot-au-feu provides a sumptuous potage and an appetizing portion of meat. All that is needed to complete the meal is some cheese and fruit or a simple compote. Plenty for a hearty meal, and a good one, too.

In traditional French homes, the ritual for serving pot-au-feu is very specific. For example, in some homes, when the menu featured roast poultry, the soup was served first, followed by the beef, while in the more modest homes, beef was generally the only meat. The bouillon was poured over thin slices of grilled bread, with the vegetables served separately, unless those vegetables were reserved to accompany the beef. This is more common, in which case a good basic tomato sauce, or even a *sauce Robert,* is served alongside the beef.

Equally quite good, the beef can be served without the vegetables, surrounded in this case by a traditional ring of bright green parsley, and accompanied with mustard, cornichons, pickled vegetables, or any other piquant bottled condiments and sauces, which the English have contributed to French eating habits.

In general, pot-au-feu provides soup to be served on the day, as well as a supply of bouillon that can be used in a variety of ways. It can be kept for a hearty potage, or for a sauce, or braising, etc. Thus, beef prepared in this way provides more than just a single meal because the leftovers have so many diverse uses.

Choice of meat: The best piece is the *rump.* It is savory by itself, and yields a good bouillon and an excellent boiled beef, easily carved. It's the same for the *silverside.* The *topside* yields a very good bouillon, but the boiled beef itself is dry and unpleasant, unless the piece is cut very high, near the rump. The *chuck* also produces an excellent bouillon, but the beef is not very presentable, although it tastes less bad. The *short ribs* are quite good, in that they are less expensive than the rump and the topside and yield very good boiled beef and bouillon. For a small pot-au-feu, it is the best piece. Choose it well marbled, and remove, *before cooking,* all the excess fat, which you can use for some other purpose, such as frying.

For a substantial pot-au-feu—that is, in the 2¼–2¾ kilogram (5–6 pound) range—the best option is to use several different cuts of meat to make up the total weight. Thus, the piece destined for the main cut of meat should be taken from the rump or the silverside. It carves well. Add a small amount of topside, which will give depth to the bouillon, and a piece of knuckle or shin because its gelatinous quality will give the bouillon a discernable smoothness.

Note that to obtain good boiled beef, the meat must be properly aged, as if it were to be used in another method of cooking. For bouillon, it is the opposite, and freshly butchered beef will provide more juices. Choose your meat with this in mind.

The bones: Bones should not be overlooked, as long as they are used in a reasonable manner. That is how it is done in professional kitchens, where there is always an abundant supply. The correct way to prepare the bones is to cook them on their own for a very long time, a whole day, in order to obtain a primary bouillon in which the meat is cooked just for the required amount of time. This technique is excellent and we recommend it, whatever the quantity of the pot-au-feu. This increases the strength of the bouillon and greatly enhances the flavor of the meat by keeping the cooking time to a minimum.

The bones should be broken into small pieces before cooking so that they can better impart their essence to the bouillon. After having broken them up like this—and the butcher will do it for you if he is friendly—you brown them lightly, in a hot oven if possible, before putting them into the pot. This adds depth of flavor to the bouillon, as well as color.

A marrow bone is, by far, the choice of gourmets, but it is cooked differently from ordinary bones, to keep the marrow intact. A piece of marrow bone must not be longer than 6 centimeters (2½ inches) if you want to be able to extract the marrow easily from the interior. It must thus be sawed into pieces. To cook it, you wrap first it in a cloth, closed up like a purse, so the marrow cannot escape. To cook it perfectly, 15–20 minutes will be enough.

The quantity of water: Generally allow *1 liter (4¼ cups)* of water for every 500 grams (about 1 pound) of meat. This is the most common proportion, indicated in *pints,* which is the measure used in the oldest cookbooks. It is the best proportion to achieve your goal, which is to make a good bouillon. But it is important to note that this proportion is intended for meat weighed *with the bone in,* which accounts for one-quarter of the total weight. This puts the proportion to about 1¼ liters (5⅓ cups) for meat without the bone.

During the prolonged cooking period, you should expect evaporation to reduce the liquid by one-third.

The vegetables: Quantity should be in proportion to quality. In other words, if you use new spring carrots, you will need more of them than carrots that are fully mature.

Cooking times vary, and also need to be calculated based on the tenderness and the type of vegetable. In winter, carrots and turnips should be put in the pot as soon as the skimming is done, at the same time as the parsnips and celery. The leeks, which are more tender, are added an hour later. The bouillon is just as good, and the vegetables thus have a better appearance when served. On the other hand, in summer, you must not put the carrots and turnips into the pot until about 2 hours before serving. In this way, they will give all their flavor to the bouillon but still remain intact. If they stay in the bouillon too long, they take on its flavor.

Preparation of the vegetables: *Carrots and turnips,* carefully scraped, are left whole if they are young and small. If not, peel them and cut them in halves or quarters according to their size. Cut them lengthwise. Carrots must always have any interior yellow part removed, which is insipid and detracts from the bouillon. Certain French carrot varieties, such as "Crecy" or "Guérande," are red on the inside, which can be left. The vegetables should, of course, always be washed after peeling. A very good technique, which adds an appreciable flavor to the bouillon, as well as color, and which does not require much work and costs nothing, involves lightly coloring the carrots and turnips before putting them in the pot. Proceed as follows: After peeling, and if they are large, after cutting, divide them into pieces about the size of a cork. Put them in a pan with a bit of fat, from the meat or elsewhere. Cook over low heat, tossing from time to time to move them about. The vegetables should take on an even, golden color, without browning, especially without blackening, which would give a bitter taste to the bouillon. When you add them to the pot, be very careful not to pour in the fat in which they have colored. You can sauté them at the same time that you skim the pot-au-feu. Set aside until needed. They do not have to be kept warm.

The *leeks* should be chosen large. Peel them and remove most of the green leaves. Then, fold the little bit that remains over the white part and tie into a bundle with kitchen string. If the leeks are very large, cut them in half lengthwise first. Use the larger stalks of *celery,* without leaves. You can add them to the bundle of leeks. Peel the *parsnips* and cut into slices. Medium-sized *onions* are peeled and left whole. Stud them with cloves like pins in a pincushion.

Bouquet garni, cabbage, garlic: An authentic pot-au-feu has only parsley, thyme, and bay in the bouquet garni. On the other hand, it is classic to include a hint of garlic. For those who find even the very word frightening, let us remark that garlic is nonetheless an ingredient in even the most refined of great consommés. We also recommend using it, while stipulating a minute quantity in the recipe. *Chervil,* in sprigs, included by classic authors, is equally recommended.

When you add *cabbage* to the pot-au-feu, which does not usually contain cabbage, you must not put it into the pot, because it will spoil the bouillon with its very particular taste. Not only will the bouillon not have its correct flavor, but any leftovers that you keep for sauces will not be usable. Should you want to add cabbage to a pot-au-feu, you must always cook it separately. Choose a small, firm cabbage. Cut it in half or quarters and take what you need. Plunge it into a pot of boiling water and cook thoroughly for a good half hour. Drain. Then cook gently, covered, in a small separate pan, with some fat taken off the top of the pot-au-feu, and just enough bouillon to cover.

What you can add to the pot: *Giblets* should always be an essential element of the bouillon. Nothing will make it more refined. It used to be that it if a whole chicken was not used, at least the giblets were never omitted, and this resulted in the most exquisite of bouillons. If you have the giblets of a turkey or chicken, add them once the skimming is completed. If using a young hen, 2 hours before serving will suffice. For preparation: Burn off the feathers, remove the tubes of the feathers, clip the beak. Separate the head and the neck into 2 pieces. Cut the gizzard in half and clean thoroughly. Wash everything. Put it all into a bundle tied with string. Reserve the liver for another use. Serve the giblets with the beef, which is a delicacy. *Chicken, turkey, or other poultry bones,* roasted, and on the condition that they are absolutely fresh, will greatly improve the bouillon. Make sure that the interior of the carcasses do not have any traces of bile, which will give the bouillon a bitter taste. It's also a good idea to add *little bits of leftover roast beef or steak,* avoiding the burned parts that could make the bouillon bitter, *rib bones from roast beef, carcasses or leftovers of roast pigeons, a small piece of beef liver.*

What you must not add to a pot au feu: Leftovers of braised meats or other dishes that have been prepared with wine or eau-de-vie, which will distort the true taste of the bouillon. No leftovers of lamb, roast or otherwise. Lamb, if it has to be used, must be used alone. No pork, lard, or ham, which are reserved exclusively for a lamb pot-au-feu. No pheasant, duck, or game. You can use these for ordinary soups, but their flavor is too particular to meld with the bouillon of the pot-au-feu, which they will spoil.

Salt: Use 7 grams (1/4 ounce) per liter (4 1/4 cups) of water. If you plan to keep a certain amount of bouillon in reserve and need to boil it several times to keep it fresh, this reduction will accentuate the salt note. You should therefore diminish the initial quantity of salt and add the necessary quantity before serving.

Cooking time: This is calculated from the moment when the skimming has been completed and the degree of boiling is regulated for the entire cooking period. Take note that this time depends on the size of the meat pieces used, and not the total weight of the meat, since a small piece will cook faster than a large one. Thus, a pot-au-feu containing many small or medium-size pieces, weighing a total of 2 3/4 kilograms (6 pounds), does not need to cook as long as a pot-au-feu containing one large piece weighing 2 3/4 kilograms (6 pounds).

The utensil: The choice is a question of budget for the purchase and staff for the maintenance. If you cannot use tin-lined copper, *choose good, thick aluminum.* Cast-iron utensils frequently impart an unattractive color to the bouillon, and enameled iron is not usable unless it is in perfect condition, because a crack will expose the iron, as frequently happens over time, and this will cause the same problem.

When you prepare a pot-au-feu, make sure that you use a utensil that is not too large for the job. The liquid should come nearly to the top to make skimming easier. However, you need to calculate that, after skimming, you will need room for the vegetables. So, because of skimming, as well as evaporation during cooking, you will need two utensils of different sizes, which you use according to the appropriate circumstances.

To degrease the bouillon: You should not transfer the bouillon directly from the cooking pot to the serving tureen. First of all, it is difficult to degrease it this way, as is necessary. Furthermore, it is much easier to keep the bouillon in a pot in advance, completely ready to be served.

Another observation: Instead of using a metal-mesh sieve for the bouillon, which is very difficult to clean thoroughly, it is better to use, as was done formerly, a towel: a piece of cloth, a napkin or whatever, that has been used but does not have holes, which you can spread over an ordinary colander with large holes. You should always keep a supply of these cloths, called "bouillon strainers," which should be washed and rinsed carefully so they do not retain any odor.

To strain the bouillon, proceed as follows: Turn off the heat under the pot containing the bouillon. Next to it, place another pot in which you put the colander with the cloth spread over it. (If the bouillon has a great deal of fat on it, you can remove the excess fat with an ordinary metal spoon before pouring it. If so, you should tilt the pot slightly. In general, the degreasing is done only in the second pot.) With a ladle, spoon out the bouillon and pour it gently through the cloth, being careful not to disturb the beef and the other solids remaining in the pot. When you near the end, carefully tip the pot itself over the cloth in order to pour the remaining liquid directly into the second pot, without using the ladle. Put the lid on the first pot and set over very low heat to keep the beef and vegetables warm.

The bouillon must be completely degreased. After removing the surplus fat with the ladle, lay a sheet of tissue paper or some other fine paper, like that used by bakers (or a paper towel), which will immediately absorb the fat. Repeat if any fat remains. Cover the pot and keep warm and boiling until ready to pour into the soup tureen.

What you put in the bouillon: General rule: No pasta on the first day, when the vegetables are often served at the same time as the soup, in the classic tradition. This is when you add bread. In metropolitan areas of France, some bakeries sell extremely long thin loaves, called "flutes for soup," which are essentially nothing more than a light crust. They also make a kind of crouton *(croûtes de soupe)*, which you can easily prepare yourself. You must use slices of white bread, which you grill in the oven until they are completely dry, crackly, and of an even, dark brown color.

To color the bouillon: If the vegetables have been previously browned, as we have advised, these will be enough to give a color to the bouillon. If not, add a few drops of caramel coloring. At any rate, the color of the bouillon should be light and clear and not excessively brown.

[Translator's note: The French differentiate between two kinds of soup, though the distinction is not always clear. Potages *tend to be more elegant, often clarified or thickened and enriched with egg yolks, cream, etc., and more characteristic of the professional kitchen. Pot-au-feu falls into the potage category because its broth is clarified.* La soupe *tends to be a more rustic, often regional preparation, usually vegetable based, but not exclusively, and is more typical of family-style home cooking.]*

Traditional Pot-au-Feu
(Pot-au-Feu Ordinaire)

This recipe offers a good balance among the various ingredients. The cooking technique, the skimming, etc., does not vary. *Time: 4–5 hours total.*

1 kilogram (2 pounds, 3 ounces) of meat (without bones); 200 grams (7 ounces) of carrots; 130 grams (4½ ounces) of turnips; 2 large leeks (about 200 grams/7 ounces total); 3 onions, one of which should be studded with 2 cloves (about 175 grams/6 ounces total); 30 grams (1 ounce) of parsnips; 25 grams (1 ounce) of celery; 2½ liters (10½ cups) of water; 15 grams (½ ounce) of salt.

PROCEDURE. Arrange the bones on the bottom of the pot and the meat on top, tied with some string to maintain an even appearance. Add water and salt.

Put the pot over moderate heat, uncovered so that you can observe the froth rise to the surface. A gradual heating of the liquid is of paramount importance here, for the clarity as well as the flavor of the bouillon. The meat is gradually penetrated by the heat, which forces out the impurities in the form of foam that would otherwise cloud the bouillon. For the quantities indicated, allow about 30 minutes before the water shows signs of an imminent boil, marked by a discernible trembling.

The first froth is dark and quite impure. Remove it with a skimmer, or a slotted spoon, which is easier to handle when the foam is level with the sides of the pot.

If the boiling becomes too rapid, pour ½ deciliter (1⅔ fluid ounces, scant ¼ cup) of water into the pot. This *cold* liquid slows down the boiling and causes a new rising of foam, which is lighter in color, less dense, and less impure than the first. Skim it again and, when the boiling resumes, pour in another 1/2 deciliter (1 2/3 fluid ounces, scant 1/4 cup) of *cold* water. Following this, a third rising of foam will be produced, this time almost white. Skim. When the liquid begins to boil again, pour in a third 1/2 liter (generous 2 cups) of water. The foam that rises, in a very small quantity, should be perfectly white and clean. Remove it.

Next, add the vegetables, *if it is winter.* Otherwise, add only turnips, onion and garlic. When the foam caused by adding the vegetables has subsided, remove it. Then, with a damp cloth, carefully wipe the interior sides of the pot, so no trace of foam remains. Then set up the pot for cooking.

Cooking: From beginning to end, this must be conducted with the most perfect regularity. That is, a very gentle boil maintained throughout the entire cooking time, *and the boiling must occur only in a specific point in the liquid.* This condition is essential for the clarity of the bouillon. This is why a gas burner is preferable to any other mode of cooking, because it allows you to regulate the heat in a controlled way, and at the same time you are assured of a partial boiling. With another mode of heating—coal or electricity—you can get the same result by sliding a flameproof object under one side of the pot. Thus, with the bottom of the pot in contact with the heat only at a single point, the boiling remains limited to that place.

Cover the pot, leaving an opening the size of two fingers, about 1 1/2 inches (4 centimeters) wide. This will promote the clarity of the bouillon. If, for any reason the boiling stops, start it again slowly, in a gradual fashion.

After skimming, the cooking time is 3 hours from the start of boiling.

Proceed for all the rest as previously directed.

Pot-au-Feu "Rapid Method" ***(Pot-au-Feu "à Chaud").*** The meat is put in the boiling liquid, without gradually bringing it to a boil and without preliminary skimming. This method is frequently practiced in home kitchens, because it results in juicier boiled beef, since the meat is not as exhausted as with the other method. However, the flavor of the bouillon is obviously affected, if the normal quantities of liquid have been added. A bouillon made like this cannot be anything but quite weak, so you must reinforce it with ground meat, proceeding as if you were making consommé.

Croûte au Pot. This is a way to serve the bouillon from the pot-au-feu in a very informal manner. The *croûtes* are made from *flûtes* (very thin baguettes) from the bakery, which have been well cooked. These are cut in half lengthwise, the soft part of the bread scooped out, then cut into sections 4–5 centimeters (1 1/2–2 inches) long.

Butter these *croûtes* and toast them briefly in the oven. (Do not use the fat from the pot in place of butter, as was sometimes done, incorrectly.) Depending on your preference, the *croûtes* can be combined with the vegetables in the soup tureen or served on the side, along with cabbage cut into quarters. Put the vegetables from the pot-au-feu in the tureen, cut into pieces, over which you pour the bouillon once it has been completely degreased.

FIG. 28. EARTHENWARE POT.

Petite Marmite. This is the name for a classic French pot-au-feu, which is served in the traditional ceramic marmite (earthenware pot) where it has been cooked, or in which it is supposed to have been cooked (*fig.* 28). Everything is served at the same time in the same receptacle; bouillon—vegetables cut into small pieces, beef in little slices and this presentation has undergone a revival in good Parisian restaurants. We say "supposed to have been cooked" in the serving marmite, because in the kitchens of these Parisian restaurants, a pot-au-feu is generally prepared in huge pots and the marmite brought to the table is really just decorative, like a soup tureen.

On the other hand, the bouillon is more concentrated than a simple homemade bouillon, because it is not made simply from water at the beginning. Half water, half bouillon is used. Under these conditions, the beef can be cooked a little less to keep more of its flavor, without the flavor of the bouillon itself being weakened.

The bouillon for a *petite marmite* is not degreased with the same meticulous care used for a bouillon that is served as a soup. It is typical of this mode of presentation to leave a certain number of small islands of fat, which is very rustic. Always serve very hot, with thin slices of toasted bread. Add a little cooked cabbage on the side and some rounds of beef marrow.

CONSOMMÉ
Le Consommé

To understand what is necessary in terms of expense and care, you must first understand the nature of a consommé. It is a *double* bouillon. That is, a bouillon made up of at least twice the amount of meat as is usual. Furthermore, poultry is used, at least in the form of giblets and uncooked carcasses, even if you are avoiding the expense of a whole chicken. Besides, you can use the whole chicken for numerous other things when you are careful not to cook it too much.

Formerly, consommé was obtained by extremely prolonged cooking, 8 hours at least, to extract the juices from the meat while progressively reducing the liquid. This ultimately yielded the desired quantities. Or sometimes, especially in professional kitchens, consommé was prepared like pot-au-feu, where the water was replaced with bouillon. Of course, this was enhanced with more fresh meat. There was always a whole chicken included, which was previously browned on the spit to give color and flavor to the consommé.

Modern cooking has introduced some changes to these methods, while still respecting the principle. These days, the double quantity of meat is made up of *raw* beef, minced fine, which is added to the pot-au-feu bouillon that has been prepared in advance. In that form, meat releases its juices faster and more thoroughly. It is therefore this procedure—the one currently used—that we give as the most practical. It allows for the use of meat that has served as a base for pot-au-feu. And it sacrifices only the beef used for the consommé, because this beef, having released all its juices, is no longer good for anything.

A method that should be followed for all consommés, whatever the garnish will be, is to bind them *very lightly with tapioca,* which has the effect of smoothing out the consommé while leaving it absolutely transparent. This tapioca is cooked separately, in some bouillon. It must be very well cooked for this use, so that it can be strained through a chinois when it is added to the consommé before serving.

Soups listed as "consommé," regardless of the other ingredients, are found mostly on the menus at large formal dinners. These days, for dinners of that kind, the usual serving for each diner is just about 2 deciliters (6¾ fluid ounces, ⅞ cup). It is on this quantity that we base our requirements, using generous proportions and keeping a little extra in the tureen for later use.

Allow, for each liter (4¼ cups) of consommé, about 375 grams (13¼ ounces) of raw beef, quite lean, preferably taken from the topside. The aromatic vegetables, carrot and leek, that are added with the minced beef enhance the overall flavor. The egg whites, used for clarification, are there to ensure a sparkling clear result. *Time: At least 5 hours. Makes 2¾ liters (11½ cups) of consommé.*

3 liters (12¾ cups) of ordinary bouillon degreased as thoroughly as possible; 1 kilogram (2 pounds, 3 ounces) of raw beef; 3 chicken giblets, and all the trimmings and carcasses you have, which should be *raw and very fresh*; 100 grams (3½ ounces) of carrot; 150 grams (5⅓ ounces) of the white part of leek; 2 egg whites.

***For the recommended tapioca thickener:* 3 level teaspoons of tapioca (30 grams/1 ounce); 4 deciliters (1⅔ cups) of ordinary bouillon, scrupulously degreased.**

If you are not using tapioca as a binder, you must still increase the amount of bouillon for the consommé, so that you always finally obtain the 2¾ liters (11½ cups) of consommé ready to serve. You should estimate that,

during the cooking of the consommé, the liquid will reduce by about 1/2 liter (generous 2 cups).

PROCEDURE. The bouillon used for the consommé should be made in advance, either that same morning, or better still, the evening before. This means that the bouillon is ready for immediate use and cooled bouillon is easier to degrease perfectly, *which is very important.*

For this bouillon, allow 1 liter (4 1/4 cups) of water for every 450 grams (1 pound) of meat. The choice of cuts is determined by how the boiled meat is to be used. Depending on the case, use silverside, chuck, rump, topside, or short ribs that are not too fatty. A bit of beef knuckle makes the bouillon smooth. So, this first bouillon is prepared exactly like an ordinary pot-au-feu, including the customary cooking times.

When the beef is not from the topside, mince it very fine, having removed all nerve tissue or fat. If you have a mechanical meat grinder, you can use it here. Mince the giblets with a cleaver. Cut the carrot and leek *en brunoise*—in other words, in small cubes—without bothering to cut too strictly or regularly.

Put the egg white in a deep, tin-lined copper pan with a 4-liter (4 1/4-quart) capacity. Beat only for a second. Add the meat, gizzard, and vegetables. Mix and mash it all with a wooden spoon. Add the lukewarm or cool bouillon, proceeding as directed for clarifying aspic (SEE CLARIFICATION OF THE ASPIC, PAGE 46).

Finally, position the pot to maintain a gentle simmer for *1 1/4 hours. Do not cover.*

If you are using chicken in the consommé, this is the time to add it.

Tapioca: A good half hour before serving, put the reserved bouillon (4 deciliters/1 2/3 cups) into a small pan. Boil it. Add the tapioca, pouring in a thin stream so that it does not form clumps. Cover. Let it cook gently.

To strain the consommé: If are using chicken, take it out now.

Spread a damp and wrung-out cloth over a large colander placed over a pot. In this particular case, the procedure is perfectly adequate and faster than the one used for aspic. Pour the consommé and all that was included in its preparation—minced meat, vegetables, etc.—into the cloth. Let it strain *without touching anything.* This takes just a few seconds.

The consommé thus strained should be perfectly clear, and perfectly salted, which you check by tasting. Boiling will have reduced the liquid by 1/2 liter (generous 2 cups), so the salt note will be stronger. Immediately add the tapioca, straining through the chinois and mixing it with a wooden spoon to help it through. Next, mix it well with the consommé, using a spoon or a silver ladle.

Keep it warm until the moment you pour it into the soup tureen, but do not let it boil.

POTAGES
Potages

Soup with Thinly Sliced Vegetables *(Potage Julienne)*

This classic potage is very representative, in its simplicity, of good bourgeois cooking at the height of great French cuisine—in other words, toward the latter half of the nineteenth century. Thus, it deserves a more thorough explanation, to ensure that it is correctly prepared as much as those of other soups in the same category.

First, it would be good to clearly define the meaning of "julienne." Contrary to what a number of people still believe, the name does not refer to the vegetables that are included in the soup, but the manner in which they are cut into small thin strips. A soup containing these same vegetables cut differently is not a *potage julienne.*

Julienne-cut vegetables must never be cooked in a liquid of any kind without having first been colored in butter. (We do not call the necessary blanching for late-season vegetables "cooking.")

The best season for julienne is when the vegetables attain their maturity. Those of early spring, in April or May, lack taste. Those that have been stored—from January, February, and March—have lost the freshness that is vital for a good *potage julienne.* They must, in this case, be blanched before braising and coloring in the butter, not so much to make cooking them easier, but to diminish the strong flavor they acquire with age. (This applies mainly to carrots.)

Cabbage is not a mandatory ingredient for the julienne; Carême, the master, and his disciple, Gouffé, did not always include it. *Peas* also remain discretionary; you could add *asparagus tips,* and a few small *flageolet beans.* What is absolutely essential is *sorrel and lettuce that have been braised in butter.* These must never be omitted.

Sometimes, as a variation, you can add a few tablespoons of *rice,* cooked separately. Or, you can serve the potage with some small *poached eggs,* one per person, served on the side. In these special cases, the amount of potage served is one-third less than for the basic julienne recipe that follows.

We do not suggest using croutons, though this used to be done. In any case, you must never use fried croutons, but *grilled croutons* that will not release any fat into the soup. The classic chefs would not have used any other kind.

Potage julienne is made both with and without meat.

With meat, it is made of bouillon that has not an atom of fat and that is crystal clear—if necessary, clarified with egg white, as used to be done. A true *potage julienne* is characterized by a broth that is perfectly clear and fat-free. Clarity and absence of fat are the defining characteristics. As for the bouillon itself, the one that must always be used for fresh julienned vegetable soups is composed of half veal knuckle, half beef, and one or two giblets, according to quantity.

Without meat, it is made either with a good vegetable bouillon, which is known in haute cuisine as "root consommé," or with the cooking water from vegetables, fresh or dried according to the season; beans, peas, lentils, potatoes, etc., always with the goal of obtaining the greatest clarity possible, especially if you are using dried legumes, which are most difficult. If you have no other liquid, simply use pure water. But in this case, the taste of the soup will obviously be much weaker.

With or without meat, the julienne can include an *extremely light purée of dried legumes:* peas, beans, lentils, broad beans (fava beans), etc., as a liquid. In this case, the potage is prepared as for basic julienne—in other words, braising in butter, then cooking in bouillon or other appropriate liquid. The purée is added at the last moment. This will have been prepared separately, according to the rules of cooking of dried vegetables, skimmed, etc. The potage then becomes a *julienne à la d'Artois,* with dried peas, or an *à la Conti* with lentils, etc. *Time: 2 hours (if using spring vegetables). Serves 6–8.*

125 grams (4$^1/_2$ ounces) of carrot, yellow core removed; 125 grams (4$^1/_2$ ounces) of turnip; 25 grams (1 ounce) of white part of the leek; 35 grams (1$^1/_4$ ounces) of celery hearts; 40 grams (1$^3/_8$ ounces) of onion; 40 grams (1$^3/_8$ ounces) of sorrel leaves and the same of lettuce leaves; $^1/_2$ tablespoon of chervil leaves; a small firm quarter curly cabbage (optional); 1 deciliter (3$^1/_3$ fluid ounces, scant $^1/_2$ cup) of fresh green peas; 60 grams (2$^1/_4$ ounces, 4$^1/_2$ tablespoons) of butter; a pinch of salt (6 grams/$^1/_5$ ounce); 8–10 grams ($^1/_3$ ounce) of sugar.

1$^1/_2$ liters (6$^1/_3$ cups) of bouillon, without a trace of fat.

The weight of all the vegetables is given as *net:* in other words, after trimming and cutting.

PROCEDURE. **Cutting the vegetables:** The consistent cut of the vegetables is of great importance. Evenly sliced strips are required not only for appearance, but also for even cooking. This is essential; otherwise some will be too cooked, others not cooked enough. The little kitchen gadgets sold for this purpose are often flawed. What you get frequently lacks clean edges and the result cannot equal the effect of using a good knife of medium size, with a good-sized, well-sharpened blade.

The carrots. These should be chosen long and as large as possible, to allow you to cut them properly with the greatest ease. If the carrots are still young, you can use all of them. But, with older carrots, only the outside orange part is used because the inner core becomes tough and bland.

Peel them carefully to retain a maximum of the exterior orange part. Square them slightly on four sides, but not at the tips. Do this so the thinner pieces will not be more rounded on one end than on the other. Having squared the carrots, cut them to the desired length for the potage, which is 3$^1/_2$ centimeters (1$^3/_8$ inches).

Place the piece of carrot in front of you, upright. With your knife, cut the orange part on each of the squared four faces, in slices 2 millimeters ($^1/_{16}$ inch) thick at the most. Stop when you reach the yellow core of the carrot.

Assemble these slices in threes or fours, stacked on top of one another. Cut them lengthwise into strips, of the same 2-millimeter (1/16-inch) thickness.

Continue to do the same with the other slices until you have the indicated weight.

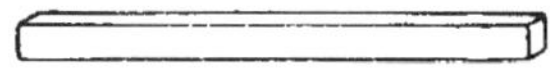

FIG. 29. FILLET OF CARROT.

The turnips. These should be chosen very firm, long, and large. To cut them, proceed as with the carrots, but without reserving the inside part, the turnip being used in its entirety.

The leek. Remove all of the green part, which must not be used. Its taste would be too dominant and it would not cook well, because it is too hard. Split the white part of the leek lengthwise. Cut rounds the thickness of the carrots and turnips.

The celery. Divide it into pieces the length of the carrots. Split them into 2–3 pieces, depending on their thickness. Then cut them lengthwise to obtain pieces the same size as the carrots and turnips.

The onion. Cut it into very fine rounds.

Assemble in one single pile: *carrot, turnip, leek, celery, and onion.* Prepare the cabbage separately.

If the vegetables are from late in the season and must be blanched, proceed as follows: Put them in a pan with cold water to cover completely. Bring to a boil for 7–10 minutes (from the moment of boiling), depending on how old they are. Drain thoroughly before braising.

The cabbage. Remove the stalk from the quarter cabbage, as well as the hard parts of the core. Cut the leaves crosswise into fine strips. Put the cabbage aside. It must be blanched before being added to the julienne. Since its flavor is much more pronounced than the other vegetables, it must previously be attenuated.

Therefore, during the following braising of the vegetables, plunge the julienne of cabbage into a pot filled with boiling water. Let it boil vigorously for 7–8 minutes. Drain, then plunge into cold water. This cabbage julienne should not be added until after the other vegetables have been braised in butter, and only when you add the bouillon, so that its flavor does not dominate the ensemble.

Cooking: *Braising.* Braising is gentle cooking without liquid. The goal of this braising is to first evaporate most of the water contained in the vegetables, and then to saturate them with butter. They cannot begin to color until they have released their water.

It is essential that the utensil chosen should be as thick as possible. After evaporation, the vegetables have to heat up enough to color, but they will burn if the pot is too thin. Good thick aluminum is preferable. Failing this, a good pot in cast iron can be used. But the problem with some cast-iron pots is that they destroy the clarity of bouillons and jus. And the clarity of the bouillon is one of the characteristics of a *potage julienne.* Use a deep pot that will be large enough to contain the liquid.

Sprinkle the vegetables with salt and superfine sugar. Mix them with your hands to combine everything thoroughly. Put them in the pot with 40 grams (1 3/8 ounces, 3 tablespoons) of butter Set over a *very moderate heat* and stir with a wooden spoon for 4–5 minutes to melt the butter and heat everything. Turn down the heat to *very low.* Do not cover. Have a wooden spoon handy to mix the vegetables from time to time. Lift them with the spoon to change their position without breaking them.

Braise gently in this way for about 20 minutes, until the vegetables have rendered their water little by little. If you heat them too much at the beginning, the vegetables will burn and darken without having released this water. They will be both raw and burned at the same time, whereas vegetables braised over low heat are practically cooked at the point when you add the liquid.

As long as white steam rises in abundance from the pot, the vegetables still contain water. It is only when this water has evaporated that they begin to color. From this moment, the vegetables run the risk of burning, and in the blink of an eye, if they are not watched very closely. You must stir them, lowering the heat as necessary, until they are *very lightly* colored and have taken on a golden tint. *Above all, do not let them brown.* This will result in a bitter taste that is difficult to correct.

Note that to obtain this uniform golden color, without burned parts, it is important that there is enough cooking fat—butter in this case—relative to the quantity of vegetables. These tend to burn when one is too sparing with the butter. This part of the cooking requires *a total of 30 minutes.*

To moisten. Pour *only half the bouillon* into the pot. Use only what you need to cover the vegetables, so that nothing sticks to the bottom of the pot. They also keep their flavor better this way, rather than being diluted in a large quantity of liquid. Add the blanched cabbage if you are using it. Bring to a boil. Lower the heat and skim carefully *for 35 minutes* (SEE SKIMMING, PAGE 16). As often as necessary, remove the foam that rises to the surface and, above all, the butter from the braising, which the boiling brings to the top. The potage must not retain the least trace of fat. This does not mean all the butter is lost because you can recover it from the degreasing pot.

Green peas, sorrel, lettuce: You could cook these different items in the soup itself, which would simplify the work, but their green color would be altered, because they would cook at a lower temperature than they should. Good cooking requires them to be prepared separately.

The green peas. If you do not have a copper pot, cook them rapidly in a small enameled pan containing 1/2 liter (generous 2 cups) of salted, boiling water. Drain them as soon as they are cooked, because they will discolor if left in water.

Sorrel and lettuce. Separate the sorrel leaves. Remove the ribs of the lettuce. Wash them and cut in thin, crosswise strips. Cook them by *braising* in a small pan with 20 grams (2/3 ounce, 1 heaping tablespoon) of butter. Soften and melt them over low heat, then add a few tablespoons of bouillon. Let it cook for *another 5 minutes.* Set aside.

To serve: At the end of the vegetable cooking time, add the rest of the bouillon, cold. Remove the trace of fat that rises to the surface just before boiling starts again. *Let it boil for 2 minutes.* Transfer to a soup tureen. Add: green peas, braised sorrel and lettuce, and chervil leaves. Serve.

Chopped Vegetable Soup *(Potage Brunoise)*

The ingredients are about the same, and the preparation is the same as for *potage julienne.* The distinguishing feature is the form of the vegetables, which are cut into little cubes. This shape is characteristic of *potage brunoise.* By extension, the culinary term *brunoise* is applied to everything cut in this way.

For all directions about the season, choice of vegetables, braising, cooking, etc., as well as the clarity and total absence of fat in the bouillon, and meat-free variations etc., we refer you to what has been said above for *potage julienne.*

Here, we give the recipe for a basic *brunoise.* But this can be varied infinitely, even more than the julienne, by adding more ingredients, such as pasta, rice, poached eggs, etc. The preparation of the soup remains exactly the same. Simply diminish the proportion of vegetables in relation to the ingredient added, and calculate this reduction for the entire dish. The soup should, in this case, appear on the menu with the name of the added ingredient—for example, "*potage brunoise* with pasta," or "with rice," etc. Alternatively, you can thicken the basic *brunoise* such as that described here with egg yolks and cream.

Everything that has been said about using a light purée of dried vegetables for a meat-free *potage julienne* is applicable to the *brunoise* as well.

A true *potage brunoise* contains green peas and string beans. This is reflected in our recipe. When fresh vegetables are not available, use canned. To avoid opening a can for the small quantities required, keep the few tablespoons necessary from the meal the evening before or from the morning. In this case, the canned vegetables should be heated in lightly salted water 7–8 minutes before being added to the tureen. *Time: 2 hours total. Serves 6–8.*

150 grams (5 1/3 ounces) of carrot, yellow core removed; 100 grams (3 1/2 ounces) of turnip; 40 grams (1 3/8 ounces) of the white part of a leek; 75 grams (2 2/3 ounces) of celery heart; 50 grams (1 3/4 ounces) of onion; 3 tablespoons of green peas; 8 good string beans; 50 grams (1 3/4 ounces, 3 1/2 tablespoons) of butter for braising.

1 1/2 liters (6 1/3 cups) of excellent bouillon, without a trace of fat; 1/2 tablespoon of chervil leaves.

PROCEDURE. **Cutting the vegetables:** This method seems complicated at first, even though it is easier than that of a julienne because the vegetables are not cut as thin. As for a julienne, the carrots and turnips should be chosen as large as possible. Peeled and squared off, not only on the four faces in length, but also *on both ends* in order to eliminate the most rounded parts.

The carrot. Place it on the table. With a good kitchen knife, cut slices no larger than 1/2 centimeter (3/16 inch) thick. As soon as you reach the yellow part of the interior core, do not cut any more slices on that side, but move on to the next side. Continue until all of the orange part has been cut away from the four sides of the carrot and all that is left is a long, square plug, which is the part of the root vegetable that is not used.

Gather the slices in twos or threes, stacking them one on top of the other, just as they were before being cut. Then, slice them lengthwise into little sticks 4–5 millimeters (about 3/16 inch) wide, which gives them the dimensions of a large matchstick. Cut these little sticks crosswise to the same width, to obtain cubes of about 1/2 centimeter (3/16 inch). You can cut the *brunoise* smaller, but the indicated size is not too large and is correct for the soup.

The turnip and the celery. For the latter, you can leave a little of the very tender green. Cut it like the carrot, and cut the onion the same way. Split the *leek* in half lengthwise. Divide it into sticks the thickness of the cubes, then cut it crosswise. For the brunoise, take only the white part of the leek.

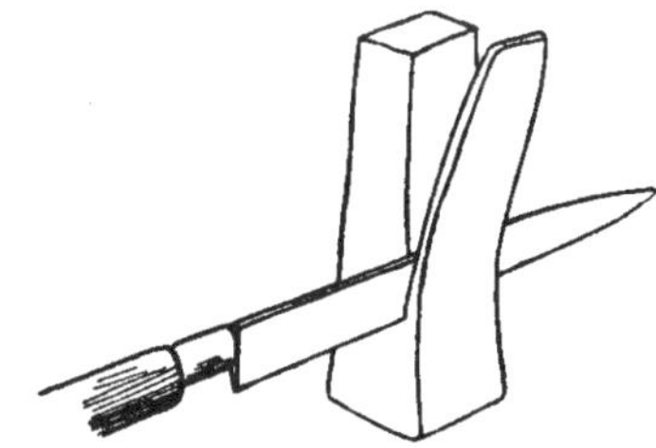

FIG. 30. CUT OF VEGETABLES IN SLICES LENGTHWISE FOR *BRUNOISE*.

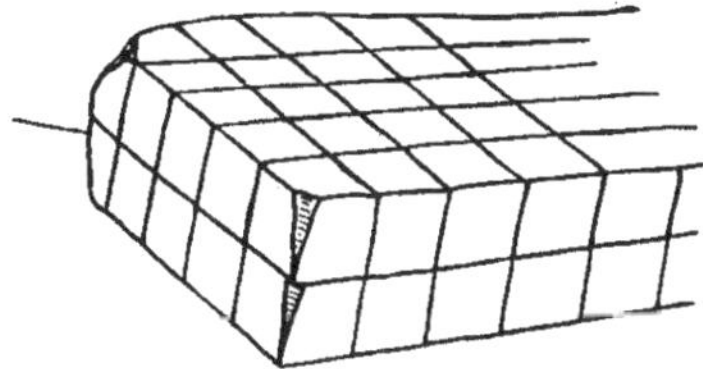

FIG. 31. SMALL, EVEN DICE, OBTAINED BY CUTTING STICKS.

Cooking: It is exactly the same as the *potage julienne.* But you should definitely be aware that the vegetables cut for a *brunoise* require a longer cooking time than a julienne, given the difference in thickness. Thus you must calculate, for young vegetables, about *45 minutes* of braising. Following this, *35–40 minutes* of cooking in the chosen liquid.

The green peas and string beans: Cut the string beans in 1/2-centimeter (3/16-inch) cubes.

Given the small quantity necessary for these vegetables and the fact that the cooking times are about the same, you can dispense with the need to cook them separately. *About 30 minutes* before serving, put them in a small pan with 3 deciliters (1 1/4 cups) of boiling, salted water (a pinch of salt). Cook, uncovered, in rapidly boiling water. If they must stand for only a few seconds, don't drain them. Keep them in their cooking water so they don't cool off.

To serve: Pour the soup into a tureen. Add the drained green peas and string beans and the chervil leaves.

When the *brunoise* contains rice or pasta, etc., these ingredients should be cooked separately in bouillon or water and added to the tureen with the peas and beans. If there are poached eggs, send them to the table separately in a small bowl, with a few tablespoons of bouillon. This is an easy way to serve them.

Springtime Vegetable Soup *(Potage Printanier)*

Essentially, a *potage printanier* is a collection of fresh vegetables in season, in equal proportions: carrots and turnips, green peas and green beans, complimented by a few leaves of sorrel and lettuce. You can also add asparagus tips and small cauliflower florets.

What distinguishes *potage printanier* from other soups with the same ingredients—for example, *potage brunoise*—is the manner in which the carrot and turnip are used. For *printanier,* it is not only the way in which the vegetables are cut, but, much more importantly from the gastronomic point of view, the different method of cooking. While the carrot and turnip are previously colored in butter for other soups of this kind, they are cooked directly in the bouillon for a *printanier,* which allows them to retain more of their natural flavor.

As far as the manner of cutting the carrots and turnips, you can choose to carve them into little balls, with a special vegetable cutting spoon; or in little round sticks, using a special tool that resembles a tube about 1/2 centimeter (3/16 inch) in diameter. For this, the vegetables are first cut into 2 1/2-centimeter (1-inch) sections, which is the length of a round stick. Both methods are equally classic.

The balls or sticks are then put into a small pan, each vegetable separately, with bouillon, a little butter, and some sugar, and cooked as directed for CARROTS GLAZED AS A GARNISH (PAGE 484).

The green peas, green beans, etc., are prepared as for *potage brunoise.* The lettuce and sorrel are cut into rounds with a pastry cutter, then blanched in boiling water. Everything is put into a tureen, into which the boiling consommé is poured. Then add the chervil, either trimmed or in whole leaves.

Rustic Vegetable Soup *(Potage Paysanne)*

This is considered more of a soup than a potage since it is characteristic of home cooking.

Potage paysanne uses all the fresh vegetables that can be used in a soup: carrot, turnip, leek, celery, or even celeriac, optional onion, potato, cabbage. In season, add green peas, green beans, flageolets, etc.

For normal proportions, the rule is to allow a total of 60 grams (2 1/4 ounces) of vegetables per person. If you are short on one vegetable, increase the quantity of the others proportionally. Do the same if, to suit particular tastes, you leave out certain vegetables, such as cabbage, for example.

As for *potage julienne,* the best time for *potage paysanne* is when the new vegetables are in season. First, because this is when they are fresh roots, carrots, turnips, etc., and also because of all the other vegetables—peas, beans, etc.—that are available to add in this season.

Potage paysanne is made with and without meat. With meat, it uses homemade bouillon, carefully degreased as always. Without meat, as for potage julienne, and depending on the season, it is best to use cooking liquid from white beans, whether fresh or dried, asparagus, green beans, dried peas, potatoes, cauliflower, etc. Or simply use warm water. In this case, add 12 grams (3/8 ounce) of salt per liter (4 1/4 cups) of water.

When the liquid used is not bouillon, add butter to the potage before serving. Allow, in addition to the 60 grams (2 1/4 ounces, 4 1/2 tablespoons) needed for the braising, 40 grams (1 3/8 ounces, 3 tablespoons) of butter added *off the heat.*

Bread, which usually is included in potages of the soup genre, can be left out. We advise, nonetheless, that you keep it, but serve it on the side, on a small plate or tray. This bread must be cut fine as lace and dried in the oven for a few moments before serving. *Time: 2 hours. Serves 6–8.*

75 grams (2 2/3 ounces) of carrots; 75 grams (2 2/3 ounces) of turnips; 40 grams (1 3/8 ounces) of the white part of a leek; 50 grams (1 3/4 ounces) of celery; 75 grams (2 2/3 ounces) of firm green cabbage; a medium potato; 30–40 grams (1–1 3/8 ounces) of green peas; same weight of green beans (the weight of the vegetables is net, after peeling); 60 grams (2 1/4 ounces, 4 1/2 tablespoons) of butter; 1 liter (4 1/4 cups) of liquid; 1/2 tablespoon of chervil; 12 rounds of lightly toasted bread.

PROCEDURE. The cut of the vegetables. Peel the *carrot,* which you have chosen long and of a good orange color. Cut in half lengthwise. Place the cut side on the table. With a good-sized kitchen knife, cut into thin and even slices, about 2 millimeters (1/16 inch) thick. Do the same with the *turnip.*

Cut the white part of the *celery* just as thinly, as well as the *leek.* The green part is not used here. (You can use it in some other dish.) Remove the rib from leaves of the *firm green cabbage.* Cut them into fine strips.

Onion is not necessary and is not included in the recipe. But you can add it, especially if it is young; use 40–50 grams (1 3/8–1 3/4 ounces). Cut it thinner than the other vegetables if possible.

If the vegetables are already mature, you must blanch them before braising. Then proceed as indicated for the *potage julienne.*

Braising: Use a thick aluminum or good cast-iron pot. Add the butter with the carrot, turnip, celery, cabbage, leek, and onion. Sprinkle with a good pinch of sugar and a small pinch of fine salt.

Put over *moderate heat.* Stir with a wooden spoon to mix well. Let it all heat well for 4–5 minutes, stirring from time to time with the spoon. Then lower the heat. Cover the pot completely. Let it braise for *a scant 30 minutes,* being sure to stir the vegetables from time to time so that they do not stick and take on a color deeper than light yellow.

In this kind of potage the vegetables do not have to take on the same blond color as for a julienne or a *brunoise;* the way they are cut is not suitable. That is why you are directed to braise them with the lid on. They are ready when, having "melted" considerably, they are soft and have an even golden color. They are, at this point, a little more than half done.

Moistening: Add *1/2 liter (generous 2 cups)* of the liquid, and salt if it's water. Bring to a boil over high heat. Then add the potato cut into thin rounds; the green peas; the green beans broken into small pieces; flageolets, if you use them, chosen small so they have enough time to cook.

Cover. Simmer for *a good 30 minutes.* Do not skim this type of potage.

To serve: When the vegetables are cooked, add the rest of the liquid (degreased bouillon or vegetable cooking water, or water), cool or hot. Let it boil for another 5–6 minutes.

If the liquid is water or vegetable cooking water, add the required amount of butter *off the heat.* Pour into the tureen. Finish with the chervil and the rounds of bread, if you do not serve them separately.

Carrot Soup *(Potage Crécy)*

Potage Crécy is prepared in diverse ways. The difference consists in the type of liaison, as well as the garnish.

Carrot, which forms the base of this dish, is a very watery vegetable and, as a result, has little consistency. Thus is it is essential to reinforce it with a thickening agent. Rice or potato are the most frequent choices, cooked and strained at the same time as the carrots. Or, bread croutons, cooked and strained likewise. Or even flour, in the form of a lean béchamel, or as a white roux in the bouillon used as a liquid.

The garnish for a *potage Crécy* can be rice cooked separately in salted water, small fried bread croutons, or cubes of potato lightly browned in butter. This garnish is added to the tureen after the soup.

Potage Crécy can be made meat-free by replacing the standard bouillon with bouillon made from vegetables, or by using the cooking water from white beans.

It's a potage for all seasons. But since carrot is the principal vegetable, this dish is naturally better when carrots are fully mature and can be used whole, rather than at the end of the winter when you can only use the exterior orange part, or even in early spring when the pulp is too watery and worthless.

The different procedures used must always lead to the same goal: a smooth, beautifully colored and well-bound purée. We have provided the most important recipes. Since the way the carrot is cut and its braising are the same for both methods, we include these directions first.

Cutting the carrot: If it is still young and mostly orange, you can use the whole vegetable. But as soon as you get into the late season, only the orange outside part can be used and not the core, which has become too hard.

Carefully peel the carrots, wipe them dry, cut them into very thin shavings of equal thickness. To do this, put the carrot on the table in front of you, standing with the point in the air. Using a small kitchen knife, mainly the tip, shave the carrot, cutting from the top to the bottom, and turning the carrot as necessary until you reach the yellow interior.

Braising: Place the carrot shavings in a heavy-bottomed pot, with a capacity of about 2 1/2 liters (10 1/2 cups) for the quantities given. If you are using onion, add it now. Add the butter (40 grams, 1 3/8 ounces, 3 tablespoons). Braise gently without coloring, as directed for *potage paysanne* (page 92).

Allow *a good 20 minutes* for this braising. It is ready once the carrots have gradually given up their natural liquid, and the shavings are softened and reduced to a coarse purée.

Traditional Carrot Soup *(Potage Crécy à l'Ancienne Mode).* *Time: 1 1/2 hours. Serves 6–8.*

300 grams (10 1/2 ounces) of carrot, yellow core removed; 200 grams (7 ounces) of bread crust, with some bread still attached (for thickening); 1/2 onion, finely minced; 90 grams (3 1/6 ounces, 6 tablespoons) of butter; 1 1/2 liters (6 1/3 cups) of fat-free bouillon; a bunch of parsley; 10 grams (1/3 ounce) of superfine sugar; 7 tablespoons of raw rice or 3 tablespoons of small cubed croutons fried in butter; 1 tablespoon of chervil.

PROCEDURE. Cut the orange part of the carrot. Finely mince the onion. Braise them with 40 grams (1 3/8 ounces, 3 tablespoons) of butter.

Prepare the crusts for thickening. It is better to use the top crust, if it is not too browned, leaving a good centimeter (3/8 inch) of bread attached. If there is no useable crust, use only the bread without crust. Cut the bread into large cubes. Dry it in the oven.

After braising, combine the bread and the carrots. Add 1 liter (4 1/4 cups) of liquid and the parsley. Boil. Cover. Cook slowly for *40 minutes.*

Prepare the garnish: rice or bread croutons, or potato croutons (SEE *CROÛTES* AND CROUTONS, PAGE 20).

Force through a drum sieve *(tamis).* Return the purée to the rinsed pot. Add the rest of the liquid. Bring to a boil. Lower the heat and skim for *15–20 minutes* (SEE SKIMMING, PAGE 16).

When ready to serve, finish with the rest of the butter, off the heat. Strain once more, this time through a chinois straight into the tureen, forcing it through with the back of a metal spoon. (Some purée will always remain in the chinois.) Add the garnish. Serve.

Carrot Soup, Housewife-Style (*Potage Crécy à la Bonne Femme).* *Time: 1 1/2 hours. Serves 6–8.*

500 grams (1 pound, 2 ounces) of the orange part of the carrot; 4 nice potatoes; 1 1/2 liters (6 1/3 cups) of bouillon or other liquid; 90 grams (3 1/6 ounces, 6 tablespoons) of butter; 10 grams (1/3 ounce) of superfine sugar; a good pinch of chervil leaves.

PROCEDURE. Cut the carrots. Braise them with 40 grams (1 3/8 ounces, 3 tablespoons) of butter, as before. Moisten with 1 liter (4 1/4 cups) of the liquid. Add the potatoes, which have been peeled and quartered previously. Bring to a boil. Cover. Let it cook slowly and regularly until the cooking of the carrots is complete, about *35–40 minutes.*

Strain through a very fine metallic drum sieve *(tamis).* Return the purée to a clean pot. Add the rest of the liquid, reserving several tablespoons for skimming. Skim for *20 minutes.* Meanwhile, prepare the potato croutons (SEE *CROÛTES* AND CROUTONS, PAGE 20).

When ready to serve, add the rest of the butter, off the heat. Strain through a chinois into the tureen. Add the hot potato crouton garnish, and the chervil leaves.

Carrot and Tapioca Soup *(Potage Velours).* This potage belongs to the repertory of modern cuisine. It's a purée of carrots, or Crécy, combined with tapioca consommé.

For the home kitchen, prepare thus: Braise the carrots with butter. Add the necessary bouillon to complete the cooking (SEE POTAGE CRÉCY, PAGE 93). Strain through a fine sieve *(tamis)* to obtain a very fine purée.

Meanwhile, cook the tapioca in the consommé or bouillon (SEE CONSOMMÉ, PAGE 86). Skim the foam if necessary. Lighten the purée of carrots with a few tablespoons of prepared tapioca before pouring it into the pot. Heat until boiling, stirring constantly. When ready to serve, mix in a bit of butter *off the heat. Time: 1 1/4 hours total. Serves 6.*

350 grams (12 1/3 ounces) of carrot, yellow part removed, braised with 30 grams (1 ounce, 2 tablespoons) of butter *for 20 minutes.* Moisten with 1/2 liter (generous 2 cups) of bouillon, cook slowly, covered, for 40 minutes. Strain through a fine drum sieve *(tamis).*

Poach 4 level tablespoons of tapioca in 1 liter (4 1/4 cups) of bouillon. Mix it with the purée of carrots. Finish with 30 grams (1 ounce, 2 tablespoons) of butter, off the heat.

Pea Soup *(Potage Saint-Germain)*

This is the name given to a potage consisting of a purée of fresh peas, garnished with small green peas. It can be made in different ways. The most popular is by rapidly cooking peas in boiling water, then puréeing them and diluting with consommé blanc. When ready to serve, add butter off the heat. You can add a bit of cream if you like.

Another method uses a good mirepoix with onion, carrot, and bacon, which is added to the peas when they are cooked in the necessary amount of water. There is also the home-style method, which consists of braising the peas before puréeing, in other words, cooking them just as you would for green peas *à la française* served as a vegetable. This latter procedure leaves more flavor in the purée, but the color of the potage is not as beautifully green as that of the peas cooked in rapidly boiling water. This can be remedied by adding some spinach leaves, lettuce, and the green part of a leek during cooking.

Whatever version you use, always add some small green peas to the potage, cooked separately in boiling water.

The peas for the purée must always be the larger peas, so they contain more starch. Small green peas, or even medium size, will not produce a purée with the correct consistency. As much as possible, you should not shell them until the time of cooking. (SEE PEAS, PAGE 529.)

Pea Soup, Home-Style *(Potage Saint-Germain, Façon Ménagère).* *Time: A scant hour. Serves 6–8.*

1 liter (4 1/4 cups) of large peas, shelled; 2 good deciliters (7 ounces) of small peas; 1 liter 4 1/4 cups) of bouillon or water; a dozen lettuce leaves; a dozen spinach leaves; 2 medium leeks; a bunch of chervil; 10 grams (1/3 ounce) of salt; 20 grams (2/3 ounce) of sugar; 100 grams (3 1/2 ounces, 7 tablespoons) of butter; a tablespoon of chervil leaves.

PROCEDURE. In a deep, heavy-bottomed pot, combine: the large peas, the green part only of the leeks, cut into thin slices; the lettuce and spinach cut into thick julienne (having first been washed and dried); the chervil; 70 grams (2 1/2 ounces, 1/3 cup) of butter; the salt and the sugar; 1 deciliter (3 1/3 fluid ounces, scant 1/2 cup) or 1/2 glass of cold water.

Bring to a rapid boil. Cover the pot in the home-style method, with a shallow soup plate into which you put several tablespoons of cold water. Cook to maintain an even, moderate boil for *about 35–40 minutes.*

The purée: Force the purée through a fine drum sieve *(tamis).* Put the purée into a pot large enough to contain the liquid. Dilute it gradually with the bouillon, which is completely fat-free, or with warm water, using a whisk or wooden spoon. Heat to boiling. Take it off the heat but keep warm until serving. Dot a few pieces of butter around the surface of the potage if it has to stand.

The small peas for garnish: Put them in a small pot of boiling water, 3/4 liter (generous 3 cups) of water, lightly salted, and cook at a rapid boil, uncovered, for *20–25 minutes.* Leave them in their water until ready to add to the potage.

To serve: Add the rest of the butter to the purée, off the heat. Check the seasoning, which will certainly need to be increased if you have used water instead of bouillon. Strain through the chinois into a tureen. Add the small peas, well drained. Serve.

Pea Soup, Restaurant-Style *(Potage Saint-Germain, Façon Grande Cuisine).* *Time: About 1 hour. Serves 6–8.*

1 liter (4 1/4 cups) of shelled peas; 2 deciliters (6 3/4 ounces, 7/8 cup) of small peas cooked separately; 1 1/2 liters (6 1/3 cups) of boiling water; 10 grams (1/3 ounce) of salt; a handful of lettuce leaves; a bunch of parsley; 60 grams (2 1/4 ounces, 4 1/2 tablespoons) of good butter; 3 tablespoons of heavy cream.

If the potage contains meat broth: add 1 liter (4 1/4 cups) of clear bouillon.

PROCEDURE. Use a copper pot (heavy saucepan or small stockpot) that is not tin-lined; or, alternatively, use an enameled utensil or a clay pot. Nothing lined with tin, so that the green color of the peas is preserved. When the water comes to a full boil, add the peas, salt, lettuce leaves, and parsley. Do not cover. Cook over high heat for a rapid boil through out the whole cooking time, *about 18–20 minutes.* The peas are ready when they squash easily between your fingers. As soon as they are cooked, drain and reserve the cooking water. If you do not use it for the potage, it will be excellent the next day for a vegetable potage. Remove the parsley.

Pour the peas and lettuce onto the drum sieve *(tamis)*. Force through rapidly to purée while they are still boiling hot. Return the purée to the pot. Dilute with the cooking water or the bouillon. Heat to the boiling point, stirring constantly. Add the sugar. If the purée is made in advance, keep it warm, dot the surface with bits of butter, and keep covered.

When ready to serve, add the cream, and, off the heat, the butter. Strain through a sieve into a tureen. Add the small peas cooked separately, then the chervil. Serve.

Lean Pot-au-Feu *(Pot-au-Feu Maigre)*

This recipe for a meat-free bouillon is always a success when made with due care. A bouillon prepared like this not only fools the tastebuds—a *trompe goût,* as it were—but at the same time it is a veritable trompe l'oeil; the carrots and leeks, served at the same time as the potage, are excellent and add to the illusion that it is a real pot-au-feu.

The grilled bread, suggested as a garnish for the broth because it is characteristic of real pot-au-feu, can be replaced by tapioca, pasta, etc. It is even possible to make a velouté with rice starch and egg yolks, or to add poached eggs. In sum, use all the methods commonly used with ordinary bouillon. The beans, which here form the base of the potage, must be the best quality—known as "Soissons" (a town to the northeast of Paris)—and rather small, because other kinds of beans cannot retain their shape during long cooking, which detracts from the clarity of the bouillon. These do not need to be soaked in advance. They can be used the next day, made into a purée with the rest of the vegetables used in the cooking. It's better to prepare this dish the night before, so that the sediment created by the cooking of the beans has time to settle on the bottom of the pot. *Time: 3½ hours. Serves 6.*

½ liter (generous 2 cups) of dry white beans; 2 liters (8½ cups) of water and 30 grams (1 ounce) of salt; 150 grams (5⅓ ounces) of onion; 200 grams (7 ounces) of carrot; 175 grams (6 ounces) of turnip; 125 grams (4½ ounces) of the white part of a leek; 30 grams (1 ounce) of celery; 15 grams (½ ounce) of turnip; 50 grams (1¾ ounces, 3½ tablespoons) of butter; a bouquet garni made of 20 grams (⅔ ounce) of parsley, a sprig of thyme, a very small piece of garlic, 2 cloves.

PROCEDURE. Put the beans into a pot, with cold water to cover. Bring to a boil over moderate heat. Let it boil only 2 minutes. Turn off the heat. Cover. Let the beans soak and swell for a good 30 minutes.

Cut the onion into rounds, not too thin. Take only half the quantity of carrot indicated, 100 grams (3½ ounces). Cut it into rounds, if the core is fresh and orange, or into slices, if the core is old and yellow, and thus flavorless. (The orange part is the only part counted for the total weight.)

Use a deep, thick-bottomed saucepan, with a capacity of at least 4 liters (4¼ quarts). When the butter has just melted, add the onions and the carrots. Do not cover. Let them cook slowly and gently over moderate heat until they turn a light golden color, stirring frequently with a wooden spoon. As they gradually turn golden, the vegetables form a light caramel on the bottom of the pot. You must be very careful that the color does not go darker because if they brown the bouillon might take on a bitter taste. Allow 15–20 minutes for this operation.

Pour 2 liters (8½ cups) of cold or hot water on these lightly colored vegetables. Add the well-drained beans and the salt. Bring to a boil. Then add the parsnip, celery, turnip, and bouquet garni. When it returns to a boil, cover the pot and lower the heat.

Let it cook at a gentle, regular, uninterrupted simmer *for 1 hour.* Just as for a pot-au-feu made with meat, the clarity of the bouillon depends on an even heat.

At the end of this time, add the rest of the carrot, cut into two or in four, as for an ordinary pot-au-feu, and the white parts of the leek tied into a bundle. Let it simmer steadily for 1 more hour.

To serve: Reheat the bouillon without letting it boil. Transfer the leeks and carrot quarters to a plate. Strain the bouillon through a fine sieve into a pan, being very careful not to mix up the beans or the sediment at the bottom of the bouillon, which is necessarily a little more cloudy. *Do not degrease.* The only grease involved here is the butter used to color the vegetables and, since it has neither overcooked nor browned, it is still very good. The little pools of liquid butter that form on the surface enhance the illusion, giving the potage the appearance of a homemade meat bouillon.

Heat to boiling. Pour into a tureen on top of toasted bread slices. At the same time, serve the leeks and carrots in a serving dish.

Oxtail Soup *(Potage à la Queue de Bœuf)*

Far from being English, as is commonly believed, the origin of this dish, according to one of our most reputed culinary authors, is French: In fact, it's a kind of pot-au-feu.

Oxtail soup is served two ways: *Clear*—in other words, with the bouillon in its natural state, as in the classic French pot-au-feu. Or, *thickened,* with brown roux, like a light sauce. In both of these cases, the garnish is composed of sections of the oxtail used in the preparation, and a *brunoise* of vegetables that has been separately prepared.

As to the final addition of port wine, this is completely optional, and of relatively recent origin, because it cannot be found in English culinary collections from the second half of the last century. Alfred Suzanne, in his excellent work on English cuisine, does not mention it either. *[Translator's note: Alfred Suzanne was the author of cookery books, most notably* L'Art Culinaire, *published in 1891.]* This addition of wine is found only in ox cheek soup, turtle soup, hare soup, etc. It thus seems that the true "oxtail soup" hardly differs from the French *potage à la queue de bœuf* except for the thickener, which is completely optional, while the cooking procedures remain the same.

The *English version* consists in first sweating the tail pieces with ordinary pot-au-feu vegetables, and adding a certain amount of beef topside, or another cut, just as when making a jus. This procedure is advocated by top French culinary professionals for the French *potage queue de bœuf.* It has the advantage of extra flavor that comes from the caramelization of the meat and vegetable juices. One can even, before adding water for the cooking, deglaze with a little white wine, exactly as for a jus. Used like this, the wine has an effect entirely different from the several tablespoons of good port that one could, in keeping with modern preferences, add just before serving.

With or without the preliminary sweating, we recommend using a bouillon prepared with gelatinous bones, which is much preferable to water. If the potage is not thickened, you can expect to obtain a crystal-clear bouillon. To this end, it must be clarified with egg white, in the usual manner.

When no other meat, except the tails, have been included when making the bouillon, it is essential to add some raw beef, which will intensify the bouillon (SEE CONSOMMÉ, PAGE 86). Use 500 grams (1 pound, 2 ounces) of *raw* beef for the quantities indicated on the following page.

In the *French version* of *potage à la queue de bœuf,* a small amount of *tapioca* lends a particular smoothness that is very appealing. A small *bit of sugar* is always indicated in the correct finish of oxtail soup.

Oxtail soup (or *potage à la queue de bœuf*) *can be prepared far in advance,* the evening before the day it is served. Both the *brunoise* and the oxtails can be kept warm after cooking if made on the day of serving, or even refrigerated to be reheated when ready to serve.

If the potage is made the evening before, for the next day, the oxtails should not be added until ready to serve, so that the bouillon is kept clear.

Finally, for thickened *oxtail soup* there is a simplified procedure, frequently used in Anglo-American cooking. Color pieces of oxtail and vegetables in fat, drain the fat. Sprinkle with flour, then let it color lightly. Moisten. Cook for 4 hours. Add, if desired, sherry or port just before serving.

Whatever the cooking method, the quantities, the preparation of the oxtails, the *brunoise* of vegetables, and the way to serve the potage are all the same.

The oxtail: The average weight of an ordinary oxtail is 2 kilos (4 pounds, 8 ounces). But you can only find nice pieces for serving in the middle part, where the thicknesses are about equal. The two extremities are either too thin or too thick, and can be used only for the bouillon and not for the garnish. Whenever possible, the middle of the tail is used, in order to get pieces that have more or less equal dimensions.

Have the butcher cut the tail into pieces demarcated by the joints. Place the pieces in a large vessel of water to soak for 2 hours, changing the water 3 times during this period. *Time: 5 hours (not counting the soaking of the tails). Serves 8–10.*

1 1/2–2 kilograms (3 pounds, 5 ounces–4 pounds, 6 ounces) of oxtail.

To strengthen the bouillon made from tails: 500 grams (1 pound, 2 ounces) of veal knuckle; 500 grams (1 pound, 2 ounces) of round roast, both cut in half; 500 grams (1 pound, 2 ounces) of gelatinous beef bones, broken into small pieces. (It is best to have all this work done by the butcher.)

A bouquet garni made up of: 2 small leeks, a branch of celery, 5–6 sprigs of parsley, a bunch of thyme, a third of a small bay leaf, all tied together with kitchen string; 3 liters (12 3/4 cups) of water, 15 grams (1/2 ounce) of salt, 2 grams (1/16 ounce) of peppercorns (about 30).

For the garnish, a *brunoise* cut into 1/2 centimeter (3/16 ounce) cubes, with, net weight: 60 grams (2 1/4 ounces) of carrots; 60 grams (2 1/4 ounces) of turnip; 60 grams (2 1/4 ounces) of the white part of the celery; 50 grams (1 3/4 ounces) of the white part of the leek; 30 grams (1 ounce, 2 tablespoons) of butter; 2 1/2 deciliters (1 cup) of bouillon from the tails.

For the roux to thicken, optional: 50 grams (1 3/4 ounces) of flour and 50 grams (1 3/4 ounces, 3 1/2 tablespoons) of butter.

PROCEDURE. **The English method:** Cut onions and carrots into large rounds and put into a good-sized pot. On top, arrange the bones, cuts of rump and knuckle, with the tails on top. Sweat it and color lightly in the oven, *about 20 minutes.* Moisten with the water or the bouillon. Bring to a boil over moderate heat. Skim. Add the bouquet garni. Cover. Allow *3 hours* of cooking from that moment. Meanwhile, prepare the *brunoise* of vegetables. SEE POTAGE BRUNOISE, PAGE 90.

If the potage must be served *clear,* clarify the bouillon with egg white and raw beef, as described previously.

If the potage is to be *thickened,* prepare a brown roux, with the indicated quantities, in a deep pot with a capacity of 2 1/2 liters (10 1/2 cups). SEE SKIMMING, PAGE 16.

Serving: The tail pieces are put directly into the tureen, with the *brunoise* of vegetables. The potage, clear or bound, is poured on top of these through a sieve. Stir gently with the ladle. Taste it to check the final seasoning, which should be zesty in a peppery sense. Use a point of cayenne (SEE PAGE 56) if necessary. This is the moment when you should add the port, sherry, or Madeira, if using—3 tablespoons for the above quantities.

You can also serve the tails separately in a *shallow dish,* with a few tablespoons of boiling bouillon. This is an easier way to serve. It is also permissible to remove the bone from each piece and to trim the meat before adding the tails to the bouillon. This is less typical, but easier for your guests. Allow 1 tail section per person.

The French method: Identical to the preparation for an ordinary pot-au-feu: the bones at the bottom of the pot with the meat arranged on top. Pour in the cold water, salt, bring to a boil, and skim carefully. Add the carrots cut into quarters, the onion studded with cloves, the bouquet of leeks, etc. Allow, after skimming, *3 hours* of cooking time.

Meanwhile, prepare the vegetable *brunoise.* Clarify and serve as previously explained.

Chicken and Rice Soup *(Potage à la Reine)*

Simply stated, this is a purée of chicken to which rice, cooked and strained at the same time, adds thickness. (In classic cuisine, crustless bread soaked in bouillon was used in place of rice.) It is finished with egg yolks, cream, and a generous amount of butter.

A potage made with these ingredients presents no difficulties. (Nonetheless, the use of a mortar is essential.) If you are making a pot-au-feu the same day, you can even cook the chicken in the same pot. In this case, the rice is cooked separately, in a small pan, with a completely degreased bouillon. Use 4 deciliters (1 2/3 cups) for each of our 100 grams (3 1/2 ounces) of rice. Cover the pan and simmer constantly for *40–45 minutes.*

The potage can be prepared several hours ahead without any problems, in terms of cooking and puréeing the chicken, proceeding as directed below. You will need about 10 minutes before serving to finish the potage. *Time: 2 scant hours. Serves 8–10.*

A nice, meaty chicken weighing 1 kilogram (2 pounds, 3 ounces) net; 2 liters (8½ cups) of very good bouillon, not colored, and perfectly degreased; 100 grams (3½ ounce) of ordinary rice for the purée; for thickening, 2 deciliters (6¾ fluid ounces, ⅞ cup) of cream and 3 egg yolks; 100 grams (3½ ounces, 7 tablespoons) of butter to finish.

PROCEDURE. Clean the bird, singe if necessary, and truss. Place it in a small pot with the bouillon. Bring to a boil. Add 2 leeks cut lengthwise and tied into a bundle with a small stalk of celery. Cover and maintain a simmer over low heat. Allow *50–55 minutes of cooking for a tender chicken, and 1¼ hours if it is a bit tough.*

Wash the rice in several changes of fresh water and drain thoroughly. You need to allow at least *40 minutes* cooking time. It must be very thoroughly cooked to be easily puréed. Consequently, to calculate when to start the cooking time, you must bear in mind the need to add the rice to the chicken at the correct time. This should start about *10 minutes* or more after the chicken is started, according to the necessary cooking time for the chicken. Take care that, when the water boils again after the rice is introduced, the grains do not stick to the bottom of the pot. Even though there is a large quantity of liquid, they can easily stick.

The purée: When the chicken is cooked, transfer it to a plate. Remove the wing and the breast fillet that is attached. Keep warm between two plates, to be used for the cubes of the garnish.

Bone the rest of the chicken, and remove the skin. Work rapidly, so the meat will still be hot when you grind it in the mortar with the pestle. Use the pestle by turning it in circles, not by tapping or crushing in place.

When the meat is thus reduced to a purée, add the rice, transferred with the skimmer. Mix it in while crushing it the same way. Transfer everything to a pot. Dilute this purée with only a few tablespoons of bouillon. Heat it slightly to make it easier to force through the drum sieve *(tamis)*. A fine metal *tamis* is essential here, to replace the muslin used in professional kitchens. Repeat this twice, proceeding as directed. SEE STRAINNG PURÉES, PAGE 14.

Place the purée in a clean pot. Stir briefly with a wooden spoon. *On the surface* pour 2–3 tablespoons of warm bouillon, and add a knob of butter the size of a walnut, divided into small pieces, to keep it from drying out. Keep warm until ready to serve.

The garnish: Use a good, thin sharp knife to avoid shredding when cutting the cubes. Slice the chicken breast into sticks of ½ centimeter (3/16 inch) per side, then cut into ½-centimeter (3/16-inch) cubes. Keep them warm between two plates, sprinkled with a tablespoon of hot bouillon.

To finish and to serve the potage: Mix together the egg yolks and cream in a bowl.

Dilute the purée with the bouillon (about 1 liter/4¼ cups), which has been previously strained. Bring to a boil, stirring constantly. Make the liaison as directed (SEE LIAISONS, PAGE 47), without letting it boil, because of the cream. Finish with the butter divided into small bits. Check the seasoning. Pour into a tureen through the chinois or a very fine strainer. Stir in the cubes of chicken breast. Serve.

Crayfish Bisque *(Potage Bisque d'Écrivisses)*

First of all, it is important to be prepared because, for this soup, a marble mortar is essential. Without it, there is no point in proceeding with the recipe.

For all the details regarding choice, preparation, etc., of crayfish, SEE CRAYFISH, PAGE 228. *Time: 2½ hours total. Allow at least 4 crayfish per person; and, in addition, the amount needed for the crayfish butter to complete the potage. Serves 8.*

40 crayfish of medium weight as indicated, of which 8 are for butter. If they weigh less, you will, of course, need more.

To cook the crayfish: **A mirepoix prepared with 60 grams (2¼ ounces) of carrot, the same of onion; 2 shallots; 2 stalks of parsley; a sprig of thyme; a fragment of bay; 50 grams (1¾ ounces, 3½ tablespoons) of butter.** SEE MIREPOIX, PAGE 21.

100 grams (3½ ounces) of ordinary short-grain rice, for the purée; 2 liters (8½ cups) of bouillon, not colored, if possible; 2 deciliters (6¾ fluid ounces, ⅞ cup) of

white wine and 4 tablespoons of cognac; 150 grams (5 1/3 ounces, 10 1/2 tablespoons) of butter, of which about 100 grams (3 1/2 ounces, 7 tablespoons) is for the crayfish butter. SEE CRAYFISH BUTTER, PAGE 79.

A good tablespoon of ground whiting, or other fish, to garnish the crayfish shells. SEE QUENELLES, PAGE 461.

We call for rice, which is more commonly used nowadays for thickening the potage than the bread croutons fried in butter and ground with the crayfish, which is the method used in classic cuisine. This procedure was very good, but more complicated.

Crayfish butter, or "red butter," should be enough to give the characteristic deep pink color to the potage. If not using butter, a few drops of red carmine food coloring are often added.

PROCEDURE. Put the sorted and washed *rice* into a deep pot to cook with 1/2 liter (generous 2 cups) of bouillon. Cover. Let it simmer for *35–40 minutes.* This rice must be cooked sufficiently to be easily puréed.

Meanwhile, in a sauté pan large enough to later hold the crayfish, gently color the mirepoix. Then, add the trimmed and thoroughly washed crayfish. From this moment, cook over high heat. Cover. Sauté everything for 2 minutes. Once the crayfish have taken on a beautiful red color, add the cognac, which has been previously flambéed, the white wine, a pinch of salt, and a point of cayenne (as much as can be held on the tip of a small knife blade). Cover tightly. Cook slowly for *about 15 minutes,* shaking the sauté pan from time to time.

When this cooking has finished, *set aside the 8 crayfish for the butter.* You will prepare them according to the first or second procedure given. Shell all the other crayfish. Keep the peeled tails warm. Reserve a dozen shells or heads, from which you completely remove the interior.

Put all the debris and shells from the crayfish, as well as the mirepoix, into a strainer, to drain completely before placing them in the mortar. If you do not do this, they will be difficult to grind. *Carefully reserve all the cooking liquid.* Grind as fine as possible. Add the rice, cooked separately. Grind everything together until you have a perfect mix. Then add the reserved cooking liquid.

Put this purée into a pot, with a cup of bouillon, and heat slightly. This will help with the sieving for the purée. If you do not have an *étamine* (similar to a jelly bag), force through a very fine metal drum sieve *(tamis).*

Return the purée to a clean pot. Add the rest of the bouillon. Bring to a boil, stirring with a whisk. Turn off the heat. To keep a skin from forming, dot the surface with bits of butter. Let stand until ready to serve.

About 10 minutes before serving, plunge the shells that have been garnished with ground fish into a pan containing lightly salted boiling water. Let them poach over very low heat, without boiling. Drain well at the last moment.

To serve: Add the crayfish butter *off the heat,* with a bit of cayenne. Pour into the tureen, straining once more through a sieve. Add the reserved tails. Serve the well-drained shells separately on a plate, or add them to the tureen.

Purslane and Fresh Pea Soup *(Potage au Pourpier et Pois Frais)*

This is essentially home cooking, which nonetheless produces an excellent potage, thanks to the extra smoothness from the purslane. The fresh peas must be perfectly tender, chosen preferably from the type known as "telephone peas," whose skins are not as hard as those of ordinary peas. *Time: 2 hours. Serves 6.*

30 grams (1 ounce) of green purslane, freshly picked, net weight; 80 grams (2 3/4 ounces) of sorrel; 10 grams (1/3 ounce) of chervil; 40 grams (1 3/8 ounces) of onion; 1/2 liter (generous 2 cups) of large fresh peas; 80 grams (2 3/4 ounces, 5 1/2 tablespoons) of butter; 1 1/2 liters (6 1/3 cups) of water; 10 grams (1/3 ounce) of salt.

PROCEDURE. Use only the leaves of the purslane. The same for the chervil. Remove the stems of the sorrel. Wash each type of herb separately. Drain them thoroughly.

With a good, large kitchen knife, first finely mince only the purslane. The thick and somewhat slimy leaves can be difficult to cut and you must be sure that the blade has completely divided them. That is why you are directed to chop them separately from the herbs. Finely mince the sorrel, chervil, and onion. Everything must be very finely minced because the potage is not strained.

Put everything into a *thick-bottomed* pot with *half* the butter. Cover. Put over very moderate heat to soften and melt the herbs in the butter, without any liquid. From time to time, mix with a wooden spoon to ensure that nothing has stuck to the bottom, then replace the lid immediately. Allow *45 minutes* for this first cooking period, for which the natural water from the herbs will suffice. When everything has softened to a purée, add the warm water. Bring to a boil over high heat. Salt. Add the peas. Return to a boil. Cover and lower the heat so it simmers slowly for *45 minutes.*

Stir in the rest of the butter divided into small pieces off the heat before pouring the potage into the tureen.

Fresh Puréed Broad Bean Soup *(Potage à la Purée de Fèves Fraîches)*

Time: 1 hour of preparation, 1 hour of cooking. Serves 6.

750 grams (1 pound, 10 ounces) of shelled beans; 1 liter (4¼ cups) of boiling water; 15 grams (½ ounce) of salt; 2 sprigs of savory, or alternatively, a sprig of *fresh* thyme; ½ liter (generous 2 cups) of milk; 30 grams (1 ounce, 2 tablespoons) of butter to finish; 1 teaspoon of arrowroot.

Optionally, you can thicken this with 2 egg yolks. In this case, reduce the quantity of arrowroot a bit.

PROCEDURE. Cook the beans in boiling water with salt, and savory or thyme. It is better not to use a utensil lined with tin, since the tin alters the green tint of the vegetables. For this same reason, do not cover, and maintain a rapid boil for about 20 minutes.

As soon as the beans are soft enough to crush easily, drain and reserve their cooking liquid. For the garnish, reserve about thirty halves of the beans that are the most intact. Force the rest through a fine drum sieve *(tamis).* Return the purée to the pot with the cooking liquid. Skim for a good 15 minutes (SEE SKIMMING, PAGE 16). Thicken with the arrowroot previously diluted in the cold milk. Boil for *2–3 minutes.* Just before serving, remove from the heat and add the butter and the reserved beans. If you are thickening with egg yolks, dissolve them first with a few tablespoons of milk taken from the quantity required for the arrowroot.

Cream of Leek Soup *(Potage à la Crème de Poireaux)*

An excellent soup, completely meat-free, which has an optional garnish of pasta, vermicelli, little croutons, or even little cubes of potato, sautéed in butter.

If you do not have crème fraîche, replace it with the same quantity of good milk. And, in this case, add 40–50 grams (1½–1¾ ounces, ⅜–scant ½ stick) of good, fresh butter just before serving, off the heat as always. *Time: One scant hour. Serves 4.*

350 grams (12⅓ ounces) of leeks (8–10 depending upon size); 40 grams (1⅜ ounces, 3 tablespoons) of butter; 30 grams (1 ounce) of flour; 1 liter (4¼ cups) of milk; 2 deciliters (6¾ fluid ounces, ⅞ cup) of cream; 20 grams (⅔ ounce) of salt.

PROCEDURE. Remove only the very ends of the leek greens. Here they are used in their entirety, the green and the white. Cut them into very thin rounds. Braise gently in butter, in a pot, for *about 15 minutes,* stirring from time to time.

When they are quite soft, sprinkle with the flour. Stir briefly over the heat to cook the flour *without coloring.* Dilute with only half the milk. Once it boils, add the salt. Simmer gently for *15 minutes* to cook the leek. Force everything through a fine metallic drum sieve *(tamis),* rubbing with the wooden mushroom-shaped pestle until absolutely nothing remains on the screen. Put the purée back into a clean pot. Dilute with the rest of the milk. Stir, over the heat, until boiling. Boil for 1–2 minutes. Turn off the heat. Add the cream.

If not serving immediately, follow the directions for sauces (SEE KEEPING SAUCES WARM, PAGE 50). When ready to serve, pour the potage over the garnish, which has first been placed in the tureen.

Potato Soup *(Potage Parmentier)*

Potato is the base, which is indicated by the name (SEE NOTE). Leek is present only to give some flavor, and its quantity must be calculated in such a way that the flavor does not dominate. This is yet another reason for using only the white part. *[Translator's note: Antoine-Augustin Parmentier introduced potatoes to France in the late eighteenth century.]*

Depending on taste and, especially, dietary restriction, the leeks can be cooked in the butter *without coloring*—in other words, gently braised, with the lid on—before adding the liquid and the potatoes. Or, simply cook them as is with the potatoes. It is this version, very healthy and very simple, that we will give here. In this way, the soup only has butter added just before serving. *Time: 50 minutes. Serves 6.*

500 grams (1 pound, 2 ounces) of potatoes, net weight; 30 grams (1 ounce) of the white part of a leek; 1½ liters (6⅓ cups) of warm water; 15 grams (½ ounce) of salt; 2 egg yolks; 1 deciliter (3⅓ fluid ounces, scant ½ cup) of good milk; 30 grams (1 ounce, 2 tablespoons) of butter to finish; ½ tablespoon of chervil; about 30 little croutons, colored in 25–30 grams (about 1 ounce, 2 tablespoons) of butter.

PROCEDURE. Peel the potatoes. Cut into quarters, then wash and drain them. Cut the leek in half or in quarters lengthwise. Slice thinly. Put everything into a pot, with the water and the salt. Cover. Boil rapidly for *20 minutes.* Make sure, by sticking a fork into a potato quarter, that they are sufficiently cooked. Set a plate under a drum sieve *(tamis)* with a metal screen. Taking only a few tablespoons at a time, while they are still hot, force the potatoes and leeks through the *tamis* with the wooden pestle.

Put the cooking water into a bowl. Rinse the pot. Add the purée. Dilute it with a bit of the cooking water. Bring to a boil. Lower the heat and arrange the pot for skimming. Skim for *about 10 minutes* (SEE SKIMMING, PAGE 16).

Combine the egg yolks and milk in a bowl for the liaison. Add the butter to the potage, divided into small pieces. Just before serving, heat the egg yolk mixture with 3–4 tablespoons of potage. Add it to the pot *off the heat.* Strain the soup through a chinois into the tureen. Add the chervil. Serve the little croutons fried in butter on the side.

Watercress Soup *(Potage au Cresson)*

In haute cuisine, this is called *purée cressonnière* or *potage de santé* (soup of health), etc. It can have a consommé base, in which case the egg yolk thickener is not used.

The recipe that we give here is a good family recipe for the home cook. The liquid used is simply water, but cooking water from vegetables would make it even better. In season, it is better to make this with the cooking water from green beans.

This potage can be served as is, with chervil leaves as the only garnish. However, it's a good idea to add vermicelli, cooked separately in salted water, about 40–50 grams (1½–1¾ ounces) for the quantities suggested here. Or, in addition, according to taste, a dozen rounds of bread, toasted and cut as fine as lace. However, we do not recommend adding bread because it distorts the flavor of this type of potage, which is very delicate yet simple.

The best time to make this is in the beginning of spring, from the middle of March to mid-April. During this period, watercress has not yet reached the bitter stage. Later, when it is no longer a new vegetable, its sap mounts faster and it takes on a distinctive, strong flavor. At this point, boiling before braising becomes essential. This is an important condition, which must not be forgotten. *Time: 45–50 minutes. Serves 6.*

A small bunch of watercress yielding 300 grams (10½ ounces) net; 2 nice potatoes; 60 grams (2¼ ounces, 4½ tablespoons) of butter; 7½ deciliters (generous 3 cups) of warm water or vegetable cooking liquid; 2½ deciliters (1 cup) of milk; 2 deciliters (6¾ fluid ounces, ⅞ cup) of cream (or milk); 3 egg yolks; a good pinch of chervil leaves.

PROCEDURE. **The watercress:** Separate the branches to make sure there are no sprigs of grass or insects. Pick about thirty of the small leaves, with no stems attached. Put them into a bowl of cool water as you pick them. Set them aside.

Trim the hard ends of the branches, where the little white filaments are found. This should give you the necessary weight. Wash the watercress. Shake it in a towel. Cut it a few times to diminish the length.

Cooking: Put it in a pot with some butter. Braise gently for about 10 minutes, so it's quite soft and melted. Add the warm liquid. If it's water, add 15 grams (1/2 ounce) of salt. Put in the potatoes, peeled and cut into quarters. Bring to a boil. Cover. Boil for *about 25 minutes.* The potatoes must give when touched, nothing more.

Force quickly through a fine drum sieve *(tamis).* Put the purée and its cooking water into a clean pot. Add the milk. Stir over the heat until it begins to boil. Lower the heat. Add the well-drained, reserved watercress. Alternatively, cut them a bit, without actually mincing. Boil *for 5 minutes more.*

Just before serving, combine the yolks and cream to thicken, and add off the heat. Pour into the tureen. Add the chervil leaves. If you are using vermicelli or bread rounds, add them at this time.

Pumpkin Soup, Housewife-Style *(Potage au Potiron à la Bonne Femme)*

Time: A little less than an hour. Serves 6.

500 grams (1 pound, 2 ounces) of pumpkin, net weight; 150 grams (5 1/3 ounces) of stale bread; 1 1/2 liters (6 1/3 cups) of water; 1/2 liter (generous 2 cups) of milk; 20 grams (2/3 ounce) of sugar (2 cubes); 80 grams (2 3/4 ounces, 5 1/2 tablespoons) of butter; 2 whole eggs.

PROCEDURE. **The pumpkin:** Remove the seeds. Cut crosswise into pieces to make it easier to peel. Remove a layer of peel about 1 centimeter (3/8 inch) thick, and cut the pieces into large squares. Put them in a deep pot with 1 1/2 liters (6 1/3 cups) of water and 10 grams (1/3 ounce) of sea salt. Bring rapidly to a boil and cook over high heat until a piece of the pumpkin squeezed between two fingers yields sufficiently so that it can be easily mashed. This should take about 12 minutes. Drain all the cooking water and *reserve it.* In the same pot, crush the pieces with the back of a large wooden spoon. Then add the bread, the milk, and the sugar.

The bread: Use ordinary bread that is stale, cut into little slices (removing any burned parts of the crust) and dried in the oven until lightly colored. You can just as easily use hard pieces of stale bread, which are often found in home pantries and normally kept for bread crumbs. In any case, break them into very small pieces, or even crush them coarsely.

The cooking: Bring to a boil. Cover the pot and let it simmer for about *22–25 minutes.* Then put everything in a metallic drum sieve *(tamis)* set over a soup bowl or a bowl. Push it through the sieve by forcing it through with the wooden pestle. Nothing should be left on the sieve. Return this purée to the pot. Add water from the pumpkin cooking, until it has reached the proper consistency. Bring it to a boil, *stirring constantly.* Turn off the heat. Add the eggs, both whites and yolks, and the butter. Check the salt seasoning. Pour it into the tureen.

Potage of Cream of Pumpkin *(Potage à la Crème de Potiron)*

Perfect up until the middle of October, when one still has fresh tomatoes. Later, they can be replaced by tomato concentrate. *Time: 1 1/2 hours. Serves 6.*

750 grams (1 pound, 10 ounces) of pumpkin, net weight; 100 grams (3 1/2 ounces) of tomato, net weight; 40 grams (1 3/8 ounces) of onion; 3/4–1 liter (generous 3–4 1/4 cups) of boiled milk; 2 egg yolks; 50 grams (1 3/4 ounces, 3 1/2 tablespoons) of fresh butter; 10 grams (1/3 ounce) of salt, and 7–8 grams (3/16 ounce) of sugar.

PROCEDURE. Peel the pumpkin and cut it into square pieces about 4 centimeters (1 1/2 inches) all around. Cut the tomatoes in half. Squeeze out the water and the seeds. Cut the onion into thin slices.

Put everything together in a thick-bottomed pot, without liquid. The moisture in the pumpkin is sufficient here. Cover with a round of baking or parchment paper placed directly on top of the pieces, as well as the lid of the pot, which should fit snugly. Put in a moderate oven for *1 hour,* during which time you must check it occasionally. Force the entire contents of the pot, the solid and the liquid, through a fine sieve. Return the purée to a clean pot. Season with salt and sugar. Dilute it with the milk, the correct amount of which depends here on the quality of the pumpkin and the quantity of the liquid that it has rendered. Bring it to a boil while stirring. Let it boil for *2 minutes.* Cover and keep it quite warm until ready to serve. Preheat the tureen with boiling water before adding the soup. Put in the butter, divided into small pieces, and the egg yolks. Mix into a fluid paste with a wooden spoon. Pour the soup gradually into the tureen, stirring it with the spoon. If you like, add some little croutons or 2–3 tablespoons of cooked rice that has been well-dried in the oven.

Pumpkin Soup *(Soupe au Potiron).* This is the simplest method, but we do not think it produces the most succulent result.

Peel the pumpkin. Cut it into pieces, and cook it with very little water, about 2 deciliters (6$^3/_4$ fluid ounces, $^7/_8$ cup) for each 500 grams (1 pound, 2 ounces). Add a walnut-sized piece of butter, some salt, and 2 sugar cubes. Cover. Let this boil slowly, about 1 hour. Strain through a strainer. Return to the pot. Dilute the purée with some milk that has previously been boiled, a good $^1/_2$ liter (generous 2 cups) at least. Bring it to a boil again, and pour it over the slices of bread in the tureen.

Pumpkin and White Bean Soup, Bordeaux-Style *(Soupe au Potiron et aux Haricots à la Mode de Bordeaux)*

If you cannot get fresh white beans, you can use dried ones for this soup. In that case, the amount must be reduced, since the volume and weight of dried beans is naturally less than those of fresh beans. About 3 good deciliters (1$^1/_4$ cups) should suffice here.

You should cook them as directed (SEE DRIED VEGETABLES, PAGE 557) in enough water to recover 1 liter (4$^1/_4$ cups) after straining the soup. *Time: 1$^3/_4$ hours. Serves 6.*

$^1/_2$ liter (generous 2 cups) of large, fresh white beans; 300 grams (10$^1/_2$ ounces) of pumpkin, net weight; 300 grams (10$^1/_2$ ounces) of tomatoes, net weight; 1$^1/_4$ liters (5$^1/_3$ cups) of boiling water; 15 grams ($^1/_2$ ounce) of sea salt; 1 small clove of garlic; 1 tablespoon of tapioca; 30 grams (1 ounce, 2 tablespoons) of butter.

PROCEDURE. Put the beans in boiling water to cook, with salt and a clove of garlic. Cover the pot. *After a half hour,* add the pumpkin, cut into pieces about the size of a walnut, and the tomatoes, which have been skinned and have had their water and their seeds removed. Let it cook for *another 30 minutes:* the beans must be able to be easily crushed into a purée. Strain the vegetables and the cooking water through a sieve in small batches. Return to a clean pot. Bring it to a boil, stirring all the while. Then add the tapioca, pouring in a constant stream. Stir with a spoon. Cover. Lower the heat to let the tapioca cook without boiling, *about 15–20 minutes.* Just before serving, stir the butter into the soup off the heat.

Jerusalem Artichoke Soup *(Potage Purée à la Palestine)*

This is a puréed soup featuring Jerusalem artichokes. Its flavor is, in effect, that of the artichoke. This very simple preparation makes for a very pleasant winter soup. This recipe includes a final thickening with egg yolks and cream, but these can be left out. However, it is absolutely essential, in this case, to include butter, adding it off the heat, just before serving, and allowing about 60 grams (2$^1/_4$ ounces, 4$^1/_2$ tablespoons) of butter. Optionally, you can add 4–5 grilled hazelnuts, which enhance the flavor of the Jerusalem artichoke. *Time: 50–55 minutes. Serves 6.*

500 grams (1 pound, 2 ounces) of Jerusalem artichokes, net; 100 grams (3$^1/_2$ ounces) of onion; 40 grams (1$^3/_8$ ounces, 3 tablespoons) of butter; $^1/_2$ liter (generous 2 cups) of warm water; $^1/_2$ liter (generous 2 cups) of boiled milk; 5 grams ($^1/_6$ ounce) of salt, and a good pinch of superfine sugar; 25 grams (1 ounce) of cornstarch; 1 deciliter (3$^1/_3$ fluid ounces, scant $^1/_2$ cup) of cold milk; 2 egg yolks dissolved in 1 deciliter (3$^1/_3$ fluid ounces, scant $^1/_2$ cup) of cream; a good pinch of chervil leaves; 2 tablespoons of small croutons fried in butter, made with 50 grams (1$^3/_4$ ounces) of stale bread without crust and 30 grams (1 ounce, 2 tablespoons) of butter.

PROCEDURE. Carefully peel the Jerusalem artichokes. Dry them with a kitchen towel. Cut them into quarters and slice thinly. Cut the onion in rounds.

Melt the butter in a heavy-bottomed pot with a 2-liter (8-cup) capacity. Add the onion; cook it slowly for about 5 minutes without allowing it to color. Add the Jerusalem artichokes; keeping the heat low, let them stew and soften, stirring occasionally with a wooden spoon for *15 minutes.*

Crush the hazelnuts. Toast them lightly near the door of the oven to make it easier to remove their skins. Crush them with the blade of a strong knife and add to the Jerusalem artichokes. Once the artichokes are stewed, add warm water. Add salt and sugar. Bring to a boil over high heat. Cover and cook gently for about *20 minutes.*

Force everything quickly through a drum sieve *(tamis)* set over a bowl. Return the purée to a clean pot. Add the boiled milk. Mix with a wooden spoon or whisk. Pour in the cornstarch, mixed into the cold milk. Bring to a boil, stirring constantly with a wooden spoon or whisk. Then let it boil gently for *5–6 minutes.*

To serve: With the help of a soupspoon, remove the foam, which has risen due to boiling. Then make the liaison (SEE LIAISONS, PAGE 47). Check the seasoning. Pour the soup through a chinois into a soup tureen. Add the croutons and the chervil leaves. Serve.

Cauliflower Soup *(Potage à la Purée de Chou-Fleur)*

In haute cuisine, the name *à la Dubarry* indicates that the dish will contain cauliflower. This soup can be made in several ways. The simplest consists in cooking potatoes with the cauliflower, which produces a purée with a consistency that the cauliflower alone would not be able to provide. *Time: About 45 minutes. Serves 6.*

350 grams (12¹/₃ ounces) of cauliflower; 200 grams (7 ounces) of potatoes, weighed after peeling; 8 deciliters (3³/₈ cups) of boiled milk; 10 grams (¹/₃ ounce) of salt; a pinch of grated nutmeg; 30 grams (1 ounce, 2 tablespoons) of butter; about 30 small croutons, fried in butter; a good pinch of chervil leaves.

PROCEDURE. Trim the cauliflower as directed (SEE CAULIFLOWER, PAGE 502). Plunge it in boiling water and boil for 5 minutes. Peel the potatoes and cut them in small pieces. Put them in a deep pot with the cauliflower, which has been well drained, and add 6 deciliters (2¹/₂ cups) of milk; salt. Bring it to a boil. Cover and cook over moderate heat until everything is tender enough to be easily puréed, which will require here about *25–30 minutes at the most.*

Force everything through a drum sieve *(tamis).* Return the purée to a rinsed pot. Dilute it with the rest of the milk; add a little more milk if it seems too thick. Bring it to a boil and keep warm. When ready to serve, add the butter, off the heat, and the chervil leaves. Pour it into the tureen on top of the croutons.

Cream of Cauliflower Soup *(Potage Velouté à la Dubarry)*

This dish is reserved for special occasions. To supplement these directions, refer to POTAGES VELOUTÉS (PAGE 114). *Time: About 2 hours. Serves about 10.*

600 grams (1 pound, 5 ounces) of cauliflower, net weight; 70 grams (2¹/₂ ounces, ¹/₃ cup) of butter and 70 grams (2¹/₂ ounces) of flour for the roux; 2 liters (8¹/₂ cups) of veal (jus) or clear bouillon; a tiny bit of grated nutmeg; a pinch of pepper; 4 egg yolks; 2 deciliters (6³/₄ fluid ounces, ⁷/₈ cup) of crème fraîche; a good pinch of chervil leaves.

PROCEDURE. Prepare the velouté with a white roux *(roux blanc)* and 1¹/₂ liters (6¹/₃ cups) of bouillon, and skim carefully (SEE SKIMMING, PAGE 16). Meanwhile, cook the cauliflower in boiling water; stop the cooking as soon as a floret yields to pressure when squeezed between your fingers. Drain; reserve 3–4 small florets for garnish; keep them warm in a little bit of their cooking water.

Put all the rest of the cauliflower in the skimmed velouté. Cover and simmer about 20 minutes. Next, force everything through a fine-mesh drum sieve *(tamis).* Return the purée to the rinsed pot. Dilute with ¹/₂ liter (generous 2 cups) of the remaining stock or bouillon. Stir until it begins to boil, then lower the heat.

Thicken with the egg yolks and the cream (there is no need to boil any further). Keep warm in a double boiler until ready to serve, with the butter dotted around on the surface of the soup. To serve, strain the soup through a chinois into the tureen, and add the reserved cauliflower florets, divided into small pieces, along with the chervil.

Cream of Rice Soup *(Potage à la Crème de Riz)*

This is a simple preparation, which is rarely successful because the rules for cooking with rice flour, sold as "Cream of Rice," are not widely known. This sort of soup can be prepared with meat bouillon, preferably veal, or without meat, prepared with milk, or with the cooking liquid from fresh and dried vegetables: cauliflower, white beans, potatoes, etc. One can add a garnish of small fried croutons or chervil leaves or sprigs. *Time: 20–25 minutes. Serves 4–5.*

1 liter (4¼ cups) of liquid; 60 grams (2¼ ounces) of rice flour; 2 egg yolks; 1 deciliter (3⅓ fluid ounces, scant ½ cup) of fresh cream; 50 grams (1¾ ounces, 3½ tablespoons) of good butter.

PROCEDURE. In a deep saucepan with a capacity of 1½ liters (6 cups), boil the liquid that you have decided to use, minus 2 deciliters (6¾ fluid ounces, ⅞ cup), which should be set aside to dilute the rice flour; put this in a bowl; dilute it gradually with the reserved liquid. Pour the diluted rice flour into the boiling liquid in a thin stream, stirring vigorously with a whisk or wooden spoon. Continue stirring until it starts to boil again.

Without covering the saucepan, and over very low heat, keep the liquid simmering—almost imperceptibly—for *12–15 minutes,* not longer. (This should have been salted according to how much liquid was required.) In the bowl where you diluted the rice flour, beat the egg yolks with the cream to make the liaison (SEE LIAISONS, PAGE 47). Give it another minute or so of boiling. Then, *off the heat,* add and stir the butter, divided into little pieces. Strain the soup through a chinois into the tureen. Serve.

Soups made with cream of oats and cream of barley are prepared in the same way.

Chestnut Purée Soup *(Potage à la Purée de Marrons)*

According to taste, this soup can be made without meat by cooking the chestnuts in water and diluting the purée with milk instead of bouillon. In this case, increase the quantity of butter added at the end ever so slightly.

The garnish can be chosen from a wide selection: Little croutons of bread, fried in butter or simply grilled; a julienne or *brunoise* of vegetables; some leek white, finely minced. We recommend celery, cut into a *brunoise* or in a fine julienne, because this vegetable marries particularly well with the chestnut, and the cooking time is more or less the same. In this case, allow 150 grams (5⅓ ounces) of celery hearts, trimmed and braised in about 50 grams (1¾ ounces, 3½ tablespoons) of butter in a small pan for *25–30 minutes,* then covered with bouillon, or with water if it's a meat-free dish, to finish cooking. *Time: 1½–2 hours. Serves 6.*

About 30 nice chestnuts; 1½ liters (6⅓ cups) of degreased bouillon; 30 grams (1 ounce) of celery hearts; half a lump of sugar; 30 grams (1 ounce, 2 tablespoons) of butter to finish.

PROCEDURE. Peel the chestnuts in one of the ways suggested (SEE CHESTNUTS, PAGE 521). Put them in any pan where they will fit snugly with the finely minced celery, *½ liter (generous 2 cups)* of bouillon and a little bit of sugar. Bring to a boil. Cover. Cook everything gently until the chestnuts can be easily puréed. Allow about *¾–1 hour* and even possibly more, depending on the kind of chestnuts you use.

Force the chestnuts, the celery, and what remains of the liquid through a fine-mesh drum sieve *(tamis)*, preferably a metallic one, because of its fine mesh (SEE TO STRAIN PURÉES, PAGE 14). Put this purée in a pan and stir with a small whisk to make it smooth. While you are stirring, thin it out a bit, gradually, with the liter (4¼ cups) of bouillon that remains. Bring it to a boil as you continue to whisk. Skim for *about 20 minutes* (SEE SKIMMING, PAGE 16).

To serve, add the butter off the heat. Strain it through a chinois into a tureen that contains the garnish of your choice.

Tomato Soup *(Potage aux Tomates)*

This is an excellent home-style preparation taken from a notebook of family recipes. Garlic is present, but it is barely noticeable and brings a subtle taste to the finished dish, rounding out the true flavor of the soup most admirably. *Time: 1½ hours. Serves 6.*

1 kilogram (2 pounds, 3 ounces) of substantial, ripe tomatoes, net weight; 60 grams (2¼ ounces, 4½ tablespoons) of butter; 1½ liters (6⅓ cups) of warm water; 15 grams (½ ounce) of salt; 1 clove of garlic; 4 level teaspoons of tapioca; 3 spoonfuls of thick cream; 2 egg yolks; a pinch of pepper.

PROCEDURE. Cut the tomatoes in half. Squeeze out the water and the seeds. Put them in a heavy-bottomed pot with a 3-liter (12¾-cup) capacity. Add the butter. Cover. Cook this slowly for *a half hour.* Then add water, salt, pepper, and the garlic clove, unpeeled. Let it cook for another *15 minutes. Remove the garlic* and force everything through a drum sieve *(tamis)* into a tureen. Return to the rinsed pot. Put it back on the heat and, when it starts to boil, add the tapioca, poured in a thin stream. Cover and simmer for *15–20 minutes.* In the serving tureen, combine the egg yolks and cream. To serve, pour the soup on top of the eggs and cream, taking due care (SEE LIAISONS, PAGE 47). Check for salt.

Tomato Soup from the Poitou Region *(Potage à la Tomate, Mode du Poitou)*

We highly recommend this dish for its simplicity and its speedy preparation. Although it is strictly meat-free, it gives the illusion of a bouillon made with meat.

It is best to make this on a day when the cooking water from white beans or flageolets is available; failing this, the cooking water from potatoes can be used. If necessary, add plain water to top up the indicated amount.

You can garnish this soup with grilled bread, vermicelli, pasta, rice, semolina, tapioca, etc. *Time: About 1¼ hours. Serves 6.*

1 good-sized onion (150 grams, 5⅓ ounces); a nice, ripe, plump tomato (at least 150 grams, 5⅓ ounces); 30 grams (1 ounce, 2 tablespoons) of butter; 1½ liters (6⅓ cups) of liquid, as directed above; if the vegetable cooking water did not include a bouquet garni, add a branch of parsley, a branch of thyme, and a bay leaf.

PROCEDURE. Cut the onion into small dice. Brown it in the butter in a heavy-bottomed pot over low heat for about 10 minutes, uncovered. Stir often with a wooden spoon.

Then add the tomato, which has simply been cut into slices. Let it melt and reduce for about 10 minutes more, still uncovered; stir it often.

Then pour in ½ liter (generous 2 cups) of liquid. Add the bouquet garni, if necessary. A little bit of salt if the liquid needs it. Cover. Boil more or less rapidly for *15–20 minutes,*. Then, add the rest of the liquid, boiling for *1–2 minutes* more.

Strain through a fine sieve, mashing it lightly with the back of the spoon, without making the onion pass through. If you are going to garnish it with grilled bread, you can put the soup directly into the tureen. If you're going to use vermicelli or pasta, strain the soup into a bowl, rinse the pot, and return the soup to it. Bring it back to a boil, then add the pasta or the vermicelli to the boiling liquid. Cover and cook gently for *15 minutes.*

Tomato soup with Vegetables, Rice, and Bacon, Portuguese-Style *(Potage à la Portugaise)*

We give the classic recipe here. The preparation is extremely simple: a purée of tomatoes enhanced with a light mirepoix and rice, cooked at the same time. Long-grain rice is cooked separately to be added just before serving, as a garnish for the soup. *Time: 1¾ hours. Serves 8–10.*

750 grams (1 pound, 10 ounces) of ripe tomatoes; a mirepoix with 60 grams (2¼ ounces, 4½ tablespoons) of butter; 50 grams (1¾ ounces) of bacon; 50 grams (1¾ ounces) of carrot and the same amount of onion; 2–3 sprigs of parsley, a bit of thyme, and a half bay leaf; 125 grams (4½ ounces) of ordinary rice; a small garlic clove; 1¼ liters (5⅓ cups) of good bouillon that has been well degreased; 10 grams (⅓ ounce) of sugar.

***To finish the soup,* 50 grams (1¾ ounces) of best-quality Carolina long-grain rice; 100 grams (3½ ounces, 7 tablespoons) of butter; a pinch of chervil leaves.**

PROCEDURE. In a deep, heavy-bottomed pot, lightly brown the mirepoix (PAGE 21). Halve the tomatoes and get rid of their water and their seeds; cut them into pieces; add them to the mirepoix that has already been lightly browned. Cover and cook over low heat to melt the tomatoes.

When the tomatoes have cooked down to a mush, add the ordinary rice, previously washed; the sugar; the crushed garlic; ¾ liter (generous 3 cups) of bouillon. Bring to a boil. Cover. Continue cooking slowly for *about 35–40 minutes*—in other words, until the rice has become a purée.

Force everything in the pot through a drum sieve *(tamis).* Nothing should be left on the sieve except the skin of the tomatoes and the fragments of thyme and bay. Put this purée into a clean pot. Dilute it with the rest of the bouillon, about 1 deciliter (3$^{1}/_{3}$ fluid ounces, scant $^{1}/_{2}$ cup). Bring it to a boil, stirring constantly. Then, over low heat, degrease it for *25 minutes.* SEE SKIMMING, PAGE 16.

Long-grain rice: Bring 1 deciliter (3$^{1}/_{3}$ fluid ounces, scant $^{1}/_{2}$ cup) of lightly salted water to the boil. Pour in the rice in a steady stream. Cook it slowly for *20 minutes.* The grains must hold their shape without bursting, while still remaining tender. If it is ready a little bit in advance, drain the water from the pan, right until the last drop, leaving the rice there. Cover and keep it in a warm place.

To serve: Melt the butter in the soup, off the heat. Strain through a chinois into the tureen. Add the rice and the chervil leaves. Serve.

Potato, Leek, and Tomato Soup *(Potage Solférino)*

This extremely good soup has become a classic, doubtless because of its many advantages: it is very easy to make, it can be prepared either with a meat-based broth or with no meat, just water, or, even better, with vegetable cooking water from white beans, green beans, etc.

The amounts given are approximate: in other words, a little bit more potato or leek doesn't really matter. But there must be enough tomato to give the soup its characteristic color and taste. We suggest serving the soup strained through a fine-mesh sieve and to garnish with little potato balls and diamond-shaped green beans; it is therefore most appropriate as an everyday soup. Alternatively, for an even easier preparation, omit the straining and serve directly, just as it is, in the tureen, where you add the green beans and the chervil. In this case, leave out the potato balls but increase ever so slightly the amount of potatoes cooked in the soup. *Time: 1 hour. Serves 6.*

About 600 grams (1 pound, 5 ounces) of potatoes; 700 grams (1 pound, 9 ounces) of tomatoes; 1 medium onion (80–100 grams, 2$^{3}/_{4}$–3$^{1}/_{2}$ ounces); the white parts of 4 medium leeks; 1 plump clove of garlic; 100 grams (3$^{1}/_{2}$ ounces, 7 tablespoons) of butter; 2 liters (8$^{1}/_{2}$ cups) of bouillon or cooking water from vegetables.

For the garnish: **3 tablespoons of green beans, cut into lozenges; a good spoonful of chervil leaves, coarsely chopped; 2 dozen little balls of potato, as well as the potato used in the soup.**

PROCEDURE. Cut the onion and the leek white into fine slices. In a deep pot, color them lightly in 50 grams (1$^{3}/_{4}$ ounces, 3$^{1}/_{2}$ tablespoons) of butter, taking care not to let anything brown. Then add the liquid; if you are using pure water only, it should be salted: 10 grams ($^{1}/_{3}$ ounce) per liter. Bring it to a boil. Once boiled, add the tomatoes, halved and cored, with the seeds and water removed and coarsely chopped. (If the soup is not strained, you must also peel the tomatoes. SEE TOMATOES, PAGE 534.)

At the same time, put the potatoes, peeled and cut into slices, and the garlic into the soup. Cover and let it boil until they are completely cooked, which should be *about a half hour.*

Meanwhile, prepare the garnish (SEE POTATO BALLS, PAGE 123). Having trimmed the green beans, gather into bunches of 4–5 on the work surface and slice diagonally, thus making diamond shapes about 1 centimeter ($^{3}/_{8}$ inch) large. Cook them as directed (SEE GREEN BEANS, PAGE 517). Then put them in cool water to keep them green: They will reheat in the soup.

When the potatoes are cooked, strain the soup through a metal-mesh drum sieve *(tamis)*, the screen of which should retain only the tomato skins. Put this purée back into a clean pot. If it seems to be a little thick at this time, dilute with bouillon or water. Bring it to a boil, stirring with a spoon. Then cover and keep warm without allowing it to boil, so that the soup does not reduce and require more liquid.

To serve: The purée should have a nice, light consistency at this point, and be *good and warm,* so stir in the butter, divided into very small bits, off the heat. Check the salt and add a pinch of pepper; a point of cayenne works very well (as much as can be held on the tip of a knife blade). Pour it into the tureen. Add the potato balls, the green beans, and the chervil. Serve.

HERB-BASED SOUPS
Potages aux Herbes

This all-encompassing name includes a wide range of soups, mostly made in the home kitchen, and prepared in many different ways depending on the season, taste, availability of ingredients, diets, etc.

By "herbs," what is generally meant is species of sorrel, chervil, lettuce, Swiss chard, watercress, spinach, and even leek. Some people even add salad burnet, celery leaves, cauliflower, and cabbage to their herb soup—but these are the exception. The herbs are not always featured together, and that's a reason for the diversity of these recipes. Sorrel is practically always used in these soups, unless it must be excluded due to dietary restrictions.

The initial cooking of the herbs is done in a little bit of butter or fat, which is called making the herbs "melt." In fact, braising reduces them: The herbs give up their moisture and lose a considerable proportion of their original volume, becoming infused with the cooking oil, because butter alone is not always used. In calling for "oil" or "fat," we have implied melted or grated lard, which is, apparently, particularly recommended for sorrel soup by Carême (SEE PAGE 110). According to this great chef, sorrel braised in lard has the greatest flavor. There is also the *question of the liquid.* The traditional family-style preparation is meat-free: either the liquid left from cooking fresh vegetables or dried vegetables, beans, peas, lentils, cauliflower, potatoes, etc.—or, for that matter, just plain water. Often, a quantity of milk is added. However, this does not necessarily rule out the use of bouillon. It is often used for herb soups in classic haute cuisine. And veal bouillon, especially, has a particular affinity for all herb soups.

The final liaison with yolks is practically essential for all soups of this kind. It is even more important when the soup has a substantial proportion of sorrel. Egg—and in this case, it is often the entire egg—is almost always used in conjunction with any dish calling for sorrel. Herb soup is often made without any other thickener, except for the liaison supplied by the egg, though sometimes it is thickened with flour after the herbs have melted in the fat, and before adding any liquid. Or it may use arrowroot, rice flour, etc., diluted in a little bit of cold liquid and poured into the soup 10 minutes before serving; this can also be done with tapioca. Another method involves potatoes, cut into quarters and cooked in the soup, then the whole thing is forced through a medium sieve for a coarse, peasant-style texture.

The optional garnish, which is often not added to soups thickened with flour or otherwise are according to taste: slices of bread, which are called *flûtes à potage* (soup sticks), and are cut fine as lace; croutons fried in butter or grilled; or pasta, vermicelli, semolina; cooked rice, etc.

Sometimes the herbs are strained, sometimes they are not. Generally, an herb soup is not strained, given the basic home-style nature of these preparations.

Herb Soup *(Potage aux Herbes)*

An excellent, classic method, which uses meat bouillon. But, as has been said earlier, the bouillon can be replaced by vegetable cooking water: in this case, we prefer the cooking water of beans. The fat, used as previously explained, can always be replaced by butter. *Serves 6.*

125 grams (4 1/2 ounces) of sorrel; 50 grams (1 3/4 ounces) of lettuce; 50 grams (1 3/4 ounces) of chervil (net weight); 30 grams (1 ounce) of fresh lard or of good bacon for the braising of the herbs; 1 1/2 liters (6 1/3 cups) of degreased bouillon; 3 egg yolks; 30 grams (1 ounce, 2 tablespoons) of butter to finish the soup; 5–6 tablespoons of very small croutons, cut into cubes and grilled.

PROCEDURE. Trim the sorrel and the lettuce; cut into very fine strips and give it a couple of crosswise slices with the knife so that the soup will be able to pass more easily through the sieve. Remove the large stems from the chervil and coarsely chop the rest. Put these herbs into a deep pot with the lard, grated: in other words, cut into pieces with the help of a knife so it can be reduced to a paste and not leave any lumps in the soup.

Soften and melt the herbs over low heat, uncovered, stirring often with a wooden spoon. Let them reduce and absorb the cooking fat for *a good half hour.* Add the bouillon. Add the sugar. Cover. Boil for *a half hour.*

To serve, thicken with the egg yolks added off the heat, then add the butter, divided into small bits. Pour it into the tureen over the croutons; or, the preferred method, set them on the table, in a separate dish, at the same time. This way, they will stay crunchy in the soup.

Herb Soup without Sorrel *(Potage aux Herbes sans Oseille)*

This recipe is for those who are not allowed sorrel in their diet. The rice used for the garnish can, depending on preference, be replaced by another garnish, according to the directions given above. *Time: 1 hour. Serves 6.*

50 grams (1 3/4 ounces) of white of leek; 60 grams (2 1/4 ounces) of spinach; 60 grams (2 1/4 ounces) of lettuce leaves (net weight); 30 grams (1 ounce, 2 tablespoons) of butter to braise them; 1 1/4 liters (5 1/3 cups) of boiling water and 10 grams (1/3 ounce) of salt; 2 deciliters (6 3/4 fluid ounces, 7/8 cup) of light cream and 2 egg yolks; 30 grams (1 ounce, 2 tablespoons) of butter to finish the soup; 3–4 tablespoons of rice, cooked in water and set aside.

PROCEDURE. Cut the leek into rounds as thin as possible. Trim the spinach and the lettuce, and chop coarsely.

Braise them in butter as above, without allowing the leek to color. Add the water; cover. Boil rapidly for *about 20 minutes.*

Strain everything through a large sieve, stirring with a spoon. Return to the pot. Bring it back to a boil. Add the rice. Boil for about 1 minute. Remove from the heat and add the cream and the egg yolks to thicken. Add the butter. Pour it into the tureen, after tasting it for salt.

Herb Soup with Fish Stock *(Potage aux Herbes à l'Eau de Poisson)*

This is a very good home-style method using a court bouillon made with shad or hake, for example, and without vinegar or wine. For the salt, do not use more than 10 grams (1/3 ounce) per liter (4 1/4 cups) of water in the court bouillon—otherwise, the soup will be over-salted. *Time: About 1 hour. Serves 6–8.*

250 grams (8 7/8 ounces) of sorrel, net weight; 100 grams (3 1/2 ounces) of lettuce, coarsely chopped; 100 grams (3 1/2 ounces) of the white part of leek, sliced into fine rounds, gently braised with 40 grams (1 3/8 ounces, 3 tablespoons) of butter for *about 20 minutes.* Add 1/2 liter (generous 2 cups) of the bouillon and strain through a sieve. At this point, add 10–15 grams (1/3– 1/2 ounce) of chervil, without the stems.

Cook gently, *for 15 minutes.* Add the rest of the liquid—which is 1 liter (4 1/4 cups) of fish bouillon. Off the heat, add a liaison of 2 eggs, both the yolk and the white. Finish with 30 grams (1 ounce, 2 tablespoons) of butter. Pour into the tureen over some slices of stale bread cut about 1 centimeter (3/8 inch) thick.

Sorrel Soup *(Soupe à l'Oseille)*

At your discretion, the butter for braising can be replaced by lard or good bacon. *Time: 45 minutes. Serves 6.*

300 grams (10 1/2 ounces) net of sorrel, chopped coarsely; 50 grams (1 3/4 ounces, 3 1/2 tablespoons) of butter; 30 grams (1 ounce) of flour; 1 1/2 liters (6 1/3 cups) of water; 3 whole eggs and 3 tablespoons of milk; 30 grams (1 ounce, 2 tablespoons) of butter for the finish.

PROCEDURE. Gently braise the sorrel with the butter or the lard, as above. Sprinkle with flour. Stir and cook over low heat, until the flour becomes a light golden color. Add the boiling liquid. Add salt and a pinch of sugar.

Cover and boil *for a good 15 minutes.* Beat the whole eggs with the milk in a bowl. Stir this into the soup. Add the butter off the heat. Pour the soup into the tureen, without straining, on top of bread slices or *flûtes à potage* (thin baguettes for soup).

Rustic-style variation: Replace the flour with peeled potatoes cut into quarters, which you add when the liquid is poured. If you prefer, you can strain the soup through a medium sieve into the tureen, or more simply, you can crush the potatoes in the pot with a wooden spoon before pouring the soup into the tureen; and in this case, on top of the eggs, which will have been beaten. If you like thick soups, you can also add some bread.

SOUPS WITH A BASE OF PURÉED DRIED VEGETABLES

Les Potages à Base de Purées de Légumes Secs

Check first for the details concerning soaking, measures, cooking, etc., in the special section on DRIED VEGETABLES, PAGE 557

When the only liquid used to dilute the purée is the cooking water for vegetables, increase the amount of the water so that it is about 4 times the volume of the vegetables.

How much liquid to use to dilute this purée is almost impossible to establish exactly. The amount varies according to the thickness of the purée. In other words, it depends on how much liquid the vegetable has absorbed during cooking, which has been more or less stopped at the desired degree. So allow, on average, for 100 grams (3$^1/_2$ ounces) of sieved purée, from 2–2$^1/_2$ deciliters ($^7/_8$–1 cup) of liquid. Also, consider the type of soup: If it has a garnish, and the type of garnish; or if it is thickened with egg yolks, as in *potage Compiègne.*

This liquid can simply be the dried vegetable cooking water, as is done in home kitchens, or it can be bouillon or milk; or, it can even be part cooking water and part bouillon or milk.

Once it has been put on the heat, the diluted purée must always be stirred gently with a wooden spoon, without stopping, until it boils. If this is not done, the soup will stick to the bottom of the pot and burn, making it fit only for the garbage can.

For any kind of soup based on a dried vegetable purée, skimming is absolutely necessary (SEE SKIMMING, PAGE 16). It should take at least a half hour. If this skimming is overlooked, or badly done, the soup will have an unattractive color and a gluey consistency, which is not very appealing.

After skimming, the soup can be kept for a rather long time in advance, warm and covered, until ready to serve. If, when ready to serve, the consistency seems a little bit too thick, you can thin it with a few tablespoons of the liquid used in the cooking, or simply a little bit of vegetable cooking water.

Any potage based on purée must be passed through a fine chinois before transferring it to the serving tureen: this is why, in haute cuisine, the garnishes are served separately. This is not always possible in the home kitchen, when the cooking of some garnishes is simplified by cooking them together with the soup.

Soups Made with a Purée of Dry White Beans *(Potages à la Purée de Haricots Blancs Secs)*

A purée of white beans is often used as a soup base, both for classic and modern soups, as well as for soups made with or without meat. In winter, the dried bean replaces the fresh; since it is the fresh bean, in fact, on which the various types of soup are based.

We provide, here, the simple, homemade method, using only the liquid from cooking the beans. But you can, if you like, modify and improve the soup by diluting the purée with some milk in place of some of the cooking liquid. If the soup has a meat base, the milk can be replaced by bouillon that has been completely degreased. In other words, a cook can take inspiration from haute cuisine and adapt the recipes according to economic limits and the whims of the cook. However, in home cooking, you must never omit the butter used to finish soup. Otherwise, the soup will lack that special something, especially since white beans, unlike red ones that can do without, need the addition of extra butter. *Time: 3–4 hours, depending upon the method. Serves 6.*

375 grams (13$^1/_4$ ounces) of beans; 1$^1/_2$ liters (6$^1/_3$ cups) of water; 15 grams ($^1/_2$ ounce) of salt; 1 medium onion (80–100 grams, 2$^3/_4$–3$^1/_2$ ounces), studded with a clove; 1 carrot (75–100 grams, 2$^2/_3$–3$^1/_2$ ounces), cut into quarters; 3 sprigs of parsley tied together; 1 branch of celery or a very small slice of celery root.

60 grams (2$^1/_4$ ounces) of butter to finish; 3 tablespoons of small croutons, fried in butter.

Necessary time, not counting soaking: about 4 hours, with a preliminary blanching recommended. At least 1 hour with the usual method.

PROCEDURE. Soak the beans as directed (SEE DRIED VEGETABLES, PAGE 557). If you have the time, blanch them as directed, especially for beans; it is particularly recommended here because the cooking water is the only liquid used for the soup, so its quality is of the utmost importance.

Put the beans in their receptacle—a metal pot or earthenware casserole—with the warm water (1 1/2 liters, 6 1/3 cups), and the salt. Bring it slowly to a boil over *very moderate heat*; skim; add the onion, carrot, parsley bundle, and celery. Cover. Adjust the cooking as directed. *After the beans have undergone a preliminary blanching, allow 1 1/2 hours of cooking.* Otherwise, at least 2 hours.

Remove the parsley, carrot, and celery; leave the onion. Force the beans through a metallic drum sieve *(tamis)*, pushing them through in small batches, without liquid. Do this while they are boiling hot (SEE STRAINING PURÉES, PAGE 14). Pour the cooking water into a bowl. Place the purée in a deep saucepan, which has been cleaned if the utensil was used for cooking the beans, and just large enough to make the skimming easy. Dilute with 1 liter (4 1/4 cups) of cooking water. Bring to a boil over high heat, stirring constantly. Then lower the heat for skimming (SEE SKIMMING, PAGE 16). Just before serving, take off the heat and stir in the butter. Strain directly into the serving tureen, add the little croutons, or serve separately, as you prefer.

Purée of Pea Soup *(Potage à la Purée de Pois)*

If you like, you can add 1 dozen spinach leaves and the green part of 2–3 leeks to impart a deeper color to the soup.

Also, if you like, you can replace the crouton garnish with 3–4 tablespoons of canned green peas, which you can keep in your pantry especially for this purpose. Heat them in lightly salted water a few minutes before serving. A potage garnished this way is an imitation of *potage Saint-Germain.* It is understood that the flavor will not be the same as a true *potage Saint-Germain,* which is prepared with fresh peas. *Time: 3 1/2 hours (not counting soaking). Serves 6.*

375 grams (13 1/4 ounces) or 4 deciliters (1 2/3 cups) of split peas; 1 1/2 liters (6 1/3 cups) of water: 15 grams (1/2 ounce) of salt.

A mirepoix, composed of: 25 grams (1 ounce, 2 tablespoons) of butter; 50 grams (1 3/4 ounces) of carrot; 50 grams (1 3/4 ounces) of onion; 50 grams (1 3/4 ounces) of good-quality bacon (do not use if the soup is meat-free); some sprigs of parsley; fragments of thyme; a quarter leaf of bay.

60 grams (2 1/4 ounces, 4 1/2 tablespoons) of butter to finish; 3 tablespoons of small fried croutons.

PROCEDURE. Soak, then cook the peas (SEE DRIED VEGETABLES, PAGE 557).

While the cooking is getting underway, prepare the mirepoix (SEE MIREPOIX, PAGE 21). Add it to the peas when they have started to boil. Cook slowly for 2 hours. At the end of this time, the peas will have been reduced to a purée. Remove only the herbs. Force everything through a drum sieve *(tamis)*, preferably with a fine mesh (SEE PASSING PURÉES, PAGE 14). Put the purée in a deep pot that has been cleaned if it was just used for cooking, and that is large enough to facilitate skimming.

Dilute the purée with 2 1/2 deciliters (1 cup) of warm water. Add a pinch of sugar. Bring it to a boil over high heat, stirring constantly. When fully boiled, position the pot for the skimming. Skim for 30 minutes, adding 1–2 tablespoons of water from time to time. Keep it warm. Just before serving, stir in the butter. Strain through a fine sieve into a serving tureen. Add the croutons, or serve separately to keep them crunchy.

Purée of Lentil Soup *(Potage à la Purée de Lentilles)*

As for the pea and dried white bean purées, lentil purée has many uses in soups. In haute cuisine, this purée is called *purée Conti. Time: 3 1/2 hours (not counting soaking).*

For details of the method for a basic puréed soup, refer to the recipe for Purée of Pea Soup: same quantities, same procedures, mirepoix, butter to finish, etc. Note that for here—as elsewhere, when using a purée—this very lightly sautéed mirepoix is much better than onion and carrot that have been added raw.

Note that the skimming of the lentil purée takes a long time: You must allow at least twice the time allotted for the dried bean purée, especially since the soup is not strained a second time before being poured into the tureen.

Prepared like this, the purée can be garnished as you like, either with croutons, or rice cooked in water, or with a chiffonade of lettuce and sorrel that has been sautéed in butter as a julienne, or even whole chervil leaves stripped from their stems, etc.

Game stock, particularly when made with partridge, goes very well with almost every lentil dish. If you should happen to have some fresh partridge carcasses—bones and leftovers of roasted partridges—add them to the lentils during their cooking.

Purée of Lentil Soup with Vegetables *(Purée Conti à la Brunoise)*

Prepare the vegetables, cut as for a potage *brunoise*. So, to 1 1/2 liters (6 1/3 cups) of purée, diluted to the proper consistency, use: 200 grams (7 ounces) of carrot; 120 grams (4 1/4 ounces) of turnip; 50 grams (1 3/4 ounces) of the white part of a leek; a little celery. Everything should be braised in 40 grams (1 3/8 ounces, 3 tablespoons) of butter. Then add at least 3 deciliters (1 1/4 cups) of bouillon to finish the cooking. Pour it into the tureen and strain the purée on top. Serve.

Purée of Lentil Soup with Sorrel *(Purée de Lentilles à l'Oseille)*

150 grams (5 1/3 ounces) of sorrel (net weight), cut into fine strips, as if for julienne, slowly softened and melted in 40 grams (1 3/8 ounces, 3 tablespoons) of butter, or even better, in a little bit of very good lard, for a good 15 minutes. Then add this to the skimmed lentil purée and cook for another 10 minutes. Pour it into the tureen with 2 egg yolks, preferably diluted with a few tablespoons of purée.

Purée of Lentil Soup with Onion *(Purée de Lentilles à l'Oignon)*

Proceed with cutting the onion as directed for ONION SOUP (PAGE 120). Color it the same way in butter. Add it to the skimmed purée and cook for 15 minutes, continuing the skimming (SEE SKIMMING, PAGE 16). According to taste, pour the soup just as it is into the tureen, or strain it first.

Purée of Kidney Bean Soup *(Potage à la Condé)*

This name designates, in an extremely general fashion, soups that are based on a purée of red beans. However, this purée can be prepared in many different ways, with many different variations, according to one's taste and means.

In haute cuisine, potage Condé is usually made with meat, as are other potages based on dried beans and pulses: you could use either ham or bacon in the cooking, or even, for special occasions, partridge. And the purée is diluted with consommé. Finish with a turn of the pepper mill and garnish with small, fried croutons.

In modern cooking, this is prepared *à la façon villageoise*, which involves adding a glass of red wine to the vegetables as they cook, the red wine being a sort of condiment for dishes made with kidney beans. In simple home cooking, potage Condé is usually made without meat—in other words, with nothing except its cooking water—and it is also excellent.

You can prepare this with a mirepoix exactly as a purée of pea soup is prepared. Or you could prepare it like a purée of white bean soup—in other words, with onion, carrot, and bouquet garni simply added to the cooking water. *In either case, the quantities and the procedures remain exactly the same.* Time: 3 1/2 hours (not counting soaking).

Let us add that a purée of kidney beans, well prepared, is particularly delicate and smooth, to the point where the amount of butter at the end could even be reduced—or left out altogether for certain days of abstinence, or for certain dietary restrictions—without detracting from the flavor of the soup.

Purée of White Bean Soup with Sorrel *(Potage Compiègne)*

This soup, a classic of the modern repertory, consists simply of a purée of white beans, dried or fresh according to season, enhanced with a garnish of sorrel. If you like, you can finish it with a liaison of egg yolks. We suggest that here; but if the egg yolks are omitted, you must replace it with butter at the end, about 40 grams (1 3/8 ounces, 3 tablespoons) added to the soup, off the heat, just before serving. *Time: 3 1/2 hours (not counting soaking). Serves 6.*

375 grams (13 1/4 ounces) of dry white beans or 1 liter (4 1/4 cups) of fresh beans; 6 good deciliters (2 1/2 cups) of their cooking water, and the same amount of boiled milk; 150 grams (5 1/3 ounces) of sorrel (net weight); 30 grams (1 ounce, 2 tablespoons) of butter to soften the sorrel in; 2 egg yolks and 1 1/2 deciliters (5 fluid ounces, 2/3 cup) of milk to thicken; a good pinch of chervil leaves.

PROCEDURE. Depending upon the kind of beans you're using, follow the directions given under DRY BEANS (PAGE 470), or under COOKING FRESH BEANS (PAGE 515). For either case, add to the cooking water: 1/2 onion, studded with a clove, a small carrot, and a bunch of parsley sprigs tied together. Drain the beans after cooking. Remove the carrot and the parsley. Force the beans through a drum sieve *(tamis)* (SEE STRAINING PURÉES, PAGE 14). Return the purée back to a clean saucepan. Dilute it with the cooking water and the milk. Bring it to a boil while stirring; then skim it for a good 20 minutes (SEE SKIMMING, PAGE 16). Meanwhile, trim and wash the sorrel; cut it into fine strips. Put it in a small pan with the butter. Let it soften over moderate heat until quite soft, or "melted," stirring often.

Just before serving, make a liaison with the egg yolk and milk. Let it boil for a few seconds. (SEE LIAISONS, PAGE 47.) Put the sorrel in a serving tureen and pour over the potage. Stir well and sprinkle with chervil leaves.

ENRICHED CREAM SOUPS
Potages Veloutés

This term "velouté" implies the preliminary use of a roux to thicken the chosen liquid, and, at the end, the addition of egg yolks, cream, and butter.

A velouté, as a cooking method applied to soups, can include a variety of ingredients, similar to those used for puréed soups (such as carrots, celery, cauliflower, beans, pumpkins, Jerusalem artichokes, etc.), or as a garnish, included in meat, poultry, fish, or game dumplings, cut into cubes or julienned, etc. It is a great vehicle for improvisation and experimentation. For the home cook, a velouté-based soup is the occasion to cut costs and reuse cooking water from vegetables—for example, from white beans, cauliflower, celery root, etc. If possible, keep a little bit of these different vegetables aside to garnish the soup.

Simple Velouté Soup *(Potage Velouté Simple)*

Time: About 40 minutes. Serves 6.

50 grams (1 3/4 ounces, 3 1/2 tablespoons) of butter and 60 grams (2 1/4 ounces) of flour for the roux; 1 1/2 liters (6 1/3 cups) of ordinary bouillon, thoroughly degreased and warm; 3 egg yolks, diluted with 1 deciliter (3 1/3 fluid ounces, scant 1/2 cup) of cream; 30 grams (1 ounce, 2 tablespoons) of good butter.

PROCEDURE. Make a light blond roux (SEE ROUX, PAGE 47). Remove from the heat and dilute it with the hot bouillon. Bring it to a boil, stirring constantly, then simmer slowly for about 20 minutes, no less, proceeding as directed. This is the minimum time, and doubling it will greatly help the purity of the velouté (SEE SKIMMING, PAGE 16). Just before serving, add the yolks and the cream (SEE LIAISONS, PAGE 47). There is no need to boil further because the heat of the soup will ensure that the eggs are sufficiently cooked. As always, check the seasoning and strain into the serving tureen through the chinois.

SOUPS
Les Soupes

Cabbage Soup *(La Soupe aux Choux)*

This soup can be made many different ways. In the most rustic version, the cabbage is divided into quarters and coarsely cut crosswise, then put in a pot of boiling water with some potatoes and some minced bacon—the cooking does not take very long. Some slices of bread are added to the tureen for serving.

Another rustic preparation is known as *potée,* in which the cabbage is similarly cut and put into boiling water, accompanied by a slab of salt pork, some carrot and turnip slices, and an onion studded with a clove. It cooks for about 2 hours, during which time some potatoes are added. To serve, bread and bacon slices are added to the tureen.

There is also a kind of soup called *garbure,* which is always made with croutons that have been gratinéed (SEE GARBURE, PAGE 117). In addition, there are all the soups based on a particular product or a regional taste preference. For example, goose is used in the Gascony region while garlic is favored in the Midi.

There is also the bourgeois method, in which the cabbage—previously blanched to take the edge off its very strong flavor—is cooked much longer in an ordinary pot-au-feu that includes some bacon. It is this recipe that we give here. At your discretion, the meat can consist of beef or lamb; at any rate, it is not included in the soup when it is served. If using mutton, keep it for the next day's lunch, breaded and grilled (SEE BREAST OF MUTTON, PAGE 321). A small, homemade sausage, with or without garlic, and cut into slices can be added to the soup just for as long as is necessary for it to be cooked. Serve in the tureen. Different kinds of cabbage are used for the soup, but the curly type, known as Savoy cabbage, is generally preferred. *Time: About 4 hours. Serves 6.*

1 small savoy cabbage; 500 grams (1 pound, 2 ounces) of breast of mutton or the same amount of beef short ribs; 150 grams (5 1/3 ounces) of salt pork; 100 grams (3 1/2 ounces) of carrots, net weight; 100 grams (3 1/2 ounces) of onion; a bouquet garni, composed of 3–4 branches of parsley, a little branch of celery, a sprig of thyme, and a quarter of a bay leaf; a clove; a small garlic clove; 3 liters (12 3/4 cups) of water.

PROCEDURE. **The cabbage:** Remove the first green leaves from the outside, to be certain that you use only the firm interior. Cut it into quarters. Cut out the root of the leaves, the stem, as well as the tough ribs of the exterior leaves. Wash in a generous amount of cold water. Check to make sure there are no snails hidden in the leaves.

Drain. Plunge the cabbage quarters into a pot of boiling water large enough for them to have plenty of room to cook. At the same time, add the salt pork. Do not cover, and watch for the moment when it returns to a boil. From that point, boil for 10 minutes. Drain. Plunge the cabbage and the bacon in a large basin of cool water, mixing them around in it. Change the water and let the cabbage soak for about 15 minutes.

Cooking the soup: Drain the cabbage and squeeze out all the liquid by pressing each quarter between your hands. Season these quarters with salt and pepper. Put them in the bottom of a 4 liter (4 1/4 quart)–capacity pot. On top of the cabbage, arrange in more or less equal layers: the carrots, previously peeled and cut in half lengthwise; the onion, peeled, left whole, and studded with a clove; the bouquet garni; the salt pork. On top of everything, add the piece of mutton. This placement of ingredients is important: it makes skimming the bouillon easier and keeps the cabbage at the bottom of the pot. Without this, it would float to the top. Pour 3 liters (12 3/4 cups) of fresh water into the pot, then proceed exactly as for an ordinary pot-au-feu, skimming, cooling off, etc.

Allow another 3 hours of tranquil and continuous simmering.

To serve: Cut as many 1-centimeter (3/8-inch)-thick slices of bread as there are guests out of a slightly stale loaf, and toast them to a beautiful light brown.

Remove all the different ingredients from the pot, leaving only the cabbage. Remove the cabbage with a skimming ladle and transfer it to the serving tureen. Give it a couple of crosswise slices with the knife, so that it is more easily picked up with a spoon. Arrange the crusts of bread on top. Over everything, pour the boiling bouillon, which *has not been degreased.* Serve immediately so that the croutons do not have too much time to become soggy.

Workingman's Soup *(Soupe du Laboureur)*

The name is indicative of the style of this dish: bucolic and substantial. It is really another sort of *potée.* The pork called for here can be fresh or salted. In metropolitan areas, butchers tend to have more fresh pork, and the pork mentioned in the recipe is the part used to make ham. In rural areas, salt pork is more frequently used. It must be soaked in lukewarm water to remove the excess salt for at least 2–3 hours in advance, and the water should be changed 2–3 times.

It should be mentioned, in passing, that the charm of such quaint country-style soups is accentuated greatly by serving them in a rustic tureen. *Time: 3 1/2 hours (from the moment when the soup has begun to cook). Serves about 10.*

500 grams (1 pound, 2 ounces) of hock of ham or pork; 250 grams (8 7/8 ounces) of bacon; 3 liters (12 3/4 cups) of water; 150 grams (5 1/3 ounces) of carrot, and the same of turnip, cut into slices; an onion of about 60 grams (2 1/4 ounces), and the same weight of the white part of leek, cut into very fine slices; 175 grams (6 ounces) of split peas, chosen from the best quality: in other words, of a large size and from a recent harvest; 10 small slices of stale bread, cut about 1/2 centimeter (3/16 inch) thick, lightly grilled and quite crispy.

PROCEDURE. Wash the dried peas. Cover them with lukewarm water and let them soak until ready to put them in the soup; that should be about 1 hour after beginning to cook the soup. If the bacon is salted, blanch it (SEE BACON, PAGE 15). In a pot, preferably earthenware, put the pork hock, fresh or already desalinated, the bacon, and the vegetables. Pour in the water. For the time being, do not salt. Bring to a boil over moderate heat. Skim. Cover partially, leaving a little space for the steam to escape, and maintain the liquid at a slow, steady simmer, *for 3 hours. After 1 hour, add the well-drained peas to the pot.* Continue cooking at the same rate for the time indicated. It can be extended, according to the requirements of serving, for another 20 minutes, without any inconvenience.

About 10–15 minutes before serving, put the ham hock and the bacon onto a plate. Remove all the bones. As much as you can, cut the meat of the hock into bite-sized pieces, so that there is no need to put knives on the table; cut the bacon similarly. Return this meat to the tureen, which you should then cover.

You can strain the soup, not through a drum sieve *(tamis)*, but through a strainer with large holes, to standardize the size of the vegetables. You could also simply squash directly in the pot with the back of a large wooden spoon and mix them well with the purée provided by the peas. Taste the soup and adjust salt as necessary. Pepper here is almost essential, but you could leave your guests the task of adding it themselves. Pour the soup into the tureen on top of the pieces of meat. Add the slices of toasted bread or serve separately to keep them crisp. *Serve the soup boiling hot.* To keep it hot, you could pass the tureen around the table so that your guests can serve themselves, and be sure to give them plates that have been well warmed.

Bread Soup *(Soupe à la Panade)*

Generally speaking, you love it or you hate it. This soup would perhaps attract less extreme reactions if its blandness were relieved by adding more interesting ingredients, such as sorrel, celery, or leek white, depending on the season. You could also replace the water with some thoroughly degreased bouillon, preferably veal bouillon, which would be more in keeping with the austere nature of this dish. Or, for a meat-free version, make it with half water, half milk. *Time: 1 hour.*

At any rate, bread soup must always be thickened with egg yolk and a final addition of a little fresh butter, sometimes replaced by crème fraîche.

The bread used must always be stale. It doesn't matter if it's an ordinary loaf of bread or a special bread, but insofar as is possible, use only the crust and especially the top crust of the bread, lighter and better cooked than that of the bottom crust. If the crust has some burned parts or parts that are simply too dark, do not include them. Break the crust into little pieces. If it is not quite dry, spread it out on a baking tray and put it in a moderate oven for a little while, or even with the oven door open for a few instants. Put the crusts in a deep, thick-bottomed pot. Pour lukewarm water on top; cover and warm over very low heat to give the bread time to be perfectly soaked before any cooking; this should take about 10 minutes.

Next, bring it to a boil, stirring constantly with a wooden spoon. Cover again, and do not go beyond a very gentle, very regular simmer for *a good 30 minutes.* For this cooking, it's best to imitate, as closely as possible, the conditions of an old-fashioned country stove, where the bread soup simmers gently over warm cinders. The disadvantage of direct contact with heat, no matter how gentle—as with gas, for example—is that the bread may stick to the bottom of the pot. For this reason, avoid stirring the bread as it cooks, which would cause the bread to attach to the bottom.

Only when the cooking is complete should you energetically stir the bread with a wooden spoon, being sure to crush any remaining little bits. You must thus obtain a cream, as smooth as possible. For babies, or the infirm, this can be strained through a medium-mesh drum sieve, rubbing it with the wooden pestle over the soup dish or tureen in which the soup is to be served. In this case, the egg yolk liaison is preliminarily done in the pot. Then there's nothing left to add but the final butter.

Bread soup with sorrel or the white part of a leek, etc.: Cut the sorrel in a large julienne, or finely mince the white part of the leek. Thus, for 6 people, 100 grams (3 1/2 ounces) of sorrel or 75 grams (2 2/3 ounces) of leek. In the pot where you will cook the bread soup, braise them with 30 grams (1 ounce, 2 tablespoons) of butter over low heat for about 10 minutes, without letting the leek color if you are using it. Then add the water and the bread, and proceed as above for the rest of the cooking.

Given the circumstances in which bread soup is often prepared, we will give the quantities of bread soup for one good serving, and you can increase it according to your needs: 40 grams (1 3/8 ounces) of stale bread; 3–4 deciliters (1 1/4–1 2/3 cups) of warm water; 1 small egg yolk, quite fresh; 10 grams (1/3 ounce) of good butter; a grain of salt.

Garbure Soup in the Peasant Style *(Soupe Garbure à la Paysanne)*

A *garbure,* whatever its composition, is always classed as a soup rather than a potage.

Actually, it is a quintessentially rustic preparation in which the ingredients vary according to the region. But the distinguishing features are the croutons, covered with cheese and browned (or gratinéed). Either the croutons are placed on top of the vegetables and bacon in the bowls and the bouillon is served separately from the tureen, or, the croutons are garnished with a purée of vegetables and served separately on a plate; or it could be that the croutons are browned right on top of the whole soup. At any rate, in the Southern French provinces, the croutons are not always browned. There, garbure is made with cabbage, or other vegetables, and arranged in the tureen with alternating layers of vegetables and thin slices of bread, without the bread being necessarily on the surface to form the final gratin.

The recipe we have given is a simple peasant garbure. The amount and choice of vegetables are not carved in stone; you can use even more than suggested here as a base, using vegetables in season—in other words, green peas, green beans, beans, string beans, etc. Preferably, the liquid used should be good bouillon or cooking water from beans or potatoes. Or, if you have neither, use warm water. In that case, add 7–8 grams (1/4 ounce) of salt to cook the vegetables, and about the same again when you begin cooking the soup. Note also that, if you are not using bouillon, the quantity of butter suggested to finish the soup must be doubled.

For serving the garbure, we will give two ways to proceed. The second, more characteristic and original—and simpler—also involves a gratinée of croutons on the surface of the soup. It requires a shallow tureen, such as a vegetable bowl or a soufflé dish, something that can withstand the strong heat of the oven. It should be in silver or some metal, or it could be in ceramic. *Time: Barely 2 hours. Serves 6.*

1 large carrot and 1 large turnip; the white of 3 good-sized leeks; 1/4 of a small, firm cabbage; 2 branches celery; 80 grams (2 3/4 ounces, 5 1/2 tablespoons) of butter to braise the vegetables; 1 glass (2 deciliters, 6 3/4 fluid ounces, 7/8 cup) of cooked white beans; 2 medium-sized potatoes; and, in season, 2–3 tablespoons of green peas and other vegetables as mentioned above.

1 3/4 liters (7 cups) of liquid: bouillon, or vegetable cooking water; 20 grams (2/3 ounce, 1 heaping tablespoon) of butter to finish the soup; a good pinch of chervil leaves. A large, thin baguette, or, failing that, a chunk of stale bread, for the croutons; 20 grams (2/3 ounce, 1 heaping tablespoon) of butter to fry them in; 40–50 grams (1 3/8–1 3/4 ounces) of grated Gruyère cheese.

PROCEDURE. Finely mince the cabbage, the carrot, the turnip, the celery, and the leek. The shape in which these vegetables are cut is not important because they must be made into a purée; but they should be cut in a consistent size to be able to cook evenly.

Braise them in a pot with the butter, a pinch of salt, and a pinch of sugar, as for *potage julienne.*

Allow *25–30 minutes* for this braising. Add only 3/4 liter (generous 3 cups) of the chosen liquid. Bring it to a boil. Then add the rest of the vegetables: in other words, the potatoes, cut into thin quarters; or the white beans that have *already been cooked;* the green peas; and any other vegetables that you have. Cover; cook gently for about *45 minutes.*

The croutons: Cut the bread into 1-centimeter (3/8-inch) slices, whether it's on a thin baguette or a piece of stale bread. In the latter case, the slices should be cut into small 5-centimeter (2-inch) squares. Sauté them lightly in the butter on both sides. Set aside.

As soon as the vegetables are cooked to the point where they can be easily puréed, remove one-third of them with the skimmer. Drain them well and purée. Put this purée into a pot set over high heat and cook, stirring constantly, until all the moisture is evaporated and it has the consistency of a thick potato purée. Used as is, directly after puréeing, it would be too thin to spread on the croutons. On each crouton, place a tablespoon of this purée. Smooth it out with the blade of a knife, mounding it in the middle; it should be just under 1 centimeter (3/8 inch) thick. One by one, arrange the croutons on a baking sheet. Sprinkle a little pinch of cheese on each one.

To brown the croutons, allow *10–12 minutes* in an oven of medium heat. They can be placed in the oven as soon as they are garnished, and you can finish the soup while they are being browned. Please note that the heat of the oven must come from the top to melt the cheese and to form the gratinéed layer; the underside of the croutons must neither brown nor dry out. If you have a broiler, it is preferable to the oven for these reasons.

Cooking the soup: Quickly strain the rest of the vegetables into a purée. Return to the heat and stir until it begins to boil. Remove from the heat and add 20 grams (2/3 ounce) of butter. (If using a liquid other than bouillon, do not forget to double the quantity of butter.) Check the salt. If you have used water as the liquid, this is the time to add 7–8 grams (1/4 ounce) of good salt. Pour the potage into the tureen. Add the chervil leaves. Serve the browned croutons on the side.

Another way of serving garbure: Here, the bread—either rounds from a thin baguette or simple slices—is cut much thinner, not even 1/2 centimeter (3/16 inch) thick. These croutons should not previously be fried in butter. But, to sprinkle them with cheese, you must anticipate twice the quantity suggested above.

Braise and cook the vegetables exactly as described above. Purée everything. With the remaining liquid, dilute this purée. Bring it to a boil. Remove from the heat, add the chervil leaves, and pour it into the tureen. Cover the entire surface of the potage with the rounds of baguette or the slices of bread. Sprinkle these with cheese. Dot the bits of butter—each about the size of a pea and about 12 in total—over the surface. Set the tureen in a shallow bowl in which you put a little bit of water. Put everything into a good, warm oven, and as close as possible to the top of the oven, so that the surface with the cheese on it takes the full force of the heat. If the oven is quite warm, the gratin should form within 6–7 minutes.

To divide the gratin between guests more easily, use the tip of an ordinary spoon when serving, preferably one of those large serving spoons, which you can use to separate the gratinéed layer. This division will be difficult using a soup ladle.

Rustic Vegetable, Bean, and Sausage Soup *(Soupe de la Mère Onésime)*

This is an incredibly lavish dish, the sort of thing that is served in the countryside for a hunter's breakfast. Extremely good reheated, it can be prepared in a quantity much larger than necessary for one meal. In sum, it's virtually identical to a rustic soup, potage paysanne, but good oil replaces the butter and you add a simple sausage to the dish.

These kinds of soups can be greatly improved, as we have previously said for pot-au-feu, by the addition of bones from roasts, carcasses of fowl, and other meat leftovers, but while the pot-au-feu has a rather limited choice of elements that can be added, this recipe gives the cook complete freedom to use mutton, pork, duck, goose, pheasant, etc., on condition that anything used is absolutely fresh.

It is important to pay attention to the bones and the carcasses and to remove any bone splinters that might be mixed up with the vegetables.

Here is how to proceed: a good 45 minutes before serving, strain the carrots, the turnips, and the leeks through a medium-sized sieve to eliminate any bone fragments. Return the purée and the cooking liquid to the rinsed pot. Bring it back to a boil and add the beans, peas, and sausage. Cook as directed. Also, you can use the cooking water from some vegetables, as directed for *potage julienne* (PAGE 87) and *potage paysanne* (PAGE 92). The bouillon produced by cooking a beef tongue or cooking veal, which has a flavor that is too mediocre to be served alone, will come into its own in a dish like this.

Bones from a leg of lamb, ham, or ham hocks are also excellent. Use them on the understanding that, as for pot-au-feu, uncooked bones must first be sautéed until browned before being added to the vegetables for the potage.

The quantities suggested for the vegetables are not fixed. They can be modified according to convenience and availability, using more of this or less of that.

Note that these kinds of soups are not skimmed. Therefore, in country-style cooking, which uses good fat or excellent butter, it is essential to be sure that the grease has not been heated too much when braising the vegetables. *Time: 2½ hours. Serves 6–8.*

100 grams (3½ ounces) of carrot and the same of turnip, net weight; 50 grams (1¾ ounces) of the white part of a leek; 60 grams (2¼ ounces) of cabbage; 1 deciliter (scant ½ cup) of fresh white beans; the same of fresh peas and the same of green beans, cut into pieces; 1½ liters (6⅓ cups) of liquid; a small, simple home-style sausage, *uncooked;* a good tablespoon of pork fat; a bouquet garni; a small cube of sugar; 10 grams (⅓ ounce) of salt, if using only water.

PROCEDURE. Cut the carrot, turnip, leek, cabbage, as for *potage paysanne* (PAGE 92). Gently braise them in the fat in a heavy-bottomed aluminum or cast-iron pot with a lid.

Add half of the liquid. It is at this point that you should put in the bones, leftovers, carcasses, etc. Bring it to a boil over high heat. Skim if necessary; add the bouquet garni; the salt, if the liquid is water; the sugar. Cover, lower the heat, and simmer gently for *45 minutes.*

Then pour in the rest of the liquid; bring it to a boil; add the beans, peas, green beans, and the sausage. After returning to a boil, give it a further *45 minutes* cooking time.

To serve, remove the bouquet garni, the bones, and the carcasses, if you have used them. You can degrease it if you like. In this case, the choice is yours. Taste it to check the salt. Cut the sausage into slices, which you then put into the tureen, after having divided them into 2 or in 4, according to the dimensions of the sausage. Or you can serve them separately on a plate. Add a pinch of freshly ground pepper to the tureen: country folk always put some into their soup, to very good effect.

Rustic Soup *(Soupe Rustique)*

All we have said about *la soupe de la mère Onésime* is applicable here regarding the use of vegetable cooking water of any kind and the addition of bones and leftovers. The base of the soup, carrots, and turnips is the same; onion replaces the leek here. And potatoes are added instead of fresh vegetables. *Time: 2 hours. Serves 6.*

100 grams (3½ ounces) of carrot and the same of turnip, net weight; 40 grams (1⅜ ounces) of onion; 60 grams (2¼ ounces) of cabbage; 75 grams (2⅔ ounces) of good pork fat or even butter; 150 grams (5⅓ ounces) of potatoes, weighed after they have been peeled; 1½ liters (6⅓ cups) of water; 10 grams (⅓ ounce) of salt; bouquet garni; a pinch of pepper.

PROCEDURE. Cut the vegetables and braise them in fat or butter, as for *la soupe de la mère Onésime.* Add half of the chosen liquid. Bring it to a boil. Add the bouquet garni, and salt if using only water. Cover. Lower the heat and simmer gently for *1½ hours.*

About 45 minutes before serving, add the rest of the liquid and the potatoes, simply peeled but left whole. To serve, first use a spoon to transfer the potatoes to a colander with good-sized holes, placed over the tureen. Mash them with a wooden pestle or the back of a large wooden spoon, wetting them with a little bit of liquid to help push them through. Then pour several tablespoons of broth only into the tureen, to dissolve the potatoes into a paste with the help of a wooden spoon. Then pour in the rest of the soup and serve it quite warm.

Celeriac Soup with Gruyère *(Soupe à la Savoyarde)*

The ingredients of this soup can vary, as can their quantities, and none require any absolute precision. Above all, pay attention to the preliminary use of butter when braising the celeriac, the leek, and the onion; this is not always done in the home kitchen, and it is a pity. One can equally use bacon grease or another good fat in the place of butter. When you have rye bread, it is preferable to the rustic whole wheat bread suggested here. *Time: 45 minutes. Serves 6.*

200 grams (7 ounces) of celeriac, weighed after trimming; the same weight in total of the white part of leek, onion, potato; 50 grams (1 3/4 ounces, 3 1/2 tablespoons) of butter or of good fat; 10 grams (1/3 ounce) of salt and a pinch of sugar; 3/4 liter (generous 3 cups) of lukewarm water; 1/2 liter (generous 2 cups) of boiled milk; a dozen small slices of whole-wheat bread, cut to a length of about 5–6 centimeters (2–2 1/2 inches), with a thickness of 1/2 centimeter (3/16 inch); 25 grams (1 ounce) of butter to spread over them; 75 grams (2 2/3 ounces) of freshly grated Gruyère.

PROCEDURE. Peel the celeriac and cut it into slices as fine as possible—as if it were paper—and of an equal thickness. Cut the potato in the same way. Also, very thinly slice the leek and the onion. Put them all together in a deep pot with 50 grams (1 3/4 ounces, 3 1/2 tablespoons) of butter or oil, salt, and sugar. Braise them over very low heat—in other words, gently cook them in the fat, either butter or grease, *without allowing them to color in the slightest.* Stir frequently with a wooden spoon. Allow *20–25 minutes* of braising, at the end of which the vegetables must be tender, without any browning. Then add the warm water. Bring it to a boil, cover, and simmer; after 10 minutes, add the milk and continue cooking gently.

The croutons: Spread the slices of bread with the butter, *on both sides.* Arrange them on a baking sheet as they are buttered and dry them thoroughly in the oven. This can be done in advance, but the dried croutons should be sprinkled with cheese *only 5 minutes before serving.* Then, drizzle them with a few drops of melted butter and put them into a warm oven, toward the top, where it's hottest, so that the cheese melts rapidly and takes on a golden color. Or, put them under the broiler.

Pour the soup into the tureen and check its seasoning. Put the gratinéed croutons on top and serve immediately.

Celeriac Soup, Served Like a Garbure *(Soupe à la Savoyarde, Façon Garbure).* All garbures are characterized by having the consistency of puréed vegetables, so here it is essential to reduce the amount of liquid or to add a little more celeriac and potato.

The vegetables are cooked as indicated, then forced through a wide-mesh sieve with their cooking liquid to obtain a coarse purée. Put everything into a pot, then bring it to a boil, and lower the heat. *About 7–8 minutes* before serving, pour this purée into a shallow ceramic tureen. Arrange the dried croutons on top of the purée, dunking them under just a little bit. Sprinkle with the cheese and drizzle them with a little melted butter. Set the tureen in a bowl filled with a little bit of water. Put into a warm oven so that the cheese melts rapidly and turns golden. Serve quite hot.

Onion Soup *(Soupe à l'Oignon)*

Certainly the simplest of homemade soups, the preparation of which can apparently be summarized in a few lines. Everyone is supposed to know how to make onion soup.

There are quite a few people who appreciate onion soup. Some have certain qualifications, and others make demands about what must be added. First of all, there are those who want only to taste the onion but do not want to find any pieces of it in their bowl: to satisfy them, simply strain the soup through a chinois or a fine-mesh sieve and pour it into the tureen. There are those who find the quantity of onion that is generally included—25–30 grams (1 ounce) per person—insufficient; increase the amount according to taste. Another group considers it onion soup only when it has cheese. Among this group, you can find those who would like it to have a gratinée on top. We indicate here the basic methods of serving onion soup, noting that the only thing that is invariable is the preparation of the onion itself. *Time: 45 minutes. Serves 6.*

2 large onions (about 200 grams, 7 ounces); 70 grams (2 1/2 ounces, 1/3 cup) of butter; 20 grams (2/3 ounce) of flour; 1 liter (4 1/4 cups) of warm water and 1/4 liter (1 cup) of boiled milk; 15 grams (1/2 ounce) of salt; a little pepper; a dozen rounds of thin baguette.

NOTES. The liquid used for this soup can be simply water. Do not add milk unless the preferences of the guests on this point are known. If you have bouillon, this would be a good replacement for the water: it is the liquid almost always used in good restaurants. In that case, it is, of course, unnecessary to add salt.

When the soup must be made with cheese, it is a good idea to check the amount of salt in the cheese: you can therefore decide if the quantity of salt prescribed has to be maintained or diminished a little bit. When bouillon is used, you can dilute it with some water if the cheese seems to be a little too salty.

PROCEDURE. **Cutting the onions:** Cut the onions in half once they have been peeled, removing the tough part of the root, unless the onion is quite young. Cut it into equal slices as thin as a sheet of paper. Two conditions of extreme importance: onions cut too thick are unpleasant to find in the soup and coloring them will take that much longer in the butter; and if the slices are of different thickness, the thin parts will brown and burn before the thicker parts are even colored.

Under no circumstances should you cut the onion while holding it up in the air between your fingers. To cut your slices, put each half of the onion with its cut side flat on the table or the board so it is secure. Then, with a very good knife, a little on the large side, you cut the slices. The way the onions are cut, in fine and equal slices, is so important. This is why we recommend using *large onions,* which are much easier to cut the proper way.

To color the onions: For this, it is absolutely essential to understand and establish that the onion, butter, and flour should never go beyond a light blond tint. In this respect, too many people believe that onion soup, particularly when made with water, contains well-browned onions to give it color. Treated thus, an onion becomes a burnt onion, and the soup takes on an unbearable bitterness. The butter, which has been overheated, also tastes burnt.

In a *good, heavy-bottomed* pot, with a capacity of about 2 1/4 liters (9 cups), heat the butter over moderate heat *without allowing it to brown.* Add the onion, and from that point on, stir with a wooden spoon, almost without interruption, until the onion turns a blond color and is uniformly golden. If you are in a hurry, you can sauté the onion over high heat, but then *do not leave it for a second* because there is the possibility that some parts will burn while others barely color.

When the onion is golden, add the flour. Mix it well, *stirring constantly* with a wooden spoon. Cook it *over very low heat,* until it turns slightly blond. Just like the onion, it must not become too brown.

Adding the liquid and cooking: Now add the water and the salt (or the bouillon). Put the pot over the heat and stir with a wooden spoon until it's boiling rapidly. Then let it boil slowly for *8–10 minutes.*

During this time, cut the 2 millimeter (1/16 inch)–thick rounds from the baguette; put them in the tureen. Sprinkle a pinch of pepper over them.

To serve: Add the boiling milk. Taste for seasoning. Pour the soup on the bread in the tureen; If you do not want to keep the onion in the soup, strain it through a *tamis,* as suggested on page 120.

Onion Soup with Cheese *(Soupe à l'Oignon au Fromage).* To obtain the stringiness that pleases the lovers of this soup so much, you must have good Gruyère cheese, fresh and with a high fat content. Grate it, or cut it in little pieces as thin as a sheet of paper. If it is too thick, it will not melt well and will require much more time. Arrange one-third of the baguette rounds in the bottom of the tureen. Cover them with one-third of the cheese, about 1 good tablespoon, and add a little pepper. Make a second layer of rounds and cheese without omitting the pepper; then a third, final layer. *In all, 3 good tablespoons of cheese.*

Pour the onion bouillon into the tureen (either straining it or not). Cover with a tight-fitting lid. Leave it in a low oven for a few minutes. Serve.

Onion Soup with Gratinéed Croutons *(Soupe à l'Oignon Gratinée).* An ordinary tureen will not allow you to obtain a good gratinéed topping. You must use something shallow, like a vegetable dish, which is much wider than it is tall, so that the heat of the oven can get to the soup more easily, and the gratin will be formed better and faster. Whenever possible, this tureen should be made of metal or be sufficiently resistant to the heat of the oven.

A few minutes before serving, pour the bouillon into the tureen, straining it or not. Arrange the rounds of baguette on top. Sprinkle them with 3 good tablespoons of freshly grated Gruyère, which you have mixed with a pinch of pepper. Drizzle the cheese with a tablespoon of melted butter.

Put the *uncovered* tureen in the oven in such a way that the surface sprinkled with cheese takes the full force of the oven's heat. Alternatively, put it under the broiler if you have room for it and if the tureen can withstand the kind of heat that comes from the broiler. Carefully watch the gratin without leaving your observation post, and serve it as soon as it is ready.

Another way of serving with gratinéed croutons: Choose a slightly larger baguette so that you can get rounds 3½ centimeters (1⅜ inches) in diameter, which you will slice to a thickness of 1 centimeter (⅜ inch). Allow 2 rounds per person. Strain the soup through a chinois, either into another pot or into the tureen. In this latter case, cover the tureen and keep it warm. Drain the strained onion and put it on a small plate. Put a little bit of the onion onto each bread round. Sprinkle it copiously with grated Gruyère that has been lightly peppered.

Arrange the rounds on the lid of a pot that has been turned upside down, or on a tart pan or baking sheet. Put a bit of butter on the cheese of each round, or use a few drops of melted butter that you have prepared. Gratinée them under very high heat. Put the croutons into the tureen and serve immediately. Or: when the onion is well drained, strain it through a sieve or a chinois, crushing it with a wooden spoon. Collect the purée in a bowl. Then spread each round with a generous portion of this purée. Sprinkle each with cheese. Gratinée as above.

VARIOUS GARNISHES FOR POTAGES
Diverses Garnitures pour Potages

Cooking Pasta and Tapioca for Potages. It is always better to cook them separately in the correct amount of liquid required. Their cooking—in effect, a kind of poaching—will thus be more consistent.

Pasta, vermicelli, pearl barley, etc.: For 50 grams (1¾ ounces) of any one of these, 3 deciliters (1¼ cups) of bouillon in a small pot, taken from the quantity of liquid required for the potage. When the bouillon boils, throw in the pasta; cover; lower the heat and maintain a slow simmer for about 20 minutes. Mix it with the potage in the tureen.

Tapioca: The quantity of liquid for the amount of tapioca has to be greater than for pasta. Allow, for 30–40 grams (1–1⅜ ounces) of tapioca, 4–5 deciliters (1⅔–generous 2 cups) of liquid. When the liquid is at a full boil, gradually pour in the tapioca, from a moderate height, so that it falls in a light shower and scatters well: otherwise, it will stick together in balls. When pouring the tapioca, stir constantly with a wooden spoon. When all the tapioca is in the liquid and the boiling has resumed, cover the pot and simmer very gently, at a *barely perceptible* boil for 20 minutes.

Royale* for Garnishing Potages *(Royale pour Garniture de Potages). In haute cuisine, the name "royale" implies a preparation very similar to a crème caramel, which is cut into small tubes or diamond shapes and used as a garnish for clear soups and consommés, among others.

The ordinary *royale,* which we give here, is the point of departure for a series of *royales* made with many different ingredients: purées of game, fowl, fish, vegetables, which are all solidified combined with egg and poached in a mold, using a bain-marie (double boiler).

A *royale* can be prepared well in advance, even in the morning. This, in fact, is the best way to ensure that it is completely chilled, which is absolutely necessary. You can also, in advance, cut it into small pieces, which are reheated the moment they are put into the potage. *Serves about 15.*

4 deciliters (1²/₃ cups) of perfectly degreased bouillon; 2 medium-size eggs and 6 egg yolks; 2 good pinches of chervil.

PROCEDURE. Boil the bouillon in a small pan. Add the chervil. Cover. Let it infuse over very low heat for about 15 minutes. Beat the eggs and the yolks in a bowl. Dilute them *gradually* with the warm bouillon. Strain this through a fine sieve into a small mold that has been buttered. With a metal spoon, remove the surface foam. Poach exactly as directed (SEE CARAMEL CUSTARD, PAGE 582). Allow 35–40 minutes for poaching. Check the total firmness by touching with your finger before removing the mold from the water. Let the royale *chill completely* before unmolding.

Invert the mold onto a clean kitchen towel. With a large-bladed knife, gently smooth the surface. Then cut the *royale* into 1-centimeter (3/8-inch)-thick slices, either horizontally or vertically. Then divide these slices into little cubes or little squares about 1 1/2 centimeters (5/8 inch) big, or in little diamond shapes, being certain to cut them accurately. As you cut them, put these cubes of *royale* into a small saucepan. Pour a little bouillon over them to keep them from drying out. About 5 minutes before adding them to the soup, heat them gently in the saucepan, but absolutely without boiling.

Potato Balls for Garnishing Potages *(Boules de Pommes de Terre pour Garnitures de Potages).* Formerly called Dutch potatoes in France, these should be cut out of large, peeled potatoes, using a tool for cutting vegetable balls. Put them into a small saucepan and cover completely with cool salted water. Bring them to a boil over high heat; watch them carefully so that you do not go beyond the point at which they are cooked, so that the balls hold their shape. Just before the cooking is complete, tip the water out of the saucepan, keeping the potato balls in by holding them back with the lid. Keep the potato balls in the covered saucepan in a warm place. They will dry out a little and become perfectly cooked.

Rice for Garnishing Potages *(Riz pour Garniture de Potages).* For this use, the rice must remain in beautiful, perfectly whole grains that are still tender: good-quality long-grain Carolina rice is the best kind to use here. For a garnish of rice only, the proportions are 1 deciliter (scant 1/2 cup) of rice, measured uncooked, for 2 liters (8 1/2 cups) of potage. To cook it, which is done separately in bouillon, allow at least three times its volume of liquid: thus, for 1 deciliter of rice (scant 1/2 cup), 3 good deciliters (1 1/4 cups) of degreased bouillon.

Before being cooked, the rice must either be blanched or washed in several changes of water, as has been indicated (SEE RICE, PAGE 561). Both procedures have the same goal, which is to get rid of the starch. Drain the rice well. Put it in a small pan with the bouillon. Bring it to a boil. Cover. Keep it at a very gentle simmer for 25 minutes without touching it during this time; at the end, the rice will have absorbed almost all of the liquid. Mix it with the soup in the tureen.

COLD AND WARM HORS D'OEUVRES

Cold hors d'oeuvres are generally not appreciated unless they are greatly varied and are presented in a way that is agreeable both to the eye and to the taste buds. They invite great creativity; with a little imagination and ingenuity, one can infinitely multiply the association of eggs, fish, crustaceans, meats, and vegetables, cooked or raw, and find unexpected uses for leftovers.

Simple and rapidly prepared hors d'oeuvres will fill out a family menu that's a little short. More refined hors d'oeuvres, longer to make and more costly as well, have the benefit of being able to be prepared in advance and make an excellent start to an elegant meal.

As for warm hors d'oeuvres, these must be light and small in size; this is why a cheese soufflé is not placed in the category of hors d'oeuvre, while little soufflés in molds are considered to be warm hors d'oeuvres. The same distinction can be applied to large and small cheese pastries, the small cheese pastry simply being a smaller version of the larger ones.

Generally, these are served at dinner, after the potage. However, warm hors d'oeuvres can be a part of a luncheon menu, particularly in winter, when cold food is less desirable.

With the current tendency to simplify menus, warm hors d'oeuvres, which were previously called *entrée volante,* often replace the classic fish or fowl entrée. In fact, it is becoming difficult to establish a precise distinction between hot hors d'oeuvres and entrées.

COLD HORS D'OEUVRES
Hors d'Oeuvres Froids

The Butter *(Le Beurre).* A good solid butter of the finest quality must be on the table at the same time as the hors d'oeuvres. For easy service, it is best to divide the butter among several small special plates—either in scallop shells, or in bowls, or in little decorative dishes, depending on the utensils at your disposal—or to simply put it out in individual ceramic molds.

Mayonnaise *(Le Sauce Mayonnaise).* Mayonnaise is frequently used when making cold hors d'oeuvres, either blended with the ingredients, as a coating, or surrounding them, as a decorative fringe. In the latter case, the mayonnaise must be made firm enough so as not to spread out on the plate (SEE MAYONNAISE SAUCE, PAGE 76).

Generally speaking, seasoning is open to the imagination: lemon, wine vinegar, tarragon vinegar, salt, pepper, sometimes spicy mustard, and depending on what the mayonnaise is accompanying, you can vary the appearance and the taste by adding, just before serving, some tomato concentrate, curry powder, anchovy purée, paprika, and crème chantilly, if seasoned with lemon.

Eggs *(Oeufs)*

Hard-boiled eggs, stuffed or not, poached, or soft boiled, lend themselves to multiple combinations.

Hard-Boiled Eggs: Deviled Eggs *(Oeufs Durs: Oeufs Farcis à la Russe).* SEE EGGS, PAGE 134. Using this recipe as a blueprint, you can vary the stuffing, replacing the fish with mixed cooked vegetables, or with cooked, cubed artichoke hearts, asparagus tips, etc. You can also: (a) cut the hard-boiled eggs in half, lengthwise, and replace the yolks with a mixture of the yolks that have been forced through a drum sieve *(tamis),* combined with a bit of butter and some puréed anchovies, and seasoned with a pinch of pepper. Spoon over some anchovy mayonnaise and garnish with anchovy fillets; (b) Crush the yolks in a bowl until smooth. Mix them with some grated Gruyère and season with a point of cayenne pepper (as much as can be held on the tip of a small knife) and add some thick crème fraîche.

Beat the mixture to give it some lightness. Fill the halves of the whites without pressing down on them. Form a dome and garnish as you like, with capers, little rounds of cornichon, or fresh tarragon leaves. Adding minced ham to the stuffing offers more variety and gives you a chance to use up a little bit of leftovers. Pipe a thin ribbon of mayonnaise all around.

Hard-boiled eggs, cut in crosswise slices, can simply be arranged on a platter and topped with mayonnaise then sprinkled with capers and olives from which you have removed the pits. This display can be enhanced by alternating the slices of egg with slices of tomato without water or seeds, or rounds of cucumber that you have previously purged of excess liquid. Pipe a ribbon of mayonnaise all around (SEE MAYONNAISE SAUCE, PAGE 76).

Soft-Boiled Eggs. These are served whole, of course, and should be rather small and very fresh. As a way of stabilizing them, as well as enhancing their appearance, you should serve them placed in artichoke bottoms that have been previously boiled and cooled; or on a bed of lettuce leaves with tiny slices of ham; or on top of a mixed vegetable salad; or over rice pilau served cold. Any of these can be garnished with thin slices of tomato, alternating with a julienne of green peppers, coated as you prefer with either mayonnaise, tartare, or remoulade sauce.

You can also put each one atop a hollowed-out half tomato that has been filled with a mixture of finely chopped tongue, ham, boiled potatoes, small, tender branches of celery, and mayonnaise. Pipe a ribbon of mayonnaise flavored with tomato concentrate all around.

Poached Eggs in Aspic *(Oeufs Pochès en Gelée)*: SEE PAGE 157.

Individual Egg Molds *(Petites Timbales d'Oeufs Froides)*: SEE EGGS, PAGE 134.

Fish, Crustaceans, Shellfish, Mollusks, Etc. *(Les Poissons, Les Crustacés, Les Coquillages, Les Mollusques, Etc.)*

Fish *(Poissons)*. In the shops, there is a good selection of fish products ready to be served as hors d'oeuvres. First, sardines or tuna in oil, which can be greatly improved with a sprinkling of vinegar and capers; many kinds of herring: salted, smoked, rollmops; marinated mackerel; smoked eel filets; caviar, which should be presented in its original container, always surrounded by crushed ice and accompanied by small, thin pieces of buttered rye toast; smoked salmon, cut into thin slices garnished with parsley or rolled to form cones, accompanied by small slices of toasted, buttered dark bread.

In addition, a fish salad can provide a very presentable hors d'oeuvre on the family table. The fish should first have its bones carefully removed, and then, according to type, be sliced thinly or cut into pieces, bound with some mayonnaise, and served in little scallop shells, covered by more mayonnaise and garnished with a few crayfish tails, anchovy fillets, or simply with rounds of hard-boiled egg. If you do not have scallop shell dishes, you can place the fish on some lettuce leaves that have been thoroughly dried and arranged on a serving dish.

Other preparations of fish for hors d'oeuvres:

Herring Salad *(Salade de Harengs)*: SEE PAGE 467.

Salted Herrings with a Piquant Sauce *(Harengs Lucas)*: SEE PAGE 188.

Salmon Trout in Aspic *(Truite Saumonée en Gelée)*: SEE PAGE 226.

Cucumbers Stuffed with Tuna *(Concombres Faris au Thon)*: SEE PAGE 506.

Crustaceans *(Crustacés)*. For crustacean lovers, we should mention: cockles, which are served the same way as oysters, and sea urchins, in the shell—the top is cut off with scissors, their water drained, and they are served garnished with parsley and lemon wedges.

Oysters *(Huîtres)*: These can be consumed from October to March; choose them absolutely fresh, whatever their variety. They should be opened only a few moments before being served. To open them: pick up the oyster and hold the concave part in the palm of the left hand, which should be protected by a thick towel, or better, by the corner of a thick cloth. Slip a strong knife with a wide and short blade between the two shells, right next to the hinge. Keeping the oyster flat, with a lateral movement of the knife, cut the ligament that keeps the shell closed, and then, with a sharp blow, spring open the hinge. During this time, be very careful to keep the oyster horizontal so that you do not lose any of its liquor. Carefully clean the edge of the shell so that there is no sand or shell fragments. Serve on a mound of shaved ice. Make sure that you have enough lemon for all of the guests, a pepper mill close at hand, and some thin slices of buttered rye bread. Some oyster-lovers like a sauce made of finely minced shallots, pepper, and good-quality wine vinegar.

Crayfish *(Crevettes):* Gray crayfish for a family meal, pink crayfish for a special hors d'oeuvre, arranged in a heap and served with parsley in the center.

Canapés of Crayfish, Langoustine, Lobster, etc. *(Canapès de Crevettes, Langoustines, Langouste, etc.):* Crayfish tails, or langoustine, can, as well as being made into a salad, be served on canapés, which enhances the quality of the selection and varies the presentation.

The canapé, in this case, is a slice of white bread cut about 1/2 centimeter (3/16 inch) thick, the crust removed and cut as a round disc or as a square or rectangle, lightly toasted and buttered while warm so that it remains moist. You can, if you like, add to the butter a point of curry powder (as much as can be held on the tip of a knife) or a soupçon of cayenne pepper, or even a teaspoon of mustard. Keep the best tails whole. Finely chop the others and mix them with butter that has been softened to a pomade (SEE PAGE 16), using just enough to hold the minced tails together. Season with a pinch of pepper if there is none in the butter you have used. Spread a layer of butter on the bread and top with the reserved tails, 3–4 if they are crayfish; 1 if it's langostine; or a nice round of lobster tail, from which you have used the meat from the claws and other parts. Keep cool until ready to serve.

Crabs *(Crabes):* SEE PAGE 227.

Langoustines: SEE PAGE 238.

Spiny lobster *(Langouste):* SEE PAGE 235. For hors d'oeuvres, choose the smaller lobsters.

Aspic of Spiny Lobster *(Aspic de Langouste):* SEE PAGE 238. This should be served molded in small individual timbales.

Crayfish Presented in a Decorative Heap *(Écrevisses en Buisson):* SEE PAGE 230.

Cold Mussels with Vinaigrette *(Moules Froides, Sauce Vinaigrette):*

1 liter (4 1/4 cups) of small mussels; 3 tablespoons of water to open them.

For the vinaigrette: 2 tablespoons of good wine vinegar; 5 tablespoons of oil; 1 teaspoon of mustard; salt; pepper; 1 level tablespoon of finely minced onion; 1 level tablespoon of minced parsley; 1 hard-boiled egg, minced.

PROCEDURE. Clean the mussels, then open (SEE PAGE 241) over high heat. Take them from their shells and put them in a strainer to cool and drain completely.

In a bowl, combine the elements of the sauce as if you were making a salad dressing; dilute the salt, pepper, and mustard with vinegar and oil and mix well, then add the raw minced onion, and the parsley and the hard-boiled egg, also minced. When the mussels are cool, add them to the sauce and mix carefully so that you do not damage them. They must be well covered with the vinaigrette without an excess of sauce. Serve in a small dish or bowl.

Charcuterie and Meats *(Charcuterie et Viandes)*

Good charcuterie shops offer a large array of products that provide the variety always desirable for hors d'oeuvres. Different kinds of hams: boiled, cured, baked, raw smoked ham; pickled tongue; sausages and mortadella, cervelas sausage, which must be cooked for 15 minutes in barely simmering water, then chilled, and finally cut into thin slices and served with a salad dressing and fines herbes; galantines; terrines: of hare, rabbit, pheasant; various patés; goose and duck rillettes; head cheese; and various sausages.

As a general rule, charcuterie should be served in thin slices, surrounded, if possible, by chopped aspic; accompanied with a variety of condiments: cornichons, onions, either pickled or *à la grecque*, green or black olives, stuffed or not, mushrooms preserved in vinegar; and also by salads and vegetables, raw or cooked.

For a home-style preparation: leftovers from a pot-au-feu can be very easily arranged in a salad if the meat does not have too much fat in it, as it would if it were a piece of rib steak. Cut it into small slices and arrange it on a plate with slices of beet, then sprinkle it with a salad dressing that has been enhanced with mustard, well in advance, so that it can be thoroughly absorbed, and, if you like, add some raw minced onion. When ready to serve, garnish with rounds of hard-boiled egg and some minced herbs (parsley, chives, chervil, tarragon).

Another use for leftovers is to make *veal paupiettes,* prepared in the Alsatian manner (SEE PAGE 281).

For other ways to use leftover beef, see the recipes for: BEEF SALAD (PAGE 465) and BEEF SALAD WITH TOMATOES (PAGE 466). Note also the ALSATIAN SALAD (PAGE 465), which contains ham, sausage, etc.

Ham lends itself to some very refined preparations such as: HAM ROLLS (PAGE 346), HAM MOUSSE (PAGE 347).

And if you have the time, you can make your own: terrines, pâtés, and galantines, which are very useful to have in reserve and for which you will find the recipes in the sections devoted to these preparations.

Foie gras, which can be found in cans or prepared fresh (SEE PAGE 428), will always be welcomed with pleasure.

Aspic of foie gras (SEE PAGE 447) could, as an hors d'oeuvre, be molded into small timbales; in this case, the slices of foie gras should be cut into sizes appropriate for the serving dish.

Duchesses of foie gras are little pastries prepared with unsweetened choux pastry (SEE PAGE 664). They must be chilled, then filled with a purée of preserved foie gras, blended with one-third of its weight of good butter. Force this through a drum sieve *(tamis)* and add a few tablespoons of crème Chantilly to the obtained purée to lighten it. You can, if you like, glaze the *duchesses* with a little meat aspic, cold but not yet completely set.

For **sweetbread aspics** (SEE PAGE 448), proceed as for the foie gras aspics, molding them in individual timbales, or in round dariole molds if you want to unmold them.

Fruits and Vegetables *(Fruits et Légumes)*

Fruits. Avocados *(Avocats):* This is a pear-shaped fruit, dark green in color, which you can find in some markets in the south of France and at exotic fruit merchants. Cut in half and remove the pit, then season the avocado with vinaigrette sauce. The flesh is not tart and has the consistency of butter.

(Melon): Clean it thoroughly, then cut the melon into slices and take out the seeds just before serving, not sooner. Serve it on crushed ice if you like: a fruit that is too cold loses some of its flavor. Arrange the slices in a decorative dish or serve each slice on a plate. At the same time, offer salt, pepper, and superfine sugar.

(Olives): These can be found ready for consumption at charcuterie and specialty shops. Depending on your preference, choose either black or green olives, large or small, stuffed or not.

Grapefruit *(Pamplemousse):* Allow 1 grapefruit half per person. Wash and dry the fruit. Cut them in half crosswise; using very clean scissors, remove the white cottony part in the center. Then, either with a stainless steel knife or with a little sawtooth knife especially made for this use, loosen each segment from the skin that surrounds it so that it will be free in its cavity. If you like, pour a tablespoon of gin over the segments and place a maraschino cherry in the middle of the fruit. Serve with superfine sugar.

Vegetables *(Légumes).* Almost all raw or cooked vegetables that can be prepared as a salad can be served as hors d'oeuvres. You will find directions and recipes on this subject in the article on simple and mixed salads (PAGE 463). We will add here artichokes for salad (SEE PAGE 473).

Artichoke Bottoms *(Fonds d'Artichauts):* Chosen small, cooked in boiling salted water with the addition of a little lemon juice and oil (SEE PAGE 471), chilled and well drained, these can be garnished with: a vegetable salad; asparagus tips; cooked mushrooms, diced or sliced; hard-boiled egg slices, mixed, if you like, with minced truffles; pickled ham, tongue, or chicken breast, mixed with mayonnaise. Arrange them on a serving platter with lettuce leaves and slices of very red tomato.

Chilled Asparagus with Mayonnaise Sauce *(Asperges Froides à la Sauce Mayonnaise):* SEE PAGE 477.

Beets ***(Betterave):*** Cut into very thin slices, these happily accompany a salad of lamb's lettuce (mâche) or endive. Their seasoning—salt, pepper, oil, and vinegar—must be made separately and well in advance so that the beet has the time to thoroughly soak up the flavors. You can add beet slices to any salad, but at the last moment, without adding the red juice that seeped out as they were standing, which would discolor the dish.

Beet prepared as a salad can be cut into rounds or in a julienne; you can add mustard and finely minced herbs to the usual seasoning, and if you like, a little bit of mild sour cream.

Raw Grated Carrots ***(Carottes Râpées Crues):*** Peel or grate the carrots, wash them carefully, wipe them dry, and grate only the outer orange part of the carrot, not the yellow core; season with salt, pepper, lemon juice, and crème fraîche. Sprinkle with minced parsley.

Celery Stalks ***(Céleri en Branches):*** Use only the white and tender part of the heart of the celery. Cut off the earthy part of the base, leaving the leaves intact, then separate the branches to wash them well, without detaching them completely from the base. Thoroughly dry and serve in a tall glass as a bouquet. As an accompaniment, serve small slices of Chester cheese. Served like this, instead of being part of an hors d'oeuvre, the celery can accompany the cheese platter at the end of a meal.

Mushrooms ***(Champignons):*** Choose 125 grams (4½ ounces) of the smallest button mushrooms. Cook them for *10 minutes* over high heat with a little bit of lemon juice, salt, pepper, and 1 tablespoon of olive oil. Let them cool in their cooking juices. Drain the mushrooms and spread them out on a plate. Mix the cooking juice with 1 tablespoon of mustard. Pour it over the mushrooms and sprinkle with minced parsley.

Cauliflower with Mayonnaise Sauce ***(Chou-Fleur à la Sauce Mayonnaise:*** SEE PAGE 403.

Red Cabbage ***(Chou Rouge):*** Divide a small red cabbage into quarters. Wash them. Remove the hard parts of the center and the large veins. Cut the leaves into a fine julienne and immerse them for 1 minute in a pan of rapidly boiling water; put them in a strainer and chill in cold water. Dry thoroughly. Season with salt, pepper, oil, and vinegar for several hours in advance.

Cucumber Salad ***(Concombres en Salade:*** SEE PAGE 506.)

Broad Beans ***(Fèves):*** Young broad beans are eaten raw simply dipped in salt; when mature, they are shelled, peeled, cooked in salted water (SEE PAGE 514), then drained well and mixed with mayonnaise.

Onions with Tomatoes and Coriander Seeds ***(Oignons à la Grecque):*** This preparation, very flavorsome without being spicy, is a pleasant accompaniment to cold meats and charcuterie.

250 grams (8⅞ ounces) of pearl onions (about 20); 2 deciliters (6¾ fluid ounces, ⅞ cup) of white wine; ½ deciliter (1⅔ fluid ounces, scant ¼ cup) of olive oil; 250 grams (8⅞ ounces) of very ripe tomatoes; 5 peppercorns; pinch of salt; a sprig of thyme; a quarter bay leaf; a small branch of celery; a sprig of fennel, or use 10 fennel seeds and about 10 coriander seeds.

PROCEDURE. Peel the onions carefully because they must remain whole; if they are not young onions, blanch them for 10 minutes in boiling water. Drain them. Put them in a heavy-bottomed pot large enough to hold the onions in a single layer and so that the cooking liquid can cover them. Add all the aromatics; the tomatoes, previously peeled and chopped coarsely; the wine; and the oil. Bring to a boil. Cover the pot and *simmer* steadily, without touching the onions, for 1 hour. They must be perfectly tender and give lightly to the touch while remaining whole.

Carefully lift them out with a slotted spoon or a skimmer and put them into a small, shallow bowl. Strain the cooking juice from the onions through a chinois, pressing it well in order to extract all the juice. Let it cool completely. Serve them in the marinade, well chilled.

Green Pepper and Tomato Salad ***(Piments Verts et Tomates en Salade:*** The tomatoes should be washed, cut in half, and emptied of their water and their seeds; the peppers, should be rubbed with oil and grilled over low heat, then peeled and the seeds removed. Tomatoes and peppers should be cut in a julienne and seasoned with salt, pepper, and vinegar, then served sprinkled with minced herbs. If you like, you can garnish them with anchovy fillets in oil.

Leeks ***(Poireaux):*** Only the white part is used.

Cut into pieces about 10 centimeters (4 inches) long, which is about 2 for a good-sized leek, and cook in boiling water for 30–40 minutes according to size and age. Drain the leeks extremely well without unraveling them. Let cool and serve drizzled with mayonnaise or vinaigrette.

Radishes *(Radis):* We mention the radish, the springtime hors d'oeuvre par excellence, if only to also mention that larger radishes can also be made into a salad; washed, drained, and cut into thin slices without peeling, a few radish leaves, coarsely chopped, can be added with a little bit of tarragon. Use the usual salad seasoning.

Niçoise Salad *(Salade Niçoise):* Subject to numerous variations, a salade niçoise always contains potatoes and green beans, cooked separately in salted water, diced, and seasoned with salt, pepper, oil, and vinegar. These are combined with slices or quarters of tomatoes without their water or their seeds, anchovy fillets, pitted olives, and capers. Sprinkle with chervil and minced tarragon. If you like, you can rub the salad bowl with a clove of garlic.

Tomatoes *(Tomates):* Aside from their preparation in a salad—for which it is particularly important to rid them of their water and their seeds before slicing, by gently pressing them between your hands—tomatoes should be chosen small and perfectly round so that they can be filled with a variety of stuffings.

Cut off the top of the tomato, where the stem is. Scoop out the flesh without damaging the skin, lightly salt the interior, and let all the water that they contain drain out by turning them upside down on a board. The stuffing can be a fish salad, shrimp, finely diced mixed cooked vegetables, cooled rice pilau mixed with a julienne of peppers, diced hard-boiled eggs, leftovers from a *salade russe,* etc. All these elements are mixed with mayonnaise. If you like, this can be flavored with tomato concentrate or anchovy paste.

Tomatoes Filled with Tuna, Mayonnaise, and Anchovies *(Tomates à la Monégasque):* Choose small, round tomatoes. Slice off the stem end to form a lid. Remove the liquid and the seeds and squash the interior divisions with the handle of a teaspoon to make little containers. Season the inside of each tomato with salt, pepper, 2 drops of oil, and 1 drop of vinegar. Prepare a stuffing with: tuna, drained of its oil, and onion, shallot, hard-boiled egg yolk, and minced parsley. (If the onions are not new, remove their acidity by putting the minced onions on a towel and wetting them with cold water, then squeezing them dry.) Add some salted anchovy fillets, either squashed under the blade of a knife or, better, forced through a sieve. Mix everything well in a bowl, and add mayonnaise seasoned with mustard. Fill the tomatoes, shaping the stuffing into a little dome over the opening. Coat them lightly with a brush dipped in oil and serve well chilled, surrounded by parsley.

HOT HORS D'OEUVRES
Hors d'Oeuvres Chauds

Deep-Fried Cheese Soufflé Fritters *(Beignets Soufflés au Fromage)*

This hot hors d'oeuvre is always appreciated and, as a practical detail, can be made 15–20 minutes in advance and kept warm in a moderate oven. You can leave the door open. *Time: 45 minutes. Makes 18 fritters.*

2 deciliters (6 3/4 fluid ounces, 7/8 cup) of cold water; 50 grams (1 3/4 ounces, 3 1/2 tablespoons) of butter; 125 grams (4 1/2 ounces) of flour; a pinch of salt; a good pinch of pepper; 4 eggs (of an average weight of about 60 grams/2 1/4 ounces each); 100 grams (3 1/2 ounces) of grated cheese, half Gruyère and half Parmesan.

PROCEDURE. For directions on how to make the dough, prepare the pastries, and how to fry them, refer to the recipe for *beignets soufflés* (SEE PAGE 601). The grated cheese is added to the dough at the last moment, when the eggs have been incorporated. Beat the dough vigorously to thoroughly mix everything.

Deep-Fried Cheese-Filled Sticks, Turkish-Style *(Beurrecks à la Turque)*

Time: 40 minutes (assuming the pasta dough is already made). Makes about 20 beurrecks.

175 grams (6 ounces) of pasta dough (PAGE 568); 5 deciliters (generous 2 cups) of sauce béchamel (PAGE 52); 200 grams (7 ounces) of Emmenthal cheese;

100 grams (3 1/2 ounces) of stale white bread, and 2 eggs for the bread crumb coating (SEE ENGLISH BREADING, PAGE 19).

PROCEDURE. With the pasta dough ready, prepare the béchamel sauce and reduce it over high heat until thick; let it cool a little, stirring from time to time to prevent a skin from forming. During this time, dice the cheese into 1/2-centimeter (3/16-inch) cubes; stir them into the warm béchamel. Spread them out on a plate in a thin layer. Brush the surface with a little butter to prevent a skin, and let it *cool completely.*

Roll out the pasta dough as thin as possible, cutting it with an oval pastry cutter, about 9 centimeters (3 1/2 inches) long and 5 centimeters (2 inches) wide. Divide the mixture of béchamel and cheese between the ovals of dough. On a floured board, roll them into cigar shapes. Enclose each one of these rolls in an oval of dough, then moisten the dough's borders with water to seal it. You thus obtain rolls pointed at both extremities, in the form of a cigar. Bread the beurrecks and deep-fry them in hot oil, which has been heated to the point where it is smoking lightly. As soon as they are golden, drain them on a cloth and serve quite hot.

Hot Cheese Puff Pastries with Cayenne Pepper *(Condés à la Diable)*

Time: 40 minutes (once the dough has been prepared). Makes a dozen pastries.

350 grams (12 ounces) of leftover of *pâte feuilletée*, or the same amount of *demi-feuillétage* (PAGE 662); 60 grams (2 1/4 ounces) of Gruyère, cut into tiny cubes; 2 good tablespoons of grated cheese, half Gruyère and half Parmesan; a generous point of cayenne pepper (as much as can be held on the tip of a knife).

PROCEDURE. With the dough ready, prepare a béchamel, then reduce this over high heat until thick to obtain a quantity of about 2 deciliters (6 3/4 fluid ounces, 7/8 cup). Put it in a bowl and dot pieces of butter over the top to prevent a skin from forming. Let it cool. Dice the cheese into cubes and mix these into the cooled béchamel sauce.

Roll out the dough in 2 strips each 20 centimeters (8 inches) long, 7 centimeters (3/4 inches) wide, and about 8 millimeters (3/8 inch) thick. Spread the mixture on the ribbons of dough. Mix the grated Parmesan and Gruyère with the cayenne pepper and sprinkle over the dough strips. Divide each prepared strip into 5 rectangles. Transfer to a baking sheet that has been lightly sprinkled with water, and cook them in a moderate oven for 20 minutes. If, after 8–10 minutes, the surface of the pastries are too colored, cover them with a dampened piece of baking parchment. Serve quite hot.

Deep-Fried Cream with Cheese *(Crème Frite au Fromage)*

Time: 2 hours (of which 1 hour is for chilling the cream). Serves 6.

***For the cream:* 100 grams (3 1/2 ounces) of fine wheat flour; 50 grams (1 3/4 ounces) of rice flour; 2 large eggs and 4 yolks; 1/2 liter (generous 2 cups) of milk; 150 grams (5 1/3 ounces) of grated cheese, half Parmesan and half Gruyère; pinch of salt; pinch of cayenne pepper; some grated nutmeg.**

***For breading:* 2 small eggs beaten with 6 drops of oil; 150 grams (5 1/3 ounces) of stale white bread in very fine crumbs, mixed with 50 grams (1 3/4 ounces) of grated cheese.**

PROCEDURE. **Cream:** Put the sifted flours in a bowl and make a well in the middle. Put the eggs and the yolks in the well with the salt, the pepper, and the nutmeg; mix with a wooden spoon, gradually incorporating the flour into the eggs. Pour in the milk, which has been previously boiled and cooled, mixing thoroughly. Pour everything into a heavy-bottomed pot large enough to permit you to stir constantly with a wooden spoon that touches the bottom of the pot, to make sure that the mixture does not stick. Cook over moderate heat until the cream thickens. Off the heat, add the grated cheese and stir vigorously. Spread the mixture thus obtained on a large buttered tray in an even layer about 2 centimeters (3/4 inch) thick. Rub a little bit of butter, stuck to the point of a knife, over the surface, to prevent a skin from forming, and let it *cool completely.*

Breading: SEE ENGLISH BREADING, PAGE 19. Divide the composition into strips 3 centimeters (1 1/4 inches) wide, then into rectangles or in squares; dip them in the beaten egg and then in the mixture of the bread crumbs and cheese; with the flat part of a knife blade, press the bread crumbs on the top and sides so that they stick perfectly to all the surfaces.

Frying: Immerse the pieces in the frying oil, which should be *lightly* smoking; in 3–4 minutes, they will have taken on a golden hue and will be perfectly done. Take them out of the oil with a skimmer and put them on a cloth, which has been spread out to absorb the grease. Quickly arrange them on a warm plate and serve.

Fried Oysters *(Huîtres Frites)*

Open the oyster shells and remove the fleshy parts, without spoiling them, and then put them in a sauté pan where they fit comfortably side by side, without overlapping. Add their liquor, poured through a muslin cloth spread out over a funnel. Cook over moderate heat. At the first sign of boiling, remove from the heat, take out the oysters carefully so as not to damage them, dry them on a clean cloth, and remove their beards.

Bread each oyster in the English style (SEE ENGLISH BREADING, PAGE 19), handling them carefully—slide 2 forks under each oyster without piercing them. Then fry them in a large quantity of hot oil that is smoking lightly. As soon as they turn golden, drain them on a cloth and serve them in a mound, piping hot. Garnish with lemon wedges.

Savory Crêpe Parcels *(Pannequets)*

Pannequets, as hors d'oeuvres, are crêpes prepared with a batter that has neither sugar nor any other flavoring, but that is instead lightly salted (SEE PAGE 602). The crêpes are spread while they are still hot with duxelles (PAGE 21) or with a mixture of ham and raw and cooked mushrooms in a reduced béchamel sauce. Roll them up, cut the ends to give them a neater appearance, and then divide them into rectangles. Serve very hot.

***Pannequets* Mornay.** The crêpes, spread with a sauce Mornay (PAGE 63) to a thick consistency, are rolled, then arranged in a gratin dish that can be brought straight to the table. Sprinkle with grated Gruyère, and drizzle with melted butter. Run under a hot broiler until browned on top.

Stuffed Broiled Peppers
(Piments Grillés et Farcis Garcia)

Time: 1 hour, 30 minutes. Serves 6.

6 red or yellow bell peppers; 6 slices of lean ham and 6 slices of good Gruyère, cut into rectangles 1/2 centimeter (3/16 inch) thick and 4–5 centimeters (1 1/2–2 inches) wide, their length being determined by the pepper; a little olive oil to coat the peppers.

PROCEDURE. Choose the peppers with the smoothest possible surface. Wash them and coat with oil, then broil under the broiler heated *to low.* When the skin becomes blistered, turn them so that all the skin becomes loose. Watch carefully to make sure they don't burn.

Leave the peppers in a warm spot under the broiler, which has been turned off, and do not take them out until you are ready to peel them, which should be while they are still warm. Proceed by turning and pulling on the skin with the tip of a small knife. You must allow almost 1 hour to broil and peel the peppers. Cut off the stem end of the pepper so that you can remove the burned stump and make an opening that is large enough to remove all the seeds without damaging the pulp, which has become soft and fragile. Wrap a slice of cheese in a slice of ham from which you will have removed the rind, and slide the whole thing inside the pepper, not allowing the ham and cheese to stick out.

Bell peppers prepared like this can be made 1–2 hours in advance, kept under a clean cloth. About 15 minutes before serving, brush the peppers again with oil on all sides, and broil them under low heat; turn once during the course of cooking and apply the oil 2–3 times, making sure that the flesh of the pepper does not darken. The cheese must be melted inside its ham wrapping. Just before serving, glaze with a piece of butter on the tip of a knife. Serve very hot. Green peppers have the same taste as red peppers, but they take on a brownish color when they are cooked, and that is not pleasing to the eye.

Puréed Roasted Veal Kidney Toasts *(Rôties de Rognons de Veau)*

Time: 1 hour.

6 slices of stale white bread, without a crust, cut about 1/2 centimeter (3/16 inch) thick and trimmed to about the size of a playing card; 100 grams (3 1/2 ounces) of cooked veal kidneys and 50 grams (1 3/4 ounces) of its fat; 2 eggs; 25 grams (1 ounce, 2 tablespoons) of butter; 3 teaspoons of white bread crumbs; salt; pepper. For the sauce: 2 hard-boiled egg yolks; 2 tablespoons of parsley and minced chervil; 1 deciliter (3 1/3 fluid ounces, scant 1/2 cup) of olive oil; 1 teaspoon of vinegar; 1/2 teaspoon of mustard; salt and pepper.

PROCEDURE. Finely mince together the kidney and its fat; an electric grinder is useful for this since it reduces the meat almost to a purée, which takes a long time to do with a knife. Put the mixture in a bowl, then add the raw egg yolks, having first removed 1 teaspoon of it to reserve in a cup. Mix and season with salt and pepper. When ready to spread the bread slices, beat the whites until they hold stiff peaks; after a few turns of the whisk, while they are still liquid, remove a small teaspoonful, then add this to the reserved egg yolk, along with a few drops of water. Beat the whites until firm, and mix them with the kidney mixture, taking due care. Spread the mixture on the bread slices. With the blade of a knife that has been dipped into the reserved egg, spread and smooth the surface of the mixture into a dome shape, without too much pressure so that you do not destroy the lightness brought to it by the egg whites. Sprinkle with the white bread crumbs made only with the *crustless part* of the dried bread, crushed and pushed through a coarse sieve.

Butter the bottom of a gratin dish that can hold the pieces without them touching one another, and cook in a *hot* oven for 10–12 minutes. The stuffing will swell and the bread must become golden and crisp; it will remain limp if the cooking is too slow and the fat in the stuffing escapes. Brush the pieces once or twice with the melted butter from the bottom of the dish. The *sauce* is a vinaigrette. Crush the cooked egg yolks in a warmed bowl, then add the finely minced chervil and parsley, and the mustard, and pour the warmed oil in a thin stream, whisking vigorously. Finally, add the vinegar, salt, and pepper. Pour this into a warmed sauceboat and serve quite warm with the kidney toasts.

To make it easier to choose warm hors d'oeuvres, whose recipes are found throughout this book in various chapters, we will give a list of them here:

Deep-Fried Anchovy Matchstick Pastries ***(Allumettes aux Anchois):*** SEE PAGE 716.

Eggplant Fritters ***(Beignets d'Aubergines):*** SEE PAGE 481.

Stuffed Artichoke Bottoms ***(Fonds d'Artichauts Farcis):*** Choose the smaller ones. SEE PAGE 475.

Hot Ball-Shaped Cheese Pastries ***(Ramequins):*** SEE PAGE 700.

Hot Triangle-Shaped Cheese Pastries ***(Talmouses):*** SEE PAGE 700.

Savory Custard Tart ***(Salée Vaudoise):*** Served as tartlettes made from demi-feuilletage or pâte à foncer. SEE PAGE 662.

Filled Pastry Shells ***(Bouchées)*** **with a Financière or Toulousaine Filling:** SEE PAGES 457 AND 459.

EGGS

SOFT-BOILED, OR CODDLED, EGGS IN THEIR SHELLS
Oeufs à la Coque

The most important thing for an egg cooked in its shell is that it should be absolutely fresh. Fresh to such a point that a true soft-boiled egg should come from an egg laid on the very same day it is cooked; this rule can only really be observed in the countryside. If the egg is more than three days old, it stops being creamy. And it is its very creaminess that is the essence of soft-boiled eggs. If the eggs have been kept in a refrigerator, which is not necessary in temperate climates, you must take them out 2 hours before using them, so that they return to a normal temperature.

The ideal coddled egg is an egg in which the white is creamy but firm. It should not set or become attached to the shell. The yolk, quite warm, should be the same temperature as the white.

The cooking methods are various. Before listing them, we shall explain certain precautions that are particular to cooking coddled eggs. Of paramount importance: never store eggs near ingredients that give off a strong odor: cheese, fish, etc., because eggshells are more permeable than most people think.

Second, when eggs are to be served in the shell, always wash them before cooking, so that they are perfectly clean. If necessary, scrub any resistant spots with a little bit of salt, which will act like cleaning powder.

For cooking eggs, you should use a pan deep enough to cover the eggs adequately with the water. *Allow 1/2 liter (generous 2 cups) of water for 2 eggs.* This quantity allows for the cooling caused when the eggs are added to the boiling water, and the cooking time is naturally based on these proportions. Serving eggs cooked in the shell can be done in a folded napkin, or a pocket of embroidered cloth decorated with lace and doubled-up for added warmth; or they can be served in a shallow silver dish, the eggs half-submerged in the warm water to maintain their temperature.

Different Cooking Procedures

First procedure: Bring the water to a boil in a pan. Turn the heat down very low. Using a soupspoon, put in the eggs gently, so that you do not break the shell. Cover, and leave for *4 minutes,* without boiling again.

Second procedure: Put the eggs in the pan, amply covered with cool water. Put over high heat. When the water begins to boil, the eggs will be perfectly cooked. Drain immediately.

Third procedure: Boil the water in the pan. Remove from the heat and add the eggs. Cover, return to the heat, and bring it to a lively boil. From this moment, allow *3 minutes* of cooking. Remove from the heat. Drain. If the eggs are quite large, leave them in the water for *1 minute* more, off the heat.

Fourth procedure: Plunge the eggs into the pan of rapidly boiling water. *Immediately* turn off the heat. Leave it thus for 10 minutes. At the end of this time, the eggs will be perfectly cooked.

Fifth procedure: Plunge the eggs into a pan of boiling water. Cover and leave it for *1 minute only* on the heat. Turn off the heat. At the end of *5 minutes,* the eggs will be perfectly cooked. This method, recommended by Gouffé (SEE PAGE 57) and other great French chefs through the years, is most advantageous because it allows the eggs to be kept warm in the cooking water for a long time without going beyond the desired cooking point.

Finally, we would also like to mention coddled eggs by steaming, for which certain special utensils are made. And let us not forget the use of old-fashioned egg timers, which are available in durations of 3–5 minutes.

FRIED EGGS, OR EGGS SUNNY-SIDE UP
Oeufs sur le Plat

The real way to cook these is in the oven, on as many individual plates as there are diners. This is why, most of the time, fried eggs are very badly made in home kitchens, because these conditions are not observed.

But first, what is a successful fried egg? It is an egg cooked to a uniform consistency: the white is just solid enough so that it can be taken on the fork, white and creamy; the yolk is runny, but slightly thickened, covered by a light veil of white that is almost reflective—hence the old French name for fried eggs, *au miroir* (as a mirror).

We say *baked in the oven* because when the cooking is done on top of the stove, the heat strikes the egg only from beneath, in a way that is partly direct and partly indirect since only the bottom of the utensil is heated. Thus, the white part firms up to a certain thickness yet stays runny on the surface while the yolk has only begun to warm when the white is already cooked. The opposite is true in the oven—which here replaces the lid filled with coals, or the radiating hearth of old fireplaces: the egg is surrounded by the heat and cooked evenly all over.

The cooking dish: Let us first of all consider the size of the dish, because this is of essential importance. For a dish that is too large in relation to the number of eggs to be cooked, the white will spread out thinly and will set before the yolk can cook. It is therefore necessary to be strict about the correct proportions relative to the size of the dish and the number of eggs.

There are individual dishes, made of ovenproof porcelain, that are generally the correct size for 2 eggs: about 13–14 centimeters (5–5½ inches) in diameter. Always allow 2 eggs per person, although there are dishes for 1 egg only. If you do not have these individual dishes, you must cook a certain number of eggs in the same dish, which should be smaller rather than larger so that the eggs are combined and concentrated, ensuring that they are thicker than they are wider. But cooking in individual dishes is the method that offers the largest number of guarantees: not only in terms of the cooking itself, but also for serving, which is infinitely more proper, and more certain, because it often happens that, when helping oneself from a communal dish, one of the guests will surely puncture a yolk, causing it to run all over, an undesirable effect.

The cooking: Here we are going to discuss eggs cooked in individual dishes. The cooking time is the same for eggs cooked two at a time in individual dishes as it is for those that are all grouped together in a single dish. The thickness of the egg, which really is the important question, is the same in both cases.

The amount of butter will be enough for 2 eggs cooked in an individual dish of the indicated diameter; which is *10–15 grams (⅓–½ ounce, about 1 tablespoon) of butter per dish.* You should arrange your dishes toward the front of the oven so that they heat for just a few seconds. Then add the butter and, when it is melted and has spread right across the dish and is good and warm, rapidly break the 2 eggs into each dish. Season with a very small pinch of salt on the white only. Do not let it fall onto the yolk because this will mar its appearance, making it spotted. No pepper: your guests can put it on if they like.

As soon as possible, put the eggs in the oven, preferably one that is too warm rather than not warm enough. The heat must come primarily from the top, the bottom of the dish having already acquired a certain degree of heat from the oven shelf. For this reason, instead of putting the eggs in the lower part of the oven, it is best to put them on a shelf in the middle of the oven, so that they get more of the heat called "top heat."

About *3 minutes of cooking, 4 at the most,* should be enough so that the white is completely set but still tender, while the yolk has a slightly mirrored finish but remains soft.

You should then, in total, allow about *6 minutes* for preparing fried eggs, broken down as: 2 minutes to heat the dishes, melt the butter, and break the eggs, and 2–3 minutes in the oven.

To serve: Arrange the dishes on a tray covered with a cloth or a napkin. If the eggs have a garnish, arrange it rapidly in the dishes because the eggs should always be served quite warm.

Main Preparations

Fried eggs *(sur le plat)* make up one of the most extensive group of dishes: at least, they do in the restaurant kitchen, where sauces and garnishes that are already made allow for imagination and improvisation. In the home kitchen, the diversity of preparations is naturally more restricted; however, leftovers can often be used in a manner that is both advantageous and original.

In principle, the garnish is spread out in the bottom of the dish in which the eggs are subsequently broken; you should use a scant tablespoon for two eggs, no matter what leftovers you are using: *green peas à la française* with their lettuce; or purée of *lentils,* or*kidney beans,* on which you can place a thin slice of cooked bacon; or chicory or spinach, adding a sprinkling of grated Gruyère on top of the eggs before sliding the dish into the oven; *asparagus tips,* mixed, if possible, with a little leftover béchamel; onion purée or leftover Brussels sprouts, mashed with a fork into a coarse purée; *minced herbs,* tarragon, parsley, and chervil; minced truffle peels, etc.

Eggs with Anchovies *(Oeufs aux Anchois).* Allow 1 salted anchovy for each egg. Clean the anchovies, divide them into 4 strips or slices; cut 3 of the fillets into small pieces to scatter them over the bottom of the plate. After cooking, encircle the yolk with the fourth fillet, rolled in a ring.

Eggs with Brown Butter *(Oeufs au Beurre Noir).* SEE PAGE 158.

Eggs with Sausage and Tomato Sauce *(Oeufs à la Bercy).* Because these are quick to prepare, they have a permanent place on many restaurant menus. In this dish, the eggs are simply garnished with small sausages and surrounded by a ribbon of tomato sauce. For serving, individual dishes are quite preferable.

Allow 2 eggs per person, for which you will need: 10 grams (1/3 ounce, 1 scant tablespoon) of butter for the dish; 1 small, long sausage, or 2 chipolatas; 1 tablespoon of tomato sauce. For this dish, you can use tomato concentrate; so, for one dish with 2 eggs, 1 teaspoon of tomato concentrate, diluted with 1 tablespoon of *bouillon,* and finished with a little brown butter, added off the heat.

PROCEDURE. In a small saucepan, heat the diluted tomato concentrate. Cook the sausages (SEE PAGE 338). Cook the eggs. As soon as the eggs are finished, arrange the dishes on a tray lined with a cloth. Place 1 sausage between the 2 egg yolks, without touching either one. Drizzle the tomato sauce in a ribbon around the edges of the dish. Serve immediately.

This garnish must be made with great celerity. Because of the heat acquired by the dish, the cooking continues for a few seconds after leaving the oven.

Fried Eggs with Bacon, Cream, and Cheese *(Oeufs sur le Plat à la Lorraine).* A delicious, rustic preparation. *Time: 20 minutes.*

100 grams (3 1/2 ounces) of bacon; 30 grams (1 ounce, 2 tablespoons) of butter; 60 grams (2 1/4 ounces) of Gruyère; 6 eggs; a good deciliter (3 1/3 fluid ounces, 1/2 cup) of heavy cream that is very fresh.

PROCEDURE. Trim the rind, then cut the bacon into very thin slices that are *not too big,* so that you will be able to loosen them from the bottom of the dish when removing the egg, without breaking the egg. Blanch them for 3 minutes (SEE BLANCHING BACON, PAGE 15). Similarly, cut the cheese into small, extremely thin slices.

With your fingers, butter a porcelain egg dish of the appropriate size. Place the slices of bacon on the bottom, and over these, the slices of Gruyère. Break the eggs over all this. Salt lightly. Add the cream. Cook in the oven: *6–7 minutes* should be enough to ensure the whites set properly.

DEEP-FRIED EGGS
Oeufs Frits

Most often, in home cooking, a "fried egg" is an egg that has been simply cooked in a frying pan, in much the same way as an oeuf sur le plat, but this is not an accurate representation of a true oeuf frit. In reality, an oeuf frit is an egg poached in hot fat instead of boiling water. The golden color is the difference, but the general consistency should be the same, with the yolk remaining quite soft within its envelope of white. Even if the question of its freshness is not as essential for an oeuf frit as for a poached egg, the eggs should still be very fresh: an egg of dubious freshness does not keep its form when poached, and it's difficult to cook it without breaking it. So, never use eggs that have been kept a long time for this method of cooking.

You can fry only one egg at a time. That is because of the rapidity—almost instantaneous—of its cooking, and because of the attention it requires, which means that you cannot ignore it for even the slightest instant. You should use no more than enough fat to cover a single egg: which is about 2 deciliters (6¾ fluid ounces, ⅞ cup). The degree of heat of the fat is thus much easier to maintain than with a large amount of fat, where the balance of cooking the egg would be destroyed. Only very highly purified fat or clarified butter can be used for this frying process; but oil is preferable. The commonly employed utensil is a small cast-iron omelet pan, well made—which implies one that is thick-bottomed, with relatively high sides. The smaller the pan, the better it will be for this operation. The egg must be completely submerged in the oil; therefore, you need a very small utensil so the oil is deep enough to cover the egg.

Frying the eggs: To fully understand why you must proceed quickly and accurately, you must realize that to break, fry, and remove each egg takes *less than 1 minute.* You can allow 8 minutes to fry 12 eggs one at a time. Thus, everything must be prepared in advance, to accommodate the necessary movements and combinations.

Put the oil into the pan (2 deciliters, 6¾ fluid ounces, ⅞ cup).

On the stovetop, prepare a baking sheet lined with a clean cloth, folded several times and warmed, on which you will place the eggs as they are fried.

Have at hand a *saucer,* into which you will break the eggs one at a time when ready to fry. At your side, *salt and pepper.* Equally at hand, *a slotted spoon* or a good *wooden spoon* that is smooth, not rough, so that you do not graze the envelope of the egg; or you can use a metal cooking spoon, which also works.

When the time to fry the eggs arrives, raise the heat of the oil right up to the point where it *smokes a little.* Now it's a matter of maintaining the oil at this exact temperature throughout the whole operation, so that when you drop the egg into the oil, it is immediately seized. Do not go beyond this correct point either, because if the oil smokes more than lightly, everything is going to burn. Therefore, make sure that you keep your pan over very low heat, so that this light smoke persists without increasing.

To ensure a deeper level of oil, tilt one side of the pan to send the oil to the opposite side, and stabilize it with some kind of wedge, a little piece of iron, a chunk of potato, etc. This will be much more practical than lifting the handle of the pan to tilt it each time you slide in an egg.

Break the egg into the saucer. Season it lightly, only the yolk, with salt and pepper (the salt has a dissolving action on the white). Slide the egg into the pan by bringing the saucer right up to the level of the oil. Quickly grab your spoon and dunk it into this burning oil, and use it to spread the white over the yolk, completely surrounding it. Immediately thereafter, turn the egg over in the oil. Leave it there *a second.* Quickly put the spoon under it and remove it to the cloth to drain it.

Do the same for the others, keeping a sharp eye on the temperature of the oil each time you are ready to add another egg. And, very importantly, always be careful to dip the spoon into the hot oil before you touch the egg, otherwise it will stick to the spoon.

Main Preparations

Fried eggs, which play a more important role in garnishes for sautéed chicken, fish stews, etc., don't really lend themselves, when served as a dish on their own, to complicated or ceremonious meals; thus, the ingredients with which they are generally accompanied are usually simple.

First comes bacon and ham. The bacon, about 25 grams (1 ounce) for each egg, is sliced thinly, blanched, browned in a pan, and then the egg is placed on top. *Cured* ham is briefly warmed in a pan with butter to heat it through before putting the egg on top of it. If you like, you can surround it with tomato sauce.

Alternatively, the eggs are placed on croutons that have been fried in butter and lightly covered with an appropriate sauce: anchovy, tomato, etc.

Or, the eggs are set on fried croutons that are set atop *potato purée*, or *braised tomatoes,* on *rice pilau* and placed on slices of bacon or ham.

Or, they are served on a *jardinière.* This involves, for 6 eggs: 150 grams ($5^1/_3$ ounces) of carrots cut into rounds and glazed (SEE CARROTS PAGE 483), then mixed with green peas and green beans, the same amount for each vegetable, cooked and drained as indicated (SEE JARDINIÈRE GARNISH, PAGE 459). Add 60 grams ($2^1/_4$ ounces, $4^1/_2$ tablespoons) of butter to this off the heat. Spread the vegetables out on a round plate. On top, arrange the eggs in a circle and add slices of bacon that have been fried until crisp.

SOFT-BOILED EGGS
Oeufs Mollets

Because of its texture, a soft-boiled egg is more like a coddled egg than a hard-boiled one. The yolk of a soft-boiled egg must still stay a bit runny within the envelope of white but be solid enough to withstand the shelling and handling that follows. You could say that a soft-boiled egg is really a coddled egg that has been cooked too much. This explains the importance of cooking eggs that are perfectly fresh and using small eggs or medium-sized eggs: eggs cooked like this retain a certain suppleness, the larger volume eggs remaining proportionally softer.

When cooking more than 1 or 2 eggs at a time, make sure that you choose the same size eggs to ensure even cooking. Also, because even cooking is so important, it's always better to put all the eggs together in a strainer or a deep-frying basket to be able to plunge them into the boiling water all at the same time. First of all, this prevents them from bumping into one another at the bottom of the pan and cracking, as happens if they are placed individually, no matter how much care is taken. Furthermore, being put into the water together and then removed together ensures even cooking. Despite a very short time between adding the first and last eggs, there will be differences, accentuated further when they are removed in the same way—that is, one by one. Now, no matter how fast you are, a minute more or less at this stage has an enormous impact: it is enough to make an almost hard-boiled egg in place of a soft one.

If you do not have a basket made especially for the task, the best utensil for keeping the eggs together is the basket from a deep fryer. A colander does not offer the same advantages because its rounded bottom will cause the eggs to pile up on one another and prevent them from coming into complete contact with the boiling water.

Have a pan over high heat, filled with enough boiling water so that the eggs are completely covered. When the water reaches a full boil, immerse the basket containing the eggs. Bring it rapidly to a boil again. From the point when the water returns to a boil, allow *5 minutes* of cooking for *very small eggs* and *6 minutes* for *medium-sized* eggs.

Remove the basket containing the eggs. Plunge it into a container of cool water, where you will leave it for *7–8 minutes.* If you do not have a basket, rapidly drain the water from the pan. Or, remove the eggs with a skimmer and put them immediately in cool water.

To shell the eggs: Take the egg in the palm of your left hand; with the flat part of a large kitchen knife blade, carefully tap on the shell all over, so that it becomes completely covered in cracks, like a mosaic. Carefully lift a little piece of the shell and remove it. Continue to detach it in strips: these strips of broken shell are very supple and do not risk damaging the egg when you peel it.

If the recipe does not call for a sauce in which you can reheat the eggs, they should be returned to warm water for a few moments before serving. Drain them well and pat them dry with a cloth before dressing them with sauce.

Main Preparations

Soft-boiled eggs can be prepared in many ways, depending as much on the resources of the kitchen as on the imagination used to prepare them. We will list here the recipes that are best adapted to the home kitchen.

First, let us note the simplest way to serve them, which is either in an individual dish or in a vegetable dish, covered by an appropriate sauce, such as: anchovy sauce, aurore sauce, béchamel, sauce crème, Mornay sauce, soubise sauce, tomato sauce, etc. If you prefer, the eggs can first be placed on croutons that have been fried in butter.

Next, you have eggs served *on any kind of purée:* we recommend a purée of white beans or a soubise purée. Cover each egg with cream sauce or béchamel, 2 tablespoons per egg, just enough to "coat" it without covering the purée. Or, eggs on *squares of toast* that have been buttered and topped with a good tablespoon of *artichoke tips,* or *green peas* mixed with butter and covered with a cream sauce. Eggs on *croutons,* topped with a round of *ham,* if you like, and then coated with tomato sauce. Or, eggs on a bed of *sauerkraut* spread evenly in the dish and with a slice of bacon or of smoked ham and sprinkled with a tablespoon of thickened *jus* to glaze them like a varnish. Or, cold eggs on *artichoke bottoms* set on rounds of boiled ham and covered with mayonnaise.

Soft-Boiled Eggs on Rice *(Oeufs Mollets au Riz).* Cook the rice in bouillon (SEE PAGE 162). Spread in an even layer in a buttered ovenproof dish. Cut the eggs in half, lengthwise. Place the egg halves on the rice, cut-side up. Sprinkle the eggs only with grated Parmesan or Gruyère, and then drizzle with melted butter. Put the dish into a very hot oven: preferably, if possible, underneath the broiler. The top should brown lightly in no more than *2 minutes,* so that beneath the gratin layer, the yolk of the egg will not harden; because of this, the rice must be quite hot when it is spread in the dish because it will not have the time to subsequently reheat. *Time: 30 minutes.*

1 egg; 60 grams ($2^1/_4$ ounces) of rice, uncooked weight; 1 tablespoon of grated Parmesan or Gruyère; 8–10 grams ($^1/_3$ ounce, 1 scant tablespoon) of butter, part of which is used to butter the dish.

Soft-Boiled Eggs with Red Wine and Shallot Sauce *(Oeufs Mollets à la Bourguignonne).* SEE PAGE 159.

Soft-Boiled Eggs with Sorrel *(Oeufs Mollets à l'Oseille).* A very home-style dish. *Time: 30 minutes.*

450 grams (1 pound) of good sorrel, net weight; 50 grams ($1^3/_4$ ounces, $3^1/_2$ tablespoons) of butter; 1 egg, for the liaison; 15 grams ($^1/_2$ ounce) of beurre manié made with 1 teaspoon of flour (SEE LIAISONS, PAGE 47); 6 croutons and 30 grams (1 ounce, 2 tablespoons) of butter to fry them; 6 soft-boiled eggs.

PROCEDURE. When the sorrel has been plucked, washed, and dried, assemble the leaves in little packets on the table and cut them, crosswise, into strips. Put them into a small sauté pan with the butter. Cook over low heat to soften and "melt" the sorrel, stirring frequently with a wooden spoon; if not, it will stick. Allow *at least 10 minutes* for it to melt.

Next, beat the egg for the liaison, both the yolk and the white, in a bowl; mix a little sorrel in to heat it before pouring it *gradually* into the pan of sorrel, which has been taken off the heat. Stir vigorously with a wooden spoon. Then add the beurre manié; salt; cover, and put it in the oven for a good 15 minutes, to finish cooking the sorrel.

The croutons: Cut them at least 1 centimeter ($^3/_8$ inch) thick and slightly oval-shaped, like an egg. Hollow out the slices a little bit, lengthwise, so that you can place the egg there. Fry them (SEE PAGE 20). Keep them warm.

To dress the plate: Arrange the croutons in a rosette on the serving plate. On each crouton, place an egg that has been thoroughly dried off. In the middle of the rosette, place the sorrel.

Soft-Boiled Eggs with Puréed Onions and Cheese Sauce *(Oeufs à la Maintenon).* For both *soft-boiled* and *poached* eggs, this is one of the best and most recommended recipes because it is so easy to prepare. It's done thus: the eggs, placed on a purée soubise, are covered with a sauce Mornay.

If you prefer, and this is true for all eggs of this type, they can be served in individual pre-baked tartlet shells, in small egg plates, in small porcelain soufflé dishes, or put in a single ovenproof dish and run under the broiler for a final glaze. *Time: 1 hour.*

For the soubise: 2 large onions (200 grams, 7 ounces total); 6 eggs; 25 grams (1 ounce, 2 tablespoons) of butter; 1 deciliter ($3^1/_3$ fluid ounces, scant $^1/_2$ cup) of milk or bouillon; 1 good deciliter ($3^1/_3$ fluid ounces, $^1/_2$ cup) of sauce béchamel.

For the béchamel: 30 grams (1 ounce, 2 tablespoons) of butter and 20 grams ($^2/_3$ ounce) of flour; 3 good deciliters ($1^1/_4$ cups) of boiled milk; a small bouquet garni.

For the Mornay sauce: **The leftover béchamel sauce; 20 grams (2/3 ounce, 1 heaping tablespoon) of butter; 30 grams (1 ounce) of grated Gruyère.**

PROCEDURE. Prepare the onions (SEE SOUBISE PURÉE, PAGE 526); strain them through a drum sieve *(tamis)* and keep them warm in a small pan. Cook the eggs. They will have to be reheated 5 minutes before serving.

Prepare the béchamel (SEE SAUCE BÉCHAMEL, PAGE 52); keep it at a very gentle simmer for about 10 minutes; stir frequently so that it does not stick, considering how thick it is. If making this in advance, dot the surface with a few pieces of butter. SEE KEEPING SAUCES WARM, PAGE 50.

Finishing: Add a little less than the half of the béchamel to the onion purée. Over high heat, stir the purée constantly for *5–6 minutes,* to make it smooth and well combined. Lower the heat and keep it warm.

Into the other half of the béchamel—which should have been kept *quite warm*—whisk in the grated Gruyère, from which you will reserve 1 tablespoon for glazing. Then, off the heat, add the butter: Now you have Mornay sauce.

If you are serving on pieces of toast, individual plates, or dishes, put the receptacles on a baking tray. Then spread out the soubise in each dish. Place the eggs on top, previously reheated and patted dry; spoon a tablespoon of sauce Mornay over each egg, then sprinkle them with grated cheese.

Glaze them in a hot oven or underneath the broiler (SEE GLAZING SAUCED DISHES, PAGE 15). *One minute* should be enough; if not, the eggs yolk will harden. Serve immediately.

Soft-Boiled Eggs with Souffléd Béchamel Sauce *(Oeufs Mollets en Soufflé).* *Time: 1 hour.*

6 eggs; 3 deciliters (1 1/4 cups) of lean béchamel sauce, well seasoned with a little mirepoix, as directed (SEE LEAN BÉCHAMEL, PAGE 53). Here, allow 8 grams (1/4 ounce) of flour for each deciliter (3 1/3 fluid ounces, scant 1/2 cup) of roux blanc: that is, 25 grams (1 ounce) of flour; 2 egg whites, beaten until firm.

PROCEDURE. Start the sauce béchamel. Cook and shell the eggs. About 25 minutes before serving, butter a soufflé dish or a shallow ovenproof dish. Place the eggs in the dish next to one another without letting them touch, in a more or less rosette pattern. Whisk the whites (SEE EGG WHITES, PAGE 8) and mix them with the sauce. Completely cover the eggs with the sauce. Put it in a moderate oven. Allow about *15 minutes:* the mixture must swell by one-third of its original height, be uniformly firm, light, and moist. Serve immediately in the dish set on a serving plate.

POACHED EGGS
Oeufs Pochés

The eggs that you are going to poach should be chosen fresh, as though you were going to serve them coddled. This is essential if you want to make the best poached eggs. When the egg is not as fresh as it should be, the white becomes tough and shriveled, resembling an old towel, while the yolk, almost fully exposed, either gets hard or bursts. It's a different matter with a fresh egg: upon contact with boiling water, the white immediately closes around the yolk, protects it, and encloses it so well that the egg resumes, so to speak, its original form.

Choose eggs that are medium in size, and when you have a large number to poach, make sure they are all as evenly and regularly sized as possible, to ensure a uniform poaching.

A sauté pan is the best thing to use, because in such a low and wide utensil the water is spread out over a much larger surface. And because it is shallow, the water comes nearly up to the top of the utensil, which allows you to easily slide the egg onto the surface of the liquid. If the egg, released from its shell, is dropped from too high up, its shape is altered by the fall, and the natural position of the white around the yolk is not perfect.

The eggs must be able to float easily in the water without touching each other. If the number of eggs that you need to poach is more than half a dozen, you would do better to put in no more than 6 at a time. Not matter how quickly you are able to work, you will be much more likely to achieve uniform poaching if you keep them to that number.

The water has to fill the pan to within 1–2 centimeters (3/8–3/4 inch) of the top. You should add

10 grams ($^1/_3$ ounce) of salt and a good tablespoon of *white* vinegar for each liter ($4^1/_4$ cups) of water: the effect of the vinegar is to strengthen and firm the egg white to help it coagulate. For 6 eggs, about $1^1/_2$ liters ($6^1/_3$ cups) of water should be enough.

To poach the eggs: When the water has come to a boil, position the pan over the heat in such a way that you can maintain the boiling *at one single place in the liquid.*

Take the eggs, one by one. Crack them on the edge of the pan by striking a sharp blow in the middle of the shell. Open the shell briskly with two hands, like a book, at the same time holding it just next to the liquid at the place where it is boiling. Placed in the liquid like this, an egg keeps its shape and the yolk remains rounded beneath the veil of white, which sets immediately.

This procedure, simple though it may be for people who have practice or a natural dexterity, seems to others to be slightly risky, in terms of the method used for cracking the shell of the egg. It takes precision to be able to crack them rapidly, leaving a large opening for the egg to pass through, so that in one single motion it slides, intact, into the boiling water.

For novices, and for the timid, professionals recommend the following procedure, which they themselves also use: simply break the eggs successively into a small saucer, from which, one by one, you can slide them into the water.

Whichever method you use, once you have placed the eggs in the water, position the pan so that the water only simmers gently.

Cover the pan. Let the eggs poach for *3 minutes*—in other words, to the point where the white has become just firm enough so that the egg can be removed from the water and handled without breaking. It is nonetheless extremely fragile, and must not be touched, except with the greatest of care.

Then, using a slotted spoon or a small skimmer, take the eggs, one after the other, and plunge them into a container of moderately warm water, which has been prepared in advance.

To trim the eggs: When, in an moment or so, the eggs are cooled slightly, take them, one by one, in your open left hand and, with the point of small knife, cut away any tiny filaments of white that you might find. This is called "trimming" the egg.

If the eggs are being made in advance, keep them warm in the warm water that has been slightly salted, or put them one by one on a napkin that has been folded in two. Pat them dry thoroughly; set them on the lid of a large pan, whose concave shape will make moving and transporting the eggs for the final preparation easier than almost any other utensil.

Main Preparations

The sauces and ways of serving poached eggs are the same as for soft-boiled eggs. They are served accompanied by the same sauces, and sometimes on top of croutons.

Poached Eggs with Red Wine and Shallot Sauce *(Oeufs Pochès à la Bourguignonne).* SEE PAGE 159.

Gratin of Poached Eggs with Cheese Sauce *(Oeufs Pochés au Gratin).* *Time: 15 minutes.*

On the bottom of an ovenproof dish that has been lightly buttered, spread a very thin layer of Mornay sauce (PAGE 63). Put the eggs on top of this; cover them with sauce; sprinkle them with grated Gruyère. Put in a very hot oven or underneath the broiler for 3 minutes to brown. If you're using the oven, set the dish on some cold bricks or put it in a receptacle of cool water to prevent the eggs from hardening.

You can put fried croutons under each egg instead of putting them directly on the sauce: this is more elegant and, at the same time, easier. Allow about $^1/_2$ liter (generous 2 cups) of sauce (SEE MORNAY SAUCE, PAGE 63) for 6 large eggs.

Poached Eggs with Anchovies *(Oeufs Pochés à l'Anchois).* *Time: 15 minutes.*

This is a really nice, warm hors d'oeuvre, with a very simple preparation that can be described as follows: take some squares of white bread, cut $1^1/_2$ centimeters ($^5/_8$ inch) thick and 7–8 centimeters ($2^3/_4$–$3^1/_4$ inches) on each side; remove any crust and trim the four corners. Grill the squares of bread under a heat that's hot enough to brown them rapidly without drying out the interior. Spread them, on one side only, with, for each piece of toast, 15 grams ($^1/_2$ ounce, 1 tablespoon) of fresh butter mixed with 20 grams ($^2/_3$ ounce) of anchovy paste. Keep them warm while you poach the eggs. Place an egg on each square of toast; serve on a plate that has been covered with a cloth napkin.

Baked Eggs with Cream *(Oeufs en Cocotte à la Crème).* This is the original, typical method for making *oeufs en cocotte.* Formerly, the recipes were complicated, using stuffings, purées, stews, and various mixtures, which made the preparation difficult and expensive for everyday cooking. A true *oeuf en cocotte,* at the beginning, was nothing more than an egg poached directly in cream; this excellent method, in its full simplicity, is the one we give here.

The baking dishes to be used—called *cocottes* in French—are the size suitable for a single egg. They should be ovenproof or made of porcelain: either completely white or colored on the exterior, with a little handle. Usually, you allow one cocotte per person; but for a family meal that needs filling out, you could allow two.

The cream to use is light. In other words, very liquid, not too thick, and absolutely fresh; you should allow 1 good tablespoon for each egg. The eggs must be as fresh as those for coddled eggs. *Time: 15 minutes.*

6 tablespoons of cream, which is the equivalent of $1^1/_2$ deciliters (5 fluid ounces, $^2/_3$ cup); 6 eggs; 25 grams (1 ounce, 2 tablespoons) of butter; fine salt, about a pinch ($^1/_2$ gram) for each egg—a total of 3 grams ($^1/_8$ ounce).

PROCEDURE. Put the cream into a small pan and bring to a boil over moderate heat so that you do not risk burning it.

Arrange the previously heated cocottes in a large sauté pan or in a large dish that can go into the oven. In each cocotte, put 1 tablespoon of boiling cream. Break the eggs by striking the shell on the edge of the pan and put one into each cocotte. Sprinkle with salt. (The egg, seized by the warmth of the cream and of the cocotte, will remain tender as it cooks: for this reason, these preliminary steps must not be neglected.) In each cocotte, add 2 pieces of butter the size of a pea.

Using your kettle, pour enough *truly boiling* water into the sauté pan to come halfway up the sides of the cocottes. Cover the entire pan with a big lid. Put it in an oven warm enough to maintain the simmering water without fully boiling. If the cocottes are made of thin porcelain, the eggs will be done at the end of *6–7 minutes,* depending on their size. With cocottes made of thick earthenware: *2 minutes* more. A properly done egg will have a lightly set white with the yolk being the same consistency of that of an egg poached directly in liquid.

As soon as they are ready, take the dish out of the oven. Remove the cocottes from the water. Carefully wipe them and arrange them on a round plate or a tray, covered with a towel or a napkin. Serve immediately.

HARD-BOILED EGGS
Oeufs Durs

When it comes to hard-boiled eggs, it is a very common error to think that there is no risk of overcooking and that it is no problem to leave them in the boiling water after they have set. A hard-boiled egg that has been overcooked is tough; the yolk is circled with green, the white gives off an unpleasant odor, and the egg gives the impression of not being fresh.

Another error: putting eggs into water that is merely warm, or even cool, and then bringing to a boil. The result is that the white sets unevenly around the yolk, which will not give you attractive rounds—or, in the case of stuffed eggs, handsome containers of egg white, each equally thick.

Cooking. Proceed exactly from start to finish as for soft-boiled eggs: put them together into a basket and plunge them into rapidly boiling water.

From the point that the water returns to a boil, allow *10 minutes cooking for medium* eggs (a weight of 55 grams/2 ounces) and *12 minutes for large* eggs (an average weight of 65 grams/$2^1/_4$ ounces).

Then plunge them into cold water and shell them as for soft-boiled eggs.

Main Preparations

The simplest way to serve hard-boiled eggs is to cut them in half, lengthwise, and place them on a sauce—aurore, anchovy, béchamel, Mornay, tomato, etc. or, cut into slices and arrange in alternate layers with the same sauce. Allow at least a good 1/2 deciliter (1 2/3 fluid ounces, scant 1/4 cup) of sauce for each egg.

NOTE. When cut into rounds and combined with an equal volume of thinly sliced boiled celeriac, the egg can be served in a shallow dish with alternate layers of brown sauce or tomato sauce, and garnished with small croutons, fried in butter. Or, the eggs can be mixed with artichoke bottoms, cut into thin rounds, and gently sautéed in butter.

Or, served on a *croûte* as a vol-au-vent, for a meat-free meal: the eggs are cut into slices, with the addition, for 6 eggs, of 125 grams (4 1/2 ounces) of mushrooms that have been boiled in water; some béchamel sauce, to which is added the cooking water from the mushrooms, using the same quantity of liquid as for a white roux (SEE BÉCHAMEL SAUCE, PAGE 52).

With Red Wine and Shallot Sauce *(À la Bourguignonne).* SEE PAGE 57.

Hard-Boiled Eggs with Cheese Sauce Served in Scallop Shells *(Oeufs Durs en Coquilles de Poisson).* A hot hors d'oeuvre and an imaginative dish. Very simple to prepare, this gives the illusion of being fish, either turbot or brill.

To summarize: hard-boiled eggs are finely minced and mixed with a lean béchamel and finished with anchovy butter. They are then packed into scallop shells—one shell per person—and sprinkled with grated Gruyère, then glazed under a hot broiler. *Time: 40 minutes. Serves 6.*

6 scallop shells; 8 eggs.

For the sauce: a little mirepoix with 60 grams (2 1/4 ounces) of carrots and the same of the white part of a leek, or you can substitute onion, 10 grams (1/3 ounce) of parsley branches, a sprig of thyme, and 30 grams (1 ounce, 2 tablespoons) of butter; 7 deciliters (3 cups) of boiled milk; 40 grams (1 1/2 ounces, 3 tablespoons) of butter and 40 grams (1 1/2 ounces) of flour for a white roux; salt, pepper, grated nutmeg; 60 grams (2 1/4 ounces) of grated Gruyère.

For the anchovy butter: 7–8 salted anchovies, or 1 tablespoon of anchovy paste; 50 grams (1 3/4 ounces, 3 1/2 tablespoons) of butter.

PROCEDURE. In a small pan, lightly color the mirepoix with the butter (SEE MIREPOIX, PAGE 21). Boil the milk, then add the mirepoix to it. Cover partly and let it simmer gently, *for 15–20 minutes,* then strain the infused milk through a chinois into a tureen. Thoroughly wash and dry the pan. Make a white roux in this same pan with the butter and flour. Dilute it with the infused milk. Stir until it boils. Add a pinch of pepper. If the sauce is made in advance, put a piece of butter on top to prevent a skin forming on the surface.

Prepare the anchovies, as directed (SEE ANCHOVY BUTTER, PAGE 78).

The eggs: As soon as the sauce is underway, cook them. After shelling, cut them in half lengthwise. Without crushing them, remove the yolks; set them aside. Divide each half of white into two—cutting lengthwise, as always. Cut these quarters across in little slices 1/4 centimeter (1/16 inch) thick, at the most. Cut the yolk a little bit thicker, being careful not to crumble it. Keep the whites and the yolks separate.

The scallop shells: Use ordinary scallop shells (coquilles Saint-Jacques), washing them, like any other cooking utensil, after each use.

Add the anchovy butter to the sauce, *off the heat.* Taste it to check the seasoning: if you prefer, add a point of cayenne (as much as can be held on the tip of a small knife). Add the minced whites to the sauce. Fill each shell with this mixture half way, smoothing it out thoroughly. On top, spread a layer of yolk: in this way, it will stay intact better than if mixed with the whites in the pan. Cover the yolk with the second part of the mixture so that you fill the shell completely, shaping it to form a dome. Sprinkle with grated Gruyère.

Put the shells on a baking tray and glaze them. (SEE GLAZING SAUCED DISHES, PAGE 15.)

Hard-Boiled Egg Gratinée with Noodles *(Oeufs Durs Gratinés au Noilles).* An old and excellent recipe that can be summarized as follows: eggs, divided into quarters and mixed with a good béchamel sauce that has been enhanced with soubise purée, are placed between two layers of noodles that have been previously cooked in cream. This entire dish is sprinkled with bread crumbs, then put in the oven to form a gratin.

This dish is even more tasty when the noodles are homemade, which of course increases the amount of eggs required. Nonetheless, it is still very successful made with store-bought noodles; for a noodle recipe, see NOODLE DOUGH, PAGE 568. The milk used must be perfect. You can even reduce it—in other words, take a larger quantity than what is required and boil it down to concentrate the milk.

The garnish of noodles described here requires 1 egg per person. *Time: 1 hour.*

250 grams (9 ounces) of noodles; 3 deciliters (1¼ cups) of light cream and 30 grams (1 ounce, 2 tablespoons) of butter to cook them; 6 eggs; 1½ tablespoons of good white bread crumbs and 30 grams (1 ounce, 2 tablespoons) of butter for the gratin.

***For the sauce:* 125 grams (4½ ounces) of onion that has been finely minced and 30 grams (1 ounce, 2 tablespoons) of butter in which to sauté it; 15 grams (½ ounce) of flour for a white roux; 3 deciliters (1¼ cups) of very good milk, boiled; salt, white pepper, grated nutmeg, and a small bunch of parsley; 20 grams (⅔ ounce, 1 heaping tablespoon) of butter to finish the dish.**

PROCEDURE. **The sauce:** In a small pan, *gently* sauté the onion with the butter without allowing it to color in the slightest, for *10–12 minutes.* Sprinkle with flour; cook 2 minutes, dilute with the boiled milk, season it, and bring it to a boil while stirring constantly. Then let it simmer *gently for 35 minutes.*

The noodles: Plunge them into a pot of boiling, salted water. Let them boil for *exactly 5 minutes.*

Meanwhile, boil the cream in a medium-sized sauté pan. Add the warm noodles, well drained, then season with salt, pepper, and nutmeg. Add the butter, divided into little bits; cover; let it boil very gently, until the noodles absorb all the cream and stick together, with the result that there is *no liquid whatsoever at the moment they are served on the plate.*

The eggs: Cook them for 15 minutes before preparing the dish. After shelling, keep them in warm water until you put them in the sauce.

Strain the sauce through a chinois into a sauté pan, stirring it so that you push through a little bit of the onion. Return to the heat and bring it to a boil. Turn the heat down very low to add the rest of the butter and the eggs, cut into quarters. Keep it warm without boiling.

To serve: Copiously butter the entire inner surface of an ovenproof dish: bowl, baking dish, vegetable dish, etc. Arrange half of the noodles in a kind of a nest.

In the middle, place the eggs and the sauce. Cover with the remaining noodles: you should now have a flat surface. Sprinkle with the bread crumbs. Drizzle with the melted butter.

Immediately put it into an oven that is sufficiently hot, if you don't have a broiler, to brown the surface of the noodles in *5–6 minutes.* If the dish stays any longer in the oven, the inside will dry out. Serve as soon as a gratin has formed.

Eggs à la Tripe *(Oeufs à la Tripe).* A very old recipe, this preparation is extremely simple and can be described as follows: rounds of hard-boiled egg, to which you add a large amount of onion slices, are served in the milk sauce known as "béchamel." This is the classic recipe—as far as the sauce goes, at least—and is the one we give here. Previously, the sauce could be made with bouillon or even wine; and instead of cooking the onions in a way that keeps them white, they were frequently browned.

To cut the onions as required, you must use rather good-sized onions. This is a very important condition; so, use onions weighing an average of about 100 grams (3½ ounces). Blanching the onion before sautéing is necessary as the season progresses. Not only is the cooking made easier but, above all, the onion is thus freed of its sharpness, which is very pronounced when it has fully matured.

Allow 1½ eggs per person for this kind of dish. For the sauce, we are giving the simplest recipe possible in this circumstance. That is, instead of adding the sautéed onion to a béchamel that has been already prepared, the two operations are carried out in the same pan. *Time: 1 hour. Serves 6.*

9 eggs; 3 nice, medium-sized onions (total of 300 grams, 10½ ounces); 100 grams (3½ ounces, 7 tablespoons) of butter, 30 grams (1 ounce) of flour; ½ liter

(generous 2 cups) of boiled milk; a bunch of parsley sprigs; salt, pepper, nutmeg.

PROCEDURE. **The onions.** If these need blanching, have a pan with 1½ liters (6⅓ cups) of salted boiling water ready (15 grams, ½ ounce of salt). Cut the onions, once peeled, in half, in the same direction as the stem; put the flat cut side on the work surface. With a good kitchen knife, cut off a slice about ½ centimeter (3/16 inch) thick at each end, because the shoot and the root both retain a great deal of sharpness. Then cut the onion into thin and even slices that are never larger than 2 millimeters (1/16 inch) thick.

If you must blanch them, immediately put them into the boiling water. Boil them over high heat for *8–10 minutes;* drain and cool them; then spread them out on a dry towel to remove all moisture before sautéing them.

In a sauté pan, heat three-quarters of the butter without allowing it to take on the slightest color; add the onions. Stir them with a wooden spoon for *5 minutes* to evaporate all excess moisture. Then cover the pan and let them cook in the butter over low heat for *15–20 minutes* without the slightest trace of browning. Stir them from time to time.

The eggs: Cook them hard-boiled, as directed. After shelling, put them into any kind of receptacle containing lightly salted warm water.

The sauce: When the onions are sautéed and have absorbed the butter well, sprinkle them with flour. Let them cook over low heat for *4–5 minutes,* stirring and taking care that they do not color. Stirring all the time, add little by little: milk, cold or warm, salt, pepper, nutmeg. Stir until it boils. Add the bunch of parsley and keep the sauce at a very gentle simmer *for 15–20 minutes.* Do not cover.

To serve: Pat the eggs dry. Slice them in rounds a good centimeter (3/8 inch) thick. Put them into the sauce from which you have removed the bunch of parsley. Shake the pan to mix everything, without stirring with the spoon. Let it simmer for *2–3 minutes.*

Just before you are ready to serve, add, off the heat, the rest of the butter, divided into very small bits. Shake the pan again to mix and melt the butter. Check the seasoning. Pour into a preheated serving dish or vegetable dish.

STUFFED EGGS
Oeufs Farcis

This dish is a universal favorite, and it has the added benefit of being very useful for those little bits of leftovers of meat, fowl, fish, and others. The egg is cut in half, but when it's stuffed, it looks like two eggs. One can thus allow only one egg per person or, according to the menu or appetite, maybe an egg and a half per person.

Generally speaking, the eggs are put into the oven only moments before serving, which serves to reheat them and form a light gratin on the surface. It is therefore necessary to watch the oven heat carefully. If the eggs are left for too long in an oven that is not hot enough, everything will dry out without browning. On the other hand, if the oven is too hot, the surface of the dish will burn before the inside has warmed.

When you brown under the broiler, which is always the most recommended way, do not turn the heat up too high at the beginning because the bottom of the dish does not heat directly and needs time to warm through at the same time that the top browns.

Main Preparations

Stuffed Eggs à l'Aurore *(Oeufs Farcis à l'Aurore).* A savory and decorative method; even though complicated in appearance, the preparation remains quite simple because béchamel sauce is used for all the steps. A small portion of béchamel goes into the stuffing, two-thirds of the béchamel mixed with Gruyère becomes the Mornay sauce, and the remaining third, mixed with tomato, becomes the aurore sauce.

The preparation can be described as follows: the egg yolks, except the third reserved for decoration, are crushed with butter and minced fresh herbs. A little bit of béchamel is added to make it light, bind it, and help it to rise when gratinéed. Once stuffed, the eggs are placed in a baking dish, covered with a layer of Mornay sauce, and gratinéed. Next, they are sprinkled with minced egg yolk and surrounded by a ribbon of sauce aurore. *Time: 45 minutes.*

6 eggs; 3 good deciliters (1¼ cups) of sauce béchamel, for which: a roux blanc, made with 15 grams

(1/2 ounce, 1 tablespoon) of butter and 15 grams (1/2 ounce) of flour; 3 deciliters (1 1/4 cups) of milk, a pinch of salt, a touch of nutmeg; 50 grams (1 3/4 ounces) of dry Gruyère, grated; 90 grams (3 1/6 ounces, 6 1/3 tablespoons) of butter; a scant tablespoon of tomato concentrate; a tablespoon of parsley, chervil, tarragon, in equal measure, minced.

PROCEDURE. Cook the hard-boiled eggs. Meanwhile, prepare the sauce in a small pan (SEE SAUCE BÉCHAMEL, PAGE 52). Once it begins to boil, lower the heat to a gentle simmer. After 5–6 minutes, transfer 2 tablespoons of the sauce to a plate, which must be just slightly warm the moment it is used with the yolks.

In a mortar—or if you do not have one, in a bowl—place the egg yolks, cut in half lengthwise; set aside 2 of the yolks to decorate the plate. Add 40 grams (1 1/2 ounces, 3 tablespoons) of butter to the mortar, a pinch of salt and a pinch of pepper, and ground nutmeg. Crush and mix. Then add the minced herbs and the 2 tablespoons of reserved sauce; crush more to obtain a perfectly smooth paste. Fill the egg white halves with this mixture: either with the help of a small spoon or by putting the stuffing in a large paper cornet with an opening snipped at the end, much like a pastry bag. The stuffing must cover the edges and be slightly domed; smooth the stuffing with the blade of a knife.

Put two-thirds of the béchamel sauce into a small pan. Add a good tablespoon of grated Gruyère; give it a few seconds to boil while you are stirring it so that it mixes and melts. Turn off the heat and finish it with 25 grams (1 ounce, 2 tablespoons) of butter. Spread this sauce in a baking dish. Arrange the egg halves one next to the other on top of the sauce. Sprinkle everything with the rest of the cheese. Melt about 15 grams (1/2 ounce, 1 tablespoon) of butter—taken from the rest of the butter—and distribute it on the eggs *only.* (Prepared thus, the dish easily can wait a half hour before being put into the oven.) *About 7–8 minutes before serving,* put the dish in a very warm oven or under the broiler.

Meanwhile, mix the tomato with the rest of the béchamel that has been kept warm in its pan; off the heat, add the little bit of remaining butter.

Finely mince the yolks using a large kitchen knife.

To serve: When you take the dish out of the oven, sprinkle the surface with the minced egg yolks, using a card, so that you do not squash them. A tablespoon at a time, drizzle the aurore sauce in a small ribbon around the eggs. Serve immediately.

Stuffed Eggs with Mushrooms *(Oeufs Farcis à la Chimay).* The dish can be described thus: eggs are stuffed with a mixture of their own yolks, minced mushrooms and onion, or duxelles, covered with a Mornay sauce, and glazed in a hot oven or under the broiler. Sometimes, instead of Mornay sauce, you can use a layer of béchamel to cover not the eggs, but the bottom of the dish in which they are to be cooked, without sauce, and then browned. In any case, the quantities remain the same. For the sauce, see the recipes for Mornay sauce or béchamel, as you prefer. *Time: 45 minutes.*

6 eggs; 15 grams (1/2 ounce, 1 tablespoon) of butter and 1 tablespoon of oil; 25 grams (1 ounce) of onion and 15 grams (1/2 ounce) of shallot, minced fine; 100 grams (3 1/2 ounces) of mushrooms, for which you can use the whole mushroom—peelings and stems; 1 teaspoon of minced parsley; 1/2 tablespoon of tomato concentrate ; 4 deciliters (1 3/4 cups) of sauce Mornay or béchamel.

PROCEDURE. Cook the hard-boiled eggs. In a small sauté pan, heat the butter and the oil; add the minced onion and shallot. Over moderate heat, mix it with a wooden spoon for several minutes, *without letting it color in the slightest.* Then add the mushrooms, minced; over high heat, stir rapidly to evaporate the liquid. Then add tomato, minced parsley, salt, pepper; stir and mix for 1 minute and remove from the heat. Cut the eggs in half lengthwise. Put the yolks in a small bowl; crush them to a fine paste with the puréed mushrooms. Mix in the minced ingredients. Grind everything together for another minute.

Fill the eggs to overflowing with this mixture, then smooth out into a dome shape with the help of the moistened blade of a large knife. The eggs can be prepared up to this point well in advance and wait on the kitchen table until ready for the sauce. If they are to be served with a Mornay sauce, you should put the eggs, as you stuff them, into a buttered baking dish.

About 6–7 minutes before serving, cover the eggs with the Mornay sauce, pouring it over them with a soupspoon. Sprinkle with grated Gruyère and put the dish into a hot oven to glaze rapidly. SEE GLAZING SAUCED DISHES, PAGE 15.

If the eggs are topped with a layer of béchamel sauce, see the directions given here for Stuffed Eggs with Fish.

Stuffed Eggs with Fish *(Oeufs Farcis au Poisson).* An excellent use for leftover cod or bream. You can even cook a little bit of cod especially for this dish. *Time: 45 minutes.*

6 eggs; 125 grams (4 1/2 ounces) of cooked cod, net weight, with all skin and bones removed; 2 level tablespoons of grated Gruyère, and 1 level tablespoon of fine white bread crumbs; 1 tablespoon of melted butter; 3 deciliters (1 1/4 cups) of béchamel sauce, thus: 15 grams (1/2 ounce, 1 tablespoon) of butter and the same of flour for the roux; 40 grams (1 3/8 ounces) of minced onion; 3 good deciliters (1 1/4 cups) of milk; a small bunch of parsley; salt, pepper, nutmeg.

PROCEDURE. Start the sauce (SEE SAUCE BÉCHAMEL, PAGE 52). Allow 20 minutes to simmer, during which time you can cook the eggs and prepare the cod, dividing it into small pieces.

To stuff the eggs: Cut them in half lengthwise. Remove the yolks and put them into a small container. With the tip of a small knife, cut some of the white from the inside of the egg halves, at the large end, to create little oval boxes with sides of equal thickness. Mince the white trimmings and add them to the yolks. Add the cod and a good half of the sauce. Mix everything well. Before stuffing the eggs, prepare the dish in which you will place them: a shallow dish that can go from the oven to the table. Spread the remainder of the sauce over the bottom of the dish.

In each egg half, put a good tablespoon of the filling mixture. With the blade of a knife, smooth out to form a dome shape so that the egg half gives the appearance of a whole egg. As each egg half is garnished, place it next to the others in the prepared dish. Sprinkle the surface of the eggs with the mixture of cheese and bread crumbs, then drizzle it with the melted butter.

Up to this point, the dish can be prepared 20–30 minutes before it is put in the oven to form a gratin.

To form the gratin: *About 5–6 minutes* should be enough in a very warm oven, or preferably, under a broiler, to obtain a light golden crust on the eggs, beneath which the stuffing remains quite moist and without the layer of sauce in any way sticking to the bottom of the dish. To achieve this, the dish must be placed on a cold brick or some other insulating device if the oven is very warm.

Stuffed Eggs with Cheese *(Oeufs Farcis Gratinés au Fromage).* A simple and attractive preparation. *Time: 30 minutes.*

6 large eggs; 75 grams (2 2/3 ounces) of half Gruyère and half Parmesan, grated; 4 tablespoons of cream, or of a good milk that has been reduced; 2 large egg yolks, raw, or 3 small ones; salt, pepper, grated nutmeg.

For the sauce: 20 grams (2/3 ounce) of flour and the same of butter (1 heaping tablespoon) for the roux; 3 deciliters (1 1/4 cups) of boiled milk; salt, pepper; 20 grams (2/3 ounce, 1 heaping tablespoon) of butter to finish.

PROCEDURE. Cook the hard-boiled eggs; shell them and cut them in half lengthwise. With the handle of a small spoon, pry out the yolk into a bowl. Completely crush the yolks using a wooden spoon. Then add 1 of the uncooked egg yolks and *all but 2 tablespoons* of the grated cheese. Finally, add the cream or the reduced milk, and work the whole thing with the spoon, stirring and beating to obtain a light and creamy paste.

Fill the egg white halves with this mixture, which must fill them completely and be slightly dome shaped. Smooth the surface with the blade of a knife and sprinkle with the reserved cheese. One by one, place the stuffed eggs on a baking sheet or gratin dish. Set aside.

Prepare the sauce, one of the fastest to cook: a little *roux blanc* (SEE PAGE 47) diluted with the milk; 5–6 minutes to boil; then the remaining butter is dotted *on top of* the sauce while it's waiting.

Five minutes before serving, slide the sheet loaded with eggs either into a *very warm* oven, toward the top near the heat source; or underneath the broiler, which is preferable. They will warm through at the same time as they brown. Do not go beyond *3–4 minutes;* otherwise the stuffing will dry out and all of your previous work will be wasted.

Quickly slide the eggs onto a serving platter. Whisk the sauce once or twice and, spoonful by spoonful, pour it around the eggs.

Deep-Fried Stuffed Eggs *(Oeufs Farcis Frits).* In this dish, the eggs are mounded with stuffing so that each egg half appears to be a complete egg, and then is covered with bread crumbs and, finally, plunged into a large quantity of hot oil, like croquettes; the egg is warmed through and the crust is formed at the same time. Refer to the directions in the section about frying breaded objects (SEE FRYING, PAGE 41).

The eggs can be stuffed well in advance so that to serve them you have only to coat them in bread crumbs and fry them. At any rate, when you come to coat them with bread crumbs, the stuffing must be thoroughly cooled.

Deep-Fried Eggs Stuffed with Mushrooms and Ham, Home-Style *(Oeufs Farcis Frits à la Ménagère).* If you like, you can accompany this with a tomato sauce. *Time: 1 hour for preparation, 7–8 minutes to cook the eggs.*

100 grams (3$^1/_2$ ounces) veal or chicken, cooked; 30 grams (1 ounce) of ham; 6 eggs; 60 grams (2$^1/_4$ ounces) of mushrooms; 1$^1/_2$ deciliters (5 fluid ounces, $^2/_3$ cup) of sauce as a thickener, made from: a little roux with 15 grams ($^1/_2$ ounce, 1 tablespoon) of butter and 12–15 grams ($^3/_8$–$^1/_2$ ounce) of flour; 2 deciliters (6$^3/_4$ fluid ounces, $^7/_8$ cup) of good bouillon or of a good boiled milk; 20 grams ($^2/_3$ ounce, 1 heaping tablespoon) of butter to finish.

To bread the eggs **(SEE ENGLISH-STYLE BREADING PAGE 19): 150 grams (5$^1/_3$ ounces) of stale white bread crumbs; 1 large egg or 2 small ones; 1 teaspoon of oil.**

PROCEDURE. Start the sauce cooking in a small pan. Make a roux and let it lightly color, then dilute it with bouillon or milk. If you do use milk, the sauce will gain a great deal of flavor if you first infuse the milk with a little bit of onion or the white part of a leek (SEE SAUCE BÉCHAMEL, PAGE 52). Season, add a small bunch of parsley sprigs; let it simmer very gently for a scant half hour.

Cook the hard-boiled eggs. Let cool, then shell and cut in half lengthwise. With the handle of a small teaspoon, pry out the yolks onto a plate and keep the white on another plate.

Cook the mushrooms without peeling them, with water, salt, lemon juice, etc. (SEE MUSHROOMS, PAGE 490). Let them cool in their liquid; then add them to the sauce.

Mince the meat and ham, not too finely, but in equal sized bits. Similarly, mince the mushrooms and the egg yolks.

Check to make sure that the sauce, which has been simmering, has sufficiently reduced to the indicated quantity, and thus become very thick: it should be more of a mush than a sauce. Strain through a chinois into a small bowl, scraping it with the back of the spoon to help push it through. Immediately add the final butter, the meat, mushrooms, and minced yolks. Stir so that all the different elements are perfectly bound by the sauce.

Check the seasoning, which should be rather spicy. If you like, you can add a point of cayenne (as much as can be held on the tip of a small knife).

Let the stuffing cook a bit; then, with a small spoon, fill each egg white half; be sure to fill the halves completely, to the edges, and mound up the stuffing so that it looks like a whole egg. Smooth the surface using a large kitchen knife, first moistening the blade with water.

Line the eggs up on a plate and allow them to *cool completely.* This gives them the necessary solidity to hold together while being breaded and to withstand the heat of deep-frying.

Bread them, and as they are breaded, arrange them on a large overturned pot lid or another flat surface from which you can easily slide them into the boiling oil.

Seven minutes before serving, plunge the eggs into the hot oil—that is, it should be smoking slightly (SEE FRYING, PAGE 40). Once they have acquired a beautiful golden color, drain them on a towel, sprinkle them lightly with salt, and arrange them on a serving plate lined with a cloth. Decorate with fried parsley if not serving with a sauce.

Stuffed Deep-Fried Eggs with Anchovies *(Oeufs Farcis Frits aux Anchois).* The procedures are the same as those above. The only difference is the preparation of the stuffing. For 6 eggs, allow 8 salted anchovies, 50 grams ($1^3/_4$ ounces) of stale white bread crumbs soaked in $1^1/_2$ deciliters (5 fluid ounces, $^2/_3$ cup) of milk; 50 grams ($1^3/_4$ ounces, $3^1/_2$ tablespoons) of butter; a level soupspoon of finely chopped parsley with a little bit of scallion.

Halve the eggs. In a small bowl, combine: the yolks; the butter; the bread, squeezed to extract the extra milk; and the anchovies, rinsed and with their bones removed. Crush and mix everything; force through a metallic drum sieve *(tamis)* to obtain a homogenous and very smooth purée. Add the parsley and scallion, previously sautéed briefly in butter over low heat. Pepper lightly. Stuff the eggs. Coat in bread crumbs and fry them.

SCRAMBLED EGGS
Oeufs Brouillés

This is the most delicate and refined preparation for eggs, regardless of the garnish that accompanies them. It would also seem to be the simplest, but like many things that are thought to be simple, it calls for extreme care to succeed: in other words, you must obtain a mass that is creamy and smooth, where the yolks and the whites mingle intimately, with sufficient consistency to be taken up on the fork, but no more.

This "no more" represents one of the difficulties of preparing this dish, as you will see by the following; if you go past this point, even eggs that have been cooked properly become dry and lumpy, no matter how creamy they were; this is because once they are removed from the heat, their own residual heat is enough to overcook them. Also, you must take great care, because if the eggs cannot be served as soon as they are cooked, they can wait for only a very short time.

The need for a cooking procedure that is very gentle, very gradual and even is such that, in earlier days, a double boiler was normally used to make scrambled eggs. This method, which has many advantages, is really quite inconvenient because it requires too much time. These days, we generally prefer to cook it directly over the heat.

When cooking with direct heat, it is absolutely vital to use a *thick-bottomed pan,* so the heat is obtained gradually. Also, the bottom of the pan must be completely smooth, because the eggs will stick to any dents or cavities. You must never, ever, use a thin-bottomed pan because the egg, in contact with the thin bottom, will be seized by the heat that cannot be controlled, and it will become lumpy. If you do not have a thick-bottomed pan, you must, without question, cook the eggs in a double boiler.

FIG. 32. SAUTE PAN.

Use a frying pan; its slanting sides and softer angle makes the operation much easier than a sauté pan. If you do not have a frying pan, a sauté pan is preferable to a pan with high sides: what is, in fact, important is that the bottom of the utensil has a large surface area so that the gentle heat is dispersed over the largest surface of egg all at once. If the egg is too deep in a high-sided utensil, the part in contact with the bottom heats up too much, while the top layer does not heat up enough, and even stirring it with the spoon or a whisk to move the eggs around cannot restore the balance.

Another condition for success: *the perfect mixture of white and yolk,* which must be achieved before they are cooked; and this must occur without creating any foam, because this foam will be transformed into lumps during cooking.

The methods to obtain a perfect mixture vary with trends and individuals. Some proceed by breaking the eggs directly into a buttered pan, then beating them. Others beat the eggs first in a bowl, like an omelet. Finally, others, and these are the most modern, beat the eggs in a bowl first and then strain them through a chinois into the pan; or, they don't beat them at all, and instead strain them through a fine cloth, twisted at both ends, right above the pan. The goal of straining the eggs is twofold: it binds the eggs at the same time as it eliminates the stringy bits of the eggs and any pieces of shell. It is irrefutable that *straining them through a chinois is useful* because afterward you will find the bits and foamy residue in the bottom of the chinois, and these spoil the purity of the eggs. So you should use this procedure, seeing as it's really quite simple.

The amount of butter is also important: it is not only flavor that you must consider here, but equally the influence of the fat on the eggs during cooking. *You must allow 10–15 grams (1/3–1/2 ounce, about 1 tablespoon) of butter per egg.*

The final addition of a little raw cream, or, lacking that, good-quality milk, is suggested, not only because the cream gives the dish a certain finesse, but also because it helps the eggs to stop cooking at the desired point. So: *2 tablespoons for 6 eggs.*

Should a whisk or a wooden spoon be used to mix the eggs as they cook? Opinions on this are divided, and the choice of one or other utensil depends most of all on how it is used.

A whisk should not be considered here except from the point of view that it makes it easy to simultaneously and quickly reach all the parts of the pan better than a spoon. But its whisking action must not be used, because that will form a mousse. And as we have previously said, that must be carefully avoided. So, you must determine clearly—before using the whisk—the style and method with which it will be used. Particularly at the beginning of the operation, it must be used like a spoon, which must be scraped across the bottom and into the angles of the pan. It should not be used as a whisk until much later, if it is needed to mix or to break up some parts that are more cooked than the others.

When you use a wooden spoon, you must choose one with a very large head that is squared on the end, so that its action will be rapid and decisive on the bottom of the pan.

PROCEDURE. *For 12 eggs, the necessary time for this operation is a half hour.* Butter the pan by spreading out the butter over the bottom and the sides using your fingers. Use *half* the butter in the recipe.

Break the eggs into a bowl. Season them with salt and pepper. Beat them rapidly with a fork or a small whisk, just to the point where the whites and yolks are perfectly mixed and you cannot see any mucous parts.

Strain the eggs through the chinois into the buttered pan. Add the other half of the butter, divided into little bits. The pan is thus completely ready to be set over the heat when you are ready.

NOTE. Some people, instead of putting the other half of the butter into the eggs immediately, prefer to keep it to one side and add it gradually during cooking; this is useful for slowing down the cooking process when excess heat poses a danger. Others, having very copiously buttered the pan, add the butter only when the cooking is complete, after the pan has been removed from the heat. All of this is optional. We indicate here the most contemporary procedure.

To scramble the eggs: Put the pan over very low heat to avoid the eggs seizing.

Stir the eggs immediately, without stopping for one second, scraping the bottom of the pan with your wooden spoon or whisk so that you are constantly moving the cooked bits of egg into the parts that are still liquid.

As soon as you perceive a light thickening of the eggs, take the pan off the heat, *stirring constantly.* From this point, the cooking completes itself, as it were, without the heat of the stove, using only the heat retained by the pan and the eggs. Continue to stir until the eggs obtain the consistency described in the beginning of this section. This is the moment to add the cream.

If, when you take the eggs off the heat, you realize that you have just gone past the point of perfect cooking and the eggs risk hardening, you should then rapidly plunge the bottom of the pan into a little bit of cool water, just for a minute, to stop the cooking process.

To serve: Because of the soft consistency of scrambled eggs, they are served in a shallow dish or a vegetable dish that has been previously heated and kept at the ready. But you must be careful not to heat this utensil to the point where it is burning hot, because the eggs will start to cook again. For this reason, you should not put it into the oven, but simply fill it with very hot water and then dry it thoroughly.

If the eggs must stand for a few moments, which is always regrettable, you must then keep the serving dish in a double boiler full of water that is a little bit more than lukewarm.

Main Preparations

As with omelets, to which we will soon come, scrambled eggs can be served in many ways and with a number of garnishes for variety. Depending on the circumstances, the garnish is either placed on top of the eggs or mixed with them; but for the latter, the mixture takes place only *after the eggs have been cooked* and just before putting them into the serving dish.

In restaurants, where there are always sauces ready, scrambled eggs are often finished with a ribbon of a very reduced and thick sauce: demi-glace or brown sauce, a thickened *jus de veau,* soubise, béchamel, tomato, etc., depending on the garnish.

Let us also mention the decorations made with boiled ham or tongue, cut into rounds with a pastry cutter, or into rectangles, which you can place right on top of the eggs or not. Equally, it is worth mentioning scrambled eggs served in large pastry shells, which are cooked *à blanc,* without other fillings, and used as edible containers. Remember to put them in the oven for a while so that they are good and warm when you put the eggs in them for serving.

Depending on the quantity and the type of garnish, as well as the size of the eggs, you should allow about 1 1/2 eggs per person, or you could also allow 2 eggs per person.

Scrambled Eggs with Croutons *(Oeufs Brouillés aux Croûtons).* SEE OMELETS, PAGE 152. Mix the croutons with the eggs that have already been scrambled.

Scrambled Eggs with Mushrooms *(Oeufs Brouillés aux Champignons).* SEE OMELETS, PAGE 152. Add sautéed mushrooms to the scrambled eggs.

Scrambled Eggs with Fresh Herbs *(Oeufs Brouillés aux Fines Herbes).* *For 6 eggs:* 2 shallots and 3–4 mushrooms or mushroom peelings, minced and quickly sautéed in butter or oil; add a good pinch of minced parsley and mix everything with the eggs *before* scrambling them.

Scrambled Eggs with Asparagus Tips *(Oeufs Brouillés aux Pointes d'Asperges).* SEE ASPARAGUS FOR GARNISH, PAGE 479. Thoroughly drain the asparagus after cooking. Mix them gently with the already scrambled eggs using a wooden spoon. Transfer them to a plate and surround them with croutons fried in butter. Allow 225 grams (8 ounces) of asparagus for 8 eggs.

Alternatively: combine the asparagus with butter, just as when serving them à la maître d'hôtel. Pour the scrambled eggs into the serving dish and arrange the asparagus in a pile in the middle of the eggs.

Scrambled Eggs with Cheese *(Oeufs Brouillés aux Fromage).* Grated Gruyère, 10 grams (1/4 ounce) for each egg, added to the scrambled eggs at the end of cooking. Do not forget to add a point of grated nutmeg (as much as can be held on the tip of a small knife) at the beginning. You can, if you like, place croutons fried in butter on the eggs: you can cut them in cubes or in rectangles.

Scrambled Eggs with Tomato and Kidneys *(Oeufs Brouillés à la d'Aumale).* This is a classic dish: it's simply a garnish of kidneys, arranged on top of the eggs, to which you add, while cooking, some concentrated tomato sauce.

For 6 people, allow 9 eggs and about 200 grams (7 ounces) of veal kidney, or, lacking that, 4 sheep's kidneys. For their preparation, consult OMELET WITH KIDNEYS, PAGE 156.

Once the kidney is cooked, keep it warm and cook the scrambled eggs, adding 2 tablespoons of very reduced tomato sauce as the eggs thicken. Pour this into the serving dish. With a spoon, make a well in the middle of the scrambled eggs for the kidneys; or, simply pile them up on top of the eggs. Sprinkle the kidneys only with minced parsley.

Scrambled Eggs with Eggplant and Tomatoes *(Oeufs Brouillés aux Aubergines et Tomates).* Prepare the tomatoes as for a fondue (SEE TOMATOES, PAGE 534): 1 large tomato or 2 medium-sized ones for 6 eggs. Cut 2 small eggplants, without peeling them, into rounds 1/2 centimeter (3/16 inch) thick. Dredge them in flour and fry them as directed. SEE NEAPOLITAN-STYLE EGGPLANT, PAGE 480.

Scramble the eggs. Transfer them to a serving dish; smooth the surface with the back of a spoon.

Make a little well in the middle and fill it with the tomato fondue. Surround it with the rounds of eggplant, which should be both dry and crisp.

Scrambled Eggs with Cheese, Mustard, and Herbs *(Oeufs Brouillés Magda).* An original dish, and one of the most straightforward. Scramble the eggs as directed. At the last moment, add, for 6 eggs, 30 grams (1 ounce) of good freshly grated Gruyère. Continue to stir, over the heat, until it is completely melted and thoroughly blended. Immediately remove from the heat and add 2 teaspoons of mixed fresh herbs that have been minced, and 2 teaspoons of good mustard. Mix everything well with your wooden spoon. Pour it into the serving dish and surround it with small croutons cut into triangles or rectangles and fried in butter.

Scrambled Eggs with Truffles *(Oeufs Brouillés aux Truffes).* In fine restaurants, truffles are cut into small cubes and mixed with eggs that have already been scrambled. Then, truffle slices that have been glazed with some *jus de viande* are arranged on top of the eggs already in the serving dish.

Things are done much more simply in home kitchens: fresh truffle, cut into small cubes or in a julienne, or just very well minced, is added to the eggs that have been beaten and strained through the *tamis;* it cooks at the same time as the eggs.

There is another method that is common in southern regions: in the sauté pan, heat the butter that you would normally use to grease the pan; add the truffle, cut into slices, for 2 minutes; as soon as you detect an aroma, add the eggs to the pan and scramble them as you usually do; finish by adding some heavy cream: a good tablespoon for 6 eggs will help give them a creamy consistency.

We would like to recommend, as we recommend for omelets, a clove of garlic, cut in half, which you can use to rub the utensil where the eggs will be beaten. The garlic, used in this discreet manner, enhances and complements the aroma of the truffle quite well, without being perceived directly. Some of the best regional French authors, and others, including Urbain Dubois, recommend this technique, which has unknown origins.

OMELETS
Omelettes

It would be nice if we had recourse to film here because the most detailed explanations for making an omelet could never match a simple demonstration. There is also an undeniable "tour de main," or technique, which comes from experience, observation, and a certain special and individual dexterity. This is the reason that some cooks, experts at complicated dishes, are often inferior to a humble village innkeeper when it comes to making an omelet.

Nonetheless, there are basic rules that must be observed when making an omelet and it is these that we specify first.

The pan: Its importance is fundamental, regardless of the ability of the cook. Always use a *thick* pan; never, for an omelet, use a *thin* one, where the heat will be too brutal. *The size of the pan depends on the amount of eggs;* in any case, it is best to have a pan that is a little too large, rather than too small, because in a small pan the eggs would be too thick and they would not cook quickly enough, resulting in a compact and heavy omelet. Let us say, for 6 eggs, a pan of 24–25 centimeters (9½–10 inches) in diameter at its top edge.

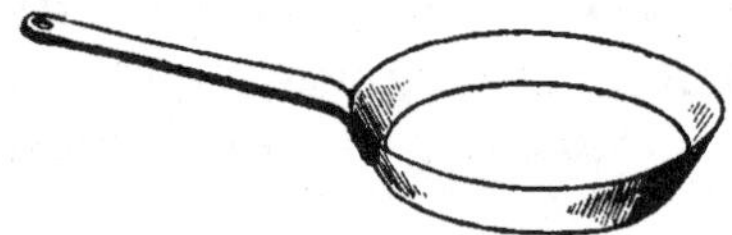

FIG. 33. OMELET PAN.

This pan must be reserved exclusively for omelets. As soon as it has been used, it is simply wiped clean and not washed. The bottom of the pan thus remains sufficiently coated with oil so that it does not oxidize between uses, making it much easier to maintain the pan in the necessary condition: that is to say, absolutely *clean and smooth, because even the smallest rough part can cause an omelet to stick.*

To justify the strictness of these recommendations, you must understand that, if, for example, you sauté some meat or other food in this very pan, some of the juice will stick to the bottom, and you must, of course, wash it off immediately. However, no matter how thorough the cleaning, you always risk leaving some indiscernible little bits, in places where the eggs will stick. If this happens, you must loosen the omelet by sliding a flexible spatula underneath it; but this will inevitably damage the outside of the omelet.

If you must wash this pan, you should scrub it a bit with a fine scouring pad or an emery cloth, or at least rub it with greased paper and a little bit of rock salt; dry it, and always keep it oiled.

The eggs: The most important point is this: *never make a large omelet,* because, unless you have extraordinary dexterity, you will not be able to mix the mass of eggs quickly enough, and the omelet will be heavy and dense. The absolute maximum amount of eggs is nine, and it's better to restrict yourself to 6.

Consequently, when the number of guests requires a larger quantity of eggs—let's say 12 eggs for 6 people—you should prepare 2 omelets of 6 eggs each. And, let us note that two small omelets, made one after the other, scarcely take any more time than making just one large one. In this case, to ensure you have the right quantities, it is best to beat the necessary amount of eggs for each omelet in a separate bowl. You should also melt and clarify all the butter required so that it is always ready throughout the course of your operation.

Beat the eggs with a fork just as you are ready to use them, no sooner; and just to the point where the whites and the yolks are well mixed, without overmixing until foamy: Four or five strokes of the fork, given judiciously, suffice. The eggs should not be broken down too far. Far from making the omelet light, any foam will on the contrary, stop the eggs from solidifying, and its effects will be even more harmful if the eggs have been beaten in advance, because it will return to the surface while the eggs are standing, making it necessary to beat the eggs again to mix them. The result will be more foam and an even greater liquefaction of the eggs.

The butter: For an average sized egg, allow 7–8 grams (1/4 ounce, 2 teaspoons) of butter. This is a good, average quantity, though numerous culinary writers call for at least 10 grams (1/3 ounce, 1 scant tablespoon). Some, like Gouffé, even go as far as 15 grams (1/2 ounce, 1 tablespoon). *[Translator's note: Jules Gouffé, 1807–1877, protégé of Carême, author of several famous cookbooks.]* You could keep a small portion, about one-quarter, broken into very small pieces, to add to the beaten eggs at the same time as the seasoning, which makes the omelet softer. In southern regions of France, and notably for omelets with anchovies, mushrooms, tomatoes, etc., the butter is replaced with good olive oil. People sometimes use half butter and half olive oil.

The milk (or, even better, light cream): This is optional. It brings some lightness to the omelet. The milk must always be *uncooked:* if boiled, it will mix badly with the egg. Allow 2 tablespoons for 6 large eggs.

The heat: For an omelet, it is necessary to get as close as possible to a "strong and lively" fire that was formerly found in country kitchens. This is not the "full blast" of a wood- or coal-fired stove from which the heat is infinitely too powerful and too brutal, unless the power of the flame has been substantially diminished by spreading cinders over the coals. If the plate of the stove is quite hot, you should put the pan on this plate. If you have gas, this is the best heat source for cooking an omelet. Use a large burner in such a way that the entire bottom of the pan is heated equally, with the flame spreading completely over the bottom, a condition of fundamental importance.

PROCEDURE. But, above everything else, is it not appropriate to understand what makes a successful omelet? The terms used to describe this are often unclear and debatable—such as the French *baveuse* ("runny"). *Baveuse,* in the exact sense of the word, describes an omelet in which some parts are extremely cooked, even hard, and others are runny. In essence, it's a badly made omelet. Furthermore, those who vaunt the merits of the *baveuse* omelet are really thinking more of a *creamy* omelet: an omelet that has the consistency of scrambled eggs inside and an exterior that is just solid enough so that it can be rolled on itself. This is the definition of a perfectly cooked omelet.

Making the omelet: Once the eggs are beaten, you will need 2 1/2 minutes at the most to cook a 6-egg omelet.

Beat the eggs as directed. Season them. Add cream or milk, if you like, and the quantity of butter indicated, according to your own taste.

Put the butter in the pan without heating it in advance, because there is a risk that it will burn partially.

The purpose of this butter is to provide a layer of fat that insulates the eggs from direct contact with the pan once they are poured into it. For that, the butter must be *quite hot.* If it is not hot enough, it mixes with the eggs and no longer provides any insulation, causing the eggs to stick. To obtain this even layer of fat, it is extremely important to set the pan on a level surface, quite horizontal, when the eggs are added.

Put the pan containing the butter over the heat and heat it until the butter is just turning blond and begins to smell faintly of hazelnut. Without waiting, because the butter will turn black, in one motion, quickly pour the eggs into the middle of the pan, upon which they will, of themselves, spread out.

With your left hand, immediately grab the handle of the pan, without shaking it, and immediately mix the eggs with the fork that you have in your right hand, scraping around the edges of the pan toward the center, without worrying about the occasional channels made by the passage of the fork. Proceed as for soft-boiled eggs, without stopping, but without brusque movements; at the end of several seconds, gently shake the pan back and forth in a movement that prevents the eggs from sticking.

As soon as the mass of eggs no longer shows any liquid parts and has taken on the consistency of scrambled eggs—somewhat firm but still quite moist—do not stir it any more. Leave it like this for *4–5 seconds* to lightly brown the bottom of the omelet, which will become the outside. Next, proceed quickly to folding or rolling, which is done not on the plate but in the pan.

Folding: The omelet will look a great deal better if it's rolled into thirds rather than simply doubled.

To fold it into thirds, tip the pan by lifting it on the handle side, and give it a good sharp blow so that the omelet slides to the opposite side. Slip your fork under the omelet on the handle side of the pan to draw about one-third of it over itself. Then tip the pan in the opposite direction and give it a sharp blow, which will make it slide toward the side of the handle. This is how professionals do it. If you don't succeed in getting it to slide over itself, use a fork as you did on the first side.

Take the handle of the pan with your right hand and the serving plate with your left. Place the edge of the pan on the plate and turn the omelet over onto the plate so that the top becomes the bottom. If you need to, adjust the shape with the back of the fork. Quickly take a small bit of butter on the fork and rub it over the surface of the omelet to give it a little shine. Serve immediately.

Various Omelets

The variety of omelets is infinite, considering that every kind of different ingredient can be added. These ingredients, previously cooked, are either put directly into the beaten eggs, which makes a *simple omelet,* or, added to the omelet before folding it over in the pan. This is called "filling" the omelet.

You could, for a filled omelet, reserve a tablespoon of its filling, and add it, as a kind of decoration, on top of the omelet before serving. Or, arrange it in a pyramid in the middle of the folded omelet, or place it in a small pocket made into the middle of the omelet.

Enhance a stuffed omelet by surrounding it with a ribbon of sauce that goes with the filling. Brown sauce, béchamel, tomato sauce, and cream sauce are frequently used for this purpose: 1 deciliter ($3^1/_3$ fluid ounces, scant $^1/_2$ cup) for a 6-egg omelet. On the other hand, omelets are ideal for using up leftovers: potatoes, artichoke bottoms, Jerusalem artichokes, etc., which you cut into small cubes and lightly brown in the pan before pouring in the beaten eggs. You can also add a little bit of leftover spinach, sorrel, chickory, green peas, green beans, etc. Or, if you prefer the stuffed omelet, these same ingredients can be mixed with a little béchamel or tomato sauce.

Note the procedure, which consists of rubbing a cut clove of garlic around the receptacle in which the eggs will be beaten. This is particularly recommended for truffle omelets, mushroom omelets, tomato omelets, artichoke bottoms, eggplant, etc.

We list the most popular omelets. *The quantity*

of ingredients in each omelet applies to a 6-egg omelet. Allow 2 eggs per person for a simple omelet, and $1^1/_2$ eggs for an omelet that has been garnished with bacon, croutons, kidneys, etc.

Plain Omelet *(Omelette au Naturel).* This consists of eggs seasoned only with salt and pepper, and, if possible, with a little cream added. So: 6 eggs, 2 tablespoons of cream, and 50 grams ($1^3/_4$ ounces, $3^1/_2$ tablespoons) of butter total. Proceed as directed to make the omelet (SEE PAGE 152).

Omelet with Fresh Herbs *(Omelette aux Fines Herbes).* Add to the beaten eggs 2 tablespoons of parsley, chervil, and chives, which have been finely minced. Proceed as directed to make the omelet (SEE PAGE 152).

Omelet with Croutons *(Omelette aux Croûtons).* Use 4 tablespoons of very small croutons cut into cubes, browned in a pan with 30 grams (1 ounce, 2 tablespoons) of butter (SEE FRIED CROUTONS, PAGE 20). Add them to the beaten eggs just as you put them into the pan. Proceed as for the omelet au naturel.

Potato Omelet *(Omelette Parmentier).* The croutons of bread are replaced by the same amount of small-diced potato (SEE POTATO CROUTONS, PAGE 20), added at the last moment to the beaten eggs. Proceed as directed to make the omelet (SEE PAGE 152).

Cheese Omelet *(Omelette au Fromage).* Cut 60 grams ($2^1/_4$ ounces) of Gruyère into very small cubes, and add the same amount of grated Parmesan. Mix the grated Parmesan into the beaten eggs. Accentuate it with a note of pepper. Make the omelet, and when it is almost ready, add the Gruyère. You can finish this with a ribbon of tomato sauce.

Bacon Omelet *(Omelette au Lard).* Blanch 100 grams ($3^1/_2$ ounces) of excellent lean bacon, rind trimmed, cut into 1-centimeter ($^3/_8$-inch) cubes; drain them on a towel. Heat 50 grams ($1^3/_4$ ounces, $3^1/_2$ tablespoons) of butter in the pan. Sauté the bacon until it is lightly browned. Pour the beaten eggs onto the bacon. Make the omelet as directed.

Ham Omelet *(Omelette au Jambon).* Cut 100 grams ($3^1/_2$ ounces) of cooked lean ham into small cubes. Add them to the beaten eggs. Add very little salt and pepper. Make the omelet as directed.

Onion Omelet *(Omelette aux Oignons).* Cut 75 grams ($2^2/_3$ ounces) of onion into thin slices, lightly brown in the pan with 30 grams (1 ounce, 2 tablespoons) of butter. Add more butter as necessary. Pour in the beaten eggs and make the omelet as directed (SEE PAGE 152).

Browned onions, with a little bit of minced parsley, added to the beaten eggs is called *à la lyonnaise.* You can also make this dish with the onions stewed in butter without browning and thereafter beaten in with the eggs. This is then called an *omelet à la bretonne.*

Mushroom Omelet *(Omelette aux Champignons).* Thinly slice 75 grams ($2^2/_3$ ounces) of raw mushrooms, sauté in the pan with 30 grams (1 ounce, 2 tablespoons) of good hot butter, until all moisture has been evaporated. Then, heat the usual quantity of butter in the pan. Add the beaten eggs and proceed as directed for omelets (SEE PAGE 152).

Omelet with Asparagus Tips *(Omelette aux Points d'Asperges).* Use a small bunch of asparagus. Cut and cook them as directed (SEE GREEN ASPARAGUS FOR GARNISH, PAGE 479). Drain them well on a towel before adding them to the beaten eggs. Make the omelet in the usual way.

Alternatively, mix the cooked asparagus with 30 grams (1 ounce, 2 tablespoons) of butter (SEE VEGETABLES À L'ANGLAISE, PAGE 470). Make the omelet, put the asparagus on the top, and roll it. Now it's a *stuffed* omelet, and you can surround it with a rope of cream sauce.

You can also keep the asparagus tips aside to put them in a sort of bouquet on the omelet. Once the omelet is arranged on the plate, you should make a little pocket in it for this.

Sorrel Omelet *(Omelette à l'Oseille).* In the rustic fashion, you first soften and melt the sorrel with butter in the pan. Cut the sorrel leaves into thin ribbons. Then add the beaten eggs and make the omelet in a customary manner.

For a less rustic preparation, fill the omelet with 2 tablespoons of sorrel purée made with leftovers from the previous day. Surround the omelet with a ribbon of cream sauce.

Tuna Omelet *(Omelette au Thon).* Cut 60 grams (2 1/4 ounces) of tuna packed in oil into very small cubes and added to the beaten eggs. Generally, you replace the butter with oil for cooking the omelet.

Tomato Omelet *(Omelette à la Tomate).* Fresh tomatoes, prepared as for fondue (SEE TOMATOES, PAGE 534), are used to fill the omelet. Surround it with a little good jus or *sauce brun* (brown sauce), replacing the demi-glace used in fine restaurants. Or, use what is called *à la Portugaise:* surround by a well-buttered tomato sauce (with butter added when the sauce has been taken off the heat).

Florentine Omelet *(Omelette à la Florentine).* This omelet is filled with spinach leaves which have been blanched and cooked gently for a few moments in butter. In a home kitchen you can use leftover minced spinach. The omelet should be surrounded with a ribbon of firm béchamel sauce (SEE PAGE 52).

Fresh Herb and Anchovy Omelet, Nimes-Style *(Omelette Nîmoise aux Fines Herbes).* Add to the fines herbs, indicated in the name, fillets of a salted anchovy that have been finely minced, and be sure to rub the receptacle where the eggs will be broken with garlic. Use oil rather than butter.

Chicken Liver Omelet *(Omelette aux Foies de Volaille).* Cut 3 chicken livers into thin slices and sauté them in butter just enough to firm them up; mix them with a little bit of brown sauce, or, if you don't have that, with a little bit of jus that has been thickened with starch. Put it on the omelet before you fold it.

Truffle Omelet *(Omelette aux Truffes).* Use the same method as for Scrambled Eggs with Truffles (SEE PAGE 152).

Kidney Omelet *(Omelette aux Rognons).* This dish, which is quite easily made in restaurants because there is always brown sauce ready, consists of: kidney, cut into small cubes of about 1/2 centimeter (3/16 inch), sautéed in butter for 2–3 minutes (SEE KIDNEYS, PAGE 329); drained and combined with a few tablespoons of Madeira sauce (SEE PAGE 54). The omelet is garnished with the kidney before folding. In fine restaurants, they set aside 1 tablespoon of the kidney mixture and put it, clearly visible, into a pouch made after the omelet has been placed on the plate.

If you have veal jus you can thicken it with starch (SEE LIAISONS, PAGE 47) in the necessary proportion and then off the heat, add some Madeira and some butter, to finish. Or, if you have meat glaze in a solid state, dissolve it in a few tablespoons of water and use in place of the jus.

For a more typical home kitchen preparation, you can use leftover kidney from a cooked veal loin. The kidney, cut into small, even cubes, is sautéed in butter for 1 minute in a pan, just enough to heat it up, sprinkled with parsley, and then spread out on the omelet before it is folded. If you like, you can surround the kidney omelet with a ribbon of tomato sauce.

Allow, for an omelet of 6 large eggs, 1/2 veal kidney or 3 lamb kidneys; 3 good tablespoons of jus or meat glaze that has been melted; 1/2 tablespoon of Madeira, and 20 grams (2/3 ounce, 1 heaping tablespoon) of butter.

Cream, Gruyère, and Potato Omelet *(Omelette à la Savoyarde).* This method is frequently used in restaurants. It is simple and primarily requires speed, because the omelet should be eaten piping hot, as soon as it is made.

Even more than other omelet recipes, this one must not be too large or it will not roll up easily. It rolls up on itself like a crêpe, which will certainly never happen if it is made with more than 5–6 eggs. For 6 people, it is necessary to make 2 omelets. Allow about 1 1/2–2 minutes, at the most, for each omelet. *For 5–6 eggs:*

A pinch of salt and a bit of pepper; 2 tablespoons of very fresh and very heavy cream; 30 grams (1 ounce) of fresh Gruyère, grated; 180 grams (6 1/3 ounces) of potatoes, weighed peeled; 50 grams (1 3/4 ounces, 3 1/2 tablespoons) of butter.

PROCEDURE. Cut the potato into cubes about 1 good centimeter (3/8 inch) all around. Cook them in the pan with 25 grams (1 ounce, 2 tablespoons) of butter until brown. SEE POTATO CROUTONS, PAGE 20.

Beat the eggs as directed, with salt and pepper. Add the cheese and the cream. Heat 25 grams (1 ounce, 2 tablespoons) of butter in a medium frying pan. Add the potatoes and the beaten eggs. Stir briskly with a fork while you shake the pan with a small back and forth movement.

As soon as the eggs have the consistency of scrambled eggs, allow the part in contact with the bottom of the pan to set. Make sure, then, that the omelet has not stuck anywhere and is easily moved; flip it over like a crêpe. Leave the pan on the heat for *2 seconds* only, then slide the omelet onto a round plate *without folding it over.* Serve.

NOTE. If you are not used to flipping the omelet in the pan to turn it over, cover it with a plate, invert the pan to put the omelet on the plate, then quickly slide the omelet into the pan to firm it up on its other side, as has been indicated.

COLD EGG DISHES
Oeufs Froids

Eggs in Aspic *(Oeufs en Gelée)*

Poached, these eggs can be served, according to personal preference, in small casserole dishes or small porcelain ramekins, or even in paper containers; in tart shells about 6 centimeters (2 1/2 inches) in diameter, which you can order from the bakery rather than making them at home; or simply in a slightly shallow dish.

The most common way to present these is decorated with a slice of truffle or a nice bit of ham; the slices should be cut paper-thin. Or even more simply, when in season, use tarragon leaves that have been dipped in boiling water to rid them of their bitterness, chilled, and well drained on a towel.

These eggs are greatly enhanced by any number of garnishes: minced ham, fowl, or fish, mixed with a touch of béchamel; foie gras; etc. You need very little, and you can thus use your leftovers. The aspic (SEE MEAT ASPIC, PAGE 45) is a simple one, which you may, if you like, enhance with a little Madeira wine. For this, the aspic should be melted—in other words, almost cool and barely liquid, just to the point where it can be easily spread over the eggs. Allow about 1/2 deciliter (1 2/3 fluid ounces, scant 1/4 cup) of aspic for each egg, plus more if you want to include a decoration of minced aspic on the plate—we cannot estimate how much you will need. *Time: 1 hour (the aspic already prepared).*

PROCEDURE. Most important, and particularly when it's warm, work in a cool environment, so that the multiple layers of aspic set quickly. Place the eggs in the chosen receptacles (the exception here is pastry shells, which would get soggy if sprinkled with liquid; in this case, the eggs are placed on any plate from which they will subsequently be transferred to the pastry shells.)

Using a kitchen brush that has been dipped in the aspic, paint the eggs with a layer of aspic about 2 millimeters (1/16 inch) thick. Let it set, then arrange your chosen elements of decoration on top of this aspic layer, dipping them in aspic first to use it as a sort of glue to stick them securely in place.

When, after a few moments, the decorative elements are adhered well enough that they will not become dislodged later, coat the eggs with aspic, pouring it over them from a spoon *drop by drop,* so that you do not disturb the decoration and to give it time to set somewhat.

If the eggs are served in tartlets, when the aspic is quite firm all around the eggs, this is the moment to put in the eggs. In order to do this, trim them with the tip of a small knife about 1/2 centimeter (3/16 inch) in from their edges so that you can loosen them from the plate; slide the round tip of a knife underneath to lift them up and put them in the pastry shells. Then they can be coated with aspic that is, as always, almost completely set, adding it drop by drop. The procedure of coating does not differ, no matter what receptacle you use. The final layer of aspic covering the eggs must be about 4 millimeters (about 3/16 inch) thick.

Molded Eggs in Aspic *(Oeufs en Gelée Moulés).* Spread a very thin layer of aspic over the bottom of some small molds or small porcelain casserole dishes. Put the decoration on top of this: truffle, ham, or tarragon leaves arranged into a star. Coat with a second layer of aspic and let it set. Thoroughly dry the poached eggs and trim every stray piece of white (use a pastry cutter if necessary), then set on top of the aspic. The most attractive side of the egg should be placed facing down, as this will appear when the egg is unmolded. Fill the receptacle with aspic and keep cool to allow it to set.

Briefly dip the mold into boiling water to loosen it, then unmold onto the serving plate. Garnish the spaces between the eggs with minced aspic. If you like, you can garnish with: salad, mixed diced vegetables (*jardinière*), etc., which has been dressed with mayonnaise.

Eggs Stuffed with Fish in Mayonnaise *(Oeufs Farcis à la Russe)*

This is typical of the home kitchen. You can use leftovers of fish—salmon or similar—or some shrimp mixed with a good firm mayonnaise. For 6 eggs, allow 125 grams (4$^{1}/_{2}$ ounces) of shrimp, net weight. And for the mayonnaise, 1 large egg yolk and 1$^{1}/_{2}$ deciliters (5 fluid ounces, $^{2}/_{3}$ cup) of oil.

The hard-boiled eggs are sliced *lengthwise* into 2 halves. Remove the yolk. Then trim the rounded bottom of each egg white half so that they will stay upright, like a little bowl: you need only trim a very small part to make the egg stable on its base.

Fill each half with the mayonnaise mixture, which must fill them completely, and then use a moistened knife blade to smooth it out into a mound. Place the stuffed eggs on a serving plate; sprinkle with egg yolks that have been pushed through a medium-sized sieve and garnish with a couple of sprigs of fried parsley.

Set aside the necessary number of shrimp to place one atop each stuffed egg. If you have enough aspic, you can arrange a border of minced aspic around the eggs. We would also like to recommend, in this case, the addition of a little bit of aspic, just as it is beginning to melt, but still cold, to the finished mayonnaise. You can then leave this to set.

VARIOUS WAYS TO PREPARE EGGS *Divers Apprêts d'Oeufs*

Eggs in Black Butter *(Oeufs au Beurre Noir)*

These are prepared according to several different methods, baked, or more frequently, fried. (For cooking the butter, SEE BLACK BUTTER, PAGE 80.)

Baked *(Sur le Plat).* Proceed as for simple baked eggs. Once they have been cooked, sprinkle them with 10 grams ($^{1}/_{3}$ ounce) of beurre noir for each egg, and a few drops of vinegar that has been heated in the pan.

Fried Eggs *(Oeufs Frits).* Heat the butter in the pan (10 grams/$^{1}/_{3}$ ounce/1 scant tablespoon per egg). When it turns a hazelnut color, break in the eggs. Season and cook. Slide them onto a warmed serving plate. Add a little bit of butter to what is already in the pan: about 10–15 grams ($^{1}/_{3}$–$^{1}/_{2}$ ounce, about 1 tablespoon) for each egg; heat until it browns. While it is piping hot, sprinkle it on the eggs. Heat the vinegar in the pan, which will still be burning hot, and pour it over everything.

Eggs with Ham and Bread *(Oeufs à la Bonne Femme)*

A very substantial and completely rustic preparation. For the toast, country-style bread with a good tight grain is most preferable. Country ham, *cooked*, is preferable to York ham. If you like, you can add a little bit of chives. *For 6 eggs:*

75 grams (2$^{2}/_{3}$ ounces) of lean ham; 30 grams (1 ounce, 2 tablespoons) of butter; 6 small slices of bread, without the crust, cut 1 centimeter ($^{3}/_{8}$ inch) thick and about 6 centimeters (2$^{1}/_{2}$ inches) in diameter.

PROCEDURE. Broil the slices of bread on both sides until they are a light golden color. Arrange them in a round ovenproof dish of the correct size that has been previously buttered.

Beat the eggs as for an omelet; add the minced ham; pour over the slices of toast. This addition of liquid will make them float, but that is not important.

Put them in a good hot oven with heat that comes mostly from the bottom. When you see the eggs swell up, make sure they are just right—in other words, good and moist, and serve.

Eggs in Red Wine and Shallot Sauce *(Oeufs à la Bourguignonne)*

The eggs can be either *poached, soft-boiled, or hard-boiled:* the sauce remains the same. When you are dealing with poached eggs, you can, in the popular Burgundy fashion, poach the eggs in the wine itself, which has first been boiled with aromatics (shallot, onion, etc.). Poach the eggs in a sauté pan, where the poaching is much easier. Then, reduce it for the sauce, which is simply, in the final analysis, a reduction of wine that has been thickened with beurre manié.

Insofar as possible, avoid the use of any tin-lined utensil for boiling the wine. It breaks down the wine and alters the color; a ceramic pan, here, is best. With the exception of hard-boiled eggs, this dish includes croutons, made in a rustic style; the bread is simply grilled and buttered. For a more sophisticated presentation, the croutons are fried in butter. You can even cut these croutons into little rings and place soft-boiled or poached eggs in the middle. *Time: 30 minutes.*

6 croutons, fried in 30 grams (1 ounce, 2 tablespoons) of butter.

For the sauce: 3/4 liter (generous 3 cups) of very good red wine; 3 shallots; 30 grams (1 ounce) of onion; a bit of garlic, optional; 3 parsley sprigs, a sprig of thyme, and a fragment of bay; 6 eggs; 15 grams (1/2 ounce) of flour and 20 grams (2/3 ounce, 1 heaping tablespoon) of butter for the beurre manié; 35 grams (1 1/4 ounces, generous 2 tablespoons) of butter to finish the sauce; salt and pepper.

PROCEDURE. **The sauce:** Put the wine into your chosen utensil with the onion and shallot, both finely minced, the garlic, thyme, bay, and a pinch of salt. Bring it to a boil. Do not cover. Let it boil rapidly until reduced by *by half*—that is, to 3 1/2 deciliters (1 1/2 cups).

As the sauce reduces, cook the eggs in the manner you have chosen and prepare the croutons. (SEE FRIED CROUTONS, PAGE 20.)

To finish: Strain the reduced wine through a fine chinois into a small pan. Thicken as directed (SEE LIAISON WITH BEURRE MANIÉ, PAGE 48). Remove from the heat and add the final butter, the pepper, and some good salt, if necessary.

To dress the dish: *Soft-boiled eggs*—Arrange the croutons in a circle on a heated round plate. You can put 3 of them in the middle. Drain the eggs on a cloth. Place them *standing up* on the croutons, which have been cut in rings to help them to stay upright. With a soupspoon, coat the eggs with the sauce; they must be completely covered by the sauce. Pour the rest into the plate. *Poached eggs*—Placed on the croutons, they are covered with the sauce in the same way as the soft-boiled eggs. *Hard-boiled eggs*—These should be served in a small dish, or failing that, in a shallow bowl. First, pour the sauce into the heated receptacle. Cut the eggs in half lengthwise. Put them on top of the sauce without covering them with the sauce.

Egg Croquettes *(Croquettes d'Oeufs)*

SEE THE ARTICLE ON CROQUETTES, PAGE 438. These are made with hard-boiled eggs, both the whites and yolks cut into cubes. To these are added some cooked mushrooms (SEE MUSHROOMS, PAGE 490), using about one-third of the weight of the eggs, plus a little bit of truffle, which sets this off quite nicely. If this is not a meat-free dish, you can add some ham or tongue, also cut into cubes. Form the croquette into the shape of the eggs. Serve with a light tomato sauce, or cream sauce, or soubise, etc.

Deep-Fried Egg-Filled Pastries *(Rissoles d'Oeufs)*

SEE THE ARTICLE ON RISSOLES, PAGE 441. Garnish the rissole with a tablespoon of the sauce that you use on croquettes. Serve with fried parsley.

Eggs in Individual Molds *(Petites Timbales d'Oeufs)*

This is a family dish that is extremely simple to make and that calls for "dariole" molds or small timbales in tin-lined steel. Otherwise, you can use small porcelain ramekins. These molds are surrounded by a tomato sauce, or a béchamel that has been heavily spiced. You can also serve them chilled with mayonnaise, tartar, or another sauce.

Time: 30 minutes. Makes 6 timbales, in molds with a capacity of about 1/2 deciliter (1 2/3 fluid ounces, scant 1/4 cup):

3 whole eggs and 1 1/2 deciliters (5 fluid ounces, 2/3 cup) of bouillon or milk; about 2 deciliters (6 3/4 fluid ounces, 7/8 cup) of sauce to surround them.

PROCEDURE. Butter the molds with a brush that has been dipped in partly melted butter, being sure to butter in the angles and at the bottom.

Beat the eggs with the milk or bouillon. Season with salt and white pepper, being generous with the pepper. Then proceed as for *crème en petits pots* (SEE PAGE 579): add the beaten eggs, then cook in a double boiler. Allow *about 10 minutes* for it to set properly.

Keep the molds in warm water *off the heat* to keep them warm right until you are ready to serve. Wipe them off thoroughly; carefully run the blade of a knife between the egg and the mold and turn it over carefully onto the serving plate. Surround with sauce.

FISH

Freshness: Freshness is most clearly manifested by a glossy eye: this must be as bright and lively as a living fish. The nice pink color of the gills and the firmness of the flesh when pressed with your finger also indicate freshness. But the most important factor to consider, the surest sign of freshness, is the sheen and clarity of the eyes.

To prepare the fish for cooking: The professional term is "dressing." *Dressing a fish* means gutting it, scaling it, removing the skin, etc. In essence, getting it ready to cook. The dressing varies, of course, according to the type of fish. We will cover the details relating to different fish in the appropriate recipes, but here we would like to give a general overview. With a good strong scissors, cut the fins and belly fins of the fish and shorten the tail. If it has to be scaled, you should do this with the back of the blade of a knife, applied flat: place the fish with the tail pointing toward you, and scrape, working toward the head. Be particularly thorough near the head and fins because these scales are more resistant.

Some authors feel that it is better not to scale large fish intended for cooking in court bouillon. Moreover, scaling the fish makes the skin more fragile, and the flesh of the fish will burst much more easily during cooking. Since a large fish is served skinned, it is better to remove all the skin after it has been cooked.

To gut the fish: Pull out the gills. Generally, these are the bronchia, or the organs suspended in the head cavity of the fish. To do this, lay the fish on its side, its head in front of you. Raise the flap that covers the gills. With the index finger of your right hand bent into a hook, slide it underneath the gills and pull it firmly toward yourself to extract them: Generally, the stomach will follow. Especially when you're first learning, it's better to do this with your finger wrapped in the corner of a cloth to avoid puncture wounds and resulting complications.

Make a small incision along the stomach to remove the intestines. To do this, use a long-handled spoon with a hook at the end. Place the fish on its back and stick the handle into the opening that you have made, pulling out the remaining intestines; scrape the spoon along the backbone, pulling it toward you, to remove any remaining blood, which will give you black lines after the fish is cooked. Then rinse the fish under running water, through the opening of the gills. Pat dry with a towel.

FIG. 34. INCISIONS OR "SCORING."

To score the fish: This term, when applied to fish, is one of the most ancient expressions in the culinary repertoire: it is frequently used in recipes from the first part of the eighteenth century. By "score," we mean to make incisions, or cuts, into the skin and also into the flesh of fish. The purpose of these incisions, or scores, is, first of all, to prevent the flesh from bursting from the heat, and above all, to help cook the fish, because the heat penetrates more easily through these cuts.

To score a fish, use a good sharp knife. Place the fish in front of you; starting from the tail, make slanted crosswise cuts about 2–3 millimeters ($^{1}/_{16}$–$^{1}/_{8}$ inch) deep, at a distance that varies depending on the size of the fish.

To determine when a large fish is done: Before removing it from the heat, insert a trussing needle into the thickest part. Leave it there for 30 seconds; take it out and press the part of the needle that was stuck into the fish on the back of your hand. If the needle is *burning hot*, the fish is sufficiently cooked. If not, the cooking must be prolonged, and you must repeat the experiment.

THE PRINCIPLE METHODS OF COOKING FISH

Fish in Court Bouillon

Under the general name of "court bouillon" we mean a liquid in which the fish is cooked.

The composition of court bouillon varies according to the type of fish; according to the different preparations for these fish and the sauce accompanying them; also, according to the cost and availability of ingredients. A court bouillon could consist simply of salted water, or of a very fine wine. The most popular is made from a base of salted water to which is added either vinegar or red or white wine and a certain amount of aromatics, such as carrots, onion, parsley, etc.

But what does not change and is much more important than the court bouillon itself is the method by which the fish must be cooked in it.

Cooking in Court Bouillon. Cooking a fish in court bouillon is done by *poaching,* which means, in culinary terms, that it is cooked without boiling: that is, the liquid must not boil strongly, it should simply simmer with a tremor that is barely perceptible. Poaching is much better than an outright boil because it ensures that the fish is heated evenly. This cooking, because it is gradual, can be nothing other than successful.

To cook the fish: Gutted and prepared, the fish is put into the cooking utensil. Cover it with the court bouillon. *Very gradually bring it to a boil. The larger the fish, the slower the process.* A hurried boil causes the skin and the flesh to shrink, which makes them burst. Furthermore, too much heat on the exterior of the flesh prevents the interior from being well cooked. (There are some exceptions for certain freshwater fish.) The interior will be only half-cooked and bloody, while the surface is perfectly done.

As soon as the boiling has begun, the court bouillon should be heated only to the point that is necessary to *poach* the fish.

If you have a *poissonière* or a *turbottière* (fish poacher) without a lid, cover the fish with cheesecloth or a thin towel, folded in half, ensuring the edges completely cover the fish in the court bouillon: this is to retain the steam and to appropriately cook the top of the fish, which must not be turned over; turning will damage it.

Cooking time for the fish: The time is calculated as for poaching time, in other words, from the moment when simmering is well established and the liquid is maintained just at the simmering point, but not briskly boiling, as described above. These times vary, depending on the kind of fish and its thickness.

For large thick fish: 10 minutes of poaching for every 500 grams (1 pound, 2 ounces) of fish whose total weight is less than 2 kilograms (4 pounds, 6 ounces); *8 minutes per pound* for fish that are larger than 2 kilograms (4 pounds, 6 ounces), as the entire fish benefits from the heat that has already been acquired.

For small fish: 10–12 minutes of poaching in total for fish that weigh 100–200 grams (3½–7 ounces); *15 minutes* for those weighing 200–300 grams (7–10½ ounces).

Slices of fish (2½ centimeters/1 inch thick): *12–15 minutes* of poaching.

Flat fish (turbot or brill): *8–9 minutes* per 450 grams (1 pound).

Use of the court bouillon (cold or hot): The court bouillon must be cold—or at the most, lukewarm—when you add the fish. If you plunge the fish into boiling liquid, not only will the flesh burst, having been brutally dilated, but the flesh will not have time to be infused by the seasoning. This is especially true with larger fish.

Exceptions are made for certain fish *au bleu,* which we will see ON PAGE 166.

Another exception is when the fish has reached the limit of its preservation, especially in summer, and particularly in stormy weather. The slow and progressive heat of the court bouillon, in this case, causes the fish to break down. Furthermore, the drawbacks of the hot liquid are not the same because the fish is not absolutely fresh and no longer has such firm flesh: the flesh has already expanded, so it cannot burst. What's more, it is easily infused with the seasoning. Thus, *whenever the freshness of the fish is in question, put it into a hot court bouillon.*

Slices of fish are also put into a *hot* court bouillon because the inconvenience of bursting is not to be feared in this case and because slices put into

SOLE (*SOLE*). Dorsal fin of an even thickness starting *anterior to* the superior eye. Oval, elongated body. Inwardly curved mouth. Dorsal and anal fins almost continuous. Rough scales. Superior eye ahead of the other. Soft teeth.

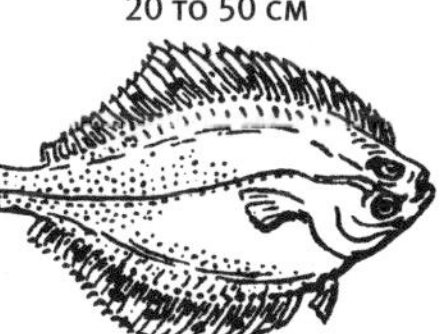

20 TO 50 CM

FLOUNDER (*FLET*). Dorsal fin starting *above* the superior eye, and larger in the middle than at the ends. Base of the dorsal fin has spiny tubercles. Generally resembles the plaice. Soft and closely set teeth.

20 TO 40 CM

Dorsal fin starts *above or after* the superior eye. Base of the dorsal fin without spiny tubercles. Dorsal fin larger in the middle than on the sides.

PLAICE (*PLIE*). Diamond shaped body with small, smooth scales. Right side of face brown with orange spots. 5 to 7 bony tubercles near the eyes. Sharp teeth.

30 TO 50 CM

LEMON SOLE (*LIMANDE SOLE*). Elongated body. Right side of face reddish yellow with blacking parts. Sharp teeth. Dorsal fin starts *behind* the superior eye.

30 CM

SAND DAB (*LIMANDE*). Oval body, right side of face yellowish grey, rough scales. Right pectoral much more developed than the other. Pointy teeth.

20 TO 30 CM

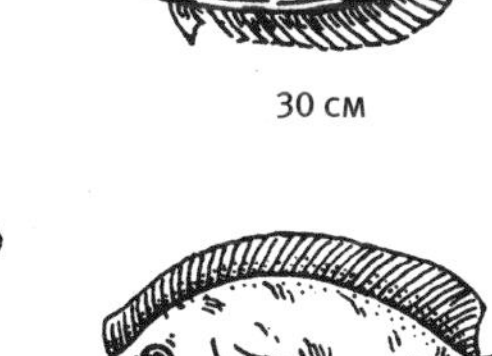

30 CM

CARDINE (*CARDINE*). Space that separates the eyes *smaller* than the vertical diameter of the eye. Anal fin *not united* with the ventral fins, placed very far in front. Dorsal fin starts in front of the anterior edge of the superior eye. Large oblique mouth, not curved in. Rather long oval body. Soft, small, hooked teeth.

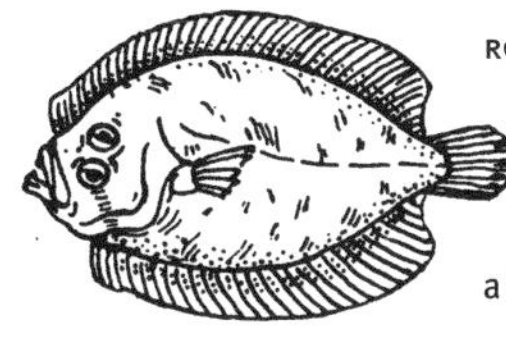

ROCK SOLE (*TARGEUR*). Anal fin *united* with the forward ventral fins. Oblique mouth, a little curved in. Dorsal fin starts before the anterior edge of the superior eye. Oval body, a little elongated. Soft teeth.

20 TO 50 CM

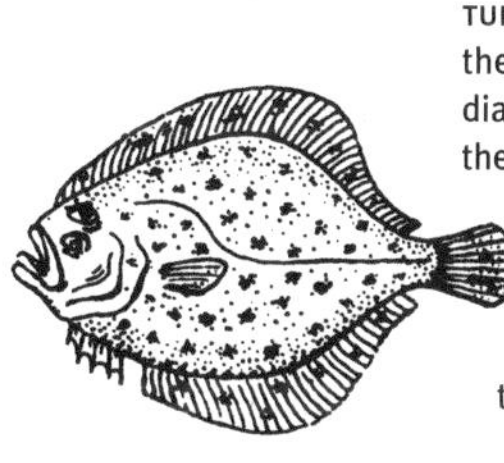

TURBOT (*TURBOT*). Space which separates the eyes *at least equal* to the vertical diameter of the eye. Dorsal fins starts at the muzzle. Conical tubercles, more or less rough, on the left side and the head. Diamond shaped body. Short muzzle, oblique mouth, very extendable. Comblike teeth. The two eyes are at the same level.

40 TO 80 CM

BRILL (*BARBUE*). Dorsal fin starts on the muzzle. No tubercles, but smooth, thin scales, rounded on the right side. Body rather oval. Short muzzle. Very extendable oblique mouth. Fine comb teeth. The inferior eye is a little more anterior than the other.

20 TO 60 CM

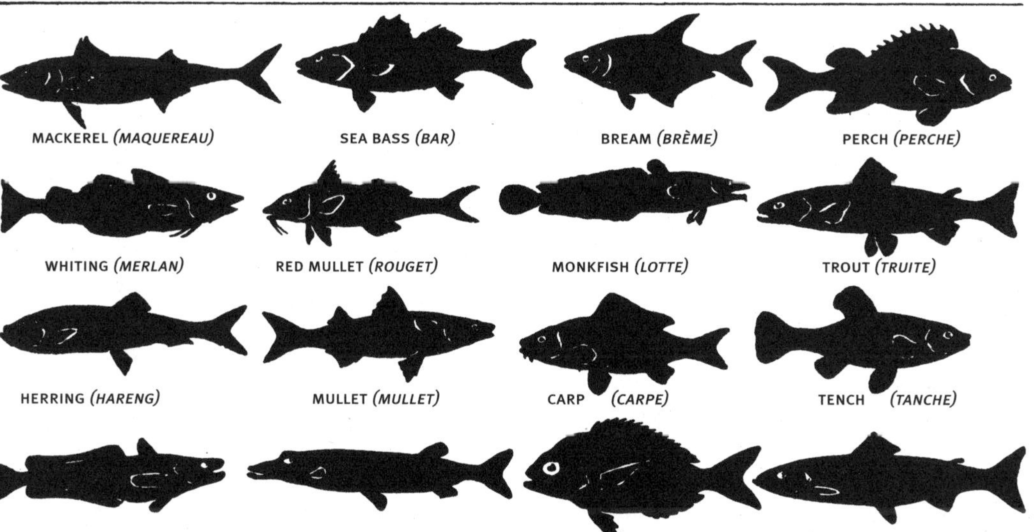

FIG. 35. HOW TO RECOGNIZE CERTAIN FISH.

cold water will allow their juice to escape, very much like the pieces of meat in a pot-au-feu.

Fish intended to be served cold must cool down in the court bouillon.

Conserving a court bouillon: A court bouillon may be used several times, and it will be tastier for it. To conserve it, you must boil it vigorously every 3–4 days, depending on the season, each time adding some water to compensate for the reduction of liquid that results from boiling (that is, a good water glass for each liter, 4 cups, of court bouillon).

Different court bouillons: We mention here, only for the record, court bouillon made with fish stock, Chambertin, or Champagne, and we give here only those most popular with good cooks.

VERY IMPORTANT NOTE. A court bouillon made with onion, carrots, etc., must be prepared in advance to allow the aromatics enough time to infuse, and it must be cooled before being used. No exception should be made, except when you are taken by surprise and time is too short or when preparing a large fish that requires a rather prolonged cooking time; the flavor of the aromatics, in that case, will have the time to develop. You can therefore overlook advance preparation of the court bouillon for a fish whose cooking requires more than 45 minutes. In this case, you should arrange the slices of onion, carrot, etc., in the bottom of the *poissonière* (fish poacher) *beneath* the grill (*fig.* 36), on which the fish is placed, and then pour the cold liquid over everything.

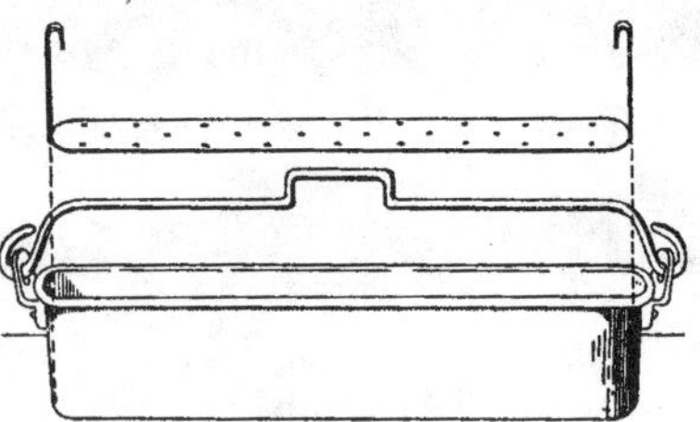

FIG. 36. POACHING PAN AND TRAY.

Court Bouillon with Vinegar *(Court Bouillon au Vinaigre)*. Used for all fish cooked *au bleu,* and for salmon, whether whole or in slices, or for trout, pike, carp, brill, eel, lobster, langoustine, etc. This is the most common recipe, mainly due to cost, and it is suitable for all fish, especially freshwater fish whose relatively bland flavor requires lively seasoning.

2 1/2 liters (10 1/2 cups) of water; 5 deciliters (generous 2 cups) of vinegar; 450 grams (1 pound) of carrots, cut into thin rounds; 300 grams (10 1/2 ounces) of onion, cut the same; a bay leaf; a sprig of thyme; 7–8 parsley sprigs, 3 shallots, 35–40 grams (1 1/4–1 3/8 ounces) of salt; 8 peppercorns.

The quantities of vinegar cited are for ordinary vinegar; but if you're using a very tart vinegar, instead of 2 deciliters (6 3/4 fluid ounces, 7/8 cup) for each liter (4 1/4 cups) of water, use only 1 1/2 deciliters (5 fluid ounces, 2/3 cup) for each liter (4 1/4 cups).

PROCEDURE. Put all the ingredients into a saucepan, except the pepper. Cover. Boil gently for *1 hour.* Add the pepper *10 minutes* before removing from the heat; longer cooking will make the court bouillon bitter. Strain the court bouillon through a fine strainer.

White Wine Court Bouillon *(Court Bouillon au Vin Blanc)*. For salmon, trout, eel, pike, etc.

1 3/4 liters (7 1/2 cups) of good white wine; 1 1/4 liters (5 cups) of water; 180 grams (6 1/3 ounces) of carrot, cut into thin rounds; 125 grams (4 1/2 ounces) of onion, cut the same; 7–8 parsley sprigs, torn into small bits; a sprig of thyme; half of a small bay leaf; 35 grams (1 1/4 ounces) of salt; 8 peppercorns.

If expense is no object, you should use a good Graves.

You could, to keep costs down, reduce the quantity of wine, using half water, half white wine; or even only one-third white wine, which is 1 liter (4 1/4 cups) of wine for 2 liters (8 1/2 cups) of water.

PROCEDURE. The same as for a vinegar court bouillon. We strongly suggest, for this court bouillon, proceeding with the classic and excellent method of lightly browning the onion, carrot, and parsley in butter before adding them to the liquid. Put the onion and carrot, cut into very fine slices, into a pan, with the parsley cut into small pieces and a little butter, about 50 grams (1 3/4 ounces, 3 1/2 tablespoons) for the given quantities. Let them soften gently. Brown only lightly over low heat, stirring from time to time with a wooden spoon. Allow about *15 minutes.* Moisten with the liquid. Add the salt, thyme, bay. Cover. Cook very gently for *45 minutes.* Do not add the pepper until

10 minutes before removing from the heat. Strain and let cool.

Red Wine Court Bouillon *(Court Bouillon au Vin Rouge).* For fish cooked *au bleu* (SEE PAGE 166): large or small carp, pike, tench, small trout.

3 liters (12 3/4 cups) of ordinary red wine; 450 grams (1 pound) of carrot, cut into fine rounds; 300 grams (10 1/2 ounces) of onion, cut the same; a bay leaf; a sprig of thyme; 7–8 sprigs of parsley; 3 shallots; 40 grams (1 3/8 ounces) of salt; 8 peppercorns.

The red wine used must be of good quality and free of preservatives. If you use a cheaper red wine, you should cut it by one-third with water.

PROCEDURE. The same as for the vinegar court bouillon and the white wine court bouillon, with the same cooking times.

NOTE. The amount of carrot and onion for these different court bouillons is not absolute. You can increase or decrease them as you wish; the quantities given here are an average.

The salt must always be calculated per liter (4 1/4 cups) of liquid: usually 12–15 grams (3/8–1/2 ounce) per liter (4 1/4 cups); the pepper must not be added until the final moment.

Do not overdo the amount of the bay leaf. Use only the stem of the parsley.

Court Bouillon with Milk *(Court Bouillon au Lait).* For turbot, brill, cod, etc.

1 deciliter (3 1/3 fluid ounces, scant 1/2 cup) of milk for each liter (4 1/4 cups) of water; 12–15 grams (3/8–1/2 ounce) of salt; 4 small slices of lemon.

Carefully peel the lemon slices to remove the *white* skin, which will make the court bouillon bitter. Remove the seeds for the same reason.

Saltwater Court Bouillon *(Court Bouillon à l'Eau de Sel).* For sea bass, mullet, cod, place, mackerel, royal sea bream, etc.

Use cold water, salting it at a ratio of 15 grams (1/2 ounce) of salt per liter (4 1/4 cups). Do not add anything else.

This is the best way to cook fish when they are quite fresh, because it allows them to retain their own natural taste.

Basic Fish Stock *(Bouillon de Poisson pour Apprêts)*

This bouillon is made with the bones, heads, and raw trimmings of fish (whiting, sole, brill, turbot), etc., as well as onion and carrot, to which you add varying amounts of white wine along with the water.

In professional kitchens, where there is a substantial quantity of these trimmings, you can allow, for 1/2 liter (generous 2 cups) of bouillon, 500 grams (1 pound, 2 ounces) of bones and heads. The result is naturally much more flavorsome and concentrated than a bouillon made in a home kitchen with only the bones and heads of fish that have been purchased for use that very day.

When preparing the bouillon to accompany a fish served whole, for which you can use neither the bones nor the head, you must purchase some ordinary fish, such as whiting. But this additional purchase, just for making a sauce, is not really much of an extravagance, though it seems so at first glance; because once you have taken what is required for the bouillon, the fish can be used in other ways. For example, whitefish fillets prepared à la Bercy, with white wine, au gratin, etc.

Furthermore, when you have the time, you can greatly enhance the flavor of the bouillon by sautéing lightly in butter, *without browning at all,* both the trimmings and vegetables before you add the liquid. In other words, a kind of "sweating," as is done with the meat for a white jus; but in this case, it is always a little bit detrimental to the whiteness of the sauce, no matter how careful you are. We will give here only the procedure for making the bouillon. The quantities necessary are in the recipes for each dish.

PROCEDURE. In a deep pot of sufficient capacity, combine the heads, trimmings, and bones, broken into small pieces; the onion and the carrot cut into fine rounds; the branches of parsley torn into little pieces; thyme and bay in a very modest proportion; mushroom trimmings, if possible; the water and the white wine; the salt.

Bring it to a boil. Carefully remove any foam that rises to the surface, using a metal spoon. Do not cover the pot, and let it boil for *a good 30 minutes, very gently and evenly.* A stronger boil would be harmful, not only because the bouillon would reduce much more than is necessary, but also because it would become cloudy, which should also be avoided. The pepper must not be added until the end of the cooking. It need only stay in the bouillon *6–10 minutes, at the most;* any longer and it will impart a bitter taste. You can coarsely crush the peppercorns, but in that case, do not leave them any more than *5–6 minutes* in the bouillon.

When the cooking is finished, strain the bouillon through a fine cloth spread out over the inside of a chinois. It is now ready for use.

Fish *au Bleu (Poissons au Bleu)*

This term is applied to the cooking of certain fish in a court bouillon, under particular conditions that cause the skin of the fish to take on a bluish color. This tint is frankly more on the violet side, especially when the fish are cooked in a court bouillon made with red wine.

The essential condition, so to speak, of cooking *au bleu* is that the fish must still be alive, *covered with their viscous coating,* which is found most notably on freshwater fish, and which contributes to the bluing. If the fish are no longer alive, they must be exceptionally fresh.

A fish intended to be cooked au bleu, *no matter what the fish, must never be scaled or washed.* Simply wipe it with a good cloth, always very lightly, to retain the viscous coating. It's gutted through as small an opening cut in the belly as possible, the gills having already been removed. All of this must be achieved with as little touching and handling of the fish as possible, in order to preserve the viscous coating.

Fish that can be cooked *au bleu:* salmon, lake and river trout; many lake fish; freshwater fish, such as pike, carp, tench, etc. It's better to cook only medium-sized fish *au bleu,* but the smaller fish suggested will also work quite well.

Court bouillon for cooking *au bleu:* There are two kinds: court bouillon made with vinegar and court bouillon made with red wine. The fish must always be completely covered by the court bouillon.

A court bouillon *with vinegar* is appropriate for all the fish listed above.

A court bouillon *made with red wine* is appropriate only for carp, both large or small; for a pike no larger than 900 grams (2 pounds); for tench; or for small trout. This is called the *court bouillon des mariniers d'eau douce* (bargeman's court bouillon). It is often served to accompany poached fish served hot, whether *genevoise* style or similar.

The preparation and cooking of the fish vary according to whether or not it is still alive.

For live fish: You can, before gutting the fish, kill it by plunging the head into boiling water. Gut it, remove the gills, lightly wipe the fish, *do not wash it.* If it is a large fish, cover it with the *boiling* court bouillon. If the fish are small, plunge them into the court bouillon, also *boiling.*

For dead fish: When fish are no longer alive, *sprinkle them generously with boiling vinegar* before putting them into the court bouillon, whatever kind it may be.

This sprinkling with vinegar develops the blue color because it dissolves the viscous coating. The way it is used here, it serves no other purpose than to develop the color, because the viscous coating does not have the same properties when the fish is dead as when it is alive.

The vinegar used for sprinkling the fish is then added to the court bouillon *when the court bouillon is made with vinegar,* and it is taken from the total quantity of vinegar used for the court bouillon. For example, if the court bouillon has 5 liters (5¼ quarts) of vinegar, you use half of this vinegar for sprinkling over the fish. There will thus only be 2½ liters (10½ cups) of vinegar for the court bouillon when you start, but you will subsequently add the 2½ liters (10½ cups) of vinegar used to bathe the fish.

Put the fish into the utensil where it is to be cooked: a *poissonnière* (fish poacher) for a large or medium-sized fish, or a suitably sized saucepan for small fish. Sprinkle with *boiling* vinegar by using a large soupspoon. Soon afterward, pour over the court bouillon that has been strained and is *cold,* or barely lukewarm. Bring to a boil, then, over very low heat, poach the fish.

If the court bouillon is made with red wine, put the fish onto a plate. Sprinkle with *boiling vinegar.* Then discard this vinegar and, as quickly as possible, put the fish in the utensil where it is to be cooked. Cover with the court bouillon that has been strained and is barely lukewarm. Bring it to a boil, then poach for the time suggested.

Serving fish cooked *au bleu:* You can serve warm or cold, as you like.

Served warm: remove the fish from the court bouillon at the exact moment; drain just before putting it onto a serving plate.

Spear a small piece of butter on the tip of a small knife and rub it all over the surface of the fish, tapping it lightly: this gives it some sheen.

If the fish has large scales, like carp, it is preferable to quickly scale it immediately upon removing it from the court bouillon, and only then to spread it with butter. Strictly speaking, carp, like all fish cooked *au bleu,* should be served as they are. In other words, with the scales. But, aside from the fact that the fish is more difficult to slice for serving, and the scales must be removed at this point, your guest will inevitably come across a few scales, which is unpleasant. It is much better to do this work in the kitchen.

Do not forget to surround the fish with a nice green border of parsley.

Served hot: The most classic is melted butter, seasoned simply with a little salt. Of course, it is understood that this butter must be of excellent quality and very fresh. You can melt it in the double boiler so that it does not heat too much: only melted, not cooked. Allow 30–40 grams (1–1 3/8 ounces) per person.

Any sauce like a hollandaise—caper sauce, cream sauce, etc.—will work equally well.

Served cold: Let the fish cool down in their cooking liquid—in other words, in the court bouillon—where they must be kept until ready to serve. Dry them off and place them on a napkin, then coat them with a little oil spread over the surface with a small brush, or a feather, to give them some gloss.

For carp, see the above on the subject of scales.

Surround with whole parsley sprigs.

Accompanying sauces: mayonnaise and its derivatives, such as tartar, green remoulade, etc., and all of the various vinaigrettes.

Fish Cooked in Butter with Lemon and Parsley *(Poissons à la Meunière)*

This is one of the simplest and best preparations that exist for small fish and slices of large fish. It consists of pan-cooking the flour-coated fish in butter and serving it drizzled with butter cooked à la noisette: in other words, just turning golden and foamy, with lemon juice and minced parsley.

It is the preparation *par excellence* for small river trout. It can also be used for gudgeon, tench, barbel, and for small eels, cut into pieces. It's splendid for sole, with or without garnish, as well as for whiting, herring, or mackerel, either in fillets or whole, and for smelt, plaice, salmon slices, and hake.

This method of cooking fish can replace grilling and can be used for fish that are not strictly served à la meunière: in other words, without the characteristic addition of noisette (hazelnut) butter. In this case, the fish can be served exactly as is, like a fried fish with a lemon half, or accompanied by an appropriate sauce, such as hollandaise, white sauce, etc., or even on a maître d'hôtel, or anchovy butter.

Unless you have excellent butter, it is always preferable to clarify it (SEE PAGE 16), when it is to be used for cooking fish, especially when preparing fish whose weight and thickness require a long cooking time. In any case, no matter how pure the butter you use, its whey will gum up when heated, making the fish stick to the bottom of the pan and tearing its skin. In homes where there is a supply of clarified butter, this is what should be used. Hazelnut butter *(beurre noisette),* on the other hand, must be made with very good, plain butter.

The amount of butter used for this cooking must be just enough to cover the bottom of the pan with a light, oily layer, and there should be no point where the bottom is not covered, because the fish will stick there. It's that simple. Here, it is not a question of frying; it's a sort of grilling, of roasting that you're looking for. Therefore, there is no reason whatsoever for the oil to overflow, and even worse, to cover the fish; use only enough butter to circulate freely beneath the fish, preventing it from sticking to the pan.

About 50–75 grams (1 3/4–2 2/3 ounces, 3 1/2 tablespoons–1/3 cup) of butter to cook enough fish to serve 6, which is about 6 small trout, or 3 small sole, or 6 slices of a larger fish.

Depending on whether the butter is more or less pure and filled with whey, you must naturally allow a bit more because you will lose some in clarification. The weight of the butter suggested refers to butter of very good quality.

The pan must be completely clean and large enough so that, when you put the fish in, particularly if you have a large amount, they all rest directly on the bottom and are not *too tightly packed.* This is to allow the steam to escape, because dry heat is the principle of this method of cooking. If the fish are piled up in the pan, the evaporation is slowed down and imperfect: the color will be bad and they will either be limp or disintegrate.

PROCEDURE. Spread some flour on a plate: 2 good tablespoons for our quantities. Season the fish with good salt and a little bit of pepper. Dredge it in the flour, making sure that all parts are well covered so that, when cooked, the flour will form a little crust. Take the fish by the tail and shake to remove the excess flour.

Meanwhile, the butter should have been put in the pan to heat. It must be quite warm when the fish is added in order to seize the fish. However, do not ever let it get too brown, so, as soon as it begins to smoke *slightly,* add the fish. As soon as the fish is in the pan, reduce the heat to low. The cooking must be done progressively so that the heat penetrates the fish gradually and evenly. Cooking and browning must go hand in hand.

After 5 minutes of cooking, turn the fish over very carefully so that you do not bruise or damage it in any way. In professional kitchens, this is done with a very large spatula, but you can replace it with a fork that has been skillfully slipped underneath the fish.

Cook the other side of the fish and let it color the same way and for the same time. According to the thickness and the type of fish, it might be necessary to prolong the cooking beyond these 10 minutes. You must then turn it over again, and again, on both sides, never letting it cook for more than 2–3 minutes on each side.

Thus, you can allow, for cooking small trout, weighing about 150 grams (5¹/₃ ounces) before it has been gutted, *a total of 10 minutes;* for sole of about 350 grams (12¹/₃ ounces), net, *a scant 15 minutes;* for medium-sized sole, about *18 minutes;* and *20–22 minutes* for a large sole.

The fish is perfectly done when you can carefully loosen one of the fillets next to the head, and it detaches cleanly from the fish bones.

For slices of fish that are no more than 2 centimeters (³/₄ inch) thick, allow *a scant 15 minutes.* The perfect cooking point is determined by forcefully sticking the point of a small knife into the middle of the central backbone and then pulling the knife out. The backbone, which must be removed in order to serve it, will come with it and detach easily. If the cooking is not sufficient, the backbone resists and does not detach, but brings along some flesh with it. It is then essential to prolong the cooking a little bit.

To serve: As a rule, any fish that is prepared à la meunière must be served straight from the pan. Suppose that, for some reason, it must stand for a few minutes and is being kept warm on its plate; only when you are ready to serve should you drizzle it with the hazelnut butter *(beurre noisette),* so that the butter is still boiling and foamy when the fish arrives in front of the guests.

Very carefully take the fish from the pan and place it on a long plate, warmed in advance. Squeeze a few drops of lemon juice on it. Sprinkle with minced parsley.

In the pan where the fish was cooked, add the raw butter, about 60–75 grams (2¹/₄–2²/₃ ounces) for 6 people. Cook as directed (SEE BEURRE NOISETTE, PAGE 80). As soon as it's ready, pour it directly, in one motion, on the fish, where its boiling will be even stronger. Serve immediately.

Fish au Gratin *(Poissons au Gratin)*

Beneath the guise of bourgeois simplicity, *poisson au gratin* results in many a disappointment at the family table. Either the fish swims in a clear liquid beneath a layer of soggy bread crumbs; or it is dry, with the fried bread-crumb coating hard, greasy, and sticking all over the serving dish. More often than not, although everyone knows that the gratin is by no means what it should be, no one particularly knows what it should have been. Let us then define it, first of all; a fish cooked perfectly beneath a layer of sauce turned into a gratin with a beautiful, uniform, *golden* hue and perfectly tender overall. *The gratin must never stick, even a little bit, to the serving dish.*

To produce this, methods may vary, but the ingredients of the dish remain the same: *mushrooms* always, because they form the base of the preparation, and are therefore essential, with onion or shallot, all minced together—"duxelles," in professional cooking terms; *white wine,* which is obligatory, plus another liquid that could be fish bouillon. In the home kitchen, you replace fish bouillon with the cooking liquid from mushrooms or with a meat bouillon, and if it is a meat-free dish, with cooking water from vegetables.

But it is important to note that the white wine, no matter how it is included in the dish, should be used in a very small quantity and quite reduced. Its role here is not to furnish the liquid element, but to impart a special flavor. Therefore, if you do not have either fish bouillon or any other liquid to replace it, you should simply use pure water, adding some white wine. Even though your intention may be to improve the dish by increasing the wine, it serves only to destroy the balance of flavors.

The procedures, as we have said, vary, to arrive at the same goal, which is, in effect, this: *make the cooking of the fish coincide with the reduction of the liquid and the formation of the gratin.*

Some culinary authors first poach the fish in wine and bouillon until it is three-quarters done; then they reduce the cooking liquid on the side, adding mushrooms that have been sautéed in butter, onions, etc. They thicken it with beurre manié, add the sauce to the fish, cover it with bread crumbs, and form a gratin quite rapidly, which takes about 4–5 minutes, in an extremely hot oven. Others poach the fish with the duxelles, thicken the cooking liquid, and rapidly form a gratin in the same way. The masters of classic French cuisine first cook their fish with wine and butter; this reduced cooking liquid is then added to a sauce *italienne,* for which duxelles is the base, and this is poured over the fish to cover. It is then topped with bread crumbs and finally gratinéed quickly in 5 minutes.

Alternatively, the fish is cooked with the sauce and the bread crumbs. The dish is prepared from the outset in such a way that the fish can be served directly in the dish. This last procedure is now used in fine restaurants; it is certainly the most practical, and advantageous, for the home cook because it allows you to do most of these preparations in advance. So it is this one that we will describe.

However, to make a successful gratin in this way, you must respect two very important conditions.

The first is to use the *exact amount of sauce:* if there is not enough sauce, it will reduce before the fish is cooked, and any liquid added subsequently would have only an unfavorable effect. If, on the other hand, there is too much sauce, the fish will cook before the sauce is properly reduced. It will then be necessary to cook it further by boiling the sauce over the heat and the steam, which is the result of this boiling, will ruin the crispiness of the gratin.

The second condition, of equal importance, is *the temperature of the oven.* The oven must always be heated high enough for a gratin of uncooked fish. But it is necessary to adjust the temperature according to the size or thickness of the fish. It should be strong and sustained for medium-sized or flat fish, and a little less so for larger fish. This is because large fish require longer cooking time than the others, and excessive heat would cause the gratin to form without allowing the fish to be cooked properly.

In any case, *the heat must be produced from the top* given the need to form the gratin. The fish cooks at the same time. When the heat of the oven is insufficient, it is essential to bring the cooking utensil as close as possible to the top of the oven, where the heat is strongest, to cause the gratin to form.

A fish that you intend to prepare au gratin *must never weigh more than 450 grams (1 pound), net;* otherwise, it will require too much cooking time. A long cooking time makes it impossible to synchronize the reduction of the liquid, the formation of the gratin, and the cooking of the fish.

In fine restaurants, they add tiny whole mushrooms or sliced mushrooms, sometimes both, to garnish the dish. The same can be done in the home kitchen because there is nothing very complicated about it. In this case, allow 1 medium cap or 2 small mushroom caps per person. These mushroom caps should be previously cooked, as instructed under mushrooms for garnish (SEE PAGE 490). Other sliced mushrooms are arranged raw around the fish, slightly overlapping, one on top of the other, to form a border.

To serve: *Poisson au gratin* should be served from the same dish in which it was gratinéed; a long metal plate, silver-plated or similar, with flat sides, or one of ovenproof porcelain. The problem with the latter is the right angle of the sides, which give some depth to the platter but are not really appropriate for the requirements of a gratin.

Grilled Fish and Fried Fish *(Poisson Grilles et Poissons Frits)*

For these two methods of cooking fish, you should refer to the chapter on cooking methods. There you will find a special paragraph: grilling fish (PAGE 37) and deep-frying fish (PAGE 40).

VARIOUS PREPARATIONS OF FISH

Freshwater Fish Stews with Wine *(Les Matelotes)*

In this section, as a matter of interest, we will concern ourselves only with recipes for sumptuous, old-fashioned matelotes. These were prepared with classic wines—Champagne, Pommard, dry Madeira, Sauternes, Rhine wines, etc.—presented on a pedestal and studded with *hâtelets* (decorative skewers), and then served ceremoniously in great silver pots à la française.

Times have changed. These days, the idea of a fish stew usually evokes the concept of a bistro; it has become a dish reserved for casual meals, which does not, in any way, mean that its excellence has been diminished.

Excluding the opulent décor, garnish, and accompaniment lavished on these preparations in the past that allowed culinary celebrities of the times to distinguish themselves from one another, there are many lessons to be learned from these ancient techniques. Furthermore, many great chefs mentioned have simplified preparations considerably for their own everyday stews.

There are many recipes for matelote. The procedures vary by region, period, personal preference, and, above all, by the ingredients that were available. But let us consider the fundamental conditions of every matelote, no matter how basic.

- Live fish.
- Excellent wine, red or white, depending on the type of stew. Consequently, never any of those sharp or unsophisticated wines known as *ordinaire.* Anyone who really loves fish stews must be prepared to devote either a Bordeaux or a Burgundy of very good quality.
- Plenty of good butter.
- High heat.
- A large, shallow dish. Above all, avoid using cast iron, which will give an unattractive tint to the sauce.
- When the stew contains different types of fish, cook the fish in the order of their tenderness.
- Cook the onion garnish separately.

Now that these points have been well established, let us examine what is optional or subject to variations.

Choice of fish: The preparation of a matelote is reserved almost exclusively for freshwater fish, as it improves their natural blandness. The range of fish available is vast, though the names often vary according to location. We will indicate here only the main varieties. According to preference and availability, either a single or several types of fish can be used. The best fish stews always contain several types.

Pride of place goes to the eel. One could even say that it is the base of any matelote, where it is appreciated even more because it doesn't have any bones. Next, by order of tenderness, and not necessarily by the fish itself but rather by its cooking time: small pike, brill, barbels, tench, perch, bream, trout, carp. In other words, for stews that include several types of fish, you first add the fish with the toughest flesh because they require longer cooking, and you add the others gradually, at intervals determined by the tenderness of the different fish.

The fish for a matelote must be rather large because they are going to be cut up, and large fish will give you pieces that are the right size and more equal.

The cooking liquid: There must always be enough liquid to sufficiently cover the pieces of fish. Wine is not always the only ingredient used.

You can, according to taste and depending on whether the stew is heavy or light, use a consommé or a very good bouillon, fish bouillon, or even water. So, roughly, half wine and half one of these liquids, depending upon circumstances.

Also bear in mind that this cooking liquid must then be reduced by about half, in order to make the sauce.

The wine: You can use, even in the same stew, both white and red wine, usually about two-thirds red to one-third white. This mixture, as well the simultaneous use of different wines of the same color, offers you the best opportunity to use the remains of your better bottles.

The liaison: The most widely used method remains beurre manié. But *roux blanc* is used just as often, both in the home and professional kitchen.

The quantity of beurre manié is 5–6 grams (1/5 ounce) of flour mixed with almost twice the amount of butter for each deciliter (3 1/3 fluid ounces, scant 1/2 cup) of reduced sauce. That is the amount of flour you must allow for the roux, if using a roux to thicken.

The sauce of a fish stew must remain light; the butter, which you add only at the last moment, *off the heat,* completes the liaison and gives it a softness and smoothness that is much finer than using a larger quantity of flour. Thus, the butter must be relied upon to enhance the consistency of the stew rather than a greater proportion of flour. This is why it is called for in rather substantial amounts and its quality is of utmost importance.

Various procedures and details: Garlic is not obligatory, but the tiny little bit that you add, and that contributes to the whole, is highly recommended. All the great chefs suggest it. In certain regions, shallot is used in place of garlic.

Carrot slices, and maybe a bit of celery, can be added, if you like, to the onion. If you do this, it is best to use butter to lightly sauté these vegetables, which are used here as aromatics, in order to develop their aroma. Sometimes they are cooked only with wine, or a court bouillon, before adding the fish.

Following this same procedure, you can prepare in advance an excellent fish bouillon using the heads and trimmings from the fish: let it boil for *20–30 minutes* in water or white wine, with onion and carrot, whether sautéed or not in butter, and bouquet garni, etc.

Anchovy butter, added at the very last moment, is also recommended by both traditional and modern chefs.

Sometimes, also, a squeeze of lemon.

A tiny pinch of sugar is always recommended by Carême (SEE PAGE 53) when beginning fish stews.

Pepper is added whole, or, if ground, only at the very end, to avoid bitterness.

Flambéing the stew is not always essential, and furthermore, is not even possible except when you use wine as the only cooking liquid. The great masters of classic French cuisine do not always include it, doubtless because they added a certain amount of fish bouillon or of consommé to their matelotes, thereby lessening the impact of the wine. The use of flambéing is employed mainly for rustic fish stews where wine is the only liquid, or where this wine, even if it's of very fine quality, is not the same as that used in the finest restaurants; so flambéing, which corrects the slight sharpness of the wine used on its own, is therefore recommended in these cases.

Some country-style and older recipes suggest cooking the crayfish used as a garnish in the stew itself, along with the fish; this makes it easier if lack of equipment is a problem. You take them out, in this case, before thickening the sauce.

Bacon sometimes is used in rustic fish stews. Cut into tiny slices, it is sautéed with the onions before adding the fish and the wine.

Among the methods of preparation differing from the most well-known, we should mention one in particular. It is a regional variation, practiced in châteaux kitchens in Poitou: the fish, cut into sections, is first deep-fried to seal only the outside. The cooking is then finished in the sauce, which has been prepared in a sauté pan with a roux, white or red wine, or water if it's a lean sauce. It is served with a garnish of croutons, poached eggs, etc. The goal of this method is to maintain the pieces of fish intact and keep them from losing their bones.

We should also mention the liaison of egg yolks, which, in some places in the Franche-Comté is characteristic of a dish known as *pochouse,* or the matelote native to that region.

The garnishes: First there are the croutons, an essential accompaniment to every fish stew, from the most rustic to the most elegant. Except for certain local country-style preparations, where the bread is grilled, these croutons are fried in butter and cut from the heart of the bread (SEE FRIED CROUTONS, PAGE 20).

The pearl onions must always be cooked separately, so that they are cooked properly, which is not possible given the temperature or cooking procedures of the stew. You put them in the sauce, along with the mushrooms, to impart their flavor, adding them only a few moments before serving. This is for everyday matelotes.

For more elaborate matelotes, where the presentation is more important, Carême (SEE PAGE 53) recommends sautéing the pearl onions in butter, then cooking them with a little bit of white wine and consommé and thickening the mixture with a tablespoon of the sauce from the fish stew before arranging them in groups around the pieces of fish. This procedure is worth remembering.

Choose and prepare them as recommended in the section on pearl onions for garnish (SEE PAGE 525.)

Presentation: This dish should be served in a shallow bowl or a low, shallow plate. It is the most practical way of ensuring quick service, so that it can be serve boiling hot, as it should be, especially when the stew does not contain a huge number of garnishes.

In the nineteenth century, when a variety of garnishes was the norm for the elaborate matelotes of the times, some of the sauce was often served in a sauceboat to make it easier to arrange the crayfish and other items around the fish. It would be a good idea, circumstances permitting, to bring this practice back into fashion as it had its merits.

With the exception of eel, you serve the fish with the heads on. Many true lovers of fish stews are extremely fond of them.

Though fish stew must be served simply and rapidly, its presentation on the plate, insofar as possible, should always be in the form of a pyramid. First, place the fish heads on the bottom of the *well heated* platter, or plate, which will serve as a support. Set aside 1 carp head if the stew contains one. On this base of heads, arrange the pieces of fish randomly without paying any attention to the different types. Put the carp head on the top. Pour over the sauce.

Arrange the garnishes in a neat pattern around the pyramid. For example, the crayfish, trussed with their large claws stuck into their tails and their tails placed in the air; a breaded fried gudgeon, and a fried crouton alternating with each crayfish. The pearl onions can also be arranged symmetrically—that is, in little groups.

For more rustic matelotes, containing toasted bread as croutons, these slices of bread are put at the bottom of the plate and the pieces of fish are placed on top with the sauce.

Basic Freshwater Fish Stew *(Matelote Simple)*

The recipe given here is an example of a straightforward, everyday matelote, and it represents a meeting point between country-style methods and those of the grandest haute cuisine. You can modify this recipe at your will in terms of the choice of fish, the garnish, and the different details, according to all the directions already given.

The use of two pots greatly facilitates the final procedure of thickening the sauce, because the fish, during this time, is also kept hot. If you do not have the necessary equipment, transfer the fish to a plate and then reduce and thicken the sauce, in which you then reheat the pieces of fish. The choice of garnishes is optional—that is, gudgeon, crayfish, and mushrooms can be left out. But the croutons, as we have already said, are absolutely mandatory for any matelote. *Time: 1 scant hour. Serves 6.*

1 kilogram (2 pounds, 3 ounces) of fish, net weight: eel, tench, pike, barbel, etc. 8 deciliters (3 3/8 cups) of wine; a Madeira glass (1 1/2 deciliters, 5 fluid ounces, 2/3 cup) of cognac or fine champagne; 150 grams (5 1/3 ounces) of onion, cut into rounds; a small piece of garlic about the size of a bean, crushed; a small bouquet garni; 20 grams (2/3 ounce) of flour, worked into 25 grams (1 ounce, 2 tablespoons) of butter; 50 grams (1 3/4 ounces, 3 1/2 tablespoons) of butter to finish the sauce.

For the garnish: 6 small croutons, fried in 20 grams (2/3 ounce, 1 heaping tablespoon) of butter; 100 grams

($3^1/_2$ ounces) of cultivated mushrooms, or preserved mushrooms, or, in season, morel mushrooms; 6 medium-sized crayfish, cooked in a court bouillon, warm; 6 small breaded and fried gudgeons; 12–15 pearl onions.

PROCEDURE. It is not essential to wait for the last moment to cook the mushrooms, gut and bread the gudgeons, and cut the croutons. All this can be done before starting the stew.

The fish should be gutted and cleaned, each one in the method that is appropriate to their type, then cut into pieces 3–5 centimeters ($1^1/_4$–2 inches) in length. The length is proportional to the thickness and to the different parts of the fish: if the fish is large, the piece must be short; the pieces closer to the tail, being thinner, should be kept longer, so that they are about the same weight.

In a sauté dish large enough to easily hold all the ingredients later on, put the onion rounds, the bouquet garni, the pieces of eel, and the wine, and add 8–10 grams ($^1/_3$ ounce) of salt. No pepper at this stage. Do not cover. Put over high heat and bring to a rapid boil. When the liquid is boiling well over the entire surface, pour in the cognac, or the fine champagne cognac. Light it carefully with a paper match and let the flames subside on their own. Add the other fish. Cover. When it returns to a boil, lower the heat and maintain a sustained and steady boil for *15 minutes.*

The sauce: Lift out the pieces of fish, one by one, on a fork, and put them in another sauté pan or on a plate. Be careful to drain them well. Do not put in the eel heads. They are used only during cooking to impart their taste.

Remove the bouquet garni and pour all the liquid through a sieve into any receptacle. Rinse the pot. Pour back the liquid that you have strained. If you have prepared a mushroom garnish, now is the moment to add the liquid from their cooking to the pot.

Boil strongly, uncovered, until the liquid has been reduced to about 4 deciliters ($1^2/_3$ cups).

Then add the beurre manié (SEE LIAISONS, PAGE 47). Mix it with a little whisk to dissolve it well. Let it boil for only *1 minute.* Check the salt seasoning. Finish with a pinch of pepper.

Pour the sauce on the pieces of fish, or put them back into the pot, depending on whether they have been kept in a pot or on a plate. Shake the pot by holding it by its handle and keeping it flat on the stovetop, swirling the contents around in a circular movement. This is to coat the pieces of fish with the sauce without having to use a spoon, which would break them apart.

Then add the garnish of onions and mushrooms. Shake the pot the same way. Cover and simmer gently, without boiling, which would reduce the sauce, for *5 minutes.* Then keep it warm.

If you have some gudgeons for the garnish, you can fry them during this time. The same is true if you are using deep-fried eggs (SEE PAGE 136).

To serve: Arrange the matelote according to the directions for presentation already given. To the sauce that remains in the pot, add the butter (50 grams/$1^3/_4$ ounces/$3^1/_2$ tablespoons), divided into pieces about the size of a bean, so that it will melt more quickly. Gently shake the pot over low heat to melt and blend this butter into the sauce *without heating it too much,* because it would lose its thickening effect. Pour the sauce through a chinois onto the pieces of fish, the pearl onions, and the mushrooms.

Quickly arrange the croutons and the garnish, if any, around the matelote, and serve immediately.

Bouillabaisse *(Bouillabaisse)*

Given the variety of fish that must be used in the preparation of a good bouillabaisse, made according to Provençal traditions, it follows that this dish cannot be made properly except when close to a seaport—moreover, a fishing port—or near enough to a sufficient source of all the different fish, which should all be absolutely fresh. Do not be at all surprised if this bouillabaisse ends up being rather expensive. Among all the recipes that we have been able to experiment with, there is one created by the Marseilles chef Reboul, which seems to us to be as perfect as possible. For a dish that is essentially regional, we are using this recipe from one of the greatest master chefs of Provençal cuisine. *Time: 1 hour of preparation; 20 minutes of cooking. Serves 8–10.*

About $2^1/_2$ kilograms (5 pounds, 8 ounces) of fish, total. Thus: a lobster of 700 grams/1 pound, 9 ounces (or 2, weighing a total of 700 grams/1 pound, 9 ounces);

2 scorpion fish, weighing a total of 400 grams/ 14$^{1}/_{8}$ ounces (or the same weight in smaller ones); 2 gudgeons, weighing about 300 grams (10$^{1}/_{2}$ ounces); John Dory, weighing about 200 grams (7 ounces); slices of whiting—400 grams (14$^{1}/_{8}$ ounces)—or hake or cod, whichever you prefer; monkfish: 500 grams (1 pound, 2 ounces), or, as a substitute, sea eel or conger eel.

1$^{1}/_{2}$ deciliters (5 fluid ounces, $^{2}/_{3}$ cup) of olive oil; 150 grams (5$^{1}/_{3}$ ounces) of minced onion; 150 grams (5$^{1}/_{3}$ ounces) of fresh tomato, or 100 grams (3$^{1}/_{2}$ ounces) of thick tomato concentrate; 20 grams ($^{2}/_{3}$ ounce) of garlic; 2 tablespoons of minced parsley.

A bouquet of aromatics, composed of: a branch of fennel; a little sprig of thyme; a medium-sized bay leaf; 2 sprigs of parsley, with their large stems. A piece of orange peel, about the size of a postage stamp, and only the part that is nice and orange, without any white skin underneath it.

15 grams ($^{1}/_{2}$ ounce) of salt; a pinch of saffron; a pinch of pepper.

2 liters (8$^{1}/_{2}$ cups) of boiling water.

A long bread in the form of a flute, to make about 20 1-centimeter ($^{3}/_{8}$-inch) slices, with a diameter of 7–8 centimeters (2$^{3}/_{4}$–3$^{1}/_{4}$ inches).

PROCEDURE. *Warning:* The success of bouillabaisse depends primarily on the manner in which the cooking is conducted and the swiftness with which the boiling hot bouillon is served as soon as the pot is taken from the heat. This can easily be understood, because after cooking, leaving the bouillon on the heat, even for a short time, will cause it to lose its texture, the velvety smoothness, which characterizes a perfect bouillabaisse. The oil, used in relatively large quantities, will separate upon standing, and not only is the flavor considerably altered, but the bouillon no longer has as an attractive appearance. It is thus vital to be extremely careful in this matter: prepare the slices of bread in advance. Have a good, strong, steady heat; and, above all, do not start cooking the fish until *15–18 minutes* at the most, before you think you will need to serve.

To prepare the fish: Scale them carefully. With kitchen shears, trim the fins and the tail. Gut them, removing the intestines and the gills. Rinse under running water, without letting them soak in it.

Cut the fish into pieces if their size is moderate. Leave whole any fish whose weight is less than 100 grams (3$^{1}/_{2}$ ounces). Put the pieces of fish on a plate. Set aside the whiting and the John Dory, which do not have the same cooking time.

Split the lobster in half lengthwise. Remove the pouch, or the stomach, which always contains some gravel. Also, remove the intestines. Divide each half so that you will have at least 1 piece for each guest.

To cook: Use a deep saucepan with a capacity of at least 5 liters (5$^{1}/_{4}$ quarts). This is necessary so that you can maintain a brisk boil without having the liquid spill over. The bottom of the saucepan must have *its entire surface placed over a heat that is as hot as possible* to maintain as strong a boil as possible during cooking.

Put the oil and the minced onion into the pot. Stir over the heat with a wooden spoon *for only 1 minute, without allowing it to brown at all.* Add the tomato, after removing its seeds and chopping it; the garlic and the bouquet garni; the lobster, the scorpion fish, the monkfish, the gurnard (essentially, all the fish with firm flesh); salt, pepper, saffron; the *boiling* water.

Bring rapidly back to a boil. Do not cover. Let it boil briskly for *10 minutes.* To avoid damaging the fish with a spoon, be sure, during this time, to gently shake the saucepan so that nothing will stick to the bottom. After the allotted time has passed, put the reserved fish on top of the fish which have been two-thirds cooked; their extremely fragile flesh would disintegrate if added at the beginning. Allow *5 minutes* of cooking for these last fish. This comes to *15 minutes* for everything.

Make sure that the liquid, while it is boiling furiously, covers the fish completely. The fish must retain the form it had when put into the pot, staying the same from the beginning of cooking until the very end, without being either mixed nor stirred. A very gentle horizontal shake of the pot from time to time should be enough to prevent the fish from sticking to the bottom. At the end of *15 minutes* of very strong and continuous boiling, the cooking is finally finished. Turn off the heat and proceed directly with the arranging of the two plates: bread and fish.

Presentation: *The bread:* In advance, you will have neatly arranged the slices of bread in a shallow bowl or vegetable dish that has been well warmed. It is not correct practice to toast this bread. Over the bread, pour *three-quarters* of the bouillon through a fine sieve. Cover. Keep it as warm as possible while you quickly arrange the fish. *Only when you are ready to send this to the table* should you sprinkle these slices of bread with parsley, after sprinkling them one last time with the bouillon that you poured on top of them. In addition to the liquid these slices absorb while you are preparing the fish, there should still be a little less than 2 tablespoons of liquid in the dish for each person.

The fish: In advance, prepare a second plate that has been well heated. Carefully remove the fish from the pot with a fork. Arrange them one by one on the plate, in a way that best reflects the diversity of fish and seafoods and makes each one sufficiently visible so that the guests can choose the pieces that they like.

Then, pour the remaining bouillon over everything and sprinkle the fish with the minced parsley. Immediately serve *both plates together.*

Individual Fish Gratins in Scallop Shells *(Coquilles de Poisson Chaudes)*

This preparation is a marvelous way to use leftover fish. It is always very popular and is also quite practical because these servings can be made with very small quantities. Thus, for 3–4 servings only, you will need about 60 grams (2¼ ounces) of fish for each dish and a good ½ deciliter (1⅔ fluid ounces, scant ¼ cup), or about 3 full tablespoons, of sauce. This is almost always a Mornay sauce, as for the fish in cream sauce au gratin or, if you do not like cheese, a good lean béchamel.

This can be made with lobster and langoustine, eel, bream, salmon, turbot, sole, brill, etc. The presentation of these dishes is greatly enhanced by surrounding the fish with a ribbon of piped duchesse potatoes, which also prevents the sauce from running out while you are glazing it.

The recipe offered here includes the border of duchesse potatoes. *Time: 30 minutes for the sauce and the fish; 45 minutes for the potatoes. Makes 6 scallop shell dishes.*

About 450 grams (1 pound) of potatoes; a walnut-sized piece of butter and 2 small eggs, from which a small spoonful is kept for glazing.

The shells used are scallop shells, which you can buy empty at a fish market if you do not already have some on hand.

PROCEDURE. Start cooking the sauce (Mornay or cream), calculating the quantities for 3 good deciliters (1¼ cups) of sauce. Prepare the duchesse potatoes (SEE PAGE 541). Rid the fish of all its skin and bones: cut it, if possible, into very small slices, or divide it into thin layers, depending on the type of fish.

The ribbon of duchesse potatoes: In fine restaurants, they use a pouch fitted with a fluted nozzle; but you can, if you do not have such accessories, make it just as well by hand. On a floured board, roll the potato dough under your two extended hands into a long sausage about the thickness of a finger. With a knife, divide it into 6 parts. Each part should be 13–14 centimeters (5–5½ inches) long. Lightly butter the edges of the shells. Arrange a sausage of dough onto each one in such a way that the two ends are joined, forming a circle. Glaze it with the beaten egg, and lightly groove it with the tines of a fork.

The fish: *About 15 minutes* before serving, put all the fish pieces into a pan. Cover with lightly salted boiling water; cover and cook over low heat or in a very low oven, without allowing the water to boil. Drain and pat dry with a towel. If you do not do this, the water will dilute the sauce.

Divide the fish and the smaller bits of fish into 6 equal portions. Fill the shells with the fish, and top each one with 3 tablespoons of sauce. Sprinkle with grated cheese. Place 2 small pieces of butter on top. Put the shells, now garnished, into a long dish, having first poured a few tablespoons of cool water on the bottom. Glaze in the oven or under the broiler (SEE PAGE 15).

As soon as they are glazed, arrange the shells on a large round plate covered by a napkin. Serve immediately.

Fish Soufflé *(Soufflé de Poisson)*

A very good recipe for the home cook, which can be used for any leftover fish, such as turbot, brill, sole, salmon, pike, etc. Or, use a fish that has been simply cooked for this purpose in a court bouillon of salted water (SEE PAGE 165) such as hake or even cod.

The béchamel can be prepared with exactly the quantity of milk needed to make the required 2 deciliters (6³/₄ fluid ounces, ⁷/₈ cup) or with a little more milk and then simmered until reduced to the right quantity; it would be greatly improved by this, particularly if you add a small bunch of parsley and a few mushroom trimmings. *Time: 45 minutes (once the fish has been prepared). Serves 6–8.*

500 grams (1 pound, 2 ounces) of fish, *cooked,* weighed without skin or bones; 5 egg yolks; 6 egg whites; 30 grams (1 ounce, 2 tablespoons) of butter.

2 deciliters (6³/₄ fluid ounces, ⁷/₈ cup) of béchamel sauce, for which you will need: 15 grams (¹/₂ ounce) of flour; 25 grams (1 ounce, 2 tablespoons) of butter; 2–3 deciliters (6³/₄–10 fluid ounces) of boiled milk.

Salt, pepper, nutmeg.

PROCEDURE. The fish must be thoroughly cleaned of the least fragment of skin and even the smallest bone. The best way to do this is to put it into a pan with some water and a grain of salt and cook it. Once heated, drain the fish on a towel and the skin will be easy to peel right off. Next, mince the fish very finely, practically into a paste. If it is cod, grind it.

Meanwhile, prepare the béchamel. Heat the milk. Then, in a small pan, make a white roux with the flour and 25 grams (1 ounce, 2 tablespoons) of butter. Dilute with the boiling milk. Season with salt, pepper, and nutmeg.

Take a reasonably large sauté pan and combine all the ingredients for the soufflé in it. Pour in the sauce, after it has been strained if it contains parsley and other ingredients. Add the fish and stir. Put in the butter, divided into small pieces. Cover. Keep the heat low enough to maintain it barely lukewarm, until you are ready to add the egg yolks and the beaten whites. Proceed as for the vanilla soufflé (SEE PAGE 634), minus the glazing. Allow *26–30 minutes* for cooking.

Kedgeree *(Cadgery de Poisson)*

This is an excellent preparation, inspired by an English recipe, in which you use the leftovers of boiled fish: turbot, brill, salmon, hake, etc. It can also be used for smoked haddock, cod, or monkfish. The fish bouillon, which is what should be used here, is replaced by ordinary bouillon in this instance. For a completely meat-free dish, you can use water, with some cooking liquor from mussels added, in the amount of about one-quarter liquid; or, the same amount of cooking water from mushrooms; or simply water alone, salted with 6–7 grams (¹/₄ ounce) of salt, and with 25 grams (1 ounce, 2 tablespoons) of butter added to it. *Time: 45 minutes. Serves 6.*

300 grams (10¹/₂ ounces) of cooked fish; 125 grams (4¹/₂ ounces) of rice; 1 good tablespoon of minced onion; 30 grams (1 ounce, 2 tablespoons) of butter; 4 deciliters (1²/₃ cups) of bouillon and water. *For the sauce:* 20 grams (²/₃ ounce, 1 heaping tablespoon) of butter and 15 grams (¹/₂ ounce) of flour for a white roux; 3 deciliters (1¹/₄ cups) of milk; a small bunch of parsley; 4 hard-boiled eggs.

PROCEDURE. In a deep pan, heat the butter over very moderate heat. Put in the minced onion. Let it brown very lightly. Add the rice, *which has not been rinsed.* Stir until it has taken on its natural color and has become a sort of porcelain white (it's the same procedure as for a pilaf or for a risotto). Pour in the liquid, either warm or cold. Bring it to a boil over moderate heat. Cover the pan and put into a moderately hot oven to maintain a slow and regular boiling for *15–25 minutes,* depending on the type of rice: long-grain rice takes longer to cook. Do not touch the rice, in any way, during this time.

The sauce: In a 1-liter (4-cup) pan, make a white roux. Dilute it with the boiled milk. Season with salt, pepper, and nutmeg. Once it has begun to boil, add the parsley. Lower the heat for a moment to allow it to finish.

Cut the fish, which has had its skin and bones removed, into large cubes, or into small slices. Cut the hard-boiled eggs into large cubes. Stir everything into the sauce after you have removed the bouquet garni. Season with a point of cayenne (as much as can be held on the tip of a small knife) or a good pinch of curry powder—whichever you prefer. Keep over low heat until the fish has completely reheated.

To serve: Place half of the rice in a small dish or shallow bowl that has been well heated. Then spread half of the fish on top of this, and the hard-boiled eggs, and the sauce. Cover it with the rest of the rice. On top of this rice, put the rest of the fish and the eggs. Serve immediately.

Fish in Cream Sauce au Gratin
(Poisson Crème au Gratin)

This recipe can be used for all fish with white flesh—that is, brill, sole, bream, eel, etc. This is an excellent way to serve the leftovers of turbot, and, after a festive meal, you can often find yourself left with plenty of this fish. Moreover, these leftovers, frequently in small pieces, cannot be used except as part of a *coquilles de poisson* or croquettes.

The dish can be summarized as follows: a border of duchesse potatoes into which you put the fish, mixed with a lean béchamel sauce. If you like, you can add some Gruyère, which would make it a Mornay sauce. The preparation is then put in the oven to color it. *Time: 1 hour. Serves 6.*

About 500 grams (1 pound, 2 ounces) of fish.

***For the border:* SEE BORDER OF DUCHESSE POTATOES (PAGE 542).**

***For the sauce:* 20 grams (2/3 ounce, 1 heaping tablespoon) of butter and 12–15 grams (3/8–1/2 ounce) of flour; 2 1/2 deciliters (1 cup) of boiled milk; a small bunch of parsley sprigs; salt, pepper, and nutmeg; 2 good-size tablespoons of grated Gruyère; 75 grams (2 2/3 ounces, 1/3 cup) of butter to finish the sauce.**

***For the gratin:* 1 tablespoon of grated Gruyère; 25 grams (1 ounce, 2 tablespoons) of butter.**

PROCEDURE. Prepare the duchesse potatoes as directed (PAGE 541).

In a small pan, cook the butter and flour into a white roux. Dilute with the boiled milk. Season and add the bunch of parsley. Let it simmer gently, at a barely perceptible simmer, for *25 minutes.*

Prepare the duchesse border (SEE PAGE 542).

Remove all fragments of skin and bones from the fish. Put the pieces that have been cleaned into a pan. Add lightly salted boiling water to cover. Heat well, but do not let the water boil.

Remove the bunch of parsley from the sauce. Add the cheese. As soon as it is mixed in, turn off the heat and finish with the butter (75 grams/ 2 2/3 ounces/1/3 cup).

Glaze the exterior of the border with beaten egg. Inside the border, cover the bottom of the dish with 2–3 tablespoons of sauce. *Thoroughly* drain the fish. If you do not do this, the sauce will be diluted. Put it on top of the layer of sauce spread over the bottom of the plate.

Cover the fish with the rest of the sauce, added by tablespoons, being careful to leave at least a good 1/2 centimeter (3/16 inch) between the edge of the border and the level of the sauce. Otherwise, the sauce will overflow while cooking and will discolor the exterior of the border, which must remain absolutely whole.

Sprinkle the sauce with the grated cheese. On top, spread the 25 grams (1 ounce, 2 tablespoons) of butter, divided into small pieces.

Immediately put the dish into a *very hot* oven, to effect, as rapidly as possible, the browning of the border and the glazing of the sauce. That is all that remains to be done, in addition to reheating the cooked ingredients in the dish. Allow *8–10 minutes* to brown the border and glaze the sauce: in other words, time for a light, golden skin to form on the surface of the sauce. Turn the dish from time to time so that it browns evenly all over. Serve straight from the oven.

Fish Gratin with Noodles
(Gratin de Poisson aux Noilles)

Because of the simplicity of its preparation, this is an excellent way to use small amounts of leftover fish, such as brill, bream, hake, cod, etc. *Time: 45 minutes. Serves 6.*

250 grams (8 7/8 ounces) of fish, net weight, with its skin and bones removed; 450 grams (1 pound) of noodles, weighed *cooked;* 75 grams (2 2/3 ounces, 1/3 cup) of butter; 40 grams (1 3/8 ounces) of the white part of a leek; 30 grams (1 ounce) of flour; 5 deciliters (generous 2 cups) of boiled milk; 50–60 grams (1 3/4–2 1/4 ounces) of grated Gruyère; salt, pepper, nutmeg.

PROCEDURE. **The noodles:** Poach them in boiling water (SEE PAGE 568). We do not give the weight of the uncooked noodles here, because it varies depending on the type of noodles you use. Some are dry, like macaroni, and some are fresh, usually found at specialty grocers or delicatessens.

The sauce: In a small pan, gently stew the leek white, which has been sliced into thin rounds, with 30 grams (1 ounce, 2 tablespoons) of butter, without allowing it to brown at all. After *7–8 minutes,* add the boiling milk. Cover and keep warm, without boiling, for about 10 minutes to infuse. Strain the infused milk into a bowl through a chinois. Rinse and dry the pan.

Make a white roux with 30 grams (1 ounce, 2 tablespoons) of butter and the flour. Dilute it with the infused milk; season; let it boil slowly, *2–3 minutes.* Keep the heat very, very low until you are ready to serve the dish.

To serve: Choose an ovenproof dish that is large enough to hold the ingredients. In the bottom of the dish, spread out one-third of the sauce, which here would be equivalent to 8 tablespoons. On top of this, arrange the fish leftovers, each piece divided into equal parts. Cover them with half the remaining sauce. On top of this layer of sauced fish, spread out an even and flat layer of the noodles, having drained them well. Cover them with the rest of the sauce. Sprinkle the grated cheese on top and place the rest of the butter, divided into pieces, on top of that.

About 5 minutes before serving, put the dish into a very hot oven so that the surface of cheese rapidly turns golden. Or, if you have a broiler, slide the dish beneath it: this is the best method. However, in this particular case, it is essential to reheat the underside of the dish on top of the stove for 1 or 2 minutes, because it is possible that the heat of the broiler will not be able to penetrate all the way to the bottom during such a short time beneath the heat.

DEEP-SEA FISH
Poissons de Mer

Sea Bass *(Bar, Loup de Mer, Loubine)*

Large sea bass are simply cooked in a court bouillon of salted water, and they are accompanied with the usual sauces for boiled fish: white sauce, caper sauce, cream sauce, shrimp, mousseline, hollandaise, etc., which are served in a sauceboat.

Small sea bass, which do not weigh more than 300–400 grams ($10^1/_2$–$14^1/_8$ ounces), are cooked in the following manner: à la meunière; deep-fried; grilled and served with a maître d'hôtel butter, or other; au gratin.

Sea Bass Cooked in Court Bouillon *(Bar Bouilli).* Trim the belly and dorsal fins, and the end of the tail; gut and wash the fish. Wrap the head with 3 turns of string and a fourth at the beginning of the body, where you will knot the two ends of the string, without pulling it too tight. This binding maintains the head after cooking and keeps it from slipping away when the fish is transferred from the *poissonière* (fish poacher) to the serving platter. To remove the head, simply snip the string, which will prevent any unnecessary jolting of the fish (for the cooking time, see the directions under court bouillons, PAGE 162). Rub a bit of butter, stuck onto the tip of a knife, over the surface of the fish to give it some shine before placing it on the serving platter.

Mullet can be prepared using the same methods that are appropriate for sea bass.

Brill *(Barbue)*

All the preparations for turbot are appropriate for brill, and vice versa. This is also true of sole. To make brill in a court bouillon, follow the directions given for turbot; the accompanying sauces are the same.

Brill with Mushrooms, White Wine, and Butter Sauce *(Barbue à la Bonne Femme).* Even though this is one of the simplest, it is also one of the best preparations for brill. It can also be used for turbot, as well as for large sole.

The white wine used in the cooking can be cut by one-third with any liquid. In haute cuisine, cooking water from mushrooms, fish bouillon, or, in a pinch, mussel cooking liquor are commonly used. In home kitchens, where these resources are generally not available, it's simply water that you add. The quantity of butter given here for the sauce might seem excessive given the simplicity of the preparation. It is, however, the amount needed to perfect the sauce that draws a considerable part of its characteristic flavor and consistency from the final addition of this butter.

Fish prepared like this are to be served in the same dish in which they have been cooked. Not only do you run the risk of damaging the fish by changing it to another plate, but you would detract from the original character of the dish. *Time: 45 minutes. Serves 6.*

A brill or a turbot, weighing 1 kilogram (2 pounds, 3 ounces), net weight; or 2 sole of the same weight; 200 grams (7 ounces) of fresh mushrooms; 25 grams (1 ounce) of minced shallot; 1/2 tablespoon of parsley, coarsely minced; 150 grams (5 1/3 ounces, 10 1/2 tablespoons) of butter; 8 grams (3/16 ounce/1 teaspoon) of flour; 2 deciliters (6 3/4 fluid ounces, 7/8 cup) of white wine and 1 deciliter (3 1/3 fluid ounces, scant 1/2 cup) of water; salt and pepper.

PROCEDURE. Gut and clean the fish as directed for turbot (SEE PAGE 213). With the tip of a knife, make an incision along the backbone, on the dark side, from the head to just a few centimeters into the tail. Detach the fillets, which have a depth of 2–3 centimeters (3/4–1 1/4 inches) from each side of the bone: this makes it easier for the heat to penetrate the flesh.

The mushrooms: Trim the stem ends. Wash the mushrooms. Do not peel them. Mince both the caps and the stems finely, at the same time.

To cook: Use an ovenproof dish long enough to comfortably hold the fish; it could be in terra cotta, fired porcelain, or in metal. It does not matter, but it should be a little bit concave. Generously butter the bottom, spreading the butter with your fingers. Sprinkle it next with the shallot and the minced parsley. Then spread the minced mushrooms on top. Place the fish on this layer, with the white side up. Sprinkle it with a pinch of good salt and a pinch of pepper. Add the white wine and the water. Dot little bits of butter over the entire surface of the fish; about 30 grams (1 ounce) in total.

Bring to a boil on top of the stove. Then immediately put a piece of oval-shaped buttered baking or parchment paper on top of the fish, extending down the insides of the dish, and completely covering and in direct contact with the fish. Immediately put into a moderately hot oven, so that the liquid will continue to boil *slowly and continuously.* Baste the fish every 5–6 minutes, and completely cover it up each time with the paper.

Cooking time: This should be calculated from the moment the fish is put in the oven; that is, for brill and turbot, at the given weight: *25 minutes* for the brill, and 6–7 minutes more for turbot. For sole weighing about 500 grams (1 pound, 2 ounces), net, *18–20 minutes.* The point of perfect cooking can be established by lifting the end of one of the fillets, which should come away quite easily from the bone.

The sauce: Prepare a beurre manié, with the flour and 15 grams (1/2 ounce, 1 tablespoon) of butter. (SEE LIAISON WITH BEURRE MANIÉ, PAGE 48). Remove the dish from the oven using a kitchen towel or oven gloves. Tilt it over a small pan, preferably a sauté pan, to pour out all the cooking liquid. Cover the fish. Keep it warm.

Reduce the cooking liquid to *2 deciliters (6 3/4 fluid ounces, 7/8 cup).* Thicken it with the beurre manié, as directed. Finally, add the rest of the butter *off the heat,* and incorporate it into the sauce just as you would for a hollandaise.

The sauce, thus finished, can be kept in a double boiler until ready to pour on the fish, which should also be kept warm. The fish must never be sauced until the precise moment before serving.

To serve: Pour the last drop of liquid remaining on the fish plate into the sauce. Spread the sauce over the fish; you can either serve it immediately just as it is, or glaze it. (SEE GLAZING SAUCED DISHES, PAGE 15).

Fillet of Brill with Mussels and Shrimp *(Filets de Barbue à la Dieppoise).* The name *à la dieppoise* implies a garnish of mussels and shrimp, with a sauce base of fish bouillon thickened with egg yolks. It is used for whole fish as well as for sole fillets. The mushrooms are optional, but some mushroom trimmings are suggested to make the sauce aromatic. The shrimp must be absolutely fresh. If not, it would be better not to use them.

We suggest using fillets here, for all recipes using sole (SEE PAGE 204). It is also a matter of simplifying the utensils, because generally, home cooking equipment does not include a *turbotière* (fish poacher) in which it is possible to cook whole fish. Fillets also enable you to use 2 medium-sized fish instead of 1 large one for the same number of guests. *Time: 2 short hours. Serves 10.*

2 brill weighing a total of 1.4–1 1/2 kilograms (3 pounds, 1 ounce to 3 pounds, 5 ounces).

***For cooking the fillet:* 30 grams (1 ounce, 2 tablespoons) of butter; 1 1/2 deciliters (5 fluid ounces, 2/3 cup) of white wine; 4 tablespoons of mushroom cooking water.**

For the fish bouillon: **the bones and head of the fish; 1 onion; 1 small bouquet garni; 4 deciliters ($1^2/_3$ cups) of water; $2^1/_2$ deciliters (1 cup) of white wine; 4 peppercorns; 3 grams ($^1/_{10}$ ounce) of salt.**

For the garnish: **about 40 medium-sized mussels, in other words, about 1 liter (4 cups); 200 grams (7 ounces) of shrimp, net weight.**

For the sauce: **30 grams (1 ounce, 2 tablespoons) of butter and 30 grams (1 ounce) of flour for the roux; 5–6 deciliters (generous 2–$2^1/_2$ cups) of fish bouillon; the poaching liquid from the fish; 4 tablespoons of mussel liquor; 3 egg yolks; 100 grams ($3^1/_2$ ounces, 7 tablespoons), of butter to finish; a bunch of parsley; pepper, grated nutmeg.**

PROCEDURE. Fillet the fish. Make the bouillon with the bones. Start the sauce. Prepare the garnish. Cook the fillets. Add the cooking liquid from the fillets and 4 tablespoons of mussel liquor to the sauce. Thicken it with egg yolks. Reduce and finish with butter. Sauce the fish. Glaze, if you like. Serve.

The fillets: Fillet the fish as directed for fillet of sole. Trim them lightly on the diagonal at both ends.

Divide the largest ones, those of the back, into 3 pieces, cutting them *on the diagonal:* this makes them longer and also better looking. For the small fillets from the belly, you can make only 2 pieces—thus, in total, you will have 20 fillets or pieces. Arrange them in a buttered ovenproof dish. Prepare the fish bouillon as directed in its section (SEE PAGE 165).

The sauce: In a medium pan, make a *light* blond roux. Dilute it with the fish bouillon. Season it with a pinch of white pepper and a hint of grated nutmeg. Bring it to a boil and add the bunch of parsley. Immediately lower the heat, position the pan as required and skim the sauce, for about *35 minutes* (SEE PAGE 16).

The mussels: Clean them (SEE PAGE 241). Open them in a covered pot over low heat, with 2 finely minced shallots, some parsley branches in pieces, a sprig of thyme, and a hint of bay. Remove them from their shells and keep warm in their cooking water, which has been decanted and strained through a cloth.

The shrimp: After peeling, keep them cool between 2 plates.

Cooking the fillets: About 20 minutes before serving, season them lightly with good salt. Add white wine, the cooking liquid from mushrooms, and the butter, divided into small pieces. Bring it to a boil. Cover it with buttered baking or parchment paper, and position the dish at the front of the oven, to poach for *8–9 minutes,* as has been directed for sole fillets.

Presentation: Arrange the fillets on a large, round serving platter; it must be ovenproof if you are going to glaze the fillets. Surround them with the mussels, *well drained,* and shrimp, mixed together. Cover everything with another platter. Keep it warm at the front of the oven.

To finish the sauce: Remove the bouquet garni. Add the cooking water from the fillets and 4 tablespoons of mussel liquor. Strain this through a chinois into a sauté pan. Thicken with the egg yolks (SEE LIAISONS, PAGE 47). Reduce it over high heat, stirring constantly, until the sauce has been reduced to 6 deciliters ($2^1/_2$ cups) or less. Add the final butter *off the heat,* and the cayenne pepper.

Keep it warm, and serve as directed for BARBUE À LA BONNE FEMME (PAGE 178).

Brill with Tomatoes, Onions, and White Wine *(Barbue à la Dugléré).* This is a simple preparation, which is equally adaptable for sole and for flat fish in general. It is a good dish both for lunches and dinners, and it is easy to make, as long as you can obtain fresh tomatoes.

This is a very popular restaurant dish, which explains why the fish is presented in slices, as they are easier to cook rapidly than fish of a certain size. This division is in no way essential in other circumstances. We suggest it nonetheless, but you have complete license to leave the fish whole. This is frequently done for sole.

This dish includes the final glazing for the sauced fish. Nonetheless, this final glazing can be omitted if achieving it proves a real difficulty: an insufficiently hot oven, or a serving platter that is incapable of sustaining the intensity of the heat, or not enough time, etc. But whenever possible, we recommend the glazing here. *Time: 40 minutes, but the tomatoes and onions can be prepared in advance; the dish, therefore, takes less time. In this case, allow 18 minutes to poach the fish, plus 12 minutes to finish the sauce in the final glazing. Serves 6.*

A brill weighing, net, 1 kilogram (2 pounds, 3 ounces); 500 grams (1 pound, 2 ounces) of tomatoes; 1 tablespoon of tomato concentrate; 100 grams (3 1/2 ounces) of onion; 3 shallots; a piece of garlic the size of a pea; 1 tablespoon of minced parsley; a fragment of thyme and bay.

2 deciliters (6 3/4 fluid ounces, 7/8 cup) of white wine; 1 deciliter (3 1/3 fluid ounces, scant 1/2 cup) of fish bouillon, or of the cooking liquid from mushrooms; or, if you have neither of those, the same amount of white wine to make up the total—in other words, 3 deciliters (1 1/4 cups) white wine; 15 grams (1/2 ounce, 1 tablespoon) of butter worked with 10 grams (1/3 ounce) of flour; 150 grams (5 1/3 ounces, 10 1/2 tablespoons) of butter; a good point of cayenne pepper (as much as can be held on a knife tip).

PROCEDURE. Peel the tomatoes (SEE PAGE 534). Squeeze them to remove the water and the seeds. Mince them thoroughly. Put them on a plate.

Finely mince the onion. Press it in the corner of a towel, having first plunged it into cool water so that it does not discolor while standing. Mince the shallot and the parsley very finely.

Crush the garlic with the blade of a knife. Tie the thyme and a third of a bay leaf with a string, leaving a bit extra so that you can easily retrieve it after cooking.

Assemble all these different ingredients on a plate.

The brill: This can be gutted and cleaned in advance, as for turbot (SEE PAGE 213).

If you want to cut up the brill to cook it, proceed as follows: split it the long way from the head to the tail, being careful to follow the backbone down the middle. Then divide each half into 6 pieces. The part of the head is only for show, so this gives you only 10 pieces in total for the entire fish.

Generously butter the bottom of an oval dish, or any ovenproof plate. In an even layer, spread half of the tomatoes, onion, shallot, parsley and garlic. Add the tablespoon of tomato concentrate.

On top of that, arrange the pieces of brill just as they were before they were cut, thus reconstructing the fish. Season with a good pinch of salt and a pinch of pepper. Then cover it with the remaining half of the different ingredients. Add the liquid and 25–30 grams (about 1 ounce, 2 tablespoons) of butter, divided into pieces, which you spread around on the surface of the dish. If white wine is the only liquid used, add an additional 25 grams (1 ounce, 2 tablespoons) of butter.

Bring it to a boil on top of the stove first, then cover it with buttered baking or parchment paper directly touching the fish. Replace the lid over that, and put the dish into a rather warm oven.

Allow *a scant 15 minutes* of cooking in the oven, and *25 minutes* if the brill is cooked whole. A whole turbot cooks *6–7 minutes* more. For a large whole sole that weighs from 500–550 grams (1 pound, 2 ounces to 1 pound, 3 ounces), allow *18–20 minutes.* The sauce is made with the cooking liquid from the fish. Before taking it out of the oven, check that it is done by lightly lifting up the flesh, which must easily come away from the bone.

Remove the pieces of brill from their cooking liquid, using a spatula or 2 forks, and arrange them on the serving platter in the same order as before. In other words, in the original shape of the fish. If the fish is to be glazed before serving, the platter must metal or some other material that can withstand the heat of a hot oven. Cover it with another plate turned upside down, keep it warm in a very low oven.

The sauce: Pour the cooking liquid from the fish into a small sauté pan. Remove the thyme and the bay. Boil over high heat until the original quantity of 3 1/2 deciliters (1 1/2 cups) is reduced to barely 2 deciliters (6 3/4 fluid ounces, 7/8 cup). Thicken with the beurre manié. Then stir, over the heat, for 2 more minutes. If you serve immediately, add the final butter *off the heat.* Check the salt. Add the cayenne pepper to spice it up, because of the tomato.

To sauce and serve: Pour the little bit of liquid that has been released by the fish into the sauce. With a metal spoon, spread the sauce on the fish. Then glaze it (SEE PAGE 15). Serve.

Brill with Shrimp, Cream, and Butter Sauce *(Barbue à la Havraise).* An exquisite regional dish. Although this is quite simple, there are three essential requirements: fish that is absolutely fresh; thick and extremely fresh cream; and shrimp cooked only when ready to use.

Large sole can be prepared in the same manner. *Time: 45 minutes. Serves 6–8.*

A brill weighing at least 1 kilogram (2 pounds, 3 ounces); 250 grams (8 7/8 ounces) of shrimp; 80 grams (2 3/4 ounces, 5 1/2 tablespoons) of good, fresh butter; 20 grams (2/3 ounce) of flour; 2 good deciliters (6 3/4 fluid ounces, 7/8 cup) of heavy cream; salt and pepper.

PROCEDURE. Clean and scale the brill as directed for the turbot. Make an incision that runs the entire length of the spine on the dark side to make it easier for the heat to penetrate the flesh.

Use a dish that can comfortably hold the fish, is not very deep, that can go both into the oven and be used to serve at the table. Generously butter the bottom with about 30 grams (1 ounce, 2 tablespoons) of butter, spread out with your fingertips. Sprinkle it with salt and pepper. Put in the brill, dark side down, and sprinkle lightly with salt. Spread about 30 grams (1 ounce, 2 tablespoons) of butter, divided in bits, over the fish. Do not add any liquid.

Cover the plate with another plate; or, if you do not have that, a good, strong sheet of baking or parchment paper, about the size of the plate, and placed directly in contact with the fish. Set the dish over low heat, simmer gently without boiling. If your oven can be regulated to a moderate heat, you can put the dish, carefully covered, in it to cook. Allow *a good 30 minutes* of cooking on top of the stove and *25 minutes* in the oven.

Baste the fish with the cooking butter every 5–6 minutes, and then recover it immediately. The dish is cooked when a matchstick inserted into the thickest part of the flesh penetrates without effort.

Meanwhile, in a small saucepan set over low heat, warm the remaining butter and mix it with the flour. Let it cook for 1 minute, without any browning, to remove the raw taste from the flour. Add the cream, tablespoon by tablespoon, stirring constantly with a wooden spoon, and heating it gently, without ever letting it boil. Finally, add the peeled shrimp. Keep everything warm until the fish is perfectly cooked.

About *5–6 minutes* before serving, add the liquid from cooking the fish to the sauce. You do this by tipping the cooking platter above the saucepan to pour out the juice right to the final drop; otherwise, any liquid left in the fish cooking dish will not mix with the sauce. Check the seasoning. Put the sauce over the brill. It must completely cover the brill in a creamy layer. If possible, glaze it (SEE PAGE 15). If not, serve good and hot and on warmed plates.

Monkfish *(Baudroie)*

Monkfish sold at the markets is offered without its head and without its skin; its flesh resembles lobster without having quite the same finesse. Usually, it's cut into slices and fried, accompanied by a well-flavored sauce: of capers, béarnaise, tomatoes, etc. The same slices, cut a little thicker, can also be cooked in a court bouillon of salted water (SEE PAGE 165); they are served warm with the same sauces, or cold, with mayonnaise or tartar sauce, etc. You can also, for monkfish cooked in court bouillon, keep the side whole, instead of dividing it into slices. For all dishes, you must carefully remove the white membrane, which is transparent and covers the back, and above all, the darkish skin covering the belly, because if you do not do this, the cooked fish will have a very unattractive, unappetizing appearance.

Monkfish with Tomatoes, Onion, Garlic, and Olive Oil *(Baudroie à la Provençale).* *Time: 45 minutes. Serves 6.*

900 grams (2 pounds) of monkfish; 900 grams (2 pounds) of tomatoes; 2–3 good tablespoons of finely minced onion; 1 deciliter (3 1/3 fluid ounces, scant 1/2 cup) of olive oil; a speck of garlic the size of a pea, crushed; 1 tablespoon of minced parsley.

PROCEDURE. Plunge the tomatoes into boiling water for several seconds to remove the skin. Cut them in half and remove the seeds and water. Cut them in slices and chop coarsely. Heat the oil in a pan with a large bottom; gently sauté the onion in the oil without letting it brown. Then add the tomatoes and the garlic. Let the whole thing cook gently, stirring from time to time, until the pieces of tomato resemble a compote.

The fish should be peeled and washed, then cut into slices. Dip it in flour, and, over high heat, brown it in a pan with a few tablespoons of very hot oil. Drain it and place it on top of the tomatoes, where you will let it stew for 10 minutes, turning it over occasionally. Serve the fish slices surrounded with tomato and sprinkled with the minced parsley.

Cod *(Cabillaud)*

In France, this fish is used fresh, when it is known as *cabillaud,* as well as dried and salted, when it is called *morue* (salt cod). Whenever possible, always choose the section from the middle of the body, going toward the tail, because it is the best part. Allow 1 kilogram (2 pounds, 3 ounces) of fish for 6 people. Since cod is one of the most ordinary of fish, its different preparations are always quite simple.

Boiled Cod *(Cabillaud Bouilli).* In salt water: accompanied by one of the appropriate sauces; hollandaise, mussel sauce, cream, capers, etc.; or, as they do in the northern part of the country, with a sauceboat of melted butter and served with boiled potatoes (*pommes de terre à l'anglaise*).

Creamed Cod au Gratin *(Cabillaud à la Crème au Gratin).* SEE CREAMED FISH AU GRATIN, PAGE 183.

Grilled Cod *(Cabillaud Grillé).* Cut into slices 3 centimeters (1¼ inches) thick. Season, flour, drizzle with melted butter, and grill gently. Serve with a flavored butter: maître d'hôtel, anchovy, etc.; or accompany it with a flavorsome sauce.

Deep-Fried and Breaded Cod *(Cabillaud Frit).* Cut into thinner slices (2½ centimeters/1 inch), then season and coat with bread crumbs. Deep-fry, taking care to observe the directions given about the thickness of the fish and the degree of heat required (SEE DEEP-FRYING FISH, PAGE 40). Serve with tartar sauce, tomato sauce, caper sauce, etc.

Baked Cod *(Cabillaud à la Ménagère).* *Time: 1 hour to marinate; 35 minutes of cooking.*

1 kilogram (2 pounds, 3 ounces) of cod; 60 grams (2¼ ounces) of carrot; 80 grams (2¾ ounces) of onion; 20 grams (⅔ ounce) of shallot; 4–5 parsley stems; a sprig of thyme; a very small half bay leaf; 3 tablespoons of oil; 2 deciliters (6¾ fluid ounces, ⅞ cup) of white wine; salt and pepper; 2 good tablespoons of bread crumbs.

PROCEDURE. With a knife, make some incisions on both sides of the fish. Put the cod into a dish with the onion, carrot, shallot, which has been finely minced, and all the rest of the ingredients mentioned above, except for the bread crumbs. Marinate for 1 hour, turning the fish at least 5–6 times.

Drain the fish and pat dry. Put it into an ovenproof dish that has been very generously buttered. Strain the marinade through the chinois and pour it *around* the fish. Bring to a boil on top of the stove. Then spread the fish with melted butter. Put it into a hot oven.

Allow *30–35 minutes* for cooking, depending on the thickness of the fish. From time to time, baste it with the liquid in the plate; 7–8 minutes before the end of this cooking process, cover the surface of the fish with the bread crumbs and drizzle with melted butter. When the gratin has formed, the fish can be kept warm toward the front of the oven for some time until you are ready to serve. At the last moment, squeeze the juice of a lemon quarter over the cod. At the same time, in another dish, serve small potatoes that have been boiled à l'anglaise, then drizzled with melted butter and sprinkled with minced parsley.

Plaice *(Carrelet)*

This is a fish much like a turbot, but flatter, and with brown skin that is speckled with orange spots. Its flesh, although tender, lacks the finesse of turbot, brill, or sole; thus, it should be reserved only for family meals.

The preparation varies according to size: small and medium-sized are best fried or à la meunière. You can also grill them, after making lengthwise and crosswise incisions, in the form of a cross, and serve with a flavored butter, such as maître d'hôtel or something similar. When it weighs more than 500 grams (1 pound, 2 ounces), cook it in white wine or serve as a gratin; or, you can cook it with onions à la lyonnaise, as hereafter described.

Plaice with Onions *(Carrelet aux Oignons).* This method is used for larger plaice, but it also works quite well for medium-sized plaice weighing around 500 grams (1 pound, 2 ounces). And you can also cook 2 medium-sized plaice in the same dish, arranging them tail to tail. *Time: 1 short hour. Serves 6.*

1 large plaice, not gutted, weighing 1 kilogram (2 pounds, 3 ounces); or 2 medium-sized ones, weighing 500 grams (1 pound, 2 ounces) each.

PROCEDURE. Thinly slice 500 grams (1 pound, 2 ounces) of fresh onion. Gently stew the slices in a sauté pan with 50 grams (1 3/4 ounces, 3 1/2 tablespoons) of butter, a pinch of salt, a little bit of sugar, and some pepper, without letting it brown at all. Then arrange the onions, which are by now quite soft, into a long ovenproof dish and spread with 25 grams (1 ounce, 2 tablespoons) of butter. Place the fish on top, dark side *down,* after first making an incision the entire length of the bone; do not remove any skin.

Add 1 1/2 deciliters (5 fluid ounces, 2/3 cup) of white wine, 1 deciliter (3 1/3 fluid ounces, scant 1/2 cup) of the cooking water from mushrooms, or, if you do not have that, water. Bring it to a boil on top of the stove. Cover with buttered baking or parchment paper and put it into the oven. Allow, from that moment, *25 minutes* of cooking for large plaice and a few minutes less for medium-sized ones. Baste every 6–8 minutes with the cooking liquid.

To serve: Drain the fish in a strainer, then put it on a serving platter. Arrange the onions all around. Thicken the cooking liquid with 25 grams (1 ounce, 2 tablespoons) of butter mixed with 10 grams (1/3 ounce) of flour (SEE LIAISON WITH BEURRE MANIÉ, PAGE 48). Pour it over the fish and the onions.

Hake *(Colin)*

This is a fish that was greatly underestimated until life became expensive after the Great War. However, no cookbook fails to mention it, if only as an ingredient for fish bouillon, for which, of course, inexpensive fish is used.

The recipes are very simple, and here they are:

Hake in Slices *(Colin en Tranches).* Cut 2 centimeters (3/4 inch) thick, *fried,* served with a flavorsome sauce: anchovy, caper, béarnaise, etc.; or *cooked à la meunière* (SEE PAGE 167). Or, even *au gratin* SEE WHITING AU GRATIN, PAGE 194).

Whole Hake or in Large Pieces *(Colin Entire ou en Gros Morceau).* Cook in a court bouillon of salted water (SEE PAGE 165). If the hake is whole, cut off the head where the body begins, the dorsal and belly fins, and almost the entire tail. Gut the fish, wash it, wipe it dry. On both sides, make some small incisions, about 1/2 centimeter (3/16 inch) deep, at a distance of about 2 centimeters (3/4 inch).

Rub the surface of the fish with good salt. Let macerate in a cool place for 30 minutes. Plunge the hake into the boiling water, salted with 15 grams (1/2 ounce) of sea salt for each liter (4 cups) of water. Once boiling has resumed, allow *10 minutes* of poaching for every 450 grams (1 pound). To serve, completely remove the skin from the fish. Place it on a long platter covered with a napkin. Decorate it at both ends with parsley, and on each side, boiled potatoes à l'anglaise. At the same time, serve one of the recommended sauces as for HAKE IN SLICES, above, or even melted butter, for which you should allow about 20 grams (2/3 ounce, 1 heaping tablespoon) per person, seasoned with salt, white pepper, nutmeg, and lemon juice.

Sea Bream, or Dorade *(Daurade, Royal)*

The different preparations of this excellent fish can be classified thus: small fish can be grilled, previously scaled and trimmed, and served with a maître d'hôtel butter or other flavored butter, or cooked à la meunière. Larger fish can be cooked in a court bouillon of salted water (SEE PAGE 165), which is the best cooking method when the bream is good and fresh, or accompanied by a sauceboat of white sauce, caper sauce, hollandaise, etc. Like whiting, it can also be prepared au gratin or à la Bercy, and *à la Portugaise,* as we describe on PAGE 186. Baked and au Chablis, the two recipes given below, are particularly recommended.

Baked Bream *(Daurade au Four)*. This is one of the simplest home-style dishes. As with every preparation of this type, its excellence is a result of meticulous attention to detail and technique, as much as the freshness of the fish. *Time: 30–40 minutes for cooking. Serves 6–8.*

A bream weighing approximately 1 1/4 kilograms (2 pounds, 12 ounces); 70 grams (2 1/2 ounces, 1/3 cup) of butter; 30 grams (1 ounce) of onion, cut into thin rounds; 3 tablespoons of water; 3 pinches of salt; a pinch of pepper; a branch of parsley.

PROCEDURE. Carefully scale the bream. Remove the gills. Then, by way of a small incision made in the belly, finish cleaning the insides by scraping the dorsal backbone with the tip of your finger to loosen the coagulated blood. Trim the fins and the end of the tail. Wash the fish under running water.

Choose a long ovenproof dish, preferably made of a good, thick, rustic clay and large enough so that the fish head fits comfortably in the dish. During cooking, the head releases more flavor and more substances to thicken the sauce than any other part of the fish. Use your fingers to spread one-third of the butter over the bottom of the dish. Sprinkle with salt.

On this buttered surface, place onion and parsley in the middle, where you're going to put the fish. Stuff half of the remaining butter in the cavity of the bream, with a pinch of salt and pepper.

Put the fish on top of the onion and parsley in the dish. With a good knife, make 4 parallel diagonal incisions, as for fish that is to be grilled, about 2 millimeters (1/16 inch) deep. This should be just adequate to split the skin from one side of the fish to the other. The tender flesh will open considerably as a result.

Divide the remaining butter in small pieces. Insert them into the deepest part of the incisions. Sprinkle everything with a pinch of salt. Add the 3 tablespoons of water to the dish. Now it is ready to put into the oven. The fish can be prepared at your leisure and can be kept in a cool place for an hour or more.

To cook: This requires a good warm oven, but not so warm that it browns the fish too early.

Depending upon how the heat is dispersed in your oven, either put the dish on the bottom of the oven, or on a shelf in the middle, so that the fish is heated mainly from above.

After 7–8 minutes, it should not yet have begun to brown. But in the incisions, which will have expanded with the heat, the flesh should already appear to be somewhat blanched. Then, move the dish closer to the front of the oven and, tilting it carefully so that you do not move the fish, use a metal spoon to baste it with 2 good tablespoons of cooking liquid.

Baste it again every 7–8 minutes. While you do this, make sure that the onions are not moved, so that they do not brown in the slightest, which is essential for the flavor of this dish.

As soon as you see the bream beginning to brown, bit by bit, baste it more often to prevent it from getting too dark. If necessary, cover with buttered baking or parchment paper laid directly on the fish.

Allow *35–40 minutes* of cooking, under these conditions, for a fish of this weight. Once cooked, the fish should be golden, firm, with a light browning. The cooking liquid is a beautiful blond juice, slightly syrupy. Serve it in the same dish, placed on a serving platter lined with a cloth.

Bream Baked in Chablis *(Daurade au Chablis)*. An excellent dish. The cooking procedure is exactly the same for ordinary baked bream; but here, white wine replaces water. This wine—used in a larger quantity than the water it is replacing in view of the final sauce—must be of very good quality—an excellent Chablis or an authentic Sauternes. *Time: 35–40 minutes for cooking.*

A bream weighing about 1 1/4 kilograms (2 pounds, 12 ounces); 150 grams (5 1/3 ounces, 10 1/2 tablespoons) of very good butter; 3 deciliters (1 1/4 cups) of dry Sauternes or Chablis; 30 grams (1 ounce) of onion and a sprig of parsley; 1 tablespoon of minced parsley and chervil; juice of 1 lemon; salt and pepper; 1 teaspoon of arrowroot or of another starch.

PROCEDURE. Clean the fish as directed in the preceding recipe.

Spread 50 grams (1 3/4 ounces, 3 1/2 tablespoons) of butter in a shallow oval baking dish, preferably earthenware, according to the directions given for the baked bream (SEE ABOVE), making sure there is not too much space around the fish, because this would require more liquid, and also because it would reduce too rapidly.

In the buttered dish, place the onion, cut into 2–3 rounds about 1/2 centimeter (3/16 inch) thick, and the sprig of parsley. Put the fish on top of that, with the head in direct contact with the bottom, for the reason given above; if the tail sticks out a little, that's no problem. *Do not make any incisions on the fish.* Add the wine, season with salt and pepper.

To cook: Proceed as for the baked bream. Above all, avoid excessive heat beneath dish, because the fish must simmer; you must not allow it to boil rapidly; this would cause it to reduce too much. This liquid, after cooking, must still be relatively abundant to make the accompanying sauce.

When the bream is perfectly cooked, remove it with a spatula, or with 2 forks, to place it on the serving platter, with all traces of onion and parsley removed. Keep it warm. If you like, you can decorate it with lemon rounds.

The sauce: Strain all the cooking liquid through a chinois into a small saucepan.

If the bottom of the dish has colored a bit too much due to excessive heat, rinse it with some of the wine, strained through the chinois, to lift off this light caramel. You should have, at this point, 2 deciliters (6 3/4 ounces, 7/8 cup) of liquid. Thicken it with the arrowroot (SEE LIAISONS, PAGE 47). Add the butter (SEE BUTTERING, PAGE 16). Finish with the parsley, chervil, and lemon. Check the seasoning. Pour it into the sauceboat and serve.

Bream with Tomatoes, Onions, and Wine *(Daurade à la Portugaise).* A flavorsome preparation in its simplest form, which does not require mushrooms as indicated for sole. For all the details of this recipe, you should refer to the two preceding recipes. *Time: 45 minutes (once the fish has been gutted and cleaned).*

A bream weighing about 1 kilogram (2 pounds, 3 ounces); 6 medium-size tomatoes; 50 grams (1 3/4 ounces) of minced onion; 100 grams (3 1/2 ounces, 7 tablespoons) of butter; 2 deciliters (6 3/4 fluid ounces, 7/8 cup) of white wine; 1 teaspoon of starch, preferably arrowroot; 1 tablespoon of minced parsley; salt, pepper.

PROCEDURE. Clean the bream as directed (SEE PAGE 185).

Remove the skin, seeds, and the liquid of the tomatoes; chop coarsely. Butter an ovenproof dish with 30 grams (1 ounce, 2 tablespoons) of butter. Spread half of the tomato, the onion, and the minced parsley in the dish. Place the bream on top. Sprinkle it with salt and pepper, and cover it with the remaining tomato, onion, and parsley. Dot 30 grams (1 ounce, 2 tablespoons) of butter divided into small pieces over the fish. Pour the white wine into the dish. Put it in the oven. Cook as directed in the preceding bream recipes, basting frequently; the time is the same, give or take a few minutes.

When the bream is cooked, remove the dish from the oven and tilt it over a small pan, making sure that the fish does not slide, to pour out all the cooking liquid. Bring it to a boil over high heat, and soon you will be able to thicken it with the starch (SEE LIAISONS, PAGE 47). Off the heat, stir in the remaining butter, divided into small pieces. Check the seasoning; pour the sauce on the bream. Return the dish to the oven for 2–3 minutes before serving in order to send it out burning hot.

Smelt *(Éperlan)*

The most popular way to prepare this fish, given its small size, is deep-frying, as for gudgeon. They can be served on skewers, like kabobs, or arranged on a platter. In both of these cases, they are served on a cloth and garnished with fried parsley and lemon quarters. They can also be cooked à la meuniére or au gratin, as for whiting, but it should be noted that smelt must be cooked *in a very hot oven,* so that the gratin forms at the same time as the fish are cooked to perfection, a point that is reached rather rapidly, this fish being smaller than the whiting.

Smelt are not washed, except when they do not seem to be clean. Simply wipe them with a dry towel once you have gutted them through the gills. The roe is left inside. You should handle this fish as little as possible, because its very delicate flesh is easily damaged.

Gurnard *(Grondin)*

Due to its red color, this fish is often wrongly confused with red mullet. There is no doubt that this is an error, because the shape of the two fish is substantially different. The gurnard has a large head, resembling a dolphin, and its flesh does not even begin to approach the delicacy of the red mullet.

The best way to prepare this is to cook it in a vinegar court bouillon (SEE PAGE 164). It can then be accompanied with a sauce of your choosing: capers, mussels, etc.

You can also cook it simply in salted water. To serve, remove the head, take off the skin, and cover it with a sauce of your choice.

Baked Gurnard *(Grondin au Four).* Cooked in the same way as for bream (SEE PAGE 185).

Gurnard in Cream Sauce *(Grondin à la Crème).* Choose small fish, each weighing about 150 grams ($5^1/_3$ ounces). Cook them in the oven covered with buttered baking or parchment paper with 1 tablespoon of white wine and 2 tablespoons of water for each fish. Make a small *roux blanc* (SEE PAGE 47), diluted with their cooking liquid; add 1 tablespoon of heavy cream for each gurnard. Cover the fish with this, and serve with potatoes that have been cut into small balls and boiled.

Smoked Haddock *(Haddock)*

Haddock is a fish that resembles hake, which is smoked in a special way, and is a great favorite in England, where it is often served for breakfast. In France, where this meal is not as important, lunch is when haddock is served. The best haddock has thick fillets that are neither dried out nor shriveled, with a yellowish-orange tint that is not too dark. The Finnan haddock, imported from Scotland, is better than all others. You can either broil it or roast it in the oven, or you can cook it in boiling water. Better yet, cook it in milk in the Scottish way, which is excellent. Then serve it with melted butter and lemon, or with a white sauce, or even an egg sauce.

Allow about 100 grams ($3^1/_2$ ounces) of haddock per person. Whichever method of cooking you use, do not rinse the haddock. Simply wipe it off with a dry cloth.

Broiled Haddock *(Haddock Grillé).* Brush the fillet with melted butter kept ready in a cup (25 grams/1 ounce/2 tablespoons of butter for 450 grams/1 pound of haddock). Put it under a broiler that has been preheated to moderate. After 3 minutes, baste again using a brush, and turn the fillets over. Allow *12 minutes of cooking* in all, turning the fillets twice and basting them each time *on both sides.* Serve them with melted butter or sauce.

Roast Haddock *(Haddock Rôti au Four).* Put the fillets on a grill set in a roasting dish, so that they do not touch the bottom. Brush them with melted butter. Put them in a good, hot oven for *10–12 minutes.*

Boiled Haddock *(Haddock Cuit à l'Eau).* Put the fillets in a long heatproof dish. Cover them generously with cool water. Bring them to a boil. Then, over moderate heat, maintain the water just at the simmering point for *about 12* minutes.

To serve: On a round plate, arrange the fillets of haddock, cooked according to one of these methods. If you like, surround them with parsley leaves. On the side, serve melted butter in a sauceboat, or an egg sauce, or simply with fresh butter. You can also serve with boiled potatoes.

Smoked Haddock, Scottish-Style *(Haddock à la Façon Ecossaise).* Divide the haddock in half lengthwise. Line them up in an ovenproof baking dish large enough so that the liquid can sufficiently cover the fish. Pour in milk that has been previously boiled *but subsequently chilled:* $^1/_2$ liter (generous 2 cups) for every 450 grams (1 pound) of haddock. Bring it slowly to a boil. Then lower the heat. Cover and simmer for *about 10 minutes.*

During this time, in a small pan, combine 30 grams (1 ounce, 2 tablespoons) of butter and 30 grams (1 ounce) of flour for a white roux. Once the fish is cooked, dilute the roux with the cooking milk while it is still quite warm. Add pepper and grated nutmeg but no salt since the haddock is already salted. Bring it to a boil. Remove from the heat and stir 50 grams ($1^3/_4$ ounces, $3^1/_2$ tablespoons) of butter into the sauce. Pour that into a sauceboat.

Smoked Haddock Soufflé *(Soufflé de Haddock).* For quantities and preparation, refer to FISH SOUFFLÉ (PAGE 175). Except in this case, it would be infinitely better to cook the haddock in milk, in the Scottish way. This milk should then be reduced to obtain the quantity needed for the béchamel, which is used to thicken the sauce. It also adds a great deal of flavor to the entire dish. Season with salt very prudently, as the milk will have absorbed a great deal of the salt from the fish.

Herring *(Hareng)*

Fresh herring is at its best when it is quite full—in other words, with its roe or its eggs. Fall is the best season for this and, consequently, that is the time of year when it is best to use them. The ways to prepare herring are simple enough, and mustard is quite important in these recipes: either in traditional broiled herring with a mustard sauce, and *herring à la portière,* which is also a classic and for both of which we give the recipes, as well as *herring à la diable.* For this, herring is brushed with mustard and sprinkled with bread crumbs, then grilled, sprinkled with oil, and served with a very piquant ravigote sauce. For something more subtle, à la meunière is also appropriate for herring: in this case, you serve it without any other accompaniment except a border of lemon slices.

Allow 1 herring per person.

Fresh Herring in Mustard Sauce *(Harengs Frais Sauce Moutarde).* *Time 25 minutes (once the fish have been gutted).*

Clean the herrings and rub them to remove the scales. With scissors, cut off the end of the tail and the fins. Wash the fish and dry with a towel. With the tip of a knife, make some diagonal incisions in the filets; this will facilitate the cooking; in other words, 5–6 incisions on each side, about 2–3 millimeters (1/16–1/8 inch) deep, running the entire length of the fish. Salt and pepper the fish, drizzle with oil, and broil under moderate heat.

Serve them garnished with several branches of fresh parsley, and with a mustard sauce in the sauceboat (SEE MUSTARD SAUCE, PAGE 69).

Fresh Herring with Mustard, Vinegar, and Butter Sauce *(Harengs Frais à la Portiere).* *Time: 15–20 minutes for cooking (once the fish have been gutted).*

Clean the herrings and cut the fillets as indicated for broiling them. Soak them in a little milk that you have poured into a shallow bowl. Season with salt and pepper. Roll them in flour, spread out on a sheet of paper, and then shake them, holding them by the tail, to rid them of excess flour.

For 4 herrings, heat 25 grams (1 ounce, 2 tablespoons) of butter in a pan. Arrange the herrings head to tail. Cook over moderate heat and turn them over from time to time to brown evenly on all sides, as for a meunière.

Arrange them on a long, warmed platter. Using a small brush, generously coat them with mustard; this doesn't have to be completely consistent, because the covering is not very thick. If necessary, you can dilute the mustard with a few drops of vinegar. Sprinkle everything with minced parsley.

In the pan where the herrings have just cooked, heat 75 grams (2 2/3 ounces, 1/3 cup) of butter over moderate heat until it is lightly colored, and gives off an odor of hazelnut. In one motion, pour the butter over the herrings. Quickly, with the pan still burning hot, pour in a small amount of vinegar, and pour it over the butter, which is already over the herring. Serve immediately, so that the butter is still foaming when the plate arrives at the table.

Salted Herrings *(Harengs Saurs).* Choose them plump and supple; dry and flat indicates that they are old and oversalted. For all preparations, you first remove the head. Then, cover the herrings with warm water, where they must soak comfortably for a good hour. Drain them on a towel; split the skin along the back and remove it; it detaches like a ribbon. Open the herrings by splitting the flesh along the entire back. Remove the dorsal bone. Carefully remove the small bones from the flesh, as well as the intestine and other debris. Reserve the roe and the eggs.

Cover the fillet, the roe, and the eggs with fresh milk. Leave them to soak and desalinate; the time will vary according to the kind of dish being prepared, but it should not be less than 3 hours. It can be as long as 24 hours, to ensure the fish are thoroughly desalinated. Now the herrings are ready for their chosen use. The milk should be discarded.

Salted Herrings with a Piquant Sauce *(Harengs Lucas).* A popular hors d'oeuvre, which is named after the famous Parisian restaurant, now called

Lucas-Carton. Choose nice salted herrings, half with roe and half with eggs.

Prepare the herrings as ON PAGE 188, alternating successive soakings (warm water and milk), each one lasting 24 hours. Drain, dry, and drizzle them with oil; 1 tablespoon for each herring. Let them soak a third time for 24 hours. Turn over once during this time. This oil is not used for the sauce, as it will have taken on an odor. Drain, and cut the herrings into thin slices. Cover them with the following sauce:

For 4 herrings, which will serve about 6 people, put 2 hard-boiled egg yolks, crushed with a wooden spoon in a small bowl with 3 teaspoons of mustard, the roe and milt of the herring, and a pinch of pepper. Gradually, and stirring constantly, as for a mayonnaise, dilute with 6 tablespoons of oil, alternating with 3 tablespoons of good vinegar. Add 3 tablespoons of minced cornichons, 1/2 teaspoon of minced shallot, 2 tablespoons of chervil leaves, and finally, 6 tablespoons of thick crème fraîche.

Add the pieces of herring to this sauce and mix well. Transfer to a shallow dish. Serve as an hors d'ouevre.

Sand Dabs *(Limande)*

This fish resembles sole only in its shape, because its flesh has none of the savoriness nor the firmness of a sole. For this reason, it's preferable to leave the dark skin on.

Generally, you fry sand dabs: either with bread crumbs or simply dipped in milk and then floured. It can also be prepared au gratin with white wine. See recipes for fish prepared like this, and proceed the same way. Recipes for plaice are also appropriate for sand dabs.

Mackerel *(Maquereau)*

The season for mackerel extends from the end of the spring to fall. Like sardines, herring, and in general, all oily fish, this has a tendency to spoil rapidly. More than any other fish, this gives it a very strong and unpleasant fishy taste. Thus, an important and essential prerequisite is that the fish must be perfectly fresh. Just as for other fish, this can be recognized by a well-rounded, or convex, clear eye, still full of life, and the firmness of the flesh to the touch. Its roe is extremely delicate: the result is that mackerel with roe is more in demand than that which has eggs.

Main preparations: The most common and, without a doubt, the best as well, is grilled à la maître d'hôtel. Therefore, we give a detailed explanation of this dish ON PAGE 190.

Grilled mackerel can be served with any number of sauces: ravigote, caper, mustard, etc. You cover the fish with sauce just enough to completely mask it, and the rest of the sauce is served in a sauceboat.

The other mackerel dishes, generally speaking, tend to involve the use of the fish cut into large pieces or separated into 2 fillets.

That's the way it is used in all recipes that call for a court bouillon, where it is rarely cooked whole; nonetheless, we will use the whole fish in the recipe for mackerel with gooseberry. The court bouillon used has a vinegar base, or is simply salted water. Always be sure, after cooking in court bouillon, to remove the skin from the pieces or the fillets.

Boiled mackerel is accompanied with a caper sauce, parsley sauce, ravigote sauce, and others. It is served in a sauceboat with the whole fish and poured over for pieces or fillets. The same is true if you serve the mackerel *cold;* in this case, it should be accompanied by an appropriate sauce: mayonnaise, tartare, remoulade, etc.

Poached Mackerel with Mussels *(Maquereau Bouilli à la Boulonnaise).* Divide it into pieces. Cook in a vinegar court bouillon (SEE PAGE 164). This should be surrounded by mussels that have been cooked separately (SEE MUSSELS, PAGE 241). Everything should be covered with a butter sauce or a white sauce, for which one-third of the liquid used is furnished by the court bouillon of the fish.

Mackerel Stew with Leeks *(Maquereau en Ragoût, aux Poireaux).* *Time: 40 minutes (once the fish has been gutted).*

About 1 kilogram (2 pounds, 3 ounces) of mackerel, washed, gutted. Remove the head and the thin part of the tail. Divide the mackerel into pieces, as if for a *matelote.* Boil the heads and the tails for about 20 minutes in 1/2 liter (generous 2 cups) of water and 2 deciliters (6 3/4 fluid ounces, 7/8 cup) of white wine, with parsley, thyme, bay, and 1 clove.

Meanwhile, in a sauté pan, soften, without browning in any way, 150–175 grams (5¹/₃–6 ounces) of the white part of a leek, cut into thin rounds, with 60 grams (2¹/₄ ounces, 4¹/₂ tablespoons) of butter. If you like, replace the butter with oil as for the Provençal method. Then add the pieces of mackerel. Sauté them for 2–3 minutes without browning to simply dry out the fish a little.

Sprinkle with 15–20 grams (¹/₂–²/₃ ounce) of flour. Stir and cook for 1 minute. Add the strained fish bouillon, then bring it to a rapid boil. Let it boil rapidly for *5–6 minutes.* Lower the heat. Keep it at a slow simmer, uncovered, for *about 15 minutes.* The leek should be perfectly cooked at the same time as the fish, and this should also coincide with the required reduction of the liquid, which should be approximately half of what you started with. Serve it in a warmed dish or shallow bowl.

Mackerel with Parsley and Lemon Butter *(Macquereau à la Maître d'Hôtel).* Generally, you serve one mackerel for two people, or a whole mackerel per person if it's a small one. Large or small, the preparation is identical. *Time: 20 minutes (1 hour for the optional marinade). Serves 2.*

A mackerel weighing about 280–300 grams (9⁷/₈–10¹/₂ ounces); 1 good tablespoon of oil; salt and pepper.

For the maître d'hôtel butter: 50 grams (1³/₄ ounces, 3¹/₂ tablespoons) of good, fresh butter; a small pinch of good salt; ¹/₂ pinch of pepper; 1 teaspoon of finely minced parsley; 4–5 drops of lemon juice, which can, if absolutely essential, be replaced by a few drops of vinegar, but lemon is preferable.

PROCEDURE. Trim the end of the tail, and the dorsal and belly fins.

Remove the gills and the intestines at the same time. Insert the tip of the knife in the hole found at the extreme end of the stomach. With this tip, pull out the intestines. Wipe off the mackerel. *Do not wash it; or if you do, it should only be the outside, and be careful not to let any water get inside.*

Put the mackerel on the work surface, the head to your right and the back turned toward you. Use a good kitchen knife with a reasonably long blade, and begin by cutting just the tip of the snout, at the place indicated by a line in the first illustration on this page (*fig.* 37). Then, from this place, split the fish all along the back by cutting it with the blade of the knife. It must penetrate the flesh by about 2¹/₂ centimeters/1 inch (this could be a little bit more or less depending on the size of the fish). To make this operation easier, keep your left hand open and lightly leaning on the fish. Follow the bone with the tip of the knife, sliding just below it until you get to the middle of the fish, in the place indicated on the drawing. At that point, cut the bone, which is not hard, being careful not to cut the flesh. Then pass the blade of the knife on top of the bone and continue almost until you have reached the tail. In this manner, each half of the fish is supported by a part of the backbone, which means there is a much lower risk of it coming apart during cooking.

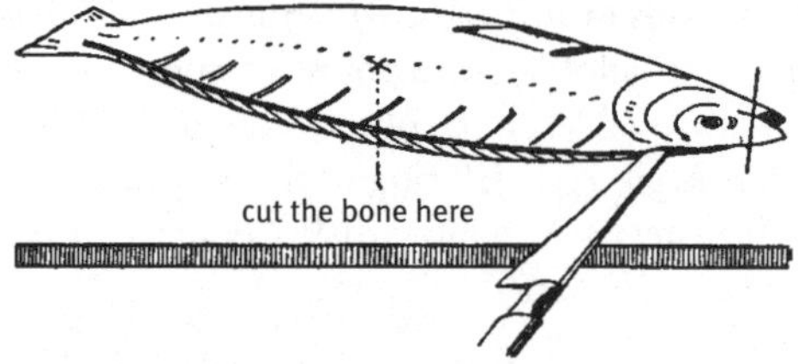

FIG. 37. TO OPEN THE MACKEREL.

Once the mackerel has been cut lengthwise, open it up. It now looks like the second illustration on this page (*fig.* 38). Season the inside and the outside with a pinch of good salt and a little bit of pepper.

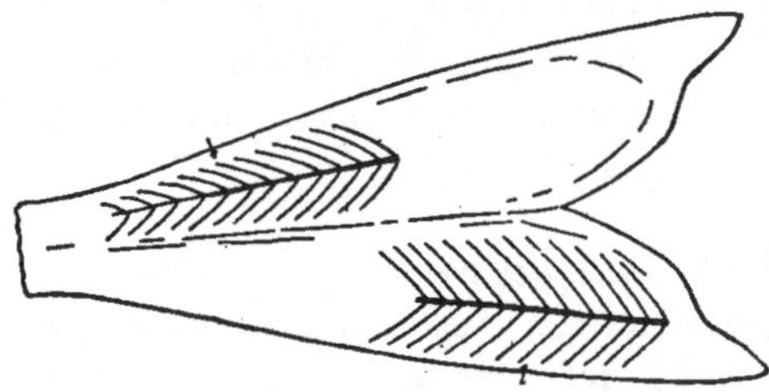

FIG. 38. THE OPEN MACKEREL.

NOTE. This cut down the back of the mackerel both facilitates and accelerates the cooking, but if you make it by going all the way to the end of the backbone without dividing it midway, all of it will remain on the same side so that one of the fillets will be extremely well supported and the other not at all. If the fish is large, you must split the fish as we have just explained, but without separating the two sides. If you simply make some slits in the sides, as for herrings, the cooking will be, first of all, very long and uneven, because of the thickness of the flesh that the heat must penetrate. Furthermore, this method of splitting the fish for cooking is widely used on the Brittany coast, whether for grilling or for cooking on the stove à la meunière.

Most of the time, you proceed immediately with grilling; but if there is time, it's better to marinate it in oil for an hour in advance; this will tenderize the flesh and aid in the cooking.

Arrange it on a long plate and drizzle with a good tablespoon of oil. Sprinkle 2–3 parsley branches, torn up, and salt and pepper. Keep it cool and turn from time to time in its seasoning.

To grill: Heat and oil the grill. If the mackerel has been marinated, remove the parsley. Place the open side of the interior on the bars of the grill. If the mackerel has not been marinated, spread oil over the interior side before putting it on the grill.

After *6 minutes,* baste the outside—that is, the skin—using a brush dipped in oil. Turn the fish over and similarly brush oil on the other side again. Let it cook for the same time. Turn it over once more. Cook it for another *3–4 minutes* on each side, constantly brushing it with oil.

To serve: Put the open mackerel on a long warmed plate, skin-side down. Spread the butter all along one of the halves, and fold over the other half to close. In other words, restore the mackerel to its natural shape once the butter has been put inside. You can also, if you like, spread the butter on the plate and simply place the mackerel, restored to its shape, on top.

Mackerel with Gooseberries *(Maquereau aux Groseilles Vertes).* A very old, classic dish. Recipes for this can be found in collections from the beginning of the eighteenth century under the designation of mackerel Flemish style. Interestingly, this dish is particularly popular in northern European countries. In England, gooseberries are also used as an accompaniment for boiled mackerel and goose; in fact, the bird is the reason for the English name of "gooseberry." Gooseberries are prepared in many ways, either as a clear purée—in other words, simply cooked with a little bit of water and sugar, then strained through a *tamis;* or, this purée is added to a butter sauce or a white sauce, which is the recipe we will give.

Fennel is the essential aromatic when cooking mackerel, which is cooked simply in salted water here. You can, if you like, add several minced leaves to the sauce.

PROCEDURE. Trim the tail and the dorsal and belly fins from the mackerel. Gut it and cut the tip of the muzzle, as directed in the recipe for maquereau maître d'hôtel. Tie a string around the head because this detaches easily from the body when it is cooked. Put the fish into the *poissonnière* (fish poacher). Cover with boiling water, salted at a ratio of 15 grams (1/2 ounce) per liter (4 1/4 cups), and add a branch of fennel. Put it over high heat and bring it to a boil, then lower the heat and simmer almost imperceptibly; timing is calculated by the size of the fish (SEE COURT BOUILLON, PAGE 162). Drain and dry off the mackerel. Coat it with the gooseberry sauce (PAGE 69).

Fillets of Mackerel *(Les Filets de Maquereau).* To cook the fillets, choose mackerel of medium size—that is, weighing about 280–300 grams (9 7/8–10 1/2 ounces), so that you will have one fillet per person; or, you can use small mackerel of medium weight, 150 grams (5 1/3 ounces), and you will then allow two per person. By "fillet," we mean each half of the fish, because the flesh of the mackerel does not lend itself to further division as does sole, for example.

Depending on the recipe, the filets are cooked in court bouillon or very little liquid, using wine or another liquid; in the latter case, this small quantity of liquid is used in the sauce with which the fish is served.

The most common and most practical method to cook fillets is in a pan. These can then be served with a highly seasoned sauce: bordelaise, anchovy, mustard, tomato, etc., served in a sauceboat or poured over the filets. For cooking them in the pan, see fish à la meunière (PAGE 167).

To prepare the mackerel fillets: Cut the head. Use scissors to remove the tail and fins. Gut the fish. Then, divide the mackerel in two halves lengthwise, as directed for grilled mackerel à la maître d'hôtel (SEE PAGE 190). Each half of the fillet therefore has a part of the backbone to serve as a support; this bone is removed after cooking, before serving.

Cooking mackerel filets in a court bouillon: A simple saltwater court bouillon (SEE PAGE 165) is generally used here. Arrange the fillets in a large, long ovenproof platter that has been buttered. Pour in the boiling court bouillon. Cover with a sheet of buttered baking or parchment paper placed directly on the fillet. Return to a boil directly on the stovetop. Then lower the heat to maintain the liquid at a simple, gentle simmer that is barely perceptible. Allow *16–18 minutes* for large fillets, and *12 minutes* for small ones.

To serve the fillets: Mackerel fillets cooked in court bouillon must never, ever be served with their skin.

Two minutes before serving, take them from the dish where they were cooked, very carefully, so that you do not break them, and put them on a folded kitchen towel. Scrape off the skin with the tip of a small knife. Arrange the fillets, as they are skinned, on the serving platter. It should be a long plate, well heated, kept warm on the side of the stove. Before adding the fillets, you should pour in about 2 tablespoons of court bouillon so that the fillets do not stick. This little bit of liquid is removed at the last moment by tilting the plate.

Depending on the dish you have chosen, garnish the plate with fresh parsley and potatoes cut into small rounds or otherwise, and serve the sauce on the side. Or, you can coat the fillet with the sauce you are using; in this case, be even more careful to make sure that the water in the bottom of the plate has been emptied right to the last drop, because it will dilute the sauce added to the fillets.

Whiting *(Merlan)*

This is one of the most popular fish with home cooks, because it lends itself to very simple methods of preparation. In haute cuisine, it is frequently used for making fish dumplings.

1 whiting per person, weighing about 180 grams (6 1/3 ounces), full weight, which generally yields about 140 grams (5 ounces), net weight. Or, if you have a good-sized whiting that weighs 320–350 grams (11 1/3–12 1/3 ounces) gross, this will serve 2.

Whiting à la Meunière *(Merlans à la Meunière).* SEE FISH À LA MEUNIÈRE, PAGE 167.

Whiting with Mussels and Shrimp *(Merlans à la Dieppoise).* The whitings, split in half along their entire back, are poached with white wine, the cooking water from mushrooms, and butter. Proceed, for the garnish and the sauce, as for BARBUE À LA DIEPPOISE (SEE PAGE 179).

Whiting with White Wine *(Merlans au Vin Blanc).* Prepared as for sole. First, cut off the head of the whiting; cook these heads with rounds of onion, branches of parsley, and white wine cut by one-third with water. With this cooking liquid, poach the whitings. Proceed as for sole.

Whiting with Wine, Shallots, Butter, and Parsley *(Merlans à la Bercy).* This very simple method, which has become a classic, is one of the best there is for whiting. It can also be used for other fish.

The liquid is white wine and the cooking water from mushrooms. The bothersome thing is that this mushroom cooking liquid is not usually available in home kitchens, and it is often necessary to do without. If you have fish bouillon, which is another rarity, you can substitute it for the mushroom cooking liquid and use the same quantities. If you have both ingredients, you can use one-half of each: that is to say, 1/2 deciliter (1 2/3 fluid ounces, scant 1/4 cup) of mushroom cooking liquid, and 1/2 deciliter (1 2/3 fluid ounces, scant 1/4 cup) of fish bouillon; this, along with the deciliter (3 1/3 fluid ounces, scant 1/2 cup) of white wine, will make up the 2 deciliters (6 3/4 fluid ounces, 7/8 cup) of liquid required. *Time: 30–40 minutes (depending on the size of the fish).*

3 large whitings weighing between 300–320 grams (10 1/2–11 1/3 ounces), or 6 small ones, weighing 160–180 grams (5 2/3–6 1/3 ounces) each (if there is a choice, it is better to use 3 larger whitings rather than 6 small ones, as the flesh of the fillets is thicker in the larger one); 2 deciliters (6 3/4 fluid ounces, 7/8 cup) of liquid, including 1 deciliter (3 1/3 fluid ounces, scant 1/2 cup) white wine and 1 deciliter (3 1/3 fluid ounces, scant 1/2 cup) from mushrooms. If you do not have this mushroom cooking liquid, or fish bouillon, allow

$1^1/_2$ deciliters (5 fluid ounces, $^2/_3$ cup) of white wine in total, and 3 tablespoons of water to make the necessary quantities.

30 grams (1 ounce) of minced shallots; 60 grams (2 ounces, $^1/_4$ cup) of butter; 1 teaspoon of minced parsley; a lemon quarter.

PROCEDURE. Clean and gut the fish. With a knife, make an incision about 1 centimeter ($^3/_8$ inch) deep along the entire length of the back, starting from the head and ending a little bit before the tail: this is to make cooking the flesh easier, and to prevent it from breaking. In this instance, this procedure is preferable to small, diagonal incisions.

Generously butter a dish that can go from the oven to the table. Sprinkle it with the minced shallot. Lay the whitings on top, placing them at a slight angle. Season with a good pinch of salt and a little bit of pepper. Sprinkle them with the liquid. Divide the butter into small bits and dot it on and around the whiting. Up to this point, the dish can be made in advance if it is kept cool, until ready to cook.

To cook: First, set the dish over high heat and bring it to a rolling boil.

Then, transfer the dish to an oven heated sufficiently to maintain the liquid at a boil. It is always necessary to be mindful here of the heat of the oven relative to the size of the whiting. For small fish, the heat should be quite strong, so that the reduction of the liquid reduces at the same time as the fish is completely cooked. For larger fish, you must use lower temperatures: because the whitings are thicker, the cooking will take longer. You must therefore moderate the heat here because if it is too hot, it will cook the exterior of the flesh without penetrating completely.

For small and large whitings, the fish should be cooked at the same time as the liquid is cooked. For medium-sized whiting, weighing about 170 grams (6 ounces), allow *18–20 minutes* of cooking in the oven. For large whiting, *25–27 minutes* in an oven with a lower temperature.

From the moment when the fish are in the oven, baste them frequently with their cooking liquid. When the cooking has finished, or is almost finished, this liquid must be syrupy, which is characteristic of whiting à la Bercy. And, in this state, there should be only a few tablespoons. If this is not the case, it is because the heat was not sufficient. You must let the liquid reduce until it is syrupy.

About 3 minutes before taking the fish out of the oven, baste copiously one last time with their reduced cooking liquid and glaze them, either in a very hot oven, or under the broiler. Finally, sprinkle them with minced parsley and squeeze a little lemon juice on them. Serve hot.

If the whiting must stand for a bit, which is always regrettable, keep them at the front of the oven, with the door left open.

Fried Whiting *(Merlans Frits).* Preferably, use whitings weighing about 150–175 grams ($5^1/_3$–6 ounces). Gut them, wash them, dry them off, and trim the fish. Dip them in milk and then flour. Fry them in a large amount of hot oil, *7–8 minutes* (SEE PAGE 40). Drain them on a towel or on a paper. Salt them moderately.

Arrange them on a long plate, on a napkin, with bouquets of fried parsley and lemon.

Breaded Whiting with Lemon and Parsley Butter *(Merlans Frits Colbert).* Cut the fish along the back, from the head to about 2 centimeters ($^1/_2$ inch) away from the tail, so that you can remove the backbone without completely separating the fish just yet. You can remove the head to make it easier to handle, but the fish will not stay closed as well if you do.

Once the backbone has been removed, gut and rinse the fish, then wipe the interior thoroughly. Remove the dark skin. Close the fish back up. Proceed to bread and fry the whiting as for sole Colbert (SEE PAGE 207).

To serve: Arrange them side by side on a long warmed platter. Put some beurre maître d'hôtel (SEE PAGE 80) inside each one—25–30 grams (about 1 ounce, 2 tablespoons) of butter for each whiting.

Whiting à l'Hôtelière *(Merlans à l'Hôtelière).* This is an excellent way to serve whiting, used frequently in restaurants. Because of its simplicity and its rapidity, it is recommended for home cooking. Duxelles, or minced mushrooms, can be prepared in advance, but it is extremely important, as in dishes prepared à la meunière, not to cook the fish until the last moment: it is therefore essential to calculate both the cooking time and serving time precisely. Thus, 10 minutes to cook them and 2 minutes to arrange them on the plate: *12 minutes* in total.

Though generally served at lunch, this dish is also suitable for a family dinner. You can decorate the edges of the dish with very thin lemon slices to make it more attractive. But the most important thing we would like to remind you is to serve it piping hot, with foaming butter, as for à la meunière. *Time: 30 minutes (once the fish have been gutted).*

6 whiting of medium weight, 180 grams (6 1/3 ounces) each.

For the duxelles: **80 grams (2 3/4 ounces) of mushrooms, net weight; 60 grams (2 1/4 ounces) of onion; 2 shallots; 1 tablespoon of oil and 25 grams (1 ounce, 2 tablespoons) of butter; salt, pepper, nutmeg.**

To flour the fish and cook them: **1 1/2 deciliters (5 fluid ounces, 2/3 cup) of milk and 2 tablespoons of flour; 50 grams (1 3/4 ounces, 3 1/2 tablespoons) of butter.**

To serve: **50 grams (1 3/4 ounces, 3 1/2 tablespoons) of noisette butter; 1 teaspoon of minced parsley; lemon juice.**

PROCEDURE. Prepare the duxelles (SEE PAGE 21). Keep it warm.

Gut the whitings, then rinse, wipe dry, and trim.

Have handy: the milk in a shallow bowl, seasoned with salt and pepper; the flour, spread out on a plate or on a kitchen towel. In an ordinary frying pan large enough to arrange the fish side by side without crowding them, you should have the warm butter. If you cannot fit all the fish into the pan, you should do this in two batches: keep the cooked fish warm in the oven.

Dip the whiting in the milk. One by one, dip them in the flour, patting them between your hands so that the flour sticks thoroughly to the fish. Put them immediately into the very warm butter in the pan; set this pan over very moderate heat.

Turn the fish after *3 minutes,* since the flesh of the whitings is extremely delicate. You should take very great care when you do this, either by turning over the fish with a spatula or by sliding two forks underneath them. At the end of *3 more minutes,* turn them over again. Finish cooking them thus; or, you can put the pan into the oven during these *remaining 4 minutes.* The whiting must be a beautiful, uniform golden color, and the butter must not go darker than the tint of a yellowish oil.

To serve: Remove the pan from the heat. With great care, remove the whiting and arrange them side by side on a long warmed platter. With a spoon, put equal amounts of duxelles on each fish; keep the plate in the oven.

Quickly add the reserved butter to the butter already in the pan and cook as directed. Pour noisette butter (PAGE 80) over the fish. Quickly sprinkle the surface with the minced parsley. Squeeze a few drops of lemon juice on each fish, and serve.

Whitefish au Gratin *(Merlans au Gratin).* See fish au gratin (PAGE 168). For the optional addition of sliced mushrooms around the plate and caps of mushrooms on the fish, allow about 250 grams (8 7/8 ounces) of mushrooms in addition to those used for the sauce.

For a lean version, ordinary bouillon is replaced by vegetable cooking water. *Time: A brief hour (once the fish have been gutted).*

6 whiting, weighing an average of 180–200 grams (6 1/3–7 ounces) each, or 3 whiting weighing about 350 grams (12 1/3 ounces) each.

For the sauce: **2 tablespoons of oil and 25 grams (1 ounce, 2 tablespoons) of butter; 60 grams (2 1/4 ounces) of onion and 25 grams (1 ounce) of minced shallot; 100 grams (3 1/2 ounces) of mushrooms that have been finely minced; 1 1/2 deciliters (5 fluid ounces, 2/3 cup) of white wine; 2 deciliters (6 3/4 fluid ounces, 7/8 cup) of ordinary bouillon; a piece of garlic the size of a pea (optional); 20 grams (2/3 ounce, 1 heaping tablespoon) of butter blended into 15 grams (1/2 ounce) of flour; salt, pepper, nutmeg.**

For the gratin: **30 grams (1 ounce, 2 tablespoons) of butter for the plate; 2 tablespoons of white wine; 2 tablespoons of bread crumbs, 30 grams (1 ounce, 2 tablespoons) of butter to sprinkle on them at the end.**

To finish: **1/2 tablespoon of minced parsley; juice of 1 lemon.**

PROCEDURE. **The sauce:** Over good strong heat, warm the oil and the butter in a small pan, preferably a small sauté pan. Add the onion and minced shallot. Lower the heat and stir until the onion is lightly colored. Add the minced mushrooms. Then return it to high heat for *3–4 minutes* to completely evaporate all the moisture. Add the white wine; let it boil rapidly, uncovered, until reduced to 1/2 deciliter (1 2/3 fluid ounces, scant 1/4 cup). Then add the bouillon; season with salt, pepper, and nutmeg. Once it has boiled again, turn the heat down very low. Thicken with the beurre manié. Let the sauce simmer gently, uncovered, while you take care of the whiting.

The whiting: Gut it, remove the fins, clean it, etc. Along the back, make a 1 1/2 centimeter (5/8-inch) incision, starting with the head and stopping 4 centimeters (1 1/2 inches) short of the end of the tail. This is to help the inside of the flesh to cook.

Butter the bottom of your chosen baking dish, a long dish. Also lightly butter the sides of the dish, which will allow you to clean it more easily when it comes out of the oven. On the buttered bottom, spread 2–3 tablespoons of the prepared sauce after having checked its seasoning. Then lay out the fish, without crowding them: at an angle for small fish, and head to tail for large ones.

If using raw mushroom slices, arrange them around the fish, laying them overlapping each other. If garnishing with mushroom caps, now is the time to arrange them on top of the fish. Completely cover the whiting and the mushrooms with the sauce, spreading it out with a spoon. Next, pour the 2 tablespoons of white wine *around* the fish, but *on* the sauce. This is so that the sauce, which will be in direct contact with a very warm plate, thus reducing even further, will not dry out or burn.

Sprinkle the entire surface of the sauce with the bread crumbs. Drizzle with the butter that you have melted; or, place the butter, divided into small pieces, on the bread crumbs. Immediately put the platter in the oven.

NOTE. You can, if you like, prepare this entire dish but not begin cooking the fish until later. In this case, garnish the plate with *chilled* sauce; add the whiting with the mushrooms. Keep it cool. Just before you put the dish in the oven, cover with the sauce that has been kept warm or reheated; then spread the bread crumbs, drizzle butter, etc.

To cook: For the directions about the temperature of the oven, see fish au gratin (PAGE 168). For medium-sized whiting, allow about *20–22 minutes* of cooking; for large whitings, about *27–30 minutes.* After 10 minutes, if the heat of the oven seems insufficient, it will be essential, particularly in the case of small fish, to get the platter as close as possible to the hot part of the oven, raising it how you can. This is to ensure the gratin forms.

To serve: Squeeze the juice of the lemon on the gratin. Sprinkle it with minced parsley. Place the platter on a serving plate covered with a cloth. Serve immediately.

Salt Cod *(Morue)*

"This is, so to speak, the beef of meatless days," says an old cookbook. Those who are in the habit of eating salt cod only once a year, at Easter, in the style that is most popular—which is à la maître d'hôtel—would hardly be able to imagine the number and diversity of its other preparations. The greatest variety is encountered in the southern provinces, where salt cod is served all the time. In northern and central regions, one scarcely sees anything other than potatoes, milk, butter, and sometimes onions used as ingredients with salt cod. In the Midi, on the other hand, many other ingredients are added: tomatoes, spinach, carrots, leeks, anchovies, peppers, pimientos, oil, red and white wine, rice, etc.

These different preparations, furthermore, are rarely precise about amounts or ingredients and, in these cases, you can let the imagination run wild. But the one thing that does not change is the initial preparation of the cod—that is, its soaking and its cooking. The choice of these ingredients is also very important because a dish made with a poor quality of cod is execrable.

Choice of the cod: When buying, base your calculations on a weight of 125 grams (4 1/2 ounces) per person; after you remove the fins, skin, etc., this will reduce to about 90 grams (3 1/6 ounces). To choose the best cod, you must learn to recognize quality.

Bad cod has flat fillets, because the fibers retract over time as they age, the surface of the flesh takes on a yellowish or reddish tinge. It loses its suppleness, and to check it, you only have to twist a fillet. If, when you do this, you see a cloud of powdery salt escape from the flesh, it is a sure sign that the cod is far too old: it will therefore certainly be rancid and tough.

Good-quality cod has thick fillets and white flesh that looks like small leaves superimposed in layers. The skin is nice and brown on the back side and silvery underneath. All this indicates, almost infallibly, that the cod comes from the most recent fishing season.

The desalination: Before being cooked, salt cod must always be desalinated, and this is achieved by soaking, for a rather long time, in cold water. The duration of this soaking varies with the quality and the thickness of the fish. Generally speaking, you can count at least an average of *18–24 hours* for good-quality cod. This time could even be reduced to *12 hours,* as long as all the necessary requirements for this soaking are meticulously observed. The problem with over-soaking is that it removes more salt than it should from the cod, which is detrimental to the flavor. But this inconvenience is much less regrettable than insufficient soaking, which leaves excess salt in the flesh. You can always add the salt that is lacking, while the problem of too much salt has no remedy.

Have a bowl or another receptacle ready, in which you can place, about halfway down, a grill or a rack to support the cod; or simply leave it suspended in the water, attaching it with a string tied to a stick placed across the top of the bowl. This allows you to keep the cod in the middle of the water, to remove the salt completely and evenly. If the cod rests directly on the bottom of the utensil, the water there will become saturated with salt and will not have the desired effect. The soaking water must be renewed completely at least twice a day.

After desalinating the cod, and before cooking, you must clean it extremely well. With good strong kitchen scissors, or a sharp knife, remove the fins, the tail, and the backbone, if they are present. Scrape the skin with a knife if it still has scales. Then, wash the fish in cool water. With your knife, divide it into pieces 6–8 centimeters (2½–3¼ inch) long, depending on the thickness, and weighing approximately 80–100 grams (2¾–3½ ounces). When the cod is divided in this way rather than left in one large piece it cooks much better. And, no matter what the recipe is, cutting it into pieces is in no way inconvenient. If, instead of being "flaked" into pieces, as is usually done, the pieces must be served whole, you should tie them crosswise with string to keep them intact.

To cook: For the amount of cod that is to be cooked, the chosen cooking vessel must always be big enough so that the pieces are not piled on top of one another and can fit comfortably. And, whatever utensil you choose, make sure it's easy to clean, because the odor of cod is particularly persistent.

Cover the pieces generously with cold water. Set the pan over extremely moderate heat. The liquid needs to heat very gradually. From time to time, shake the pan a little bit to move the pieces around and to mix the layers of water that are unequally heated. Watch for the moment when the boil is about to begin, because it takes only that little bit too much, once it starts to boil, to toughen the fish and make it curl up. The onset of boiling will be indicated by a rising white foam that becomes increasingly thicker and which you must carefully remove, because if it hardens, it will stick to the cod. This foam will boil over like milk if you keep the heat high once boiling has begun.

Therefore, the fish need just *1 second,* not 1 minute, of boiling, or even simmering, after which you must lower the heat to very, very low so that the liquid stays as warm as possible without boiling: a faint simmer will suffice, and indicates the degree of heat that is necessary to "poach" the cod. It is best not to cover the pan at any time: it is easier to keep an eye on the degree of boiling this way.

The poaching time varies with the recipe. If we assume that the cod will be served with a sauce that has been prepared on the side and does not have to be cooked further after poaching, allow *15–20 minutes.* In other cases, evaluate the time according to whether the cod has to be subsequently heated, and for how long, not to mention how strongly.

Provided it is simply kept hot, but not boiling or simmering, the cod can be kept in its cooking water after poaching.

Cod au Naturel *(Morue au Naturel).* This cod—removed from its cooking water, like all fish cooked in a court bouillon—is served as follows: carefully patted dry with a towel, arranged on a napkin-covered plate and surrounded by boiled potatoes. It can be accompanied by sauce in a sauceboat: butter that has simply been melted, as it is in Northern regions, or white sauce, capers, cream, eggs, hollandaise, tomato, vinaigrette, remoulade, etc.

Or, thoroughly pat dry, place directly on the plate while still piping hot, and drizzle well with maître d'hôtel butter (SEE PAGE 80). Allow 100 grams (3 1/2 ounces, 7 tablespoons) of butter for 450 grams (1 pound) of cod, net weight.

Cod with Beurre Noir *(Morue au Beurre Noir).* This is prepared as for skate (SEE PAGE 200).

Cod Fritters *(Beignets de Morue).* After cooking, the cod is divided into relatively small pieces, marinated in lemon juice, pepper, and salt, then dipped in batter and deep-fried in hot fat.

Fish Balls *(Croquettes de Morue à l'Américaine).* Use 300 grams (10 1/2 ounces) of cod that has been poached, ground, and mixed with the same amount of potato purée, with the addition of 30 grams (1 ounce, 2 tablepsoons) of butter, 1 1/2 deciliters (5 fluid ounces, 2/3 cup) of *extremely thick* béchamel, and 2 raw egg yolks. Shape into patties or balls, and cover with bread crumbs. Deep-fry in hot fat until golden brown. Serve a tomato sauce on the side. *Serves 6.*

Salt Cod with Béchamel in Pastry Cases *(Vol-au-Vent de Morue).* Cod mixed with a béchamel sauce that has been enhanced with a mirepoix of onion, carrot, etc., and served in a vol-au-vent crust with slices of truffle.

Cod Soufflé *(Soufflé de Morue).* SEE FISH SOUFFLÉ, PAGE 175.

Salt Cod Served with a Border of Duchesse Potatoes *(Morue en Bordure de Pommes de Terre Duchesse).* Salt cod beneath a cream sauce, gratinéed if you like, and surrounded by a border of duchesse potatoes (SEE PAGE 542).

Salt Cod Served in a Timbale or in a Shallow Bowl *(Morue Servie en Timbale ou en Plat Creux).* Beneath a sauce of your choice: béchamel, Mornay, soubise, tomato, etc., with or without the addition of another ingredient, usually potatoes, and subsequently gratinéed, if you like.

The advantage of this technique is that it allows you to reheat the cod perfectly, which is then arranged in alternating layers with the sauce. Begin at the bottom of the plate with a first layer of sauce; then half the cod; a second layer of sauce; the other half of the cod; a third layer of sauce; and then finally sprinkle with bread crumbs if you want a gratinée. When you add sliced potatoes, they are placed directly on top of the cod before covering it with sauce.

Allow 3–4 deciliters (1 1/4–1 2/3 cups) of sauce for 500–600 grams (1 pound, 2 ounces to 1 pound, 5 ounces) of cod, net weight.

Salt Cod Salad *(Morue en Salade).* Served warm, with one-third of its volume of potatoes, and optionally, some garlic; either rubbed on a piece of bread, or rubbed in the salad bowl.

Salt Cod, Southern-French Style *(Morue à la Façon Méridionale).* This recipe is the exception, for the cod is fried without previously being poached: that is, after soaking, it is cut into pieces that are dipped in flour and deep-fried, then simmered 10 minutes or so in a sauce—tomato or other—to finish cooking.

Sautéed Salt Cod *(Morue Sautée).* With parsley, chives, finely minced anchovies and cornichons, egg yolks, and a nice piece of butter, which must not be heated too much to maintain its creaminess.

Salt Cod with Fried Onions *(Morue à la Lyonnaise).* Optionally, you can use oil or butter. So, for 500 grams (1 pound, 2 ounces) of cod, heat 60 grams (2 1/4 ounces, 4 1/2 tablespoons) of butter or 1 deciliter (3 1/3 fluid ounces, scant 1/2 cup) of oil in a pan. Lightly brown 250 grams (8 7/8 ounces) of onion, finely minced. Add the cod, once it has been poached and flaked. Sauté everything together for *7–8 minutes* to brown well. Before serving, check the seasoning. Sprinkle with pepper and minced parsley and lemon juice.

Salt Cod with Mashed Potatoes *(Morue à la Brandade).* We are not going to give the recipe here for *brandade,* because even in the Midi, it is not prepared at home but is obtained from specialty food stores.

Salt Cod with Fresh Herbs *(Morue aux Fines Herbes).* An excellent dish. You must follow the directions for the sauce quite carefully; it must not be heated before the pieces of salt cod have been added. *Time: 45 minutes.*

500 grams (1 pound, 2 ounces), net, of cod, weighed after cooking, without bones or skin; 60 grams (2 1/4 ounces, 4 1/2 tablespoons) of fresh butter; 2 large uncooked egg yolks; 1 good deciliter (3 1/3 fluid ounces, 1/2 cup) of boiled milk that has been left to cool; a good pinch of fines herbes that have been finely minced; 10 grams (1/3 ounce, 1 scant tablespoon) of butter blended with 6–7 grams (scant 1/4 ounce) of flour, to make beurre manié; 4 tablespoons of olive oil; juice of 1/2 lemon.

PROCEDURE. Cook the cod, divided into relatively large pieces. Meanwhile, in a sauté pan, combine, without heating: the butter, the egg yolks, the fines herbs, and the beurre manié. Off the heat, add the pieces of cod. Then put the sauté pan over moderate heat and shake it gently to mix everything up and to coat the pieces of cod with the seasoning—if possible, without using a spoon, which risks breaking them.

As the preparation heats, the sauce will begin to thicken. Little by little, add the oil, which will bind the sauce. Be careful, in heating the pan, not to let the mixture boil. Finish with the lemon juice. Check the seasoning. Serve burning hot in a warmed dish.

Breaded and Fried Salt Cod *(Morue Panée et Frite).* This is served on a napkin with the accompanying sauce on the side: tomato, caper, soubise, etc. Or, arrange the pieces in a circle around a garnish of vegetables bound with butter—a *macédoine,* for example—or around a soubise purée; or, even better, with spinach prepared à la crème because spinach goes particularly well with the flavor of the cod.

750 grams (1 pound, 10 ounces) of cod, net weight; 1 whole egg; 225 grams (8 ounces) of stale bread (SEE ENGLISH-STYLE BREADING, PAGE 19).

To fry the cod: 3 good deciliters (1 1/4 cups) of oil.

PROCEDURE. Make sure that before putting the cod into the cooking oil you divide it into even-sized pieces, allowing 1 piece for each person. After poaching, remove the pieces, one after the other, with a skimmer and place them on a towel that has been spread out on the counter. Remove the skin, the bones, etc.

Taking great care not to break the cod, and using a fork, proceed as directed for breading. Arrange them on the upside-down lid of a pan.

The pan must be large enough to hold the pieces without crowding; otherwise, work in batches. Heat the oil just until it smokes. Arrange the pieces in the oil and immediately lower the heat; otherwise, the breaded part, which touches the bottom, will burn.

After *8 minutes,* turn them and brown them on the other side, turning once again if necessary.

Arrange in a circle on a round plate.

Salt Cod Fritters, Antilles Style *(Acras de Morue).* A flavorsome dish from the French Antilles. This is a kind of beignet or fritter, rather than croquette, and this recipe comes from a private collection from an old Creole family. *Time: 1 hour.*

500 grams (1 pound, 2 ounces) of cod, weighed after desalination and skinning; 60 grams (2 1/4 ounces) of flour; 4 deciliters (1 2/3 cups) of good milk that has been boiled; 2 good tablespoons of olive oil; 2 egg yolks; 4 egg whites that have been whisked until they hold stiff peaks; 1 tablespoon of minced parsley; a bit of garlic and a bit of cayenne pepper (optional).

PROCEDURE. Put the soaked cod into the cold water, turn on the heat, then drain it once the water has boiled. Flake it, then pound it in the mortar into a fine paste until you can no longer see any individual pieces. Transfer this paste to a bowl large enough to stir it comfortably with a wooden spoon, and add the oil, the sifted flour (in a thin shower), the egg yolks, and the milk; the ingredients are added one after the other. Finish with the parsley, the cayenne pepper, and the garlic crushed into a paste. You could also, for the garlic, simply rub inside the mortar with a garlic clove.

Just before you are ready to fry the fritters, combine with the egg whites, (SEE EGG WHITES, PAGE 8).

In a large quantity of oil that is moderately hot, fry a fritter the size of a small egg, which you form with a soupspoon. Proceed as for beignets soufflés (SEE PAGE 601). The cooking time and frying technique are the same. Drain on a towel. Serve quite hot on a plate covered with a cloth.

Salt Cod Bouillabaisse *(Bouillabaisse de Morue).* This recipe has many variations, but they all require the main aromatics characteristics of a bouillabaisse: onion, tomato, garlic, and saffron, to which you can add, in the authentic Marseilles style, a branch of fennel and a small piece of orange peel. The white part of a leek is often added. Potatoes are often called for in a cod bouillabaisse. The slices of toasted bread are, in any case, absolutely essential. The cooking procedure scarcely varies, no matter what recipe has been chosen. This recipe was inspired by the Provençal master chef, Reboul. *Time: 45 minutes. Serves 6.*

600–700 grams (1 pound, 5 ounces to 1 pound, 9 ounces) of cod, dry weight; 5–6 tablespoons of olive oil; 1 large onion that has been finely minced (125 grams, 4½ ounces); 2 medium-sized tomatoes, or 2 tablespoons of tomato purée; 1 clove of garlic; 1 bunch of parsley branches; a sprig of thyme, a bay leaf, a fennel branch; 1 gram of saffron; 1 tablespoon of minced parsley; ¾ liter (generous 3 cups) of boiling water; pepper; 6 round slices of stale bread about 1½ centimeters (⅝ inch) thick and approximately 7–8 centimeters (2¾–3¼ inches) in diameter. If you add potatoes, allow a weight equal to the cod, and diminish the proportion of cod; in other words, for the same number of people, allow 350 grams (12 ounces) of each.

PROCEDURE. The cod should have been soaked to remove the salt, as directed. Scrape it to remove the scales if necessary. Wash it again carefully, and divide it into square pieces about 6–7 centimeters (2½–2¾ inches) on each side.

In a pot with a wide bottom, combine the oil and the minced onion. Stir with a wooden spoon over high heat, uncovered, until it is *very lightly* browned. Above all, do not let it darken. Immediately add the fresh tomato, which will have previously been peeled, seeded, and cut into pieces. Or, failing that, use tomato purée. Reduce it, stirring constantly.

Once all the humidity has evaporated, and before the tomato begins to stick, add boiling water. Add the parsley, the clove of garlic crushed to a paste, the saffron, and a good pinch of ground pepper. Do not cover. As soon as it boils, add the pieces of cod: they must be completely covered by the bouillon. If, because of the dimensions of the pot, the cod has not been covered completely by the liquid, add a little more liquid. You will then have to reduce it when you finish the cooking.

Boil constantly and vigorously, over high heat that must be sustained so that it thoroughly heats the entire bottom of the pot to maintain an even boil. Allow *10 minutes* of rapid boiling, which should be accentuated, if possible, toward the end. This will help to ensure the sauce thickens perfectly, because slow boiling causes the oil to separate, and it will then float to the surface. Check the final seasoning in case you need to add salt.

To serve: You can serve the cod in a single round, shallow dish, on top of the slices of bread—which you can toast, if you like—and then serve the bouillon on top of that. Sprinkle everything with the minced parsley. Or, you can serve the cod on a separate plate, and the slices of bread in a shallow bowl, moistened with the bouillon so that they become quite soaked. Serve both plates at the same time. The plates should be quite hot.

Salt Cod with Rice, Tomatoes, and Chile *(Morue à la Valencia).* For this particular dish, allow a minimal amount of cod for each person, because the rice that is used increases it considerably. *Time: 45 minutes. Serves 6.*

400 grams (14⅛ ounces) of cod; 180 grams (6⅓ ounces) of rice (or 2 deciliters/6¾ fluid ounces/⅞ cup); at least 2 deciliters (6¾ fluid ounces, ⅞ cup) of tomato purée; 3 medium onions; 2½ deciliters (1 cup) of oil; 75 grams (2⅔ ounces, ⅓ cup) of butter;

1 small dried pepper, or, as a substitute, a point of cayenne (as much as can be held on a knife tip);
1 tablespoon of fine white bread crumbs.

PROCEDURE. Poach the cod for about 15 minutes, as directed.

At the same time, prepare the rice as for risotto (SEE PAGE 449), with 1 deciliter (3 1/3 ounces, scant 1/2 cup) of oil, and 6 deciliters (2 1/2 cups) of water; add 7 grams (1/4 ounce) of salt, the pepper, or the cayenne pepper. Put it in the oven: *20–25 minutes* for cooking, according to the quality of the rice. Simmer the tomato purée in a small pan with the salt, the pepper, and a piece of crushed garlic the size of a pea. Cut the onions into rounds scarcely 1/2 centimeter (3/16 inch) thick; season them with salt and pepper, and dip them in flour. Fry in the pan in the remainder of the oil. Drain.

In a round, shallow dish, or a timbale, arrange in alternating layers, one-quarter of the rice, one-third of the onion rounds, and one-third of the cod, divided into little pieces and with the bones completely removed. Taste the cod to check that it is salty enough, and if you need to, add some salt. Sprinkle it lightly with pepper. Cover the cod with tomato. Continue in the same order, finishing with the rice. Thus: 4 layers of rice, 3 layers of onions, 3 layers of cod, 3 layers of tomato. Put the dish or the timbale in a very moderate oven for *5 minutes* to make sure that the whole thing is heated.

In a small pan, heat the butter until foaming. Throw in the bread crumbs and let them fry for only 2 seconds. Pour everything over the layer of rice, and serve immediately.

Skate *(Raie)*

Unlike other fish, which must be eaten as freshly caught as possible, skate should stand for a while before being eaten—from 1 to 3 days depending on the season and the temperature. Used too fresh, it is tough and hard; you must use it the moment it begins to deteriorate without actually decomposing.

Fish markets generally supply us with skate at the right point. To be good, it must be covered with a viscous coating that is somewhat gelatinous. If the coating is dried out, the skate is bad; in this case, you would do well not to use it because it may be dangerous. It has an odor of ammonia, which should make you reject it without hesitation. You should choose skate that is slightly curled with light spots across its back.

In cooler weather—and only in cooler weather—you can buy more than is necessary for one meal, because cooked skate keeps for several days when cooked in aspic; the leftovers can be reheated outside of the aspic in salted water. When the weather is warm or humid, the ammonia odor, which has been mentioned previously, comes on rapidly even after it has been cooked; the fish must then be thrown away because eating it might be harmful.

Small skates that weigh 1–2 kilograms (2 pounds, 3 ounces to 4 pounds, 6 ounces) are generally sold whole or in halves. Each half is called a "wing." Larger skates are divided into ribbons and cut in the direction of the fibers of the fish. Allow about 1 kilogram (2 pounds, 3 ounces) of skate, more or less, for 6 people.

The liver of the skate, a delicate morsel, has its fans. It can be served together with the skate, or it can be made into very exceptional hot hors d'oeuvres. Just like the fish itself, it should be kept in cool water until the moment it is cooked—remember to remove the bile first.

Preparing the skate: Whatever means of preparation is chosen for the skate, it must first be cleaned, carved, or divided up and cooked in court bouillon, as follows:

Plunge the skate into a receptacle filled with cold water.

Either with your hands or with a scrubbing brush, scrub off the mucous covering it. Rinse it again in clean water. If you are not cooking it immediately, leave it in the water or under the faucet with the water running slowly over it.

You can cook either the wing, or a skate in its entirety, but dividing the skate to serve is harder after cooking than before, so it's better to cut it raw. Furthermore, you can always reconstitute the wing or piece on the plate, putting the sections next to each other.

First trim the end of the wing—in other words, the very thin part. This is nothing but cartilage, which is good for nothing and contains gelatin that will spoil the cooking. Then, divide the wing of the skate into pieces that are more or less square, cut in the direction of the flesh. Rinse them one last time.

To cook: Arrange the pieces next to one another in a pan that has a rather good size bottom; a sauté pan is recommended. Cover with enough cold water to have at least a good centimeter (3/8 inch) above the skate, so that it is thoroughly immersed.

For each liter (4 cups) of water add: 15 grams (1/2 ounce) of salt; 1 deciliter (3 1/3 fluid ounces, scant 1/2 cup) of vinegar; 100 grams (3 1/2 ounces) of onion, cut into rounds; 5–6 parsley stems without their leaves; 1 sprig of thyme and a small bay leaf.

Do not cover the pan. Bring it to a boil over moderate heat. Immediately lower the heat, then cover. Maintain the liquid at a slow simmer, as for all poaching.

From this point, allow *25 minutes* of cooking, no matter the amount of skate; the same cooking time is applicable because the thickness of the fish remains the same.

Cleaning the pieces of skate: Remove them one by one from the pan with a skimmer; place them on a cloth that has been folded in quarters. Pour the court bouillon into a bowl.

With the back of the blade of a knife, lightly scrape the skate to remove the skin from both sides. Now, depending on the chosen recipe, keep the pieces warm either on the serving dish or put back into the rinsed sauté pan and covered with their strained court bouillon; cover the pan and keep it warm.

Aside from the traditional skate with beurre noir, its main preparations are as follows:

Skate with Caper Sauce *(Raie à la Sauce Câpres).* The skate, drained well of its court bouillon, is placed on a cloth and surrounded with fresh parsley and accompanied with a caper sauce. For this caper sauce, you can use a court bouillon made from skate instead of water, keeping in mind that this is a very salty solution.

Deep-Fried Skate *(Raie en Fritot).* After cooking and removing the skin, etc., cut the ray into smaller pieces and marinate it for 2–3 hours in salt, pepper, lemon juice, oil, and onions sliced into small rounds. Then dip it in a batter (as for salsify) and deep-fry it in a large quantity of oil. Place it on a cloth with fried parsley and onion rounds taken from the marinade and dipped in flour, then fried.

Skate with Black Butter *(Raie au Beurre Noir).* Once the skate has been cooked and skinned, drain the pieces thoroughly. On a round, warmed plate, arrange them one by one, next to each other, thereby reconstituting the fish as if it were whole. Sprinkle with salt, pepper, and minced parsley. Keep warm.

Cook the butter. Use 80 grams (2 3/4 ounces, 5 1/2 tablespoons) for 1 kilogram (2 pounds, 3 ounces) of skate (SEE BEURRE NOIR, PAGE 80). Pour it over the skate. Heat 2 tablespoons of vinegar, and pour it over everything. Serve immediately.

Red Mullet *(Rouget)*

The red mullet, or small mullet of the Mediterranean, should not be confused with the grondin, which has a large head; by its shape and size alone, the red mullet, which is a brilliant red color, resembles the small river trout.

To gut or not to gut a red mullet? Carême proclaimed that: "Just like the woodcock, this fish is never gutted." Others suggest, after taking out the intestines, that you put the liver back into the body. Some do not mention this at all, implying that the fish needs to be cleaned out in the usual way. There is no precise rule regarding this matter.

Red mullet is prepared in many ways but always using a rather aromatic seasoning, which is apparently due to the southern origins of the fish; tomatoes play a large part in most dishes. Almost without exception, the recipes call for fish that has been previously grilled or sautéed in butter or oil. Among the main preparations, we mention: à la meunière, grilled with a maître d'hôtel butter or other butter; grilled or sautéed and accompanied with a tomato sauce, bordelaise sauce, Italian sauce, etc., served in a sauceboat; or the mullets are covered with a sauce, as in the Livorno style or the Provençale style, or the Oriental or Siberian style in the following recipes; au gratin as for a whiting; in pastry shells, a dish that is appreciated as much for its originality as for its convenience of service. Further on we will give more information on the subject.

Per person, allow 1 mullet weighing about 125–150 grams (4 1/2–5 1/3 ounces) per person.

Red Mullet Gratin with Tomatoes, Garlic, and Wine *(Rougets à la Livournaise).* One of the simplest preparations: a gratin that does not require mushrooms and where tomatoes are the main ingredient. Whenever possible, choose a fresh tomato over concentrate. *Time: 45 minutes.*

6 mullets weighing about 125 grams (4 1/2 ounces) each.

***For the sauce:* 4 medium tomatoes that are nice and ripe or 2 1/2 deciliters (1 cup) of tomato purée; 25 grams (1 ounce, 2 tablespoons) of butter and 2 tablespoons of oil; 150 grams (5 1/3 ounces) of finely minced onions; a pea-sized piece of garlic; 1 deciliter (3 1/3 fluid ounces, scant 1/2 cup) of white wine.**

***For the gratin:* 1 1/2 tablespoons of fine bread crumbs; 3 tablespoons of oil; a good pinch of minced parsley; the juice of a quarter lemon.**

PROCEDURE. If you believe that you should gut the fish, be careful to make only a very small opening in the belly and then immediately put the liver back inside. The gills should have been removed first. Wipe the mullets with a towel; do not wash them. Make 5 or 6 incisions on each side so that they will not break up during cooking. Arrange them in an ovenproof dish (metal, porcelain, or terracotta) with a low side that has been generously buttered.

In a small, heavy-bottomed saucepan, gently heat the butter and the oil. Cook the minced onions in it very gently for *7–8 minutes* without letting them brown. Add the white wine. Boil strongly to reduce it by about half. Then add: either the tomato purée, or the tomatoes that have been peeled, seeded, had their water squeezed out, and then been minced fine; the garlic, crushed under the blade of a knife; salt and pepper. Let it boil for *10–12 minutes,* until it has thickened sufficiently.

Season the mullets with salt and pepper; cover them with the sauce. Sprinkle with bread crumbs and drizzle with the oil. Then immediately place them in a *hot,* but not extremely hot, oven. Allow *18–20 minutes* of cooking. Beneath the perfectly gratinéed surface, the sauce must be well bound. Squeeze the lemon on the gratin, and sprinkle the minced parsley over it. Put the oven plate on a serving platter covered with a cloth. Serve.

Red Mullet with Tomatoes and Saffron *(Rougets à la Provençale).* According to the excellent recipe from the famous Provençale cook Reboul, mullets prepared like this can be served either on the plate or in paper pouches (SEE PAGE 203). *Time: 1 1/4 hours.*

8–10 mullets; 1 deciliter (3 1/3 fluid ounces, scant 1/2 cup) of oil; 150 grams (5 1/3 ounces) of finely minced onion; 500 grams (1 pound, 2 ounces) of tomatoes; 1/2 liter (generous 2 cups) of fish bouillon; a pinch of saffron; salt and pepper; the juice of a small lemon; a pinch of minced parsley.

PROCEDURE. Clean the mullets, roll them in flour, heat the oil in a pan until lightly smoking. Arrange the mullets side by side. If the pan is not large enough, work in batches. Turn them after 2–3 minutes to cook them evenly on each side. That makes *5 minutes* total; you do not cook them completely at this point.

Sprinkle the mullets with salt and pepper at the last moment. Line them up in a long gratin dish that has been oiled and is large enough so that the fish are not too crowded. Keep them warm, but do not overheat. Pour the oil from the pan into a heavy-bottomed pot with a capacity of about 1 1/2 liters (6 1/3 cups). Add the minced onion and sauté gently without allowing it to brown in any way. Add the tomatoes, which have been first peeled, seeded, and minced. Let it all cook gently, uncovered, stirring often for *a good 30 minutes* at least.

Meanwhile, prepare the fish bouillon (SEE PAGE 165). Add it to the tomatoes. Let everything cook *20 minutes,* uncovered. The tomatoes must then have a good, thick consistency. Add the saffron and a pinch of pepper. Check the seasoning, which should be rather spicy. Using a spoon, spread the sauce over the mullets so that they are completely covered on the sides as well as on top. About 10 minutes before serving, put the dish in a good, hot oven, but not too hot. Here, the point is *a simple simmering to finish cooking the fish in the sauce* and not to make a gratin. When you take it out of the oven, sprinkle it with lemon juice and minced parsley. Serve on very hot plates.

Serving mullets in paper cases: Line the cases on a plate. In each case, place a mullet that has first been fried in a pan. Cover with the tomato sauce. Put it in the oven as above. To serve, arrange the cases on a plate covered by a napkin (SEE BELOW).

Poached Red Mullet with Shallot, Butter, and Cream Sauce *(Rougets à la Sibérienne).* This is a cold dish, which is best for the summer. It is chic to serve it on a bed of ice. *Time: 2½ hours. Serves 6.*

6 small mullets put in a heatproof dish with 3 deciliters (1¼ cups) of white wine, and the same amount of water, packed tightly so that the liquid is enough to cover them. Add some branches of parsley, a sprig of thyme, a piece of bay the size of a fingernail, a pinch of salt and a pinch of pepper.

PROCEDURE. Put the dish, uncovered, over low heat. Wait until it begins to boil and, as soon as it begins, lower the heat. Cover and keep the liquid as hot as possible *without boiling.* This poaching requires special attention because, if the liquid starts to boil both when it begins to poach and during the poaching, the mullet will almost instantly break. The skin will come away, the head will come away, and the appearance of the fish, as well as its flavor, will never be the same.

Allow *10 minutes* of poaching from the moment the heat is lowered. Then, drain the mullets, sliding them out one by one on a skimmer. Arrange them on a long serving platter, all in the same direction, crosswise and a little bit on an angle. Let cool.

In a small pan, lightly brown 7–8 grams (¼ ounce) of shallot, which has been coarsely minced, with 15 grams (½ ounce, 1 tablespoon) of butter. Add the strained cooking liquid from the mullet. Boil until it has been reduced by half. Thicken with 3 egg yolks diluted in 3 tablespoons of good, fresh, thick heavy cream (SEE LIAISONS, PAGE 47).

Add 30 grams (1 ounce, 2 tablespoons) of butter off the heat. Check the salt and pepper. You can add a point of cayenne (as much as can be held on a small knife tip). Strain everything through a chinois into a bowl. Pour out the little bit of liquid that escapes the mullets by tilting the plate. Then, with a spoon, cover the fish with the sauce under which their beautiful red color will show. Chill them as thoroughly as possible.

You must allow 30 minutes for the cooking and 2 hours to chill them perfectly.

Red Mullet Cooked in Paper Cases *(Rougets en Caisses).* Use only small red mullets for this, measuring 12 centimeters (4½ inches) in length at the most and weighing about 100–200 grams (3½–7 ounces).

Use good, strong paper, preferably. Make the cases the same size as the shape of the mullets. Dip a brush in the oil and brush the entire inside surface of the paper case. Arrange them on a baking sheet and put them in a moderate oven for *10 minutes.* The paper should stiffen and become somewhat waterproof, thus becoming tougher. Above all, avoid any form of browning because the effect will be entirely contrary to what is desired and will substantially diminish the resistance of the paper.

Generally speaking, the mullets are not put into the cases until they have been previously grilled or sautéed in oil as *à la provençal.* The classic method consists of coating the bottom of the pouch with a layer of *sauce italienne* and placing the mullet on top. The fish is then covered with the same sauce and sprinkled with fine bread crumbs. Then, drizzle with melted butter and put in the oven for *7–8 minutes* to form a gratin. For each mullet, allow a good ½ deciliter (1⅔ fluid ounces, scant ¼ cup) of *sauce Italienne* (SEE PAGE 61). You can also serve the mullet in paper cases prepared with another sauce, as directed in Provençale Style (PAGE 202).

Sardines *(Sardines)*

We will give the most popular methods of cooking.

Grilled Sardines *(Sardines Grillées).* In this case it is not necessary to scale them or gut them if they are quite fresh; sardine lovers prefer them this way. Be sure to wipe them and gut them when necessary and to remove the head. Grill them over a hot fire and serve them just as they are, with fresh butter on the side.

Sautéed Sardines *(Sardines Sautées).* These should be sautéed in a pan with a little bit of butter. In this case, they are scaled first. Serve straight from the pan.

Sardines in Butter with Lemon and Parsley *(Sardines à la Meunière).* SEE FISH À LA MEUNIÈRE, PAGE 167.

Fried Sardines *(Sardines Frites).* Scale, flour, coat with bread crumbs and put into a large quantity of hot oil.

Sardines with an Herb and Bread Crumb Coating *(Sardines à la Façon Provençale).* Scale, remove the heads, and arrange in an oiled dish with minced fines herbes, then drizzle with oil and top with a layer of very fine white bread crumbs; put in the oven for *about 10 minutes* to form a gratin.

In addition to these practical and fast ways of cooking, which are certainly the best and bring out the true flavor of the fish, there is an entire series of recipes for stuffed sardines, in which the sardine is stuffed with a fish stuffing and other ingredients that, at first glance, seem quite eclectic, such as, for example, spinach, which is prepared in the Provençal manner, as follows.

Sardines with Spinach *(Sardines aux Épinards).* Scale and wash the sardines and remove the heads. Open them, their entire length, from the belly side. Spread them out on a towel with the open side up; remove the backbone. Fill with a scant tablespoon of spinach that has been cooked and seasoned well. Close the sardines up, returning them to their original shape. Arrange them in a buttered gratin dish on top of a layer of spinach. Sprinkle with a light coating of white bread crumbs and drizzle with a little oil. Cook in a hot oven for 15 minutes to form a gratin.

The spinach, blanched and minced as directed (SEE PAGE 511), should be sautéed in a pan with a little bit of oil in place of butter, a little minced onion. Then add a pinch of flour and milk in the usual quantities. You can add a hint of garlic, which has been crushed under the blade of a knife. Serve very hot.

Sole *(Sole)*

This is one of the fish that lends itself to the largest variety of recipes, either cooked whole or in fillets. Among its numerous merits is the fact that it stands up much better than any other sea fish to the higher temperatures of the summer months. This does not, of course, preclude either the need for using it as fresh as possible or the care you must take to preserve it.

The best sole, which has the most delicate flesh, is the medium sole, with a net weight of 300–350 grams (10½–12⅓ ounces) before being gutted or scaled. It is the best kind for all recipes: fried, á la Bercy, au gratin, etc. This is what is offered in restaurants "for two," either served whole or in fillets, because it is enough for two people. For one person, you need a sole weighing 200 grams (7 ounces) net.

Preparation of sole for all dishes: Place the sole on its white side lengthwise in front of you. Begin by cutting the head *below* the gills, cutting on the bias from the stomach side and taking great care not to touch the flesh of the large fillets.

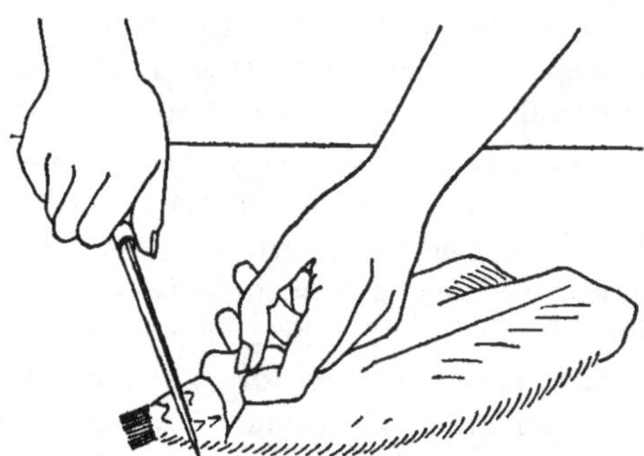

FIG. 39. INCISION ON THE TAIL OF THE SOLE.

Next, remove the brown skin of the sole. You can do this in two ways, both equally simple and rapid. Using the point of a knife, raise the corner of the skin where the head has been cut off and carefully detach several centimeters (at least 1 inch). Then, with your right hand, take the end of the skin in a corner of a kitchen towel and, while holding down the sole on the table with your left hand, rip off the skin in one motion with the other, pulling it backwards in a brisk movement. Alternatively, use the point of the knife to make an incision across the tail of the sole (*fig.* 39), and then carefully turn back the cut skin. Grab this part with a corner of a towel and tear off the skin as described above.

In both cases, how easily the skin peels off is determined by how fresh the fish is. If the sole is not very fresh, the skin will detach with the least effort.

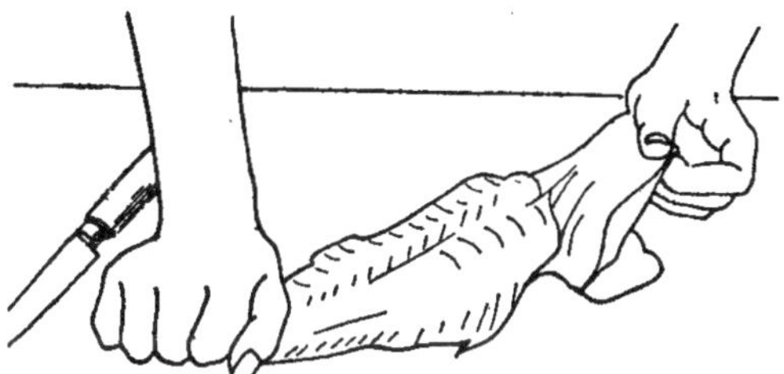

FIG. 40. REMOVAL OF THE SKIN.

The white skin is generally left on the fish because it supports the flesh; carefully scrape it with the knife to remove the scales. You may prefer not to eat this skin; it can be removed in the same way as the dark skin.

With a good pair of scissors, cut off the fins and the frilled edges. Trim the tail. Make a small opening on the side near the head, which is the location of the stomach. With the end of a knife handle, push on this part to expel the entrails. You must gut the fish very carefully to remove the coagulated blood, which will ruin the flesh. Next, wash the sole under running water to rinse the inside clean. Sponge it off on a dry towel.

Finally, with the point of a small knife on the side where the dark skin was, make an incision the entire length of the bone. Slide the blade of the knife under each side of the backbone, which will allow you to carefully remove the fillets, particularly on the upper side, so that the thickest part of the flesh cooks properly; otherwise, the tail side will be overcooked while the flesh toward the head will still be bloody.

To remove the fillet from the uncooked fish: Cut off the head and remove both skins. Place the sole directly in front of you, with the tail toward you. Using a good knife with a flexible blade, make an incision all along the dorsal bone from the head to the tail. As you bring the knife down, raise the flesh of the fillets, turning them *toward your left.* By scraping the blade on the backbone (which avoids cutting the flesh), carefully let the knife cut no more than about 2 centimeters ($^1/_2$ inch) under the fillet. While doing this, keep the sole in place by pressing on the fillet with the tips of your left fingers (*fig.* 41).

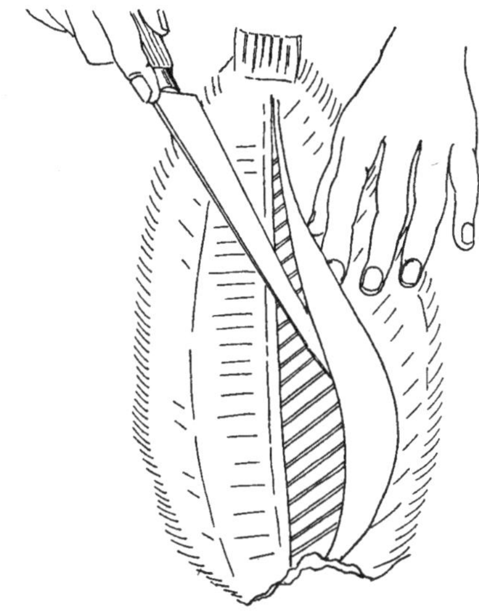

FIG. 41. REMOVING THE FILLET.

Repeat a second time, always cutting from the head to the tail on the same fillet, using the same precautions to avoid ripping the skin and maneuvering the knife always toward your left. Then do this a third time exactly the same way. The fillet has now been cut free.

Turn the fish so its head is closest to you. Do this so that you can maneuver the blade of the knife underneath the fillet that you are detaching in the same direction, toward your left. Proceed exactly as described above, moving the knife from top to bottom. However, now you begin at the tail and move toward the head with the knife, always cutting the flesh toward your left. Turn the fish over to remove the fillet from the other side, proceeding in the same manner.

With the flat of a cleaver that has been moistened with cold water, gently hit the fillets a couple of times, not to flatten them but to break the fibers of the flesh so that they will not shrink while cooking. For the same result, some cooks make several very small incisions across the fillets on the skin side instead of using blows from the cleaver.

Finally, with a sharp knife, trim the fillets at the end and on the sides so that they are more or less equal in size and only the white, thick meat remains. The fillets must have only white, thick meat and all of the shredded and thin parts of the edges are removed. Use the trimmings and the bones to make fish bouillon.

Fillets of sole: Fish, particularly sole, is traditionally served in fillets when it is accompanied by a sauce such as *à la Normande* (SEE PAGE 209) or when the sauce is simply poured directly onto the fish. This makes serving the dish much easier and less awkward, for both server and guest. What's more, it looks more elegant, even to the last piece served.

In haute cuisine the fillets are always removed *raw.* This is particularly necessary for recipes such as paupiettes and garnish for timbales, when they must be rolled up on themselves. It also has the advantage that the bones can be used to make fish bouillon when it is necessary for the dish. This is economical too, since you will not have to buy more fish just to make a small quantity of bouillon.

Preparing raw fillets of fish is both quick and easy for whoever has previously removed them raw. However, you may think that this is too difficult, so if the recipe does not require fish bouillon, you can first cook the sole whole and then remove the fillets before pouring over the sauce. We will describe later on, this page, how to do this.

The Choice of Sole for Fillets

The average gross weight before a fish is gutted and skinned is about 300 grams (10$^{1}/_{2}$ ounces). For current tastes, you should allow 2 fillets per person. However, if you are offering several courses to a large number of guests and do not intend to offer seconds, you can figure on a less generous amount.

Fillets taken from large soles are too large for most people, so these fillets are normally cut diagonally in half before cooking them.

Cooking the Fillets

Only a scant amount of liquid is used—in fact, hardly any liquid—and the fillets are poached in the oven without letting the liquid boil. If it does begin to boil, the fillets will twist and lose their shape.

We would like to make the point that the best way of cooking the fish is to poach the fillets in butter with just a few drops of lemon juice. However, the amount of butter needed means that this is not at all economical because of the substantial quantity of butter necessary. So, use some liquid to reduce the amount of butter. That is, for 4 fillets of 1 sole, use 20–25 grams ($^{2}/_{3}$–1 ounce, about 2 tablespoons) of butter, $^{1}/_{2}$ deciliter (1$^{2}/_{3}$ fluid ounces, scant $^{1}/_{4}$ cup) of water, and just 3 or 4 drops of lemon juice. This is the best way to ensure nice, white fillets.

If you cook with white wine, you must always dilute it with water, using 2 tablespoons of water for 1 tablespoon of wine. This ensures that the fillets will not darken; but if the wine is not of very good quality, then it is better to leave it out altogether. There is no need to use lemon with the wine; the wine serves only to add flavor to the water.

Put the platter over moderate heat without parchment paper or a cover over it. Watch carefully, and as soon as a few bubbles appear, put the platter into a moderate oven, covered with buttered paper. Make sure that the liquid maintains a gentle simmer while the fillets are cooking, to ensure that they remain straight and whole.

To poach or cook fillets from a sole weighing 250 grams (8$^{7}/_{8}$ ounces) requires *4–5 minutes; 8 minutes* for fillets from a sole weighing 350 grams (12$^{1}/_{3}$ ounces). Any longer, and the fillets will darken.

If the Fillets Are Removed after Cooking the Sole

Prepare the fish as if they were going to be served whole; make sure you remove the white skin.

Arrange the sole side by side on an ovenproof plate that has been generously buttered, the split side touching the plate. Pour the liquid you are going to use over them, and then cook as for fillet of sole. However, allow a little more time for the entire sole: *10 minutes* for a sole of 300–350 grams (10$^{1}/_{2}$–12$^{1}/_{3}$ ounces). You will know the fish has been properly cooked because the fillets will easily come away from the bone.

To Serve the Fillets

Carefully remove the fillets using a large-bladed knife. Make sure you remove only the fillets and not the roe or the frayed edges, which often come along with the rest.

Then arrange the fillets with the inner side on top: a little on the bias, one next to the other, and slightly overlapping in two rows.

Grilled Sole *(Sole Grillée).* If you wish, season the sole, then simply brush with oil and grill over very moderate heat. Alternatively, bread the sole (SEE BREADING, PAGE 19), then sprinkle with melted butter and grill: *15–18 minutes* according to their size. To serve, surround them with lemon wedges. You can also serve a caper sauce or a tartar sauce with breaded sole; in that case, do not serve the lemons, and garnish with fresh parsley.

Sole in Butter with Lemon and Parsley *(Sole à la Meunière).* As described earlier (SEE PAGE 167), sole cooked à la meunière can be accompanied by any number of garnishes, according to taste and season: cèpes cut into slices and sautéed in butter; cultivated white mushrooms cut into thick slices and also sautéed; fresh morels, also sautéed; eggplant in slices 1 centimeter (3/8 inch) thick, coated in flour and fried in butter just before serving; or slices of tomato, also sautéed in butter. Arrange these garnishes either around the fish oron lined up top of it and sprinkle with minced parsley: then pour over butter cooked à la noisette.

Sole Saint-Germain *(Sole Saint-Germain).* Dip the sole in bread crumbs and grill, then surround with small potato balls (SEE PAGE 123) and olives. Serve sauce béarnaise in a sauceboat for guests to help themselves.

Dieppe-Style Sole *(Sole à la Fieppoise).* Cook as for brill: whole or in fillets.

Sole with Mushrooms, White Wine, and Butter Sauce *(Sole à la Bonne Femme).* Cook as for brill (PAGE 178). The directions are given there for the necessary cooking time for sole.

Fillet Orly *(Filets Orly).* This is traditionally prepared by marinating the fillets for 1 hour with lemon juice, oil, a few slices of onions, salt and pepper. Next, bread the fillets or dip in a light batter. Fry in a large quantity of hot oil, then arrange on a napkin and serve with a tomato sauce on the side.

Sole au Gratin *(Sole au Gratin).* SEE FISH AU GRATIN (PAGE 168) AND WHITING AU GRATIN (PAGE 194).

Sole Colbert *(Sole Colbert).* The best sole for this dish are medium-sized fish weighing about 350 grams (12 1/3 ounces), which is the right amount for two—and is used in the following recipes. *Time: 45 minutes.*

We would like to emphasize that these quantities are based on sole weighing 350 grams (12 1/3 ounces).

For the breading: **1 whole egg; 1/2 tablespoon of oil; salt and pepper; 80 grams (2 3/4 ounces) of bread crumbs (SEE BREADING, PAGE 19).**

For the maître d'hôtel butter (PAGE 80): **60 grams (2 1/4 ounces, 4 1/2 tablespoons) of good butter, the juice of 1/2 lemon, 1 tablespoon of minced parsley, salt and pepper.**

PROCEDURE. Cut the head on the bias. Remove the dark skin. Scrape the white skin. Trim, gut, and clean the sole as described (SEE PAGE 204).

With the point of a knife, make an incision along the entire backbone on the side where the skin has been removed. On each side of this incision, cut into the flesh for 1 centimeter (3/8 inch).

Having thus loosened the backbone, break it on both ends with the point of a knife, 2 centimeters (3/4 inch) from the tail and about the same distance from the head, to make it easier to remove this bone *only after* cooking.

Prepare the bread crumbs as described (SEE PAGE 19). Spread the crumbs out on the corner of the table. In addition, you will need 2 or 3 tablespoons of milk in a saucer, as well as a little bit of flour spread out on a corner of a napkin.

Dip the sole in the milk and drag it through the flour, then shake it lightly to remove any excess. Just a light dusting of flour is needed to dry the flesh so that it will take a coating of egg, in which it is dipped next. Make sure that the fish is uniformly covered with egg, including the edges. Finally, dip it in the bread crumbs, turning to coat both sides. Once the sole have been breaded, do not let them stand for more than a few minutes because the bread crumbs will dry out and their effect will not be the same. You can prepare the maître d'hôtel butter while you are cooking the sole.

To fry: Put the sole into a large quantity of hot oil (SEE DEEP-FRYING FISH, PAGE 40). Allow *8–10 minutes* of cooking, according to the size of the fish. You will not need to turn it. The fish is done when the sole floats to the surface of the oil and its crust is a beautiful golden color.

Lift it out carefully, making sure you do not break it, then put it on a towel, its open side up. If cooked properly, the crust will be nice and dry. If not, sponge off the sole with a towel. Salt lightly.

Cut the backbone loose with the point of a small knife, then lift it out with your fingers. Quickly put the maître d'hôtel butter into the opening, using a metal spoon. Then turn the sole over and arrange on a warm plate. Serve immediately so the butter is still creamy when it arrives at the table.

Sole Mornay *(Sole à la Mornay)*, Whole or in Fillets. Whether you use sole whole or in fillets, the method is exactly the same. No fish bouillon is required, so you can serve the fish whole, removing the fillets after cooking rather than doing so when the fish is raw (SEE FILLETS OF SOLE, PAGE 206). Whichever way you serve them, the quantities of fish and sauce remain the same.

For this preparation, glazing the dish before serving is just about *derigueur.* At any rate, a good glaze forms, thanks to the grated cheese sprinkled over the surface of the sauce. *Time: 50 minutes. Serves 6–8.*

3 sole, each weighing about 300 grams (10 1/2 ounces).

To cook them: **1 1/2 deciliters (5 fluid ounces, 2/3 cup) of white wine; 40 grams (1 3/8 ounces, 3 tablespoons) of butter.**

For the Mornay sauce: **25 grams (1 ounce, 2 tablespoons) of butter and 25 grams (1 ounce) of flour for the roux blanc; 5 deciliters (generous 2 cups) of boiled milk; a bouquet of parsley branches; 6 grams (1/5 ounce) of salt, a pinch of white pepper, a little bit of grated nutmeg; 50 grams (1 3/4 ounces) of a half-and-half mixture of grated Gruyère and Parmesan; 50 grams (1 3/4 ounces, 3 1/2 tablespoons) of butter to add to the sauce just before serving.**

To glaze the plate: **25 grams (1 ounce) of mixed cheese; 10–15 grams (1/4–1/2 ounce, 1 tablespoon) of melted butter.**

PROCEDURE. **The sauce:** Boil the milk. Meanwhile, in a small pot with a capacity a little bit more than 1/2 liter (generous 2 cups), make a *roux blanc.* Dilute it with the hot milk. Season it with salt, pepper, and nutmeg. Bring it to a boil; add the parsley bouquet and let it boil (very gently) without a cover for a good half hour.

The sole: Prepare them to be cooked whole if you do not remove the fillets when they are raw (SEE PREPARATION OF SOLE, PAGE 204). Refrigerate for at least 15 minutes before poaching them. Cook them with the wine and the butter. Allow *8 minutes* for the fillets and *10 minutes* for the whole sole. Next, carefully arrange on the serving plate: make sure that the plate is ovenproof; do not use a bowl, which will make it difficult to create the glaze. Keep the fish warm. Reserve the cooking liquid.

To finish the sauce: Pass it through a chinois into a small sauté pan. Add the cooking liquid from the sole. Then reduce the sauce over high heat, mixing it constantly with a whisk until it has been reduced to 4 deciliters (1 2/3 cups) or less.

Off the heat, add the grated cheese (50 grams, 1 3/4 ounces). Mix well, then put it back on the heat, mixing constantly with a whisk for only a few seconds: just long enough to melt the cheese.

Turn off the heat, then add the final butter. Check the seasoning, which may need to be adjusted according to the amount of salt in the cheese. Next, pour in the few drops of liquid that have escaped from the fish while they were kept warm.

Pour on the sauce, making sure that it is spread in equal thickness over the fish. Sprinkle with the grated cheese, then pour over the melted butter. Immediately put the plate in the oven to glaze, as described (SEE PAGE 15). Serve immediately.

Fillet of Sole Marguery *(Filets de Sole Marguery).* The same as Dieppe-style sole, but without the mushrooms and with a garnish of mussels and shrimp only. Glaze before serving (SEE PAGE 15).

Normandy-Style Fillet of Sole *(Filets de Sole à la Normande).* Normandy-style sole, whether it is served whole or in fillets, is distinguished by its garnish of gudgeon or fried smelt, shrimp, croutons, and sometimes oysters, mussels, and mushrooms. In fact, this is the garnish that accompanied the superb matelotes (fish stews) served a hundred years ago; the anthologies included: sole in a Normandy Matelot. In those days, the preference was for a very large sole, which was served whole; this was the era of service à la française, when the guests admired with great anticipation the beautiful piece of fish placed on the table on a large silver hot plate.

In some regions, crayfish are included in the garnish, but this is not traditional. Also, the truffle slices are optional. When you have a white meat glaze, it is usual to finish the plate with a thin ribbon of this glaze drizzled over the sauce with a small brush. This is very appealing to the eye but is not absolutely necessary.

See the article on fillet of sole regarding the choice of preferring the whole fish to the fillets (PAGE 204). The dish is prepared in the same way in both cases; but if the fish is served whole, you will need to buy extra fish not indicated in the recipe to make the bouillon; or substitute for the fish bouillon some of the liquid used to cook the mussels or some mushroom and white wine cooking liquid. You first poach the sole in whatever you have chosen, and then use the same liquid for the sauce. *Time: 2 hours. Serves 6.*

3 medium sole, each weighing about 300 grams ($10^1/_2$ ounces).

To cook them: About $1^1/_2$ deciliters (5 fluid ounces, $^2/_3$ cup) of fish bouillon; 25–30 grams (1 ounce, 2 tablespoons) of butter; lemon juice.

For the Normandy-style garnish: 18 nice mussels (about 1 liter/$4^1/_4$ cups); 12 oysters, Portuguese or others, inexpensive; 10 small mushrooms; 6 medium crayfish; 6 gudgeons or 6 small smelt; 6 croutons fried in butter.

For the fish bouillon: The bones and heads of the sole; 60–75 grams ($2^1/_4$–$2^2/_3$ ounces) of carrot and the same of onion; 2 shallots, 7 or 8 sprigs of parsley; 1 small bay leaf; 1 sprig of thyme; 2 deciliters ($6^3/_4$ fluid ounces, $^7/_8$ cup) of white wine and 2 deciliters ($6^3/_4$ fluid ounces, $^7/_8$ cup) of water; a pinch of sea salt.

For the sauce: 30 grams (1 ounce, 2 tablespoons) of butter, and 20 grams ($^2/_3$ ounces) of flour for the roux; $2^1/_2$ deciliters (1 cup) of fish bouillon; 2 tablespoons of cooking water from the mussels; 4–5 tablespoons of cooking water from the mushrooms (that is $3^1/_2$ good deciliters/$1^1/_2$ cups of liquid total); 2 egg yolks; for the liaison to thicken the sauce the cooking liquid of the sole and 100 grams ($3^1/_2$ ounces, 7 tablespoons) of butter for the final finish.

PROCEDURE. Everything except the gudgeons and the croutons must be prepared in advance so that when you are ready to serve you have only to fry the gudgeons and the croutons, finish the sauce, and dress the plate.

The sole fillets: Remove these in the usual way. Keep them cool and ready in a buttered ovenproof dish. You don't have to worry about anything else but poaching them 10–15 minutes before serving.

The fish bouillon: Prepare this according to the directions in the section on bouillon (PAGE 165).

The mussels: Prepare as described (SEE PAGE 241). When they are open, you can take them out of their shells immediately and keep them warm in the liquid that they have yielded, which should be completely decanted from the pan. Or you may leave them as they are under very, very low heat and take them out of their shells at the last moment.

The oysters: Prepare as described under oyster sauce (PAGE 66).

The mushrooms: Turn them (SEE PAGE 491) or skin them. Cook them as described with water, butter, and lemon (SEE MUSHROOMS, PAGE 490).

The crayfish: Prepare and cook them as described. Keep them warm. SEE CRAYFISH, PAGE 228.

The gudgeons: Prepare them "in a sleeve," as described on PAGE 221.

The croutons: Cut them from a piece of stale bread, either in a rectangle or a long heart shape, about 5 centimeters (2 inches) long and

1/2 centimeter (3/8 inch) thick. Keep them between two plates so they don't darken.

Prepare these ingredients while the fish bouillon, which you have already started, is slowly cooking. Thus, it will be ready when you need to make the sauce.

The sauce: In a small pot, make a *roux blanc.* Dilute it with the fish bouillon, the cooking water of the mussels, and the water from the mushrooms. Return almost to a boil. Add a pinch of white pepper, a hint of nutmeg, and some of the mushroom peelings. Let it simmer gently for *20 minutes,* skimming it from time to time.

Cooking the fillet of sole: Moisten the fillet with the rest of the bouillon. If there is not enough, add 2 or 3 tablespoons of the mushroom cooking water. Squeeze 10 drops of lemon juice on the fillet. Spread 25–30 grams of butter (1 ounce, 2 tablespoons) divided into small bits over the surface. Cover with buttered parchment paper.

Poach for *6 minutes.* Then take the dish out of the oven and keep it warm, without letting the liquid simmer, until you are ready to arrange it on the plate.

Final preparation: Pass the sauce into another small pot and thicken the sauce with the egg yolks (SEE LIAISONS, PAGE 47). Arrange the fillets of sole on a long service platter. Surround them with the mussels and oysters and arrange the mushrooms in a line on top of the fillet. Put the dish in a very moderate oven to keep it warm.

Deep-fry the gudgeons and sauté the croutons in butter.

Add enough of the cooking liquid from the fillet to the sauce to bring it to the right consistency. Heat it well, then *turn off the heat* and add the butter.

To serve: Take the plate out of the oven. Tilt it over the sauce to pour out those few drops of liquid that have escaped. Otherwise, the liquid will subsequently float to the top of the sauce. Cover the fillets and the garnish with the sauce, spreading it on top by spoonfuls and as quickly as possible.

Arrange the crayfish (well drained) around the plate, alternating them with the gudgeons and the croutons. Serve.

Portuguese-Style Fillet of Sole *(Filets de Sole à la Portugaise).* A lunch dish that is particularly good when tomatoes are in season. You can replace the fish bouillon with the cooking water from the mushrooms for poaching or cooking the fillets. You don't need to remove these fillets from the raw fish if you don't need the bones for the bouillon. You can then cook the soles whole and later remove the fillets to arrange on the serving dish. This should then be glazed if possible (SEE PAGE 15). *Time: 35 minutes. Serves 6–8.*

3 medium sole, each about 300 grams (10 1/2 ounces); 6 medium-sized ripe tomatoes; 40–50 grams (1 3/8–1 3/4 ounces) of finely minced onions; 100 grams (3 1/2 ounces) of mushrooms; 1 1/2 deciliters (5 fluid ounces, 2/3 cup) white wine; 1 good deciliter (3 1/3 fluid ounces, 1/2 cup) of mushroom cooking liquid; 125 grams (4 1/2 ounces, 9 tablespoons) of butter total; 12 grams (3/8 ounce) of flour; the juice of 1/4 lemon; a pinch of minced parsley.

PROCEDURE. Put the onion in a small pan with 20 grams (2/3 ounce, 1 heaping tablespoon) of butter. Sauté it on very low heat without letting it color at all.

Meanwhile, prepare the tomatoes. Plunge them for 2 seconds in boiling water to remove the skin. Cut them in two. Squeeze out the water and the seeds. Then cut into small slices and press these in a towel to remove their excess water.

Add the tomato to the sautéed onion. Add a pinch of salt, a pinch of pepper, and, if you wish, a piece of garlic the size of a pea, crushed into a fine paste. Cover the pan; let it simmer on very low heat, mixing from time to time.

The mushrooms: Prepare them and cook them with lemon, butter, and water as described (SEE MUSHROOMS FOR GARNISHES, PAGE 490). Put them aside.

The sole: Either immediately remove the fillets from the raw fish, or prepare the sole to cook them whole (SEE PAGE 204).

Begin to cook the fish a good 15 minutes before serving a whole sole, and a little less than 15 minutes if using fillets. Add the liquid and 20 grams (2/3 ounce, 1 heaping tablespoon) butter to the fish on the platter. Bring to a boil; put the platter into the oven with parchment paper placed directly on top of the fish.

Allow *8 minutes* of poaching (more or less) for the fillets; *about 10 minutes* for the whole fish.

Once cooked, immediately take the fish out of the oven and pour all the cooking liquid that is going to be used for the sauce into a bowl.

The sauce: Prepare in advance a *roux blanc* in a small pot with 15 grams (1/2 ounce, 1 tablespoon) of butter and the flour. Then dilute it with the cooking liquid from the fish. Let it boil *2–3 minutes* on very gentle heat. Season immediately with a pinch of good salt and no more than a small knife point of cayenne, which you will use with extreme prudence.

To dress and serve: If glazing the fillets before serving, use a long serving dish that can be placed in the oven. Arrange the fillets as described (SEE PAGE 206). Quickly cut the warm prepared mushrooms into fine slices. Add to the pan with the tomatoes. With a spoon, place this garnish on each side of the fillet of sole.

Add the remaining butter to the sauce. Taste and correct the seasoning if it is not sufficiently spicy. Pour this sauce on the fillets *without putting any on the garnish of tomatoes and mushrooms.*

Glaze quickly and serve immediately.

Russian-Style Sole *(Sole à la Russe).* Make this recipe in the summer months, when you can find very tender carrots. There's no need to complicate this dish with fish bouillon, which would barely add to its flavor. Even the finest chefs are careful to maintain the simple home-cooking style of this recipe. To summarize, this is sole served with the vegetables from its own cooking court bouillon. *Time: 1 1/4 hours. Serves 6–8.*

2 sole, each weighing about 500 grams (1 pound, 2 ounces).

75 grams (2 2/3 ounces) of carrots, net weight, long, thin and *quite red inside;* 75 grams (2 2/3 ounces) of onions; a good pinch of parsley leaves; 150 grams (5 1/3 ounces, 10 1/2 tablespoons) of butter; 2 1/2 deciliters (1 cup) of water; the juice of 1/4 lemon; salt and pepper.

PROCEDURE. **The vegetables:** Carefully peel the carrots. Cut them into rounds that are 4 millimeters (1/8 inch) thick. The equality of their thickness is important for the unity of their cooking, and the thickness indicated must not be diminished or the rounds will break while they are being cooked. Cut the onions into rounds of the same thickness.

Put everything into a small sauté pan with 30 grams (1 ounce, 2 tablespoons) of butter. Sauté on gentle heat for *a little less than 15 minutes,* until the vegetables are nice and soft but have not colored in any way.

Next, add the liquid and a pinch of salt. Bring to a boil on lively heat, then immediately turn the flame down very low. Add another 25 grams (1 ounce, 2 tablespoons) of butter and let it cook gently without covering the pan for about 20 minutes. This is the time necessary to cook the vegetables thoroughly without the rounds of carrots becoming deformed.

Break the parsley leaves into small fragments, and make sure there are no stems left. This parsley will be added to the vegetables only *5 minutes before taking them out of the pan.*

The sole: Prepare these as soon as the vegetables have been started (SEE PREPARATION OF SOLE, PAGE 204). When the fillets have been removed, lightly season them with salt and pepper. Slide a piece of butter as big as a walnut under each fillet. Put them back in the skillet.

Take a long metal or porcelain plate that is ovenproof and that can easily hold the 2 sole placed head to tail. With your fingers, spread out a layer of butter, about 40 grams (1 3/8 ounces, 3 tablespoons). Arrange the soles on the plate, then pour on top of them carrots, onions, and parsley with their cooking liquid. You should have about 2 deciliters (6 3/4 fluid ounces, 7/8 cup) or less of liquid. If there is more liquid than this, boil it to reduce before pouring it over the fish.

To cook: Bring to a boil. Then turn the heat down low enough so that the liquid only slightly simmers. Cover the dish *as tightly as possible,* then poach for *20–25 minutes.* Baste the sole frequently while cooking. You can also cook or poach the sole in the oven; the heat of the oven will allow you to keep the liquid simmering at the perfect temperature. In this case, it is even more important to keep the plate well covered and to baste frequently so that the vegetables do not dry out at all. Five minutes before the end of the cooking, divide the remaining butter into bits and spread it over the sole. Baste one or two times more.

Wipe the edges of the dish clean. Squeeze the lemon over the sole. Serve in the same oven dish.

Sole with White Wine *(Sole au Vin Blanc).* This recipe may not seem very complicated, but there are nonetheless quite a number of variations. Some classic authors suggest cooking the sole with white wine, adding the cooking liquid to a butter sauce or a white sauce and then simply pouring it over the sole. More modern authors suggest poaching the sole with a fumet of white wine or a concentrated bouillon of fish and the cooking liquid from mushrooms; the fish is then coated with a white wine sauce, which can be prepared in a number of ways. However, it is always based on a fumet of fish, with a liaison of egg yolks and a final addition of a substantial quantity of butter.

For cooking this at home, where you may not have at hand a fish bouillon or the cooking liquid from mushrooms, the recipe has been simplified. But this does not mean that the quality of the ingredients should be compromised. Indeed, the reverse is true; thus, we particularly recommend that you use a good, nonacidic white wine, a Bordeaux, preferably a Graves. You will need very little. Use a very good butter to add to the sauce just before serving; its flavor will then be much more obvious. Or, you can cook the sole with a few onion rounds; you do not serve these, but they will contribute substantially to the overall flavor of the dish. *Time: 25–30 minutes.*

1 sole of 350 grams (12 1/3 ounces), 1 1/2 deciliters (5 fluid ounces, 2/3 cup) of white wine; 4 or 5 extremely thin rounds of onions; 75 grams (2 2/3 ounces, 1/3 cup) of butter; 10 grams (1/3 ounce) of flour; 2 egg yolks.

PROCEDURE. Prepare the sole (SEE PAGE 204). Salt it lightly on both sides. Butter a long, large ovenproof plate and cover with onion rounds, then arrange the fish, cut side down. Moisten with the white wine.

Put the plate on very moderate heat. As soon as it boils, cover with parchment paper, laying it directly on the fish. Then put the dish into the oven. Allow about *10 minutes* of cooking or poaching, without boiling.

The sauce: Meanwhile, mix 15 grams (1/2 ounce, 1 tablespoon) of butter with the flour in a small pot. Cook for 1 minute on very gentle heat, without letting it color, to remove the raw taste of the flour.

Once the sole have been cooked to perfection, pour all the cooking liquid into the chinois. Keep the sole warm. Then dilute the *roux blanc* with this liquid, using a whisk and keeping the pot off the heat. Add the egg yolks (SEE LIAISONS, PAGE 47), then boil for about 1 minute. Turn off the heat. Divide the remaining butter (about 2 ounces, 1/4 cup) into bits, and add to the pot. Verify the seasoning and add just a few drops of lemon juice. (Do not add this butter until the very last moment, just before pouring the sauce over the fish, because the sauce must not be returned to the heat.)

To serve: Slide the sole onto a warm plate. Do not let the rounds of onions fall onto this plate. Pour the sauce over the sole, completely covering it.

Sole with Red Wine *(Sole au Vin Rouge).* The best sole for this dish, whether served in restaurants or at home, are medium-large sole: that is, sole weighing 550 grams (1 pound 3 ounces) each.

The wine used—Burgundy or Bordeaux—must be good. If you wish to be ceremonial you can put the name of the wine on the menu. *Time: 30 minutes (once the sole have been cleaned and made ready). Serves 6–8.*

2 sole of the weight specified above; 4 deciliters (1 2/3 cups) of red wine; 125 grams (4 1/2 ounces, 9 tablespoons) of butter; 12 grams of flour (3/8 ounces); 1/4 lemon; salt and pepper.

PROCEDURE. Prepare the sole (SEE PAGE 204). Generously butter a roasting dish (use about 40 grams/1 3/8 ounces/3 tablespoons of butter, and spread it out with the tip of your finger). Arrange the sole side by side, with the open, cut side down. Cover with a white oval of buttered parchment paper, placing it directly on top of the fish. Prepared thus and kept cool, they can be left to stand for 1 or 2 hours before being cooked.

To cook: About 30 minutes before cooking, take off the paper. Sprinkle the sole with a pinch of good salt. Pour the wine over them. Add about 30 grams (1 ounce, 2 tablespoons) of butter divided into pieces. Heat the dish on the flame until it starts to boil. As soon as it boils, put the plate into the oven, placing the buttered paper on top of the fish. Poach for *about 20 minutes,* keeping the liquid at an imperceptible simmer without a pronounced boiling. If you are using a dish that is a little too large for the sole to be completely covered by the wine, make sure you baste them two or three times during this poaching.

To check if the fish has been perfectly cooked, lift a corner of the fillet near the head. It should cleanly detach from the backbone. Take the dish out of the oven and carefully slide the sole onto a flat spatula to transfer them to an ovenproof serving plate. Cover the sole with an inverted plate. Keep warm.

The sauce: Pour the cooking wine into a small sauté pan. Boil it strongly, uncovered, to reduce it by half. Prepare a beurre manié with the flour and about 15 grams ($^1/_2$ ounce, 1 tablespoon) of butter. Make the liaison as described (SEE PAGE 47), then remove from the heat. Finally, add the rest of the butter divided into small bits; a pinch of ground pepper; and 5 or 6 drops of lemon juice. Taste to check the salt. Do not turn the heat back on.

To sauce and glaze the sole: Uncover the sole. Tip the plate to pour out every last drop of liquid that has seeped into the sauce. Spoon the sauce over the sole to cover, then glaze (SEE PAGE 15).

Serve immediately.

Tuna *(Thon)*

All of the following recipes use tuna that has been cut into slices or "rounds" about 3 centimeters ($1^3/_8$ inches) thick. No matter how you cook it, you can tell that the tuna is perfectly cooked when the central backbone comes away easily from the flesh.

Tuna Cooked in Court Bouillon *(Thon au Court Bouillon).* This tuna is cooked simply, just covered with liquid. To serve, glaze the flesh with a little melted butter and remove the dark skin. Serve on a napkin and accompany with a sauce of your choice: white sauce, caper, anchovies, tomato, etc.

Grilled Tuna *(Thon Grillé).* Marinate the round or steak for 1 hour with salt, oil, a few rounds of onions, and some parsley. Grill it on gentle fire for *25–30 minutes.* Remove the skin and then serve with maître d'hôtel butter or anchovy butter, or accompany with a rémoulade sauce, caper sauce, or any other sauce, offered in a sauceboat.

Baked Tuna *(Thon au Four).* Arrange the fish on a gratin plate. Simply season with salt and pepper and sprinkle with oil, then coat with fine bread crumbs and cook in a hot oven, basting it frequently with its cooking liquid. It cooks in about the same time as grilled tuna. and is subject to the same test for being perfectly done. Serve on an ovenproof plate accompanied with a tartar sauce or a rémoulade sauce.

Braised Tuna *(Thon Braisé).* This is a recipe using meat juices, in which the tuna is treated as if it were veal. Some authors even suggest larding the tuna steak with lardons. To cook the round, proceed exactly as for the fricandeau (SEE PAGE 277). Sweat it the same way, then add just enough bouillon and white wine to cover, the white wine making up one-quarter of the liquid. Allow for *$1^1/_2$ hours* of gentle cooking. Carefully remove the skin from the round. Bind the braising juice with starch. Just as with fricandeau, surround the braised tuna with a garnish of sorrel, chicory, spinach, or cooked tomatoes.

Tuna in Chartreuse *(Thon en Chartreuse).* This is cooked exactly as in the previous recipe, taking care to cut the carrots for the bottom of the pot to a thickness of 1 centimeter ($^3/_8$ inch). That is about 150 grams ($5^1/_3$ ounces) of carrots for 1 kilogram (2 pounds, 3 ounces) of tuna divided into rounds. Surround the tuna with 6 small blanched lettuces (SEE BRAISED LETTUCE, PAGE 519) and then cook it. To serve, arrange the fish on a plate and surround it with carrots and lettuces. Moisten it with the cooking liquid, having first skimmed the fat from the surface. Then degrease and thicken it.

Turbot *(Turbot)*

Traditionally, turbot is reserved for sumptuous meals; and whichever sauce you choose to accompany it will enhance the impression of opulence that is created by the appearance of such a beautiful piece of fish. That said, you should avoid getting too large a turbot because the flesh is often tough. Choose a fish of medium weight: the flesh is infinitely more delicate.

The trimmings from the turbot—the guts, the head, the tail, the skin, the bone, etc.—generally account for a loss of one-third of the gross weight. Thus you should allow a net weight of 100 grams (3½ ounces) of fish per person for a generous serving. That works out as 1 gross kilogram (2 pounds, 3 ounces) for seven people. If you want to offer seconds, count on 1 gross kilogram (2 pounds, 3 ounces) for five or six people. Any leftovers can be put to good use, so you may prefer not to limit yourself to the minimum weight required.

In the extravagant days of the Master Carême, turbot was sometimes cooked in white wine, either a Sauternes or Chablis. Nonetheless, some people prefer that it be cooked in saltwater, which lets the turbot keep its natural flavor and also keeps the flesh white and firm. These days, turbot is always boiled either in saltwater with milk added to it or in a court bouillon made with milk.

Use a sauceboat to serve any one of several sauces as an accompaniment: hollandaise, mousseline, cream sauce, caper sauce, shrimp sauce, Nantua, oyster sauce, etc. As with all fish dishes prepared this way, accompany it with potatoes cut into pieces the size of a large olive, cooked in salted water or steamed.

Any leftovers can be used in a gratin, made into croquettes, served in little shell dishes *(coquilles)*, as soufflés, as a garnish for a vol-au-vent, and to edge duchess potatoes (SEE PAGE 541). It is worth mentioning the smaller turbot, which can be used in all of these recipes: boiled, grilled, gratin, meunière, etc. For the different ways to prepare this, refer to the directions given for sole and brill. Always taking the greatest care, make an incision on the dark side or the back of the fish, both to facilitate its cooking and to make sure the flesh keeps its shape.

Preparation of the turbot: With a pair of large kitchen scissors, cut off the fins, the barbs, and everything around the fish, cutting about 1 centimeter (3/8 inch) equally into the body of the fish. Cut off one-third of the tail. Wrap a towel around the index finger of your right hand. Lift up the gills with your left index finger and then put your right finger in to pull them out; use your finger like a hook.

Put the turbot on its stomach, on its white side. With a knife, cut into its skin at the intestinal pouch: high up on the body on the dark side, it is easily recognizable. An incision of 2 to 3 centimeters (3/4–1 1/8 inches) will let you put in your bare index finger to tear out the guts, pulling them toward the top. Alternatively, to be absolutely sure of gutting the fish, cut a larger opening in the pouch so that you can more easily remove the guts and the coagulated blood inside of the pouch, because it will darken when it is cooked.

Place the turbot under cold running water to wash it on the outside and, above all, on the inside, to thoroughly clean the pouch. Place it in a fish poacher covered with very cold water and a very small handful of sea salt. Allow it to disgorge at least 2 hours before cooking it. This will ensure that the fish remains perfectly white and any bloody matter dissolves. During the summer, keep everything as cool as possible. Before cooking the turbot, there are some precautions to take so that the fish does not lose its shape:

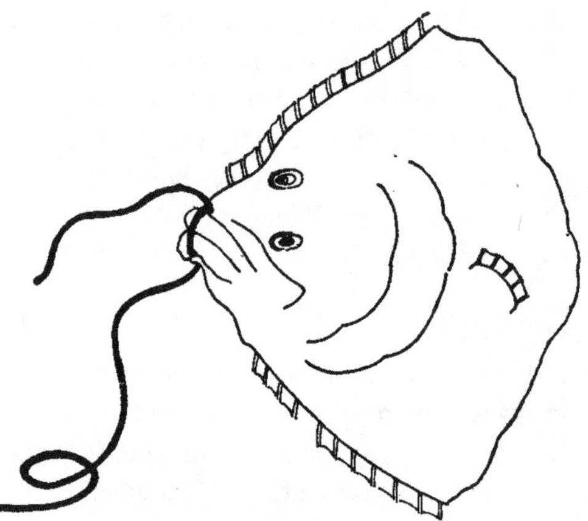

FIG. 42. HOW TO THREAD THE STRING TO SUPPORT THE MUZZLE.

For a very large turbot: With the point of a good, strong knife and on the dark side of the fish, make an incision about 6–7 centimeters (2¼–2¾ inches) along the backbone, where the skin is thickest. Push aside the flesh to expose the large backbone. Break the backbone by carefully bending the fish back on itself, which is much easier than cutting it, which you can also do. Take out a piece of bone that is two or three joints long. This ensures that the backbone does not fight against the natural shrinkage of the fish while it cooks.

For a medium-size turbot: It is enough to make a double incision on each side of the backbone without breaking it. This gives some flexibility to the fish and helps it keep its shape. Note that the flesh is much more likely to burst when the fish is fresh; the incisions also help the heat penetrate the thick flesh.

Always try to avoid the fish losing its shape. Secure the head by stitching in a triangle with a cooking needle threaded with fine thread. Stick the needle several times into alternate ends of the jaw and the muzzle and then join these two parts by making a simple knot, leaving a length free to attach it to the end that has been threaded through the needle (*fig.* 42). Then stick the needle in the white side a little behind the opening where you have gutted the fish. Push the needle through and stick it through the other side of the backbone to come out of the white side a little behind the gills. Finally, tie the string to the place where it has already been tied to the muzzle (*fig.* 43 and *fig.* 44).

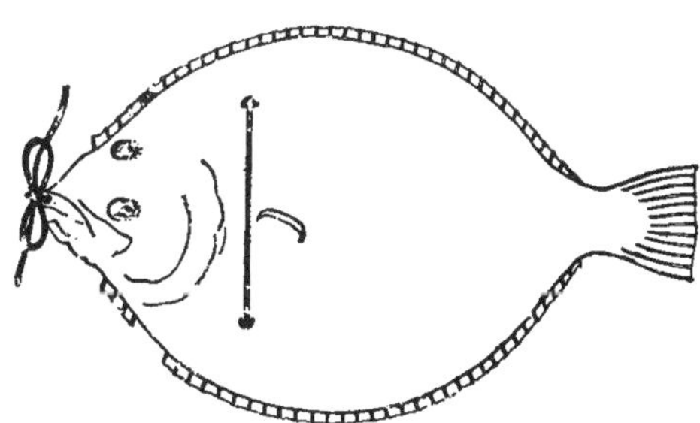

FIG. 43. PASSAGE OF THE STRING UNDER THE TURBOT.

To cook: A fish poacher, or *turbotière,* is absolutely essential for cooking a medium-sized turbot (*fig.* 45). Not only is this utensil the right shape to hold the fish, but it also contains a wire rack or pierced metal plate, which facilitates the removal of the turbot after it has been cooked, lets it drain completely, then helps you transfer it to the service plate—all of these operations can be difficult given the fragility of the cooked flesh.

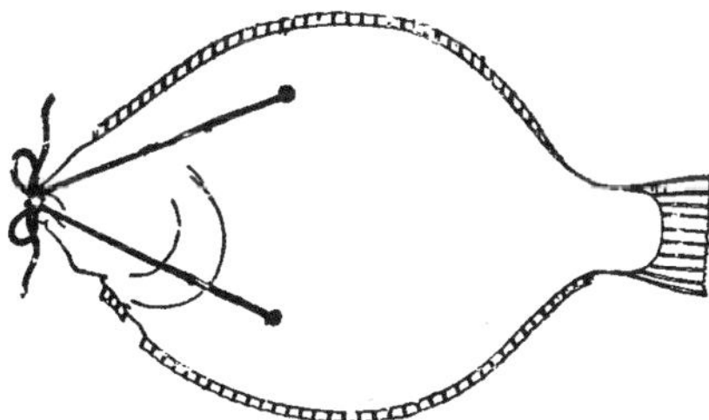

FIG. 44. TRUSSING COMPLETED, VIEWED FROM THE WHITE SIDE.

Place the turbot on the metal plate of the fish poacher with the white side up. Put the rack or grill into the fish poacher. Pour in enough cold water to completely cover the fish. Add milk and salt in the given quantities (SEE COURT BOUILLON MADE WITH MILK, PAGE 165) and the rounds of lemon.

Put the fish poacher on a strong heat.

Remove the foam produced as the liquid begins to boil. As soon as it starts to boil, immediately turn the heat down under the fish poacher. From this moment keep it at a simple, barely perceptible simmer and maintain it until cooked, as described in the section on court bouillon (SEE PAGE 162).

Once the turbot has been perfectly cooked, you can leave it for up to a half hour to keep warm in the fish poacher until you are ready to serve; do not let it simmer.

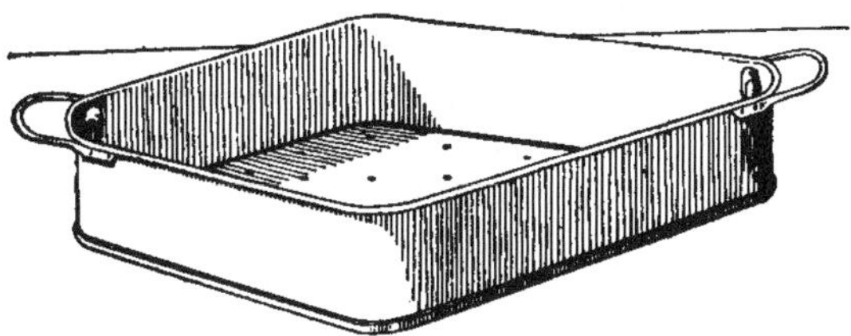

FIG. 45. TURBOTIÈRE.

To serve: Traditionally, this is served on an oval plate covered by a heavy cotton cloth on which the fish is laid. This is because even the largest service plate is not large enough for a fish this size. When you are ready to serve, lift the metal grill supporting the turbot out of the poacher and set it diagonally over the poacher or *turbotière.* Let the fish drain for 1 minute so that you do not drench the cloth on the serving dish. Slide the turbot, white side up, right onto the middle of the serving platter by shaking it off the metal grill. Cut the string on the head with scissors. Surround the fish with groups of potatoes cut into small balls, alternating with sprigs of parsley, or serve the potatoes in a vegetable dish and surround the fish with parsley, placing some into the openings of the gills.

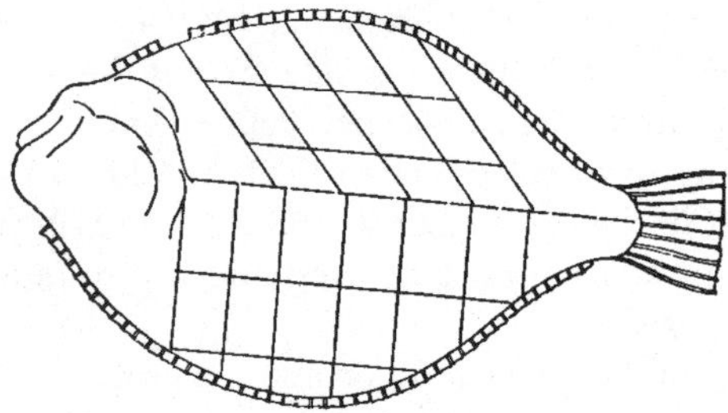

FIG. 46. CARVING THE TURBOT.

To carve: First remove the white skin. With a silver-bladed knife, make an incision down the middle of the entire backbone. Depending on the size of the fish, mark 2 or 3 parallel incisions along the backbone and then divide it crosswise in squares or in rectangles (*fig.* 46) so that each guest can easily use a fish spatula to help themselves. Before everyone has done so, you should quickly remove the backbone and then cut the bottom half of the fish into fillets as you have with the top part.

Turbot Croquettes *(Croquettes de Turbot).* See the article about croquettes (PAGE 438). Bind the flesh of the fish with a light béchamel sauce, then thicken with egg yolk, using 1 yolk for each 1½ deciliters (5 fluid ounces, ⅔ cup) of sauce. Add a little bit of anchovy paste. Surround with fried parsley.

FRESHWATER FISH
Poissons d'Eau Douce

Shad *(Alose)*

The true season for shad is from the middle of April to the end of June. This fish deteriorates very quickly, and even faster in warm or humid temperatures. So check that it is fresh, and if you are not going to cook and serve the shad as soon as possible after buying it, keep it in a very cool environment wrapped in sorrel leaves.

Whenever possible, buy it when it contains soft roe. The weight recommended for the different recipes described below is at least 1 good kilogram (2 pounds, 3 ounces).

Shad is mostly *grilled,* then served on a traditional purée of sorrel or with anchovy butter, ravigote sauce (herbs and shallots), shallot butter, etc. You can also *stuff it* with its own roe; it is then either *grilled* or *poached.* Less frequently, shad is cooked in a court bouillon: in wine or in saltwater. In this case, the scales are traditionally left on, not only for the sake of appearance but also to preserve the unctuousness of the flesh by retaining the oil that is characteristic of the fish. Some chefs then use the court bouillon—without the wine, of course—to make a peasant sorrel soup.

Preparation of the fish: Gut and scale the fish as described (SEE PAGE 161). Completely remove the tail. If the fish is full of roe, carefully set this to one side. (Poached in a court bouillon, it will be excellent used in an omelet.)

Grilled Shad *(Alose Grillée).* According to preference, you can grill shad whole or cut it into slices: use slices if you buy the fish already cleaned, Choose slices weighing 125–150 grams (4½–5⅓ ounces) per person.

The flesh of the shad is quite oily and is greatly improved by being marinated before being grilled. Marinate for 1 hour for a whole fish and 20 minutes for the slices.

Once the fish have been prepared, make incisions 5 millimeters (¼ inch) deep and about 1½ centimeters (⅝ inch) apart on each side. Arrange the fish on a plate and season with salt and pepper. Sprinkle with 4 tablespoons of oil and the juice of half a lemon. Then spread over the slices a finely minced medium-size onion, and some sprigs of parsley, thyme, and bay leaf broken into fragments. Let stand in a cool place to marinate, as above.

To grill: SEE GRILLING, PAGE 35. Drain the marinade from the fish. Brush it generously with oil and put it on the grill.

The cooking time is *35–40 minutes* for a whole fish with a gross weight of about 1¼ kilograms (2 pounds, 12 ounces). Turn it at the end of *10 minutes* and brush the side that you have turned over with oil. Turn and brush with oil at least three times. Reduce the heat after you have turned the fish for the first time.

If you are grilling slices, cook for *15–18 minutes* at medium heat. Turn over the slices after *5–6 minutes,* being sure to brush them with oil.

Serve the fish or the slices on a long plate that has already been spread with your choice of butter or the sorrel purée.

Stuffed Shad *(Alose Farcie).* **The stuffing:** With a wooden spoon, mix 150 grams (5⅓ ounces) of bread crumbs soaked in ½ glass of milk and chilled; 2 tablespoons of minced onions, cooked without being allowed to color in 20 grams (⅔ ounce, 1 heaping tablespoon) of butter, then chilled; the roe, minced; 2 or 3 chopped mushrooms; a small tablespoon of minced parsley; 1 whole egg, or 2 eggs that have been previously mixed in a bowl and added little by little; 30 grams (1 ounce, 2 tablespoons) of melted butter; a good pinch of salt; a pinch of pepper; and a bit of grated nutmeg.

Put the shad on a kitchen towel on its back. With a spoon, put the stuffing into the belly, pushing it down with your finger. Stitch the opening closed completely, using a cooking needle and good strong cooking thread. Grill or poach the fish. After cooking, do not forget to remove the thread.

Shad Cooked by Poaching. Place in a thoroughly buttered ovenproof plate with about ½ liter (generous 2 cups) of court bouillon made with white wine. Bring to a boil on the stove, then put the plate in a moderate oven to maintain a very gentle simmer. Allow *15 minutes* of simmering for a fish that weighs from 1–1¼ kilograms (2 pounds, 3 ounces–2 pounds, 12 ounces). Baste frequently.

Pour the liquid into a small pot over a blond roux that has been prepared in advance; use 15 grams (½ ounce) of flour and 15 grams (½ ounce, 1 tablespoon) of butter for 3 deciliters (1¼ cups) of reduced cooking liquid. Finish with butter, about 75 grams (2⅔ ounces, ⅓ cup), added off the heat. Serve the sauce separately.

Home-Style Shad with Melted Bones *(Alose à Arêtes Fondues, Recette Familiale).* An excellent dish, in which the fish is braised to keep it succulent and to soften the bones so much that you can swallow them without any discomfort. *Time: 7–8 hours of gentle cooking.*

1 shad weighing 1½ kilograms (3 pounds, 5 ounces); 150 grams (5⅓ ounces) of onions; 150 grams (5⅓ ounces) of carrots; 30 grams (1 ounce) of shallots; a clove of garlic; 60 grams (2¼ ounces) of raw Bayonne ham; 30 grams (1 ounce) of flour; 4 substantial tablespoons of good oil; ½ liter (generous 2 cups) of good bouillon or jus of veal; ½ liter (generous 2 cups) of Bordeaux wine, preferably white; 2 tablespoons of vinegar; 1 deciliter (3⅓ fluid ounces, scant ½ cup) of cognac; a bouquet garni; salt and pepper.

PROCEDURE. **The sauce:** Cut the onion and carrot into a mirepoix (SEE PAGE 21). In a tall pot, gently heat the oil and cook the mirepoix until lightly colored. Toward the end, add the minced shallot, barely letting it color. This will take *a good half hour.*

After this, sprinkle with the flour and stir with a wooden spoon. Cook until a blond roux forms. Moisten first with the veal bouillon, which has been degreased and warmed, and then with the wine. Add the garlic, crushed with the blade of a knife.

Bring to a boil, then turn down the heat. Cover the pot. Simmer very slowly for at least *a good half hour.* Absolutely do not shorten the cooking time, which allows the flavors of the aromatics to infuse the liquids. They are cooked alone instead of with the fish because the long cooking time would make it too difficult to take them out without damaging the fish slices.

The shad: Clean, scale, and gut the fish. Cut it into equal slices 2½ centimeters (1 inch) thick. If the shad has roe, reserve it. Arrange the slices side by side and close together in a large sauté pan that has been well oiled on the bottom and on the sides. Place the head of the fish in the middle.

With a chinois, strain the sauce—*without first removing the fat*—directly onto the slices, and then the vinegar (you will need only 1 tablespoon if it is very strong). Add the Bayonne ham cut into long strips and a pinch of ground pepper. Add the bouquet garni, putting it near the head. Bring it to a boil on high heat without stirring and then cover the pan as tightly as possible. Now you are ready to cook the fish.

To cook: You need a consistent heat that warms all the parts of the utensil equally, keeping the liquid at a gentle simmer for *6 hours.* In other words, use a low oven. But if you absolutely must cook the pan on the stove, use a heat diffuser.

Two hours before serving, add the cognac. Now there is nothing more to do except watch carefully. Any sudden rush of heat that would cause a lively boil would make the fish burst.

If you have the fish roe, add it to the pan right at the very end so it can poach there for a few minutes without boiling.

To serve: Once cooked, carefully use a fish spatula or a skimmer to remove the slices of fish, making sure you keep them *absolutely intact, exactly as they were put into the cooking dish.* Arrange them in a shallow bowl in a crown shape or overlapping each other. Do not serve the head.

Deglaze the sauce, which should have reduced by half. Check the seasoning. Strain through the chinois onto the slices of fish. Serve on hot plates.

Eel *(Anguille)*

You really need to buy eel alive, because its flesh is firmer and more flavorsome than an eel that has been out of the water for a long time. Furthermore, an eel can stay alive for a long time if it is surrounded by herbs, so an eel sold dead is likely to have been caught several days ago.

Be careful choosing the eel and make sure that you do not get one that has come from stagnant waters; it will be inedible because it will taste of sludge. An eel that has been caught in running water, a good eel, can be recognized by its light brown color, greenish reflections on the back, and a silver wash on the belly. The color of an eel from stagnant water is a somber brown on the back and a dirty yellow under the belly.

A nice eel weighing 600–700 grams (1 pound, 5 ounces–1 pound, 9 ounces) will weigh about 550 grams (1 pound, 3 ounces) when it is skinned and gutted. The largest weigh up to 1 kilogram (2 pounds, 3 ounces); their flesh is generally tough. It is better for today's recipes to use 2 small eels rather than 1 large one.

To kill and skin the eel: Grab it by the tail after wrapping a towel around it to stop it from slithering away and escaping. Bang it violently on the head with a stone, on the sink, or against the wall to stun it. With the point of a small knife, make an incision in the skin completely around the head, deep enough to reach the flesh, just below the gills, which can be found near the head.

Turn back the skin where you have just cut it. Grab the head of the eel with a towel held in your left hand and, with another towel, held in your right hand, grab the skin and tear it off in a single motion.

An alternative, which might be easier, is to hang the eel from a nail by the head, using a string that has been tied around the gills. Cut the skin as above, then turn it back on itself and, using a towel, tear it off. It comes away easily, turning back on itself and sliding off like the finger of a glove. The most difficult part of the operation is turning back the skin at the beginning where it has been cut.

Next, cut off the barbs, the gills, and the end of the tail. Make a small opening in the belly to gut the eel and then run the end of your finger along the dorsal bone to detach the clotted blood; if it coagulates while cooking, it makes the pieces appear most unappetizing.

Finally, wash the eel and thoroughly rinse the inside with running water to remove the blood. Drain it and dry with a towel.

PRINCIPAL RECIPES

For details of preparation and cooking times, see the directions under tartar-style eel (PAGE 219).

Eel Stew *(Anguille en Matelote).* With white or red wine. SEE FRESHWATER FISH STEWS WITH WINE (PAGE 170).

Eel in Butter with Lemon and Parsley *(Anguille à la Meunière).* Small eels are best. They should be skinned, cleaned, and cut into pieces and the head removed. Cook them as directed (SEE FISH À LA MEUNIÈRE, PAGE 167).

Fried Eel *(Anguille Frite).* This method is primarily used with small eels. Soak them in milk, dip them in flour, and arrange them in a circle, the head joined at the tail, or in a figure eight twisted onto a skewer. Then deep-fry.

Eel in Rich Mushroom Sauce *(Anguille à la Poulette).* This method of cooking can be used for several small eels as well as for one large one. The poulette sauce is prepared with the cooking liquid of the fish, but you can use meat bouillon or even just water for a strictly meatless dish. A *sauce poulette* is, especially in this case, thickened with egg yolks and characteristically flavored with lemon juice (SEE POULETTE SAUCE, PAGE 61).

Divide the fish into pieces; then just cover with two-thirds bouillon and one-third white wine. Add slices of onion, bouquet garni, and a touch of garlic. Cook it as for TARTAR-STYLE EEL (SEE BELOW). Strain the cooking bouillon. Bind it with a blond roux, using 6 grams (1/5 ounce) of flour for each deciliter (3 1/3 fluid ounces, scant 1/2 cup) of sauce. Degrease it for 15 minutes, then make the liaison with the egg. Pour it on the pieces of eel, the head excluded, which have been kept warm in a sauté pan. Immerse them well in the sauce. Finish with lemon, minced parsley, and butter, adding more if the cooking liquid is water.

Tartar-Style Eel *(Anguille à la Tartare).* Though detailed, this preparation is one of the simplest.

Breaded eel is rarely grilled these days: today, it is fried, which is the best way to ensure a crusted coating. That said, you can place it on a grill to completely remove the grease from the coating of egg and bread crumbs. Serve a tartar sauce on the side in a sauceboat. *Time: 1 hour (plus 1–2 hours for cooling, to room temperature). Serves 6.*

1 eel weighing 750 grams (1 pound, 10 ounces).

For the court bouillon: 6 1/2 deciliters (2 3/4 cups) of water; 1/2 liter (generous 2 cups) of white wine; 100 grams (3 1/2 ounces) of minced onions; 75 grams (2 2/3 ounces) of minced carrots; a bouquet garni; 12 grams (3/8 ounce) of salt; 6 peppercorns.

For breading: 1 egg; 1 teaspoon of oil; a pinch of good salt and a little bit of pepper; 150 grams (5 1/3 ounces) of stale bread crumbs passed through a sieve; 1 tablespoon of flour.

PROCEDURE. The court bouillon requires about a half hour of boiling. It must be *almost cold when it is used.*

The eel can be rolled into a circle or cut into pieces—your choice. If the eel is to be served at the table, arrange it in a ring with a bouquet of dried parsley that is nice and green in the middle. But if you are going to serve it directly to the guests, cutting it into pieces is more practical.

To roll it into a ring: Remove the head (which is never left on), then tuck the pointed end of the tail inside, making a circle. Tie with two or three pieces of string to hold it together in this shape, which you will remove when you coat it in bread crumbs.

If it is in pieces: Cut it into pieces 5 or 6 centimeters (2–2 1/2 inches) long, cutting them on a diagonal, which is more attractive.

Whether the eel is in a ring or in pieces, always make a few cuts in the flesh so that it does not burst and crack while cooking.

Place the eel pieces or ring in a sauté pan large enough to contain the eel, which can then be entirely covered with the court bouillon. Bring it to a boil, then cover and let it cook over gentle heat for *20 minutes,* keeping the liquid at a very gentle simmer.

Transfer to a tureen and let the eel cool completely *in its cooking liquid.* Even if you are pressed for time, you must let it stand in its court bouillon for at least 15 minutes after it is cooked. Drain the eel and dry it off with a dry towel. Roll it in the flour, then dip it in beaten egg and the bread crumbs (SEE ENGLISH-STYLE BREADING, PAGE 19).

Plunge the eel into a large quantity of *smoking* oil. Immediately turn the heat down and cook for *8 minutes.* Meanwhile, heat the grill. Fry the eel, then drain it on a towel. Next, put it on the grill and turn after 2 minutes. The point of cooking the eel on the grill is to completely eliminate the grease that has seeped into the egg and bread-crumb coating. It will need only *4–5 minutes.*

While the eel is on the grill, heat some oil for deep-frying and, as soon as it is smoking, plunge in the parsley. Drain on a towel and sprinkle very lightly with finely ground salt. Serve on a round plate garnished with a towel or a napkin. If the eel is rolled into a ring, place the parsley in the middle in a small pyramid; if it is in pieces, arrange them next to each other, the fried parsley on each side. Serve the tartar sauce in a sauceboat.

Barbel and Small Barbel *(Barbeau et Barbillon)*

Barbel is usually cooked in a court bouillon made with vinegar or *grilled* like shad. Sometimes it is gently simmered with wine, herbs, butter, and a cooking liquid bound with a roux or beurre manié.

The little barbels or small barbels are used in matelotes or cooked à la meunière.

The roe of barbel are unhealthy to eat and should not be used.

Bream *(Brème)*

This fish is rarely cooked in a court bouillon unless it is being used as an ingredient in a matelote. Cooked on its own, it is usually *grilled.* Follow the same directions used for cooking whole shad, including the initial marinade; allow *25–30 minutes* of cooking for a bream of the same weight as the shad.

Pike *(Brochet)*

The oldest collections of recipes feature a remarkable number of preparations for this fish.

In earlier times, pike were frequently cut into slices to be cooked in a pan. They were also prepared in the same way as a fricassee of chicken—that is, cut into pieces, sautéed in butter with mushrooms, and sprinkled with flour, then moistened with white wine and bouillon, cooked over high heat, and finished with a liaison of egg yolk and cream. It was also served with a sauce Robert, the pieces having first been marinated, coated in flour, and fried. Also popular was to prepare it as a ragoût with turnips. Indeed, there are many ways to cook pike, and each has its merits.

These days, the medium-sized pike is primarily prepared au bleu (SEE FISH COOKED AU BLEU, PAGE 166). It is then served warm or cold with an appropriate sauce (SEE BEURRE BLANC, PAGE 80). Large pieces are cooked in a court bouillon and are accompanied by boiled potatoes and with a sauce of your choosing: capers, genevoise, hollandaise, etc.

The pike can be stuffed, if you wish, and cooked in the oven with white wine and aromatics. You can also cut it into slices and fry it after first marinating it, as described for the shad accompanied with hollandaise sauce; or, if you do not want to marinate it, cook the slices in a court bouillon.

Small pike are also used in matelotes. Pike is also used for a fish stuffing, whether cooked in dumplings or in a loaf.

Carp *(Carpe)*

Traditionally, carp was served in as many different ways as pike. The following are the most common recipes used today:

Carp au Bleu *(Carpe au Bleu).* Served warm or cold with an appropriate sauce.

Carp Matelote *(Carpe en Matelote).* Prepared on its own or with other fish.

Grilled Carp *(Carpe Grillée).* Like shad, but without the marinade. Served on an anchovy butter (or, indeed, any other butter) or with a sauce; or on a purée of sorrel.

Carp Roasted in the Oven *(Carpe Rôtie au Four).* Make incisions 1 centimeter (3/8 inch) deep on the cleaned fish. Put the carp on a large heatproof plate, placing it on its belly so that it cooks evenly. Keep it in that position using pieces of raw potato to support it. Moisten with melted butter. No other seasoning is required except salt and pepper. *A fish of 1–1 1/4 kilograms (2 pounds, 3 ounces–2 pounds, 12 ounces) will need 40–45 minutes* to cook in a good, medium oven. Serve as for grilled carp.

Stuffed Carp *(Carpe Farcie).* Stuff it with a home-style stuffing, as used for shad, and then grill or poach it; use a stuffing of fish, pike, or whatever you prefer. You can also braise it in a fish poacher with red wine, herbs, bacon, etc.

Carp à la Bonne Femme *(Carpe à la Bonne Femme).* Poached in the oven in an ovenproof dish with wine, onion, carrot, etc. Bind the cooking liquid with a beurre manié (SEE PAGE 48), adding a nice piece of butter right at the end.

Fried Carp *(Carpe Frite).* SEE FRYING (page 37). When the carp are small, fry them just as they are, either coated in flour or dipped in a batter. Larger fish weighing about 450 grams (1 pound)—must be split down the back and opened out like a book before frying, the two parts remaining joined on the belly side. To open them, use the same technique used for mackerel (SEE PAGE 190). The fish is floured or breaded before being deep-fried.

Carp à la Chambord *(Carpe à la Chambord).* This recipe is used for fish of at least 2 or 3 kilograms (4 pounds, 6 ounces–6 pounds, 10 ounces). It can be found in recipe collections dating from the first half of the thirteenth century. At that time, it was served with a gargantuan accompaniment of pigeons, sweetbreads, truffles, crests, kidneys, fois gras, roe, mushrooms, etc.

Through the centuries, Carp à la Chambord has been modified. It is now made in the following way: Stuffed with a stuffing of fish and studded with truffles, then braised in a fish poacher with wine (generally red), fish bouillon, and strips of bacon. Reduce the cooking liquid, then bind it with a roux and add a meat glaze. Strictly speaking, the garnish for carp à la Chambord includes fish dumplings, mushrooms, truffles, roe, crayfish, but it can also be augmented with veal sweetbreads, rooster crests, and kidneys, in which case it is known as *à la financière.* It is always served with fried croutons.

For a completely modern touch, add anchovies to the sauce, in the form of anchovy butter or extract.

An authentically bourgeois recipe is to clean and scale the carp, but not stud or stuff it, then place it on its belly in a fish poacher. Add a good mirepoix that has been sautéed in butter, and some red wine and bouillon to come halfway up the fish. The bouillon should make up a third of the liquid. Bring to a boil on high heat. (This type of cooking always requires high heat.) After this, cover the fish with a buttered parchment paper and place the fish poacher in the oven to continue cooking at a regular simmer, frequently basting the fish with its cooking liquid.

Allow *1 hour* to cook a fish of 1.8–2$^{1}/_{4}$ kilograms (4 or 5 pounds). You know the fish is perfectly done when it yields easily under the finger. Reduce the cooking liquid, then bind it with a light roux (4–5 grams/$^{1}/_{7}$–$^{1}/_{6}$ ounce of flour for each deciliter/3$^{1}/_{3}$ fluid ounces/scant $^{1}/_{2}$ cup) and add the butter. Arrange the carp on its serving plate and surround it with the garnish, then pour a light covering of sauce over everything. Serve the remaining sauce in a sauceboat.

Carp Roe *(Laitances de Carpe).* What makes this recipe so special is its particular delicacy. When it is not being used to accompany the fish, you can make special dishes from it: fritters, pastry shells, etc.

Sturgeon *(Esturgeon)*

Because of its size, this fish tends to be prepared only in thick slices or steaks. It is often barded with bacon, then braised with mirepoix, wine, and bouillon. Thicken with beurre manié (SEE PAGE 48).

Gudgeon *(Goujon)*

Gudgeon is usually deep-fried: it may be served as a fish entrée. as a garnish or in a matelote, or with any entrée prepared like sole Normande (SEE PAGE 209). Large gudgeons also can be cooked à la meunière.

For a garnish, these are often coated in bread crumbs, except for the head and tail, then fried. Proceed as follows: gut the fish, then dip in some milk; drain, roll in flour, then dip first in beaten egg and then into bread crumbs (SEE ENGLISH-STYLE BREADING, PAGE 19). Roll them in the palm of your hand to remove excess bread crumbs. With your fingers, wipe off the bread crumbs from the head and tail. The fish will thus look as if they are wrapped in a sleeve of bread crumbs. Fry in a very hot oil (SEE PAGE 40) for *4–5 minutes.* Serve the gudgeon piled on a napkin-covered round plate, surrounded by fried parsley and lemon.

Perch *(Perche)*

Fish lovers swear that after the salmon trout, the river perch, also called the yellow perch, is the most delicate freshwater fish there is. But you should handle it with great care, particularly when it is alive, because of the spines in its dorsal fin. Protect your hand by wrapping it in a towel.

Small perch are generally deep-fried or cooked à la meunière. A medium-sized fish should be cooked in a slightly vinegary court bouillon. A wonderful method from the Alsace is to cook them with very little liquid in the serving dish, which we will describe. Although a perch weighing as much as 450 grams (1 pound) is unusual, it is good roasted in the oven on a plate coated with butter.

Perch Cooked in Court Bouillon *(Perches au Court Bouillon).* If they are alive, kill the perch by banging their heads on the sink. Cut off the fins, then gut and scale the fish. However, when cooking in a court bouillon, you can leave the scales on to prevent the flesh bursting during cooking. Arrange them in a shallow oval plate big enough to hold them. Cover them with *hot* court bouillon and bring it to a boil. Turn down the heat, then poach for *25 minutes* for perch weighing about 250–275 grams (8⁷/₈ ounces–9²/₃ ounces).

After they have been cooked, carefully scrape the fish, moving from the tail to the head, to take off both the skin and the scales with one stroke, completely exposing the flesh. Rinse them in the court bouillon and arrange them on a long plate covered with a napkin garnished with parsley and lemon quarters. Serve with a sauceboat of melted butter or even a hollandaise sauce.

Perch Cooked the Alsatian Way *(Perches à la Façon d'Alsace).* Scale them carefully, then gut and wash them. Put them in an ovenproof plate, on some large onion slices and some parsley; add a good chunk of butter, divided into pieces and spread between and on top of the fish; some peppercorns; salt; a little water. Thus, for 6 small perch: 100 grams (3¹/₂ ounces) of onion; 3 sprigs of parsley; 75 grams (2²/₃ ounces, ¹/₃ cup) of butter; 1 deciliter (3¹/₃ fluid ounces, scant ¹/₂ cup) of water; a good pinch of salt; 7 or 8 peppercorns.

Traditionally, this is placed on a good, solid, thick clay platter and cooked on hot coals for *a good half hour.* To cook at home means imitating this method as best you can. That is, you need to maintain a gentle, regular simmer throughout the cooking time, frequently basting the fish with its cooking liquid. Serve the dish exactly as it is, on a serving plate.

Salmon *(Saumon)*

The modern way to serve salmon is to place one large piece on the table, but a family home will rarely have the opportunity to serve an entire salmon, even a small one. You should allow a net weight of 100 grams (3¹/₂ ounces) of salmon for each person. Since the weight of a small salmon is not less than 3 or 4 kilograms (6 pounds, 9 ounces–8 pounds, 12 ounces), the following recipes will use it cut into pieces.

Whether buying or preparing it yourself, a salmon is always carved up into the following parts: the head; steaks; slices; tail.

The head part is the head plus about one-third of the body. The tail part contains about the last third of the fish. The darne, or steak, comes from the very middle of the salmon.

The precise meaning of the word "darne" is: a slice of fish whose thickness frequently varies according to the number of guests. Thus, a darne of steak can weigh from 600 grams to a kilogram (1 pound, 5 ounces–2 pounds, 3 ounces). By extension, the term "darne" on a menu applies to pieces weighing at least 1¹/₂ kilograms (3 pounds, 5 ounces), and indicates more of a chunk than a slice of fish. To clarify the differences in modern cooking, the word "slice" means a piece of salmon weighing no more than 200 and 250 grams (7–8⁷/₈ ounces) and with a thickness of 2¹/₂ to 3 centimeters (1–1¹/₄ inches). The best steaks or fillets come from a small or a medium-sized salmon. Fillets weighing the same but from different size fishes will vary in thickness. The slices from smaller fish will be thicker than those taken from the larger fish.

Boiled Salmon *(Le Saumon Bouilli).* Today, the court bouillon used to boil salmon is one made with vinegar or, more simply, salted water. Indeed, both modern and ancient authors have suggested cooking it this way—and those we have mentioned were never suspected of parsimony. After all, it is not cheap to cook a fish that is to be chilled in its court bouillon of white wine.

To cook the piece of salmon you do not need to scale it. The scales protect the flesh and prevent it from falling apart. The fish is often currently served skinned, which is far less difficult if the scales have not been removed before cooking. When using the head of the salmon, make sure you support the gills and the mouth by tying them with string.

To prepare and cook the court bouillon, see the directions given in the section on court bouillon (PAGE 162).

The *hot* sauces that should accompany boiled salmon are: anchovy, caper, shrimp, genevoise, hollandaise, oysters, mussels, mousseline, etc. For *cold* salmon: mayonnaise and all its variations, tartar sauce, *sauce verte,* etc.

The Darne *(La Darne).* This is the section chosen for special occasions. If the number of guests is limited to twelve—fifteen at the most—you can buy a large darne, which is practically the size of a log. For more than this number of guests you will need 2 darnes. In this case, you will need to allow more than 100 grams (3 1/2 ounces) per person so that you have a presentable size of salmon. The leftovers from salmon can be used in so many ways that this is certainly not an extravagance.

We will consider here a recipe for a darne that will feed twelve to fifteen people. Cut from a small salmon, it must be at least 12–14 centimeters (4 3/4–5 1/2 inches) long to look right (The length here is determined by the thickness of the piece.) This will mean that it weighs about 1 1/2 kilograms (3 pounds, 5 ounces).

For a nice darne of this weight you will need 2 1/2 liters (10 1/2 cups) of whichever court bouillon you intend to use (SEE COURT BOUILLON, PAGE 162). Remember that this should be prepared in advance and *chilled* if you are not simply using salted water.

To prepare and cook: Remove anything left inside, running your finger along the middle backbone to remove the clots of blood.

Before starting to cook the piece of fish, wash it off again in cold water, then sponge it off with a towel. Tie four or five rounds of string around it without pulling too tightly, otherwise the strings will mark the flesh as it swells during cooking. Tie a knot in the string on the top of the darne.

A *daubière* or a long saucepan is the most accommodating utensil to cook this piece. Otherwise you can use a high-sided pot that is just large enough to contain the darne, especially if the court bouillon has white wine in it, because the liquid must completely cover the fish; otherwise it will be necessary to add more liquid. For a court bouillon made with vinegar, this economic consideration has less importance, and none at all if you are using salted water.

Place the darne in the pan on its belly. To hold it in place, prop it up with 2 large carrots that have been cut square to serve as supports. Pour the chilled court bouillon over the fish and bring to a boil. Then turn the heat down low as instructed in COOKING FISH IN COURT BOUILLON (PAGE 162). Cover with a fine napkin folded in half. For a darne weighing 1 1/2 kilograms (3 pounds, 5 ounces), poach for *30 minutes,* or *10 minutes* per pound.

Drain and remove the skin. Place the darne on a plate covered with a napkin. At each end, arrange potatoes cut into small balls and boiled. Surround with parsley. Serve the chosen sauce on the side in a sauceboat.

Darne of Cold Salmon *(Darne de Saumon Froide).* This is a dish that is particularly welcome in the summer for lunches and is equally good for dinners. Since the darne must be chilled in its court bouillon to better absorb the flavors, it is essential that you cook it the previous evening. Take it out of the bouillon to decorate it 1–2 hours before serving. Court bouillon made with a white wine is recommended here because it is particularly flavorsome. Proceed as described above.

Once poached, carefully transfer the darne to an appropriate clay receptacle and pour the court bouillon over the top.

To decorate the cold darne: Use a dozen anchovies in fillets that have been divided into fine slices; 2 large cornichons that have been cut into extremely thin rounds; 1 good tablespoon of large capers; about 50 tarragon sprigs taken from the plant; 7 or 8 hard-boiled eggs and some fried parsley for the border.

If you like, replace the border of hard-boiled eggs with a border of very small *raw* tomatoes; you will need about fifteen very small tomatoes hollowed out and deseeded, then filled with 3 chopped hard-boiled eggs mixed with 2 or 3 tablespoons of a good, stiff mayonnaise.

How to decorate is a matter of taste. The most classic way is to lay the anchovies in a crisscross halfway up along the length of the darne, which should first be wiped dry and skinned. Next, place the rounds of cornichons on top of this grid to form a border, and underneath the rounds place the tarragon leaves, pointing down.

With a small kitchen brush, brush a little bit of oil on the darne without destroying the arrangement, paying particular attention to the two cut ends that are not decorated. Between the little crosses of anchovies, place the capers like large periods.

Carefully place the darne on the serving plate. Surround it with hard-boiled eggs that have been cut in half and slightly trimmed to give them some stability, and a border of fried parsley. Or, instead of the eggs, use little tomatoes, but always include the parsley.

Serve a mayonnaise sauce or a *sauce verte* on the side, if you like.

Slices of Salmon *(Les Tranches de Saumon).* Slices tend to be used for simple, quick dishes that are served for family meals. For lunch, it is *grilled* or *cooked à la meunière*, and for dinner it is cooked in a court bouillon, preferably a white wine court bouillon, then accompanied by an appropriate sauce.

We have previously said that by slice we mean a piece of salmon weighing no more than 250 grams (8⁷/₈ ounces). Its thickness naturally varies with the size of the fish. If the fish is large, the slice will be very thin; taken from a medium-sized salmon, it should be about 12 millimeters (1/2 inch) thick. If the salmon is small, the slice will be thicker; in all cases, the weight will be somewhere between 200 and 250 grams (7–8 7/8 ounces).

Grilled Slices of Salmon *(Tranches de Saumon Grillées).* For this type of cooking, use slices that are 2 centimeters (3/4 inch), with an average weight of about 250 grams (8 7/8 ounces). One slice will serve two people.

To be thick enough but not overweight the slices must come from a small salmon, as we have just said. Thinner slices will break when you turn them on the grill. Any thicker, and they will need a longer cooking time at the end of which the outside flesh, which is protected by skin, will have colored too much and darkened.

If the slices have been taken from the stomach side, make sure you remove the little clot of blood that is usually found right along the backbone underneath a small membrane, which you should also remove. Do not wash the fish, but use a towel to wipe everywhere that you find blood, which will darken the flesh when it is cooked.

If you wish, and when you have the time, you can marinate the slices with salt, oil, and rounds of onions 1 hour before putting them on the grill. If they have not been marinated in this way, you should, before putting them on the grill, dip both sides in a little bit of oil poured on a plate.

After you have removed all fragments of the marinade from them, lay the slices on a grill that has been well heated in advance. It should be a low heat. After 5 minutes, turn them using a fish spatula or the large blade of a knife.

Cook for the same time on the other side. Turn them a second time, then turn down the heat. Grill for 2 more minutes, then turn them for the last time and let them cook another 2 minutes on this side. Grilling for 5 minutes each side at first, and then for 2 minutes for each side means a total cooking time of *14 minutes.*

You can check that the salmon is done by sticking the point of a small knife into the very middle of the backbone and pulling on it slightly by inclining the knife toward you. If the backbone comes away easily, the fish is cooked. If not, let it cook a few minutes more.

Arrange the slices on the same plate in which they were dipped in the oil. The remaining oil will give them some gloss. Remove the backbone, using the same technique as previously described. If the slices are served on a maître d'hôtel butter or any other butter, you can now remove the skin. Spread half the butter onto a long plate, which is warm but not so hot that the butter turns to oil, and then spread the other half on the slices and serve immediately.

If serving the slices with a béarnaise sauce, anchovy sauce, or warm ravigote, you do not need to take off the skin, but make sure you remove the bone. Arrange on a plate covered with a napkin, and then, if necessary, gloss again by rubbing a small piece of butter on their surface. Surround with fried parsley. Serve the sauce on the side.

NOTE. Instead of grilling, you can roast slices of the same thickness; the fish tastes exactly the same. Wash the slices, then put them in an ovenproof dish; cook them in a hot oven, allowing a little more time than if grilling, and check that the fish is done by lifting up the backbone, as described above.

Slices of Salmon in Butter with Lemon and Parsley *(Tranches de Saumon à la Meunière).* For this kind of cooking, the slices must be thin—scarcely 1 centimeter (3/8 inch) thick—so that the heat can easily penetrate the flesh. According to the size of the salmon from which they have been taken, you can use 1 slice for two people, or if the salmon is very small, one slice per person, always allowing a net weight of 100 grams (3 1/2 ounces).

Clean the slices as if to grill them. Season with salt and pepper; turn them in the flour and proceed as described (SEE FISH À LA MEUNIÈRE, PAGE 167). Cook them for *4–5 minutes* on each side, then turn them over and give them a further *2 minutes* on each side. Because they are so thin, be very careful not to break them when turning them. If you do not have a fish spatula to slide under the slices, you can use two forks to lift them.

Arrange the slices on a warmed serving plate previously decorated with slices of lemon. Remove the backbone. Heat the hazelnut butter (75 grams/ 2 2/3 ounces/1/3 cup for 6 people). Pour it over the slices; add lemon juice and minced parsley. Serve very hot.

Slices of Salmon Cooked in Court Bouillon *(Tranches de Saumon au Court Bouillon).* When cut a good 2 1/2 centimeters (1 inch) thick, these can, as we have said previously, be cooked in saltwater or in a court bouillon made of vinegar or wine.

Place the slice, cleaned as described on PAGE 224, in a correctly sized pan. Cover it with *hot* court bouillon. Place it on a slow fire. Cover. Poach for *12–15 minutes.* The time reflects the thickness and not the weight of the fish. You can tell when the salmon is done by how easily the backbone comes away from the flesh, just as for the grilled slices.

Drain the slices on a napkin. Remove the backbone. You can leave the skin on if it is not going to be masked with sauce. If the sauce is going to be served on the side, it is essential to varnish the surface of the slice with butter or oil to offset the grayish tint on the outside of the flesh that was not protected by skin. This tint is the result of cooking the fish in a liquid; it is inevitable and more or less pronounced according to the quality of the salmon.

Lightly brush oil on the slice or use a knife to rub a piece of butter on the surface. Place the fish on a serving plate; surround it with fried parsley and boiled potatoes. Serve one of the sauces suggested for *boiled salmon* (SEE PAGE 222).

Salmon Croquettes *(Croquettes de Saumon).* See the article on croquettes (PAGE 438). Serve with a light béchamel sauce, thickened with egg yolks, 1 yolk for each 1 1/2 deciliters (5 fluid ounces/ 2/3 cup) of sauce. You can add to the salmon flesh half its volume in rice cooked *à la Indienne* and a little bit of curry powder.

Tench *(Tanche)*

Mostly used in matelotes, it can also be prepared à la meunière, au bleu, au gratin, deep-fried.

To fry it: remove the head; completely split the fish from the head to the tail on the belly side, leaving the two parts connected on the other side. Coat in flour and deep-fry.

Trout *(Truite)*

Trout in Court Bouillon *(Truite au Court Bouillon).* This recipe calls for a court bouillon made with white wine. For details of how to make this and then cook the trout in it, see COURT BOUILLON (PAGE 162).

PROCEDURE. Cut the fins and only 1 centimeter (3/8 inch) of the tail. Make an incision 4 or 5 centimeters (1 1/2–2 inches) long on the belly, thus lengthening the little natural opening located near the tail. Then gut the fish (SEE PAGE 161).

Place the trout on its side on the grill of the fish poacher; pour in the chilled court bouillon, which must completely cover the fish.

Cook as described (see COOKING IN COURT BOUILLON, PAGE 162). Seven to eight minutes before serving, raise the metal plate or grill on which the trout is lying and rest it diagonally on top of the fish poacher so that the fish drains. Then take the grill by its handles and with one sharp movement slide the trout onto a serving dish held parallel with the grill. Traditionally, the serving dish is covered with a napkin. If the trout is large, serve it on a plank of light colored wood completely covered with a doubled napkin that is fixed in place on the underside of the plank. Quickly remove the skin and varnish the flesh with a little piece of butter stuck on the end of a knife. Surround with parsley and boiled potatoes, or serve them alongside in a vegetable dish. Serve with a sauceboat of sauce genevoise (PAGE 65), hollandaise (PAGE 72), or mousseline (PAGE 75).

Cold Salmon Trout en Gelée *(Truite Saumonée Froide en Gelée).* In haute cuisine, the gelée is obtained only from a bouillon or fumet made from the fish. You need about 1 kilogram (2 pounds, 3 ounces) of bones for each liter (4 1/4 cups). This is clearly inappropriate for cooking at home, but the following recipe for gelée, which is an old family recipe, is excellent and is particularly good for such dishes. Serve the trout with or without its skin, according to individual taste and preference. Accompany with a green sauce or with a mayonnaise in a sauceboat.

The veal foot used to prepare the gelée can then be served either cold in a vinaigrette or hot, deep-fried.

1 small trout weighing about 750 grams (1 pound, 10 ounces).

For the court bouillon: 1 bottle of good white wine; 2 deciliters (6 3/4 fluid ounces, 7/8 cup) of water; 75 grams (2 2/3 ounces) of carrot and the same of onion cut into thin slices; 3 or 4 sprigs of parsley; 2 cloves; 12 grams (3/8 ounce) of sea salt; 5 or 6 peppercorns.

For a gelée made with a veal foot: 1 veal foot; 75 grams (2 2/3 ounces) of very fresh lean bacon; 1 egg white with its shell; and juice of 1/3 of a lemon to clarify the gelée.

To be prepared the day before its use.

PROCEDURE. **To make the gelée:** Wash and blanch the veal foot (SEE PAGE 307). Put it in a pot with 1 good liter (4 1/4 cups) of cold water. Bring it to a boil. Cover the pot, putting the lid on askew so the pot is not completely covered, and turn the heat down very low so you can maintain a very gentle, uninterrupted and steady simmer for *4 hours.*

Strain the cooking liquid. Carefully degrease it. The easiest way to do this is first to let it chill and then remove the fat that has solidified on the surface. Then quickly wipe a napkin, dampened in warm water, over the surface of the gelée to remove the final traces of fat.

The court bouillon: Prepare this in advance (SEE COURT BOUILLON, PAGE 162), so that it can be chilled before it is poured on the fish.

The trout: Prepare it and gut it as for the trout in court bouillon (SEE PAGE 225). Handle it carefully so you do not damage the skin, which you must neither scrape or scale before cooking.

Place the trout on the grill of an appropriately sized fish poacher. Wrap string two or three times around its head, then cross it around the body and underneath the grill. Knot the ends around the place where you have made the cut so the heat of the liquid does not make it any larger. Do not tie it too tight; the flesh swells when it is cooking and the string may leave a mark.

Pour the strained and *chilled* court bouillon over the trout, which should just completely immerse it. Once it is boiling, allow the fish to poach for *15 minutes.* Then allow the trout to cool in its court bouillon.

The gelée: Once it is strained, you will have no more than 3 deciliters (1 1/4 cups) of gelée because it will have reduced considerably while the veal foot is cooking. Add court bouillon to make this up to a liter (4 cups). Thus, you will need 7 deciliters (3 cups) of court bouillon and 3 deciliters (1 1/4 cups) of gelée, which has been reduced back to its liquid state.

Pour both liquids into a pot. Add the lemon juice, a pinch of salt, a few grains of pepper, 1 egg white beaten into foam, and the empty egg shell. Clarify the liquid, as described (SEE MEAT GELÉE, PAGE 45). Let the gelée chill, but do not let it solidify.

To serve: Drain the trout thoroughly, which will have produced a little more liquid after being removed from the fish poacher. Untie it carefully, cutting the string with your scissors. If you are going to serve the trout without its skin, do not let it drain for too long; the skin will dry out and it will be much more difficult to remove. Lightly pass the blade of a small knife between the skin and the flesh and pull carefully so that you do not damage the flesh.

With or without skin, place the trout on a long, narrow serving plate. Cover it with the gelée, adding it little by little, 1 tablespoon at a time, so that it sticks to the surface of the fish to create a golden varnish. If you have any leftover gelée after the fish has been completely covered, let it solidify, then chop it up and place it around the trout before serving.

Keep the plate cool for about 8 hours, or 2 hours on ice, so that the gelée solidifies. When you are ready to serve, decorate the head and the tail with bits of fried parsley.

River Trout *(Truites de Rivière)*

Before they are gutted, river trout weigh an average of 150–200 grams (5¹/₃–7 ounces). The two ways of preparing them are *au bleu* and *à la meunière.* Both recipes rely on fish that are absolutely fresh, Indeed, for trout au bleu, live fish are preferable. You can keep the fish alive for a few hours in a large receptacle of cold water. You should prepare the fish to be boiled in court bouillon no more than 15 minutes before serving. Before gutting the trout, kill the fish by plunging their heads into the boiling water, or stun them with a blow to the head.

With scissors, quickly cut the fins and the end of the tail. Remove the gills and at the same time pull out the intestines. You may need to cut into the belly, but make the opening quite small, just large enough so you can put your finger in it. Carefully wipe the fish.

Trout au Bleu *(Truites au Bleu).* SEE FISH AU BLEU, PAGE 166. If you like, plunge the cleaned trout just as they are into the court bouillon. Alternatively, form them into a circle, their head joining the tail: hold them in this position either with ordinary string or by using a matchstick to pin the head and the tail together.

Plunge the trout into the boiling court bouillon; inevitably, the flesh will burst. As soon as the liquid returns to a boil, cover the utensil. Turn the heat down very low to let it poach for *5–7 minutes* (for trout of the preferred weight). Drain. Arrange the trout on a plate garnished with fried parsley. Accompany with any of the sauces served in a sauceboat with trout au court bouillon or with good quality melted butter and some lemon quarters.

Trout á la Meunière *(Truite à la Meunière).* SEE FISH À LA MEUNIÈRE (page 167). Gut the trout as above. With the point of a knife, make oblique cuts 2 or 3 millimeters (¹/₈ inch) deep on each side of the fish, spacing them about 1¹/₂ centimeters (⁵/₈ inch) apart, to help the fish cook and hold its shape. Turn the trout only once while cooking, which takes *about 10 minutes.* Serve them arranged on the bias on an oval plate.

Trout in the Manner of Alsace *(Truites à la Façon d'Alsace).* SEE PERCH, PAGE 222.

CRUSTACEANS, SHELLFISH, SNAILS, FROGS
Crustacés, Coquillages, Escargots, Grenouilles

Crab *(Crabe)*

The species of crab that the French think is worth cooking is known as *tourteau* or *poupard.* The very small crabs that kids like to fish for at the seaside are cooked like crayfish, in seawater or in salted water.

Do not choose a crab that is too large, because its meat will be tough and stringy; medium and small ones are preferable. As for all crustaceans, it is essential to use crab that are still alive. If the crabs are small, use three for two people.

The most practical dish is crab à la anglaise, described below. For a warm dish, we can only suggest crab *à la diable,* also described below. Whatever the recipe, the crab must first be boiled in water, salted with 15 grams (1/2 ounce) of seawater for each liter (4 1/4 cups) or in a very simple court bouillon made with the same amount of salt and 1 tablespoon of vinegar per liter (4 1/4 cups), adding some parsley sprigs, 1 sprig of thyme, and 1 bay leaf.

Scrub the crabs with a scrubbing brush while washing them in generous amounts of fresh water. Plunge them into a boiling court bouillon; they must be completely immersed in it. As soon as the liquid returns to a boil, cook at a rolling boil for *20–30 minutes,* according to the size of the crab. Drain, then let them completely cool.

Take off the claws. Break the shell with a small hammer to create an opening that will allow you to extract the flesh without splinters. Open the crab by inserting the point of a knife between the carapace (the upper shell) and the plastron (the lower shell). Do this carefully to preserve the carapace, which should be kept intact as a serving dish. Wash the carapace and dry thoroughly.

Completely empty the carapace. Use a spoon to take out the creamy and yellowish substance first, and put this into a small bowl. Then take out the little bit of flesh left clinging to the shell; cut it into small cubes and combine it with the flesh from the claws. Break all the legs to extract everything that is edible.

Add a little salt, mustard, and pepper to the creamy material in the small bowl. Mix it with a wooden spoon or a small whisk. Then pour in some oil, drop by drop at first, proceeding exactly as if making a mayonnaise sauce; here, the creamy parts replace the egg yolk. Finish with a good dose of vinegar. Mix the diced flesh into the sauce along with some hard-boiled egg, also cut into dice. Use both yolk and white, and allow 1 egg for each crab.

Spoon this into the carapaces, forming it into a slight dome. Decorate it with chopped egg white and yolk and minced parsley. Keep it cool until ready to serve.

Crab à la Diable *(Crabes à la Diable).* This is cooked and cut as above, and the creamy parts and meat are mixed with a cream sauce that has been strongly spiced with cayenne pepper (SEE CREAM SAUCE, PAGE 63). Fill the carapaces. Sprinkle with fine, freshly grated bread crumbs, and moisten with melted butter. Brown in a hot oven or under a broiler for 4–5 minutes. Serve very hot.

Crayfish *(Écrevisses)*

Whatever recipe is chosen, the crayfish *must be alive.* There are no exceptions to this rule. The best crayfish are those with a carapace that is brown tending toward black because these will take on a bright red color. The shell of the gray and bluish crayfish will not take on the same bright color, but will only go a dull pink.

If you have bought your crayfish in advance and are not planning to use them for a while, do not put them in water to conserve them, but simply keep them in a basket full of herbs, preferably nettles, and store in a cool place or cellar. You can keep them very well like this for 7 or 8 days, checking on them each day and pulling out any that have died. If the weather is not stormy, you will lose very few.

Commercially and culinarily, crayfish are classed into three categories:

Small crayfish, which are reserved for bisques and weigh from 25–40 grams (1–1 3/8 ounces), that is, an average of 32 grams (about 1 1/8 ounce);

Medium-sized crayfish, which are used for garnishes and weigh an average of 50–60 grams (1 3/4–2 1/4 ounces);

Large crayfish, which are the best crayfish and are reserved for entrées and prepared à la meunière, à la bordelaise, etc. They weigh an average of 75–80 grams (2 2/3–2 3/4 ounces).

Removing the intestines: Before cooking, the *crayfish must always have their intestines removed*—in other words, cleaned of their guts, which have a bitter taste. This is particularly true in spring, when the crayfish eat certain plants that give them a strong, bitter, unpleasant taste. You cannot do this in advance, because the crayfish will dry out very quickly unless they are cooked immediately. That does not happen when they are opened and then *immediately seized by the strong cooking heat.*

Begin by washing the crayfish in cold water. Drain well, then keep them in a drum sieve *(tamis)* or a terrine. Prepare the pot with the court bouillon or seasoning in which the crayfish are cooked, and then add the crayfish as soon as they are cleaned. The pot must be large enough so that you can toss the crayfish during the cooking.

To clean: Insert the point of a small knife in the end of the intestine, an opening at the base of the phalanx (or fin) in the middle of the tail. Seize this end between the point of the knife and the end of your thumb, then gently pull to extract without breaking it. Alternatively, you can pull on the phalanx itself or the fin in the middle of the tail, but this is not the best method since the gut may not come out or may break in the process. It also mars the appearance of the crayfish.

To cook: *A very strong heat* is absolutely essential when cooking crayfish. This is to ensure that the crayfish are instantly killed, because *they must always be put into the cooking liquid alive.* This is not to mitigate the torture but because the flesh would otherwise allow the juice to escape and then be insipid and dull; another benefit is that it serves to cauterize the wound made removing the gut, through which the crayfish would lose its juices. Crayfish must be cooked in *as little liquid as possible.* Indeed, for some recipes crayfish is cooked with only a little butter, a little cognac, and seasoning. The flesh of a crayfish that is cooked almost dry keeps its quality and flavor and better absorbs the seasonings in which it is cooked.

You must always use *a pot large enough* to let you easily toss the crayfish. This also means that they will all touch the bottom of the pot where the heat is stronger, and also helps the flesh to absorb the seasoning.

Crayfish Cooked in Court Bouillon *(Écrevisses au Court Bouillon).* Entirely contrary to what many believe, the term "court bouillon," when used in reference to cooking crayfish, does not mean cooking them in a generous amount of liquid, as is required for large crustaceans. Instead, the crayfish are sautéed in a pot and exposed in turn to the strong heat at the bottom of the pot and do not require so much liquid. The term "court bouillon" applied to crayfish mostly indicates the method of cooking. Only a small amount of liquid is used for the court bouillon, just enough to cook the aromatics, onions, parsley, etc., and to moisten the bottom of the pot during cooking. Thus the classic chefs use a glass of liquid for 2 dozen crayfish.

A court bouillon is appropriate for: crayfish to be served *en buisson* (in a pile); crayfish for garnishes; crayfish served *à la marinière* with their cooking liquid. The composition of the court bouillon can vary: first according to the recipe for which it is used, next according to taste and resources. Choose any of the following: a pure white wine; white wine diluted with water; white wine with vinegar added; pure vinegar; vinegar diluted with water. Never use red wine, which would spoil the crayfish.

Onions should always be used. Carrot can be used, but only when the court bouillon is made in advance (which is always preferable if possible), otherwise it will have no effect given the short cooking time. Other ingredients include parsley, always taken from the stems and not the leaves; salt; whole peppercorns, which are preferable to ground pepper, which will stick to the carapace of the crayfish and destroy the neat appearance of the dish. You should almost always add thyme and bay and a touch of garlic, whose taste will not be discernable but will complement the other flavors.

A court bouillon with just a small amount of liquid not only helps the crayfish to absorb its seasonings better, but is also more economical since you can use white wine, which you might hesitate to sacrifice in larger quantities, even when the crayfish are to be served only as a garnish or *en buisson,* when the cooking liquid will not be used.

White wine diluted with a little water is best for a court bouillon to cook crayfish that are served *en buisson.* Vinegar is generally used for court bouillon to cook crayfish as a garnish.

Crayfish for Garnishes *(Écrevisses pour Garnitures).* *Time: 1 hour (including the preliminary cooking of the court bouillon).*

12 medium crayfish; about 30 grams (1 ounce) of onions and the same of carrot cut into thin rounds; 2 sprigs of parsley; 1 sprig of thyme; 1/2 of a small bay leaf; 1 small garlic clove; a pinch of salt; 1 1/2 deciliters (5 fluid ounces, 2/3 cup) of water; a good 1/2 deciliter (1 2/3 fluid ounces, scant 1/4 cup) of vinegar; 4 peppercorns.

PROCEDURE. Put all the ingredients together in a pot. Bring to a boil and then keep on a low boil on medium heat. Wash and trim the crayfish. Tie them up. That is to say, pierce the end of both claws, taking great care so that you do not detach these limbs. If you think this seems too difficult, don't bother, because it is better to leave the claws free rather than risk breaking them. Put the crayfish in the pot. Cover. Cook on a good, strong heat for *7–8 minutes,* stirring them from time to time. Then keep them warm in the court bouillon until you are ready to serve.

Crayfish in a Buisson *(Écrevisses en Buisson).* Always choose the most attractive crayfish for this recipe, in which they are most on show. Generally, you need 2 large or 3 medium crayfish per person. *Time: 30 minutes of cooking (3–4 hours cooling).*

12 crayfish or 18 medium-sized ones; 50 grams (1 3/4 ounces) of carrots, 50 grams (1 3/4 ounces) of onion cut into fine slices; 1 shallot; 1/2 clove of garlic; 4 sprigs of parsley; 1 sprig of thyme; 1/4 of a bay leaf; 6 peppercorns; a knife point of cayenne if you want a rather spicy cooking liquid; 1 deciliter (3 1/3 fluid ounces, scant 1/2 cup) of white wine and 1 deciliter (3 1/3 fluid ounces, scant 1/2 cup) of vinegar.

PROCEDURE. You can use white wine only or vinegar cut in half with water, according to your taste and your means.

In a sauté pan large enough to contain the crayfish, put all the ingredients for the court bouillon. Put it over a strong heat. Cover. Once it is boiling rapidly, toss the washed and gutted crayfish into the sauté pan. Cover and cook over a strong heat, mixing from time to time, for a good 15 minutes if they are large and for 10–12 minutes if they are of medium size. Overcooking for 1–2 minutes is better than undercooking for the same amount of time.

Let them cool in their cooking liquid. Just put everything into a tureen and then cover it.

Dressing the dish: Serve this on a dish covered by a napkin. In the middle, place a large bunch of parsley and then place the crayfish on the parsley, leaning one against the other.

Crayfish à la Bordelaise *(Écrevisses à la Bordelaise).* This very well known recipe may vary in detail, but the final result always remains the same. Here, we are going to give a recipe by the Master Philéas Gilbert, simplified enough so that it can be executed anywhere by anyone prepared to spare the expense. Remember, that none of the ingredients can be left out: a meat glaze, or the reduced meat juices, is essential here, as is an excellent cognac or fine champagne. If you do not have one of the white wines suggested here, substitute with a wine of similar quality. It is well known that the sauce for crayfish *à la bordelaise* must be spicy; but keep this in sensible limits, remembering that cayenne pepper should only ever be used sparingly. If necessary, it can be replaced with ordinary black pepper *ground at the time of use.*

We suggest flaming the cognac or fine champagne in advance: just put it into a very small pan, heat it, then light it and let it flame. Once the flames have died out, pour it over the crayfish. When the flaming is done directly with the crayfish, it often happens that the extremities of the small claws and antennae are scorched, which makes the sauce bitter, so be sure to wait until the flame has extinguished.

We also recommend that you use very little salt at the beginning, a necessary precaution for any recipe that includes a glaze or meat jus. There is always time to adjust the seasoning at the end, but it is difficult to rectify if too much has been used in the first place. Choose some nice, large crayfish. Allow at least 2 crayfish per person. *Time: A brief hour.*

12 crayfish; a mirepoix (the traditional condiment for crayfish à la bordelaise) composed of: 25 grams (1 ounce) of the red part of the carrot; 25 grams (1 ounce) of onion; 8–10 grams (1/3 ounce) of shallot; 3–4 grams (1/8 ounce) of parsley sprigs; a small pinch of dried thyme; a bit of bay leaf the size of a fingernail.

Plus: 125 grams (4 1/2 ounces, 9 tablespoons) of butter; 5 tablespoons of excellent cognac or fine champagne; 2 deciliters (6 3/4 fluid ounces, 7/8 cup) of white wine of Bordeaux (Graves or Petit Sauternes); 1 level teaspoon of concentrated tomato purée; 1/2 tablespoon of melted meat glaze or 1 tablespoon of very good veal

juice that has been reduced—either the juice from a braised fillet or the liquid from a braised dish (use 4 tablespoons, then reduce to make 1 tablespoon); a good pinch of coarsely chopped parsley; salt, cayenne pepper; sprigs of fried parsley.

PROCEDURE. **The mirepoix:** Cut the following into an extremely fine *brunoise* (cubes no bigger than 1 millimeter/less than 1/16 inch): carrot, onion, shallot, and parsley. Next, mince everything together briefly so that the vegetables are almost reduced to a sort of vegetable bread crumb. Add the thyme and the bay, reduced to a powder.

In a very small pot, gently heat 25 grams (1 ounce, 2 tablespoons) of butter. Add the mirepoix. Cook *very gently for about 10 minutes,* mixing it often enough so that the ingredients are equally cooked. The vegetables should virtually melt and just begin to color but not brown at all.

Meanwhile, before cleaning the crayfish, take out a sauté pan of the appropriate size. Heat 30 grams (1 ounce, 2 tablespoons) of butter in it. As you clean the crayfish, put them in the pan. Then cover the pan and put it on *strong heat.* After each minute, take the cover off to mix the crayfish until all of their carapaces have become uniformly red: this should take *about 7–8 minutes.* Then add the cognac or the fine champagne, which you have flamed in advance to the pan, along with the white wine; the purée of tomato; the prepared mirepoix; a pinch of salt; the cayenne pepper, no more than you can hold on the point of a small knife. Cover the pan tightly and, once the mixture begins to boil, continue to cook on low heat *for 10–15 minutes.* While cooking, stir the crayfish around from time to time.

Take the crayfish out of the pan one by one to place them on a silver tray or in a vegetable plate. Keep them warm.

On strong heat, reduce the sauce that remains in the pan, mixing it with the wooden spoon until there only remains about 1 3/4 deciliters (6 fluid ounces, 3/4 cup). Turn off the heat, then add: the meat glaze, which has been diluted in advance, or the veal juice; and the rest of the butter, 70 grams (2 1/2 ounces, 1/3 cup), in pieces about the size of a small walnut. Mix with a whisk.

Taste carefully to check the seasoning. If needed, added a little bit of salt and a hint of cayenne or of ordinary black pepper. Pour the sauce onto the crayfish. Sprinkle with the coarsely chopped parsley. Serve immediately.

Supreme of Crayfish *(Suprême d'Écrevisses).* An excellent traditional recipe from Alsace. It's a *crème renversée* infused with the flavor of the crayfish, served warm surrounded by crayfish tails and covered with sauce finished with crayfish butter.

To prepare and cook crayfish, refer to the directions given at the beginning of this section. For the entire dish, allow *2 1/2 hours* at the most. But you can cook the crayfish well in advance, prepare the butter, etc., and then turn your attention to the cream and the sauce just 1 hour before serving. *Time: 2 1/2 hours. Serves 7–8.*

1 1/2 kilograms (3 pounds, 5 ounces) of small crayfish.

***For cooking the crayfish:* 1 deciliter (3 1/3 fluid ounces, scant 1/2 cup) of white wine; 1/2 deciliter (1 2/3 fluid ounces, scant 1/4 cup) of cognac; 40 grams (1 3/8 ounces) of minced onions; 20 grams (2/3 ounce) of parsley sprigs; 1 small bay leaf; 1 sprig of thyme; 2 level teaspoons of salt; 2 good pinches of ground pepper.**

***For the cream and the crayfish butter:* 1/2 liter (generous 2 cups) of excellent milk; 75 grams (2 2/3 ounces, 1/3 cup) of butter; 4 nice eggs.**

***For the sauce:* 25 grams (1 ounce, 2 tablespoons) of butter and 25 grams (1 ounce) of flour for a white roux; 1/2 liter (generous 2 cups) of good bouillon that has been thoroughly degreased; 1/2 deciliter (1 2/3 fluid ounces, scant 1/4 cup) of very good white wine; 1 small onion stuck with a clove, 1 small bouquet garni; 2 egg yolks mixed with 3 tablespoons of fresh, heavy cream.**

PROCEDURE. Cook the crayfish as described.

Peel and reserve the tails. Prepare the crayfish butter with the heads, shells, carapaces, etc., and all the other debris with the butter recommended on PAGE 79. Add the *boiling* milk. Let it simmer for 15 minutes. Pass it through a fine chinois. Set this red butter to one side.

The cream: As if preparing an omelet, beat, but not excessively, the whole eggs seasoned with salt, pepper, and nutmeg. Add the milk. Pass it through a mousseline or fine cheesecloth sieve. Pour the mixture into a 1-liter (4-cup) charlotte mold that has been carefully buttered. Poach it in a double boiler (bain-marie) in the oven, exactly as for a *crème renversée*, for *40 minutes.* After cooking, remove the mold from the double boiler and wait 15 minutes before turning the cream out of the mold.

The sauce: Start this as soon as the cream is in the double boiler. In a small pot, cook the white roux for 5–6 minutes. Dilute it with the hot bouillon. Add the white wine; any cooking liquid remaining after the crayfish have been drained; the small onion with the clove; the bouquet garni; salt, if the bouillon is not salted. Bring it to a boil and then, on gentle heat, degrease it (SEE PAGE 16) for *a half hour.*

Remove the onion and the bouquet garni. Make the liaison with the egg yolks and the cream, then let it boil for a few moments. Turn off the heat to add the reserved red butter to the sauce. Keep it in the double boiler until ready to serve.

To serve: Turn out the crème onto a warmed plate. Surround it with the crayfish tails, which have first been reheated in a few tablespoons of sauce. Pour the sauce, which should have a beautiful rose-colored tint, over everything.

Lobster *(Homard)*

For the best lobster, cook it in court bouillon, proceeding as described for the spiny lobster (SEE PAGES 235).

Lobster à l'Américaine *(Homard à la Américaine).*

Because this is primarily a dish offered by the great restaurants, the difficulties of preparing it at home have been greatly exaggerated.

In reality, it is not that the ingredients are difficult to obtain; rather, it is the method that is likely to cause problems at home. For success, follow the procedure precisely; prepare everything in advance; and do not overlook anything, even if it seems unimportant,

To avoid confusion, the necessary techniques will be explained here before describing the recipe itself. The recipe for lobster à l'américaine is equally good used to prepare a spiny lobster weighing no more than 800–900 grams (1 pound, 12 ounces–2 pounds). Lobster is preferable because of its excellent meat, but spiny lobster makes a good enough alternative. The lobster or spiny lobster must be *alive when cooked:* this is essential for the taste and so that the meat remains firm. If possible, choose a lobster with a brown carapace, which will turn bright red when cooked. Lobsters with a bluish carapace are as good in terms of taste, but the carapace only turn pink when they are cooked. So that the following directions are clear, let us explain that the lobster or the spiny lobster is composed of two parts: the rigid part, which, in culinary terms, is called the shell, and the flexible tail.

Let us also insist that it is essential to *carve the lobster while it is alive.* Not only will the flesh of the animal killed in such a way be firmer when it is sealed by the hot oil, but you will not risk seeing the lobster void itself, which often happens when it is plunged into boiling water in order to kill it before carving it, as is sometimes recommended. It might perhaps be better to stick a cooking needle into its flesh, but this does not really lessen the suffering inflicted on the lobster, which is unfortunate but necessary. Rapid carving in effect ultimately provides the same result.

We will explain below the procedure used in professional kitchens. The one used by the classic master, Colombié, is described here. With your hands above a bowl, hold the lobster with your left hand by the shell and slide a small knife between the carapace and the tail to make a circular incision. Then pull apart the two parts. Keep them suspended over the bowl, holding the open, cut parts downward to collect the colorless liquid that escapes. This is the lobster's blood, which will add to the color and taste and also thicken the sauce. Afterwards, divide the lobster as described in the recipe. This preliminary procedure is an indication of the care you must take to gather all the liquid that escapes from the beast when you carve it. You should always use this method. Still on the topic of carving, let us consider the contents of the shell. Known as *coral,* this soft substance is a greenish color in the male and a grayish color in the female. This same substance can be found solidified after cooking lobsters and spiny lobsters in court bouillon, when it will be solidified and a very beautiful red color, hence the name "coral." It plays a very important role in the preparation of lobster à l'américaine, as much for the red color it gives to the sauce (especially when it comes from a male), as for its particular flavor and even more for its role in thickening the sauce.

The grayish substance of the female lobster does not give as bright a color, but you can reinforce it with the *eggs,* which you may find accumulated under the tail. If so, remove them and squash them into a purée through a drum sieve *(tamis)* before mixing them with the coral.

For cooking lobster, professional kitchens use not just white wine, which makes up two-thirds of the cooking liquid, but also some fish fumet or bouillon or even the water used for cooking the mushrooms. This last one is very simple to make. Nonetheless, you can, if you prefer, use a similar quantity of a bouillon that has been completely degreased; or, for a meat-free meal, a white wine diluted half and half with water. For a meat-free meal, you should also leave out the meat glaze.

It is sometimes suggested that butter should be used with the oil to sauté the lobster, but oil is the only thing that should be used, because this type of cooking spoils it and it cannot be re-used. The cognac, which is an integral element of the dish, must be flamed. This is traditionally done after first draining the oil by basting the lobster with cognac to remove the oil, then lighting it. But this method requires a great deal of care so that you do not char the little feet or the antennae, which would then make the sauce sharp. If you are not used to doing this, it is better to flame the cognac in advance on the side.

The cayenne pepper so essential to this dish must be used sparingly. It is better to have to add some at the very end than to add too much at the beginning. We suggest using no more than can be held on the point of a small knife, probably no more than 1/3 gram (less than 1/14 ounce).

If you are not sure that your guests will be on time, do not finish the sauce until you are ready to serve. Given the large amount of butter that is added to the sauce at the end, the sauce cannot be kept very warm without risking it turning into oil.

The traditional way to serve lobster à l'américaine is to leave the pieces of lobster in their carapace. But some restaurants now prefer to serve the meat of the lobster removed from its carapace. We will describe how to do this, though it is, of course, optional. *Time: 35 minutes.*

1 live lobster weighing from 900 grams–1 kilogram (2 pounds–2 pounds, 3 ounces); 1 1/2 deciliters (5 fluid ounces, 2/3 cup) of oil to color and firm it.

For cooking: 20 grams (2/3 ounce) of minced shallot and 25 grams (1 ounce, 2 tablespoons) of butter; 3 medium fresh tomatoes (about 300 grams/ 10 1/2 ounces net weight); or, when out of season, 2 good tablespoons of tomato paste (double that if it is ordinary, or unconcentrated, purée); 1 piece of garlic the size of a pea; a Madeira glass (1 1/2 deciliters, 5 fluid ounces, 2/3 cup) full of cognac; 2 deciliters (6 3/4 fluid ounces, 7/8 cup) of white wine; 1 deciliter (3 1/3 fluid ounces, scant 1/2 cup) of mushroom cooking liquid (but bear in mind what has already been said); salt and ordinary pepper; a point of a knife of cayenne pepper.

To correct and finish the sauce: 1 good tablespoon of melted meat glaze; 125 grams of butter (4 1/2 ounces, 9 tablespoons); 1 scant tablespoon of minced tarragon and chervil, half of each; a pinch of minced parsley.

PROCEDURE. **The preparations:** *The herbs:* Finely mince the shallot. Also finely mince the mixed chervil and the tarragon. Coarsely chop the parsley. Gather these elements on a plate in little separate piles.

The tomatoes: Peel the tomatoes and thoroughly remove their seeds and their water. Chop them finely. Keep them on a plate.

The cognac: Put it into a small pan. Heat it and light it with a piece of paper. Let it flame and then go out. Reserve.

The cooking liquid of mushrooms: SEE MUSHROOMS (PAGE 490).

The sauté pan: A heavy-based sauté pan in which the pieces of lobster can fit without being too crowded. Pour in the oil. Put it on a low heat to begin warming. You will then need no more than a moment to heat the oil to the right temperature, ready for cooking the lobster as soon as it has been carved.

Carving the lobster: With your left hand, keep the lobster laid out on the table. With a large knife, first cut off the 2 claws. Divide the tail into 5 or

6 pieces by cutting it cleanly with your first blow in order to avoid splinters.

Then split the carapace lengthwise. Immediately remove and toss aside the little membranous pouch just by the head, which always contains some gravel. Then, with great care, pick out the coral and put it on a plate.

With the side of a cleaver, break the carapace and the claws so that you can easily extract the meat after cooking. Separate the phalanx from the claw.

To cook: As soon as the lobster is carved, turn the heat up very high under the sauté pan. As soon as the oil begins to smoke, arrange the pieces in it, then season with salt and pepper. Turn them over from time to time until the carapace has taken on a beautiful red color and the flesh has begun to shrink: *4–5 minutes* on a good heat.

Then put a cover on the pan to hold in the pieces while you tilt the pan to pour out every last drop of oil.

Next, mix the minced shallot and the piece of butter with the lobster. Mix everything together for a few seconds. Then add the flamed cognac; the chopped tomatoes or the tomato purée; the garlic squashed into a paste under the blade of a knife; the white wine; the mushroom cooking water or the liquid replacing it; a pinch of salt; a bit of pepper; a hint of cayenne pepper.

Bring it to a boil. *Cover the pan.* Let it boil rapidly for *15 minutes.*

Finishing the sauce and serving: While the lobster is cooking, finely mince the coral, adding to it a piece of butter the size of a walnut. Keep everything ready on a plate. If there are eggs, squash them completely by passing them through the *tamis* with a little bit of butter. Add them to the coral.

At the end of 15 minutes of cooking, pick out the pieces of the lobster with a fork and place them in a silver timbale or a small heated vegetable dish: arrange the pieces of the tail on the bottom; on top of those, the 2 half shells, facing each other. Put the 2 claws on each side, standing up; keep warm in a very mild oven. Then put the pan, uncovered, on very high heat to reduce the sauce to less than 2 deciliters (6¾ fluid ounces, ⅞ cup). At this point, add the coral and the purée of eggs, if there are any (SEE PAGE 232). Mix together over the heat for no more than 2 minutes to cook the coral, which will then take on a vermillion tint and also bind the sauce. Immediately turn the heat off. Add and mix the rest of the butter, divided into small pieces, the meat glaze (previously melted in a small pot), the chervil and tarragon. Check the seasoning and, if you need to, add a little bit of cayenne. Pour this on the pieces of the lobster. Sprinkle the surface with the minced parsley. Serve immediately on very hot plates.

An alternate method of serving lobster à l'américaine: Carve the lobster as described, being careful to completely break the carapace and the pinchers so you can rapidly extract the meat when you dress the dish.

Cook as described above. Once the pieces have been cooked, lift them out and put on a plate. Remove the pieces of flesh from the tail with a fork. Arrange them in a serving dish. Add the flesh from the claws. In the middle, stand the 2 halves of the shell.

Reduce the sauce and add the coral as previously described. Pass the sauce through a fine chinois so that you remove any splinters, beating it vigorously with the whisk. Rinse the sauté pan in hot water, then put the sauce back into it. Heat it until it boils. Finish the sauce, adding butter to it *off the heat* as has been previously described. Pour it on the pieces of the lobster; sprinkle with parsley.

Lobster à la Newburg or à la Van Der Bilt *(Homard à la Newburg ou à la Van der Bilt).* This can be prepared two ways: carved raw as for lobster à l'américaine, or carved after cooking in a court bouillon, which itself has several variations. Whatever the method, it always includes cream, which is characteristic of this dish; since the result is the same, we offer here the most practical recipe, modeled after Philéas Gilbert.

Nonetheless, the recipe requires great care, particularly for the final addition of cream and egg yolks; in effect, what you are doing is preparing a crème anglaise, then heating it strongly to reach the thick consistency required, all the while preventing it from boiling, which would curdle the sauce. To make things easier, you can add a little béchamel, and the flour in it will let you heat the sauce strongly without curdling. In this case, proceed as follows: dilute 2½ deciliters (1 cup) only of cream with 4 egg yolks. When you pour it on the slices of lobster, add 1½ deciliters (5 fluid ounces, ⅔ cup) only of boiling béchamel sauce. Then cook as directed. *Time: 35 minutes (once the lobsters have been cooked). Serves 6.*

2 live lobsters, each one weighing about 550 grams (1 pound, 3 ounces).

For the court bouillon: 3 liters (12¾ cups) of water; 40 grams (1⅜ ounces) of salt; 2½ deciliters (1 cup) of vinegar; 12 sprigs parsley, 2 small bay leaves, and 1 sprig of thyme.

For the sauce: 50 grams (1¾ ounces, 3½ tablespoons) of butter; 2½ deciliters (1 cup) of very good Madeira; 3 deciliters (1¼ cups) of cream, quite thick and perfectly fresh; 5 egg yolks; a good pinch of fine salt and a pinch of pepper.

PROCEDURE. **The lobsters:** In a deep pot, put all the ingredients for the court bouillon; bring to a boil.

With string, securely bind the end of the lobster's tail, drawing it under the belly. Plunge it into the court bouillon, which should be at a rolling boil. From this point, allow *20–22 minutes* at a rolling boil.

Then take the lobsters out of the court bouillon. Let them cool for about 1 hour before carving the flesh. If, however, you are pressed for time, the flesh can be carved while lukewarm.

Place the lobsters on their backs. Using scissors or the point of a small knife, cut away from the carapace on each side the membrane situated under the belly. Then gently pull on the tail to make it come out, twisting the shell. Cut 8 or 9 slices or medallions from each tail, cutting them on a slight bias to improve their appearance. Then carefully break the carapace and the claws using the flat end of small cleaver, taking care so that you will be able to extract the flesh intact.

Get a sauté pan of a large enough capacity so you can arrange the medallions and the claw meat each beside the other. Spread the butter on the bottom of the pan. Arrange the pieces on top. Season with salt and pepper. Do not cover. Put the pan on a gentle fire that will heat the flesh *without coloring it:* this allows the lobster's epidermis to redden. Allow about *6–8 minutes* for this and turn the medallions over once during this time.

Then add the Madeira. *Cover the pan.* Boil moderately to reduce it only slightly and to give the Madeira time to flavor the lobster meat. Allow *16–18 minutes* to reduce the wine to about 3 tablespoons.

The sauce: While the Madeira is reducing, dilute the egg yolks in a bowl with the cream. Once the Madeira has reduced, pour the egg and cream onto the lobster. Then shake the pan vigorously, holding it by the handle and shaking it on top of the burner until the sauce has thickened to the consistency of a crème anglaise. At this point, check the seasoning and rapidly pour everything into a dish that has been well heated in advance. Serve quickly.

Spiny Lobster *(Langouste)*

The spiny lobster *must always be alive* when it is cooked. The flesh of a spiny lobster, dead before it has been cooked, is flaccid and tasteless. It must also be whole, without having lost its claws or received any wounds through which it would lose its juices during cooking. When choosing them, make sure that they are heavy in the hand for their size.

Cooking the spiny lobster in court bouillon: When you are by the seaside, the best court bouillon to use is seawater without any seasoning. Below, we will give a recipe for a court bouillon that works as well for the spiny lobster as it does for the lobster. The amount of liquid depends on the size of the utensil you are going to use for the cooking. This utensil must be higher than wider so that the spiny lobster can be completely immersed.

You should use only a minimal amount of vinegar in a court bouillon for lobster and spiny lobsters because its acid affects the coloration of the carapace, which will remain pale instead of taking on a beautiful light red tint; furthermore, the vinegar is not absolutely necessary, so it can be left out without ill effect. The same is true for ground pepper, which will leave an acrid taste in a court bouillon after it has been boiled for a long time. Notice the substantial quantity of salt: 15 grams (½ ounce) for each liter (4¼ cups) of water.

You should allow *35 minutes* to cook a spiny lobster that weighs about 1 kilogram (2 pounds, 3 ounces). For a lobster weighing 1 1/2–2 kilograms (3 pounds, 5 ounces–4 pounds, 6 ounces) allow *38–40 minutes because the heat will be cumulative and not exactly proportional to the weight of the lobster.*

Spiny Lobster with Mayonnaise Sauce *(Langouste Sauce Mayonnaise).* *Time: 35 minutes to cook the spiny lobster, counting from the moment you plunge it into the court bouillon and the liquid returns to a boil. About 1 1/2 hours, to cool it outside the court bouillon. Serves 6.*

1 spiny lobster of 1–1 1/4 kilograms (2 pounds 3 ounces–2 pounds, 12 ounces).

***For the court bouillon:* 3 liters (12 3/4 cups) of water and 45 grams (1 1/2 ounces) of salt; 15 grams (1/2 ounce) of parsley sprigs; 1 sprig of thyme; 1 bay leaf; 3 tablespoons of vinegar (optional).**

PROCEDURE. In your chosen cooking utensil, put in all the ingredients for a court bouillon. Bring it to a boil.

Plunge the spiny lobster into a bowl of cold water. Lightly brush its carapace with a scrubbing brush and rinse it for a second time in clean water. Bind the lobster so that when you plunge it into the boiling water it does not struggle and splash you with burning liquid. Bend the tail underneath the belly of the beast and tie it securely, then fold the horns toward the back. Fix them along the body with a double turn of string that has been knotted and tightened.

Immediately plunge the spiny lobster into the *boiling* court bouillon: in order to seal it and kill it instantly, the court bouillon must be at a rolling boil. Keep the pot on high heat so that it returns to a boil as quickly as possible. From the moment it returns to a boil, *allow a good 35 minutes* to cook. Maintain a rolling boil throughout. Avoid overcooking, which will make the flesh of the spiny lobster tough.

As soon as the time is up, remove the spiny lobster from the court bouillon. Insert the point of the knife between the two horns to help the lobster drain. Lean it against something standing up with the head facing down. Let it drain and cool in this position.

To serve: Remove the strings. With the point of a good, strong knife, split the underneath of the spiny lobster, cutting from the head to the tip of the tail without completely separating the two halves, so that you can open them like a book. Remove the gut found right in the middle of the tail.

If carving the spiny lobster at the table, place it open side up on a long plate covered with a napkin, surrounded with leaves of fried parsley and served with a mayonnaise sauce on the side.

If carving the spiny lobster in the kitchen, remove the flesh of each half tail by taking it out of the shell. Cut the flesh of each half tail in slices, cutting on the bias (as when cutting a sausage) to make it appear larger. Make the cuts an equal size. Divide each half of the shell into 2 pieces. Leave everything inside them. Do the same for the claws.

On the plate, rearrange the shell and the carapaces of the tails just as they were when the spiny lobster was split. Fill the interior of the tails with lettuce cut into a julienne and seasoned with salad dressing. On top of this, place the slices of lobster, leaning them one against the other. Garnish the space between the 2 halves of the lobster with parsley. Accompany with the mayonnaise sauce in a sauceboat.

Spiny Lobster in Bellevue *(Langouste en Bellevue).* This is also called "à la parisienne": it is a cold spiny lobster whose empty carapace is arranged along the plate to hold the medallions of lobster, which are lined up on its back and covered with a gelée. Around the spiny lobster is arranged a *macédoine* of vegetables, either bound with mayonnaise and served on artichoke bottoms or molded in a high, narrow *dariole* mold, which would allow you to eliminate the artichoke bottoms. This garnish is completed with halves of hard-boiled eggs and lettuce quarters.

Generally, a light, well-spiced mayonnaise is served alongside in a sauceboat. *Serves 6–8.*

1 live spiny lobster weighing from 1–1 1/2 kilograms (2 pounds, 3 ounces–3 pounds, 5 ounces).

1/2 liter (generous 2 cups) of colorless gelée.

***For the garnish:* carrots, turnips, green peas, green beans, potatoes—80 grams (2 3/4 ounces) each; 3 med-**

ium truffles, cooked; 6 hard-boiled eggs; 6 hearts of lettuce; 2$^1/_2$ deciliters (1 cup) of mayonnaise.

PROCEDURE. Prepare the gelée the evening before (SEE MEAT JELLY, PAGE 45).

At least 3 hours before dressing the spiny lobster, prepare the court bouillon as instructed for spiny lobster with mayonnaise (PAGE 235). Before plunging the beast in it, you must first attach the lobster to a plank to hold its tail completely straight; without doing this, it will be impossible to keep the tail in the right position after chilling. Use a plank 8 to 10 centimeters (about 3–4 inches) wide and about the length of the spiny lobster. Securely tie the animal onto this plank.

Plunge everything into the boiling court bouillon. Cook and drain as described for the spiny lobster with mayonnaise (PAGE 236). Let the beast cool completely on the plank.

Garnish of vegetables: Prepare as described for the garniture jardinière (PAGE 459).

The mayonnaise: SEE PAGE 86.

The truffles: You need about 15 extremely thin medallions, cut, if possible, in graduated sizes to complement the slices of lobster. Coarsely chop any peelings and add to the vegetables.

To cut and decorate the slices of spiny lobster: Untie the spiny lobster. Place it on its back. With a small knife or scissors, make an incision in the membrane underneath the tail, where it is attached to the carapace, cutting the entire length of each side so that you are able to extract the meat. Remove this meat by twisting it lightly to take it out of the shell, working carefully so that you can keep it as intact as possible.

Use a very good knife to trim the side of the tail that was attached to the shell. Divide the tail in medallions or slices cut slightly on the bias the way you would slice sausage, with a standard thickness of 1 good centimeter ($^3/_8$ inch). This bias cut gives them a better appearance. Arrange them piece by piece on a long plate, and side by side in the order in which you cut them, so that they are arranged in order of size.

Melt 3 deciliters (1$^1/_4$ cups) of gelée: it must be completely cool before being used. With a small brush, paint the jelly on the surface of the slices. Put a round of truffle on each slice. Lightly baste with the gelée. Put the plate in a cool place so that the jelly sets. Then baste again. Repeat each time the jelly has solidified, which will take a rather long time if you do not have a refrigerator or icebox.

The garnish: Extract everything you can from the head or shell of the spiny lobster. Cut this into little dice along with the trimmings from the tail. Mix into the mayonnaise 1 scant deciliter (3$^1/_3$ fluid ounces, scant $^1/_2$ cup) of melted but cold jelly. Immediately add to it the little cubes of spiny lobster and the prepared vegetables: carrots, turnips, green peas, green beans, potatoes cut into dice, $^1/_2$ tablespoon of minced chervil, and the truffle peelings. If you are going to serve this in artichoke bottoms, keep it in a cool place until the salad has solidified. Then arrange in a pyramid on the artichoke bottoms and keep it in a cool place. Glaze it with melted cold gelée several times, as with the slices, in order to give a gloss to the salad.

Dressing the spiny lobster: Some form of pedestal or base is needed to raise the spiny lobster to an elevated position, which is better than simply placing it flat on a plate. Make this base from stale bread cut into a wedge 8 centimeters (3$^1/_4$ inches) wide and 20 centimeters (8 inches) long. The top of the wedge where you place the head of the spiny lobster should be 8 to 10 centimeters (3$^1/_4$–4 inches) in height, and the bottom should be only 2 centimeters.

Generously spread the surface and the sides of the wedge base with softened butter. Onto this, spread some small, extremely thin shavings cut from the leaves of nice green lettuce, pressing them in firmly with the blade of a knife. Place this green base in the center of the plate from which the spiny lobster will be served, where a little softened butter has been spread out which will act as glue when it cools. Keep this in a cool place.

Fill the empty carapace of the tail with lettuce leaves cut into a coarse julienne. Place the spiny lobster on the base so that it is half standing. Brush the entire carapace with a brush dipped in oil to give it a luster. To secure the spiny lobster, stick the point of a skewer between the horns and sink it into the bread base.

Next, arrange the slices of spiny lobster symmetrically on the carapace. Detach them first from the plate by passing a small knife around each one. Place the largest closest to the horns of the spiny lobster. Then, working in decreasing order of size, place the second, with about 1 good centimeter (1/2 inch) of it leaning on the first—and so on until you reach the tail.

On each side of the plate, arrange the artichoke bottoms that have been garnished, alternating them with the half hard-boiled eggs: these should have been lightly trimmed on the large end to enable them to stay standing.

Cut the hearts of lettuce in quarters and arrange these quarters behind the eggs and artichokes, leaning them along the base of the bread pedestal. Complete the arrangement with little sprigs of parsley or watercress placed between the artichokes and the eggs. Keep the plate in a cool place until ready to serve.

Aspic of Spiny Lobster *(Aspic de Langouste).* As has been explained elsewhere, aspic can be molded in a cylindrical mold, a ring mold, a Charlotte or other mold, or put in a low timbale or shallow bowl. For directions, SEE ASPICS, PAGE 445.

If the aspic is molded in a ring mold, you can put a vegetable salad in the center, adding the trimmings from the spiny lobster, divided into small cubes. To the mayonnaise for the salad, you can add the creamy interior of the shell after you have made it into a fine purée by passing it through a drum sieve. If you use another mold, this same salad can be served alongside as an equally good accompaniment to the aspic. *Time: 1 1/2 hours for cooking the spiny lobster and the gelée; 6 hours, at least, to clarify, cool, and chill.*

1 spiny lobster; approximately 1 1/2 liters (6 1/3 cups) of fish gelée, for which you must allow 1 1/2 kilograms (3 pounds, 5 ounces) of the bones, heads, and trimmings of raw fish. However, as is often the case in home kitchens, you may not have such a large quantity of bones. So use inexpensive fish to make the bouillon for the gelée: for example, eel, guenard, heads of hake, etc. Allow 1 kilogram of fish for each liter of finished gelée.

PROCEDURE. Prepare the fish bouillon (SEE PAGE 165). Put the fish and the vegetables straight into the liquid, without first sweating them: use at least 1 1/2 liters (6 1/3 cups) of water and 2 1/2 liters (10 1/2 cups) of white wine, preferably Graves, which will not be spoiled by cooking; if you do not have Graves, leave the wine out altogether.

To cook the bouillon, allow at least *1 hour* at a slow simmer. Then put 1 deciliter (3 1/3 fluid ounces, scant 1/2 cup) of bouillon in a small mold and chill it. Once it is chilled, you will have some idea of the gelée's consistency and can judge if you need to add more gelatin. If more is needed, add it before clarifying (SEE GELATIN, PAGE 18).

Then clarify the bouillon in the same way you would for meat jelly. In this case, you will need to repeat the clarification several times to produce a gelée that is perfectly clear and brilliant. This will mean carefully straining the gelée through the napkin several times.

The spiny lobster: Cook in the court bouillon as described. As soon as it has been cooked, stick a large needle in its horns as described in previous recipes for spiny lobster. Break the shells of the claws to extract the meat. With scissors, cut the interior carapace of the tail along its entire length on 2 sides so that you can remove the meat. Cut this meat from the tail, slicing straight and not cutting on the bias, making each slice 2 millimeters (less than 1/8 inch) thick. Mold the aspic according to your preferred method.

Croquettes of Lobster or Spiny Lobster *(Croquettes de Homard ou de Langouste).* See the article relating to croquettes (PAGE 438). Use the same sauce for the liaison as that used for FOWL CROQUETTES (PAGE 440).

Norway Lobster *(Langoustine)*

Norway lobster look more like large shrimp than like spiny lobsters. They are sold uncooked in the markets; choose them heavy and firm. First, wash them quickly in cold water and brush off their shells and underneath their tails.

Generally, they are prepared in a saltwater court bouillon. Plunge them in a court bouillon that is at a rolling boil, and boil for a good 15 minutes. Drain the Norway lobsters. Let them cool completely for 1 hour and serve them in a *buisson* with an accompanying sauce, mayonnaise, or rémoulade.

Menton-Style Langoustine *(Langoustines à la Mentonnaise).* *Time: 40 minutes.*

1 dozen langoustine: 1 deciliter (3 1/3 fluid ounces, scant 1/2 cup) of olive oil.

For the mirepoix: 1 medium onion; 1 carrot; 1 white celery stalk; 3 or 4 sprigs of parsley; 2 medium-sized tomatoes that are good and ripe; 1 sprig of thyme, of sage, and 1/4 of a bay leaf; 2 deciliters (6 3/4 fluid ounces, 7/8 cup) of white wine; 1/2 liter (generous 2 cups) of cognac, previously flamed; 1 piece of a garlic the size of a pea.

For the liaison: 25 grams (1 ounce, 2 tablespoons) of butter worked with 20 grams (2/3 ounce) of flour.

PROCEDURE. In a pan with a large bottom big enough to hold the langoustine without them piling up, heat the oil and gently sauté the elements of the mirepoix (SEE PAGE 21). Add the langoustine and the pea-sized piece of garlic, squashed, and sauté them on strong heat, stirring them for 5 minutes. Then moisten them with the white wine and the cognac. Cover the pan and let everything cook gently for 15 minutes. Take out the langoustine, draining them well. Put them on a plate and keep them warm. Pass the cooking liquid through a chinois into a small saucepan, stirring it with a wooden spoon; put it back on the fire to heat the sauce sufficiently and then make your liaison with the buerre manié (SEE PAGE 48). If you wish, you can serve this sauce on the side, or—which is typical of this recipe—pour it over the langoustine; but they are somewhat difficult to shell and some of the sauce will be lost under the carapace.

Scallops *(Coquilles Saint-Jacques)*

Each person is served 2 scallop shells, so to make sure that the shells are properly filled, you will need at least 3 scallops per person. This is because the scallops are trimmed of the stringy and tough muscles that attach them to the shell and also because the mushrooms used are not enough to boost their quantities. Choose scallops that are heavy in your hand and are also tightly closed, which means the mollusk inside is alive and—more important—fresh. If you see that the shells are slightly open, tap on them or slip in a knife blade; the scallop will immediately close if the animal is alive.

As well as the recipes described here, we wish to recommend several different methods: à la Mornay (SEE SOLE, PAGE 204), in which the cooking liquid from the scallops is added to the sauce; *with anchovies,* in which the scallops are served with a light béchamel flavored with either a little anchovy butter or a bottled purée of anchovy; *with white wine,* where the scallops are cooked in white wine diluted with one-third water, which is then bound with a white roux and thickened with egg yolks and butter, just like recipes for fish made with white wine.

Generally speaking, mushrooms, or if you do not have them, the cooking liquids from mushrooms, are used to prepare scallops.

Prior preparation of the scallops: Briskly brush them off in fresh water. Open them either by sliding a knife between the two shells or by putting them on top of a stove on gentle heat; the heat affects the living mollusk and you will see the shell open up a bit and the flat part lift. You then easily detach this flat shell, which you will not use; only the hollowed shell is kept for serving. Remove the meat of the scallop by passing the point of a supple knife blade under the meat. This meat looks like a large flat cork surrounded by tendons—the curly gray part, which cannot be used. It is surrounded by the coral, the red part. Remove the small blackish pouch that is attached to the meat.

Wash the meat in abundant cool water; dry it well before preparing it in one of the following ways. Brush and wash again the empty shells; drain them and wipe them dry.

Home-Style Scallops au Gratin *(Coquilles au Gratin à la Ménagère).* *Serves 6.*

9 scallops; 150 grams (5 1/3 ounces) of fresh mushrooms; 100 grams (3 1/2 ounces, 7 tablespoons) of butter; 50 grams (1 3/4 ounces) of finely minced onions; 3 deciliters (1 1/4 cups) of white wine; 1 good tablespoon of tomato paste; 3 good tablespoons of fine white stale bread crumbs (SEE PAGE 19); 1 tablespoon of minced parsley; 1 piece of garlic the size of a pea and 1 small shallot, optional; salt and pepper.

PROCEDURE. Put the flesh extracted from the scallops in a pan with the white wine and a pinch of salt. Slowly heat it. As soon as it begins to boil, turn the heat down to let it poach or cook without boiling *5–6 minutes.* Drain and reserve the cooking juice.

The sauce: In the same pan, gently soften the onion with 50 grams (1 3/4 ounces, 3 1/2 tablespoons) of butter, without letting it color at all, *for about 10 minutes.*

Remove the mushroom stems. Wash them in plenty of water; mince them finely. Add to the onion along with the minced parsley. Cook on strong heat *for 4–5 minutes,* stirring continuously to evaporate the mushroom juices. Add the cooking liquid from the scallops after it has been carefully decanted and strained, along with the tomato and half of the bread crumbs. Let it boil gently until it thickens.

Cut the scallops into small dice, removing the tendons and reserving one of the best crescents of coral for each shell. Mix the diced scallops into the sauce; turn off the heat. Butter the empty shells and garnish. Sprinkle with bread crumbs and baste with melted butter. Thus prepared, the scallops can wait a while before being put in the oven to brown.

To gratinée: Place the scallops on a baking sheet. Put them under a hot broiler to brown *for a good 10–12 minutes.* Alternatively, broil or brown on the top shelf of a hot oven.

To serve: Arrange the scallops on a platter covered with a napkin.

Simplified Home-Style, without Mushrooms or Wine *(Façon Ménagère Simplifiée, sans Champignons ni Vin).*

PROCEDURE. Put the flesh of the scallops into a pan fully covered with cool water. Bring it to a boil; let it poach for *4–5 minutes* just to firm the flesh. Drain and remove the barbs.

The sauce: Add 25 grams (1 ounce, 2 tablespoons) of butter. Gently sauté 1 tablespoon of minced parsley and the same amount of shallot (or of onion, if preferred) without letting it color. Sprinkle with 20 grams (2/3 ounce) of flour, barely letting it color. Moisten it with 4 deciliters (1 2/3 cups) of bouillon that has been perfectly degreased. Season it with pepper and, if necessary, with salt. Let it simmer gently for just a few minutes. Put 1 tablespoon of sauce at the bottom of each shell. Fill the shells with the flesh of the scallop cut into large cubes. Cover them with sauce. Sprinkle with bread crumbs. Put a piece of butter the size of a hazelnut on each shell.

A scant 15 minutes before serving, put the scallops into a *hot oven for 12 minutes* to cook and brown. Serve on a plate as above. If necessary, you can keep the scallops warm for a short time before serving.

Prepared with Cream *(Apprêt à la Crème).* Mushrooms are not necessary here, but their flavor would complement the recipe—hence their inclusion here. *Time: 45 minutes.*

The same number of scallops as above; 2 1/2 deciliters (1 cup) of white wine and 1 deciliter (3 1/3 fluid ounces, scant 1/2 cup) of mushroom cooking liquid; 1 deciliter (3 1/3 fluid ounces, scant 1/2 cup) of crème fraîche; 25 grams (1 ounce, 2 tablespoons) of butter and 25 grams (1 ounce) of flour for the roux; 60 grams (2 1/4 ounces, 4 1/2 tablespoons) of butter to add at the end; salt, pepper, and a point of cayenne (no more than can be held on the tip of a knife).

PROCEDURE. Poach the flesh of the scallops in white wine and mushroom cooking water seasoned with salt and pepper. Let poach for *10–12 minutes* because there will not be any other cooking. Drain and reserve the liquid, passing it through a strainer and decanting. Divide each scallop in 2 or 3 rounds and cut the coral into small cubes.

The sauce: Make a light blond roux. Dilute it with the reserved cooking juice and the cream. Once it has begun to boil, let it cook for 3–4 minutes more. Turn off the heat, then add the remaining butter, divided into small pieces. Check the seasoning and add the cayenne pepper.

Spread 1 tablespoon of sauce on the bottom of each shell. On top, arrange the scallop rounds and coral cubes in the quantity appropriate for each shell size, then cover everything with the sauce. In this state, the scallops can be set aside.

Put the scallops into a very hot oven to heat them well and rapidly glaze the surface of the sauce (SEE PAGE 15). Arrange the scallops on a platter and serve *immediately.*

Mussels *(Moules)*

Choosing them: Medium-sized mussels are the best and the most delicate. But absolutely essential, for health reasons more than anything else, is that they should be *fresh.* This means not only that the mussels should be *alive* (without exception) but also that they should have been harvested recently enough that they retain their liquor. Once this has escaped, the mussel is still alive, but in a sorry state. For this reason, an open mussel is unlikely to be fresh. Remember this when buying them, and also bear in mind that a fresh mussel is relatively heavy.

Several markets sell mussels that have already been cleaned; you may be tempted by these, thinking they will save you both time and trouble, but remember that mussels that have been mechanically cleaned are likely to have lost most of their water.

Cleaning them: Whether or not the recipe uses their shells, they must be cleaned meticulously. The way to open mussels is to cook them in their shells. Cook them in the purest water possible, not only to preserve the mussel itself but also so that the cooking liquid is as pure and clear as possible because it is such an important element in any recipe. *Mussels must never be left in the water used to wash them. And they must be cleaned one at a time.*

Using a knife with a short, strong blade, first rip off the "beard" that is found along the mouth of the mussels. Thoroughly scrub any mussels whose shells are covered with a calcareous coat. As you clean them, put them in a tureen *without water.*

If some mussels seem of an unusual weight—that is, very heavy—be careful and do not hesitate to open slightly to check the contents. Heavy mussels may sometimes be filled with sludge or sand, around which the mussels have closed. Note that if you miss just one bad mussel, all will probably be lost, because apart from the sand, which will spread among the other mussels, the sludge will seep out, mixing with the mussel liquor and giving it an extremely unpleasant taste. It is impossible to be too careful about this; any suspect mussel must be rigorously examined.

The shells must be tightly closed. If you see one that is even slightly open—that is, you can slide a knife blade inside—tap the shell lightly with the knife. The noise and the shock should cause the mussel to close again if it is alive. If the shell remains open, the mussel is dead. It is essential that you throw it out because it is bad and is likely to make anyone eating it ill. Once the mussels have been cleaned, fill the tureen with water and toss them vigorously, mixing well. The shock and the noise will keep them from opening. Take them out by handfuls with your two hands and put them in a strainer or another receptacle. Throw out this water and rinse the tureen. Rinse the mussels again another two or three times, always taking them out with your hands to drain them, thus leaving the sand at the bottom of the tureen. The last time you rinse them, the water should be absolutely clear. Then they are ready to cook.

Cooking the mussels: Regardless of the recipe, the method of cooking mussels remains the same.

It does not matter what utensil you use. At the seaside, fishermen use a frying pan as long as it's big enough that the mussels are not overcrowded; so try to be sure to use a utensil that has a rather large bottom and that is big enough for the volume of mussels put into it. You want to be able to stir the mussels easily as they open; otherwise those underneath will become tough while those on top will scarcely open. For this reason, if you do not have a utensil that is big enough, cook the mussels in two or three batches. You can keep the opened mussels warm while you cook the rest.

The seasoning added to the mussels while cooking includes: parsley, thyme, bay, pepper, and generally onion and sometimes garlic. Often a bit of white wine is added, not to flavor the flesh of the mussels (the cooking time is too short), but to flavor the water, which is used later in the recipe. When white wine is not used, the mussels are usually put into a pot with their seasonings, without liquid. That said, some people add a very little cold water, which boils rapidly at the bottom of the pot, releasing a hot steam, which causes the shells to open. This is an excellent method.

For 2 liters (8½ cups) of mussels, add: 1 medium onion cut into thin rounds; 5 or 6 sprigs of parsley; 1 sprig of thyme; ⅓ of a bay leaf; a speck of a *whole* white peppercorn or, if you do not have that, a pinch of ground white pepper and 2 deciliters (6 3/4 fluid ounces, 7/8 cup) of water. Tightly cover the pot. Place it on high heat. Shake the mussels at the end of 2 minutes, and do this another two or three times.

A total of *5–6 minutes* should be long enough for the shells to open and the mussels to be well cooked: indeed, the former is an indication of the latter. As soon as the shells are spread wide apart and the mussel can be easily pulled off, remove it from the heat. Overcooking will make the mussels turn a yellowish color and will stiffen them and make them tough. Mussels should be white and juicy. On the other hand, if the mussels are not cooked for long enough or heated sufficiently, the shells will not open completely and the mussels will remain stuck. It will be difficult to pull the mussel off and the flesh will be soft and unpleasant under the tooth.

Immediately take the pot off the heat in order to remove the shells. It is only when mussels are used as a garnish for a stew or a sauce, or are fried inside a batter, that they are served with their shell or a part of the shell—the part to which it naturally clings.

Detach the empty shell, holding the mussels directly over the pot to avoid losing any of their liquor. As you work, put the mussels on a plate. Cover and keep it warm.

Mussels à la Marinère *(Moules à la Marinière).* This preparation has a few variations: with or without white wine; with or without lemon; and with a different liaison. Only the shallot, a characteristic element of the "marinière," always remains.

Of the different recipes for the marinière, we give the simplest, which is also the best. In this, the sauce is bound with bread crumbs. If you prefer a liaison with buerre manié, you should replace the bread crumbs with 10 grams of flour (1/3 ounce) worked with 20 grams (2/3 ounce, 1 heaping tablespoon) of butter. *Time: 1 brief hour. Serves 6.*

2 liters (8 cups) of mussels cooked as above; 3 deciliters (1 1/4 cups) of cooking liquid; 1 1/2 deciliters (5 fluid ounces, 2/3 cup) of white wine; 20 grams (2/3 ounce) of shallot, finely minced; 2 good pinches of minced parsley; 75 grams (2 2/3 ounces, 1/3 cup) of butter; 2 good soupspoons of bread crumbs ground into a fine semolina.

PROCEDURE. In order to use the same pot used for cooking the mussels, decant the liquor that they have released, carefully pouring it into another container to eliminate the sand.

Rinse the pot. Add the white wine and shallot. Reduce it vigorously until about 3 tablespoons are left. Then add 3 deciliters (1 1/4 cups), carefully measured, of cooking water from the mussels. Make sure that it is not too salty, or you will have to add some water, thereby diluting the cooking liquid. Boil it for only a few *seconds* without reducing it. *Turn off the heat.*

Next, add to the sauce, always off the fire, the pepper, if this has not already been included as peppercorns; and the butter, divided into very small pieces the size of very small hazelnuts. Sprinkle over the bread crumbs, mixing well and shaking the pot to melt the butter; and then some minced parsley; and some lemon juice, if using.

Put the mussels back into the pot. Shake them in the sauce for a few seconds only *without putting them directly over the heat.* The point is to heat the mussels thoroughly and to cover them completely with sauce, but not to allow this to boil *or even overheat,* because the butter just added would lose its creaminess and turn to oil.

Then pour everything in a pile, pell-mell, into a warm timbale or onto a warm plate. Serve on very warm plates.

Marinière-Style Mussels from the Charente Coast *(Façon Marinière du Littoral Charentais).* Cooked as above, but you leave out the wine and the shallots. Use nothing but the liquor from the mussels, plus the minced parsley, as well as some scallion and a bit of crushed garlic, added at the same time as the butter and the bread crumbs. No lemon.

Mussels à la Bordelaise *(Moules à la Bordelaise).* A delicious dish. Indeed, one that is "finger-licking good." Do not even think of using less than the amount of butter indicated because this replaces the meat glaze more commonly added. In fact, if this recipe is carefully followed, the dish is entirely meat-free. *Time: 1 1/2 hours. Serves 5–6.*

2 liters (8 1/2 cups) of small mussels; 2 deciliters (6 3/4 fluid ounces, 7/8 cup) of white wine, used to open them.

For the sauce: **A little mirepoix with 50 grams (1 3/4 ounces) of onion, 50 grams (1 3/4 ounces) of carrot, 10 grams (1/3 ounce) of shallot, 1 sprig of parsley and 1/4 of a bay leaf, 50 grams (1 3/4 ounces, 3 1/2 tablespoons) of butter, 2 deciliters (6 3/4 fluid ounces, 7/8 cup) of white wine. The cooking water from the mussels; 1 tablespoon of tomato paste; 10 grams (1/3 ounce) of minced parsley; a small pinch of cayenne pepper; 100 grams (3 1/2 ounces, 7 tablespoons) of butter added at the end.**

PROCEDURE. SEE MIREPOIX, PAGE 21. Put all the ingredients for the mirepoix into a small pot. Cover and cook *for a half hour,* letting it gently soften and melt without going beyond a slight yellowish. Moisten with the white wine and bring to a boil. Then keep it at a very gentle simmer *for 1 hour.* At this point, the liquid will have completely reduced and the mirepoix will look like and have the consistency of a moist marmalade.

Meanwhile, clean and open the mussels (SEE PAGE 241). You will have poured the white wine into the bottom of their pot before placing it over heat. Once all the mussels are open, remove the shells to which they are not attached, working right over the pot.

To decant the cooking liquid, carefully pour it into a bowl. Taste it to be sure that it is not too salty, particularly since it must be reduced later. Keep the mussels warm in their pot.

Pour this mussel water into a sauté pan or, if necessary, a good frying pan. Add the mirepoix and the tomato. Boil it uncovered on a high heat, stirring with a wooden spoon until the liquid has reduced to 1 scant deciliter (3 1/3 fluid ounces, scant 1/2 cup).

Immediately add the mussels and the minced parsley. Toss everything to cover the mussels entirely in the sauce: only 1 minute. Turn the heat down very low. Then add the butter, divided into pieces the size of a walnut. Shake the pan in a circular motion to mix and melt the butter. Do not heat it to the point that it curdles, because the butter will turn into oil, but make sure that the mussels are still quite hot. Check the seasoning and finish with the cayenne pepper, *added sparingly.* Pour it into a warm timbale or vegetable dish or onto a warm shallow and serve very hot.

Mussels in Rich Mushroom Sauce *(Moules à la Poulette).* Two liters (8 1/2 cups) of mussels. Pour 3 deciliters (1 1/4 cups) of white wine into the pot used for opening the mussels.

Prepare the sauce (SEE SAUCE POULETTE, PAGE 61) with 25 grams (1 ounce) of flour and 35 grams (1 1/4 ounces, generous 2 tablespoons) of butter made into a blond roux.

Moisten with the mussel water, which should be 4 deciliters (1 2/3 cups) of liquid. Bind it with 2 egg yolks. Off the heat, add 30 grams of butter (1 ounce, 2 tablespoons) and the lemon juice. Put the mussels into the sauce in their shells. Serve in a shallow bowl or vegetable dish. Sprinkle with minced parsley.

Mussel Pilaf *(Pilaf de Moules).* This is a recipe that we particularly recommend. Refer to PAGE 451 to learn how to cook the rice. The liquid used is either bouillon or water with the mussel cooking water added to it. How much of this cooking water you will have is extremely variable; mussels that are not cooked the moment they are caught will inevitably have opened a little and lost some of their liquor. The water must be carefully collected because it lends a characteristic flavor to the dish. You should always make sure that it is not too salty.

You can, if you wish, replace the butter here with 2 tablespoons of olive oil. *Time: 1 scant hour. Serves 6.*

1 1/2 liters (6 1/3 cups) of small mussels; 175 grams (6 ounces) of Indian rice; 1 good tablespoon of minced onion; 50 grams (1 3/4 ounces, 3 1/2 tablespoons) of butter; 4 1/2–5 deciliters (about 2 cups) of liquid total; 1 tablespoon of tomato paste; a small clove of garlic; a bouquet garni; a pinch of saffron and a pinch of pepper.

PROCEDURE. Clean and open the mussels as has been directed, by adding 1 1/2 deciliters (5 fluid ounces, 2/3 cup) of water to the bottom of the pot. Then take the mussels out of their shells, holding them directly above the pot so that you do not lose any of their liquor. Gather the mussels that have been taken out of their shells on a separate plate. It is not essential to keep them very warm, which would risk toughening them; the rice will reheat them sufficiently. Decant the mussel water through a fine strainer into a bowl.

The rice: Sauté the minced onion and the rice as described. Moisten with the mussel water and complete it with bouillon or water in order to get the quantity of liquid necessary. Add the tomato paste, garlic, saffron, bouquet garni, pepper, and a little bit of salt since the mussel water will be salty enough.

Once the rice has been properly cooked, remove the bouquet and the clove of garlic, which will have risen to the surface. Using a wooden spoon, mix the mussels and the rice, stirring carefully so that you do not bruise the grain. Dress the pilaf in a warmed timbale or on a round plate, and serve very hot.

Snails *(Escargots)*

To satisfy those who truly appreciate snails and know how excellent they can be, snails should be prepared only when they are "sealed"—that is, from the end of October to the middle of March. If snails are harvested outside that time, it is essential before using them to make them fast for about fifteen days; otherwise, you risk being made ill by the plants they have eaten. So, during the summer, you can gather the snails as and when you need them, keeping them in a box and feeding them with salad (lettuce or chicory) to fatten them up. Snails that have withdrawn into their shell can easily be preserved during the winter, buried in sand.

There are different kinds of snail: The best, particularly for the dish à la bourguignonne, is the vineyard snail, which can be found under grapevines from Indian Summer (early fall) onward. When preparing this snail, it is customary to remove the black part, or "cloaca," at the end of the tail. We recommend doing this for snails à la bourguignonne, which is an authentic regional recipe. We must, however, record the opinion of a true connoisseur of snails, Dr. C—, who considers this black part of the snail to be one of its most delicate parts, because it is actually the snail's liver. Consequently, he thinks it should not be removed, particularly because he believes the best recipes to be those in which the shell of the snail is not removed. Furthermore, this is the methods used by the people of Poitou, as we will describe below.

Different snail recipes generally feature a sauce based on the court bouillon used to cook them. The ingredients for this court bouillon vary by region and, of course, preference: sage, mint, celery, fennel, etc., can be used as you choose, while thyme, bay, and parsley are the usual herbs. As for garlic, it is the essential condiment, and is readily available. We particularly recommend wild garlic, whose aroma is considered superior to cultivated garlic by true connoisseurs.

Whatever your chosen recipe, *the snails must always be previously washed and disgorged,* as described below. They do not always need to be blanched afterward, though this is recommended because it ensures that they are perfectly clean before being cooked in the court bouillon.

To clean the snails: Put the snails into a large receptacle, either a basin or terrine. Cover them with generous amounts of cold water and scrub the shells thoroughly to rid them of all traces of dirt. Take them out of the receptacle with your hand, and then put them in a large strainer or in a basket. Pour out the water. Rinse the receptacle, add the snails and cover with fresh water, then wash them a second time. If this water is a little unclear, rinse for a third time in fresh water.

Drain the snails. If they are blocked, detach their partition with the point of a small knife. Then one by one, throw them in a terrine where they can be easily stirred. Sprinkle them with gray sea salt (two handfuls for 4 dozen snails) and pour some vinegar on top of them (a large glass).

Stir quickly with the handle of a wooden spoon in the center of the tureen to mix the snails and to spread the salt and the vinegar thoroughly. Let them stand *for 2 hours.* During this time, stir them several times more so that they will absorb the salt and the vinegar, which causes the snails to release their slime and silt in the form of foam. At the end of this time, wash them again in two changes of water, stirring them around with the spoon to completely rinse the shells of the mucus that covers them. A properly cleaned snail will have no slimy traces at the opening of its shell. Once they are clean, drain them.

To blanch: Put the snails in a pot or a container of an appropriate size for cooking: for 4 dozen snails, you will need a container of 7 or 8 liters (7½–8½ quarts). Cover with a generous amount of cold water and heat everything slowly to bring to a boil. As it does so, remove the scum produced by the remaining silt released by the snails. Let it boil for *8–10 minutes,* then drain them and rinse again in fresh water.

Snails à la Bourguignonne *(Escargots à la bourguignonne).* *Time: 7 hours (of which 3 hours is preparation).*

To prepare the snails, clean them, disgorge, and blanch, then cook them in a court bouillon. Take them out of their shells and sauté them in the pan with butter and seasoning. This is to flavor the snails, which will have absorbed little flavor from the court bouillon. It also has the benefit of helping to preserve the snails for a long time, since the butter coating them acts as an insulator. The snails are then put back into their shells and stuffed with "snail butter," which is butter mixed with shallot, garlic, parsley, etc. Lightly coated with bread crumbs and moistened with white wine, they are then put into a very hot oven for 7–8 minutes before serving. The recipe given below is by the famous chef Philèas Gilbert, who is from Burgundy.

Allow about 6 snails per person. This naturally assumes that you use the nice large snails that are best for this recipe.

For the court bouillon: 4 dozen snails; 1¼ bottles of ordinary white wine; 2½ liters (10½ cups) of water; 30 grams (1 ounce) of gray sea salt; 10 peppercorns; 8 shallots; 5 cloves of garlic; 1 nice carrot (150 grams/5⅓ ounces) cut into thick rounds; a large onion (150 grams/5⅓ ounces) stuck with a clove; a substantial bouquet of parsley branches with their leaves, garnished with 1 sprig of thyme and 1 bay leaf.

To cook: Once the snails have been blanched, put them back into their rinsed pan. Add the rest of the ingredients and bring it to a boil. Skim and then cover the pan and set it up so that you can maintain a very gentle, uninterrupted steady simmer for *3½ hours.*

For sautéing the snails in the frying pan: Fifty grams (1¾ ounces, 3½ tablespoons) of butter; 10 grams (⅓ ounce) of fine salt; a good strong pinch of pepper; a pinch of spices; 5 shallots finely minced; a clove of garlic crushed under the point of a knife.

Once the snails have been cooked, put them in a drum sieve *(tamis)* while they are still burning hot. In order not to bruise, pull them out of their shells using a cooking needle. Immediately cut off the black end and put them on a plate.

Heat the butter in a pan. Throw in the snails. Add the rest of the ingredients listed above. Sauté the snails *for 5 minutes without letting them color,* then pour them into a small terrine and cover them with a round of buttered paper. Keep them cool until you are ready to stuff them.

To stuff and serve the snails: Once you have pulled them out of their shells, wash the shells thoroughly and shake them so that all the water runs out of them. Then place them with the opening facing down in a large drum sieve *(tamis)* or on a rack in order to dry them.

Snail Butter *(Le Beurre d' Escargots).* This can be prepared in advance and kept cool. For a very fine and smooth butter, use a mortar and a pestle to mix the different ingredients. Otherwise, knead all the ingredients until thoroughly mixed.

4 dozen nice snails; 400 grams (14⅛ ounces, 1¾ cups) of butter; 80 grams (2¾ ounces) of shallot and 60 grams (2¼ ounces) of parsley leaves that have been very finely minced; 25 grams (1 ounce) of garlic smashed with the blade of a large knife; 25 grams (1 ounce) of fine salt; 7 grams (¼ ounce) of pepper; 2 grams (1/14 ounce) of spices.

To stuff: First insert a piece of butter about the size of a small bean into the bottom of a shell, then put the snail back in. Plug the opening of the shell with butter, tapping it down firmly with your thumb. If you keep them cool, you can store the snails like this for as long as is possible without the butter going rancid.

To serve: If you do not have the particular serving dish known as an "escargotière," use either an ovenproof porcelain plate, or another plate that can be taken to the table. Egg plates are appropriate for this use; a plate that holds 2 eggs is just the right size for 6 snails.

Arrange the snails on the plates with the opening facing up, leaning them against the other so they do not tip over. Sprinkle over a small amount of fine bread crumbs. On each snail, put a small piece of butter the size of a pea and moisten it with a little bit of white wine (use about 1 good tablespoon for 6 snails).

Put the plate into a good hot oven for *7–8 minutes.* Serve immediately because the butter must still be sizzling when the snails arrive at the table.

Snails in the Style of Poitou *(Escargots à la Mode du Poitou).* This traditional rustic recipe is one of the simplest and one of the best because the snails are not taken out of their shells. The sauce is so flavorsome that it can be eaten separately by dipping your bread into it.

For this dish the large vineyard snails are preferable. They must be cleaned meticulously because the snails are not first cooked in a court bouillon, which releases their mucus and allows it to be skimmed off. *Time: 5 hours (of which 3 hours is preparation).*

4 dozen large snails: 125 grams (4 1/2 ounces, 9 tablespoons) of butter; 20 grams of flour (2/3 ounce); 25 grams (1 ounce) of stale bread (about the size of an egg); at least 10 grams (1/3 ounce) of garlic (2 cloves); 15 grams (1/2 ounce) of fine salt; 2 bay leaves; 3 or 4 sprigs of parsley; 8 deciliters of boiling water (4 ordinary glasses; 3 3/8 cups); a nice pinch of ground pepper.

PROCEDURE. Clean and disgorge the snails completely, as previously described. After washing them, dry them one by one by tapping each to remove the water and the mucous threads. Then place them one by one on a kitchen towel.

The seasoning: Prepare this while the snails are disgorging. Use only the *leaves* of the parsley. Add them to the grated bread crumbs. Squash the garlic with the blade of a large knife. Chop everything together very carefully to make it as fine as a powder. Mix in the flour and hold it on the side.

To cook: Use a pan large enough so that the snails are not too crowded. Heat the butter in it and then put in the snails. On low heat and without a cover, let them sauté *for 8–10 minutes* while frequently shaking the pan. You need enough heat to seal the snails, but the butter must not color.

Once they have absorbed the butter, the snails will begin to give off a wonderful characteristic odor. Sprinkle them with the prepared minced ingredients. Shake the pan sufficiently to mix everything. Let it cook for *3–4 minutes,* shaking it throughout. Then, while shaking the pan, add the boiling water. Add salt, pepper, bay. Once it has started to boil, turn the heat down very low. Cover and leave a small opening between the cover and the pan so that the liquid will reduce: about the width of a finger. Cook for *2 1/2 hours* at a very gentle, steady simmer that is apparent in only one or two places in the liquid.

During this time, mix the snails four or five times to bring those at the bottom to the top. Toward the end of the cooking time, the reduced sauce will expose the snails on the top; you will therefore need to mix them a little more often, although the shells will have absorbed enough liquid to cook the snails. By the time they are ready to serve, the sauce will have been reduced by about half and will attach to the shells like a syrup. Taste, and add more salt if needed. Serve in a timbale or on a very well heated plate.

Frogs *(Grenouilles)*

The only edible part of frogs are the hindquarters, which is how you buy them, strung on wooden skewers. Freshness is of paramount importance, and can be judged by the appearance of the skin, which should be taut and shiny. As well as the classic recipe *à la Poulette,* you can prepare frogs in several ways. Whatever the recipe, you always cut off their webbed feet with scissors.

Sautéed Frog's Legs *(Grenouilles Sautées).* *Time: 30 minutes.* Season with salt and pepper, then sauté in butter in a pan over a strong heat to season and color them well. Arrange on a plate or a timbale and moisten with lemon juice, then finally, sprinkle with freshly chopped parsley.

Or, dip in flour and sauté in the pan, using a

few tablespoons of good olive oil instead of butter. If you wish, add a little bit of garlic.

Fried Frog's Legs *(Grenouilles Frites).* Marinate for 1 hour in advance with salt, pepper, lemon juice, a little bit of oil, some minced parsley, and, if you wish, a small bit of garlic crushed under a blade of a knife. Then dip into a light frying batter and deep-fry. Serve with fried parsley. Or do not marinate, but dip in flour and bread crumbs (SEE PAGE 19). Deep-fry, then serve with lemon quarters.

Frog's Legs in Fines Herbes *(Grenouilles aux Fines Herbes).* Soften some minced onion in butter over low heat; add the legs and sauté them to a golden color with the onion. Season with salt, pepper, and nutmeg; add 1/2 of a bay leaf and a touch of garlic. Sprinkle with white wine (2 deciliters/6 3/4 fluid ounces/7/8 cup for 3 dozen frogs). Reduce it on a strong heat. Serve the frog's legs sprinkled with minced parsley and lemon juice.

Frog's Legs in Rich Mushroom Sauce *(Grenouilles à la Poulette).* Put the frog's legs in a tureen of cold water with a little bit of milk. Let them disgorge for 1 good hour.

To cook: Prepare a court bouillon with carrot and onion, gently sautéed in butter, using 40 grams (1 3/8 ounces) of each and 20 grams (2/3 ounce, 1 heaping tablespoon) of butter, without letting the vegetables color. Add the white of a leek. Moisten with 7 1/2 deciliters (generous 3 cups) of warm water and 2 1/2 deciliters (1 cup) of white wine. Add 12 grams of salt (3/8 ounce) and a bouquet of parsley.

Drain the frog's legs well, then plunge into the court bouillon. Bring it to a boil. Then turn the heat down very low. From this moment, simmer gently for *25 minutes.* At the end of 15 minutes, add 4 or 5 peppercorns; do not add earlier because they will make the dish too acrid. Before taking out the legs, check that they are done by lightly pinching the flesh, which should be tender.

Sauce poulette: Make in the same way as SAUCE POULETTE (PAGE 61). But for the liquid, use the court bouillon from cooking the frogs. Thus, for 3 dozen frogs: a little white roux with 20 grams of butter (2/3 ounce, 1 heaping tablespoon) and the same of flour diluted with 3 deciliters (1 1/4 cups) of bouillon. Add pepper and nutmeg. Let simmer *for 10–12 minutes.* Make the liaison with 2 or 3 egg yolks mixed with 3 tablespoons of crème fraîche, if possible, though it is not essential. Off the heat, add 30 grams (1 ounce, 2 tablespoons) of butter and the juice of 1/4 lemon.

This sauce should be prepared in a small sauté pan, which lets you more easily mix and sauté the frog's legs. Drain them carefully just before serving, then pour into a timbale or a well-heated shallow bowl. Sprinkle 1 teaspoon of minced parsley on everything.

NOTE. These are excellent served in a vol-au-vent shell.

MEATS

BEEF
Boeuf

Beefsteaks and Rib Steaks
(Bifteks et Entrecôtes)

These are always lunch dishes: both in the restaurant and at home. There is no difference between an *entrecôte* (rib steak) or a *biftek* (beefsteak); both refer to a beefsteak. In fact, *biftek* is an example of the French adopting an English term and making it their own. It seems particularly apt for describing meat that is grilled and simply served on a maître d'hôtel butter, accompanied only by potatoes: the popular beefsteak with French fried potatoes is simply a variant of this. The rib steak can be sautéed as well as grilled, and prepared in many different ways, all simple enough, with a sauce and a garnish.

Choosing the steaks: From what part of the beef should the steak come? It doesn't really matter because any tender part of the beef can furnish them. Normally a classic beefsteak is cut on the fillet, but, in practice, for reasons of economy, it is often substituted with sirloin or rump steak. Rump steak comes from the croup along the spine between the sirloin and the tail.

No matter what part of the beef it is cut from, a beefsteak should be around $2^1/_2$ centimeters (1 inch) thick. Thinner than that, the meat dries out on the inside before the outside has had time to acquire that beautiful crispness that is one of the pleasures of grilled meat.

The rib steak is meat taken from between the two ribs, but it is a rather large piece and should not be used when serving two or three people. This is simply because you will need too much meat for slices of the optimal thickness—at least 2 or 3 centimeters ($^3/_4$–$1^1/_4$ inches). If you tried using less meat, it would have to be cut very thin, producing only a meat without juice, which would be dried out even by the most careful cooking.

Furthermore, there is no advantage in using a rib steak since there will be a lot of waste, particularly when the meat is of a good quality—in other words, marbled with fat. For these reasons, a sirloin is often substituted for a rib steak even when the menu refers to "rib steak."

When the number of guests means that you need a large quantity of meat, do not choose one large piece of meat but two or three pieces, each of the proper thickness (never more) Choose steaks from a medium-sized sirloin. Grill or sauté the meat according to the recipe, which is usually simple, and also according to the equipment in your kitchen.

For beefsteaks and rib steaks, you should allow 125 grams ($4^1/_2$ ounces) of meat per person, trimmed of all waste. "Waste" means both the nerves and the fat. True steak lovers can, of course, leave a little bit of the fat on the meat—on a rump steak, for example, or a fillet, where there is not a great deal of fat. Never leave fat on a sirloin steak, but take off the fatty part running along the edge.

To sauté beefsteaks, rib steaks, rum steaks, tournedos, cutlets, etc.: You can, as described in the article about fats, use a good oil or clarified butter. But nothing is better than sustained by oil; so to sauté a rib steak or rump steak, use 30 grams of butter (1 ounce, 2 tablespoons) and 40 grams ($1^3/_8$ ounces) of oil.

It is the thickness of the steak, and not the total weight, that determines the cooking time here. The time indicated is applicable for meats that are no more than $2^1/_2$ centimeters (1 inch) thick.

Heat the pan on a rather strong heat until a *light* smoke rises from the pan: this indicates that the fat is now hot enough to seal the meat, thus preventing any of the juices inside from escaping.

Lightly sprinkle the meat with salt and pepper, then put the meat into this smoking oil. Keep the sauté pan on the same heat. Leave the meat there without turning it *for 4 minutes* if you want it bloody and very red; and *for 5 minutes* if you want it medium-rare—that is, nice and rosy and juicy. You can lift it up with a fork to ensure that the hot oil has spread equally under it, but do not turn it over.

At the end of the cooking time, check that the meat on the underside is a beautiful brown, then turn the meat to seal it on the other side and cook for the same time: thus, *4 or 5 minutes.* Turn the heat down a little bit when you notice that the oil in the sauté pan has gotten hotter than required.

To turn the meat over, do not use a fork, which would pierce the meat, thus releasing all the juices we have tried so carefully to contain. Either lift it with two forks or, better still, a spatula.

Checking that the meat has been properly cooked is the same as for grilled meat: drops of juice forming on the surface of the meat indicate that it is cooked medium-rare, meaning that the inside of the meat will be rosy and juicy. And when you push your finger on the meat, you will feel some resistance. Meat that is still red and bloody on the inside does not release pearls of juice, and when you touch it, it is soft and yielding.

Bitoques, or Russian Beefsteaks *(Bitoques, ou Bifteks Russes).* This is a hash of raw beef, which is formed into little beefsteaks, and these are then sautéed in the pan. We suggest serving the *bitoques* with sour cream, as the Russians do. If you do not have sour cream, add a few drops of lemon to crème fraîche. *Bitoques* may also be served with a pepper sauce, a tomato sauce, sauce béarnaise, etc. *Time: 45 minutes (of which 12 minutes is cooking). Serves 6.*

400 grams (14 1/8 ounces) net weight of a good lean beef in slices; 125 grams (4 1/2 ounces, 9 tablespoons) of butter; a good pinch of salt and a pinch of pepper; 6 good teaspoons of stale bread crumbs soaked in milk; 3 tablespoons of sour cream and 3 tablespoons of bouillon.

PROCEDURE. Mince this meat by hand with a good knife. Do not use a grinder or food processor because it grinds the meat too fine and squashes it.

Cut the meat into small bits; remove all the nerves, skin, fat. Add salt and pepper and start to chop it coarsely. Add the bread crumbs, which have been soaked and then well squeezed, and the butter divided into small bits. Continue to mince until you have a fine hash in which all three ingredients are thoroughly mixed.

Generously sprinkle the board with flour. Divide the hash into 6 equal parts. Roll each part into an egg shape with the floured palm of your hand. Flatten the eggs to make an oval about 1 1/2 centimeters (5/8 inch) thick and turn them over on the floured board once or twice.

Heat either clarified butter or oil in a sauté pan until it gives off a light smoke. Arrange the *bitoques* side by side, then turn the heat down, allowing them to cook gently, turning them over from time to time.

As soon as they are ready, arrange the *bitoques* on a warmed plate, then quickly drain the grease from the sauté pan. Pour in the cream and the bouillon. Scrape the bottom of the pan with the wooden spoon to loosen and dissolve any crispy bits. Boil for only *2 or 3 seconds* and pour it over the *bitoques,* arranged in a crown.

Steak Tartar *(Biftek Tartare).* Tartar steak is a culinary fantasy made of raw ingredients.

150 grams (5 1/3 ounces) of fillet or of sirloin of beef; 1 egg yolk; salt; pepper; mustard; 1 tablespoon of oil and 1 tablespoon of vinegar; 1 level tablespoon of minced onion; 1 tablespoon of parsley and minced capers; Worcestershire sauce and whiskey.

PROCEDURE. Remove the fat and the nerves from the meat and chop it finely with a cleaver, a good kitchen knife, or a hand chopper (do not use mechanical choppers, which tear the meat and let the juice escape). Place the hash in a bowl and then with 2 forks, one in each hand, break up the hash. Add the egg yolks and all the seasoning, which can be adjusted to taste. Mix everything thoroughly. Then use a fork to reform the hash into the shape and thickness of a beefsteak, and slide it onto the serving plate.

Chateaubriand *(Le Chateaubriand).* *Time: 20–24 minutes. Allow* 20–24 minutes *for the chateaubriand to be fully cooked: rosy and quite juicy in the center.*

The chateaubriand (or *châteaubriant*) is a dish somewhere between a beefsteak and a roast, and it

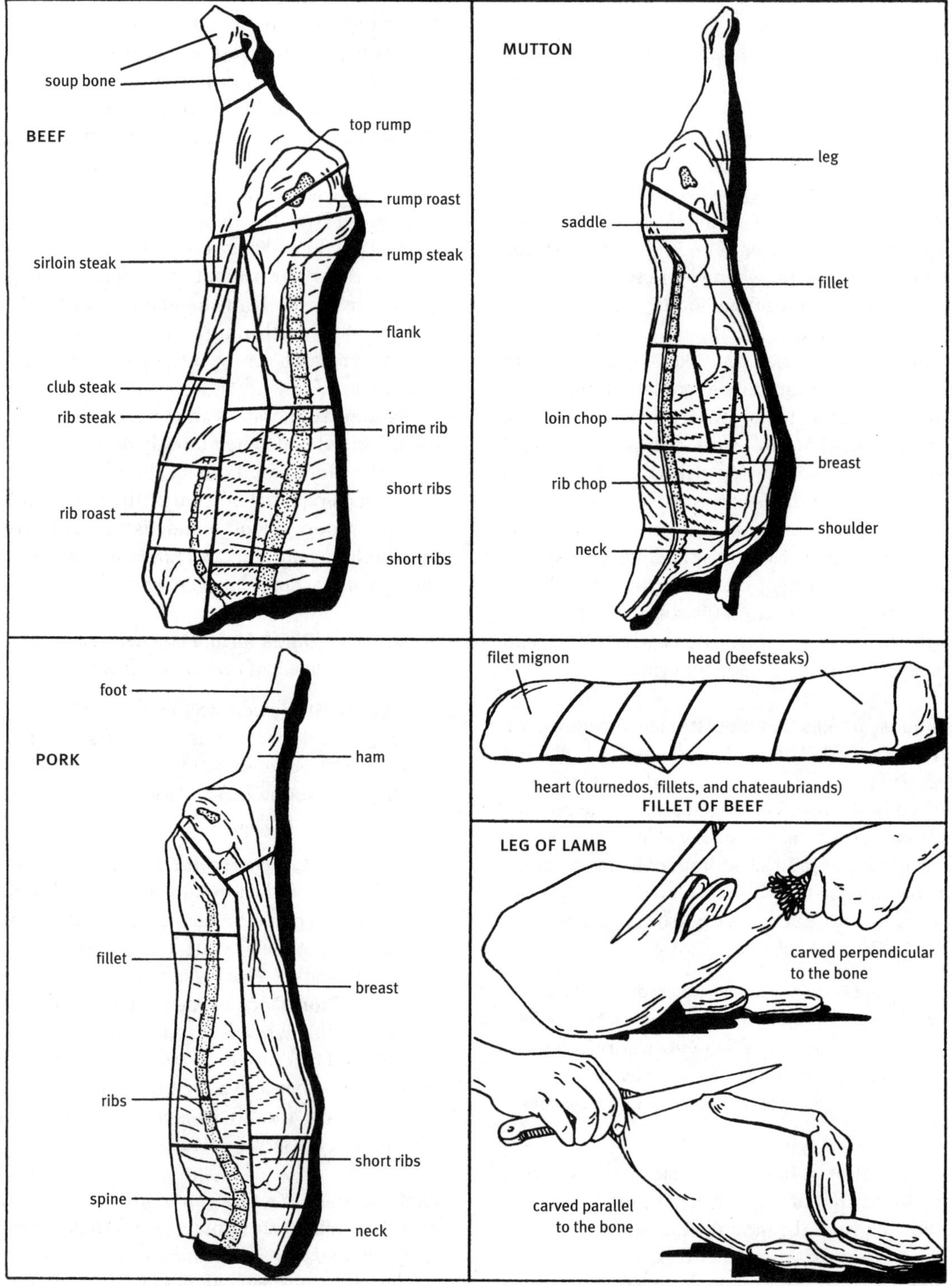

FIG. 47. DIFFERENT PARTS OF BEEF, MUTTON, AND PORK.

has long been the pièce de resistance at lunch, when traditionally, large pieces of roast meat are not served. So be generous calculating the quantities.

The chateaubriand is a piece of fillet taken "from the heart," as the professionals say. That is, from the absolute middle of the very center of a fillet of an entire beef. You should cut it to double the thickness of an ordinary beefsteak: that is, 4 or 5 centimeters (1½–2 inches) thick. Any thicker, and when you cook it on the grill, it will be difficult to ensure that the meat is perfectly cooked inside without the outside drying out.

To make sure that the fillet is the correct size for a chateaubriand, you must allow 500–600 grams (1 pound, 2–5 ounces) of trimmed meat. Less than this weight and the meat will be thinner than required, making it no more than a simple grilled fillet.

By "trimmed fillets", we mean fillets from which the stringy meat attaching it to the backbone or spine has been removed, along with all the skin and fat.

To grill the chateaubriand: Hit it several times with the blade of a cleaver to flatten and compact the meat. Moisten with melted butter. Grill it as directed (PAGE 35). Remember that the thickness of the chateaubriand means that, once it has been sealed on both sides, it must be grilled *on low heat.* Otherwise, given the length of cooking time needed for a piece of meat this thick, the browned layer will burn, preventing the heat from reaching the inside; the result will be meat that is charred on the outside and raw inside. While cooking, brush the meat with melted butter to prevent charring.

Chateaubriand can be served in the same way as rib steaks and tournedos. The most current and the most classic is to serve it on maître d'hôtel butter, offering on the same plate "château" potatoes, which are named after the dish.

Different Ways of Serving Rib Steak

In its many variants, rib steak is usually covered or surrounded by the sauce. However, if preferred, you can serve the sauce alongside in a sauceboat.

To serve rib steaks and beefsteaks with any kind of butter, including maître d'hotel: First soften the butter in a cup to make a paste. *Gently* warm the plate; if the plate is burning hot, the butter will melt into an oil instead of staying creamy. Spread half the butter on a plate. Place the beefsteak on top and cover it with the rest of the butter.

To serve the grilled rib steak with sauce accompanying it: In fine restaurants serving haute cuisine, the steak is lightly covered with a melted glaze of meat to give it some shine. Instead of this glaze, you could spread the meat with a bit of butter stuck on the tip of a knife.

Rib Steak Béarnaise ***(Entrecôte à la Béarnaise).*** Grilled. Served on a long platter with potatoes sautéed in butter at either end. Sauce béarnaise is laid in a thick ribbon around the rib steak or served on the side in a sauceboat. SEE SAUCE BÉARNAISE (PAGE 75).

Rib Steak à la Bercy ***(Entrecôte à la Bercy).*** Grilled. Served with Bercy butter (PAGE 79) using 50 grams (1¾ ounces, 3½ tablespoons) of butter for a rib steak weighing 400 grams (14⅛ ounces).

Rib Steak à la Bordelaise ***(Entrecôte à la Bordelaise).*** Grilled or sautéed. Place rounds of poached beef marrow on top. Cover everything with sauce bordelaise (SEE PAGE 57).

Rib Steak with Mushrooms ***(Entrecôte aux Champignons).*** Sautéed. Proceed as for tournedos (SEE PAGE 259).

Rib Steak à la Maître d'Hôtel ***(Entrecôte à la Maître d'Hôtel).*** Sauté, then deglaze. That is, for a rib steak of 400 grams (14⅛ ounces), add 3 tablespoons of white wine to the browned juices in the sauté pan and reduce to 1 tablespoon; put the maître d'hôtel butter on top of the rib steak, then spoon over the juices.

Rib Steak à la Mirabeau ***(Entrecôte à la Mirabeau).*** Grilled. Served on an anchovy butter and garnished with fillets of salted anchovies, pitted olives, and leaves of tarragon, with a tuft of watercress at either end.

Rib Steak with Tomato ***(Entrecôte à la Tomate).*** Sautéed or grilled. Surrounded with a fondue of tomatoes (SEE PAGE 534).

BEEF À LA MODE
Le Boeuf à la Mode

Beef à la mode has variations, but the basis is always the same: a piece of beef, preferably taken from the rump, larded throughout with large lardons and cooked with onions, carrots, and one veal foot. The last ingredient is essential, giving the juices that jellied texture so characteristic of beef à la mode; a roux is never used for thickening. To stop the beef from drying out, add bouillon or even water mixed with red or white wine. The key to this dish is slow and prolonged cooking with a heat source both above and below—in other words, in the oven.

In very simple home cooking, the onions and the carrots of the stock are cooked with the meat. But the long cooking time means they lose their juices, diminishing their flavor, and the onion itself dissolves and is no longer attractive.

This is why the more refined chefs will serve Beef à la Mode accompanied with a garnish of onions and carrots that have been prepared separately and that have not been cooked with the beef; those vegetables that are cooked with meat are there only to provide flavor. The garnish is added to the beef long enough only to, as it were, blend with the juices. Make sure you do this for the onions, at least. If necessary, serve the carrots cooked with the meat, as long as you have cut these large enough to withstand the long cooking time.

An initial marinade in the wine and the aromatics used for the cooking will give the beef a pleasant flavor. This marinade does not require additional expense because all the ingredients will be used in the cooking; the variable is how they will be used. The only drawback is the time needed. Allow at least 6 hours for the meats to be sufficiently impregnated; but if circumstances and the temperature allow, you can let it marinate for up to 24 hours, being careful to turn the meat from time to time.

In modern kitchens, the beef is usually lightly browned before any liquid is added to moisten it.

Use a bouillon, prepared in advance with the bones and trimmings from the beef (SEE POT-AU-FEU, PAGE 81). This is preferable to adding the raw bones straight to the meat, which requires using a pot that is too large and also uses too much liquid.

The pan: See the article on braising (PAGE 26). Remember that the meat will shrink a great deal while cooking, so choose a pan of the right size.

Choice of the cut: The unanimous preference is rump. This meat is the least dry, the most savory, and the most likely to be able to provide one whole piece; it also has a light layer of fat, which improves both the appearance and the flavor. Have the piece cut a little long but thick; thickness is essential so that the volume of the meat does not diminish too much during the cooking and it also keeps enough of its juice.

It is always preferable to lard the piece at home because then you can season the lardons, which the butcher would not do. If you let him prepare the meat for you, do not allow him to surround this piece with lard or other fat, which would keep the meat from browning. Use string to tie up the meat, turning it tightly four or five turns crosswise and lengthwise to make a dome that will become less pronounced when the meat shrinks due to compression of the flesh during cooking.

The weight of the piece: This should not be less than 1.3 kilograms (2 pounds, 14 ounces). For such slow and prolonged cooking, a smaller piece will not give a good result. If the amount is too large for one meal, you can serve the leftovers in a gelée for a cold meal, which many prefer to warm beef.

You will have the best result with a piece that weighs about 2¼ kilograms (5 pounds), but you must not exceed this weight by much, or both the preparation and cooking will become more complicated.

The juice or the sauce for the beef: Generally, for home cooking it is sufficient to degrease the cooking juice without reducing it before you pour it over the beef and vegetables. However, this will not give you the syrupy consistency desired, nor is it flavor strong enough, particularly if the dish has been moistened with water instead of bouillon. This is why reducing is so important. If you do not care that much about the consistency of the warm juices, and if you wish to keep some of the juices to make the gelée that accompanies the cold leftovers, you can abridge the reduction. The minimum requirement is that the liquid used will have reduced by *half* at the end of the cooking time, which is the normal proportion for reductions.

In haute cuisine, the juices are considerably reduced after cooking. The purpose of this is to give the juice the consistency of a demi-glace without the addition of starch: assume 1 good deciliter (3 1/3 fluid ounces, 1/2 cup) of reduced juice for every 450 grams (1 pound) of meat.

To thicken juices that you have not reduced, make a liaison with starch or arrowroot before serving (SEE LIAISONS, PAGE 47). Put the juice into a small saucepan and thoroughly degrease it. Thicken as directed, using scant 1/2 teaspoon of arrowroot for each deciliter (3 1/3 fluid ounces, scant 1/2 cup) of juice. Do not forget that a *light, barely syrupy* consistency is the hallmark of the juice of a good beef à la mode.

Cooking time: In the following recipes, we have allowed *about 4 hours* of braising—slow cooking in the oven—for 3 pounds of meat. For a larger piece of meat, say 2 1/4–2 3/4 kilograms (5–6 pounds), allow a half hour to an hour more.

NOTES. Before straining the juice, always make sure that the meat has been properly cooked: check by sticking a cooking needle into the meat; it should pierce the meat easily and also come out equally easily.

Once the beef has been properly cooked, it can wait for a rather long time kept warm in its pan. You then have plenty of time to strain the juice and proceed with the final preparations.

Home-Style Beef à la Mode *(Boeuf à la Mode à la Ménagère).* A very simple method, which uses the vegetables from the cooking to garnish the beef. *Time: 4 1/2 hours (once the beef has been prepared for cooking).*

1 1/2 kilograms (3 pounds, 5 ounces) of beef, net weight without bone; 150 grams (5 1/3 ounces) of fatback bacon for larding; 250 grams (8 7/8 ounces) of carrots; 150 grams (5 1/3 ounces) of onions; 1 medium-sized veal foot.

1 liter (4 1/4 cups) of water or of bouillon prepared with the bone; 1 deciliter (3 1/3 fluid ounces, scant 1/2 cup) of red or white wine; 1 small glass of eau de vie; a bouquet garni; 10 grams (1/3 ounce) of salt and a pinch of pepper; 2 tablespoons of fat taken from a marmite or a previous roast or stock.

PROCEDURE. Lard the piece as directed (SEE PAGE 11).

Heat the fat in the pan that you are planning to use. Brown the beef to a nice color on all sides; this should take about 20 minutes.

Meanwhile, prepare the veal foot (SEE PAGE 307).

Once the beef has been browned, drain all the fat from its pan. Pour the wine and cognac on the beef. Boil it without a cover on strong heat, turning the piece of meat until this liquid is reduced to 1 or 2 tablespoons.

Then add the veal foot, the bacon rind, the onion, the bouquet garni, pepper and salt, and either the water or the bouillon made from the bones. The liquid must reach to about half the height of the piece of meat.

Bring it to a boil on strong heat. Skim it, then cover the pan tightly. Put it in the oven. From this point, allow 4 hours at a gentle, constant, regular simmer.

During this time, make sure you turn the meat at least three or four times.

The carrots: Grate or peel the carrots, depending on their quality, then cut into quarters, and divide each quarter into two lengthwise. Remove all of the inner yellow part.

According to whether or not they are new or late season, add the carrots to the beef in the middle of the cooking: that is, after 1 or 2 hours. This will disrupt the simmering, so make sure that it starts again.

To serve: Put the beef on a good, hot plate. Remove the string. Lightly trim the fat. Then surround it with the onions and the carrots, well drained of any fat in a small strainer, and the veal foot, cut into small pieces, if your guests will appreciate it; otherwise, leave it in the pan. Keep it warm.

Strain and degrease 1/2 liter (generous 2 cups) of the cooking juice. Boil it rapidly, uncovered, to reduce it to about 3 deciliters (1 1/4 cups). If the consistency does not seem sufficiently syrupy to you, thicken it as described above. Pour it over the beef and the carrots to glaze. Serve.

The leftovers: In the pan containing the rest of

the juices and the veal foot (if it has not been served immediately), add about 3 deciliters (1 1/4 cups) of water and a pinch of salt. Cover and boil it gently for 1 good hour. Degrease and pour it over the beef that has been cut and surrounded by vegetables. Keep it cool.

Beef à la Mode à la Bourgeoise *(Boeuf à la Mode à la Bourgeoise).* This recipe, a classic of haute cuisine, has a separate garnish of onions and carrots as well as a marinade of wine and aromatics, including onions and carrots, etc., which are used only to cook the beef. *Time: 5 hours at least (once the beef has been larded and marinated in advance).*

1 1/2 kilograms (3 pounds, 5 ounces) of beef, net weight without bones; 1 large veal foot; 150 grams (5 1/3 ounces) of fatback bacon for barding; 1 liter (4 1/4 cups) of bouillon, very little salted or not at all salted; 2 tablespoons of fat taken from a marmite or previous roast or stock.

***For the marinade:* 4 deciliters (1 2/3 cups) of wine (white or red); 150 grams (5 1/3 ounces) of onion and 200 grams (7 ounces) of carrots cut into rounds; 3 or 4 stems of parsley without leaves; a small sprig of thyme; 1/2 of a bay leaf; salt, pepper, spices; that is: 10 grams (1/3 ounce) of salt mixed with 2 grams (1/14 ounce) of pepper and 2 grams (1/14 ounce) of spices.**

***For the garnish:* 2 dozen small onions; the same amount of carrots cut in the shape of an olive or small new carrots in season; 1/2 liter (generous 2 cups) of bouillon to cook them.**

PROCEDURE. Cut the lardons for the length of the piece of beef into pieces about 1 centimeter (1/2 inch) thick—a half dozen of these large lardons will suffice. Roll them in the salt, pepper, and spices mixed on a plate—along with, according to preference, a piece of garlic the size of a pea, crushed under the blade of a knife, as well as a little bit of parsley that has been very finely minced. Lard the piece as described (SEE PAGE 11).

With your hands, rub the meat with the salt and spices to well season all its surfaces. Tie the piece and put it in a terrine; you'll probably have to squeeze it in. Moisten it with the wine. Put on top and all around the rounds of onion, carrots, thyme, etc.

To cook: Remove the beef from the marinade. Drain it and wipe away all traces of the aromatics. Then rub the meat with a towel to dry it thoroughly. If you do not do this, it will not color in the hot fat and will boil instead of browning. In the chosen utensil, heat the fat. Color the beef to a nice tint on all of its surfaces. Meanwhile, prepare the veal foot (SEE PAGE 307).

Once the beef has been colored, drain all the fat from the pan. Pour in the marinade with all its ingredients. On strong heat and without a cover, boil it while turning the meat over several times so that it completely absorbs the seasoning. When all the liquid has been reduced, pour in the bouillon. Add the bound veal foot. Bring everything to a boil on strong heat. Skim, then tightly cover the pan. Put it in the oven. From this point, allow *4 hours at a regular, uninterrupted simmer,* turning the meat three or four times.

Also, remember that the veal foot cooks faster than the beef, so take it out as soon as it is tender when you touch it with your finger. Then cut it into small pieces about 2 centimeters (3/4 inch) square. These will be returned to the pan later, and it is not worth trying to keep them warm in the meantime.

While the beef is cooking, prepare the garnish of small onions and carrots (SEE SMALL ONIONS COLORED FOR GARNISH, PAGE 525, AND CARROTS FOR GARNISH, PAGE 484). Make sure they are slightly undercooked, because they will be added to the pan to finish cooking in the beef cooking liquid about a half hour before serving.

Final preparation: Once the beef has been cooked properly, take it out of the pan and put it on a plate. Lightly trim its fat, scraping it with a good, large knife. Pass the juice through the chinois into a bowl. Return the beef, with the fat part facing up, to the pan used to cook it, having first removed what's left of the vegetables but without having rinsed the pan.

Completely degrease the juice. You should find you have at least 5 full deciliters (generous 2 cups). Pour the juice on the beef. Surround the meat with the carrots and onions and the pieces of veal foot.

Return the pan to the oven without a cover to glaze the meat and also so that the vegetable garnish finishes cooking in the juice. *Allow just a scant half hour for this,* and baste the meat frequently with the juice. The juice will now reduce to about 3 good deciliters ($1^1/_4$ cups), just enough to sauce the meat and its garnish. It should then have a light, syrupy consistency; if you do not think it is syrupy enough, add a hint of starch (SEE LIAISONS, PAGE 47). Arrange the meat on a warm plate. Place the garnish all around it. Pour the juice over everything. Serve.

Leftovers: Line up the pieces of beef in a shallow plate or in the bottom of a terrine; arrange the vegetables around it. Pour the juice over everything, then put it somewhere cool to gel. To serve, very briefly heat the bottom of the utensil just enough to unmold it onto the serving plate.

Cold Beef à la Mode *(Boeuf à la Mode Froid).* If you intend to serve the beef cold, prepare it the same way as for warm beef à la mode. After cooking, trim the piece. Arrange some of the vegetables and veal foot symmetrically on a salad plate or in a tureen or any mold, then put the meat on top; arrange the rest of the vegetables and veal foot around the meat. Straining them through a strainer, pour the completely degreased but not reduced juices over everything. You can, if you like, add a little Madeira wine at this point. Let it gel. When ready to serve, unmold it onto a serving plate. For the gelée, the juices do not need to be clarified, particularly if they are not cloudy—which they will not be if this dish has been cooked with due care.

Fillet of Beef *(Le Filet de Boeuf)*

For a meal with many guests, a nice fillet of beef is a perennial favorite, roasted or braised and accompanied by a seasonal garnish. Choose a large, whole fillet. If you have fewer than 15 people to serve, it is best to use only the middle, thickest part and to reserve the thinner ends for other preparations like tournedos, fillets, etc. This is to ensure that the meat cooks evenly; otherwise, the thinner parts will be overcooked and the rest undercooked.

If you are going to trim the fillet yourself at home—that is, remove the membrane and fatty parts—remember that you will lose, on average, about a third of its weight. Remember, too, that this average varies, depending on whether or not the fillet has a lot of fat, which is actually an indication of the meat's excellence. Always take great care, whether braising or roasting the meat, to weigh it once it has been trimmed so that you can calculate the exact cooking time.

The amount of meat per person varies a bit according to the rest of the menu, and also the age and sex of the guests. It can range from 80 grams to 100, 110, and even 120 grams (from $2^3/_4$ ounces to $3^1/_2$, $3^7/_8$, even $4^1/_4$ ounces), according to the circumstances. This difference may seem insignificant in terms of one serving, but for a piece of meat for 12 or 15 people, it is something to consider. Relatively speaking, you need a larger piece of meat for 7 or 8 people than for 15 or 18 given that a meal for a large number of guests usually has more courses, and some guests may abstain.

When, as is frequently the case, the fillet of beef is served as an entrée or second main dish, we recommend braising it rather than roasting it. This is because braising gives the fillet and its juices a flavor that is much appreciated by gourmets and that harmonizes particularly well with the garnish that accompanies the meat. Indeed, in earlier times, the meat would only have been braised, and it is mistake to assume that the effect of cooking in the oven is identical to that of braising. That said, making the stock for braising was an expense, and you may not have the appropriate utensil.

The inside of a braised fillet of beef must always be rosy pink. Indeed, this is what differentiates the fillet from all other braises of meat, white or red, which are completely colored by the cooking, and for which a little overcooking will make no difference. For a fillet, it is essential to weigh the fillet *after* trimming to establish the exact braising time needed for a roast.

Preparation of the fillet: You can easily trim the fillet yourself. Just be careful, and use a large knife with a thin blade.

First, take off all the fat. Then remove the shiny skin covering the meat, taking it off sheet by sheet; the flesh is thus entirely uncovered without being damaged. Also, trim the piece of meat that adheres to the fillet for its entire length. Then lard the fillet with lardons cut as thick as a matchstick and 3 centimeters long ($1^1/_4$ inches) (SEE LARDING MEAT, PAGE 11). Tie five or six turns of string around the fillet to maintain its shape but without pulling it too tight, because the meat will swell when cooking and the string would therefore leave marks.

Carving the fillet in the kitchen, and serving it: When you take the fillet from the roasting dish or the oven, put it on the cutting board. Cut the strings with *scissors.*

With a good carving knife, cut thin slices and leave them on the cutting board instead of putting them one by one on the serving plate. After this, slide a knife blade under them to pick them all up at the same time and transfer to the plate. Arrange them in a straight line on a long, preheated serving plate, stacking and overlapping them, allowing only the part stuck with lardons to show; in effect, you more or less reform the original fillet. Moisten it with the juices that have escaped during the carving. Never add these to the cooking juice or into the sauce, because they will dilute it and cause it to clump.

Then arrange the garnish on each side of the fillet.

Braised Fillet of Beef *(Filet de Boeuf Braisé).* We will summarize here the procedure described for braising red meats (SEE PAGE 30). You can check there for all the details. *Serves 12–15.*

2 1/2 kilograms (5 pounds, 8 ounces) of fillet, gross weight; 150 grams (5 1/3 ounces) of fatback bacon for barding.

***For the braising stock:* 80 grams (2 3/4 ounces) of bacon strips; 150 grams (5 1/3 ounces) of carrots cut into rounds and 150 grams (5 1/3 ounces) of onions cut the same way; 2 tablespoons of fat; a bouquet garni; 1 liter (4 1/4 cups) of veal juice, either unsalted or hardly salted, because it will be reduced.**

PROCEDURE. Prepare, bard, and tie the fillet. Place it in a roasting dish, supported on a rack as for an ordinary roast. Since the fillet has been barded, it cannot be browned on all of its surfaces in a pot. Moisten it lightly with fat or with melted butter and put it in a *very warm* oven for about 10 minutes to seal it: that is, to color the outside flesh on all sides and also to keep the juices inside.

Meanwhile, in a pan, lightly color the rounds of carrots and the onions used for the braising stock.

Take a braising pot or other utensil of appropriate dimensions (SEE BRAISING, PAGE 25). Spread out the bacon rinds; on the top, sprinkle the browned carrots and onions and the bouquet garni. Place the browned fillet on top of it. Add at least *1 full deciliter (3 1/3 fluid ounces, scant 1/2 cup) of juice.*

Put the utensil on the heat without a cover and bring it to a lively boil until the liquid has almost completely reduced. Then add the rest of the juice and bring to a boil. When the boiling has begun, put a sheet of buttered parchment paper right on top of the fillet. Cover the utensil. Put it in the oven at a heat that is just strong enough to maintain a very gentle simmer, steady and uninterrupted. Moisten the fillet every 10 minutes with its cooking liquid.

Including the final glazing, which will require 7 or 8 minutes, *allow 12 minutes of cooking per pound from the time that the pot has been put in the oven, if you like your fillet rare; a brief 15 minutes for medium-rare—that is, pink.*

To glaze: About 8 minutes before the end of the cooking time, put the fillet on a roasting dish, then moisten it with a few tablespoons of the braising juice. Put it back in the oven to glaze it and to color the lardons, which will also finish cooking.

Strain and degrease the braising juice. Boil it to reduce it to 3 deciliters (1 1/4 cups). Pass it again through the chinois; keep it warm in a small saucepan.

Another Procedure for Braising a Fillet. This is a classic and extremely good technique; it is simpler but nonetheless requires the use of an excellent juice because none of the braising stock, which adds to the flavor, is used. *Time: 45 minutes. Serves 8–10.*

1 1/4 kilograms (2 pounds, 12 ounces) of fillet, net weight after trimming; 75 grams (2 2/3 ounces) of fatback bacon for barding; 1 teaspoon of arrowroot.

***For braising:* 6 deciliters (2 1/2 cups) of excellent jus; 1 deciliter (3 1/3 fluid ounces, scant 1/2 cup) of good white wine; 2 tablespoons of cognac; shortening.**

PROCEDURE. Bard the fillet as indicated. Put the

meat, barded part up, in a small braising pot of the appropriate size, on the bottom of which you have spread the bard of fatback bacon, to completely surround the fillet.

Pour 2 deciliters ($6^3/_4$ fluid ounces, $^7/_8$ cup) of jus and the cognac into the utensil. Put the uncovered pot on *high heat.* As soon as this little bit of liquid boils, baste it over the surface of the fillet with a spoon, and do this continuously while the liquid reduces; this should take *7–8 minutes.* As soon as the liquid is completely reduced, with no moisture left in the pot, pour in the rest of the juice and the wine. It should reach to about halfway up the fillet. Add 2 tablespoons of good pork fat. Season with salt and pepper. Boil.

Once boiling has started, cover and put it in the oven. *Including the final glaze, allow a scant 15 minutes of cooking per pound.* Maintain a regular simmer throughout. Meanwhile, baste the surface of the fillet three or four times. Seven to eight minutes before serving, put the fillet on an ovenproof plate. Baste it with 3 or 4 tablespoons of its degreased juice and then put it back in the oven to color it and glaze it, as has been described previously.

Degrease the cooking juice. Reduce it to $2^1/_2$ deciliters (1 cup) and thicken it with the starch (SEE LIAISONS, PAGE 47).

Roast Fillet of Beef *(Filet de Boeuf Rôti).* SEE ROASTS (PAGE 30).

If roasting in the *oven,* place the fillet on a roasting dish. Pour 2 or 3 tablespoons of water onto the plate, *no more;* as previously mentioned, this water is only to keep the bottom of the dish from burning. Baste the fillet with melted butter. Put it in a good, hot oven to seal it and to form a brown crust so that the meat retains its juices.

For cooking, allow *10–12 minutes per pound for a rare* fillet; *11–13 minutes for medium-rare; 13 minutes for well done.* When it is cooked, put it on a long serving plate. Keep it warm. To deglaze the plate, proceed as indicated. SEE JUS OF ROASTS (PAGE 33).

Sirloin or Porter House Roast *(Contre-Filet Rôti).* Bard it. Roast it as indicated above: *13–15 minutes* per pound.

Garnishes for Fillet of Beef

The principal garnishes for braised fillet of beef are also good for roast fillet served as an entrée or a second entrée. For the quantities, preparation, etc., refer to the different sections describing these garnishes and how to make them.

Fillet of Beef à la Dauphine *(Filet de Boeuf à la Dauphine).* Surround the fillet with pommes dauphine (croquettes). Serve Madeira sauce alongside in a sauceboat.

Fillet of Beef à la Financière *(Filet de Boeuf à la Financière).* Arrange the different elements of the garnish in separate groups. Lightly moisten them with just enough sauce to cover. Serve them with the remainder of the sauce, alongside either Madeira or Périgueux sauce.

Fillet of Beef à la Jardinère *(Filet de Boeuf à la Jardinère).* Arrange the garnish in bouquet. The juices from roasting or braising the fillet should be served in a sauceboat.

Fillet of Beef with Madeira and Mushrooms *(Filet de Boeuf au Madère et aux Champignons).* Surround the fillet with a few mushrooms and a few tablespoons of sauce. Serve the rest on the side in a sauceboat.

Fillet of Beef Nivernaise *(Filet de Boeuf Nivernaise).* Glaze carrots and onions and arrange in a bouquet. The juice from braising the fillet should be strained and degreased, then served in a sauceboat.

Fillet of Beef Renaissance *(Filet de Boeuf Renaissance).* Broadly speaking, this garnish is a jardinière of new vegetables, with the addition of new potatoes sautéed in butter. Serve the juices from roasting or braising the fillet in a sauceboat.

Fillet of Beef Richelieu *(Filet de Boeuf Richelieu).* Glazed turnips and carrots; green peas and green beans in a butter sauce; braised lettuce; potatoes sautéed in butter; and stuffed tomatoes and mushrooms. Serve the juices from roasting or braising the fillet in a sauceboat.

Fillet of Beef Saint-Florentin *(Filet de Boeuf Saint-Florentin.* Garnish the fillet, preferably roasted, with potatoes and cèpes. Serve Bordelaise sauce (PAGE 57), made with white wine, alongside.

Fillet of Beef Saint-Germain *(Filet de Boeuf Saint-Germain).* Roast the fillet. Garnish with a purée of peas, glazed carrots, and pommes fondants (potatoes cut to olive size and baked in butter). Serve béarnaise sauce (PAGE 75) alongside.

Tournedos *(Les Tournedos)*

A tournedos is a kind of small, thick beefsteak taken from the fillet, which is about the size of the center of a nice lamb chop. A tournedos can be grilled, but the most usual method is to sauté it in a sauté pan on very strong heat: its inside must stay nice and pink and juicy.

It is a very common dish in good restaurants because it is quick and easy and can be served in a hundred different ways. In addition, it is very easy to serve: the portion for each guest is already cut, so no carving or preparation need be done. Another advantage is that it can be served fast and hot, so if you don't know when your guests will arrive or of they are late, you will need only about 10 minutes to cook the tournedos.

For all of these reasons, the tournedos are particularly good when planning a menu for a very elegant luncheon, or even a ceremonial lunch.

Tournedos are frequently arranged on a "plinth" made from a fried crouton, a potato croquette that has been flattened into a palette, or even an artichoke base, sautéed in butter. No matter how you cook it, the tournedos must never be allowed while cooking to be in contact with any liquid, even its own escaped juices. This is the true way to sauté.

Preparing the tournedos: Tournedos are exactly 5½ centimeters (2¼ inches) in diameter and 2½ centimeters (1 inch) thick, never less; its weight is an average of 100–110 grams (3½–3⅞ ounces).

You can buy tournedos ready-trimmed by the butcher, though this is, of course, more expensive than buying a whole fillet. You will lose about one-third of the fillet's weight when the meat is trimmed of its fat and membrane, but the trimmings can be put to good use, so it is always better to buy a whole piece of fillet and trim it yourself. However, make sure you get meat from the thin end, or tail, of a small fillet, because meat taken from the middle, thickest part of the fillet or even from the end of the large fillet would have to be severely trimmed to produce tournedos of the right diameter (5½ centimeters/2¼ inches).

Remove the band of meat that runs along the fillet, which is never employed in the tournedos. Slide a slim, sharp knife blade under the fine nerve membrane covering the meat and take it off layer by layer. Also trim the bottom of the fillet.

Now divide the trimmed meat into slices exactly 2½ centimeters (1 inch) thick. Carefully trim all around them. Be careful to keep them in regular rounds. To keep the tournedos in this round form, tie string around the middle, like the bands on a cask, which will keep the flesh compacted. Keep them in a cool place until you are ready to cook them.

Cooking the tournedos: For directions, SEE SAUTÉING (PAGE 34). Heat the oil and the butter in a sauté pan until a light smoke comes off it. Lightly season the tournedos with salt and pepper, then place in the pan. Maintain a strong heat on the pan to brown the side of the meat sitting on the bottom of the pan. Turn them over at the end of *4–5 minutes* to brown them on the other side for an equal amount of time.

So, in total, you need *10 minutes* to cook the tournedos perfectly, when the meat inside will be pink. You can judge this by pushing the tip of your finger against the surface of the meat; it should offer some resistance. If you prefer the tournedos very rare, reduce the cooking time to *8 minutes:* 4 minutes on each side. In this case, the meat will yield a bit when you prod it. Immediately take them out of the sauté pan and keep them between two plates while you quickly prepare the final ingredients.

The croutons: These are the most common base for tournedos. Cut them from a loaf of stale bread (SEE CROUTONS, PAGE 20), using a cookie cutter with a diameter of 6½ centimeters (about 2½ inches) so that they are slightly bigger than the tournedos. The croutons should be 1 centimeter (⅜ inch) thick. If you do not have a cookie cutter this size, mark the flat piece of bread with the circumference of a glass and cut it with the point of a small knife.

Fry the croutons, then use a small brush to cover the croutons with melted meat glaze on one side only, the side upon which the tournedos will be placed. The meat glaze forms a barrier that prevents the bread from being soaked by the juices escaping from the meat, which would soften the croutons while you are finishing the sauce. (You can buy meat glaze in small quantities at certain select gourmet stores. You dilute it in a little bit of warm water.)

If you do not have any meat glaze or even a jus reduced to a similar consistency, do not place the tournedos on the croutons until the last second so that there will not be time for the bread to soak up the juice.

PRINCIPAL RECIPES FOR TOURNEDOS

There is an infinite number of recipes, varying only according to your imagination and the promptings of the season, not to mention the stocks, juice, sauces, and garnishes available in the kitchens of the great restaurants. Apart from the two most classic recipes, we are limiting ourselves to describing only the most modern recipes and those best adapted to home cooking.

As elsewhere, we'll also describe several more ways to serve tournedos:

- Garnish with a round of *fried eggplant,* without croutons, arranged in a circle with a *fondue of tomatoes* (PAGE 534) in the middle, allowing 1 tablespoon of tomato for each tournedos.
- Without croutons, arrange in a circle, adding to each one a piece of maître d'hôtel butter. Put French fries in the middle.
- Without croutons, with Vichy carrots.
- On croutons with Bordeaux-style cèpes. Or, similarly, with a little stew of morels.
- On croutons with a slice of truffle on each tournedos and a Périgueux sauce.
- On artichoke bottoms and a purée soubise, etc.

Tournedos with Béarnaise *(Tournedos à la Béarnaise).* On croutons with a garnish of "château" potatoes. Pour BÉARNAISE SAUCE (PAGE 75) in a ribbon around each tournedos or serve in a sauceboat. If possible, put a little meat glaze on the tournedos.

Tournedos à la Bordelaise *(Tournedos à la Bordelaise).* Without croutons and with a large round of marrow placed on each tournedos. Pour BORDELAISE SAUCE (PAGE 57) around the meat or serve in a sauceboat.

Tournedos en Chevreuil *(Tournedos en Chevreuil).* On croutons. Marinate the tournedos beforehand. Serve with venison sauce *(sauce chevreuil)* and a purée of chestnuts served on the side.

Tournedos à la Choron *(Tournedos à la Choron).* On croutons. Serve with a Choron sauce—a sauce Béarnaise prepared without minced herbs and to which a thick tomato purée is added.

Tournedos with a Garnish of Seasonal Vegetables *(Tournedos avec Garniture de Legumes de Saison).* Brussels sprouts or green peas or green beans or asparagus tips, etc. Arrange the tournedos on croutons in a circle, and put the vegetables in a butter sauce in the middle.

Tournedos à la Paysanne *(Tournedos à la Paysanne).* Without croutons and arranged simply on top of a mixture of vegetables: green beans, rounds of carrots, green peas, small onions, all cooked together in a stew of butter, salt, and very little water.

Tournedos Sautéed Hunter-Style *(Tournedos Sautés Chasseur).* The recipe given here is particularly appropriate for home kitchens, which, unlike the great kitchens, do not have most basic sauces at hand. Even so, and despite the limitations of a family kitchen, you can achieve good results. *Time: 25 minutes (once the tournedos have been trimmed and prepared).*

6 tournedos of the recommended size and weight; 2 tablespoons of oil and 30 grams (1 ounce, 2 tablespoons) of butter for the sauté; 6 croutons and 30 grams (1 ounce, 2 tablespoons) of butter to fry them; 75 grams (2 2/3 ounces) of fresh mushrooms, 2 tablespoons of oil and 20 grams (2/3 ounce, 1 heaping tablespoon) of butter to sauté them separately; 2 medium shallots; 10 grams (1/3 ounce) of flour; 1 1/2 deciliters (5 fluid ounces, 2/3 cup) of light veal juice or of bouillon and the same amount of white wine; 1 tablespoon of tomato paste; 1 teaspoon of minced chervil and tarragon; a pinch of parsley, coarsely chopped; 20 grams (2/3 ounce, 1 heaping tablespoon) of butter to finish the sauce.

If possible, though it is not essential, 20 grams (2/3 ounce) of meat glaze melted in 1 good tablespoon of warm water to dress the tournedos.

PROCEDURE. Cut off the earth end of the mushrooms, then wash the mushrooms, drain, and wipe dry. Without peeling them, cut lengthwise through the head and the stem, in equal slices about 3–4 millimeters (1/8 inch) thick. Mince the shallots as finely as possible. In a small sauté pan, heat the oil until a light smoke escapes. Put in the sliced mushrooms. Sauté them on strong heat until they are lightly colored, then pour out all the grease, holding a cover on the pan to retain its contents.

Add the shallot. Sauté it for a moment with the mushrooms, being careful not to let it burn. Sprinkle everything with the flour. Cook this gently without a cover for 4–5 minutes. Then add the veal juice or bouillon, the tomato, and a pinch of pepper; do not add salt if the juice or bouillon already contains salt. Mix and bring it to a boil. Let it simmer very gently while you are preparing the rest of the dish.

Prepare the croutons (SEE PAGE 20). Keep them warm in their pan until ready to serve.

The tournedos: About 15 minutes before serving, heat the butter and the oil in a sauté pan, then cook them as described.

Dressing the dish: If using melted meat glaze, brush the croutons with it and arrange them in a circle on a round plate. Remove the string from the tournedos and place on each crouton. Then glaze the tops of the tournedos. Keep them warm while you finish the garnish. If you do not have any meat glaze, keep the tournedos warm between two plates.

The sauce: Once the tournedos have been either dressed (or kept warm), completely drain the grease from their sauté pan. Pour in the white wine to deglaze and to dissolve the little bit of the juice that has caramelized on the bottom of the pan. Boil rapidly to reduce the quantity to *4 or 5 tablespoons,* then add their mushrooms and their sauce. Let it boil just for a few seconds. *Turn off the heat.*

Quickly add 20 grams (2/3 ounce, 1 heaping tablespoon) of butter to the pan, and then the chervil and the tarragon. Pour the sauce in the middle of the circle formed by the tournedos. Sprinkle the pinch of parsley over it. Serve quickly.

Tournedos Rossini *(Tournedos Rossini).* A recipe that has become a classic and that is one of the best; it's among the richest, despite its apparent simplicity. The best time to serve it is from November to March, preparing it with fresh fois gras and fresh truffles. You can use preserved truffles; in this case, gently heat the slices of fois gras with a little bit of cooking liquid from the mushrooms. *Time: 25 minutes (once the tournedos have been cut and prepared, and the truffles scrubbed and cleaned).*

6 tournedos of the recommended size and weight; 2 tablespoons of oil and 30 grams (1 ounce, 2 tablespoons) of butter to sauté them; 6 croutons and 30 grams (1 ounce, 2 tablespoons) of butter to fry them; 6 slices of fois gras and 30 grams (1 ounce, 2 tablespoons) of butter to cook them; 6 truffles the size of a chestnut cooked in 3 tablespoons of Madeira and the same quantity of white wine; 1 good deciliter (3 1/3 fluid ounces, 1/2 cup) of veal juice; 1 good tablespoon of melted meat glaze: that is 25 grams (1 ounce) of meat glaze dissolved in 1 tablespoon of warm water; 1 small teaspoon of arrowroot; 4 or 5 tablespoons of Madeira; 30 grams (1 ounce, 2 tablespoons) of butter.

PROCEDURE. From one half of a small fois gras weighing about 275 grams (9 2/3 ounces), cut 6 rounds 1 centimeter (3/8 inch) thick from the thickest part. Trim carefully to make neat rounds 5 centimeters (2 inches) in diameter: either with a round cookie cutter that has been dipped in warm water, or if you do not have one, with the blade of a small knife, also moistened. Keep these slices of fois gras ready on a plate.

Clean the truffles (SEE PAGE 537). Peel them carefully, then cut them into slices about 3–4 millimeters (1/8 inch) thick: 4 slices for each tournedos. Put them in a small saucepan with 3 tablespoons of Madeira, the same amount of white wine, a bit of fine salt, a touch of spice, a very small sprig of thyme, and a bit of bay. Cook this for 5 or 6 minutes, then turn off the heat. If using preserved truffles, heat them in their juices *without boiling.*

Cut the croutons. Dissolve the meat glaze with minimal heat.

About 15 minutes before serving, start cooking the tournedos and the fois gras at the same time.

The tournedos: Sauté them as previously described (PAGE 258).

The fois gras: In another sauté pan, heat 30 grams (1 ounce, 2 tablespoons) of butter. Season the slices of fois gras with salt and pepper. Dip them in flour. Place them in a sauté pan. Cook them gently, turning them from time to time. If using preserved fois gras, you must heat the slices carefully on a plate in a low oven, sprinkled with a little cooking liquid from the mushrooms.

Meanwhile, fry the croutons. SEE CROUTONS (PAGE 20).

The sauce and dressing: Arrange the croutons in a circle on a round plate. Brush them with the meat glaze. Remove the string from the tournedos and arrange them on the croutons. Keep the plate warm in a low oven.

Drain the grease from the sauté pan in which you cooked the tournedos. Pour in the Madeira to dissolve the little bit of juice that is caramelized at the bottom of the sauté pan. Let it reduce almost completely. Add the veal juice and the cooking liquid from the truffles (fresh or preserved). Boil it rapidly to reduce it to a little more than 1 deciliter (3 1/3 fluid ounces, scant 1/2 cup).

Thicken it with the starch diluted in 1 or 2 tablespoons of cold bouillon. *Off the heat,* add the rest of the butter. Take the plate from the oven. Place a round of fois gras on each tournedos. On top of this round, place 4 slices of truffle. Pour the sauce on the tournedos and serve immediately. The plates should be quite hot.

Braised Beef à la Flamande
(Boeuf Braisé à la Flamande)

This recipe *à la flamande* is defined by its garnish of cabbage, carrots, turnips, potatoes, bacon, and sausage.

The recipe given here produces a garnish in which each vegetable is cooked separately to retain its own flavor. You can also use turnips and potatoes without risking their absorbing the flavor of the cabbage, which not everyone likes; the cooking juice is also unaffected. The execution of Beef à la Flamande is thus divided into two distinct parts: braising the piece of beef and preparing the garnish.

The cut that this dish requires is the rump or sirloin. Ask the butcher to cut it as evenly as possible so that it will cook uniformly. The weights given for the trimmed piece are more than you will need to serve 10 or 12 people, but remember that you will get a better result with a large piece than a small one. And any leftovers can be put to good use, served cold or reheated with any sauce, thus saving you both time and trouble. *Time: 4 1/4 hours.*

2 kilograms (4 pounds, 6 ounces) of sirloin weighed trimmed and without bones.

To braise: 150 grams (5 1/3 ounces) of rounds of carrots and the same of onion; a bouquet garni; 2–3 tablespoons of good skimmed cooking grease; 100 grams (3 1/2 ounces) of pork rind; 2 deciliters (6 3/4 fluid ounces, 7/8 cup) of white wine; about 1 deciliter (3 1/3 fluid ounces, scant 1/2 cup) of light veal juice or of a good bouillon that is very lightly salted; 1 teaspoon of starch.

SEE GARNISH À LA FLAMANDE, WHICH FOLLOWS.

PROCEDURE. First start braising the beef. While it's cooking, you will have time to make the garnish.

Tie up the piece of meat, to help you handle the meat, without pulling the string too tight, which would leave marks. Its length means that a braising pot is the best utensil to use, if you have one, but you do not want one that is too large, because the cooking liquid must come halfway up on the piece of meat.

Brown the beef as described (SEE BRAISING RED MEAT, PAGE 30), in whatever way is easiest for you, either in a very hot oven or in the braising pot itself. Allow *about 20 minutes* for this. Meanwhile, lightly color the vegetables, which are the basis of the braising in the pan.

Into the braising pot, first put the bacon and the browned vegetables, etc. Put in the piece of beef and moisten it with the white wine. Do not cover. Boil rapidly to completely reduce the wine. Then add 1$^1/_2$ deciliters (5 fluid ounces, $^2/_3$ cup) of bouillon. Reduce this to a glaze.

Finally, moisten well, adding the rest of the liquid, juice, or bouillon. Bring to a boil. Cover it first with parchment paper and then with the cover. Put it in the oven. From this point, cook for an additional *3$^1/_4$ hours.* At the end of *2 hours,* the liquid will have reduced substantially so that it no longer covers the meat, so be careful to baste every 10–12 minutes thereafter.

Strain the juice through a fine strainer into a small saucepan. You should not have more than *4 deciliters (1$^2/_3$ cups)* if the recipe has been correctly followed. Degrease it thoroughly. If you glaze the piece, use 4 or 5 tablespoons of this juice.

Thicken the juice with the starch diluted in a bowl with 3 tablespoons of bouillon (SEE LIAISONS, PAGE 47). Keep it warm while you dress the beef and its garnish.

Garnish à la Flamande *(Garniture à la Flamande).* This garnish is principally intended for a piece of braised beef, but it also works for a braised beef or veal tongue, as well as a braised loin of veal. *Time: 2$^1/_2$ hours. Serves 10–12.*

850 grams (1 pound, 14 ounces) of firm Napa cabbage, weighed after you have removed the stems and rough leaves; 250 grams (8$^7/_8$ ounces) of nice red carrots, weighed after they have been peeled; 250 grams (8$^7/_8$ ounces) of turnips, also weighed after peeling; 5 medium Holland potatoes (or other good quality potatoes); 250 grams (8$^7/_8$ ounces) of *very lean bacon;* an ordinary sausage (or one with a bit of garlic) weighing 200 grams (7 ounces); 1 liter (4$^1/_4$ cups) of very lightly salted bouillon; 2 nice tablespoons of beef fat; 40 grams (1$^3/_8$ ounces, 3 tablespoons) of butter.

PROCEDURE. **The cabbage:** To make up the right weight, use 2 small cabbages. Cut them in two. Remove the stems, the outer leaves, and the ribs of the leaves. Wash them. Plunge them into 5 liters (5$^1/_4$ quarts) of boiling, salted water (30 grams of salt). Boil for 15 minutes. Drain; cool them in a large amount of cool water, changing it several times. Let them stand in the water while you peel and blanch the vegetables. Blanch the bacon for 15–20 minutes.

After soaking, drain the cabbage as much as possible. Take off and reserve about 20 leaves, taking them from the outside.

Coarsely chop the rest of the cabbage and season with salt and pepper. Divide the chopped cabbage into 8 or 10 parts. Wrap each one in 2 of the reserved cabbage leaves, to make a little package. Next, shape these into a ball by placing each package on a corner of the towel and folding the towel over it, like a purse. Then twist the towel to squeeze the package; any water left in the cabbage will come out. Unwrap the towel, and you will find the cabbage has been pressed into a compact ball.

Arrange these balls of cabbage side by side in a sauté pan, separated by the sausage and the blanched bacon, trimmed as necessary. Pour $^1/_2$ liter (generous 2 cups) of bouillon over this. Add the purified beef fat.

Bring it to a boil, then cover and put in an oven that is just warm enough to keep the liquid in a gentle simmer for *1$^1/_2$ hours,* or put on a moderate heat if the oven is already being used to braise the meat. *The sausage should be removed at the end of 35–40 minutes; the bacon at the end of 1 hour.*

The carrots: Prepare and cook them as described (SEE CARROTS FOR GARNISH, PAGE 484) with 2$^1/_2$ deciliters (1 cup) of bouillon, 20 grams ($^2/_3$ ounce, 1 heaping tablespoon) of butter, and 2 lumps of ordinary sugar. Keep the carrots warm in their pot until you are ready to dress the plate.

The turnips: Peel them and cook them exactly like the carrots. Blanch them, too, if necessary. For cooking quantities and time, proceed as for the carrots, leaving out the sugar.

The potatoes: Cut them in quarters; trim the two ends. Peel and pare each quarter to make little boats. As you peel them, put them in a terrine of cool water. You can do this in advance, but the potatoes must not be cooked until they are needed, because they should not be left to stand before serving.

Put them in a high-sided pot covered with cool salted water. Put the pot on a good heat *25 minutes before you dress* the plate. Cover and boil rapidly. As soon as they are cooked, pour the water out of the pot and keep it warm until the moment that you place the potatoes on the plate.

Dressing the plate: Arrange the garnish as you like; just use your imagination. The most important thing is to work with enough speed so that everything is hot when it arrives at the table. This is particularly important if the piece of meat has not been carved in advance.

To simplify matters, we suggest the following method: place the piece of beef, carved or not, in the middle of a long plate that has been thoroughly heated in advance. At each end of the plate, arrange the small cabbage balls in a half circle. In the middle of the plate and on each side of the beef, put the carrots. On one side of the carrots, place a pile of turnips, and on the other side, a pile of potatoes. Surround all the ingredients with thin bacon slices alternating with rounds of sausages, making a border around the plate. Serve the juice on the side in a sauceboat. The plates should be quite hot.

Rib Roast *(Côte de Boeuf)*

Whether roasting or braising, you need a good, thick piece of meat, so do not try to cook anything less than 2 kilograms (4 pounds, 6 ounces). Remove the backbone.

Accompany a rib roast, roasted or braised, with all the usual garnishes: *flamande,* macaroni or noodles, purées of fresh or dried vegetables.

Beef in Terrine *(Boeuf en Terrine)*

A recipe that is excellent for home cooking: The simple ingredients and method put it within the reach of everyone. Quite simply, slices of beef alternated with slices of bacon; in 10 minutes, the terrine is ready to put in the oven; especially good for housewives looking to prepare cold dishes good for hunters. *Time: 4 hours (12 hours for chilling). Makes enough for a terrine 10 centimeters (4 inches) high and with a diameter of 22 centimeters (8½ inches):*

1 kilogram (2 pounds, 3 ounces) of beef rump, net weight, trimmed of membrane and skin; 300 grams (10½ ounces) of good bacon; 50 grams (1¾ ounces) of pork rind; 12 grams (3/8 ounce) of salt; 2–3 grams (1/14–1/10 ounce) of salt and pepper; 3 medium-size bay leaves, depending on whether or not you like it spiced; 4 sprigs of thyme; grated nutmeg, as much as can be held on the point of a knife; 1 good deciliter (3⅓ fluid ounces, ½ cup) of fine bouillon.

PROCEDURE. Cut the beef in slices parallel to the grain of the meat about ¾ centimeter (5/16 inch) thick. Cut the bacon in similar slices, but thinner. In a cup, mix salt, pepper, and nutmeg.

Garnish the terrine with alternate layers of bacon and beef, beginning and finishing with the bacon; for the quantities given, the terrine should be filled with 5 layers of bacon and 4 layers of beef. Be careful to disperse the seasoning among the different layers. Finally, pour the bouillon over everything and put the salt pork on top, then cover. The terrine is now ready to be put into the oven.

Cook it in a very gentle oven *from 3–3½ hours.* Do not let it cook at more than an imperceptible simmer. Take off the cover from time to time to see if you need to add a couple of tablespoons of bouillon and to check that the liquid is not reducing in an oven that is a little too warm, causing a simmer that is a little too strong.

While cooking, the meat shrinks, leaving an empty space around the perimeter of the terrine, so put the bits of bacon there so that they will release their gelatinous elements into the liquid.

Once the cooking is done, pour the juice into a cup. Degrease and then pour it back into the terrine; you should have the same amount as at the beginning. Place a plate on top of the meat and weigh down with 2 kilograms (4 pounds, 6 ounces), then let it stand overnight.

Accompany the terrine with a seasonal salad.

Hochepot of Short Ribs of Beef *(Hochepot de Plat de Côtes de Boeuf)*

The hochepot (or hotchpotch), for which there are numerous, often contradictory recipes in eighteenth-century cookbooks, is a mixture of various meats and vegetables. It is well suited for home cooking, being both simple and generous. It is cooked very slowly and very gently to mimic the traditional way of cooking: in the ashes of the fireplace, carefully watched.

The short ribs suggested here can be replaced by the same quantity of beef tail or oxtail. Also, you can replace the bacon with 2 small pig's feet, and you can also add a few potatoes. Use 8 Holland or good quality potatoes of medium size, peeled and put into the marmite a good half hour before serving. Be careful to push them well down into the cooking liquid so that they will cook properly.

If you use beef tail, you must allow a little more cooking time since it will take longer to cook than the ribs. So add it 2 hours before adding the vegetables.

A good method for short ribs, and we recommend it here, is to color them by sautéing them before putting them in the cooking pot. This will enhance the dish's overall flavor. *Time: 3½–4 hours. Serves 6.*

1–1¼ kilograms (2 pounds, 3 ounces–2 pounds, 12 ounces) of short ribs; 1 salted pig's ear, if possible, which has been well cleaned; 200 grams (7 ounces) of bacon, the leanest possible; 2 medium carrots (200 grams/7 ounces); 2 medium turnips (200 grams/7 ounces); 1 small firm green cabbage weighing about 500 grams (1 pound, 2 ounces); 1 onion stuck with a clove; 100 grams (3½ ounces) of celery; 2 tablespoons of purified fat from degreasing to color the meat; 6 small, long sausages; salt, pepper. About 1 liter (4¼ cups) of water.

PROCEDURE. **The short ribs:** Carefully saw the rib bone into pieces 5 centimeters (2 inches) long, but without cutting into the meat that covers the bone on one side: it will then be much easier to cut into the pieces when you dress the plate.

Heat the purified fat in a good, thick pan. Brown the short ribs in it on moderate heat, gently and without haste; if you need to, do this in two batches if your pan is not large enough. Drain the grease from the meat. Put the ribs in a cooking pot, preferably an earthenware marmite, of an appropriate size.

Pour enough warm water into the marmite so that the meat is well covered. It's impossible to be exact about the amount you will need because this will depend on the size of the cooking pot. Allow at least 1½ liters (6⅓ cups), salted with 10 grams (⅓ ounce) per liter, but this may vary by as much as 2 deciliters (6¾ fluid ounces, ⅞ cup).

The pig's ear: Add this at the same time as the meat. It should be quite clean: If it is salted, wash it first thoroughly in lukewarm water; and if a few hairs remain on the interior, burn them off. You can cut the ear in two lengthwise to place it more easily near the meat.

Put the marmite on the fire to bring it to a boil. Skim. Turn the heat down quite low to maintain a gentle and regular simmer, and cook for *a good 1¼ hours.*

The garnish: You can take care of this during the first stage of cooking the meat.

The cabbage: Remove the shriveled outer leaves. Divide it in two. Cut each half into 3 or 4 pieces (take off the stem pieces and the rough ribs of the first leaves). Wash them, then put them into a pot of boiling water. Drain them after about 10 minutes. It is not necessary to chill them. Keep them on the side.

The bacon: Blanch it as indicated (SEE PAGE 15). It should not be added to the vegetables until *1¼ hours* before serving. Otherwise, it will be overcooked.

Carrots and turnips: Cut into pieces 3 centimeters (1¼ inches) long. Divide each piece into 4 or 6 parts, according to their size. Peel them and trim them into the shape of a large pod. After the meat has been cooking for 1¼ hours, add: carrots, turnips, cabbage, the onion with the clove in it and the celery, placing them around the meat. Add a nice pinch of pepper. Rapidly bring it to a boil; cover the marmite and continue at the same slow and uninterrupted simmer. From this point, allow another *2 good hours of cooking.*

Add the bacon to the marmite at the appropriate time, making sure it is well buried under the vegetables. Do the same for the potatoes if you are going to use them. Finally, about 20 minutes before the end of the cooking time, add the sausages, having first immersed them in boiling water for 2 or 3 seconds to firm up their casing and to prevent them from bursting.

To serve: Remove all the meat from the marmite. Take the cabbage out with a slotted spoon and press it against the side of the marmite to extract the liquid from it. Put it on a long plate. At each end, make two heaps of carrots and turnips and add the potatoes if there is space.

Quickly cut up the pieces of short rib, then arrange them on top of the cabbage. Divide the pork ear into thin strips and place these between the pieces of rib. On each side of the plate, place the sausages and the bacon, cut into small, even pieces.

This allows the guests to help themselves and suit themselves, but you must proceed rapidly so that the dish can be served *very hot.*

Beef Bourguignonne *(Boeuf à la Bourguignonne)*

Despite the name, this is not a regional specialty. In modern cooking, this term designates a dish composed of red wine—very good red wine—with a garnish of small onions, mushrooms, and bacon.

For a beef bourguignonne, you can prepare the ingredients in two ways. Either cut the meat into pieces and cook as for a ragout or stew, or leave the meat whole, and lard it, then cook it exactly like a braised beef. The second method lets you serve it for a nice little dinner.

Cooking it as a stew is an advantage when there are not a great number of diners, because you will not need a large piece of meat, as is needed for braising. However, do remember that a small piece of meat will not produce a good result, no matter what you do. In this case, your best bet, both in terms of time and trouble, is to use enough meat for two meals, as beef bourguignonne reheats easily. In fact, many people find it better reheated. Either leave the entire leftover piece whole, or cut it into slices

The initial marinade suggested for the large piece is equally recommended when cooking the meat as a stew. The difference in flavor is notable when the meat is not marinated before cooking.

Large Piece of Beef Bourguignonne *(Pièce de Boeuf à la Bourguignonne).* The rump (sirloin) is the best piece to use here, as is true for all recipes that call for braising. However, it could be replaced with the part of the rump called "silverside." In both cases, the meat must be cut lengthwise, rather than sideways, to make cutting the slices easy.

For the cooking, a light veal jus is preferable to a beef bouillon, no matter how good it is. The jellied element of the veal jus produces a sauce that is smoother and has a better sheen. And it would be much better to prepare the small quantity of veal jus needed the evening before, rather than to prepare beef bouillon. After all, it would be rather inconvenient to have to make a boiled beef dish so near to serving a beef bourguignonne. *Time: 8 hours (including the marinade). Makes 2 servings for 8–10.*

1 piece of rump sirloin with a net weight of a good 1.8 kilograms (4 pounds); 200 grams (7 ounces) of fresh fatback bacon for larding; 3 tablespoons of cognac, salt, pepper, and spices to marinate the bacon pieces.

To marinate the beef: 7 1/2 deciliters (generous 3 cups) of very good red wine; 1 medium onion cut into thin rounds; 1/2 of a bay leaf; 4 sprigs of parsley, 1 sprig of thyme; 2 tablespoons of oil; salt and pepper.

For the cooking: 3 tablespoons of good fat; 30 grams (1 ounce) of flour for the roux; 5 deciliters (generous 2 cups) of veal jus or beef bouillon; the wine from the marinade; 30 grams (1 ounce) of mushroom peelings; a bouquet garni; a clove of garlic.

For the garnish: 250 grams (8 7/8 ounces) of lean bacon; 24 small onions; 375 grams (13 1/4 ounces) of fresh mushrooms; 90 grams (3 1/6 ounces, 6 1/3 tablespoons) of butter in total.

PROCEDURE. Cut the lardons into pieces *7 millimeters* (3/8 inch) thick and the same length as the beef. Put them on a plate, then sprinkle them with salt, spices, and cognac. Let them marinate for 15 minutes, turning them over from time to time in the cognac. Then lard the beef as indicated (SEE PAGE 11).

In an appropriately sized terrine, place half the onion and the aromatics used for the marinade.

Add the beef seasoned with salt and pepper. Put the rest of the aromatics on top, with the wine, the oil, and what remains of the cognac used to marinate the bacon pieces. Let the beef marinate in a cool place for *at least 3 hours*. Turn it from time to time without touching it with your hands, which would sour the meat.

To cook: Remove the piece from the marinade. Completely dry it off. In a thick, tall pot of the proper size, heat the fat until it begins to smoke. Brown the beef on all sides over a high heat to compensate for the moisture of the marinade.

Next, put the meat on a plate. Turn down the heat under the pot to low. Add the flour and cook it slowly until you have a deep brown roux (SEE PAGE 47). Dilute with the jus or the bouillon and the wine from the marinade, straining it first through a chinois. Bring to a boil over strong heat, stirring with a whisk. Turn down the heat to low, and place the meat in this sauce along with the juice that has escaped onto the plate. At the same time, add: the bouquet garni, crushed garlic, and mushroom peelings. Cover the pot. Let it boil for *5 or 6 minutes*. Place the pot in a moderate oven so that the sauce maintains a regular and continuous gentle simmer *for 3½ hours*, then add the garnish.

The garnish: Prepare this while the beef is under way.

The mushrooms: Clean, wash, peel, and turn them as described (SEE PAGE 490). Cut the stems into 2 or 3 pieces, and the heads into 2 or 4, according to size. Sauté them in a pan over high heat with 30 grams (1 ounce, 2 tablespoons) of butter. Drain them and reserve on a plate.

The onions: If they are no longer young, plunge them in a pot of boiling water for 2 minutes. Peel them and color them gently with 30 grams (1 ounce, 2 tablespoons) of butter in a small sauté pan. Then put them next to the mushrooms.

The lean bacon: Trim the rind. Cut the bacon into small 1-centimeter (½-inch) cubes. Put them in a small pot of cold water. Boil them for 5 full minutes. Drain them on a towel. Heat 30 grams (1 ounce, 2 tablespoons) of butter in a skillet. Brown them lightly over strong heat. Drain and put them with the mushrooms and onions.

To add the garnish: Turn off the heat under the pot. Let the sauce rest for about 10 minutes. With a metal spoon, degrease it completely by tilting the pot. Pass the sauce through a chinois into a terrine. Rinse the pot with hot water. Put the meat back in the pot. Surround it with the onions, bacon cubes, and mushrooms. Add the sauce. Bring it back to a boil. Cover the pot and put it back in the oven, or over gentle heat. From this moment, allow *40 minutes* at a regular and steady simmer to finish cooking the meat and the garnish.

To serve: Place the meat on the serving dish. Arrange the garnish around the meat. If you are carving in the kitchen, cut the required number of slices, then arrange them around the plate and place the garnish in the middle. Check the seasoning for the sauce, which should measure a good 6 deciliters (2½ cups). Cover the meat and the garnish with only one-third of this sauce. Serve the rest in a sauceboat.

Beef Bourguignonne Cooked as a Stew *(Boeuf à la Bourguignonne Façon Civet).* Both economical and simple, this method requires only one pot. *Time: 6 full hours (including the marinade). Serves 6.*

1 kilogram (2 pounds, 3 ounces) net weight of rump sirloin, cut into 5-centimeter (2-inch) cubes.

For the marinade, garnish, and cooking liquid, use half the quantities given for the previous recipe.

PROCEDURE. Blanch the bacon. Peel the onions and the mushrooms. Brown the bacon and the onions with 1 good tablespoon of fat for about *2 minutes*, in the sauté pan where the beef will be cooked. Put them on a plate. Sauté the mushrooms over strong heat and add them to the onions and bacon.

In the same fat, brown the pieces of beef, which have first been dried thoroughly. Drain the fat from the pan. Sprinkle the pieces of beef with the flour.

Little by little, on low heat, brown the pieces of meat, mixing them from time to time with a wooden spoon. Then add and combine the bouillon and the wine from the marinade. Bring to a boil. Cover and cook gently *for 2 hours.* After this, degrease the sauce, which should have reduced by half. Add the garnish. Cover and let it simmer for *another full half hour.* Serve.

Salted Beef *(Boeuf Sale)*

A home-style dish and an excellent standby for all seasons, which you can vary with different sauces and your choice of garnish: sauerkraut, braised stuffed cabbage, macaroni, noodles, purées of fresh or dried vegetables, etc.; piquante sauce, soubise sauce, tomato sauce, etc.

There are two ways to salt the beef: either dry, with sea salt mixed with saltpeter; or in a liquid brine. Brine, which is neither more costly nor more complicated than using the salt and saltpeter rub, is preferable because the brine acts more rapidly and effectively on the meat. We will therefore give this method first; it is equally good for ham, beef tongue, and all large cuts of meat.

A cut of meat, the sirloin or rump, will produce very beautiful slices of an equal thickness; if you prefer a fattier piece of meat, use the short ribs. Saw into the bones only, lengths of 5 or 6 centimeters (2–2 1/4 inches), taking care not to cut into the meat at the same time. This prepares them to be carved when you are ready to serve.

After the beef has been salted, it is cooked like a pot-au-feu. Take the meat out of the brine or clean off the salt, then wash the meat in cold water; next, put it in a marmite with carrots, onions stuck with a clove, and a bouquet garni. Do not add salt. Bring it slowly to a boil. Cook as for a pot-au-feu, allowing *3 hours* for a piece weighing about 1 1/2 kilograms (3 pounds, 5 ounces).

Salting with a Cooked Brine. The following proportions are appropriate for a cut of beef weighing from 1 1/4–2 kilograms (3 pounds, 5 ounces–4 pounds, 6 ounces); or for a tongue that weighs about 1 1/4 kilograms (3 pounds, 5 ounces).

2 liters (8 1/2 cups) of water; 900 grams (2 pounds) of gray sea salt; 60 grams (2 1/4 ounces) of saltpeter; 120–150 grams (4 1/4 to 5 1/3 ounces) of soft brown sugar; 5 peppercorns; 5 juniper berries; 1 sprig of thyme; half of a bay leaf.

PROCEDURE. Assemble all the ingredients in a pot. Bring to a boil and let boil gently for 5 minutes. Let it chill completely.

Using the cooked brine: Any meat that is to be put into brine must first be pierced deeply and all over with a large cooking needle. This helps the brine to penetrate the flesh.

After this, rub the meats vigorously and for a long time with a mixture of gray sea salt and saltpeter, using your hands. For a piece of meat weighing 1 1/2 kilograms or so (3 pounds, 5 ounces), use 100 grams (3 1/2 ounces) of gray sea salt and 30 grams (1 ounce) of saltpeter crushed and mixed on a plate. Then put the piece of meat into a marmite or other utensil that is higher than wide so that the meat will be well bathed in the brine. Cover it with the *very cold* brine. Place a round wooden board, or something similar, right on top of the meat, so that you can put a weight on top to make sure the meat remains completely immersed.

Keep it in a cool and dry place. Every 2 or 3 days, no matter what the time of year, turn the meat over in the brine using a couple of wooden spoons. *Do not put your hands in the liquid,* which might affect the brine.

To conserve the brine while salting the meat, it must be boiled. Do this every 8 days in mild winter weather and every 4 or 5 days in the summer. Pour it into a pot, leaving the meat behind. Boil it strongly for 2 minutes, then let it completely chill before pouring it back over the cut of meat. The brine can be cooled and boiled several times.

If, for any reason whatsoever, the brine is no longer enough to completely cover the meat, top it up with more, making it as described above.

How long to salt meat in brine: For a piece of short ribs weighing about 2 kilograms (4 pounds, 6 ounces): 8 or 9 days during the winter and 6 days during the summer. For a beef tongue: 12–15 days in temperate weather; 15–18 days when the weather is very cold; 8–10 days in very warm weather.

Dry Salting. Here, too, saltpeter is essential; not only does it give the meat a characteristic red tint, but it also plays an important role in attacking the germs that cause fermentation.

1 cut of beef weighing 1 1/2 kilograms (3 pounds, 5 ounces); 75 grams (2 2/3 ounces) of saltpeter; 750 grams (1 pound, 10 ounces) of gray sea salt; about 10 peppercorns; 2 sprigs of thyme; 1 bay leaf.

PROCEDURE. Crush the saltpeter with a rolling pin; mix it with the salt. Pierce the meat and rub it with the combination of salt and saltpeter, as described above, but for even longer.

Spread about a third of the salt into a bowl. Put in the meat; cover it with the rest of the salt (above all, make sure that the meat is completely covered with salt; add more if you need to). Add the pepper, the thyme, and the bay. Keep it in a cool place that is *completely dry—nothing is more important than this.*

Turn over the piece every 2 days using two wooden spoons, and *without touching it with your hands,* for the reason already given. For a dry salting, allow 7–8 days in temperate weather, and 10–12 days when it is cold.

Leftovers

Boiled Beef à la Crème *(Boeuf Bouilli à la Crème).* This method is appropriate for a leftover piece of beef that can be divided into slices. *Time: 40 minutes.*

250 grams (8 7/8 ounces) of beef net weight; 60 grams (2 1/4 ounces) of minced mushrooms; 1 teaspoon of chopped shallot (optional); 1 teaspoon of minced parsley; 20 grams (2/3 ounce, 1 heaping tablespoon) of butter; 8–10 grams (about 1/3 ounce) of flour; 1 deciliter (3 1/3 fluid ounces, scant 1/2 cup) of white wine; 1 deciliter (3 1/3 fluid ounces, scant 1/2 cup) of bouillon; 3 nice tablespoons of thick cream.

PROCEDURE. Cut the beef into slices 5 millimeters (1/4 inch) thick. Arrange them on an ovenproof dish, then moisten with 3 tablespoons of white wine and the same amount of bouillon. Season with salt and pepper. Cover the plate and put it on very, very low heat so that the beef gradually absorbs the liquid as it warms up.

In a small sauté pan, heat the butter. Put in the mushrooms and the minced shallot. On strong heat, mix it with a wooden spoon until you have evaporated all the mushroom juices.

Then sprinkle with the flour; cook it for a minute over low heat without coloring. Dilute it with the rest of the bouillon and the white wine and let it simmer for a few moments. The sauce should be quite thick. Check the salt note, then sprinkle with the parsley. Spread the sauce on the slices of beef. Cover the plate. Put it in a very low oven so that the beef, which is already warm and softened, can become moist *without browning.*

Two or three minutes before serving, pour the cream on the beef. Leave the plate in the oven just long enough to heat the cream without boiling. Serve.

Beef Hash au Gratin *(Hachis de Boeuf au Gratin).* An attractive use of the leftovers of a beef from a pot-au-feu, making use of meat that could not be divided into regular-sized slices. Coarsely chop the meat, then moisten with a little tomato sauce and cover with a light purée of potatoes. Then put in a very hot oven or, preferably, under a broiler, to brown. Allow about 80 grams (2 3/4 ounces) of meat per person. *Time: 45 minutes.*

500 grams (1 pound, 2 ounces) of beef.

***For the sauce:* 120 grams (4 1/4 ounces) of onions that have been finely minced; 40 grams (1 3/8 ounces, 3 tablespoons) of butter; 20–25 grams (2/3–1 ounce) of flour; 2 deciliters (6 3/4 fluid ounces, 7/8 cup) of white wine and 2 deciliters (6 3/4 fluid ounces, 7/8 cup) of degreased bouillon; 1 tablespoon of tomato paste; 1 tablespoon of minced parsley.**

***For the purée:* 500–600 grams (1 pound, 2 ounces–1 pound, 5 ounces) of nice Holland or other good-quality potatoes; 50 grams (1 3/4 ounces, 3 1/2 tablespoons of fresh butter; 2 deciliters (6 3/4 fluid ounces, 7/8 cup) of boiled milk; salt, pepper, and a pinch of nutmeg.**

***For the gratin:* 60 grams (2 1/4 ounces) of fresh grated Gruyère; 1 good tablespoon of bread crumbs; 10–15 grams (1/3–1/2 ounce, 1 scant tablespoon–1 tablespoon) of butter.**

PROCEDURE. Put the onion and the butter in a small saucepan. On low heat and without a cover, let it gradually color a little. Then sprinkle it with the flour. Mix it with the wooden spoon for 2 or 3 minutes until the flour has taken on a yellow tint. Dilute it with the wine, the bouillon, and the tomato paste. Bring it to a boil. Turn the heat down low. Cover and maintain a gentle simmer for *about 10 minutes.*

While the onions are cooking, start to make the puréed potatoes. Prepare it as described (SEE PAGE 540). The amount of milk here is a little more than usual since the dish is to be cooked as a gratin.

Take a heatproof serving dish that you can serve at the table. Add the beef. Skim the sauce with a metal spoon, then pour it over the meat, mixing well. Check the seasoning. Cover with a plate that has been turned over and keep it on very low heat for *6–7 minutes* at a very gentle simmer so that the beef is well flavored by the sauce as it heats.

Next, add the minced parsley. Spread out the beef in an equal layer over the plate. Cover it with the purée of potatoes in an even layer. Mix the grated cheese and bread crumbs on a plate; sprinkle them over the purée. On top of this, spread the butter, divided into little pieces. Put it immediately into the oven or under the broiler. If you are using an oven, keep the dish at the top so that the strong heat crisps and browns the potato for a perfect gratin. Allow *8–10 minutes* at the most.

Only the surface of the purée must brown; the rest of the dish should be nice and moist on the interior, the sauce having moistened the beef.

Beef Gratinée with Cheese *(Boeuf Gratiné au Fromage).* An excellent method of preparing the remains of boiled beef, provided it is in a state to let you divide it into regular slices. The dish, while it is extremely appetizing, does not contain onion or shallot or spiced seasoning. If you like, you can use either Gruyère without Parmesan or only Parmesan, but this makes the flavor a little strong. *Time: 30 minutes. Serves 6.*

500 grams (1 pound, 2 ounces) net of boiled beef; 60 grams (2¼ ounces) of grated Parmesan and the same of Gruyère; 15 grams (½ ounce) of flour and 15 grams (½ ounce, 1 tablespoon) of butter for a roux; 2½ deciliters (1 cup) of well degreased bouillon; ½ deciliter (1⅔ fluid ounces, scant ¼ cup) of white wine; pepper and nutmeg.

PROCEDURE. Cut the pieces into slices at least 1 good centimeter (⅝ inch) thick. Remove all the parts that are tough, darkened, hard, and fatty. If the piece has been larded, use the interior parts, which are excellent.

In a very small pan, make a light brown roux. Dilute it with hot or cold bouillon and wine. Mix it until it boils, then let it boil on low heat for 5–6 minutes. Remove the foam. Season with pepper and nutmeg. Check the salt level.

Pour half of the sauce into an ovenproof serving dish large enough so that the slices will not be too crowded. First, sprinkle the sauce with half of the mixed cheeses. Next, put the meat slices on top of this, arranging them so that each slice will get an equal covering of gratin. This should form a surface that is as flat as possible; otherwise, any meat sticking out will color before the rest of the dish, and therefore darken and dry out. Cover the slices with the rest of the sauce. Sprinkle with cheese.

This can be left to stand until you are ready to put it into the oven. You only put it into the oven for long enough to reheat the beef, so that the cheese melting on the surface takes on a beautiful color. The oven must be hot enough that this takes no more than *8–10 minutes.* If it is cooked for a longer time in an oven that is not hot enough, the dish will dry out before it colors. Put it in the oven where the surface receives the strongest heat while the bottom of the plate heats as little as possible.

To serve: Place it on a serving plate covered by a napkin.

Beef Miroton *(Boeuf en Miroton).* Onions, and a considerable quantity of them, are the characteristic ingredient for this dish. Certain authors also include mushrooms, but that is an exception. Others add some lemon juice or reduced vinegar as a final condiment. The recipe here includes a border of potatoes, which augments this dish, which is a classic of home cooking: the border and the gratin are not essential, and the beef can simply be served reheated in the sauce, having let it simmer for 10 minutes or so. *Time: About 1 hour. Serves 6, allowing 80–90 grams (2¾–3⅙ ounces) of beef per person.*

500 grams (1 pound, 2 ounces) of beef; 300 grams (10½ ounces) of onions net weight; 10 grams (⅓ ounce) of flour; 1 deciliter (3⅓ fluid ounces, scant ½ cup) of white wine; 2 deciliters (6¾ fluid ounces,

7/8 cup) of bouillon; 40–50 grams (1 3/8–1 3/4 ounces, 3–3 1/2 tablespoons) of butter; 3 large, long potatoes; 2 good tablespoons of fine bread crumbs.

PROCEDURE. **The onions:** Mince the onions evenly. If the onions are old, first throw them into a pot of boiling water and boil them for 8–10 minutes. Drain and then dry on a towel. If they keep their moisture, they will not subsequently color.

In a sauté pan, heat the butter strongly, particularly if the onions have been blanched. Add the onions, but do not cover. Over heat that is not too high, stir frequently with the wooden spoon until they have taken on an equal light golden color. Sprinkle with the flour. Let them gently color for *5–6 minutes,* stirring them from time to time.

Add wine, bouillon, pepper. Stir until it boils, then let it simmer for *25 minutes.*

The potatoes: Cook them in salted water with their skins on. They can be cooked in advance and kept warm in their pot.

The beef: Remove the membrane and fat. Cut the beef as best as you can into small, thin slices. Put these, along with the trimmings, into the pan with the cooked onion. Let simmer for another *7–8 minutes.*

To dress and make the gratin: Peel the potatoes. Cut them into rounds a good 5 millimeters (3/16 inch) thick.

Butter an ovenproof dish. Arrange the rounds of potatoes in a crown or circular shape, leaning one up against the other. Take the pieces of beef with a fork and arrange them in the middle of the potatoes.

Check the seasoning for the sauce. And if the sauce is not thick enough, reduce it over strong heat for a few minutes. Pour the onions and the sauce on top of the beef. If you do not want to eat the pieces of onion, strain the sauce and the onion through a strainer, pushing it through with a pestle, and then pour this sauce over the beef. Sprinkle the beef with bread crumbs. Put the rest of the butter, divided into pieces, over this. Put the dish in a very hot oven for *8–10 minutes,* with a strong heat from the top to make the gratin.

Hash from Meat Cooked to Prepare Jus. With these meats and the vegetables, especially carrots (which are particularly appropriate here), you can make a very good hash.

At the same time as the meat, chop the raw onion (using as much or as little as you want) and a little bit of parsley. If you have a small grinder, pass this mixture through the large disc. Depending on the amount of hash, add 1 or 2 tablespoons of finely ground white bread crumbs. To enrich the hash, you can add a quarter of its weight in sausage meat; I recommend this highly.

In a pot, reduce 3 or 4 tablespoons of very good vinegar to just 1 tablespoon. Lightly color the sausage meat, while stirring. After this, add the hash of cooked meat, onion, etc. Continue to color it. Moisten it with a little bouillon or water; use about 3 deciliters (1 1/4 cups) per 450 grams (1 pound) of hash, just enough to moisten it, but no more. Spread the hash in a gratin pan. Put it in a very hot oven or under the broiler so that the surface browns rapidly while the inside does not dry out: approximately *7–8 minutes.*

Leftovers of Roast Beef. If you have a large quantity of leftovers, these can be quite nicely used in thin slices, which can be served cold with an appropriate sauce (tartar, rémoulade, etc.), or served hot with any sauce (piquante, peppery, chasseur, etc.).

There are two points to note: first, cut the slices no larger than 3 millimeters (1/8 inch) thick so that they will reheat quickly; second, make sure the meat does not boil, which will harden any roast meat.

Allow 3 slices per person, which will be about 80 grams (2 3/4 ounces), and 1/2 deciliter (1 2/3 fluid ounces, scant 1/4 cup) of sauce. Arrange the slices in a crown or in a circle on a round plate, or in one long line on a long plate. Make sure that the slices are barely overlapping so that the meat reheats without being slowed down. Cover with a *boiling* sauce and heat the bottom of the plate thoroughly for a few seconds. Serve immediately.

Beef Tongue *(Langue de Boeuf)*

Beef tongue is, above all, a recipe for home cooking; it is excellent if you take the time and trouble to braise it, though more often it is cooked simply and well as a pot-au-feu; the bouillon used for cooking can be used in a soup, so the tongue ends up providing two dishes. Tongue cooked thus can be accompanied by your choice of sauce—tomato, piquante, a sauce Robert, etc.—served on the side. Cut into slices, it can also be served in a stew, the sauce having been prepared separately with this recipe in mind.

You get a much better result when braising, so once the pot has been set up for cooking, it is just a simple matter of keeping an eye on it from then on. We therefore recommend this method above all others. Furthermore, this is the method used in fine classic cooking, the braised tongue going well with very different garnishes, and the leftovers lending themselves perfectly to being reheated in all kinds of recipes. So it is to your advantage to buy a piece substantially larger than what you need for one meal.

As for cooking the tongue in a pot-au-feu or braising it, it is worth mentioning the method used in some regions: that is, to cook the tongue three-quarters of the way through in a marmite and then to finish cooking it in an ovenproof pot, to give it color and taste. We give the recipe for this below.

Let's also mention the method of cooking the tongue in a pot-au-feu and then cutting it in half and finishing it on the grill (or under the broiler), serving it with an anchovy butter or any other butter. Or just finish cooking it in the oven. You can lard it, as you would for a roast, and baste it with the juice. Larding the tongue with large lardons is, at least in classic cooking, very common, not just for braising but also for a tongue that has been cooked in a marmite, especially when the cooking has been finished in a pot or as a roast.

If you have to buy the tongue several days in advance, and particularly if it is summer, you can preserve it better by putting it in salt. What's more, in certain countries, tongue is never used unless it has first been half-salted (known as *demi-se* in France)—in other words, kept for several days in a terrine covered with salt. This method is very good; remember to wash it completely before you start cooking it, and remember, too, that the meat is already salted.

The principal garnishes that are suitable for a braised tongue are mostly purées: potatoes, beans, and peas, either fresh or dried; chestnuts, sorrel, chicory, spinach, etc.; noodles and macaroni, cabbage and sauerkraut; and a garnish à la flamande, etc. The stock or juice from the cooking is carefully degreased and bound with arrowroot to be served on the side. You can also prepare beef tongue à la bourgeoise by adding, after two-thirds of the cooking time, a garnish of carrots and small onions, as for beef à la mode.

To accompany braised tongue, choose from mushroom sauce, piquante sauce, tomato sauce, sauce soubise, etc.

There is another sauce worth mentioning because it is extremely good as well as simple. *After* the tongue has been cooked, strain the cooking liquid and degrease it, then add fines herbes, some cornichons cut into rounds, capers, a little bit of white wine, and some bouillon. Let simmer for a while to reduce. The tongue can, if you like, be put back into this sauce and kept warm at a very low simmer until you are ready to serve. *Off the heat,* add a piece of fresh butter that has been divided into fragments, and pour it over the tongue on a serving plate.

Let us say in conclusion that braised tongue is an excellent cold plate with a seasonal salad.

To lard the tongue: Even if it must be cooked in a court bouillon as a pot-au-feu, you must first blanch the tongue so that it will be firm enough to let you put in the lardons. Then cook as for braised tongue.

For a tongue weighing net about 2 kilograms (4 pounds, 6 ounces), use 100 grams ($3^1/_2$ ounces) of fresh fatback bacon or half fatback and half raw ham. Cut the lardons 10 centimeters (4 inches) long and about 1 centimeter ($^3/_8$ inch) square. Roll them on a plate sprinkled with salt, pepper, and spices. Using a large larding needle with a gutter shape (SEE LARDING, PAGE 11), lard the tongue crosswise, directing the larding needle a little bit on the bias, which makes a better pattern when you cut up the tongue.

To serve the tongue: There are several ways to serve tongue, depending more or less on the garnish.

With a purée, cut the tongue in half lengthwise; put the halves on each side of a long plate. Place the purée in the middle in a dome shape. Or: cut a whole tongue into slices 7–8 millimeters (about $^5/_{16}$ inch) thick, cutting on a light bias, just as butchers cut sausages to give them a larger surface area. Arrange them on a round plate in a tight circle so there is only a little bit of empty space in the middle. Fill this empty space with the purée, mounting it into a pyramid tablespoon by tablespoon.

Boiled Beef Tongue *(Langue de Boeuf Bouillie).* You can use different methods for this dish.

The simplest is surely this one: Take out the nasal bones and the glands. Thoroughly brush the tongue with a scrubbing brush to remove the black material found among the buds on the tongue. Soak it in cold water for 1 hour before cooking.

Once cleaned, put the tongue into a marmite or some other pot.

1 tongue with a net weight of 2 kilograms (4 pounds, 6 ounces); 4 liters (4$^1/_4$ quarts) of cold water; 2 medium-sized onions, a total of 120 grams (4$^1/_4$ ounces) into which you will stick 2 cloves; 2 bouquets garnis; 25 grams (1 ounce) of sea salt (7 grams/$^1/_4$ ounce per liter/4$^1/_4$ cups); 3 or 4 peppercorns. If the tongue has been put in salt (SEE PAGE 271), do not use salt when cooking.

PROCEDURE. Bring to a boil, then skim. After this, completely cover the utensil and regulate the heat to maintain the liquid at a very gentle, regular simmer for *3 hours.*

Once you have skimmed the court bouillon, you should allow a cooking time of about *40 minutes* per 450 grams (1 pound). That said, the age and the quality of the animal that provided the tongue will affect the cooking time. Overcooking a tongue from a choice animal will make it soft and insipid, but undercooking will leave the tongue dry and tough. You can judge when it is perfectly cooked by sticking a cooking needle into the tongue, which it should easily pierce right through.

Now drain the tongue. Take off the skin covering it, lifting it at one end and pulling it off carefully so that you do not damage the flesh. The skin comes off easily if the tongue has been properly cooked.

Serve the tongue as you would for beef in a pot-au-feu, offering the appropriate sauce in a sauceboat.

The court bouillon used for cooking the tongue can be used as a vegetable soup.

Another method. This is simply a refinement of the first dish. Instead of being satisfied with a simple court bouillon, you cook the tongue as if it were a pot-au-feu—and as you can imagine, this produces a much better bouillon for your soup than the first method. If possible, the bouillon used here should include some bones, previously browned like the bones used for a pot-au-feu.

1 tongue with a net weight of about 2 kilograms (4 pounds, 6 ounces); 120 grams (4$^1/_4$ ounces) of carrot and the same of turnip; 100 grams (3$^1/_2$ ounces) of leeks and an onion stuck with a clove; 10 grams ($^1/_3$ ounce) of celery; a nice bouquet garni; 3 or 4 liters (3$^1/_5$–4$^1/_4$ quarts) of water salted with 7 grams ($^1/_4$ ounce) of salt per liter (4$^1/_4$ cups).

PROCEDURE. Take out the bones of the tongue and the remains of the glands, then blanch as described for braised tongue. Remove the skin and plunge it into boiling liquid with the browned bones and the vegetables. Once it has returned to a boil, arrange the marmite or the pot as for a pot-au-feu, with the cover slightly open to let the steam escape: this is for the benefit of the soup later, because it allows a slight reduction and thus strengthens the bouillon, which has too few ingredients to produce much flavor.

The same gentle and regular simmer; the same cooking time. The same test to see if it is properly cooked, and the same service.

Braised Beef Tongue *(Langue de Boeuf Braisée).* For all the details of cooking, refer to the section on braising (SEE PAGE 25). The method used here for tongue is the same for braising all white meats. *Time: 1 scant hour to blanch and clean the tongue, which can be done in advance; 3$^1/_4$ hours for braising. So, in total, 4$^1/_4$ hours. Once the tongue has been perfectly cooked, it is not at all inconvenient—in fact, far from it—to leave it standing until you are ready to serve. This gives you time for other last-minute preparations.*

1 tongue weighing about 2 kilograms (4 pounds, 6 ounces) before it is trimmed; 50 grams (1$^3/_4$ ounces) of pork rind; 125 grams (4$^1/_2$ ounces) of carrots cut into rounds; 125 grams (4$^1/_2$ ounces) of onion cut the same; a nice bouquet garni; $^1/_2$ deciliter (1$^2/_3$ fluid ounces,

scant 1/4 cup) of white wine; about 1 liter (4 1/4 cups) of bouillon very lightly salted and very well degreased.

PROCEDURE. Take out the bones and the glands (the useless fatty parts) that cling to the "heel" (the large end) of the tongue.

If you bought the tongue a few hours in advance, leave it to disgorge, trimmed as it is, in a large quantity of cold water. Change the water from time to time. The tongue can be left like this for an entire day or an entire night.

To blanch: Put the tongue into a large ovenproof receptacle: enameled steel or whatever else. Pour over enough cold water to completely cover.

Bring it quickly to a boil, then simmer gently for *15–20 minutes.* During this time, a foam will appear and rise to the surface, and this is how the tongue is cleaned. Remove this foam, which will otherwise attach itself to the tongue. Remove the tongue from the water after 20 minutes. Submerse it in cold water, and let it stand there to thoroughly chill.

Drain and then remove its white skin. This is simple enough to do: start at the pointed end, where the skin is very thick, using the point of a knife. As you reach the heel, you will find that you can only remove small parts of the skin; scrape it with the knife blade, holding the knife at right angles to the surface.

Cooking the tongue: Use a thick pot, as used when braising, or even a good pot made of enameled steel. You will have to curl the tongue slightly, but make sure that it has enough room.

Put the tongue into the pot. Place the *covered* pot on moderate heat. Allow it to sweat for *10–20 minutes* and firm up. Turn off the fire to add the white wine. Put it back on the heat without a cover to reduce it completely.

Then add the hot or cold bouillon, to cover up to two-thirds of the tongue. Bring it to a boil, then put a round of buttered parchment paper directly on top of the tongue. Cover tightly with the cover and immediately put it into a medium-hot oven. Allow for about *3 hours of cooking* at a moderate, regular simmer.

During the first 2 hours, turn the tongue three or four times in its braising juice. For the rest of the cooking time, you need only baste it occasionally. At the end of the indicated time, check to see if the tongue is properly cooked by sticking it with a cooking needle. If the needle pierces it without difficulty, the tongue is properly cooked. If not, leave it and let it cook for another 20 minutes or so.

To serve: Strain the cooking juice into a small saucepan. You will not really need to degrease it because the tongue and the cooking stock barely yields any grease. There should be about 3 deciliters (1 1/4 cups). If there is more, reduce it by boiling it uncovered over strong heat. Thicken with starch (SEE LIAISONS, PAGE 47). If desired, and if it suits the garnish, dress the tongue with a few tablespoons of juice added to the dish. Serve the rest of the juice in a sauceboat.

Home-Style Beef Tongue *(Langue de Boeuf à la Ménagère).* This is the method we mentioned earlier; it is a cross between boiled tongue and braised tongue.

PROCEDURE. Cook the tongue in the court bouillon as described in the previous recipe. But leave it there for only *2 hours.* If you have made a pot-au-feu on the same day, then the simplest thing to do is to cook the tongue right in this boiling liquid and to leave it there for the time suggested. You can cook it like this the evening before you are planning to serve it.

Remove the skin. Lard the tongue, as described, when it has cooled.

In a thick pot or a good enameled pot, put 1 good tablespoon of nice fresh fat from a roast or stock with 1 or 2 onions, depending on their size—at least 100 grams (3 1/2 ounces) in all—cut into thick rounds. This is enough for a tongue with a net weight of 2 kilograms (4 pounds, 6 ounces). Let it stew on low heat for about 10 minutes, simply to soften the onion and to color it slightly.

Then put the tongue on top of the onion. Cover. Let the tongue slightly color underneath for *8–10 minutes,* shaking the pot two or three times to move the onion and to keep it from burning.

Turn the tongue over and color on the other side. As soon as the onion starts coloring beyond golden, pour 1 tablespoon of water into the pot and cover it immediately. Two or three minutes later, add 3 or 4 tablespoons of vinegar. Let it boil without covering the pot to reduce the vinegar and increase its acidity. Add two glasses, 4 deciliters ($1^{2}/_{3}$ cups) of jus, if you have it, or of bouillon. Once it has begun to boil, cover it and leave a small opening for the steam. Cook it very gently for *45 minutes.*

During this time, turn the tongue once and frequently baste it with its cooking juices, being careful that it does not stick to the bottom of the pot. Strain the juice into a small bowl, then degrease it and thicken it with a little bit of starch (SEE LIAISONS, PAGE 47). Serve it on the side.

Gras-Double *(Gras-Double)*

Culinarily speaking, you must not confuse *gras-double* with ordinary tripe. Certainly both make use of a beef stomach, but while the name "tripe" refers to the stomach and anything wrapped in it, *gras-double* makes use of the stomach only as a kind of thick sheet.

We give here no directions for preparing tripe. Tripe, and particularly tripe à la mode de Caen, can be prepared only in very large quantities; it also involves a large amount of work, which is complicated further by the difficulties of a cooking process that involves very special conditions. So we will concern ourselves only with *gras-double* itself.

In the villages and at butchers in most parts of the country, *gras-double* is sold already cooked, ready for use. When you cannot find it precooked, you must wash it and then soak it well in cold water for about 6 hours, changing the water frequently. Afterwards, you immerse it in a generous amount of cold water, which has been salted with 7–10 grams ($^{1}/_{4}$–$^{1}/_{3}$ ounce) of salt per liter ($4^{1}/_{4}$ cups). Bring it to a boil and maintain the liquid at a gentle simmer for at least *5 hours.*

The *gras-double* sold by tripe sellers is rolled up on itself like a big sausage. You can cut this sausage into slices 7–8 millimeters ($^{5}/_{16}$ inch) thick, which you can then divide lengthwise, in effect, making a short julienne. This is much quicker than unrolling the *gras-double* and then cutting it into small rectangles.

Gras-Double with Sauce Robert *(Gras-Double à la Sauce Robert).* Simmer the *gras-double* in the sauce for a half hour before finishing it with mustard. Allow 3 deciliters ($1^{1}/_{4}$ cups) of sauce for 450 grams (1 pound) of *gras-double.*

Gras-Double à la Poulette *(Gras-Double à la Poulette).* Simmer it in the sauce, then thicken with egg yolks.

Gras-Double with Parmesan *(Gras-Double au Parmesan).* Arranged in a shallow bowl in layers, alternating with tomato sauce and grated Parmesan, as for Neapolitan-style macaroni.

Grilled Gras-Double *(Gras-Double Grillé).* Cut into rectangles, then dip in melted butter or oil and coat with bread crumbs (SEE PAGE 19). Grill (or broil) gently, sprinkle with butter or oil. Serve arranged in a circle, with piquante sauce, rémoulade, tartar, tomato, etc.

Fried Gras-Double *(Gras-Double Frit).* Cut into rectangles and marinate with a dash of vinegar, salt, and pepper. Coat in bread crumbs (SEE BREADING, PAGE 19), then deep-fry in very hot fat. Serve with one of the sauces suggested for grilled *gras-double.*

Lyon-Style Gras-Double *(Gras-Double à la Lyonnaise).* Cut into a large julienne, then season with salt and pepper. Sauté it in smoking lard in a pan on strong heat to brown it to a beautiful golden color. Meanwhile, in a second pan, sauté and color some onion, which has been cut into very thin slices; use the same weight of onions as of *gras-double.* Bring together both ingredients into one of the pans, then sauté to brown thoroughly.

Pour into a timbale or warmed plate. Sprinkle with 1 tablespoon of vinegar, which you have first swirled around the pan. Sprinkle with minced parsley and serve quite hot.

Beef Heart and Veal Heart *(Coeur de Boeuf et Coeur de Veau)*

Many people have never eaten this in their life. Properly speaking, this part of the beast is not a culinary delight, but rather a practical use of this part. We will confine ourselves to just a few directions, observing that the heart of a young calf is preferable to that of an adult, as is also true of the kidneys. Both should be chosen as fresh as possible and be nice and fatty.

The beef heart: Usually only prepared by braising—in other words, whole, larded, and cooked like BEEF À LA MODE (PAGE 252). To prepare, slit the heart from the top to the bottom without separating it completely, to extract the clots of blood. Wash it carefully, then lard and marinate, and finally bind it with a few turns of string. Or cut into large square pieces and brown in some minced bacon, then sprinkle with flour, moisten with red wine, add a nice bouquet garni, and, when it is half cooked, add some small onions, previously browned in butter. Whichever cooking method you use, allow at least 3 hours at a gentle regular simmer, in the oven if possible.

The veal heart: Cut lengthwise into thin slices, as when preparing veal kidneys and veal liver, then sauté. And take the same care when cooking: that is, sauté the slices over strong heat, and when you add the sauce in which they will be served, do not let it boil.

Veal heart can also be braised. If you wish, you can stuff it: use 3 tablespoons of finely chopped and slightly browned onion with 25–30 grams (1 ounce, 2 tablespoons) of butter, then add 150 grams (5¹/₃ ounces) of very fine sausage meat; minced parsley; a portion of bread crumbs the size of an egg, moistened with bouillon; a whole beaten egg; salt, pepper, and grated nutmeg. Open the heart, extract the clotted blood from it, season it lightly, and fill it with the stuffing. Close it and tie it up. Cook as for braised veal liver. You can also add a garnish if you wish: a little onion, new carrots, mushrooms, etc. Once the heart has been browned and the court bouillon has begun to boil, allow almost *3 hours* to cook.

VEAL
Veau

Round Roast of Veal *(La Noix de Veau)*

The piece known as round roast in a calf corresponds to a round roast of beef. It is that part of the leg that is all meat without fat or nerves (as for a leg of lamb or ham). Taken from the outside of the haunch, it is consistently thick; two-thirds of this is covered with a light layer of fibrous meat, which is tough and a little fatty.

This meat is the best part of the haunch, and it is the meat used for fricandeaux, grenadins, and scallops. Never confuse it with the rump roast, a piece cut across the haunch with the bone running through it.

Braised Round Roast of Veal *(Noix de Veau Braisé).*

For details on how to braise white meats, SEE BRAISING (PAGE 25). *Time: 3 scant hours (once the meat has been larded and is ready to be cooked).*

1 round roast of veal weighing 1¹/₂–2 kilograms (3 pounds, 5 ounces–4 pounds, 6 ounces); 150 grams (5¹/₃ ounces) of fatback bacon for barding.

For braising: 100 grams (3¹/₂ ounces) of fresh pork rind; 120 grams (4¹/₄ ounces) of carrot; 120 grams (4¹/₄ ounces) of onion; a bouquet garni; ¹/₂ glass of white wine; 1 liter (4¹/₄ cups) of veal jus or excellent bouillon, either unsalted or only lightly salted.

PROCEDURE. Bard the veal round roast on the uncovered part with fat, bacon lardons 3–4 millimeters (¹/₈ inch) thick and no longer than 4 centimeters (1¹/₂ inches) (SEE LARDING, PAGE 11). Thus, you'll end up with four or five rows of lardons crisscrossing each other and sticking out by about 1 centimeter (³/₈ inch) on either side.

Line the ovenproof pot with salt pork, onions, carrots, and bouquet garni. Put in the round roast, barded part up. Sweat it for *15–20 minutes.* Add the white wine; let it reduce to a glaze. Then add 1 deciliter (3¹/₃ fluid ounces, scant ¹/₂ cup) of jus, and let this reduce to a glaze, too. Moisten it with the rest of the jus. Bring it to a boil. Cover with buttered parchment paper and then the cover. Put the pot in the oven and cook as described.

At the end of 1 hour of cooking, baste the meat every 10–12 minutes for another hour. Thus, cook for a total of *2 hours* in the oven.

Strain the juice. Degrease it. It should have reduced to 3 deciliters (1¹/₄ cups).

Glaze the roast on the barded side. Even though this is optional in many cases, glazing is particularly essential for white meats when they are barded.

The garnishes: A number of different kinds of garnish suit a braised round roast of veal. We will simply list them here and you can refer to the appropriate sections for how to prepare them.

In the first place, we would like to mention purées—of chicory, sorrel, or spinach—which are good whether used to garnish the veal directly or to serve apart in a separate vegetable dish.

- Braised cabbage. A braised sauerkraut, garnished with rounds of sausage, etc., in the Alsatian manner.
- Carrots à la Vichy or with cream.
- Chinese artichokes, bound with a little béchamel sauce.
- Pommes dauphines (croquettes).
- Green beans; white beans; flageolets; green peas—any one of these vegetables cooked in water and bound with butter.
- Braised lettuce, stuffed or not.
- Macaroni or noodles sautéed in butter, with cheese added, and if you wish, a little bit of chopped ham.
- Surround the meat with a very reduced juice from the braising. Serve a more or less light tomato sauce alongside.
- Nevers-style; glazed carrots and onions.
- Risotto with a tomato sauce.
- Stuffed tomatoes.

Depending on the kind of garnish and also on whether it is served with the roast or alongside, the braising juice is served in a sauceboat once it has been thoroughly degreased and strained. Or reduce it greatly and then pour around the meat.

Round Roast of Veal à la Bourgeoise *(Noix de Veau à la Bourgeoise).* The garnish is very simple to prepare, being partially cooked with the veal. The veal is braised the same way as all white meats (SEE PAGE 28); the veal foot completes the garnish.

From March on, you can use new vegetables for the garnish. But the pot for braising the veal should be lined with winter vegetables, since new vegetables are delicate and will not give the cooking juices a strong enough flavor.

Like classic braising, the cooking time here is rather lengthy. Also, the meat is a little more difficult to cut into thin slices, so you must use a good knife. *Time: 3 hours (once the roast has been barded and the pot completely prepared).*

1 veal roast weighing from 1½–1.8 kilograms (3 pounds, 5 ounces–4 pounds); a small veal foot; 125 grams (4½ ounces) of fatback bacon for barding.

***For braising:* the same quantities of ingredients given in the previous recipe.**

***For the garnish:* 4 medium-sized carrots; 15 small onions; 125 grams (4½ ounces) of lean bacon; ½ teaspoon of starch to bind the juice.**

PROCEDURE. Bard the roast as above. Split the veal foot lengthwise and then blanch. Line the ovenproof pot. Put in the roast, the barded part facing up. Put a half foot and the bacon trimmings on either side.

Sweat for about 20 minutes. Add ½ glass of juice or bouillon; quickly reduce it to a glaze. Add the rest of the liquid, which must reach halfway up the roast. If the pot is a little bit larger than necessary, you must add a little more liquid.

Bring it to a boil, then cover with the parchment paper and the cover. Put it in the oven and let it gently simmer for *1 hour.* After this, baste every 10 minutes and cook for a second hour. In other words, the meat should cook for *2 hours* before adding the garnish, which you have prepared in the meantime.

The garnish: Cut the *carrots* in rounds 4 centimeters (1½ inch) thick. Divide these into small quarters, then trim into the shape of an elongated olive, removing as much as possible of the heart of the carrot, which is worthless.

Put them in a pot covered with cool water and a pinch of salt. Let it boil gently for 20 minutes. Drain them, then set aside on a plate.

Peel the *small onions* carefully (SEE PAGE 525). Brown them in a pan with 30 grams (1 ounce, 2 tablespoons) of butter on low heat, tossing them from time to time. Add them to the carrots.

Cut the *bacon,* trimmed of its rind, into lardons 1½ centimeters (⅝ inch) square. Put them in a small pot of cold water. Boil for 5 or 6 minutes. Drain them well. Add these to the vegetables. After the roast has been cooking for *2 hours,* turn off the heat. Put the meat on a plate. Strain the juices into a terrine, which should have reduced to 6 or 7 deciliters (2$^1/_2$–3 cups).

Take out of the pot what's left of the braising vegetables. Then put back the strained juice, *without degreasing it,* and the veal. Around the veal, put carrots, onions, lardons, and the veal foot cut into small pieces. Replace the circle of paper and cover. Turn the heat back on and return to a gentle simmer, then cook for another *45 minutes.*

About 10 minutes before serving, remove the veal roast and put it on an ovenproof dish. Put it into a very hot oven, so that the heat of the oven colors the lardons: you want a nice golden color without letting them brown too much. Meanwhile, strain the cooking juice into a small saucepan. Degrease it and reduce it to at least 3 good deciliters (1$^1/_4$ cups). Thicken it with the starch (SEE PAGE 48).

To serve: *If you are carving at the table:* Place the veal roast on a round plate. Place the garnish in little piles all around it. Moisten with the thickened juices.

If you are carving in the kitchen: Cut the necessary number of slices *very thin.* Arrange them in a half oval at the end of a long plate. Place the remaining piece of veal on the other end of the plate. Put the garnish in the middle; don't worry about arranging this too carefully. Baste with the juices. This second procedure is the best for serving hot.

Fricandeau (Braised Veal) *(Le Fricandeau)*

Fricandeau with sorrel! For those of a great age, this is a reminder of a time very long ago when there was no advice to eliminate sorrel from the diets of those with gout—otherwise known as gourmets; a time when chefs in white hats, who could not even read, prepared this recipe with the time and care required to make it excellent. The fricandeau is a kind of braise, but a methodical and patient way of braising. At the end the meat is rich and soft, a beautiful golden blond with a jus like a succulent amber syrup, which, according to tradition, can be "cut with a spoon."

The round roast of veal is the only part of veal that can supply a proper fricandeau: a long piece 3 or 4 centimeters (1$^1/_4$–1$^1/_2$ inches) thick *at the most,* cut along the length of the piece and barded on its entire surface with tiny lardons. Here, the importance of this larding means dividing the piece in the direction of the grain of the meat, as has been explained in the article on barding.

The garnishes that accompany the fricandeau, after the classic purée of sorrel, are those made from chicory and spinach: either baste the purée with the cooking jus, then arrange the meat on top; or (which is more convenient) serve the fricandeau surrounded by its juice and the purée in a serving dish. You can serve all other garnishes in the same way, including: jardinière, macédoine, braised lettuce, green peas, asparagus tips, glazed carrots, Brussels sprouts, mushrooms, purées, soubise, tomato fondue, etc.

We have stated that the usual thing is to divide the fricandeau with a spoon instead of a knife. That is why it is better to serve it by itself on a plate, so that guests can help themselves. If the fricandeau is served on its garnish, it must first be divided into slices about two fingers thick. In this case, do not use a spoon to carve but a very fine-bladed knife, so that you do not crumble the slices and you can then put them back together again to reshape the fricandeau. *Time: 3$^1/_2$ hours (once the fricandeau has been barded and put on the fire). Serves 8–10.*

1$^1/_2$ kilograms (3 pounds, 5 ounces) of round roast of veal; 150 grams (5$^1/_3$ ounces) of fatback bacon for larding; 60 grams (2$^1/_4$ ounces) of fresh pork rind; 90 grams (3$^1/_6$ ounces) of onion and 90 grams (3$^1/_6$ ounces) of carrot; 1 deciliter (3$^1/_3$ fluid ounces, scant $^1/_2$ cup) of good white wine; 6 deciliters (2$^1/_2$ cups) of veal jus or bouillon, barely salted (if using bouillon, double the quantity of pork rind to make up for the absence of gelatin).

A bouquet garni.

PROCEDURE. Cut the veal round roast in even slices of the recommended thickness—or have the butcher do it for you. Bard one side of each slice with lardons 3 centimeters long (1$^1/_4$ inches) and 2 millimeters (about $^1/_{16}$ inch) on each side at intervals of 1 centimeter ($^3/_8$ inch). SEE BARDING (PAGE 11).

Use a thick pot with a good flat bottom to hold the slices next to each other; don't worry if they are a little crowded, because the meat will shrink soon enough in the cooking. Line it with pork rinds and vegetables—one of the basics of braising, as described (SEE BRAISING, PAGE 25). Put in the fricandeau with the barded part facing up. Cover the pot.

We will only summarize the techniques here. For further details, refer to the directions on braising white meats (PAGE 28).

Thus, on extremely low heat, sweat the meat gently for *about 20 minutes;* do not let it shrink. Pour in the white wine, then cover again. Let it reduce gradually until it is a glaze; about another 20 minutes. Add another deciliter (3 1/3 fluid ounces, scant 1/2 cup) of jus or bouillon, then cover and repeat the procedure. Finally, moisten it with the rest of the jus or the bouillon, about 5 deciliters (generous 2 cups), which must come halfway up the meat without covering it.

Bring to a boil on strong heat. Then place a round of paper right on top of the meat. Cover it tightly. Put it in a medium oven.

From this point on, cook for another *2 hours* at a gentle simmer. Every 15–20 minutes, raise the paper and the cover to baste the meat in its cooking juice, without moving anything in the pot.

At this point, keep the pot warm until you are ready to glaze as directed. With great care, use a skimmer to lift out the veal slices onto a plate; they will be extremely fragile. Pass the juice through the chinois into a small terrine and take out the cooking liquid and vegetables from the braise. Put the meat back in, then degrease the juice. Pour it on the fricandeau, then put this into the oven or under a medium-hot broiler, proceeding as described for glazing. Baste every 3 minutes for *10–12 minutes.* Avoid too strong a heat or too direct a heat, which will burn the lardons. What you want is the meat to brown lightly to a beautiful brilliant color.

Glazing naturally reduces the juice, which will now be barely more than 1 1/2 good deciliters (5 fluid ounces, 2/3 cup). This is just the right amount either for basting the garnish or for surrounding the fricandeau if it is served by itself. In the latter case, 1 tablespoon per person will suffice, enough just to moisten only the meat, which will already have absorbed the cooking juices.

Grenadins *(Les Grenadins)*

The *grenadin* is like the scallop and the fricandeau: like the scallop because it uses the same weight of meat and is taken from the same part of veal; and like the fricandeau because it is barded and it is prepared the same way. Thus, the *grenadin* is a fricandeau in miniature.

The essential difference between the *grenadin* and the scallop is that the scallop must be flattened so that it can be rapidly sautéed while the *grenadin* retains a certain thickness and is cooked slowly; finally, the scallop is served only at lunch while the *grenadin* is a dinner course and can form part of a serious menu, though not one for official occasions.

A *grenadin* that has been completely trimmed is an oval slice 8–9 centimeters (3 1/4–3 1/2 inches) long, 4–5 centimeters (1 1/2–2 inches) wide, and 1 1/2 centimeters (5/8 inch) thick. The round roast veal is the only part used for a *grenadin,* which is cut from it in the direction of the grain of the meat, like a fricandeau.

You always allow 1 *grenadin* per person, but it is usual to prepare a few more than are strictly necessary. Any leftovers make such a good, popular cold entrée that you can prepare the *grenadin* just to make a nice, cold entrée, serving it with a jardinière garnish and a gelée.

Grenadins are always accompanied with a garnish and particularly with a garnish of vegetables. Use any of the garnishes that are appropriate for a round roast of braised veal and a fricandeau.

Dressing *grenadins:* Do this according to taste and your choice of garnish: arrange them in a rose pattern on the purée, or put the purée in the center of the plate and arrange the *grenadins* around it, still in the rose pattern; or, if you are offering several different garnishes, as for a dish à la jardinière, arrange them in bouquets between each *grenadin* with a bigger pyramid in the center. Or, the *grenadins* can be arranged in a tight turban—that is, leaning against each other in the center, with the garnish arranged in as high a pyramid as possible, or on a long plate. The *grenadins* can be arranged in one single line in the middle, slightly overlapping each other, and the garnish arranged in a border on either side.

In any case, use the reduced cooking juice only for basting the garnish; the *grenadins* have been previously glazed, so they do not need to be basted when they are served.

You can enhance the dish by placing slices of *hot boiled* tongue between the *grenadins*. To heat them, cover them with cold water in a small sauté pan; heat them just to the point where your fingers cannot support the heat (hotter than this, and the slices will toughen). Drain them afterward on a towel. *Time: 2 1/2 hours. Serves 6.*

8 scallops of an average weight of 150 grams (5 1/3 ounces) *untrimmed* (that is to say, 1 1/4 kilograms/ 2 pounds, 12 ounces of veal round roast); 150 grams (5 1/3 ounces) of fatback bacon to bard them; 50 grams (1 3/4 ounces) of fresh salt pork; 75 grams (2 2/3 ounces) of carrot and the same amount of onion; a bouquet garni; 1 deciliter (3 1/3 fluid ounces, scant 1/2 cup) of white wine; 5 deciliters (generous 2 cups) of light veal juice, barely salted. If you do not have veal juice, use the same quantity of bouillon, very lightly salted, and 30–40 grams (1–1 3/8 ounces) of salt pork as well, to make up for the lack of gelatin in the ordinary bouillon.

PROCEDURE. Pare the meat—that is, use a good knife to trim all around the scallops to make uniformly-sized slices. Doing this reduces the weight of the scallop from 150 grams (5 1/3 ounces) to 110–120 grams (3 7/8–4 1/4 ounces).

Bard the slices on one side only, as for a fricandeau, with four rows of small lardons, each 3 centimeters (1 1/4 inches) in length and 2–3 millimeters (scant 1/8 inch) square.

Use a sauté pan large enough to hold the *grenadins* side by side. Garnish the bottom with salt pork, onions, and carrots, as when braising (SEE BRAISING, PAGE 25). Put the *grenadins* on top with their barded side facing up.

Then follow all the directions given for cooking a fricandeau (PAGE 277). The only difference is that the meat is thinner, so it needs to sweat for a slightly shorter time: just *12–15 minutes.* Also, the total cooking time is reduced to *1 3/4 hours.*

Dress the *grenadins* and the garnish accompanying them according to preference. Baste the garnish with the cooking juice, which has been strained through a fine strainer and which should have the consistency of a light syrup. There should be only about *1 1/2 good deciliters (5 fluid ounces, 2/3 cup).*

Stuffed Veal Scallops *(Les Paupiettes)*

A very old dish, which can be found in cookbooks dating back more than a century and a half, referred to as *poupiettes, polpettes,* or "headless birds." It means a ribbon of raw veal meat spread with stuffing on one side and then rolled up on itself to make a large cylinder. By extension, you can apply this procedure to beef, and even fillet of sole or other fish. But when it was invented, and for a long time afterward, it was prepared with veal.

Braising is used to cook the paupiettes. The accompaniment is usually a purée of sorrel, chicory, spinach, or fresh or dried beans, etc., and noodles or macaroni with tomato sauce, on which you serve the paupiettes. You can also accompany them with a jardinière garnish, including asparagus tips, flageolet beans, etc. In short, use any of the garnishes that go well with braised meats.

These paupiettes are made from a long scallop weighing about 125 grams (4 1/2 ounces) and, when possible, cut from a fillet of veal. If not, take it from the round roast. They must be at least 15–17 centimeters (6–6 1/2 inches) long and only 6–7 centimeters (2 1/2–2 3/4 inches) wide: however, it is often difficult to get these from the butcher, who is more used to cutting ordinary scallops for sautéing. But if the scallop for the paupiette is not thin and very long, it is very difficult to roll up once you have stuffed it, and the stuffing will come out while cooking and spoil the look of the paupiette.

Do not make the mistake of thinking that a simple sausage meat will give the same results as a stuffing that has been specially prepared. Do not take off the bacon strip that is tied around each paupiette while cooking: this nourishes the meat and prevents it from browning. A paupiette, like a fricandeau and a grenadin, must retain a light color, and the meat should be as tender on the outside as on the inside. Given the thinness of the meat, it could dry and harden if it browns. Furthermore, the paupiettes are colored by the final glazing. *Time: 2 scant hours (once the paupiettes have been prepared).*

8 scallops of the suggested weight.

For the stuffing; **60 grams (2 1/4 ounces) of fine white stale bread crumbs; 1 scant deciliter (3 1/3 fluid ounces, scant 1/2 cup) of boiled milk; 120 grams (4 1/4 ounces) of fresh bacon; 15 grams (1/2 ounce, 1 tablespoon) of butter; half of a whole beaten egg; the trimming from the scallop.**

To wrap the paupiette: **150 grams (5 1/3 ounces) of bard of bacon cut thin as paper, to supply ribbons about 10 centimeters (4 inches) long and 5 centimeters (2 inches) wide.**

For cooking: **75 grams (2 2/3 ounces) of fresh salt pork; 60 grams (2 1/4 ounces) of carrot; 60 grams (2 1/4 ounces) of onion; a small bouquet garni; 1 deciliter (3 1/3 fluid ounces, scant 1/2 cup) of white wine; 4 deciliters (1 2/3 cups) of light veal juice or bouillon very lightly salted and well degreased; salt, pepper, nutmeg.**

PROCEDURE. With the bread and the milk, prepare the panade for the stuffing (SEE PANADE, PAGE 21).

Trim the scallops. Lay them out on your board, dampened. With one or two blows from the flat of a dampened cleaver, flatten them to reduce them to an even thickness of 6–7 millimeters (that is, a little bit more than 1/2 centimeter/about 3/16 inch).

Next, trim the ends and the sides to make a neat ribbon squared at both ends. The trimmings are needed for the stuffing, so you do not have to worry about waste.

The stuffing: Finely mince the trimmings from the meat and the bacon (without the rind). Gather everything into a terrine. Add the panade (when it is quite cool), salt, pepper, and a hint of grated nutmeg. Mix everything well with a wooden spoon. Then add the butter and the egg and stir vigorously. Finally, pass the stuffing through a metallic strainer. Then stir it again with a small wooden spoon to smooth it out.

The paupiette: Spread the 8 ribbons of veal in front of you. Divide the stuffing into 8 parts. Put some of it on each ribbon; spread the stuffing out in an equal layer with a moistened knife. Then roll the scallops on themselves, closing the stuffing inside. Rolled up like this, this meat looks like a large cylinder or small barrel—the paupiette.

Wrap each paupiette in a strip of bacon. Finally, surround each one with three turns of string.

Thus prepared, the paupiettes can be left for a rather long time, kept cool, until they are ready to be cooked.

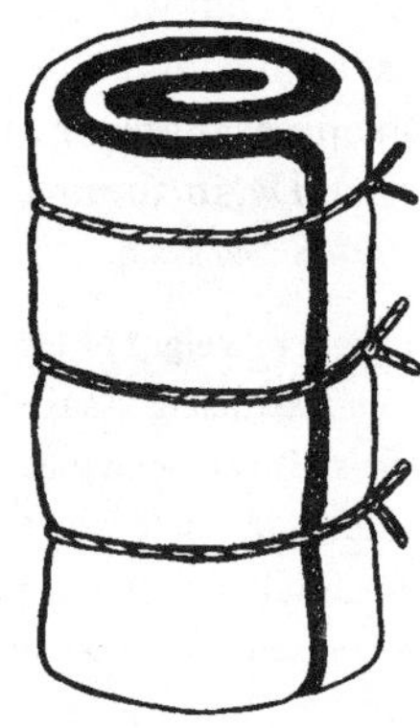

FIG. 48. PAUPIETTE.

Cooking the paupiette: Use a sauté pan large enough so that you can arrange the paupiettes either standing up or lying down, one next to the other, without being crowded.

Line the pan as directed (SEE BRAISING, PAGE 25). Arrange the paupiettes in the pan. Then cook exactly as has been described for braising white meats and, in particular, a fricandeau. Sweat it for *12–15 minutes.* Once you put the pot into the oven, allow *1 1/4 hours* of cooking before you are ready to glaze the paupiettes. At the end of a half hour, start basting them with their cooking juice.

A good 15 minutes before serving them, take the pan out of the oven and put the paupiettes on a plate. Strain the cooking juice into a bowl to degrease it: If the paupiettes have been properly cooked, you should have about 2 deciliters (6 3/4 fluid ounces, 7/8 cup). Pour it back into the pan once it has been strained.

Remove what remains of the bacon around the paupiettes. Put them back into the pot. Moisten them with their juice. Glaze in the oven for 7–8 minutes, as suggested for the fricandeau.

To serve: With scissors, cut the strings from the paupiette. Arrange them in a circle around the chosen garnish. If you have used simple bouillon for cooking, thicken the juice with 1/2 teaspoon of starch (SEE LIAISONS, PAGE 47). After glazing, you should have 1 1/2 good deciliters (5 fluid ounces, 2/3 cup) of juice. Pour it over or around the paupiettes, depending on how you want to serve them. Serve at once.

Veal Paupiette in the Manner of Alsace *(Paupiettes de Veau, Façon Alsacienne).* An excellent recipe taken from an Alsatian family notebook, where it is known as "roulettes of veal." The paupiettes are extremely simple and do not require any stuffing. Instead, a very thin slice of *smoked* bacon is used. This smoked bacon gives a particular flavor to the dish; so make sure you do not use ordinary bacon in its place.

These roulettes are also excellent cold, cut into rounds like a sausage and served as an hors d'oeuvre. *Time: 1 1/2 hours (once the paupiettes have been prepared for the oven).*

6 scallops; 150 grams (5 1/3 ounces) of smoked bacon; 2 tablespoons of minced parsley with, if you wish, a little shallot; 50 grams (1 3/4 ounces, 3 1/2 tablespoons) of butter; 30 grams (1 ounce) of onion; 5 grams (1/6 ounce) of celery; 5 or 6 parsley sprigs; 1 deciliter (3 1/3 fluid ounces, scant 1/2 cup) of bouillon.

PROCEDURE. Once the veal scallops have been cut as described above, lightly sprinkle them with salt, pepper, and the minced parsley. Place a strip of smoked bacon, cut extremely thin and only slightly longer than the scallop on each one. At one end, line up the scallop and the bacon, then roll the scallop up to enclose the bacon. In this way, the bacon is perfectly wrapped and hidden in its paupiette. Tie it as indicated.

Meanwhile, in the sauté pan where you will cook the paupiettes, heat the butter. Add the onion and celery, cut into small cubes; the parsley sprigs, chopped; and the trimmings from the smoked bacon and the scallops. Gently color the ingredients in the uncovered pan, stirring from time to time with a wooden spoon, for about 10 minutes.

Then place the paupiettes in the sauté pan, one next to the other. Do not cover them. Still on low heat, leave them in the pan for *7–8 minutes,* turning them one or two times, so that they lose the rosy tint of raw meat and take on the white color of cooked veal flesh—*nothing more,* no golden coloration. Cover it tightly. Let it cook steadily on very moderate heat for *1 1/2 hours.* Turn it two or three times during the second half of the cooking to ensure they cook evenly and color gradually.

Five minutes before serving, take the paupiettes out of the dish and put them on a heated round plate. Remove the string and keep them warm. Pour the bouillon into the pan. Scrape with the wooden spoon to dissolve the caramelized juice. Boil for just 1 minute; with a metal spoon, remove the excess grease, and then pour the juices through the chinois on the paupiettes.

Inevitably, you will have just a very small amount of juice; you want it to be concentrated. That said, you can add another 2 or 3 tablespoons of bouillon. If so, thicken it with the recipe given above. But doing so would not be faithful to the original and simple recipe.

Cutlets or "Chops" of Veal *(Les Côtelettes ou "Côtes" de Veau)*

A cutlet with a gross weight of 350–400 grams (12 1/3–14 1/8 ounces), and of 250–300 grams (8 7/8–10 1/2 ounces) when trimmed, is enough for 2 people. A rib-eye, supplying 1 cutlet per person, weighs about 180 grams (6 1/3 ounces) gross weight and 130 grams (4 1/2 ounces) when trimmed. It is always better when the recipe allows 1 cutlet per person. For the recipes mentioned below, remember that we are talking about gross weight.

Trimming the cutlets: Remove what remains of the spine with a cleaver: removing this bone is extremely important because, being thicker than the meat, it rests on the bottom of the pan, stopping the cutlet from contacting the surface and therefore ensuring the meat colors evenly. Using a good knife, detach the ribbon of nerve membrane surrounding the meat on the rib, which would warp the meat during cooking.

Then expose the end of the bone—as is done for mutton cutlets—to reveal 2 1/2 centimeters (1 inch) of bone: do this by cutting the flesh from the bone and pushing it back with the point of a knife. When putting a paper sleeve on the bone, cut the bone on the bias to facilitate its introduction into the paper sleeve. After this, using the flat of the cleaver or butcher's hammer, hit the cutlet one or two times to flatten the meat. The cutlet is then ready for all recipes.

Breaded Veal Cutlets *(Côtes de Veau Panées).* If you like, and for some recipes, you can bread the cutlets in the English style—that is, dipped in beaten egg before being covered with freshly grated bread crumbs. Indeed, people who love this recipe prefer this, because it keeps the meat more tender. Serve it with an appropriate sauce: tomato, Italian, etc. And, if you like, with a garnish, as for cutlets à la Milanaise, or simply in the manner described below.

The fat used for cooking them should be butter, preferably clarified butter. This is essential here; otherwise, the bread coating will be strewn with black lumps or risk coming off in patches if some impurity from the unclarified butter sticking to the bottom of the pan attaches to the coating when you try lifting it from the pan.

You can replace the clarified butter with pure fat, but it is a good idea to understand the differences and also to make sure you have some reserves. Clarified butter is preferable because the cutlets must be cooked gently and gradually. The layer of bread crumbs absorbs the fat, for an effect that is a little bit like pastry. There is also this to consider: Any fat that can reach a temperature substantially higher than butter without burning must be much more carefully watched so that it does not get hotter than you want for cooking the cutlets and risks turning the cutlets brown.

If then, instead of clarified butter, you use oil with a bit of butter, you will have to take care that the cutlets are cooked as gently as with the butter alone. *Time: 2$^{1}/_{2}$ hours (of which 1$^{1}/_{2}$ hours is for cooking).*

6 small cutlets.

For the breading: 1 large egg beaten as for an omelet with salt, pepper, and 5 or 6 drops of oil; 2 tablespoons of flour; 150 grams (5$^{1}/_{3}$ ounces) of freshly grated stale bread.

To cook them: 100 grams (3$^{1}/_{2}$ ounces) of clarified butter (SEE PAGE 16).

PROCEDURE. Bread the cutlets as described (SEE ENGLISH-STYLE BREADING, PAGE 19), making sure that they are completely covered with bread crumbs on their edges as well as on their two sides. Press down on the bread crumbs with the blade of a knife, making a sort of yellow paste that sticks well to the meat.

Use a thick sauté pan large enough to put the cutlets in without crowding so that the hot fat, as little as it is, will be able to circulate. Strongly heat the clarified butter until it begins to give off a very light smoke, so that when you put in the cutlets the coating dries immediately. *As soon as the cutlets are placed in the hot fat, turn the heat down to moderate.* Do not cover. At the end of 3 or 4 minutes, when the side in contact with the butter has been seared and lightly colored, turn over the cutlets; do this either by sliding a fork under them or grabbing them by the end of the bone. Color them the same on the other side.

Continue cooking under the same conditions for *18–20 minutes;* the cooking should be rather gentle, the fat remaining at the same heat so that the bread crumb coating is not too colored and the meat cooks perfectly. Thus, a total cooking time of *25–30 minutes.*

Serve them immediately, according to your chosen recipe.

Breaded Veal Cutlets, Simple Method *(Côtes de Veau Panées, Simple Façon).* Once the breaded cutlets have been cooked, arrange them on the plate. Keep them warm. Drain the butter from the sauté pan, which you can use to sauté again. Then, for 6 cutlets, pour in 2 deciliters (6$^{3}/_{4}$ fluid ounces, $^{7}/_{8}$ cup) of white wine and 1 scant deciliter (3$^{1}/_{3}$ fluid ounces, scant $^{1}/_{2}$ cup) of juice. Boil it briskly without a cover to reduce this liquid by half. *Turn off the heat* and then melt 60 grams (2$^{1}/_{4}$ ounces, 4$^{1}/_{2}$ tablespoons) of butter, divided into small pieces, while you shake the pan. Add some lemon juice. Pour over the cutlets. Serve.

PRINCIPAL RECIPES FOR VEAL CUTLETS

You can prepare veal cutlets in many ways; they are most frequently sautéed, then served with any garnish or sauce. This is preferable to grilling: besides other advantages, it provides a jus after the pan has been deglazed, and this is an advantage that should not be overlooked, particularly when cooking at home. Braising—in other words, cooking in their juices—is equally good for cutlets. Independent of the recipes given below, we will summarize here the principal recipes. You can also use the different garnishes that accompany veal round roasts for the cutlets.

Veal Cutlets Not Breaded *(Côtes de Veau Non Panées).* These are gently sautéed in a pan. Drain the fat from the sauté pan. For 3 cutlets, deglaze using 1 deciliter (3 1/3 fluid ounces, scant 1/2 cup) of white wine, and 3 or 4 tablespoons of jus or bouillon. Add lemon juice and 30 grams (1 ounce, 2 tablespoons) of butter off the fire.

Breaded Veal Cutlets *(Côtes de Veau Panées).* Fried in butter; sautéed as for VEAL SCALLOPS À LA VIENNOISE (SEE PAGE 288). Serve sprinkled with beurre noisette and with any one of many garnishes.

Braised Veal Cutlets *(Côtes de Veau Braisées).* Choose rather large cutlets. Bard them, then cook as for a fricandeau. Serve with a garnish of vegetables, purée of sorrel, noodles, etc., and tomato sauce.

Veal Cutlet Casserole *(Côtes de Veau en Cocotte).* **À la bonne femme:** Choose cutlets weighing 350–400 grams (12 1/3–14 1/8 ounces). Season. First color the meat in a ceramic casserole dish with 50 grams (1 3/4 ounces, 3 1/2 tablespoons) of butter. Then add, for 1 cutlet, 6 small onions, previously sautéed in butter in a pan until golden, and 100 grams (3 1/2 ounces) of raw potatoes cut into rounds. Cover and cook gently for *1 good hour.* Serve just as it is in the casserole dish.

Veal Cutlets à la Paysanne *(Côtes de Veau à la Paysanne).* Choose cutlets weighing 400 grams (14 1/8 ounces). In a casserole dish, brown the cutlet with 4 slices of blanched lean bacon and 30 grams (1 ounce, 2 tablespoons) of butter. Then add 6 small onions, previously sautéed in a pan with butter until golden, and 100 grams (3 1/2 ounces) of raw potatoes cut into slices. Cover and finish by cooking gently for 45 minutes. Serve in the casserole dish.

Veal Cutlets with Noodles *(Côtes de Veau aux Nouilles).* Choose cutlets weighing 400 grams (14 1/8 ounces). Season and sauté in butter in the casserole dish. Cover with veal jus, or, if you do not have that, bouillon. Surround it with noodles that have been half-cooked—that is, poached for 10 minutes in boiling water. Cover. Finish by cooking until the noodles have absorbed the cooking juice. Pour over a little bit of tomato sauce to serve. Serve in the casserole dish.

Grilled Veal Cutlet au Vert-Pré *(Côtes de Veau au Vert-Pré).* Grill on moderate heat from the start, given that it is not necessary to seal the meat. On the contrary; the meat should color as it cooks. Dress on a plate: cover with maître d'hôtel butter and on each side, place a bouquet of straw potatoes and a bouquet of watercress.

Veal Cutlets in Their Juice *(Côtes de Veau dans Son Jus).* For a nice cutlet: heat 30 grams (1 ounce, 2 tablespoons) of butter in a sauté pan; add the cutlet, seasoned with salt and pepper. Cover. On moderate heat, let it gently color; turn it over to color the other side. Add bouillon or water: 4 or 5 tablespoons. Finish cooking gently; *1 good hour in total.*

Veal Cutlets à la Gendarme *(Côtes de Veau à la Gendarme).* An agreeable lunch dish that is simple to make and not very expensive. Here the breaded cutlets are first marinated, which adds a great deal to the general flavor of the dish, which is a bit spicy, though not excessively.

If you do not cook this in butter only, use for the 6 cutlets only 40 grams (1 3/8 ounces, 3 tablespoons) of butter and 1 1/2 deciliters (5 fluid ounces, 2/3 cup) of oil. *Time: 1 1/2 hours (of which 30 minutes is for cooking).*

6 small cutlets.

For the marinade: juice of 1 lemon; 6 tablespoons of white wine; 2 tablespoons of oil; a pinch of salt and a pinch of pepper; 4 parsley sprigs, chopped; 1 small onion; 1 small bay leaf; 1 sprig of thyme.

For breading: the same quantity as for breaded cutlets.

For the sauce: 1 small onion (50 grams); 2 shallots; a bit of garlic the size of a pea; 2 deciliters (6 3/4 ounces, 7/8 cup) of white wine and the same quantity of bouillon; beurre manié made with 20 grams (2/3 ounce, 1 heaping tablespoon) of butter worked with 12 grams (3/8 ounce) of flour; 1 teaspoon of parsley and tarragon, minced; 20 grams (2/3 ounce, 1 heaping tablespoon) of butter to finish the dish.

PROCEDURE. Arrange the cutlets in a large shallow bowl, seasoned with salt and pepper on both sides. Sprinkle the chopped parsley over them, then the onion minced fine as lace, the thyme and the bay leaf, crumpled and torn into bits. Sprinkle with the wine, the oil, and the lemon juice. Let it marinate for *at least 1 hour,* and longer if possible. Turn frequently during this time, being careful always to cover the meat with onion.

Before breading them, dry the cutlets on a kitchen towel. Dip them in the flour and proceed as described to bread and cook them.

The sauce: Prepare this while the meat is cooking. In a small saucepan, add the finely minced onion and shallot to the wine. Reduce by a good half. Add the bouillon and bring it to a boil. Immediately thicken it with the beurre manié, and add the garlic, which has been crushed with the blade of a knife. Let it stew until ready to serve. Turn off the heat and finish the sauce with the butter, parsley, and minced tarragon, as well as a pinch of pepper. Check the salt. Arrange the cutlets in a circle and pour the sauce in the middle. Serve.

Veal Cutlets à la Milanaise *(Côtes de Veau à la Milanaise).* We include this recipe because it is equally suitable for lunch and dinner; the macaroni garnish (SEE GARNITURE À LA MILANAISE, PAGE 458) makes a dish that is both substantial and elegant. *Time: 1 hour (including preparing the garnish). Serves 6.*

6 small cutlets or 4 medium-size ones.

To bread them: Use the same quantities as those indicated for the breaded cutlets. You can add 2 tablespoons of grated Parmesan or, if you do not have that, Gruyère, mixing well with the bread crumbs.

To cook the cutlets: 100 grams (3 1/2 ounces, 7 tablespoons) of clarified butter.

For the Milanaise garnish: the quantities given on PAGE 458.

In addition: 1 good tablespoon of tomato purée; 1 deciliter (3 1/3 fluid ounces, scant 1/2 cup) of bouillon and 10 grams (1/3 ounce, 1 scant tablespoon) of butter to dress the plate.

PROCEDURE. Clarify the butter to be used for cooking the cutlets. Trim and bread the cutlets so that they are ready when you need them.

Start cooking the macaroni for the garnish. As soon as you have started, heat the clarified butter and cook the cutlets in it as directed.

While cooking the cutlets, take care of the various elements of the garnish. In a small saucepan, heat the tomato purée and the bouillon for dressing the plate. Finish it, off the heat, with the butter; keep it warm.

To dress the cutlets: Drain well, then arrange in a circle on a round plate. With a spoon, put the garnish in the middle. Pour the sauce in a ribbon *around* the cutlets without letting any actually fall on them.

If you like, put a paper sleeve on the bone of each cutlet. Serve.

Veal Cutlet Foyot *(Côtes de Veau Foyot).* A creation of this celebrated restaurateur in the rue de Tournon, the Veal Cutlet Foyot is an example of excellent home cooking. The recipe is simple, but nonetheless requires minute and meticulous attention. It is, in fact, a veal cutlet coated with Parmesan and fine bread crumbs that has been slowly gratinéed and served surrounded by a Périgueux sauce.

To make this sauce at home might be complicated if you follow the usual method. You can avoid some of this difficulty by using an excellent veal jus thickened with starch and to which some minced truffle is added. However, ordinary veal jus prepared for everyday use is not sufficiently concentrated; you must use the juice from a braised veal, which is not usually prepared in a home kitchen. So use a good meat glaze to supplement the ordinary jus or use any bouillon that you have; for the given quantities, use 20 grams (2/3 ounce) of an excellent meat glaze. Parmesan is essential; it cannot be replaced by Gruyère, whose flavor does not have the same effect. *Time: 21/2 hours. Serves 6.*

3 veal cutlets taken from the middle of the rib roast, sometimes called "the butcher's cut." They are cut short and at least 2 centimeters thick (3/4 inch), and they should weigh at least 400 grams (141/8 ounces) each. Expose the bone to about 4 centimeters (13/8 inches) above the central part and remove the end of the backbone.

60 grams (21/4 ounces, 41/2 tablespoons) of butter; 50 grams (13/4 ounces) of onion, finely minced; 50 grams (13/4 ounces) of grated good Parmesan; 20 grams (2/3 ounce) of freshly and finely grated stale bread crumbs; 11/2 deciliters (5 fluid ounces, 2/3 cup) of white wine; and 11/2 deciliters (5 fluid ounces, 2/3 cup) of good bouillon.

***For the sauce:* 40 grams (13/8 ounces) of black truffle that has been finely minced; 4 tablespoons of Madeira; 11/2 deciliters (5 fluid ounces, 2/3 cup) of jus; 10 grams (1/3 ounce) of arrowroot.**

PROCEDURE. Use a sauté pan where the cutlets can be placed next to each other without being crowded, but with not too much space between them. Heat 40 grams (13/8 ounces, 3 tablespoons) of butter in the pan. Add the cutlets, lightly seasoned with salt and pepper. Color them on both sides over strong heat. Take them out and put them on a plate. To the oil in the sauté pan, add the minced onion. Then, on low heat, let it color until *lightly golden,* no more, while you prepare the cutlets. The bread crumbs (SEE BREADING, PAGE 19) and grated cheese should have been prepared in advance. Mix them together on a plate.

Melt the rest of the butter, 20 grams (2/3 ounce, 1 heaping tablespoon), in a small cup. Have a small kitchen brush ready.

One after the other, press the cutlets into the mixture of cheese and bread crumbs *on one side only.* Put them on a plate and then sprinkle on each one the remains of the cheese left on the plate. Press it down with the side of a knife blade to make it stick. Put the cutlets back into the sauté pan, with *the side sprinkled with cheese facing up.*

Pour the white wine and the bouillon into the pan. Dip the brush into the melted butter and paint it over the layer of cheese and bread crumbs. Bring it to a boil. Then immediately put the pan into the oven *without covering it.*

To cook: The heat of the oven must be extremely moderate: just hot enough to maintain the simmer, which must be very gentle and constant. Once the cutlets are in the oven, let cook for *2 hours.* There is no way to shorten the cooking time. It is essential so that the cutlets are cooked correctly; like a fricandeau, they must be so well cooked that you can cut them with a spoon.

Every 15 minutes, baste the cutlets with their cooking liquid, tipping the pan and using a metal spoon. You should do this for the first 11/4 hours of cooking: in other words, *5 times.*

After this, do not baste them with the liquid, but for the last 45 minutes, paint the cheesed surface occasionally with the melted butter. It will therefore gradually take on a beautiful golden color.

If the liquid reduces too much while cooking, add a few tablespoons of bouillon, so that you always have about the same quantity of liquid that you started with.

The sauce: In a small saucepan, boil the truffles with the Madeira until it has been reduced to 1 tablespoon. Add the veal jus; let it boil for just a few minutes. Thicken with arrowroot (SEE LIAISONS, PAGE 17). Once this is done, add the meat glaze and allow it to dissolve completely. Keep it warm.

To serve: Carefully remove the cutlets from the sauté pan; by now, they will be extremely fragile. Arrange them side by side on a long, warmed platter.

Boil the cooking liquid from the cutlets over strong heat to reduce it to 2 or 3 tablespoons. Then mix it with the Périgueux sauce you have just improvised. Pour the sauce *around* the cutlets without letting it fall directly on top of the cutlets. Serve on very hot plates.

Veal Cutlets in Papillotes *(Côtes de Veau en Papillotes).* Whatever the method used, you cannot hope to complete cooking the cutlets in the papillote: the heat would reduce the paper to cinders before the meat is thoroughly cooked. The paper is really only a holder for the duxelles—minced mushrooms and fines herbs—which garnish the cutlets.

For home cooking, the cutlets are first sautéed in butter and oil until they are a little more than half-cooked. Then, covered on both sides with a thin layer of duxelles, they are put into the papillote. After this, they are put on the grill to finish cooking on very gentle heat so that the paper does not burn, which is rather difficult to avoid. Because of this, the great restaurants have introduced a few modifications, which we describe here, below.

The cutlet is sautéed in butter and oil to cook completely; after this, it is garnished with duxelles and wrapped in some very thin slices of ham, which, as it were, reinforce the paper wrapping. It should be noted that this ham is the finishing touch for the cutlets and should not be left out, either for reasons of economy or to simplify. Put the cutlet inside the papillote in the oven, not so much to finish cooking the meat and the duxelles, which are both, in fact, done, but to swell up the paper and to color it a little. In other words, to enhance its presentation.

Allow 1 cutlet per person, each weighing about 170–180 grams (6–6$^1/_3$ ounces). Trim them carefully, completely removing the spine and exposing the end of the rib from the meat for a good 2 centimeters ($^3/_4$ inch); then lightly flatten them with a kitchen hammer.

For each cutlet, allow: 2 slices of lean ham already cooked and cut as thin as possible, which should be about the same size as the cutlet but a little bit larger on the edges; 2 tablespoons of stuffing (SEE DUXELLES, PAGE 21), with the ham trimmings added. (The duxelles should be very reduced, to the consistency of a thick stuffing. Otherwise the mixture will slide off the meat, touch and moisten the paper, and eventually cause the papillote to burst.) A sheet of strong paper—butcher's paper—is needed for each cutlet.

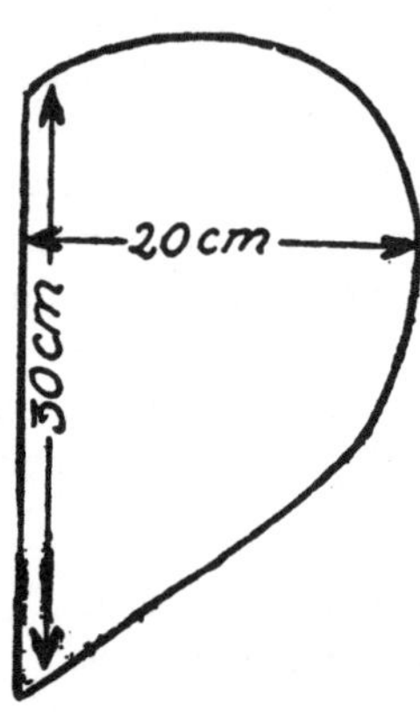

FIG. 49. FOLDING PAPER FOR PAPILLOTE.

Fold the sheet of paper in two. Cut it into the shape of the dimensions indicated in *fig.* 49. Open it out on the work surface and rapidly brush it with a small brush that has been dipped in oil. This strengthens the resistance of the paper. On the table, line up the oiled papers, opened, with the pointed part pointing up. On the right half, place a sheet of ham; spread it with 1 tablespoon of *warm* duxelles without going all the way to the edge, so that the mixture does not touch the paper. Then put the veal cutlet on top, cooked as has been directed and still warm (*fig.* 50). Cover equally with duxelles and ham. Do this for all the cutlets. Act quickly, so that you do not let them cool.

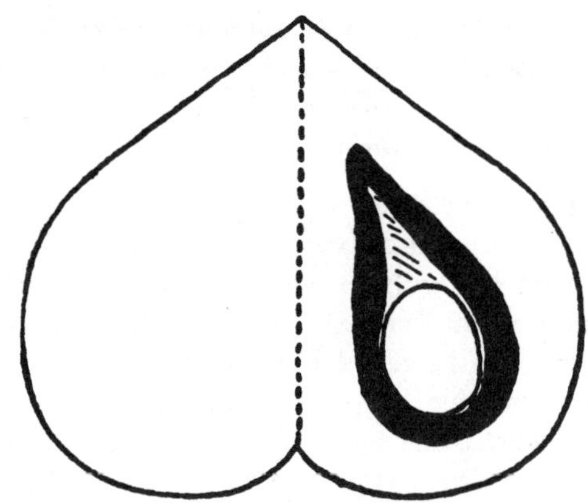

FIG. 50. PLACING THE VEAL ON THE PAPER.

After this, fold over the left-hand sheet so that the edges of the two sheets join. Close up the papillote by folding back the edges of the paper on each other, creasing them obliquely as you go, as shown in *fig.* 51.

FIG. 51. CLOSING UP THE PAPILLOTE.

(At this point, let me interrupt myself to explain how professionals make the papillote swell. Fold back the paper as described, but when you reach the very tip of the pointed edge, and before you fold it over, insert a straw or a piece of macaroni. Blow through it to inflate the papillote, then quickly take out the straw, and twist the paper to close the papillote. We would rather not comment on this technique.)

Put the cutlets on an ovenproof plate that you can serve at the table, because after all this time in the oven the paper will be extremely fragile and will break if handled. They must not be touched, and you should put only 2 on a plate.

Quickly, so that the papillotes do not lose their heat, put them into the oven. A medium oven, hot enough so that at the end of *1 minute* the paper is a beautiful golden color and nicely swollen. Serve.

Veal Scallops *(Les Escalopes de Veau)*

These are a good standby, particularly for lunches. Usually they are breaded, but they can also be sautéed without any breading, depending on the recipe. Below, we offer a standard recipe for each method. In both cases, sauté the scallops in a fat that can take strong heat: normally butter and oil. But you can also use clarified butter; it is just that this is more expensive. Or use a good purified fat. Essential here is that the fat used must get extremely hot without burning, so that the meat can be thoroughly sealed. For all cooking details, see sautéing (PAGE 34).

Breaded or not, the scallops can be served on a purée—potatoes, sorrel, chicory, spinach, green peas, etc. Serve with a garnish of fresh vegetables—green beans, carrots, peas, etc., sautéed in butter; a fondue of tomatoes; and noodles, macaroni, or risotto with tomato sauce on the side.

Or serve *breaded* with a sauce on the side: a bordelaise made with white wine, tartar sauce, soubise, tomato, etc.

How the scallops must be cut: The fundamental and principal condition is that the scallops must be cut *across the grain of the meat.* Otherwise, it will be impossible for you to obtain a good result no matter how carefully you flatten the meat with the cleaver: as soon as the meat begins to warm in the pan, it will swell and lose its shape; it will not color or cook evenly; and its juices will escape, resulting in a meat that is dry and stringy.

Normally, scallops should be taken from the fillet or loin, or even from a rib roast with the bones removed. Not only are these cuts of meat fine and tender, but also, and most important, it is natural to slice this meat across its grain. The only drawback is that amount of meat lost to trimming considerably increases the price for the necessary quantity of scallops.

The scallop is normally taken from the round roast of veal, the meatiest and also the most tender part of the haunch. But you will have great difficulty getting the butcher to cut the scallops across the grain of the meat, particularly when you want just a small quantity, because he will be reluctant to cut into the fillet, reducing the size of roast he can sell.

The direction in which the scallops must be cut is so important that if you cannot get them from the round roast, it would be better to take them from rump roast. The drawback is that this meat is not as good: nerves run through it and it is a bit tough. Also, the shape of the piece forces you to cut slices that are longer than you need.

A real scallop must not be more than 1 good centimeter (3/8 inch) thick when you first cut it. Its gross weight is therefore 110–120 grams (3 7/8–4 1/4 ounces), reduced to no more than 90–100 grams (3 1/6–3 1/2 ounces) after trimming.

With a butcher's mallet lightly moistened with water, begin by flattening the scallops until they are no thicker than about *7 millimeters (a generous 1/4 inch).* This makes the meat more tender by breaking the fibers. The reduced thickness also means the meat cooks more quickly—and speed is essential when cooking scallops.

Scallops of Veal with Tarragon *(Escalopes de Veau à l'Estragon).* One of the best and simplest recipes when tarragon is in season. For home cooking, replace the concentrated veal jus used to finish these scallops with the same amount of bouillon and 25 grams (1 ounce) of meat glaze; this glaze is easily available nowadays in gourmet food shops. *Time: 25 minutes.*

6 veal scallops of a medium size; 30 grams (1 ounce, 2 tablespoons) of butter and 3 tablespoons of oil to cook them; 1 good deciliter (3 1/3 fluid ounces, 1/2 cup) of white wine; 1 scant deciliter (3 1/3 fluid ounces, scant 1/2 cup) of bouillon and 25 grams (1 ounce) of meat glaze; 1 scant tablespoon of minced tarragon; 24 whole tarragon leaves; 20 grams (2/3 ounce, 1 heaping tablespoon) of butter to finish.

PROCEDURE. **Cooking the scallops:** Use a sauté pan that is large enough so that the whole of the scallop can completely touch the bottom. Given that each scallop has been flattened out, they are rather large. So, if the pan is not big enough to let you do this, you will have to sauté the scallops in two batches. Cover the first ones with a plate to keep them warm. Remember, though, that this will add an extra 10 minutes or so to the cooking time.

Heat the fat you are using in the sauté pan until it gives off a light smoke. Arrange the scallops, seasoned with salt and pepper, in the pan. On strong heat, let them cook for *4 minutes* without turning them over. Then, if they are well colored all over, lift them up with a fork without piecing them. Let them cook for another *5 minutes* on the other side, being careful to watch that the meat colors evenly—which means that it is properly cooked. Lift out the scallops onto a plate, then cover and keep them warm.

Drain all the fat from the sauté pan. Pour in the white wine; with the back of a fork, dissolve the crusty bits on the bottom. Boil it without a cover over strong heat to reduce the wine a little bit: by about a third. Add the bouillon and the meat glaze, divided into small fragments. Heat it gently to dissolve and mix the ingredients.

Put the scallops back into the juice and add the juice that they have released while standing. Cover and reheat it for only 4–5 minutes without boiling, which would toughen the meat. They were thoroughly cooked when they were sautéed, so they do not need any more cooking.

The tarragon: Prepare this while cooking the scallops. Immerse the whole leaves for 1 minute in boiling water to make them more flexible, then drain on a plate. Mince the rest of the tarragon. Have it ready so that you can add it to the juice at the very last moment, because this herb does not tolerate boiling when chopped.

To serve: A minute before serving, dress the scallops in a circle on a nice, hot plate, leaning them lightly one against the other. On each one, place 4 tarragon leaves in the shape of a cross.

Put the juice over strong heat. As soon as it begins to boil, turn off the heat. Add the minced tarragon and the last bit of butter; shake the sauté pan and pour the buttered juice in the middle of the scallops.

Veal Scallops à la Viennoise *(Escalopes de Veau à la Viennoise).* A recipe that is both one of the simplest and one of the most practical, and is a particular favorite at lunches.

Their extreme thinness is what characterizes these scallops; they are thinner than other scallops, so their cooking time is even more rapid. Speed is essential when making this dish, which cannot be left standing. You must serve them as soon as they are ready and eat them while they are piping hot and while the bread crumb crust is still crisp. If they are left standing, the crust softens and the dish is not the same at all. All this should be taken into consideration and everything prepared in advanced so that as soon as they are sautéed the scallops can be placed on a plate, sprinkled with noisette butter, and served immediately. *Time: 1 hour (10 minutes for cooking).*

6 scallops of the suggested weight; 30 grams (1 ounce, 2 tablespoons) of butter and 3 tablespoons of oil to cook them.

***For the breading:* 1 raw egg; about 125 grams (4 1/2 ounces) of stale bread crumbs.**

***To serve them:* 2 hard-boiled eggs, warm; 1 tablespoon of minced parsley; 1 1/2 tablespoons of capers; a good pinch of paprika; 1 small lemon; 50 grams (1 3/4 ounces, 3 1/2 tablespoons) of butter for the noisette butter.**

Paprika, or red pepper, from Hungary is used a great deal in today's cooking and has no similarity to cayenne pepper except for its red color. The flavor is infinitely less violent than cayenne and, actually, very pleasant; use it in about the same amounts as ordinary pepper.

PROCEDURE. Flatten the scallops with a butcher's mallet so that you make them equally thick, 6–7 millimeters (about 1/4 inch) at the most. Then bread them, as described previously on PAGE 282.

Prepare the breading (SEE ENGLISH-STYLE BREADING, PAGE 19).

Before dipping the scallops in the beaten egg, season them on both sides with salt and paprika, which, here, replaces ordinary pepper.

Prepare the serving dish: take a round plate and place the capers in a small mound right in the middle. Chop the hard-boiled eggs, the whites and the yolks separately. Circle the yellow egg yolks around the pile of capers. Surround this with minced parsley and then with a circle of egg white. On the edges of the plate, arrange some half slices of lemon in a circle.

Heat the oil and the butter in a large sauté pan on strong heat until it gives off a light smoke. Put in the scallops.

At the end of *3 1/2 minutes (4 minutes at the most)*, turn them with a spatula, if possible, or a fork. In either case, take care, as with all breaded foods, not to damage the crust. Then cook the scallops for the same amount of time on the other side. They are then properly cooked.

Arrange them in a turban or ring on the plate, leaned up one against the other, without disturbing the arrangement in the middle of the plate.

In a small, clean pan, briskly cook the reserved butter (SEE BUERRE NOISETTE, PAGE 80). Pour it on the scallops. Serve immediately.

Roast Veal *(Le Veau Rôti)*

To roast veal, the oven is much preferable to the spit, or any similar form of cooking. Like pork, veal is much better when roasted right in the oven dish: either simply basted with butter or placed on a bed of onion rounds and carrots, which is then basted with fat from time to time, and to which a little warm water is added by tablespoons if the vegetables are in danger of burning.

When the piece of meat is taken from a lean part—the fillet, for example—and when it is a certain size, it must cook for a longer time in the oven. In that case, wrap it with very thin sheets of bacon or some sheets of buttered parchment paper so the meat does not dry out. Ten minutes before serving, take off the bacon or the paper so that the meat colors.

You can also roast veal in the way known in haute cuisine as *poêler*—that is, with the meat resting on a bed of rounds of onions and carrots and slices of bacon in a covered utensil without any liquid, copiously basted with melted butter and cooked gently in the oven. In other words, it is cooked like a braise, but without any liquid from the beginning of cooking to the end. When the veal is cooked, remove the cover to give the meat a beautiful color. Take it out and put it on a warm plate. For the remaining vegetables that have not burned but that have cooked in the fat and juices from the veal, pour in a little bit of jus or bouillon, then boil it for 10 or 12 minutes so the liquid absorbs the flavors of the vegetables, which have been released by the cooking. Strain it and degrease it before serving in a sauceboat.

Cooking time: You should count on an average of *20–25 minutes* per 450 grams (1 pound) to roast in an oven at a good, even, and moderate heat. Veal is a white meat, so it must roast gently but thoroughly; when you stick a kitchen needle into the meat, the juice that escapes should be absolutely white.

The cuts of meat appropriate for this roast are the *saddle*, which is the animal's entire set of ribs on both sides (you trim the bones from these ribs and remove the spine or backbone); the *loin*, boned and rolled as directed; and the *fillet or loin steak*, taken from the end of the loin. Boning a loin requires a few directions: these follow.

Veal Loin *(Le Longe de Veau)*

The loin is the half of the saddle that, cut in 2 lengthwise, gives 2 identical loins: these correspond to the part of the beef called the "sirloin." The loin is recognized as one of the finest cuts of veal, as good to roast as to braise or to cook in its juice. It is generally boned and the kidney is often left on the piece, which makes this cut even more of a delicacy.

To bone and trim the loin: Lay it out flat on its back lengthwise in front of you. Take off the kidney and remove its fat, leaving only the little bit of fat that covers the kidney. Using a good medium-size knife, cut off the filet mignon, trimming it right next to the small bones. Once you have reached the end, turn over the loin with the back now on top. Slide the blade of the knife between the flesh and the backbone, following its entire length and trimming it well, so that you allow as little meat as possible to stick to it. The loin is now completely boned.

Spread it out on its back. With the point of a knife, pierce the surface here and there along the entire length of the ribbon called the flank. This is always bloated and full of air, so hit it a couple of times with the flat of a cleaver to expel this air.

Put the kidney back in its place; sprinkle with fine salt. Then roll the loin on itself, thoroughly enveloping the kidney and the filet mignon in the flank. Trim any excess once the kidney and the fillet are thoroughly covered.

Then trim the outside of the loin on the side opposite the flank, sliding the blade of the knife along the entire length of loin between the flesh and the nerve membrane to remove a long ribbon of membrane. Then, on top of this, put the slices of fat you have taken from the kidney. Tie up the rolled loin, with turns of string about 2 centimeters (3/4 inch) apart, so that it looks like a long bundle or a galantine.

Veal Casserole *(Le Veau à la Casserole)*

This is an old and excellent recipe, a form of roasting that substitutes the casserole dish for the oven. The veal is cooked in its juice without anything other than butter or fat and, toward the end, only a few tablespoons of water.

This cooking method is one of the best for a cut of medium size or one that is not very thick. Meat cooked in this manner is very moist and the juice keeps its natural flavor. It is perfect for older people, people of delicate health, and lovers of simple and carefully crafted dishes. But its excellence depends entirely on the care you take, and people today do not seem to understand how very closely it needs to be watched. That is why we are going to give some directions here that this simple dish wouldn't seem to require.

For this method of cooking, choose a cut of meat that is not too dry and that naturally has a certain amount of fat: either in the loin or in the saddle. A boneless piece of meat should weigh no more than 1 kilogram (2 pounds, 3 ounces). Of course, if you are choosing a large cut, make sure that the rib is shortened and the backbone removed.

Use a *thick* casserole dish made from good aluminum; cast iron frequently spoils the color of the juices. Spread a good lard all over the bottom of the utensil: 30 or 40 grams (1–1 3/8 ounces) for the quantities indicated above. You might prefer to use butter instead of pork fat; if so, use melted butter or clarified butter, otherwise it will burn while cooking. Leftovers of fresh bacon are very good here. For this type of recipe, the juice is not thoroughly degreased before serving, so the choice of cooking fat is important.

Put the piece of veal into the greased casserole and *cover it immediately.* Put it on very moderate heat, heating the entire bottom of the casserole equally. Do not turn over the meat until the end of *a half hour* and turn down the heat after the first *10 or 15 minutes.* At this point, the casserole is heated through, and if the heat gets too high the meat will brown instead of sweating. The effect of sweating is that the juices escape and then, without burning, reduce on the bottom of the casserole. They color there as they concentrate, and are then reabsorbed by the dilated flesh.

When you turn it over, the meat must be slightly golden on the side in contact with the bottom of the casserole; the other side will have gradually taken on a whitish color. Cover the casserole again and cook for the same amount of time, until the second side also becomes golden. After this, salt the meat and turn the fire down very low, keeping the casserole covered.

Now there will be only pure fat in the bottom of the casserole with a small amount of juices: those produced by the meat as it sweats and then condensed into a sort of soft colored crust. By reducing the heat, the steam given off by the meat no longer dries it out but dissolves the gratin. This last effect explains the need for keeping the cooking very gentle at this point, for which you can allow another *scant hour.*

Nonetheless, the moisture from the meat will not be quite enough and you will need from time to time to add 1 or 2 tablespoons of warm water—7 or 8 in total—spreading the water around the bottom of the casserole. Each time you do this, make sure you then baste the meat with its juice.

To serve: Half degrease the jus and then use it to glaze the meat by basting after you have placed it on the serving dish.

Sautéed Veal *(Le Veau Sauté)*

Veal Sautéed Chasseur *(Veau Sauté Chasseur).* Actually, veal sautéed chasseur style is—like veal Marengo—a ragout: the term "sauté" refers only to the method used to initially color the meat. It is true, however, that it is extremely important for the recipe as a whole, as you will see in the course of our directions.

The ingredients characteristic of a dish prepared chasseur style are minced and colored mushrooms, shallot, and a quantity of white wine. The tomato is used here only in a very small quantity as a condiment. *Time: 2 scant hours. Serves 6.*

750 grams (1 pound, 10 ounces) of veal flank or meat from cutlets; 30 grams (1 ounce, 2 tablespoons) of butter and 3 tablespoons of oil to sauté the meat; 125 grams ($4^1/_2$ ounces) of fresh mushrooms; 15 grams ($^1/_2$ ounce) of flour; 2 deciliters ($6^3/_4$ ounces, $^7/_8$ cup) of white wine; 4 deciliters ($1^2/_3$ cups) of bouillon; 2 or 3 tablespoons of tomato purée; 3 minced shallots; a bouquet garni; 1 tablespoon of minced chervil.

(See details and the instructions for the pan, procedure, etc., under SAUTÉING, PAGE 34).

PROCEDURE. Divide the meat into small pieces weighing 40–50 grams ($1^3/_8$–$1^3/_4$ ounces) each.

Cut off the bottom of the stem of the mushrooms. Do not peel them. Wash them. Cut them in two and put the flat part on the table, then cut them into slices 1 millimeter thick, cutting them lengthwise through both the head and stem. Keep them on one side.

Heat the oil and butter in the sauté pan until a light smoke is given off. Put in the pieces of veal without stacking them up, so that each piece is in contact with the bottom of the pan and they are not too crowded. If you cannot put them all in at the same time, cook in two batches: both times, the fat must be heated until it is smoking before you add the pieces of meat; otherwise, the meat will fray into shreds and you will not be able to sauté them to a golden color. Keep the pan on strong heat and let the pieces color well on one side before turning them over: allow 6 or 7 minutes. If you move them during this time, the meat will color badly.

Turn them over to color them the same way on the other side. You can now turn the heat down a little because everything is good and hot in the pan.

Once the meat has been well colored without going as far as a dark brown, add the mushrooms. Sauté them and mix everything with a wooden spoon for 2 or 3 minutes to evaporate all their juices. As long as they are continuing to give off a great deal of steam from the pan, they have not been properly cooked. Drain the grease by keeping the cover partially on the pan and then tipping it. Add the minced shallot. Sprinkle everything with flour and mix it well over very moderate heat. Let it cook continually for 5 minutes so the flour takes on a light golden color.

Then pour in the wine and the cold or hot bouillon little by little, dissolving the crusts at the bottom of the pan with the spoon. Add the tomato purée and bouquet garni. Bring to a boil. Cover with a tight-fitting lid.

Put it into a moderate oven, hot enough to keep the liquid at a gentle simmer, uninterrupted for *$1^1/_2$ hours.* If you do not have an oven, you can cook the pan on the stove, but it must likewise be done very gently.

To serve: Turn the heat off under the pan for a few minutes so that the grease mounts to the surface; then remove it as completely as possible with a metal spoon. At this point, you should have about *3 deciliters ($1^1/_4$ cups)* of sauce. Taste to check the salt, then add a pinch of pepper.

Dress the pieces on a serving dish, a timbale, or a vegetable platter. Pour the sauce over the top without straining it. Sprinkle over the minced chervil.

Veal Sauté Marengo *(Veau Sauté Marengo).* What differentiates this from the veal sauté chasseur is the dominant note of tomato, which is used in substantial quantities, either fresh or canned, and the more discreet, but still essential, note of garlic. Oil is the only thing used for coloring the meats. Shallots are replaced by onion and the mushrooms are added uncooked.

Cooking this in the oven, in the same way as veal sauté chasseur, is essential, particularly so that the liquid reduces as expected. If you absolutely must cook this dish and you do not have an oven it can be cooked on a stovetop, but you will have to turn over the meat a couple of times during this cooking time, because the action of the heat is primarily on the bottom of the pan. *Time: 2 scant hours. Serves 6.*

750 grams (1 pound, 10 ounces) of flank or half flank and half rib-eye; 1½ deciliters (5 fluid ounces, ⅔ cup) of oil; a large minced onion (100 grams, 3½ ounces); 15 grams (½ ounce) of flour; 1½ deciliters (5 fluid ounces, ⅔ cup) of white wine; 5 deciliters (generous 2 cups) of bouillon; 500 grams (1 pound, 2 ounces) of fresh tomatoes or 1½ deciliters (5 fluid ounces, ⅔ cup) of concentrated tomato purée; 10 grams (⅓ ounces) of garlic; 150 grams (5⅓ ounces) of mushrooms; a bouquet garni; 6 fried croutons cut into triangles about 6 centimeters (2⅜ inches) long on each side; 1 tablespoon of minced parsley.

For details of the appropriate utensils and methods, etc., see SAUTÉING PAGE 34.

PROCEDURE. Divide the meat as directed for veal chasseur. To color it, proceed in the same way: use oil, 1 deciliter (3⅓ fluid ounces, scant ½ cup) of it, heated to the point where it gives off a *light* smoke.

Once the meat is well colored, drain the oil from the sauté pan. Add the chopped onion. Sprinkle it with the flour; mix on very moderate heat for 5 or 6 minutes to give the onion a nice golden color.

Then add the bouillon and the white wine. Stir to dissolve the roux and, while stirring constantly, bring it to a light boil on strong heat. Turn the heat down low and add: a pinch of salt and pepper; the garlic, crushed with the blade of a knife; the bouquet garni; and the tomato.

If using use fresh tomatoes, cut them in half and squeeze them with your hands to expel the water and the seeds. It is pointless to peel them because the sauce must be strained.

Once you have added the fresh tomatoes or the tomato purée and everything has returned to a boil, carefully cover the pan and put it in a moderate oven, hot enough to maintain a very slight, continuous simmer for *1½ hours.*

You can prepare the croutons and the mushrooms in advance.

The mushrooms: Leave them whole if they are quite small. Otherwise, cut them into halves or in quarters, depending on how large they are. Make sure you remove the earthen part and wash them without peeling them.

The croutons: These should be cut 5 millimeters (3/16 inch) thick (SEE CROUTONS, PAGE 20). Fry them in butter as directed, just a few moments before serving.

To finish cooking: Put the meat pieces onto a plate. If the sauce is now *more than 3 good deciliters (1¼ cups),* boil it over strong heat without a cover to reduce it to this amount. Pass it through the chinois into a bowl. Quickly rinse the sauté pan. Put back the veal *with the mushrooms* and the sauce. Cover. Put it into the oven to cook for another *15 minutes* at a regular simmer.

To serve: Take the pieces out with a fork to put them in a little pile in a timbale or on a serving dish. Pour the sauce over them: it should be concentrated, a nice reddish-brown color, and a bit on the spicy side. Sprinkle it with minced parsley. Surround it with fried croutons. Serve.

Veal Flank with Tarragon *(Tendrons de Veau à l'Estragon)*

Here we offer a method that is entirely home style and economical, given that water will be used as a cooking liquid rather than jus. However, if you are going to use jus, leave out the roux, and thicken the juices with starch after the veal is cooked and ready to serve: so, for 3 deciliters (1¼ cups) of sauce, use 1 good tablespoon of arrowroot (SEE LIAISONS, PAGE 47).

The flank, as we have said before, is the cartilaginous part tying the short ribs to the ribs. (Do not confuse it with rib-eye, which also contains the bone, because a true flank has the advantage that it can be eaten whole.) Cut it into squares about 6–7 centimeters (2½–2¾ inches) long on each side; remove the membrane that covers one side of the flank, a simple and rapid operation using a good kitchen knife. *Time: 2 hours. Serves 6.*

750 grams (1 pound, 10 ounces) of veal flank; 1 deciliter ($3^1/_3$ fluid ounces, scant $^1/_2$ cup) of oil to color the pieces of veal; 15 grams ($^1/_2$ ounce) of flour; 1 deciliter ($3^1/_3$ fluid ounces, scant $^1/_2$ cup) of white wine; $^1/_2$ deciliter ($1^2/_3$ fluid ounces, scant $^1/_4$ cup) of water; 4 or 5 sprigs of parsley and 1 sprig of tarragon; about 20 nice tarragon leaves detached from their stems; salt and pepper.

PROCEDURE. Heat the oil until quite hot in a sauté pan and color the veal, proceeding as for VEAL SAUTÉED CHAUSSEUR (PAGE 291). Above all, make sure you do not let the bottom of the pan burn: the light crust that forms there will color and flavor the sauce. You should not allow it to go beyond a light brown tint.

Then drain every last drop of oil from the sauté pan by tilting it, keeping the cover about two-thirds on so that it retains the meat.

Sprinkle the pieces of meat with flour. On gentle heat, mix constantly with the wooden spoon for 3 or 4 minutes until the flour is a light yellowish color. Dilute it little by little with the wine and the water, either cold or hot, making sure that at the same time you dissolve the crust in the bottom of the pan. On a higher heat, bring it to a boil, stirring constantly. Then add the bouquet, the salt and the pepper. Cover the pan.

Put the pan into an oven at very moderate heat. Otherwise, put it over very controlled heat. In both cases, the boiling must be maintained at a very gentle pace. It must be extremely regular and spread evenly over the entire surface of the liquid. From this point, cook for *$1^1/_2$ hours.* During this time, if you are not cooking in the oven, the pieces must be turned over at the end of 45 minutes.

To serve: A few moments before serving, coarsely chop the tarragon leaves. Put them in a strainer and submerse them in boiling water for *1 minute* only to remove their natural bitterness. Dry them on a kitchen towel.

Using a fork, take out the pieces of veal and arrange them on a warmed plate or timbale. Remove the little bit of fat that rises to the surface of the sauce, which should have reduced by half to the consistency of a light syrup, with a beautiful golden color. If it is more dilute than this, boil it rapidly, uncovered, to reduce to this state: you will end up with about 3 deciliters ($1^1/_4$ cups).

If, on the other hand, you have boiled the sauce too much during cooking and you do not have enough, add as much water as necessary, then boil for another minute.

Pass the sauce through the chinois onto the veal pieces, arranged in a pyramid. Sprinkle the tarragon over everything. Serve hot.

Blanquette of Veal *(La Blanquette de Veau)*

This recipe is equally applicable to all white meats: lamb, fowl, rabbit, etc.

The blanquette can be served just as it is, with only the meat and the sauce; or it can be served with a garnish, the most common and, in a way, the most traditional one being small onions and mushrooms; equally you can use artichoke bottoms, celery, endive, etc. Depending on the vegetable used for the garnish, it can be cooked with the meat; if it is cooked separately, you add it at the end to the sauce. You can also accompany the blanquette with noodles or with rice served on the side.

The recipe for blanquette is the same for the different meats; the only difference lies in the cooking time. For veal, you can assume at least *$1^1/_4$ hours* after skimming; for lamb, 40–50 minutes will suffice.

Below, we give the recipe for blanquette à l'Ancienne—with small onions and mushrooms, this is considered the classic one. The method described here is the best and, in any case, typical of a blanquette. That is, the meat does not cook in the sauce, like a fricassee, and the sauce, though well thickened, must be kept light and thinner than a fricassee. That is why it must be skimmed, as described. This should not be overlooked, because the resulting sauce is much better than a sauce prepared at the last minute, which will be gluey and stick to the plate.

The small onions are cooked separately. Since they are an important part of the blanquette, they must keep their shape and all their aroma, which will not be possible if they are cooked in a large amount of liquid in the same amount of time as the meat. Allow 2 small onions per person.

The mushrooms stand up to being cooked in a lot of liquid, but to keep their shape and whiteness, it is better to cook them separately. Allow 1 mushroom per person.

The veal: The flank is the part of the veal generally used for a blanquette and is the part best suited for this recipe. By the flank, we mean the cartilaginous part at the top of the veal breast. The breast and the shoulder, though a little bit dry, can also form the basis of a blanquette. You can even use different cuts. But the flank is always the best cut.

In any case, choose quality veal—in other words, *quite white* because neither preliminary soaking nor any cooking method can make a meat that is red when raw anything other than a meat that has a grayish tint when cooked and that is stringy and tasteless. Preliminary soaking is useless here; the care taken while cooking is sufficient.

Allow 125–150 grams (4½–5⅓ ounces) of meat. Whatever part of the veal you use, flank or breast, the meat must be cut into squares about 4–5 centimeters (1½–2 inches) on each side, weighing from 50–60 grams (1¾–2¼ ounces). *Time: 2½ hours. Serves 6–8.*

1 kilogram (2 pounds, 3 ounces) of veal flank.

For the cooking: 1 onion weighing about 80 grams (2¾ ounces), stuck with half a clove; 60 grams (2¼ ounces) of carrot, cut into very thin quarters and using only the red part; a bouquet garni including leafy celery branches; 1 good liter (4¼ cups) of water; 8 grams (⅓ ounce) of salt.

For the sauce: 40 grams (1⅜ ounces, 3 tablespoons) of butter and 35 grams (1¼ ounces) of flour for a white roux; 7–8 deciliters (3–3⅜ cups) of bouillon from veal; the trimmings from the mushrooms; 2 nice egg yolks, for binding the sauce; 1 deciliter (3⅓ fluid ounces, scant ½ cup) of crème fraîche; a little pinch of grated nutmeg; juice of 1 lemon; 1 tablespoon of minced parsley.

For the garnish: 8 medium-size mushrooms of equal weight; 10 grams (⅓ ounce, 1 scant tablespoon) of butter; juice of 1 lemon; 12–15 very small onions and 20 grams (⅔ ounce, 1 heaping tablespoon) of butter to cook them.

PROCEDURE. The utensil you use to cook the meat must be deep and big enough to contain the meat pieces stacked one on top of the other. This is so that you use only the amount of liquid strictly necessary to cover the meat; if you use too much, the bouillon will be diluted and the sauce weakened. Do not use cast iron here, which often creates a grayish off-color tint; good aluminum or enameled cooking ware is appropriate.

Put the meat into the pot, then pour over the suggested amount of cold water. If the size of your pot is such that 1 liter (4½ cups) of water is not quite enough to cover the meat well, add a little extra. Add the salt at the same time as the water.

Slowly and gradually bring it to a boil on moderate heat; this gentle cooking means that the meat will not be sealed by the heat and will thus discharge any foam. Mix the pieces from time to time with a wooden spoon to encourage this discharge. Remove the foam with a metal spoon, and as you do so add a few tablespoons of cold water so that the meat releases even more. In all, you will use about 1 deciliter (3⅓ fluid ounces, scant ½ cup) of cool water.

Allow *a good half hour* from the time that you begin cooking to do this, to ensure a thorough skimming.

Then add the carrot, the onion with the clove, and the bouquet garni.

When the liquid has returned to a boil, put the lid on to cover the pot by three-quarters, then regulate the heat so that it maintains a very gentle, uninterrupted simmer for *1 good hour.* The meat, though well cooked, must stay a little bit firm.

Meanwhile, prepare the mushrooms and the small onions as described (SEE MUSHROOMS, PAGE 490; SMALL ONIONS FOR GARNITURE, PAGE 525). Cook the mushrooms first, which take very little time. You then put them in a bowl and use the same pot for cooking the small onions.

The sauce: Use a pot with a capacity of a little more than 1 liter (4¼ cups). With the butter and flour, make a white roux and cook well (SEE PAGE 47), which will take about 10 minutes.

While the roux is cooking, quickly pass the veal bouillon through a chinois into a terrine (leave the pieces of veal in their pot or put them into a sauté pan as described below. Keep them warm and covered).

You should have about *7–8 deciliters (3–3³/₈ cups)* of veal bouillon for the sauce. If you have less, this indicates that the meat was not cooked as gently or regularly as described, and the liquid reduced too much. If so, add warm water to bring it up to the required amount.

Dilute the roux with the veal bouillon. Bring it to a boil. Add the peelings from the mushrooms, pepper, and nutmeg. Turn the heat down very low to skim the sauce (SEE PAGE 16) for *15–20 minutes.* Little by little, in several stages, add the *cold* cooking liquid from the already cooked mushrooms.

Once the sauce has been skimmed, bind with egg yolks, cream, and lemon juice (SEE LIAISONS, PAGE 47). Then check the seasoning.

To hold and serve: There are several options.

First: If you have enough cooking utensils and do not mind washing one more, the simplest thing to do is to lift out the pieces of veal with a fork, let them drain, then put them in a sauté pan. Add the cooked onions and mushrooms. Cover tightly and keep warm. When the skimmed sauce has been bound, pour it through a chinois over the pieces of veal and the garnish. Put the sauté pan on the heat for just long enough to completely reheat the pieces of veal, but without allowing the sauce to boil, which would reduce it. Keep it in a double boiler covered with pieces of butter on the surface.

Second: Put the drained pieces of veal on a plate. Rinse the pot, then put the pieces back and add the mushrooms. Keep the onions separate because they would lose their shape when stacked into a high-sided pot. Keep it covered and warm. Pour the sauce, skimmed and bound, on the pieces. Continue as above.

Dressing the plate: A round shallow bowl is better than a timbale for easy serving. Put the pieces into the bowl, not arranging them carefully but in sort of a little pile. Over the middle, spread the minced parsley. Serve immediately.

A Blanquette with Leftover Roasted or Braised Meat *(Blanquette avec Viande de Desserte, Rôtie ou Braisée).* The sauce is prepared exactly as for the standard blanquette, but you replace the bouillon used for cooking the veal with ordinary light bouillon.

The amount of sauce needed is dependent on the amount of meat. If you like, add a garnish of small onions and mushrooms, or any garnish you prefer.

Cut the meat into slices that are not too thin. Remove any hard, overbrowned parts.

After thickening the sauce, strain it into a sauté pan. Put in the meat to gently reheat it *without boiling,* which would toughen the meat, particularly a roast meat.

Stuffed Veal Breast *(Poitrine de Veau Farcie)*

An attractive recipe from the home kitchen. Stuffed veal breast, served hot the first day, also yields the ingredients for a good cold dish, a kind of homemade galantine.

The ingredients for the stuffing vary according to taste and, above all, to what is available: the most common is chopped pork or sausage meat, to which you can add minced onion and mushroom. You can use the leftovers of roast meats, thus reducing the amount of sausage meat. Do not chop the roast meat, but cut it into small cubes to better preserve its flavor. When you are not limited by economy, you can use some pickled tongue in the stuffing. Cut into small cubes. This is very good, particularly when the breast is served cold.

Generally, a stuffed breast veal is braised and served with many different garnishes (braised cabbage; a purée of fresh or dried vegetables; green vegetables; noodles), basted with a reduction of its cooking juice; or it is served without a garnish and accompanied by a tomato sauce, a sauce soubise, or a sauce Robert. It can also be cooked in a pot of boiling water just as a pot-au-feu is cooked with carrots, turnips, etc.; you can serve it with one of the sauces listed above, either in a sauceboat or covering the meat.

Here we give the method taught us in former days by the classic master Columbié. According to taste, either shallot or garlic is used to "season" the stuffing, very subtly. *Time: 3 hours.*

1 piece of boned veal breast weighing 1¹/₂ kilograms (3 pounds, 5 ounces); 300–400 grams (10¹/₂–14¹/₈ ounces) of sausage meat, or a mixture that is half meat

leftovers and half sausage meat; 20 grams (2/3 ounce, 1 heaping tablespoon) of finely grated bread crumbs; 5 grams (1/6 ounce) of minced parsley leaves; a whole egg; 3 tablespoons of white wine; shallot or garlic; salt, pepper, nutmeg.

PROCEDURE. If you use garlic, rub the bowl where you will mix the stuffing with a clove that has been cut in two. Then add the egg, white wine, pepper, nutmeg, and salt, remembering that you must be mindful that the sausage meat is already salted. Add parsley and bread crumbs, then the sausage meat and the leftover meats, if you are using them. When using shallot instead of garlic, finely mince it and add it now.

To stuff the veal: This recipe uses the veal as a kind of pouch or sack that holds the stuffing. This piece, just as it is gotten from the butcher, should be rather flat and cut into a rectangle 25–30 centimeters long (10–12 inches) by 18 to 20 wide (7–8 inches). With a good kitchen knife, carefully slice into and along the longest side, right in the middle of the piece, easing the meat apart on either side; stop at least 2 good centimeters (3/4 inch) from the other three sides, to form the bottom and side of the pouch.

Before inserting the knife into the side of the piece, remember that the front and back of the pouch should be equally thick. Do not come too close to the skin with your knife or the pouch might break. A certain amount of meat must remain there to give the pouch strength.

Then put the stuffing in the pouch, tapping it down into the corners. With a kitchen needle and string, sew the two sides of the opening of the pouch together tightly so that they touch. Do not draw the string too tight and do not tighten the skin, because its tension will increase while cooking, and the juices soaking into the meat will cause the pouch to swell; under this double pressure, the skin might break.

Cooking the breast of veal: For all details, refer to BRAISING OF WHITE MEATS (PAGE 28). Do not omit the pieces of salt pork lining the pot; and, given the size of the meat, it would be better to use a braising pot. Sweat the meat as described and let it contract. Pour over bouillon up to half its height. Allow at least 2 hours of cooking from the moment when the liquid begins to boil. Finally, glaze the breast by basting it with its juice as directed.

Take the meat out of the oven and allow it to lose much of its heat before cutting the string; otherwise, the pouch risks opening up. Serve in one of the ways described in this section.

Calf's Liver *(Le Foie de Veau)*

To be the best quality—fine, tender, and soft—the calf's liver should be a very light color, described by professionals as "blonde"; livers of a reddish brown or a reddish violet are not good. It goes without saying that you must be absolutely sure it is fresh.

Prepared in slices or sautéed or grilled, calf's liver makes a special lunch. For dinners, it is properly served only as a large piece, braised or roasted.

Because it is so fresh, calf's liver must always be marinated before being braised or roasted; more or less for a long time, according to the type of recipe for which it is going to be used. The type of marinade also depends on the circumstance: most often it consists of aromatics (onions, thyme, etc.), white wine and oil, as described further down for braised liver; for home cooking, you can also use vinegar. It can also be marinated with Madeira strengthened with cognac; in this case, leave out the onion. So for a liver of the weight given below, use 1 good deciliter (3 1/3 fluid ounces, 1/2 cup) of Madeira, a small glass of cognac, parsley sprigs, salt, pepper, spice powder. Allow it to marinate for at least *1 1/2–2 hours.*

A piece of liver for braising or roasting must be as evenly thick as possible; so, remove the thin part of the liver. Trim the little bits of fat that might cling to it and remove the skin covering the liver.

Braised Calf's Liver *(Foie de Veau Braisé).* One of the advantages of braised calf's liver is that it can be reheated, but it also makes a very pleasant cold plate. For this reason, it is a good idea not to reduce the quantities for a lesser number of guests because, as with all braised meats, you will be able to serve it at other meals. The thorough cooking also lets you keep it for several days. If you like, braised calf's liver can be served with a purée of fresh or dried vegetables, according to the season. *Time: 2 1/2 hours (once the liver has been barded, marinated, and tied up). Serves 8.*

$1^1/_4$ kilograms (2 pounds, 12 ounces) of liver, net weight; 150 grams ($5^1/_3$ ounces) of fresh fatback barding bacon to bard the piece; 1 piece of pork caul big enough to wrap the liver. This pork caul avoids the need for barding: it preserves the liver and the fat nourishes it at the same time.

To marinate the liver: **1 large onion (125 grams, $4^1/_2$ ounces) minced fine; 5 or 6 sprigs of parsley, 1 sprig of thyme, $^1/_2$ of a bay leaf; 2 deciliters ($6^3/_4$ ounces, $^7/_8$ cup) of white wine; 2 tablespoons of oil; salt and pepper.**

Cooking the liver: **30 grams of butter (1 ounce, 2 tablespoons); 20 grams ($^2/_3$ ounce) of flour for the roux; 5 deciliters (generous 2 cups) of bouillon; a marinade; 3 fresh tomatoes or 1 nice tablespoon of concentrated tomato purée.**

PROCEDURE. Cut the bacon into large lardons about 1 centimeter ($^3/_8$ inch) thick and the length of the piece of liver: 6 or 7 lardons of this size will be enough. Season them with salt, pepper, and minced parsley and lard the liver (SEE LARDING, PAGE 11), inserting the lardons symmetrically.

Put half of the ingredients of the marinade into a shallow bowl. Put the liver on top of this, seasoned with salt and pepper. Cover with the rest of the ingredients, the wine, and the oil. Keep in a cool place. Turn it over from time to time in the marinade.

At the end of the time indicated (at least 2 hours), take the liver out of the marinade and wipe it clean of any ingredients attached to it. *Dry it well with a kitchen towel.* Wrap it in the caul, holding it in place with a few turns of string.

In a deep sauté pan of the right capacity, heat the butter. Put in the liver. Do not cover. Keep it on high heat *for 5 minutes* to heat everything up well. Then turn down the heat and for *15–20 minutes* let it gradually take on a beautiful golden color, turning it over from time to time, keeping the pan uncovered throughout.

Then remove the liver onto a plate. Mix the flour in the butter in the pan. Cook it gently until it turns a dark blond color (SEE LIAISON WITH A ROUX, PAGE 47). Then add the bouillon to dissolve the flour mixture. Add the marinade with all its ingredients, the pinch of pepper, and either the fresh tomatoes, squeezed and deseeded and then cut into pieces, or the tomato purée. Bring it to a boil, stirring constantly. Then put the liver back into the pan. Place a round of greased paper directly on top of the liver. Cover the pan. Continue cooking in the oven with a *very moderate* heat to maintain a very slow and regular simmer for another *2 hours.*

To serve: Place the liver on a round plate. With scissors, remove the string holding the caul in place. Degrease the sauce. Pass it through the chinois onto the liver, serving it either whole or cut into thin, even slices.

Calf's Liver à la Bourgeoise *(Foie de Veau à la Bourgeoise).* In other words, with a garnish of carrots and small onions. The recipe is exactly the same as for braised calf liver. *Time: $2^1/_2$ hours.*

Prepare the carrots and onions as described under ROUND ROAST OF VEAL À LA BOURGEOISE (PAGE 276). At the end of 1 good hour of cooking the liver, take it out of the pot and put it on a plate. Pass the sauce through a chinois into a terrine. Rinse the pot; put the liver back in. Surround it with carrots and onions, both previously sautéed until lightly colored. Pour the sauce over everything. Bring it back to a boil. Cover the pot and continue cooking—very gently in order not to damage the vegetables—for *at least 1 hour.*

To serve: Arrange the vegetables around the whole liver; or, if it has been carved, in the middle of the circle formed by the slices. Pour the boiling sauce over everything.

Braised Calf's Liver with Fresh Cèpes *(Fois de Veau Braisé aux Cèpes Frais).* The same recipe as above. Allow 1 good pound of small cèpes, the earth end trimmed. Carefully peel the stems and heads without washing them. Wipe them with a kitchen towel. Cut them into slices 1 centimeter ($^3/_8$ inch) thick. Mince 4 shallots.

Strongly heat 2 deciliters ($6^3/_4$ ounces, $^7/_8$ cup) of oil in a pan. Sauté the cèpes in it on strong heat to color nicely on the outside. Put them in a strainer. Drain all the oil from the pan, then put the mushrooms back in. Add the minced shallot. Sauté for a moment. Keep it on the side.

A half hour before serving, pass the sauce as described in LIVER À LA BOURGEOISE (PAGE 297). Arrange the cèpes and the shallots around the liver. Continue cooking for *another half hour.* Dress as described above. Pour the degreased sauce over everything. Serve boiling hot.

Burgundy-Style Stewed Calf's Liver *(Foie de Veau Étuvé à la Façon de Bourgogne).* Prepared in this way, the liver is cooked in thick clay pots, which were used in earlier days throughout the countryside. If you do not have a clay pot, you can use a good pot made of thick cast iron: The thickness of the pot is very important here because the cooking must be very gentle and uninterrupted. The pot must be exactly the right size so that you can pack down both ends of the liver—not too deep, and with a rounded bottom if possible. The leftovers of the liver are excellent cold or reheated. *Time: About 4 hours.*

1 kilogram (2 pounds, 3 ounces) of liver, net weight, after it has been prepared; about 10 large lardons for barding; 1 piece of caul or veal fat to wrap it; 1 good tablespoon of fresh fat from lard (shortening); 200 grams (7 ounces) of carrots, cut into quarters and using only the red part; 125 grams (4 1/2 ounces) of onions, cut into 2 or 4 depending on their size; a bouquet garni with a clove of garlic enclosed; 15 grams (1/2 ounce) of salt; a pinch of pepper; the trimmings from the liver, and the rind from the lardons; a small glass of cognac.

PROCEDURE. Bard and wrap the liver in the caul as for braised calf's liver.

In the pot, heat the fat. Put in the liver with its trimmings. Color it briskly on high heat to seal the liver before it has the time to let its juices escape. After 10 minutes, it should have the color of a finished roast.

Turn down the heat to put in the vegetables and the bouquet garni around the liver and on top of the liver, piling them up. Season with salt and pepper. *Add no liquid.* Tightly cover the pot. Turn the heat back up to begin cooking again. As soon as you hear boiling, turn the heat down to a steady and gentle medium heat—this is the substitute for the hot coals used to surround the pot in the fireplaces of rural Burgundy.

Allow *3 hours* of cooking. At the end of 1 1/2 hours, turn the liver over and add the small glass of cognac. At this point, both the liver and vegetables will have cooked and shriveled a bit and rendered their juices, which will reach more than halfway up the liver. Recover the pot tightly and continue cooking as above.

To serve: Untie the liver and keep it warm on its plate. Degrease the juice. With the vegetables, pass it through a fine strainer over a small saucepan, pressing with the back of the spoon to crush the vegetables: you will get a sort of coulis out of it. If the cooking has been properly done and if the carrots used are new season, this sauce will thicken to a consistency that flows smoothly. Otherwise, correct by adding 1 or 2 tablespoons of bouillon or of water. Boil for another minute, check the seasoning, and then pour it boiling hot over the liver.

Roast Calf's Liver *(Foie de Veau Rôti)*

Always marinated, as has been mentioned, larded on the inside to nourish it with fat, and then surrounded by a caul or with bards of fatback bacon, the liver is roasted either on the spit or in the oven. It is generally accompanied by a moderately spicy sauce: poivrade, bordelaise, and at the same time, with its degreased juice.

Here again, it is better to use a rather large piece. The leftovers do not reheat like those of a braise, but when cut into thin slices, they make a good cold plate with any salad or with a cold sauce.

Home-Style Roasted Calf's Liver *(Foie de Veau Rôti)* à la Ménagère. The juices from the cooking are made into a sauce to accompany the liver. *Time: About 4 1/2 hours (of which 45 minutes is for cooking). Serves 7 or 8.*

1 kilogram (2 pounds, 3 ounces) of liver trimmed completely; 150 grams (5 1/3 ounces) of fresh fatback bacon; 1 piece of caul to envelop the liver.

For the marinade: 60 grams (2 1/4 ounces) of onions cut into rounds; 3 or 4 sprigs of parsley; 1 sprig of thyme; 1/2 of a bay leaf; salt, pepper, spice powder; 2 tablespoons of vinegar; 2 tablespoons of oil.

For the sauce: 1 tablespoon of good lard to baste the roast; 2 tablespoons of vinegar; 2 deciliters

(6$^{3}/_{4}$ ounces, $^{7}/_{8}$ cup) of bouillon; 1 small teaspoon of starch.

PROCEDURE. Lard the liver in the same way as for braised liver. Marinate it and likewise wrap it in the caul.

Put it on a small rack in a roasting dish. Pour the marinade into the bottom of the dish. Put it in a hot oven, but not too hot, because the liver must be cooked more like a white meat than like a red meat. In the initial stages of cooking, baste the liver in the melted fat, turning over the piece. Then, as the cooking advances, baste it with a little bouillon. For the weight suggested, allow *45 minutes* of cooking. The roast liver must be cooked *à point*—that is, uniformly pink throughout, neither bloody nor too cooked. When you stick a cooking needle into the center of it, the juice that bubbles at the opening must be neither red nor golden blond but lightly pink.

A few minutes before checking for this, remove the caul so that the liver colors. After this, keep it on its plate in a very warm spot or in a very, very low oven for the 2 or 3 minutes you take to prepare the accompanying sauce.

The sauce: In a very small saucepan on strong heat, boil the 2 tablespoons of vinegar until there is less than $^{1}/_{2}$ tablespoon. Meanwhile, pour the bouillon into the roasting plate. With the back of a spoon, scrape it to deglaze and dissolve the crust that has formed from the juices during the cooking. Pass everything, both the liquid and the aromatics, through the chinois into the saucepan with the vinegar while you whisk it. Degrease it. Boil. Bind it with a little bit of starch (SEE LIAISONS, PAGE 47), until this sauce has the consistency of a syrup. Check the seasoning. Pour into a warmed sauceboat. Serve immediately.

Roast Calf's Liver à la Crème Poivrade *(Foie de Veau Rôti à la Crème Poivrade).* Proceed exactly as above, but deglaze with a few tablespoons of bouillon only. Strain and degrease the juices, then pour onto the reduced vinegar and add 2 deciliters (6$^{3}/_{4}$ ounces, $^{7}/_{8}$ cup) of heavy cream, which has gone a little sour. Boil for 5 minutes on very gentle heat. Bind it with the starch. Check the seasoning, which should be somewhat spicy. Baste the roast liver with a few tablespoons of this sauce and send the rest to the table in a sauceboat.

Sautéed Calf's Liver for All Preparations *(Foie de Veau Sauté pour Tous Apprêts)*

For each person, allow a slice of liver weighing from 100–110 grams (3$^{1}/_{2}$–3$^{7}/_{8}$ ounces). The slices should be of equal thickness, about a little less than 1 centimeter—that is, 8 or 10 millimeters ($^{3}/_{8}$–$^{3}/_{8}$ inch). They should also be the same thickness throughout—a point we insist upon because when slices are cut on the bias they are often much thinner on one side than on the other. This is an absolutely defective procedure because it means that the liver will not cook uniformly, the thin part being dried out and tough while the thick part is still half raw. It is always better to cut the slices yourself; if you need only 1 or 2 slices, ask the butcher to cut them, but make sure he follows these directions.

To get slices that are more or less uniform and without too many trimings, it is important to choose the part used for the slices carefully. They must be cut right *in the very thickest part of the liver*—that is, almost on the middle. Slices from the thin end of the liver that has been cut on the bias can only give you slices of an uneven thickness. On the contrary, the other end is too thick to cut the slices in the size and weights necessary without there being considerable waste.

Cooking the liver: This is generally done in a good clean pan with, depending on the recipe, butter, lard oil, or butter and oil. You need about 60 grams (2$^{1}/_{4}$ ounces, 4$^{1}/_{2}$ tablespoons) for 6 slices.

A scant 15 minutes before serving, spread 1 tablespoon of flour on a plate. Season the slices of liver generously on both sides with salt and pepper to counteract the natural blandness of the liver. Coat both sides in flour. When cooked, this flour will produce a light crusty layer on the slices and it will also retain the juices.

Heat your chosen fat in the pan. When it is nice and hot, arrange the slices in it *one next to the other* (SEE SAUTÉING, PAGE 34). Keep the pan on a nice high heat and let it cook for *4 minutes* on one side. Then turn them over to let them cook for *4–5 minutes* on the other side. This should be enough time to cook the liver properly—that is, *à point* and still tender.

Slide a fork under the slices of liver to transport them without piercing them, which would allow the juice to escape. Put them on a well-heated plate. Then add your chosen sauce. Serve.

Italian-Style Sautéed Calf's Liver *(Foie de Veau Sauté à l'Italienne).* The sauce to accompany this liver requires a little time: *35–40 minutes.* It can be prepared in advance at no inconvenience and kept warm, then brought back to a boil before serving. *Time: 45 minutes. Serves 6.*

6 slices of liver of the suggested weight; 30 grams (1 ounce, 2 tablespoons) of butter and 2 tablespoons of oil to sauté them.

For the sauce: 50 grams ($1^{3}/_{4}$ ounces) of fresh mushrooms; 20 grams ($^{2}/_{3}$ ounce) of onions; 15 grams ($^{1}/_{2}$ ounce) of shallots; 30 grams (1 ounce, 2 tablespoons) of butter; 1 tablespoon of oil; 10 grams ($^{1}/_{3}$ ounce, 1 scant tablespoon) of butter; $^{1}/_{2}$ deciliter ($1^{2}/_{3}$ fluid ounces, scant $^{1}/_{4}$ cup) of white wine; $2^{1}/_{2}$ deciliters (1 cup) of bouillon; 1 tablespoon of a good tomato purée; 40 grams ($1^{3}/_{8}$ ounces) of pickled tongue or lean cooked ham; 1 teaspoon of parsley, chervil, and tarragon, minced and mixed; salt, pepper, and nutmeg.

PROCEDURE. Make the sauce as described (SEE ITALIAN SAUCE, PAGE 61). Cut the ham or the tongue into small cubes 2 millimeters ($^{1}/_{16}$ inch) long on each side. They should be added to the sauce only a few seconds before serving.

A scant 15 minutes before serving, flour and sauté the slices as has been described. Arrange them in a circle on the plate. Pour the sauce in the middle, not allowing it to fall on the slices. Serve with well-heated plates.

Grilled Calf's Liver *(Foie de Veau Grillé)*

Time: 45 minutes. Serves 6.

6 slices of liver weighing from 100–110 grams ($3^{1}/_{2}$–$3^{7}/_{8}$ ounces) each, cut $1^{1}/_{2}$ centimeters ($^{5}/_{8}$ inch) *equally thick throughout.* For this weight, they should be a maximum of 12 centimeters long ($4^{3}/_{4}$ inches) and $5^{1}/_{2}$ centimeters ($2^{1}/_{8}$ inches) wide. They should be no thicker, and not much thinner, because slices that are too thin will toughen when they are grilled.

40 grams ($1^{3}/_{8}$ ounces, 3 tablespoons) of melted butter to baste the slices during cooking.

PROCEDURE. For details of how to grill, SEE GRILLING (PAGE 35).

Please note that the liver must be cooked rather gently; and this is not simply to keep the juices in the flesh, as when cooking beef steaks or cutlets, but to ensure that the liver cooks gradually and thoroughly. This means watching carefully because if the cooking goes on too long, the liver will harden instead of being tender, and it will become utterly insipid. There is another point of great importance: As soon as it is grilled, the liver must be served immediately. Allow 10 minutes *of cooking* on a coal fire, and be prepared so that you can serve right away.

Line up the slices of liver on a plate. Sprinkle them lightly with salt and pepper. Heat the butter in a small pan to melt it. With a kitchen brush, apply the melted butter on both sides of the slices and arrange them on a preheated grill. *After 3 minutes* of grilling, brush the surface of the slices and turn them over; also brush the side that was in contact with the grill. Turn the slices over again *at the end of 3 minutes,* brushing them one more time, then let them grill for another *4 minutes.* In all, then, a total of 10 minutes of cooking.

Calf's Liver Grilled à la Bercy *(Foie de Veau Grillé à la Bercy).* This is a popular lunch plate in good restaurants. It is very simple but requires a speedy technique so that it can be served *very hot.* This is essential for this kind of recipe. *Time: 30 minutes. Serves 6.*

6 slices of calf's liver, of the weight suggested above. See Bercy butter (PAGE 78) for details of how to prepare the butter and also of the quantities needed, which will correspond to the amount needed here.

PROCEDURE. Prepare the Bercy butter 5 minutes before putting the slices of liver on the grill.

Spread the butter on a long plate. Arrange the slices of grilled liver on the plate and turn them over so that the side facing up will also be well covered with butter. Serve.

If the plate must be left standing (which is most unfortunate), keep the liver on its own in a warm place between 2 plates and let the butter stand in a double boiler.

Brochettes of Calf's Liver *(Brochettes de Foie de Veau).* In haute cuisine, rounds of mushrooms are added to the brochettes along with the bacon that plays a supporting but essential role. Everything is covered in a duxelles sauce before being breaded and grilled. The brochettes are then served with a duxelles or Italian sauce, or a maître d'hôtel butter.

For home cooking, the mushrooms are left out and the liver alternates only with the bacon. But one practice that should be retained from haute cuisine is to first sauté the liver in the pan; this firms up the liver, making it easier to handle, and also shortens the cooking time, which is just as well since it is difficult to maintain a regular heat when grilling for a long time. *Serves 6.*

1 nice pound of calf's liver; 250 grams (8⁷/₈ ounces) of lean bacon; 30 grams (1 ounce, 2 tablespoons) of butter and 2 tablespoons of oil for frying in the pan; 2 nice tablespoons of bread crumbs; 30–40 grams (1–1³/₈ ounces, 2–3 tablespoons) of melted butter or 2 tablespoons of oil for the breading; salt, pepper.

PROCEDURE. **The bacon:** Trim the rind, then cut the bacon into slices about 8 millimeters (5/16 inch) thick. Divide these into squares at least 3 centimeters (1 1/8 inch) long on each side. Allow for *4 squares of bacon per brochette.* Blanch them (SEE BACON, PAGE 15). Drain and reserve.

The liver: From slices that are 1 1/2 good centimeters thick (5/8 inch), cut the liver into squares 3 1/2 centimeters (1 3/8 inch) long on each side. These dimensions are not absolute: it is enough that the squares are more or less the same size. In any case, try not to be wasteful when trimming. *Allow for 5 squares of liver for each brochette.*

Strongly heat the butter and the oil in a clean pan until the oil starts to smoke. Put in the liver squares, seasoned with salt and pepper. Sauté them over high heat for *3 or 4 minutes,* to firm them up nicely.

You could also sauté the squares of blanched bacon, adding them 2 minutes before the liver, but this is not absolutely necessary. The essential thing is to nicely firm up the squares of liver, and for this you have to seal them with very high heat. Drain them.

The brochettes: On each brochette, thread a square of liver and a square of bacon, alternating them and ending with a square of liver. Dip it into melted butter or oil and roll it in the bread crumbs. Keep it in a cool place on a plate until the moment you grill it.

To grill and serve: Fifteen minutes before serving, have your grill ready if you are grilling over coals (SEE GRILLING, PAGE 35). Sprinkle the breaded surface of the brochette with the remaining butter or oil. Put it on the grill and turn it from time to time. Allow *12–14 minutes* over a hot grill fire. Serve the brochettes without taking them off the brochette on a long heated plate. If accompanying them with a maître d'hôtel butter, spread this butter out on the bottom of the plate first. In fact, do this for any sauce.

If not, baste the brochettes with a little melted butter and a little lemon juice and sprinkle freshly minced parsley over them. Whichever way you plan to serve them, serve burning hot.

Calf's Sweetbreads *(Les Ris de Veau)*

Usually sweetbreads are larded, braised, and glazed like a fricandeau, then served with one of the garnishes that accompany a fricandeau. This garnish varies according to the seasons and the circumstances.

That said, there are two garnishes that are particularly appropriate to veal sweetbreads—so much so, in fact, that they have more or less becomes classics: sweetbreads à la financière and sweetbreads à la Toulouse. Prepared in this manner, they have a place on fine menus. But for the recipe à la Toulouse, cooking differs because the sweetbreads must, like any preparation au blanc, be cooked without coloring. Here we will give the two methods of cooking appropriate for whichever recipe you choose.

In haute cuisine, the sweetbreads are often prepared like scallops, sautéed in butter: in this case, they are blanched a little longer than needed when just firming them up.

You can also grill them, divided in half, but make sure they are always blanched first. Thus, they can be accompanied with a sauce of your choosing; béarnaise, Italian, tomato, etc.; or with a maître d'hôtel butter. And if you wish, you can add an appropriate garnish: potato sautéed in butter, carrots, fresh sautéed vegetables, etc.

Dressing the dish: This depends not only on the garnish but also on taste and circumstance. Thus, for sweetbreads à la financière and à la Toulouse, you can proceed in different ways. Put the sweetbreads on a long plate surrounded by only a few tablespoons of their cooking juice, which has, of course, been strained, degreased, and reduced; the garnish in its sauce is served on the side. Alternatively, you can arrange the sweetbreads in a cross, with their open sides facing up along one direction of the cross and facing down along the other; put 5 or 6 slices of truffle on each piece, and put the garnish, lightly sauced, in between; the rest of the sauce for the garnish should be served on the side. Or you can put the sweetbreads in a circle, then pour the garnish and the sauce into the middle. But whichever way you choose to dress the dish, take great care to prevent the sauce from falling on the sweetbreads. By "sauce," we do not mean the juices from cooking the sweetbreads, which can be reduced to a glaze and then used to baste the sweetbreads.

Be inspired by these dressings to think of other ways to dress the dish. Try something like a garnish à la jardinière, which includes different ingredients; or serve only one vegetable or one purée. Whatever dressing is easiest and quickest, the important thing is to always serve it very hot.

The cooking juice, degreased, reduced, and lightly bound with a little starch can be served on the side or in a sauceboat, or you can use it to baste the garnish: in this case, it must be reduced further.

Sweetbreads are only carved with a spoon—never with a knife. And they are always served on hot plates.

Preparation of Calf's Sweetbreads *(Préparation des Ris de Veau).* Whatever recipe and cooking method is chosen, the sweetbreads must first always undergo the following: soaking, blanching, pressing.

To soak: The reason for this is to disgorge the sweetbreads and dissolve every last droplet of blood. Keep the sweetbreads in a terrine of cold water for at least 4 hours in advance, and change the water each time it turns red. Three hours would be enough under running water.

If not enough time and care is taken for soaking, the inside of the sweetbreads will remain slightly pink after cooking, and they should never be presented like that. So, do not begin the following stages until the sweetbread is *absolutely white* without any red blemish.

To blanch: Here the intention is not to clean or begin cooking the sweetbread, but to firm it up. Even if the sweetbread does not have to be larded, blanching is essential given the handling required for trimming and cooking, etc.

Put it in a pot large enough so that you can cover it completely with cold water. Heat it very slowly so the heat can penetrate gradually. Boiling it too quickly and intensely would inflate the skin and make it burst and the inside would become soft; having badly released its foam, the sweetbread would be left with an ugly tint.

As soon as it has begun boiling, boil for only *2 minutes.* At this point, the sweetbread will be sufficiently firm. Furthermore, it will be a little bit swollen. Take it out with a skimmer and plunge it in cold water, changing the water so that it cools more quickly.

Drain it on a clean towel. Using a knife, separate it into 2 lobes, the rounded side and the grooved. Then carefully remove all the skin and fat, as well as the strings that held them together. While you are doing this, take great care not to harm the light and transparent film that covers the sweetbread like a taut rubber balloon. This is essential for holding together the sweetbread flesh, which would crumble without it.

Lay out a towel and arrange the sweetbreads on one half, side by side. Then cover them with the other half of the towel. Make sure that the towel is very clean and has no odors, because this delicate meat can be easily spoiled. On top of this, place a board or a large plate directly onto the sweetbreads, and load it with 1 or 2 weights totaling 2 kilograms (4 pounds, 6 ounces). This will flatten out the sweetbreads to give them a good appearance and will make them spread out. Let them stand like this for at least 1 hour.

Blanched, pressed sweetbreads can be prepared very much in advance. You could do this in the morning, so they are ready when you lard them or start cooking them for dinner.

Braised Calf's Sweetbreads *(Ris de Veau Braisés).* This is the fricandeau method, the most popular for most circumstances. *Time: 1½ hours to braise and glaze the sweetbreads. Serves 6–8.*

2 veal sweetbreads weighing 800–900 grams (1 pound, 12 ounces to 2 pounds), gross weight; 200 grams (7 ounces) of fatback bacon for larding; 7½ deciliters (generous 3 cups) of jus; 1½ deciliters (5 fluid ounces, ⅔ cup) of white wine; 50 grams (1¾ ounces) of fresh pork rind; 150 grams (5⅓ ounces) of carrots cut into rounds ½ centimeter (¼ inch) thick, and 150 grams (5⅓ ounces) of onions cut similarly; a bouquet garni.

PROCEDURE. For all cooking details, refer to BRAISING WHITE MEATS (PAGE 28) and particularly to FRICANDEAU (PAGE 277). We will summarize here only the stages that follow.

First, disgorge and blanch the sweetbreads and then put them under the press. Next, lard each part of the sweetbread with 5 rows of lardons 3 centimeters long (1¼ inches) and 3 millimeters (⅛ inch) on each side. Leave just under 1 centimeter (⅜ inch) between each lardon (SEE LARDING, PAGE 11). When larding, you must be very careful to avoid any direct contact with your hand, which risks spoiling the sweetbread, the most delicate meat of all.

As described under BRAISING (PAGE 25), line a sauté pan large enough to place the sweetbreads side by side without squeezing them together too closely, and with the larded side up. Place the bouquet garni among the sweetbreads. Sweat for 10 minutes and then pour in the white wine. Reduce. Then add *1½ deciliters (5 fluid ounces, ⅔ cup) of jus;* reduce it again to make a glaze. Then finally add the rest of the jus, about 6 deciliters (2½ cups). Bring it to a boil. Cover with a round of paper placed directly on top of the sweetbreads and cover. Put it into a medium hot oven to maintain a slow, regular simmer for *35 minutes.*

Glazing the sweetbreads is essential for every piece that has been larded. A good 15 minutes before serving, remove the sweetbreads from their pan, taking care because of their considerable fragility. Use a spatula or a skimmer, or 2 forks, then place them either in another sauté pan or in a shallow bowl, proceeding as has been described for the fricandeau.

Strain the jus. Degrease it completely. You should have 2 deciliters (6¾ ounces, ⅞ cup); pour this directly on the sweetbreads to baste them. Glaze them as described, basting 3 times with the juice at 3-minute intervals. Finally, turn up the heat to color the lardons nicely. Then serve the sweetbreads the way you like.

Sweetbreads Braised à Blanc *(Ris de Veau Braisés à Blanc).* Actually, this is more a question of poaching. The sweetbreads are cooked so that their final tint is a very light gold. They are served like all recipes *à blanc:* either with a garnish à la Toulouse or with a similar dish.

Here the sweetbreads are blanched, as always, but not larded. At least, the larding is not essential any more than the truffles used in haute cuisine for dishes made à la Toulouse. *Time: 1¼ hours. Serves 6–8.*

The weight of the sweetbreads and the ingredients for their cooking are the same as for the ordinary braised sweetbreads. The major difference is that *the juice used must not be colored.* In addition, *a very thin slice of bacon* must be used to wrap each sweetbread that has not been larded.

PROCEDURE. Cover each sweetbread with a bard of bacon kept in place with a few turns of string. Put them in a sauté pan that has been lined with pork rind, carrot, and onion, as for a standard braise. Add the white wine immediately.

Put the pan, *without a cover,* over good heat. Boil until the wine has completely reduced. Watch it carefully so that nothing sticks to the bottom or colors, because the cooking juice must remain white.

Then pour in the jus to cover the sweetbreads. Bring it to a boil. Then put a round of white buttered parchment paper on the sweetbreads and *cover the pan.* Immediately put it into a moderate oven so that the liquid does not go beyond a light simmer, which is all that is needed for poaching. Make sure that the liquid does not boil any more strongly for the entire duration of the cooking: *poach for 45 minutes.*

After this, proceed to the glazing. As for all glazing, glaze just before serving. If the sweetbreads are ready a little in advance, you should keep them warm in their pan, waiting for the moment to start glazing them, about 10 minutes before serving. Take them out of the pan and put them into a sauté pan or plate, as described above. Remove the bards of bacon. Baste them with a few tablespoons of their juice *once it has been degreased.* Put them in the oven or under the heat of a very moderate broiler. After 3 minutes, baste them again. From this moment, watch them carefully so you can take them out as soon as their surface has taken on a very light golden tint. Above all, do not let them brown; since they are served with a white sauce, as for that of the garnish à la Toulouse, the sweetbreads must be barely colored. For this recipe, it is simply a matter of letting them take on a brilliant skin of a pale golden tint. Then serve them according to your choice of dressing.

Marshal-Style Sweetbreads *(Ris de Veau à la Maréchale).* The name does not imply a recipe from haute cuisine but rather a family recipe that is extremely good for a special dinner.

The sweetbreads—larded, braised, and glazed—are served surrounded by a cream sauce. For details about quantities and preparing and cooking the sweetbreads, you should refer to the recipe for sweetbreads braised like a fricandeau.

For a sauce for a pair of medium-size sweetbreads, you need about 30 grams (1 ounce) of flour and 30 grams (1 ounce, 2 tablespoons) of butter to make a white roux. Dilute this with 4 deciliters (1 2/3 cups) of crème fraîche, then add a pinch of salt and a pinch of white pepper. Boil it up a little bit. Off the heat, add 30 grams (1 ounce, 2 tablespoons) of butter.

To serve: Place the sweetbreads on a warmed plate. Surround them with a ribbon of sauce. Cover the sweetbreads, already glazed, with a few tablespoons of their reduced cooking juice, which should overflow a little bit onto the cream sauce.

Calf's Head *(La Tête de Veau)*

The preparation and the initial cooking are the same for all the recipes that follow.

When the calf's head is cooked and chilled in its jelly, it keeps perfectly for several days. It would thus be sensible to buy a whole head, because even if you use only a part of it the first day, the extra work of preparing the whole head is not considerable.

No matter what the recipe, there are two essentials to note: *maintain the whiteness of the meat; serve very hot.* Calf's head is unpleasant to eat when it is cold. For this reason, it is never served whole. The difficulty of carving makes it difficult to serve quickly, which is obligatory, so calf's head is always carved into pieces before being cooked.

Choosing the head; disgorging it: Choose a head that is as fatty as possible, a medium size, and very white: that is, that has been thoroughly disgorged in cold water and has no blemishes. It goes without saying that you must buy the calf's head with its skin on, known as the hide. It must be boned before being cut into pieces and the simplest thing is to have the butcher do this.

Once the head has been boned, keep it in cold water until you are ready to cook it. In the major cities, where calf's head is generally sold only after it has already been disgorged for some time, you will need only a few more hours to disgorge it; otherwise, you must let the head disgorge in cold water overnight, and even longer. However much time is needed, make sure the head does not sit right at the bottom of the utensil, where the water will quickly become saturated with blood, nor float on the surface, where it will spoil.

Use a utensil, a pail or basin, large enough so you can generously bathe the head. Put a clay tablet or a board right on top of the meat, which should be lightly weighed down so that the head is always partially submerged in the water. Renew the soaking water several times; or leave the utensil under a faucet of running water.

To blanch: This firms up the meat and also serves to clean it so that carving is easier.

A large utensil is essential here so the head is generously bathed. An earthenware marmite would work very well and keep the meat white. Put in the head and cover it with cold water. Bring it to a boil slowly. Skim it and then allow it to boil for 5 or 6 minutes from the time the boiling has begun. Plunge the head in cool water; clean it well, brushing the hide if necessary to remove the foam that could attach to it.

The *blanc* for cooking: Calf's head is cooked in a *blanc* (SEE PAGE 42), the seasoning varying slightly in different recipes. It always contains onions, but some people add carrot and garlic, using lemon instead of the vinegar. When the cooking liquid is used, which is unusual in this dish, the flour is left out, because it produces a gluey effect; and lemon replaces the vinegar.

At home, the cooking liquid from the calf's head can be put to good second use as a soup. But in any case, you must not leave out the fat used when cooking *en blanc,* its function being to prevent the meat from spoiling by keeping out the air.

We give here the most modern recipe for calf's head in its various recipes.

For a half head: **2 1/2 liters (10 1/2 cups) of water; 35 grams (1 1/4 ounces) of flour; 20 grams (2/3 ounces) of sea salt; an onion with a clove stuck in it; a large bouquet garni; 6 peppercorns; 4 good tablespoons of vinegar; 3 generous tablespoons of fat.**

For a whole head: **Increase these quantities by 1 1/2 liters (6 1/3 cups) of water; 20 grams (2/3 ounces) of flour; 10 grams (1/3 ounce) of salt; 1 tablespoon of fat; and bring up the rest of the seasoning a bit.**

PROCEDURE. Prepare the *blanc* before carving the veal head so that you can put the pieces immediately afterward into the *blanc.* A high-sided cooking pot in thick aluminum is the best utensil to use.

To carve and cook: Take off the ear by cutting around the base in a circle, using the point of a small kitchen knife. Cut off the muzzle and divide the rest of the cheeks into 3 pieces. Rub these pieces with a quarter of lemon on the skin side; the acid of the lemon preserves their whiteness.

As you cut them, put them in the *boiling blanc.* Add the fat, then cover the pot. From the moment when it starts boiling, *allow to cook for 1 1/4–1 1/2 hours,* keeping the liquid at a simple, even, uninterrupted simmer. You can tell when it is properly cooked by using your finger to touch the skin of a piece of the cheek. Then turn the heat off under the pot, but keep it covered. Do not take out the pieces of head until the moment you are ready to use them.

PRINCIPAL RECIPES FOR CALF'S HEAD

Calf's Head au Naturel *(Tête de Veau au Naturel).* Reserved for lunches, this is always served cold with a cold sauce, presented in a sauceboat, or made by the guests on their own plates, where you present not only the oil cruet but also the ingredients for the cold sauce on a small plate. In other words: capers, onion, parsley, cornichons, etc., all minced.

Calf's head au naturel can also be served with a tomato sauce served aside in a sauceboat.

Calf's Head à la Poulette *(Tête de Veau à la Poulette).* The pieces are cut into small scallops while they are still burning hot and sautéed in a sauce poulette. Serve on a plate or timbale.

Calf's Head Fritters *(Tête de Veau en Fritot).* Cut small pieces about 5 centimeters (2 inches) square from the skin part. Marinate them in lemon juice, minced parsley, and pepper for at least 1 hour. When you are ready to fry, dry off the pieces and dip them in a light frying batter. Dress them on a napkin with fried parsley. Serve a Madeira sauce or a tomato sauce on the side.

Calf's Head en Tortue *(Tête de Veau en Tortue).* Traditionally, this was served thusly: the head, carved and cooked in a *blanc,* was covered with a *financière* garnish of a Madeira sauce strongly flavored with tomato and spiced with cayenne. This whole dish was decorated with crayfish alternating with fried eggs on croutons or balls of hard-boiled eggs; the rest of the sauce and garnish was served in a sauceboat. Note the inclusion of cornichons in the garnish, which were a traditional part of the financière and characteristic of a recipe *en tortue;* all the authors, both ancient and modern, indicate this.

These days, the preparation is the same; but in imitation of the English "mock-turtle," aromatic herbs are introduced: basil, sage, rosemary.

These herbs should be added carefully; otherwise, you will get an unpleasant pharmaceutical taste. Some people do not like this innovation at all, and it remains optional. *Serves 10–12.*

1 half calf's head.

For the garnish: coxcombs, cock's kidneys, mushrooms, olives, dumplings, in the quantities given for the financière garnish (SEE PAGE 457). Add 6 small, green cornichons cut into cubes or into large rounds. In addition: crayfish, croutons, fried eggs in equal proportions; allow 1 of each per person. Or, if you feel that some of your guests will not want them, you can restrict yourself to 8 or 9 of each.

For the sauce: good 1/2 liter (generous 2 cups) of Madeira sauce, including a concentrated tomato purée, no more than 1 scant deciliter (3 1/3 fluid ounces, scant 1/2 cup) for these. (Note that, as well as flavor, the tomato adds consistency and color to a sauce whose characteristic tint is a brownish red; in consequence, you should use good red tomatoes in a very concentrated purée like that of a good preserve.)

For the aromatic herbs: 1 gram of each (1 gram is 1/28 ounce) basil, marjoram, sage, thyme, and bay leaf; 2 grams rosemary; about 12 parsley leaves. Everything is put into 1/2 deciliter (1 2/3 fluid ounces, scant 1/4 cup) of boiling bouillon. Cover it tightly and let it infuse off the heat for 15 minutes. Strain it through a fine cloth and reserve it for a final addition in the sauce.

(Quantities from the recipes of chef Philéas Gilbert.)

PROCEDURE. Because of the many steps involved in making the garnish, the work should be divided into 2 parts. Do all that you can in advance, and leave yourself free to work on the last-minute steps, which are the most critical part of the work.

Prepare the stuffing for the dumplings *the night before,* and also the sauce without the infusion. The calf's head can be cooked and kept in its cooking liquid; it can be reheated there and made ready a half hour before dressing the plate.

The same day you serve the dish, poach the dumplings. The mushrooms, truffles, and olives should also be prepared as described for the *financière* garnish.

Use a pot with a capacity of about 1 liter (4 cups), into which you will put the various ingredients of the *financière* garnish as they are prepared and to which the sauce will be added at the last moment. Everything should be kept warm, at an imperceptible simmer, during the last-minute preparations and until you are ready to dress the dish.

The sauce: If it does not include the herbal infusion, this is mixed just as it is into the pot, *reserving the Madeira,* which will be added at the last moment. If it does include the herbal infusion, the sauce is first reduced to *4 deciliters (1 2/3 cups),* boiling it strongly before adding the infusion to it; this is so that it remains as thick. As above, the Madeira is not added until the last moment.

Final preparations: Reserve for the décor as many truffle slices as you have fried eggs. These should be lightly heated in a bowl with 1/2 tablespoon of Madeira and the same of bouillon. Cook and prepare the crayfish as for garnishes (SEE PAGE 229). Cut the croutons in small triangles 5 millimeters (3/16 inch) thick then round them into a heart shape.

Dressing the plate: Use either a large silver tray with low sides or, simply, a round serving dish, warmed under boiling water.

Two or three minutes in advance, drain the pieces of cheek and muzzle on a towel. Let the ear stand in the warm liquid until the last moment. Separate the gelatinous part or the part that resembles the tortoise meat from the fatty part. Scrape off the white skin on the muzzle. Cut these pieces into cubes 3 centimeters (1 1/4 inches) long on each side. Arrange these on the bottom of the plate. Cover them with half the garnish and the sauce. On top of them, put the crayfish and croutons, alternating them. Put the fried eggs on the croutons and on each egg a slice of truffle.

The ear is a part of the decoration, and is put in the middle; drain it first on a kitchen towel. To remove the skin from the inside, scrape it off. On the gristle part, make some incisions with the knife; then fold the gristle part back on itself and stand the ear in the middle of the plate.

The rest of the garnish and the sauce are served separately. Make sure you use burning hot plates.

Calf's Tongue *(Langue de Veau)*

2 tongues; 1 piece of salt pork to garnish the bottom of the pot; 1 carrot; 1 onion; a bouquet garni; 2 deciliters (6 3/4 ounces, 7/8 cup) of white wine; 4 deciliters (1 2/3 cups) of bouillon.

PROCEDURE. Trim the tongues, removing the horn (the bony part) and the gristle (SEE BOILING BEEF TONGUE, PAGE 271). Blanch them for 10 minutes. Chill them in cool water and remove all traces of foam. In a pot with a thick bottom, put the salt pork on the bottom, then the carrot and the onions cut into slices, and then put the tongues on top of everything without peeling them. Let them sweat. Baste them with the white wine, and then reduce this by half on high heat, proceeding as for all braises of white meats (SEE PAGE 28). Pour over the bouillon, then add the bouquet garni; bring it to a boil and cook in the oven for *2 hours* without going beyond a slight steady simmer.

To serve: Take the tongues out of the pot, drain them well and remove the skin quickly with a small knife. Split them down the middle lengthwise and place them on a plate. Keep them warm. Quickly reduce the cooking liquid over strong heat until it has the consistency of a light syrup, then pass it through a chinois onto the tongues. Veal tongue can be accompanied by an Italian sauce, tomato sauce, a warm ravigote sauce, or a piquante sauce, served in a sauceboat, and with a *jardinière* garnish or a purée of vegetables: fresh or dried peas, chestnuts, etc.

Calf's Caul *(Fraise de Veau)*

Calf's caul is sold disgorged—that is, having already been soaked. However, if it is not cooked immediately, it should be kept in cool water, which should be changed if left to stand for a few hours.

The way that it is most commonly served is also the simplest: taken hot from its cooking liquid and quickly divided into pieces, the caul is placed in a vegetable dish or a low soup tureen, moistened with 2 cooking ladles of its cooking liquid, about 1 tablespoon per kilo (2 pounds, 3 ounces), and accompanied by a sauceboat filled with a vinaigrette sauce made with fines herbs minced and served aside on a plate.

If you like, you can also accompany it with a warm and very spicy sauce; a tomato sauce; or even a sauce poulette; or it can be breaded and fried; dipped in a batter and also fried; or served au gratin. Thinking ahead, you can also cook more caul than is necessary for one meal; always remember, though, that it cannot be kept for more than 2 days in summer; in winter it can be kept a little longer.

Whatever the recipe, the caul is cooked in the same way. First you must blanch it to clean it thoroughly. Put it in a marmite and bathe it in a generous amount of cold water; bring it to a boil and let boil for about 10 minutes. Drain it and then cool it in substantial water. Once the boiling has firmed the tissues, you can check to see if the caul is clean by scraping off the yellowish material that you find in the folds.

After this, put the caul in a *blanc* and prepare it as directed (SEE BLANC, PAGE 42). Once the *blanc* has started to boil, put in the caul. Cook as directed, allowing *at least 2 hours.*

For 1 or 2 kilograms (2 pounds, 3 ounces or 4 pounds, 6 ounces) of calf's caul, you need 5 liters (5 1/4 quarts) of water for the *blanc.* Add the other ingredients in proportion to the quantities given for a *blanc.* Also add 2 good onions, stuck with 2 cloves and 5 or 6 peppercorns (not more).

The final point to make is that veal caul must be eaten very hot.

Calf's Foot *(Les Pieds de Veau)*

In the major cities, tripe sellers weigh the calf's foot once it has been cleaned, flamed, and disgorged in cold water and will even, if you ask, separate it into 2 parts, removing the large middle bone. If you want to remove the bone yourself, first take off the 2 hooves, then make an incision on and under the foot for its entire length, cutting right to the bone. Spread the heels to dislocate them; with the blade of a knife and following the incision, trim along the bone to detach the skin. This produces 2 half feet, with only 2 small bones left at the end, which cannot be removed until after a thorough cooking.

To blanch: This complements the cleaning and cannot be overlooked, no matter what recipe the foot is to be used for, whether added to a jus or braised or cooked in a *blanc.*

Put the foot or the feet into a pot so they are covered with cold water. Gradually bring it to a boil, which will be obvious because a large amount of foam will be released. Let it boil rapidly for 2 minutes. Turn off the flame and plunge the feet into cold water. Wipe them off and remove any remaining hairs. Before cooking them, tie them together, folding the two cut sides back over themselves. This is to avoid the foot breaking after lengthy cooking, which makes it fragile.

PRINCIPAL RECIPES FOR CALF'S FOOT

Allow a foot or a half foot per person, depending on the size of the foot.

No matter how they are prepared, they must first be cooked in a *blanc* (SEE PAGE 42), for which you can allow 5 liters (5 1/4 quarts) of water for 6 feet. You can braise them, but the *blanc* is simpler and more economical. Allow at least *2 hours* of gentle cooking, at the end of which the small bones must easily detach from the meat.

Cooked thus, then well drained, the feet can be served just as they are in a tomato sauce, a piquante sauce, or a sauce poulette, etc., or dressed on a napkin surrounded with fresh parsley and eaten *à la vinaigrette.*

Fried Calf's Foot *(Pieds de Veau Frits).* Cooked in a *blanc,* well drained and dried, they can then be prepared a number of ways.

Cut each half foot into 4 pieces. Marinate it for 20 minutes or so with a little oil, lemon juice, salt, pepper, nutmeg, and minced parsley. Bread these pieces (SEE BREADING, PAGE 19); for 6 feet, allow 2 complete eggs (beaten with 2 tablespoons of oil and 2 tablespoons of water) and around 250 grams (8 7/8 ounces) of fine bread crumbs. Deep-fry in very hot oil (SEE PAGE 37), then dress on a napkin and accompany it with a tomato or béarnaise sauce.

Alternatively, the pieces can be coated with mustard instead of being marinated, and then breaded and fried.

Calf's Foot Fritters *(Fritot de Pieds de Veau).* The half feet are divided into 4 or 5 pieces as above and marinated the same way. Prepare a batter for frying (SEE BATTER FOR FRYING, PAGE 19); for 6 feet, allow 2 egg yolks, 2 tablespoons of oil, 300 grams (10 1/2 ounces) of flour, and about 4 deciliters (1 2/3 cups) of water. Let it rest for 3 or 4 hours, and then, just before using it, mix in 2 or 3 egg whites, which should make the batter very light.

Drain the marinade from the pieces and dip them one by one into the frying batter, and then plunge them one by one into very hot oil to deep-fry. Dress them in a pyramid as above and serve a tomato sauce on the side; according to culinary tradition, this accompaniment of tomato sauce is essential to calling the preparation a "fritter" when it is among this genre of beignets.

Grilled Calf's Foot *(Pieds de Veau Grillés).* Divided in two, then coated with mustard, these are dipped in melted butter, rolled in white bread crumbs, and grilled gently. Serve alongside your choice of sauce, from tomato sauce, diable sauce, béarnaise sauce, etc.

Calf's Heart *(Coeur de Veau)*

SEE BEEF HEART (PAGE 274).

Calf's Brains *(Cervelle de Veau)*

SEE BRAINS AND KIDNEYS (PAGE 328).

Calf's Kidneys *(Rognon de Veau)*

SEE BRAINS AND KIDNEYS (PAGE 328).

Croquettes of Calf or of Calf Sweetbreads *(Croquettes de Veau, de Ris de Veau)*

Follow the same recipe as for fowl croquettes. Serve a sauce périgueux, soubise, or tomato on the side. SEE CROQUETTES (PAGE 438).

Pâté of Veal, Veal Loaf *(Pâtés de Veau, Pain de Veau)*

SEE PÂTÉS AND TERRINES (PAGE 434).

MUTTON
Mouton

Leg of Mutton *(Le Gigot de Mouton)*

No matter which way this is cooked, a leg of mutton must come from a young beast and be correctly aged to be tender. It is easy to recognize the best mutton: it has a light red tint rather than a brownish red, and the meat is firm. Also, be wary of the taste of suint, which is more pronounced in the first months of the year, so before buying, make sure you sniff the leg at the point where the bone crosses the fillet.

You will have to ask the butcher how long the meat has been hung to age. If a meat is too fresh, no matter its providence, it will be rubbery when cooked. What's more, a leg of mutton must be well cured, particularly if braising or cooking in a pot rather than roasting. To ensure that it is very well cured, you can always keep a leg of mutton at your house for several days without risk, up to 5 or 6 during the winter: in this case, let it hang it in a place that is airy, dry, and cool.

It is only when you are ready to cook it that a leg of mutton should be trimmed—that is, rid of its excess fat and the fillet bone, which makes carving difficult. If the butcher sells you a leg of mutton sufficiently aged to be cooked immediately, he will take care of this for you, and also shorten the knucklebone. If not, proceed thus: Begin by shortening the leg of mutton by sawing the knucklebone just behind the bit of meat attached to it, at a distance of 5 or 6 centimeters (2–2 1/4 inches) from the joint. This is a job that you can always let the butcher do, because removing this little end of bone does not affect the leg's keeping qualities. Then take out the bone that goes through the fillet, which is attached to the knuckle, by detaching it with the point of a small knife to remove it as far as the knuckle.

Using a large kitchen knife, scrape the excess fat from the inside of the leg of mutton. For some dishes, the leg must be larded with small lardons, so remove the fatty and nervous membrane that covers it by sliding the flexible blade of a large knife beneath it and removing layer by layer until the flesh of the leg is completely exposed. The work takes a bit of time if you are not used to it, but it is not at all difficult.

Roast Leg of Mutton *(Gigot de Mouton Rôti)*. For a long time, it was usual when roasting a leg of mutton to slide a clove of garlic into the meaty part of the knuckle. Today this is optional, and nothing more than a matter of taste and tradition. Refer to the section on roasts (PAGE 30) for all details about cooking the leg of mutton: brushing with good fat, serving the degreased juices separately, etc. For roasting in the oven, allow *9 minutes* per 450 grams (1 pound) for a rare leg of mutton; *a good 10 minutes* for medium, *à point* (with the juice pink); *13 minutes* for well done.

To make certain that the bone in the leg of mutton does not break when it is carved, it is a good idea to wrap this bone in strong greased paper before putting the leg of mutton to roast.

An old custom, which continues to this day, is to accompany the roast leg of mutton with white beans or flageolets, prepared as you like and served in a vegetable dish.

Leftovers of Roast Leg of Mutton *(Restes de Gigot Rôti)*. SEE LEFTOVERS OF ROAST BEEF (PAGE 270). The same directions apply to all leftover roast mutton large enough to be cut into regular slices.

Venison-Style Marinated Roast Leg of Mutton *(Gigot de Mouton Rôti Marine en Chevreuil)*. No matter how fine the leg of mutton prepared in this manner, it may not be as excellent as venison. All the same, it makes a lovely second entrée for a ceremonial summer dinner. And it is just as good for simple family meals. There are several possibilities for preparing the marinade, depending on the circumstances: for example, out in the country, where you have to stock up with all your supplies well in advance, including getting the meat from the butcher and then preserving it.

The leftovers of a leg of mutton prepared this way are excellent, served cold with a tartar sauce or another sauce of the same type; or minced and reheated, either with the same sauce or with another spicy sauce.

How long the leg stays in the marinade is determined by the temperature at the time. The meat is impregnated by the marinade much more quickly in the summer, especially during stormy weather. If the weather is muggy, 2 days of marinating will suffice; otherwise, you should allow 3 full days and sometimes 4 if the weather is temperate and if you are not ready to use the leg. *Time: 50 minutes for cooking. Serves 12.*

1 medium-size leg, rather short than long, with a gross weight of approximately 2 1/2 kilograms (5 pounds, 8 ounces), or, when trimmed, 2 1/4 kilograms (5 pounds); 200 grams (7 ounces) of fatback bacon for larding; 3 tablespoons of oil for basting during cooking.

For the cooked marinade: **100 grams (3 1/2 ounces) of carrot; 125 grams (4 1/2 ounces) of onion; 40 grams (1 3/8 ounces) of shallot; 40 grams (1 3/8 ounces) of celery if possible; 1 sprig of thyme; 1/2 of a small bay leaf; 6 peppercorns; 8 juniper berries; 7 1/2 deciliters (generous 3 cups) of ordinary white wine; 5 deciliters (generous 2 cups) of very good vinegar; 2 deciliters (6 3/4 ounces, 7/8 cup) of oil.**

For the accompaniment: **6 deciliters (2 1/2 cups) of sauce chevreuil (SEE PAGE 55).**

PROCEDURE. **The marinade:** Cook it as directed and chill it. SEE MARINADES (PAGE 18).

The leg: Once it has been trimmed, lard it with lardons 4 centimeters (1 3/16 inches) long and 3 millimeters (1/8 inch) thick (SEE LARDING, PAGE 11).

To marinate the leg: Put the leg in a clay or earthenware utensil that is long, deep, and narrow so that the leg bathes in the liquid. Season with a pinch of salt and a pinch of pepper. Pour the marinade over it with its vegetables and its condiments, *well chilled.* Put it in a cool place immediately.

While it marinates, turn the leg once or twice a day.

Cooking the leg: A few minutes before putting the leg of mutton in the oven, take it out of the marinade. Remove all bits of vegetables and aromatics. Dry it thoroughly on a kitchen towel: any moisture that remains will prevent it from coloring. Put it on a roasting dish with a rack (SEE ROASTING, PAGE 30). If the oven is very hot, put 1 tablespoon of marinade in the dish to prevent the juice that falls to the bottom from burning.

Baste the leg with the oil. Put it into a good hot oven. A high heat at the beginning is essential here. The mutton may have been well dried off, but it will nonetheless have kept some of the moisture from the marinade, which you must rapidly evaporate.

Turn it over from time to time while it is cooking and brush it everywhere with oil. At the end of 8 or 10 minutes, when the outside has been colored, turn down the very strong heat a bit, still maintaining a high temperature. For cooking time, calculate as for the roast leg of mutton, and make sure the lardons are well colored.

To serve: Place the leg of mutton, carved or not, on a long, well warmed plate. Garnish the bone with a sleeve of paper. Serve the sauce separately in a sauceboat without adding the juice from the carving, which would dilute it rather than making it better. Carve it in very thin slices with all possible celerity.

Braised Leg of Mutton *(Gigot de Mouton Braisé).* This recipe takes a long time. The cooking of the braised leg of mutton requires *40 minutes per 450 grams (1 pound)* from the moment when the cooking liquid has begun to boil. As for all braised meats, the result is always better with a larger piece, so we suggest using a medium-size leg rather than a small one; the leftovers keep very well and can be used in different ways.

There are many garnishes for a braised leg of mutton: purée of potatoes, of white beans, of chestnuts, of onion soubise, of cauliflower, etc., served separately in a vegetable dish; equally, Brussels sprouts, and duchess potatoes. The leg of mutton is basted with several tablespoons of its cooking juice, and the rest is served in a sauceboat.

A braised leg can sometimes be cooked homestyle, or à la bourgeoise, by adding the ingredients for the garnish at the appropriate time while the mutton is cooking: for example, use turnips and carrots. *Time: 4–5 hours. Serves 10–12.*

1 well-aged leg of mutton weighing 2 1/4–2 3/4 kilograms (5–6 pounds).

For braising: **150 grams (5 1/3 ounces) of salt pork; 150 grams (5 1/3 ounces) of rounds of carrots; the same of rounds of onion; a bouquet garni; 4 tablespoons of good fat; 2 deciliters (6 3/4 ounces, 7/8 cup) of white**

wine; about $1^1/_2$ liters ($6^1/_3$ cups) of ordinary veal juice or good bouillon.

PROCEDURE. For the details, refer to BRAISING (PAGE 25).

For this recipe, use a narrow pot, a small braising dish, or an oval casserole. It should not be too large because the cooking liquid must almost completely cover the piece of meat, and you would therefore need more than the amount suggested, which is itself only approximate.

Partly bone and trim the leg. If you have only a round pot, cut the knucklebone even shorter to help it fit into the pot, particularly if you are going to carve the meat before serving.

Color it in a very hot oven or in the braising dish. Allow *about 20 minutes* for this coloring.

Line the braising dish or the casserole, as described, with the salt pork, the sautéed vegetables, etc. Put in the leg; pour over the white wine; boil it rapidly without a cover to completely reduce the wine. Immediately add $1^1/_2$ deciliters (5 fluid ounces, $^2/_3$ cup) of bouillon; reduce it to a glaze.

Finally, cover it with the remaining bouillon; bring it to a boil. Cover with a paper and with the cover. Put it into the oven. From that point, allow *40 minutes of cooking per 450 grams (1 pound),* maintaining a gentle, regular simmer as directed. After $1^1/_2$–2 hours of cooking, the meat will no longer be completely submerged in the liquid, so be careful to baste it every 10–12 minutes.

Check when the cooking is complete with a kitchen needle. Strain the juice through a fine strainer into a small saucepan. Degrease it. If the leg must be glazed, reserve a little bit of this juice for the glazing: that is, 1 or 2 deciliters ($3^1/_3$–$6^3/_4$ ounces, scant $^1/_2$–$^7/_8$ cup). Boil the rest rapidly in the saucepan, uncovered, to reduce it to 5 deciliters (generous 2 cups). If you judge that it is not thick enough, bind it with some starch. SEE LIAISONS (PAGE 47).

Boiled Leg of Mutton à l'Anglaise *(Gigot de Mouton Bouilli à l'Anglaise).* A leg cooked in this way keeps its juices better than a roast leg; the meat does not shrink at all and remains uniformly pink. But you must be scrupulous about calculating the cooking time in proportion to its weight.

The essential accompaniment for a boiled leg of mutton à l'anglaise is a garnish of boiled potatoes, a caper sauce served in a sauceboat, and the turnips from the cooking served alongside in a small dish.

For this preparation, the leg must be well aged, trimmed of its surplus of fat as for roasting, and the knuckle partly detached so that you can later place a paper sleeve on it. *Time: 15 minutes of cooking per 450 grams (1 pound) of leg of mutton, calculated from the moment that the liquid has returned to a boil after the leg was plunged into it.*

1 leg of mutton weighing about $2^1/_4$ kilograms (5 pounds); 5 liters ($5^1/_4$ quarts) of *boiling* water; 140 grams (5 ounces) of onions; 500 grams (1 pound, 2 ounces) of turnips; 150 grams ($5^1/_3$ ounces) of carrots; 50 grams ($1^3/_4$ ounces) of salt (10 grams/$^1/_3$ ounce for each liter/$4^1/_4$ cups); 1 large bouquet of parsley sprigs with 1 sprig of thyme and 1 bay leaf; a clove stuffed into 1 of the onions; 5 or 6 peppercorns.

PROCEDURE. Take a utensil, either a marmite or a braising pan, in which the leg can be soaked so that all its parts are mostly covered by the liquid: this is essential for this type of cooking.

Pour in the boiling water, or bring it to a boil in the pot, adding the vegetables, bouquet, salt, and pepper only when the water is already warm. The vegetables should be prepared as for a pot-au-feu: carrots split lengthwise, onions left whole. According to the utensil employed, you can remove the main bone through the fillet or leave it in. The leg soaks better, particularly in a marmite, if the bone is removed, which also makes it easier to pack down the meat. In this case, tie up the leg to hold the flesh in place. Once the leg of mutton has been completely trimmed and there is nothing left to remove, weigh the leg of mutton. Work out exactly what time you will serve it, and work backward to calculate the cooking time needed.

Once the water has reached a rolling boil on good, high heat, add the leg of lamb, which should be completely immersed. Cover. Carefully watch for the point when it returns to a boil and *look at the clock.* Turn down the heat when the entire surface of the liquid is bubbling, and always keep the utensil tightly covered.

Maintain a moderate boil that is not too strong and is well distributed throughout the liquid. You do not want the slow simmering of a pot-au-feu. Note that keeping the utensil tightly covered means that the liquid continues to boil on a more or less moderate heat.

Prepare the sauce as described (SEE CAPER SAUCE, PAGE 69) 10 minutes before service.

To serve: As soon as the cooking time is complete, remove the leg of lamb from the utensil and keep it warm on its serving plate, surrounded by potatoes. Serve the sauce in a sauceboat and the turnips, lightly crushed, in another dish.

Saddle of Mutton *(La Selle de Mouton)*

The saddle includes the 2 joined fillets of the sheep and the part of the spine that divides the legs, adjoining the first ribs.

For serving about 10 people, choose a saddle that is not cut too large, with a gross weight from 2–2½ kilograms (4 pounds, 6 ounces–5 pounds, 8 ounces).

Saddle of mutton makes a very nice roast and is also frequently included as an excellent second entrée on formal menus. Many of the garnishes can be adapted to suit the seasons and the circumstances. The principle ones are, in the summer, jardinière, macédoine; in fall, stuffed tomatoes and mushrooms, braised lettuce, etc.; in the winter, croquette à la dauphine and other croquettes, and also noodles and macaroni sautéed in butter with cheese, tomato purée, and, optionally, a little minced ham.

With the vegetable garnishes, serve the juices from the saddle separately in a sauceboat. It should be strained and degreased. With the garnishes of mushrooms, lettuce, dauphine, etc., serve a Madeira sauce. And serve a tomato sauce with macaroni and noodles.

When served as a secondary entrée with a garnish, the saddle is almost always roasted and it is this recipe we shall give below, but you can equally braise it like a leg. On menus, saddle will always be described as *pré-salé,* because such a recipe requires meat of the finest quality. Be equally careful that it has been well aged, so order it or buy it in advance.

In Paris and in the major cities, the butcher trims the saddle. This is not true in the countryside, so directions for this appear below.

Preparation of the saddle: Prepare it in the morning for serving that evening. The piece is kept cool until the moment it is put in the oven.

Remove the block of fat inside the saddle. Remove the kidneys. Cut off the 2 little flaps on each side of the saddle, leaving them no more than 5 or 6 centimeters (2–2½ inches) in length. Remove the thin skin that covers the layer of fat enveloping the saddle so that the fat is completely exposed. If this layer of fat is too thick, remove some of it by scraping its surface with a good knife, leaving only the thickness of 1 full centimeter (⅜ inch).

With the point of a small knife, make some little square incisions on the surface of this fat, close together, about 1 centimeter (⅜ inch) apart and barely 3 or 4 millimeters (⅛ inch) deep. This is to help the heat penetrate the meat while cooking. Lightly salt and pepper the inside of the meat. Roll the flank of each side on itself and push it toward the inside of the piece, then surround the saddle with five or six turns of a good string and knot securely.

Cooking the saddle: Cooking in the oven, especially for such a piece of meat, is so common now that we will give directions here for this, although we should add that we prefer roasting on a spit whenever possible.

Put the saddle on a roasting platter fitted with a rack (SEE ROASTS, PAGE 30). You should know as accurately as possible precisely when you want to serve it; and having weighed the piece, you should work out the cooking time so you can put the saddle in the oven at exactly the right moment. Use a good, hot oven, and maintain a consistent heat for the entire cooking period. Allow 10 minutes *per 450 grams (1 pound)* if you would like the meat to be a little bloody; and *12 minutes* if you would like it to be medium—that is, only pink and a little juicy. If you know that you are going to have to let the meat stand for a while, cook it until it is more or less bloody and then keep it warm in a very mild oven, where the cooking is prolonged and is completed by the effect of the heat concentrated inside the meat.

Copiously brush the saddle with good fat or melted butter. Do not salt it. Put it into a very hot oven to seal the meat completely—that is, to color it. Once it is colored, the heat of the oven should be kept quite strong and be completely consistent. While cooking, turn the saddle 2 times, brushing it each time with fat, using a kitchen brush. Follow all the directions given on this subject for roasts and particularly for oven roasts.

To carve: The practice of carving meats in the kitchen is now universal, so you should proceed in the following manner: Carve just as you would at the table, separating the meat from the bone, but do not bother with a formal serving and carving board. Before carving, make sure you heat the serving dish so that it is burning hot when the slices are placed upon it.

Remove the string from the saddle and place the meat on the cutting board. With a carving knife that has a long, thin blade, quickly remove the small fillets or filet mignon. Turn the saddle over. On each side of the spine, make a cut as far as the bone. Slide the blade of the knife underneath the fillet, scraping along the bone to detach the fillet. Do the same on the other side.

Put these large fillets on the cutting board. Cut them quickly into very thin slices, cutting them a little on the bias just as when cutting a slice of sausage, to make it larger. Be careful not to move the slices out of alignment: this allows you subsequently to pick up all the slices at the same time by sliding a knife blade underneath them. You can then put them back in their proper place on either side of the backbone, which has been placed on the serving dish. Add the filet mignons on each side and moisten them with the juice that has run out while carving.

Put the plate in a moderate oven for a few moments to give the meat the necessary heat. Then rapidly arrange the garnish around the saddle if it is to be served as a second entrée.

Mutton Cutlets *(Les Côtelettes de Mouton)*

These are cut from the rack. A normal rack of mutton includes three kinds of cutlets. The cutlets of fillet closest to the saddle are considered the best quality in France *(les premières)*; *les secondes* are fattier and have more veins of fat running through them; and *les decouvertes* (bare) are the cutlets taken from under the shoulder and up to the neck, which are much less attractive but extremely juicy.

When the rack comes from a good-size animal, each bone of the rib produces a cutlet, so there are: 5 *premières*; 4 *secondes*; and 6 "bare" ribs. But if the sheep is not strong or fat, you will need 2 bones and even sometimes 3 to make a nice cutlet.

The weight of a nice cutlet is about 160 grams (5 2/3 ounces) *gross* and about 125 grams (4 1/2 ounces) *net:* that is, after trimming. However, this is not a weight currently carved by the butchers. In Paris, a "première" cutlet, cut and trimmed by the butcher, weighs hardly 90 grams (3 1/6 ounces). And—an important detail—the butcher cuts it slightly on the bias. This is a professional procedure designed to give more surface area to the fillet and also a better look for the *uncooked* cutlet, but it is very inconvenient: the cut goes against the grain of the meat, the fibers will return to their proper direction when heated, and they swell and burst, letting all their juices escape, so that their final look and size is unfortunately very different from the way they were in their raw state.

So, if the butcher cannot supply you with cutlets of the weight specified and cut *exactly parallel to the bone,* you must cut them yourself at home. Let us repeat here that for good cutlets from a sheep that is not very large, it is essential to cut at least 1 or 2 cutlets fewer than the actual number of ribs. To put it another way, ignore the position of the bones in the rack and divide the cutlets in as many parts as you need in order to get the necessary weight; you might find that 1 or 2 of them have two bones.

FIG. 52. TRIMMING THE CUTLETS.

Procedure: With a large kitchen knife, make the divisions by cutting the meat until the point that the knife reaches the spine. Remove one of the ends of the ribs from the cutlets that have two. Use a blow of the cleaver to remove the spine, and keep only the rib bone. With a good kitchen knife, completely remove the skin covering the entire rib bone. Then strip the end of the bone: that is, scrape away 2 centimeters (3/4 inch) of the flesh around it, so that you can, if you like, put on a paper sleeve.

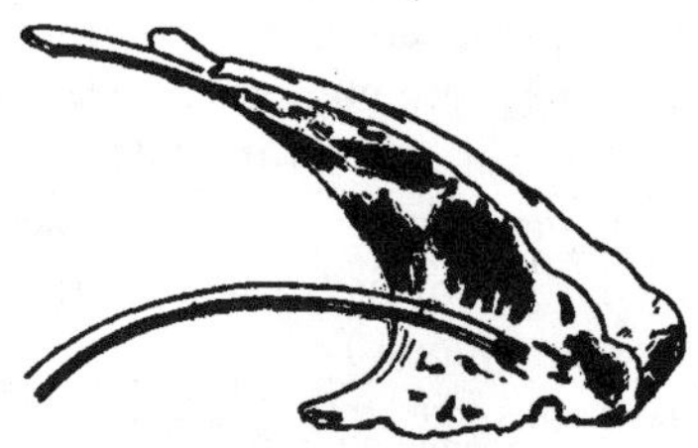

FIG. 53. SUPPRESSION OF SECOND BONE.

With the flat side of the cleaver, hit the cutlet one or two times to flatten the fillet to a thickness of 1 1/2 centimeters (5/8 inch). Finally, with a good knife, scrape almost all the fat from around the cutlet: most particularly toward the top and the bottom of the bone, to give a rounded shape to the cutlet.

Cut and trim "bare" cutlets in the same way, but before putting the knife into them, remove the cartilaginous ribbon of flesh that joins the shoulder and covers the top of the cutlet.

To grill and serve: SEE GRILLING, PAGE 35. As long as possible in advance, the cutlets should be generously covered with oil to make them more tender and to prevent them from drying out. Grill them as described: *6, 7, or 8 minutes,* according to thickness *before turning them.* Cook for about 1 minute less on the other side. Remove them to a warm plate and season with salt only at this point. If you like, put a paper sleeve on the bone. If they are accompanied with a garnish, some purée, potatoes, etc., put this on the same plate, arranging it as appropriate.

Navarin or Mutton Stew
(Le Navarin ou Ragout de Mouton)

This holds such an important place in home cooking that it merits a long, detailed explanation. This is one of those simple, excellent plates that requires the same time and meticulous care as a dish of haute cuisine. Letting it stand once it has been cooked is very bad for the dish: it is not the meat that suffers but all the other ingredients. The potatoes disintegrate, thickening the sauce, the little onions begin to come apart, and, if the navarin contains fresh vegetables, they lose a great deal of their special qualities.

The ragoût of mutton must be served boiling hot, so you must know when you want to serve it and calculate how long you need to prepare it accordingly. And only make enough for the number of guests, because its garnish is not worth much reheated.

As for the ingredients for the garnish, the navarin varies: thus, it can contain only potatoes with or without small onions; an assortment of vegetables, as in a *navarin printanier;* a garnish of turnips only; white beans fresh or dried, etc. But whatever the adopted garnish, the method of preparation remains the same, and the ragoût is cooked in two distinct stages. So, for the *first part:* the meat is colored in the fat and then sprinkled with flour, then covered with the cooking liquid and cooked for 1 good hour, after which the pot is completely emptied. And the *second part:* the meat is put back in it with the strained cooking juice. The garnish of vegetables is added to the meat to finish cooking together.

Straining the cooking liquid—a step that is too often overlooked by time-pressed home cooks wanting to simplify things, but that is nonetheless essential. It allows you to remove the shards and splinters of bone, which, although invisible, present some serious dangers to both the teeth and stomachs of the guests; under no pretext should this straining be overlooked. In haute cuisine, the meat is put into another casserole and the juice is strained directly onto it. In home cooking, where the number of casseroles is limited, use the same utensil, previously rinsed, to complete the second stage of cooking.

At this point, we would like to say that the utensil used is of fundamental importance, as much for coloring the meat as for the flavor and appearance of the subsequent sauce. Ideally, use a pot or sauté pan made of good aluminum *with a thick bottom.* The sauté pan must be large enough so that the pieces of meat are not heaped up together when they are being sautéed to color; like all sautés, all the pieces must be fully in contact with the bottom of the pan. This is an essential point. If your pan is a little small, sauté the pieces in two batches in order to give them their necessary space. Remember too that the utensil used must also be big enough to hold the garnish that is added later.

As for the *choice of the meat,* it is recommended to use different parts of the beast, because they complement each other: thus, shoulder, chest, fillet and neck, in equal proportions. The pieces of breast that are a bit fatty, for example, correct the dryness of the pieces of shoulder, and the guests can thus serve themselves according to their tastes. The more choice morsels, notably the fillet of mutton, do not produce the same result. In other words, it is not for reasons of economy that the lesser cuts are used here.

The liquid for cooking is generally water; bouillon will undoubtedly improve the recipe, but it is not essential, and even in haute cuisine water is also used.

Do not add white wine. If possible, use some tomato for an excellent effect. Garlic is absolutely indispensable here; the small amount means that it is not perceptible in the ensemble, but it plays an "incognito" role in flavoring of the ragoût. Take assurance from knowing that it is used in all the navarins of haute cuisine.

To brown—that is, to color—the pieces of mutton, we suggest using fat instead of butter. Economy is not the principle reason for this. Good, fresh cooking fat, well purified, is preferable to butter because it can be heated to a point where butter will burn. This fat is later drained and the sauce is completely degreased again, so none of it remains in the ragoût.

The navarin does not contain any bacon, which is reserved for a more rustic kind of ragoût called "haricot of mutton."

The sauce: It is impossible to estimate accurately what the final quantity of the sauce for a navarin will be. The potatoes thicken it, but to a variable extent. Thus, the sauce will be less thick when cooked with new potatoes, which have practically no starch. And it will be thicker, even too thick, with the starchier kind of potato.

But what can be said is that the sauce will be more or less concentrated, because it gradually reduces while cooking. It will not be thick, but only the consistency of a well-thickened jus, and as transparent as a varnish. If it is too diluted and too light, you will have to remove the meat and the vegetables from the pan, then reduce it by boiling it on strong heat without a cover before degreasing it.

As for dressing the dish, whatever your chosen garnish, the most important thing is not to delay serving the dish, so that it reaches the table burning hot.

Navarin *(Navarin).* This is the recipe for a simple navarin. *Time: 2½ hours. Serves 6.*

1¼ kilograms (2 pounds, 12 ounces) of mutton: shoulder (weighed after it has been boned), breast, the top of the cutlets next to the breasts. Cut everything into pieces weighing 60–70 grams (2¼–2½ ounces). The butcher will usually do this.

40–50 grams (1⅜–1¾ ounces) of fat; 30 grams (1 ounce) of flour; about 1½ liters (6⅓ cups) of water or bouillon; a nice bouquet garni; a clove of garlic; 2 nice tablespoons of concentrated tomato purée or, in season, 4 ripe tomatoes with their seeds and water removed, and cut into pieces.

For the garnish: a dozen small onions the size of hazelnuts and 30 grams (1 ounce) of fat to color them; 1 good kilogram (2 pounds, 3 ounces) of potatoes.

PROCEDURE. **First part of the cooking:** Put the fat in the sauté pan to heat. Season the pieces of mutton with 2 pinches of salt, a pinch of pepper, and a pinch of superfine sugar (about 1 teaspoon). The reason for this is that the sugar melts onto the bottom of the casserole when you color the meat and caramelizes there. A little later, when you put in the liquid, it helps to color the sauce.

Put the seasoned pieces of meat into the smoking fat. Do not cover. Keep it on lively heat. Mix from time to time with a wooden spoon until the pieces have taken on the coloring of a roasted piece of meat or one that has been grilled to perfection. Moderate the fire as the cooking proceeds.

Put a cover on the pan to hold in the contents, then tilt it to pour out three-quarters of the fat.

Sprinkle the pieces of the meat with the flour. Turn down the flame. Mix the pieces again until the flour has gradually taken on a light brownish tint.

Add the warm water or the bouillon. The quantity indicated here can only be approximate; it depends on the contents of the pan. At any rate, the liquid must be enough so that all the pieces are more or less covered.

Bring it to a boil on strong heat, stirring it continually. This is to prevent the flour from falling to the bottom of the utensil and sticking there and burning, and also to thoroughly mix and dissolve the roux that has attached to the meat. Once the liquid has begun boiling, continue cooking on low heat. Add: a pinch of salt; a pinch of pepper; tomato; garlic crushed with the blade of a knife; and a bouquet garni.

Cover the pan. Let it cook for *1 good hour* at a gentle simmer, both slow and continuous, either on the heat or, preferably, in the oven. This assumes, of course, that the oven can be adjusted to maintain a gentle simmer and not surpass that point.

This full hour for simmering the meat is the first part of the cooking. During this time, prepare the garnish. Here it will be onions and potatoes.

The onions: Carefully peel the onions so they remain intact. Heat the fat in a good, clean pan. Put in the onions. Sauté them over moderate heat to color them. When they are nice and golden, remove them with a small skimmer. Keep them on a plate.

The potatoes: Peel them. Shape them into pieces the size of an elongated pigeon egg. New potatoes are obviously the best, but make sure you peel them completely. If using other potatoes, you must cut them into pieces and then trim them into the desired shape. Be careful when you do this to cut off any sharp angles: the thinner part of the potato will cook much faster than the rest, crumble off, and then be diluted into the sauce. As you peel them, put them into a bowl of cold water. Leave them there until you are ready to add them to the ragout.

Second part of the cooking: At the end of the time indicated, remove the pan from the oven or turn off the heat. Put it on the table. Remove the bouquet garni.

Remove each piece of meat with a fork, checking as you do that there is no debris attached to them. Put them into a bowl. Tilt the pan to concentrate the fat in a smaller area, and remove as much as you can with a metal spoon; if the mutton is a little fatty, this first degreasing diminishes by some degree that which you must do before serving.

Pass the degreased sauce through the chinois onto the pieces of mutton. Quickly rinse the pan. Put back the pieces of meat and the sauce. Bring it back to a boil.

Cover the pan. Put it back into the oven or onto the heat to return to the same cooking temperature, a gentle and uninterrupted simmer. Add the little onions. *At the end of 20 minutes,* add the potatoes, dried off on a towel first. Push them into the sauce as much as possible. Place a round of white greased paper directly on top of the meat and the vegetables, then put the cover back on. Continue cooking at a gentle simmer for *45 minutes.* (It is important to note here that the potatoes will cook more slowly in the sauce than in boiling water. According to their type, you can even put them in with the mutton immediately after the sauce has been strained and begun simmering again.)

To serve: A few minutes beforehand, remove the pan from the oven or turn off the heat. Let it rest off the heat for a few moments so that the fat comes to the surface.

Using a soupspoon, remove this fat, leaving no trace.

For a little sophistication, take out the pieces of meat with a fork and put them in the middle of the plate, arranging the vegetables around them. Then pour the sauce over everything. Serve on very hot plates.

To serve more quickly with a view to serving the navarin hotter, you can simply pour it directly from the pan into a warmed timbale or a bowl.

Spring Navarin *(Navarin Printanier).* The name indicates the best time of year for making this recipe, because all the vegetables used for the navarin are from the new season. When these are no longer available or you do not have any green peas or fresh green beans, you can replace them with canned vegetables. In this case, the vegetables have already been cooked, so add them to the ragoût only a few moments before serving to reheat them there.

The recipe for a *navarin printanier* is exactly the same as for an ordinary navarin, which is described in the previous recipe: use the same proportion of meats and elements to cook it, and cook for the same time, etc. It is thus only the garnish that differs. *Time: 3 hours.*

For the garnish: 20 small new potatoes (about 500 grams/1 pound, 2 ounces); 12 pearl onions the size of a hazelnut; 150 grams (5 1/3 ounces) of carrots and the same of turnips; an ordinary glass full of medium-size green peas; 100 grams (3 1/2 ounces) of green beans; 30–40 grams (1–1 3/8 ounces) of fat to color the turnips.

PROCEDURE. Refer to the exact directions given in the recipe for ordinary navarin (SEE PAGE 315). Likewise, prepare the garnish during the first part of the cooking.

The carrots: According to their size, cut them in 2 or in 4. Carefully peel each half or quarter. Lightly trim each corner. As you trim them, put them into a small bowl of water.

The turnips: Cut them into pieces 3 1/2 centimeters (1 3/8 inch) long. Divide each piece into 2 or 4 according to size. Peel them and trim the corners to give each piece the shape of a large clove of garlic. Do not wash them. Simply wipe them to remove any moisture, which would slow down their coloring.

(Toward the end of the season, you must first blanch turnips and carrots. That is, cook them first in boiling water for about 10 minutes; with new-season vegetables, blanching is not necessary.)

The onions: Color them in the pan as for a simple navarin. Remove them and keep them on a plate.

In the same fat where the onions have been colored, and which has been heated to the point where it smokes lightly, put *the pieces of turnips* after they have been thoroughly wiped dry. Sprinkle them with 1 scant teaspoon of superfine sugar. Sauté them over strong heat until they have turned a blond color. Then pour them into a strainer to drain off the fat.

The potatoes: Prepare them as for an ordinary navarin.

The green beans: Break off the ends and cut them into diamond shapes 2 centimeters (3/4 inch) long. Keep them ready on a plate with the green peas.

Cooking the vegetables: Once the first stage of cooking the meat has been completed as described and the pieces of mutton have been put back in the pan into the degreased sauce, bring it back to a boil. Add the carrots and the turnips at the same time, pushing them down into the sauce. Maintain a slow and regular simmer, as directed. *At the end of about 20 minutes* add: onions, green peas, green beans, and potatoes, always pushing them down into the sauce as much as possible. Cover with a round paper placed directly on top of the vegetables. Put the cover back on the pan. Continue cooking under the same conditions for *45 minutes.*

To serve: Proceed according to the directions already given for the simple navarin.

Haricot of Mutton *(Haricot de Mouton).* If we refer to one of its earliest descriptions—a recipe dating from the seventeenth century—this is a ragoût made with mutton or veal cut into pieces. You can make a haricot of pike, of duck, etc.

To justify the name of "haricot" (beans), modern authors have believed that it is necessary to replace all the standard ingredients in a ragoût of mutton or navarin with beans only. But this shows a lack of understanding, because a haricot of mutton has nothing in it that cannot be altered; according to the times, region, your taste and means, you can add other elements to it. As, in fact, we have suggested after the first recipe, which is popular today. The haricot of mutton is, then, a country-style dish that is very appetizing and lavish, and in which you find everything, vegetables of all kinds, including, of course, beans.

The recipe with beans only: The parts of the mutton employed are those used, at least as far as the present recipe goes, for navarin, to which you can refer for preparation and cooking details. *Time: 2 1/2 or 4 hours, according to the method.*

1 kilogram (2 pounds, 3 ounces) of mutton; 125 grams (4 1/2 ounces) of bacon cut into large cubes; about 12 small onions; 30 grams of lard; 20 grams (2/3 ounces) of flour; 1/2 liter (generous 2 cups) of dry white beans;

1/2 liter (generous 2 cups) of water; a bouquet garni; a clove of garlic; salt, pepper.

PROCEDURE. In a thick sauté pan, heat the lard and color the lardons, which have first been blanched with the onions. Drain them on a plate. In the same fat, color the meat as for a navarin. Pour out half of the fat from the pan. Sprinkle the pieces of mutton with the flour. Mix and cook 2 or 3 minutes. Add: water, salt, pepper, bouquet garni, garlic clove; mix until it boils. Cover and let cook for *1 hour* on gentle heat.

Meanwhile, begin cooking the dried beans as described (SEE DRIED VEGETABLES, PAGE 557). When they are half-cooked, drain them.

With a fork, lift out the pieces of meat and place them in a shallow bowl or salad plate. Add the lardons and the onions. Pour the sauce over everything, passing it through a very fine strainer. Rinse the pan. Put back the meat, the lardons, the onions, and add the half-cooked beans. Cover and finish cooking the meat and the beans very gently, in the oven if possible, for *1 scant hour.* Serve on a round, shallow plate that has been well heated, or better still, as is now fashionable, in small terrines.

You must allow 2 1/2 hours after the beans have been soaked.

Country style: The parts of the mutton used are the shoulder and the breast in equal proportions.

1 kilogram (2 pounds, 3 ounces) of mutton; 175 grams (6 ounces) of carrots and the same of turnips, cut into rounds 1/2 centimeter (3/16 inch) thick; 75 grams (2 2/3 ounces) of onion cut the same; 1 small Napa cabbage weighing about 350 grams (12 1/3 ounces) after it has been trimmed, or 1/4 of a larger cabbage; 2 1/2 deciliters (1 cup) of dry white beans blanched in advance; a walnut-size piece of good, fresh fat from a roast or some lard; 3/4 liter (generous 3 cups) of warm water; a bouquet garni; a clove of garlic; 7 grams (1/4 ounce) of salt and a nice pinch of ground pepper.

PROCEDURE. Use a pot with a capacity of at least 3 1/2 liters (14 3/4 cups), which is also *thick.* Spread the fat in it. Place the pieces of mutton in it and then put the onion on top. Cover it. On very moderate heat, sweat it for about 20 minutes, frequently shaking the pot. After this, turn the heat up; remove the cover, and for *7–8 minutes* completely reduce the liquid that has gathered at the bottom of the utensil and allow the meat to lightly color.

Then pour in 1 or 2 tablespoons of cold water to dissolve the juice that has formed a crust on the bottom. Turn down the heat. Place the cabbage, which has first been blanched (SEE CABBAGE, PAGE 496), and tied tightly into a ball, in the middle of the meat. In the gaps, place the beans: these have been subjected, as described, to a preliminary boiling (SEE DRIED VEGETABLES: WHITE BEANS, PAGE 515). Add the carrots and the turnips and the bouquet garni; moisten with the cold water and add the salt. Bring it to a boil. Cover and turn the heat down to maintain a gentle and steady simmer for *3 1/2 hours* from that moment on. Every half hour, carefully pass a spoon under the meat and the vegetables to turn them over.

You must allow 4 1/2 hours in total to cook.

An hour before serving, add the potatoes, cut into thick rounds, but do not change the position of the vegetables.

To serve: Remove the string from the cabbage and place it in the center of the plate. Scatter the meat and the vegetables pell-mell all around, taking them out with a slotted spoon. Degrease the cooking juice, of which there should remain only *1 good deciliter (3 1/3 fluid ounces, 1/2 cup).* If not, you must reduce it. Pour it over everything, then serve burning hot.

Shoulder of Mutton *(L'Épaule de Mouton)*

We must first make it clear that no matter how it is prepared, a shoulder of mutton can only be served as a simple home-style dish.

It can be roasted in the oven, boned or not. But different methods of braising are particularly apt for this cut; and even though it is generally reserved for a lunch, it makes a good evening meal for the family, accompanied with a garnish.

We recommend stuffing the inside of the shoulder with a stuffing that is a little on the fatty side, not to increase the size of each serving, but more because the fat of the stuffing will nourish the meat, which is both dry and nervy. Furthermore, this is work that can be done very much in advance: the stuffed shoulder, completely ready, is kept cool until the moment of putting it to the flame.

When you cook mutton as a braise, it is very important that the meat be of good quality. It should also be aged: in other words, rested, and not too freshly killed. Otherwise, despite its good quality and all the care taken in its cooking, it will remain tough.

The different forms of braising adapt well to cooking a shoulder of mutton. You can, in fact, use any of the classic methods, such as is used for a leg of lamb (SEE BRAISING, PAGE 25); for example, the braising liquid will make the meat a lot more succulent. The garnish is then prepared separately—either a seasonal vegetable or some purée—and the cooking juices are served on the side. Or, if the garnish will improve by being cooked with the piece of meat, the meat is removed from its braising liquid when it is three-quarters cooked and then put back into the pot or pan with the degreased and strained cooking liquids; the garnish can be added at this point.

The home-style method is much more simple because it leaves out the braising stock, straining the juice, etc. For some recipes, like a good ragoût, you proceed with the piece of meat left whole. Below, we provide a good recipe for this method, emphasizing again that shoulder of mutton is essentially a dish for home cooking. We describe separately the methods for boning, stuffing, and rolling the shoulder. These are the same for the different recipes and methods of cooking.

A last observation: shoulder of mutton requires a very thorough cooking. And, as for every type of braising, it gets better when you prolong the cooking.

To bone the shoulder: It is easiest to allow the butcher to do this work, but ask him not to tie up the piece of meat subsequently. That said, it is one of the simplest things to do yourself.

Put the shoulder in front of you, upside down. With the point of a medium-size kitchen knife, detach the flesh from the palette or the flat triangular bone. Then detach the meat underneath to remove the palette from the rib bone. Scrape your knife along the 2 bones retaining the flesh and remove them. Thus, the shoulder will be completely boned.

Be careful during this work to destroy the skin of the shoulder as little as possible; it acts as an envelope for the stuffing.

To stuff the shoulder: The quantities below are given for a shoulder of mutton weighing from 1¼–1½ kilograms (2 pounds, 12 ounces–3 pounds, 5 ounces) after it has been boned; this is enough to serve 6 to 8 people.

Given the very small amount of sausage meat needed for the stuffing, you can simply purchase it ready-made. In this case, ask for it to be very finely minced.

200 grams (7 ounces) of sausage meat; but if you have a machine to grind it, you can prepare the meat yourself with 100 grams (3½ ounces) of fillet of pork and 100 grams (3½ ounces) of fresh bacon. In both cases, you must add, for this quantity, 50 grams (1¾ ounces) of finely minced onions; 50 grams (1¾ ounces) of bread crumbs into which you will add several tablespoons of hot bouillon; 2 tablespoons of minced parsley; 1 small raw egg.

PROCEDURE. Put the stuffing into a small terrine. Add: the bread crumbs, well squeezed out, and the onion, parsley, and the egg, beaten in a bowl and added not all at once but in 3 batches. Mix everything until it is homogenous.

Lightly season the inside of the meat. Spread the stuffing on the top. The method of rolling the shoulder depends on the utensil that will be used for cooking it.

To leave the shoulder in a long form, it is almost essential to employ a long or oval utensil, a small braising pan, or a cocotte. In an ordinary casserole, the space between the walls of the casserole and the shoulder will be too large. And for all the reasons given under BRAISING (PAGE 25), it will cook badly there: the sauce will reduce too rapidly, etc.

With a long pan, the shoulder can be rolled in its longest form like a galantine, completely enclosing the stuffing inside, and then firmly tied with double string.

With an ordinary pot, the shoulder must be rolled in the form of a thick pancake. Gather the edges of the meat into the middle to completely enclose the stuffing. Tie it crosswise with a string to secure the bundle, leaving one end of the string very long. Use this to continue binding the bundle, moving always in the same direction—in other words, tie the string crosswise between the previous turns of string. It will end up looking like the ribs of a flattened melon. Be sure that you tighten the string, because the meat will shrink during the cooking.

Shoulder of Mutton à la Boulangère *(Épaule de Mouton à la Boulangère).* A very simple recipe that makes a good lunch dish in all seasons.

When the onions and potatoes are new, you can leave the potatoes whole. If they are large, cut them into thick rounds. In any case, they must always be sautéed with the onions to brown them slightly before arranging them around the shoulder. Mutton shoulder *à la boulangère* is served in the same earthenware pot that has been used for its cooking. *Time: About 1 hour.*

1 medium-size mutton shoulder with a gross weight of around 2 kilograms (4 pounds, 6 ounces); 5 large Holland or good-quality potatoes in order to have about 750 grams (1 pound, 10 ounces) after peeling; 2 nice onions totaling 250 grams (8⅞ ounces); 50 grams of lard; 60 grams (2¼ ounces, 4½ tablespoons) of butter; 2 pinches of coarsely minced parsley; salt and pepper.

PROCEDURE. Bone the shoulder and season the inside with salt and pepper. Roll it up as tightly as possible. Bind it with a string both length and width completely to make a cylinder.

In a long earthenware receptacle big enough to hold the garnish, spread out half the lard. Place the shoulder, seasoned lightly with salt and pepper, in the dish. Cover it with the rest of the fat. *No liquid of any kind is added at any time during the cooking.*

Put the receptacle into a medium oven. The cooking should be rather slow, particularly when the vegetables are added, tucked around the shoulder. Let it color gradually and evenly on all sides by turning it often. Allow a *half hour* for cooking the shoulder on its own, before adding the garnish.

Potatoes and onions: Peel the potatoes and cut them into equal pieces, about 6 from each large potato; put them into cold water. Cut the onions into fine rounds.

Heat the butter in a pan. Sauté the onions in it on a strong heat to slightly color them, but do not let them darken. Drain the potatoes and sponge off, then add to the pan. Shake the pan in order to mix everything well. Season with salt and pepper. Keep them warm if they are ready before the end of the first stage of cooking the shoulder.

At the end of this stage, distribute the onions and the potatoes around the shoulder. Let the meat and the vegetables cook for *a good half hour,* during which time you should baste it 3 or 4 times with the cooking fat, tilting the pan slightly to let you spoon it over the meat. If the vegetables are new, 20 minutes of cooking with the shoulder will suffice.

To serve: Make sure you arrange things so that the shoulder can be eaten *burning hot.* It can, without inconvenience, be held in the oven for a few more minutes after it has finished cooking.

When you take the plate from the oven, cut the string with your scissors in 5 or 6 places to let you work more quickly; remove it without damaging the shoulder. Spread the parsley on the garnish. Serve just as it is with very warm plates, no matter what the season.

Home-Style Shoulder of Mutton with Turnips *(Épaule de Mouton aux Navets, Façon Ménagère).* (This is the simplest recipe, which does not include stock for braising.) *Time: 2½ hours (once the shoulder has been boned and stuffed and is ready to be put on the heat). Serves 6–8.*

1 shoulder weighing 1.1–1.3 kilograms (2 pounds, 7 ounces–2 pounds, 14 ounces) after boning, stuffed as directed; 3 good tablespoons of cooking fat or lard to color the meat and the onion; 15 grams (½ ounce) of flour; 7 deciliters (3 cups) of very, very slightly salted bouillon; a bouquet garni; salt, pepper, spices.

For the garnish: **500 grams (1 pound, 2 ounces) of turnips, net weight, peeled and trimmed; 50 grams (1¾ ounces, 3½ tablespoons) of butter to color them; 12 small onions the size of a hazelnut.**

PROCEDURE. In the chosen utensil, rapidly heat only half the fat. The other half is used to color the onions. Add the shoulder. Keep it on high heat for 5 minutes to seal the meat completely. Do not cover. Turn the heat down to medium so that the meat continues cooking without burning. Turn the shoulder over to color on all its surfaces.

Once well colored, take it out and put it on a plate. Drain almost all the fat, leaving only about 1 tablespoon for the roux. On a very gentle heat, mix in the flour; cook it to make a brown roux (SEE LIAISON WITH ROUX, PAGE 47). Dilute with the bouillon; stir until it boils. Add pepper and bouquet garni. Put the shoulder back into the pot along with the juice that has escaped while standing. Cover. Put it in the oven if possible or on the heat; in either case, use very, very moderate heat; No matter which method you use, only a small, gentle simmer is necessary.

Allow a total of *2 good hours* for cooking, toward the end of which you need to add the garnish of turnips and onions, as explained further on. While waiting, baste the shoulder every 15 minutes with its cooking juice; and, meanwhile, prepare the garnish.

The turnips: Choose them long and firm. Divide into rounds 3 centimeters ($1^1/_4$ inches) thick, and then divide these into 4 or 6 segments, depending on the size of the turnip. Peel and trim each segment into the shape of a large olive. As you trim them, dry them on a dry towel without washing them.

If the turnips are from late in the season, blanch them before coloring for 10 minutes in boiling water. Chill them in cool water. Dry them thoroughly in a kitchen towel; otherwise, they will not color.

In a nice, clean pan, briskly heat the butter, previously clarified (SEE CLARIFIED BUTTER, PAGE 16). Add the turnips. Sauté them on strong heat until they are a little bit colored. Then sprinkle them with a good pinch of superfine sugar and sauté them again, still on very high heat, until they turn a reddish-blond color. Then drain them well in a strainer. Keep them until you are ready to add them to the shoulder, but do not keep them warm.

The onions: Peel them as directed (SEE PAGE 525). Heat the rest of the fat in the pan. When it smokes lightly, put in the onions. Sauté them on strong heat until they are evenly colored. Drain them in a strainer. Keep them on the side in a plate. The moment to add the garnish to the shoulder varies, according to whether the vegetables are new season or not.

If the turnips are new season, it will be enough to put them into the pan *35 minutes* before serving; and if they are from late in the season, you should allow 1 scant hour.

For new-season onions, *25–30 minutes* of cooking is enough; late-season onions require 1 scant hour.

Arrange the turnips and the onions around the shoulder in the sauce. Cook for the necessary time in the same slow and regular manner.

To serve: Dress the untied shoulder on a long or round plate, depending on how it was rolled up. Thoroughly degrease the sauce and check the seasoning. Arrange the turnips and the onions around the shoulder. Pour the sauce all around. Make sure the plates are burning hot.

Grilled Breast of Mutton *(Poitrine de Mouton Grillée)*

Apart from its use in ragoûts, navarins, cassoulets, etc., breast of mutton is only served grilled; but it is always cooked first, and then grilled only at the end.

The initial cooking is done by braising with a small amount of water and white wine; or home-style, as a pot-au-feu, in which the bouillon becomes the base for a good soup made with the vegetables from the pot.

No matter how it is initially cooked, the breast is subsequently boned, put under a press, chilled, and divided into pieces before it is breaded and grilled. You can accompany it with a sauce of your choice, though this should be rather spicy: piquante, à la diable, Robert, etc. Or, depending on the season, serve with a purée of potatoes, lentils, etc., or with fresh vegetables sautéed in butter; or even without a sauce or garnish but with a good-quality mustard.

A sheep breast is a thin cut that contains a range of flat bones. These are the continuation of the rib bones from the cutlets of the rack, so the French also call it *hauts de côtelettes*—"top of the cutlets." The amount of bone means that you must allow about 150–160 grams ($5^1/_3$–$5^2/_3$ ounces) of breast, gross weight, for each person.

Whatever the mode of cooking used, the meat is

sufficiently cooked when you can easily detach it from the bone. Do not overcook because this makes carving even pieces difficult.

Under the press: This operation is essential to compact and thicken the meat, without which you would not be able to carve it or bread the pieces easily.

Once the breast has been cooked, put it on a plate. Remove the bones, which should come off easily, while the meat is still burning hot. Place the breast flat on one half of a kitchen towel laid out on a table, then fold the other half of the kitchen towel over it. On this, place a board to completely cover the breast on top. On this board, put a weight of 5 kilos (11 pounds). *Let it cool completely: 2 hours at least.*

To carve the breast: Carve into pieces weighing about 80 grams (about 2³/4 ounces), shaping them into rectangles, diamond shapes, or even triangles. Try to keep the pieces neat and the same size, but at the same time you must be careful to avoid losing too much meat by trimming. Possibly the most attractive method, and one that avoids any loss, is to cut them into sharp triangles with a base of about 6 centimeters (2¹/2 inches): what you do is to cut a series of opposing triangles into the meat, the points coming alternately at the top and the bottom of the breast.

To bread and grill: SEE BREADING, PAGE 19. For this recipe, the meat should always be breaded (*à l'anglaise*). It is an unbreakable rule that you must first dip the pieces in melted butter before rolling them through the finely grated white bread crumbs. These must always be freshly grated and never replaced by stale, dried-out bread crumbs.

Put the breaded pieces on a preheated and oiled grill (SEE GRILLING, PAGE 35). Use a very moderate heat so that the bread-crumb coating colors gradually and the heat gradually penetrates to the interior of the meat. Lightly baste the pieces with melted butter. Allow *about 20 minutes* for grilling. Do not go beyond a nice, even golden color.

Mutton in the Manner of a Braise *(Mouton à la Façon d'un Braisé)*

Many people think that this cooking method is a form of braising. However, as it does not include a jus or bacon, the result is far less succulent than what is produced by a true braising. But you can get a perfectly good meal for a family dinner by following the directions given exactly. So it would be wrong to try to simplify things by leaving out the final stage, in which the cooking juices are degreased in a small saucepan, thereby purifying them. Note, too, that the meat will not release its fats into the juices if left to keep warm in its pot. So both the meat and the juices can be kept warm as long as necessary without inconvenience, which means it can even be prepared rather far in advance. *Time: 2¹/2 hours. Serves 6–8.*

1–1¹/4 kilograms (2 pounds, 3 ounces–2 pounds, 12 ounces) of mutton, weighed after it has been boned and trimmed (shoulder or fillet or other part).

For the cooking: **The bones and the lean trimmings of the meat; 120 grams (4¹/4 ounces) of onions and the same of carrots cut into large rounds; 10–12 grams (¹/3–³/8 ounces) of flour; 3 deciliters (1¹/4 cups) of warm water; a bouquet garni; salt, pepper; 1 tablespoon of cooking fat.**

PROCEDURE. If you are using a shoulder, make sure it has first been boned, lightly seasoned on the inside with salt and pepper, and then tied into a round ball like a melon. If using a fillet, remove the excess fat and shorten the tail; squash the piece by rolling it with the tail on top, then shape it into a square bundle by tying it with a couple of turns of string in a cross shape. This will make it easier to put the piece into a pot that is not very large.

In a thick pot of just the right size, heat the fat until it begins to smoke; then add the meat and put the bones and trimmings around it. Do not cover.

Gradually color all the surfaces of the piece on a rather high heat and brown the bones and the trimmings. Take them out at the end of *about 10 minutes.* Turn the heat down a little, because the utensil will now be hot enough.

At this point, if the mutton is very fatty, pour off the fat that it has released; otherwise, the meat would effectively be deep-fried. (Do this by tipping the pot, using the cover to keep its contents inside.)

In the place of the bones and trimmings, add the onion and carrot. Cook for about another 10 minutes to color, mixing it often. Turn the fire down a little during this operation. Then drain the excess fat, leaving only 1 or 2 tablespoons at the bottom of the pot.

Turn down the heat *very low.* Put the meat on a plate. Sprinkle the vegetables with the flour. Mix and let it color gradually until it becomes a hazelnut color, no more; this should take *4–5 minutes.* Moisten with warm water and bring to a boil, mixing with a wooden spoon to completely dissolve this roux. Put the bones and the trimmings back in the pot and place a bouquet garni in the middle. On top of this, put the meat with the fatty side facing down. The liquid thus contains bones, trimmings, and vegetables, all of which will flavor the meat without soaking it: let us not forget that this cooking liquid is not a jus. Add salt and pepper.

Once this has returned to a boil, cover the pot tightly. Place it in the oven if possible; if not, on a very moderate heat. In either case, the liquid must be kept at a very moderate uninterrupted simmer for *1³/4 hours.* Every 15 minutes, baste the meat with its cooking juices without changing its position. Finally, check that the cooking is done by sticking a cooking needle into the center of the piece; it should come out easily.

To strain the juice: Take the meat out of the pot. Put it on a plate for a moment. Pour the cooking juice into a small saucepan through the chinois.

Put the meat back into the pot as before. Cover. Keep it warm. With a metal spoon, completely degrease the juice in a small saucepan. After degreasing, you should have almost the same quantity of liquid as at the start. Boil it and skim it carefully for *12–15 minutes* (SEE SKIMMING, PAGE 16). You should have only 2 good deciliters (7/8 cup) of juice left. Keep it warm and covered until the moment of service with a few bits of butter on the surface.

Cut the strings with scissors when the meat is placed on the serving plate. If it is a fillet, place it with the fatty side *up.* Baste it with the juice. Serve on burning hot plates.

Sheep's Trotters *(Les Pieds de Mouton)*

These are served at lunch only. No matter what the chosen recipe, the trotters must first be cleaned and cooked in the manner described below. In cities, the tripe sellers sell the feet already scalded; in the country, the butcher will do this if you ask him to, a procedure that is, in effect, the first stage of cleaning.

Choose nice white feet without any blemish. Avoid buying feet that come from animals that are already old, because these, too, are offered for sale. You can tell by pinching the skin of the feet; the older feet will be much harder than those of young sheep. The normal cooking time, which is already long, would not be enough and would have to be prolonged: either by putting them to cook before the others or letting them cook longer after the others are done.

In a cool season, the feet keep very well in their cooking juices, which form a gelée or aspic. You can therefore prepare enough for a second meal, and thus vary the recipe.

On average, you should allow 2 feet per guest.

Preparation of sheep's trotters: Even though they have already been scalded and thus partly cleaned, there will always be several hairs left, which you should flame, either over a flame or over an alcohol burner. With the point of a small knife, remove the small woolly ball between the two hooves.

Wipe off the trotters with a towel. Put them in a pot, amply covered with cool water. Gently bring it to a boil. Let it boil for *4–5 minutes.* Drain. Cool. Put them in a strainer and examine them carefully one by one to ensure that they are well cleaned. After this, disengage the bone, either by taking the foot in the left hand and turning the bone with the right hand, or by splitting the skin with the point of a knife on the interior side of the foot.

Cooking the trotters: This is done in a *blanc* (SEE PAGE 42), which you can prepare a little bit in advance so that once the trotters have been blanched and inspected, you have nothing left to do except put them in the *blanc. Time: 1 hour of preparation, 4 hours of cooking.*

12 trotters; 40 grams (1³/8 ounces) of flour; 2³/4 liters (11¹/2 cups) of water; 15 grams (¹/2 ounce) of salt; 1 large onion stuck with a clove; a bouquet garni; 3 tablespoons of vinegar; 50 grams (1³/4 ounces) of white cooking fat.

PROCEDURE. Prepare the *blanc* as directed in a pot with a capacity of 5–6 liters ($5^1/_4$–$6^1/_4$ quarts). Once it is boiling, add the trotters at the same time as the salt, vinegar, onion, bouquet garni. Let it slowly come back to a boil. Then put in the fat. Cover with a lid without completely closing it.

From this point, allow about *3–4 hours* at a very gentle, regular simmer that is hardly perceptible under the layer of liquid fat. The exact time needed depends on the tenderness of the feet. Before taking them off the heat, check by touching: if they are a little firm under the finger, continue cooking until you feel them completely tender. Without letting them cook to the point of excess, it would nonetheless be better for them to be overcooked than undercooked.

Sheep Trotters à la Poulette *(Pieds de Mouton à la Poulette).* This is the recipe that is most common and is something of a classic.

12 trotters; 5 deciliters (generous 2 cups) of sauce poulette; 150 grams ($5^1/_3$ ounces) of small, fresh mushrooms; 2 nice pinches of minced parsley.

PROCEDURE. Clean, blanch, and cook the trotters as directed.

Turn the mushrooms and cook them as directed. SEE MUSHROOMS FOR GARNISH (PAGE 490).

Prepare the sauce (SEE SAUCE POULETTE, PAGE 61).

Five minutes before serving, remove the feet with a skimmer and put them on a large plate. Finish the sauce with butter and lemon juice; add the mushrooms.

Immediately pick up the trotters one by one with a fork and put them in the pan with the sauce. Sauté them, and cover them completely with the sauce. Then pour everything into a timbale, a vegetable dish, or a bowl; whatever you use, make sure it has been well heated. Sprinkle the minced parsley on the feet. Serve with very hot plates.

If the trotters mixed with the sauce must be left standing for several minutes, keep the pan in a double boiler.

Fritters of Sheep's Trotters *(Pieds de Mouton en Fritot).* While they are still warm, the trotters are marinated for *20–25 minutes* with lemon juice, a little oil, pepper, salt, minced parsley; then dipped before serving in a light frying batter (SEE BATTER FOR FRYING, PAGE 666) and deep-fried in hot fat. Serve dressed on a towel with fried parsley and accompanied with a tomato sauce in a sauceboat.

Sheep's Trotters in Vinaigrette *(Pieds de Mouton en Vinaigrette).* After being drained and while still hot, the trotters are arranged on a plate garnished with parsley. Serve sauce vinaigrette aside in a sauceboat.

Grilled Sheep's Trotters *(Pieds de Mouton Grillés).* Once these have been cooled and drained, coat the trotters with mustard. Bread them by passing them through melted butter and freshly grated white stale bread crumbs (SEE BREADING, PAGE 19). Sprinkle them with melted butter and gently grill them. Serve a *sauce à la diable* (SEE PAGE 60) on the side.

Sheep's Brains *(Cervelles de Mouton)*

SEE BRAINS AND KIDNEYS (PAGE 328).

Sheep's Kidneys *(Rognons de Mouton)*

SEE BRAINS AND KIDNEYS (PAGE 328).

LAMB
Agneau

In culinary terms and butcher's terms, the name "lamb" refers to an animal during the whole of its first year. But during this time, the flesh undergoes several transformations, resulting in very marked differences. So two and even three different kinds of lamb are offered for sale: "milk–fed," or "baby," lamb, which is not older than two months and which has a viscous flesh that is appreciated both for its whiteness and tenderness; "spring" lamb, which is still milk-fed lamb, but no older than four or five months and not yet weaned, with a more developed flesh that is, nonetheless, very white with a very fine grain; and, finally, "salt marsh" *(pré salé)*, which has been weaned but is not yet fully developed, with a flesh that is very pale pink, but that darkens as the animal ages.

Regular or *"pré salé"* lamb is, in general, used more than spring lamb, but never confuse this with young mutton, which is a red meat, while regular lamb, classed as milk-fed lamb, is a white meat. This distinction is extremely important from the point of view of cooking it.

For a cut of lamb roasted in the oven, allow about *12–15 minutes per 450 grams (1 pound)* if the piece is larger than 2 kilograms (4 pounds, 6 ounces). For a shoulder that has not been boned, this will be no more than 30 minutes *total.* For a leg, *15–20 minutes,* and the same for the rack. SEE ROASTING, PAGE 30.

It is important to note that lamb, like all white meat, must be roasted in a slow and gradual fashion and cooked to the point where the juice that is released by deeply piercing the meat with a cooking needle is absolutely white.

The time given here cannot be anything but approximate: it will vary according to the method of roasting, as for all roasts.

Only milk-fed (baby) lamb is served roasted. Older lamb is very good for other recipes; we will suggest further on how to prepare cutlets and cuts of breast. Here is a summary of the other recipes that are suitable.

Sautéed Lamb *(Agneau Sauté).* If you use the recipe for a veal sauté, allow *50 minutes* of cooking from the time that the liquid has begun to boil. But it is much better to prepare lamb using the recipe for sautéed chicken rather than veal, to produce more of a ragoût. That is, the lamb is cooked in butter without any liquid during this time. Only at the last moment do you add a concentrated sauce, which you must not let boil. Refer, then, to sautéed chicken and its various recipes.

Blanquette of Lamb *(Blanquette d'Agneau).* Proceed exactly as for veal, reducing the cooking time to *1 hour* (SEE PAGE 293). The parts of the lamb that are to be used are half shoulder, half breast by weight.

Grilled Breast of Lamb *(Poitrine d'Agneau Grillée).* Proceed as for mutton and accompany it with a tartar sauce.

Pilaf of Lamb or Curry of Lamb *(Agneau en Pilaf et en Curry).* Refer to these two recipes (SEE PAGE 451).

Lamb Chops *(Côtelettes d'Agneau).*

It is only rarely that these chops are grilled, and when they are, they are served only as a simple family lunch. In one contemporary recipe, they are sautéed, but more often they are breaded à l'anglaise; the breading does not create a lot of work and it has the advantage of making the chops look better, keeping them tender and letting them be served as a small dinner entrée.

They are served with a garnish as follows: either around a purée shaped into a dome, leaning against it with the bone in the air, and side by side overlapping slightly; or arranged in a circle, into the middle of which you can put any garnish: green peas, asparagus tips, flageolet beans bound with butter, perhaps maître d'hôtel; artichoke quarters à l'italienne; tomato fondue; mushrooms; morels; or a Milanaise garnish.

We mean here rib chops, the "première" cutlets, taken from the middle of the rack. Not only are these the more delicate, but they are also a good shape for cooking. It's preferable to buy the chops completely prepared and trimmed rather than to cut them out of the rack yourself. Hardly having any fat, they do not need to be trimmed except to give them a small handle on the end, which could later be garnished with a little curly paper sleeve.

Unless they are part of a rather substantial menu, you must generally allow for 2 lamb chops per person.

Preparation of the chops: Before breading the lamb chops, they should first be slightly cooked quickly so that the heat firms up the flesh and does not swell subsequently underneath the bread coating, bursting it. In a sauté pan, heat some clarified butter, 50 grams ($1^3/_4$ ounces, $3^1/_2$ tablespoons) for some 10 chops, or some good lard, or even some butter and oil; as soon as this fat is warm, arrange the chops one next to the other, alternating bones and fillet. If the sauté pan is not large enough, cook them in two batches. A few good minutes of heat for each side on moderate heat is enough to firm the meat. Turn off the heat. Place the chops on a plate to cool slightly.

Bread them à l'anglaise (SEE PAGE 19).

About 10 minutes before serving, put the sauté pan back on the heat with the same fat. Heat it until it begins to smoke and then lower the heat. Replace the chops in the same position as before. The strong heat will instantly solidify the layer of bread crumbs; cook them on this side *3 minutes* only. Turn them over carefully. Let them cook for 3 more minutes on the other side. As soon as possible afterward, put the sauté pan into the oven to finish cooking for *3–5 minutes,* depending on the thickness of the chops. This is the best way to finish them. Do not cover them: the steam would soften the bread coating, which would then come off in patches.

If the chops have to be left standing before serving, do not keep them in the sauté pan, where they will absorb the fat. Drain them and keep them warm on a plate without covering them.

Stuffed Lamb Chops *(Côtelettes d'Agneau Farcies).* You can stuff them with finely ground sausage meat or with a veal stuffing prepared for the dish. Thus, for 10 chops: 150 grams ($5^1/_3$ ounces) of fillet of veal uncooked, minced, and pounded in a mortar. To thicken, add some *panade,* preferably made with flour (SEE PANADE FOR STUFFING, PAGE 21), in the following proportions: $^1/_2$ deciliter ($1^2/_3$ ounces, scant $^1/_4$ cup) of water; 10 grams ($^1/_3$ ounce, 1 scant tablespoon) of butter; a grain of salt; 25 grams (1 ounce) of flour; chill the panade before using. Then add to the stuffing 2 egg yolks, 50 grams ($1^3/_4$ ounces, $3^1/_2$ tablespoons) of butter, and finally, a little cold béchamel, which makes the stuffing lighter and more tender; you should prepare it immediately after the *panade* and in the same pot with 10 grams ($^1/_3$ ounce, 1 scant tablespoon) of butter and 1 tablespoon of flour mixed over the heat and diluted with 1 scant deciliter ($3^1/_3$ fluid ounces, scant $^1/_2$ cup) of milk; season with salt and boil for about 1 minute.

Pass the stuffing through a metallic strainer. Beat it with a wooden spoon to make it light and smooth. If you add some minced truffles to it, stuff the chops as soon as the truffles have been mixed into the stuffing.

The chops should first have been firmed up in the same way as those that are breaded. So proceed as directed, but leaving them for a little longer on the heat; *3 minutes on each side.*

Spread a clean towel on a large plate. Arrange the chops one next to the other on one half of this towel. Draw the other half on top. Cover with another plate or a board; place a weight of 2–3 kilograms (4 pounds, 6 ounces–6 pounds, 10 ounces) on top. Leave them under the press for a half hour.

After this, uncover them and arrange them on a plate, with all the bones facing in the same direction: if the chops are not all stuffed from the same side, it would be impossible to arrange them evenly on the serving plate.

On each chop, place 1 good tablespoon of stuffing in a mound, and press it down lightly in the middle, spreading it with the blade of a small knife dipped into cold water. As they are stuffed, place the chops on a large ovenproof plate or on a dish that can go into the oven. Keep it in a cool place.

About 10 minutes before serving, put the chops in an oven at a good medium heat for the chops to finish and for the stuffing to cook. As soon as the stuffing has firmed, cover the chops with a sheet of buttered parchment paper to prevent the stuffing from coloring; it should remain white. At the end of *8–10 minutes,* when the stuffing feels firm to the touch, open the oven door and leave the chops standing there, without removing the paper, until ready to serve.

When you are ready to serve, put them on a heated plate, in a circle, almost standing side by side. Pour a few tablespoons of sauce in the middle. Put a small sleeve of paper around each chop bone. Serve the rest of the sauce in a sauceboat.

Accompany with your choice of sauce: Madeira, Périgueux, soubise, tomato, etc.

Lamb Chops à la Villeroy *(Côtelettes d'Agneau à la Villeroy).* As for all dishes with this name, lamb chops à la Villeroy are prepared thusly: coat an already cooked, or partly cooked, ingredient in a thick parisienne sauce and then in a coating of bread crumbs à l'anglaise; fry it in deep fat or sauté it in clarified butter to both color and reheat the food.

If you wish, accompany it with a sauce or a garnish of vegetables, as has been suggested previously.

Allow for a small lamb chop from a baby lamb, 1/2 deciliter (1 2/3 ounces, scant 1/4 cup) of parisienne sauce that has been very reduced; that is, use 8 grams (1/3 ounce) of flour for each deciliter (3 1/3 fluid ounces, scant 1/2 cup) of sauce ready to be used. See SAUCE ALLEMANDE also called PARISIENNE (PAGE 52).

Grill the chops for *3–4 minutes* on each side. Put them on the press as with the stuffed chops and let them cool the same way. Dip them in the warm sauce. Arrange them on a lightly oiled plate. Let the sauce completely solidify. Then remove the chops and wipe off any smudges of sauce with the point of a small knife. Bread them à l'anglaise (SEE PAGE 19).

In a sauté pan, heat some clarified butter until it gives off a light smoke; this is better than deep-frying. Arrange the cutlets in the sauté pan and reduce the heat. Let them color for 5 minutes on each side. Dress them as has already been directed.

Épigrammes of Lamb *(Épigrammes d'Agneau)*

More commonly applied to lamb than to mutton, an *épigramme* is made up of pieces of breast of lamb that have been breaded, alternating with an equal amount of chops. Some authors describe pieces of breasts alone as *épigrammes,* but these are the exception. Normally, the name suggests a piece of breast served with a cutlet.

Before being divided into pieces, the breast is first cooked, either braised (which is the most popular way, the simplest), or as a pot-au-feu. If you have made a pot-au-feu that day, you can even cook the breast in it, the lamb not in any way harming the flavor of the bouillon, as would mutton.

Before breading the pieces of breast, you can, if you like, coat them with a very thick *Sauce Allemande* as for preparations *à la Villeroy.* Also, if you like, and according to your resources, these breaded pieces of breast can be grilled, sautéed, or fried in deep fat.

According to some authors, the chops may be left without saucing and then, after cooking, covered with a meat glaze. Generally, they are simply breaded with fine bread crumbs, then subsequently grilled or sautéed.

Cutlets and pieces of breast are arranged in a turban or a circle, in the center of which is placed a garnish of your choice: green peas, asparagus tips, a macédoine of vegetables, various purées, chicory, etc.

PROCEDURE. The breast of lamb must be cooked well in advance or even the evening before. This is to ensure that it has completely cooled by the time you divide it into pieces.

Whatever the cooking method used, you can tell that the breast is done when the bone can be easily pulled back from the flesh. So allow 45 minutes to 1 hour at a very gentle simmer.

Then proceed as directed (SEE GRILLED BREAST OF MUTTON, PAGE 321) for the *pressing.* Reserve the bone from the breast. Cut on the bias at either end, they are then stuck back into the pieces of breast, imitating the chop bones.

Divide the chilled breast into triangles, as directed. Then cut off the three corners so that each piece looks the size and shape of a chop. Bread these pieces à l'anglaise (SEE PAGE 19) and keep them cool.

Lightly season the chops with salt and pepper. Brush them on both sides with melted butter. Roll them in the bread crumbs (SEE BREADING, PAGE 19). Gently grill them *5 or 6 minutes* on each side. Or you can sauté them in clarified butter. At the same time, in a second sauté pan, also heat some clarified butter until it smokes. Arrange the pieces of breast in this pan. Color them nicely on both sides; this will also reheat the chops.

To serve: Into each piece of breast, stick the end of one of the reserved bones and leave the part protruding that you will garnish with a piece of curly paper.

Dress the chops and the pieces of breast as directed. Put the garnish in the middle. Put a sleeve of curly paper on each chop bone. Serve immediately on good, hot plates.

BRAINS AND KIDNEYS
Cervelles et Rognons

Brains *(Les Cervelles)*

Before cleaning, these must be submersed in a large amount of cold water for at least 2 hours, with the water being frequently changed. The goal is to dissolve the clotted blood and bits of bloody tissue as well as to soften the membrane surrounding the brain.

Remove the membrane thus: take a fragment of the membrane between the thumb and the index finger of the left hand, then carefully detach it with the end of the index finger of your right hand. Make sure no fragments remain. Although this takes a little time for the brains of veal or beef, this procedure is much more difficult for the brains of sheep, which have a thinner membrane. Then put the brains into a container of water at room temperature to dissolve any bloody parts remaining in the crevices, which would darken while cooking.

For most recipes using brains, these are previously cooked in a court bouillon, the most modern recipe for which is given below. Most often, the brain is put into a court bouillon made at the moment of use, and it follows that this fresh court bouillon will not have been thoroughly infused with the taste of the aromatics, meaning that the brain itself will be less flavored. When you have the time, it is better to cook the court bouillon beforehand.

Court bouillon for brains: The quantities are for 1 beef brain, 2 medium-size veal brains, or 6 mutton brains:

1 liter (4 1/4 cups) of water; 10 grams (1/3 ounce) of sea salt; 1 onion stuck with two cloves; 2 tablespoons of vinegar; a bouquet garni; 4 or 5 peppercorns (pepper becomes bitter when cooked for a long time, so do not add to the court bouillon until halfway through the cooking: that is to say, after about 10 minutes).

If the court bouillon is prepared in advance, put all the ingredients into a pot. Bring it to a boil, then cover and let it boil gently for *20–25 minutes.* Then allow it to almost completely cool.

Cooking the brains: Once the brains have been cleaned as directed, put them in a pot and cover them with a *lukewarm* court bouillon, strained through a fine strainer.

(If the court bouillon has not been prepared in advance, put all the elements together in it except for the pepper, then put in the brains.)

In either case, bring it to a boil. Cover and immediately turn down the heat very low for the brains to poach—that is, cook in a liquid at a very gentle simmer. From this point, allow *20–25 minutes* for a small beef brain or a veal brain; *15 minutes* for a mutton brain.

Once the brains have been poached and are ready to be used, they should be lifted from the court bouillon with a skimmer and very carefully drained.

PRINCIPAL RECIPES FOR BRAINS

Brains with Black Butter *(Cervelle au Beurre Noir).* Once the brains have been poached and thoroughly drained, they are dressed on a round plate, either whole or cut into scallops—that is, relatively thin slices. Season with salt and pepper. Pour the *beurre noir* over it (SEE PAGE 80).

Brain Beignets *(Cervelle en Beignets).* Cooled in their court bouillon, then cut into scallops. Dip in a light batter and deep-fry at high heat.

Deep-Fried Brains *(Cervelle en Fritot).* Cut the poached and the cooled brains into scallops. Marinate them for a half hour with lemon juice, salt, pepper, minced parsley, and a bit of oil. Bread them à l'anglaise (SEE PAGE 19). Deep-fry at high heat. Accompany with a tomato sauce.

Brains in Shells *(Cervelle en Coquilles).* The brains are poached, chilled, and cut into small cubes, then mixed with a béchamel sauce, using 1 scant deciliter (3 1/3 fluid ounces, scant 1/2 cup) of sauce for each 100 grams (3 1/2 ounces) of cooked brain (you can, if you wish, add a little bit of cooked fines herbes). Fill the shells. Sprinkle grated Parmesan and Gruyère over them. Put the shells in the oven or under the broiler for just long enough to heat the inside and to color the surface gold.

Stewed Brains *(Cervelle en Matelote).* The brains are cooked in a court bouillon, made of a good red wine and prepared in advanced so that it is strongly flavored. Salt very slightly, bearing in mind that the court bouillon is reduced after the brains have been cooked in it to make a sauce: it is then bound with beurre manié (SEE LIAISONS, PAGE 47) and poured over the brains, cut into scallops after cooking. As for all matelotes, add a garnish of small onions and fried croutons.

Brains à la Poulette *(Cervelle à la Poulette).* Cut into scallops after cooking. Simmer for a moment in a SAUCE POULETTE (SEE PAGE 61), then serve.

Brains with Sauce Piquante *(Cervelle à la Sauce Piquante).* Follow the same procedure as above (SEE SAUCE PIQUANTE, PAGE 58).

Sautéed Brains *(Cervelle Sautée).* Once the brains have been cleaned, they are only blanched—that is, plunged into boiling water that has been salted and acidified with a bit of vinegar, for 3 or 4 minutes. After this, cut into long scallops, then marinate for about 20 minutes with salt, pepper, and lemon juice. Then dip in flour and sauté in butter or oil (SEE SAUTÉING, PAGE 34). Dress in a circle on a heated plate with *sauce Italienne,* tomato sauce, or another sauce in the middle.

Brains in a Vol-au-Vent *(Cervelle en Vol-au-Vent).* This is a recipe with a garnish à la Toulouse, the brains here replacing the veal sweetbreads. But for simple home cooking, you prepare the garnish only with mushrooms, and none of the other ingredients. Allow about 4 deciliters (1²/₃ cups) of parisienne sauce for 500 grams (1 pound, 2 ounces) of brain. The brain is first poached, then cut into small scallops and simmered in the sauce with the garnish before it is poured into the vol-au-vent crust.

Finally, we note for the record a very ancient recipe that has now been abandoned. This consists in blanching the brains for *3 or 4 minutes* only in boiling, salted, and vinegared water, and then cooking it in some *very good jus.* The brains are then served under an appropriate sauce.

Kidneys *(Les Rognons)*

In order of excellence, kidneys are classified thus: mutton, veal, beef. Pork kidneys have a particular taste, which not everyone likes; you prepare them in the same way as veal kidney.

To compare the weights of the different kidneys: a mutton kidney weighs about 50 grams (1¾ ounces); a medium-size veal kidney weighs about 260 grams (9⅕ ounces); a small beef kidney weighs from 550–600 grams (1 pound, 3–5 ounces).

No matter the type of kidney used, it is essential that it should be fresh. The smell is an indication. It is also prudent to smell the kidneys, particularly those of the sheep, when the skin covering them is flaccid and dull. The various recipes for kidneys follow:

Sheep kidneys: On a brochette and with a *vert-pré* garnish: two classic methods, whose recipes follow.

Brochette: You cook as for veal liver; refer to the recipe. The kidneys are cut into slices about 7–8 millimeters (¾ inch) thick and then, as for veal liver, are firmed up in warm butter and strung onto brochettes, alternating with pieces of bacon, etc.

Au gratin: Divide the kidneys in two. Firm them up on the cut side in warm butter and place them on a purée of your choice. Cover everything with a brown sauce and put in the oven to form a golden-brown crust.

Sautéed: Recipes and instructions are given below.

Veal kidneys: *Grilled:* Proceed as directed for sheep kidneys on a brochette. In this case, leave a thin layer of fat on the kidney. Keep the 2 halves of the split kidney open by sticking 2 little skewers through, in parallel. Grill gently while basting with melted butter. Serve with a maître d'hôtel butter or another butter.

In a cocotte: A recipe is given below.

In a casserole: Served without any garnish, which is characteristic of the method of cooking known as "en casserole." The chosen utensil should be earthenware: a pan, cocotte, or any terrine.

The kidney is left whole and gently cooked in nothing other than butter seasoned simply with salt and pepper. Thus, for one single veal kidney, 30 grams (1 ounce, 2 tablespoons) of butter.

As when cooking "en cocotte," leave a thin layer of fat on the kidney, which replaces a bard. Do not color it first. Immediately put the *covered* utensil in the oven: *25–30 minutes of cooking,* frequently turning the kidney. At the very last moment, baste it with 1 tablespoon of good veal jus. Serve in the same utensil.

Sauté: Directions and recipes are given below.

Beef kidneys: This is only prepared as a sauté, and it demands a certain amount of care, as described below—refer to the directions for sautéed kidneys.

Sheep Kidneys à la Brochette *(Rognons de Mouton à la Brochette).* *Time: 30 minutes (including 10 minutes for cooking).*

Allow for this dish 2 kidneys per person, and for each kidney allow 10 grams (1/3 ounce, 1 scant tablespoon) of butter, maître d'hôtel butter, or other (SEE MAÎTRE D'HÔTEL BUTTER, PAGE 80, OR BERCY BUTTER, PAGE 79).

For cooking kidneys, you should have some small stainless steel skewers specifically for this use, which are removed just before serving.

If you like, kidneys *à la brochette* can be breaded. That is, after they have been oiled and seasoned, you sprinkle them with bread crumbs, then moisten them with oil before putting them on the grill. This coating does not, in fact, add anything to the flavor of the dish and it even complicates the grilling, since bread crumbs burn easily, so the kidneys have to be watched more closely. For this reason, breaded kidneys should be grilled on a gentler heat.

PROCEDURE. Remove the membrane of the kidneys. If their surface is a bit dried out, which would make removing this membrane much more difficult, soak the kidneys for a second in fresh water. Wipe them off thoroughly.

Split them along the convex surface right in the middle, about *three-quarters of the way through,* so that the 2 halves do not separate. Then string them in pairs on a skewer, threading it through the part of the kidney that forms a bridge; do this in such a way that the kidney stands completely open.

FIG. 54. KIDNEY BROCHETTES.

With a small brush, coat the kidneys with oil. Season with salt and pepper.

Prepare a *maître d'hôtel* butter. Heat the plate. Preheat the broiler, or, if grilling on coals (SEE GRILLING, PAGE 35), these must be burning well, because cooking kidneys requires *high heat.*

Put the kidneys on the grill, with the open side of the kidney exposed to the heat when you start. If the kidneys are of a medium size, turn them *after 3 minutes of cooking* and cook them for the same amount of time on the other side.

As soon as they are ready—that is, lightly shriveled, and forming a little bowl—put them on a serving dish. Remove the brochettes. In the hollow of each kidney, put 10 grams (1/3 ounce, 1 scant tablespoon) of *maître d'hôtel* butter or another butter than you have chosen. Serve immediately on very hot plates.

Sheep's Kidneys Vert-Pré *(Rognons de Mouton au Vert-Pré).* *Time: 40 minutes (including 10 minutes for cooking).*

These are prepared exactly like Kidneys à la Brochette. You simply add a garnish of straw potatoes and fresh watercress. (A vert-pré is a garnish of watercress and is typically Parisian.) All of this is quite simple. At home, the difficulty lies not so much in the execution of each detail, but in the need to conduct several operations at the same time so that everything will be ready together and at the right moment. Here, nothing can wait. So, as in the restaurant kitchens, you must prepare the different elements in advance, and make sure they are ready at hand.

The elements: *the potatoes,* cut up, washed, dried, and ready to be deep-fried (SEE STRAW POTATOES, PAGE 553); *the watercress,* which takes a long time to carefully pluck; *the maître d'hôtel butter* (which can be difficult to soften in the winter); *the fat for frying* (melted so that it can be heated rapidly when needed); the grill preheated; *the kidneys:* prepared as brochettes, as already described.

We simply summarize here the work order.

Eight minutes before serving, the frying fat must be hot enough to fry the potatoes. As soon as they are in the pan, put the kidneys on the heat.

Once cooked, arrange the grilled kidneys on a long warmed plate. At this point, following the standard procedure for straw potatoes, put them back into the *smoking* deep fat for the 7 or 8 seconds needed to dry them.

Garnish the inside of the kidneys with the maître d'hôtel butter. Surround them on each side with the straw potatoes. On each end of the platter, place a bouquet of watercress, seasoned with a little bit of salt and vinegar. Serve immediately.

Sheep's Kidneys Turbigo *(Rognons de Mouton Turbigo).* This dish is one of the simplest to make; it is as quick as preparing the kidneys themselves. The mushrooms and croutons are prepared in advance and can be left until you need them, with no risk. *Time: 40 minutes. Serves 6.*

6 nice sheep's kidneys; 30 grams (1 ounce, 2 tablespoons) of butter to sauté them.

For the garnish: 12 small mushrooms or 6 medium-size; 6 small sausages known as *chipolatas*; a dozen croutons and 20 grams (2/3 ounce, 1 heaping tablespoon) of butter to fry them.

For the sauce: 1 deciliter (3 1/3 fluid ounces, scant 1/2 cup) of white wine; 1 1/2 deciliters (5 fluid ounces, 2/3 cup) of very good veal jus; 1 teaspoon of tomato purée; 1 small teaspoon of arrowroot; 1 teaspoon of coarsely chopped parsley; 30 grams (1 ounce, 2 tablespoons) of butter for finishing.

PROCEDURE. **The mushrooms:** According to their size, leave them whole or cut them in 2. Cook them as directed (SEE MUSHROOMS FOR GARNISH, PAGE 490). Then keep them on the side.

The croutons: With a cookie cutter, cut them 5 centimeters (2 inches) in diameter, 6–7 millimeters (1/4 inch) thick. Then cut them in 2. With the point of a small knife, trim them around the edges so that they look like a rooster's crest.

Color them (SEE CROUTONS, PAGE 20). Keep them warm on a plate.

The sausages: Prepare these at the same time as the kidneys. Usually grilled, they can just as well be cooked in the oven—whatever is easiest at the time (SEE SAUSAGES, PAGE 338).

The kidneys: Remove the membrane. Cut them in half lengthwise. Heat the butter in a sauté pan. Put in the kidneys. Sauté them over strong heat until they are lightly colored on the outside and have firmed up. Take them out with a skimmer and put them on a plate; cover them and keep them warm.

The sauce: Completely drain the butter from the sauté pan. Pour in the white wine. Bring to a strong boil until the wine is reduced to *2 tablespoons.* Then add the veal jus, the tomato purée, and the mushrooms, and bring to a boil. Let it simmer on gentle heat for *4–5 minutes.*

Thicken the sauce as directed (SEE LIAISONS, PAGE 47) with arrowroot dissolved in 1–2 tablespoons of the cooking liquid from the mushrooms. Put the kidneys back into the pan with the blood that they have released, to heat them for a couple of seconds without boiling.

To serve: Arrange the kidneys in a circle, in a shallow vegetable dish or on a round plate, leaning them one against the other and putting a crouton between each kidney. In the middle, put the sausages. Briskly mix the final butter into the sauce. Pour it with the mushrooms on the sausages. Sprinkle the parsley on top. Serve on very hot plates.

Veal Kidneys à la Robert *(Rognons du Veau à la Robert).* Cooked whole in a casserole dish, the kidneys are then carved and their cooking completed with mustard, fresh butter, lemon juice, and minced parsley. This final cooking is done at your will and according to the circumstances, either at the table itself or in the kitchen. In either case, this must be rapid: about *3 minutes,* so that the kidneys hardly have time to cool. Plates that are *very hot* are essential here. If the final cooking is done at the table, put the casserole dish on a spirit stove or hot plate, to keep the kidneys warm.

The amount of mustard suggested here assumes you are using ordinary mustard. If it is not very strong, you can use 1 1/2 tablespoons. Beyond its role as a condiment, the mustard also acts as a thickener. *Time: 20 minutes. Serves 6.*

2 medium-size veal kidneys; 40 grams ($1^3/_8$ ounces, 3 tablespoons) of butter to cook them; 1 deciliter ($3^1/_3$ fluid ounces, scant $^1/_2$ cup) of white wine.

To finish the cooking: **1 good teaspoon of mustard; 30 grams (1 ounce, 2 tablespoons) of fresh butter; a pinch of minced parsley; juice of a quarter of a lemon; salt and pepper.**

PROCEDURE. In your chosen utensil—a heat-proof porcelain or an earthenware dish—heat the butter as strongly as possible to completely seal the kidneys. But do not let them darken, because this butter is not drained after cooking the kidneys and it will be used in the reduced sauce.

Put the kidneys into this very hot butter, side by side, seasoned with salt and pepper. On rather strong heat, lightly brown them, turning them at the end of a few minutes. Without covering the utensil, continue cooking at a more or less hot temperature. If you have a very hot oven, you can put the casserole dish at the bottom.

Either way, allow *12–15 minutes* of cooking so the kidneys are perfectly done: neither too cooked nor bloody.

Then remove them to a plate. Pour the white wine into a pot; boil it strongly to dissolve the little bit of juice that has caramelized on the bottom of the pan and, at the same time, to lightly reduce this wine. If the cooking is to be finished at the table, put the kidneys back into the pot to bring them, just as they are, to the dining room. If not, proceed as necessary.

To finish cooking: Whether this is done at the table or in the kitchen, you must have prepared all the ingredients in advance and have them on hand. Place the kidneys on a *hot* plate. Quickly cut them into very thin slices. Cover them with a *hot* plate.

In the juice in the pot, and *off the heat* if you are doing this in the kitchen, add the mustard, the butter divided into pieces, the minced parsley, the lemon juice, and salt and pepper. With a fork, mix everything well, to thicken the juice. Then pour in the slices of kidney with the juice that they have rendered while standing. Mix everything well with a spoon. Send it immediately to the dining room or pass it to your guests.

SAUTÉED KIDNEYS
Les Rognons Sautés

In restaurant kitchens, where basic sauces, stocks, or very reduced juices are readily available, sautéed kidneys can be prepared quickly. The veal stock needed for kidneys sautéed in Madeira, with mushrooms, will be on hand, ready to add to the pans, as the starch for thickening will also be. Since a home kitchen is unlikely to have either ingredient, use the substitutes suggested in the recipe for kidneys sautéed in Madeira.

In any case, remember that the following procedure is absolutely forbidden for home cooks: coating the sautéed kidney with either flour or a roux, and then covering it in liquid and boiling it. This is not so much because boiling, a direction often given, is bad in itself; it is more that for every recipe using sautéed kidneys, there are two points that must be obeyed to the letter.

First: Sauté the kidneys quickly over strong heat. If cooked too slowly, the kidney simmers in its juice, which makes it tough.

Second: Never allow the kidney to boil in the sauce, for the same reason. It is not added to the sauce to finish cooking—it is already perfectly done—but simply to reheat and to be thoroughly impregnated by the sauce.

To sauté, use either a sauté pan or a good skillet. A good skillet was often suggested by the great master Urbain Dubois for this dish.

To prepare the kidneys for sautéing: *Sheep kidneys:* Make an incision in the membrane covering them to tear it off. If the kidney has dried out a little, despite being very fresh, dip it for a second in some cool water to help remove this membrane.

Remove the cord if it remains, as well as the little button of fat in the middle. Divide each kidney in 2 lengthwise. Cut each half into 5 pieces, slicing across and on a diagonal to give a larger surface area to the slices.

Veal kidneys: Remove the fatty skin covering them. Divide the kidney down the middle lengthwise. Remove the fat from the crack in the middle of the kidney.

Cut each half into slices 6–7 millimeters ($^1/_4$ inch) thick.

Beef kidneys: These require several supplementary preparations, due to the odor of ammonia so often given off by them, which is much stronger in an older animal; a reddish brown color, in addition to the ammoniac odor, also indicates age. First, remove the skin that covers the kidney, which is easy to do for a fresh kidney. Divide it in two, as directed. Remove every last vestige of fat from the fold in the middle of the kidney; this fat in particular has a marked alkaline odor.

Divide each half into 2 again. Cut each part into slices 4–5 millimeters (scant 1/4 inch) thick.

If the kidney gives off a very perceptible odor of ammonia, put the slices in a colander, then immerse for *only 1 second* in a pot of boiling water. Drain well. Spread the kidney on a towel and dry it off *completely* before sautéing. Any remaining moisture would stop it from being sealed by the hot fat.

Because of the odor of ammonia it is essential to completely drain the blood that escapes from the kidney after sautéing because it also smells. (Note that this precaution applies only to beef kidneys.) So, once the kidneys have been sautéed, take them out with a skimmer and place in a strainer to drain more easily.

To sauté beef kidneys, a *good skillet* is preferable to a sauté pan.

PRINCIPAL RECIPES FOR SAUTÉED KIDNEYS

The following dishes are for 6 people. You should allow: 10 sheep's kidneys, 2 veal kidneys, or 1 small beef kidney.

Kidney Sautéed in Madeira *(Rognon Sauté au Madère).* A home-style recipe suitable for sheep, veal, and beef kidney. *Time: 25 minutes.*

To sauté the kidneys: 25 grams (1 ounce, 2 tablespoons) of butter and 2 tablespoons of oil.

For the sauce: 15 grams (1/2 ounce, 1 tablespoon) of butter and 10 grams (1/3 ounce) of flour for the roux; 2 deciliters (6 3/4 fluid ounces, 7/8 cup) of veal jus or a well degreased bouillon; 3 good tablespoons of Madeira; 30 grams (1 ounce, 2 tablespoons) of butter; a good pinch of minced parsley.

PROCEDURE. Prepare the kidneys as directed. Season them lightly with salt and pepper. Strongly heat the butter and oil in a sauté pan. Put the kidneys into this *smoking* fat. Sauté them over very strong heat until the slices are quite firm and a uniform grayish color. This takes only a few minutes; you are not trying to color the kidneys, which would require a degree of heat that would harden them.

Take them out with a skimmer to put them in a shallow bowl. If using beef kidneys, put them in a colander. Cover with a plate and keep warm.

The sauce: Drain the fat (butter and oil) in which the kidneys have been sautéed. Replace it with the butter to make the roux, then add the flour. On gentle heat, carefully cook it to make a lightly brown roux (SEE PAGE 47). Dilute it with jus or bouillon. Bring to a boil, stirring constantly with a whisk or spoon. Cook for *4–5 minutes* at a gentle simmer.

Next, put the sautéed kidneys into the sauce. At the same time, add the blood that has escaped from them while they were waiting, unless you are using *beef kidneys* (for the reason given above). Also add the Madeira. Cover the pan. Keep the kidneys on extremely low heat for 2 minutes, making sure, above all, *not to let it boil,* which is sometimes recommended.

Add butter to finish the sauce, dividing it into fragments the size of beans. Then, without touching the sauce, encourage it to melt by shaking the pan in a circular movement on top of the burner. Check the seasoning.

To serve: Pour it into a well-heated timbale or a shallow bowl. Spread the minced parsley over the kidneys. Serve immediately with very hot plates.

Peasant-Style Kidney Sauté *(Rognon Sauté à la Paysanne).* This method is equally suitable for sheep, veal, or beef kidneys. For beef, its particular odor means that the procedure must be modified a little bit; sauté the kidneys first, then drain the fat and put some new butter back into the pan again to color the onion and make the sauce. For this peasant style of cooking, use a good skillet. *Time: 25 minutes.*

50 grams (1$^3/_4$ ounces, 3$^1/_2$ tablespoons) of butter to sauté the kidneys; 2 tablespoons of finely minced onions; $^1/_2$ glass (1 deciliter/3$^1/_3$ fluid ounces/ scant $^1/_2$ cup) of good white wine, which is not acidic, and a glass of completely degreased bouillon; a small garlic clove; $^1/_2$ of a bay leaf; beurre manié made from 20 grams ($^2/_3$ ounce, 1 heaping tablespoon) of butter worked with 10 grams ($^1/_3$ ounce) of flour; 1 scant tablespoon of minced parsley.

PROCEDURE. Prepare the kidneys to be sautéed, as directed.

Heat the butter in the skillet and lightly color the onion. Turn up the heat when you add the kidneys, salt, and pepper. Shake the skillet as soon as the kidneys appear to have firmed up and are a uniform grayish color. Take them out with a skimmer and keep them between 2 *hot* plates.

Pour the white wine and bouillon into the pan. Add garlic and bay. Once it has begun to boil, put a cover on the skillet and simmer gently for *6–8 minutes*. After this, remove the garlic and the bay. Put back the kidneys into the skillet with the juice that they have released. Add the beurre manié (SEE LIAISONS, PAGE 47). Shake the skillet to mix the contents, then let heat for 1 or 2 minutes *without boiling*. Pour onto a heated plate and sprinkle with minced parsley. If you like, surround with large croutons fried in butter.

Kidneys Bercy *(Rognon Bercy).* What characterizes a Bercy preparation is shallot. So, for the quantities given for kidneys cooked in Madeira: sauté the kidney and remove from the sauté pan, then drain the fat and add 1 tablespoon of finely minced shallot with 1 deciliter (3$^1/_3$ fluid ounces, scant $^1/_2$ cup) of white wine. Boil it rapidly to reduce it by half. Add 2 or 3 tablespoons of veal glaze and the juice of $^1/_4$ lemon.

Put the kidneys back into the pan with the juice that they have rendered while they were waiting (except for beef kidneys). Heat it without boiling. Add 50–60 grams (1$^3/_4$–2$^1/_4$ ounces, 3$^1/_2$–4$^1/_2$ tablespoons) of butter divided into small bits, and mix them by shaking the pan in a flat, circular movement on the burner. Pour into a timbale or heated plate. Sprinkle with a pinch of fresh, minced parsley.

Bordelaise-Style Kidneys *(Rognon à la Bordelaise).* Prepare the sauce bordelaise on the side (SEE PAGE 57): that is, 2 deciliters (6$^3/_4$ fluid ounces, $^7/_8$ cup) for the same quantity of kidneys suggested above. Sauté the kidney; drain all the fat from the pan. Add all the bordelaise sauce and 3 tablespoons of small cubes of poached marrow. Heat the kidney in this without boiling.

Kidney with Mushrooms *(Rognon au Champignons).* Proceed as for kidneys sautéed in Madeira. Prepare in advance 150 grams (5$^1/_3$ ounces) of mushrooms divided into quarters and sautéed on the side in a pan with 30 grams (1 ounce, 2 tablespoons) of butter and 2 tablespoons of oil until they are lightly browned. Keep them warm. Put them in the sauce, previously drained, so they can stew there for 5 minutes before the kidneys are added.

Kidneys in White Wine *(Rognon au Vin Blanc).* This uses the same procedure as KIDNEY TURBIGO (PAGE 331), as well as the same ingredients for the sauce, minus the tomato purée. So: sauté the kidneys and drain, then drain the fat from the pan. Reduce the white wine in the pan; add the jus; thicken with arrowroot. Put back the kidney. Add 30–40 grams (1–1$^3/_8$ ounces, 2–3 tablespoons) of butter for the finishing.

PORK
Porc

Fresh Roast Pork *(Le Porc Frais Rôti)*

Large pieces of fresh pork are cooked only by roasting. But pork should be roasted under different conditions than those generally observed for other meat. The spit is preferable for other roasts. Pork, on the other hand, improves by being cooked in the oven and directly on the roasting pan, in its own fat and juice. And unlike other meats, pork is basted with water, because the meat itself always contains a substantial amount of fat.

Country earthenware is the best utensil for roasting pork. A garnish of vegetables, cooked separately three-quarters of the way through, can be added to the pork to finish: so use beans, cabbage, etc., or even raw potatoes, as when cooking shoulder of mutton à la boulangère. Pork prepared thus can be served as an entrée.

You can also serve it in a vegetable dish with an accompaniment of a purée of dried potatoes or dried vegetables. The piece is dressed on a serving plate with its cooking juices, which are degreased only about three-quarters, or served alone with a spicy sauce presented on the side in a sauceboat—a piquante sauce, a pepper sauce, a sauce Robert, etc. The piece that is most generally appropriate for roasting is the fillet, also called the loin, and the rack. The latter should be boned, which lets the initial seasoning better penetrate the meat and also makes the carving much easier. If you leave the bones in, the ribs should be shortened and the spine removed. You can also roast two lesser cuts, the shoulder and the spare ribs, which should both also be boned.

Pork meat, which always needs spicy seasoning, improves by being marinated before cooking. At the very least, it should be macerated with salt and spices at least 3 hours before cooking. Whatever the piece and recipe chosen, make sure that the pork is completely cooked; otherwise, the flesh is indigestible.

Roast Pork *(Porc Rôti)*. Country style. *Serves 7 or 8 people.*

1 kilogram (2 pounds, 3 ounces) of pork without the bones, taken from the parts indicated above.

To macerate it: 30 grams (1 ounce) of gray sea salt; a pinch of dried thyme flowers; a pinch of spice powder; 1 bay leaf; a dozen peppercorns.

PROCEDURE. Lay out all the ingredients on a board. Crush them by rolling a well-cleaned empty bottle over them so that you reduce everything to a fine powder. Then rub it rigorously into the pork with your hands so that the seasoning penetrates the entire surface of the piece, and rub it even more carefully into the part from which you have removed the bones. Then put the pork on a plate, laying it down on the boned side. Keep it cool and dry for 1–2 days.

After this time, put the pork in a roasting pan with a few tablespoons of water. Cook it in a moderate oven for at least *1 hour,* turning the piece over from time to time and basting it with a few tablespoons of warm water as the liquid added at the beginning reduces.

Once the pork is cooked, put it on a serving plate while it is still warm. Drain almost all the fat from the cooking utensil, but make sure you retain all the crusty bits. Pour 3–4 tablespoons of white wine and the same amount of water into the utensil. Bring it to a boil for 1 minute, using a spoon to scrape the brown crust that has formed on the bottom while cooking. This deglazing concentrates the cooking juices, which are subsequently poured over the piece or served in a sauceboat.

Pork Fillet with a Cream Poivrade Sauce *(Filet de Porc Sauce Poivrade à la Crème)*. Cooked in the way of the Provençal chef Reboul. A savory recipe for good home cooking, which is simple to make. Make sure that the cream used is thick and lightly soured. You will not get the right flavor for the sauce if the cream is sweet. You can be sure it is sour enough by buying it in advance—the evening before or even earlier—and leaving it in a cool place. Note that if it is too cool, it will sour less efficiently. *Time: 24 hours for the marinade; 2 hours for cooking the sauce. Serves 10.*

1½ kilograms (3 pounds, 5 ounces) of pork fillet, not too fatty, boned.

For the marinade: 4 deciliters (1⅔ cups) of white wine; 2 deciliters (6¾ fluid ounces, ⅞ cup) of good vinegar; 100 grams (3½ ounces) of onion and the same amount of carrots, cut into slices; 1 bay leaf, 1 sprig of thyme, some celery; a garlic clove; about 20 peppercorns; a pinch of salt.

For cooking: the marinade; 3 deciliters (1¼ cups) of jus or bouillon.

For the sauce: 1 deciliter (3⅓ fluid ounces, scant ½ cup) of vinegar; a dozen peppercorns, crushed; the cooking juice from the pork; 3 deciliters (1¼ cups) of heavy cream, lightly soured; 1 teaspoon of arrowroot.

PROCEDURE. Once the fillet of pork has been boned, remove the excess fat so that a thickness of only 1 centimeter (3/8 inch) is left. Then roll the piece tight and truss it. Put it in a terrine with all the ingredients for the marinade, turning it over to impregnate it well with the marinade. Let it stand for 24 hours, turning it occasionally.

To cook: Two hours before serving, drain the marinade from the pork. Put it in a deep pot made of thick aluminum or in a good casserole dish made of enameled steel. Around this meat, laid fatty side up, arrange the vegetables from the marinade *without the liquid;* at this point, do not add anything else.

Put the uncovered pot or casserole dish in a hot oven. After a few moments, the meat will have already released some fat and also some of the marinade that it absorbed. Let it cook in this juice, turning it over from time to time until the juice has reduced and the vegetables begin to brown. The add all of the marinade: not just the liquid but also all that remains of the aromatics.

Let it cook, basting it from time to time with the cooking juices, until the liquid has reduced to *one-quarter* of its original quantity. Then add the jus or the bouillon. Cover and cook very gently, without letting the liquid reduce any further. From the moment when the pork has been put in the oven, allow it to cook for *1 1/2 hours.* To check that it is well cooked, stick a kitchen needle into the thickest part of the flesh: the needle should go in and come out without much resistance, and no drop of juice should pearl at the opening.

Remove the piece of meat to an ovenproof platter. Cover it and keep it warm in a very moderate oven while preparing the sauce, which takes *25 minutes.*

The sauce: Pour the entire contents of the pot used for cooking the pork into a small tureen. Into the same *empty* pot and without rinsing it, put the vinegar and the pepper. Boil it briskly to reduce it to 1 tablespoon.

Completely degrease the cooking juices that you have poured into the terrine, then pour it back, with its vegetables and aromatics, into the pot where you have just reduced the vinegar. Add the cream. Bring it to a boil; do not cover it, and let it simmer gently for *a scant 45 minutes.* Next, pass the sauce through the chinois into a small saucepan. Bring it back to a boil to bind it with the starch (SEE LIAISONS, PAGE 47). It should cover the spoon like a layer of varnish. Check the seasoning; you may need to add more. At this point you should have at least 5 deciliters (generous 2 cups) of sauce.

To serve: Untie the pork and wipe it clean of any fragments of vegetables, then arrange it on a plate. If you are carving in the kitchen, join the slices back together to reform the fillet. Carved or whole, use a spoon to pour part of the sauce over to coat it. Serve the rest of the sauce in a sauceboat.

Pork Chops *(Les Côtelettes de Porc)*

These should be taken from the rack. You can also cut them from the fillet; but when cut as chops, this piece of meat can be a little bit dry.

A nice chop taken from the rack and correctly trimmed—that is, with the rib bone is shortened and the spine removed—weighs around 200 grams (7 ounces). But chops that are less thick, weighing 150–180 grams (5 1/3–6 1/3 ounces), are appropriate for most guests. Whatever their weight, make sure the chops have been taken from the rack. Charcuteries and butchers have a habit of cutting them a little bit on the bias to make them look better, but flesh cut this way tends to warp while cooking and also colors badly.

The chops, seasoned with salt and pepper and basted with melted lard, can be gently grilled just as they are; fried in butter; sautéed as they are, or even breaded à l'anglaise (PAGE 19). They are always improved by being marinated with lemon juice and a little bit of oil, well in advance; they can also be bought the evening before for using the next day. The sauces suggested for roast pork are equally appropriate for chops. If not accompanying with a sauce, serve at the same time with mustard and the usual pickles: cornichons, etc.

Pork Chops à la Charcutière *(Côtelettes de Porc à la Charcutière).* So called because they are prepared just like the chops that Parisian charcuteries sell already hot. *Time: 1 hour.*

6 chops; 30–40 grams (1–1 3/8 ounces) of good lard to cook them.

For the sauce: 1 large onion (125 grams/4 1/2 ounces); 25 grams (1 ounce) of good lard; 15 grams (1/2 ounce) of flour; 2 deciliters (6 3/4 fluid ounces, 7/8 cup) of

white wine; 4 deciliters (1 2/3 cups) of bouillon; 1 teaspoon of mustard of your choice; 2 good-size soupspoons of rounds of cornichons.

PROCEDURE. **The sauce:** Cut the onion into small cubes. To do this, peel it first, then cut it in two. Cut each half into slices, but do not separate, holding them one against the other to cut them into cubes. Put these cubes in a small saucepan with the fat. On gentle heat, soften the onions without letting them color at all.

Next, mix in the flour using a wooden spoon; cook gently for *6 or 7 minutes* without letting it color beyond a tint that is only slightly yellow. Dilute it little by little with the wine and bouillon. Mix continuously on a slightly higher heat until it boils. Add a pinch of pepper, but no salt if the bouillon is salted, because the sauce must be reduced by half. Keep it at a gentle simmer and skim as needed (SEE SKIMMING, PAGE 16). Allow *about 40 minutes* of cooking from this point.

The chops: Sprinkle them lightly with salt. In a sauté pan where all the cutlets can be arranged one next to the other, placed close together if necessary, heat the fat. As soon as it is good and hot, put in the chops. Do not cover the chops. Leave them on strong heat, without turning them, for *5–6 minutes,* until the side touching the bottom of the pan is lightly golden. The fire must be hot enough to seal the meat and to ensure that their juices do not escape in a large amount of white foam.

Turn the chops over and color them on the other side for a little less time. Once they have been sealed, turn down the heat to finish cooking gently, turning them over from time to time. Allow, according to the thickness of the chops, about *12–15 minutes* at this gentle cooking. In total, then, *about 20–25 minutes* of cooking.

To serve: Skim the sauce one last time; there should be no single drop of fat left. Having been reduced by *half* during its cooking, it should have the consistency of light syrup and the onion should be thick like a preserve. Off the heat, add the rounds of cornichons and the mustard. As soon as they are incorporated, they must not boil or even heat too much. Check the seasoning for salt and pepper.

Drain the fat from the chops in the sauté pan. Arrange them on a well-heated plate. Cover them with sauce. Serve with hot plates.

Pork Chops with a Cream Poivrade Sauce *(Côtelettes du Porc avec Sauce Poivrade à la Crème).*

The recipe is the same as for pork fillet (PAGE 335). *Time: 1 hour.*

6 chops.

For the marinade: **1 deciliter (3 1/3 fluid ounces, scant 1/2 cup) of white wine and the same of vinegar; 1 medium-size onion and 1 carrot, cut in cubes; 1 sprig of thyme; 1 bay leaf; 1/2 clove of garlic; salt and pepper; 30–40 grams (1–1 3/8 ounces) of good lard to color the chops; 2 deciliters (6 3/4 fluid ounces, 7/8 cup) of juice or bouillon; 2 deciliters (6 3/4 fluid ounces, 7/8 cup) of heavy cream that is slightly soured; 1 nice teaspoon of starch.**

PROCEDURE. Trim the chops completely, removing excess fat, and then marinate the chops for 12 hours in a large shallow bowl.

To cook: *About 40 minutes before serving,* drain the chops and sponge them off well with a towel. Color them and cook them as directed for PORK CHOPS À LA CHARCUTIÈRE (PAGE 336). When done, remove them from the pan and keep them warm on a plate.

The sauce: In the fat of the pan where the chops have just been cooked, put all the ingredients from the marinade, well drained of their liquid. On strong heat and without covering the pan, color everything, mixing it well with the wooden spoon.

Drain all the fat, then add the liquid of the marinade, loosening the crispy bits from the pan with the spoon. Boil it strongly without a cover until this liquid has reduced to no more than 1/2 deciliter (1 2/3 ounces, scant 1/4 cup). Add the juice or the bouillon and the cream. Let it simmer gently for another 7–8 minutes, removing the fat and the foam that rises to the surface of the sauce. Assume 3 deciliters (1 1/4 cup) of sauce will be enough for the 6 chops.

Make the liaison with starch (SEE LIAISONS, PAGE 47). Pass the sauce through the chinois onto the chops or serve it on the side in a sauceboat.

Sausages *(Les Saucisses)*

Here we are just dealing with recipes that use them, not explaining how to make them. We mean the ordinary sausages sold fresh by all butchers. The same pork stuffing is used for the flat sausages called *crèpinettes,* so called because the stuffing is wrapped in a caul *(crépine)* rather than gut, but these do not lend themselves to all the recipes that are suitable for ordinary sausages.

The sausage most generally used for all dishes is 10–12 centimeters (4–4 1/2 inches) long. In this case, you should allow 2 sausages per person; if the sausages are served on a purée or on another accompaniment that makes the dish more substantial, you can allow 1 1/2 of each for each person, and even 1 if the menu is large.

Cooking ordinary sausages: The way to cook sausages can vary according to the type of recipe and also the facilities available. But whatever mode you use, the sausages should, as for all pork meats, be "well done"—no matter which way they are cooked, or even if they are begun one way and ended a different way. It is better to slightly overcook than slightly undercook fresh sausages.

Grilled: To stop the skin of the sausages from bursting while cooking, plunge them into boiling water for *2 seconds* only, then prick them in several places with a pin. The number of times depends on the size of the sausages, so count on about 5 or 6 pricks per sausage.

Baste them with melted fat, butter, or lard. Arrange them on a previously heated grill and grill them *on a slow heat,* turning them, *5 or 6 minutes.*

In the skillet: Use a skillet when you do not have a grill or when you are using the fat they release in the recipe. Quickly plunge the sausages into boiling water; drain them on a towel and pierce them as above.

In a small, very clean skillet, heat the butter or the fat: about 25 grams (1 ounce, 2 tablespoons) for 6 small, ordinary, long sausages. Arrange them in the skillet. Cook them gently on very low heat.

In the oven: Prepared as above, arranged on a buttered baking sheet. Distribute a few pieces of butter among the sausages and cook them in a moderate oven.

Cooking flat sausages *(crépinettes)*: Cook as above, but do not blanch or pierce, which is not necessary thanks to the covering of caul fat.

Cooking frankfurters and similar types of sausages: Plunge them in a pot of boiling water. Cover and maintain them on very gentle heat so that the liquid maintains a simple simmer. Allow 10 minutes of cooking without a full boil. Prolonged cooking should be avoided with this kind of sausage.

PRINCIPAL RECIPES FOR SAUSAGES

The sausages can be served just as they are—that is, grilled or sautéed in the skillet, and in this case drained of all fat—with an accompaniment of mustard, cornichons, pickles, etc. But most often they are served on a purée: potato, dried vegetables, chestnuts, etc. If they have been cooked in a skillet or sauté pan, baste them with part of their cooking fat.

Or even better, serve them au gratin: that is, the sausages are first firmed up in hot butter in the skillet and are then arranged on top of the purée, shaped into a dome; the entire thing is sprinkled with grated Parmesan mixed with a very fine bread crumb (SEE BREADING, PAGE 19), basted with the fat of the sausages and then put into a hot oven or under a broiler to crisp and brown in 6–7 minutes.

Sausages with Beans *(Saucisses aux Haricots).* Cooked in the skillet or in the oven, then gently simmered for about 10 minutes in the white beans (SEE BEANS, PAGE 557).

Sausages with Cabbage *(Saucisses aux Choux).* Braise the cabbage (SEE PAGE 496). A scant half hour before serving, lightly brown the sausages in the skillet in butter or lard; then simmer them in the cabbage, basting them with their fat until you are ready to arrange both ingredients in a serving dish or shallow bowl.

Sausages with White Wine *(Saucisses aux Vin Blanc).* One of the most popular dishes. The recipe varies according to the sauces, stock, meat glazes, etc., that are available. Here we give the recipe that we feel is the most appropriate for good home cooking. We recommend serving the sausages on croutons fried in butter. *Time: 40 minutes. Serves 6.*

1 dozen ordinary sausages about 10–12 centimeters (4–4½ inches) long and weighing a total of about 500 grams (1 pound, 2 ounces): 40–50 grams (1⅜–1¾ ounces) of lard or butter; 2 deciliters (6¾ fluid ounces, ⅞ cup) of white wine.

For the sauce. **A roux made with 20 grams (⅔ ounce, 1 heaping tablespoon) of butter and 20 grams (⅔ ounce) of flour; 3 deciliters (¼ cups) of bouillon; reduced white wine; an egg yolk; lemon juice.**

PROCEDURE. Blanch the sausages in boiling water; prick them. In a sauté pan, preferably a skillet, heat butter or fat. Arrange the sausages in the skillet one next to another. Color them on gentle heat, turning them often.

In a small saucepan, make a white roux (SEE PAGE 47); dilute it with the bouillon; stir until it boils; then keep it at a gentle simmer.

Once the sausages have been colored, pour all their fat out of the skillet and set aside to use for other things. Pour in the white wine. Let it simmer for *about 10 minutes.* Do not cover the skillet so that the wine will have reduced *by half* at the end of this time.

Then add the reduced wine to the sauce; keep the sausages warm in the skillet while you prepare a liaison with egg yolk (SEE LIAISONS, PAGE 47). Add the lemon juice.

Pour the sauce over the sausages in the skillet. Keep warm until ready to serve. You can sprinkle the surface with bits of butter (SEE KEEPING SAUCES WARM, PAGE 50), mixing them in before serving by shaking the skillet in a flat, circular movement.

Sausages with Rice *(Saucisses au Riz).* An excellent dish that is simple and economical. If you like, the rice can be prepared with a meat bouillon or as for a risotto; the sausages, either grilled or cooked in fat, are then arranged on the rice; you can finish the plate with a ribbon of tomato sauce at the base of the rice or cover the entire thing with a white wine sauce. For the different ways of cooking the rice, you should refer to that particular section (SEE PAGE 561). The risotto method is preferable here. *Time: 45 minutes. Serves 6.*

1 dozen ordinary sausages, average weight 50 grams (1¾ ounces); 50 grams (1¾ ounces, 3½ tablespoons) of lard or butter; 1 nice tablespoon of minced onion; 250 grams (8⅞ ounces) of rice; 6–7 deciliters (2½–3 cups) of bouillon; a bouquet garni, including 1 stalk of celery; salt, pepper, grated nutmeg.

PROCEDURE. In the skillet, or preferably in a sauté pan, melt the fat or butter. Arrange the sausages there, one next to the other, after they have been pricked and boiled. Do not cover. Let them gently color while turning them. Then drain all of their fat into the pot where you will cook the rice. Keep the sausages warm in their covered skillet or sauté pan.

Into this sausage fat, put the minced onion and proceed exactly as directed for making risotto (SEE PAGE 449), allowing the same amount of time to cook. Once the rice has been cooked, arrange it on a plate and place the sausages on top. Add or do not add sauce, but, most of all, serve it burning hot.

Cooking Boudins, Andouillettes, and Breaded Trotters

Grilled Boudins *(Boudins Grillés).* On both sides of the pieces of boudin, and from one end to the other, make incisions on the bias about 2 or 3 millimeters (scant ⅛ inch) deep. This is to prevent the skin from bursting while cooking.

Heat the grill in advance. Grill the boudin on gentle heat: 5 minutes on each side.

Grilled Andouillette *(Andouillettes Grillées).* Same procedure and time as for boudins.

Grilled Breaded Pig's Feet *(Pieds de Porc Panés Grillés).* Baste with butter or good lard. Put them on a heated grill. Grill them gently: the heat must reach the center of the foot before any color appears on the bread crumb coating. Allow about *12–15 minutes* total.

Stuffed Feet, Head Cheese, and Gayette *(Pieds Farcis, Hure et Gayettes)*

Truffled Stuffed Pig's Feet *(Pieds de Porc Farcis Truffés).* This recipe was taken from a gourmet's notebook. It gives you stuffed feet vastly superior to most of those you can buy, in which the stuffing dominates too much in proportion to the size of the foot and also the quantity of truffle. The preparation here is not complicated, and the recipe follows after a few preliminary observations.

Stuffed, truffled pork feet are served only at lunch. You never serve them with mustard: you accompany them with an excellent purée of potatoes; and, if you like, for a meal of some ceremony, they can be served with a sauce Périgueux.

Since they are meatier, choose nice front feet. In the countryside, those who butcher the pig know how to clean the feet, which must be heated and scraped before being cooked to get rid of all their hairs. In the cities, the butcher will take care of that if you ask him to do so. *Time: 3 1/2 hours for cooking the feet; 45 minutes to stuff and grill them.*

4 nice medium-size stuffed feet; 2 pig's feet weighing 1 1/2 kilograms (3 pounds, 5 ounces).

To stuff them: 400 grams (14 1/8 ounces) of pork meat, comprising equal proportions of lean and fatty (preferably taken in the fillet); if there is not enough fat, add some fresh bacon to make up the right amount; 10 grams (1/3 ounce) of salt; 1 gram at least of finely milled white pepper; 80 grams (2 3/4 ounces) of truffle; 4 squares of pork caul, about 20 centimeters (8 inches) on each side.

We give the size rather than the weight of the caul, because the weight varies, depending on the amount of fat it contains. Divide it into squares when you are ready to stuff the feet. When buying this caul, if it is not completely intact, make sure that you buy a larger amount so that you can double over any holes.

For the preliminary cooking of the feet: 3 1/2 liters (14 3/4 cups) of water; 30 grams (1 ounce) of sea salt; 10 grams (1/3 ounce) of parsley sprigs; 2 grams (1/14 ounce) of thyme and 1 bay leaf; 1 onion stuck with 2 cloves; a dozen peppercorns.

PROCEDURE. **The feet:** Once these have been perfectly cleaned and scalded, put them in a pot or a marmite with all the other ingredients. They must be completely covered. Cover the pot, then bring it to a boil on moderate heat. Let it cook very gently, like a pot-au-feu, until the meat comes away easily from the bone. You can allow at least *3 hours* for this slow cooking. Throughout this time, the liquid should completely cover the feet. If it reduces, add some hot water.

When they are completely cooked, let them partly cool in their cooking juices. Cooler than that, they will be harder to bone. Drain them.

Split the feet lengthwise only. Handle them carefully so that they do not break crosswise, and so that the meat is kept intact. Then lay out each half of the foot on the table; remove the bones so that you are left with a piece of flesh that is all in one piece. Be careful to remove the number of small bones hidden in the thick part of the meat.

Then divide each half lengthwise into strips about 1 centimeter (3/8 inch) wide.

The feet are ready to be stuffed.

The stuffing: Prepare this while the feet are cooking.

The truffles should be brushed and cleaned as directed (SEE TRUFFLES, PAGE 537). Peel them and give them an even shape so that you can then cut them into rounds at least 1 millimeter thick. Too thin and they will burn on the grill. Add the trimmings to the mixture.

Cut the pork into pieces the size of a walnut. Remove all skin or any filaments you might find there depending on which part of the pork you are using. Pass them through a small mechanical grinder along with the truffle peelings. If you do not have a grinder, chop them very, very fine and then grind them in a mortar until extremely fine. Season with salt and pepper, and mix well.

To stuff: Soak the caul for about 10 minutes in water that is a little warmer than lukewarm, to soften it nicely. Spread out a clean towel on the table. Carefully stretch out the caul, blotting it to dry it. Cut the 4 pieces to the size indicated. If the caul has holes in it, place a piece of caul larger than the hole over it as a patch. If it has a series of tears, cut it large enough so that you can double it over, wrapping the foot; it is then protected by a double thickness, both lengthwise and crosswise.

Cut the rounds of truffle into 4 pieces. On each square of caul, arrange *half* of these pieces in the shape of the stuffed foot.

Also divide the hash into 4 quarters. Taking only *half* of each quarter, shape it in your hands into a sort of evenly thick patty 14 centimeters

(5$^{1}/_{2}$ inches) long by 6 or 7 centimeters (2$^{1}/_{2}$–2$^{3}/_{4}$ inches) wide. Place this patty on the square of caul that is sprinkled with truffles.

Then take the half pork foot. Arrange it on the layer of stuffing, and, if the strips are too long, bend them over. Remember that this layer of pig's foot should be of equal thickness. Cover it with a layer of stuffing prepared in a patty like the first but with even more care, because once you have placed it there, it cannot be rearranged without ruining the arrangement of pig foot layers. Sprinkle the remains of the truffle rounds on the stuffing. Fold up the caul lengthwise. Slide your left hand underneath the stuffed pig's foot so that you can finish wrapping it with your right hand.

Maintain a gently rounded form at each end of the stuffed pig's foot. Pull gently on the caul to pack everything down, and fold back the ends on the feet without allowing any opening for the stuffing to escape. Place the foot on the table. Give it a few blows with the flat side of the cleaver, to flatten it to about 2$^{1}/_{2}$ centimeters (1 inch) thick.

Thus prepared, the feet can be left in a cool place for 1–2 days.

To grill them: Lightly and evenly grease each foot with a little bit of lard; then roll them in freshly made bread crumbs (SEE BREADING, PAGE 19). Grill them on gentle heat 10 minutes *on each side* so that the heat penetrates completely to gradually cook the stuffing and reheat the foot.

Serve on burning hot plates.

Pork Head Cheese *(Hure de Porc ou Fromage de Cochon).* A home-style preparation of absolute simplicity, made in the shape of a kind of galantine or cheese, which gives you several options for a cold plate. In a cool season, the head cheese can keep for over a week: you therefore save yourself both time and trouble by making a rather large amount. If not, you can use half the quantities given here.

We give the most common recipe here. Some recipes include white wine, and the cooking liquid is made into a geleé to accompany the head cheese. But the wine, even in small quantities, will sour rapidly, so is only appropriate if eaten immediately. We would also like to add that the bouillon of the cooking liquid is best used for a good soup.

The pork head should be sold by the butcher completely cleaned and ready to be cooked: that is to say, scraped, flamed, and even boned, which is the easiest method of proceeding. If you are planning to mold it in a galantine, ask the butcher to bone and skin it in such a way that the skin remains completely intact, because it is used as a wrapper for this recipe.

If you are using half the suggested quantities, buy a half head divided down the center. It should be boned with the same care, then pickled, cooked, and molded the same way. For the additional lean pork meat, we suggest buying the neck or the knuckle, both parts that are less dry after cooking. Make sure the salt pork is absolutely fresh or it will give a rancid flavor to the entire dish.

You can mold the head cheese in either of two ways. First, as a galantine, in its own skin, and molded into a round or cylindrical form. Shaped like this, it keeps longer and better; the skin provides an envelope that shields the inside from being spoiled. Or, second, in some mold or terrine; this procedure may be preferable, since it is easier and also because the addition of cooking bouillon gives the cheese a certain smoothness. However, the cheese not keep as long, since elements of the bouillon will soon begin to ferment. *Time: 3 hours and 35 minutes (for cooking).*

1 pig's head of a medium size and including the tongue, which should weigh, once completely boned, about 3 kilograms (6 pounds, 10 ounces); 1 kilogram (2 pounds, 3 ounces) of meat, preferably from the neck or knuckle; 500 grams (1 pound, 2 ounces) of very fresh pork rind.

For pickling: 200 grams (7 ounces) of fine salt; 10 grams ($^{1}/_{3}$ ounce) of pepper and grain; 5 grams ($^{1}/_{6}$ ounce) of spice powder; 3 bay leafs; 2 sprigs of thyme.

For the cooking: 1 onion (120–130 grams/4$^{1}/_{4}$–4$^{1}/_{2}$ ounces) stuck with a clove; 2 medium-size carrots; a bouquet garni; sprigs of parsley, 1 celery stalk, 1 sprig of thyme, and part of 1 bay leaf.

PROCEDURE. On the board or on a very clean table, lay out the salt. With your hand, vigorously rub it into the pork head, both on the flesh side and on the skin side. Similarly, rub in the salt on the tongue and over all the flesh. Put everything into a terrine with the pork rind. Then add the pepper, thyme, bay, and spices. Keep it cool in a dry place for *4–5 days.*

To cook: Clean the aromatics off the meat; dry everything with a towel because the salt will now have liquefied.

Put the meat pieces in a pot and cover completely with cold water. Add vegetables and a bouquet garni. On moderate heat, gradually bring to a boil. Skim. Then cover the utensil and regulate the heat so that you maintain the liquid at a gentle simmer that bubbles at only one point, as for a pot-au-feu.

Allow from that moment *a little more than 3 hours.* The toughest parts of the meat must be cooked; check by sticking a cooking needle into them. Avoid overcooking, which would rob the meat of some of its flavor.

To mold: With the skimmer, remove the pieces of meat from the utensil and place them on a large plate.

Galantine method: Cut the ears off at their base to reduce the thickness of the skin there. Also, detach all the flesh sticking to the inside of the head under the skin, so that you keep an almost equal thickness of skin everywhere.

Cut the tongue and the lean meat into large cubes, about 2 centimeters (3/4 inch) on each side. Cut the salt pork and the inside meat from the head into strips 2 centimeters (3/4 inch) wide; the ears into fine strips only *5 millimeters (3/16 inch)* thick, the cartilaginous parts remaining crispy after cooking. Season everything with coarsely milled pepper. It should already be salty enough, but do check. Mix all the meats well.

Dip a clean napkin into some cool fresh water; wring it out and spread it flat on the table. On top of it, lay out the skin of the head, *interior side up.* In the middle, place the whole mixture of meats. Gather the borders of the napkin together, making sure that the skin of the head completely encloses the cut meats. Give the bundle a round shape by tying the napkin tightly with string: this gives the head cheese a round shape. You can also give it the slightly elongated form of a true galantine by tying up the napkin at the two ends and also encircling it with a turn of string in the middle of the bundle, without tying it too tight.

Then place a board on top, putting on it a weight of 2 kilograms (4 pounds, 6 ounces), no more, because the head cheese must retain its juices so that it is not too dry. Do not untie it until at least 12 hours have passed, when it should be completely chilled.

Another way to mold: Cut all the flesh, including the head *with its skin,* into large squares about 2 centimeters (3/4 inch) on each side. Put everything into a pot. Add pepper and 500 milliliters (generous 2 cups) of cooking bouillon from the head, then mix with a wooden spoon. Pour it into a mold or some pot with an opening sufficiently flared to allow unmolding. *Do not weight it down.* Let it cool completely. To unmold, dip the mold for 2 or 3 seconds in warm water and immediately turn it over onto a plate.

Home-Style Gayettes of Pork *(Gayettes de Cochon à la Ménagère).* Thus named around 1830 by the Nîmes cook Durand, gayettes are one of the most popular recipes from the Midi. These are large *crèpinettes* or meatballs made of pork liver, which you can serve either hot or cold: today, they are most often served cold, and generally are kept in a container of lard, from which you can take them out as you need them.

Their preparation is very simple and so are their elements: Pork liver and fat. We summarize here the method used by families in Nîmes. Garlic is not included, although we think it could feature discreetly. It would be enough in this case to rub a cut garlic clove all around the bowl where you mix the chopped meat.

For the fat, we recommend, as Reboul also recommends, using the fat that envelops the intestines of the pig, which is finer and more easily melted then the ordinary fatback found under the rind. *Time: 1 1/2 hours for cooking; 7 1/2 for preparation and chilling.*

8–10 gayettes, according to their size; 500 grams (1 pound, 2 ounces) of pork liver; 250 grams (8 7/8 ounces) of pork hash in equal quantities of fat and lean meat or sausage meat; 250 grams (8 7/8 ounces) of pork fat taken from the intestines; 250 grams (8 7/8 ounces) of pork caul; 30 grams (1 ounce) of good fine salt; 2 grams (1/14 ounce) of

spice powder; a nice pinch of pepper; 1 tablespoon of finely minced parsley.

PROCEDURE. Mince the pork fat very finely, and also, if you have not purchased sausage meat, the pork meat. Put it into a shallow bowl.

Cut the liver into pieces to remove all skin, fat, and fibers, and check carefully to remove all the parts that the spleen might have reached: then chop the liver similarly. It will quickly reduce to a liquid hash. Pass it through a simple strainer with medium holes, crushing it with a mortar, and allowing the strainer to retain all the filaments. Add it to the fat and the minced pork. Season it and mix it with a wooden spoon to combine everything perfectly. Then let it firm up in a cold place for at least 5 or 6 hours.

To make the gayette: Divide your minced meat and fat into similar piles about the size of an orange. Put the caul into tepid water without unfolding it, to soften it. Drain it and dry it off carefully on a towel. Spread it out on the table, stretching it. With a large knife, divide it into as many squares as you have minced meat piles. It is essential that the mince or stuffing be wrapped in a double thickness of caul; if this is not absolutely intact and there are some holes in it, spread a little piece of caul over them to serve as a patch.

On each square, place a heap of minced meat. Fold the caul over it. Having done this, do not stretch it too much: the swelling of the stuffing while cooking would make it burst. Quickly shape everything into balls, which will nonetheless want to flatten out because of the heat from your hands. It is therefore better, so that they maintain their spherical form, to let them firm up a little bit in a cool place before cooking them. They can easily be left until the following morning; in a very cool place, 2 hours will suffice.

To cook: In the classic method, as we have described, the gayettes are placed one next to the other, without crowding them too much, into a sauté pan whose bottom is covered with a thick layer of lard. On top of them, place a few tablespoons of cool lard; cover and then cook very carefully on gentle heat. Allow, according to the size of the gayettes, *1–1½ hours* of gentle simmering from the moment when the fat has begun bubbling.

Today, now that all home kitchens have an oven, gayettes are gently cooked in the oven, though the cooking time is a little bit shorter. Whether shaped into balls or small squares, a modern gayette (which uses the liver and fat cut into lardons or cubes) can be arranged side by side in a roasting pan; basted with lard, they are put into a hot oven. Allow about *30–35 minutes* for cooking, and baste them several times with their fat. These kind of gayettes are served very hot on a purée or completely cooled, with mustard and cornichons.

Ham *(Le Jambon)*

Served whole, whether hot or cold, a ham is an elegant part of any important meal. And in a house with few people, it's also a bargain because the leftovers make a useful reserve for the pantry, its keeping time being quite long and its uses numerous.

In general and, indeed, for all dishes, the best ham is the kind called "York," which is prepared in a superior manner and whose meat is remarkably fine. An average weight of a York ham is 4–5 kilograms (8 pounds, 13 ounces–11 pounds). This is what you need for serving 12–15 people and will give you a nice piece.

The ham is first soaked to desalinate the meat. The time needed varies because it very much depends on the type of ham and the age of the ham. Ham that has been substantially pickled, like those from Germany, require a prolonged soaking. It is the same thing for aged hams, which have acquired a particular dryness. These should be soaked for 2 days, and frequently more, to penetrate the hardened flesh; you can then see them gradually swell over time and regain their original elasticity.

For a York ham of a good quality, an average of 12 hours of soaking is more than enough; you can even, if you need, reduce this time by a few hours. Soak in cool water in a container large enough so that the ham is completely covered with the water, which you should change several times.

To serve ham warm, when circumstances allow, finish cooking the ham by braising in a good wine—Madeira, Marsala, port, sherry, etc.—which also flavors the meat. In this case, first cook the ham in water, using a simple method we will explain below. Once it is three-quarters cooked, take it from the water, remove the skin, trim the ham as described for glazing it, and then put it in a braising pan or other pan utensil of *exactly the right capacity* with a half bottle of one of the wines mentioned above. Put the pan, tightly covered, in a gentle oven, for the ham to finish cooking. Reduce the braising wine and then add to the accompanying sauce—financière, Milanaise, etc.—or the sauce for the garnish.

For the final flavoring with Madeira or other wine, there is a special procedure that is simpler than the braising used in haute cuisine, and we will give this further on.

The *cooking time* varies not only with the weight of the ham, but according to its source and even its quality. Allow about *15 minutes per 450 grams (1 pound)* for a York ham of good quality of the medium weight suggested above; remember that you must always consider the size of the piece and give more time *per 450 grams (1 pound)* for a large piece than a small one. Check to see that the cooking is complete by inserting a kitchen needle into the thickest part of the meat; it should go in and come out without resistance.

Hot Ham. For cooking a York ham, use only water; for another ham, the longer cooking time includes the addition of aromatics as directed further on for cold ham.

PROCEDURE. Once the ham has been soaked, take it out of the water when you want to cook it. Brush it carefully on all sides. Remove the brown parts, and, if it is an aged ham, also remove the parts that are rancid and soiled. Rinse it again through clean water.

After having drained the ham, cut off the protruding bone; then remove the shank bone, which is attached to the leg bone. Do this carefully, scraping the point of a knife along the bone so that you do not leave any meat there. If you must, you can take the leg bone out only after cooking, but you may as well get rid of all the bones beforehand since they are useless and impede carving.

To cook the ham: Use a braising pan if possible or a tinned copper pan long enough to let you put the ham in it. The pan must be large enough so that the ham is not restricted and remains completely covered by the liquid. If you do not have a braising pan, use an ordinary pot that is deep enough so that the ham can be put in it almost standing up—traditionally, a ham is not cooked lying down. Here, too, the piece must be completely immersed in the water. To keep the ham standing, you can securely attach the bone to a wooden spoon placed across the pot. Thus, the ham is suspended in the middle of the pot and completely surrounded by water; this also prevents the bottom of the pan from sticking to the part in contact with the ham (a necessary precaution for an earthenware pan). Another, older, method is to place the ham on a cloth folded 4 times and laid on the bottom of the pan.

Whatever pan you use, put in enough cold water to basically cover the ham. Bring it to a boil on strong heat. As soon as it boils, turn the heat down very low to maintain a *simple simmer* until the end. A stronger boil would not speed up the cooking: on the contrary—the sealed flesh would not be equally cooked on the inside and the rind could burst.

Calculate the cooking time from the moment the simmering starts. If, while cooking, the water reduces by evaporation and no longer covers the ham completely, add more water, but make sure that it is *boiling.*

To trim the ham: At the end of the cooking time, take the ham out of its pan and place it on a carving board. Completely remove the rind, pulling it in the direction of the narrow end. Trim it using a good large knife, scraping everywhere to leave no browned part. Take off some of the fat from the top and leave only a layer about 1 centimeter (3/8 inch) thick on the meat.

Trim the narrow end, or sleeve, as you would a leg of lamb, cutting the meat from around the bone.

If you glaze the ham, put it on a long roasting plate and baste it with several tablespoons of veal jus. Put it into a rather hot oven so that a small reddish layer forms on the surface of the ham, which should be slightly browned. This should take a *scant 15 minutes.*

To replace braising with Madeira or other wine: Cook the ham as above, but allow only *12 minutes* per 450 grams (1 pound). Trim it as directed. Put the ham on a long oven plate; for a ham of 4–5 kilos (8 pounds, 12 ounces–10 pounds, 15 ounces), add at least 3 deciliters ($1^1/_4$ cups) of one of the wines suggested above (PAGE 343). First bring it to a boil on the stove, then put it into a moderate oven. Frequently baste the ham with the wine for the *first 20 minutes,* but do not baste it any more after that. And place it on the top shelf of the oven to *glaze* it, as suggested above.

To serve: *If carving is done at the table:* place the ham on a large, long plate and put a large sleeve of curled paper around the bone, then surround the ham with several tablespoons of the accompanying sauce.

Carving: You begin with the narrow end, or sleeve, of the ham. First carve a rather thick piece, and put to one side. This will make it easier to cut the wider slices, which should be as thin as a sheet of paper. It is essential to use a particular knife, with a blade that is rounded on the end and is rather long, thin, and flexible; make sure that it is sharp.

If carving is done in the kitchen: Put the sliced pieces one on top of the other to reform the ham. Put everything in the oven to heat it. Be careful to remove the first slice before passing the plate.

THE PRINCIPAL GARNISHES AND SERVING HOT HAM

Ham with Spinach *(Jambon aux Épinards).* A classic spring dish. Madeira sauce is the essential accompaniment. Thus, for a ham of the kind mentioned, $2^1/_2$kilograms (5 pounds, 8 ounces) of very fresh spinach prepared as instructed (SEE PAGE 511) with 2 deciliters ($6^3/_4$ fluid ounces, $^7/_8$ cup) of good veal juice to braise them; and at least 500 milliliters (generous 2 cups) of Madeira sauce (SEE PAGE 54), prepared at the same time as the ham. You can take care of the spinach while the ham is cooking.

Serve the spinach on the side in a vegetable dish and the sauce in a sauceboat. For easy serving, particularly if you are using 2 plates, you can arrange the slices of ham in a circle on a round plate and put the spinach in the middle. Or, better still, arrange the spinach in a little mound at the end of a long plate on which the entire carved ham rests. For a fancy arrangement, you can also put the spinach in little shells of puffed pastry and surround the ham with them. The sauce in all of these cases is always served in a sauceboat.

Ham à la Financière *(Jambon à la Financière).* Very common in the rich and savory cuisine of the nineteenth century, this method is always to be recommended. The ham must finish cooking with Madeira wine as directed, and any remaining wine is reduced, if necessary, and then added to the sauce for the garnish (SEE FINANCIÈRE GARNISH, PAGE 457). The garnish is in part arranged around the ham and the rest is served in a sauceboat.

Ham with Braised Lettuce; Ham with Sauerkraut; Milanaise-Style Ham (with Macaroni, Cheese, Tomato); Ham Risotto *(Jambon au Laitues Braises; à la Choucroute; à la Milanaise; au Risotto).* These are accompanied by a very clarified brown sauce (SEE PAGE 50), to which is added the reduced wine from the braising. SEE LETTUCE (PAGE 519), SAUERKRAUT (PAGE 454), RISOTTO (PAGE 449).

A garnish of fresh vegetables in season is equally good with hot ham: beans or peas, cooked in water, bound with butter; or prepared as a purée.

We also suggest here a garnish known as *à la maillot,* which is particularly appropriate to hot ham. It includes either carrots or turnips, carved to the size of an olive and cooked with consommé; small glazed onions; braised lettuce; green peas and green beans bound with butter. For all details, refer to the appropriate sections.

COLD HAM
Le Jambon Froid

A ham in aspic, surrounded or not with vegetables, always looks good for breakfast, a buffet lunch, or an evening meal. The choice of a York ham of fine quality is just as appropriate here, but its cooking requires an aromatic court bouillon, which can also be used for any ham served hot, as we have suggested above.

Desalinate the ham *24 hours in advance,* then put it in a braising pan or a pot covered with cold water. Bring it to a boil. Soon after, toss this water away. Then cover the ham with water, boiling this time. Add carrots; an onion stuck with cloves; some leeks whose green part has been removed; and 2 bunches of parsley with a sprig of thyme and a suggestion of bay. No pepper for the moment. If possible, add some *white wine,* which substantially enhances the ham: the necessary quantity is not considerable, requiring only 1 bottle for each 3 liters (12¾ cups) of water.

Bring it to a boil. Then turn the heat down low to regulate the cooking, as directed. Allow *a good 15 minutes per pound (450 grams).* A few minutes before turning off the heat, add a few peppercorns. After the ham has completely cooled, remove the rind from the ham and trim as directed above. Remove the shank bone.

After this, baste the ham with a few tablespoons of melted aspic to which you have added a good quantity of gelatin. Only a small amount of this gelée is needed, but it gives the meat an attractive luster, and the gelatin guarantees that the gelée sets quickly. The minced gelée used to surround the ham does not need added gelatin.

Next, arrange the ham on a long, large plate, standing it on a base cut from a piece of stale bread; this is so that the meat stands out from the garnish that surrounds it, but no one should see this support, which should be hidden under a ribbon of minced gelée. If you like, surround it first with more gelée cut into decorative patterns and then with a garnish of vegetables arranged in groups, alternating the colors. These vegetables can then be placed in a salad bowl and bound with a loose mayonnaise. The carved ham is served with the salad and with a mayonnaise sauce offered in a sauceboat.

Ham Cornets *(Cornets de Jambon).* Depending on circumstances, cornets can be served alone as an hors d'oeuvre or as part of the garnish of a cold dish. They can be filled with an infinite variety of ingredients: all kinds of salads bound with mayonnaise or a Russian sauce, a macédoine of vegetables, tomatoes, cèpe mushrooms, chopped lettuce, fish leftovers, fowl, etc. Or a fois gras in a mousse, minced gelée, or a mousse of ham featuring the trimmings left over from making the cornets.

We suggest using a round slice for making cornets: it is the most practical. The size of a cornet differs according to its use. To determine the size, roll different sizes of rounds of paper into the shape of a cornet. Note that you can make the cornets more or less flared by the way you fold the round slice; the less the 2 sides come together at the top of the cornet, the larger is the opening. The flared form is better when the garnish has the right consistency to stick to the sides of the cornet and not fall out when the cornets are served as they should be, leaning against the plate or against the food that they are accompanying.

FIG. 55. HAM CORNET.

When you have worked out the right size for the cornets, note the diameter and then make a round of paper to serve as a template for cutting the ham into round slices. For smaller cornets, use a cookie cutter, which avoids the need for a knife and is much simpler than a paper template.

For salads, use a spoon to fill the cornets. For mousses, a pastry bag is preferable.

Cornets are always made with a cooked York ham, without any fatty parts and cut into *very thin* slices; its size should let you cut 1 or 2 rounds, depending on how big the cornets are. The trimmings from cutting the rounds can be used in a number of ways: minced in the garnish or used for other recipes.

PROCEDURE. The cornets should be prepared at least 1 hour before they are filled, and during this time they should be kept in the refrigerator.

Have the slices of ham ready on a plate. Have ready too a piece of butter—rich, *firm* butter, the size of a pigeon's egg—and squeeze it in a towel to soften it. Put this butter on a plate and keep it on the side while you roll the cornets. Have a small kitchen knife ready, both to cut the ham and for the butter. Also have ready an empty jar with a wide neck, which will act as a support.

To cut and make the cornets: Cut rounds from the slices of ham, either placing them on the cardboard template or using a cookie cutter. Place the rounds on a plate, then roll each round into a horn and hold it in your left hand. With your right hand, use the kitchen knife to pick up a little butter on the end. Slide this butter under the point where the meat folds over to close the cornet, using the butter as a kind of glue. Then lightly squeeze to make it stick.

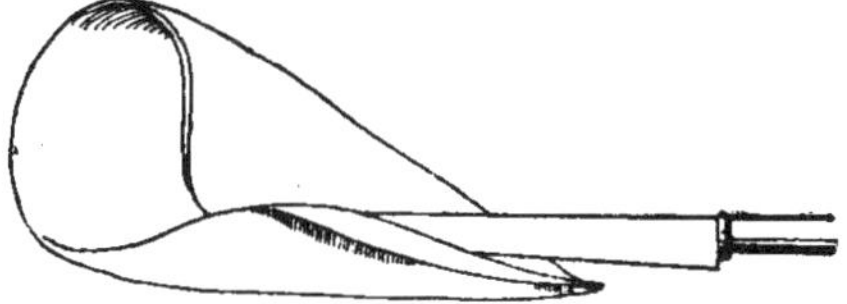

FIG. 56. PASTING THE CORNET.

Immediately place the cornet into the neck of the jar to hold it and maintain its shape. Start again and do the same for the second cornet: place it in the first cornet already in the jar and so on, for about a dozen cornets. Be careful when doing this not to squeeze the cornets against each other so that you do not have any difficulty separating them later on. Now put them somewhere cold so that the butter can become as firm as possible and therefore keep the edges of the round of ham stuck together.

Cold Ham Mousse *(Mousse Froide de Jambon).* Use York ham that has been cooked nice and red, the lean part without any vestiges of fat.

The best mold to use is the charlotte or timbale mold—that is, one with straight sides and with a smooth bottom. If you like, this can be lined with a geleé and decorated (SEE ASPICS, PAGE 445); or simply oiled; or even lined on the inside with a round of paper on the bottom and strips of this paper on the sides up to the top of the mold. This procedure allows you to unmold without any preliminary dipping in hot water.

Use either a Madeira-based gelée, as given in the aspics section, or a simple gelée, as described under meat gelée (PAGE 45). The choice is yours.

For the mousse to set, allow 2 hours in a refrigerator, or 5 hours in a cool place. The surface of a mousse should have a certain consistency while the inside remains soft, even though solidified. *Time: 1 hour (plus 2–5 hours for chilling). Serves 8–10.*

400 grams (14 1/8 ounces) of ham, net weight; 1 deciliter (3 1/3 fluid ounces, scant 1/2 cup) of thick béchamel; 3 deciliters (1 1/4 cups) of very fresh heavy cream for whipping; 3 deciliters (1 1/4 cups) of gelée reduced to 1 deciliter (3 1/3 fluid ounces, scant 1/2 cup); salt, pepper, cayenne. About 3/4 deciliter (2 1/2 fluid ounces, scant 1/3 cup) of geleé to garnish the mousse; a mold with a capacity of 1 1/4 liters (5 1/3 cups).

PROCEDURE. Prepare the béchamel—that is, make a white roux with 10 grams (1/3 ounce, 1 scant tablespoon) of butter and 10 grams (1/3 ounce) of flour diluted with 1 1/2 deciliters (5 fluid ounces, 2/3 cup) of boiled milk; a pinch of salt, grated nutmeg. Let it cook gently and reduce to 1 scant deciliter (3 1/3 fluid ounces, scant 1/2 cup). Spread it out on a plate to chill.

In a small saucepan, boil 3 deciliters (1 1/4 cups) of gelée to reduce it to 1 1/2 deciliters (5 fluid ounces, 2/3 cup). Allow it to cool without becoming completely solid.

Cut the ham into large cubes; grind them in a mortar into a fine paste. Add the cooled béchamel tablespoon by tablespoon, continuously crushing with the pestle. Pass it through a fine metallic drum sieve; pour this paste into a terrine and keep it in the refrigerator or in a cool place.

Whip the cream to very firm (SEE PAGE 586).

Using a wooden spoon, vigorously work the paste for 2 minutes to make it light and smooth. Add the gelée, reduced almost to liquid, by half tablespoons at a time, continuously working it with the spoon. After this, add the seasoning, keeping in mind that the addition of whipped cream lends a certain blandness to the mousse: the quantity of salt depends on how salty the ham is; it should be 6–7 grams (1/5–1/4 ounce).

Finally, add the whipped cream, following the same procedures as for egg whites (SEE PAGE 10). Taste it one last time to check the seasoning, which is particularly important in a mousse; it must be more or less spicy, principally from pepper, but without excess.

Pour this composition into the mold and let it solidify there. When you are ready to serve, but no sooner, unmold onto a plate covered with a napkin; surround the base with a geleé chopped using the back of a knife blade dipped in warm water.

Home-Style Ham Hors d'Oeuvres *(Croûtes au Jambon à la Ménagère).* A hot hors d'oeuvre that is simple to make. You must fry these in a *very hot* deep fat (SEE PAGE 40). *Time: 20 minutes. Serves 6.*

250–300 grams (8 7/8–10 1/2 ounces) of stale bread; 100 grams (3 1/2 ounces) of well cooked lean ham; 25 grams (1 ounce, 2 tablespoons) of butter; 100 grams (3 1/2 ounces) of flour; 1 good deciliter (3 1/3 fluid ounces, 1/2 cup) of boiling milk; salt, pepper, nutmeg; 2 egg whites whipped into a firm snow.

PROCEDURE. Remove all the crusts of the bread. Cut about 10 slices, each 1 centimeter (3/8 inch) thick. Divide them into rectangles or squares about 7–8 centimeters (2 3/4–3 1/4 inches) wide. Mince the ham fine.

In a small saucepan, mix the butter and the flour over moderate heat without letting it color at all. Add the boiling milk. Work this mixture with a sauce whisk to obtain a nice, smooth paste. Season with salt, pepper, and nutmeg, then heat it, stirring continuously until it reduces by about half and takes on a very thick consistency. Turn off the heat. Mix in the ham. Put it to one side while you whisk the egg whites. Add them to the batter, taking the usual precautions (SEE PAGE 10).

Garnish one side of the slices of bread with the paste, spreading it evenly right to the edges, and to a completely equal thickness of about one finger. Smooth the batter with the back of a spoon or the blade of a large knife. As you do this, put the slices on a baking sheet.

Slide the *croûtes* into the frying mixture. They must be completely covered. Turn them carefully: 5–6 minutes will be enough to swell the batter and color the bread. Turn off the heat, then quickly drain the *croûtes* on a towel or on a paper. Put them on a napkin-covered plate and sprinkle with fine salt. Serve immediately.

FOWL

PREPARATION OF FOWL

To pluck the fowl: This is much easier when the beast has just been killed and not yet refrigerated. You start at the head, tearing out the feathers in small clumps, pulling in the opposite direction to the feathers: you will rip the skin if you pull the feathers out in their natural direction.

If you are short of time to cook the fowl, you can soak it for about 30 seconds in boiling water before pulling out the feathers. This makes plucking the feathers so much easier they almost come out by themselves when you touch them; the boiling and scalding also tenderizes the flesh of the fowl. But never do this when you have to keep the beast for some time before cooking it, because it accelerates the speed at which the flesh begins to rot.

Fowl bought in town have usually already been plucked, although the large wing feathers are usually left. If so, remove the feathers one by one. Dip the wings in boiling water to take out the smaller feathers more easily, a pinch at a time. And afterward, make sure that you remove the little tubes of the feathers using the point of a knife.

The feet: To pull off the skin, dip the bird for 30 seconds in boiling water. Wrap a towel around your right hand; take first one foot and then the other in this hand, pulling it toward you: the skin comes off like a glove. Grilling the feet should be avoided; they are virtually fleshless and the operation gives off a strong burnt smell.

To flame the fowl: Flaming removes the long hairs found all over the skin of the beast.

It requires a lively flame that does not give off any smoke. Smoke not only blackens the bird, but an even greater inconvenience is that it communicates an odor that does not disappear during cooking. Burning paper in particular has this disadvantage.

If you do not have a gas flame, use a little bit of burning alcohol in a container and light it with a piece of paper to avoid the sulfurous odor of the match.

Quickly pass every bit of the bird over the flame. For a beast with a skin that is considered a particular delicacy—a young hen, say, or a pheasant—the flaming should be done even more rapidly and skillfully; you must do it very gently so the skin does not shrink under the heat, which would cause it to break.

To gut the fowl: When you buy a bird that has already been plucked and gutted, a lateral incision will have been made along the length of the body under the thigh. This enables the merchant to present the bird in a more attractive way; but the cleanliness of the bird inside is less certain. In good kitchens, the method is different, and it is this method we will describe, which is in every way preferable to the other (see *fig.* 57).

Put the chicken on its breast, its head in front of you on the table. Take its head in your left hand; with a good kitchen knife of medium size—that is, with a blade 25 centimeters (10 inches) long—split the skin on top of the neck from the head to the stomach. You leave this skin sticking to the head so that you have more leverage when you gut the beast.

With thumb and index finger of the left hand, loosen the skin from the neck. Pull on the gut and the crop *slowly* to avoid breaking the crop. Pull out the crop—a more or less swollen pouch of partially digested food—and the gut, which looks like a large macaroni, at the same time.

Once this entire package has been loosened and lifted out but not cut, slice at the point of the beak. This way, you cut both the canal of the crop and the extreme end of the gut right at their ends. Both are linked to the lungs, the gizzard, and the intestines. To remove these different parts,

CLEANING A CHICKEN.

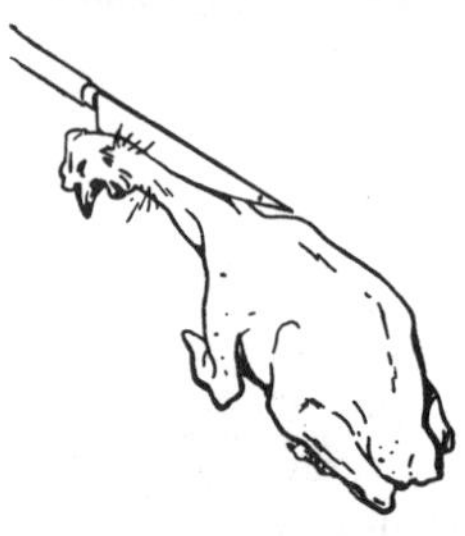

A. Cut open the entire length of the neck.

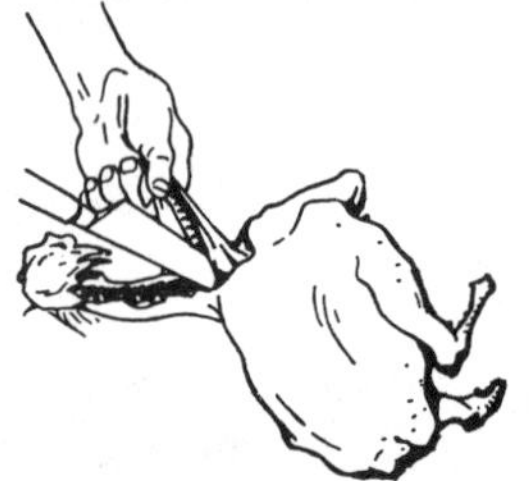

B. Detach the crop.

C. Place the chicken on its back and cut open the rump.

D. Remove the intestines.

CARVING A RAW CHICKEN.

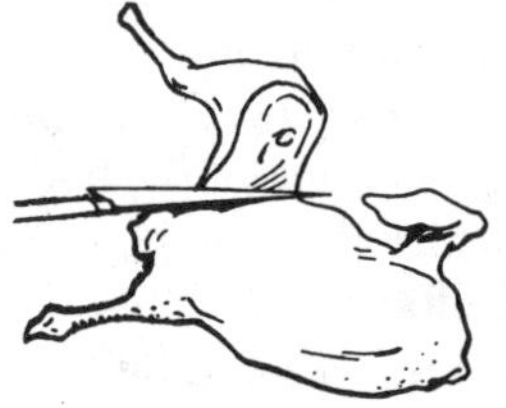

A. Remove the right drumstick.

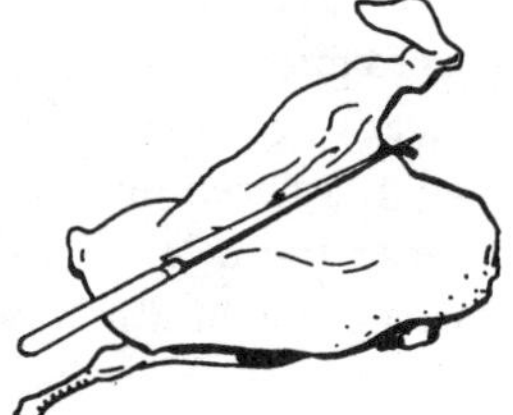

B. Remove the right wing.

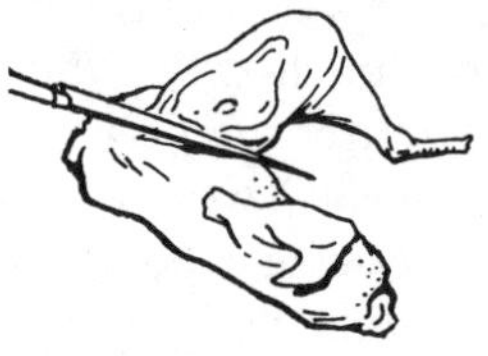

C. Remove the left drumstick (chicken resting on its right side).

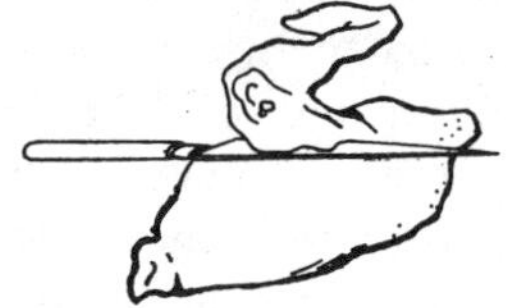

D. Remove the left wing.

CARVING A DUCK.

A. Detach the two thighs.

B. Make an incision the length of the breastbone.

C. Slice the breast fillets.

D. Remove the wings.

FIG. 57. CLEANING A CHICKEN; CARVING A RAW CHICKEN; CARVING A DUCK.

proceed as follows: put your index finger into the opening where the crop is, then ease your finger down the vertebral column and detach the lungs and the gut from the inside of the beast; a bent finger pressed against the carcass should be enough to guide you.

NOTE. If the bird has been purchased already killed, be careful when you stick your finger inside; because the kidneys may have been squashed when the bird was flattened with a blow of a hammer to give it a better appearance. Also, you may cut your finger on the broken bones.

After this, turn the bird on its back. With a knife, trim the anal orifice or rump so that you can pull away a thin round that looks like a ring, and then enlarge the opening to remove all the "waste" as well as this part, which is not dainty.

Then press on the lower part of the wishbone with the thumb and the index finger to make the gizzard come out of the same orifice. Grab the gizzard with your fingers to pull it out. The intestines and the liver will follow. The crop and the large intestine, etc., which has already been loosened on the other side, can then be pulled out through the same opening.

At this point, everything that can be described as "waste" has been removed from the bird. The only thing worth keeping is the liver and the gizzard, if it is a young chicken. If it is a rooster, keep the kidneys, too, to which you will later add the crest. With one cut of the knife, immediately remove the *bile pouch* from the liver. This is a small bluish vessel, which you must be very careful not to break because of the unpalatable bitterness of its contents. If it is broken, the liver is tainted and you will have to throw it out.

The final operation is to cut the skin from the neck just under the head, and then to cut off the neck itself, *leaving its skin,* all the way up to the breast. Fold this skin back down the bird, or roll it up and stuff it in the opening of the crop. If the head and neck are left on the beast, loosen the skin all around the head with a knife; then, with your fingers, pull this skin, which easily lifts away, taking with it the little bits of feather. Finally, with a cut of the knife, remove the tips of the claws from the feet so that the only thing left are the stumps.

The bird is now ready to be trussed.

To gut a fowl so that you can stuff it: A fowl that is to be stuffed or garnished with truffles is not gutted via its anus. (Or, if it is, you must make only a very small opening in the rump and then close it back up with a strong thread so that the stuffing does not escape when the bird is stuffed.) It should be gutted via an opening at the front of the bird (see below). After this, the stuffing is introduced into the beast from this same large front opening.

Once the large intestine and pouch have been removed, continue as follows:

Cut off the neck, *leaving the skin,* at body level. Cut the skin at the level of the head to keep it as long as possible. This skin of the neck has a very important role in all stuffed fowl: It is folded back over the back of the beast after it has been filled to close it and keep all the stuffing inside the body. You must therefore keep the whole length of it intact.

Using the point of a small knife, first detach and remove the small fork-shaped bone at the front of the breast. Then, with the point of a larger knife, raise the flesh of the breast and cut the wishbone. Put your fingers into this opening to pull out the heart, liver, gizzard, and intestines; if necessary, use the hook on the handle of a kitchen spoon or other kitchen utensil. Take great care not to break the bile pouch. If you do, you will have to wash the inside of the bird in several changes of warm water and then dry it subsequently by pushing a corner of a towel inside the beast.

How to Truss and Secure a Fowl

Trussing is the method in which the position of the limbs of the bird are arranged for cooking: securing them is the way the limbs are tied down with string to keep them in the correct position.

To roast: Trussing for roasting keeps the wings and legs of the bird. When the spit was the sole method of roasting, the head and the neck were also left: these helped to secure the bird better on the spit, and many people also appreciated the meat. Once ovens began to be used, they were removed, because trussing does not sufficiently secure them, and they do not stay in a fixed position when heated, so the bird is not stable on the rack of a roasting pan.

For demonstrating, we will use a chicken as a typical bird. The procedures are the same for all fowl and game birds.

You need a steel kitchen needle about 25–30 centimeters (10–12 inches) long threaded with $1^1/_2$ meters (5 feet) of kitchen string. Put the bird on its back, with the rump of the bird facing you. Stretch out your left hand to squeeze together the two thighs, keeping them at the same height on either side of the beast. Stick the needle into the left drumstick *under the bone* (see *fig.* 58A), then go right through the bird in order to make the needle come out of the other drumstick corresponding to the point where it entered. Turn the chicken onto its left side and stick the needle into the right wing. Turn the chicken over to push the needle through the left wing, going through the flesh of the back. Return the chicken to its back. Forcefully pull the two ends of the string together to tighten it before tying a knot: cut the ends.

Again, squeeze the thighs with your left hand. Stick the needle into the base of the drumstick, but this time *above* the bone. Push the needle through to make it come out *on top* of the bone on the other drumstick. Then turn the chicken with its head toward you, lying on its back. Pierce it with a needle through the carcass at the point indicated (see *fig.* 58C-D) at the height of the oyster, to meet the other end of the string, with which you will tie a knot once you have turned the chicken over.

Note that the direction of the trussing leaves the two knots on the same side of the beast; this makes it easier to remove the strings after cooking. Do this by cutting the string with scissors opposite the knots, and then pull the knots toward you; the bird will be untrussed in the blink of an eye.

To bard: Use a bard of fatback bacon sliced thin and big enough to cover the bird from one end to the other, and also to protect the tender and delicate parts of the wings and the white meat. Secure it by tying string three or four times around the bird, crossing it over and knotting the two ends (see *fig.* 58H). The bird is now ready to be cooked.

To truss the bird as an entrée: The classic method simply involves folding back the legs of the bird to arrange them against the body after having cut the tendon of the joint. But today, when the bird is not presented at the table before being carved, the problem of appearance is no longer the same. Thus, these days you remove the feet and the wing tips as well as the giblets that will be used in the jus. Trussing the bird remains the same, except instead of passing the string through the wing tips, you pass it under the bone of the wings.

How to Carve a Raw Chicken for Sautéing

The way to cut up an uncooked chicken is essentially the same as for a roast chicken, the fingers of your left hand replacing the service fork used in carving. But it is important to equip yourself with a good kitchen knife whose blade is wider and stronger than that of a carving knife since a raw chicken is naturally tougher than a cooked bird. The blade of the kitchen knife must be about 20–25 centimeters (8–10 inches) long. To understand the following explanations, note that we say the "heel" of the knife when we mean the part of the blade next to the handle.

Let us also remark that *all of the pieces of a sauté chicken must retain their skin.* You must pay attention to this when you are carving.

Lay the chicken on its side. With your left hand, take hold of the thigh in front of you, pulling it open to pass a knife under it, then cut the skin, holding it to the body. Pull on the thigh to detach it from the carcass, passing the blade of the knife into the joint (see *fig.* 59); turn back the thigh in order to detach it, and pull back, taking off at the same time the little piece of flesh sticking to the carcass. Place the thigh on the table; with the heel of the knife, cut off the end of the bone of the drumstick.

Now you must trim the thigh. In professional kitchens, the thigh is left whole—that is, the drumstick and fleshy part of the thigh are not separated, which makes arranging it on the plate easier and which is also more correct. In contemporary home cooking, it is often better to separate these two limbs, thus getting two pieces instead of one. The choice is yours, but whether the thigh is left whole or divided, the largest part of the bone should always be removed: this gives the meat some flexibility, which lets it take on a better form when it is cooked. To remove a part of this bone, place the thigh flat on the table with the flesh side up and use the back of the knife blade to give it a

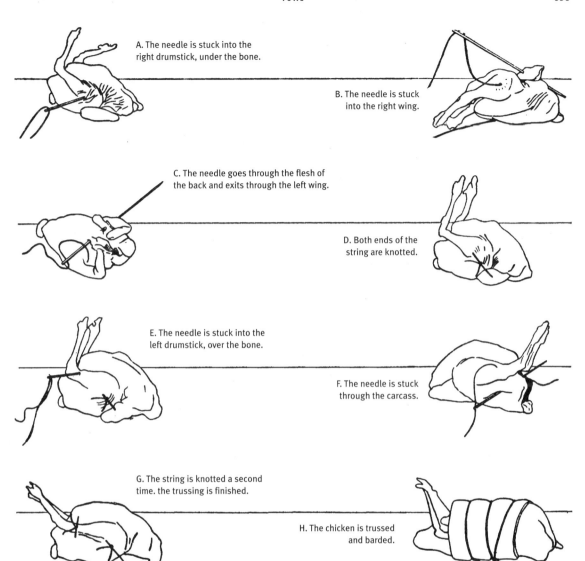

A. The needle is stuck into the right drumstick, under the bone.

B. The needle is stuck into the right wing.

C. The needle goes through the flesh of the back and exits through the left wing.

D. Both ends of the string are knotted.

E. The needle is stuck into the left drumstick, over the bone.

F. The needle is stuck through the carcass.

G. The string is knotted a second time. the trussing is finished.

H. The chicken is trussed and barded.

FIG. 58. BARDING THE FOWL.

FIG. 59. CUTTING THE THIGH.

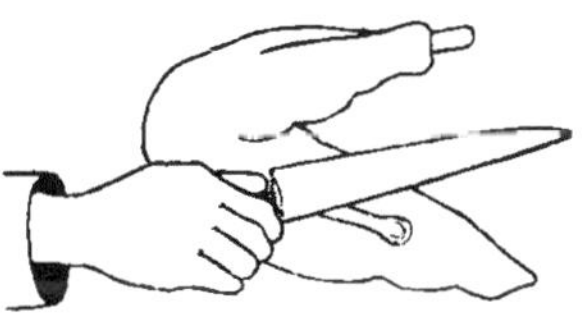

FIG. 60. BONING THE THIGH.

sharp blow around the middle of the bone (see *fig.* 60), rather than near the joint with the drumstick, in order to leave as little of the bone there as possible. Then remove the end of the broken bone without leaving any meat on it. Trimmed in this way, when swollen by cooking, the whole drumstick will take on the shape of a small ham instead of remaining rigid and extended. If the thigh is separated from the drumstick, it too will take on a good shape when cooked, which it would not be able to do if the bone is left there whole.

With the point of the knife, make an incision or a light cut along the entire length of the drumstick on its interior side. This helps the heat reach into the meat of the drumstick, which is more difficult to cook.

Next, detach the wing as you do for a roast chicken. That is, pass the knife into the joint attaching it to the body. Be careful with the skin along the entire length of the wing. With one blow of the knife, separate the tip of the wing from the bone of the wing; with the back of the blade, break the main bone of the wing to prevent the flesh from warping while cooking.

Do exactly the same on the other side of the bird. After this, use a knife to detach the parts of the carcass to which the fillet or white meat are attached. With the heel of the knife, remove the clavicles and the little bits of bone sticking out from it.

Divide the carcass at the back in two, cutting crosswise. With some strong scissors, level up the edges of the pieces of carcass. With one blow of the knife, remove the rump, which is oily and has an unpleasant odor.

You should have a total of 9 pieces. The neck, divided in two, can be used mostly to give a foundation for dressing the bird; if not, combine it with the head, the feet, and the gizzard, and put it into the soup stock or a jus.

Finally, push back the flesh around the bones of the drumstick and the wings, which will let you more easily place a sleeve of curly paper there when dressing the bird to serve.

Boning the Fowl for Galantine

All fowl or game birds are boned in the same way. The most important point to note is to keep the skin of the bird perfectly intact, because it acts as an envelope to contain all the ingredients of the galantine. To avoid damage, it is essential to possess a special knife for boning not only fowl but also meat. This has a blade that is half rounded at the end and is from 20–25 centimeters (8–10 inches) long.

We will use here a chicken as a model for boning.

Clean the beast (SEE PREPARATION OF FOWL, PAGE 349). With a good ordinary kitchen knife, split the skin of the neck on the back side from the head to the thighs. Note that this neck skin plays a very important role in a galantine, as we will see later. *So leave it sticking to the rest of the body and absolutely intact for all its length.*

Empty the crop. Cut off the neck, separating it from the skin at the level of the carcass. Cut off the head, cutting the skin next to the head. Remove the legs and the wing tips at the first joint that leaves the body. With the point of a knife, split the skin of the legs from the claws up to the knees. With your index finger, lift up the package of nerves that you find on the bone, pulling them one by one toward you to make them come out. Then use the back of the knife to strike the base of the thighbone to separate it from the leg.

Now the actual boning begins. Place the beast on the table with its back in the air and rump toward you. Take the special knife and separate the skin on the back from the neck to the rump. From this point, all the work is done on the flesh, always pressing with the rounded point of the knife on the carcass and the bone. Proceed first on the left side of the beast, scraping the carcass to detach the bones up to the joint of the wing. As you go, turn back flesh and skin, holding both in your left hand. Cut the nerves tying the wing to the body. Always scrape on the bone, continuing to detach flesh and skin, reaching as far as kidney level. Do the same on the right side of the animal.

Once the two sides are detached, fold back the flesh and skin on each side of the carcass. Take both wings in your left hand. In your right hand, grab the carcass near the neck. Pull it back, thus exposing the white meat, which remains attached to the wishbone. Stop there. Grab first the right thigh and turn it back, pulling it from the carcass. Do the same for the other thigh. With your knife, separate the thighs from the carcass.

Continue to detach the flesh, scraping the carcass right up until the rump. You now have two absolutely distinct parts. On your left, the flesh has been almost completely removed, with the bones of the wings and the thighs remaining; on your right is the carcass, with the breasts, or white meat, still clinging to the wishbone. The inside has not yet been gutted. With your knife, remove the breasts. With your hands, one holding the wishbone and the other the back, separate the carcass. Take out the lungs, the liver, and the gizzards and put them to one side with the carcass. Throw out the rest. The liver can be added to a hash; the carcass, bones, etc., are added to the bouillon for cooking the galantine.

Finish boning the carcass. Turn it over to expose the bones of the stump of the wings. Cut the nerves there in order to detach this bone from the flesh and then remove it. Do the same for the bones of the thighs, always scraping on the bone. At this point, you can remove about half the flesh from the top of the thigh and the drumstick, then add it to the hash mixture.

The boning is now complete. Return the skin into its original form, which during all this time has been turned back like a glove turned inside out. Put the end of the wings and thighs back inside the flesh to reconstitute these parts into their original appearance. The piece is ready to be made into a galantine.

Truffling a Piece of Fowl

To truffle: To serve an appropriate portion, you must allow 35–40 grams (1¼–1⅜ ounces) of truffles per person, whether it be 2 small truffles or three-quarters of a truffle. This is the net weight after trimming (SEE TRUFFLES, PAGE 537).

Rounds of truffles are often inserted between the skin and the flesh of chickens that are displayed for sale. This is a commercial practice, and they have no reason for being there other than to dress the bird traditionally or even to fool customers into believing the birds have actually been truffled. However, these rounds do not add much aroma to the flesh; and as far as appearance goes, they are useless, since the bird is not normally presented at the table before being carved. Nonetheless, we will explain how to make them.

Use only the fat of pork or grated bacon for truffling. Never use any other stuffing, no matter what it is, because it would absorb all the aroma of the truffle at the expense of the flesh of the bird. The pork fat acts as a liaison for the truffles, and at the same time nourishes them and concentrates their aroma during the cooking. It can be replaced for all small pieces by grated bacon, as long as it is very fresh. For a more elegant truffling, add a little *raw* foie gras to the fat, in the proportion of a fifth for a fattened chicken and a good third for a pheasant or partridge. But this is not essential.

Truffling is done *hot* or *cold* according to circumstance. When the bird must be served the same day or the next day, it is essential to truffle *hot*. The aroma of the warmed truffle spreads more rapidly and thus affects the flesh more quickly. When the piece is prepared in advance, it is better to truffle *cold*, so that the flesh is infused by the odor gradually in a more normal manner. For truffling *cold*, allow at least five days in cool temperatures and three days in moderate and humid weather. Keep the truffled piece in a cool place and, above all, away from any humidity.

PROCEDURE. **The fowl:** Flame it and clean it out as directed for fowl to be stuffed or truffled.

The truffles: Clean them as directed. Peel them as finely as possible. Gather the trimmings to add them to the fat, which you will pass through a drum sieve.

If you use rounds of truffles, first choose 2 of the most attractive and blackest, to cut a dozen rounds from them about 5 millimeters (⅜ inch) thick; put these to one side.

Depending on the size of the truffles, cut the small ones into 2, and the medium and large ones into 3 or 4 pieces. Do not make them too thin, so you make 3 or 4 quarters for each guest. Put them on a salad plate with cognac, Madeira, oil, a pinch of pepper, salt, spices, etc. Let them marinate while you are preparing the pork fat. Mix them around from time to time so they are equally infused.

The fat: Divide the fat into very small pieces. Remove the skin and filaments. Put it in the water and crush it to a fine consistency. When it has been reduced to a purée, add the foie gras, if using it. Gather everything onto a plate. Let stand for a scant half hour in a warm place until the purée softens, so that it can then be passed through a metallic drum sieve. Add the truffled peelings or trimmings so that you pass everything together.

Truffling cold: Once the fat has been passed through the drum sieve, put it in a terrine with the truffles and their marinade, from which you will remove the thyme and bay. Add the rest of the seasonings of salt, pepper, and spices. Mix everything well.

The rounds of truffles: Raise the skin of the beast by sliding your fingers between the breast and the skin, taking great care not to break the skin while doing this. Then introduce the rounds of truffles, reserving 3, to arrange on the breast.

Then proceed to fill up the bird. For this, place the beast on a napkin folded in quarters in front of you. Have the terrine with the mixture on one side. With a soupspoon, introduce it into the bird through the opening of the crop, spreading it around with your fingers. Keep a little bit of fat to fill the hole in the crop. All of the truffles should be placed inside the body.

When the body is filled, finish by filling the hole in the crop with the fat. On top of this fat, place the 3 truffles you have reserved. Fold back the skin of the neck over the back so that you close everything well. Truss the beast thoroughly with a double string as if you were going to roast it. Pass the string around the skin covering the back to fix it firmly there.

Truffling hot: Put the fat, once it has been passed through the drum sieve, into a sauté pan with the rest of the seasoning of salt, pepper, and spices. Gently heat and melt. Add the truffles and the marinade: cover and warm for 10 minutes, but at a temperature no warmer than is comfortable when you dip your finger into it. Let the fat cool until completely solid. Then introduce the mixture, proceeding as for truffling cold.

Crests and Kidneys of Cock for Garnish

The crests: They are better and whiter if you have been able to soak them for 3 or 4 days in cool water, changed 2 or 3 times each day. Choose ones that are nice and pink with long intact barbs.

Once they have disgorged, put them in a small pot, generously bathed in cold water. Heat *very gently.* As soon as the water is warm enough not to allow you to dip your finger into it, drain it. If the crests are sealed, or if the water boils, they will remain red and have no taste: there is nothing you can do about this. But if they have been properly cooked, the crest will have lost all traces of blood and have taken on a uniform gray tint.

Drain them. Rub them in a towel with sea salt to remove the epidermis. Put them back to soak in cold salted water for at least half a day. Then wash them in several changes of cold water, lightly pressing them with your hand to squeeze out all the bloody parts. They should then be a pure porcelain white. Lightly scrape the points that are too thin, and similarly trim the side where they were attached to the head.

To cook: Put them in a boiling *blanc* (SEE PAGE 42). Thus, for 150 grams (5 1/3 ounces) of crest, 1 level tablespoon of flour, 1 1/4 liters (5 1/3 cups) of water, a good pinch of salt, 1 tablespoon of vinegar, and 1 tablespoon of cooking fat. Boil very gently for *35 minutes.*

The kidneys: It is enough to allow them to disgorge in fresh water for 24 hours. Do not peel them: it is enough just to remove the string. They need to cook for no more than 10 minutes in the same *blanc* used for cooking the crest.

If you use preserved kidneys and crests, drain the crests and kidneys, then heat them in a little salted water.

FATTED CHICKENS, HENS, YOUNG CHICKENS
Poularde, Poule, Poulet

Truffled Fattened Chickens *(Poularde Truffée)*

For truffling the chicken and all points to note, SEE PAGE 355. Here we will consider a chicken that is ready to be cooked and will not concern ourselves with either the ingredients for truffling or the actual cooking of the chicken.

You can serve a truffled chicken accompanied with a sauce Périgueux: the trimmings of the truffles are then reserved for the sauce. But the simple roasting juices remain the best accompaniment. Truffled dishes are never surrounded with watercress. *Time: About 20 minutes of cooking per 450 grams (1 pound). Serves 10–12.*

1 fattened chicken with a net weight of about 1.8 kilograms (4 pounds) and 1.4 kilograms (3 pounds, 1 ounce) when gutted; 500 grams (1 pound, 2 ounces) of pork fat; 125 grams (4 1/2 ounces) of *raw* foie gras or 125 grams (4 1/2 ounces) of additional fat; a bard of fatback bacon large enough to wrap the piece or 2 medium pieces; 550 grams (1 pound, 3 ounces) of truffles, net weight; 4 tablespoons of cognac; 3 tablespoons of Madeira; 2 tablespoons of oil; 20 grams (2/3 ounce) of salt; 3–4 grams (1/10–1/8 ounce) of pepper; 2 grams (1/14 ounce) of spices; 1 sprig of thyme; 1 small bay leaf.

PROCEDURE. Before you put the chicken on the fire, surround it with the bards, without pulling them too tight so that the heat does not break them when they shrivel; secure them with the string. Weigh the chicken. *The cooking time of a truffled bird is based on the weight of a bird that has been completely truffled and barded.* Wrap the bird in 2 sheets of paper that have been generously buttered, one doubling over the other, for more resistance. Secure them with the string.

In the oven: This is the most common method of roasting and it gives an excellent result for a large bird like this.

Place the bird on a rack in a roasting pan. Just before you put it in the oven, baste it with some good melted lard. It is useless to baste it further while cooking. Turn it only when necessary. Use a medium oven, maintained at the same temperature throughout the cooking time. The heat must penetrate the flesh gradually, which also determines the melting of the fat and the cooking of the truffles. If the heat were too strong, the bird would be too dry on the outside while the inside would be undercooked.

Allow *18–20 minutes* of cooking per 450 grams (1 pound), the bird having been weighed *completely truffled,* as directed. *About 8 minutes* before the cooking time is over, remove the paper and the bards so that the chicken can take on a light coloration without completely browning. Check the cooking by sticking a cooking needle deeply into the thigh at the thickest point. If the juice pearls pink, leave it for another 8 or 9 minutes.

On the spit: The beast should be barded and wrapped the same way. If you do not have a cage to support the roast, avoiding the need for piercing it with the spit, make sure you take great care not to tear the skin of the neck around the hole where the spit passes through. Both holes might let all the stuffing escape: a veritable disaster. Attach the legs to the spit with a string. Surround them with greased parchment paper.

Roasting on the spit requires a little more time than in the oven (SEE ROASTS, PAGE 30). So allow *20–22 minutes* per 450 grams (1 pound).

To serve: Untie the bird. Place it on a long plate, either whole or carved with the truffles in the middle. Partially degrease the juice and pass it through a chinois into a pan. If the amounts seems a little scarce, add several tablespoons of veal juice to the roasting pan, or simply some water to deglaze it—that is, detach and dissolve the gratinée parts. Boil it for a minute before passing it through the drum sieve.

Chicken with Sea Salt
(La Poule au Gros Sel)

Even though this seems the simplest method for cooking chicken, there are still difficulties with it, as will be explained.

To improve a bouillon, and at the same time to make the best possible use of a chicken that is no longer young, the classic procedure is to cook it barded with bacon in the marmite of a pot-au-feu with beef, mutton, or veal, according to choice. Submerge it in the pot-au-feu, having first calculated the time needed for cooking the chicken, which is, of course, determined by its age and quality. Nonetheless, be aware that prolonged cooking cannot make an old and tough bird tender; only the bouillon is improved by this.

A chicken cooked in this manner is simply served basted with 3 tablespoons of completely degreased bouillon with a few grains of sea salt on its breast. *Time: About 1 hour for cooking.*

For a young chicken or a pullet, you can proceed according to the recipe by Gouffé. Put the fowl in a pot with 1/2 liter (generous 2 cups) of bouillon, an onion stuck with a clove, and a bouquet garni. Bring it to a boil. Cover with buttered parchment paper underneath the cover itself.

Cook it on top of the stove at a gentle and regular simmer for *45 minutes to 1 hour.* Turn the bird over in the middle of cooking to completely reach the part that has not been submerged in the liquid. Pass the juices through a drum sieve and reduce the cooking liquid. Pour it on the chicken. Serve gray sea salt on the side.

The jus resulting from this reduction must be light, clear, and without any element of thickening: this is the characteristic of a dish served with sea salt. There should be only enough to thoroughly moisten the bird. In other words, about 1½ deciliters (5 fluid ounces, ⅔ cup) of reduced juice. Note: because of this reduction, use only a bouillon that is very lightly salted. If the bird has been carved in the kitchen, you should likewise baste the pieces.

For a young chicken, there is another method used by commercial restaurants. It simply includes the use of a *font blanc:* that is, a good veal jus that has not colored. The bird is poached in it at the same time as a garnish of small carrots and small onions, as with the vegetables in a pot-au-feu. Then it is served surrounded by vegetables, with the sea salt served apart and the juices from the cooking, reduced and not thickened, in a sauceboat.

Allow for this dish: 2½ liters (10½ cups) of bouillon *blanc;* 12 small onions; 12 small quarters of carrots taken from the red part; 4 good deciliters (1⅔ cups) of cooking liquid reduced to 2 deciliters (6¾ fluid ounces, ⅞ cup); a bard of fatback bacon. The bird must be covered by the liquid, which you pour in cold. Bring it to a boil. Skim. Add the garnish of vegetables. Cover and leave a small opening for the steam. Once boiling has resumed, keep it at a very gentle and regular rate for *1 scant hour* for a young chicken of good quality.

Fattened Hen à l'Ivoire
(Poularde à l'Ivoire)

A generous quantity of heavy cream is characteristic of a sauce ivoire, as is the fact that it is not bound with egg yolks, unlike the sauce for fowl *au blanc.*

At any rate, the sauce must use only the liquid in which the bird was cooked. In haute cuisine, professional kitchens will always have stock ready, so the procedures are different from those of home kitchens: the sauce can be bound with a sauce béchamel added to the reduced cooking juices from the hen. Here, we limit ourselves to the simplest recipe for making the sauce. *Time: 50–55 minutes to cook the hen; 10–15 minutes for the sauce. Serves 6–8.*

1 nice fattened hen weighing about 2 kilograms (4 pounds, 6 ounces); a half lemon to rub it; 2 large bards to enclose it.

The ingredients for cooking are the same as for CHICKEN AU BLANC (PAGE 361).

***For the sauce:* A white roux with 25 grams (1 ounce) of flour and 25 grams (1 ounce, 2 tablespoons) of butter; 3 deciliters (1¼ cups) of reduced cooking juice from the hen; 3 deciliters (1¼ cups) of very fresh, heavy cream.**

PROCEDURE. **The fatted hen:** Prepare it as directed for the hen *au blanc,* with the one extra detail that you rub it with lemon before wrapping it in the bards. This helps to keep the flesh as white as possible. To cook it, proceed as for a hen *au blanc.*

The sauce: Strain the cooking liquid of the hen into a terrine. Degrease 6–7 deciliters (2½–3 cups) of it, and boil rapidly to reduce it by half: to at least 3 deciliters (1¼ cups). Pour this reduced jus into a bowl.

In the same sauté pan, make a white roux with butter and flour (SEE LIAISON WITH ROUX, PAGE 47). Dilute it in the warm juice using a whisk. Then put it back on strong heat. Stirring continuously, add the cream gradually—that is, in 4 or 5 additions—adding a fresh amount only when it has resumed boiling; this takes just a few minutes. The sauce should be perfectly smooth and just thick enough with a beautiful white matte tint to justify its name. It can also be kept warm in a double boiler until you are ready to serve. SEE KEEPING SAUCES WARM (PAGE 50).

To serve: You should always carve this dish in the kitchen because the skin should be removed from the pieces. Take off the bards. Detach the thighs and separate the drumstick from the upper thighs. Detach the wings at the same time that you cut the breast, or *blanc (as it is known in France;*

literally "white meat"). Divide each wing into 3 pieces cut on the bias. You will have 6 pieces in total. Arrange them on a round plate that has been well warmed. Cover it with a few tablespoons of sauce and serve the rest in a sauceboat.

Chicken with Rice *(La Poule au Riz)*

There are many ways to make this, depending on the type of bird available and also your preferred way of preparing rice, not to mention the time, trouble, and expense you are willing to undergo.

So a chicken with rice can, if it is a beast that is already somewhat old and tough, be cooked for a long time in the same pan as a beef pot-au-feu, right along with the beef, and then simply served just as it is. Or, if it is a young hen, it can be poached for no more than 1 hour in a light veal bouillon and then served with a sauce made from its cooking juices; bound with egg yolks as for a hen *au blanc;* or it can be braised and served with its reduced cooking juices.

On the other hand, the rice can, according to the situation and taste, be cooked with the chicken itself; or separately, using the cooking liquid from the chicken; or *à l'indienne* in a large amount of water; or in the manner of a risotto. And it can be served underneath the chicken; as a border; or on the side. Below we will describe the principal recipes. If you like, you can modify both the way you make the rice and the way you serve it. SEE RICE (PAGE 561).

You generally allow 200 grams (7 ounces) of rice to serve with a fowl. This amount can be reduced or increased, depending on the way the rice is presented. When it is served underneath the fowl, it can probably be reduced. Generally speaking, and if you are cooking for French tastes, the rice served with the chicken must be very moist, with a little bit of excess of its cooking liquid, though this should not prevent the grains from being distinct and intact.

Chicken with Rice *(Poule au Riz).* This is the simplest home-style method. *Time: From 1½–2 hours, depending on the condition of the hen.*

1 medium-size chicken; 750 milliliters (generous 3 cups) of bouillon that has not been degreased (only a light bouillon is needed, so you can dilute it by half with water); 1 medium-size onion (80 grams, 2¾ ounces), stuck with a clove; a bouquet garni; 200 grams (7 ounces) of good Carolina rice.

PROCEDURE. Use a good, deep pot, not too large, but with enough room for the rice to swell as it cooks. Put in the chicken, the bouillon, the onion, the bouquet; do not salt it if the bouillon is already salted.

Bring to a boil. Place buttered parchment paper right on the breast of the beast and a cover that closes tightly on top. If you have a medium-heat oven, put the pot there. If not, place it over *moderate* heat. Either way, make sure the liquid is bubbling gently but regularly. If you are not cooking in the oven, but on the stove, make sure that you turn the chicken in the pot so that the heat reaches every part of it.

The length of cooking time is proportional here to both the weight and the quality of the beast. It will also take a bit longer when the chicken is not cooked in the oven, where the heat envelops the entire pan. While 45 minutes of gentle boiling could suffice for a very young chicken, you must allow an hour for a larger bird, and 1½ hours if the bird is also older.

It would, therefore, be sensible to take precautions when you are not certain of the necessary cooking time for a chicken that is neither young nor very good. That is, begin cooking sufficiently in advance to prolong it if necessary; it will not be inconvenient if the chicken has to stand in the pot, keeping warm, until you are ready to serve.

The rice: Once the rice has been previously washed, blanched, and cooled, allow *15–25 minutes of very gentle, regular boiling for its cooking.* So however long the chicken takes, do not add the rice until the exact moment when its cooking will not exceed this scant half hour. Although chicken can stand for a long time without spoiling, the same is not true of rice.

Simply add the rice to the pot on each side of the chicken. For 200 grams (7 ounces) of rice, you need *at least a good half liter (generous 2 cups)* of liquid. If the cooking for the chicken has been prolonged and the liquid has been greatly reduced, you can simply top it up with bouillon or even with water.

To serve: Place the chicken on the plate. Remove the onion and bouquet. Tilt the pot to remove the little bit of fat that has risen on the top of the rice. Check to see if salt is needed. Arrange the rice around the chicken. There should be whole, completely intact grains, separated but very moist.

Chicken with Rice in the Method of a Chicken au Blanc *(Poule au Riz Façon Poulet au Blanc).* Proceed exactly the same as for cooking CHICKEN AU BLANC (PAGE 361): the same quantities, the same procedures, only leave out the mushrooms.

Wash, blanch, and completely drain the rice. Put it in the pot with 2½ times its volume of cooking liquid from the chicken, *which has not been degreased.* So, for 180 grams of rice (6⅓ ounces), you need 5 deciliters (generous 2 cups) of bouillon. You can take out this bouillon 10–15 minutes before the chicken has finished cooking, so that the rice is ready when the sauce is and there is no delay in serving. SEE RICE WITH MEAT BOUILLON (PAGE 563).

The sauce: 3 deciliters (1¼ cups) will suffice. Thus: 20 grams (⅔ ounce, 1 heaping tablespoon) of butter and 20 grams (⅔ ounce) of flour for the roux; 3 good deciliters (1¼ cups) of degreased bouillon from the chicken; 1 egg yolk with 1 tablespoon of cream; 15 grams (½ ounce, 1 tablespoon) of butter to finish.

To serve: Degrease the rice if necessary. Arrange it on a plate, either under the chicken or on each side; or molded in a round buttered mold. Pour the sauce over the chicken, either left whole or carved in the kitchen.

Braised Chicken with Rice *(Poule au Riz Façon Braisée).* *Time: About 1½ hours. Time varies a little according to the weight and quality of the beast. It also varies according to the method by which the rice is prepared. See below for further comments on this subject. Serves 6.*

1 medium-size chicken not older than 2 years; a bard of fatback bacon; 100 grams (3½ ounces) of fresh bacon; 60 grams (2¼ ounces) of onions; 60 grams (2¼ ounces) of carrot, only the red part; a bouquet garni; 7½ deciliters (generous 3 cups) of ordinary bouillon.

For the rice: **150 grams of Patna or Carolina rice (5⅓ ounces); 3 deciliters (1¼ cups) of ordinary bouillon; and 1 deciliter (3⅓ fluid ounces, scant ½ cup) of cooking liquid from the chicken to cook it (you should allow here 2½ times liquid for the volume of rice).**

PROCEDURE. Truss the chicken as for an entrée. Cover the breast with the bard; secure it with two turns of string without pulling too tight, because the flesh will swell when it's cooked.

Cut the bacon into slices as thin as possible. Cut the onion into *thick* rounds and the carrot into thin slices taken from the red part.

Use a pot made of thick aluminum; avoid cast iron, which will give the cooking juices an unpleasant color. Spread the slices of bacon over the bottom of the pot; on top of it, spread the onion and the carrot; on top of everything, place the fowl with the barded side up. Completely cover the pot. Put it over very moderate heat to sweat the chicken and vegetables for *about 20 minutes.*

Raise the cover from time to time to see how the "sweating" is progressing. Little by little, the chicken swells and whitens, and a white steam escapes from the pot. While the steam rises, you know that nothing has stuck to the bottom; as soon as it disappears and you also see a *very light* caramel—an indication of *pinçage* (as professionals call it)—sweating is complete. SEE BRAISING WHITE MEATS (PAGE 28).

Pour the bouillon into the pot. The liquid must come up to half the height of the bird and cover the thick part of the thigh. Bring it to a boil. Place buttered parchment paper right on top of the chicken underneath the cover. Put it in a medium oven so that you maintain the liquid at a gentle simmer, which should not vary throughout the cooking time.

A scant hour should suffice for a medium-size bird of good quality.

The rice: Begin to take care of this about 45 minutes before you are ready to serve. Prepare it and cook it as directed (SEE RICE COOKED WITH MEAT BOUILLON, PAGE 563). The bouillon from the chicken should be taken from the fattiest part. Add a little bit of grated nutmeg.

To finish and serve: Once the chicken has been properly cooked, remove it to a plate, draining it well by the rump. Strain the cooking juice into a small container. Remove the strings and the bard from the chicken. Put it back into its pot. Cover it. Keep it warm.

Completely degrease the cooking juice. Pour it into a small saucepan. Boil it and skim it. Once it has reduced to scarcely 3 deciliters ($1^1/_4$ cups), bind it lightly with starch or arrowroot (SEE LIAISONS, PAGE 47). Remove the little bit of fat that remains on the surface of the rice. Place it on the serving plate, either underneath the chicken or on each side. Place the chicken on the serving plate. Pour the thickened juice on everything.

NOTE. Once you have cooked the chicken, you can also use its cooking juice to cook the rice. In this case, do not bind the juice, as directed. And cook the chicken a half hour in advance for its cooking juices. Then keep it warm in its pot with a few tablespoons of juice while the rice cooks. Do not degrease the juice for cooking the rice.

Chicken Casserole in Aspic *(Poule en Daube à la Gelée)*

What is known in families as *daube* is usually a cold preparation, *en gelée* (in aspic); and when it refers to fowl, the name tends to be reserved for a bird that is rather old and consequently not very tender. In this case, the best recipe is for STUFFED DUCK IN ASPIC (PAGE 384).

The recipe for a cold daube includes some variations; it can prepared as a type of braised dish, with a veal foot added to the braising liquid to provide the gelatin to set it. You first sweat the chicken, to obtain the light *pinçage* or shrinking (SEE BRAISING WHITE MEATS, PAGE 28), and then add the cooking liquid. Or, for home cooking, put the chicken immediately into this cooking liquid, which should be made up of juice that is more veal than beef (SEE SIMPLE ASPIC, PAGE 46).

If the fowl is young, and if its cooking does not exceed $1^1/_2$ hours, the braising liquid can be prepared far enough in advance so that the meat has released its juices and the veal foot its gelatin by the time that the chicken is submerged in it. Bring it back to a boil and continue boiling very gently, almost imperceptibly.

It is not possible to be exact about the quantity of cooking juice because this will depend on how much it has reduced while cooking the chicken, which could take up to *3 hours*. In any case, whatever liquid is used, it must completely cover the beast throughout the entire cooking time.

Once the chicken has been cooked and the string from the trussing removed, drain it thoroughly, holding it by the rump, and then place it on a plate, breast down. Strain the cooking juice, then clarify, as described under aspic.

To simplify, you may prefer to eliminate this clarification. If so, the juice, which has already been scrupulously degreased by being strained through the chinois and rested, should be strained again by carefully decanting it through a moistened towel. That is, pour it slowly so that you do not also pour out any of the solid matter that sank to the bottom while the liquid was resting; otherwise the limpidity of the liquid will be affected. For that reason, it must be said, that clarifying with egg white is preferable. Let the liquid get almost cold; you should have at least 1 liter ($4^1/_4$ cups). Add 3 tablespoons of Madeira, then pour it on the chicken. Keep it in a very cool place until the next day. Unmold it when you are ready to serve. Accompany it with a salad.

Chicken au Blanc *(Le Poulet au Blanc)*

A recipe that comes from good, old-fashioned home cooking, for which each family believes it has the best recipe. The lengthiest ones often contain some absolutely useless directions—for example, enclosing the fowl in cloth to preserve its whiteness—as well as some that are simply mistaken, such as those for cooking the sauce.

The sensible recipe for chicken *au blanc* can be summarized thus: cook gently or poach the fowl in its cooking liquid, fully covered so that there is no contact with the air. Cook the garnish of mushrooms on the side. Make a blond sauce with a white roux, using the cooking bouillon from the fowl, and prepare a liaison with egg yolks and cream.

For a chicken *au blanc,* the fowl is cooked whole, even if the chicken is carved in the kitchen before being brought to the dining room. If it is carved before it is cooked, it becomes a fricassée of chicken. Not only do pieces of chicken cooked this way look different, having more or less shriveled up and warped during cooking, but the flavor is not the same: the wing of a chicken *au blanc* is much tastier, its flesh having stayed much more moist than a wing from a fricassée.

The fowl chosen for this dish must be of a very good quality, fleshy rather than fatty, preferably a nice young hen, tender and with a white skin and flesh. Chickens from Nantes, as good as they are, are not recommended here because of their black feathers, and the small tubes that can sometimes be left after plucking.

The liquid used for cooking the chicken must be a light jus made with veal only, and not beef bouillon, which is so frequently and incorrectly used: even diluted half and half with water, as it often is for this type of cooking, the flavor is not delicate enough for recipes like this. If you do not have veal bouillon, it is much better to improvise, as we have suggested, using a light bouillon made with the intestines of the bird.

Do not put little onions in the chicken *au blanc;* these are reserved for a fricassée. But mushrooms are essential here. It is better to cook them separately, for the reasons already given (SEE MUSHROOMS, PAGE 490). In addition to mushrooms, chicken *au blanc* is sometimes accompanied by little dumplings bought at the pâtisserie and made of veal sweetbreads, which are not very expensive. Thus prepared, chicken *au blanc,* which was such a feature of Sunday family dinners, was a home-cooked adaptation of fowl *à la toulousaine,* a nod to the haute cuisine of the time. Sometimes cream was added to the liaison made with egg yolks, and we suggest adding it here, even though this is similar to the sauce for a fricassée; the recipe for chicken *au blanc* is not unchanging, and it is simply a matter of taste. You can replace the cream with 2 or 3 tablespoons of reduced milk and add a little more butter to the sauce after thickening it with the egg yolk liaison.

Some recipes suggest cooking the chicken in boiling liquid to seal the flesh and thus concentrate the juices in it. The suggestion is a good one, and it certainly works, but at the expense of the sauce; the fowl will not release its juices to the liquid as generously as when it is put into cold liquid. And in this recipe for chicken *au blanc,* the sauce is particularly important.

Throughout the cooking time, the liquid must cover the chicken, so it is important, particularly for the sauce, that the casserole chosen be the right size. A large utensil would need more liquid: the taste that it would communicate to the chicken would therefore be weakened, and this in turn would reduce the sauce's flavor. Make sure that there is a space of 2 centimeters (3/4 inch) between the wall of the utensil and the fowl, so that the bird is surrounded on all sides by liquid; this is quite enough space. Always use a deep casserole in good aluminum. If not, use a good enameled steel casserole or even a good clay pot, a little marmite, or a deep pot. But never use cast iron, which can disagreeably tint the chicken and affect the juice. *Time: 1 1/2 hours (once the bouillon has already been prepared). Serves 6.*

1 fowl plucked and gutted without any organs left inside, weighing 1 good kilogram (2 pounds, 3 ounces); a bard of fatback bacon of about 100 grams (3 1/2 ounces) to completely cover the chest of the beast.

For the cooking: About 1 1/2 liters (6 1/3 cups) of bouillon made with the giblets; 125 grams (4 1/2 ounces) of carrots; 100 grams (3 1/2 ounces) of onion; 15 grams (1/2 ounce) of celery; 15 grams (1/2 ounce) of parsley sprigs; 10 grams (1/3 ounce) of salt; 3 deciliters (1 1/4 cup) of white wine; some trimmings of bacon; 1 piece of lard or butter the size of a walnut; the peelings from the mushrooms, and a clove.

For the sauce: 40 grams (1 3/8 ounces, 3 tablespoons) of butter and 30 grams (1 ounce) of flour for the roux; a good half-liter (generous 2 cups) of bouillon from the cooking; 3 egg yolks; 1 scant deciliter (3 1/3 fluid ounces, scant 1/2 cup) of fresh heavy cream; 30 grams (1 ounce, 2 tablespoons) of fresh butter to finish the sauce; 250 grams (8 7/8 ounces) of mushrooms cooked separately.

PROCEDURE. **The bouillon:** If it contains a little bit of veal foot—which would, of course, be preferable—prepare the bouillon well in advance so that it can cook for hours. If not, and only if the carrot used is not old or hard, you can start cooking it a brief hour before cooking the fowl.

In the casserole, spread out the lard or the butter; the trimmings from the fatback bacon; the carrot, cut into very thin and equal slices; the onion, cut into quarters; the celery; the parsley; and the giblets. Cover and place it on very gentle heat to sweat it *without letting it color.* If necessary, add 1 tablespoon of water from time to time. You can allow a *scant half hour* for this sweating. Once the vegetables have been softened enough, as if part of a compote, add just enough water to cover them. And if you have the time, continue cooking them for a moment longer with just this little bit of liquid. If not, you can immediately add the fowl.

To cook: Lay the fowl on its back in the casserole on top of the vegetables. Add the lukewarm bouillon and the wine, enough so that there is 1 centimeter (3/8 inch) above the bird. Bring it to a boil on moderate heat. Remove the little bit of foam that rises to the surface when the liquid starts to boil. Add the mushroom peelings, clove, and salt. Cover the casserole, leaving a very small opening for the steam. From this point, the liquid should not boil but *barely simmer,* so that the chicken is cooked by poaching for *50–55 minutes.*

Check that it is done by piercing the flesh of the drumstick joint, which takes the longest to cook. The pearl of juice released must be completely white. Strain the cooking bouillon into a terrine. Leave the fowl in its casserole to keep it good and hot while preparing the sauce.

The sauce: In a 1-liter (4-cup) casserole, make a *white* roux that is well cooked (SEE LIAISON WITH ROUX, PAGE 47). Dilute it with at least 5 deciliters (generous 2 cups) of bouillon from the chicken, which must still be hot. Mix it with the whisk until it boils. Turn the heat down and carefully skim the sauce for about another 20 minutes. From time to time add some of the cold cooking liquid from the mushrooms: in all, 3 or 4 tablespoons (SEE SKIMMING, PAGE 16).

Make the liaison with egg yolks and cream (SEE LIAISONS, PAGE 47). After letting it boil for 2 minutes, turn off the heat. Spread a few pieces of butter on the surface of the sauce. You will add the rest at the time of serving. Cover, and keep it warm in a double boiler to avoid boiling, which would reduce the sauce. If you think the sauce is too thick, you can dilute it with a few tablespoons of well-degreased bouillon from the fowl.

To serve: Cut the strings and remove the bard from the fowl, then carefully drain the liquid that remains in the interior by the rump. Place it on a heated serving plate. Arrange the mushrooms, well drained, all around it or in groups. Cover everything with the sauce, applying it 1 tablespoon at a time. Pour the rest of the sauce into the sauceboat.

If the chicken is carved in the kitchen, place the pieces one next to the other on a plate, arranging the mushroom garnish as you like, and then covering everything with sauce, serving the rest in a sauceboat.

Fricassée of Chicken *(La Fricassée de Poulet)*

The different recipes for a fricassée of chicken are as diverse as those for a chicken *au blanc.* But the basics remain the same, whatever the method of cooking: the chicken, carved into pieces before cooking, is served surrounded by its garnish with a sauce made from its cooking liquids and bound with egg yolks and cream. It is in the actual method of cooking that differences appear: we are not going to describe all these here, but confine ourselves to just the two best recipes.

The liquid used in haute cuisine is a white stock—that is, a bouillon or light jus that includes only veal as its meat. In home cooking, it is more often water. Everything we have said under chicken *au blanc* about the use of beef bouillon and how to make a light bouillon from vegetables and giblets is equally true for a fricassée of chicken. Some people add some white wine to it in the amount of 2 deciliters (6 3/4 fluid ounces, 7/8 cup) for 8 deciliters (3 3/8 cups) of water or bouillon.

Serve the fricassée by itself or surrounded by a garnish, cooked separately: the classic garnish, and the one most often served, is mushrooms and small onions. Also good are crests and kidneys, slices of truffles, crayfish, veal sweetbreads, olives, etc. Or try a vegetable garnish: either carrots or turnips cut into balls, braised in butter or cooked in bouillon; or celery stalks or artichoke bottoms or green peas, asparagus tips, green beans, etc., cooked à l'anglaise (blanched).

Choose a nice fleshy chicken, grain fed if possible, for a fricassée. It is better to use aluminum pans if you do not have tinned copper. No cast iron, which often lends a gray tint to this type of recipe.

To carve the bird for cooking: You can do this in two ways, whichever you prefer.

Either carve as *for sautéing;* but in this case, you must always separate the drumstick from the upper part of the thigh. Or carve *à vif:* that is, leaving a piece of the carcass attached to the carved flesh. This is the best way, and you proceed as follows.

Take a very good kitchen knife, with a large blade that must measure at least 25 centimeters (10 inches) in length. Pass the blade through the joint of the thigh; but instead of drawing it toward you to detach the thigh, as you would usually do, push the knife into the carcass, continuing in the same direction until you reach the rump; in other words, you are including the part of the carcass on which you find one of the oysters. Cut the joint of the thigh to separate it from the drumstick; carve 2 pieces from the upper part of the thigh by cutting it a little bit on the bias lengthwise after removing a part of the bone; do the same operation on the other side. Also remove the wing, cutting into the carcass along the breast until the end. Be careful not to cut the fillets of the breasts, which must remain intact. Leave each wing whole, but remove the wing tips. Cut the breast in 2 pieces across its length. Cut the back the same way.

This will make 14 pieces in total: 2 drumsticks; 2 wings; 2 wing tips; 4 pieces from the top of the thigh; 2 pieces of breast; 2 pieces of back. Each piece of chicken must be covered with its skin. The neck, head, legs, and giblets are reserved to add to the bouillon and are not served in the fricassée.

Classic Chicken Fricassée *(Fricassée de Poulet à l'Ancienne Mode).* This preparation is like chicken *au blanc,* applied to a chicken that has been cut into pieces. *Time: 2 hours. Serves 6.*

1 chicken gutted and plucked, etc., weighing a good kilogram (2 pounds, 3 ounces).

Cooking: 1 liter (4 1/4 cups) of water; 1 medium-size onion stuck with a clove; the red part of a medium-size carrot sliced into thin slices; a bouquet garni; 10 grams (1/3 ounce) of salt.

For the sauce: 50 grams of butter (1 3/4 ounces, 3 1/2 tablespoons) and 50 grams (1 3/4 ounces) of flour; 7 1/2 deciliters (generous 3 cups) of cooking bouillon; a liaison of 3 egg yolks and 3 tablespoons of good, thick cream; the juice of 1/4 lemon.

For the garnish: 125 grams of mushrooms (4 1/2 ounces) cooked separately; 12–15 small onions and 20 grams (2/3 ounce, 1 heaping tablespoon) of butter to cook them on the side.

PROCEDURE. In a deep casserole made of good aluminum, put the pieces of chicken, carrot, onion, bouquet garni, and salt. Pour in the *hot* water.

Bring it to a boil, but not too quickly, on very moderate heat. Remove the little bit of foam. Once it has begun to boil, cover the casserole, leaving a small opening for the passage of steam. Turn the heat down very low. Let it cook no longer than a *scant hour* at a very regular mild simmer.

In 2 small separate casseroles, prepare the small onions (SEE PAGE 525) and the mushrooms (SEE PAGE 490). Once the sauce has started to cook, you can add 2 or 3 tablespoons of it to the onions to finish cooking. Put the trimmings from the mushrooms into the casserole with the chicken.

The sauce: Once the chicken has been cooked for the time suggested, pour all its cooking liquid into a receptacle, without disturbing the chicken in its casserole. Cover tightly and keep it warm without cooking it further.

Take a casserole with a 1-liter (4-cup) capacity. With the butter and flour, make a well cooked white roux (SEE LIAISON WITH A ROUX, PAGE 47). Dilute it with the hot cooking liquid of the chicken. Whisk it and stir it until it boils. On low heat, skim it (SEE PAGE 16) for *about 20 minutes.* While skimming, add a total of *3 tablespoons* of the cooking liquid from the mushrooms. Finally, make the liaison with egg yolks and cream (SEE LIAISONS, PAGE 47).

Waiting until ready to serve: Put the pieces of chicken on a plate. Thoroughly rinse the casserole with warm water. Put the pieces back into the casserole, having checked that they are clean, free of any fragments of skin, of foam, parsley, etc. Then pour the thickened sauce over them, passing it through the chinois or a very fine strainer. Add the mushrooms, well drained. Keep the onions on the side so they do not lose their shape. Check the seasoning and add a pinch of white pepper.

Put the completely covered casserole into a low casserole full of boiling water to serve as a double boiler. Keep it over gentle heat until ready to serve.

To serve: In a shallow bowl or in a large serving dish, arrange the pieces in a dome, reserving the breast and wings for the top of the dome. Pour the sauce over it. Surround it with mushrooms and onions as a double ring. Serve.

Home-Style Fricassée of Chicken *(Fricassée de Poulet à la Ménagère).* This method is excellent, and is often considered to be the one most in keeping with this type of preparation. So much so that it is equally used in haute cuisine.

The fricassée here is served au naturel—that is, without any garnish and with less sauce. But all sorts of garnishes can be added to it if you like, including those for the classic fricassée, as described above. If so, you need only to increase the quantity of sauce, counting 6 or 7 grams (1/5–1/4 ounce) more for the roux for each deciliter of liquid (3 1/3 fluid ounces, scant 1/2 cup) added for the cooking of the chicken, an additional egg yolk for the liaison, and a little more cream, which is typical of this kind of preparation. *Time: A good hour. Serves 6.*

1 chicken, cleaned, without giblets, weighing about a good kilogram (2 pounds, 3 ounces); 40 grams (1 3/8 ounces, 3 tablespoons) of butter; 30 grams (1 ounce) of flour; 7 1/2 deciliters (generous 3 cups) of light "blanc" bouillon or water; 8 grams (1/3 ounce) of salt.

If cooking in water, add an onion of about 30 grams (1 ounce) stuck with a clove; a bouquet of 6 or 7 parsley sprigs attached with a double turn of string.

For the liaison: 2 nice egg yolks; 1 deciliter (3 1/3 fluid ounces, scant 1/2 cup) of *very fresh* heavy cream.

PROCEDURE. Use a thick-bottomed sauté pan just large enough to contain the pieces of chicken without their being too crowded or squeezed together.

Gently heat the butter. Arrange the pieces, seasoned with salt and white pepper, the skin side touching the bottom of the pan. Cover. Place the casserole on very moderate heat.

The pieces of chicken should simply tighten up *without coloring.* This preliminary sautéeing is intended to firm up the flesh and dry out the bloody parts, which would color the sauce. The pieces are thus nice and white, puffed up, with a good shape. You should turn them once carefully, without piercing them with the fork, during this braising, which requires *at the most about 10 minutes.*

You can make the roux in two ways: either sprinkle the pieces of chicken with the flour and cook it *without allowing it to color,* mixing the pieces to coat evenly with the flour; then add the warm liquid and mix continuously until it boils to detach the flour from the pieces and the bottom of the utensil. Or—and this is always better—remove the pieces from the plate to make a white roux with the fat that remains in the casserole (SEE LIAISON WITH ROUX, PAGE 47). Not only does the roux itself cook better, but it is easier to mix the liquid, particularly if you are not used to doing this.

Dilute the roux with the bouillon. Bring it to a boil. Immediately put the pieces of chicken into the casserole, adding onion and parsley if you are cooking with water. Add the juices that have been released by the pieces onto the plate. Once it has returned to a boil, cover the casserole. Turn the heat down very low so that you maintain a very gentle, regular simmer for *45 minutes.*

Be careful during this time that nothing sticks to the bottom of the casserole, particularly toward the end of the cooking when the sauce has reduced and become thicker. It must at this moment not be more than 5 deciliters (generous 2 cups).

The liaison of yolks and cream can be made as soon as the cooking is complete, keeping the covered casserole in a double boiler; or you could make it just before serving, keeping the casserole warm until then. Make the liaison in the casserole itself where the pieces of chicken are, as described (SEE LIAISONS, PAGE 47). Check the seasoning.

To dress the plate and serve: Proceed as for the classic fricassée, straining the sauce through the chinois on the chicken.

Tarragon Chicken *(Le Poulet à l'Estragon)*

There are no fixed rules for this preparation. According to taste, the other courses on the menu, the means at your disposal, and the nature of the beast—whether it be a young chicken, a fattened hen, or a chicken that is already somewhat old—you can poach it or braise it; accompany it with a blond sauce bound with egg yolk or simply the reduced cooking juices thickened with starch; or, following a classic recipe, cook the bird on the spit or in the oven, wrapped in bards of fatback bacon and parchment paper, and serve with a clear jus flavored with tarragon leaves.

Whichever recipe you choose, the chicken must always be cooked carefully to preserve its whiteness. This is helped by the bard of bacon protecting the bird, which also nourishes the flesh. For both reasons, this should never be neglected.

When the fowl is served before carving, decorate its breast with blanched tarragon leaves. If it is carved in the kitchen, you can decorate the larger pieces after having placed them on the serving plate. But it is enough to cover them with a little bit of sauce or jus.

The tarragon must, of course, always be fresh. For the decoration, take a dozen of the nicest leaves detached from the stem. Put them in a small strainer with a flat bottom, then plunge them into boiling water for 1 minute; drain them. Lay the leaves out on a plate, then pierce them with the end of a cooking needle to lift them up and put them on the fowl.

The chopped tarragon should contain only the leaf, without any part of the stem, which is tough. Add it to the boiling sauce without blanching it first.

Chicken Tarragon, Simple Method *(Poulet à l'Estragon, Simple Façon).* Cook as for the CHICKEN AU BLANC (PAGE 361), leaving out the mushroom trimmings. Salt it only lightly, bearing in mind the final reduction of the sauce that accompanies it. You can add a bunch of tarragon leaves to the bouillon, but remember that you do not need all the cooking bouillon for the sauce that accompanies the chicken, and any remaining bouillon cannot easily be used for other recipes.

Put 7 deciliters (3 cups) of cooking bouillon into a casserole; add a bunch of tarragon, about 15 grams (1/2 ounce); boil it strongly, without a cover, to reduce it by half; take out the bunch; bind it with arrowroot (SEE LIAISONS, PAGE 47). Serve the juice on the side in a sauceboat, adding 1 scant tablespoon of minced tarragon.

Tarragon Chicken, Sauce Blonde Method *(Poulet à l'Estragon, Façon Sauce Blonde).* Proceed as for the CHICKEN AU BLANC (PAGE 361), leaving out the mushroom trimmings. Add a bunch of tarragon to the sauce while you are skimming it. Make the liaison with egg yolks but without cream or lemon. Add 1 tablespoon of minced tarragon and 30 grams (1 ounce, 2 tablespoons) of butter to the thickened sauce.

Lightly cover the chicken with sauce. Serve the rest in a sauceboat.

You can also make this recipe by braising the fowl as directed for CHICKEN WITH RICE (PAGE 360) and taking the cooking juice from it for the sauce, which you prepare as above.

Tarragon Chicken, Restaurant Method *(Poulet à l'Estragon, Façon des Restaurants).* Braise it as for the CHICKEN WITH RICE (PAGE 360) with lightly salted, slightly colored veal juice. Then keep the bird warm in its casserole, having strained its cooking juice.

Put the juice into a small sauté pan with 1 tablespoon of tarragon leaves, which have been coarsely chopped, and 1 scant deciliter (3 1/3 fluid ounces, scant 1/2 cup) of Madeira. Boil until this quantity is reduced to 3 good deciliters (1 1/4 cups); thicken it with arrowroot (SEE LIAISONS, PAGE 47). Decorate the bird with tarragon leaves. Serve the juice in a sauceboat.

Sautéed Chicken *(Les Poulets Sautés)*

The list is rather long, and one can always improvise new dishes by combining the garnishes; but whatever the garnish, the procedure for cooking the chicken remains the same. It is the invariable starting off point for sautéed chicken—refer to the general principles for sautés (PAGE 34).

For this dish, get a nice young chicken that has a fine and white skin, and that is, above all, not too fatty and well fleshed. "Grain-fed" fits all these criteria and is the best. By "grain-fed" chicken, we mean a chicken that has not yet reached the end of its growth, and that has been nourished, for a certain period, in a special way to develop the production of its flesh without fattening it.

The weight of a nice grain-fed chicken is about 1 kilogram (2 pounds, 3 ounces) and about 800 grams (1 pound, 12 ounces) when it is gutted, which is enough for 4 people. The following recipes assume this weight and this number of guests. For 6 people, you should use 2 chickens, each weighing a little bit less, rather than 1 very large fattened hen.

The cooking time varies according to the delicacy and tenderness of the bird. For the type of chicken we have suggested, the chicken will generally need no more than *20–25 minutes* on the heat.

The method of carving the chicken for sautéing is of real importance, as much as for determining whether the parts of the beast are more or less well cooked, as for the style of presentation. SEE PREPARATION OF FOWL (PAGE 349).

In the great restaurant kitchens, where there are basic sauces, jus, and garnishes always on hand, recipes featuring a sautéed chicken are the simplest and most rapid. For home kitchens, where such sauces are not available, we will compensate by giving directions that will allow us to obtain nearly the same results.

Cooking the chicken: Use a sauté pan with a bottom big enough that the pieces can fit side by side without being squeezed together. Thus, for a medium-size chicken, you need of a sauté pan of about 22 centimeters ($8^1/_2$ inches) in diameter.

Heat the fat you are using on a strong heat, but not too strong. When the fat begins to give off a *light* smoke, a sign that the right temperature has been reached, arrange the pieces in the sauté pan. Lightly season them with salt, with their skin side against the bottom of the utensil. As soon as you have placed all the pieces in the sauté pan, turn the heat down quite low, so that once they have been sealed by the heat of the fat, they can then cook without burning. Do not cover the casserole; do not touch the chicken.

At the end of *5 or 6 minutes,* lift up one of the pieces with a fork, without piercing it, to check how much it has browned. If the skin side is nicely golden, you can turn them. If not, wait another minute. Begin with the smallest pieces, those that have cooked most quickly. Brown the other side.

As soon as the wing tips are nice and firm and colored on the side, which should be at the end of *about 6 minutes,* lift them out onto a plate, covering it immediately with another turned over plate. *Three or four minutes later,* you can take out the breast; but be sure first that it is properly cooked.

The flesh of the thighs is thicker and tougher, so it requires a longer cooking. If your oven is already good and hot, you can put the casserole in it, still without its cover, to finish this cooking. If not, which is most often the case, turn the heat down very low and put a fire spreader under the pan. Allow *8–10 minutes* for the thighs to finish cooking, or, at least, to be properly done. To assure yourself that this is so, pierce the flesh of the drumstick on its interior part near the joint of the thigh; if the juice that pearls out is clear, the cooking is done; if it is pink, continue cooking for a few more minutes.

Then take out the thighs, carcass, and neck. Put them on the plate with the other pieces.

Dressing the chicken: Serve on a round plate, not a bowl, well heated in advance.

First place the 2 pieces of carcass in the middle, 1 next to the other; on each side, put the wing tips, neck, and feet if you cooked them (see *fig.* 61, BELOW). These will provide a base, a support even, for the good pieces of chicken, which should be arranged *thighs* first, crossed over each other; the breast; and finally, the wings.

If you put little curly paper sleeves on them, do this only after pouring sauce over the chicken and precisely at the moment that you send them to the table, placing them on the ends of the wing bones and thighs, as shown. Keep the plate warm near a hot stove or in an open oven while you proceed with these last preparations.

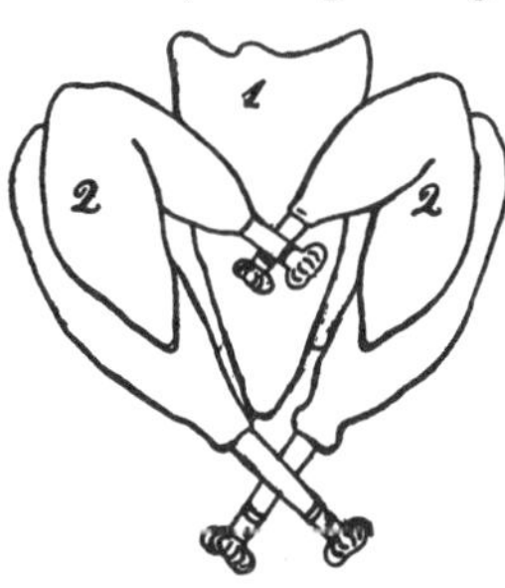

FIG. 61. DRESSING A SAUTÉED CHICKEN.

NOTE. The little paper sleeves at the end of the thigh and wing bone are completely optional. In modern-day serving, the most important thing above all is to simplify things so that you can serve food good and hot, and sautéed chicken must be served burning hot.

Hunter-Style Chicken Sauté *(Poulet Sauté Chasseur).* Chicken sautéed in the hunter style is one of those dishes that is always better in restaurants than at home, because at home it is all too easy to leave out one of the elements that is so characteristic of the dish. Cooking the mushrooms in the fat used to sauté the chicken, and seasoning with shallot, tomato, cognac, etc., are typical of the hunter-style preparation: one can therefore not leave out any of them. *Time: 35–40 minutes (once the chicken has been gutted and carved). Serves 4.*

1 chicken of the quality and weight indicated;
100 grams (3 1/2 ounces) of fresh mushrooms; 25 grams (1 ounce) of shallot (3 medium-size); a small liqueur glass of cognac, flamed in advance; 1 deciliter (3 1/3 fluid ounces, scant 1/2 cup) of white wine; 2 scant deciliters (6 3/4 fluid ounces, 7/8 cup) of veal jus, or, if you do not have it, bouillon; 1 teaspoon of flour; 2 level tablespoons of *concentrated* tomato purée, nice and red; 1 teaspoon of chervil and tarragon, minced (half of each); a pinch of parsley, coarsely chopped; 50 grams (1 3/4 ounces, 3 1/2 tablespoons) of butter; 2 1/2 tablespoons of oil; salt and pepper.

NOTE. If you use ordinary tomato purée, increase the amount by a tablespoon. When tomatoes are in season, you can use a few fresh tomatoes peeled, pressed, and chopped. If so, these are the amounts to use: 1 tablespoon of purée and 2 tablespoons of very red and ripe tomatoes.

PROCEDURE. The elements of the hunter-style garnish can be prepared in advance if you like. Before starting to cook the chicken, you can mince the shallot, parsley, etc., and wash and mince the mushrooms. (You can also make these preparations at the last moment while you are monitoring the cooking of the chicken.)

The chicken: Sauté it as described (PAGE 366) in 25 grams (1 ounce, 2 tablespoons) of butter and 1 tablespoon of oil. Then keep it warm on a plate.

Hunter-style garnish: Here the mushrooms are cut into slices—and absolutely not divided into quarters. Remove the sandy part and wash them, then meticulously dry them on a kitchen towel, since any moisture will prevent their browning. Do not peel them and do not separate the head from the stem. Put the mushrooms on the table and with a good medium-size knife, slice them—that is, divide them lengthwise, cutting both the head and the stem into thin slices of equal thickness.

In the casserole from which you have just taken the pieces of chicken, add to the cooking fat the rest of the oil, which should be a little more than 1 tablespoon. Heat it until it smokes lightly. Put in the sliced mushrooms; sauté them over strong heat until they are a little brown. Then add the chopped shallot. Sauté the mushrooms for another few moments.

After this, drain almost all the fat from the casserole. Sprinkle the mushrooms with the flour; mix it well. Cook it gently for 2 or 3 minutes. After this, add the cognac, flamed in advance; the white wine; the jus or the bouillon; the tomato purée (or purée the fresh tomatoes); and a pinch of pepper. But no salt, because the jus or bouillon is salted. Bring it to a boil on strong heat, mixing it continuously with the wooden spoon. As soon as the boiling begins, turn down the heat. Cover it. Let *simmer* gently for *6 or 7 minutes.*

At the end of this time, put the pieces of chicken in the casserole, being careful to insert them down into the garnish. Add the juice that they have released while waiting. Cover the casserole; allow it to simmer, *but not to boil,* which would toughen the flesh, for 5 or 6 minutes: that is, just the time needed to thoroughly reheat the pieces of chicken.

To serve: A few minutes before serving, dress the chicken as directed. Leave the plate near a hot stove or in a very moderate oven while you finish the sauce as follows.

Put the uncovered casserole on high heat and boil it rapidly until the sauce is reduced to *about 1 1/2 deciliters (5 fluid ounces, 2/3 cup).* Then *turn off the heat* immediately. Add to the sauce: minced chervil and tarragon, the rest of the butter, divided into pieces the size of a bean. Take the casserole by the handle; shake it on the stovetop with a circular movement to encourage the rapid mixing and melting of the butter in the sauce.

Check the seasoning. Pour the sauce on the chicken. Sprinkle the minced parsley on everything. Serve immediately.

Chicken Marengo *(Poulet Sauté à la Marengo).* There are many recipes for this. Without going back to the legendary origins of this dish, we will state what essentially characterizes this dish: oil, tomato, garlic. The garnish of fried eggs and crayfish is an invention consecrated by time and habit, and to which we must now conform. The recipe we are going to give is for the Chicken Marengo that has become a sort of classic, such as that served in fine restaurants. We would like to point out that it is common now to leave out the olives, whose effects are nonetheless excellent. Generally, slices of truffles are added to the ingredients listed below; it is always excellent to include the truffles. You can also make rounds of ham as part of the garnish, placing fried eggs on top.

In commercial kitchens, where a very concentrated veal jus is always on hand, it is easy to thicken the sauce; in home kitchens, it is often necessary to use a little bit of beurre manié instead, as we explain further on. *Time: 1 hour. Serves 4.*

1 chicken of the quality and weight indicated; 3 good tablespoons of *olive oil* to sauté it; a clove of garlic, squashed under the blade of a knife; 2 nice medium-size tomatoes, peeled and perfectly ripe, deseeded and cut into small pieces; 1 tablespoon of tomato purée; about 20 pitted olives lightly desalinated in warm water; a dozen small cooked mushrooms, nice and white (SEE MUSHROOMS FOR GARNISHES, PAGE 490); 1 scant deciliter (3 1/3 fluid ounces, scant 1/2 cup) of cooking liquid from the mushrooms; 1 deciliter (3 1/3 fluid ounces, scant 1/2 cup) of white wine; 1 deciliter (3 1/3 fluid ounces, scant 1/2 cup) of jus of veal; 1 teaspoon of coarsely chopped parsley.

Plus, for the garnish for each person: 1 small fresh egg, 1 fried crouton and 1 crayfish.

PROCEDURE. To proceed in the right way and with the necessary speed, the elements of the garnish must be prepared and within reach before the chicken is put on the fire. Keep the crayfish warm in the casserole where they have been cooked (SEE CRAYFISH FOR GARNISH, PAGE 229). The croutons and eggs should be fried in the oil used for sautéing the chicken.

The chicken: Carved in advance and sautéed as directed. Once the pieces have been browned and cooked properly, take them out and put them on a plate. Cover them and keep them warm.

The sauce: Drain the grease from the skillet where the croutons and eggs were fried.

Put the tomato and the garlic into the sauté pan. On moderate heat, stir with the wooden spoon, pressing on the bottom of the pan to dissolve the crisp bits that have formed on the bottom. As soon as the tomato has softened a little, add the white wine, jus, and cooking liquid from the mushrooms. Reduce for a few moments to about a third: 2 deciliters (6 3/4 fluid ounces, 7/8 cup) of liquid will suffice. Add the tablespoon of tomato purée. Keep everything at a gentle simmer while you are busy with the other preparations. Cover the casserole.

The croutons and the eggs: Add a little more oil to that already in the small pan. Fry the croutons there: 1 minute should suffice to brown them. Replace them with the eggs (SEE FRIED EGGS, PAGE 135). As soon as they are poached in the oil, place them on a kitchen towel in a warm spot, where they can drain while being kept warm.

Before serving: Be sure that the sauce is done regarding consistency and seasoning. If the juice that you have used is thin, you will have to bind it with beurre manié—a piece of butter the size of a walnut combined with 1 teaspoon of flour. Divide it into pieces, then add it to the casserole off the heat, mixing it well to combine it. Do not let the sauce boil any more. Put the pieces of chicken into the casserole, with the olives and the mushrooms. Cover it and reheat everything without letting it boil *for 2 or 3 minutes.*

Meanwhile, drain the crayfish on a towel and prepare the plate: use a round and rather large plate, considering the garnish.

To dress: Place the pieces of chicken on the plate as directed; on top, pour the sauce and sprinkle the minced parsley. All around the base of the chicken, alternate the eggs, the croutons, and the crayfish, their heads pointing out. Put a small curly sleeve of paper on the bones of the thighs and wings. Serve on burning hot plates.

Chicken Sautéed Parmentier *(Poulet Sauté Parmentier).* So called because it contains potatoes, this preparation is certainly one of the simplest for sautéed chicken. It is most appropriate for lunch.

If you like, the potatoes can be formed into large olive-size pieces, using a cutting spoon, or simply into cubes, as we suggest here. *Time: 35 minutes. Serves 4.*

1 chicken of the weight indicated; 300 grams (10 1/2 ounces) of potatoes, net weight; 80 grams (2 3/4 ounces, 5 1/2 tablespoons) of butter; 4 tablespoons of white wine; 4 tablespoons of veal jus, or, if you have none, bouillon; salt and pepper; a nice pinch of coarsely chopped parsley.

PROCEDURE. Cut up the chicken as directed.

Cut the potatoes: use 3 nice potatoes, medium-size, which have been carefully peeled. Begin by squaring a potato on 4 sides and on 2 ends. Cut it into slices 1 good centimeter (3/8 inch) thick, and then divide into squares of the same thickness. You can just as easily do this before you cut up the chicken; if so, keep the cubes in cold water until you are ready to cook them.

Heat half the butter in a sauté pan. Arrange the pieces of chicken seasoned with salt and pepper in it. Keep it on moderate heat without covering it.

As soon as the chicken is put in the casserole, take care of the potatoes. The two must be prepared at the same time so that they finish cooking together. If the potatoes have been kept in water, drain them and completely dry them in a towel. Heat the rest of the butter in a very clean pan. Add the potatoes, lightly seasoned with salt and pepper; sauté them on strong heat until they are equally brown.

Meanwhile, proceed as directed for cooking the chicken. As soon as the wings and the breast are nicely colored, take them out and put them on a plate. Cover them and keep them warm. Cook and gently color the thighs on their interior side for a few more minutes. Then add the potatoes to the chicken. *Cover* the casserole; put it in the oven. At the end of *8–10 minutes,* put the wings and the breast with the other pieces. Continue cooking for another 8 minutes.

To serve: Arrange the pieces of chicken as directed. Surround them with the potatoes or arrange the potatoes in a heap on each side. Keep it in the dish in a very moderate oven.

Place the casserole on strong heat and add the white wine. Reduce it to *2 tablespoons,* gently shaking the casserole during this time to deglaze—that is, to dissolve the juices that have caramelized at the bottom of the pan. Then add the veal jus. Let it boil for a second, then pour some of these juices on the pieces of the chicken: it is enough just to moisten them, so allow about 1 tablespoon per guest. Sprinkle the parsley on the potatoes only and serve.

Sautéed Chicken à la Portugaise *(Poulet Sauté à la Portugaise).* Any recipe *à la Portugaise* is one in which tomato is the most important ingredient, as much in the sauce as in the garnish. Small stuffed tomatoes provide the garnish, which surrounds the chicken in the service. However, for a family meal, you can leave out the garnish. *Time: 1 1/2 hours (including preparation). Serves 4.*

1 chicken of the weight suggested; 75 grams (2 2/3 ounces, 1/3 cup) of butter; 3 tablespoons of oil; 100 grams (3 1/2 ounces) of mushrooms; 60 grams (2 1/4 ounces) of finely chopped onions; 3 large ripe tomatoes; 1 1/2 deciliters (5 fluid ounces, 2/3 cup) of bouillon and the same quantity of white wine; 1 level tablespoon of concentrated tomato purée; 1 piece of garlic the size of a pea; 1 teaspoon of flour; a nice pinch of coarsely chopped parsley; salt and pepper; 12 small stuffed tomatoes (SEE TOMATOES STUFFED FOR GARNISH, PAGE 535).

PROCEDURE. **The stuffed tomatoes:** These should be prepared in advance and ready on the plate to be cooked when needed.

The chicken: Sauté it as directed with 2 good tablespoons of oil. Then keep it warm on a plate.

The sauce: You will have prepared the ingredients while the chicken was cooking. Cut the *mushrooms* as directed for HUNTER-STYLE CHICKEN SAUTÉ (PAGE 367), but in thick slices of about 5 millimeters (3/16 inch). Peel the *tomatoes.* Eliminate the seeds and the water; chop the tomatoes fine.

Add the rest of the oil to the little remaining in the sauté pan. Heat it until it gives off a light smoke. Lightly color the mushrooms on strong heat, then drain them thoroughly in a strainer.

Pour all the oil out of the casserole. Put the minced onion into the casserole with 25 grams (1 ounce, 2 tablespoons) of butter. Cook for a few moments without coloring at all. Then add the tomatoes; do not cover; cook for *5 minutes.* Add the white wine; boil it vigorously to reduce it completely.

Then add: the colored mushrooms; the garlic, squashed with a blade of a knife; the bouillon; the tomato concentrate purée; salt and pepper. Cover, then cook gently for 8–10 minutes.

To serve: Put the pieces of chicken back into the casserole along with the juice that has escaped while it was waiting; shove them completely into the sauce; cover and reheat everything for *5 or 6 minutes* without letting it boil. Prepare a little beurre manié with the flour and 15 grams (1/2 ounce, 1 tablespoon) of butter (SEE LIAISONS, PAGE 47). Reserve it. Dress the chicken. Keep it warm.

Bind the sauce, as directed. Turn the heat off under the casserole to add the rest of the butter. Pour the sauce on the chicken. Sprinkle it with the minced parsley and surround it with the stuffed tomatoes. Serve.

Archduke Sautéed Chicken *(Poulet Sauté Archiduc).* Archduke chicken, once the classic of Maire, a famous Parisian restaurant, has undergone some modifications since then. Briefly, it is a chicken that is sautéed *à blanc,* that is, without any coloration, and covered with cream sauce. Originally, this sauce was a sort of crème anglaise whose elements consisted of 3 deciliters (1 1/4 cups) of crème fraîche, a glass of cognac, the same of whiskey, the same of red port, and 3 egg yolks. No garnish.

In the new recipe given here, which is by the respected authority chef Philéas Gilbert, egg yolks are not used for the liaison, but are replaced by béchamel, and the note of liquor and wine includes fine champagne cognac and Madeira. What's more, you can add some thin rounds of truffles to the dish.

Archduke chicken can be made in any season. The onions are used just as they are, if they are fresh or spring onions; when they are mature, or if it is toward the end of the season, blanch them first to rid them of all their bitterness and at the same time begin their cooking. *Time: 1 hour. Serves 6.*

1 medium-size chicken, completely cleaned out, weighing a good kilogram (2 pounds, 3 ounces); 40 grams (1 3/8 ounces, 3 tablespoons) of butter to cook it; 150 grams (5 1/3 ounces) of finely minced onion and 30 grams (1 ounce, 2 tablespoons) of butter to cook the onions.

For the sauce: 8–10 grams (about 1/3 ounce) of flour and 10 grams (1/3 ounce, 1 scant tablespoon) of butter for a little white roux; 1 generous deciliter (3 1/3 fluid ounces, 1/2 cup) of good boiled milk. A liqueur glass of fine champagne cognac; 1 1/2 deciliters (5 fluid ounces, 2/3 cup) of crème fraîche; 2 tablespoons of Madeira; the juice of 1/4 lemon, and 40–50 grams (1 3/8–1 3/4 ounces, 3–3 1/2 tablespoons) of butter for the final finish.

PROCEDURE. **The onions:** In the sauté pan where you will later cook the chicken, gently heat the 30 grams (1 ounce, 2 tablespoons) of butter for the onions. Put the rounds of onion in the pan and cook them gently, stirring them frequently without allowing them to color at all. When they are almost cooked, put them on a plate. Keep them on the side.

The chicken: While the onions are cooking, carve the chicken as directed for sauté.

In the same casserole where the onions were cooked, gently heat the 40 grams (1 3/8 ounces, 3 tablespoons) of butter. Arrange the pieces in the casserole. Put them on very gentle heat. For *7–8 minutes,* allow the wings to firm up a little bit without any coloring whatsoever. Then lift them out onto a plate. Turn the other chicken pieces at the end of *3 or 4 minutes,* and also take out the breast. Continue cooking the thighs for *8–10 minutes;* do not allow them to color.

Then put the breast and wings back into the casserole and add the onions. Cover it and put it in the oven for *10–12 minutes* to finish cooking there: that is, 20–25 minutes total cooking time. Then take out the pieces of chicken and put them on a plate, making sure that no piece of onion is attached. Cover the plate and keep it nice and warm. Keep the onion in the sauté pan.

The sauce: Start cooking this while the chicken is cooking. In a small casserole, make a white roux. Dilute it with the milk. Season it with salt, pepper, and grated nutmeg. Once it has boiled, allow it to simmer until you are ready to add this little bit of béchamel to the onion.

As soon as you have taken out the pieces of chicken and put them on a plate, pour the fine champagne cognac into the sauté pan with the onion. Without covering, boil it rapidly until there is complete reduction of the liquor. Then add the béchamel and the cream. Let it boil for only *3 or 4 minutes.*

Pass the sauce through a fine chinois into a bowl, squeezing it and beating it with a wooden spoon to pass as much of the onion as possible; this is a substitute for the drum sieve so commonly used in professional kitchens.

Rinse the little casserole with warm water. Pour the sauce into it. Heat it to the point where it is just about to boil. Immediately *turn off the heat* to add the final butter, the Madeira and the lemon juice. Check the seasoning. Keep it in the double boiler until ready to serve.

To serve: Dress the pieces of chicken on a round heated plate. Cover them with the sauce. *If you are using truffles,* these should have been previously cut into fine rounds and heated without boiling with a little bit of their juice from the can or 1 tablespoon of Madeira. You then scatter them on the sauce. Serve very hot.

Chicken in a Pot *(Les Poulets en Cocotte)*

Brought into fashion by the deluxe restaurants in the final years of the nineteenth century, this way of serving chicken in a pot did not take long to be adapted by homemakers—with a success that remains undiminished. This is explained in particular by the capital advantage that it can be served burning hot, the pan having stored enough heat so that when it arrives at the table you can often see it quivering slightly inside.

The garnish for Chicken in a Pot varies according to the season and your means: fresh vegetables in the spring and in the summer; artichoke bottoms, various mushrooms in the fall; Chinese artichokes, chestnuts, salsify, Brussels sprouts, etc., in the winter. For every season, try potatoes, little onions, bacon, etc. For Chicken in a Pot, the garnishes are unlimited.

A grain-fed chicken that weighs a little more than 1 kilogram (2 pounds, 3 ounces) before being gutted, and about 800 grams (1 pound, 12 ounces) once cleaned out, is the one generally used for this recipe.

The bird is trussed as for an entrée, with the head and the neck cut and the feet tied along the body. SEE PREPARATION OF FOWL (PAGE 349).

The utensil called the *cocotte,* or pot, is available in all kinds of special models: faience, earthenware, porcelain, and even special ovenproof glass. The different cocottes can be put directly on the plaque of a coal oven. For gas or electricity, however, it is essential to put an insulating plate between the gas flame or the electric plate and the cocotte, or to use a pot made out of enameled steel; these are made in an oval shape, supplied with a cover, in exactly the right size for a chicken.

In professional kitchens, the diverse elements are half-cooked separately and then put in the pot together to finish cooking. The time taken to color the chicken, which is longer when done in the pot itself, can be shortened by roasting the chicken in the oven to half-cook it. This is how it is done in the great restaurants, where diners must be served within 25–30 minutes: the chicken half-roasted is quickly stuck into the pot so that it looks good. This is why people who have been served it in restaurants have concluded that cooking it in for an hour at home is excessive.

If you wish to shorten the time you can also color the chicken in a sauté pan. But these different procedures do not conform at all to the principles of the original recipe; and let us mention too that country kitchens do not have such utensils or conveniences, so it is always in the pot itself that the chicken is colored, while that of the garnish, if it is necessary, is done in a pan. It is better not to resort to shortcuts or to try to avoid the need for cooking it at a slow, gentle simmer, the cooking method so characteristic of Chicken in a Pot. In short, this recipe is a sort of braising *à la bonne femme.*

When the preliminary coloring of the chicken is not done in the pot itself, make sure the pot is quite hot, ready for the moment when the chicken is put in it: either by standing it for about 10 minutes in advance in a warm spot or by putting some boiling water in it at the last moment.

The cooking of the chicken after it has colored is always done in the oven so that the cooking utensil is completely surrounded by the heat—essential for this recipe. In the country, the pot was put inside the large fireplace, surrounded by a wall of hot coals and cinders: it is this form of heat that the oven is intended to replace. The oven must be of a good, strong heat.

Always check that the chicken has been properly cooked: stick a kitchen needle into the fleshiest part of the thigh and pull it back immediately. The pearl of juice that escapes should be absolutely clear.

The veal jus: In professional kitchens, it is usual to add 3 or 4 tablespoons of very concentrated veal jus to the chicken in the pot *after cooking.* This refinement is not within the reach of all home kitchens and it does not conform to the original recipe, veal jus being nonexistent in country kitchens. Nonetheless, when possible, it is recommended.

Carving the chicken in the pot: This must be done at the table itself if you want to retain the recipe's character and all its advantages. Furthermore, this is what is done in the fine restaurants, where the maître d'hôtel does this in front of the guests. If the carving is done in the kitchen, the pieces must be put back into the pot, which is kept hot and everything served as if it has just come out of the oven.

To serve: Remove the trussing strings. Wipe the pot with a damp cloth. Place the *covered* pot on a plate that is covered with a folded napkin. (If you must wait, keep the covered pot in a very moderate oven, or in the oven with the door open.)

Stuffed Chicken in the Pot *(Les Poulets en Cocotte Farcis).* Chicken in the pot is often stuffed. This is very close to the original recipe, and also has its advantages; a chicken that ordinarily serves 5 people can, when it is more or less generously stuffed, be enough for 7 or 8 people.

The type of stuffing is dependent on both taste and means. The base of it is the liver of the bird, and you can add, if you like, either other livers from fowl or a mince of pork, cultivated mushrooms or cèpes, morels, etc., some soaked bread crumbs, egg, onion, shallots, garlic, etc. All of this is optional.

The chopped pork mixture should always have an equal proportion of fat and lean, no matter how much of it you are using; you can add the interior fat of the chicken when you find it. The minced pork is put into the bird *uncooked.* If it contains onions, shallots, or garlic, these elements are first gently cooked without coloring in a little bit of butter, then *cooled* before being mixed with the uncooked pork mixture; it's the same for the mushrooms. The chicken can be stuffed well in advance, even the evening before, and kept cool until it is cooked. SEE STUFFING AND PREPARATION OF FOWL (PAGE 351).

The cooking time is naturally longer for a stuffed chicken. Once the chicken has cooked, allow, *1 hour of cooking* at a good sustained heat for a chicken that contains about 250 grams (8 7/8 ounces) of minced uncooked pork.

Chicken in a Pot *(Poulet en Cocotte).* This simple method is either simply called *poulet en cocotte, poulet en cocotte bonne femme* ("wife"), or *poulet en cocotte grand-mère* or *mère grand* ("grandmother"). Its garnish includes salt pork, small onions, and potatoes.

The small onions are optional. They should be very small, about the size of a mirabelle, the small yellow plum. You can color them in the casserole dish itself at the same time as the bacon, or separately in a small pan, where you can add them just as they are. When they are not new, you must first half-cook them in boiling water before adding them to the chicken.

Make sure you choose potatoes that have a yellowish flesh. In this recipe, white potatoes end up like boiled turnips. At the start of the season, they can be used whole if they are about the size of a medium-size plum. Later in the season, you should cut them into quarters, trimming these quarters into elongated pieces the shape of large garlic cloves. Usually, they are added uncooked into the pot; you get a much better result when you blanch them first, as directed. Cooking them in the pot is made easier if you do so, and the end result is potatoes that are golden and melting. *Time: 1 1/4 hours.*

1 grain-fed chicken of a medium weight; 150 grams (5 1/3 ounces) of lean bacon; 350 grams (12 1/3 ounces) of potatoes, net weight; 12 small onions; 50 grams (1 3/4 ounces, 3 1/2 tablespoons) of butter; a small bouquet garni; 1 tablespoon of minced parsley.

PROCEDURE. Cut the *lean bacon,* trimmed of its rinds, into large cubes. Blanch it for 5 minutes. Drain.

Peel, cut, and wash the *potatoes.* Put them in a small casserole covered with cold water. Keep them on the side.

Heat half of the butter in the pot on very moderate heat. Color the bacon pieces in it, mixing it from time to time with a wooden spoon, then take them out and put them on a plate.

Put the chicken in the fat they rendered when they browned and shriveled. The pot should always be uncovered on moderate heat when you color it, keeping the breast and the thighs mostly toward the bottom of the pan. Do not turn it over onto another side until it has been well browned on one side. And do not stick it with a fork while doing this: instead, use 2 wooden spoons to move it. You need to allow *15–20 minutes* for the chicken to color to a golden blond. The fat in the casserole must not go beyond a beautiful light yellow color.

Meanwhile, when the chicken has almost colored, put the potatoes on lively heat. *They must only boil once.* As soon as they begin to boil, immediately turn off the heat. Put a cover on the casserole to keep the potatoes in it as you tilt the casserole to drain all the water. Keep them warm and dry in the casserole for just enough time to drain the chicken.

Put the chicken on the plate with the cubes of bacon. Pour all the fat from the casserole dish into a bowl and let it rest there for an instant; then pour the fat back in, keeping back the brown sandy deposit on the bottom. Add the rest of the butter; heat it on moderate heat; remove the foam, which will create new brown residues if allowed to solidify.

Once the fat is again good and hot, put in the drained potatoes carefully. Let them heat uncovered *2 minutes,* stirring them and rolling them about to evaporate the rest of their moisture. Push them aside to put the chicken back into the pot, its breast facing up. Surround it with the potatoes, small onions, and bacon cubes. Add the bouquet garni. Sprinkle with a good pinch of salt. Replace the cover. Put it in the oven.

Allow about 30 minutes at a gentle regular simmer. Every 10 minutes, shake the pot to move its contents about.

To serve: Remove the bouquet. Sprinkle the minced parsley over the chicken. There should not be any juices in the casserole dish: only a stock of clear, golden fat.

Chicken in a Pot à la Fermière *(Poulet en Cocotte à la Fermière).* *Time: A solid hour.*

1 grain-fed chicken of a medium weight; about 100 grams (3 1/2 ounces) of lean *uncooked* ham cut into slices the size of a playing card and about 3 millimeters (1/8 inch) thick; 75 grams (2 2/3 ounces) of young carrots cut into rounds 1 or 2 millimeters (1/16 inch) thick; 40 grams (1 3/8 ounces) of small onions cut the same way; 40 grams (1 3/8 ounces) of celery that has been finely minced; 60 grams (2 1/4 ounces) of green beans cut into small pieces 1 centimeter (3/8 inch long), cut on the bias; 1 deciliter (3 1/3 fluid ounces, scant 1/2 cup) of fresh green peas; 80 grams (2 3/4 ounces, 5 1/2 tablespoons) of butter; 1 deciliter (3 1/3 fluid ounces, scant 1/2 cup) of bouillon.

PROCEDURE. **The chicken:** On gentle heat, melt 30 grams (1 ounce, 2 tablespoons) of butter in the pot. When it is nice and warm, put in the chicken and color it gently, as previously directed. Meanwhile, prepare the vegetables.

The vegetables: In a small sauté pan, melt the rest of the butter. Add only the onion to it. Let it color for *4–5 minutes,* no more than a straw yellow. Add carrot and celery. Braise it gently on very low heat for *15 minutes*; toss them, so that you do not break them as when you mix them with a spoon. They must be nice and tender, but not at all browned; the onion should have taken on a golden tint and the butter have kept its light color.

To cook: Remove the chicken from the pot and then line the utensil with the sheets of ham. Put the chicken into the pot on its back. Surround it equally with all the mixed vegetables, cooked and raw. Add the bouillon. Cover.

Put the pot in the oven; from this point, allow *45–50 minutes.* Make sure that the heat does not go higher than a good medium heat, because if the liquid reduces, the surrounding vegetables might burn and the cooking of the chicken would be accelerated.

Check that the chicken is done and then serve as directed.

Roast Chicken *(Le Poulet Rôti)*

As for any fowl destined to be roasted, the quality of the chicken must not be in any doubt: you can recognize a good chicken by the thickness of its legs, and a fine and transparent skin on the body, under which you should be able to see a light pink flesh that is not too fatty in the breast. It is on the back that you should find fat, though not too much. On this point, you are looking for a golden mean: when choosing a chicken to roast, you will not get a good result from a beast that has too much fat; it will melt during the cooking process. On the other hand, for a bird that has no natural fat, using a bard or any other fat would have no effect on the flesh, which would remain dry and stringy.

You do not have to bard a chicken that is roasted on a wood fire spit, a charcoal spit, or a gas flame in open air. In this case, baste it with melted butter, using about 50 grams of butter ($1^3/_4$ ounces, $3^1/_2$ tablespoons) melted into a cup and applying it with a metal spoon or, better still, a large kitchen brush to brush the chicken each time you turn it. SEE ROASTS (PAGE 30).

If the roasting is done in the oven, it is always better to lard it with bacon than to baste it with butter. First of all, the strong surrounding heat of the oven might dry out the fillet of the bird. Also, butter does not hold up well to a very high temperature, and will burn or at least turn brown in the plate, while bacon fat does hold up.

For roasting in the oven allow about 18–20 minutes per 450 grams (1 pound) and about 20–22 minutes on the spit. You can be certain it is cooked properly by sticking a kitchen needle into the thickest part of the thigh; the pearl of juice that escapes must be absolutely clear and not at all pink. This is equally true for the juice that escapes from the rump when you tilt the beast. If the liver has been put back into the chicken, the juice will not be absolutely clear, nor will it be tinted with red.

Note that a perfectly cooked roast chicken, in which the flesh of the breasts and wings has retained its juices, will have thighs whose inside meat is pink when carved. If it were otherwise, the breast would be overcooked by the prolonged heat and therefore dry and stringy when carved. You can, when carving in the kitchen and for guests who like their upper thighs well cooked, expose the inside of the thighs to the heat of the oven or a broiler for 2 minutes.

To serve: Cut and remove the strings and sprinkle the chicken with salt; put it on a heated plate with a bunch of watercress. Serve the jus on the side, lightly degreased if roasting has been done on a spit.

Chicken in a Casserole *(Poulet à la Casserole).* Under this name, the modern cuisine of the great restaurants have made fashionable this type of preparation, a form of cooking in a *cocotte,* which is equally good for pheasants, partridges, etc.

This same preparation was once practiced in home kitchens, usually when a spit was not available for roasting the bird. The procedure, as simple as it was, was very well thought out: heat some butter in a casserole (which at that time was always tinned copper) and once both the butter and the utensil were nice and warm, put in the chicken; *cover immediately.* On moderate heat, allow the chicken to cook gradually and to be slowly penetrated with the butter, which should not color at all during the cooking. Finally, remove the cover to color the chicken on all sides, turning so that they are in contact with the bottom of the casserole. Take out the chicken and then lift off the light crust from the bottom of the casserole with a little bit of water; thus, and without practically any degreasing required, a jus is produced to accompany the roast.

These days, the kitchens of the great restaurants continue to operate the same way, this being the sole difference: that the entire cooking is done in the oven in an earthen vessel to which the chicken is returned after adding a little bit of liquid. It is then served like any chicken in the pot.

Grilled Chicken *(Poulet Grillé).* This preparation is used only for very young grain-fed chickens, whose weight once gutted is about 500 grams (1 pound, 2 ounces). Truss, split, and flatten the chicken as for TOAD-STYLE GRILLED SQUAB (PAGE 389). Season it with salt and pepper and brush it with melted butter. First put it in a relatively hot oven for *10 good minutes.* After this, bread it like the squab and grill it the same way on a more or less gentle heat for *20–25 minutes.* Serve with a sauce diable or tartar sauce.

Curried Chicken *(Poulet en Curry).* SEE CURRY (PAGE 451).

Chicken Made with Blood *(Poulet au Sang).* An essentially country dish, based on using the blood of the beast for the final liaison of the sauce, just as for a civet of hare. Depending on the region, and notably in Burgundy, the liquid used includes wine: two-thirds for one-third of bouillon; and, like civet, you add a garnish of bacon, small onions, and even mushrooms. We give here the simplest method, from Berry, where bouillon and water are the only liquids used, and no garnish is served.

Bleed the chicken, reserving the blood in a bowl, and add 2 tablespoons of vinegar to it to prevent clotting. Keep it cool. Carve up the chicken as for a sauté, but separate the drumstick from the upper thigh, making 2 pieces from each wing; make 2 pieces from the neck; you can keep the head, but make sure you remove the beak.

In a sauté pan, heat half butter, half good pork fat—using a total about the size of an egg. On strong heat, brown the pieces, seasoned with salt and pepper: *8–10 minutes.* Turn the heat down in order to powder the pieces with 1 tablespoon of flour (20 grams, 2/3 ounce). Allow it to lightly brown, moving it with the wooden spoon. Dilute with 2 glasses (4 deciliters/1 2/3 cups) of bouillon or water; mix it until it begins to boil. Add the bouquet garni, an onion stuck with a clove; a pinch of salt, if only water is used; cover the casserole three-quarters of the way with a lid. Put it on moderate heat in order to maintain the liquid in a gentle, regular simmering. Allow *35–40 minutes* for a young bird of good quality and *1 hour* for a fowl that is older and less fine.

Five minutes before serving, make the liaison with blood, proceeding as for Civet of Hare. *Off the heat,* mix a piece of fresh butter the size of a pigeon egg into the sauce before pouring it over the pieces arranged on the plate.

TURKEY
Dinde

Turkey with Chestnuts *(Dinde aux Marrons)*

Turkey with chestnuts is a modest replacement for truffled turkey. It is a classic and traditional dish at family meals for Christmas and New Year's Day. Its garnish of chestnut stuffing ensures that it will serve a relatively large number of guests.

It would be more accurate here to say young turkey, since only birds born the same year are used, and you are therefore likely to find many young turkeys. Furthermore, the term is without importance, because the difference from the point of view of quality and flavor is not appreciable. For a turkey of the right size, you need to allow a gross weight of 4 kilograms (8 pounds, 13 ounces), which would have a net weight of 3 kilograms (6 pounds, 10 ounces). Generally, you will lose about a quarter of the weight of the beast once it is gutted, but a part of this—neck, giblets, liver—can be used in a ragoût.

The chestnuts should be very nice chestnuts, allowing 30–35 chestnuts per 450 grams (1 pound). For this recipe, we are allowing about 60, which can make as much as 1 kilogram (2 pounds, 3 ounces). You can buy the chopped stuffing readymade as long as you get it from a very good charcuterie. Order it cut extremely fine so that you do not have to mince it again later; you then only have to add the cognac and a pinch of spiced salt, since readymade stuffing does not generally have enough seasoning. There is no reason to wait until the last moment to stuff the turkey; you can do this a few hours in advance, as long as you keep the bird in a cool place. Cook it in the oven, allowing about *23 minutes* of cooking per kilo (2 pounds, 3 ounces): relatively speaking, cooking a large piece in the oven takes less time than a small or medium piece. *Time: 1 3/4 hours in the oven (**SEE ROASTS, PAGE 30**). The cooking time of a stuffed piece is calculated by the weight of the beast once it has been completely stuffed, ready to be put into the oven. Serves 12–15.*

1 turkey of the weight suggested; 1 kilogram (2 pounds, 3 ounces) of fine pork hash, purchased ready; or 500 grams (1 pound, 2 ounces) of pork fillet and 400 grams (14 1/8 ounces) of *very fresh* fatback bacon; 300 grams (10 1/2 ounces) of bards of bacon cut thin; 1 deciliter (3 1/3 fluid ounces, scant 1/2 cup) of cognac; 750 grams (1 pound, 10 ounces) of carefully selected chestnuts; 7 1/2 deciliters (generous 3 cups) of bouillon to cook them.

If the pork hash is made at home: **25 grams (1 ounce) of spice salt, which consists of 20 grams (2/3 ounce) of**

fine salt, 3 grams (1/10 ounce) of pepper and 2 grams (1/14 ounce) of spices.

PROCEDURE. **The chestnuts:** Peel them as directed (SEE PAGE 521). Put them in the casserole with the bouillon. Bring it to a boil, then cook gently for *about 25 minutes.* Drain and spread them out on a plate so they can cool.

The pork hash: Remove the nerve membrane covering the flesh of the pork. Cut this flesh into large cubes. Cut the bacon into cubes of the same size, having first removed the rind. If you have a small mechanical grinder, first grind the flesh and then the bacon. Then pass these together through the finest cutter and repeat two more times. Then grind it a bit in the mortar, adding cognac and spiced salt.

If you do not have a machine, first chop the meat with a cleaver or a large, strong knife; then the bacon; mix them; add the spiced salt; chop it again to mix it well, crush the hash in the mortar a little at a time; finally add the cognac.

Put the hash into a terrine. Mix in the chilled chestnuts, being careful not to break them.

The turkey: Prepare it as directed for stuffing (SEE PREPARATION OF FOWL, PAGE 349). For a turkey, it is also necessary to remove the nerves from the thigh. With the point of a knife, split the skin of the foot near the place where it joins the drumstick. Using a large kitchen needle, lift the pack of nerves resting on the bone of the foot. Take hold of each nerve, one by one, and roll it up on the end of the needle; then turn it carefully like a capstan to pull and to detach the end of the nerve, which is lodged in the drumstick. When they are all pulled out and hanging like strings, cut them at foot level with a knife.

Stuff the beast as for TRUFFLED CHICKEN (SEE PAGE 355). In the same way, pull the skin of the neck onto the back. For a bird this large, ordinary string is not good enough. You must truss it with a double string, and use a very solid one. Bard and envelop the turkey with buttered parchment paper before putting it in the oven.

To cook: Put the turkey on a strong rack placed in a roasting dish. Pour only 2 or 3 tablespoons of bouillon or water into the bottom of the dish. This may seem to run contrary to all the rules laid down in the chapter on roasting: but the turkey requires a very long time to cook, and this little bit of liquid is put there to prevent the juices that fall from the turkey from sticking there and burning on the bottom of the platter; remember that the jus will be the only accompaniment for the roast, so it must be very carefully preserved. In other words, the turkey needs a medium-hot oven that maintains a constant temperature.

An hour after the bird has been put into the oven, take off the paper. From this point, brush it rather frequently with melted butter, using a kitchen brush or a feather. Twenty minutes after you remove the paper, remove the bards. From then on, check the coloration, turning the beast over on all sides. Brush it frequently with melted butter; above all, do not baste it with the juice from the cooking in the oven dish. Do not allow the coloration to go to a brown tint. Check that it is properly cooked and then prepare the jus as for TRUFFLED CHICKEN (SEE PAGE 355).

To carve: The art of carving a turkey consists of obtaining the largest number of slices from the breast, each as thin as possible. Unless you have a large number of guests, the thighs are rarely cut off and eaten the same day. What's more, the procedure is not like that for a chicken, taking off the joints one by one, but rather the slices are carved right off the beast as you would do for a piece of meat—veal, for example.

Now that this principle has been established, the one point to consider is the way in which these slices should be carved. On this point, advice differs. In England, the country par excellence for producing and eating turkey, where carving is done at the table and is considered an art itself, the slices are cut from the top part (*fig.* 62) being always careful not to make them too long. To do it this way you must have an excellent knife, and also

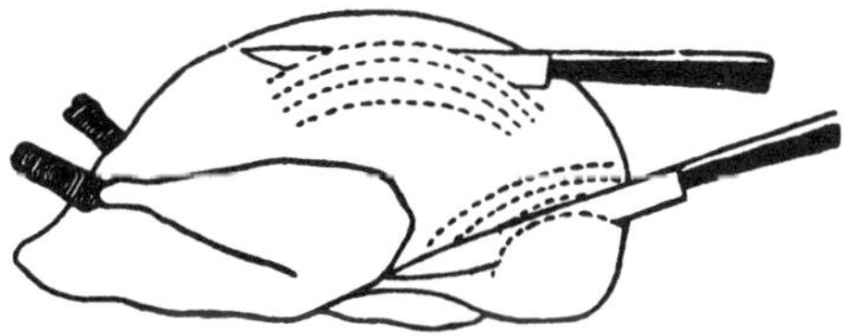

FIG. 62. CARVING A TURKEY.

experience with carving very thin, regular slices.

In the French method, the slices are cut smaller and in the direction marked at the bottom of the same illustration. This is easier, since you are cutting a bit on the bias.

In both methods, the thigh is not removed but must first be somewhat detached so that it does not interfere with the movement of the knife. The English method of carving better preserves the part of bone that touches the wing, and the bone itself is highly esteemed.

Truffled Turkey *(Dinde Truffée)*

Proceed as for TRUFFLED CHICKEN (SEE PAGE 355), increasing the quantities for the truffling ingredients according to the size of the turkey. For serving about 20 people, allow about 3 kilograms (6 pounds, 10 ounces) net, and to truffle it, double that amount for the chicken. Also regulate the time and the conduct of the cooking. If you like, serve it with a Périgueux Sauce on the side. For carving, see turkey with chestnuts (PAGE 376).

Roast Turkey *(Dinde Rôti)*

Proceed as for ROAST CHICKEN (PAGE 375).

Turkey Giblets à la Chipolata *(Abatis de Dinde à la Chipolata)*

Giblets prepared in this manner make an excellent home-style dish. It is prepared like a navarin-style ragoût, the sauce being half-cooked, then strained and put back on the giblets, to which are added the rest of the garnish, previously half-cooked. Bear in mind that for the chestnuts in particular, this method of starting the cooking separately in the bouillon must not be modified: this is because chestnuts, which are put uncooked into the sauce, would cook very badly there, no matter how long you leave them, as in any liquid that includes a liaison of flour. *Time: 2 hours. Serves 6.*

Giblets including the neck, wing tips, feet, gizzard, liver.

40 grams (1 3/8 ounces) of good fat, either lard or fat from roasting; 1 large onion; 35 grams (1 1/4 ounces) of flour for the roux; 2 deciliters (6 3/4 fluid ounces, 7/8 cup) of white wine; 7 1/2 deciliters (generous 3 cups) of bouillon; a bouquet garni and a small clove of garlic.

For the garnish: **100 grams (3 1/2 ounces) of lean bacon; 12 small onions; 12 small chestnuts; 200 grams (7 ounces) of carrots; 6 chipolata sausages.**

PROCEDURE. **The lardons:** Cut to 1 scant centimeter (3/8 inch) on each side. Blanch them, as directed (SEE PAGE 11).

The giblets: Clean and flame the neck, head and feet, as directed for preparing fowl. Remove the beak. Scrape the claws. Cut the head and neck into 4 pieces. Cut the legs and wingtips in 2. Split the gizzard; take out the stony pouch. Remove the thick skin from the inside and clean it, then divide it in four. Carefully examine the liver; with a knife, remove any part of the bile that might have tainted it. Keep it cool.

To cook: Use a deep casserole in thick aluminum, or if you do not have that, a good cast-iron pot. Heat the fat strongly in it. Then lightly brown the *lardons*; drain them on a plate. Replace them with the *small onions* (SEE PAGE 525). Color them gently, turning down the heat at this point; shake the casserole from time to time, to move them around. Then put them next to the bacon. Again, strongly heat the fat. Put in the pieces of giblets except the liver. Add the onion, cut into six parts. Mix everything with a wooden spoon on strong heat for *8–10 minutes,* until the giblets are lightly browned on all surfaces. Sprinkle them with the flour; mix it well. Now on very moderate heat, continue to mix until the flour has taken on a nice brown color.

Then add the white wine and the bouillon (minus about a glass, which you need to reserve for cooking the chestnuts). On strong heat, bring to a boil, stirring continuously with a wooden spoon to completely dissolve the roux. Cover and immediately turn down to very moderate heat—or better yet, put it into a medium heat oven. One way or another, the sauce must be kept at a gentle, tranquil, and regular simmer for *1 1/4 hours.* Meanwhile, prepare the rest of the garnish.

The carrots: Cut them into pieces 3 centimeters (1 1/4 inches) thick. Depending on the size of the vegetable, divide each piece into 4 or 6 parts to get 18 pieces—that is, 3 per person. Trim them into the shape of a large, long olive. Put them into a small casserole covered with cold water with a pinch of salt. Bring them to a boil, then maintain a gentle simmer for *about 20 minutes;* at this point, they are half-cooked. Drain, then keep them on a plate.

The chestnuts: Peel them (SEE PAGE 521). Put them in a small casserole with the reserved bouillon. Cook them gently for *about 20 minutes.*

To finish cooking: Turn off the heat. Wait 5 minutes to degrease it thoroughly, using a metal spoon. With a fork, lift out the pieces of giblets and put them in a sauté pan large enough to contain them with all the garnish and the sauce: in a deep casserole, it is hard to divide the garnish and finish the cooking.

On top of the pieces, spread out the carrots, the chestnuts, the bacon, and the small onions. Pass the degreased sauce through the chinois on everything. Check the salt. On strong heat, bring it back to a boil; cover. If possible, finish the cooking in the oven, which is better once the garnish has been added; if not, cook on gentle heat. Allow about *35 minutes* for this.

About 10 minutes before serving, cut each part of the liver into 4 scallops, cutting them on a bias. Drop the sausages into boiling water to stretch the skin and to prevent it from bursting; then put the liver and the sausages into the sauce.

(The liver must not cook any longer because it will become tough}. Without dressing the plate, pour it into a timbale or a heated shallow bowl. Serve boiling hot.

DUCK
Canard

Roast Duck *(Canard Rôti)*

Invariable rule: only a young and tender duck is good to roast.

Prepare it and truss it as a roasting chicken without barding it. Brush it with melted butter. Roast it in a very hot oven to seal it well and continue to brush it every time you turn it. This should take about *15 minutes* in the oven, keeping in mind that the flesh of the roast duck must not be bloody, as for a Rouen duck, but *very slightly pink.*

Carve the duck by first cutting long, thin slices from the entire length of the breast by holding the blade of the knife perpendicular to the carcass. After this, take off the thighs, dividing them as for the other fowl, and then remove the stumps of the wings.

Serve surrounded with watercress or with rounds of lemon, with the juice in a sauceboat.

Duck with Turnips *(Canard aux Navets)*

An excellent classic of home cooking. Even though this dish is good for all seasons, it is better to make it at the beginning of the summer when the duck is well fleshed but still very tender, and when the turnips are new. *Time: 1³/₄ hours for cooking.*

1 nice farm-raised duck, fleshy rather than fat, weighing 1 kilogram (2 pounds, 3 ounces) gross weight and 700 grams (1 pound, 9 ounces) when it has been gutted; 40 grams (1³/₈ ounces) of fresh fatback bacon, finely minced, to color the duck; if you do not have that, the same quantity of lard or butter; 15 grams (¹/₂ ounce) of flour for the roux; a half-liter (generous 2 cups) of excellent bouillon; a bouquet garni; a pinch of pepper.

400 grams (14¹/₈ ounces) of turnips, gross weight; 40 grams (1³/₈ ounces, 3 tablespoons) of butter to color them; a good pinch of superfine sugar.

PROCEDURE. Clean the duck meticulously after it has been gutted, flamed, etc. Remove the neck while preserving the entire length of the skin in order to draw it over the back. Truss it carefully with string. Use a deep, thick aluminum casserole of the right size so that the liquid is enough to cover the turnips.

Melt the bacon in it on gentle heat. Put the duck in it; do not cover. Keeping the heat low, color it gently for *15–20 minutes,* turning it from time to time so that it can gradually take on the golden tint of a roast duck. Then take it out and put it on a plate.

In the fat where it was colored, mix the flour. Turn the heat down more. Cook it gently (SEE ROUX, PAGE 47) until it has taken on a light, reddish color. Dilute it with cold or warm bouillon; add the pepper—but no salt, because the bouillon is salted. Bring it to a boil on strong heat, stirring constantly. Then let it boil gently for *about 10 minutes;* with a metal spoon, remove the fat that has risen to the surface of the sauce.

Then pass the sauce through a chinois into a bowl. Rinse the casserole with hot water. Put the sauce back in the casserole, having first removed any burned pieces of duck and bacon. Bring it back to a boil with a strong heat. As soon after as possible, put the duck into the casserole with the juice that has escaped while resting and add the bouquet garni. Put a round of buttered parchment paper right on top of the duck, well down into the casserole.

Put the cover on. If possible, put the casserole into a moderate oven so that the sauce maintains an uninterrupted, gentle simmer. If you do not have an oven, put the casserole on a gentle heat, observing the same conditions for cooking. A boil that is too lively would not only spoil the duck, but would also mar the sauce. From this point, allow *25 minutes of cooking.*

The turnips: As soon as the duck is in the oven, prepare them as directed (SEE TURNIPS FOR GARNISH, PAGE 525), making them the size of a nice olive.

At the end of *25 minutes of cooking,* add the drained turnips, pushing them down into the sauce. Cover everything with the paper and the cover. Continue cooking for *35–40 minutes.* Thus, a total of *1 good hour* calculated from the moment the duck was put into the sauce.

To serve: Remove the casserole from the heat. Take out the duck, draining it well by the rump. Put it on a warmed round serving plate, not a bowl. Cut the string with scissors. Remove the bouquet garni. Remove the turnips with a slotted spoon, or, if you do not have one, put a fork under them so that you do not remove the fat at the same time, and arrange them around the duck. Keep the plate in a warm place.

With a metal spoon, degrease the sauce as much as possible. At the most, you need *3 deciliters (1¼ cups).* If there is more than this, boil it on strong heat, uncovered, to reduce it. Check the seasoning. Pour it on the duck and the turnips. Serve on very hot plates.

Olive Duck *(Canard aux Olives)*

Use exactly the same cooking procedure and the same quantities as for DUCK WITH TURNIPS (SEE PAGE 379). Follow every point of the directions, replacing the turnips with olives. In other words, use 4 dozen *nice round olives,* pitted and blanched as directed (SEE PAGE 22), which you add to the sauce for the duck only a few moments before serving, just long enough to heat them.

Without changing any part of the cooking or the quantities, we suggest adding 1 tablespoon of concentrated tomato purée at the same time as the bouillon; and a small refinement also practiced by Mme. Sainte-Ange, 1 scant tablespoon of Madeira wine mixed into the sauce at the last moment, off the heat.

Duckling with Green Peas *(Caneton aux Petits Pois)*

Calling this dish "duckling" is to indicate that the chosen beast must be young and tender. Proceed as directed for SQUAB WITH GREEN PEAS (PAGE 390). The quantity for 2 pigeons is enough for 1 duck. As recommended for pigeons, take all the time needed for coloring the onions, the bacon, and the duck. Conduct your cooking gently without haste. Allow *1½ hours* of cooking in total.

Duck à la Orange *(Canard à l'Orange)*

According to different epochs and authors, there are several dishes that deserve this title. Some say that the duck is roasted and accompanied by a bigarade ("bitter orange") sauce: this sauce is a very reduced brown sauce to which orange juice is added, to return it to its original consistency, and then orange peel, cut in julienne, is added. Or, more simply, the juices from roasting the duck are thoroughly degreased and then diluted with ordinary juice; starch is added to make a liaison, then orange juice and a julienne of the orange peel are added. As for every roast duck, this method can only be used on a young and tender duck.

Other authors suggest braising, which does not require a beast that is quite so tender. The procedure of braising can vary according to your means. When you have brown sauce, add this to the duck, which has first been colored in butter; later, the sauce is reduced, then finished with orange juice and the julienne of orange peel. If you do not have this brown sauce ready in advance, proceed as described further down. But one way or the other, note that the duck must be cooked long enough so that it reaches the point where it could be, as the

French say, "carved with a spoon": this is the characteristic of duck that has been braised à l'orange. You should also observe that, for juice or sauce, you must not let it boil after adding the orange juice and the zest; and roasted or braised, the duck should be surrounded by orange quarters, which are trimmed of all their membranes *(pelés à vif). Time: 2½–3 hours. Serves 4–6.*

1 nice fleshy duck; 50 grams (1¾ ounces) of good lard; 80–100 grams (about 2¾–3½ ounces) of carrots and the same of onions cut into slices 5 millimeters (3/16 inch) thick; 2 deciliters (6¾ fluid ounces, ⅞ cup) of white wine; 6 deciliters (2½ cups) of veal jus, or, if you do not have it, good bouillon; 1 teaspoon of starch, preferably arrowroot; the juice and the zest of an orange; 2 oranges divided into quarters.

PROCEDURE. In a deep casserole made of good thick aluminum, heat the lard. Put the duck in with the carrots and the onions; on very moderate heat, color it, turning it as necessary. Then baste it with the white wine; on strong heat and without a cover, bring it to a boil until this wine is reduced to 3 tablespoons. Add the jus or the bouillon; season it with a pinch of pepper and salt depending on how more or less salted the bouillon is. Bring it to a boil. Cover first with buttered parchment paper placed right on top of the duck and then with the cover. Put it in an oven at a heat that is just sufficient to maintain the liquid at a gentle, regular simmer (as for the pot-au-feu), for at least *2 hours* or more, according to the tenderness of the bird.

During the cooking, finely peel the orange so that you take only the orange part of the skin without allowing the least bit of white to stick to it. Then cut this peel into julienne as thinly as possible. Throw these into a small casserole of boiling water and let boil 5 or 6 minutes to tenderize. Dry on a kitchen towel.

Meanwhile, peel the 2 oranges *à vif*: separate the quarters and remove the membrane that covers them in such a way that the flesh, or pulp, is completely exposed.

Once the duck has been properly cooked, strain all the juice from cooking into a small casserole. Completely degrease it. Here you will need 3 deciliters (1¼ cups) of juice; depending on whether you have more or less, either boil it for a moment to reduce it, or increase the quantity with a little bit of bouillon. Bind it with the starch (SEE LIAISONS, PAGE 47). Finally, mix in the orange juice that has been previously strained, a pinch of superfine sugar, and the zest of the orange. Dress the duck on a round heated plate surrounded by orange quarters. Send the cooking juice to the table in a sauceboat.

Rouen Duck *(Canard à la Rouennaise)*

Generally speaking, at least on menus, the word *caneton* ("duckling") replaces *canard* ("duck"), thus indicating a young and choice beast. A Rouen duck is unique in that it is not killed like other ducks, which are bled, but is killed by suffocating it: this conserves all its blood, so the flesh takes on a darkish tint. This means that a Rouen duck must, uniquely, be cooked rare. That is why, when it is served warm, it can only be cooked by roasting, though there are, nonetheless, different ways of doing this.

A Rouen duck can be prepared in two ways: stuffed or not, roasted on the spit or in the oven, and served with an accompanying Rouen sauce, which is nothing other than a bordelaise with some purée of liver added to it. But even though this is the way that it is most often done in home cooking, this is not the real method *à la rouennaise.* The real method tends to be practiced in the great restaurants, which possess the necessary ingredients. What you need to know: The first requirement is a red-hot oven, one that can generate an extreme heat so that the duck is immediately sealed, to hold the blood in its flesh; the second requirement is a press to extract the juice from the duck; and the third, a sufficiently experienced maître d'hôtel so he can rapidly carve the duck into extremely thin slices, taking a dozen slices from each side. Here we will follow the directions of the chef Philéas Gilbert, who is particularly qualified for this operation. *Serves 10.*

1 nice Rouen duck weighing 1½ kilograms (3 pounds, 5 ounces), completely gutted.

PROCEDURE. Once the duck has been gutted and flamed with alcohol, wipe the duck with a dry towel. Scrape the claws and clean the bottoms of the feet. Using a small knife, detach the forked bone at the beginning of the breast to make it easier to carve these slices.

Prepare a grill fire in advance, the grill greased first so that the bars are very hot by the time you have carved the duck and the grill is then ready to have the thighs placed on it.

Put the duck into a small roasting plate: brush it lightly with melted butter. Put it into a red-hot oven; in a professional restaurant oven, just *10 minutes* of cooking will suffice. For home cooking in an ordinary oven, this time must of course be prolonged, and you should allow *16–18 minutes.* In each case, the actual time will depend on the particular oven and the degree of heat it can achieve.

Meanwhile, have at hand: a long, large plate—made of silver, metal, or other—that can go from the oven to the table, and spread the bottom with a piece of butter the size of a walnut, then sprinkle with 20 grams (2/3 ounce) of finely minced shallot and season with salt, pepper, etc.; mix in a saucer: 7 grams (1/4 ounce) of sea salt, crushed into a powder, a good pinch of ground pepper, a small pinch of grated nutmeg and the same amount of spiced powder: 30 grams (1 ounce, 2 tablespoons) of butter divided into pieces; 1 full deciliter (3 1/3 fluid ounces, 1/2 cup) of *good* red wine; a duck press with the recipient to gather the juice; a carving knife with a thin, sharp blade.

At the end of cooking, remove the duck from the oven. Allow it to *rest 5 minutes* before carving. Detach the thighs; on the interior and very rare part, make a few cuts with the point of the knife. Lightly season this side and put the thighs on the grill, the interior side exposed to the heat.

Cut thin slices along the entire length of the flesh on the breast. As you cut them, put them on the prepared plate, previously sprinkled with shallot, salt, pepper, etc. Lay them down a little bit on the bias. Finally, detach the stumps of the wings; season them, and put them on the grill.

Sprinkle the slices with a pinch of seasoning; spread some pieces of butter on top of them. Cover them with an upside-down plate.

Coarsely chop the carcass. Put it in the press; close the press. Open it to add the wine; press again even more strongly to extract all the juice from the carcass. Stir to mix the juices and the wine. Pour this jus onto the slices. Place the metal plate on the stovetop to heat the juice thoroughly *without boiling.* Put the plate into a very hot oven to glaze it (SEE PAGE 15). If the oven is not hot enough to complete this glaze in just a *few seconds,* it would be better to heat the jus and the slices, without boiling, for an moment. To serve, put a thigh and a wing piece at each end of the serving plate. Use burning hot plates.

Duck à la Villageoise
(Canard à la Villageoise)

A home-style dish that is particularly apt for a duck that is not very young but is very well fleshed; for sumptuous meals in the countryside, this is a dish that is always very much appreciated. *Time: 2 1/2 hours. Serves 6.*

1 nice duck weighing, gutted, about 1 1/2 kilograms (3 pounds, 5 ounces); 30–40 grams (1–1 3/8 ounces, 2–3 tablespoons) of good lard or butter; 200 grams (7 ounces) of lean bacon; 15–20 grams (1/2–2/3 ounce) of flour for the roux; 200 grams (7 ounces) of carrots and the same of turnips; 1 deciliter (3 1/3 fluid ounces, scant 1/2 cup) of white wine; 1/2 liter (generous 2 cups) of bouillon; a small bouquet garni; a pinch of pepper; a small curly cabbage weighing, completely trimmed, about 500 grams (1 pound, 2 ounces); 150 grams (5 1/3 ounces) of bacon; 3 deciliters (1 1/4 cups) of bouillon and 2 tablespoons of fat (fat from a stew or a roast, except for mutton).

PROCEDURE. **The cabbage:** Peel it, blanch it, cool it as directed (SEE PAGE 496). The cabbage should have been previously divided into 4. Cut the bacon into thin slices and blanch it (SEE PAGE 11). Line the bottom of a small sauté pan. Put in the cabbage, coarsely chopped with just a few knife cuts. Add the bouillon and the fat. Bring it to a boil on strong heat. Cover with greased parchment paper placed directly on top of the quarters of the cabbage and with a tightly fitting cover. Put it into a very moderate oven. Be sure that this cooking is maintained at a gentle and regular pace for *2 hours.*

Carrots and turnips: Peel them and divide them in quarters. Remove the inside yellow parts of the carrots. Make 2 or 3 pieces of each quarter, depending on how large they are. Trim the two ends with the knife to shape them like a large clove of garlic. Throw them into a casserole of boiling salted water (10 grams/1/3 ounce of salt per liter). Let them boil for *10–15 minutes*, depending on how early or late in the season it is. Then drain them.

The bacon: Remove the rind. Cut it into slices about 4–5 centimeters (1 1/2–1 3/4 inches) square and 1/2 centimeter (3/16 inch) thick. Blanch it.

Take a nice thick casserole—a good cast-iron pot if you do not have tinned copper—that is big enough to hold not just the duck, but also the garnish of carrots and turnips. Heat the butter or the fat in it. Add the slices of bacon. On moderate heat, brown them lightly. Remove them with a small skimmer so that all the fat is left in the casserole; replace them with the duck.

The duck: Like all the previous recipes, this should have been meticulously cleaned, gutted, etc.; with the neck and feet removed. Carefully truss with string.

Color it as directed for DUCK WITH TURNIPS (PAGE 379). Then make the roux. Dilute it with the white wine and bouillon and continue in just the same way, until the duck is put back in the rinsed utensil.

Then add the bacon around the duck, and also the carrots on one side and the turnips on another; plus a bouquet garni. Cover with a buttered parchment paper placed directly on top of everything, then close with the cover and put it in the oven. Cook as for the DUCK WITH TURNIPS (SEE PAGE 379), basting it from time to time with the cooking juice. Allow *1 1/2–2 hours* of cooking, depending on the tenderness of the beast.

To serve: Drain the cabbage in a strainer placed over a bowl, pressing gently with a spoon to extract all the liquid from it: even the smallest amount would later spoil the garnish.

Remove the duck from its casserole, draining it well. Put it on a round heated plate. Cut the strings with a scissors. With a small skimmer, take out the cooked vegetables and put them on each side of the duck. Arrange the slices of bacon on top. Place the cabbage at each end of the duck. Keep the plate hot. Using a metal spoon, degrease the cooking juice of the duck; if necessary, reduce it so that there is no more than *3 deciliters (1 1/4 cups)*. Check the seasoning. Pour it on the duck and the garnish. Serve with burning-hot plates.

Stuffed Ducks *(Canards Farcis)*

This is an excellent recipe in that it makes the bird go further, and the flavor of the stuffing adds to its savoriness. The ingredients for the stuffing are about the same for all the recipes listed below; garlic is almost always used as a discreet complement, so it is added in an infinitesimal amount, or cut a clove in half and rub it on the inside of the bowl where you mix the stuffing. When you have mushroom trimmings, these are excellent to use; you color them with minced onion before adding them to the mix. *Serves 6.*

1 good, mature duck, still sufficiently tender and nice and fleshy, and weighing about 2 1/2 kilograms (5 pounds, 8 ounces) gutted. This can be accompanied by any garnish, as you will see below.

For the stuffing: 125 grams (4 1/2 ounces) of good pork, minced, or sausage meat, containing equal amounts of lean and fat; 60 grams (2 1/4 ounces) of finely minced onion; 20 grams (2/3 ounce, 1 heaping tablespoon) of butter; 50 grams (1 3/4 ounces) of stale bread crumbs; an egg; 1/2 tablespoon of minced parsley; 1 piece of garlic the size of a pea; a pinch of salt, a pinch of pepper, and some spice powder.

PROCEDURE. In a small casserole, put the butter and minced onion. Cook the onion gently, letting it scarcely color. Pour it onto a plate to cool it. Put the bread crumbs to soak in a bowl, moistened with several tablespoons of bouillon at room temperature.

To stuff: Gut the duck as directed (SEE PREPARTION OF FOWL, PAGE 349). Flame it and then clean it, particularly under the wings, wiping it there with a dry towel.

Remove the bile sack from the liver, taking great care not to allow any green part to remain on the liver, which would make the stuffing bitter. Finally, mince the liver; put it into a terrine with: the minced pork; the bread crumbs, thoroughly squeezed to completely extract the liquid; the onion, which has been left to cool; the parsley; the garlic, squashed under the blade of a knife; a pinch of salt, a pinch of pepper, and a little pinch of spice powder; and the egg, already beaten into a foam in a cup. With a wooden spoon, mix it well until perfectly combined.

Place the duck in front of you, standing it on its rump, and leaning up against something for support. Take the stuffing with a metal spoon and spoon it into the neck opening, pushing it in with your finger. Stretch the skin from the neck over the back to completely close the opening. Carefully bind the beast, tying the neck skin with the string that passes underneath the wing, and fold the legs along the breast, turning them front to back. The duck is then ready to be cooked.

Stuffed Duck in the Limousin Style *(Canard Farci à la Façon du Limousin).* The quantities for the stuffing, and how to prepare it, are the same as those given above. *Time: 2 hours (the duck already having been stuffed). Serves 6.*

For garnish and cooking: 125 grams (4½ ounces) of bacon with the rind removed, cut into small lardons and blanched (SEE PAGE 11); 15–20 very small onions; 40 grams (1⅜ ounces, 3 tablespoons) of butter and 20 grams (⅔ ounce) of flour for a roux; ½ liter (generous 2 cups) of bouillon and ½ deciliter (1⅔ fluid ounces, scant ¼ cup) of white wine; a bouquet garni; about 30 nice chestnuts and ½ liter (generous 2 cups) of bouillon to cook them; 1 stalk of celery.

PROCEDURE. In an appropriately sized thick aluminum casserole, heat the butter. Lightly brown the lardons on strong heat. Drain them and put them on a plate. Replace them with small onions (SEE SMALL ONIONS FOR GARNISH, PAGE 525). Once they are colored, drain them and put them with the lardons. In the same butter and on very moderate heat, gradually color the duck as for DUCK WITH TURNIPS (PAGE 379). Take it out and put it on a plate. Still in the same butter, make a dark blond roux with the flour (SEE ROUX, PAGE 47). Dilute with the bouillon and the wine; bring it to a boil, constantly stirring with the whisk.

Put the duck in the sauce with the juices that have escaped from it and the bouquet garni. To simplify things, you do not need to strain the sauce as for DUCK WITH TURNIPS (SEE PAGE 379). Cover the casserole. Then keep the sauce at a gentle, regular simmer, either by putting the casserole into a medium oven or keeping it on low heat. From this point, allow *1¼ hours* of cooking. At the end of *a good half hour,* add the onions and the lardons to the duck; *and 40 minutes later,* add the chestnuts (that is, 20 minutes before the end of cooking).

Meanwhile, as the duck is coloring, peel the chestnuts (SEE PAGE 521). Put them in a small casserole with the celery cut into small pieces and the bouillon; no salt. Bring it to a boil, then cover and cook gently for *a good half hour*—that is, cook them two-thirds of the way through and they will finish cooking with the duck. Then drain them in a strainer, take out the celery, and put them in the sauce around the duck.

To serve: For the duck, the garnish, and degreasing and reducing the sauce, etc., proceed as for DUCK WITH TURNIPS (SEE PAGE 379). Allow here *3½ deciliters (1½ cups)* of sauce. If carving in the kitchen, take out the stuffing and divide it to accompany each slice of duck along with the garnish.

Stuffed Duck in Aspic *(Canard Farci en Gelée).* This is an excellent home-style recipe for preparing a very young duck.

Prepare the stuffing with the liver of the duck, finely minced; 125 grams (4½ ounces) of minced pork or sausage meat, truffled, and 125 grams (4½ ounces) of non-truffled meat; 60 grams (2¼ ounces) of stale bread crumbs mixed with a whole beaten egg; 2 tablespoons of Madeira; pepper and a little bit of salt, depending on whether the meat is more or less salted. Knead everything into a homogenous mixture.

Thoroughly clean the duck, then stuff, proceeding as directed for stuffed duck; truss it in the normal fashion. Cook it in a deep casserole or in a *daubière* with a half veal foot, carrots, leeks, onions, garlic cloves—exactly as for a pot-au-feu; 2 good glasses of white wine; very little salt, some coarsely ground pepper and enough water to cover the duck.

When it comes to a boil, cover and cook very gently for *3–4 hours,* depending on your estimate of the firmness of the meat according to the age of the duck. Lift it out onto a plate and immediately untie it. Reduce the cooking liquid if there is still too much. Clarify it as directed (SEE MEAT GELÉE, PAGE 45). Allow it to gel, and with this gelée decorate the duck according to your taste.

Duck of the Green Monkey *(Le Canard du Singe Vert).* Here garlic is not included in the sauce except to rub the bowl where the stuffing is mixed; add 1/2 tablespoon of cognac and an extra egg. Out of season, replace both the fresh tomato and the fresh beans with canned tomatoes; if you have only tomato concentrate, dilute it with enough water to make an amount of liquid equivalent to that from a fresh tomato. Use the same amount of stuffing as above. *Time: 2 hours (the duck having already been stuffed).*

For cooking and garnish: 1 good tablespoon of lard; 3 nice tomatoes; 1 medium-size onion stuck with a clove; a bouquet garni; 1 liter (4 1/4 cups) of fresh, white beans; or, according to the season, about 1/2 liters (generous 2 cups) of dried beans; 2 deciliters (6 3/4 fluid ounces, 7/8 cup) of cooking water from the beans.

PROCEDURE. In a good cast-iron pot, heat the lard. Gently color the duck in it.

Peel the tomatoes; remove the water and the seeds; cut them into pieces. Put them around the colored duck along with the onion and clove and the bouquet garni. Once it has come to a boil, cover it tightly and put it in a moderately hot oven, which here replaces the burning cinders of the old country fireplaces. Allow *1 hour* of cooking at a small, regular simmering.

Meanwhile, cook the beans so that they can be added to the duck at the end of this time (SEE COOKING FRESH BEANS, PAGE 470, OR COOKING OF DRIED VEGETABLES, PAGE 556). Once the duck has been cooked for the given time, add half a glass of the water from the beans to dilute the little bit of juices from the duck; if has reduced too much, add a little more water from the beans. Put the beans around the duck; place the cover back on the pot and put it back into a mild oven to maintain a very gentle simmer for *25–30 minutes.*

To serve: Put the duck on a warmed round plate. Cut the strings. Remove the bouquet and the onion. With great care, mix the beans into the cooking juice and pour everything around the duck. Leave behind the cooking fat: it has not been overheated at any time, so it is extremely good.

GOOSE
Oie

No matter how it is presented, goose must never be considered anything other than a dish suitable for home-style cooking, and even to country-style cooking, given the use made of it on farms in particular.

For all goose recipes, always use a young beast whose flesh is tender but sufficiently mature: thus, at Christmas, the traditional time for roast goose in the country, you should use a bird born the previous May. In this case, it is more of a "gosling," and this is what is recommended in the very oldest recipes. Such a goose weighs around 3 kilograms (6 pounds, 10 ounces), and when plucked, gutted, with its giblets removed, about 2 1/4 kilograms (5 pounds). It will serve about 10 people.

Roast Goose *(Oie Rôti)*

Trussed as usual and prepared as directed (SEE ROASTS, PAGE 30). Allow, for roasting a young, well-fleshed goose, about *15–18 minutes per 450 grams (1 pound);* and *20 minutes per 450 grams (1 pound)* for a fatted goose. Degrease the juice after cooking and reserve the fat for a preparation of your choice.

Goose with Turnips *(Oie aux Navets)*

Proceed as for DUCK WITH TURNIPS (SEE PAGE 379). Increase the amounts a bit for all the ingredients. Allow *1 1/4 hours* for cooking after the goose has colored. The degreased sauce should provide about 4 deciliters (1 2/3 cups).

Goose with Chestnuts *(Oie aux Marrons)*

Proceed in every way as for TURKEY WITH CHESTNUTS (SEE PAGE 376).

Cold Goose in Casserole *(Oie aux Daube Froide)*

Proceed as for CHICKEN IN A CASSEROLE (SEE PAGE 375) à la ménagère, or as for STUFFED DUCK IN ASPIC (SEE PAGE 384).

Ragoût of Goose *(Oie en Ragoût)*

Bought retail and cut into pieces of 50–60 grams (1 3/4–2 1/4 ounces). Season with pepper and salt and gently color it in a sauté pan with minced bacon or good lard: so, per kilogram (2 pounds, 3 ounces) use 30–40 grams (1–1$^3/_8$ ounces) of chopped bacon. Drain the fat; sprinkle with 20–25 grams ($^2/_3$–1 ounce) of flour; let it gently color. Add 2 deciliters (6$^3/_4$ fluid ounces, $^7/_8$ cup) of white wine and $^1/_2$ liter (generous 2 cups) of bouillon or water; bouquet garni; an onion stuck with a clove. Cover and cook it at a very gentle simmer for *a good 1$^1/_4$ hours.* At the appropriate time, add the vegetables of your choice: salsify, which has first been blanched for a half hour, and which should cook here for 45 minutes to 1 hour. Or chestnuts cooked three-quarters of the way through and then marinated in the sauce for 15–20 minutes. Or celery stalks or celery root; the root should be half-cooked when it goes into the ragoût.

Carefully degrease the sauce before serving. The final quantity can scarcely be estimated here, because it depends on the kind of vegetables, but there should be relatively little.

Stuffed Goose *(Oie Farcie)*

Mince finely and separately: the liver of the beast, a medium onion, 2 shallots, some parsley, about enough for 1 good teaspoon. Soak 50 grams (1$^3/_4$ ounces) of stale bread crumbs in a few tablespoons of bouillon; then press it thoroughly. Assemble these different ingredients in a terrine; add a whole egg to it; season with a pinch of salt, some pepper, and a little pinch of spice powder. A little bit of garlic, squashed under the blade of a knife, is optional.

Mix everything well. Put this stuffing into the bird, through either an enlarged rump opening or a small opening on the side of the breast. Sew with strong string. Cut the head, but keep the skin that is close to the body. Stretch the skin over the back; truss the animal securely with a double string. Place the goose in a roasting pan, then brush it with good fat. Put it into a *very hot* oven and turn it as it colors: this should take about *15 minutes.*

Next, scatter a few rounds of onion and carrot underneath the goose, having first colored them in a little bit of fat in a pan. Add a bouquet garni and three-quarters of a glass of bouillon. From this point, allow for *1$^1/_4$ hours* of cooking; given the time needed for coloring the goose, this means a total of *1$^1/_2$ hours* of cooking. Note that you should also turn down the heat of the oven at this point, keeping it at a consistent temperature until the end.

Frequently baste the goose with its cooking juices: this type of roasting does not follow the principles of other roasts. Turn the bird from time to time.

To serve: Cut the string with scissors. Pass the juice through a chinois and degrease it only partially. Serve it on the side.

Goose in the Alsatian Manner *(Oie à l'Alsacienne)*

Soak and wash 1.3 kilograms (2 pounds, 14 ounces) of sauerkraut. Put it in a thick casserole with about 200 grams (7 ounces) of good fat; 4 deciliters (1$^2/_3$ cups) of white wine; $^3/_4$ liter of light bouillon that is lightly salted; a bouquet garni; 15 juniper berries enclosed in a little bit of cheesecloth. Cover with greased parchment paper, putting it directly on top of the sauerkraut, and then put on the lid. Cook gently in the oven *3 hours.* When the cooking is half done, add to the sauerkraut 400 grams (14$^1/_8$ ounces) of *smoked* bacon that has been previously blanched for a good 15 minutes.

Stuff the goose with its liver, shallots, and minced parsley. Put it in a casserole that has been lined as for braising (SEE PAGE 25) with about 100 grams (3$^1/_2$ ounces) of salt pork, and rounds of onion and carrots. Put the uncovered casserole in an oven that is hot enough to give a nice color to the bird, turning it on all sides; then pour 4 deci-liters (1$^2/_3$ cups) of bouillon and 2 deciliters (6$^3/_4$ fluid ounces, $^7/_8$ cup) of good white wine into it. Once it has begun boiling, place a round of buttered parchment paper right on top of the bird. Cover. Place the casserole in a gentle oven to maintain a very steady, gentle simmer for *2 hours.* Baste frequently.

To serve: Pour the juice used for braising the goose into a small casserole; it should now be reduced by a good half. Degrease it and bind it with starch (SEE LIAISONS, PAGE 47). Place the sauerkraut in a circle on a round plate: do this either by molding it first in a round mold or place it there tablespoon by tablespoon. It is possible that the sauerkraut may have absorbed all its liquid during its long cooking, so that there is no excess; put the bacon cut into thin slices on top. Keep it warm;

rapidly carve the goose. Arrange it inside the border of sauerkraut. Pour the bound juice on the pieces. Serve burning hot.

Flemish-Style Goose *(Oie à la Flamande)*

Braised as above and surrounded with a garnish *à la flamande.* SEE GARNITURE À LA FLAMANDE (PAGE 262).

English-Style Goose *(Oie à l'Anglaise)*

Blanch a few leaves of sage, fresh or dried, taking care to reduce the amount if they are fresh, because their odor is stronger. Mince them finely; also mince 3 large onions; blanch them for 5 minutes and drain them well. Color them with the sage in a casserole in butter for a few minutes. Add a good teacup of stale, fine bread crumbs, and salt and pepper; be generous with the pepper. Stuff the goose with this mixture. Roast it in front of a good fire for 1 hour or more, depending on the size of the bird. Accompany it with its juice and applesauce in separate dishes.

Applesauce is a purée of apples to which very little sugar is added. You can even dispense with the sugar so that you do not destroy the predominately acid flavor of the apples, which is a good counter to the fatty goose.

Foie Gras

Terrine of Foie Gras. SEE PATÉS AND TERRINES (PAGE 424).

Foie Gras with Madeira *(Foie Gras au Madère)*. The Madeira can, if you like, be replaced by port and the foie gras can be truffled or not; the preparation remains the same. We describe here the simplest method for the liaison of the sauce; it is increasingly being used in professional kitchens. We insist only that it is essential to use a very good veal jus, which is only *lightly salted* given the final reduction that takes place. The quality of this jus is all the more important because the sauce for the foie gras is nothing other than the reduced juices used to cook the liver, and most of its flavor comes not from the liver—which, in fact, does not flavor it at all—but from the cooking liquid itself—in other words, from the veal jus. Refer to jus of veal (PAGE 45). *Time: 1 1/4 hours for cooking and then correcting the sauce. If the liver is truffled, it is a good idea to prepare it 2 hours in advance and then keep it cool in a terrine before cooking it. Serves 8.*

1 foie gras weighing about 800 grams (1 pound, 12 ounces); 1 large bard or 2 of medium-size cut as thin as a sheet of paper.

For the cooking: 20 grams (2/3 ounce) of fresh salt pork; 80 grams (about 2 3/4 ounces) of carrot and the same of onions, cut into fine rounds; 3 finely minced shallots; 25 grams (1 ounce) of fresh mushroom trimmings; a small bouquet garni; 3 deciliters (1 1/4 cups) of veal jus; 1 deciliter (3 1/3 fluid ounces, scant 1/2 cup) of Madeira; salt, pepper, spices.

For the liaison and to finish the sauce: 12 grams (3/8 ounce) of arrowroot; 1/2 deciliter (1 2/3 fluid ounces, scant 1/4 cup) of Madeira; 25 grams (1 ounce, 2 tablespoons) of good butter.

If you truffle the foie: 2 medium-size truffles (about 75 grams/2 2/3 ounces gross weight).

PROCEDURE. Clean the liver as directed for terrine of FOIE GRAS À L'ALSACIENNE (PAGE 428). Season it lightly with salt, pepper, and a hint of spice. Enclose it in sheets of fatback bacon.

Use an oval cooking utensil, pot, or pâté terrine just large enough so that between the liver and the walls of the pan there is just 1 centimeter (1/2 inch) of space. Line the bottom with the salt pork (the fat part down), carrots, onions, shallots, mushroom trimmings, bouquet garni. Place the liver on top. Add the veal jus and the Madeira. If the utensil or the terrine are of the right size, this amount of liquid will be enough so that the liver is lightly immersed; but if the pan is too big, you will have to add a little more jus and Madeira.

Bring it to a boil on strong heat. Then cover the utensil with its cover and put it in the oven. The heat of the oven must be moderate, just sufficient to maintain the liquid not at a boil, but at a simple simmer for *45 minutes.* At the end of this time, take the pan out of the oven. Put the liver on a plate. Cover it and keep it warm.

Strain the cooking liquid through a fine chinois into a small sauté pan. Boil it strongly, uncovered, to reduce it to *2 1/2 deciliters (1 cup).* Dissolve the arrowroot in a bowl with 2 or 3 tablespoons of jus or bouillon. Pour it into the reduced juices, mixing it with a whisk. Allow it to boil scarcely *10 seconds.* Turn off the heat. Add the 1/2 deciliter (1 2/3 fluid ounces, scant 1/4 cup) of Madeira.

Remove the bards from the liver. Put the liver in the sauce. Keep it on very gentle heat in the covered casserole for *10–12 minutes* without allowing the sauce to boil. At the end of 6 minutes, turn the liver over in the sauce.

To serve: Place the liver on a round plate *that is very hot.* Heat the sauce on strong heat for a few moments, but do not let it boil because the Madeira would lose its aroma. *Off the heat,* mix in the butter. Pour only a few tablespoons on the liver. Serve the rest in a sauceboat.

Truffled liver: Once the liver has been cleaned, use the point of a small knife to make a dozen incisions *on a bias,* about 1 centimeter (3/8 inch) deep and about 1 1/2 centimeters (5/8 inch) apart.

Clean the truffles (SEE PAGE 537). Cut them in rounds about 1/2 centimeter (3/16 inch) thick. Cut them on the bias on one side. Slip them into the prepared incisions, letting them stick out by about 1 good centimeter (3/8 inch) so that they look a little bit like large scales. Season and surround the liver with bards, as already directed. For cooking the sauce, proceed exactly the same way. If you do not have any use for the trimmings and peelings from the truffles, they can be put into the cooking water of the liver.

Mousse of Foie Gras *(Mousse de Foie Gras).* According to preference, you can use a liver from a terrine or one that has been canned, or you can even use fresh *foie gras* cooked in Madeira. The truffle can also be preserved or fresh and cooked in the Madeira. The quantities we give are for cooked liver: if you use fresh liver, you must take into account the weight loss caused by cooking.

For the kind of aspic, the time needed, and other directions, refer to COLD HAM MOUSSE (PAGE 347). *Time: 1 hour (once the aspic has been prepared). Serves 8–10.*

300 grams (10 1/2 ounces) of *cooked* foie gras; 100 grams (3 1/2 ounces, 7 tablespoons) of good butter; about 10 grams (1/3 ounce) of salt; 3 deciliters (1 1/4 cups) of gelée reduced to 1 1/2 deciliters (5 fluid ounces, 2/3 cup); 2 1/2 deciliters (1 cup) of fresh, heavy cream to be whipped; a point of cayenne pepper, as much as can be held on the point of a knife blade; 3/4 liter (generous 3 cups) of gelée to garnish the mold and then decorate the mousse; a charlotte mold with a capacity of about 1 1/4 liters (5 1/3 cups).

PROCEDURE. Line the mold with the gelée and decorate the bottom of it with patterns of truffles. Crush the foie gras in a mortar, chilled if it has been cooked in Madeira, and add the butter to it. Pass it through a fine metal drum seive. Incorporate the reduced and chilled gelée. Season. Add the whipped cream. Carefully check the seasoning. Pour it into the mold. Let it set for the time suggested. Dip the mold into warm water to unmold on a napkin-covered plate. Surround it with aspic decorations or minced aspic (SEE PAGE 445).

SQUAB
Pigeon

Stewed Squab *(Pigeon en Compote)*

This preparation is quite old. The recipes from different authors scarcely vary, and apart from a few details of execution, are always the same: the pigeon is colored in the casserole and cooked with a brown sauce, to which is added at the same time a garnish of mushrooms, lardons, and small onions. In some areas, stewed pigeon is prepared like a fricassée, but this is an exception.

We are going to give the classic recipe. The only modification is to the length of the cooking time. Today, the squab is first colored and put in the sauce, then cooked for an average of 25 minutes, but previously it was braised, like a red meat for at least 2 hours. It's true that, at the time, the directions for squab stew were to make sure that the bird absorbed so much of the cooking liquid that it could almost be cut with a spoon. The sauce was a sort of a light, exquisite syrup, in which the small onions seemed almost to have been preserved.

It is this classic form of cooking that we describe here: the quantities for the different ingredients are the same as the more recent recipes, and so are the preparations. It is only the cooking time for the squab, a slow and prolonged braising, that differs. Squab cooked thus can be cooked and held warm in its casserole for a very long time.

It is best to choose common squab for this dish. Do not buy them too young or too fat. The squab sold as a "squab hen" is not appropriate. *Time: 3 scant hours. Serves 6.*

3 ordinary squabs; 175 grams (6 ounces) of lean bacon; 200 grams (7 ounces) of very small onions; 200 grams (7 ounces) of small mushrooms; 6 deciliters (2$^1/_2$ cups) of light veal jus; 2 deciliters (6$^3/_4$ fluid ounces, $^7/_8$ cup) of white Bordeaux wine; 30 grams (1 ounce, 2 tablespoons) of butter and 20 grams of flour ($^2/_3$ ounce) for the roux.

PROCEDURE. Cut the *lardons,* having first removed the rind, into pieces 1 centimeter ($^3/_8$ inch) thick and 2 or 3 centimeters ($^3/_4$–1$^1/_4$ inch) long. Blanch them as directed (SEE PAGE 11).

In a thick aluminum casserole with high sides, just large enough to contain the squabs and their garnish, place the squab side by side; heat the butter and put in the lardons. On moderate heat, sauté them or move them around until they are lightly colored; drain them on a plate.

Put the *small onions* in the fat, and still without a cover color them gently, shaking the casserole to move them around without touching them directly, which would risk stripping their layers. To be properly cooked, they must be able to be stacked without their layers coming off, and they should have a golden tint that is stronger at their two ends. You can sprinkle them with some superfine sugar when they begin coloring to assist with that process. Drain them and put them with the lardons.

Clean the *mushrooms.* Cut them in half lengthwise without peeling them. Put them in the fat. On strong heat, lightly color them. Drain them thoroughly and put them with the lardons and the onions.

Meanwhile, the squab should have been cleaned, trussed, etc. Put the livers back into their bodies.

You can cut off their heads and add the heads to the cooking liquid.

Put the squab in the fat where the lardons, mushrooms, and onions have been colored. Do not cover. Color them gradually on all of their surfaces with very moderate heat. Take them out and put them on a plate. Make a dark blond roux with the flour, using the fat remaining in the casserole (SEE LIAISON WITH ROUX, PAGE 47). Dilute with the veal jus and the wine. Stir and bring to a boil; strain the sauce through a chinois into a small terrine. Rinse the casserole; pour the sauce back in. Once it has returned to a boil, put in the squab, lardons, mushrooms, and onions. Put buttered parchment paper right on top of the squab and cover tightly.

Put the casserole into a slow oven so you can maintain a simple and uninterrupted simmer for *2 hours.* You can monitor the cooking as it progresses by listening to the gentle bubbling from the casserole. You can also, from time to time, take the casserole out of the oven, uncovering it for a second to be sure that the liquid maintains a very small bubbling at the edges. Put the casserole immediately back into the oven without moving anything around in it.

To serve: Remove the squab carefully; put them on a plate, or, preferably, a shallow bowl. Cut the strings. Keep warm. Completely degrease the juice. There should be about *4 deciliters (1$^2/_3$ cups).* If there is more, remove the onions with the skimmer, then reduce it over strong heat. Pour it, with the garnish, on the pigeons. (Always be careful to detach the crust that has formed on the inside of the casserole, to mix it with the jus.)

Toad-Style Grilled Squab *(Pigeons à la Crapaudine)*

This recipe can be summarized as follows: the squab is split and flattened, thus taking on the shape of a toad, and then is breaded, grilled, and accompanied by a very spicy sauce—generally a sauce diable, which you can replace with a tartar sauce, if you like, or a remoulade sauce, a *sauce piquante,* etc. If the squab is very young and very tender, as it should always be, it should be entirely cooked on the grill. If not, it is better to half-cook it in a sauté pan with butter, then bread it to complete its cooking and coloration on the grill. *Time: 1 hour (including 25 minutes for cooking).*

3 squab; 75 grams (2$^2/_3$ ounces, $^1/_3$ cup) of butter; 6 good tablespoons of finely grated stale bread crumbs (SEE PAGE 19).

PROCEDURE. Once the squabs have been gutted, cleaned, etc., cut off their heads near the body.

Scrape the claws and insert the end of the feet into a small incision you make in the skin of the breast on each side of the thighs. With a good kitchen knife, split the pigeons on the back lengthwise completely. Open them without separating the 2 parts. Then give a couple of blows with the flat of a large cleaver to flatten the pigeon so that it looks like a level pancake.

Spread the bread crumbs on a plate. On another plate, melt the butter. Mix in the 2 pinches of salt and the 2 pinches of pepper. Dip one side of the squab into the melted butter; then place this buttered side onto the bread crumbs. Do the same on the other side. With the blade of a good-sized knife, press down on this breading to thoroughly amalgamate the bread crumbs and the butter.

To grill: Grilling on charcoal is better here than any other method. The squab must be grilled on a gentle fire and colored very gradually. Allow *20–25 minutes* according to the type of fuel you are using. Meanwhile, moisten the pigeons 2 or 3 times with melted butter, turning them over carefully on the grill so that you do not tear off the breading.

Serve burning hot on a warm plate with the sauce in a sauceboat. You can surround the squab with rounds of cornichons.

Squab with Green Peas *(Pigeons aux Petits Pois)*

Menus generally claim to offer squab because it looks better than young pigeons. But in reality, young adult pigeons are used rather than true squabs.

Let us explain ourselves. In fact, a young pigeon that is a true squab should have left the nest only scarcely a few days before; its excessive tenderness cannot stand up to prolonged cooking. But a squab, as we understand it, is a bird that has been self-sufficient for several months and whose flesh has developed and acquired a good flavor. As for an old pigeon, there are very few recipes that make use of it: certainly not this one.

This recipe with green peas can made in several ways. In the restaurants, the usual method is to cook the pigeon by itself, either in the oven or in a casserole with butter but no liquid. The peas are cooked separately and then poured on the squab just before serving. This procedure is particularly appropriate for true young squab, which should not cook for more than 18 minutes, while cooking the peas requires at least thirty. You can also apply this to an adult pigeon, and some people prepare it this way, which conserves its own juices and flavor.

In professional kitchens, the squab and the peas are cooked in the same pan, given that stock is already on hand. In old-fashioned home cooking—which always tends to follow the lessons of haute cuisine—it is the same. It is thus the simple method of very attentive bourgeois cooking that we recount here.

For the peas, note that you should choose medium-size peas of uniform size. Tiny peas are too tender for this recipe and large peas have a skin that is too thick, which prevents the heat from penetrating them in a limited cooking period. You should allow 1 deciliter (3 1/3 fluid ounces, scant 1/2 cup) of green peas per person. We recommend extremely fresh peas: do not shell them until the moment you are going to cook them.

You can omit the garnish of small onions. Indeed, it is not recommended by every author, but it is a nice addition to the dish. *Time: 1 1/2 hours. Serves 6.*

3 *nicely fleshed* squab; 150 grams (5 1/3 ounces) of *very lean* bacon; 18 small onions the size of a hazelnut or 9 the size of a small walnut; 9 deciliters (3 3/4 cups) of medium-size peas; 45 grams (1 1/2 ounces, 3 tablespoons) of butter; 20 grams (2/3 ounce) of flour; 4 1/2 deciliters (scant 2 cups) of completely degreased bouillon; a small bouquet garni; a pinch of pepper.

PROCEDURE. Bacon and onions. Remove the rind from the bacon and cut it into lardons a little more than 1 centimeter (3/8 inch) thick and 2 centimeters (3/4 inch) long. Blanch them as directed (SEE PAGE 11).

In a good aluminum casserole with deep sides, big enough to hold the pigeons and the peas, melt the butter. Add the lardons. On moderate heat, sauté them and mix them until they are lightly colored. Then take them out and put them on a plate, draining them well so that you leave all the butter in the casserole. Replace them with the small onions. Color the onions gently with the casserole still uncovered; do not touch them, but make them roll around the casserole by shaking it lightly: the color should be a uniform gold without any brown stains. Drain them: put them with the lardons.

The squab: Prepare these while cooking the lardoons and onions. Gut them, flame them, wipe them dry, and then put back the liver, which has no bile, inside the bird. Tuck the legs back in or flatten them, then truss the birds with string.

As soon as the onions are drained, put the squab into the casserole. Color them gradually, gently, on moderate heat without covering them, turning them over successively.

The peas: These can meanwhile be shelled.

The sauce: Once the squabs have been colored, take them out and put them on a plate. Carefully examine the butter that remains in the casserole before making the roux. If the lardons, the onions, and the squab have been gently colored, as recommended, the butter should not have burned and its color should be a beautiful yellow, resembling olive oil. Then you can add the flour. But if you heated it too much and the butter has browned, you must pour it completely out of the casserole and replace it with 20 grams (2/3 ounce, 1 heaping tablespoon) of new butter. Mix in the flour. Let it cook gently to form a small amount of roux that takes on dark blond color.

Dilute it with warm or cold bouillon. Add the pepper; no more salt, because of the bacon and bouillon. Bring it to a boil on strong heat, stirring continuously. Let it boil for 2 minutes; then strain the sauce through the chinois into a small terrine. Rinse the casserole with warm water to get rid of any residue. Pour in the strained sauce and bring it back to a boil on strong heat.

Then put the pigeons back into the sauce with the little bit of juice they released while standing, the bacon, the onions, the peas, and the bouquet garni. Cover the casserole. Once it has returned to a boil, turn down the heat very low. The sauce must continue to boil in a rather lively fashion, and not as for an ordinary braising. That said, the boiling must not be excessive.

Allow from this moment *a good half hour of cooking.* It is the peas that dictate the cooking time, which will always be enough for the pigeons. If the peas are not perfectly done at the end of this time, let everything cook for a few more minutes.

To serve: Place the pigeons on a round serving plate. Cut the strings with scissors.

Remove the bouquet. Tilt the casserole so that, with a metal spoon, you can *completely* remove the fat that has risen to the surface. The sauce should have reduced by a good third, giving a scarce *2 deciliters (6 3/4 fluid ounces, 7/8 cup).* If it seems a little diluted and does not bind the peas sufficiently, put the casserole, uncovered, on high heat, and boil it strongly for *2 minutes.* Pour the peas, the bacon, and onions over the squab. Serve.

To carve: At the table or in the kitchen, carve in the shape of a cross—that is, in 4 parts. First in half lengthwise, then divide each half widthwise, a little bit above the thigh. Carved like this, one of the pieces will include the largest part of the wing and the breast; the other, the thigh and the end of the breast.

Squab à la Valenciennes
(Pigeons à la Valenciennes)

Here we give the simplest recipe for this excellent dish, which has become a classic. You can replace the bacon with raw ham if it is available. In any case, the bacon used must be as lean as possible. Instead of the white wine suggested, you can replace it with the same amount of bouillon. *Time: 1 hour. Serves 6.*

3 squab; 200 grams (7 ounces) of very lean bacon; 60 grams (2 1/4 ounces, 4 1/2 tablespoons) of good lard or butter; 1 1/2 deciliters (2/3 cup) of white wine; 3/4 liter (generous 3 cups) of well degreased bouillon; a bouquet garni.

3 deciliters (1 1/4 cups) of nice Carolina or Indian rice; 18 small chipolata sausages; 50–60 grams (1 3/4–2 1/4 ounces) of butter to finish the rice; a pinch of pepper or, if you like, cayenne pepper.

PROCEDURE. Gut and clean the pigeons and put their livers back into the body; cut off the heads; scrape the bottoms of the feet. Truss them as for an entrée (SEE PAGE 352). Remove the rind of the bacon. Cut it into cubes about 2 centimeters (3/4 inch) on each side. Blanch it (SEE PAGE 11).

Take a good thick aluminum casserole of the right size so that the squab will not be too squeezed together in it. On moderate heat, warm the fat or the butter. Add the well-drained lardons; color them lightly. Take them out with a skimmer, leaving all the fat in the casserole. Add the squab in their place. Turn up the heat and color them, turning them over as necessary until they have taken on the golden tint of roasted squab. This should take *15 minutes.*

Pour all the fat from the casserole. Into this, pour the wine. Still without a cover, boil and reduce this wine until it is scarcely 1 or 2 generous tablespoons. Then add the bouillon; it must come halfway up the squab. Put back the lardons and add the bouquet garni. Bring it to a boil. Cover the casserole. Let it cook gently on moderate heat for *about 10 minutes* before adding the rice to it.

The rice: Wash it as directed (SEE PAGE 562). Completely drain. Add it to the squab, spreading it around until it is completely covered by the liquid. Return to boiling with strong heat. Then immediately cover the casserole and put it in an oven hot enough to maintain a gentle, uninterrupted simmer for *25 minutes,* which is the normal time for cooking rice this way and also corresponds to the time needed to completely cook the squab. During the entire cooking period, do not stir the rice. It should have gradually absorbed all the liquid and be dry at the end of the given time, with its grains intact and tender.

The sausages: Grill them or sauté them in a pan (SEE PAGE 338).

To serve: Place the squab on a plate. Remove the bouquet from the rice. With a fork, loosen up the grains carefully. Mix in some butter. Add a nice pinch of pepper or cayenne pepper, with extreme prudence regarding its quantity. Check the salt.

On a round heated plate, dress the rice in an elevated dome, with the cubes of bacon spread around here and there. On top of the rice, place the squab cut into 4 pieces. Surround them with the small sausages. Serve burning hot.

Roast Squab *(Pigeon Rôti)*

Only young and tender squab are good for roasting. You should figure on a half squab per person. Gut, clean, and then put their liver back into the body; be certain the liver has no bile; truss them as for a roast chicken, and cover the breast with a bard of bacon, then secure this with two turns of string. Roast them on a spit in front of strong heat or in a hot oven (SEE ROASTS, PAGE 30), brushing them with melted butter for *15, 20,* or even *25 minutes,* according to the size of the squab and the method of cooking you are using.

As with roast partridge, remove the bard at the end of cooking to allow the squab to color, but put it back before serving. Carefully monitor the cooking of the squab so that it does not go beyond the proper degree. Roast squab must be "perfectly cooked." Serve it surrounded by watercress with the juices on the side. If you like, you can stuff the squab like duck.

Squab with Olives *(Pigeon aux Olives)*

Proceed as for OLIVE DUCK (SEE PAGE 380).

Fricassée of Squab *(Pigeon en Fricassée)*

Follow the same recipe as for chicken (SEE PAGE 363), but do not carve the squab first.

Squab Salmis *(Pigeon en Salmis)*

It is better to use woodpigeons (wood squab). Proceed as directed (SEE SALMI, PAGE 395), preferably using red wine.

Squab in a Pot *(Pigeon en Cocotte)*

Just as for CHICKEN IN A POT (PAGE 372).

Stuffed Squab *(Pigeon Farcis)*

Allow for each squab at least 40 grams ($1^3/_8$ ounces) of very fine sausage meat mixed with 10 grams ($^1/_3$ ounce) of stale bread crumbs moistened with bouillon, the minced liver of the squab, a little bit of minced onion that has been colored in butter, and minced parsley. Squab stuffed like this can be cooked either in a pot or in a ragoût, or as a casserole with no liquid but with butter or good cooking fat, and can be served on many kinds of garnish: braised cabbage, purée of dried vegetables, etc.

Pigeon Pie *(Pâté de Pigeon à l'Anglaise)*

This kind of pie has a crust only on the part that forms the cover: the pie is cooked and served in a special dish, preferably an earthenware terrine. These plates are now sold everywhere in heatproof porcelain. They have a large border upon which you attach the dough. The quantities given here are for a plate measuring about 22 centimeters (8 1/2 inches) long, 16 centimeters (6 1/4 inches) wide, and 6 centimeters (2 1/4 inches) deep. You can, if you must, use an oblong faïence pâté terrine, and not use its cover.

Making this pie is simple for anyone familiar with working dough. The recipe given here is strictly an English one, but it produces a very substantial hot entrée that is much appreciated in France; pigeon pie can also be served cold. No liquid is added to the pie, so the juice from the meat forms a light gelée. *Time: 2 1/2 hours (including 1 1/2 hours for cooking). Serves 6.*

2 squab weighing about 175 grams (6 ounces) each, gutted and plucked; 375 grams (13 1/4 ounces) of lean rump steak; 175 grams (6 ounces) of raw ham, with equal parts of lean and fat, net weight without rind; 60 grams (2 1/4 ounces) of fatback bacon; 4 hard-boiled egg yolks; pepper, salt, and spices.

***For the dough:* 250 grams (8 7/8 ounces) of flour; about 1 deciliter (3 1/3 fluid ounces, scant 1/2 cup) of water; 7 grams (1/4 ounce) of salt; 150 grams (5 1/3 ounces, 10 1/2 tablespoons) of butter.**

PROCEDURE. Prepare the dough as directed (SEE PASTRY DOUGH, PAGE 658). With the flat part of a cleaver, flatten the slice of rump steak to a thickness of 1 centimeter (3/8 inch). Then cut it into squares about 5 or 6 centimeters (2–2 1/2 inches) on each side. Use them to line the bottom of the plate, which has first been sprinkled with a small pinch of pepper and spice powder, making sure that they are next to one another and coming up a little bit on the side of the dish.

Gut and clean the squab, then cut into 4 pieces. Remove the beak; cut off the feet and put those aside. Lightly season the inside of the pieces. Place them on the layer of beef, reconstituting the whole squab; between each piece, slip a slice of fatty bacon that has been cut as thin as possible. Place a slice of bacon between the squab and the sides of the dish and another between each squab; this is to stop the squab from drying out. Divide the hard-boiled egg yolks into 4 and distribute them into the empty spaces. Season with pepper or spice powder and a little salt, depending on whether or not the ham is salty. Cover the squab with the ham cut into slices 1/2 centimeter (3/16 inch) thick.

To cover the dish: With a rolling pin, roll out the dough into a sheet 1/2 centimeter (3/16 inch) thick, the same shape as the plate but slightly larger, so that you can, before cutting out the cover, cut out 2 strips to garnish the outer edge of the dish. The cover is then stuck down onto these strips.

With a large knife, cut these strips 2 centimeters (3/4 inch) wide and longer than the outer edge of the dish. Put them down flat on this edge, *moistening it first with water,* allowing 1 good centimeter (3/8 inch) to overlap the edge.

The overlap is then folded back inside the plate. Moisten the ends of the strips where they join, and squeeze them lightly together. Moisten the dish thoroughly at every point where it comes into contact with the dough, pressing it everywhere with your fingers to fasten it. If not, it will come away during the cooking and let too much steam escape.

With a brush, moisten the strip of dough. Place the dough cover on top; it should more or less extend beyond the dough strip. With scissors, cut the sheet all around to make it equal with the edge of the strip. With the end of your fingers, squeeze together the dough of the cover and strip to fasten them thoroughly. Then make a light scallop pattern by squeezing lightly with your thumb and index finger on the edge of the dough so that it extends beyond the border of the platter by *scarcely 1/2 centimeter (3/16 inch).*

If you like, place some small decorations on the cover, cut from the trimmings of the dough. At the very center of the dish, make an opening the size of a pencil; stick a rolled piece of cardboard into it as a chimney, so that the steam can escape. Brush it with egg yolk diluted with a little bit of water.

Put it in the very bottom of a good, hot, even oven. Avoid too much heat on the top, because it will color the dough too quickly. If, after about 10 minutes and when the dish has begun to rise, you see it begin to color, protect it with a piece of parchment paper. Allow about *1 1/4–1 1/2 hours* of cooking. Toward the end of the cooking time, allow the dough to color. Remove the cardboard chimney and replace it with 2 or 3 feet of the squab, stuck in with their claws in the air.

GUINEA FOWL
Pintade

Its flesh is such that the guinea fowl occupies a position between game and fowl; furthermore, it is prepared more like a pheasant or partridge. So among the most appropriate recipes to suggest are: cooked with cabbage in a salmi, for which you should refer to the recipes for game; or cooked in a *cocotte* (casserole), a recipe we give here and which is equally good for pheasant and the partridge.

As with game, choose a guinea fowl that is young and tender, but do not use it too soon after it has been killed: this is not to give it a taste of aging, but to lightly deteriorate and tenderize the flesh. Thus, in summer, leave it for 2 days, hanging it unplucked in a good dry place where the air moves. Just as for game, it should not be plucked until the last moment.

Roast Guinea Fowl *(Pintade Rôtie)*

More than for any other recipe, the guinea fowl must be chosen young—that is, having just reached full growth. Generally the breast is entirely studded with fine lardons rather than barded by wrapping a sheet around it. Truss it tightly like a partridge to squeeze the fillets until they bulge; salt the inside. The best way to cook it is to roast it on a bright fire on a spit, frequently basting it with melted butter. Allow *15–20 minutes per 450 grams (1 pound),* with the beast having been weighed and gutted. The flesh of a young guinea hen, like that of a roast pheasant, must always be very lightly pink.

Serve with lemon, watercress, and buttered toast if you like. The juices from the dripping pan, melted with 2 or 3 tablespoons of bouillon and slightly degreased, is served on the side.

Guinea Fowl in Cream Sauce *(Pintade en Cocotte à la Crème)*

This very simple dish is particularly appropriate for lunches, but it can also be used for family dinners or intimate meals. As with every recipe *en cocotte,* the guinea fowl is served in the same utensil in which it is cooked (SEE CHICKEN IN A POT, PAGE 372). If, instead of sour cream, you use crème fraîche, add a little bit of lemon juice to the crème fraîche when you pour it on the guinea hen. *Time: 40 minutes (once the guinea fowl is ready for cooking). Serves 4.*

1 nice fleshy young guinea fowl; 40 grams (1 3/8 ounces, 3 tablespoons) of butter; 1 onion weighing 80 grams (2 3/4 ounces); 2 deciliters (6 3/4 fluid ounces, 7/8 cup) of sour cream; salt and pepper; 1 nice teaspoon of lemon juice, if necessary.

PROCEDURE. Truss and bind the guinea fowl as directed, after having put the liver back into the body with a few grains of sea salt.

Heat the butter in the pot, making sure it does not color. Put in the guinea fowl surrounded by onion divided into 6 parts; cover the pot and put it in a medium-hot oven. Let it cook for *20–25 minutes,* turning the guinea fowl often enough so that it takes on a golden color all over.

Meanwhile, boil the cream in a small casserole and add a good pinch of fine salt and a pinch of white pepper. At the end of the suggested time, once the guinea fowl are nicely colored, pour the *boiling* cream onto the guinea fowl. Cover again and continue cooking in the oven for *15–20 minutes:* so, a total of *40 minutes* to cook.

During this second period, generously baste the bird in cream at least *3 times.*

GAME

SALMI

Salmis

These days, there is a tendency to regard a salmi as a way of using leftovers, the sauce making any bird acceptable. This is a regrettable deviation from the real aim of the salmi, which is an excellent method of preparing feathered game, because it perfectly fuses the aroma and the flavor of the bird and combines an excellent sauce with the taste of roast game.

It is the value of roasting the game that is too often forgotten. A salmi made with leftover game cannot produce the same result as a salmi made with game that was specially roasted for the dish: that is, to a point slightly below being cooked since it has to be reheated. The ideal recipe would be one when there was plenty of game available, so that the coulis could be prepared in advance using carcasses of the same type of bird, and then poured on top of a bird that has been perfectly roasted and carved as soon as it is taken off the spit.

So, to make a good salmi, you must be both a skilled roaster and talented sauce chef.

The recipe for a salmi is equally good for pheasant, partridge, woodcock, snipe, thrush, grouse, hazel grouse, plover, and little bustard; for the different kinds of wild duck, teal, etc.; and, by extension, for guinea fowl, domestically raised duck, and squab, preferably wood pigeon.

The different procedures: The origin of salmi is ancient and its principle has not changed: it is always a bird cooked on a spit, then carved and served under a coulis made from carcasses and trimmings.

Every cooking procedure, except for roasting the whole bird on a spit, differs from a true salmi. And it is only the coulis that varies, the details changing over time and according to region and means.

In the olden days, when the cooking equipment generally used was a mortar, the carcasses were crushed, but now it is easier to chop them before putting them in the sauce. Also in this epoch, one frequently used a liaison made with crusts of bread in home cooking; this procedure, still followed in certain regions, is worth retaining. The procedure is: slices of bread roasted in the dripping pan are added to the carcasses.

These days, the recipe for the coulis of any salmi can be summarized as follows: carcasses and trimmings are chopped and then cooked with wine, shallot, and other aromatics, then passed through a drum sieve and squeezed to extract the essence from them. To the resulting purée is added an appropriate quantity of brown sauce; in professional kitchens, this is an *espagnole* or demi-glace prepared with a game stock. For home cooking, this is normally a *brown sauce* prepared when needed, although it is an advantage to prepare it in advance; use only veal jus, since unlike a bouillon or ordinary jus, it has a neutral flavor that allows the characteristic taste of the bird to dominate, which is particularly important for pheasant or partridge.

Aside from truffles and mushrooms, which are essential, as are croutons, a salmi is not accompanied by a garnish. Nonetheless, in the Midi, one often adds olives, and the famous chef Durand also introduced some celery root.

Truffles, cut in slices after cooking, are added to the pieces of game as soon as they are carved, so that they infuse them with their flavor while they are standing; their finely minced trimmings are added to the strained sauce. The *mushrooms* must be very small and left whole: if you cannot get small ones, you can cut them into quarters. The trimmings and cooking liquid are reserved for the sauce.

The *croutons* are not quite as essential as they were once considered, particularly in terms of appearance. The need to serve this dish burning hot—an important point—often means that people leave them out, particularly the croutons stuffed with liver or, for woodcocks, with the intestines of the bird. Nonetheless, there is a type of crouton that is very good in a homemade salmi, particularly for one made with leftovers: these are slices of bread cut to a thickness of about 1 centimeter (3/8 inch), all crusts removed, then gently colored in butter; these are put at the bottom of the plate, and dressed with the pieces of game. Infused with sauce and very tender, these croutons are excellent.

The wine. In principle, white wine is used for a salmi; but you can also use red wine. Carême suggested using Sauternes or Château-Lafite; Gouffé suggests Madeira and Burgundy. Indeed, Champagne has sometimes been used.

Whatever it is, the wine must always be reduced in the sauce and used in a small proportion relative to the amount of sauce. It is not used in the salmi as a moistening agent, as it is in a civet; its role is to lend an aroma to the recipe without dominating it. And that is why you must use very good wine.

The necessary time for preparation: It is difficult to establish this because a coulis always benefits from prolonged cooking; on the other hand, the roast bird will always lose something from waiting. Note, too, that you must wait until the bird is no more than warm before carving it; if it is carved just as it comes off the spit, all the juices will escape from the meat.

In trying to balance these things, the roast and the coulis, without going beyond a certain point, you can allow about *45 minutes to 1 hour* to prepare the coulis before the carving of the bird.

Roasting: The bird is trussed, barded, etc., exactly as if it were to be served as a roast (leave the head on and take out the liver), following the rules for roasting it, and if you have only an oven rather than a spit, with all due care for the requirements of replacing roasting on the spit.

Roast the bird to cook only a little more than *three-quarters of the way through.* It will finish cooking when the sauce is reheated, all the more so since the limbs are cut up, which also allows the heat to penetrate more effectively. If the bird is roasted to completion, it will be dry when it is served.

Carving: This is done as for any roasted fowl. That is, 5 or 6 pieces, depending on the size of the bird: 2 wings, 2 thighs, and the breast left whole or divided in 2 lengthwise. The wing tips, the feet, the head, and the neck are removed and added to the carcasses of the coulis. The smallest birds are divided in half lengthwise.

The skin is always removed from the pieces after carving, then added to the carcasses in the coulis. An exception is made for the skin of *waterfowl game,* wild duck, or others, which must be thrown out after it is removed because of its strong odor.

Serving: You can use a round plate, a shallow bowl, or a *timbale.* This is a large silver plate with low sides; heat it well.

Arrange the pieces of the bird in a heap, stacked on one another, or lay out the thighs first, then the pieces of breast, and finally the wings. The essential thing is to proceed quickly so you do not allow them to get cold.

Salmi of Partridge
(Salmis de Perdreaux)

We give here the most practical recipe for salmi. It is good for all the game and fowl for this preparation, and can thus serve as a typical recipe.

The quantities of the coulis are determined by the number of guests, above all: so allow for an average of 3 generous tablespoons per person, bearing in mind what you will lose when you transfer things from pan to pan. *Serves 4.*

2 partridges.

For the brown sauce: A roux made with 20 grams (2/3 ounce) of flour and 25 grams (1 ounce, 2 tablespoons) of butter; 4 deciliters (1 2/3 cups) of veal jus or bouillon; 1 scant deciliter (3 1/3 fluid ounces, scant 1/2 cup) of cooking liquid from mushrooms (or, if you do not have it, replace it with the same quantity of jus or bouillon). SEE BROWN SAUCE (PAGE 50).

For the carcasses: A mirepoix made with carrot, onion, shallot, mushroom peelings (25 grams/1 ounce of each), 1 fragment of thyme, only 1 square centimeter (3/8 square inch) of bay leaf, 4 or 5 parsley sprigs, 30 grams (1 ounce, 2 tablespoons) of butter. SEE MIREPOIX (PAGE 21).

2 scant deciliters ($6^3/_4$ fluid ounces, $^7/_8$ cup) of wine, 4 tablespoons of cognac that has been flamed to baste the pieces while they wait; 30 grams (1 ounce, 2 tablespoons) of butter, fresh and good quality, to finish the sauce; 125 grams ($4^1/_2$ ounces) of mushrooms; 4 croutons.

PROCEDURE. Use 2 small saucepans: one for making the brown sauce *(sauce brune);* the other for reducing the wine with the mirepoix and the carcasses. Plus a sauté pan to keep the cut pieces warm while making the coulis and in which they will be thoroughly reheated just before serving.

If possible, take care of everything that can be prepared in advance: pluck, gut, truss the birds; cook the mushrooms (SEE PAGE 490); cut the croutons, flame the cognac, prepare the brown sauce. Also, if you do not have the necessary amount of brown sauce (4 deciliters, $1^2/_3$ cups), use a little dark, blond roux diluted with jus or bouillon; let everything simmer gently and keep it on the side, ready for the right moment to combine the sauce with the carcasses; the skimming will be done afterward.

Put the bird on to roast. Meanwhile, gently color the mirepoix. When the birds are roasted to the appropriate point, carve them when they are medium-warm. Arrange the pieces in the sauté pan; add the cooked mushrooms. Baste them with the flamed cognac. Place a round of buttered parchment paper directly on top of it. Tightly cover the sauté pan. Keep it warm.

Rapidly and very finely chop or crush in the mortar the carcasses and all of the trimmings. Also chop the livers. Combine everything with the mirepoix. Add the wine. Bring it to a boil on strong heat to reduce it *by half.* Then add the brown sauce. Let the whole thing simmer for *a good 20 minutes.* At the end of that time, pass everything through a fine *drum sieve* by rubbing and pressing on it to extract the essences from the carcasses and vegetables. Add a pinch of pepper. Bring it back to a boil, and on gentle heat skim for *a good 15 minutes,* adding as you go about 3 tablespoons of cooking liquid from the mushrooms or cold veal jus (SEE SKIMMING SAUCES, PAGE 16). Finally, you should have *3 good deciliters ($1^1/_4$ cups) of brown sauce.*

Five or six minutes before serving, pour only half of the sauce onto the pieces that you have kept in the sauté pan, passing it through the chinois. Place the sauté pan on extremely low heat so that everything is thoroughly heated, but above all *without allowing the sauce to boil at all:* if the sauce were to boil, the flesh would not reheat any faster and would, in fact, harden. A few seconds before serving, add the butter to the sauce in the small saucepan *off the heat.* Dress it rapidly as directed. Pour the rest of the sauce through the chinois onto the pieces. Serve.

Salmi made with leftovers from roast game. Make the coulis sauce in just the same way as for a fresh roasted bird. But since you do not have to worry about reducing the time that the fresh roast stands, you can let the coulis cook as slowly as you like: it will only get better for it.

Choose, if possible, the thighs of the bird, which are thicker and less cooked than the other parts. Put them in a sauté pan with wine or jus to reheat them on very gentle heat before adding the sauce.

WOODCOCK AND SNIPE
Bécasse et Bécassine

An exceptional gift for lovers of game, woodcock is only roasted or prepared in a salmi. To develop its aroma, it should be lightly "cured" *(faisandée).* However, at this point the term should be explained, because many people wrongly assume that this implies an extreme state of decomposition; in reality, it implies the point just before mortification immediately preceding this extreme state. Between killing the woodcock and cooking it you must allow several days to pass, the number generally dictated by the temperature and also by different tastes and curing methods.

Roast Woodcock *(La Bécasse Rôtie)*

As for all delicate game, this should only be roasted on a spit. Only when this is absolutely impossible should you use the oven. Make sure that the roast woodcock is cooked not bloody but pink: *above all, never too cooked,* because the meat would considerably lose its flavor.

Usually, 1 woodcock will serve 2 or 3 people, depending on the size of the menu. Cut it into 4 pieces: that is, the thighs and the wings, including the meat from the breast. You can also make 6 pieces by dividing each wing into 2 pieces cut on the bias.

Usual procedure: Do not pluck the woodcock until the last moment. Cut the skin on the neck to withdraw the pouch. With the point of a small knife, detach the eyes. Remove the skin from the head. *Do not gut the woodcock.* Just pull out the gizzard through the pouch or through a small opening made in the side at the height of the thigh.

Quickly flame it with your alcohol lamp, then rub it with a soft kitchen towel. Turn back the legs, crossing one over the other. Turn the beak of the bird toward you and push it into its body, in between the thighs. There's no need to truss the woodcock with string unless you found it difficult to turn back the legs. In this case, simply push the beak into the body and truss the bird in the normal fashion.

Cover the woodcock with an extremely thin bard of fresh fatback bacon, about 12 centimeters (4½ inches) long and 9 centimeters (3½ inches) wide. Secure it with two turns of kitchen string.

Cut a slice of bread without a crust 1 centimeter (3/8 inch) thick by about 12 centimeters (4½ inches) long and 6–7 centimeters (2½–2¾ inches) wide. Spread it with butter.

Put the woodcock on the spit. Completely brush it with melted butter.

Put the buttered piece of bread underneath the woodcock in front of the spit. Roast it in front of a hot fire, allowing *18–22 minutes of cooking* depending on the size of the bird. (This is about less than half the time for a snipe.)

As soon as it is properly cooked, take the woodcock off the spit. Remove the bard of bacon and the string if it has been trussed. Lightly salt it. Put it on a long plate with the bread slice underneath; this will be divided at the table into as many pieces as the woodcock. Serve.

Another method: *Gut the woodcock.* Truss it as above and roast it the same way.

Cut a slice of bread of the suggested size. Color it well on both sides in butter (SEE CROUTONS, PAGE 20). Heat a piece of butter the size of a walnut in a small saucepan; *add the intestines to it* and season it lightly; cook them on gentle heat. Then squash them into a purée with the back of a fork. Spread this purée on the fried crouton, then put the woodcock on it. Keep the platter in a very mild oven.

Quickly pour 1 tablespoon of water and ½ generous tablespoon of cognac into the drip pan to dissolve the caramelized juice. Pass it through the chinois and send this juice to the table in a sauceboat.

Flamed Woodcock *(Bécasse Flambée)*

Roast the woodcock *without gutting it,* following the normal procedure. Then carve it into 6 pieces. Put the intestines to one side. Arrange the pieces as well as the head in a small pot. Cover and keep warm. Pour 1 tablespoon of water and 1 tablespoon of eau de vie into the drip pan to loosen the crust; reserve.

If you have a meat press, press the carcass there. If not, chop it and crush it to extract all the juice possible.

Crush the intestines into a purée, then put in a small saucepan and dilute with the juice from the carcass and the juice from the drip pan. Add salt, pepper, and 4 or 5 drops of lemon juice. Heat this coulis well *without allowing it to boil.*

To serve: Baste the pieces of woodcock with 3 or 4 tablespoons of fine champagne cognac, which has been previously heated. Cover the pan and serve immediately with the coulis made from the intestines on the side in a sauceboat.

As soon as the woodcock is on the table, light the fine champagne cognac, allow it to burn out, then pour the coulis on the pieces. Serve with very hot plates.

Salmi of Woodcock *(Salmis de Bécasses)*

Proceed as directed for SALMIS OF PARTRIDGE (PAGE 396). But make sure that the woodcocks are cooked *very rare* during the preliminary roasting. Carve them as directed for roast woodcock.

Pick up the reserved intestines; these can be immediately added to the carcass and to the debris and the trimmings for the sauce, but it is much better to add them only at the last moment to the coulis, because that way they will communicate a tastier note. In this case, you can: either gut the woodcocks before roasting them and proceed for the intestines as directed; or remove the intestines only after roasting—they will still be quite bloody because the woodcock in this instance is very rare.

Transport them quickly to the skillet, which has been very well cleaned, and cook them in a little bit of good and hot butter, but do not let them color. Put them on a plate. Detach the crust from the pan with 1 or 2 tablespoons of Madeira and add it to the intestines; pass it through the drum sieve as for a purée. Add this purée to the coulis sauce that is ready to be served.

Sautéed Woodcock with Champagne *(Bécasse Sautée au Champagne)*

A common preparation in fine restaurants, which it is appropriate to describe here. The bird is carved *uncooked*. Season the pieces and sauté them briskly in 30 grams (1 ounce, 2 tablespoons) of butter, taking them to the point where they are just cooked; then put them in the dish where they will be served and keep them good and hot.

In the same sauté pan, put the carcass and the intestines, which have been finely minced; mix them for a few moments on strong heat; add 2 deciliters ($6^3/_4$ fluid ounces, $^7/_8$ cup) of Champagne. Boil it strongly until it reduces by half. Pass this through the chinois into a very small saucepan, squeezing it strongly; a fine drum sieve would be better. What you are aiming for is a type of coulis. Warm this and then add, off the heat, 20–25 grams ($^2/_3$–1 ounce, 1 heaping tablespoon–2 tablespoons) of butter and a bit of lemon juice. Pour it on the pieces of woodcock and serve.

QUAIL
Caille

These should only be fresh, white, and plump with good firm fat: this means cooking them as soon as possible after they have been butchered. The proper way to cook them, the ones that amateurs prefer, is to roast them on a spit. Nonetheless, there are other preparations, and we will give the best of these.

Roast Quail *(Caille Rôties)*

Pluck them *at the last minute.* Gut them. Flame them quickly with an alcohol flame: if not, they become greasy. Truss them. Wrap them first in a buttered grape leaf and then in a very thin sheet of fatback bacon. Stick them onto a skewer, which you will then put on a spit. Roast them with a lively flame *from 10–12 minutes.* Dress on fried, buttered croutons. Surround them with half lemons. Serve the juices, which should be very reduced, on the side.

Quail with Lettuce *(Cailles aux Laitues)*

This is one of the most delicate game entrées of classic French cooking, even though it is very simple to make. No matter how succulent the birds, it is essential to use the jus described below: this is neither complicated nor time-consuming to prepare, and it can even be made the evening before. The lettuce leaves can also be prepared earlier than is strictly necessary and kept warm in their pan. So the time needed for preparing the dish can be reduced to between *25 and 30 minutes* for cooking the quail and *7–8 minutes* for finishing and dressing on the plate. *Time: $2^1/_2$ hours. Serves 6.*

6 quail; 6 small studs of fresh fatback bacon; 4 deciliters ($1^2/_3$ cups) of jus for the cooking; 2 small teaspoons of starch; 6 nice firm lettuce; 3 deciliters ($1^1/_4$ cups) of rich bouillon to braise them; a slice of bacon for the bottom of the sauté pan.

***For the jus:* 150 grams ($5^1/_3$ ounces) of lean veal; 150 grams ($5^1/_3$ ounces) of lean, uncooked ham, preferably Bayonne ham; 60 grams ($2^1/_4$ ounces) of fatback bacon; 60 grams ($2^1/_4$ ounces) of onions and the same of carrots; 20 grams ($^2/_3$ ounce, 1 heaping tablespoon) of butter; 1 very small piece of bay leaf; 1 liter ($4^1/_4$ cups) of bouillon very lightly salted and degreased.**

PROCEDURE. **The jus:** Cut the veal and the ham into small pieces; finally mince the bacon. Cut the onion and carrot into thick slices. In a deep, thick pot, melt the butter; add the meat and the vegetables. Do not cover. On moderate heat, allow it to color gently, mixing frequently for *about 20 minutes.* Moisten with the bouillon, dissolving the crust on the bottom of the pot. Bring it to a boil.

Cover. Turn down the heat. Maintain the liquid at a regular simmer for *$1^1/_2$ hours.* After this, strain it without degreasing it. It should have reduced by about half. Reserve it.

The lettuce: Proceed by peeling them, blanching them, and trussing them as directed in the recipe for BRAISED LETTUCE (SEE PAGE 519).

Spread the bacon in the bottom of a sauté pan; put in the little thyme packages one next to the other; pour in the bouillon, which should cover the lettuce by about the width of a finger. Bring it to a boil. Cover the pan; put it into a very moderate oven and let it simmer gently until you are ready to begin cooking the quail; then continue braising the lettuce on very gentle heat, the oven rarely being large enough to hold 2 sauté pans. Allow *about 2 hours* at a gentle and regular simmer.

The quail: Pluck and flame them. Gut them, leaving the liver inside. Truss them, tying the legs along the body. You can leave the head on and tuck it underneath the wings, but it is usually removed. Wrap each one in a bard, attaching it with a few turns of string.

Use a sauté pan of the right size so that the liquid will reach to at least half the height of the birds, which should be placed side by side. Pour the non-degreased juice over the quail. Bring it to a boil. Cover with buttered parchment paper, placing it right on top of the birds, and then with a tightly fitting cover. Put the pan into a very moderate oven: from this point, allow *25 minutes* at a very gentle simmer.

To serve: Thoroughly drain the lettuce in a large strainer, squeezing it with the back of the spoon to extract all of the liquid. Untie it. Gently scrape each leaf on both sides with the back of a blade of a knife to make them look good and then lightly fold under the end. On a warmed round plate, arrange them in a rosette, with the point toward the center of the plate. Keep them warm in a very moderate oven.

Remove the quail from their bards by cutting the string with scissors, and arrange them, draining them as you go, on the lettuce. Quickly pass the juice through the chinois into a small saucepan. Completely degrease it. Boil it for a few moments uncovered to reduce it to *$3^1/_2$ deciliters ($1^1/_2$ cups).* Bind it with the starch (SEE LIAISONS, PAGE 47). Put it on the quail and lettuce by tablespoons and serve.

Quail with Rice *(Cailles au Riz)*

Also called a "pilaf," this is one of the simplest recipes to make, and relatively rapid, too. You can cook the rice in two ways: either using the method described below or as a pilaf. In both cases, the quail are colored and half cooked, and then added to the rice halfway through its cooking. For details of how to treat the rice, see PAGE 561. If you use the pilaf method, the onion should be chopped and lightly colored in the fat after the browning of the quail. *Time: 35 minutes (once the quail have been prepared). Serves 6.*

6 quail; 270 grams ($9^1/_2$ ounces) of Indian or Carolina rice; 150 grams ($5^1/_3$ ounces) of uncooked ham; 3 small onions; a bouquet garni; 40–50 grams ($1^3/_8$–$1^3/_4$ ounces) of good lard; 7 deciliters (3 cups) of bouillon; a pinch of pepper.

PROCEDURE. Gut, flame, and truss the quail as directed for the other dishes. Do not bard.

In a thick, deep pan, thoroughly heat the lard. Put in the onion, the ham cut into small lardons, and the quail. Do not cover. On strong heat, color the quail until golden for *7–8 minutes.* Take them out of the pan and put them on a plate. Keep them warm.

In the pan with the lardons and onions, pour the bouillon. Bring it to a boil. Put in the rice, which has been previously washed in several rinses of water and drained, etc., as directed (SEE PAGE 561). Add the bouquet garni.

On strong heat, mix it until it returns to a boil. Cover the pan. Turn the heat down very low; alternatively, it is much better to put it in a very moderate oven to keep the liquid at a very gentle simmer for *10–15 minutes,* the time depending on the quality of the rice.

At the end of this time, add the quail to the pan, but *very carefully.* Throughout the cooking time, *the rice must not be touched.* You must therefore be very careful about placing the quail on the surface of the rice without mixing it at the bottom, because disturbing the liquid will cause the rice to stick. Cover it again and cook it for another *10 minutes or so.* The rice should then be tender and soft, having absorbed all the liquid.

To serve: With a fork, gently mix the grains of rice to mix in the fat that has risen to the surface. Remove the onions and the bouquet. Pour the rice into a serving dish or simply onto a round plate; arrange the quail next, untied and left whole or divided in 2. Serve burning hot.

WILD DUCK AND TEAL
Canard Sauvage et Sarcelle

Both these game birds are considered low fat and particularly good for dieters: teal is, in fact, a kind of wild duck. These are only prepared as roasts or in a salmi. *Scoter* (a wild sea duck) can also be prepared in a matelote, cut into pieces with its skin and fat carefully removed before being cooked.

Roasts: After gutting them and thoroughly wiping them clean inside, put a bunch of parsley into the body with a little piece of butter and their liver—a procedure that can be highly recommended. For a meatless preparation, baste the birds with melted butter while roasting; you can also wrap them in buttered parchment paper. Otherwise, cover the breast with a thin sheet of bacon. Roast on strong heat. For a duck, allow *18–20 minutes;* a scant *15 minutes* for the teal. Degrease the juice of the drip pan and dissolve the crust with a little bit of white wine. Serve with a bunch of watercress and lemon wedges.

In a salmi: Proceed as directed in the relevant article (SEE SALMI, PAGE 395). *Be very careful never to add the skins of the birds to the carcasses for the sauce:* the skin of game waterfowl has a taste that is rather "wild."

For meatless recipes, replace the ordinary bouillon with the cooking water used for vegetables, dried beans, or peas, or a bouillon of vegetables. If possible, include in this liquid some cooking water from the mushrooms. The juice and zest of an orange is the best complement for this game, whether roasted or made as a salmi. For details, refer to DUCK À LA ORANGE (PAGE 380).

PHEASANT
Faisan

Pheasant must be hung for some time before being used: a pheasant freshly butchered is no match for a good chicken. During this time, the flesh breaks down, which develops the gamey flavor. But if the pheasant is left for too long, the flesh actually starts to rot, and the process called *faisandage* (ripening) by the French changes to simple putrefaction. This should be absolutely avoided, and it would be a grave imprudence to attempt to use corrupted game.

Pheasant should not be hung for more than 4 days in humid weather. In cold weather, it can be left for 8–10 days. During this time, the beast should be kept in a dry place with good circulation. As with all feathered game, the pheasant should not be plucked until it is ready to use; this is to allow the special sap absorbed in the tubes of the feathers to expand into the flesh, giving it its characteristic taste; the feathers also protect the beast against insects.

The weight of a very nice pheasant cock is 1.1–1.2 kilograms (2 pounds, 7 ounces–2 pounds, 10 ounces) plucked, and about 900 grams (2 pounds) after it has been gutted. A pheasant of this weight can serve 4–5 people, and 6 if it is stuffed.

The most popular preparations for pheasant, and the best, are: roasted, either truffled or not, and for which we will give directions further down, and in a salmi (SEE SALMI, PAGE 395) with cabbage as for a partridge; and in a cocotte à la crème (SEE GUINEA FOWL, PAGE 394).

Roast Pheasant *(Faisan Rôti)*

If you like, you can bard it or stud the entire breast with small lardons. It was the classic masters of haute cuisine who taught chefs to use lardons, and the practice was adopted by their successors. Roasting a piece that is studded does, of course, require much more care and attention to ensure that the bird colors gradually. For details of how to stud it, refer to the article (SEE BACON, PAGE 13), and for details of roasting to the recipe for ROAST PARTRIDGE (PAGE 404), the details being the same except for the use of the grape leaf. The cooking time varies depending on the size of the piece. On average, it takes about *22–24 minutes per 450 grams (1 pound)* on the spit. In a hot oven, *20–22 minutes.*

Serve the jus on the side, not degreased.

Truffled Pheasant *(Faisan Truffé)*

For all details about truffling, enclosing the piece in paper, etc., refer to TRUFFLED CHICKEN, COLD OR HOT (PAGE 356).

1 nice cock pheasant; at the most 350 grams (12 1/3 ounces) of pork fat and 150 grams (5 1/3 ounces) of uncooked foie gras (if you do not use foie gras, make up the weight with an extra 150 grams/5 1/3 ounces of pork fat); 375 grams (13 1/4 ounces) of truffles; 18 grams of fine salt (2/3 ounce); 2 grams (1/14 ounce) of pepper; 1 gram (1/28 ounce) of spices; 3 soupspoons of cognac and the same of Madeira; 1 tablespoon of oil; 1/2 of a bay leaf; 1 sprig of thyme; a thin slice of fatback bacon weighing 150–180 grams (5 1/3–6 1/3 ounces) to wrap the pheasant.

PROCEDURE. Allow for cooking time: *On the spit, 23 minutes* per 450 grams (1 pound) if it is a game bird that you want to cook to a light pink; and *24 minutes* if you prefer it well cooked.

In the oven, 20–22 minutes per 450 grams (1 pound). Six minutes before the end of the cooking, remove the paper and the bard to lightly color the piece.

The best accompaniment is the completely degreased juices, as for chicken; but you can also serve a sauce Périgueux: In this case, reserve some of the trimmings from the truffles for the sauce. This should be kept a little bit light, rather like a jus that has been bound as a sauce.

THRUSH
Grive

It's in October, at the very height of the harvest, that the thrush is at its most excellent: past October, connoisseurs do not rate it as highly.

A thrush should be nice and plump; and it must be eaten freshly butchered, without being left to hang. It must not be gutted. Do not pluck it until the very last moment, and then be very careful to remove the gizzard. You can remove the head and neck, but it is more usual to leave them. Turn the legs backward, and cross them one over the other, then bend the head back to the level of the thighs and stick the beak into the breast. There is no need to truss it.

Juniper berries are an almost essential element of all recipes for thrush, bringing a characteristic note that complements the particular flavor of this game. (Juniper can be bought at all the herbalists and specialty food shops.)

Generally, you allow one thrush per person for all recipes.

Roast Thrush *(Grives Rôties)*

Put a small juniper berry in the body of each one. Wrap them with bacon. String them one next to the other sideways on a skewer, and then attach this to a spit. Roast them on strong heat for *10–12 minutes.* Serve on a crouton fried in butter.

Thrush Salmi *(Grives en Salmis)*

Follow the directions already given (SEE SALMI, PAGE 395). Roast the thrush and then cut it in two pieces. Take out the intestines, the liver, the head, and the feet for use in the coulis, and add a couple of whole thrushes to it, which will then be chopped and put through a drum sieve with the rest. Use Bordeaux wine, white or red. Cook on gentle heat for *a half hour.* Bind with beurre manié.

Thrush in a Pot *(Grives en Cocotte)*

In a clay pot, briskly heat some butter (10 grams/1/3 ounce, 1 scant tablespoon per bird), and briskly color the thrushes there without allowing the butter to brown. Salt. Cover halfway; finish the cooking on gentle heat. In all, this should take *about 20 minutes.* Some 3 or 4 minutes before serving, sprinkle some finely minced juniper berries over the thrushes (2 berries per bird) and add only a few drops of water to dissolve the little bit of caramelized juices at the bottom of the pan. Around the birds arrange some small croutons that were fried in butter while the thrushes were cooking: 1 small crouton per bird. Serve burning hot in the covered pot.

Thrush à la Bonne Femme *(Grives à la Bonne Femme)*

Time: 30 minutes (once the thrushes have been prepared).

6 thrushes; 60 grams (2 1/4 ounces) of butter; 100 grams (3 1/2 ounces) of bacon cut into small lardons of 1 centimeter (3/8 inch) on each side; about 30 small cubes of stale bread the same size as the lardons fried in butter; 8 or 10 chopped juniper berries; 3 tablespoons of cognac.

PROCEDURE. Blanch the lardons (SEE BACON, PAGE 11). In a small sauté pan where you will also cook the thrushes, heat 30 grams (1 ounce, 2 tablespoons) of butter. Lightly color the lardons there.

Meanwhile, mix the chopped juniper berries with 30 grams (1 ounce, 2 tablespoons) of butter, and salt and pepper. Divide this paste into 6 parts, and put 1 inside each bird. Then truss them as already directed.

Remove the lardons to a plate. Replace them with the thrushes and color them well, turning them often. Salt them lightly. Put the lardons between the birds. Cover and put into a relatively hot oven. From this point, allow *12 minutes* for the thrushes to finish cooking.

To serve: Arrange the thrushes in a warmed small pot or porcelain terrine. Add the lardons. Keep it warm in a moderate oven. Pour 1 tablespoon of warm water and the cognac into the sauté pan. Boil it for a few minutes to dissolve the crust on the bottom. Pour this juice into the pot. Spread the croutons there. Cover and serve burning hot.

LARK
Mauviette

A mauviette is a lark that is edible. It is only edible for a very short period: the end of November to the first days of January, after it has fed on the autumn seeds. After this time, it is a skeletal bird. So choose a lark that is well fleshed and fattened.

These days, you can allow 2 larks per person; but according to the circumstances, this number can be increased to either 3 and even 4 larks.

For lark, the principal recipes are the same as for quail and thrush. They are also roasted on skewers or cooked in a pot using the *bonne femme* method and with the cooking time regulated according to their size.

Preparing the birds for their different dishes: A rather long time is needed to pluck them, so be sure to start well in advance. To flame them afterward without burning yourself, you should string them in twos or threes on a large cooking needle.

After flaming them, remove the gizzard, piercing it with the point of a kitchen needle to take it out; this does less damage to the skin of the belly. It is important to not gut larks any more than this. Using the point of a small knife, pop out the eyes. Push the head, beak first, into the opening of the breast. Turn back the feet, crossing them over the breast, one on top of the other; there is no need to truss them with string.

YOUNG AND ADULT PARTRIDGE
Perdreau et Perdrix

First, it is important to understand the difference between the two. A young partridge is the bird born this year; older partridges are its parents. Between both of them there is the *pouillard,* a bird that was born the previous year but that has not grown sufficiently during the hunting season. It is not considered very good. Let us also add that partridges reach their full growth in October. At this time, the underside of their crop is filled with reddish feathers. Tender young partridges can be distinguished from the tougher adult by the end of the large wing feathers, which are pointed on the young partridge and rounded on the older partridge. And the young partridge, unlike the older partridge, does not have its eyes circled with red.

The principal and best recipes beyond those described further down are:

In a Salmi *(en Salmis)*

You can find the recipe in the particular section (SEE SALMI, PAGE 395).

In a Pot à la Crème *(En Cocotte à la Crème)*

Proceed as directed for the guinea fowl (SEE PAGE 394).

With Olives *(Aux Olives)*

Proceed as for the duck (SEE PAGE 380). For cooking young partridges, allow *25–30 minutes* after they have been colored in the fat or butter.

On the Grill *(À la Crapaudine)*

Proceed as for a squab (SEE PAGE 389). For this dish, choose the young partridge known as a *pouillard.*

In a Casserole *(À la Casserole)*

Proceed as for a chicken (SEE PAGE 375). Add a bit of cognac to the casserole with the tablespoon of jus before serving.

Roast Partridge *(Perdreau Rôti)*

Let us repeat here that the spit—and, what's more, a spit with a wood-burning fire—is the only way a partridge should be roasted, as is true for all feathered game. But no matter how you roast it, there is one thing that you really must remember: to preserve its flavor, the flesh of the partridge should remain pink. And it's a pity to have to report that a well-roasted partridge is an extremely rare thing; it is almost always overcooked.

Should a partridge intended for roasting be freshly killed, or should we let it hang for a while? Roasted soon after it has been killed, as frequently happens in the country and at hunting lodges, a partridge is certainly tender, but it has only very little of its characteristic flavor. This does not develop unless the flesh has been allowed to begin breaking down; this is not, however, the same as *faisandage,* the point at which the flesh begins rotting. The length of time required is dictated by the temperature at the time: In hot weather, it should not exceed 24 hours, and the bird must be kept suspended in a draft.

We recommend that, whenever possible, you wrap the partridge in a grape leaf before wrapping it in a sheet of bacon. This leaf concentrates the flavor of the partridge in the flesh; bacon alone cannot do this, because it is used to protect the partridge from coloring and to offer the necessary fat during the cooking.

Real gourmets insist that the grape leaf be served with roasted partridge so that they can assure themselves that it has been cooked under the proper conditions; for this reason, serving the grape leaf with the partridge has become standard practice.

Also, as much as possible, the partridge should be served as soon as it is taken off the spit or taken out of the oven. *Time: 20 minutes for cooking. Serves 2.*

1 nice partridge that weighs about 225 grams (8 ounces) once gutted; 1 large fresh grape leaf; 1 very thin sheet of fatback bacon around 9 centimeters long (3 1/2 inches) and 7 centimeters (2 3/4 inch) wide; 1 crouton of bread 10 centimeters (4 inches) long, 6 1/2 centimeters (2 5/8 inch) wide, and 1 centimeter (3/8 inch) thick; 30 grams (1 ounce, 2 tablespoons) of butter; a nice lemon; a half bunch of watercress.

PROCEDURE. Pluck the partridge at the last moment, as described and for the reasons given already (SEE PHEASANT, PAGE 401). Gut it; put the liver back into the body with a grain of salt; flame it over an alcohol lamp; wipe it with a dry kitchen towel; remove the neck; truss the partridge in the normal fashion.

Generously butter the exterior side of the grape leaf and stick it onto the partridge. Cover this with the sheet of bacon. Secure everything with a string crossed on the breast and knotted. We say "cross" to ensure that the sheet of bacon cannot rise when it warps under the heat, as would happen if you used two parallel turns of string.

To roast on the spit with wood: The fire must be prepared far enough in advance so that you get a good foundation of coals, to reinforce the heat of the flames. Put enough wood into the fireplace so that you do not have to put more in during the cooking; if you do, the fire will flame up. Use good, dry wood, preferably vine clippings; above all, make sure no resinous woods are used.

Put the partridge on a spit. Fix it on the shaft by attaching it with its feet, so that you do not have to pierce it with a skewer. Generously brush it with melted butter; the surplus will fall into the drip pan. Put the studded side forward closest to the heat. *Allow to cook for 20 minutes.* During this time, do not baste it at all. Make sure you turn it from time to time. About 5 minutes before the cooking ends, remove the sheet of bacon and the grape leaf so that the bird will color; keep both the bacon and the leaf warm.

Check that the bird is done by sticking a kitchen needle into the thigh, where it joins the drumstick. The pearl of juice that escapes should be a *very pale pink,* almost clear.

Do not salt it until you have taken it off the spit. At this point, add 1 tablespoon of warm water to the drip pan to dissolve the caramelized juices from the partridge.

To roast on a spit on a rotisserie: Fill the firebox with coals that are burning hot, and use enough that you do not have to replenish them while cooking. Put the partridge on a spit and proceed just as above.

To roast in the oven: Place the partridge in a small roasting pan or a small sauté pan with flat sides, *always making sure that it is raised on a rack.* Baste it with melted butter. Put it in a *very hot* oven. Turn it over when the sheet of bacon is nicely browned. Do not baste it. As when cooking on a spit, remove the sheet of bacon and the grape leaf 5 minutes before taking it out of the oven. Allow *18–20 minutes for cooking,* depending on the heat of the oven. Do not add the tablespoon of water to dissolve the crust on the pan until *after* you have taken out the partridge.

To dress and serve: Prepare the fried crouton as directed (PAGE 20). The crumbly sharp corners should first have been removed.

To remove the trussing string, cut it with scissors. Put the partridge on the crouton in the middle of a long, small heated plate and put the sheet of bacon and the grape leaf back on the partridge. Place a bunch of watercress at each end. If you like, the watercress can be seasoned with a little salt and a few drops of vinegar. On each side, put as many lemon slices as there are guests. Serve the juices separately in a small sauceboat. Just a few drops per person will suffice.

A partridge should be carved into 5 pieces, including the carcass: 2 thighs, 2 wings, and the breast. Also divide each crouton, the sheet of bacon, and the grape leaf into 5.

Partridge with Lentils *(Perdrix aux Lentilles)*

A very excellent home-style dish dating from the time when earthenware pots simmered in the glowing cinders of the great kitchen fireplaces. The preparation of the partridge remains the same if you decide to replace whole lentils with puréed lentils. In that case, increase their amount by 4 deciliters (1 2/3 cups). For details, see PURÉE OF LENTILS (PAGE 559). *Time: 2 hours, 30 minutes. Serves 4–6.*

2 partridges; 50 grams (1 3/4 ounces) of fatback bacon for studding, cut into small lardons about 3 centimeters (1 1/8 inch) long by a little less than 1/2 centimeter (3/16 inch) thick; 40 grams (1 3/8 ounces) of onions and the same of carrots, cut into rounds that are not too thin; 3 deciliters (1 1/4 cups) of good degreased bouillon; a bouquet garni; pepper; a little bit of salt; 3 deciliters (1 1/4 cups) of lentils; 175 grams (6 ounces) of lean bacon; 50 grams (1 3/4 ounces, 3 1/2 tablespoons) of fresh butter to finish.

PROCEDURE. **The lentils:** Soak them and cook them with water and bacon as directed (SEE DRIED VEGETABLES, PAGE 557).

The partridges: Once these have been gutted and flamed, cut off their necks; scrape the end of the claws. Fold back the legs onto the thighs. Truss them and bind them before studding them.

With the lardons, make a single transverse row along each fillet. Insert the lardons deeply into the flesh; unlike the studding normally used for meats, these should be almost invisible on the surface of the meat. This is because it is the inside of the rather dry partridge flesh that must be nourished by the fat.

Use a small pot made of enameled steel or fireproof glass, which can hold the 2 partridges side by side. Garnish the bottom with the trimmings and leftovers from the bacon, the rounds of onion and carrots. Put the partridges on top. Put the bouquet garni between them.

Put the open pot on moderate heat to sweat the dish for about 10 minutes; do not stir anything during this time. When you smell a very light caramel odor, you can tell that the vegetables on the bottom have begun to color, so pour the white wine into the pot. Allow it to reduce almost completely. Then add the bouillon. It must reach to almost two-thirds the height of the partridges. Cover as tightly as possible. Put the pot in a very moderate oven so that it only receives enough heat to maintain a regular, uninterrupted simmer that is almost imperceptible: this should last *1$^{1}/_{2}$ hours.*

About 10–15 minutes before serving, pour all the cooking juices from the partridges into a cup: do this by tilting the pot and sliding the cover off a little to let the juices out. The amount should equal that of the bouillon added at the beginning. Degrease. Drain the lentils. Put them back into their rinsed pot with the juices and the bacon from the breast, having trimmed the rind and divided it into small, thin slices. Allow it to simmer, without a cover, on gentle heat for *8–10 minutes,* during which time the lentils should almost completely absorb the juices.

To serve: Untie the partridges. Put them on a well-heated round plate. *Off the heat,* add the butter divided into little pieces to the lentils; shake the pot to mix it well without crushing the lentils. Also add the little bit of the juice that remains in the pot used for cooking the partridges. Check the salt.

Surround the partridges with the lentils and spread 1 tablespoon on their breast. If the partridges are carved before serving, take off the thighs and then split each bird in 2 lengthwise. Then put the 2 sides back together and place the thighs on each side to reconstitute the partridges, which have been divided into 4 pieces. Arrange the lentils as directed.

Partridge with Cabbage *(Perdrix aux Choux)*

In professional kitchens, this recipe has few variations: the cabbage is braised on its own for a long time and then added to the partridge, which has either been braised or roasted on the spit. There are more variations for home cooking, where the necessary ingredients may not be available, and bouillon is used instead of jus, and where cooks will factor in the time and trouble as well as the cost.

What's more, the recipe for partridge with cabbage does not mean the same thing to everyone. Some consider it to be a good recipe for using a tough old beast; indeed, for them, using an old partridge is as essential as using cabbage. But this ignores the fact that the quality of the bird cannot be affected at all, and the partridge will remain tough; only the cabbage benefits from the association. Others are better advised, and they sacrifice the old partridge, using it only to lend the cabbage its characteristic taste, and then replacing it with a young, tender partridge, cooked separately.

This second procedure is what professional kitchens do, which produces a much more succulent bird. But it is only practical in houses and homes where there's plentiful game, and these are the exception. There is a method that combines the best of the two: that is, you choose a bird young enough that the flesh is still tender; cook it in the cabbage to flavor it; and then take it out after the time needed for cooking in order to preserve all of its qualities.

It is on these principles that the following recipe is founded. If, nonetheless, you have an old partridge, you can put it in the cabbage to lend its flavor, but it should not be served. Use it later in croquettes or in some hash with a spicy sauce.

For the recipe we are now describing, the birds must be just "done." That is, they should not be too fresh nor should they have actually reached the point of *faisandage:* so leave 2–3 days to hang, depending on the temperature. Do not pluck them until you are ready to cook them, or at least do so only a very short time in advance.

To the carrot you can also add some *turnip,* particularly if you intend to mold the partridge like a *chartreuse* (a molded dish shaped into a dome with multicolored layers). Small *sausages (chipolatas)* add to the pleasure of the dish and also stretch it further; for 2 partridges, allow about 10 small sausages. You can cook them gently in a pan 7–8 minutes before dressing the plate.

In dealing with cabbage, you cannot be generous enough using *bacon* in the form of studs and rinds. The bacon listed in the ingredients is lean bacon, which will not supply all the necessary fat. You can also use some *white wine:* about 1 quart of liquid. So, 2$^{1}/_{2}$ deciliters (1 cup) of wine for $^{3}/_{4}$ liter (generous 3 cups) of bouillon. *Time: 2 hours, 30 minutes. Serves 6.*

2 nice partridges; 1 kilogram (2 pounds, 3 ounces) of curly cabbage, weighed after trimming; 200 grams (7 ounces) of very lean bacon; 1 small *uncooked* sausage of 125 grams (4$^{1}/_{2}$ ounces); 1 rind of fresh fatback bacon for the bottom of the pot, or a sheet if possible; 200 grams (7 ounces) of carrots; 30 grams of

lard to color the partridges; a large onion stuck with a clove; a bouquet garni; 1 liter (4¼ cups) of bouillon; 5 or 6 tablespoons of good cooking grease or, if you do not have it, of good lard; 10 grams of arrowroot to bind the cooking juices; 30 grams (1 ounce, 2 tablespoons) of fresh butter to finish.

PROCEDURE. Here everything must be perfectly ready so you do not lose time. As soon as the partridges are plucked, gutted, trussed, etc., you should turn to the cabbage. While it blanches and cools, blanch the bacon, color the partridges, and prepare the carrots, the bouquet, and the onion. In this way, everything is ready to be added together to the casserole used for the cooking.

The partridges: Cut the neck at its root. Scrape the claws. Truss and bind the bird with its legs folded back over the breast.

The cabbage: Trim it, blanch it, and cool it as directed (SEE CABBAGE FOR GARNISH, PAGE 496). When they have been wiped dry and unfolded, lightly season the leaves with salt and pepper.

The bacon: First remove the rind. Blanch the piece and the rind for *8–10 minutes.*

The pot: This should be made of thick aluminum, be higher than wider, and also large enough so that the different ingredients for the recipe do not fill it by more than two-thirds.

Rapidly heat the lard, but make sure it does not turn yellow. Color the partridges: *5 minutes* on the back and *4 minutes* on each side. You should use strong heat, being careful that the fat does not brown. Color the heads and neck at the same time. If you are adding an old partridge for its flavor, it should also be colored the same way afterwards in this fat.

Take out the partridges. If you have *fresh* rinds, put them in the bottom of the pot with the fatty side facing down, or put in a sheet of fatback bacon. Then spread out a layer of cabbage on top, about a third of the total quantity. On top of that, place the partridges, the heads, and necks, and add the carrots all around them, simply peeled and left *whole.* Cover with a layer of cabbage. Then add the bacon, the sausage, the onion with the clove, and the bouquet garni. Add the rest of the cabbage, the bouillon, the fat (either cooking fat or lard). It is not essential that the cabbage be immersed in the liquid. Bring it to a boil. Put a round of well-greased white parchment paper right on top of the cabbage. Cover the pot. Since an all-enveloping heat is needed, put it in a moderate oven. Make sure that the liquid maintains a very small, regular simmer that bubbles all across the surface. From time to time, shake the pot a little bit to move the cabbage around without touching anything on the interior.

Allow to cook for 1½–2 hours: at least, this is the time needed for the cabbage; the other ingredients do not require all this time and should be removed as soon as they are done. So, counting from the moment the pot has been put into the oven, remove: *the sausage* at the end of 30–35 minutes, depending on its size; *the partridges* at the end of 35 minutes (the old partridge, if there is one, should be left in the cabbage); *the bacon* at the end of 45 minutes; keep everything in a shallow covered bowl.

To dress the dish: Unless you can keep the partridges, the bacon, and the sausages quite warm, put them back into the cabbage 7–8 minutes before dressing the dish; this is the best way to ensure they completely reheat. After this:

Cut the *bacon* into small rectangles ½ centimeter (3/16 inch) thick. Cut the *sausage and the carrot* into fine rounds. If carving the *partridge* in the kitchen, cut each one into 5 pieces.

Drain the cabbage in a large strainer over a terrine. Take out all of the different ingredients: onions, bouquet, etc. Press lightly on the cabbage with the back of a skimmer to squeeze out as much liquid as possible.

Dress the cabbage in a dome on a heated round plate. On top of it, place the partridge, either in pieces or the whole bird with its breast facing up. Surround with rounds of carrots, sausage, and slices of bacon. Keep it warm while you bind the juice.

The juice: Pour 6 deciliters (2½ cups) of the cooking juice into a small saucepan. Boil it strongly to reduce it by half. But taste it first; if it is salted perfectly, you should use only *3 deciliters (1¼ cups)* to bind it without reducing it, because less concentrated juices are better for this recipe.

Bind it as directed (SEE PAGE 48). Add a couple of drops of liquid caramel to color it. Off the heat, finish it with the extra butter. Pour a little bit of the bound juice around the cabbage. Serve the rest in a sauceboat.

VENISON
Chevreuil

A cut of venison that comes from a young animal and that is meant to be roasted does not need to be marinated. At the very most, you can brush it with cognac and oil when you are not going to let it stand for longer than 24 hours. In this way, the meat will be able to keep its unique flavor.

A marinade is required for an older beast—not so much to tenderize the flesh, which is already naturally tender, but to give it an aroma—or for a cut that will be kept for a couple of days. If the meat will not be left for a long time, use an uncooked marinade. If leaving it for more than 3 days, the marinade must first be cooked (SEE MARINADES, PAGE 18). In both cases, the marinade should include only a small amount of vinegar, since the acid corrodes the delicate flesh of the deer.

The sauces appropriate for venison are; *à la française, poivrade, venaison, grande veneur* served on the side in a sauceboat. Chestnuts are probably the best garnish. You can also use a purée of lentils, of celery root, or onions soubise.

Leg of Venison *(Gigot de Chevreuil)*

Time: 18–24 hours for marinating; 1 good hour for roasting; about 50 minutes in the oven. Serves 15–18.

1 leg of venison, skinned and trimmed, weighing 2 1/2 kilograms (5 pounds, 8 ounces); 250 grams (8 7/8 ounces) of fatback bacon for studding.

***For the marinade:* 100 grams (3 1/2 ounces) of carrot; 125 grams (4 1/2 ounces) of onion; 20 grams (2/3 ounce) of shallots; 30 grams (1 ounce) of celery; 2 bunches of thyme; 1/2 of a bay leaf; 4 sprigs of parsley; 4 deciliters (1 2/3 cups) of white wine; 2 deciliters (6 3/4 fluid ounces, 7/8 cup) of good natural vinegar; 3 tablespoons of oil.**

PROCEDURE. Very carefully remove the fur; the hairs are like down and stick to everything. Remove the foot by sawing the bone above the shin. With a dry, fine kitchen towel, remove the hairs that have stuck to the flesh. But make sure you do not wash the leg. Remove the thigh bone. Remove the nerve membrane covering the leg by sliding the blade of a knife underneath it and then removing the layers one by one to expose the flesh. Proceed carefully, particularly on the side of the fillet, where this skin is very fine.

Stud the leg with 4 or 5 rows of lardons that are 3 centimeters (1 1/8 inches) long by 3 millimeters (1/8 inch) thick (SEE STUDDING, PAGE 13). The most delicate part of the fillet improves by being studded with 3 smaller rows of lardons, which are 2 1/2 centimeters (1 inch) long and only 2 millimeters (1/16 inch) thick. Do this in the direction of the grain of the meat, of course, and use a very fine studding needle so that you do not damage the flesh, which is incredibly tender and delicate.

To marinate: *If it is uncooked:* The carrot, onion, celery, and shallot are finely minced; the sprigs of parsley are broken into small pieces; and the thyme and bay are divided into fragments. All of these ingredients are mixed and half of them are scattered over a long, shallow plate, which should be made of earthenware or faience. Put the leg on top of them, seasoned with salt and pepper. Cover it with the rest of the vegetables and aromatics. Add wine, vinegar, and oil.

Add also to marinate with the leg all the trimmings, the nerve membranes, and the thigh bone, which will be used in the accompanying sauce.

With cooked marinade: Cook it first as directed (SEE MARINADES, PAGE 18). When it is well chilled, pour it over the leg and the other ingredients. In both cases, keep it cool and turn the piece over from time to time.

To cook: Whatever method of cooking is used, begin by wiping the leg clean of all fragments of aromatics and vegetables. Thoroughly dry it off in a clean dry towel, since any moisture on the meat will prevent it from browning.

In the oven: Place the leg on a roasting pan fitted with a rack. Brush it with the oil. Put it into a very hot oven to thoroughly seal the outside of the meat. This is very important: no matter how well it has been dried off, there will nonetheless be some moisture near the lardons. The heat must counter this. Do not add any liquid to the pan unless the lower part of the oven is very hot; in this case, put 1 tablespoon of marinade in it to prevent the juice from burning on the bottom.

Turn the leg two or three times while you brush it with oil. At the end of 8–10 minutes, when the meat has browned, reduce the heat of the oven a little bit, though keeping it at a high temperature (SEE ROASTS, PAGE 30).

To serve: Put the cooked leg on a long plate; keep it in a very low oven. Immediately pour 5 or 6 tablespoons of marinade into the roasting pan. Boil it quickly to deglaze it: that is, to dissolve the crust in the utensil. You will add this deglazed mixture to the sauce, which should be prepared separately.

Surround the leg with a few tablespoons of sauce and serve the rest in a sauceboat. If the dish includes an accompaniment of chestnuts, serve these on the side.

Venison Stew *(Civet de Chevreuil)*

This is an excellent way to use the second best bits of a deer: that is, the shoulders, the neck, and the ends of the rib steaks. As for the blood that you should use—and it is an essential ingredient if the dish is to deserve its name—you should use the blood of a hare or even an ordinary rabbit, though the latter is definitely inferior. If you have neither, prepare the venison in the same manner; then it will just be a good stew and not a real civet. *Time: Allow a* scant 2 hours *of cooking.*

PROCEDURE. Proceed as for a civet of hare (PAGE 416). Cut the deer into squares weighing 50–60 grams (1 3/4–2 1/4 ounces) each, then marinate for 8–10 hours in the wine that will be used for the civet, with minced shallots and onions, parsley, thyme, bay, and pepper.

Roast Saddle of Venison *(Selle de Chevreuil Rôtie)*

Time: 15 minutes of cooking per 450 grams (1 pound).

PROCEDURE. Cut the flaps on each side to within 1 centimeter (3/8 inch) of the fillet. Remove the skin as directed for the leg. Stud 2 or 3 rows of lardons, depending on the size of the piece. Marinate it or not. Roast as directed for the leg (PAGE 408) for *15 minutes per 450 grams (1 pound).* Serve with the same accompanying sauces.

Shoulder of Venison *(Epaules de Chevreuil)*

The flesh is a little bit sinewy and it is not as good as the leg, but it nonetheless makes a simple family meal. Allow 2 shoulders for 6 people. When possible, they should be placed for 24 hours in a marinade that has been previously cooked and chilled; use the same quantity as for the leg. *Time: 30 minutes for cooking.*

PROCEDURE. Completely bone the shoulders, as for a shoulder of mutton. Lay them out in a large shallow bowl. Season with salt and pepper and pour the chilled marinade over them. Turn them two or three times while they are marinating.

Before roasting, drain and dry them off, as directed for the leg. Roll them up and keep them in their shape with a few turns of kitchen string. Roast them in a very hot oven. Allow *30 minutes* of cooking and *5 minutes more* to have them well done. Proceed with the deglazing of the roasting plate as directed for the leg.

Venison Chops *(Côtelettes de Chevreuil)*

When you buy venison chops, it is better to ask the butcher to cut them, and in front of you, to make sure that they are as thick as you want—that is 2 centimeters (3/4 inch). Then trim them just like lamb chops; reserve the trimmings to use in the sauce. With the flat of a cleaver, flatten the chops to the thickness of 1 1/2 centimeters (5/8 inch).

To cook: This can be done in different ways, the most popular being to sauté them (SEE SAUTÉING, PAGE 34). So, for 6 chops, use 20 grams (2/3 ounce, 1 heaping tablespoon) of butter and 6 grams (1/5 ounce) of oil heated in a sauté pan. Once the fat has started to lightly smoke, arrange them side by side, seasoned with salt and pepper. Use a relatively high heat and no cover. Turn them at the end of *2–3 minutes,* when the side resting on the pan is nice and brown. Let them cook on the other side for *3–4 minutes,* turning the heat down a little bit; allow 2 minutes more if you want the chops to be well done. Note, however, that the meat must always be just a little pink.

Take the chops out, then put them on a plate and keep them warm. Immediately and completely drain the fat from the sauté pan. Put in a little bit of jus and white wine to dissolve the little bit of crust at the bottom of the pan. This deglazing must not be omitted because, when it is put into the sauce, it adds a great deal of flavor. Three tablespoons of veal jus and the same of white wine is enough, reduced to 2 tablespoons.

If you like, the venison chops can be studded: use 6 miniscule lardons stuck on one side of the chop and very near the surface; hidden under too much meat, the lardons cannot cook or brown. You can also sauté them as directed above, with the studded side first put on the hot fat. Or arrange the chops on a gratinée plate with the studded side up, baste them with melted butter, cover with buttered parchment paper, put them in a hot oven, and allow to cook for *15 minutes.*

Thus studded, they can also be cooked in the sauté pan in the oven with a little bit of good jus and glazed as for a fricandeau or a grenadine.

The principal preparations: Almost always, they are accompanied by a purée of chestnuts, of lentils, and of celery, which makes the plate more substantial; either the chops are dressed around the purée or the purée is served on the side. The dish is then completed with a sauce: the most common one is a *sauce poivrade,* allowing 1/2 deciliter (1 2/3 fluid ounces, scant 1/4 cup) per chop. When dressed, the chops are alternated with croutons cut into a heart shape and fried in butter.

We note the following recipe as a quick dish: once the chops have been sautéed, deglaze the sauté pan with, for 6 chops, 2 deciliters (6 3/4 fluid ounces, 7/8 cup) of very good veal jus and 1 deciliter (3 1/3 fluid ounces, scant 1/2 cup) of white wine. Boil it for barely 1 minute; bind it with starch and add, off the heat, 50 grams (1 3/4 ounces, 3 1/2 tablespoons) of butter and a few drops of lemon juice. Arrange the chops in a turban with croutons and then lightly cover with the sauce, pouring the rest in the middle. You can also use crème fraîche instead of white wine.

WILD RABBIT
Lapin de Garenne

This is one of those game animals that offers the greatest number of possibilities for adapting to many recipes. Before giving the main recipes, we should make it clear that, as a rule, a rabbit must be eaten fresh. True lovers of rabbit stew put it into the pot as soon as it is killed; and another essential condition is youth, which guarantees that the rabbit is tender.

When you don't have an immediate use for the rabbit, the best thing to do is always to skin it and gut it and then marinate it until you are ready to cook it. The kind of marinade varies a little according to the final preparation: usually, it will include oil, cognac, lemon juice, parsley, and thyme.

A young rabbit grown to its normal size will have a gross weight of about 1–1.2 kilograms (2 pounds, 3 ounces–2 pounds, 10 ounces) and weigh 650–700 grams (1 pound, 7 ounces–1 pound, 9 ounces) when it is skinned and gutted. You can allow 1 rabbit for 4 or 5 people, depending on its weight.

HOW TO SKIN A RABBIT OR A HARE

With a good strong knife, first cut the 4 legs, trimming them above the knee so that there is no longer any bone sticking out.

Then place the beast on its back, its tail toward you: make an incision about 2 centimeters (3/4 inches) across the belly close to where the thighs begin. Raise the skin at the place where you have cut and then pull it back, so that you free the thighs one after the other by pulling the skin off them. They will leave a hole in each piece of skin where you have first cut the legs.

Continue to pull back the skin so that you pull it off the tail; use a knife to help separate the skin from the flesh. Now that the rear part of the beast has been completely skinned, turn it around so that the head is now turned toward you, always keeping the breast in the air. With your left hand, grab the back part of the skin and with your right hand placed on the back of the beast, strongly pull the skin toward you. It should come off all by itself until the front legs stop you.

Then disengage the legs one by one and pull again until you reach the ears. With a knife, trim all around the head of the animal, carefully detaching the skin at the ears. Now you only have to pull a little bit and the skin will come off to the end of the muzzle, where a last cut of the knife will detach it. Finally, remove the eyes and the teeth.

Now put the animal back into its original position: that is, with the tail turned toward you and on its back. Split the skin of the belly to remove the intestines. Then cut out the diaphragm (which is the stretched skin in front of the breast), and take out the heart and the liver.

Gather every last drop of blood, and also the clots if there are any. Sometimes all the blood has clotted, but it is better to have blood like this than to have none at all. You need only to gather these clots in a bowl and to dissolve them with a little red wine, then strain this blood through a chinois or a fine strainer. Add 1 tablespoon of red wine even when the blood is liquid.

As a precaution, immediately remove the bile from the liver, as well as any part of the liver that has turned greenish after contact with the bile. Immediately put the liver and the blood in a cool place.

PREPARATIONS FOR WILD RABBIT

You can prepare rabbit in any number of ways, just as imagination and circumstances dictate. Mushrooms always enhance these dishes; either cultivated mushrooms or morels, or even cèpes. Cèpes are cut into scallops and firmed up in a pan in hot oil.

Besides the traditional rabbit cooked in wine, for the recipes described in detail below, the principal preparations for rabbit, can be summarized thusly:

Roast Rabbit *(Lapin Rôti)*

Whole or simply the saddle and thighs. Studded or not, as you like. Push the forward legs into the interior of the chest. Cross the hind legs by placing them one over the other and tying them with a string. Roast in a hot oven for *20–25 minutes* (SEE ROASTS, PAGE 30).

Stuffed Rabbit *(Lapin Farci)*

Stuff it with a truffled pig's foot or flat truffled sausages. Sew the belly of the beast closed. Roast, allowing *20 minutes* per 450 grams (1 pound) with the beast weighed stuffed. Serve with the sauce on the side: *poivrade* or soubise.

Mustard Rabbit *(Lapin à la Moutarde)*

Brush the outside of the rabbit with a good layer of ordinary brown mustard (neither Dijon mustard nor English mustard is appropriate for this dish). Wrap the rabbit with 2 large thin sheets of fatback bacon secured with a string. Baste it with melted butter and roast it in the oven for *20 minutes* per 450 grams (1 pound).

Rabbit Salad *(Lapin en Salade)*

Cut the leftovers of the roast rabbit into small pieces. Season as for a beef salad. You can also add a fine julienne cut from slices of smoked tongue and fresh chopped tomato.

Grilled Rabbit à la Tartar *(Lapin Grillé à la Tartare)*

Divided into pieces as for sautéing and then marinate for *1 hour* with oil, parsley, chopped scallion, and salt and pepper. Bread it *à l'anglaise* (SEE PAGE 19). Grill it on gentle fire, basting it with the oil from the marinade. Serve it in a pyramid. Surround it with a ribbon of tartar sauce.

Rabbit Stew *(Lapin en Blanquette)*

Same as a blanquette of veal (PAGE 293).

Braised Rabbit *(Lapin Braisé)*

Only the rear of the beast is used. Cut the legs above the saddle and tie them together in a cross. Stud the top of the back and the legs. Braise and glaze as for a fricandeau (PAGE 277), for *1 hour* total. Serve on a purée of soubise or chicory or chestnuts, etc., with the juice reduced and bound with starch.

Studded Fillet of Young Rabbit *(Filets de Lapereau Piqués)*

This is an excellent dish, particularly recommended when rabbit is abundant. Take off the fillets from the carcass. Trim them into a neat shape. Stud them with 2 rows of good bacon; marinate them with a little oil and lemon juice. Prepare a jus with the carcass, juice, etc., and all the other trimmings plus a small mirepoix. Everything should be covered in butter or lard and moistened with veal jus. In a roasting plate or sauté pan, reduce the juices of the young rabbit to the consistency of a light syrup; gently cook and glaze the fillet in the oven. *Fifteen minutes* should be enough to cook completely. Dress on a soubise purée or other. Serve the rest of the juice on the side bound with arrowroot.

Hunter-Style Sautéed Rabbit and Marengo *(Lapin Sauté Chausseur et Marengo)*

If the rabbit is very young and tender, proceed as for a chicken. If not, proceed as for veal: that is, color the pieces of rabbit first and then finish cooking them in the sauce. Allow in this case *1 hour in total,* including 10–15 minutes for the initial coloring.

Sautéed Rabbit in One Minute *(Lapin Sauté à la Minute)*

Choose a *young* rabbit. If you do not have a sauté pan, use a good, thick skillet, as they do in the countryside. If you do not have already have some clarified butter, which is common in provincial households, clarify the amount you need, about 60–75 grams (2 1/4–2 2/3 ounces) (SEE CLARIFIED BUTTER, PAGE 16), because this butter can be heated more strongly without burning.

Sauté the pieces of rabbit in it, proceeding in exactly the same way as for a sautéed chicken. When the cooking is complete—*15–18 minutes* should suffice—and the pieces are a nice color, season and add a finely minced shallot.

Mix and cook for 1 minute. Put 1 tablespoon of bouillon or water into the pan to dissolve the crust in the bottom of the pan. Immediately dress the rabbit on a heated plate. Add a few drops of lemon juice to the butter and the cooking juice; pour it on the pieces. Sprinkle with minced parsley and serve burning hot.

Flemish-Style Rabbit *(Lapin à la Flamande)*

Cut it into pieces. Marinate it with a few tablespoons of red wine, thyme, and bay, for 12 hours. Wipe off the pieces with a kitchen towel before coloring them in 40 grams (1 3/8 ounces, 3 tablespoons) of butter. Then sprinkle them with 15 grams of flour (1/2 ounce); color them lightly.

Moisten them with 3 deciliters (1 1/4 cups) of white wine and 2 deciliters (6 3/4 fluid ounces, 7/8 cup) of bouillon; season. Add 225 grams (8 ounces) of prunes, which have been soaked in advance until swollen. Bring it to a boil, then cover and continue cooking in the oven for *1 scant hour.* The sauce must be reduced to 3 deciliters (1 1/4 cups) before serving.

Rabbit à la Poulette *(Lapin à la Poulette)*

Carve the rabbit into pieces. Lightly sauté it without coloring it at all in 40 grams (1 3/8 ounces, 3 tablespoons) of butter. Sprinkle it with 15 grams (1/2 ounce) of flour and let it color a light blond. Dilute with 1/2 liter (generous 2 cups) of bouillon. Add mushroom cooking liquid or trimmings of mushroom. Once it has begun to boil, cover. Cook gently for *1 hour.* Once the sauce has been reduced to 3 deciliters (1 1/4 cups), bind it with an egg yolk (SEE LIAISONS, PAGE 47). Add lemon juice and, on the pieces that have been dressed and covered with sauce, a pinch of minced parsley.

Wild Rabbit with Chipolatas *(Lapin de Garenne à la Chipolata)*

This is the original way of serving a stuffed rabbit; for family meals, it provides a good, inexpensive dish that is simple to make, because when stuffing and sewing up a rabbit, not even a beginner can go wrong. *Serves 4–6, depending on how large the menu is.*

1 medium-size rabbit; about 20 small *chipolata* sausages; 30 nice chestnuts; 40 grams (1 3/8 ounces, 3 tablespoons) of butter; 15 grams (1/2 ounce) of flour; 2 deciliters (6 3/4 fluid ounces, 7/8 cup) of white wine;

4 deciliters (1 2/3 cups) of degreased bouillon; 1 good teaspoon of concentrated tomato purée; a bouquet of 3 or 4 sprigs of parsley, 1 sprig of thyme and some wild thyme; salt, pepper, spice powder.

PROCEDURE. Once the rabbit has been skinned, split the middle of the breast up to the beginning of the chest. Gut it and leave only its liver in the body.

The chestnuts: Peel them as directed (SEE CHESTNUTS, PAGE 521). Then put them in a saucepan covered with water. Bring it to a boil and cook gently for about 20 minutes. Drain immediately.

The sausages: Prepare them as directed (SEE PAGE 338) and lightly brown them in a pan for *3–4 minutes.* Reserve.

To stuff the rabbit: Place the rabbit on its back on the table. Cut off the head where it joins the body because many people find it repugnant.

Season the inside with salt, pepper, and spice powder. Then stuff the sausages first in the upper parts of the body near the shoulders; add about 10 chestnuts, alternating with the sausages and spreading them throughout the insides of the rabbit without pushing them too close together. Also reserve about a dozen sausages and the same number of chestnuts, choosing the best ones, to garnish the plate.

Thread about a meter (40 inches) of heavy thread into a fine cooking needle or even a large sewing needle; the needle should be a fine one so that you do not destroy the very delicate flesh of the beast. Bring the two sides of the belly together, pulling one over the other; secure them with some large stitches, reforming the belly, and do not pull the thread too tight, then knot it right at the end.

With an ordinary kitchen needle threaded with a string, secure the thighs and the shoulders of the animal, pulling them in underneath so that the beast is in the position of a resting rabbit. Tighten them as much as possible lengthwise, pulling the rump of the beast underneath the body to curve the back a little bit more; this shortens the beast so you can put it into an ordinary pot. Otherwise, you would have to use a very long braising pan.

To cook: Heat the butter on strong heat in a thick casserole. Place the rabbit in it on its back. Turn it over at the end of 5 minutes, when it has taken on a golden color. Then successively color all of its surfaces, which will take *15–20 minutes,* during which the butter should not brown at all. The head, cut in half, can be put in with the rabbit for its juices.

Sprinkle the rabbit with the flour. Mix and allow it to cook on gentle heat for *5–6 minutes* without going beyond the color of a very light brown roux. Dilute it little by little with the wine and the bouillon. Bring it to a boil on strong heat, shaking the pot. Then add the tomato, the bouquet garni, the sprig of thyme and wild thyme. Cover the pot. Put it into an oven sufficiently hot to maintain the liquid at a small, gentle simmer for *1 hour. At the end of a half hour,* add the sausages and the chestnuts around the rabbit. Cover again and continue cooking.

To serve: Put the rabbit on a well-heated plate. Remove all the strings with scissors. Take out the chestnuts and the sausages with your skimmer and place them in little individual piles, using them to support the rabbit in its natural position.

With the back of a spoon, loosen the crust from around the perimeter of the pot in order to dissolve it in the sauce. This should have been reduced by half. If there is more than 3 deciliters (1 1/4 cups), boil it briskly to reduce it to this quantity. Strain this sauce through the chinois, putting 2–3 tablespoons on the rabbit and its garnish just to give it a sheen. Serve the rest in a sauceboat. Carving it and serving it is much easier this way.

Wild Rabbit à la Crème
(Lapin de Garenne à la Crème)

Taken from the notebook of Countess of R— F—, this makes an exquisite dish even though it is a very simple, home-style recipe.

1 rabbit weighing around 750 grams (1 pound, 10 ounces), net weight; 50 grams (1 3/4 ounces, 3 1/2 tablespoons) of butter; 60 grams (2 1/4 ounces) of onions cut into thick rounds; 1 tablespoon of concentrated tomato purée; 1/2 liter (generous 2 cups) of well-degreased bouillon; 1 tablespoon of flour; 8–12 tablespoons of thick crème fraîche; salt, pepper; and, if you like, a point of cayenne, the amount that can be held on the point of a knife.

PROCEDURE. Heat the butter in a sauté pan over strong heat. Put in the rabbit, which has been carved into pieces, and the onion at the same time. Color it as directed for sautés (SEE PAGE 34). Then add the bouillon, the tomato, salt and pepper. The liquid must just cover the pieces.

Once the boiling has begun, cover the pan and turn the heat down to medium, so that you maintain a sustained and regular simmer over the entire surface of the liquid for *1 hour of cooking*. At the end of this time there should not be more than *1½ deciliters (5 fluid ounces, ⅔ cup)* of sauce.

Ten minutes before serving, dilute the flour, little by little, with the cream in a small cup. Then pour it over the rabbit, shaking the pan to be sure it is mixed. Heat it *without allowing it to boil,* and detach the crust around the circumference of the pan with the spoon to mix it into the sauce. Add a few drops of vegetable color or caramel to modify the grayish tint of the sauce into a café au lait color.

Check the seasoning for the salt, which is particularly necessary because of the substantial amount of cream. If the rabbit must wait, keep the pan warm.

Remove the pieces of rabbit one by one on a fork, and be certain that all the pieces of onion are removed from them, then dress them in a pyramid on a round, heated plate. Pass the sauce through a chinois, lightly stirring it with a spoon. Serve on burning hot plates.

Sautéed Young Rabbit with White Wine *(Lapereau Sauté au Vin Blanc)*

A typical recipe for sautéed rabbit, one of the most rapid and simple, but for which a young and tender rabbit is essential. If you like, you can use some mushrooms in this dish; in this case, finely chopped. They should be added at the same time as the white wine. These should, of course, be cultivated mushrooms; Or, in season, morel mushrooms. *Time: 35 minutes (the rabbit having been carved and made completely ready). Serves 4.*

1 young rabbit, gross weight 1 kilogram (2 pounds, 3 ounces); 100 grams (3½ ounces) of lean bacon; 2 tablespoons of chopped onion; 1 piece of garlic the size of a pea; 70 grams (2½ ounces, ⅓ cup) of butter; a nice pinch of minced parsley; 3½ deciliters (1½ cups) of white wine.

PROCEDURE. Remove the rind from the bacon; cut it into cubes of scarcely 1 centimeter (⅜ inch) on each side; blanch them (SEE PAGE 11). Drain. In a sauté pan with a thick bottom, or in a good cast-iron pot, or even, as used in rural areas, a medium-size thick-bottomed skillet, heat 30 grams (1 ounce, 2 tablespoons) of butter. Lightly color the lardons. Drain them on a plate.

Put in the pieces of butter in the same fat. Color them on strong heat (SEE SAUTÉS, PAGE 34). At the end of *about 8 minutes,* add the chopped onion and the garlic. Mix it for another 5–6 minutes, reducing the heat a little so that the onion does not brown: it must simply be nicely golden.

Add the white wine and the lardons. Put a round piece of buttered parchment paper right on top of the pieces and then close it well with a cover. Put it into the oven, or, if you do not have an oven, on moderate heat to maintain a sustained boil for *15–20 minutes.* Meanwhile, finely mince the liver: for a finer purée, you can then pass it through a metallic drum sieve. Keep everything ready on a plate.

About 4–5 minutes before serving, dress the pieces of rabbit on a round heated plate. The lesser pieces—head, neck, and front feet—are put underneath, and the thighs are put on top. Cover. Keep warm.

The cooking liquid must be reduced to *2 scant deciliters (6¾ fluid ounces, ⅞ cup).* If there is more than this, boil it rapidly, uncovered, for 1–2 minutes. Add the purée of liver, mixing it rapidly, letting it cook for scarcely 30 seconds. *Off the heat,* melt and mix the rest of the butter (40 grams, 1⅜ ounces, 3 tablespoons), divided into pieces, moving and shaking the pan on the stovetop: added like this, the butter lightly binds the sauce, which must not be returned to the heat. Pour the sauce on the pieces of rabbit. Sprinkle with minced parsley. Serve.

Rabbit Stewed in Wine *(La Gibelotte)*

This is a simple rabbit ragoût, which can be varied depending on the circumstances and, above all, the kind of rabbit: the recipe is equally good for a wild rabbit as a domestic rabbit.

A classic *gibelotte* includes a garnish of lardons, mushrooms, and small onions; a spicy seasoning; white wine. It is primarily used for wild rabbit, but it is also appropriate for the domestic rabbit. Also classic, but not appropriate for a domestic rabbit, is the home-style recipe in which potatoes replace the mushrooms and the garnish. And in this case, red wine, not white wine, is used.

Always use a young rabbit so that it will be tender. Avoid the rather popular mistake of overcooking the rabbit, the idea being that if it is not well done, it will remain tough. However, too much cooking makes the flesh stringy and flabby without tenderizing it.

A domestic rabbit that has almost reached full growth weighs around 2 kilograms (4 pounds, 6 ounces) gross. The trimmings represent nearly 40 percent of this weight, so the skinned and gutted beast weighs about 1 good kilogram (2 pounds, 3 ounces). The following recipe for rabbit cooked in wine is good for both categories of rabbit. *Time: 1 hour, 30 minutes (once the rabbit is ready to be cooked). Serves 6–8.*

1 rabbit weighing (gross) 1.8–2 kilograms (4 pounds–4 pounds, 6 ounces).

40 grams (1 3/8 ounces) of fresh grated lard, or 25 grams (1 ounce, 2 tablespoons) of butter and 2 tablespoons of oil; 200 grams (7 ounces) of lean bacon; 15 small onions; 200 grams (7 ounces) of mushrooms; 30 grams (1 ounce) of flour.

5 deciliters (generous 2 cups) of white wine; 3 deciliters (1 1/4 cups) of bouillon; a bouquet garni with a generous quantity of thyme; 1 piece of garlic the size of a pea (optional).

PROCEDURE. Skin and gut the rabbit, then carve it, as directed for a civet (PAGE 416), into pieces that are not too large and as equal as possible, using a good sharp cleaver to avoid bone shards. Cut the bacon into cubes of 1 good centimeter (3/8 inch) on each side. Blanch them. Peel the small onions.

In a sauté pan or another utensil with a thick bottom, first heat the grated lard or the butter and the oil. Gently color the cubes of bacon and color the onions using moderate heat. Drain them on a plate. In the same fat heated again, put the pieces of rabbit seasoned with salt. Mix them constantly with the wooden spoon, keeping the pan on a strong heat until the flesh has firmed up and is a beautiful golden color.

Sprinkle with the flour and mix it well. Immediately turn the heat down to allow the flour to gently cook for *about 10 minutes* to turn a golden blond. Add the white wine and bouillon, a good pinch of salt, and a pinch of pepper. Stir until it reaches a boil. Put in the bouquet garni and the crushed garlic. Put buttered parchment paper right on top of the pieces. Cover the pan. Put it in the oven, if possible, which should be just hot enough to maintain a gentle simmer.

At the end of a good half hour of cooking, add the lardons and the onions to the rabbit, which you have prepared at the beginning. At the same time, add the mushrooms, cleaned and simply cut into 2 or 3 according to their size. Push them down completely into the sauce. Continue cooking for another *good half hour.*

Completely and thoroughly degrease. Take out the bouquet. Pour the rabbit cooked in wine into a shallow round bowl or another serving dish. Serve boiling hot.

Home-Style Rabbit Cooked in Wine *(Gibelotte Ménagère)*

The quantities and procedures are the same as for the stew in wine. The difference is that you omit the mushrooms and then add 500 grams (1 pound, 2 ounces) of potatoes for 1 kilogram (2 pounds, 3 ounces) of rabbit.

The potatoes are cut into pieces the size of a walnut and rounded off at the corners. You can add them to the rabbit at the same time as the small onions, pushing them well down into the sauce at the end of *a half hour* of cooking. Continue cooking for another *good half hour.*

To serve: Dress the pieces of rabbit into a pyramid and surround them with the potatoes and onions.

HARE
Lièvre

For all recipes using this game, you should choose the type of hare that the French call *trois quarts* (literally, "three-quarters"): in other words, a hare from a litter born at the beginning of the year that is approaching its full growth but has not yet made it. The weight is enough to identify it. It is never more than 2.25 kilograms (4 pounds, 15 ounces) gross weight, while older hares reach an average weight of 3.1–3.8 kilograms (6 pounds, 13 ounces–8 pounds, 6 ounces). Expect the waste from the skin, entrails, etc., to account for almost one-third of the gross weight.

Jugged Hare *(Le Civet de Lièvre)*

The principle element of all wine stews (civets) is a *liaison made with blood.* Without this blood liaison, a civet is simply an ordinary stew: in fact, for a civet of venison, where using the animal's own blood is not possible, this liaison is made with the fresh blood of another animal.

It is therefore of fundamental importance that the blood of the hare is conserved. This can be supplemented to some extent by using the liver, as we will indicate; this liver is no longer generally used in the civet, though it is very much sought after by some gourmets. Consequently, when buying a hare, you should carefully note where the animal has been pierced by the lead of the hunter; if it's a full side shot, there is a very good chance that you will not find a single drop of blood inside the beast.

Understand that we are referring here to a civet that uses the entire animal—which is the only way to obtain a good civet—and not simply the front part of the beast. Furthermore, a reheated civet is excellent, even after 2–3 days.

If, as in hunting parties, the hare is cooked as soon as it is killed, the flesh will still be warm when it is put into the pan to brown in the fat, and the civet is only the better for it. But if the hare is chilled, the flesh contracts, which means it cannot be immediately used, except under exceptional circumstances. You must then hang it for at least 2 days, in a place where a brisk current of air passes through, so that the tissues relax.

When the hare is not cooked as soon as it is killed, the civet gains a great deal if these pieces are marinated for at least 2 or 3 hours: if the civet is destined for a lunch, the pieces should be put into the marinade the evening before. This step is frequently neglected, and wrongly, because meat flavored thus is much better.

The different procedures. We give the classic recipe for civet further on down. But the recipe for a civet can differ in some details according to regions, circumstances, and particular tastes. Here we will describe the variations.

Thus, bacon or lard frequently replaces butter. As to home-style cooking, the *croutons,* instead of being fried, can be grilled and then, to the delight of some gourmets, rubbed with garlic. The garnish of *mushrooms* can, in the Languedoc style, be replaced by *cèpes,* which have been first sautéed in butter, fat, or oil, and added at the last moment. You can also use dried mushrooms instead of fresh. The preliminary marinade frequently contains red wine instead of cognac.

Above all, never leave out the garlic. It is inseparable from the ingredients of a real civet: its taste, without being discerned, combines with the other aromatics and completes, one might say, the perfect harmony of the flavors.

For his *home-style civet,* the celebrated Nîmes chef Durand suggests barding the pieces of hare with a large spiced lardon and cooking them on a slow heat with a little bit of salt pork, some lard, and carrot, in a earthenware pot that is tightly sealed and surrounded by burning cinders; the final liaison is made with blood.

As for the famous hare "in a cauldron," the recipe can be summarized thus: kill the hare, then skin and carve it while it is still quivering, and put the still warm pieces in a small cauldron with bacon and aromatics and a red wine that has a very high alcohol content. Bring it to a boil over a fire whose flames envelope the pan, which is easy to do in country fireplaces, using a chimney hook and a fire burning large pieces of very dry wood. Flame the wine; and as for a matelote, add some butter that has had flour added to it (or beurre manié) once the hare is cooked and the sauce is reduced after the blood has been added to it.

For this same method "in the cauldron," Durand indicates a procedure that is less rustic. The cauldron here can be replaced by a deep pot. The pieces of hare are put in melted fatback bacon with carrot, onion, and garlic; once they are well sealed, moisten it to cover them with wine, half cut with boiling water. Bring it to a strong boil. The hare, which must be young and tender, cooks at the same time as the liquid reduces. The liaison is made with blood and the addition of 2 tablespoons of very pure olive oil: this is an entirely regional method, and it replaces the piece of butter used for the finishing.

This *butter,* added to the sauce *when it is ready to serve,* should be included no matter what recipe is used to make the civet; and it is even better when the liquid used for moistening the civet is only wine. The butter should be added off the heat, of course, and the sauce should not be heated any further because the creamy effect of the butter would be destroyed.

And let us also suggest, which you might easily have thought of yourself, adding *a glass of heavy cream* to the blood liaison.

The *Lyon* method includes a garnish of chestnuts cooked separately like small onions, with a little bit of butter and bouillon added instead of the mushrooms; or, in home-style cooking, these are half-cooked in the oven and then finished in the civet.

Made in the *Flemish* style, a civet includes a little bit of brown sugar; no garnish of mushrooms or small onions, but a substantial quantity of onions cut into rounds in the sauce, which are then pressed to make a kind of soubise coulis. It is accompanied by red currant jelly.

Let us indicate, to finish, that in certain rustic recipes, the roux is left out at the beginning and replaced by *flour dissolved in a little bit of water* and added only at the end of the cooking. In this case, allow a level soupspoon per glass of liquid: the equivalent to 5 grams (1/6 ounce) of flour for each deciliter of sauce.

Liaison with blood; the liver. Depending on the amount of blood available, the methods are different. At any rate, you make the liaison 8–10 minutes before serving.

The normal quantity of blood gathered from a hare is about 1 deciliter (3 1/3 fluid ounces, scant 1/2 cup). Once you have this amount, proceed as follows: dilute the blood little by little with 4–5 tablespoons of sauce from the civet so that it heats gradually. If you do not do this, the heat of the boiling sauce causes the blood to clot; the sauce is then granulated rather than being smooth. Pour the heated blood into the civet, shaking the pot with a back and forth movement to mix it well, without using your spoon, which would risk damaging the pieces of hare and the garnish.

The liver, cut into 4 scallops, is subsequently added just as it is, or firmed up in the pan with a little bit of fat. Cooking it for more than 5 minutes would toughen it and make it inedible.

If you have only a little bit of blood and clots: Break up the clots as much as possible with a fork. Dilute them with a few tablespoons of red wine; pass it through the chinois, with half of the liver, which you have previously firmed up in the pan and then crushed with a mortar and passed through a drum sieve. Heat everything with a little bit of sauce before mixing it in the civet. Add the rest of the liver cut into escalopes as above.

If you have almost no blood: Use the entire liver. Divide it into escalopes and firm them up in the pan; crush them with the mortar; pass them through the drum sieve. Add them to the civet, taking the suggested precautions.

No matter how the liaison is made, the sauce must only very gently simmer on very low heat until you are ready to serve.

PRINCIPAL RECIPES

Classic Wine Stew *(Le Civet Classique)*

This includes bacon, small onions, mushrooms if possible, and croutons fried in butter. In a good, careful cooking procedure, the small onions are cooked separately and are not put into the civet until the sauce has been bound: this way, they preserve their own flavor and shape. This is the method we give here. However, if we follow the home-style method, or try to simplify things, the small onions can be cooked in the civet from the beginning. For all the rest, the ingredients and the steps are the same in both cases. *Time: 2 scant hours (the pieces of hare having been marinated in advance). Serves 8.*

1 *trois quarts* (young) hare with a gross weight of 1.8–2.25 kilograms (4–4 pounds, 15 ounces).

For the marinade: 3 tablespoons of olive oil; 5 tablespoons of eau de vie; a large onion (120 grams/4¼ ounces) cut into rounds; 3 medium shallots; 3 sprigs of parsley; ½ of a bay leaf; a pinch of powdered thyme.

For the garnish: 250 grams (8⅞ ounces) of lean bacon; 24 small onions about the size of a large hazelnut; 250 grams (8⅞ ounces) of fresh mushrooms; 12 croutons fried in butter.

For the civet sauce: 50 grams (1¾ ounces, 3½ tablespoons) of butter; 2 medium onions (180–200 grams/6⅓–7 ounces total) cut into quarters; 40–45 grams of flour (1⅜–1½ ounces); 1 liter (4¼ cups) of *good* red wine; 2½ deciliters (1 cup) of bouillon; a small garlic clove; a bouquet garni; 10 grams (⅓ ounce) of salt; a nice pinch of pepper; a small pinch of spice powder.

PROCEDURE. **The hare:** Skin the hare as directed (SEE PAGE 410).

First cut off the thighs from the saddle and divide them into 3 pieces: cut the drumstick and the upper thigh in two Detach the front legs and cut into 2 pieces. Cut the neck into 2 or 3 pieces. Split the head in two; remove the eyes and teeth. You can cook them, but they are not generally served because they repulse many people.

Divide the chops. Cut the saddle crosswise into 4, 5, or 6 pieces depending on the size of the animal; put the pieces in a pan with all the ingredients for the marinade. Keep it cool. Toss it from time to time so that the pieces are equally impregnated by the flavor of the aromatics.

The first part of cooking: *The bacon.* Remove the rind. Cut the bacon into large cubes. Blanch it (SEE BACON, PAGE 11).

Use a pot in good aluminum, with high sides *and a thick bottom* (this is extremely important), and make sure that it is the right size, so that the amount of liquid indicated is enough to just cover the pieces of hare. A pot with a diameter of 22–23 centimeters (8½–9 inches) would be appropriate here.

Gently heat the butter. Put in the lardons. Lightly color them on medium heat, mixing them from time to time. Then take them out with a skimmer and put them on a plate. In the same butter, now augmented by the fat rendered from the bacon, gently color the onion quarters. Then add them to the lardons.

Meanwhile, while you are watching the lardons and the onions, remove the pieces of hare from the marinade. Rid them of all fragments of their seasoning, then thoroughly wipe them off with a dry kitchen towel. Any moisture that remains on the meat will prevent them from browning by forming a steam.

The roux: In the same butter used for the lardons and the onions, gently cook the flour as if for an ordinary light brown roux (SEE LIAISON WITH ROUX, PAGE 47), then put the well-dried pieces of hare into this roux. On medium heat, mix it continuously, being careful to scrape the spoon on the bottom of the pot, where the roux sticks; it will burn there unless it receives some moisture from the sweating meat, which should also be stirred constantly. At the end of about 10 minutes, the pieces of hare should be nicely sealed and colored.

For the roux and to color the hare, you can also proceed in an inverse manner: that is, first put the pieces of hare in warm butter; on strong heat, mix them around for about 10 minutes. Then turn down the heat and sprinkle them with the flour, mixing them constantly until little by little they have taken on the light brown tint indicated.

When, by whatever method, the hare and roux have reached the right color, add the wine and the bouillon. Mix it on strong heat to completely dissolve the roux, and do not stop until it is boiling strongly. Add salt, pepper, and spices first, then the little bit of marinade that remains, and all its ingredients, the clove of garlic having been squashed under a blade of a knife.

Place a round of buttered parchment paper right on top of the civet; cover the pot. If possible, put it in a very moderate oven; this replaces the gentle heat that completely surrounded the utensil in the old fireplace. Cooking the civet can also be done on the stove, as long as you only maintain a very small, tranquil, and regular simmer. Do the same if you use the oven. For either method, allow

1 hour for this first part of the cooking. Meanwhile, prepare the small onions (SEE SMALL ONIONS FOR GARNISH, PAGE 525).

The second part of cooking: Take the pot out of the oven. Use a fork to pick up the pieces one by one, and then put them in a terrine or shallow dish. Add the *bacon.* Strain the sauce over everything through a very fine strainer, pressing down a bit on the aromatics with the wooden spoon. Rinse the pot. Put everything back into it. Add the *mushrooms;* to prepare these, remove the end of the stem, wash them, and then cut them into 2 or in 4 pieces, depending on their size, without peeling them.

Bring it back to a boil. Cover it again with the paper and the cover. Put it back in the oven or over the heat for *15–20 minutes,* always maintaining a very small simmer.

Meanwhile, prepare the croutons as directed (SEE PAGE 20).

Once the civet has been cooked, make the liaison with the blood. Add the *garnish of small onions.* Then let the whole thing gently simmer on the stove until you are ready to serve.

To serve: Before dressing the dish, turn the heat off for a few minutes to give the fat time to rise to the surface. With a soupspoon, completely remove this fat. Lift out the pieces of hare and the small onions with a skimmer and put them on a plate, making sure that you put the most presentable pieces aside so you can put them on top: this would be the saddle and the thighs. Put the plate in a very mild oven.

With a small whisk or a wooden spoon, mix the sauce over strong heat for *2–3 minutes* to reheat it thoroughly. Pour it over the pieces. Then place the fried croutons all around it. Serve it on burning hot plates.

Home-Style Wine Stew
(Civet Façon Ménagère)

This uses the same quantities for all the ingredients as the classic method. The difference is that you leave out the mushrooms as well as the onion used for the sauce; this is replaced by small onions put into the sauce at the beginning.

PROCEDURE. Heat the butter or the same quantity of good pork fat in a pot. Brown the lardons there, which should first have been blanched. Take them out and put them on a plate and replace them with the small onions. Gently color them: add them to the lardons.

In the same butter or fat, color the flour and firm up the pieces of hare in one of the ways suggested. Add the liquid, marinade, seasoning, lardons, and the *small onions that have been colored.* Cook as directed; put the pieces of hare back into the sauce, which should first have been strained, also adding the lardons and the small onions. Continue with the cooking. Bind and dress in the same way. Dip the fried croutons on both sides into the sauce just before placing it on the civet.

Civet Bonne Femme
(Civet Bonne Femme)

This is a simple procedure of home-style country cooking that produces an excellent civet without trouble or expense, because wine is not used in it, and only vinegar is used as a condiment for the sauce. However, it is absolutely essential to use good wine vinegar, a rather strong one. It should, of course, be understood that a hare cooked in this way is best when it is cooked straight after being killed, as is usual in hunting parties, and without the preliminary marinade. *Time: 2 hours, 30 minutes at least. Serves 8.*

1 *trois quarts* (young) hare weighing about 1.3 kilograms (2 pounds, 14 ounces) net; 200 grams (7 ounces) of bacon; 200 grams (7 ounces) of onions (2 nice medium-size onions); 40 grams (1 3/8 ounces, 3 tablespoons) of butter (about the size of a pigeon egg) or the same amount of good pork fat; 20 grams of flour (2/3 ounce); 1 scant liter (4 1/4 cups) of bouillon; 4 good soupspoons of vinegar; a bouquet garni with a little clove of garlic.

PROCEDURE. Prepare the hare as directed in the classic recipe, and also the lardons.

If you do not have a thick aluminum deep pot, use another pan of the right size. Lightly color the lardons in the butter. Take them out to replace them with the onion cut into segments (8 segments per onion). Color them; drain them and put them with the lardons.

In the good hot fat on strong heat, firm and color the pieces of hare, starting with the largest.

Then sprinkle them with the flour; on gentle heat, let them color slowly, mixing continuously.

Then pour in the hot bouillon and the vinegar; dilute it and mix it until it boils. Add the lardons, the onions, the bouquet, and the lungs and heart of the hare; very little salt if the bouillon is salted; a pinch of ground pepper.

Cover the pot. Put it on extremely low heat, which here replaces the heat from the fireplace or the charcoal fire found in some country kitchens, so that the civet very gently simmers for *2 hours.*

To serve: Degrease the sauce. Make the liaison with the blood. Keep it warm on very gentle heat until serving in a very well heated shallow bowl.

Strictly speaking, the expression "saddle" includes the part near the kidneys from the first ribs to the tail, which you should be careful to keep, without the thighs. These are eliminated, cutting them off on the bias.

A saddle taken from a 2.25-kilogram (5 pound) hare weighs a little more than 400 grams (14 1/8 ounces) and feeds 4. When the number of guests is larger, you can leave the thighs: then the piece becomes the "hindquarters" and not the true "saddle." The weight of the cut is more than doubled, to at least 900 grams (2 pounds); it can serve 8. The recipe for the "saddle" or the "hindquarters" is the same. You simply double the necessary quantities for the hindquarters.

Carving the saddle after cooking: Normally, you detach the fillets from the bone and also the filet mignon situated underneath it. Then each fillet is divided into scallops cut on the bias: that is, 3 scallops from the large fillet and 2 from the filet mignon. Each guest should always have 1 scallop from the filet mignon.

But given the fact that many of those who love this dish prefer meat that is still attached to the bone, you can satisfy them by cutting the saddle crosswise. In this case, cut 6 pieces and then place them back together to remake the saddle in its original shape.

Roast Saddle of Hare *(Râble de Lièvre Rôti).* The roasting is done by whichever method is available, either on the spit or in the oven. This second system is actually the more widespread, and we will give here the time appropriate for it; on the spit, or roasting in the open air with a gas flame, it will take a few minutes longer. At any rate, the preliminary preparation of the saddle—the studding, the marinating, etc.—remains the same. A roast saddle of hare is generally accompanied by a *sauce poivrade.*

The saddle can be prepared and put into the marinade the evening before, or at least early in the morning of the same day if it is to be served at dinner. You should figure out exactly when the saddle will be served so that it does not have to stand, or at least so that it will stand for as little as possible. Even though it has been perfectly roasted, the juices will run out of it while it waits; but when it is served as soon as it is cooked, the flesh will remain juicy. *Time: 30 minutes of cooking (once the saddle has been studded and marinated in advance).*

1 saddle; 80 grams (2 3/4 ounces) of fresh bacon to stud it; 25 grams (1 ounce, 2 tablespoons) of butter to baste it.

For the marinade: 3 tablespoons of vinegar; 1 tablespoon of oil; 6 very thin rounds of carrot and the same number of thin rounds of onion; 2 finely minced shallots; 2 sprigs of parsley broken into small pieces; 1 sprig of thyme, some bay; salt and pepper.

PROCEDURE. Remove the shiny skin that covers the saddle, using a thin, sharp knife, which you slide underneath this skin to remove it bit by bit. Then remove the nervous membranes sticking to the flesh, being very careful not to damage the meat.

Stud the saddle with 3 rows of very fine lardons on each fillet (SEE STUDDING, PAGE 13). Then put the saddle to marinate in a small round bowl, seasoned and covered with the ingredients needed for its marinade. Keep it cool and baste it frequently.

To cook: You need *25 minutes* to cook the saddle and *5 minutes* to finish the sauce: so, *a total of 30 minutes.* Take this into account when deciding when to put the roast into the oven.

A few moments before, remove it from the marinade and clean off all the fragments. Wipe it thoroughly with a *dry kitchen towel:* any remaining moisture would prevent the meat from being well sealed.

Place the saddle in a roasting pan fitted with a rack (SEE ROASTS, PAGE 30). Baste it with the *melted* butter. Put it into a good hot oven. Baste the saddle from time to time with its melted butter. If, at the end of *20 minutes*—that is, 5 minutes before the cooking time has expired—the lardons are not perfectly colored, move the roasting pan to the hottest part of the oven.

Serve the cooking juices separately in a sauceboat if the saddle is not accompanied with a *sauce poivrade* or another appropriate sauce. Otherwise, pour the cooking juices around the saddle.

Saddle of Hare Cream Sauce *(Râble de Lièvre à la Crème).* Sour cream, which is used widely in the northern countries of Europe, with an accompaniment of red currants or apple compote, is the hallmark of this dish. When you do not have sour cream, replace it with crème fraîche that has been acidulated with a little bit of lemon juice.

An apple compote must be very lightly sugared; you serve it in a little dish or sauceboat. Present the red currant jelly in a nice little pot or a small crystal bowl. Serve both at the same time as the hare.

The recipe and the quantity of ingredients are the same as for the roast saddle. What is added is the cream for the sauce: that is, 2 deciliters ($6^3/_4$ fluid ounces, $^7/_8$ cup) of thick cream and 2 good tablespoons of cooking juice that has been reduced.

PROCEDURE. To roast the saddle, put it in a sauté pan, directly on the bottom of the pan. This will prevent using a second pan for the sauce. Baste it with the melted butter and proceed as has been explained to cook it.

The sauce: Once the saddle has been cooked for the given time, proceed as follows: *first* strain the liquid remaining from the marinade into a bowl; add the veal jus. Keep it ready.

Remove the saddle from the sauté pan and dress it on its plate. Keep it warm and covered. Drain the butter from the pan, leaving only the caramelized jus from the hare. Note that we say "caramelized": that is, the jus should be colored a *light* golden brown at the bottom of the casserole. If the jus is a darker brown, even blackish, it will be burned and will give the sauce a bad taste: this means you cannot use the same pan.

Then pour the liquid from the marinade into the pan to deglaze the bottom, stirring with the wooden spoon to detach and dissolve the caramel. Then add the cream. Boil it strongly, continually stirring until it reduces to *$1^1/_2$* deciliters (5 fluid ounces, $^2/_3$ cup). Turn off the heat; add 6–7 drops of lemon juice to the sauce. Pour it immediately through the chinois *around* the saddle and not at all on top of it. Serve it immediately.

OTHER PREPARATIONS OF HARE

Bourbon-Style Hare *(Lièvre à la mode du Bourbonnais)*

This is an excellent home-style recipe, appropriate for a hare of any age. It is particularly good for a large hare, which is never tender enough to roast; but when possible, it is better to get a medium-size hare, or a *trois quarts* hare, weighing about $2^1/_4$ kilograms (4 pounds, 15 ounces).

The same preparation is good for a saddle of wild rabbit or a simple domestic rabbit that has been well fed. If using a domestic rabbit, skin it and gut it the evening before and then fill it with wild thyme, which you should also spread all over it; keep the rabbit like this until the next day.

The following quantities are appropriate for a medium-size hare. These can be modified a little bit, particularly as far as the liquid goes, depending on the size of the hare that you use. For a large hare you should allow $^3/_4$ liter (3 cups) measured generously; and, for a small hare, not even a half-liter (2 cups). *Make sure that this liquid contains an equal amount of bouillon and vinegar.* Use a good vinegar that is not too acidic.

There are similar differences in the time needed to cook the hare: while 2 scant hours are appropriate for a medium-size hare, you must allow $2^1/_2$ hours for a large hare and only $1^1/_2$ hours if the animal is small and tender. *Time: 3 hours total.*

1 medium-size hare: 3 deciliters ($1^1/_4$ cups) of bouillon and the same of vinegar; 125 grams ($4^1/_2$ ounces) of good lard; 250 grams ($8^7/_8$ ounces) of bacon; 250 grams ($8^7/_8$ ounces) of large onions, net weight; a bunch of parsley and wild thyme; if you do not have wild thyme, a small sprig of fresh thyme.

PROCEDURE. Skin and gut the hare, then put its liver back into its body, but only after having carefully checked that it no longer has any trace of bile. Roll the beast into a round shape with its head between its 4 legs, thighs up, tying it securely. If the hare is large, remove the head. If you are only using the hindquarters, roll it and tie it the same way.

The bacon and the onions: Leave the rind on the bacon. Cut it into 5 or 6 long thin slices. Blanch it as directed (this bacon is not served with the hare and can be used in other ways). Cut the onions into cubes about the size of playing dice.

Use a thick pot that is just big enough to contain the rolled hare. Heat the fat in it. Put in the slices of bacon, which have been thoroughly drained; color them lightly. Take them out and put them on a plate. Replace them with the onions. Color the onions, mixing them frequently with the wooden spoon to ensure they color equally, being careful they do not burn: otherwise, they will turn bitter, which would ruin the sauce, and nothing would be able to correct it. Then remove it with a skimmer and put it with the bacon.

Now heat the fat remaining in the pot until it gives off a very light vapor. Put in the hare. On strong heat, color it, turning it as it gets well colored on one side by lifting it with a fork, which you pass underneath the string without piercing the flesh. Color the back part equally well.

Once the hare has taken on the nice color of a roast, put in the bacon and the onions, the bouillon, the vinegar, the bunch of parsley, and a good pinch of pepper; add no salt for the moment if the bouillon is salted. Bring it to a boil. Cover the pot, leaving a very small opening so that the steam can escape. Turn the heat down low so you maintain a regular, small simmer for *2 scant hours.*

Meanwhile, turn the hare over to change the side every half hour; baste it every 15 minutes with its cooking juice. Toward the end of the cooking, loosen the string a little bit to allow the inside of the beast to be thoroughly reached by the liquid.

To dress and serve: Take the hare out of the pot, draining it thoroughly; remove all fragments of onion. Put it on a round, heated plate. Cut the strings with scissors; leave the hare in its round shape. Keep the plate in a very warm place.

Strain the cooking juice into a small saucepan through the chinois or through a very fine strainer. Completely degrease it. At this point, the juices should be half the amount you started with: so, for the quantities above, 3 deciliters ($1^1/_4$ cups). If there is any more than this, boil it strongly to reduce the juice. If not, let it boil for just a few seconds so that you can pour it very hot on the hare, which will become glazed as if with a light syrup. Serve immediately.

Hare à la Royale *(Lièvre à la Royale)*

Professionals insist that they do not know of a classic definitive formula for Hare à la Royale: on the other hand, the recipes for this dish, as supplied and vaunted by amateurs and by more or less qualified gourmets, are both numerous and varied, frequently bordering on fantasy. A choice must be made. Here we give a recipe drawn from a manuscript collection supplied to us by a veritable gastronome, who is thoroughly acquainted with the rules for cooking it and who conforms to them. The recipe is reduced to the essential points. *Time: 2–3 hours of cooking (once the hare has been prepared in advance).*

PROCEDURE. After having gutted the skinned hare, cut the feet near the shin. Remove and preserve the liver. Then, through a small hole made between the ribs, push the front legs into the chest.

Chop 500 grams (1 pound, 2 ounces) of pork, as much fatty as lean, with the liver of the hare, which has been well cleaned. Then add, in a quantity equivalent to the minced meat, some stale bread crumbs that have been soaked in bouillon and then thoroughly pressed, parsley, garlic (about the size of a bean, and squashed), shallot, pepper, salt, and nutmeg. Crush everything in the mortar, then add at least 1 egg, both the white and the yolk, and pass the mixture through a metallic drum sieve.

Introduce this stuffing into the body of the hare and close the opening with some heavy cooking string. Bind the hind legs and stick a small *hâtelet* (skewer) through the thighs to support them and to give a good shape to the beast.

To cook: Use a *poissonnière,* or fish poacher, that can hold the stretched-out hare, which you place on its back on top of a few slices of raw ham laid on the bottom of the utensil. Season it with a few onions cut in slices, some parsley, thyme, a little bit of bay, basil, garlic, 2 cloves, 1 tablespoon of jus, 1/4 liter (1 cup) of white wine, and 1 small glass of eau de vie.

Cook it in the oven for *2–3 hours,* basting it from time to time with the cooking juices.

To serve: Dress it carefully on a serving plate, because the hare will be very fragile at this point. Degrease and strain the cooking juices, and make a sauce using butter mixed with flour; if there is some blood from the hare, add it. Remove the *hâtelet* (skewer) from the thighs. Strain the sauce, then pour it on the hare. Serve very hot.

WILD BOAR
Sanglier

This is not really a game animal that is current today; so we will confine ourselves to just a few brief instructions. First of all, let us say that for culinary use, only a young wild boar (or *marcassin*) is appropriate. Do not go beyond one year for an adult boar.

A young wild boar does not need a marinade unless this is necessary to preserve the meat. For the chops, it is enough to season them with salt, pepper, and to infuse them with lemon juice a few hours before cooking them. The same is true of a haunch, for which you should use a simple marinade of lemon juice, a small glass of white wine and the same amount of eau de vie, salt, pepper, thyme, and powdered bay. Roll the meat in this and turn the haunch 3 to 4 times a day.

If the haunch or quarter will be kept for several days, a more thorough marinade is essential, and it is a *cooked* marinade that is required (SEE PAGE 18). For a quarter or a haunch of young wild boar, this might include the following: 100 grams (3 1/2 ounces) of carrots and the same of onions; 3 shallots; 2 cloves of garlic; 3 or 4 sprigs of parsley, 1 bay leaf, 1 sprig of thyme; 6 peppercorns; 2 cloves, 12 grams (3/8 ounce) of salt; 3/4 liter (generous 3 cups) of white wine and 1/4 liter (1 cup) of good vinegar; 1 1/2 deciliters (5 fluid ounces, 2/3 cup) of oil. If you are using an older and tougher boar, leave out the wine and put in only vinegar: that is, about 1 liter (4 1/4 cups).

Allow for cooking the quarter or the haunch of a young wild boar in the oven: *20–25 minutes* per 450 grams (1 pound); as for pork meat, the meat of the boar must be thoroughly cooked. For all other recipes and ways to cook wild boar, remember that the different recipes for venison are applicable to wild boar.

The sauces to accompany it are: *poivrade, venison, grande veneur,* etc., served separately, or simply a jus prepared thus: drain all the fat from the roasting pan; pour in a part of the marinade to dissolve the crust on the bottom; boil it strongly to reduce the liquid; pour it into a dish. This is particularly good for a wine marinade.

PÂTÉS AND TERRINES

The composition of both is identical. The only difference is the crust: in fact, they are so similar that you could describe terrines as being nothing but a pâté without a crust. Consequently, the instructions given for quantities, the type of meat, the method of cutting them up, the stuffing, the bards, the working order for all these steps, etc., are the same for both pâtés and terrines. A recipe for a pâté can also be applied to a terrine, and vice versa. Only the receptacle, which is dictated by whether you want a crust or not, and the method of cooking, differ.

The elements of pâtés and terrines are divided into two parts: *the garnish* and *the stuffing.*

The garnish: The garnish is made from the best pieces of meat cut into pieces, with the addition of lardons, ham, etc., depending on the case. Everything should be arranged in a distinct and decorative manner.

The stuffing: Whatever the ingredients, the stuffing must always be minced very finely: this is essential. The common French saying, "minced as fine as pâté meat," does not even begin to describe the finesse that the stuffing should have; the more finely the different ingredients are minced, the more completely they combine.

The stuffing is really a purée of raw meat. A good, general recommendation is to crush all the ingredients with a mortar and then pass them through a metallic drum sieve to retain and eliminate all the nerves and tough parts. With a mechanical chopper, this work is greatly simplified; it produces a stuffing that is perfectly fine and homogenous; and because all the scraps have been retained by the round cutter, there is no need to pass the ingredients through the drum sieve.

If you do not have a grinder to grind all the meat together, you should proceed as follows: cut the meat into very small pieces, having first removed all nerves and filaments. These should be minced separately, which is easier and less tiring; be sure to mince them as finely as possible. Put everything back together and mince some more for a perfect mixture. If you have a mortar, you can crush the different minced pieces separately, a little at a time. Finally, crush the different meats together, to combine them well. After this, pass the stuffing through a drum sieve a little at a time.

The stuffing for pâtés and terrines should be seasoned with 12–13 grams (about 3/8 ounce) of spiced salt for each pound of stuffing. The proportions of spiced salt are: for 10 grams (1/3 ounce) of salt, 2 grams (1/14 ounce) of pepper and 1 gram (1/28 ounce) of spices. In humid weather you can augment this normal dose by 2 grams of salt (1/14 ounce) per 450 grams (1 pound) of stuffing.

NOTES. Game used in a pâté or in a terrine should be used only if it is absolutely fresh: that is, very recently slaughtered, and not having had the time to even start the process of *faisandage* (curing by hanging).

Do not cut into pâtés and terrines until these are thoroughly cooled; otherwise, they will disintegrate when you cut them.

Pâtés en croûte, no matter what type, do not keep for as long as terrines. Nonetheless, if a pâté is kept in a cool and dry place, it can be preserved for at least 8 days, and can be kept as a reserve.

When a pâté or terrine is being eaten over a period of several days, it is essential that you put a piece of bacon or lard, or a piece of aluminum foil or plastic wrap, on the cut part, to avoid contact with the air, which will cause browning, and this part will be wasted each time you cut a new slice.

A gelée is used for pâtés and terrines made from game, not only to strengthen the flavor—it is very like the "fumet" prepared in haute cuisine—but also because when it sets, it binds together the different elements of the pâté and makes cutting the slices much easier.

Cooking terrines: This is done in a bain-marie

in the oven. The heat of the oven must be rather strong, a little bit hotter than the degree appropriate for roasts, and it must also be consistent.

A bain-marie is used because it releases steam around the terrine; there is absolutely no need for it to be a deep utensil; and depending on the shape of the terrine, you can use an oval roasting pan, a low pot, or a sauté pan. The water, which should be boiling when it is poured in, should reach around the terrine to a height of about 3 centimeters (1¼ inches), which is about a third of the way up the side of modern terrines.

Make sure that you bring this water immediately back to a boil. The effect of the steam is to prevent any of the stuffing that is in direct contact with the walls of terrine from drying out or burning: this is both around the sides and on the bottom. Also, there is always a certain risk that the terrine will take on the abominable taste of burned earth or stale grease. In a baker's oven—that is, a gentle oven—you can cook a terrine by placing it directly on the floor of the oven, where it will not risk drying out or burning, as in a normal kitchen oven; but you must always remember that an unpleasant earthy taste is very easily produced when the pan is in direct contact with the heat source.

It is absolutely essential that the water is maintained at a *constant boil* to produce the steam throughout the cooking period. You must therefore watch carefully that it does not completely dry up, and so you must always add a little bit of water as it evaporates.

Cooking time: Allow 32–35 minutes per 450 grams (1 pound) of the total weight of the ingredients making up the terrine. Beyond that, you can check that it is perfectly done by sticking a cooking needle into the middle of the terrine, which should come out absolutely burning hot. You can also examine the liquid that rises to the surface and simmers and boils at the edges of the terrine. As long as this liquid is unclear and milky, you know that the juices coming from the stuffing and mixing with the fat have not yet been cooked and reabsorbed. As soon as the liquid appears clear and consists only of a liquid fat, this is a certain sign that all the juices are absorbed, so you can conclude that the cooking is complete.

Pressing after cooking: The point of this is to seal the stuffing mixture and the various ingredients, which are somewhat loosened by the effect of the cooking.

For this, you need a small plank cut in the shape and size of the terrine, which can be placed into the terrine itself, fitting right in. When the terrine is taken out of the oven, let it rest for a scant 15 minutes, then cover it with the plank and place a weight on top of it. This can vary depending on the size of the terrine, but should never be excessive; 2–3 kilograms (4 pounds, 6 ounces–6 pounds, 10 ounces) is good. Let it cool until the next day without touching it.

Conservation of terrines: For terrines that you want to keep preserved for two or three months (closed tightly), and also for those that are eaten gradually over the course of more than a few days, there are some precautions you must take.

First of all, remove the juice that has turned into a gelée in the terrine, because eventually this ruins everything with which it comes in contact. Then you need a layer of fat to cover the contents of the terrine entirely, forming an isolating layer against air, humidity, bacteria, etc. Use a good lard; nothing else is appropriate for conserving terrines.

When making terrines that are to be kept for a long time, note that the cooking time must be a little bit prolonged to completely reduce the juices that cause deterioration, as we have just explained. Thus, during the last 15 minutes of cooking, remove the terrine from the bain-marie and leave it to dry in the oven until the sizzling of the grease on the surface of the terrine indicates that the juice is totally reduced. The fine odor escaping from the crust is another indication. But pay close attention so that the process does not go beyond the point of completion and burn the terrine. And remember, you do this only for terrines you are intending to keep for a longer period of time. It is not necessary for terrines that are to be eaten immediately or kept in the pantry already cut, held in supply for the next few days.

To remove the juice and cover with fat, proceed as follows: Once the terrine has been pressed and completely cooled, dip the receptacle in hot water or place everything in a hot oven for a moment and then unmold. Remove the juice that has set to a gelée in the utensil. Wash this utensil carefully and then dry thoroughly.

If the terrine is to be preserved: Remove the bacon surrounding it and wipe it off with a very dry kitchen towel if there is any moisture remaining, despite all the care you have taken to dry it out at the end of the cooking time. Any moisture will, in the long run, cause mold. Put the block back into the terrine. Fill the empty space that has formed between the container and the block by pouring in some good melted lard. Gently raise the block with a fork so that the lard runs completely underneath it on the bottom of the utensil. Pour a layer of lard about 1 scant centimeter (3/8 inch) thick on top of the terrine. Let it solidify.

For terrines that must be preserved, put a round of white paper on top of the lard once it has set. The next day, close the terrine with its cover, which must fit perfectly. Glue a ribbon of paper at the junction of the cover and the mold. Keep in a cool place and, above all, keep it quite dry.

Terrine of Domestic Rabbit *(Terrine de Lapin Domestique)*

Time: 2 hours for preparation (once the rabbit has been skinned and gutted), and 35 minutes per 450 grams (1 pound) of the total weight of the terrine for cooking. Serves 10–12.

1 rabbit yielding, after boning, 800–900 grams (1 pound, 12 ounces–2 pounds) of meat.

300 grams (10 1/2 ounces) of pork, net weight, containing about 60 grams (2 1/4 ounces) of fat in the total weight; 400 grams (14 1/8 ounces) of fatback lard of which 200 grams (7 ounces) should be cut into very thin sheets to line the terrine; 150 grams (5 1/3 ounces) of lean, uncooked ham; a small glass of cognac and the same of Madeira; 5 grams of spices (1/6 ounce) and 15 grams (1/2 ounce) of salt or 20 grams (2/3 ounce) of spiced salt. A terrine with a capacity of at least 1 1/4 liters (5 1/3 cups).

PROCEDURE. Once the rabbit has been skinned and gutted, reserve the liver, after having carefully eliminated the bile. Remove and separate the 2 thighs, then take off all the fleshy part of the upper side and cut it into 3 pieces; be careful to remove the nerves. Take off the saddle; remove all the fleshy part as well as the filet mignon and the kidneys. Put these pieces of meat on a plate: this is for garnish. Take off and bone the shoulders of the beast. Remove any flesh remaining on the carcass; remove the nerves. Gather these pieces on another plate. Add the meat from the bottom of the thighs and the liver. Add the pork and 100 grams (3 1/2 ounces) of bacon. This is for the stuffing.

The garnish: In a sauté pan, heat 50 grams (1 3/4 ounces) of grated or finely minced fatback bacon. On strong heat, rapidly firm up, but do not cook, the meat for the garnish. This step is to develop the flavor of the meats and to prevent the meat shriveling up in the course of cooking, which would cause some empty spaces in the stuffing. Then put everything on a plate to let it cool down.

In the same fat, color the liver, cut in 2 or 3 pieces, then put the liver and the fat on the plate of meat for the stuffing.

Once the pieces of rabbit for the garnish have cooled, divide them into fillets the thickness of a finger. Add the ham and 50 grams (1 3/4 ounces) of bacon cut into small 1-centimeter (3/8-inch) cubes. Put everything on a plate. Season with one-quarter of the seasoned salt. Moisten this with the cognac and the Madeira. Mix it well and allow it to marinate for 1 hour, turning everything over from time to time.

The stuffing: Finally, mince all the meat destined for the stuffing. Season it with the 15 grams (1/2 ounce) of seasoned salt that remains. Lastly, beat the stuffing with a wooden spoon to make it smooth.

Putting it into the terrine: Cut a sheet of bacon that is the same size as the bottom. You can also, depending on the pieces of bacon that you have, cut it into triangles and arrange the triangles so that the bottom of the terrine is perfectly covered. Line the sides of the terrine with sheets of bacon cut as high as the walls. With moistened fingers, so that the stuffing does not stick, apply a layer of stuffing 1 1/2 centimeters (5/8 inch) thick on the bottom and against the walls of the terrine that have been thus lined.

Then arrange a layer of garnish on the bottom of the terrine, spreading out a few fillets of rabbit mixed with a few cubes of ham and bacon. Above this layer of garnish, lay out a layer of stuffing 2 centimeters (3/4 inch) thick, packing it down with your fingers. Make a new bed of garnish, then cover with a layer of stuffing and continue alternating garnish and stuffing, ending with a layer of stuffing. Finally, on top of the terrine lay a bard of fatback bacon cut in the shape of the utensil, then put the cover on top of everything. The terrine is now ready to cook as directed.

After cooking and cooling, proceed as directed in terms of how long the terrine is to be preserved. If it is to be consumed the same day, take off the sheets of bacon and surround it with good chopped aspic.

Terrine of Hare *(Terrine de Lièvre)*

This is a very simple method, the garnish and the stuffing being mixed instead of being arranged in alternate layers. And the result is just as good in terms of flavor and appearance, because the slices, when you cut them, will look as good marbled with the lardons as when the garnish has been arranged in layers.

The best way of using an old hare is to put it into a terrine or a pâté. "Old" means a beast that has reached an average weight of 3 1/2 kilograms (7 pounds, 11 ounces), neither skinned nor gutted; here, we will take this as the typical weight. Keep the saddle for other uses, and use only the forward parts and the thighs of the hare in the terrine. Be very careful to reserve the blood of the beast, which is almost as important in a terrine as in a civet.

Let us repeat here that the hare used must be freshly killed, and must not in any way have begun the process of *faisandage. Time: 1 hour for preparation and 35 minutes per 450 grams (1 pound) of the total weight for cooking. Serves 12.*

The front part and the thighs of the hare; 200 grams (7 ounces) of fillet of pork; 200 grams (7 ounces) of veal round cut across the leg; 1 kilogram (2 pounds, 3 ounces) of fresh fatback bacon; 150 grams (5 1/3 ounces) of good, lean uncooked ham, or, if that is not available, cooked ham; 300 grams (10 1/2 ounces) of extremely thin sheets of bacon; 3 eggs; 2 1/2 deciliters (1 cup) of cognac; 4 tablespoons of oil; 1 sprig of thyme and 1 bay leaf; and 55 grams (2 ounces) of fine salt, 10 grams (1/3 ounce) of ground pepper, and 5 grams (1/6 ounce) of spices mixed together, which makes 70 grams (2 1/2 ounces) of spiced salt (seasoned salt).

A terrine about 22 centimeters (8 1/2 inches) long and 16 centimeters (6 1/4 inches) wide in the middle and 9–10 centimeters (3 1/2–4 inches) deep.

PROCEDURE. Skin and gut the hare, then break the pouch of the stomach and gather the blood in a bowl. Take out the liver and carefully remove the bile. Take out the lungs and the heart; put them with the liver on a plate. This will be used for the stuffing.

Cut out the saddle by taking it from the first ribs to the thighs, where you will cut it in a diagonal. The front part of the hare will thus be left for the terrine; its flesh, combined with that from the end of the thighs, is used for the stuffing. The flesh of the thighs is reserved for the garnish.

Bone the front part, scraping the bones clean. Remove, for the stuffing, the tongue and the brain.

The garnish: Using a small knife with a thin and sharp blade, remove the membrane and the nerves from the meat of the thighs. Cut this meat into small 2 1/2-centimeter (1-inch) squares: it is not essential that they all be the same size. Cut the ham the same way.

Remove the rind from the piece of bacon and take about 150 grams (5 1/3 ounces) of bacon from the part that was nearest the rind. Cut this into long lardons, and then cut these into small cubes about 1 1/2 centimeters (5/8 inch) on each side, but not much larger.

In a bowl, assemble the squares of hare, ham, bacon, the thyme, and bay. Sprinkle with a good pinch of seasoned salt. Pour over the cognac and the oil. Let it marinate, turning it over from time to time while you proceed with the other preparations.

The stuffing and mixing it all together: Finely mince the hare, pork, veal, and bacon. Mix everything together and add the remains of the seasoned salt and the heart, the liver, and the lungs, also minced fine. Take the thyme and bay out of the garnish, then add the stuffing mix. Also add the blood, which should have been strained first if there were any clots. Add the eggs one by one, vigorously mixing the contents of the bowl with a wooden spoon.

Then completely mix all the elements in the

bowl so that the garnish is equally distributed throughout the stuffing. It is almost essential to do this using your hands, but dip them first in cold water.

Putting it in the terrine: First cut a sheet of bacon into an oval, and reserve this to cover the terrine when you have filled it. With the rest of the sheets of bacon, line the bottom and the walls of the terrine. Add the mixture of stuffing and garnish, about 450 grams (1 pound) at a time, which will allow you to pack it down better. As you fill it, press it down with your hand, which should first have been dipped into cold water. This is important if you want to avoid empty spaces.

Once the terrine has been filled, cover it with the sheet of bacon that you have reserved. Sprinkle a pinch of spiced salt on top of it, and a few bits of thyme and bay. Put on a cover. Solder this shut with a ribbon of dough made with flour diluted with water into a rather stiff paste. The terrine is then ready to cook as directed (SEE PAGE 424).

Terrine of Foie Gras *(Terrine de Foie Gras)*

A succulent method, including only the liver of the goose, without any addition of stuffing, such as practiced by an old Alsatian family.

Do not add any other condiment. The salt and pepper are here only to counter the blandness of the liver, whose delicate taste should marry with the flavor of the truffle and the scarcely definable aroma of the cognac. Since large and small truffles are of equal quality, and the price of the same weight of truffles increases with their size, it is better to get small truffles, which can be left whole. They should be peeled after they are cleaned.

These quantities fill a "Strasbourg"-type terrine, a number 4; that is, a cylindrical earthenware terrine from Sarreguemines, which is brown on the outside and yellow on the inside, with an inside diameter of 11 centimeters (4¼ inches) and 18 centimeters (7 inches) high. These dimensions mean a capacity of about 12 deciliters (5 cups). *Time: 1 hour of preparation; 1 hour, 15 minutes for cooking. Serves 10–12.*

2 nice livers, chosen white and firm, weighing gross 700–725 grams (1 pound, 9 ounces–1 pound, 10 ounces) each; 250 grams (8⅞ ounces) of truffles; about 125 grams (4½ ounces) of sheets of very thin bacon; 15 grams (½ ounce) of salt; 1 gram (1/28 ounce) of pepper; 1 tablespoon of excellent cognac.

PROCEDURE. **Cleaning the liver:** This is a meticulous and long operation. First, with a knife, detach the packet of fibers found between the 2 lobes. Separate the lobes. Then remove all the parts of the liver that are near the spleen and that have a green or darkish tint. Do not just simply scrape the blotched surface, but assiduously dig in to remove a piece the size of a walnut from the liver, because this part is contaminated and bitter.

Similarly, remove any reddish part on the surface or on the sides. Then break the liver into small pieces; remove the light membrane covering it; then, using a small pointed knife, remove the fibers and traces of blood. This step will leave you with about 150 grams (5⅓ ounces) of trimmings for 1.4 kilograms (3 pounds, 1 ounce) of liver.

Clean the truffles (SEE PAGE 537).

To fill the terrine: Once the liver has been trimmed and the truffles peeled, cover the bottom of the terrine with a sheet of fatback bacon cut in a round. Line the terrine with the sheets of bacon, making sure they are long enough to be folded back on the liver, and cover it completely after the terrine has been filled.

Press the liver down into the terrine, twisting it strongly with your fingers so that you do not leave any open space. While you are doing this, spread around the salt and the pepper, as well as the truffles, placing these into the mixture as you go. Once the terrine has been filled, pour the cognac on the liver. Then fold back the sheets of fatback, which must completely cover it. Close the terrine with its cover and seal the joint with a thick strip made of dough worked with a bit of water, pasting it down all around.

Cooking it: Put the terrine in a pot containing warm water, so that the water comes up to a point just below the strip of dough. For this dish, it is not just a question of producing steam: rather, it's about poaching the liver.

Put it in a moderate but rather warm oven. The water must only simmer. When its level drops, add hot water. Let it cook for exactly *1¼ hours.* Overcooked liver lacks subtlety and is not tender. Don't worry about the fat that escapes through the small hole at the top of the cover.

Toward the end, check the degree of cooking. As it is almost impossible to determine this by piercing it with a knitting needle, open the terrine and probe it with a knife or small spoon, without worrying about making a hole, which will close up immediately. If it is not sufficiently cooked, you simply close up the terrine with its cover, not bothering to seal it with the ribbon of dough for the few minutes more that the terrine will remain in the oven.

A correctly cooked foie gras should have a light pink, putty color.

After cooking: Put the terrine in a shallow bowl and let it rest for about 10 minutes.

Open it and press down on it with a spoon to make the fat come to the surface, which will abundantly overflow onto the bowl. Then place an inverted saucer with a diameter slightly smaller than the terrine on the top of the liver, still enveloped by the bards. Place a weight of 2–3 kilograms (4 pounds, 6 ounces–6 pounds, 10 ounces) on top of the saucer, and leave it for 12 hours. The fat will continue to rise to the surface and overflow, little by little, and then congeal on top of the liver.

At the end of 12 hours, take off the weight and cut the bards at the top of the liver. Smooth out and equalize the surface with a spoon. Wait at least 48 hours before eating the terrine, which you should keep in a cool place.

If you want to preserve it, fill the empty spaces of the terrine with barely warm lard; cover with aluminum foil and paste paper around the rim of the cover.

To carve the terrine, use a silver spoon to scoop out shell shapes from the foie gras.

Hare Pâté en Croûte
(Pâté de Lièvre en Croûte)

The proportions given here were supplied by M. Philéas Gilbert; they provide a very nice pâté that makes a good cold entrée for a formal menu and will serve 25–30 guests. Prepared for everyday consumption in the home and carefully kept as we suggest, it will supply, over the course of 8 days or more, the same number of servings.

As well as the gelée prepared with the bones and trimmings of the hare, which is added to the pâté after cooking, it would be wise to take the precaution of making a simple gelée to accompany the slices of pâté on the serving plate.

Truffles are optional as an element of the garnish; but whenever they are available we strongly recommend using them. In this case, allow 100 grams (3 1/2 ounces) net weight—that is, after cleaning. Peel them, then divide into quarters, and add the trimmings to the stuffing.

An oval mold is the best for game pâtés. This kind of mold does not have a bottom; it is divided into sections linked together with hinges and pins, which you withdraw to unmold the pâté. You can also open the mold while it is in the oven to check the degree of cooking, then close it again. The size of the mold for the quantities given is: 25 centimeters (10 inches) long, 14–15 centimeters (4 1/2–6 inches) wide at the middle, and 9 centimeters (3 1/2 inches) high. If the mold is round, it should be 17 centimeters (6 1/2 inches) in diameter and 10 centimeters (4 inches) high. For details of how to line it—that is, to garnish the mold with the dough—see DOUGH FOR PÂTÉS AND TIMBALES (PAGE 671). *Time: Once the dough has been prepared, 1 1/2 hours for preparing the pâté; 2 1/4 hours to cook it.*

1 nice *trois quarts* (young) hare weighing around 3 1/2 kilograms (7 pounds, 11 ounces), from which only the saddle and the thighs are used for the pâté.

175 grams (6 ounces) of fillet or round of veal; 175 grams (6 ounces) of fresh pork fillet; 150 grams (5 1/3 ounces) of cooked ham, only the lean part; 1 kilogram (2 pounds, 3 ounces) of fresh fatback bacon; 1 1/2 deciliters (5 fluid ounces, 2/3 cup) of cognac; 2 sprigs of thyme and 1 small bay leaf; 45 grams (about 1 1/2 ounces) of spiced salt; 2 eggs; 3 tablespoons of hare's blood for the stuffing; optional truffles.

***For the dough:* 600 grams (1 pound, 5 ounces) of flour; 175 grams (6 ounces, 3/4 cup) of butter; 2 1/2 deciliters (1 cup) of cold water; 15 grams (1/2 tablespoon) of salt; an egg for the glaze.**

PROCEDURE. Make the dough the evening before, if possible: if not, at least 2 hours in advance. Proceed as directed for lining dough *(pâte à foncer)*, rolling it out 2 times.

Once the hare has been skinned and gutted and the blood and the liver reserved, cut off the hindquarters at the level of the last rib. This is the part that will provide the meat for the stuffing and the garnish.

Take off in layers the nerve membrane covering the meat, by sliding the thin blade of a knife under it. Cut off the ends of the thighs at the level of the first joint; this part is nerve. Put it with the front part of the hare for a civet. Bone the thighs and saddle, scraping the bones thoroughly. Detach the filets mignons. Finally, remove the fillets from the thighs, the most tender part; cut them into fillets the size of a finger. Cut the fillets at kidney level in half lengthwise.

The garnish: This is made with the fillets from the thighs, the kidney-level fillets, and the filets mignons, some large lardons, 1 good centimeter (3/8 inch) square, and some cubes of ham the same size.

First take 3 bards from the piece of fatback bacon, each thin as a sheet of paper, and that have a total weight of 200–300 grams (7–10 1/2 ounces); reserve them for lining the mold. Use 150 grams (5 1/3 ounces) of fatback bacon for the large lardons; then about 50 grams (1 3/4 ounces) to stud the hare fillets.

Cut these 50 grams (1 3/4 ounces) of fatback bacon into fine lardons and stud each hare fillet with 5 or 6 of these lardons. Put the studded fillets on a plate; add the large lardons and ham cut the same way as the fatback bacon. Season with spiced salt (10 grams, 1/3 ounce). Add a few bits of thyme and bay. Baste with *half* the cognac. Marinate until you are ready to fill the pâté, turning the pieces over from time to time in the cognac.

The stuffing: This is made of the rest of the meat from the thighs, the veal, and the pork, with all nerves removed. Mince everything as finely as has been recommended. Season with the rest of the spiced salt—that is, 35 grams (1 1/4 ounces). Add, mixing thoroughly: the 2 eggs, one after the other; 3 tablespoons of blood from the hare, one by one; the rest of the cognac, plus what was used in the marinade for the garnish. Put this stuffing into a cooking utensil.

To line the pâté: With a piece of butter the size of a nice walnut, coat the inside of the mold; make sure the grooves are well coated. Close it with the pins.

Use *three-quarters* of the dough to garnish the mold; the rest is for covering the pâté. Make the dough as directed. If the mold is oval, make sure that the "cap" or pouch of dough is also oval; placed in the mold, it must be longer than the border by *1 1/2 centimeters (5/8 inch).*

Put the pouch of dough in the mold. As we have described for lining circular tarts, it is better not to place the mold on the baking sheet until after you have lined it—that is, after you have adjusted the dough there. Be careful, when you press the dough at the bottom and in the angles, not to reduce the thickness of the dough, which would risk letting the juices from the pâté escape during cooking.

Once the pâté has been lined, place it on a thick, black steel baking sheet.

To garnish the pâté: Out of the bards, cut 2 pieces in the shape and size of the mold. Place 1 at the bottom; the other will be for the cover. Completely line the walls of the mold with the rest of the bards.

Dipping your fingers from time to time in cold water, spread a layer of stuffing 2 centimeters thick (3/4 inch) at the bottom of the mold. Also spread a layer on the walls, but thinner. On this first layer of stuffing, place a few studded fillets of hare, some lardons of bacon and ham, as well as the quarters of truffle, if you are using them. Cover with another layer of stuffing the same thickness as the first and then a new bed of fillets and lardons until you have used up all the garnish and stuffing. Finish with a layer of stuffing molded into a dome. Cover with the reserved bard. Sprinkle the rest of the spiced salt on top, and sprinkle with a few bits of thyme and bay.

With the reserved dough, cover the pâté, as directed for the decorated cover (PAGE 673).

Cooking it: To cook a piece this size, you must have a very good oven that will provide a strong heat from the bottom—that is, from the floor of the oven. However, a good, medium radiant heat will always suffice if the heat coming from the bottom of the oven is strong enough. *Cook for 35* *minutes per kilogram (2 pounds, 3 ounces).* Maintain a rigorously even heat from beginning to end. After some time in the oven, cover the pâté on top with a heavy moistened paper; if not, the pâté will turn from colored to burned, because of the long cooking time. A little before you take it out of the oven, check the degree of cooking of the crust by slightly opening the mold on both sides, using the hinges.

Once the pâté has been cooked and taken out of the oven, wait a little before taking out the pins to unmold it. When it is no more than *slightly lukewarm,* add the gelée prepared while it was cooking in the oven.

The gelée to pour into the pâté: You will need a total of *1 1/2 full deciliters (5 fluid ounces, 2/3 cup).* There are two ways to proceed. Put in a pot: the bones of the hare, broken into small bits, the trimmings of the hare, veal, and pork, with a bouquet garni, and 2 deciliters (6 3/4 fluid ounces, 7/8 cup) of veal jus, very little or not at all salted. Boil gently for *a half hour.* Then add 2 deciliters (6 3/4 fluid ounces, 7/8 cup) of ordinary gelée. Continue cooking until everything is reduced to the necessary 1 1/2 deciliters (5 fluid ounces, 2/3 cup). Strain though a fine cloth; keep it to one side until the moment you put it in the pâté.

Or, if you do not have any gelée ready, with the carcass and trimmings put 4 1/2 deciliters (scant 2 cups) of veal jus, and add 60 grams (2 1/4 ounces) of pork rind, with all the fat scraped off and then cut into small cubes (this rind replaces the gelatin of the gelée). Let it cook gently for *1 1/4 hours.* This gelée will remain unclear and is inferior to the real thing.

When the pâté is "scarcely lukewarm," stick a small funnel or cornet of paper right into the pâté through the opening of the chimney. Pour in the gelée. Then keep the pâté for at least 24 hours before cutting into it.

To serve: A good sharp knife with a long, thin blade is essential here. First detach the cover, raising it with the point of the knife. Cut the pâté from the top to the bottom, in the middle, and lengthwise if it's an oval shape. Cut thin slices. Arrange them in a circle on a round plate covered with a napkin. Put the minced gelée in the middle of the circle.

Veal and Ham Pâté
(Pâté de Veau et Jambon)

Suitable for all seasons, this is the most current, and even, perhaps, the most popular *pâté en croûte.* If you like, you can either make it molded or dressed in the method known as *pantin,* which is the simplest of all: it is the one we will explain here. Below, we give several directions for molded pâté.

The *pantin* method, so popular in the countryside and for home cooking, consists in rolling out the dough in a ribbon and placing the pâté ingredients on top, and then folding the dough back on itself to envelop everything. This produces a kind of thick bar, its length varying with the amount of pâté.

The ingredients for the pâté vary somewhat in quantity and methods, according to tastes and means. As in all such preparations, the ingredients are the garnish and the stuffing. The garnish is an equal quantity of sheets, or large lardons the size of a finger, cut from the round of veal and from lean ham: this can be raw or cooked according to availability.

Optionally, you can add some fillet of pork, cut the same way, and a smaller amount of fatback bacon, cut a little smaller. Marinate everything in a little cognac, salt, pepper and spices.

Classically, the stuffing is made with veal and pork in equal quantities, and fresh fatback bacon. The amount of this depends to a great extent on the fat used to enclose the meats. However it is made, the stuffing must contain a quantity of fat at least equal to, and sometimes more than, the lean meat. We cannot be exact about the amount of salt, because it depends on the kind of ham used. If you like to bind the stuffing, you can add whole egg. Finally, let us say that, to save on work for the stuffing, some people replace the stuffing with sausage meat bought ready-made at the charcuterie and then finely ground.

Pantin pâté does not have added gelée. For a simple recipe for home cooking, this would be an unnecessary complication. And if the pâté is to be preserved, it risks causing fermentation.

The dough is here lining dough *(pâte à foncer),* for which you could either use butter or good lard. For details on how to make it, refer to the appropriate section. You can establish the quantities by allowing for about 2 kilograms (4 pounds, 6 ounces) of meat: 600 grams (1 pound, 5 ounces) of flour; 250 grams (8 7/8 ounces, about 1 cup plus 2 tablespoons) of butter or lard; 15 grams (1/2 ounce) of salt; and about 2 deciliters (6 3/4 fluid ounces, 7/8 cup) of water.

Making the *pantin* pâté: Use the amount of dough indicated ON PAGE 431.

Sprinkle the table with flour. With the rolling pin, roll out the dough in a rectangular sheet about 45 centimeters (17 3/4 inches) long and about 30 wide (12 inches) by 1 centimeter (5/8 inch) thick. You can also, instead of a rectangle, roll it out into a completely symmetrical, very elongated oval. Put one-third of the stuffing in the middle, spreading it out about 12 centimeters wide (4 1/2 inches) and stopping 3 or 4 centimeters (1 1/4–1 1/2 inches) from either end of the dough. Then spread out on top of it about half of the slices or large lardons of garnish, mixing them together. Cover with the second third of stuffing. Then put the other half of the garnish on top of that, and cover it with the rest of the stuffing. Level it out with the 4 fingers of your right hand, sliding and pressing on top of the stuffing. First dip your hand in cold water.

Close the pâté by first pulling over one of the *long* sides of the dough onto the block after having lightly thinned the edge of the dough with the rolling pin. Moisten this thinned-out edge with water. Then fold the other edge on top of it, also having first thinned it out with the rolling pin the same way, and stick them together by pressing on them. The flap should overlap by 1 or 2 centimeters (5/8–3/4 inch).

At this point, the pâté forms a thick bar, with 2 ends of dough that do not have stuffing under them. With the rolling pin, thin out this dough to lengthen it and reduce its thickness: these ends are folded back onto the pâté; they are not joined together but are folded back just enough to seal the package shut. (When doing this, note that each piece of folded-over dough must be thinned so that when placed on top of each other they are not thicker than the dough envelope itself.) Cut off the excess from the thinned-out dough; fold the ends back over the pâté, moistening them so that they will stick together.

Make a ball out of a little bit of the dough that you have cut; roll it out very thin. Cut a ribbon from it, which can join together the 2 ends that have been folded back, hiding the seam. This replaces the puff pastry that charcutières and others use for covering this type of pâté. Instead of this ribbon, you can decorate with leaves, stars, or other motifs cut from this leftover dough.

Give an even shape to the pâté, either with your hands or by correcting it with the flat of a large knife blade. If you like, you can make some patterns with a patisserie pincers. Brush it with beaten egg. In the middle of the pâté, make a small hole with the point of a knife. Make it larger with the end of your little finger, then put a piece of rolled-up cardboard in it to make a chimney.

To cook: Place the pâté on a metal baking sheet covered with a good, strong, buttered parchment paper. Cook it in a moderately hot oven, allowing for these quantities *about 2 hours* at a regular simmer. Make sure that the juices do not come out of the chimney, which would indicate that the boiling inside is too lively.

Molded pâté: For details of making this, you can refer to the recipe for HARE PÂTÉ EN CROÛTE (PAGE 429). Normally only veal and ham is used for its garnish, but pork is also frequently used. When truffles are available, these are excellent in it. A little bit of Madeira added to the cognac for the marinade is definitely to be recommended.

When the pâté is half cooled, pour in some lukewarm gelée that has been prepared with the trimmings and bones of the meat, pork, feet, etc., and flavored at the last moment with 1 or 2 tablespoons of Madeira. Then let the pâté cool until the next day.

Galantine of Fowl *(Galantine de Volaille)*

Recipes differ, not just in terms of the ingredients chosen but also in the way they are used. In every galantine, it is essential, as for all pâtés and terrines, to distinguish two separate elements: the stuffing and the garnish. This last is made up of meat, cut either in large cubes or in lardons. This could be pork, ham, veal, pickled tongue, and the fillets from a fowl. If you like, the veal can be left out and you can use only pork; it is less dry than the veal, but its color is a little less grayish. Truffles, which were formally considered essential for a galantine, are now an exception because of their high price; and this is also true for pistachios.

As a good, general rule, the stuffing and the garnish should be of equal weight; and the fat supplied by the pork should be half of the weight of the stuffing. As for pâtés and terrines, season with about 12–13 grams (3/8 ounce) of spiced salt per 450 grams (1 pound) of stuffing. Thus, for 10 grams (1/3 ounce) of fine salt, 2 grams (1/14 ounce) of pepper, and 1 gram (1/28 ounce) of spices (in humid weather, increase the salt by 2 grams (1/14 ounce) for each pound of stuffing).

As a typical fowl, we will here use a chicken. The most important point is to choose one that is good and fleshy, rather than fatty, and not too young because its skin would not be strong enough for this use. Furthermore, you should, as a general rule, use rather old chickens for the galantine. We allow here a beast weighing plucked, gutted before being boned, 1.1–1.3 kilograms (2 pounds, 7 ounces–2 pounds, 14 ounces).

This recipe, which is one of the most practical, can serve as a typical one for all galantines of fowl or feathered game. The skin is not completely stripped, as on other occasions. The amounts given below for the ingredients are an average only. Just make sure that the proportions remain the same, as we have said above. If truffles are added, figure about 125 grams (4 1/2 ounces) and for the pistachios 15–20 grams (1/2–2/3 ounce). *Time: 1 hour, 30 minutes to prepare (2 hours, 30 minutes for cooking). Serves 12–15.*

For the garnish: **400 grams (14 1/8 ounces) of fillet of fresh pork taken from the tender and thin part (or use only 200 grams/7 ounces with 200 grams/7 ounces of veal); 150 grams (5 1/3 ounces) of good, red, cooked ham; 150 grams (5 1/3 ounces) of pickled tongue; 150 grams (5 1/3 ounces) of very fresh fatback bacon; the filet mignon of the fowl; a small glass of cognac and the same of Madeira for the marinade.**

For the stuffing: **800 grams (1 pound, 12 ounces) of fresh pork with an equal quantity of fat and lean; if not, complete with fresh fatback bacon. Also, the trimmings of ham, bacon, meat from the carcass, and the chicken thighs; and the peelings of the truffles if the galantine is truffled.**

For the cooking and the gelée: **1 kilogram (2 pounds, 3 ounces) of veal knuckle, a small veal foot, pork rind, onion, carrot, bouquet garni as directed (SEE JUS, PAGE 43); a half bottle of white wine; water as you need it.**

PROCEDURE. Once the fowl has been boned (SEE BONING FOWL, PAGE 354), put it on a plate. Season the meat with salt, pepper, spice powder, and moisten it with 1 tablespoon of cognac and the same of Madeira.

The garnish: Cut the pork into 2-centimeter (3/4-inch) cubes. Similarly, cut the fillet of the chicken. Cut the ham, the pickled tongue, and the fatback bacon into smaller cubes about 1 centimeter (3/8 inch) on each side.

If you use truffles, clean them and peel them as directed (SEE PAGE 537). The pistachios should have their skin removed in the same way as almonds.

Put all these diverse elements in a terrine. Sprinkle them with spiced salt; moisten with cognac and Madeira, turning everything over as if it were a salad. Cover; keep cool.

The stuffing: Combine the trimmings left over from cutting the meat into cubes. Take out the nerves, skin, and rinds to add to the cooking juice.

Mix the trimmings with the ingredients given in *quantities for the stuffing.* Pass everything through a grinder, first through the large disc. Season with seasoned salt, then mix everything in a terrine. Pass it through the machine a second time with the fine disc.

Then add the garnish to this hash, mixing it and combining everything with your hands, moistening them first so that you can mix as well as possible the various elements of the garnish with the stuffing. This thorough mixing creates the beautiful mosaic look that the slices have when they are cut.

To form the galantine: Lay out the skin of the fowl on the table. Put in the contents of the terrine. Pack it down with your hand, pushing everything toward the rump without letting any of it enter the open part of the thighs. Bring together the 2 sides of the opening with the 2 edges of skin almost touching. Then fold back the skin of the neck over everything; this will only cover half of the beast; the other half at the rump is left bare. It is not necessary, though it is often assumed to be, to hold the edges of the skin together by sewing them, because everything will be gathered into a cloth for the cooking. This does require some care, so proceed as follows.

Take a napkin or preferably a good cotton cloth, percale perhaps: whatever you use, the cloth must be perfectly clean and white *without any odor.* Spread it out on the table. Place the chicken at one end so that you can then roll it in the same way you roll a sleeping bag or a bolster in a sheet. On this part of the cloth, spread a little bit of butter with your finger. Place the chicken on it with the breast down. Fold the edge of the cloth over the beast so that the edge or hem lies right on the back. Then slowly roll the chicken in the cloth without squeezing it, making sure you avoid pleats, which would leave grooves on the skin of the galantine. This is particularly important for the breast, where it would be most apparent and should therefore be the most protected. And for this reason, when you have finished wrapping the bird, fold the end of the cloth over on the back of the beast when the end of the cloth would normally terminate on the breast. With some good string, securely tie the 2 ends of the cloth as if it were a large sausage. Then surround the package with 2 or 3 turns of string, without pulling it too tight, because the galantine will swell when cooking. It is then ready to cook.

To cook: The best utensil is the *braisiére,* or braising pan, because its shape is appropriate for a galantine. The problem with a round pot that is large enough to hold this piece is that it requires too much liquid.

Line the utensil as directed for the jus with bacon rind, rounds of onion, and carrot. Place the galantine on top of it. Add the veal knuckle and the veal foot, the carcass and bones of the chicken, the debris of the meat, and the bouquet garni. On very moderate heat, sweat it for *about 10 minutes* (SEE JUS, PAGE 44). After this, moisten it with the white wine—a half bottle—and enough water to cover everything. The liquid must come about 3/4 inch higher than the galantine. The amount of water required cannot be precisely given here, because it depends on the volume of the piece and the capacity of the utensil. *Salt it very lightly* in view of the later reduction.

Bring it to a boil. Skim. Cover tightly and cook it very gently as a pot-au-feu for *1 1/4 hours.* At the end of this time, turn the galantine upside down. Recover it to let it cook for another *1 hour.* In total, you should count here *2 1/4 hours* of cooking. Generally, calculate the cooking time as being 15–20 minutes per 450 grams (1 pound).

Take it out carefully to avoid breaking it, and put the galantine on a plate. At the end of 3–4 minutes, cut the strings *with scissors.* Unbind it very carefully on the table or on a very clean board. Then squeeze the cloth into the pan so that you do not lose the juices in it. Dip it into cold water. Twist it. Next, lay it out completely flat on the table. Then again roll the galantine in it, still being careful to avoid folds of the cloth on the breast of the beast, where it will make grooves. Tie the 2 ends of the cloth again as in a sausage form, but do not tie it in the middle. Put the galantine on a large plate, breast down. Put a board on top of the galantine that is larger than it, and on the board, some weights: 2–3 kilograms (4 pounds, 6 ounces–6 pounds, 10 ounces) in all. Keep the galantine cool for 12 hours.

The gelée: Reduce the cooking juice to 1 1/2 liters (6 1/3 cups). Strain it, degrease it, clarify it as directed (SEE MEAT GELÉE, PAGE 45).

To serve: When the entire galantine is to be eaten at one time, cut it in half lengthwise. Put each half cut-side down on the board, for appearance's sake. Then cut slices—which are, of course, half slices of the whole galantine. Dress it by lightly leaning 1 slice up against the other, either in a line on a long plate bordered with chopped gelée, or in a circle on a round plate with the chopped gelée in the middle.

Chop the gelée with the back of the blade of a large knife, passing it lightly through the jelly so that you do not reduce it to a mush.

Cold Veal Loaf *(Pain de Veau Froid)*

This is a family recipe that is much simpler preparation than that of a pâté or a galantine and that furnishes a good plate that can be easily taken to picnics and lunches in the country. *Time: 30 min-*

utes of preparation; 3 hours for cooking; 4 hours for the gelée. Serves 12.

1 loaf about 18 centimeters (7 inches) in diameter by 10 centimeters (4 inches) high.

1 1/2 kilograms (3 pounds, 5 ounces) of veal, net weight, without skin or fat and preferably taken from the filet; 250 grams (8 7/8 ounces) of *uncooked* ham, not smoked; 180 grams (6 1/3 ounces) of home-style cooked sausage; 125 grams (4 1/2 ounces) of sausage meat; 125 grams (4 1/2 ounces) of salted fatback bacon; 15 grams (1/2 ounce) of fine salt; 2 tablespoons of finely minced parsley with a small shallot; ground pepper.

For the jus: A half veal foot; the bones and trimmings of veal (if possible, add a round of beef shin to concentrate the juice); 150 grams (5 1/3 ounces) of carrot and the same of onions cut into rather thick rounds; a bouquet garni; 2 cloves; 1 tablespoon of fat; 3/4 liter (generous 3 cups) of water.

PROCEDURE. First trim the meat; the trimmings are necessary for the jus.

Remove all fat, nerves, and skin from the veal; using a good, large kitchen knife, cut it into slices as thin as possible.

Cut the *fatback bacon* similarly after you have removed the rind. Cut the *sausage* in rounds as fine as sheets of paper, and remove the skin. Also cut the *raw ham* the same way.

Garnish the bottom of a charlotte mold, or if you do not have one, a deep pot about 18 centimeters (7 inches) in diameter by 10 centimeters (4 inches) high with a third of the bacon. Then put the slices of veal on top of that in a layer equally thick. Sprinkle with salt, pepper, and a good pinch of minced parsley. On top of this veal, put a layer of rounds of sausage placed one next to the other, lightly overlapping each other. Then a second layer of veal, sprinkled with the seasoning; on top of this, a light layer of sausage meat; and then a layer of veal; and so on, noting that each layer of veal is alternated with a layer of one of the different elements (ham, sausage, or sausage meat) and that the seasoning of salt, pepper, and parsley is reserved only for the veal.

When you have reached exactly halfway up the mold, place the second third of the fatback bacon on a layer of veal. Continue to fill the mold, proceeding in the same manner. Finish with a layer of veal. Cover with the rest of the bacon. Press on it lightly with your hand to pack everything down to an equal level.

Cover the mold as tightly as possible. Put it into a very moderate oven, proceeding as directed for terrines (SEE PAGE 425) and renewing the hot water as it reduces by evaporation.

Allow *3 scant hours of cooking.* Just as for terrines, you can tell when it is done by uncovering the pan and seeing that the fat is completely liquid.

Allow it to firm up before unmolding the loaf; but first pour out all the juice released during the cooking, while it is still good and hot, into the pot used for making the gelée.

Turn it out of the mold onto a plate. Let it cool completely.

The gelée: Color the bones, meat and trimmings, and the vegetables, in the fat as directed (SEE HOME-STYLE JUS, PAGE 44). Moisten with the water. Add the blanched veal foot, the rind of the ham and the bacon, the bouquet garni, and the clove. Boil for 4 hours. Strain.

When the gelée has cooled and firmed up, remove the little bit of fat that has risen to the surface with a cloth dipped in warm water. Heat the gelée just enough to melt it. And then glaze the loaf: that is, baste it tablespoon by tablespoon as the gelée sets on the loaf. Put the rest of the gelée around it. Or better, cut the loaf first and serve with the gelée in the middle.

To take the veal loaf to a picnic or on a hunting expedition, you can put the loaf back in a mold and the gelée in a bowl. Or: hollow out a round loaf of country bread; put in the veal loaf cut into slices and cover with gelée.

DIVERSE PREPARATIONS

Soufflés *(Soufflés)*

"A soufflé can be waited for, but it can never wait." This is an absolute rule that has become an axiom with gourmets and professionals. All guests should conform to it, showing neither impatience nor surprise. This does not, of course, mean that the cook should not take care to arrange things so that guests wait for the soufflé for as little time as possible, or even, if everything is well arranged, so that they do not wait at all. We shall see further on how to manage this.

Every soufflé includes two elements that are equally important: first, the base composition, which flavors it; second, the whipped and beaten egg whites, which give the soufflé its characteristic lightness and are the very essence of a soufflé.

The base composition varies with the type of soufflé: a flavored floury mixture or a purée of fruits or vegetables; or a finely ground hash of fish meat, etc., bound with a thick béchamel sauce, which gives the soufflé a moistness it would otherwise lack. Egg yolks are added for consistency, usually in a lesser amount than the whites. They can be totally left out of some soufflés.

Why is it that soufflés fail in most home kitchens? So many people ask, "Why do restaurant soufflés expand fully and have a consistency that is both light and solid, which soufflés at home do not have?"

There are several reasons for this:

First, most home kitchens do not have the right utensils to whisk the egg whites to the degree of firmness and resistance necessary. The more the whites are whisked into a snow, or *neige,* the greater will be the effect (SEE EGG WHITES, PAGE 8).

Second, the egg whites were not mixed properly. Now, however well whisked egg whites are, maladroit mixing destroys all their effects (SEE MIXING EGG WHITES, PAGE 10).

Third, the soufflé was not cooked correctly. For a soufflé, the heat of the oven plays a very important part. The soufflé may have been well prepared up to that point, but if the cooking is faulty, all the trouble taken will have no effect (SEE THE OVEN AND COOKING THE SOUFFLÉ, PAGE 437).

Fourth, the cooking time is not closely controlled. This means that the soufflé is insufficiently cooked in the center, or collapses with the first touch of the cutting spoon, allowing a liquid mass to escape; or that it is overcooked and dried and flat.

For any type of soufflé, the way to prepare the egg whites and mix them in, then cook and serve the soufflé is identical. So, for every recipe, refer to the same directions for these steps, except when glazing certain soufflés (SEE VANILLA SOUFFLÉ, PAGE 634), for which we will give a detailed recipe.

The utensil: For people who are totally ignorant of kitchen manners, let us specify that the soufflé can only be served in the utensil in which it has been cooked.

In well-equipped houses, there are metal molds for this that fit into a silver serving dish. Not only are they more convenient, but these dishes also have an infinite number of other uses. If you do not have a silver serving dish, a round dish in grooved porcelain, so often used today, works very well; and the soufflés also rise in it perfectly, because the heat rapidly penetrates the sides, which are very thin.

Finally, if you do not have a special soufflé dish in metal or a timbale or a porcelain dish, you can use a very deep bowl that can go into the oven. *Whatever the utensil chosen, the inside must always be thoroughly buttered.*

For small soufflés, there are small utensils in silver-plated metal or small round dishes in ribbed porcelain, both of which are very convenient; you can even use containers of ribbed paper. These containers cannot be too small: it is best to choose them with a diameter of 7 centimeters ($2^3/4$ inches) and a height of $3^1/2$ centimeters ($1^3/8$ inch). They hold 1 deciliter ($3^1/3$ fluid ounces, scant $^1/2$ cup). You can arrange them on a baking sheet to put them in the oven.

To serve: Put the timbale, plate, or soufflé dish on a serving plate, on top of a folded napkin or kitchen towel. Do the same for the small soufflés, putting them together on 1 large plate.

For houses with long corridors to travel down to reach the dining room, there are large metal covers that you heat before covering the plate on which the soufflés are standing.

To ensure that guests do not wait too long for the soufflé: Calculate exactly the time needed for its preparation plus cooking, so that you know the precise moment for sending it to the table.

Fillings, purées, etc.—in other words, the ingredients of the soufflé base—can always be prepared sufficiently in advance, because they only need to be lukewarm to mix them with the whites. This is why it is necessary to calculate exactly the time needed for the various steps: that is, 6–7 minutes to whisk the egg whites; 5–6 minutes to mix them and to dress the soufflé; about 25 minutes for cooking, which gives a total of 40 minutes.

How to check when the soufflé is perfectly done: To know if the soufflé is perfectly cooked inside, you stick a kitchen needle into the middle. It must come out totally clean. If, on the contrary, it comes out wet and covered with egg, prolong the cooking for 2–3 minutes.

The oven and cooking the soufflé: The timbale or the plate containing a soufflé must always be placed directly on the very bottom of the oven, or on the hearth, never on a shelf in the middle of the oven; indeed, remove every shelf from the oven.

The heat of the oven must be a medium heat. And, *most important, it must come from the bottom of the oven, because it is the direction of the heat, of down to up, that causes the soufflé to rise.*

This condition is so essential that, in small stoves where the oven heats a lot less well from the bottom than from the top, this lack of heat from the bottom has to be countered using the following method: before putting the soufflé in the oven, first place the utensil containing the soufflé *on top of the stove.* Not over high heat, but a moderate one; put a heat diffuser between the recipient and the heat. On an electric stove, put the utensil on a moderately warm burner; leave it there for 2 minutes, giving it time to thoroughly heat the bottom. The soufflé will subsequently rise much more easily in the oven.

The heat coming from the top of the oven will color the soufflé, but this is often too strong in small ovens.

The right time to put the soufflé into the oven is *not* when you have checked that the oven has reached the right temperature. In fact, the oven should have reached the right temperature before you began to whisk the egg whites.

If the heat is too strong at this point, leave the oven door open for a few minutes. If it is too weak, turn up the heat. Either extreme has disadvantages. When the heat is too strong, particularly the heat from above, a crust immediately forms on the soufflé, creating a barrier that prevents the heat from penetrating the inside. This means that it will cook superficially and not rise well. When the heat is too weak, the soufflé languishes and risks running over the sides of the dish when it rises, because the heat is not strong enough to solidify the ingredients as the soufflé rises.

If you have taken all precautions and the heat of the oven is too strong and comes from the top, then it will be necessary, as soon as the surface of the soufflé solidifies, to cover it with a sheet of paper: this must be a very pure paper, cut round and covered with melted butter using a brush or feather. Put the buttered side down on the soufflé. Note that many papers available today contain certain materials that, when exposed to the heat, release an odor that would mar the soufflé.

NOTES. Whatever the consistency of the soufflé base and the method you use for dressing it, either in a dome or a pyramid, never let it run over the sides of the utensil. You must always leave at least 2 centimeters ($^3/4$ inch) of space between it and the top of the utensil. If the utensil is filled more than this, the first effect of the heat will be that the base swells and runs over the sides, not having the time to set; and then the soufflé will lean sideways as it rises. When the utensil is not completely filled, the base is already quite firm by the time it has reached the top due to the heat, so it continues to rise without running over or leaning to the side.

Sometimes, the consistency of the base is not firm enough to let it be dressed in a pyramid, the ingredients being a little moist and spreading out in the utensil. This could mean that ingredients were not properly mixed. If so, it is even more important to ensure the proper cooking conditions and that you regulate the heat of the oven. If these are well controlled, the soufflé will rise just the same.

A soufflé prepared in a dish requires less time to cook than a soufflé made in a timbale: it spreads out over a larger surface, thus becoming thinner and less resistant to the effect of the heat of the oven. Thus, allow *18–20 minutes* of cooking for a soufflé, which, when prepared in a timbale, would require almost 25 minutes.

Cooking small soufflés in small dishes requires only *10–14 minutes.*

Croquettes *(Croquettes)*

Time: 1 hour for preparing; 2 hours for cooling; 10 minutes for cooking.

These are usually classed as warm hors d'oeuvres, but when accompanied by a sauce, croquettes make a light and delicate dish that guests will gladly accept in place of a small entrée of meat or fowl. They are very inexpensive, because one can always use leftovers for them. Nonetheless, the time and meticulous trouble needed to make croquettes mean that they frighten, wrongly, a good many people. In reality, there is nothing easier than succeeding with a croquette, but do not confuse these with meatballs, which are much simpler to make.

In haute cuisine, every recipe for croquettes includes, as a general rule, a very substantial amount of mushrooms: almost half the weight of the main ingredient. It is also a rule to add another element, but in a lesser quantity—about a third or quarter the amount of mushrooms. For example, for veal croquettes: 200 grams (7 ounces) of veal, 100 grams ($3^1/_2$ ounces) of mushrooms, 50 or 60 grams ($1^3/_4$–$2^1/_4$ ounces) of ham or of pickled tongue.

In home cooking, these rules can be relaxed; fresh mushrooms are hard to find far away from centers of food supply, and their price becomes extremely high, which goes beyond the normal budget for everyday meals, when croquettes are often made as a way to use up simple leftovers. So, do as well as resources and inspiration permit: creativity, as far as croquettes go, is not only permitted but is very much appreciated.

When served as entrées, croquettes can be enhanced by dressing them around a purée or a vegetable chosen according to the kind of croquette. Thus, for game, a purée of chestnuts, of lentils, of potatoes, etc.; for white meats, a purée of fresh peas, of fresh white beans; a jardinière of vegetables, peas, or flageolet beans sautéed in butter, etc. They should always be accompanied by an appropriate sauce served in a sauceboat.

The proper way to make croquettes is founded on the four following fundamental principles:

1. *Be absolutely accurate about the proportions of the sauce for the liaison.* In other words, be rigorous about the amount of flour in the sauce, and following that, the amount of the sauce in the croquette mixture. Making them is absolutely impossible with a sauce that is too light; and it is difficult with too much sauce, no matter how good its consistency. On the other hand, a sauce that is too thick makes the croquettes too heavy, almost like paste; and too little sauce, even though its consistency is perfect, will produce a dry and flavorless composition.

2. *Allow the mixture to completely cool before making the croquettes.* You can hasten the cooling by putting it on ice if you have any; but to shape the croquettes, and then dip them in egg, etc., it is essential that the sauce has set around the ingredients, and the sauce will do this only when it is cool.

3. *Use the egg and bread-crumb coating known as breading à l'Anglaise in sufficient quantities, which is rarely done.* This breading for the croquette is essential because when it is fried in the deep fat it will be transformed into a solid crust, which

holds in the semi-liquid elements, in effect functioning as a receptacle. So note this recommendation well: be sure that the amount of breading is sufficient for making croquettes by having not enough of it but too much. You should always expect there to be bread crumbs and egg left over when the last croquette is finished.

4. *Fry in abundant and very deep fat.* Deep-frying at too low a temperature produces limp, cracked, and greasy croquettes. Use a frying fat that is not too old so that you get a nice light color for the croquettes.

The sauce for the liaison: This sauce varies according to the croquettes; but unless accompanying game, and mostly in the "bourgeoise" culinary tradition of fine home cooking," it is generally a thick béchamel, or even a type of velouté, to which you add, depending on the case, a liaison of egg yolk.

This sauce must be thicker than usual. The quantity of the flour in it should be *8 grams (1/3 ounce) per deciliter (3 1/3 fluid ounces, scant 1/2 cup) of sauce used.*

In professional kitchens, which always have the principal sauces in reserve, chefs take a certain amount of sauce and then reduce it, so that they have the right proportion for the flour. In the home kitchen, where the sauce is prepared at the moment it is used, you can easily base it on these proportions, as will be explained here.

How much sauce is necessary: 8 centiliters (1/3 cup)—that is, not quite 1 deciliter (3 1/3 fluid ounces, scant 1/2 cup) of sauce for each 100 grams (3 1/2 ounces) of total weight of solid ingredients used. (The meats, mushrooms, etc., are known as the *salpicon,* as is explained further on.) This calls for some math on your part.

It is always better to prepare the sauce in advance so that it is infused with the seasoning and can also be skimmed, if necessary. In this case, calculate the amount of flour used in the roux *with a view toward the final amount of sauce needed.* Example: for 3 deciliters (1 1/4 cups) of sauce, 25 grams (1 ounce) of flour, 500 milliliters (generous 2 cups) of liquid, and the sauce reduced finally to 3 deciliters (1 1/4 cups).

The salpicon: This is a very ancient culinary term describing a ragoût made of foods cut into *small dice* for making croquettes, the garnish for timbales, etc. All the elements of the *salpicon,* no matter what they are, must be *cooked* before being cut into dice.

Using a good kitchen knife, cut these elements—meat, fish, mushrooms, macaroni, vegetables, etc.—into regular size, 1-centimeter (3/8-inch) cubes, *no larger.* Remove the skin and all the tough parts of the meat, along with the parts that are too browned. Keep them between 2 plates so that they do not color.

With the sauce for the liaison already prepared, mix the *salpicon* in the same saucepan where you have made the sauce. Do not put the pan back on the heat. Keep it on a warm place for 5–6 minutes simply so the ingredients of the *salpicon* can be well penetrated by the warm sauce.

Then spread the *salpicon* on a buttered plate in an even layer about 2 centimeters (3/4 inch) thick. With a small knife with a little butter stuck on the end of it, dab the surface of the *salpicon:* this light layer of melted butter prevents the cooled ingredients from hardening and a skin from forming on them. Cover and put aside to cool. *The mixture must be absolutely cool when you make the croquettes. It can therefore be made well in advance.*

Making the croquettes: The shape of the croquettes varies according to their type and also according to individual preference. The most popular is a long, large cork; the most practical, perhaps, is a flattened ball. You can make them also in a pear shape, in an apple shape, as a chop, in rectangles, etc. A croquette should weigh an average of *60 grams (2 1/4 ounces),* and be about the volume of an ordinary egg.

With a large knife, divide the mixture, which should be *completely cooled,* into as equal quantities as possible, each one enough for 1 croquette, so that you do not have to add or trim, which would weaken them.

As you cut them, put the portions on a tray that has been sprinkled with flour. Then roll each portion into a ball in the flour, very lightly. This flouring allows you to then shape the croquette without it sticking to your fingers.

To make it into a *cork,* put the floured piece in

your left hand and use the fingers of your right hand to roll it there, without leaning too hard. For a croquette shaped into a large puck, which is the simplest form, roll the portions into balls, then flatten them lightly with the side of the blade of a large knife. To make them into *chops,* hold it in the floured palm of your left hand, then elongate the ball into a large comma. With the side of the blade of a large knife, give it the slightly curved shape of a chop. When you dress it, stick in a little piece of macaroni with a sleeve of paper around it to represent the bone.

Once you have formed the croquettes, bread them *à l'Anglaise* (SEE BREADING, PAGE 19). Do not do this too much in advance. More so than for any food breaded *à l'anglaise,* you must carefully follow the directions to achieve a perfectly regular layer of egg and bread crumbs. This layer forms a crust that, let us repeat, serves to contain the various ingredients, which are half liquid.

So take great care to coat the entire surface of the croquette with egg and bread crumbs. If even the smallest place is insufficiently coated, this will become the point through which the ingredients can leak into the frying oil. Make sure the coating layer is perfectly uniform, with neither slits nor dents: any irregularity will cause cracks in the frying process; and be as careful when you roll the croquette in the flour as you are when you roll it through the egg and the bread crumb: an egg that soaks the croquette will create an uneven surface.

With the flat of the blade of a large knife, press on the layer of bread crumbs, as described in the section on *breading.* This also lets you correct, if you have to, the shape of the croquette. Place each croquette as you make it on an upside-down tart pan or on a large, overturned pot cover; you can slide them into the deep-frying fat more easily from this than from a plate. Covered with a paper and kept cool, they can stand for a half hour and even more.

To fry the croquettes: Begin to heat the fat in enough time so that it is *very lightly* smoking *8 minutes* before serving. Gently slide in the croquettes. Follow the directions given in the section on *frying* (SEE PAGE 41).

As soon as the croquettes have taken on a beautiful golden color, lay them out on a towel to dry them of all fat. Salt them very lightly.

Dressing them: This depends on the kind of croquettes. If they are served with a garnish, vegetables, or purée, dress them in a circle or turban shape, and put the garnish in the middle in a pyramid. If the croquettes are served alone, put them on a napkin on the serving plate; arrange them as you like. Cork-shaped croquettes are piled on each other like logs.

The accompanying sauce is always served on the side in a sauceboat.

Croquettes of Fowl *(Croquettes de Volaille).* This recipe can serve as the template for making other croquettes, veal croquettes in particular. The liaison sauce is an improvised Parisienne sauce. If you want a less formal meal, the croquettes can be made in the shape of chops and the ham replaced by truffles. The croquettes are then listed on a menu as "Chops of Fowl." They can also be accompanied by a Périgueux sauce.

Here we will summarize the operations: for the details on croquettes, you can refer to the preceding directions. *Time: 2 hours. Serves 6.*

225 grams (8 ounces) of flesh of fowl, roasted or boiled, weighed without bones or skin; 100 grams (3½ ounces) of fresh mushrooms; 40 grams (1⅜ ounces) of very lean, cooked ham.

For the sauce: **25 grams (1 ounce) of flour and 25 grams (1 ounce, 2 tablespoons) of butter for the roux; a half-liter (generous 2 cups) of completely degreased bouillon if you do not have a light veal jus; a small bouquet of parsley; mushroom trimmings; salt, pepper, nutmeg; 2 small egg yolks or 1 large one for the final liaison.**

To bread the croquettes: **2 small, whole eggs beaten as for an omelet with a pinch of fine salt, a pinch of pepper, 1 scant teaspoon of oil; 250 grams (8⅞ ounces) of fine bread crumbs that have been freshly grated.**

PROCEDURE. First of all, start the sauce, working as follows: make a light blond roux (SEE LIAISON WITH ROUX, PAGE 47), diluted with the bouillon; season; bring it to a boil, stirring constantly; add the bouillon and the mushrooms as soon as they are trimmed. Then set up the saucepan to skim the sauce as directed (SEE PAGE 16) for *35–40 minutes.*

Clean and cook the mushrooms (SEE PAGE 490).

Cut the chicken, ham, and mushrooms as directed previously for the *salpicon.*

Once the sauce has been skimmed, pass it through the chinois into a small sauté pan. Dilute the egg yolks in a bowl with 2–3 tablespoons of cooking jus from the mushrooms. Bind the sauce (SEE LIAISONS, PAGE 47). Reduce it to the desired quantity (3 deciliters, 1 1/4 cups). Mix in the *salpicon* and proceed for all the rest as directed.

Game Croquettes *(Croquettes de Gibier).* The sauce used for the liaison is a brown sauce that is very reduced to ensure the amount of flour in the roux corresponds exactly to the amount indicated: 8 grams (1/3 ounce) per deciliter (3 1/3 fluid ounces, scant 1/2 cup) of sauce that is *ready to be used.* And this proportion must be much more rigorously observed for this recipe, which does not include a liaison made with egg yolk. Consequently, the sauce must be very thick, and the amount of 8 grams (1/3 ounce) of flour per deciliter (3 1/3 fluid ounces, scant 1/2 cup) can even be exceeded. For how to make it, see brown sauce (PAGE 50). A little bit of Madeira wine added at the end, off the heat, has a good effect here. But remember that it will dilute the sauce, and therefore reduce it first accordingly.

Accompany it with a chasseur sauce, a Périgueux sauce, a poivrade sauce, soubise, etc.

Rissoles *(Rissoles)*

Rissoles differ from croquettes only in as much as an envelope of dough that replaces the breadcrumb coating: in every other respect, the preparation of both is identical. So you can refer to the article concerning croquettes for all directions for preparing the base for rissoles, as well as for the choice of its various ingredients. For the rissoles, note that the liaison sauce of the base can be slightly less thick than for the croquettes because it is not used to hold the ingredients together.

The rissoles can be garnished with a cooked stuffing: leftovers of terrines of foie gras or others—made without any liaison sauce—making a sort of small hot pâté. You can also prepare them as warm desserts, garnishing them as you wish with a cream, with a compote of fruits, of preserves, etc. The dough is the same, as well as the method of making them.

For the dough for the rissoles, you have several choices. Use trimmings of puff pastry or of *demi-feuilletage* prepared expressly for them; or a *pâte à foncer* or fine tart dough. The trimmings of pastry dough or *demi-feuilletage* give a lighter, more raised crust; the *pâte à foncer* furnishes a crust that is more crisp and is also much easier for inexperienced cooks to make. Here we give the proportions for the necessary quantities for each dough at your choice.

Cooking rissoles is always done in a large quantity of hot fat. *Makes about 15–25 rissoles, depending on the shape adapted.*

For a demi-feuilletage: **350 grams (12 1/3 ounces) of flour; 175 grams (6 ounces, 3/4 cup) of butter; 10 grams (1/3 ounce) of fine salt; 1 1/4 deciliters (4 1/4 fluid ounces, 1/2 cup) of water. Proceed exactly as directed (SEE PUFF PASTRY DOUGH, PÂTE FEUILLETÉE, PAGE 658), being careful to give only it 4 turns.**

For the pâte à foncer: **325 grams (11 1/2 ounces) of flour; 170 grams (6 ounces, 3/4 cup) of butter; a small egg weighing 50 grams (1 3/4 ounces); 8 grams (1/3 ounce) of fine salt; 1 scant deciliter (3 1/3 fluid ounces, scant 1/2 cup) of water. Proceed as directed (SEE PÂTE À FONCER, PAGE 662).**

For garnish: **For each rissole, 1 scant tablespoon of the garnish or the ingredients you are using, prepared as directed above and always *well chilled.***

PROCEDURE. **To make the rissoles:** You can make them in different shapes, which we will describe below. Whatever the dough used—*demi-feuilletage* or *pâte à foncer*—the method will be the same.

Lightly flour the board. Place the ball of dough on it, with the seam on the bottom. With the rolling pin, roll it out to an equal thickness of 1/2 centimeter (3/16 inch) The dough is then ready to be trimmed according to your chosen shape.

In a half moon or little boot. This is the simplest and most common method (see *fig.* 63). With a round pastry cutter that has ridged sides and is 8–9 centimeters (3¼–3½ inches) in diameter, press on the dough and cut rounds from it, lining them up on a board sprinkled with flour. On each of these rounds, place 1 tablespoon of garnish. With a small brush dipped in cool water, moisten the borders of the rounds around the garnish. (Just moisten it without making it too wet.) Then fold each round in half; press on the borders with the thumb and index finger to thoroughly enclose the garnish by sticking the 2 layers of dough together. Having done this, pinch the border with your fingers to thin this place where there is a double thickness of dough, while lightly pushing the dough toward the middle of the rissole where the garnish is, so that the dough is thick enough to protect the garnish.

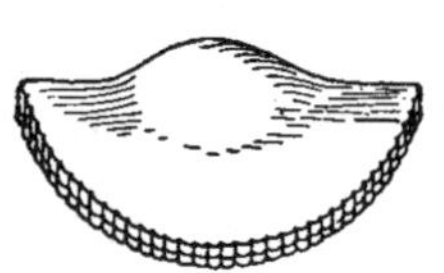

FIG. 63. RISSOLE IN THE SHAPE OF A SLIPPER.

Make sure the dough is perfectly sealed to keep the garnish absolutely enclosed; otherwise, the heat would cause the rissole to open and the fat would penetrate to the interior while the garnish would also escape.

As the rissoles are made, arrange them on a baking sheet covered with white parchment paper and lightly sprinkled with flour. Prepared thus and kept cool, they can stand for 1 hour before being fried in the deep fat.

In the form of small pâtés. With a pastry cutter that is about 6 centimeters (2½ inches) in diameter and has a jagged edge, cut rounds of dough, figuring 2 rounds per rissole. Moisten the perimeter of only 1 round. In the middle of this round, place the garnish. Cover it with the second round. Join the 2 rounds by pressing all around the rissole on the edges.

In the form of a purse. Cut the rounds of dough with a fluted pastry cutter about 11–12 centimeters (4¼–4½ inches) in diameter. On each round, place 1 tablespoon of garnish. Moisten the border of the rounds. Next, gather together the edges of each round, just like closing a purse, to thoroughly enclose the garnish. Squeeze the dough between your fingers for about 1 centimeter (⅜ inch) on the edges, pulling it to thin it out at this place. This is where you place the drawstring in a fabric purse; the jagged edges stick out and spread over, making the ridge of the drawstring (see *fig.* 64).

FIG. 64. RISSOLE IN THE SHAPE OF A PURSE.

NOTE. After the rounds have been cut in the dough, gather together the scraps and rapidly knead them, then roll them out again with the rolling pin so you can cut the rest of the rounds.

To fry the rissoles: For all the details, see deep-frying (PAGE 37). Bear in mind that you will need *7–8 minutes* for cooking the rissole; and if the cooking utensil is not very large, they will have to be fried in two batches. So calculate when the frying fat will be at the right temperature: that is, hotter than "moderate," but without getting to the point where it smokes, which would seize the dough, causing it to cook very badly.

Once all the rissoles have been put in the deep fat, turn up the heat. The added rissoles will have cooled the fat, which must be returned to its original temperature. Maintain it subsequently at the same point during the cooking, and even *turn up the heat a little bit toward the end* to finish coloring the rissoles, which will turn over by themselves; do not use a skimmer for anything except to remove them from the cooking utensil.

The dough should be a nice color and dry to the touch. Place the rissoles on a napkin to drain them thoroughly; salt them lightly and dress them surrounded by fried parsley on a napkin-covered plate; proceed with these last steps as rapidly as possible so that the rissoles can be eaten burning hot.

Chauds-Froids *(Chauds-Froids)*

The recipe for a chaud-froid varies depending on whether it is game that is being used or a bird with white meat.

With a young chicken, the chaud-froid is a kind of cold fricassée covered with gelée. With game, the chaud-froid is a cold salmi: indeed, the masters of classic cuisine described it as *"salmis de chaud-froid à la gelée."*

And actually the sauces known as "chaud-froid," whether white or brown, are the same as those used for a fricassée (in the case of a white sauce), and a salmi (for the brown sauce), with a certain amount of gelée added to each one: this gelée sets the sauce and makes it a "chaud-froid" for the meat. In other words, it coats them in a thick layer of sauce.

Clearly, one cannot classify *chauds-froids* as simple recipes, because all the details involved make their preparation time-consuming; but they are no longer dressed with the complicated decorations that were previously used. Today the meat pieces of a *chaud-froid* are arranged in a bowl or a plate, then simply covered with a layer of gelée; there are no other accessories.

Chaud-Froid of Young Chicken *(Chaud-Froid de Poularde)*. *Serves 10.*

1 nicely fleshed young chicken weighing about 1.8 kilograms (4 pounds) before being gutted; 2 large sheets of fatback bacon cut very thin to wrap them; almost 4 liters (4¼ quarts) of jus of which about 2½ liters (10½ cups) is for cooking the chicken and a good 1¼ liters (5⅓ cups) for the gelée; 750 milliliters (generous 3 cups) of chaud-froid sauce prepared with the cooking liquid from the chicken; 2 fine truffles or 3 medium ones cooked and nice and black.

PROCEDURE. **Summary:** *The evening before:* prepare the jus. *The morning of the same day the chaud-froid will be served:* clarify the jus for the gelée. Cook the chicken; allow it to completely cool. Meanwhile, prepare the chaud-froid sauce from the cooking liquid from the chicken.

Carve the chicken; prepare the pieces as a chaud-froid; let it solidify. Dress by basting them with more gelée.

Jus and gelée: For its double use, the jus must be clear. Proceed as directed (SEE ORDINARY NON-COLORED JUS, PAGE 45, AND SIMPLE GELÉE, PAGE 46). The quantities of meat indicated for the jus are here slightly reduced. So, 1 kilogram (2 pounds, 3 ounces) of beef will suffice with 1½ kilograms (3 pounds, 5 ounces) of veal knuckle.

The gelée should be clarified with raw beef: so, for the quantity of gelée expected, 100 grams (3½ ounces) of very lean beef; the gizzards from the chicken; 2 egg whites; 1 deciliter (3⅓ fluid ounces, scant ½ cup) of very good white wine. Check the consistency: in hot weather it would be sensible to add some gelatin, about 5 or 6 sheets.

The young chicken: Once the bird has been gutted and flamed, and the neck, feet, and wingtips removed, truss it. Wrap it entirely in the bards of bacon and secure them with a string.

If you do not have a small utensil known as a *daubière,* put the chicken in a deep saucepan that is just large enough, leaving a space of no more than 1 or 2 centimeters (⅜–¾ inch) on each side of the beast; this is so that the amount of jus suggested will be enough to cover it by about 4 centimeters (1½ inches). If the utensil you use is too large, you will need to add too much water; the fowl will be bathed in it and the cooking liquid, which is later used for the sauce, will have less value. That said, the jus used here is very gelatinous, so you can dilute it with a little bit of warm water so that you have just enough to cover the chicken.

Bring it to a boil. Skim. Add a medium-size onion stuck with a clove. Turn the heat down very low. Cover it, leaving a small opening for the steam to escape. *Allow 55 minutes for poaching:* that is, for cooking in the liquid at a very gentle simmer, which should be no more than a simple, uninterrupted trembling.

To tell if the flesh is done, use the same method as for a roast or a braised dish, piercing one of the thighs close to the drumstick; the pearl of juice that escapes should be clear; if it is lightly pink, let it cook for another 5 minutes. Then take the chicken out of the pan. Allow it to cool without taking off the bards. Carving when the bird is cooled offers greater precision and neatness but also helps the flesh to better conserve its juices. (Meanwhile, prepare the *chaud-froid* sauce as directed.)

White Chaud-Froid Sauce *(Sauce Chaud-Froid Blanche)*. *Time: About 3 hours. Makes 750 milliliters (generous 3 cups).*

60 grams (2¼ ounces, 4½ tablespoons) of butter and 50 grams (1¾ ounces) of flour for the roux; 9 deciliters (3¾ cups) of the jus used to cook the chicken; 25 grams (1 ounce) of mushroom trimmings; a small bunch of parsley; pepper and grated nutmeg; 3 egg yolks;

2 deciliters (6$^3/_4$ fluid ounces, $^7/_8$ cup) of cream that is not too thick and very fresh; 4 deciliters (1$^2/_3$ cups) of melted gelée.

PROCEDURE. Use a deep pot in thick aluminum with a capacity of 1$^3/_4$ liters (7$^1/_2$ cups) for the quantities given above: its size is important in view of the particularly delicate skimming operation.

Make a roux in it that colors to a light blond tint (SEE PAGE 47). Dilute it little by little with the jus, either lukewarm or hot. Add the pepper and the nutmeg. Bring it to a boil, stirring it with a small whisk. Then add the mushroom trimmings and the bunch of parsley, and skim it for *1$^1/_4$ hours* (SEE PAGE 16).

At the end of this time, pass the sauce through a chinois into a sauté pan. Keep the cream and the melted gelée handy. Dilute the egg yolks with half of the cream. Make the liaison, taking the necessary care (SEE PAGE 47).

Next reduce the sauce. For this, put it on strong heat, and from this point do not stop stirring with a wooden spatula, scraping across the bottom of the pan to stop anything from sticking, or use a wooden spoon with a large head. Minute by minute, and stirring constantly, add 2 or 3 tablespoons of gelée and a little bit of cream until you have used up both ingredients. Then continue to reduce the sauce until you are left with 750 milliliters (generous 3 cups). At this point, it should be thick and smooth and have a beautiful white tint.

Taste it to perfect the seasoning. Pass it into a small, shallow pan through a piece of cheesecloth that is twisted at two ends.

The sauce, when you use it, should be *scarcely* lukewarm. To prevent a skin from forming, which would oblige you to strain it again when you need to use it, it is essential to mix it very vigorously and frequently, using a small wooden spoon left in the pot, until it has cooled down enough. Then use the sauce immediately.

Preparation of the Chaud-Froid. Carving the chicken: Remove the bards. Lightly wipe the chicken with a good kitchen towel. Detach the thighs and take off all the meat along the carcass. With the point of a small knife, make a cut in the very middle of the breast, and then remove the 2 wings; then detach the filet mignons on each side of the wishbone.

Remove the skin from the thighs and the wings. Divide each wing into 3 long scallops; remove the end of the wing bone. Cut the thighs in two at the point where they join the drumstick. Trim each drumstick into the shape of a little ham. Take out the thighbone and make 2 pieces out of each thigh.

To chaud-froid the pieces: When it is used, the chaud-froid sauce must be nearly cold, runny, and quite smooth. If it is still lukewarm, it will not settle on the pieces in a sufficiently thick layer. If it is too cold, it will settle in clots.

In addition to the sauce terrine, have close at hand one or two large pot covers that have been turned over, so that you can put the pieces on them once they have been sauced. Dip the drumsticks in the sauce, holding them by the end of the bone. Put them on the cover. Then spear the other pieces with the end of a kitchen needle to dip them in the sauce. Arrange these, too, side by side on the cover. Make sure that the layer of sauce covering the pieces is *about 4 millimeters (scant $^1/_4$ inch) thick;* at any rate, a little less than 5 millimeters ($^1/_4$ inch).

The truffles: Cut these in very thin rounds and trim them with a pastry cutter, fluted or in a star shape, to a diameter of 2$^1/_2$ centimeters (1 inch). Place a round on each piece that has been sauced, basting it with 1 tablespoon of cold, melted gelée to attach it there. Then put the cover loaded with the pieces into a very cool place until the sauce has entirely set.

Dressing the plate: This can be done as you wish, either in a bowl or in a shallow plate made of metal, porcelain, or crystal, and round, long, or square. While the chaud-froid pieces are chilling, lightly heat the rest of the sauce and spread it over the bottom of the receptacle you are going to use. Let it set, then cover it with a few tablespoons of melted gelée and let that also solidify.

Once the layer of sauce on the chaud-froid pieces has set sufficiently so that it will not be damaged by the next steps, proceed as follows. Pass the point of a small knife around each piece to detach the excess sauce that has fallen all around the piece. Under each piece, slide the end of a blade of a large knife to transfer them to the prepared plate, placing them side by side.

Meanwhile, have the rest of the gelée ready, *just melted and chilled.* Tablespoon by tablespoon, baste the pieces with only half the gelée. Leave it there to set. After this, similarly baste the pieces with the other half, thus forming a transparent layer on the pieces.

Put it back in the refrigerator or, if not, in a very cool place, until this layer of gelée has set. When the chaud-froid must stand on the table for a buffet, lunch, or other occasion, you should put it on top of a larger plate that holds ice.

Chaud-Froid of Game, Duck, Etc. *(Chaud-Froid de Gibier, Caneton, Etc.).* In professional, modern cooking, the brown chaud-froid sauce is a *demi-glace* sauce, which is used instead of the "coulis sauce" described by the classic authors. To this is added a fumet of game, gelée, Madeira, etc. There are several ways to adapt this for home cooking, and we will give the more practical one. This is the salmi, but with the difference that the "coulis" obtained by pressing the debris and carcasses is replaced by the same recipe unpressed: the result is a less thick sauce.

The proportions of sauce and gelée are the same for game as for the chicken; the work order is equally the same. The game can even be roasted the evening before making a chaud-froid. In any case, do not carve it until it has been completely cooled.

Roast it until it is perfectly done, and do not overcook. Carve it as usual for a roasted bird; if it is a duck, you cut the fillets from the breast. Remove the skin from all the pieces. Then make a chaud-froid from the pieces, dressing them, etc., as directed for a chaud-froid of chicken.

Brown Chaud-Froid Sauce *(Sauce Chaud-Froid Brune).* *Time: 2 hours. Makes 750 milliliters (generous 3 cups).*

For the fumet of game: **a little mirepoix with 30 grams (1 ounce) of fresh lard; the same of onion and carrot; the trimmings, the carcasses, etc., after carving the bird (pheasant, quail, thrush, partridge, duck, etc.); a glass of white wine; 2 tablespoons of tomato paste; 1 good liter (4$^1/_4$ cups) of juice; 1 sprig of parsley, thyme, bay; 2 minced shallots; pepper, nutmeg.**

60 grams (2$^1/_4$ ounces, 4$^1/_2$ tablespoons) of butter and 50 grams (1$^3/_4$ ounces) of flour for the roux; the juice or fumet of the game, which has been prepared as above; 4 deciliters (1$^2/_3$ cups) of gelée; 4 tablespoons of port or Madeira wine; 1 teaspoon of lemon juice.

PROCEDURE. In a thick pot, gently color the mirepoix (SEE PAGE 21), adding to it all that remains of the bird after carving—carcass, gizzards, bones, and skin, which should be struck several times with a cleaver—and also add the finely minced liver. When everything is about to stick to the bottom, moisten it with the white wine and add the tomato. Let it reduce completely. Moisten it with the juice. Bring it to a boil; add the rest of the aromatics. Cover and cook gently for *1 hour.*

Meanwhile, prepare a dark blond roux in a deep saucepan with a 1-liter (4-cup) capacity. Dilute it with the jus prepared above, strained through the chinois. Bring it to a boil and skim the sauce for *1 hour* (SEE PAGE 16).

Once the sauce has been skimmed, add the melted gelée to it. Boil it on strong heat until there are no more than *7 deciliters (3 cups).* At this stage, the reduced sauce should have a good consistency and mask the spoon with a brilliant varnish. Off the heat, add the port or Madeira and the lemon juice. Strain it through a cheesecloth, which is twisted at both ends, into a small saucepan that is relatively shallow. Allow the sauce to cool to the point where it is *scarcely lukewarm* before dipping the pieces in it. While you wait, mix it frequently to avoid a skin forming on the surface.

Aspics *(Aspics)*

Aspic is a cold dish characterized by the gelée that covers the ingredients; so much so, in fact, that a professional author has given this imaginative definition: "a gelée is an aquarium for foie gras, fowl, game, or fish, etc."

A deluxe dish, aspic has for a long time now been made only in a mold. The mold can be whatever you like, a high-sided dome-shaped mold, smooth-sided, fluted, or even a charlotte mold; or, more commonly, a mold known as a "bavarois," which is a cylinder or a cylindrical mold with an open center, this being a design that enables the jelly to set more quickly. Or you can even use a circular or border mold, rather high-sided; this has a larger opening than an ordinary cylindrical mold, allowing you to serve the aspic with a salad or some kind of a garnish placed in the middle.

The inconvenience of molding is that it requires making a very strong gelée to keep the aspic solid, and this means adding a much larger amount of veal foot, pork rind, and often gelatin: all are ingredients that reduce the delicacy and succulence of the jelly. Then there is all the trouble you have to take and the risk that the aspic will collapse when unmolded.

For this reason, molds tend not to be used in modern cuisine, which has done away with finicky, time-consuming decorations. Instead, all the ingredients are put into a bowl or a low timbale, or even in a shallow plate, and then covered with gelée. We will describe these different ways of dressing the plate.

The amount of gelée for an aspic intended to serve 8–10 people can be calculated as 1 1/4 liters–1 1/2 liters (5 1/3–6 1/3 cups): thus 1 1/2 liters (6 1/3 cups) of jus.

Anticipating that you may need more jus for cooking the ingredients, you should prepare 2 liters (8 1/2 cups) of jus using the following proportions:

1 kilogram (2 pounds, 3 ounces) of top rump and the same of veal knuckle; 250 grams (8 7/8 ounces) of veal bones; 1 large veal foot or 2 small ones; 125 grams (4 1/2 ounces) of fresh pork rind; 2 poultry gizzards; 125–150 grams (4 1/2–5 1/3 ounces) of carrots; 175–200 grams (6–7 ounces) of onions; a bouquet garni; 2 leeks split and tied with a small branch of celery; 2 3/4 liters (11 1/2 cups) of water; 12 grams (3/8 ounce) of salt.

***To clarify the jelly:* 150 grams (5 1/3 ounces) of very lean beef; 2 egg whites; a pinch of chervil leaves and a few leaves of tarragon.**

***To add after the clarification of the gelée:* 1 deciliter (3 1/3 fluid ounces, scant 1/2 cup) of Madeira.**

PROCEDURE. **To make the gelée:** Proceed as directed (SEE PAGE 45). The gelée for an aspic should barely be tinted, so the jus should be prepared only by sweating the meat and the vegetables for about 10 minutes at the most, without letting them color; you should then immediately moisten them with the water. All this is described in the article to which we have already referred. Note, however, that in this case the clarification of the gelée does not use white wine; and remember that the Madeira is added *after* this, when the gelée is almost cold, so that its aroma will be completely preserved.

When dressing the aspic, even if perfectly melted, the gelée must be *cold.* To achieve this, do not heat it directly, but allow the receptacle holding it to become lukewarm. This should be done sufficiently in advance that it dissolves progressively, without having any clots remaining.

To decorate: Apart from the truffles, which are part of the decoration for most aspics, it is customary to use egg white cut into very thin patterns, pickled tongue, cornichons, radish cut the same way; capers; tarragon leaves; chervil leaves, etc.

The truffles. Use either preserved or fresh; and if fresh, cook them in advance (SEE PAGE 537). These can be peeled and cut into extremely thin slices, then kept between 2 plates until ready to use.

The egg whites for decoration. Beat them without making them foam and pass them through a cloth twisted at both ends. Put them in a lightly buttered mold, a *génoise* mold or another, with a large enough surface to obtain a thin layer. Solidify them in the double boiler. Detach the circumference with a knife. Turn it over on the table and cut it in rounds with a fluted pastry cutter.

The gelée decorations surrounding the unmolded aspic. In haute cuisine, these are called "gelée croutons." Pour some gelée into a receptacle, either a low mold or a small, hollow bowl, large enough so that the gelée does not reach higher than 1 1/2 centimeters (5/8 inch). Let it solidify completely, and then turn it over on a cloth extended on the table, from which you will then cut this layer of gelée into squares or regular rectangles with your knife; or even into small rounds, smooth or fluted, using a pastry cutter.

Or more simply, you can surround the aspic with chopped gelée. Simply chop it coarsely with the back of a knife. There is no need in this case to make it in a thin sheet.

Molded Aspic *(L'Aspic Moulé).* Using ice makes it considerably easier to dress an aspic, the jelly setting well and much faster in a very cold mold; it is sufficient that the mold be surrounded to half its height by the ice. But do not add sea salt to this ice, as for making ice cream: the salt increases the cooling power of the ice, but in this case the effect would be to cloud the gelée, which must, we know, be as transparent as possible.

Without ice, the aspic must be finished and put into a cool place 4 hours before being served. With ice, you can begin to dress it only 2 hours before serving, 1 1/2 hours being enough for the jelly to set.

There are several ways to dress a molded aspic, depending on whether you want the decoration to be more, or less, complicated. If you confine yourself to decorating the top of the aspic, you need only put the decoration at the bottom of the mold; if, however, you want to decorate the entire shape, apply it to the sides of the mold. In this case, the mold must first be lined with gelée: that is, the whole inside of the mold must be covered with a light layer of gelée.

As for the actual pattern of the decoration, this is a matter of skill and taste, and it cannot be truly, precisely defined. All that we can describe here is the method of attaching the decoration in the mold.

To unmold an aspic: Do not wait until the last moment. Dip the mold into a bowl of water that is a little more than lukewarm for 2 or 3 seconds, just enough time to put it in and take it out. Quickly wipe off the mold. Put a napkin-covered plate on top of it, and then invert the mold. Surround with cut or chopped gelée.

To line a mold with gelée: Pour 3 or 4 tablespoons of gelée into the mold and turn it in every direction to spread the gelée around (in the same way as when lining a mold with caramel), so that this gelée sets in a very thin layer on the entire interior of the mold. If you can roll the mold on a pile of ice, the gelée will set in a few seconds.

To place the motifs or decorations, truffles, egg whites, etc., pick them up carefully with the end of a kitchen needle and place them symmetrically at the bottom of the mold that has been coated with gelée. Baste them with just a few drops of gelée, so that when they set the decoration will hold fast. Work cautiously, because this liquid gelée might make the decorations slip. To decorate the walls of the mold, press the decorations into the half-set gelée.

When the decorations are well adhered, pour enough gelée into the mold to form a layer on the bottom 2 centimeters (3/4 inch) thick. Let this set completely before beginning to assemble the aspic: that is, before putting the other ingredients into the mold.

Aspic That Is Not Molded *(L'Aspic Non Moulé).* At the bottom of the receptacle you are going to use—a timbale, bowl, or plate—put a layer of gelée 1 centimeter (3/8 inch) thick and let it solidify. On top, place some of the elements that will be included in the aspic—foie gras, lobster, veal sweet breads, etc.—cut into slices: arrange them either in a turban shape or superimposed circles, and spread the truffles around. This is a matter of taste and skill.

No matter how they have been arranged, completely cover the slices with gelée. When this gelée has set, decorate the top with pieces of truffles cut into rectangles, either a row in the middle surrounded by a circle, or any pattern you like. Baste this decoration with a few drops of gelée, just enough to attach it. When this little bit of gelée has set, cover the decoration with a layer of gelée 1 centimeter (3/8 inch) thick.

Allow it to set in a cool spot or by surrounding it with ice. Serve it just as it is. If the aspic includes a decoration of egg white, pickled tongue, etc., place these directly on top of the various aspic ingredients.

Aspic of Foie Gras *(Aspic de Foie Gras).* This is one of the most current and most popular dishes. Depending on the season and circumstance, you can use foie gras braised at the moment of use, or foie gras prepared as a preserve. Molded or not, the foie gras can be simply cut into slices, which are then placed just as they are; into rectangles; or, using a pastry cutter, into rounds 3 1/2 centimeters (1 3/8 inches) in diameter. You can even make little shells by scraping the liver with a spoon that has been dipped in warm water. To cut the foie gras more cleanly, lightly heat the blade of the knife by dipping it in hot water.

The molded aspic can be dressed in a circular mold lined with gelée, as suggested below for the veal sweetbreads aspic. As a different kind of molding, which is equally good for other aspics, we suggest here a way to dress it in a mold that is not lined with gelée, and for which a charlotte mold can be used instead of a circular mold. The capacity of the mold, whatever its shape, should be approximately 1¼–1½ liters (5⅓–6⅓ cups). *Time: 3 hours (once the foie gras has been cooked and chilled). Serves 8–10.*

1 goose liver weighing 700 grams (1 pound, 9 ounces); 2 medium-size truffles; about 1½ liters (6⅓ cups) of Madeira-flavored gelée, some of which will be used to surround the aspic.

PROCEDURE. Cook the liver as directed for foie gras with Madeira. Drain it and chill it with its bard still around it to prevent it from browning. Next, cut it into even slices about 1 centimeter (⅜ inch) thick. In the bottom of the mold, place a layer of gelée 5 millimeters (¼ inch) thick. Decorate with truffled slices cut into rounds or rectangles. Then gently pour in 3 or 4 tablespoons of gelée to hold this decoration when it sets. Next, add more gelée to form a layer about 1 centimeter (⅜ inch) thick. Once this layer has set, put on top of it the third part of the liver slices, alternating it with truffles—about 5 or 6 slices—being careful to leave enough space between the liver and the borders or walls of the mold so that there is space for the gelée that is poured in. Pour 4 tablespoons of gelée around the slices. Allow it to set. Then add 4 other tablespoons of gelée and also allow that to gel. Then pour the right amount of gelée to come up to the edge of the slices, but without covering them.

Once this last layer has set, add a second row of liver and then pour in the gelée exactly the same way. Then a third layer of liver: finish by filling the mold with gelée, always observing the same precautions. The essential thing, as for every mold, is to pour in the gelée cold and in small quantities at a time, so that it sets little by little and does not float up to the surface of the mold.

Allow it to set on ice or in a refrigerator. A cool place will not be sufficient, because the gelée of the aspic must be perfectly set without allowing the foie gras, which has softened during these preparations, to firm up again.

Unmold and garnish with gelée as directed.

Aspic of Veal Sweetbreads *(Aspic de Ris de Veau).* The method described here to mold the aspic is a kind of preparation in a mold lined with gelée, and it is applicable to all aspics in general. Of course, the aspic can, if you like, be simply dressed in a timbale or a shallow bowl. *Serves 8–10.*

1 medium-size veal sweetbread; 200 grams (7 ounces) of pickled tongue; 2 medium truffles cut into thin slices; 2 poached egg whites; about 1¼ liters (5⅓ cups) of gelée mixed with Madeira, part of which will be used for the decoration surrounding the aspic. Use a cylindrical mold with a hollow center (an angel food mold) with a capacity of 1¼–1½ liters (5⅓–6⅓ cups).

PROCEDURE. For details of how to prepare the sweetbreads, SEE PAGE 302. Cook them as directed for sweetbreads braised *à blanc,* but without the bard or the white wine, and simply covered by a clear jus; allow no more than a half hour for poaching in the oven. The sweetbreads must here be kept rather firm, so that you can subsequently cut them into slices without them crumbling. Let the sweetbreads cool in the cooking juice.

Dry them on a towel; divide them into a dozen slices after lightly trimming the rounded part of the ends. Also cut the tongue into a dozen slices 5 millimeters (¼ inch) thick.

Line the mold with gelée. Decorate the bottom of it, and the side, with small decorations of truffle, tongue, and egg white. On the layer set in the bottom, arrange a row of slices of sweetbreads and tongue. Use 4 slices of each, alternating with the slices of truffles, and basting them with a little bit of gelée, and then allow it to set.

Then add enough gelée to make a layer 2½ centimeters (1 inch) thick. Once this has set, place on top a second row of alternating slices, then proceed as before. Before pouring on a new layer of gelée, make sure you first baste the slices with a very little bit of gelée and let it set to hold them fast. If not, these slices will move.

Again, make a third row and finish by filling the mold with the gelée. Then put it on ice to set, or in a very cool spot, as directed.

Risotto *(Risotto)*

You can serve risotto alone, either as a vegetable or even as a kind of informal entrée; and it can also be served as an accompaniment to meats, generally veal (as in Italy), or mutton or lamb chops, sausages, and small game, such as quail and other small birds, etc. The principal preparation is always the same, but depending on the recipe, you can add ham or pickled tongue, purée of tomatoes, white truffles or piedmont mushrooms, etc., or combine it with a garnish, as with risotto à la Milanaise.

The principle of cooking risotto is that the rice *is not washed first* and is colored—in other words, heated in hot butter—*before* any liquid is added. This procedure eliminates the need for washing or any other preparations. It is also very rapid and, for that reason alone, can be highly recommended for home cooking. You need only sort through the rice for bad grains; washing it, no matter how briefly, will spoil the dish because the moisture sticks the rice together, meaning that the hot fat does not reach every grain. This means that the grains will not be separate after cooking, and the dish will be pasty. If the rice is particularly dirty and you really must wash it first, pass it quickly through the water and drain it completely, then dry it immediately afterward *with absolute thoroughness* so that the grains will be as separate and as dry as before the washing.

To estimate the amount of liquid needed for cooking the rice, the simplest way is to do as the Italians do: measure the rice, not by weight but by volume, using the same cup or deciliter measure with which you will subsequently measure the liquid. This is to calculate on volume instead of weight. All directions for variable quantities are given in the special section (SEE RICE, PAGE 561). It is essential here to have knowledge of that section.

The amount of *chopped onion* seems large by comparison with other recipes but is fixed at about 25 grams (1 ounce) for each 100 grams (3½ ounces) of rice used; it is one of the essential ingredients of a risotto. Onion cooked like this is not actually perceptible in the completed dish. The amount of *butter* used to color the onions and rice can be calculated at about 20 grams (⅔ ounce, 1 heaping tablespoon) for each 100 grams (3½ ounces) of rice. Although we say butter, this can just as well be replaced, wholly or in part, with animal or vegetable fat, which is now increasingly used given the high cost of living. It is also a good idea—and not for reasons of economy—but for a felicitous effect, to mix in some melted beef marrow with the butter. This lets you reserve the fresh butter for adding to the risotto right at the end, at the same time that you add the cheese.

As much as possible, get your timing right so that you can serve the risotto as soon as you have added the butter and the cheese. At any rate, it is not a good idea to let a risotto stand too long because it will become dense. *Time: 45 minutes. Serves 6.*

250 grams (8⅞ ounces) of rice; 60 grams (2¼ ounces, 4½ tablespoons) of butter; 75 grams of onion (2⅔ ounces), very finely minced; 7½ deciliters (generous 3 cups) of degreased bouillon; a bouquet garni; 30 grams (1 ounce) of grated Parmesan and the same of Gruyère (or 50 grams/1¾ ounces of Gruyère if you do not have the Parmesan); 45 grams (1½ ounces, 3 tablespoons) of final butter; pepper and grated nutmeg; a pinch of saffron (optional).

PROCEDURE. In a medium-size pot with a thick bottom, heat the butter over very moderate heat. Add the chopped onion; stir it continuously with a wooden spoon until the onion is softened, almost melted, nearly yellowish but not at all browned; otherwise, it will be bitter, and this will communicate the taste to the risotto.

Add the rice. *Stir continuously with the spoon* until it has taken on a milky white tint and has absorbed the hot butter; this should take *about 2 minutes.* In effect, the rice is undergoing a sort of roasting in the hot fat. So make sure the rice is *burning hot* when the liquid is added to it.

Then pour in the bouillon, either cold or hot; add pepper, nutmeg, saffron, a bouquet garni, etc. On stronger heat, bring it to a boil, mixing carefully so that the rice does not stick to the bottom of the pot. As soon as it is boiling, cover the pot and put it in a very gentle oven, which is just hot enough to maintain a very gentle simmer. From this moment on, do not touch the rice: you might make it stick.

If you do not have an oven, put the pot, very well covered, on extremely moderate heat, to maintain this same gentle simmer. But cooking in an oven, where the utensil is surrounded by the heat, is the best method.

As soon as the pot is put into the oven, figure on *15–20 minutes of cooking,* depending on the method of cooking and the quality of rice. In the article on rice (SEE PAGE 561), we have explained the differences to note for cooking times; short-grain rice cooks more rapidly, so check to see if it is done at the end of 15–18 minutes. Properly cooked rice must be absolutely tender and should have absorbed all the bouillon.

To finish the risotto: Remove the bouquet garni. Using a fork, so that you do not crush the rice, begin to stir it before adding the grated cheese and the final butter, divided into pieces, into the same pot . Do this quickly so that you do not allow the rice to cool at all, and you must be very skillful so that you do not break the grains.

Check the seasoning. Pour it into a timbale or a dish that has been heated in advance, without heaping it up or smoothing the surface of the risotto. You want it to have a lightness of being.

Milan-Style Risotto *(Risotto à la Milanaise).* A recipe that can be highly recommended, producing a dish that is both attractive and excellent. *Time: 1 hour, 30 minutes (once the brain is ready to be cooked). For 10–12:*

For the rice: **600 grams (1 pound, 5 ounces) of good rice; 100 grams (3 1/2 ounces, 7 tablespoons) of butter; 150 grams (5 1/3 ounces) of onion; 1 1/4 liters (5 1/3 cups) of degreased bouillon; 2 tablespoons of thick tomato purée; a bouquet garni; salt, pepper, nutmeg; 50 grams (1 3/4 ounces) of Parmesan and 50 grams (1 3/4 ounces) of Gruyère, both grated.**

For the ragoût of the garnish and the sauce: **1 veal brain; 100 grams (3 1/2 ounces) of mushrooms; 100 grams (3 1/2 ounces) of *cooked* lean ham; 30 grams (1 ounce, 2 tablespoons) of butter and 15 grams (1/2 ounce) of flour for a white roux; 3 deciliters (1 1/4 cups) of bouillon; 1 deciliter (3 1/3 fluid ounces, scant 1/2 cup) of cream or good milk; 2 egg yolks; lemon juice.**

PROCEDURE. Once the *brain* has been disgorged, cleaned, etc., put it in a pot and cover completely with cool water, then add a bay leaf, 1 sprig of thyme, a bit of vinegar, and salt. Boil and skim. Cook gently for *a half hour.* Allow it to cool in its cooking juice. Then cut it into 1/2 centimeter (3/16 inch) thick, about the size of a one-franc piece. In the same way, cut *the ham,* but thinner. Cook the *mushrooms* as directed, with butter and lemon juice (SEE MUSHROOMS FOR GARNISH, PAGE 490). Cut them into thin slices. Reserve the little bit of juice from their cooking.

Assemble all these different elements on a plate, warm and covered, so that they do not dry out.

The sauce: In a small sauté pan, make a white roux (SEE PAGE 47). Dilute it with the bouillon. Let it cook 5 minutes. Bind it with the egg yolks diluted with the cream or milk (SEE LIAISONS, PAGE 49). Add nutmeg and lemon juice.

Reserve, in a very small saucepan, *a quarter* of the sauce. Add the juice from cooking the mushrooms. This small amount of sauce is used to cover the risotto just before serving.

In a pot, mix the brain, ham, and mushrooms, which you have kept warm. Keep this ragoût covered in a double boiler.

The risotto: Prepare it and cook it as described, adding the tomato purée at the same time as the bouillon.

Generously butter a charlotte mold with a capacity of 2 1/2 liters (10 1/2 cups). Fill to three-quarters with the risotto. Using a metal spoon, pack the risotto on the bottom and against the walls into a layer that is an even thickness all the way around, making a hollow that can contain the ragoût. Add the ragoût into this cavity, then cover it with the rest of the risotto. Pack it down with the spoon. Put the mold, without a cover, into a gentle oven for 2 minutes. Unmold it on a round plate. Baste it with the reserve sauce. Serve immediately.

Pilaf *(Pilaf)*

This is also called "pilau," and is a recipe of Turkish origin. The base is rice. Diversely interpreted by professional chefs in other countries, its simplest form is often modified by professional kitchens for the tastes and whims of the public. Some chefs cook the rice like a risotto; some add it to the meat ragoût without first cooking it in hot butter. It is worth noting here that rice cooked by this last method—in fat, *not* blanched—produces grains that are even more expanded than those of a risotto.

Whatever cooking method is used, it is understood that all pilafs include rice with separate intact grains that have completely absorbed all of the cooking liquid. For all details about the rice and the amount of cooking liquid to use, refer to the special section (SEE PAGE 561).

A pilaf can include very different ingredients: meat, fowl, game, fish, shellfish, and even vegetables such as eggplant, tomatoes, artichokes, etc. All sorts of things end up going into a pilaf: either the ingredients listed above are partly cooked with the rice, or the ingredients are added at the last moment, which is a valuable use of leftovers. Either way, the principles for cooking the rice should always be observed.

Here we summarize how to make a mutton pilaf, the best recipe for home cooking. Cut meat from the shoulder into small cubes; color them gently in butter in a sauté pan or in a pot with chopped onion; then add water or, if possible, bouillon made with the mutton bones and trimmings, using enough liquid to come right to the top of the meat; add a bouquet garni. Cover and let it cook as for an ordinary mutton ragoût.

About 15–20 minutes before serving, depending on the quality of the rice, add the rice, which should first have been *washed well.* Then add hot water or bouillon, to reestablish the amount of liquid needed for cooking the rice. For this, you should allow almost three times the volume of rice, given the surface of the utensil used. Season with pepper, nutmeg, and, if you like, a pinch of saffron; and salt, depending on the liquid used. Cover and cook gently in the oven if possible. To serve, remove the bouquet; lightly fluff the rice with a fork, being careful not to break it, and mix the rice well with the pieces of mutton, which have separated out from it while cooking. Pour everything immediately into a timbale or a heated plate.

The same procedure is used for *lamb* pilaf, with the difference being that the lamb cooks more rapidly, so the rice (and all the liquid) is added as soon as the meat has colored in the hot fat, and the two then cook for the same length of time; allow *25 minutes.* Serve them the same way as mutton.

Rice cooked as a pilaf on its own—that is, without meat or any other ingredient added to it—is prepared more or less in the same way as risotto (PAGE 449). The procedures and quantities are identical, although the cheese is, of course, left out. The mutton bouillon is replaced with beef bouillon. If you like, you can add a seasoning of tomato and saffron. If you have some leftovers to use—meat, fowl, fish, etc.—reheat them with 2 or 3 tablespoons of liquid, just enough to moisten them, and then cover them and keep them warm. To cook the rice, use a liquid that is suitable for the leftovers. So, for fowl, use a bouillon made with the carcass; for fish, the liquid from the court bouillon, salted water, or water from mussels, etc.

Curry *(Curry)*

"Curry" is the English spelling; the French write "kari," "cary," or "carry." Curry is a dish imported from India by the English, who are great lovers of spicy food: it is a fricassée of meat, fowl, or rabbit spiced with a special curry powder and inevitably accompanied by rice à l'Indienne.

Curry powder does not come, as was sometimes believed, from an Indian vegetable of this name. It is a combination of spices and it includes very different formulas: turmeric or saffron from the Indies, ginger, cumin, coriander, ordinary pepper and also cayenne pepper, cinnamon, nutmeg, mustard seeds, fennel, etc.

Here we give a recipe for curry, which was kindly given to us by an Indian cook. *Time: Serves 4–6 people, depending on how large the menu is.*

450 grams (1 pound) of meat (mutton, veal, chicken, rabbit); 1 medium-size onion; 1 carrot; 2 stalks of celery (without leaves); 100 grams (3 1/2 ounces, 7 tablespoons) of butter; 1 1/2 tablespoons of curry

powder; 100 grams (3 1/2 ounces) of purée of tomato concentrate; 1 tablespoon of water; 1 1/4 deciliters (that is, 4 1/4 fluid ounces/1/2 cup) of coconut milk, or, if you do not have it, the same quantity of crème fraîche; if you like, 1 tablespoon of Smyrna raisins, from which you have removed the stems.

PROCEDURE. In a thick-bottomed pot, heat the butter and color the onions on gentle heat until they are lightly golden. Also include the carrot and the celery, both *very finely* minced; add the curry powder and the water; mix everything well and let it cook for *5 minutes.* Add the tomato purée and mix again with your wooden spoon, then let it cook gently for *15 minutes.* Add the meat: cut into pieces weighing about 50 grams (1 3/4 ounces), if it is mutton or veal; cut as for a fricassée or a stew if it is chicken or rabbit that you are using; and add the raisins, if using them. Cover *tightly* and continue cooking *on very gentle* heat for *1–2 hours,* depending on how tender the meat is. Turn the pieces over one or two times while cooking.

To serve: Add the coconut milk or the cream and heat without allowing it to boil.

At the same time, serve a plate of rice à l'Indienne (SEE PAGE 563) and also, so that everyone can help themselves, a small cup of grated coconut, a cup of minced hard-boiled eggs with the whites and yolks separated, and a jar of chutney (found at specialty merchants, as are the grated coconut and curry powder); the amount of curry powder can be reduced for a less spicy dish, or if the curry powder is itself very strong.

Cassoulet *(Cassoulet)*

A famous dish from the Languedoc, cassoulet has gradually spread into other regions and become very popular, but generally speaking, it has not retained all its distinct characteristics everywhere: for example, confit (preserved goose meat) and goose fat, which plays such a large role in the Toulouse and Castelnaudary cassoulets, is not found everywhere.

That said, there are some elements that define the dish and that should therefore be included in all cassoulets: the dry white beans that form the base must always be cooked in the particular way described (SEE COOKING DRY VEGETABLES, PAGE 557); fresh pork rinds, previously blanched, are always used, and a raw garlic sausage. A clove of garlic must be included in the bouquet garni.

First, we will give a recipe for the "Castelnaudary" cassoulet, which comes from the classic master Colombié, himself a native of that area. This is an authentic home-style dish and it can serve about 10 people. Thus: 1 liter (4 1/4 cups) of dry white beans; 300 grams (10 1/2 ounces) of fresh bacon rinds, not too fatty, blanched and tied into a package; a sausage of 250 grams (8 7/8 ounces); 500 grams (1 pound, 2 ounces) of goose confit; 1 piece of shoulder of mutton or a leg of mutton, roasted either at that moment or the previous evening; 2 large tomatoes or 2 large tablespoons of concentrated tomato purée; 100 grams (3 1/2 ounces) of goose fat, or, if you do not have that, of melted lard.

Put the beans, blanched and soaked as directed, into a small earthenware casserole with 2 liters (8 1/2 cups) of *boiling* water. Add the rinds, the goose, the roasted mutton, the fat, and the bouquet garni. Season it very lightly with salt. Let it cook very gently for *2 hours;* it should bubble at only one point on the surface of the liquid. Then add the sausage and the tomatoes, which have had their seeds and water removed. Allow it to simmer for another *1 hour.*

Garnish an earthenware plate, a deep bowl—or, if you do not have one, a clay baking dish or a very shallow casserole dish—with the rinds. Alternate layers of beans and meat, including the sausage, both cut into slices. Powder it with bread crumbs and baste it with the goose fat or other fat. Brown the top gently, preferably in the oven. Leave enough time, at least a good 45 minutes, so that even the entire interior of the dish is absolutely burning hot at the instant that it is served.

To this recipe we will add an equally simple method, also from Castelnaudary, which includes duck instead of mutton. Cook the beans as directed, with the rinds, and toward the end, with the sausage. Color the duck in the fat in a pan; then separately color 250 grams (8 7/8 ounces) of fresh sausages and the same amount of pork. For this dish, there is a special terrine shaped like a truncated cone, but you can use a deep bowl instead.

Line it with the rind, then add the duck and cover it with beans. Add the other meats. Then cover it with more beans. Spread minced parsley over everything, along with 2 cloves of garlic mixed with a little bit of bread crumbs. Put it into the oven for about *4 hours.* From time to time, add a little bit of the cooking water on the side from the beans to keep the inside nice and soft and humid. Serve in the terrine, which should be brought to the table smoking. To make serving easier, you can carve the duck, the sausage, and the pork before putting them in the terrine. It seems that this type of Castelnaudary cassoulet does not include tomato.

The chef Reboul has a recipe that is more refined than the preceding ones. It is particularly good for duck, but, if you like, it can be replaced by goose, either fresh or in a confit, or even a piece of leg of mutton; in every case, the meat is initially cooked in the same way. So, for 6 people: 500 grams (1 pound, 2 ounces) of dry white beans; 200 grams (7 ounces) of fresh pork rind; 200 grams (7 ounces) of lean bacon; 1 small home-style sausage; 1 duck; 1 liter (4¹/₄ cups) of bouillon; 2 glasses of white wine; 100 grams (3¹/₂ ounces) of goose fat or melted lard; 2 tablespoons of tomato purée; 1 tablespoon of fine white bread crumbs; 1 tablespoon of minced parsley; 2 chopped garlic cloves.

Work in the following order:

1. Cook the beans as directed with a pinch of salt, an onion stuck with 2 cloves, carrot, rinds, sausage, and bacon; you should just cover it with water, not to excess, and then cover the casserole. Take out the sausage and bacon when they are cooked and turn the heat down as low as possible under the beans when they are ready.

2. While the beans are cooking, cook the duck as follows: color it in the casserole with some bacon trimmings, an onion, and a carrot cut into rounds, seasoned with salt and pepper. Moisten it with white wine and let it reduce to 2–3 tablespoons. Then moisten it with the bouillon; add the bouquet garni; cover; let it cook gently for about *1 hour* for a medium-aged duck. At any rate, make sure that it is tender enough. Strain the cooking juice without degreasing it and reserve.

3. Now that the cooking of the beans and duck is under way, prepare the sauce in a third casserole, where you will later put the beans. Slowly and gently color a finely minced onion on very low heat in 1 tablespoon of goose fat. Add the tomato purée, then a glass of white wine; let it reduce almost entirely in an uncovered casserole. Then moisten it with the cooking juice from the duck and add the beans, which have been completely drained of their cooking liquid, to the sauce. Let them simmer there for a few minutes.

4. Take an earthenware receptacle or a heatproof porcelain receptacle, as described in the previous directions. In the bottom, put half of the beans. Then arrange the duck on top, cut into 6 pieces; around it place the sausage and bacon, cut into slices ¹/₂ centimeter (³/₁₆ inch) thick; and the rind cut into small dice. Cover with the rest of the beans. Then, on top of it all, spread the chopped garlic and the parsley mixed with the bread crumbs. Finally, moisten it with 2 tablespoons of goose fat or melted lard. Then brown it gently, as previously directed. Since the meat and beans were quite hot when put into the receptacle, 15 minutes or so should be enough so that the inside is cooked by the simmering. At any rate, make sure that you can serve it *burning hot.*

To finish, let us finally note the procedure used in the kitchens of the famous Tivollier hotel in Toulouse, which was once kindly given to us by its proprietor: 500–600 grams (1 pound, 2 ounces–1 pound, 5 ounces) of white beans, always cooked as directed, but *only three-quarters of the way through.* In the fat, color a quarter of the duck confit, a boned shoulder of mutton, a "mountain-type" or dried sausage, pork, a pig's knuckle, and a partridge. After this, add 1¹/₂ liters (6¹/₃ cups) of jus or very good bouillon and also cook these *only three-quarters of the way through,* keeping the casserole covered.

In a large terrine—preferably the specific type of casserole already mentioned for the Castelnaudary preparation—spread a layer of previously blanched pork rinds. Over the pork, put a layer of beans; then alternate these with the meat, which has been cut into 4–5 centimeter (1 1/2–2 inch) squares, and do this just until the terrine is three-quarters full. Then pour, to the height of the last layer formed by the beans, the cooking bouillon from the meat; this should first have been reduced and had 1 tablespoon of tomato and a small pinch of dry mint leaves added. Check the seasoning for pepper and salt. As before, cover with a mixture of bread crumbs and chopped garlic.

Simmer this without a cover for about *3 1/2 hours* in the oven, to very gently reduce and form a brown crust. When this recipe was invented—in an era that is already an age away for today's youth—the oven used for cooking a cassoulet was the old model, which was directly heated by wood; dried, hard wood was burned in it, and before the cassoulet was put in the oven, a couple of handfuls of juniper were tossed onto the cinders. Is it not this last detail that makes for a truly authentic recipe?

Sauerkraut *(Choucroute)*

No matter how the sauerkraut is served, it is always prepared the same way. To summarize, the cabbage is, in effect, braised, using a very large amount of fat: either lard, duck fat, goose fat, or the fat from a roast, which is particularly good. Salted pork is also used, taken from the following pieces; the knuckle, the shoulder, the leg, the part just below the thigh, as well as from an ear or a muzzle. You can add, according to the case, some smoked bacon, or large and small sausages. Some recipes include carrots cut into quarters, an onion stuck with a clove, and a bouquet garni. And juniper berries are always used, their unique flavor being essential here. The liquid used, in home cooking, is water, with some white wine added. In restaurants, where bouillon is always available, this is used instead.

We give here the current home-style recipe for sauerkraut. Depending on the case, it is served with a garnish of meat, as a vegetable, or as plate by itself, known as *choucroute garnie.* In this case, you add sausages of various kinds and bacon, as already mentioned; thus, small, dry, home-style sausages, chipolata sausages, smoked Frankfurt sausages, etc.—whatever you like. At the same time, you can, if you like, serve baked potatoes in their skins, but chose a floury type: the round and red potato from Vosges is particularly good. The flavor of sauerkraut depends on its freshness and its quality. Do not buy it from a merchant who sells only a little a time, and who therefore keeps it in the barrel for too long.

The cooking time for sauerkraut need not be closely observed. In families in eastern Europe, where this is a standard recipe, they estimate that up to *about 5 hours* is needed to ensure the perfect digestibility of the cabbage. *Time: About 5 hours. Serves 6–8.*

1 1/2 kilograms (3 pounds, 5 ounces) of sauerkraut; 250 grams (8 7/8 ounces) of smoked bacon; 500 grams (1 pound, 2 ounces) of salted pork taken from the parts listed above; 175–200 grams (6–7 ounces) of fat; 1/2 liter (generous 2 cups) of white wine; 10 juniper berries.

PROCEDURE. **Washing the sauerkraut:** Although fresh, sauerkraut must always be washed first to rid it of all the brine. Put it in a terrine of fresh water, mix and separate it out, so that each bit is equally soaked. Let it soak there for 15 minutes. Then drain it in a strainer and renew the water 2 or 3 times, until the water is completely clear. Drain it again. Pick it up in small handfuls and squeeze it as tightly as possible to extract all the water from it; there will be a surprising amount that it has retained. As you do this, place each handful on a plate. Finally, separate and spread out in a strainer.

To cook: Put the sauerkraut in a deep casserole with water that comes right up to its level. Add the fat, the juniper berries tied securely in a small piece of cheesecloth, and the white wine. Bring it to a boil. Cover it with a round of strong greased parchment paper placed right on top; close it with the cover as tightly as possible. Preferably cook it in a medium oven and maintain a regular, gentle, small simmer during the time given.

If you do not have an oven, put the casserole on gentle heat; you will simply have to turn over the sauerkraut at least two or three times so that it cooks evenly, given that the part touching the bottom of the casserole will be cooked more strongly than that on top. After 3 hours, add the bacon, the salted pork, and the sausages if using, pressing them down well into the sauerkraut, then recover with the buttered paper and continue cooking for 2 hours. Frankfurters should be cooked separately (SEE PAGE 338), and small chipolata sausages should be added to the sauerkraut 30 minutes before serving.

The sauerkraut should have absorbed all the cooking liquid when it has finished cooking; it should then be just properly moist, fatty (but not excessively so), and nice and unctuous. It is possible that all the liquid will have reduced a little before the end of the cooking period, depending on the rate of boiling, which might sometimes have been a little too strong. For this reason, you should watch it toward the end of the cooking time, so that if you need to, you can add a little bit of liquid. At the most, just a full glass, half water and half wine, added cautiously, in small quantities at a time. You can, without any problem, cook the sauerkraut in two stages. Cook the sauerkraut for only 3 hours, then put it in a faience or earthenware receptacle to keep warm and keep it covered until ready to start cooking again. Bring it to a boil progressively on gentle heat and then add the salt pork, the bacon, etc. Before cooking, the pieces of salt pork must be soaked in frequent changes of cold water for anywhere between 30 minutes and 2 hours, depending on how long they have been in the brine. Generally, charcuterie merchants can advise you how long you will need to soak them, in order to remove the excess salt, which would ruin the dish.

To serve the *choucroute garnie:* Place the sauerkraut on a heated, round plate. (If it seems too fatty, take a skimmer and press it lightly on the top to run off the surplus fat.) Cut the bacon into small, even pieces 1 centimeter (3/8 inch) thick; cut the salted pork into small slices of the same size, and also the sausage. Put them on the sauerkraut and surround everything with small chipolata sausages. Serve the potatoes at the same time.

Fondue *(Fondue au Fromage)*

A regional specialty of the Franche-Comté and of the Swiss Romande, the fondue has variations in both the way it is made and in the cheeses used in its confection. The essential equipment is always a pan-shaped casserole made of earthenware, enameled steel, or special heatproof glass. Also, a wooden fork and a heater with an adjustable flame: while you are eating it, a fondue should maintain a temperature close to boiling, but it is essential that too much of a crust does not form on the bottom of the pan. For some people, a fondue is a meal in itself, and for others it would be a substantial entrée.

We give here a simple recipe of easy execution. *Serves 1.*

150–200 grams (5 1/3–7 ounces) of cheese, either Comté or authentic Gruyère (not Emmenthal, which is twice as thick as Gruyere and has many holes, but which is often sold in France under the name of Gruyère); 1 deciliter (3 1/3 fluid ounces, scant 1/2 cup) of white wine; 1 liqueur glass of kirsch; 1 level teaspoon of flour; 1 clove of garlic; baking soda (bicarbonate of soda), as much as can be held on the point of a knife for the whole fondue.

PROCEDURE. Rub the inside of the pan with the garlic clove. Add the cheese, cut into fine slices, and the white wine (it is sensible to keep a little bit in reserve to dilute the mixture if it gets too thick while cooking; the amount of liquid needed varies with the quality of the cheese). Put the pan on *gentle heat* and mix it continuously with a *wooden* fork—or, if you do not have that, a wooden spoon—by lifting the mixture (never stirring it in a circle) until completely combined. Do not raise the heat to melt the cheese more quickly, because a fondue, just like hollandaise sauce, will "turn" with too strong heat. Boil it gently. Season with pepper and then, while mixing continuously, add the kirsch, in which the flour has been dissolved. Finally, when it has returned to a boil, add the baking soda and mix, then serve immediately, putting the utensil on the heater, placed in the middle of the table. At the same time, serve some large dice of stale bread, which each guest will stick onto the end of a fork and then plunge into the fondue.

If this rustic style of serving does not appeal, follow the Valaisanne fashion and serve potatoes in their skins with the fondue. Each guest peels and cut these into slices on a heated plate, and then a *heated* ladle is used to pour over a portion of fondue. A successful fondue should have the consistency of a perfectly smooth crème anglaise.

Note the local custom of the *coup du milieu* ("the midway shot"), a liqueur glass of kirsch served, as its name indicates, when about half the fondue has been consumed.

Milan-Style Timbale *(Timbale Milanaise)*

This is a pastry shell filled with macaroni to which a garnish *à la financière* has been added, and in which the dominant note is tomato. In classic cuisine, which was richer than today, this garnish was augmented with chicken breasts cooked separately and cut into scallops, then placed on top of everything when it was dressed for serving. These days, generally, this is left out.

In modern cuisine, the timbale shell is generally never eaten, and may even be used several times for similar uses. Why not simply serve the garnish in a silver timbale?

Well, the best way of cooking this dish is in the shell, the aroma of the different elements of the garnish concentrating inside the dough. This is why we give the method here, which was taught by the best masters, Philéas Gilbert among others. It is listed on menus and in the culinary repertoire as "classic timbale," or *timbale à l'ancienne:* whether the timbale shell is cooked like this (with the garnish in it) or *à blanc* (that is, individually, on the side), the initial preparation of the garnish is the same, as is the method of placing it in the timbale. *Time: 3 hours (once the veal sweetbreads have been blanched). Serves 10–12.*

For the timbale shell: **300 grams (10½ ounces) of flour; 175 grams (6 ounces, ¾ cup) of butter; 1 egg; 7 grams (¼ ounce) of fine salt; a little more than 1 deciliter (3⅓ fluid ounces, ½ cup) of water; a timbale mold or a charlotte mold of 13–14 centimeters (5–5½ inches) in diameter and 11 centimeters (4¼ inches) high. And some pasta dough for decoration in the quantities given.**

For the macaroni: **200 grams (7 ounces) of fine macaroni, about 1 centimeter (⅜ inch) in diameter; 60 grams (2¼ ounces) of grated Gruyère and 60 grams (2¼ ounces) of grated Parmesan; 1½ deciliters (5 fluid ounces, ⅔ cup) of tomato purée; 50 grams (1¾ ounces, 3½ tablespoons) of butter; a pinch of salt, a pinch of pepper, and grated nutmeg.**

For the financière garnish: **150 grams (5⅓ ounces) of veal sweetbreads (use the long and less choice part of a small sweetbread); 150 grams (5⅓ ounces) of crests and 50 grams (1¾ ounces) of kidneys from a rooster; 150 grams (5⅓ ounces) of fresh mushrooms; 150 grams (5⅓ ounces) of pickled tongue; 75 grams (2⅔ ounces) of truffles; 2 tablespoons of Madeira.**

3 deciliters (1¼ cups) of tomato-flavored brown sauce, made from: a small mirepoix; plus 20 grams (⅔ ounce) of flour for the roux; 5 deciliters (generous 2 cups) of veal jus; 1 deciliter (3⅓ fluid ounces, scant ½ cup) of white wine; 1 good deciliter (3⅓ fluid ounces, ½ cup) of purée of tomato concentrate; 3 tablespoons of Madeira, added off the heat.

In addition, for dressing the dish: **1 deciliter (3⅓ fluid ounces, scant ½ cup) of tomato purée; 3–4 tablespoons of bouillon; 20 grams (⅔ ounce, 1 heaping tablespoon) of butter.**

PROCEDURE. This varies depending on the skill of the person making it. A professional would get the sauce underway and prepare all the elements for the garnish and would then have the time, while the macaroni was cooking, to work the pastry—always made well in advance—into the cap, or *calotte,* and then decorate the mold and fill it. But this would be too much for many people, no matter how skilled they were. Simply line the timbale at the most convenient moment, so that it is ready when you need to fill it with the garnish.

It is essential to put a timbale in the oven *as soon as it is filled.* If not, the garnish would soften the dough. To cook the timbale, allow *1 scant hour.* So note the order of the menu and put it into the oven so that it will be ready when it is due to be served. It can stand for a few minutes in a very mild oven.

You should proceed as directed (SEE CRUSTS OF TIMBALE, PAGE 671). First make the cap with the *pâte à foncer,* then use the pasta dough to decorate the inside of the mold. Put in the cap of dough. Gather the trimmings and flatten them into a pancake 16 centimeters (6¼ inches) in diameter by 5 millimeters (3/16 inch) thick.

The garnish: Begin by preparing the *financière* garnish, its preparation taking much longer than the macaroni, which requires only 20 minutes.

Follow the directions for beginning cooking the sauce, as well as for preparing the mushrooms, crests, kidneys, etc. (SEE FINANCIÈRE GARNISH, PAGE 457). The veal sweetbreads, here previously blanched, are cooked with a little bit of bouillon (about 1 1/2 deciliters, 5 fluid ounces, 2/3 cup) for *25 minutes.*

The tongue. Cut into slices barely 1/2 centimeter (3/16 inch) thick, then cut with a pastry cutter into rounds of 2 1/2 centimeters (1 inch) in diameter.

The truffles. Cut into slices 1/2 centimeter (3/16 inch) thick. Reserve 12–15 of the most attractive for decorating; keep them in a small receptacle with a little bit of their cooking juice and 2 tablespoons of Madeira. Add the rest to the rounds of tongue.

The macaroni. Break them into fragments 5–6 centimeters (2–2 1/4 inches) long and cook them as directed (SEE PAGE 565).

To finish the garnish; to fill and cook the timbale: At this point, 2 casseroles are essential: before being added to the timbale, the macaroni must be separate from the financière.

The macaroni. Drain thoroughly. Put them in a sauté pan without adding anything yet; sauté them on the heat to first evaporate any moisture, which would impede their liaison with the sauce. Season with a pinch of pepper and 2 grams (1/14 ounce) of grated nutmeg and add the Gruyère and Parmesan. Melt them, stirring carefully, using a fork. Then add the tomato purée and the butter, divided into small pieces. Stir it over very gentle heat.

The financière. In another casserole, combine: the veal sweetbread, previously cut into fine scallops; the mushrooms, crests, and kidneys, all well drained; the rounds of tongue and the slices of truffle, except those reserved for the final decoration.

Then add to the sauce, reduced now to 3 deciliters (1 1/4 cups), the rest of the Madeira; taste for a final seasoning. Then pour it, straining it one more time, onto the above ingredients. Toss everything for a moment to mix it.

You can now *fill* the timbale. This operation must be done very quickly so that the heat of the garnish does not have time to soften the crust before putting it in the oven.

Pour three-quarters of the macaroni into the timbale. Make a space in the middle with a fork. In this space, pour the sauced *financière.* Cover with the rest of the macaroni. Moisten the borders of the timbale. Put the cover of prepared dough on top. Fasten it; trim the excess dough. Make a hole in the middle so that the steam can escape.

Put it in the oven immediately—an oven hot enough for roasting red meat. The heat should be even throughout the cooking period. Allow 1 scant hour: thus, *50–55 minutes.*

Dressing the timbale: A few moments before taking the timbale out of the oven, put the tomato purée diluted with the bouillon and seasoned with salt and pepper into a small casserole. Bring it to a gentle simmer. Add butter to it only when you are about to use it.

To unmold the timbale, put a serving plate on top of the mold and turn it over. Thus, *the bottom of the timbale becomes the cover* and the round of dough placed on the timbale to cover the garnish is now on the plate, forming the bottom of the timbale.

With the point of a knife, trim around the bottom (now the top) to detach it from the shell. Divide it into triangles and arrange these around the timbale on the plate. Spread the tomato sauce onto the exposed macaroni. Make a circle with the reserved truffles on top of this. Serve immediately.

Financière Garnish
(Garniture à la Financière)

Classic and traditional, this garnish has numerous uses: either to accompany meats, fowl, and game or to garnish the shell of a vol-au-vent, a timbale, or a border of rice—or "a rice casserole," as it is known in traditional cuisine. A traditional financière garnish includes: dumplings, mushrooms, rooster's crests and kidneys, sweetbreads of veal or lamb, truffles, often olives. The sauce is always a brown sauce made with Madeira, known as a "demi-glace."

It is worth noting that the size of the ingredients of the garnish corresponds to their use. For example, dumplings will be smaller for a fowl, for veal sweetbreads, and for a vol-au-vent than for a large fillet of beef. The same will be true for the mushrooms.

The ingredients for stuffing the dumplings must also be modified according to use. Veal is the usual ingredient, but without changing the actual quantity of meat used, it is replaced by chicken meat to accompany fowl or by pheasant or partridge meat for feathered game.

When you do not want to go to the expense of truffles, you can leave out truffling the dumplings. Instead, use a little jar of truffle peelings, mincing them finely and then mixing them into the stuffing.

Let us also remark that for a *financière* garnish, brains should not replace veal sweetbreads, which some people do for reasons of economy. *Time: 2 hours (once the veal sweetbreads have been blanched and the dumplings prepared). Serves 12.*

25 small dumplings (PAGE 461); 12 small scallops of veal sweetbreads; 250 grams (8 7/8 ounces) of small mushrooms; 200 grams (7 ounces) of rooster's crests and 100 grams (3 1/2 ounces) of kidneys (or, if you are using preserved ones, a 1/2-liter/2 cup jar or can); 2 dozen olives; 3 small, fresh truffles and 1 1/2 deciliters (5 fluid ounces, 2/3 cup) of white wine or Madeira to cook them (or a 1/4 liter/1 cup jar or can); 7 deciliters (3 cups) of sauce, ready to serve, made from: 5 deciliters (generous 2 cups) of *reduced* brown sauce, 1 1/2 deciliters (5 fluid ounces, 2/3 cup) of cooking juice from the truffles; 4 tablespoons of excellent Madeira.

PROCEDURE. **The sauce:** Prepare as directed (SEE BROWN SAUCE, PAGE 50), anticipating that the addition of the truffle juice and Madeira will dilute it, as explained in the recipe for Madeira sauce. To ensure that the amount of flour in the roux remains the same—that is, 5 or 6 grams (1/6–1/5 ounce) for each deciliter (3 1/3 fluid ounces, scant 1/2 cup) of sauce—you must reduce the brown sauce. So take 7 deciliters (3 cups) of brown sauce, and boil strongly to reduce the quantity to *5 deciliters (generous 2 cups),* before adding the truffle juice and the Madeira.

The dumplings: Preferably the stuffing should have been prepared the evening before, so you have nothing left to do but make the dumplings the same day (SEE PAGE 461). About 20 minutes before putting together the garnish elements, you should poach them as directed.

The crests and the kidneys: Prepare them as directed (SEE CRESTS AND KIDNEYS, PAGE 356).

The sweetbreads: These will have been braised in advance as for sweetbreads *à blanc* (SEE PAGE 303); or simply gently cooked with a little bit of bouillon for *25 minutes.*

The olives: SEE OLIVES FOR GARNISH, PAGE 22.

The mushrooms: Only the heads are used. If these are not small enough, cut them after cooking into 2 or 4, depending on their size. Cook the mushrooms as directed (SEE MUSHROOMS FOR GARNISH, PAGE 490).

The truffles: Peel them as directed. Cut them into rounds 3–4 millimeters (about 1/8 inch) thick. Cook them (SEE PAGE 537).

Once the sauce has reduced sufficiently, take it off the heat, then add the Madeira, the cooking juice from the truffles, or the juice from the can, if using preserved truffles. This tops up the sauce to the right amount.

Drain the ingredients for the garnish and put them into a deep casserole with high sides, then strain the sauce onto them, through a chinois. Simmer it for 5 minutes, but *without boiling,* because of the Madeira. Then keep it in a double boiler until ready to serve, as directed (SEE KEEPING SAUCES WARM, PAGE 50).

Milan-Style Garnish
(Garniture à la Milanaise)

This is the garnish used for meats, particularly veal: breaded and sautéed chops, grenadins, braised fillets, sweetbreads, stuffed scallops, etc. Its preparation is simple and it provides a plate that is both substantial and elegant.

If you do not have Parmesan cheese, it can be replaced by the same quantity of Gruyère: thus, a total of 125 grams (4 1/2 ounces). Always use cheese of the finest quality. For an ordinary meal, the truffle can be omitted. Or, if using it and you wish to display it, do not mix it with the other ingredients but place it on top of the garnish; cut it, then heat it with 1 tablespoon of Madeira and the same amount of bouillon. *Time: 40 minutes. Serves 6.*

200 grams (7 ounces) of fine macaroni no larger than 1/2 centimeter (3/16 inch) in diameter; 60 grams (2 1/4 ounces) of pickled tongue or half tongue and half lean, cooked ham; 30 grams (1 ounce) of cooked mushroom; a truffle, 30–35 grams (1–1 1/4 ounces) (optional); 2 tablespoons of purée of tomato concen-

trate; 60 grams (2$^1/_4$ ounces) of grated Gruyère cheese and 60 grams (2$^1/_4$ ounces) of grated Parmesan cheese; 60 grams (2$^1/_4$ ounces, 4$^1/_2$ tablespoons) of butter; salt, pepper, nutmeg.

PROCEDURE. **The macaroni:** Put a 2-liter (8$^1/_2$-cup) saucepan on the heat, and in it bring 1$^1/_2$ liters (6$^1/_3$ cups) of water to a boil, salted with 15 grams ($^1/_2$ ounce) of salt. Gather the sticks of macaroni by 5 or 6 and plunge them into the depth of the casserole so that they soften in contact with the boiling liquid and *do not break.* Once the water has returned to a boil, turn down the heat. From this point, allow it to boil gently. This could take from *10–20 minutes,* depending on the macaroni. The macaroni should be firm rather than overcooked—in other words, *al dente.*

Once cooked, drain in a colander. Put them on a towel spread out on a table. Arrange the sticks one next to the other, so that with one cut of the knife you can cut them into pieces 4 centimeters (1$^1/_2$ inches) long. Put this macaroni into a sauté pan large enough so that the macaroni will not be too piled up.

The julienne: This complements the garnish and should be prepared while the macaroni is cooking. Cut the tongue and the ham, if using, into a fine julienne: that is, into pieces 2–3 centimeters ($^3/_4$–1$^1/_4$ inches thick) and 3 centimeters (1$^1/_4$ inches) long.

Also cut the cooked mushrooms (SEE MUSHROOMS FOR GARNISHES, PAGE 490). The length of the pieces is determined by the size of the mushrooms, but they must be the same thickness as the tongue. Also cut the truffle. Mix together all the ingredients on a plate.

The liaison of the garnish: Season the macaroni with salt, pepper, and grated nutmeg. Add about one-third of the butter. Heat it, tossing the casserole. When the macaroni is *very hot,* sprinkle it with the cheese. After this, turn the heat down and mix it with a fork to melt and mix the cheese; but take care not to break the macaroni.

Then add the purée of tomato and the julienne. Toss the macaroni to mix, or use a fork. Finally, add the rest of the butter, divided into pieces. Keep it warm without letting it boil any further.

Toulouse Garnish
(Garniture à la Toulousaine)

The ingredients are about the same as for the financière. The difference is the sauce, which is brown for the financière, and white or velouté for the toulousaine, is bound with egg yolks and known as "Parisienne sauce." The various uses of the Toulouse garnish are equally numerous, and can be applied to all white meats, fowl, vol-au-vent, rice borders, duchesse potatoes, tomatoes, etc.

The same is true for these dumplings as is true for *financière* dumplings: for vol-au-vent or veal sweetbreads, the dumplings are made with veal. For a fowl, you should, of course, use fowl meat. But the need for economy often intervenes, and sometimes the rule must be renounced.

Use the same ingredients, leaving out the olives, and the same quantities as for the *financière* garnish. 7 deciliters (3 cups) of Parisienne sauce (SEE PAGE 52).

PROCEDURE. For the different elements of the garnish, proceed as directed for the *financière* garnish. If you are using veal sweetbreads, these should be braised without coloring (SEE PAGE 303). Start the sauce a good 1$^1/_2$ hours in advance; butter it and pass it through the chinois onto the garnish. Keep it warm in a double boiler.

Jardinière Garnish
(Garniture à la Jardinière)

The true jardinière garnish to accompany cuts of meat or other foods requires a specific dressing for each one of its elements. That is, all the ingredients must not only be separately cooked, but must also be separately bound and then arranged in their own groups around the piece they are garnishing. For this reason, each vegetable requires its own saucepan, but in a kitchen that is not well supplied with small saucepans, you may not have all the cooking utensils you need. If so, we suggest mixing the ingredients and placing this mixture in groups separated by cauliflower florets; all things being equal, the effect will be the same. *Time: 1 hour, 30 minutes. Serves 12–15.*

100 grams (3$^1/_2$ ounces) of carrots and 100 grams (3$^1/_2$ ounces) of turnips, net weight; 125 grams (4$^1/_2$ ounces) of fresh green peas; 100 grams (3$^1/_2$ ounces) of green

beans; 100 grams (3½ ounces) of small, green flageolets; and a head of cauliflower, very white, weighing about 400 grams (14⅛ ounces); ½ liter (generous 2 cups) of bouillon, very lightly salted, to cook the carrots and turnips; 125 grams of butter (4½ ounces, 9 tablespoons) for the liaison of the peas and beans; 2½ deciliters (1 cup) of béchamel sauce to cover the cauliflower florets: thus, 15 grams (½ ounce, 1 tablespoon) of butter and 10 grams (⅓ ounce) of flour for the white roux; 3 deciliters (1¼ cups) of boiled milk, a bouquet of parsley sprigs, grated nutmeg, and salt and pepper.

PROCEDURE. You can cook all of the ingredients at the same time. Here, we obviously have to list one thing at a time, but you do not have to follow this order.

The carrots: These can be prepared in advance and then kept in cool water.

Clean and peel them, then cut them into pieces 2 centimeters (¾ inch) thick and arrange on a towel that is folded in quarters. Use a steel corer 3 millimeters (⅛ inch) in diameter. Push it through to the bottom of each piece of carrot so that you remove a small cork-shaped cylinder of carrot. Do this again immediately next to it. Cut each cylinder of carrot as close as possible to the previous one, leaving the least amount of space possible between the holes. When the corer is full of little cylinders of carrot, empty them into a terrine of cool water and continue the same way until you have the right amount of little cylinders—that is, 100 grams (3½ ounces).

Put these little rounds into a small casserole with 2½ deciliters (1 cup) of bouillon, 25 grams (1 ounce, 2 tablespoons) of butter, and a piece of ordinary sugar. Bring it to a boil and let it boil rather quickly until the liquid combines with the butter and the sugar is reduced to a thick syrup. The carrots cook as the liquid reduces. Once the carrots have been cooked, keep them on the side until you have finished the garnish.

The turnips: You can also cut these in advance, keeping them with the prepared carrots. Cook exactly the same way, but leave out the sugar, since the turnip is already sugary.

The green peas, the green beans, and the flageolets: These are cooked separately; and, if you like, one by one in the same utensil, but renew the water for each vegetable. Proceed as directed (SEE COOKING FRESH VEGETABLES, PAGE 470). Do not chill them. Drain them thoroughly and reserve them on a plate. To prepare the *green beans,* simply break the ends before plunging them into boiling water. Make sure they are not overcooked but remain slightly firm; after cooking, they are cut into small, even size diamond shapes.

The cauliflower: Divide it into medium-size florets, about a dozen, then remove the stem close to the head. Remove the little leaves from the inside. As you prepare each floret, put it into cool water that has been lightly vinegared. Then boil the cauliflower in a casserole containing 1½ liters (6⅓ cups) of boiling water and 15 grams (½ ounce) of salt. Cook rapidly and keep the florets slightly firm, then keep them warm in the pan of cooking water.

The béchamel sauce: Prepare this as directed (SEE PAGE 52) in a very small casserole and then cook on very gentle heat.

To finish the garnish: *About 5 minutes before serving,* strain the béchamel sauce through a fine chinois into another small casserole. Keep it warm.

In a sauté pan, assemble: the carrots and the turnips, taking them out with a pierced spoon or a small skimmer; then the green peas, the green beans cut into diamonds, and the flageolets. Season with a pinch of fine salt and a pinch of superfine sugar. Sauté these vegetables over strong heat for a few minutes, in order to heat them. Completely evaporate any remaining moisture. Dry them well; take them off the heat and add the rest the butter—that is, 60 grams (2¼ ounces, 4½ tablespoons) divided into pieces. Once the butter has been well stirred in, add *2–3 generous tablespoons* of béchamel sauce to the vegetables to complete the mixture; they do not have to go back on the heat.

Dressing the plate: Place the cut of meat on the serving plate. Drain the cauliflower in a colander.

Add the vegetables to the plate, arranging them more or less in heaps, using a soupspoon and scooping out *3 tablespoons* for each pile: so, in all, about 12 bouquets or piles, 6 on each side of the fillet or other cut. For a pleasing effect, make sure you arrange them regularly and at equal distance one from the other. Between each bouquet of vegetables, put a cauliflower floret and cover with 1/2 tablespoon of béchamel sauce. Serve.

Dumplings for Garnishes *(Quenelles pour Garniture)*

A large mortar with a good wooden pestle is the essential utensil for this recipe. If you have a small mechanical grinder, pass the meat through it first, which will make it much easier to grind in the mortar. But in any case, it must be worked in the mortar, because this alone can bind the different elements together and give the stuffing the finesse that is so essential. Also necessary is a good metallic drum sieve, made of fine wire, and, for fish stuffing, a drum sieve made of horsehair or linen.

In terms of the quantity of meat or fish needed, you should anticipate some inevitable waste in the purchase of meat or fish whose net weight is given under "quantities," particularly when you use a mechanical grinder for the meat, which always traps something in its gears; hence, the amounts listed are net weights. Except for fish dumplings, it is better to prepare the stuffing the evening before its use.

Small dumplings for garnishes are molded by hand with a spoon or with a pastry bag. The same is true for large dumplings, or they can be made in molds of tinned steel, shaped like a half egg. But here we are concerned only with dumplings for garnishes.

Dumplings for Financière, Toulousaine, Etc. *(Quenelles pour Financière, Toulousaine, Etc.).* *Time: About 1 hour. Makes 25 dumplings.*

175 grams (6 ounces) of round of veal, net weight, trimmed of all excess and fat; 100 grams (3 1/2 ounces) of breading made with flour (that is, 4 tablespoons of water, 10 grams/1/3 ounce/1 scant tablespoon of butter, 30 grams/1 ounce of flour); 50 grams (1 3/4 ounces, 3 1/2 tablespoons) of butter; 3 egg yolks; a pinch of salt, a small pinch of pepper, and some grated nutmeg.

PROCEDURE. Prepare the breading as directed (SEE BREADING FOR STUFFINGS, PAGE 21). Spread it out on a plate and chill it completely.

Cut the veal into large cubes. Pound them in a mortar into an extremely fine paste, with salt, pepper, and nutmeg. Then add the chilled breading. Grind it again to mix it well. (When you are working on large quantities, crush the meat and the breading separately before combining them. The paste is finer this way and it takes less time.) Add the butter, and then the egg yolks, one after the other, constantly working the mass with the mortar as you do so.

Pass through the fine metallic drum sieve. Put the stuffing in a small terrine, working it for a moment with the wooden spoon to combine completely and make it nice and smooth. Next, poach 1 piece of stuffing about the size of a walnut in a small casserole, to check the seasoning and the degree of firmness. If the *quenelle* is not firm enough after poaching, add a little bit of egg to the stuffing, which will give it the necessary support.

Prepared thus, the stuffing can wait until the next day, covered with a buttered parchment paper and kept cool. Then mold the *quenelle* using one of the methods described below. You can mold them 1 hour in advance and keep them as above in a cool spot, covered with the buttered paper until you are ready to poach them.

Fish Dumplings for Garnishes *(Quenelles de Poisson pour Garnitures).* The fish generally used is either whiting or hake, or for freshwater fish, pike. *Time: 45 minutes. Makes about 2 dozen dumplings.*

150 grams (5 1/3 ounces) of *uncooked* fish, net weight, without skin or bones; 89–100 grams (about 2 3/4–3 1/2 ounces) of breading; 75 grams (2 2/3 ounces, 1/3 cup) of butter; 2 egg yolks; a small egg white; 5 grams (1/6 ounce) of salt; a pinch of pepper and grated nutmeg; 2–3 tablespoons of thick cream.

If you like, make the breading with flour or bread crumbs: the latter produces a finer and lighter stuffing.

With flour: 1/2 deciliter (1 2/3 fluid ounces, scant 1/4 cup) of water, 10 grams (1/3 ounce) of flour; 30 grams (1 ounce, 2 tablespoons) of butter.

With bread crumbs: 4 tablespoons of boiling milk; 45–50 grams (1 1/2–1 3/4 ounces) of stale white bread crumbs. For both, proceed as directed (SEE BREADING FOR STUFFINGS, PAGE 21).

PROCEDURE. Prepare the breading and chill it completely. Remove all the skin and bones from the fish. If some of the skin and bones are missed, they will later be retained by the drum sieve. Cut the flesh into large cubes and grind them in the mortar to a very fine paste with salt, pepper, and nutmeg. (Avoid directly touching the mortared flesh of the fish with your hand, because you may spoil it.) Then add the breading. Add the butter, the egg whites, and the yolks. Pass through a horsehair drum sieve.

For a fine dumpling, the stuffing must be a rather soft consistency. However, if it is too soft, the dumplings will burst during cooking; that is why it is a good idea before adding the cream to test it by poaching a walnut-sized piece. Depending on the result, add all or part of the cream, little by little, constantly and vigorously working the paste, because this helps the paste to absorb the cream and makes it lighter.

Then keep the stuffing in a cool place for at least 1 hour if you cannot refrigerate. It can stand for much longer without spoiling. Mold the dumplings using one of the methods described below. The poaching takes *10 minutes.*

Godivau for Dumplings *(Godivau pour Quenelles).* An ancient and unchanging garnish for vol-au-vents and tourtes (tarts), the *godivau* differs from other stuffings because it is made with a very large amount of beef fat: it also invariably contains lean veal and raw eggs. The preparatory steps can vary slightly, the goal being to keep the ground fat in the right state for cohesion. Once it has been worked as required, it has the consistency of a more or less homogenous pomade, and this, particularly in summer, tends to both liquefy and granulate at the same time. We will describe below the most practical way to counter this effect, which involves using a little bit of breading.

A *godivau* must be prepared well in advance, preferably the evening before. A long rest in a cool place is essential before working the stuffing so that it is firm enough to be made into dumplings. Poach or cook in boiling water, like all other dumplings; or cook it dry, in a gentle oven, which is considered the best way by professional chefs. *Time: 1 hour. Makes about 30 dumplings.*

125 grams (4 1/2 ounces) of veal, net weight; 200 grams (7 ounces) of fat from the beef kidney, *quite dry,* net weight (after all the nerves, skin, and so forth have been carefully removed); 6 grams (1/5 ounce) of salt, and a pinch of pepper and grated nutmeg; 2 small whole eggs; 1 deciliter (3 1/3 fluid ounces, scant 1/2 cup) of milk, 10 grams (1/3 ounce, 1 scant tablespoon) of butter and 25 grams (1 ounce) of flour for the breading.

PROCEDURE. Prepare the breading. Cut the veal into large cubes. Break the fat into small pieces; remove its skin and even the smallest fibers. Put the veal into the mortar with salt, pepper, and nutmeg, and crush it into an extremely fine paste. Then add the fat and crush it similarly; then the chilled breading; then crush everything together; add an egg, beaten in a bowl as if for an omelet. Grind it until it is completely mixed and then add the second egg.

When thoroughly mixed, it will be the same color throughout and you will not be able to make out the various ingredients, so pass it through a metallic drum sieve. Gather the stuffing on a plate. Spread it out in a thin layer; cover it with buttered parchment paper. Keep it cool.

Molding and Poaching the Dumplings *(Moulage et Pochage des Quenelles).*

1. **Molding by hand:** Divide the dough into parts the size of an egg; on a floured board, roll each part into a sausage shape the size of your thumb. With a knife, cut each sausage into small pieces resembling large hard candies that weigh about 12–15 grams (3/8–1/2 ounce). With your fingers dipped in flour, roll each small piece again to make equal shapes the size of a small, elongated cork. As you do this, arrange them on a large cover of a casserole that has been turned over and sprinkled with flour or on a flat cooking sheet that has also been floured. If you do not poach the dumplings immediately, keep them cool.

Poaching. In a large sauté pan, in order to have a large surface, boil water that has been salted with 8 grams (1/3 ounce) per liter. Slide in the dumplings. Do not add more than will cover the bottom of the casserole without touching too closely, bearing in mind that they will swell when they poach.

As soon as the water comes back to a boil, turn down the heat; cover and keep the liquid at a simple simmer, for 10–15 minutes, the time depending on the composition of the dumplings. It is better to cook for a little more than a little less time; as soon as they are firm to the touch, take them out with a skimmer and carefully drain them on a kitchen towel before putting them in the sauce.

2. **Molding with a spoon:** If you do not have a heatproof dish large enough and deep enough to hold the dumplings side by side without touching, completely covered with water, replace it with a sauté pan. Butter the bottom. Meanwhile, have at hand 2 teaspoons, a small knife, and a bowl of warm water.

   Put the heatproof dish in front of you. Fill one of the small spoons with the stuffing with the spoon held in your *right hand.* Pass it, filled, into *the left hand.* With the blade of a knife held in your *right hand,* smooth out the stuffing that spills over the edge of the spoon into a dome shape. Next, take the second teaspoon in your right hand; dip it in the warm water and then slide it under the stuffing in the full spoon to detach the dumpling from it, then immediately place it in the buttered dish.

Poaching. After molding all the dumplings like this, pour boiling salted water into the heatproof dish or sauté pan, completely covering the dumplings. Keep the dish on very gentle heat to maintain the liquid at a gentle simmer, and poach for the same time.

3. **Molding with the pastry bag:** Put the stuffing into a pastry bag equipped with a nozzle 1/2 centimeter (3/16 inch) in diameter. Or, if you do not have that, make a large paper cone and cut off the pointed end with scissors. Dress the dumplings in a buttered receptacle as above, manipulating the pastry bag as directed (SEE PAGE 15). Poach as above.

4. **Dry poaching:** For a *godiveau,* the dumplings should be molded *by hand* as directed, so that each is an average weight of 15 grams (1/2 ounce). As you make them, put them on a baking sheet covered with sheets of white buttered parchment paper, so that they do not touch each other. Put it in a very moderate oven. Allow *about 10 minutes* for this kind of poaching. The dumplings are done when the fat lightly sweats in small drops, and when the dumplings are elastic to the touch. Take them out of the oven and allow them to cool on the paper if you are not going to use them immediately.

SALADS
Salades

Salads fall into two categories: simple salads and mixed salads.

For simple salads, we mean those that have only one single element, with nothing else added: green salads like lettuce, chicory, etc., as well as salads of potatoes, fresh and dried beans, lentils, cauliflower, etc.

Mixed salads combine different ingredients: Russian salad is one example. The series of mixed salads is infinite, varying only according to what your imagination, taste, and available ingredients can make from combinations that are more or less sensible or bizarre.

Generally speaking, the ingredients that most often play a supporting role in mixed salads are potato, celeriac (celery root), raw or cooked tomato, beet, and hard-boiled egg. Beside these, you can also include: artichoke bottoms, cooked or raw; raw Belgian endive, Chinese artichoke, salsify, rice, macaroni, cooked or raw mushrooms, anchovies, herring, shrimp, caviar, salmon, tuna, poached oysters, mussels, crayfish tails, apples, nuts, cucumbers, bell peppers, bananas, etc. And let us not forget truffles! For these salads, your imagination has a free run.

Some of these salads, such as Russian salad, are classics. But any ingredients can be combined in a salad, and when given a name, this usually has a contemporary relevance, whether private or public.

Seasoning simple salads: Strictly speaking, this includes only oil, vinegar, salt, and pepper. And on this subject, the popular axiom is worth repeating here: "It takes four men to make a salad: a prodigal for the oil, a miser for the vinegar, a wise man for the salt, and a madman for the pepper." For current tastes, this translates as 3 tablespoons of oil for 1 tablespoon of good medium-strength vinegar; 7–8 grams ($^1/_4$–$^1/_3$ ounce) of salt and a pinch of pepper. The generosity of this "pinch" naturally depends on personal preferences.

The addition of herbs and condiments goes beyond seasoning, in the strict sense of the word. These are frequently added but are subject to individual tastes as well as availability and the type of salad.

The chopped herbs that can be added to simple salads, particularly lettuce salad, are: chervil, tarragon, chive, burnet, and marjoram. Quarters of hard-boiled egg placed on a salad are also popular.

It should be noted that the quantities given above are an average only, and there are times when the vinegar can be increased or reduced: not only because of its strength, but also according to the salad ingredients, or when mustard, wine, or lemon juice is added to the seasoning, or has been used as a preliminary marinade.

Seasoning mixed salad: Depending on the case, season in the same way as simple salad, or use a mayonnaise. Everything that has been said about simple salads is equally true for mixed salads. The mayonnaise used in salads should be fairly light, and it, according to the nature of the ingredients of the salad, can have mustard, tomatoes, and even crème fraîche added to it. These last elements will affect its consistency, so if you are just using it *nature* ("as is"), make it looser with a little bit of warm water (SEE MAYONNAISE SAUCE, PAGE 76).

For mixing and seasoning the different elements of a salad, we recommend always working in a terrine or a kitchen bowl, then pouring the salad into the bowl that you will use for serving. This means that the serving bowl will arrive at the table with clean and shining edges.

Potato Salad
(Salade de Pommes de Terre)

Time: 45 minutes.

Generally eaten cold, potato salad is preferred, by some people when it is rather hot, or at least lukewarm, especially in the winter. But it must always be seasoned while *hot:* this enables the seasoning to better penetrate the potato.

For two reasons, you should choose the Vitelotte potato or, if you cannot, new potatoes with an elongated shape: first, so that you can cut rounds that will not be too large and can remain whole; and second, because this kind of potato is less fragile and will not turn so rapidly to mush.

When you have a steamer, you can cook the potatoes in it without peeling them, but they should have been carefully washed first. Otherwise, put them in a casserole, covered with cold water, and then cover with a cloth that has been folded over several times, placing it directly on top of the potatoes. Cook them on moderate heat for about *a half hour.* Drain and immediately peel the potatoes while they are still burning hot. Cut them into rounds $^1/_4$ centimeter (less than $^1/_8$ inch) thick, and as you cut them, put them into a kitchen salad bowl.

The seasoning should be ready in a separate bowl, on the side. Prepare this in advance using the following quantities for every 750 grams (1 pound, 10 ounces) of potatoes: 4 tablespoons of olive oil and 1 tablespoon of vinegar; 2 tablespoons of white or red wine (the quality of this wine will affect the quality of the salad); 3 or 4 tablespoons of cold bouillon or water; 1 teaspoon of salt and a good pinch of freshly milled pepper. Add: 1 tablespoon of minced parsley, and, if you like it, a bit of chive, also minced; and when in season, some chervil and tarragon. The mustard is optional but by no means "classic."

Then beat everything together to mix it and baste the potatoes with it, which should be as hot as possible. To spread the seasoning through the salad, toss it, turning it over carefully with a fork or a spoon. There must be no excess liquid at the bottom of the salad bowl. The potatoes should have absorbed everything, and should be shiny and tender.

Just before serving, pour the salad into the service salad bowl.

Another procedure: Peel and slice the burning-hot potatoes. Marinate them with about 10 tablespoons of wine, preferably white wine, per 450 grams (1 pound) of potatoes. Then season them as you ordinarily do: that is, with oil, vinegar, and chopped herbs. Mix carefully so that you do not break the slices.

Alsatian Salad *(Salade Alsacienne)*

This is taken from the precious notebook of recipes belonging to an old Alsatian family. The potato is puréed and makes up half the weight of the salad ingredients (not including the seasoning, of course). This salad is an authentic dish that is both original and nourishing. Serve it at room temperature. *Time: 30 minutes. Serves 6.*

500 grams (1 pound, 2 ounces) of nice potatoes with a yellowish pulp and quite farinaceous, weighed when cooked; 125 grams (4 1/2 ounces) of smoked ham; 75 grams (2 2/3 ounces) of sausage from Lorraine (or, if you do not have it, sausage from Cervelas); 75 grams (2 2/3 ounces) of pickled tongue; 60 grams (2 1/4 ounces) of beet; 1 salted anchovy; 30 grams (1 ounce) of cornichons; 30 grams (1 ounce) of capers; 2 hard-boiled eggs; 1 tablespoon of minced parsley.

***For the seasoning:* 3 tablespoons of vinegar; 3 tablespoons of red or white wine; 1 tablespoon of hot water; 6 tablespoons of olive oil; salt and pepper.**

PROCEDURE. Peel the potatoes. For a weight of 500 grams (1 pound, 2 ounces) when cooked, allow about 750 grams (1 pound, 10 ounces) uncooked and peeled. Cut them into 2 or 4, depending on how large the potatoes are, and make sure that all the pieces are the same size. This is very important to ensure even cooking. Wash them; put them in a casserole; cover them with cold water *(1 liter, 4 1/4 cups)*, and add 10 grams (1/3 ounce) of salt. Maintain a sustained boiling for *about 15 minutes.* These must be cooked to perfection, and you can tell when that point has been reached because a cooking needle easily penetrates the pieces.

Drain all the cooking water (which can be used for a soup) by tilting the casserole three-quarters of the way and using the cover to keep the potatoes inside. Put the casserole, still covered, in a very moderate oven. Allow the potatoes to finish cooking in their own steam and progressively dry out in this manner for about 10 minutes: a little more or less, depending on the heat of the oven.

While the potatoes are cooking and drying, prepare the different salad ingredients.

The eggs: once these have been hard-boiled and shelled, cut them into fine rounds.

The anchovies: wash them, scrape them off, and remove the bone. Mince them fine.

The sausage, the tongue, and the ham: remove the skin and rinds; mince them fine.

The beet: peel it, and cut it into thin slices. *The cornichons:* cut into thin slices.

Assemble all these elements in a terrine that is big enough to hold the potatoes. Add the minced parsley and the capers.

Once the potatoes have dried out, pass them through a metallic drum sieve placed over a clean towel (SEE TO PASS PURÉES, PAGE 14). Proceed quickly, as much to make the job easier as to obtain a snowy purée that is still warm and that will better absorb the seasoning.

Weigh it so that you have no more than is needed. Add it to all the ingredients in the terrine. Immediately add the seasoning. The salt is calculated by the degree of saltiness of the ham and the tongue. The amount of pepper depends on how peppery the sausage is, but a substantial quantity is always required. Then add the wine, the vinegar, the warm water, and, lastly, the oil.

Toss the salad well. Serve it in a salad bowl that has been lightly heated, and serve on warm plates.

Beef Salad *(Salade de Boeuf)*

When you do not have fresh tomatoes, these can be replaced by a good preserved purée that has first been mixed with the seasoning. *Time: 40 minutes. Serves 6.*

200 grams (7 ounces) of boiled beef, net weight; the same weight (200 grams/7 ounces) of small, boiled, peeled potatoes; 150 grams (5 1/3 ounces) of tomatoes, net weight (without their water or their seeds); 60 grams (2 1/4 ounces) of watercress leaves without their stems; 2 hard-boiled eggs; 10 grams (1/3 ounce) of salt; 1 tablespoon of vinegar; 4 tablespoons of oil; and 1 tablespoon of minced tarragon and chervil. Pepper and, if you like, the amount of cayenne pepper that can be held on the point of a knife.

PROCEDURE. Cut the *beef* into small slices a little less than 1/2 centimeter (3/16 inch) thick. Remove all the fatty, muscular, and grayish parts. Cut the *potatoes* the same way. We suggest choosing small potatoes so that the rounds are the right size; they will crumble if their diameter is too large. Plunge the *tomato* into boiling water for *1 minute,* then peel it. Divide it into 4 parts. Eliminate the water and the seeds. Cut the pulp into small pieces. Cut the *hard-boiled eggs* into thin rounds.

Once everything has been well chilled, combine the different ingredients in a terrine to season them and to mix the salad. Then turn it, more or less casually, into the salad serving bowl.

Beef Salad with Tomatoes *(Salade de Boeuf aux Tomates).* Here, the beef is very much a feature of this dish, cut into lovely slices no thicker than 3 millimeters (1/8 inch). For this preparation, you must thus have a piece that is large enough, and firm enough, to cut small oval or rectangular slices from it, each weighing about 15–20 grams (1/2–2/3 ounce). You should allow 4–5 slices per person. *Time: 40 minutes. Serves 6.*

6–8 small potatoes, each weighing about 50 grams (1 3/4 ounces); 1 1/2 deciliters (5 fluid ounces, 2/3 cup) of good white wine and 1 tablespoon of oil to marinate them; 3–4 small tomatoes about the size of a peach; 1 fresh onion; 1 good tablespoon of minced chervil; oil, vinegar, and salt and pepper.

PROCEDURE. Quickly cook the potatoes in salted water (20 minutes). As soon as they are cooked, peel them, then cut them into regular rounds and put them in a salad bowl. While they are still burning hot, season with a pinch of salt and a pinch of pepper. Sprinkle them with the white wine and the oil. Move them around from time to time so that they will have absorbed the liquid ingredients by the time they have cooled.

Cut the *beef* as directed. Cut the tomatoes *into slices* as thin as paper. Slice *the onion* into rounds as thin as possible; they must, so to speak, pass unnoticed in the salad.

In the salad serving bowl, arrange the marinated potatoes in a dome. Then around them place the slices of beef, arranging them close together and overlapping. Surround these with a circle of slices of tomatoes. On each slice, place a little ring of onion. Place the chervil, which has been minced, in the middle on the potatoes. Whisk together the oil, vinegar, salt, and pepper, then pour over the salad. After it has been presented to the guests, the salad is tossed.

Celeriac (Celery Root) Salad *(Salade de Céleri-Rave)*

Very simple to make, and with ingredients that are relatively inexpensive, this salad is always a real success.

There will be a lot of waste from peeling the celeriac, so allow about a third above the net weight indicated.

Note that for an authentic celeriac salad, the mayonnaise sauce used must be exceptionally vinegary. In fact, tasted on its own, it is almost inedible. So the vinegar used must be rather strong; if not, the quantities described below may not be sufficient. *Time: 30 minutes. Serves 4–6.*

500 grams (1 pound, 2 ounces) of celeriac (celery root), net weight once peeled; 2 hard-boiled eggs.

***For the mayonnaise:* 3 small, uncooked egg yolks; 2 good deciliters (6 3/4 fluid ounces, 7/8 cup) of oil; 4 tablespoons of vinegar; 1 teaspoon of mustard; salt and pepper.**

PROCEDURE. Peel the celeriac until you have completely eliminated the stringy parts. Cut each celeriac into 2 or 3 pieces, then slice into very thin and even slices. Plunge these slices into 2 liters (8 1/2 cups) of strongly boiling water, salted with 10 grams (1/3 ounce) per liter (4 1/4 cups). Cut this thin. Celeriac cooks very quickly, so check at the end of 5 minutes to see if it is cooked. It is done when the teeth of a fork pierce it very easily. Drain it without cooling it: its own heat will dry it out.

While it dries, cook the hard-boiled eggs (SEE PAGE 142) and prepare the mayonnaise sauce as directed (SEE PAGE 76).

Shell the hard-boiled eggs. Cut them into two. Separate the whites from the yolks. With a wooden pestle, crush them through a medium-sized sieve, first the whites and then the yolks, without mixing the yolks with the whites.

In a terrine, mix the cooled and very dry celeriac with the mayonnaise and the egg whites. Put it on a plate or in a shallow salad bowl. Sprinkle a circle of egg yolk over it. Keep it at moderate temperature until ready to serve.

Herring Salad *(Salade de Harengs)*

Can be served as an hors d'oeuvre on small hors d'oeuvres plates; or as a salad on a larger plate or in a salad bowl. *Time: 40 minutes (once the herrings have been soaked and desalinated). Serves 6.*

6 nice potatoes, boiled, peeled, and still hot, cut into rounds; the fillet of 3 sour herrings cut into strips; 1 hard-boiled egg, chopped; 3 medium cornichons; half a nice rennet apple, which has been finely sliced as thin as a sheet of paper; 2 tablespoons of thick cream. The typical seasoning of vinegar, oil, and pepper, but no salt, because the herring is already salted.

Before dividing the herring into strips, prepare it as directed (SEE SALTED HERRINGS, PAGE 188).

Madras Salad *(Salade Madras)*

With a rather exotic flavor, this salad can either accompany a cold meat or be served as an hors d'oeuvre. It has a unique, attractive look thanks to the mixture of different colors of its three ingredients: white, red, and green. The peppers used should be green bell pepper, perfectly sweet in spite of its name. *Time: 1 hour, 30 minutes. Serves 6.*

150 grams ($5^1/_3$ ounces) of Carolina or Patna rice; 500 grams (1 pound, 2 ounces) of nice tomatoes, perfectly ripe (gross weight); 150 grams ($5^1/_3$ ounces) of bell peppers, gross weight; 10 grams ($^1/_3$ ounce) of English mustard; 3 tablespoons of oil; 1 tablespoon of vinegar; salt and pepper.

PROCEDURE. Cook the rice in plenty of water (SEE INDIAN-STYLE RICE, PAGE 563). Dry it. Take it from the oven and allow it to cool.

The tomatoes. Peel them; cut them into 4 or 8 pieces, depending on their size. Remove the water and the seeds. Then divide each quarter into small slices; these will be a noticeable feature of the salad. The total volume of the tomatoes must be more or less equal to that of the rice.

The bell peppers. Cut them into two. Remove their grains and the interior whitish part. Cut them lengthwise into very thin strips, thin as blades of grass.

In a terrine, dilute the English mustard (which is simply mustard ground to a powder) with 1 tablespoon of cold water. Add salt and pepper; the oil, little by little, stirring it with a spoon; and finally the vinegar. It should be thoroughly homogenized and have a good consistency. Into this seasoning, add first the bell peppers, then the tomatoes, and finally the rice. Toss everything. Let it rest *in a cold place for a half hour.* To serve, pour it into a salad bowl or into a small bowl.

Spaghetti Salad *(Salade de Spaghetti)*

This salad can be part of a very elegant meal; it is particularly appropriate for a supper menu. Original, very pleasant in look and taste, it can be modified a little bit for a less formal meal. Of course, the truffle can be omitted in the first place, as can the artichoke bottoms; but the celery and the tomato must always be a part of it. Preserved artichoke bottoms are more practical to use than fresh artichokes and are therefore preferable. Fresh artichokes bottoms are infinitely more trouble to prepare: they are not as white as the preserved bottoms and the price is about the same, unless you grow your own.

Note that this salad must be served at room temperature. *Time: 45 minutes. Serves 12.*

175 grams (6 ounces) of spaghetti; 60 grams ($2^1/_4$ ounces) of leftover chicken, roasted or boiled; 30 grams (1 ounce) of lean ham; 80 grams ($2^3/_4$ ounces) of celery stems, from the nice, white, and tender part on the inside of the foot; 6 medium-size artichoke bottoms; 1 nice truffle; 2 hard-boiled eggs; 1 tablespoon of minced parsley.

***To marinate the artichokes and the celery:* 2 tablespoons of white wine; 1 tablespoon of medium strength vinegar; $^1/_2$ tablespoon of olive oil; a pinch of salt, a pinch of pepper.**

***For the mayonnaise*; 1 nice egg yolk; $1^1/_4$ deciliters ($4^1/_4$ fluid ounces, generous $^1/_2$ cup) of oil; about 2 tablespoons of vinegar; 1 deciliter ($3^1/_3$ fluid ounces, scant $^1/_2$ cup) of very concentrated tomato purée.**

PROCEDURE. Drain the *artichoke bottoms.* Divide them into horizontal slices to get large rounds that are as thin as possible. Cut the *celery* crosswise, as fine as playing cards. Put the artichokes and the celery in a shallow bowl with the marinade ingredients. Leave them there for at least a half hour, turning them over from time to time.

Cut the *chicken* into a julienne and the *ham* into small cubes.

Prepare the mayonnaise (SEE PAGE 76). Finally, mix in the tomato purée.

Break the spaghetti into small pieces about 5–6 centimeters (2–2½ inches) long. Throw them into a large casserole of boiling water (2 liters/8½ cups of water and 15 grams/½ ounce of salt). Quickly bring it back to a boil and maintain that boil for *8–10 minutes.* The spaghetti must be kept a little bit firm. Drain them in a colander. When they have cooled a little, sprinkle them with a pinch of pepper.

In a *warm* terrine that is big enough to be able to mix everything easily, combine the spaghetti and the mayonnaise, mixing well. Add: artichoke, celery, chicken. Mix cautiously to combine everything well, without making a purée out of the artichoke and the chicken. Check the seasoning, which is particularly important here.

Keep the terrine in a warm place to maintain the spaghetti at a lukewarm temperature until serving.

Dressing the plate: Pour the salad into a shallow bowl, or a wide and low salad dish. Smooth the surface while shaping it into a dome with the blade of a large knife. In the middle, put a little pile of minced parsley. Completely around it and right up to the edge of the bowl, arrange in circles next to one another: chopped egg yolk, chopped egg white, chopped ham, and chopped truffle, if using it.

Until serving, keep the salad bowl in a warm place, so that the spaghetti will be eaten *lukewarm,* and serve with heated plates.

NOTE. To make the preparation easier, the spaghetti can be cooked well in advance; but it must be kept at more than a lukewarm temperature until you are ready to season it. For this, proceed as follows: put the colander over a large casserole containing the cooking water. Cover the spaghetti, and it will stay warm in the colander thanks to the steam coming off the hot water.

It is absolutely essential that when the spaghetti pieces are mixed with the mayonnaise, they are well separated from one another and still warm. If they are stuck together, they will remain glued together in the salad. To counter this, you can plunge them into their very hot cooking water for just enough time to bathe them, and then take them out.

Russian Salad *(Salade Russe)*

Many people confuse a macédoine of vegetables bound with mayonnaise with a true Russian salad: Russian salad is much more than a macédoine of vegetables and always contains fish and meat. Indeed, it is this combination of very different ingredients that is characteristic of a Russian salad.

There is nothing fixed about its composition. The main ingredients are: carrots, turnips, green peas, green beans, potatoes, ham or pickled tongue, and fillets of herring and anchovies. To these, you can add whatever you like, depending on the season, your resources and your own tastes: spiny lobster, lobster or salmon, chicken breasts or partridge breasts, sausage, olives, truffles, beets, cornichons, capers, mushrooms, asparagus tips, cauliflower, artichoke bottoms, hard-boiled eggs, chopped gelée, etc. One ingredient can easily be substituted for another. The essential thing is to have a variety of ingredients, and the seasoning is also important and should be quite spicy. If you have no leftovers of spiny lobster, lobster, or salmon, replace them with canned fish. In winter, you can also use canned green beans and peas.

As for every jardinière, the vegetables are cut *before* being cooked and are cooked separately: *carrots, turnips, and potatoes* are cut into little balls and sticks or more exactly into cubes about 5–6 millimeters (about 3/16 inch) on each side; *green beans* into rectangles; and *asparagus tips* into little logs.

Ham, tongue, chicken, and partridge are cut into a julienne as fine and even as possible, or into little cubes. Do the same for *lobster or spiny lobster,* as well as *salmon. Herring* is divided lengthwise into fine strips; the same is true for *anchovies.*

Beet, preferably cooked in the oven, should be cut into fine rounds, using a pastry cutter with a diameter of 2½ centimeters (1 inch). *Truffles* and *cornichons* are also cut into rounds. Truffle trimmings are minced and then either mixed in with the salad itself or scattered onto the salad. *Mushrooms* are first cooked, then cut into fine julienne.

Artichoke bottoms are *cooked,* then cut into small cubes. *Olives* are cut in spirals. Cut *sausage* into slices as thin as lace. *Hard-boiled eggs* should either be cut into thin slices or chopped, as you wish. *Time: 1 hour.*

Always use equal amounts of each ingredient, whether vegetables or fish and meat.

We will give here quantities for the traditional ingredients of a Russian salad, which will serve 10 people. You can add, if you like, other things according to the directions given above. Use 100 grams (3 1/2 ounces) each of carrot, turnip, and potato, weighed once peeled; 100 grams of *each* of the other vegetables: green beans, green peas, cauliflower; chicken breasts, if possible; 50 grams (1 3/4 ounces) of fillets of smoked herring; 60 grams (2 1/4 ounces) of sausage from Lyon or Arles; 3 medium-size cornichons.

For the mayonnaise sauce for the seasoning: 3 deciliters (1 1/4 cups) of oil; 2 egg yolks; a pinch of salt; cayenne pepper, as much as can be held on the point of a knife; 1/2 tablespoon of vinegar.

PROCEDURE. *Carrots and turnips* are cut and cooked differently, and should therefore be cooked separately. As you cut the carrots, put them in a small casserole of cold water so that they are completely covered. Add: a pinch of salt, 1/2 a sugar cube, and a walnut-sized piece of butter. Cook it until the carrots yield under the finger. The time needed depends on how tender the vegetables are. Cook the *turnips* the same way, but leave out the sugar. As soon as they are cooked, drain them and put them on a plate.

If the potatoes are in little balls or sticks, cook them quickly in boiling, salted water. Drain them and put them to one side. If they are in cubes, cook the potatoes, with their skins, in salted water. *Let them cool before cutting them.*

Cut the *green peas and green beans* and cook separately in salted boiling water at a lively boil (SEE FRESH VEGETABLES À L'ANGLAISE, PAGE 470). Drain them, do not chill them, and put them to one side.

Divide the *cauliflower* into florets. Remove almost all the stems of the florets. Cook them in salted water, leaving them a little bit firm. Divide them into small fragments.

Dressing the plate: Decoration has fallen from favor in modern service, even if the salad is served as part of a buffet table. Still, if you do want to decorate the salad, simply keep back 1 scant tablespoon of each ingredient, and then arrange them here and there on top of it in whatever way you like.

At any rate, all the salad ingredients are mixed together in a terrine with mayonnaise, then poured into the salad serving bowl and the surface of the salad smoothed out with a large knife blade. A step worth recommending is to lightly season the elements in the terrine with vinegar and oil *before* incorporating the mayonnaise. Leave them to infuse with this mixture for a good 15 minutes, and be careful to drain them well before adding the mayonnaise.

⁂ VEGETABLES ⁂

COOKING FRESH VEGETABLES
Cuisson des Légumes Frais

Green Beans, Flageolet Beans, Fève Beans, Green Peas, Snow Peas, Asparagus Tips, Etc.
The essential condition for cooking vegetables like this and retaining their flavor is to cook them for the correct time so that they can be served immediately.

To preserve their nice green color, take a tip from professional kitchens and use a pot that is made from red copper and not lined with tin. Tin, particularly if it is poor quality, destroys the main chemical that makes vegetables green. If you do not have an untinned copper vessel, use an enameled or aluminum utensil.

In your chosen utensil, boil the water: 2½ liters (10½ cups) for 500 grams (1 pound, 2 ounces) of vegetables. You need this amount to ensure that the vegetables have enough water throughout the cooking period, despite the evaporation that results from rapid boiling. Salt with sea salt, at the rate of 7 grams (¼ ounce) per liter (4¼ cups). Once the water is fully boiling, plunge in the vegetables—well drained if they have been washed, since you do not want to further cool down the water, which will lose heat in any case, when the vegetables are added. Bring it back to a rapid boil immediately—that is, as quickly as possible—in order to ensure a full boil from the beginning to the end of the cooking. *Never cover the utensil.*

Once they have been cooked, drain the vegetables in a colander and prepare them for immediate use.

Keep the water to use in a potage.

Cooling the vegetables: This helps to keep them green when they cannot be seasoned and served as soon as they have been cooked: vegetables that have to wait for a long time when they are moist and warm will spoil and turn yellow; and cooling takes away much of their flavor. If, however, you cannot serve immediately, proceed as follows: once the vegetables are properly cooked, drain them in a colander. Immediately plunge them into plenty of cold water or put them under the tap to completely cool the vegetables. Drain them again. When they are ready to serve, plunge them in boiling water for just enough time to completely reheat them. Drain them and prepare them the same way as vegetables that have not been cooled.

Vegetables Prepared à l'Anglaise with Butter, and à la Maître d'Hôtel
(Légumes à l'Anglaise au Beurre, et à la Maître d'Hôtel).
Frequently, instead of being presented in a well-bound mass, vegetables prepared in this way exude a kind of greasy water onto guests' plates, and do not retain any seasoning, like something that has been washed. Or they are sometimes dry and brown, as if they were prepared with oil rather than butter. In the first case, the vegetables have not been drained well enough; in the second, they have not been correctly sautéed in the butter.

Draining in a colander, no matter how carefully, is not enough to remove all the moisture from the vegetables. Now, any moisture makes a liaison with butter impossible, because butter cannot attach to a wet vegetable; it melts, slides, and ends up on the bottom of the plate. That is why you must do more than simply drain the vegetables; you must also dry them.

To dry the vegetables: Take a sauté pan. A utensil with low sides is virtually indispensable—at least, it is better than any other—to evaporate any moisture quickly.

Put the well-drained vegetables into the pan without adding anything at the moment. Heat them thoroughly on strong heat, shaking them around to move them and encourage the release of steam. The sauté pan and the vegetables must be absolutely burning hot, without, of course, allowing the vegetables to brown. It is only when all the moisture has gone and there is no more steam that the butter should be added.

Preparation with butter: *Immediately turn off the heat.* Season the vegetables with a pinch of salt and a very small pinch of white pepper. Add the fresh butter divided into small pieces so that it will melt more quickly and mix better.

Immediately take the handle of the pan in two hands to shake it, *keeping it flat* on the stove so that you circulate the butter in the vegetables without touching them with a spoon, which would crush them, or even with a fork, which might break them. It is not a question of "tossing" the pan, which would not mix the butter nearly as well or quickly as moving the pan in a circular motion on the burner. In just a few seconds, the vegetables will be properly bound.

Above all, do not turn on the heat under the pan, because the butter will turn to oil if heated too much. This would spoil the vegetables, as described above. Just the heat of the burning-hot vegetables should be enough for mixing the butter. Serve them in a warm vegetable dish or other warm serving dish.

Preparation with maître d'hôtel butter: Proceed exactly as above. At the same time as you season with the salt and pepper, add a few drops of lemon juice. Once the vegetables have been put into the serving dish, sprinkle over some minced parsley; but if the parsley is not absolutely fresh, it is better not to use it.

Preparation à l'Anglaise: Once the vegetables have been dried and seasoned as directed, pour them into the vegetable dish. Butter, in the shape of little shells or rounds, is placed on top of the vegetables, or served separately on another plate.

FRESH VEGETABLES
Légumes Frais

Artichoke *(Artichaut)*

The season for artichokes is from May to October, at least outside the hotter, southern regions. This is an excellent vegetable, but in homes it is usually only boiled and then served hot with a white sauce and cold with oil; or even, but rarely, stuffed. Its quarters and bottoms tend only to be used in haute cuisine; and yet, in this form, the artichoke can be prepared in many different methods, all of which are suitable for home cooking.

Whatever the method, it should be adapted as much as possible to the type of artichoke; large artichokes from the North require more care than smaller artichokes from the Midi, on which almost everything is edible.

In any case, always pick artichokes that have been recently harvested, which you can tell from the stem, and that are not too old. An old artichoke is full of fibers and can barely be used except in purées, the stringy parts being eliminated by passing the artichoke through a drum sieve.

Preparation of artichokes: Generally, home cooks do not know the technique for trimming raw artichokes; and when they use only the bottoms, they tend to remove the leaves after cooking. This is the wrong way to do it, because each leaf carries away with it part of the bottom, and the leaf itself cannot be used. So an artichoke bottom must always be trimmed before cooking and blanching and the leaves removed *uncooked.*

The stem: Instead of cutting it off at the bottom, it is better to break it. At the same time, tear out the hard fibers from the bottom. In order to do this, put the artichoke on the table, holding it in your left hand, with the stem sticking out over the edge, and break it by twisting it to tear it out.

The leaves: Remove these either partially or totally, depending on whether you are dealing with whole artichokes or artichoke bottoms. Do not tear them off here and there, because they will carry away much of the bottom even when uncooked. Break the leaves by proceeding as follows: hold the artichoke in your left hand, with the bottom turned toward you; between your right index finger and thumb, grab the leaf at its base; turn it back on itself, twisting it to break it and pulling toward your right. At the same time as the leaf breaks, tear off and detach the hard skin covering it. All the good parts of the leaf will be left adhering to the bottom. Once all the leaves have been detached, remove the choke by scraping the bottom of the artichoke with a metal spoon, so that the surface will be completely clean and smooth.

The bottom: Now trim around the bottom of the artichoke on the stem side to remove everything that is hard, stringy, and too green. For a smooth surface without the ridges that would be produced by successive knife cuts made as you moved the knife toward yourself, "turn" it (a professional term). That is, turn the bottom underneath the knife blade, *which should remain absolutely immobile from beginning to end of the operation.*

To do this, take the blade of a well-sharpened kitchen knife between your right thumb and index finger. With the end of the fingers of your left hand, hold the bottom of the artichoke; with your thumb and your middle finger turn it to pass it underneath the blade, holding the blade at a slightly oblique angle, then start turning the artichoke, moving slowly in a spiral toward its stem. The procedure is very simple; it is much easier to understand when you actually do it.

There are certain recipes, particularly for artichoke bottoms, where the vegetable's whiteness is important. However, raw artichoke spoils when it is cut and exposed to the air, thanks to the acid it contains. Vinegar, and even better, lemon juice, neutralizes the action of this acid.

So, have ready a terrine of cold water with 2–3 tablespoons of strong vinegar added. Alternatively, and this is preferable, do not put any vinegar in the water, but take a quarter of a lemon and rub each part of the artichoke before putting it in the water.

PRINCIPAL RECIPES

We will summarize these briefly here, including the most current recipes and those that are most appropriate for home kitchens.

Recipes for artichoke *quarters* are just as good for *bottoms,* which are more appropriate for formal meals. You should allow 2 very small bottoms per person; the bottoms of large artichokes should be divided into large slices before cooking, and you can allow 1 bottom for 2 or even 3 people, depending on whether or not the menu contains other vegetables.

Artichoke bottoms lend themselves to being stuffed in many different ways, both for meat and meatless dishes; and with a little bit of ingenuity, you can use all kinds of small leftovers for them. They can also be served as a vegetable or a small entrée. When they are filled with a garnish, they can be used around a cut of meat or other entrée. Small bottoms are first cooked in a *blanc* (SEE PAGE 42); or in water that has lemon juice and oil added to it, a procedure we can recommend since the oil acts like a *blanc* to form a barrier that keeps the artichoke from spoiling when exposed to the air. Thus for about 12 or 15 bottoms, 750 milliliters (generous 3 cups) of boiling water, 5 grams (1/6 ounce) of salt, the juice of 1 small lemon, and 3 tablespoons of oil. Allow *15–20 minutes* at a very gentle boil.

Fried Artichokes *(Artichauts Frits).* Small artichokes from the Midi are divided into quarters, blanched, seasoned, dipped in batter, and then fried in deep fat.

Lyon-Style Artichokes *(Artichauts à la Lyonnaise).* Small artichokes from the Midi are divided into quarters and blanched, sautéed in butter with well-browned minced onions, then finished with lemon juice and fines herbes.

Artichokes to Garnish Chicken Fricassée, Blanquettes, White Ragoûts, Etc. *(Artichauts pour Garniture de Fricassées de Poulets, Blanquettes, Ragoûts Blancs, Etc.).* The bottoms are cooked in a *blanc* and kept a bit firm, then they are added to the sauce.

Artichoke Croquette *(Croquettes d'Artichauts).* See the article on croquettes (PAGE 438). Cook the artichokes in boiling water. Cut the bottoms into cubes after having thoroughly trimmed the stem so that you do not leave any fibers there. A lean béchamel is used for a liaison, bound with egg yolks; 1 yolk for each 1 1/2 deciliters (5 fluid ounces, 2/3 cup) of sauce. An excellent method is to add ham: that is, about half of the total weight of the artichoke and about a quarter in mushrooms, accompanied with a soubise sauce.

Artichoke Purée *(Purée d'Artichauts).* The bottoms are blanched, and stewed with bouillon and butter. They are then passed through a fine drum sieve, and some potato purée is added, in the proportion of one-third potato and two-thirds artichoke, measured by volume.

Artichokes for Mixed Salads Composed of Diverse Elements *(Artichauts pour Salades Composées d'Eléments Divers).* The bottoms are cooked in a *blanc* and kept a little firm.

Boiled Artichokes au Naturel *(Artichauts Bouillis au Naturel).* *Time: 35–45 minutes of cooking.*

These are accompanied by a white sauce made of cream or a vinaigrette.

Tear off the stem and remove the two rows of lower leaves, proceeding as directed. Cut the upper leaves about 2 centimeters (3/4 inch) from their ends. Cut off the ends of the lower leaves with scissors. Trim the top and the bottom of the artichokes by "turning" them.

To cook: Plunge the artichokes into a receptacle full of boiling water, salted with 7 grams (1/4 ounce) per liter. Make sure they are fully covered. The length of cooking time varies according to the size of artichokes: *35–45 minutes,* and more. They are done when the leaves come away immediately or when a kitchen needle is stuck into the bottom and pierces it easily.

To serve: Carefully drain them. Remove the small leaves and take out the choke with a small spoon. Put them on a napkin-covered plate. Serve the sauce in a sauceboat.

Artichokes à la Barigoule *(Artichauts à la Barigoule).* Recipes for this are found in menu collections from 1750. There are some minor variations in the method of preparing this reputed dish, but what never changes is the composition of the stuffing, which is characteristic of a preparation *à la barigoule.* This is a special stuffing known as "duxelles," which contains only grated fatback bacon as the element of fat, and no chopped meat at all: however, it can include a small quantity of minced ham, or ham that has been cut into very fine cubes.

The following recipe is excellent. Preparing the artichokes is quite time-consuming because it requires minute attention, so it can be partly or even entirely done in advance: that is, either just trim and blanch the artichokes, if necessary; or stuff and bard them, too, then keep them cool until you are ready to cook them.

Use medium-size artichokes, so that there is 1 artichoke per person and you do not have to cut them up to serve. If they were harvested several days prior to use, make sure that after you have trimmed them and before you have removed the choke, they are plunged into a pot of boiling water to boil for 10 minutes. *Time: 2 scant hours. Serves 6.*

6 medium-size artichokes.

For the stuffing: 50 grams (1 3/4 ounces) of onion; 30 grams (1 ounce) of shallots; 250 grams (8 7/8 ounces) of very fresh mushrooms; 1 tablespoon of minced parsley; 1 piece of garlic the size of a pea (optional); 150 grams (5 1/3 ounces) of freshly grated fatback bacon; 25 grams (1 ounce, 2 tablespoons) of butter and 2 tablespoons of oil; 7–8 grams (1/4 ounce) of fine salt; 3 grams (1/9 ounce) of pepper and 1 gram (1/28 ounce) of grated nutmeg; 12 small bards of bacon, thin as a sheet of paper, which measure 12 centimeters long (4 1/2 inches) and 6 centimeters (2 1/2 inches) wide.

To braise them: 100 grams (3 1/2 ounces) of rind of pork, thick and fresh; 150 grams (5 1/3 ounces) of carrots and the same of onions cut into rounds 1/2 centimeter (3/16 inch) thick; the usual bouquet garni; 2 1/2 deciliters (1 cup) of white wine; 7 deciliters (3 cups) of light veal jus, or, if you do not have that, bouillon that is only very lightly salted given that the sauce will be reduced; 12–15 grams (3/8–1/2 ounce) of arrowroot to bind the sauce.

PROCEDURE. **The duxelle stuffing:** Prepare it as directed (SEE PAGE 21). When the duxelles is cold or nearly cold, mix it with the grated fatback bacon (SEE PAGE 11) and the chopped parsley.

The artichokes: Remove the outer, large leaves and trim the bottom and the top as directed. With one blow of the knife, trim the ends of the leaves—that is, cut off about a third. Cut the ends of the lower leaves with a scissors.

Remove the small central leaves surrounding the choke. (If the artichokes have to be blanched, put them into boiling water at this point.) Using the handle of a metal spoon, carefully remove the choke. Then lightly pull back the large leaves near the top so that you can put a little stuffing between them.

To stuff: The quantity of duxelles prepared should be 2 tablespoons per artichoke. Put 1 1/2 tablespoons in the hollow that was formed by removing the choke. Spread the rest in the middle between the leaves at the top of the artichoke.

Wrap each artichoke in two 2: place the first one *under* the artichoke, and bring either end up each sides, reaching up to the top of the cut leaves. The second bard goes on *top* of the artichoke, covering the first one. Thus, the artichoke is nearly completely wrapped in fatback bacon. Secure the bards with a string passed over them in the shape of a cross and tied on top of the artichoke.

To braise: In a pan, lightly color the rounds of carrot and onion with 2 tablespoons of some good fat.

Take a pot large enough so that the artichokes can be placed in it, next to each other, without being too crowded. Garnish the bottom with the rind, the fatty part facing down, and with the carrots and the onions already colored. Add the bouquet garni. Then arrange the artichokes on top. Add the white wine. Boil it strongly without a cover until the wine has reduced to 2 tablespoons, then pour in the bouillon or the jus. The liquid must reach *halfway* up the artichokes. If the pot used is a little bit larger than appropriate, there will not be enough liquid and it will have to be slightly increased.

Bring it to a boil. Then cover the pot and put it into a moderate oven so that it simmers uninterrupted at a gentle pace. Once you put it in the oven, allow *45 minutes* for cooking very fresh artichokes, *or 1 hour if they were harvested some time ago.*

A good 15 minutes before the cooking is complete, uncover the pot so that you can brown the part of the bard covering the artichokes.

To dress the dish: Put the artichokes on the serving plate.

Cut the strings with scissors and remove the bards. Cut off the brown part from each bard; there should be a square about 5–6 centimeters (2–2 1/2 inches) long on each side. Reserve these pieces on a plate. Keep everything warm in a very moderate oven.

Strain the juice through the chinois into a small saucepan. Let it rest for a few minutes so that you can completely degrease it. If you have more than the *3 deciliters (1 1/4 cups)* necessary, boil it to reduce it to this amount. Bind it with the arrowroot starch (SEE PAGE 48). Check the seasoning. Pour the juice onto the artichokes, straining it again through the chinois. Place 1 of the squares of browned bacon on each artichoke. Serve.

Old-Style Stuffed Artichokes *(Artichauts Farcis à l'Ancienne Mode).* Differing from artichokes à la barigoule, notably in the stuffing, which is more substantial, as well as in the way it is cooked, these artichokes make a good, elegant dish for home cooking. They can also be used on a family table, either at the beginning of a meal as an entrée or, even better, as a vegetable dish at the end: this depends on the menu.

The artichokes can be stuffed in advance and kept in a cool place until they need to be cooked. *Time: 1 hour, 30 minutes (once the artichokes have been stuffed). Serves 6.*

3 nice medium-sized artichokes.

To stuff them: 300 grams (10 1/2 ounces), net weight, of fillet of pork with an equal proportion of fat and lean; 40 grams (1 3/8 ounce) of flour; 30 grams (1 ounce, 2 tablespoons) of butter; 1 scant deciliter (3 1/3 fluid ounces, scant 1/2 cup) of bouillon; 1 whole large egg or 2 small ones; 3 very small squares of fatback bacon, 6–7 centimeters (2 1/2–2 3/4 inches) each side; salt, pepper, etc.

For the cooking: 40 grams (1 3/8 ounce, 3 tablespoons) of butter; 25 grams (1 ounce) of flour; 7 1/2 deciliters (generous 3 cups) of bouillon; a small bouquet garni.

PROCEDURE. **The artichokes:** Remove the tough leaves and trim the bottoms as directed. Cut 2 centimeters (3/4 inch) from the upper leaves. Cut only the sharp point of the lower leaves.

Plunge them into a large pot of boiling, salted water; cover. Boil for *15 minutes.* Drain them and cool them. Press them between your fingers lightly so you do not crack the bottom. In order to remove it, pull the little violet tuft from the leaves in the middle. Using the handle of a small spoon, remove the choke; the small insignificant leaves will come off at the same time. Sprinkle the bottom with a pinch of salt and pepper.

The stuffing: Prepare this while you are blanching the artichokes. In a small saucepan and on very gentle heat, mix the butter and the flour. Cook it gently for *7–10 minutes* without allowing it to color. Add the bouillon. Stir with a wooden spoon on the heat until it has the consistency of a thick batter that slides easily off the spoon. Spread it out on a plate so that it will cool.

Meanwhile, prepare the chopped pork. Remove all the skins and filaments. Pass the meat twice through the fine cutter of a small mechanical grinder: the result is a stuffing that is as fine as a pomade. If you do not have a mechanical grinder, you must mince it very finely with a knife. Mince only the lean part. Do not mince the fat part, which does not produce a good result, but grate it instead (SEE BACON, PAGE 11). Put everything into a small terrine: the minced meat, the chilled batter, the whole egg, the salt, the pepper, and the spice powder. Work everything with the wooden spoon to mix it perfectly.

Using a metal spoon, fill the cavity of the artichokes, packing down the stuffing so that you make a small dome above the level of the top leaves. Place a bard on top of it; fix it in place with a string tied crosswise.

To cook: Use a thick-bottomed sauté pan, or, if you must, a good pot made of cast iron, in which the artichokes can be placed right next to one another. On moderate heat, melt the butter in it, and immediately place the artichokes in the pan on their bottoms. Without covering it, let the bottoms of the artichokes lightly color for *about 10 minutes,* moving them from time to time so that the hot fat circulates completely underneath them. This firms the bottoms and enhances their flavor.

Take the artichokes out and put them on a plate. The butter should not have browned because it has been only moderately heated. In this warm butter, make a small amount of a dark blond roux with the flour (SEE PAGE 47). Dilute it with the bouillon. Once it has begun boiling, put the artichokes back into the bouillon so that the liquid comes up to about half of their height. Add the bouquet garni. Bring it back to a boil. Cover. Put it into a very moderate oven. Maintain a regular, very gentle simmer for *1 hour.*

From time to time, uncover it to baste the artichokes with their cooking juice, and make sure that their bottoms do not stick to the pan by moving the pan around in a circular movement. Fifteen minutes before cooking ends, uncover the pan to color the bards.

To serve: Cut the strings. Put the artichokes on a serving dish. Keep them warm. Thoroughly degrease the jus: it should have reduced by half. Pour it through the chinois onto the artichokes and serve.

Stuffed Artichoke Bottoms *(Fonds d'Artichauts Farcis).* Use this entirely home-style recipe as the basis of all other stuffings for artichoke bottoms, which include meat or rice and other ingredients, all previously cooked. *Time: 2 hours. Serves 6.*

6 medium-size artichoke bottoms (6 centimeters/ 2 1/2 inches in diameter): a mirepoix with 50 grams (1 3/4 ounces) of carrot, 50 grams (1 3/4 ounces) of onion, 20 grams (2/3 ounce, 1 heaping tablespoon) of butter, 1 sprig of parsley, 1 sprig of thyme, 1 fragment of bay; 5 deciliters (generous 2 cups) of degreased bouillon or vegetable bouillon.

***To garnish the bottoms:* 100 grams (3 1/2 ounces) of mushrooms; 150 grams (5 1/3 ounces) of cooked noodles; 15 grams (1/2 ounce, 1 tablespoon) of butter; 5–7 grams (1/4 ounce) of flour; 1 good deciliter (3 1/3 fluid ounces, scant 1/2 cup) of milk; a pinch of minced parsley; salt, pepper, nutmeg.**

PROCEDURE. In a sauté pan or pot, prepare the mirepoix (SEE PAGE 21).

Trim the artichoke bottoms, as directed. If the artichoke bottoms are new and very tender, there is no point blanching them; if not, plunge them in salted boiling water and then boil for *5–10 minutes,* depending on how tender. Put the bottoms in the pan with the mirepoix. Add the bouillon. Bring it to a boil and cover, then turn down the heat. Allow *1 scant hour* at a regular and gentle simmer.

The garnish: In a small saucepan, heat the butter; add the chopped mushrooms. On strong heat, mix it until all their moisture has evaporated and they are lightly colored. Add the parsley and mix; then add the flour. Cook it for a minute without allowing it to color while you stir it. Dilute it with the milk and let it simmer *4–5 minutes.* After this, add the noodles, which have first been cooked in water and well drained, then cut into small pieces about 1½ centimeters (⅝ inch) long. Season with salt, pepper, nutmeg.

Thoroughly drain the artichoke bottoms. Garnish them with the mixture. Put them on an ovenproof plate. Strain their cooking liquid through a chinois into a small, rinsed out saucepan. Pour *half* of it onto the artichokes.

Put it into a very moderate oven for about *10 minutes* so that a light crust forms on the surface and colors; baste them frequently with their liquid. Bind the rest of the liquid with the starch (SEE PAGE 48) and pour it over the artichokes just before serving.

Braised Artichokes *(Artichauts à l'Étuvée).* Given to us directly by the celebrated Provençal chef Reboul, this is one of the best recipes for artichokes. It also allows you to use large artichokes, which are already somewhat tough, but actually these are preferable here, as long as they are not too old. *Time: At least 2 good hours. Serves 8.*

6 large artichokes; 3 tablespoons of olive oil; 125 grams (4½ ounces) of finely minced onions; ½ deciliter (1⅔ fluid ounces, scant ¼ cup) of white vinegar; 1 deciliter (3⅓ fluid ounces, scant ½ cup) of white wine; 3 deciliters (1¼ cups) of water; 2 small garlic cloves; 1 bay leaf; 1 teaspoon of rice flour or other starch.

***The oil* can, without great disadvantage, be replaced with the same quantity of butter or melted lard. *The garlic* may be left out, but that would be a shame because artichoke is one of the vegetables most complimented by it; instead of eliminating it entirely, add piece the size of a pea, crushing it under the blade of a knife; its flavor absolutely completes the dish.**

PROCEDURE. Trim the artichokes and remove *all* the leaves, proceeding to tear them off as already described. Cut each artichoke into 6 pieces. With a small knife, remove the choke and scrape off anything remaining that is hard and stringy. As you go, put the pieces into a terrine of cold water that has been acidulated with a little bit of white vinegar.

Use a thick pot of thick aluminum or any good pot that can be tightly closed. Heat the oil in it with the onion. Immediately arrange the pieces of artichoke in it, which have been previously well dried in a towel. On moderate heat and with the pot uncovered, cook them gently on all sides *without allowing them to color.* The onion must be nice and softened, but not at all brown.

Add salt, pepper, vinegar, and white wine. Let it boil until the liquid reduces to 2–3 tablespoons. Then moisten it with the boiling water. Add the bay and garlic. Cover it tightly. Let it simmer for *1½ hours.* The simmering must be scarcely apparent, so that it causes only minimal reduction and thus conserves the necessary liquid to sufficiently sauce the artichokes after cooking.

The artichokes are done when a fork pierces them easily. Remove the garlic and the bay, and 2 or 3 minutes before serving, make the liaison with starch (SEE LIAISONS, PAGE 47). Shake the pan in a circular movement to mix the ingredients for the liaison without touching the artichokes, which would break.

Arrange the artichokes in a circle, pouring the sauce on top of them, or, if you wish, serve them in a vegetable dish. Serve burning hot.

NOTE. If you use small artichokes from the Midi, cook the bottoms without cutting them up after trimming them. Take out the choke with a vegetable spoon or the end of a rounded knife blade. For very young artichokes that have not developed a choke or barb in the middle of the heart and whose leaves are edible until halfway up the artichoke, it is enough to trim them a very little bit at the base by turning them, and then to cut the top part of the leaves, giving the artichoke the shape of a large egg. Put them, as you do this, into acidulated water. Cook them in the same way, but for a much shorter time: that is, *30–40 minutes* at the most.

Artichoke Quarters à l'Italienne *(Quartiers d'Artichauts à l'Italienne).* *Time: 1 hour, 15 minutes. Serves 6.*

4 medium artichokes; a carrot; a large onion; a bouquet garni; a few rinds of bacon; 1 deciliter (3⅓ fluid ounces, scant ½ cup) of white wine; 3½ deciliters (1½ cups) of light jus made with veal, slightly salted; 3½ deciliters (1½ cups) of Italian sauce (SEE PAGE 61).

PROCEDURE. **Preparing the artichoke quarters:** Tear off the stem, remove the large leaves at the top, and trim the bottoms, proceeding as directed. Divide the artichokes in 4 parts as you go, to be certain that they do not spoil. Cut the ends of the leaves, remove the choke from the interior, immediately rub the quarter with the lemon, and then put it in the cold water.

As soon as all the quarters are ready, plunge them into a large pot full of boiling water, salted with 7–8 grams (1/4 ounce) per liter; cook at a rolling boil for *8 minutes* without a cover. Drain them in a drum sieve.

To cook: In a sauté pan of the right size, lay out the rinds, the fatty part down. On top of them, place the onion and the carrot cut into rounds, and the bouquet garni; and on top of everything, put the artichoke quarters *one next to the other.*

Put the pan on moderate heat without a cover *for 10–15 minutes* to first sweat the vegetables and the artichoke quarters. When no more white vapor is given off, add the wine. Reduce it entirely on strong heat. Finally, pour in the veal jus. As soon as boiling has resumed, cover with a round of buttered paper and the cover. Put it in the oven. Maintain a slow and regular simmering for *35–40 minutes.*

To dress the dish: One by one, lift out the artichoke quarters with a fork and arrange in a circle on a vegetable dish, in 2 or 3 rows, leaving the middle open for the sauce. This is finished with the cooking juice from the artichokes, once it has been degreased, strained, and reduced to 3–4 tablespoons. When pouring the sauce, make sure you do not pour any on the leaves, which will, of course, be eaten with the fingers.

Asparagus *(Asperge)*

Asparagus season is April and May. The best type is from Argenteuil and has a violet-pink tint. Whatever the type, the most important quality of asparagus is its absolute freshness. You can recognize fresh asparagus by its shininess, its whiteness, and its stiffness; a bunch should feel good and tight and heavy in the hand and you should also be able to pierce the nonedible part with your fingernail. By contrast, asparagus that has been harvested a long time ago has lost much of its water; its tint is a dull yellow; the stems will be shriveled; and a bunch will feel flabby.

In addition, be careful to choose them when they are properly ripe. That is, the heads that reached just above the soil should be lightly pink. Heads that are all white are not sufficiently mature, while green heads are overripe, having been overlooked in the previous harvest. To be appreciated at their best, asparagus must be eaten the very same day that they have been harvested. To keep them fresh for the next day, preserve them from contact with the air by wrapping them in a damp towel and keeping them in a cool place.

The size of the asparagus determines their number per guest. Depending on whether they are very large or medium size, you can normally allow 8–10 per person.

Preparation of asparagus: If they have a lot of dirt on them, begin by rinsing them in cold water to get rid of the dirt, and trim the soil-stained ends. You can later adjust their length when you put them into packages.

Generally, people have been happy just to scrape asparagus, which is not sufficient. This is what you should do. First, with the point of a small knife, remove all the little separate leaves around the heads and also a little further on down toward the stem. You will find grains of sand, which neither washing nor cooking will eliminate, because it was trapped there while the asparagus was growing. It is extremely unpleasant to feel it on the teeth. So, trim 1 millimeter from the tip, which will probably contain some sand.

Now, instead of raking them over the grater as people often do, *peel them,* starting at the point where the head stops and the white part begins. As they are peeled, put the asparagus into a large receptacle of cold water, and wash them very well there before draining.

Once drained, sort the asparagus according to their size: small, medium, large. This is to help determine how long they should be cooked, which will be proportional to their size and also to the way that you dress the plate. Assemble the stems into bunches of 6, 8, or 10 asparagus depending on their size. Tie them with two turns of string: one about 5 centimeters (2 inches) from the head, the other 8 centimeters (3 1/4 inches) further down.

Place all the heads at the same level, and then, with one cut of a good large knife, trim the ends of the stems so that the asparagus is a uniform length, no more than 18 centimeters (7 inches).

Always tie the asparagus together to cook them, even if they are the same size, and particularly if you do not have an asparagus steamer, because you risk breaking their heads when taking them out of the water with the skimmer if they are a little overcooked.

This preparation can all be done in advance, as long as you keep the bunches in a cool place, wrapped in a moist kitchen towel.

To cook asparagus: An asparagus steamer is certainly very handy, both because of its size and because, like a fish poacher, the inner container lifts out, allowing you, as with a *poissonnière,* to remove the asparagus easily and then drain them without damaging them; but it is by no means essential, and you can easily use a saucepan of the appropriate size.

What is most important is that the bunches are comfortably and completely immersed in the pans, and that the amount of water is sufficient: so, *for each kilogram (2 pounds, 4 ounces) of asparagus,* 3 1/2 liters (14 3/4 cups) of boiling water and 7 grams (1/4 ounce) of salt *for each liter of water.*

Cooking time: Work this out as follows: keep the salted boiling water on strong heat and plunge the asparagus, in bunches, into it. You can expect that it will take 4–5 minutes to return to a boil. (The water will, of course, have been cooled when the asparagus was added to it.)

From the moment when the boiling resumes, allow *12–14 minutes,* depending on the size of the asparagus. That is, *12 minutes* if it is a nice, *medium-size asparagus.* In addition, allow 3 minutes to drain the asparagus and dress them on the serving dish. You can easily calculate the cooking time by working back from the time when you want to serve the asparagus.

When the boiling has resumed, keep it regular and moderate. A rolling boil will not advance the cooking time by 1 second.

NOTE. There are two essential points. First, it is very important *not to overcook* the asparagus. They should be a little bit crunchy rather than overcooked. The reason is that if they are overcooked, they absorb their cooking water and lose their flavor.

The second point, always worth observing to preserve their flavor, is to ensure that they stand for as short a time as possible after they have been cooked. Cooking the asparagus in advance, then reheating them in their cooking juice just before serving, which is mostly done by restaurants, is bad: an asparagus saturated with water loses its delicacy.

If there is some reason why the asparagus must stand, a warm and *dry* place is essential. In this case, you must pay particular attention to make sure they are not overcooked.

As soon as they are properly done, drain all the cooking water. Leave the asparagus absolutely *dry* in the same receptacle. Spread a folded kitchen towel over them to absorb the steam escaping from the asparagus, which would otherwise soften them. Cover the receptacle and put it in a warm place. The asparagus does not have to be served burning hot.

For the same reasons as above, we advise you to not refresh the cooked asparagus—that is, plunge it into cold water. This obviously removes their flavor. And it should only be done in regions where the asparagus is too bitter.

To serve: First drain the asparagus on a spread-out kitchen towel so that the water runs out of them. Dress them on a long plate garnished with a napkin, placing the bunches one on top of the other. Cut the strings with scissors or a good sharp knife so that you do not pull on the strings and risk breaking the asparagus.

Serve the accompanying sauce separately. Asparagus presented like this will appear on menus as asparagus *en branches,* followed by the name of the sauce.

The accompanying sauce: The one most often used for home cooking is butter sauce or white sauce, as well as fresh butter simply melted, which is common in the North. Then come the more refined sauces: hollandaise, maltaise, mousseleine, and cream sauces.

When asparagus is served cold, it is accompanied with a sauce made with oil, or a mayonnaise, to which you can, if you wish, add some cream to make a mayonnaise à la Chantilly.

Green Asparagus, Known as "Asparagus Tips" and Used as a Garnish. Lightly grate the asparagus to remove the small leaves, which will otherwise come off in cooking and form a mush that would spoil the sauce.

Do not cut them: asparagus are green from the stem to the tip, so you cannot simply, by looking at them, figure out what is and is not good to eat, and you risk cutting off too little or not enough. So hold the asparagus in your left hand; then, with your right hand, grab the end of the tip side and bend it until the stalk breaks; it will break just at the point where it stops being edible.

Having washed the asparagus in cool water, let it soak for a little bit to remove the sand. Then cut the end of the tips to a length of about 3 centimeters (1¼ inches) and tie them up into little bundles, fastening them with one or two turns of kitchen string. Then cut the rest of the stalks into little pieces no larger than 1 centimeter (⅜ inch) long, somewhat like large fresh peas.

Cook in ample salted water (SEE PREPARED VEGETABLES À L'ANGLAISE, PAGE 470) for *10 minutes.* Drain them as soon as they are cooked.

Eggplant *(Aubergine)*

There are several types of eggplant: all are good and appropriate for the recipes below, assuming that the eggplants are fresh and have not gone beyond their appropriate degree of maturity. Their good season is July and August: then they have no seeds, which should always be removed when preparing eggplant since they will always spoil the flesh, or pulp, of the eggplant.

A fresh eggplant can be identified by its smooth skin, which should be shiny and tight; and by the firmness of the flesh, so press it between your fingers. A dull skin, and swollen and soft flesh, indicates that it was harvested some time ago: in this state, the result can only be mediocre, so it is better not to even try to use it.

For home cooking, eggplants are mostly stuffed. The methods of stuffing them vary according to the circumstance and the regions; but the vegetable is always prepared the same way, so we will explain how to do it. As for the composition of the stuffing you can refer to the different methods indicated for the tomato, beyond the steps we outline below for preparing the eggplant itself. If you use meat, cooked mutton is the most appropriate. The method known as "Turkish" uses mutton and rice bound with a little bit of brown sauce.

Eggplant can also be fried: either in fritters, as described below, or cut into fine slices, seasoned and floured, then plunged into a large quantity of smoking oil. You can prepare them also with a sauce: béchamel, velouté, tomato, italienne, etc. In this case, the eggplant, cut into rounds ½ centimeter (3/16 inch) thick, can be disgorged with salt, then gently braised in butter before binding it with the relevant sauce.

Preparation of eggplant for stuffing: You should allow 1 small eggplant or half a large one per person.

Whatever the stuffing you use, deep-fry the eggplant first.

Small eggplant: Cut off one-third lengthwise; this third is not used, but the waste is insignificant, containing very little flesh. With the point of a small knife, make some incisions in the flesh crosswise, cutting right through the flesh. The goal of these incisions is to help the heat penetrate and thus facilitate the cooking.

Large eggplant: Cut them in 2 right down the middle and in the same direction as the small ones—that is, lengthwise. On each half, make the same incisions.

To cook: Heat the oil for deep-frying until smoking. Add the eggplants, putting in the cut side first, so that the heat of the oil works more strongly on the flesh. At the end of *6–8 minutes,* check to see if the flesh has softened under the finger. Then drain them on a kitchen towel. Immediately scoop out the pulp with the handle of a metal spoon. Leave a thickness of barely ½ centimeter (3/16 inch) on the inside of the skin. The pulp you have taken out is for the stuffing.

To stuff: Use a gratin plate that can be taken to the table. Generously butter the bottom with the end of your finger. Then place the eggplant shells on top of it, slightly on the bias if it's a long plate. With a soupspoon, fill the eggplants with the stuffing. Sprinkle them with bread crumbs. Spread some melted butter over the top.

To gratinée: Do this in a good hot oven, as for all rapid gratins. Thus, allow *7–8 minutes,* and a hotter temperature from on top than from the bottom.

Eggplant Stuffed with Tomato and Rice *(Aubergines Farcies à la Tomate et au Riz).* This preparation is meatless. *Time: 1 scant hour. Serves 6.*

6 small eggplants or 3 large ones; 750 grams (1 pound, 10 ounces) of firm tomatoes; 1 medium-size onion; 1 clove of garlic the size of a bean; 3 generous tablespoons of rice; 1 good tablespoon of fine bread crumbs; 75 grams (2 2/3 ounces, 1/3 cup) of butter for everything; salt, pepper.

PROCEDURE. **The tomatoes:** Remove the skins. Cut them into two. Squeeze them to completely extract the water and the seeds. Divide each half into 4 or 6 pieces.

In a medium-size saucepan, heat 30 grams (1 ounce, 2 tablespoons) of butter. Gently soften the chopped onion without coloring it for 5 minutes. Then add: the tomato and the garlic, crushed under the blade of a knife, as well as 2 pinches of salt, a pinch of pepper, and a good pinch of superfine sugar. Cover. Allow the tomato to melt into a compote for *1 scant half hour.*

The rice: If you have some leftovers of cooked rice, particularly if it has been cooked à l'Indienne, this is a good time to use it. If not, just cook it in salted, boiling water.

The stuffing: Chop the flesh from the eggplant, which you have prepared as directed. Put it in a terrine. Add the rice, well drained, and the tomato, from which you keep a third to make a sauce to surround the eggplants once they have been put in the oven to brown. Fill the eggplants and brown as directed.

Neapolitan-Style Eggplant *(Aubergines à la Napolitaine).* An excellent recipe that is completely suitable for home cooking and that was given to us by the great chef M. Philéas Gilbert. *Time: 1 hour. Serves 6.*

3 medium-size eggplants or 4 small ones; 3 tablespoons of flour to coat them; 2 1/2 deciliters (1 cup) of oil to fry them; 100 grams (3 1/2 ounces) of Parmesan or of good fresh Gruyère; 20 grams (2/3 ounce) of fine white bread crumbs.

For the tomato sauce: 800 grams (1 pound, 12 ounces) of nice tomatoes; 30 grams (1 ounce) of chopped onions; 2 parsley sprigs; 1 fragment of thyme; 1 piece of bay the size of a fingernail; 12 grams (3/8 ounce) of garlic; 10 grams (1/3 ounce) of sugar; a good pinch of salt and a pinch of pepper.

75 grams (2 2/3 ounces, 1/3 cup) of butter for everything.

PROCEDURE. **Starting the tomato sauce:** In a medium-size saucepan, heat 25 grams (1 ounce, 2 tablespoons) of butter. Lightly color the onion; add the parsley sprigs broken into fragments; add the tomatoes, which have had their water and seeds removed and then been cut into quarters; the garlic, crushed and minced; thyme, bay, salt, pepper, and a bit of sugar. Cover the pan. Let the tomato gently melt. Cook for about *35 minutes.*

The eggplants: There is no point peeling them. Wipe them thoroughly. Remove the green stem from the end. Cut them into rounds scarcely 1 centimeter (3/8 inch) thick. Then arrange them on a large plate without piling them up; sprinkle them with fine salt. Let them disgorge in a cool place for *25 minutes.*

The cheese: Grate about a third of it. Cut the rest into little ribbons as thin as a sheet of paper.

The tomato purée: Once the tomatoes have thoroughly broken down, push them through a drum sieve. Put the purée into a rinsed saucepan. Reduce it on strong heat, stirring continuously, to *about 2 deciliters (6 3/4 fluid ounces, 7/8 cup).* Turn off the heat. Taste it; add 30 grams (1 ounce, 2 tablespoons) of butter.

To fry the eggplants: Drain them and dry them thoroughly in a towel. Spread out the flour on a plate and roll the eggplant in it.

Heat the oil in a sauté pan until it lightly smokes. Arrange as many of the rounds in the pan that it can hold, placed *side by side.* Turn them over after a few seconds. Once they have been well dried out and turned a golden color, quickly drain them on a spread-out towel and put them onto a large plate in a very low oven. Cook another batch of rounds, proceeding in the same way, until you have used them all up, and working as quickly as possible so that the ones that have already been fried do not soften too much.

The gratin: Use an ovenproof plate that can also be taken to the table. On it, spread out 2 tablespoons of the tomato purée and a third of the cheese ribbons. On top arrange a third of the eggplant. Cover with tomato and cheese. Then arrange 3 layers of eggplant in the same manner; then finally cover it with the tomato. Sprinkle it with the bread crumbs and the grated cheese. Moisten with 20 grams (2/3 ounce, 1 heaping tablespoon) of melted butter.

Put it into a *very hot* oven so that it browns and crisps as rapidly as possible on the surface and the cheese shavings on the inside melt at the same time. Serve immediately.

Eggplant Fritters *(Beignets d'Aubergines).* *Time: 1 hour, 30 minutes.*

Make sure they are not too ripe. Allow 1 eggplant for 2 or 3 people, depending on the rest of the menu and your guests' appetites.

Peel them, then cut them into thin rounds about 1/2 centimeter (3/16 inch) thick; spread them out on a towel; sprinkle them with fine salt; cover them with a towel. Let them disgorge for 1 hour. Then thoroughly wipe them clean, lightly squeezing them to extract all their moisture. About 5–6 minutes before serving, dip the slices one by one into batter, and then immerse them in a large quantity of very hot fat. Drain them on a towel. Serve burning hot on a napkin.

The batter used can include, if you like, and according to your taste and means, a whole egg or an egg yolk with the white whisked into a snowy mass, or simply just the whisked egg whites (SEE BATTER FOR FRYING, PAGE 666).

Ribs of Swiss Chard *(Côtes de Bette ou Poirée)*

Because of its ribs, Swiss chard is reminiscent of celery stalks and cardoons. Both the stems and the leaves can be eaten, which is why it is generally known in France as *poirée à chardes* (leaves and stalks); but its taste is completely different from those two vegetables. Actually, the taste of chard is somewhat insipid, and most of the flavor comes from the sauce with which it is served. But since it is a healthy and inexpensive vegetable, it has become increasingly popular, which it never used to be.

You can prepare Swiss chard without meat and with a béchamel sauce, Mornay sauce, cream sauce, etc., or with meat and with a poulette sauce, an Italian sauce, etc., or even au gratin. Allow 1 deciliter (3 1/3 fluid ounces, scant 1/2 cup) of sauce for each 100 grams (3 1/2 ounces) of cooked Swiss chard. For all recipes, the ribs must first be cooked in generous amounts of boiling water. For the number of guests, allow 2 ribs per person. As much as possible, Swiss chard should be freshly harvested.

PROCEDURE. Carefully trim the muddy part. Then neatly remove all the green part on the top. (The leaves are best used in an herb soup.) Divide each rib into pieces 8–10 centimeters (3 1/4–4 inches) long. With a small knife, remove the skin that covers them; as you do this, put them in cool water.

Drain them and put the pieces into a pot of rapidly boiling water that has been very slightly salted: use only 5 grams (1/6 ounce) of salt per liter because this vegetable very easily absorbs salt. Cover and allow it to cook until, when you pick up a piece, it easily yields under the pressure of your finger and does not snap when you bite it. Allow *at least 40 minutes* to cook.

Drain them in a strainer without cooling them. The best way to eat them with sauce is to alternate the layers of chard and the layers of sauce, in the vegetable dish or the service plate, finishing, it is understood, with a layer of sauce.

Cardoons *(Cardon)*

Cardoons only look like celery; the taste resembles artichoke, of which it is a variety.

Cardoon is considered something of a luxury: first because of its high price, which is compounded by the enormous waste; then because of the special care required to peel it before cooking; and finally because of the cost of its accompanying sauce, which includes nothing that was also used to cook the cardoon itself. The waste is more than two-thirds of the stalk of the cardoon. The only usable part is the white of the inside branches, which are not hollow and spongy; all the rest is good for absolutely nothing. A stalk weighing around 3 kilograms (6 pounds, 10 ounces) does not even give 1 kilogram (2 pounds, 3 ounces) net weight of cardoon, and it is the net weight that you must take into account when buying it. Below, we give the principal recipes for cardoon. It can also be served accompanied with a hollandaise sauce, a mousseline, a cream sauce, or with butter, but there is no doubt that it is most often prepared au jus (in a jus) and with marrow, which is the most popular recipe.

Preparation of cardoons: Before doing anything else, start the *blanc* so that the cardoons can be plunged into it as soon as they are peeled: even when rubbed with lemon, they risk browning if having to stand for too long. So, for a cardoon stalk weighing about 3 kilograms (6 pounds, 10 ounces), prepare 2 liters (8½ cups) of *blanc* as directed (SEE PAGE 42), replacing the vinegar, if possible, with juice squeezed from half a lemon.

Before peeling the cardoon, have at hand a cut lemon and a terrine of fresh water that has been lightly vinegared. It is absolutely essential to rub the peeled cardoon with the lemon, for this reason: the cardoon contains an acrid juice, just like the artichoke from which it is derived; when this acrid juice comes into contact with air, it darkens the cardoon unless you do not immediately counter it with lemon juice and then plunge the pieces into cold acidulated water.

Remove the branches surrounding the base of the cardoon, which are hollow and stringy. Cut off all the other branches at their base until you get to the heart. If the ends of the first branches taken off are hollow, do not use them. It is the largest branches in particular that supply the waste. As you get to the center, the branches are firm from end to end and completely usable.

Divide the branches into pieces 8–10 centimeters (3¼–4 inches). With the point of a small kitchen knife, peel both the inside and outside of the branches and remove the skin, which comes away in filaments. Do this as rapidly as possible because the cardoon will darken almost immediately on contact with the knife. As each piece is peeled, immediately rub it with a piece of lemon, kept close at hand, and then plunge it into the terrine of vinegared water. With the same speed, remove the kind of woody peel that surrounds the heart as if it were a thick skin, which is the most delicate part of the cardoon. Rub it with lemon and plunge it in the water.

As soon as you have finished peeling them, plunge the drained cardoons into the boiling *blanc.* Rapidly bring it back to a boil. Add the fat. From this moment allow to cook for *1¼ hours* at a very gentle simmer: cover the pot, but leave a slight opening so that the steam can escape. Before taking them out of the *blanc,* make sure that the cardoons yield under the finger. If they seem firm, keep them in the cooking liquid for up to another 15 minutes.

If you do not use them immediately, you can keep them very well in the *blanc,* making sure they are immersed so that they have no contact with the air. Cover them with greased parchment paper.

PRINCIPAL RECIPES

For 6–8 people, you need a cardoon stalk weighing about 3 kilograms (6 pounds, 10 ounces), previously cooked in a *blanc* as directed.

Cardoons in Juice *(Cardons au Jus).* Recipes vary. Depending on your means, you can use a very reduced excellent veal jus, bound at the last moment with starch; or use a brown sauce made with a very good homemade jus that has been well skimmed and is light and transparent. At any rate, we recommend stewing the cardoon in the jus or the sauce before serving it. *Time: 2 hours (the jus and brown sauce already having been prepared).*

4 good deciliters (1⅔ cups) of veal jus and 8 grams (¼ ounce) of arrowroot or 4 good deciliters (1⅔ cups) of brown sauce prepared in advance (SEE PAGE 50); 30 grams (1 ounce) of fresh butter for finishing the sauce or jus.

PROCEDURE. Take the cardoons out with a fork, *draining them thoroughly.* Arrange them in a sauté pan. Pour the veal jus or brown sauce on them. Cover. Stew them gently for *15–20 minutes.*

Arrange the cardoons on a vegetable plate or on any heated plate, draining them thoroughly if the jus is not yet bound. On top, arrange the heart, cut into rounds, so that each guest can take a piece.

If you have used jus, make the liaison with the arrowroot and the jus remaining in the sauté pan (SEE LIAISONS, PAGE 47). Into the bound jus or the brown sauce, add the final butter, off the heat. Pour it on the cardoons. Serve.

Cardoons with Marrow *(Cardons à la Moelle).*
Time: 2 hours (the jus and sauce already having been prepared).

You can serve these cardoons in two ways, depending on how formal the meal is: you can either simply arrange the cardoons with the marrow on top, cut into rounds, or you can surround them with little puff pastry boats containing the marrow, cut into dice and bound with a little bit of sauce from the cardoons. Whatever method you use, the amount of marrow and its preparation remain the same.

The recipe is the same as for cardoons au jus but with marrow added and a stronger seasoning to sharpen the sauce's flavor given the inclusion of marrow. So, if you like, add a little bit of reduced Madeira and a very small amount of tomato; or you can replace the jus with the same quantity of a bordelaise sauce, whose strong flavor complements the flavor of the marrow more than the flavor of the cardoon.

Thus prepared, the cardoon should simmer *15–20 minutes* in the jus or in the sauce.

The marrow: Use 150 grams (5 1/3 ounces) of very fresh beef marrow. Use a small saucepan filled with about 3 deciliters (1 1/4 cups) bouillon or salted water that is boiling. With the end of the blade of a knife dipped into the boiling water, cut the marrow into rounds 1/2 centimeter (3/16 inch) thick; or into small dice 1 scant centimeter (3/8 inch) on each side, if you are going to garnish it with the little boats of puff pastry. Put the rounds or the dice into the pan of boiling liquid. Maintain it at a simple simmer for *10 minutes.*

If the marrow is in *rounds,* and the cardoons are to be served on a vegetable plate, lift out these rounds with a fork, draining them thoroughly; spread them around on the cardoons so that they can easily be picked out by your guests. Cover the cardoons and the marrow with the sauce.

If the marrow is to be served as *dice* in pastry shell boats, drain them quickly and thoroughly. Put them into a small, rinsed out and dried saucepan and then bind them with a few tablespoons of sauce. Immediately take them out with a spoon to fill the warm pastry shell boats. Pour the rest of the sauce on the cardoons. Surround them with the pastry boats.

Cardoons à la Mornay *(Cardons à la Mornay).*
Time: 1 hour, 30 minutes.

4 deciliters (1 2/3 cups) of Mornay sauce (SEE PAGE 63); 20 grams (2/3 ounce) of grated Gruyère (or half Gruyère and half Parmesan, which is preferable); 10 grams (1/3 ounce, 1 scant tablespoon) of butter.

PROCEDURE. Use an ovenproof plate. Spread out a layer of sauce over the bottom of the plate. On this sauce, arrange the pieces of cardoons once they have been *well drained.* If the cardoons have been cooked in advance and kept in their *blanc,* you must first reheat them in it. Cover them with the rest of the Mornay sauce. Sprinkle with the cheese.

Spread the butter on top of them, divided into small pieces.

Glaze rapidly (SEE GLAZING SAUCED DISHES, PAGE 15). When the surface of the dish is nice and golden, serve immediately.

Cardoons with Hollandaise Sauce or Other Sauce *(Cardon Sauce Hollandaise au Autre).* Cook the cardoons in the *blanc* until they are nice and tender. Since they will not be simmered in the sauce, as in other recipes, it is even more important to make sure they are properly cooked. Once the pieces have been drained, arrange them on a napkin-covered plate. Send the chosen sauce on the side in a sauceboat.

Carrots *(Carotte)*

The good time for carrots is from the end of May to September.

New carrots do not need to be blanched. When fully grown, or if the carrots come from late in the season, it is essential to blanch them first: this is to lessen their pronounced bitter taste as well as to help their cooking. In this case, trim the carrots and cut them according to the recipe, then put them in a pot of cold water and bring it to a boil.

Depending on how old the vegetable is, boil it for a shorter or longer time: 5–6 minutes, 10–12 minutes depending on the case. Drain the carrots and cook them as directed.

The different recipes for carrots that are presented not so much as an accompaniment but as a dish in their own right are almost always cooked in a water or bouillon base that includes butter and sugar, like GLAZED CARROTS AS A GARNISH. This is why we place such importance on that particular recipe.

Carrots Glazed as a Garnish *(Carottes Glacées pour Garnitures).* By "glazed," we mean that the carrots are covered with a brilliant film, like a sugar syrup, which makes them look like a beautiful compote. Indeed, Carême, the master chef, defined "glazed" vegetables—carrots, turnips, and onions—as the "compote" of the kitchen. The term compote implies, in all cases, that the fruit or vegetable is left whole.

Preparation of the carrots: For this recipe, the carrots, even new or small carrots, are not scraped clean nor are they rubbed in a towel with sea salt to remove their fine skin. They must always be very, very finely peeled.

If the carrots are young and very small, keep them whole and "turn" them when peeling them, using the same method as for mushrooms (SEE PAGE 490). Larger ones are cut into 2 or 4, depending on their size, and trimmed to eliminate the corners.

If using mature carrots, cut the larger ones into rounds 3½ centimeters (1⅝ inches) thick. Then divide each round into small quarters, and then trim into the shape of a large, elongated garlic clove, eliminating as much of the yellow inside part as possible, which is bland.

Cooking the carrots: The liquid used is generally water, occasionally replaced by a bouillon that has been perfectly degreased: in this case, omit the salt. The carrots must always be covered by the liquid. *Time: 35–40 minutes. Serves 6.*

500 grams (1 pounds, 2 ounces) of carrots; 6 deciliters (2½ cups) of water; 30 grams (1 ounce) of sugar; 60 grams (2¼ ounces, 4½ tablespoons) of butter; a good pinch of salt (6–8 grams/⅕ ounce).

PROCEDURE. Put the carrots and the other ingredients into a small, deep saucepan, piling them up so that you do not need a large amount of liquid to cover them. Bring it to a boil. Cover. Now let them cook very gently.

After 10 minutes, shake the pan lightly. Repeat after 7–8 minutes. Do not touch them again, because when they are finally done they may break if you mix them.

The carrots should be done at the same time that the liquid has almost completely evaporated. In fact, this liquid, combined with the butter and the sugar, should be a thick syrup. During this last stage, you must watch very carefully because this syrup can burn quickly. What's more, the carrots should be glazed only *just* at the moment before serving, because if they are left to wait, they will lose their shine. So, when the carrots are done and the liquid reduced appropriately, turn the heat way down so that they no longer boil but nonetheless stay warm.

Just a few moments before dressing the plate, lightly shake them in their syrup to envelop them in a light shining layer, like a varnish.

Carrots à la Bourgeoise *(Carottes à la Bourgeoise).* An excellent recipe, formerly produced by the famous cook Durand of Nîmes. We suggest butter for stewing the vegetables, but it can be replaced by lard or even olive oil. Choose carrots that are long and nice and red. *Time: 1 good hour. Serves 6.*

400 grams (14⅛ ounces) of carrots, net weight; 200 grams (7 ounces) of onions; 60 grams (2¼ ounces, 4½ tablespoons) of butter; 5–6 grams (⅕ ounce) of flour; 4 deciliters (1⅔ cups) of bouillon that has been completely degreased; 2 deciliters (6¾ fluid ounces, generous ¾ cup) of good milk; 2 nice egg yolks; 1 good teaspoon of minced parsley; salt, a pinch of superfine sugar, pepper, and grated nutmeg.

PROCEDURE. Scrape the carrots. Wash them. Cut them into thin, perfect rounds that are equally thick. *Blanch* them if necessary if they are mature. Cut the onion into fine slices. Put the carrots and the onions into a thick pot where they will not be too heaped up. Add butter, salt, and sugar. Do not cover. On gentle heat, braise them slowly, mixing the vegetables frequently so that they do not stick together.

They must not color at all, but soften and become a little golden as their own moisture evaporates. Allow *a good half hour* for this braising. Then sprinkle with the flour And mix carefully because the carrots will have become fragile. Let them cook gently for 2–3 minutes, then dilute them with the bouillon and the milk. Bring them to a boil, stirring continuously. Add pepper and nutmeg.

Turn the heat way down. Do not cover. Let them braise *for 15–20 minutes:* during this time, the vegetables will finish cooking and the sauce, infused with their flavor, will lightly reduce, gaining its final consistency. If you are not ready to serve, cover the pot to keep it warm until the moment the sauce is bound.

Some 5 minutes before serving, make the egg yolk liaison (SEE LIAISONS, PAGE 47). Check the seasoning. Add the minced parsley. If you like, add, off the heat, a walnut-size piece of fresh butter; or, as is done in Nîmes, 1 tablespoon of olive oil, mixing it in by shaking the pan that contains the carrots. Serve good and hot.

Carrots à la Vichy *(Carottes à la Vichy).* This relatively modern name is, in fact, applied to carrots prepared using the same recipe given for garnishes. The recipe is most appropriate for new carrots—that is, young carrots. Use long or half-long carrots, which are red on the inside. Add Vichy salt or baking soda (bicarbonate of soda) to the ingredients, not for medicinal reasons, but to replace the natural mineral water of the Vichy region, which is low in calcium and therefore cooks carrots to perfection. *Time: At least 1 hour. Serves 6.*

500 grams (1 pound, 2 ounces) of carrots; 1/2 liter (generous 2 cups) of water; 50 grams (1 3/4 ounces, 3 1/2 tablespoons) of fresh butter; 15 grams (1/2 ounce) of sugar; 5 grams (1/6 ounce) of salt; a pinch of bicarbonate of soda (baking soda); 1 small teaspoon of minced parsley.

PROCEDURE. Peel the carrots, eliminating all the greenish parts of the stem. Cut them into rounds at least 1/2 centimeter (3/16 inch) thick so they will cook evenly.

Put them in a thick pot where they will have enough room to be easily moved about without having to touch them with a spoon, which might break them. Add the butter, divided into pieces; salt; sugar; water; and baking soda. *Cover.*

Bring to a boil. Turn the heat down very low and maintain a small, regular simmer for *a half hour.* During this time, and once the water has substantially reduced, toss the carrots very carefully so that you do not break them.

Do this 3 times during the following 15 minutes: that makes a total of *45 minutes* to cook. Once the liquid has been quite reduced, turn the heat down very low, so that, like glazed carrots, they are done at the same time as the liquid is fully reduced and has turned into a *very thick* syrup.

Just before serving, and only then, toss them in order to glaze them, very carefully, given their fragility. Pour them into a heated vegetable plate. Sprinkled the minced parsley on top. Serve immediately.

Carrots à la Crème *(Carottes à la Crème).* *Time: 1 hour.* There are two ways to add the final cream. But the carrots are initially cooked the same way.

The carrots are cut into rounds or, if you are using new carrots, turned. Cook them exactly as for the garnish. Once their liquid has been reduced to a syrup, add, for 500 grams (1 pound, 2 ounces) of carrots, 2 1/2 deciliters (1 cup) of heavy cream. Boil on strong heat to reduce the cream to the point where it completely envelops the carrots without excess sauce.

Alternatively: prepare a little bit of béchamel sauce without any other flavoring except a bunch of parsley and some grated nutmeg. That is, 2 deciliters (6 3/4 fluid ounces, generous 3/4 cup) of sauce, to which you will add 1 scant deciliter (3 1/3 fluid oucnes, scant 1/2 cup) of heavy cream for the quantities above. Mix this sauce with the glazed carrots and toss everything for a moment to mix it thoroughly.

Celery *(Céleri)*

Celery is a rather important winter vegetable, not only in its own right, but also as a garnish for braised meats. Here, we give the principal recipes; it can also be served in a fritter and in a purée with potatoes added to it.

No matter which recipe is used, celery must

always be initially braised, using generous amounts of fat, because celery is greedy for fat just as spinach is greedy for butter. A meatless braise will always give poor results: the celery will always remain slightly dry from its initial cooking, and this cannot be compensated for by the butter added at the end.

Since this preliminary braising takes a rather long time, we suggest preparing the celery in quantities that can provide enough for 2 or 3 meals, even though put to different uses; it really does not take that much more time to cook 8 or 10 stalks instead of 3 or 4; and aside from the purchase of a stalk of celery, the additional expense is insignificant. The leftover celery can be kept for a rather long time; it is enough to thoroughly drain the stalks of celery and to keep them on a plate in a very cool spot, simply covered by buttered parchment paper placed directly on top of them to keep off the dust.

Preparation of celery: The bunches of celery should have nice, white ribs; any green stalks will remain stringy despite prolonged cooking. For braising, choose stalks from small and medium bunches; very large ones are hardly appropriate. This is not only because the smaller ones are more tender, but because their size allows you to keep them in their original shape: that is, with all the branches attached to the root, which is the best part of the celery.

Begin by removing all the outside branches, which are green, hollow, and tough. Then cut off the branches (the green end) at the place where the white stops. That is about 15 centimeters (6 inches) above the root. The white part could be a little bit longer or a little bit shorter: it depends on how the celery was grown. In all cases, it is the white part you want, though this must not be more than 18–20 centimeters (7–8 inches) long.

Depending on the size of the stalk, and if the white part is rather long, you can even cut it into 2 pieces, each part no shorter than 10 centimeters (4 inches); the choicest part is always, of course, the part near the root. Let us note in passing that some of the stalks you have not used can still be good for a pot-au-feu or for a mixture of cooked vegetables.

Peel the root, trimming it and cutting it to a point like the point of a large square nail.

Wash the stalks of celery in plenty of water, separating the branches one by one, almost right to the heart of the vegetable, because they may contain small stones or pebbles.

Drain them and plunge them in a large pot or stockpot of boiling water. When it returns to a boil, let them boil strongly for *10 good minutes.*

Remove the stalks with a skimmer and plunge them into cold water, changing it to cool them more quickly. Drain them by shaking them and then put them on a towel to finish draining. Surround the stalks of celery with a few turns of string, but do not pull too tight.

Cooking Celery. You can allow one-half stalk of celery for 2 people. *Makes 6 medium stalks of celery.*

100 grams (3½ ounces) of fresh fatty bacon, or use the equivalent of trimmings; ½ carrot; 1 large onion; a bouquet garni; 1 good liter (4¼ cups) of bouillon that is very lightly salted; 4 tablespoons of cooking grease.

PROCEDURE. Use a sauté pan that is large enough to hold the celery stalks one next to the other, but not too large. On the bottom of the sauté pan, spread out the bacon, coarsely chopped. Spread out the carrot and the onion on top, cut into rounds. On top of this, arrange the celery stalks, placing them head to tail. Put the bouquet garni in the middle; season with a small pinch of pepper. Add the bouillon and the cooking grease. If the pan is the right size, there will be *just* enough bouillon to more or less bathe the celery stalks. If there does not seem to be enough liquid, add a little bit more bouillon or water.

Bring it to a boil. Right on top of the celery, put a round of white greased paper. Cover the pan. Put it into a medium oven, which is just hot enough to maintain the liquid at a constant, very gentle simmer. From this moment allow it to cook for *1¾ hours.* At the end of 1½ hours, you can check to see if it is cooked by lightly pinching a stalk; it is particularly important to do this because some celery plants cook more easily than others.

Once the celery has been cooked, take them from the pan with a skimmer, being careful not to break them; drain them in a drum sieve (at this point, set aside the celery you wish to reserve for another meal, as suggested above).

For the celery that is to be used immediately: untie them. Cut them into 2 or 3 lengthwise, depending on their thickness, so that each piece includes a part of the root. Drain them carefully so that there is no liquid left among their leaves, which would dilute the sauce that is poured on the celery to serve it. Arrange them on a warm serving plate. To shorten the length of the celery stalks and to make it easier to serve them, fold back the ends onto the root. Keep them warm while you finish the sauce.

PRINCIPAL RECIPES

Celery au Jus *(Céleri au Jus).* *Time: 2 hours.* Prepare this according to your resources: that is, use a brown sauce or a veal jus, or be more economical and use only their cooking liquid for their sauce. We will indicate these two last methods, establishing the quantities for 3 bunches of celery stalks, which will serve 6 people.

Once the celery has been untied, divided, and kept warm, strain the cooking liquid through a fine chinois; thoroughly degrease it.

If using veal jus: In the pan used for cooking the celery, which should first be rinsed and dried, pour 4 deciliters (1²/₃ cups) of the cooking juice. Boil strongly, uncovered, until the liquid is reduced to *2 deciliters (6³/₄ fluid ounces, generous ³/₄ cup).* Add *1 deciliter (3¹/₃ fluid ounces, scant ¹/₂ cup)* of good veal jus. Let it boil for 2 minutes. Bind with 8 grams (¹/₃ ounce) of starch diluted in 2 tablespoons of bouillon or cool jus. Finish with 30 grams (1 ounce, 2 tablespoons) of butter off the heat.

If you are not using veal jus: In the same way, reduce 6 deciliters (2¹/₂ cups) of the degreased cooking juices to a quantity of 3 deciliters (1¹/₄ cups).

Make the liaison however you like, either with starch, as above, or with a roux (SEE LIAISONS, PAGE 47). If the latter, prepare a brown roux in a small saucepan, with 15 grams of butter (¹/₂ ounce, 1 tablespoon) and 10 grams (¹/₃ ounce) of flour; simmer this roux while reducing the cooking liquid. Then dilute the roux with the reduced liquid. Bring it to a boil; let it very gently boil for *7–8 minutes.* Off the heat, add the butter. Then pour it on the celery, which should be well drained and arranged on a plate or on a vegetable dish.

If you cannot serve the celery immediately, it would be better to put it in a pot and cover it with the sauce, then let it simmer there very gently until you are ready to serve; the butter should, of course, be added only at the very last moment.

Celery with Marrow *(Céleri à la Moelle).* As for the celery au jus, but with rounds of marrow: use 100 grams (3¹/₂ ounces) of good, fresh beef marrow for 3 bunches of celery. Cut the marrow into rounds ¹/₂ centimeter (³/₁₆ inch) thick, using a good knife with a large blade, dipped in warm water. Some *10 minutes* before serving, put the rounds into a small pot filled with boiling water, turning down the heat very low, making sure that the water only slightly simmers.

Once the celery has been dressed and sauced, spread the well-drained marrow rounds on top and serve.

Celery with Sauce Mornay *(Céleri Sauce Mornay).* Prepared as previously directed, sauced with *3 deciliters (1¹/₄ cups)* of Mornay sauce, made with the cooking liquid reduced as above and then added in the proportion of one-third (SEE MORNAY SAUCE, PAGE 63).

Celeriac *(Céleri-Rave)*

The very strong flavor of celeriac is like celery, and the two vegetables are prepared the same way. That is, raw or cooked, in a salad; in an hors d'oeuvres; or cut into a large, raw julienne seasoned with an oil-and-vinegar sauce strongly flavored with mustard. Or as a vegetable dish, served with a béchamel sauce, a cream sauce, Mornay sauce, Italian sauce, bordelaise sauce, etc., according to whether or not the recipe includes meat. The celeriac is first cooked three-quarters of the way through in boiling water, and then is finished in the sauce at a very gentle simmer, just as for BORDEAUX-STYLE CELERIAC (PAGE 488). You can also stuff a celeriac in the same way as a cucumber.

Choose celeriac with small- or medium-size bodies: large ones are often hollow and their pulp is porous. You want the celeriac to be quite firm with a rather yellowish pulp, and bear in mind that you will lose about one-third of its weight by peeling it.

Preparation of celeriac: Peel the celeriac. That is, remove the outside part so that you have a flesh that is thoroughly clean and smooth with no woody fibers remaining.

The celeriac can be cut into rounds, quarters, or pieces shaped like large garlic cloves: the most suitable shape depends on the size of the celeriac heads. For rounds, slices are cut about 1 good centimeter (3/8 inch) thick; if you use a pastry cutter, you should cut them about 5 good centimeters (2 inches) in diameter. So, 750 grams (1 pound, 10 ounces) of celeriac net weight would give you about 30 rounds.

Once the celeriac has been cut, put it into a saucepan amply covered with cold water and salted at the rate of 7 grams (1/4 ounce) per liter. Cover. Let it cook until a fork can easily pierce a piece. The cooking time varies a little bit depending on the way it is cut and, of course, on the thickness of the celery; and also according to its quality. You should allow about *45 minutes.* The time is somewhat shorter when the celeriac is simmered in the sauce to finish cooking.

Drain the celeriac thoroughly in a colander, and even wipe it off afterward so that it retains no moisture, which might dilute the sauce.

Bordeaux-Style Celeriac *(Céleri-Rave à la Bordelaise).* *Time: 1 hour, 30 minutes. Serves 6.*

750 grams (1 pound, 10 ounces) of celeriac, net weight after skinning and peeling; about 4 deciliters (1 2/3 cups) of bordelaise sauce; 30 grams (1 ounce, 2 tablespoons) of butter for the final finishing; lemon juice.

PROCEDURE. First prepare the sauce (SEE BORDELAISE SAUCE, PAGE 57). Cook the celeriac as above. Put it in a sauté pan. Skim the sauce, then strain it through a chinois onto the celeriac. Cover. Simmer it for *15–20 minutes* on gentle heat.

To serve: In a well-heated timbale, vegetable dish, or shallow bowl, place the celeriac pieces, taking them out of the sauce one by one. Next, place the uncovered sauté pan on strong heat. Boil the sauce strongly for a few minutes while you stir it continuously, until it takes on a consistency that is thicker, though still quite light; there should be at least 3 deciliters (1 1/4 cups). Off the heat, mix in the butter and lemon juice. Check the seasoning and pour it on the celeriac.

Purée of Celeriac *(Purée de Céleri-Rave).* This is excellent as a garnish for braised or sautéed meats—veal, mutton, or pork—and especially for sausages that have been grilled or pan-fried.

A celeriac purée always has steamed or boiled potatoes added to it. In haute cuisine, the celeriac and potatoes are cooked separately, and the proportion of potato used is one-third of the weight of the celeriac, both weighed after cooking.

In home kitchens, you can simplify this by cooking the two vegetables together, but not for the same length of time; that is, cooking the celeriac takes longer than the potatoes, which should be added only at the right time—say, *20–25 minutes* before straining everything into a purée. Cooked longer, they absorb too much water and give you all the disadvantages explained in the section on potato purée. *Time: Serves 6.*

500 grams (1 pound, 2 ounces) of peeled celeriac, net weight; 175–200 grams (6–7 ounces) of potatoes, net weight; 60 grams (2 1/4 ounces, 4 1/2 tablespoons) of butter; about 1 deciliter (3 1/3 fluid ounces, scant 1/2 cup) of milk; a pinch of salt and a pinch of sugar.

PROCEDURE. Peel the celeriac; divide it into slices that are scarcely larger than 1 good centimeter (3/8 inch) at their widest part. Cook them as directed for *about 30 minutes,* then add the potatoes: these should not be too large, so that you do not have to divide them into too many pieces, the disadvantage being that the thin parts are overcooked before the thick parts are cooked at all. Cover. Let it cook for *20–25 minutes.*

Pass everything into a purée through a metallic drum sieve (SEE PURÉES, PAGE 14).

Gather the purée in a sauté pan. Add the butter and dry it out on strong heat, as directed (PAGE 14). Sprinkle with salt and sugar. Add the warm milk, proceeding just as you would for potato purée.

Cèpes *(Cèpe)*

The season of the common cèpe is from the end of August to the middle of October. Like mushrooms, they should be used only when they are very fresh and when the flesh is firm to the touch. If it is soft, and if your imprint remains when you press your finger on it, it would be prudent to reject it.

These can be made au gratin, à la crème, with tomato, with ham, grilled, etc. But the two most common methods, and the most popular, are those known as "à la bordelaise" and "à la provençale." They are prepared in more or less the same way. The difference is that in "à la bordelaise," the shallot is the essential ingredient; while in "à la Provençale" it is onion and garlic. In both cases, use oil for cooking. However, when making cèpes bordelaise, you can use oil and butter to finish. The best oil is olive oil, whether "fruity" or not, depending on your preference.

Bordeaux-Style Cèpes *(Cèpes à la Bordelaise).*

First we will give the recipe for fresh cèpes. *Time: 25 minutes. Serves 6.*

750 grams (1 pound, 10 ounces) of fresh cèpes; 2 deciliters ($6^3/_4$ fluid ounces, generous $^3/_4$ cup) of oil; 30 grams (1 ounce, 2 tablespoons) of butter; 25 grams (1 ounce) of finely minced shallot; a good pinch of minced parsley; a lemon quarter; salt and pepper.

PROCEDURE. Cèpes soften very quickly after cooking if left to stand; so, instead, make your guests wait for them. Put them on the heat knowing that you will be able to serve them as soon as they are ready: they should take a good 15 minutes.

Preparation of cèpes: If you are able to choose, pick out medium-sized ones rather than large ones with very short stems.

Do not wash fresh cèpes. If they have been harvested the same day, do not peel them either: just wipe them with a dry towel. If the skin is a little bit spotted, remove it with the point of a small knife without going into the flesh. Then wipe off the cèpe.

With the point of a knife, begin by removing the very ends of the stem of the cèpes, which were in the soil, peeling them so they are pear shaped, with rounded ends. Then cut the tails off level with the cap. From each one, cut a round that is at least 1 centimeter ($^3/_8$ inch) thick and taken from the tender part right next to the cap. This part is reserved for the minced hash: the rest of the tail is rather woody and holds lots of water, so it is not generally used for cèpes à la bordelaise. That said, you can use the stems for another stuffing, so preserve them by chopping them with a little bit of onion and cooking them in butter or oil.

When the cèpes are small, it is better to "scallop" them—that is, to cut them in completely even slices, cut on the bias. They must be 1 good centimeter ($^3/_8$ inch) in the thickest part. Cut rounds from the stems. Finally, mince the shallot. Put everything on a plate.

Cooking cèpes: In a medium-sized pan that is quite clean, put $1^1/_2$ deciliters (5 fluid ounces, $^2/_3$ cup) of oil. Heat it just to the point where it is *smoking*. Put in the scalloped cèpes (without seasoning them, which will be done a little bit later). Keep the pan on a rather strong heat. After *2 minutes,* they should be completely brown on one side, so quickly turn over the cèpes with a fork and let them color the same way on the other side.

(You can also brown the cèpes by tossing them in the pan, but given the amount of oil used, this is rather dangerous for anyone not overly familiar with managing a pan, and it is more sensible to turn them over as we suggested.)

When the cèpes are well browned, turn the heat down quite low to let them cook for *5–6 minutes.* After that, if you find they have softened a little bit, put the pan on strong heat to stiffen them up and then turn them over one more time with the fork.

Having done this, loosely cover the pan with a pot cover held in your left hand. With your right hand, pick up the pan by the handle and then tip it, so that you make all the oil run out. Then season the cèpes with a pinch of fine salt and a pinch of pepper. Toss them for an instant to thoroughly mix the seasoning. Then pour them into a timbale or into a vegetable dish, heated in advance. Keep them warm.

NOTE: Do not put pepper in at the beginning because it will burn, making the cèpes bitter. The oil used to cook the cèpes is not lost; add it to a meatless fat for a deep-frying mixture.

To finish and serve: Quickly put the remaining oil and the butter in the pan (or a little more oil and no butter; it's purely a matter of taste.) Heat it on strong heat until the mixture begins to smoke lightly, and then add the hash of cèpes and shallots. Sauté everything on strong heat until it is slightly browned, which barely takes a minute if the heat is rather strong. Then immediately pour the entire contents of the pan onto the cèpes. Squeeze the lemon quarter over it; sprinkle with the minced parsley. Serve immediately with *very hot* plates.

Cèpes à la Bordelaise Made with Preserved Mushrooms. *(Les Cèpes à la Bordelaise avec de la Conserve).* A half can will be enough for 6 people.

Open the can, then pour the cèpes into a colander to get rid of some of their gluey coating. Put them in a terrine with rather hot water (not boiling). Mix them for a few moments in this water to remove their coating; drain them by taking them out in your hand. Wipe them thoroughly with a clean and dry towel. Then divide them into scallops as above.

Reserve about 40 grams ($1^3/_8$ ounces) of the stem (or cèpe if there is no stem) and chop. To this mixture, add the shallot, just as for fresh cèpes.

Heat about 1 deciliter ($3^1/_3$ fluid ounces, scant $^1/_2$ cup) of oil in the pan (use less rather than more for this recipe). Sauté the cèpes over strong heat and turn them over with the fork until they are browned and nice and firm. No special attention is required when cooking. All you have to do is make sure that they brown properly. Then proceed as directed for seasoning, browning the hash mixture, and adding lemon juice and parsley.

Provençal-Style Cèpes *(Les Cèpes à la Provençale).* For both fresh and preserved cèpes, the recipe is the same as à la bordelaise except for these small differences:

Only oil is used, and it must be *olive* oil. The shallot is replaced by *onion and garlic.* Thus, for the given quantities: 20 grams ($^2/_3$ ounce) of finely minced onion; 5 grams ($^1/_6$ ounce) of garlic, first crushed under the blade of a knife and then subsequently finely minced. The amount of garlic can be increased according to taste.

For all other directions, refer to cèpes à la bordelaise.

Mushrooms *(Champignon)*

Mushrooms for Garnish *(Champignons pour Garnitures).* A frequent error made in home kitchens is to add mushrooms directly to sauces and ragoûts and then to cook them for far too long. Treated this way, mushrooms become bland and leathery and lose their value as part of the dish. When used in sauces, they contribute more than their flavor, becoming themselves an important element. Mushroom trimmings, which are practically unknown in home kitchens, are enough to flavor a sauce. You should also, of course, use the liquid used for cooking the mushrooms, a veritable essence.

To preserve their quality, mushrooms must be cooked separately, at full boil, with little liquid. The extra work cooking them separately is no more than cleaning the small pan used.

Choosing: We are dealing, of course, with cultivated mushrooms. These must be fresh. You can recognize this by the whiteness of the cap, the firm texture, and the shape: the cap must be connected directly to the stem and not be opened out like a parasol.

Mushrooms for garnish should be as equal as possible in size and quite small so that they can be served whole. This makes for a more attractive dish. When it is impossible to get small mushrooms, cut them into halves or quarters, but only *after* cooking.

Cleaning: Cut off the grainy part at the bottom of the stem. Lightly scrape the stem.

Put the mushrooms into a container of cool water; mix them vigorously, rubbing them with your hands to remove the sand and dirt that is sometimes found under the caps. Wash them in a second container of water, picking them out from the first with your hand to leave behind the dirt and sand. Don't leave them in the water too long or they will lose their aroma and become flaccid. Dry them in a strainer or with a towel, so they can be immediately peeled and cooked.

Have a pot ready to put the mushrooms in as you peel them. *For 225 grams (8 ounces) mushrooms, put a scarce half glass (1 scant deciliter/$3^1/_3$*

fluid ounces, scant 1/2 cup) of fresh water in the pot, a pinch of salt (3 grams/ 1/10 ounce), and the juice of half a lemon. The lemon juice keeps the mushrooms white.

Peeling and turning the mushrooms: Cut off the stems level with the cap. In fine restaurants, the stems are not used in a garnish; they are considered mushroom "trimmings," used only for cooking sauces, unless included in a dish with minced mushrooms or in a gratin. In home cooking, you can add them to the caps if you have no better use for them.

The next step is to peel the mushrooms. Do this not with the defective technique of incompetent cooks—which consists of tearing and scraping the skin with the knife as if flaying an umbrella, which leaves a cottony and unequal surface—but by *turning* them. The culinary operation known as "turning the mushroom" is one of the most simple. The mushroom is peeled in a spiral, just the way you peel an apple, with the knife cutting only slightly into the mushroom. This way, you obtain a smooth, clean, and attractive surface.

To "turn" the mushroom, take the cap between three fingers of the left hand (including the thumb). Turn it into the blade of a small sharp knife held in your right hand. *The knife itself must not move.* Take off about 1–2 millimeters (no more than 1/16 inch) of skin. With a little practice, you will produce perfectly smooth mushroom caps without any knife marks. But the knife must be sharp!

As you peel them, throw them in the pot, mixing them so that the lemon juice in the water bathes them completely, keeping them from discoloring. Keep the peelings for sauces; they are added raw.

To cook: When all the mushrooms are in the pot, add *30 grams (1 ounce, 2 tablespoons) of butter* (a piece the size of a walnut). Put the covered pot on strong heat; boil strongly, making sure the boiling liquid covers the mushrooms. Cook for 4–5 minutes, shaking the pot a few times. Take them off the heat and keep them warm until adding them to the dish. Strain off all the liquid before adding them to a sauce or stew.

Prepared this way, mushrooms can keep until the next day, immersed in their cooking liquid and covered. Don't forget that this cooking liquid is itself a veritable essence that should be carefully preserved for a number of uses if it is not required for the dish you are preparing.

Stuffed Mushrooms *(Champignons Farcis).* These are, of course, cultivated mushrooms. Make sure you choose the largest and freshest available, and as equal as possible in size. Stuffed mushrooms are used primarily as an accompaniment to large roasts, but they can also be served as a vegetable. Serve them on a round plate surrounded by a few tablespoons of brown sauce or a light tomato sauce and sprinkled with minced parsley.

If convenient, the mushrooms can be stuffed well in advance so that all you have to do at the last moment is put them into the oven. They must be served as soon as they come out of the oven. *Time: 30 minutes to prepare the mushrooms; 15 minutes to brown and crisp them. Serves 6–8.*

15 mushrooms, with their stems and peelings; 60 grams (2 1/4 ounces) of onion and 40 grams (1 3/8 ounces) of shallots, minced; 30 grams (1 ounce, 2 tablespoons) of butter and 4 tablespoons of oil; 1 scant tablespoon of minced parsley; 1 clove of garlic; 1 1/2 deciliters (5 fluid ounces, 2/3 cup) of white wine; 1 deciliter (3 1/3 fluid ounces, scant 1/2 cup) of bouillon; 2 tablespoons of concentrated tomato purée; 1 good teaspoon of flour worked with 10 grams (1/3 ounce) butter; 60 grams (2 1/4 ounces) of stale French bread, the crust trimmed and crumbled for breading; 2 tablespoons fine bread crumbs; salt and pepper.

PROCEDURE. Trim the grainy end of the stem. Do not peel the mushrooms. Wash and dry them. Remove the stems, and, with the point of the knife, cut out the inside of the cap. When you are finished, the caps must be like little bowls. Trim the edges smooth. Put the trimmings to the side with the stems.

Arrange the hollowed-out mushrooms on a plate, the open side up. Sprinkle each mushroom with a few drops of oil. Put them in a warm oven for 7–8 minutes to evaporate their moisture. When you take them out of the oven, turn them upside-down on the plate. Set aside.

The stuffing: Prepare as directed (SEE DUXELLES, PAGE 21), with the onion, shallot, and mushroom stems and trimmings. When there is no more steam rising from the pot, which indicates that their moisture has been sufficiently reduced, add the white wine. Keep the heat strong and let it reduce completely. Then add the bouillon, tomato purée, the crushed garlic, and the butter, mixed with the flour and then divided into small pieces so that it will integrate easily.

Simmer gently on low heat for 5–6 minutes; finish with the crumbled bread, which is used to thicken the stuffing. (If it's not thick enough, add more crumbled bread.) Add the parsley.

To stuff the mushrooms: The fastest and easiest way to do this is by using a pastry bag with a large nozzle. Or, failing that, a cone of strong paper with the tip cut to create an opening at least 1 centimeter (3/8 inch) big. Put the stuffing inside the cone. Arrange the mushrooms side by side on the plate. Fill them with the stuffing, which will form into a ball inside the mushrooms. They are then ready for the oven.

If you are using a spoon, put a good spoonful into each mushroom. Smooth it into a dome with a small knife that has been dipped in water. As the mushrooms are stuffed, arrange them on the plate. When they are finished, sprinkle them with the fine bread crumbs.

To *gratinée:* This will take 12–15 minutes, depending on the heat of the oven. Just before serving, put a dab of butter on each mushroom, or sprinkle them with a few drops of oil. Keep them in the oven until ready to serve.

Mushroom Purée *(Purée de Champignons).* Use cultivated mushrooms, as above. This purée is an excellent garnish for sweetbreads, stews, fowl, game, etc. The recipes vary; in the classic method, the mushrooms are cooked in the usual way with water, butter, and lemon juice (SEE MUSHROOMS FOR GARNISH, PAGE 490), then forced through a sieve. The purée is then bound with a very reduced béchamel. Modern cooks pass the raw mushrooms through the sieve, then heat this mixture in a sauté pan for a few moments to evaporate the moisture. Then you add the béchamel. You may also simply add butter to the minced mushrooms and cook for a few minutes, then add the béchamel and simmer for a few more minutes before making the purée.

No matter what the method, allow for every 500 grams (1 pound, 2 ounces) of mushrooms 2 deciliters (6 3/4 fluid ounces, generous 3/4 cup) of very reduced béchamel. (The reduced béchamel will include a total of 10 grams/ 1/3 ounce of flour per deciliter/scant 1/2 cup.) Adding some cream to the béchamel will make the dish more succulent. Alternatively, you could add 50 grams (1 3/4 ounces, 3 1/2 tablespoons) of butter after the dish is off the heat, just before serving. And don't forget a pinch of grated nutmeg when you add the salt and pepper.

Mushroom Shells *(Croûte aux Champignons).* To summarize, the mushrooms are cooked as usual with water, butter, and lemon juice; then mixed with a "parisienne" sauce, to which their cooking liquid is added, and served in a crusty shell of French bread that has been hollowed out, buttered, and dried in the oven.

The bread can be replaced by a vol-au-vent shell, a tart shell, or a shell cooked "à blanc" as for a raspberry tart; or by any of the other shells described (SEE CROÛTE À LA CRÈME, PAGE 674); or even in little shells or tartlets cooked à blanc; it's easier to serve like this. For shells made from bread, allow 1 shell per person.

Choose cultivated mushrooms that are so small you can leave their heads whole; and above all, make sure they are very fresh—that is, not opened out. But in spring and fall out in the country, you can use mushrooms from the fields and the woods, such as morels, St. George's mushroom, chanterelles, and cèpes, as long as they are always absolutely fresh.

Whatever the kind of mushroom you use and the kind of shell that you use, the sauce remains the same. We have given the minimum time for its preparation; a real allemande sauce takes longer to cook, so, if you have the time, start this dish further in advance (SEE SAUCE ALLEMANDE KNOWN AS PARISIENNE, PAGE 52).

The cream listed is not absolutely essential, but if you can get some we advise you not to leave it out because it refines the sauce and makes it smooth. *Time: 45 minutes. Serves 6.*

300 grams (10 1/2 ounces) of small mushrooms.

To cook them: 1 scant deciliter (3 1/3 fluid ounces, scant 1/2 cup) of water; 3 grams (1/10 ounce) of salt; 35 grams (generous 1 ounce, 2 tablespoons) of butter; juice of 1/2 lemon.

For the sauce: 20 grams (2/3 ounce) of flour and 20 grams (2/3 ounce, 1 heaping tablespoon) of butter to make a small blond roux; 4 deciliters (1 2/3 cups) of clear bouillon; a *small* bouquet garni; 2 nice egg yolks; the cooking liquid from the mushrooms; 4 tablespoons of cream, if possible; 25 grams (scant 1 ounce, 2 tablespoons) of butter to finish, with 1 teaspoon of lemon juice; pepper and grated nutmeg.

For the shell: 1 long demi-baguette (about 550 grams/ 1 pound, 3 ounces); about 45 grams (1 1/2 ounces, 3 tablespoons) of butter to butter the shells (thus, for the entire quantity of the dish, a total of 125 grams/ 4 1/2 ounces/ 9 tablespoons of butter).

PROCEDURE. **The sauce:** In a medium-size, thick aluminum pot, cook the blond roux (SEE PAGE 47). Dilute it with the bouillon, mixing with a small whisk. Season with pepper and a little bit of grated nutmeg, but not salt, because the bouillon has been salted. Bring it to a boil, stirring continuously with the whisk. Then turn the heat down; add the small bouquet garni and let it cook gently while the other parts are being prepared. As soon as the mushrooms have been turned, or "peeled," add 20 grams (2/3 ounce) of mushroom trimmings.

The mushrooms: "Turn" the heads as directed, or otherwise peel them in a home-style method. Cook in the same way as mushrooms for garnishes.

The shell: The most popular procedure is to cut them out from a long, special bread that is well risen. A long bread, split, or even a homemade bread can be used; both should be a little bit stale, without large holes in the bread. To cut the shells from them you should use the same directions as for the other breads.

With special breads: Cut 6 pieces 5–6 centimeters (2–2 1/2 inches) thick. Remove the bread from the inside, leaving a layer about 7–8 millimeters (1/4 inch) thick on one of its sides. Hollowed out thus, each piece becomes a kind of box, the bottom being the side with the layer of bread that was not removed.

With split bread: On 1 of the halves of the bread, cut 6 pieces 5 1/2 centimeters (2 1/4 inches) thick; remove the bread from the inside, again leaving a layer the same thickness as above on the side of the piece that will form the bottom.

Whatever kind of bread is chosen, butter the shells on all sides and particularly on the inside. Arrange them on a baking sheet and put them in a medium oven so that you can dry them out thoroughly and give them a golden sheen at the same time. While they are in the oven—they should take about *8 minutes*—watch carefully because they burn quickly.

Perfecting the sauce: Dilute the egg yolks in a bowl with the cream: or, if you do not have cream, with 4 tablespoons of the cooking liquid from the mushrooms. Then proceed for the liaison as directed for the parisienne sauce. Add all the juice from the mushrooms to the sauce, and boil, stirring continuously, until it has reduced to about *4 deciliters (1 2/3 cups).*

Check the seasoning and strain this sauce through a chinois into the pot that holds the mushrooms. Simmer the mushrooms in the sauce: simmer, but do not overtly boil, or they will harden up too much, for *4–5 minutes.*

To serve: Finish the sauce by adding, *off the heat,* butter and lemon. Mix everything by alternately tossing the mushrooms and gently shaking the pot.

Arrange the shells on a quite warm round plate. Using a metal spoon, fill the shells, being careful not to spread the sauce on the plates. Serve immediately on hot plates.

Chicory (Curly Endive) *(Chicorée)*

The masters of classic cuisine dedicated time, of which there is too little these days, and care, which is seldom taken now, to preparing their chicory dishes. They allowed 1–2 hours for braising the chicory—a cooking term signifying a very slow, regular simmer. The liaison was made with a few tablespoons of base sauce chosen according to the dish (velouté, béchamel, etc.), which is still done today in professional kitchens. In home kitchens, this liaison is replaced by a simple roux, which is added directly to the chicory.

Whether it is a matter of a garnish for a braised

meat or whether the chicory is to be presented as a vegetable plate, the preparation is the same. Served as a vegetable, prepared with a meat base and basted with a good veal juice, it appears on menus as chicory au jus. Prepared without meat and basted with cream in the place of jus, it appears as chicory à la crème. The recipe below is for braised chicory, which is appropriate as both a garnish and vegetable; in the latter case, you can, if you like, finish it with a veal jus. But even without this, it is already an excellent dish.

Here, we do not suggest passing it through a drum sieve; instead, it should be finely minced. Passing chicory through a drum sieve makes it less apt to pick up the flavors of the ingredients with which it is braised.

The chicory referred to here is, of course, frisée chicory. This is taken from the green part in the middle of the bunch, which is found between the outside limp leaves and the heart, which has a yellowish tint and is generally reserved for a salad. That said, the heart can be cooked with the rest if you do not want to reserve it.

If you buy chicory by weight, remember that after trimming it diminishes by almost half: a nice head weighs 500–600 grams (1 pound, 2 ounces–1 pound, 5 ounces), but when the stem and the hard leaves have been removed, it will give you only about 280 grams (9⁷/₈ ounces).

Braised Chicory for All Recipes. *Time: For trimming, blanching, etc., the chicory, a good 30 minutes; for braising it, 1³/₄ hours. Serves 6.*

> **About 1 kilogram (2 pounds, 3 ounces) of chicory, weighed after trimming; 30 grams (1 ounce, 2 tablespoons) of butter and 25 grams (about 1 ounce) of flour for the roux to make the liaison; 4 good deciliters (1²/₃ cups) of light jus or, if you do not have it, of very good degreased bouillon; 1¹/₂ deciliters (5 fluid ounces, ²/₃ cup) of very fresh heavy cream; 30–40 grams (1–1³/₈ ounce) of fine butter as a final complement. Pepper, grated nutmeg; a pinch of superfine sugar; and salt, depending on how salty the jus or bouillon is.**

PROCEDURE. **Trimming, blanching, chopping:** Tear apart the stalk of chicory where the leaves begin, and rather a bit higher than lower, because the rib is tough and bitter. Remove all the outside, shriveled leaves. The second and third layer should also be removed if they seem tough because they will not cook in the same way as the tender leaves, and you will find them clumped together later. With scissors, cut off the ends of the spoiled and shriveled leaves. Check carefully between the leaves; you will almost always find soil and small stones. If the stalks are large, cut them into quarters. As soon as the leaves are peeled, put them in a terrine of cold water. Wash them again for a second time; drain them in a towel.

During these preparations, put a large pot or basin of water on to boil, ready to *blanch* the chicory: so, for the quantities above, *3 liters (12³/₄ cups) of water and 25 grams (1 ounce)* of sea salt. There are two reasons for *blanching:* to reduce the bitterness, which is pronounced in late season; and to begin cooking the chicory, which makes it easier to chop.

Once the water is boiling, rapidly plunge in the chicory. Bring it quickly back to a boil, which will have been arrested by the cold vegetables. When boiling resumes, allow it to boil rapidly for *12–15 minutes,* and even a little bit more, depending on how tender the chicory is, and also how bitter. As soon as it is good and tender, take it out of the boiling water; prolonging its braising is preferable, if necessary.

Then drain the chicory; refresh it with large amounts of water. Drain it again. Squeeze handfuls of it strongly, little by little between your hands to express all the water. As you do this, place it on the cutting board (by now, the weight of the peeled chicory will have reduced by about a third.) With a large knife or a cleaver, finely and evenly chop the chicory. Then put it in a towel, and twist strongly to make the rest of the water come out. This elimination is particularly important because it means that the chicory will more thoroughly absorb the braising liquid.

Thus prepared, the chicory can stand for a few hours covered with parchment paper and left in a cool place, ready to be put into the braising pan.

Braising: Here it is essential to use a *thick* pot of very strong aluminum. Mix the butter and the flour in it to make a small, blond roux (SEE ROUX, PAGE 47). Add the chicory. Mix it well with the roux. Stir it continuously with a wooden spoon on strong heat for *4–5 minutes* so that you dry out the chicory.

After this, gradually pour the liquid into it, stirring continuously. Add pepper, sugar, and nutmeg, and salt if necessary. Stir, until bubbles indicate that it is boiling. There is a strong risk that the chicory will stick to the bottom of the pot and burn there if it is not constantly stirred with a spoon. Turn the heat off and place a round of white parchment paper, which has been buttered or greased, right on top of the chicory. Then put the cover on. Place the pot in a very moderate oven to maintain a gentle and regular simmer, for *1½ hours.* A stronger heat will be of no benefit and will also risk causing the chicory to stick to the pot. So keep a close eye on it, and always immediately recover with the paper and the cover. If, unfortunately, you do not have an oven, this cooking can, with great effort, be done on very low heat. But the all-around heat of an oven is preferable.

To finish and serve: Take the pot out of the oven. Mix the cream into the chicory, which will dilute its thick consistency. Heat it and boil for a few moments, or a little longer if the consistency of the chicory does not seem thick enough. What you want is to be able to dress the chicory in the salad bowl and keep the imprint of the tines of the fork, which you use to trace decorative lines on it.

Working *entirely off the heat,* complete the dish with the fine butter, divided into small pieces so that it mixes in more rapidly. Check the seasoning. Dress as above. Decorate, if you like, with a dozen small golden croutons cooked in butter, quite warm and arranged in a circle.

Meatless chicory: The recipe is the same as the previous one, replacing the jus or bouillon with *very good milk* for the braising. Use double the quantity of butter to finish. If you like, you can baste it with 1 deciliter (3⅓ fluid ounces, scant ½ cup) of cream that has been previously boiled and lightly salted. Garnish with small fried croutons.

Chicory au Gratin *(Chicorée au Gratin).* You can use chicory leftovers, adding about one-third of their volume of potato purée: this is an extremely good vegetable dish for lunch. Thus, for about 225 grams (8 ounces) of braised chicory: 150 grams (5⅓ ounces) of potatoes (weighed peeled), 15–20 grams (½–⅔ ounce, 1 tablespoon) of butter, 2–3 tablespoons of their cooking liquid. Prepare the purée as directed (SEE POTATO PURÉE, PAGE 540). Mix it with the chicory. Put it on very low heat for 5–6 minutes to heat everything.

Then put the chicory in a shallow, ovenproof bowl, which is buttered and sprinkled with grated Gruyère. Smooth the surface with the back of a spoon or the blade of a knife. Sprinkle it with 15 grams (½ ounce) of grated Gruyère and 1 tablespoon of fine bread crumbs, mixed together on a plate. Generously spread with melted butter or oil, according to taste. Put it in a hot oven with the dish on the top shelf or even under a broiler so that its surface receives the greatest heat. *Eight to ten minutes* should be enough to form a nice golden crust on the chicory. Serve immediately.

Chicory Loaf à la Crème *(Pain de Chicorée à la Crème).* For meat-free meals, this loaf is both decorative and substantial, and it is extremely simple to make. *Time: To prepare the chicory, a good 1½ hours; to poach the loaf, 45–50 minutes; 2½ hours total. Serves 6.*

About 750 grams (1 pound, 10 ounces) of chicory (net weight); 20 grams (⅔ ounce, 1 heaping tablespoon) of butter and 15 grams (½ ounce) of flour for the roux to make the liaison; 1½ deciliters (5 fluid ounces, ⅔ cup) of milk; a pinch of salt; a pinch of pepper; some grated nutmeg; 3 whole eggs and 2 yolks.

For the sauce: 20 grams (⅔ ounce, 1 heaping tablespoon) of butter and 15 grams (½ ounce) of flour for the white roux; 2½ deciliters (1 cup) of boiled milk; 1 deciliter (3⅓ fluid ounces, scant ½ cup) of very fresh light cream.

PROCEDURE. Prepare and cook the chicory exactly as directed for braised chicory (PAGE 494), observing only that the roux here is a white roux (roux blanc), that the *milk* replaces the *jus* or bouillon, and the cooking time is only *1 good hour.*

Use a charlotte mold or a timbale with a 1-liter (4-cup) capacity. With the end of your fingers, spread a nice chunk of butter the size of a walnut in it, being sure that you have spread it everywhere, particularly in the corners: otherwise, unmolding it will be difficult, even impossible.

Beat the whole eggs and the yolks as if for an omelet. Make the liaison of the chicory with the necessary precautions (SEE LIAISONS, PAGE 47). Taste it to see if you need to accentuate the seasoning, because it becomes more bland whenever you add egg. Then pour the chicory into the mold. Poach it in the bain-marie (double boiler) for 45–50 minutes (SEE PAGE 42).

Meanwhile, prepare the sauce as directed (SEE CREAM SAUCE, PAGE 63).

To serve: Remove the mold from the water; but do not unmold the loaf immediately. Wait 6–7 minutes so it shrinks a bit. Meanwhile, finish the sauce and add the cream to it. Unmold the loaf on a round, heated plate. Cover with the sauce. Serve immediately.

Chicory Soufflé *(Soufflé à la Chicorée).* Proceed as for a SPINACH SOUFFLÉ (PAGE 513), having first braised the chicory.

Cabbage *(Chou)*

Cabbage for Garnishes. The usable part of the cabbage is only the heart—that is, the firm part whose leaves are a pale yellow, scarcely tinged with green on the ends.

To peel and blanch cabbage: Divide each heart into 4–6 pieces. Remove the stem as well as the large exterior ribs of the leaves.

Wash the pieces in plenty of water, spreading apart the leaves to check if there are any stones hidden there. Drain in a drum sieve so that you do not chill the boiling water too much when you immerse them. So, for 2 medium-size cabbages, use 4 liters (4 1/4 quarts) of water at a rolling boil in a large pot or other utensil. Once you have added the cabbage and the water has returned to a boil, allow *10–15 minutes* at a strong boil, depending on whether or not the cabbage is young or old. The older the cabbage is, the longer it must be blanched.

Drain the cabbage in a drum sieve. Then soak it in a large amount of cold water and let it disgorge for about 10 minutes. Drain it again. Squeeze each piece between your hands to completely extract the water. Place it on a table. Remove the leaves and spread them out on a towel. With a small knife. remove the hard part left on the ribs.

To braise cabbage: Lightly season with salt and pepper. Arrange in a sauté pan lined with a bard of fatback bacon; add a carrot cut into quarters, an onion stuck with a clove, a bouquet garni, and 1/2 liter (generous 2 cups) of bouillon that has not been degreased; cover everything with a bard of fatback bacon. Bring to a boil. Cover, then put it in an oven *for 2 hours* at medium heat to maintain the liquid at a simple simmer.

NOTE. Depending on the case, you can also shape the cabbage into balls, as directed for the GARNISH À LA FLAMANDE (PAGE 262).

Stuffed Cabbage. Stuffed cabbage is a recipe that belongs to home cooking: if you like, you can stuff it with a hash of pork or with leftover meats; or even a meat-free stuffing, as we will also indicate.

For a meat stuffing, using leftovers is the most economical method and also produces excellent results, as long as you choose the appropriate meat. Generally speaking, this means that roasted meats should not be used: the stuffing is dry and granular. In preference, use braised or boiled meats; indeed, the best cooked meat stuffing is the beef from a pot-au-feu, as long as it comes from a piece that is not too dry. The top rib of beef is perfect because of the large amount of fat that it contains, which is excellent for the cabbage: the resulting stuffing is unctuous and smooth.

Above all, it is essential that the stuffing include a substantial quantity of fat, whether from the meat itself or from the fatback bacon that is added. The amount of fatback bacon must be increased when you use a meat that is a little bit dry—the leftovers of a braised shoulder of mutton, for example.

If using pork meat purchased specifically for the stuffing, the quantity of fat and lean should be equal. To this hash of pork meat, bread crumbs are usually added, having been soaked first in bouillon and egg. So, for 225 grams (8 ounces) of pork, use a nice whole beaten egg and the same volume as the egg of stale bread, plus 1 tablespoon of finely minced onion and the same amount of parsley. Add garlic or shallot, if you like. The stuffing does not need to be browned first—that is, colored in hot fat or butter. It can be put uncooked into the cabbage.

As a final direction, let us advise you to prepare the cabbage well in advance—always the night before if serving at lunch. This means that you can take the necessary care and will also be able to devote enough time to cooking the dish. Stuffed cabbage can never be overcooked, and it can stand, simmering, for as long as you like. It is excellent reheated with a few tablespoons of bouillon.

Home-Style Stuffed Cabbage *(Chou Farci à la Ménagère).* The method of blanching the cabbage—that is, cooking it first in boiling water—differs slightly from other methods. It comes from an experienced practitioner, who considered it more practical since the tough, interior parts of the cabbage are cooked better by the gradually heating liquid. *Time: 4 hours (the cabbage having been stuffed and prepared in advance). Serves 6–8, depending on the size of the menu.*

1 Milan cabbage or a firm Napa cabbage of medium size, weighing, when completely trimmed and cleaned, 1 good kilogram (2 pounds, 3 ounces).

To stuff: 250 grams (8⁷/₈ ounces) of boiled beef; 50 grams (1³/₄ ounces) of fatback bacon; 5 grams (¹/₆ ounce) of salt; a pinch of pepper; a pinch of spice powder; 1 tablespoon of minced parsley; 1 deciliter (3¹/₃ fluid ounces, scant ¹/₂ cup) of white wine; a little bit of garlic or shallot according to taste; 2 large bards of fatback bacon to wrap the cabbage.

Cooking the cabbage: An onion and a carrot cut into rounds; ¹/₂ liter (generous 2 cups) of bouillon; 2 tablespoons of fat from a pot-au-feu.

PROCEDURE. Cut the stem of the cabbage level with the head. Remove any leaves that are too green or spoiled. Using a good kitchen knife, make an incision all around the stem, cutting deeply to remove as much as possible of the stem without detaching the leaves. This helps the hot liquid to penetrate into the heart of the cabbage.

Put the cabbage into a basin full of *cold* water so that it is completely covered. Cover the pan. Put it on moderate heat so that the liquid heats gradually: almost 45 minutes will be needed before the water begins to boil. Then immediately remove the cabbage, which must not boil. Drain it in a sieve, and allow it to lose its most intense heat.

The stuffing: Start preparing this as soon as you have put the cabbage into the water.

If you have a small mechanical grinder, grind the meat in it, as well as the fatback bacon, which has been cut into little pieces. Otherwise, use a good large knife. For the fatback bacon, it is impossible to cut it as finely as needed with a knife: scrape it with the blade of a knife so that you obtain a pomade, which is essential for a perfect mixture with the stuffing (SEE PAGE 17).

Squeeze the cabbage between your hands to extract the excess liquid. Put it on a towel and pat it with another kitchen towel to dry it.

On a table, lay out 4 pieces of string each 50 centimeters (20 inches) long, crossing them over each other to make a simple cross. In the center of the cross that is formed, put 1 of the bards of fatback bacon, then place the cabbage on top, on its stem side. Carefully fold down the leaves one by one, spreading them out without detaching them, and going all around the cabbage until you reach the heart, where the leaves are too small to be folded back. With the point of a knife, trim the heart and then lift it out. This allows you to remove the hard parts that you were not able to reach when you detached the stem.

To easily handle the fatty stuffing, first dip your hands in cool water. Put a little bit of stuffing into the hollow of the cabbage and then put the tuft of heart back on top. On this, place a little bit of stuffing, without going as far down as the beginning of the leaves, and then smooth it out with your hand. Fold back up the first 2 or 3 leaves, packing them tightly one on the other into their natural position. Cover them with a little coating of stuffing, always without allowing it to get down near the beginning of the leaves, which must remain free of stuffing. Continue like this to garnish the cabbage with a series of small, successive coatings, folding back up 2 or 3 leaves as you go. Finish with a final layer of leaves to cover everything.

This method allows you to return the cabbage to its original form: nice and round and firm. While doing this, use a kitchen towel, as you go, to dry any leaves that are still wet. Place the second bard over the cabbage that has been stuffed. Raise the 2 ends of one of the strings that you have placed under the cabbage, also raising up the corners of the bard from underneath. Tie the string a little bit tightly. Do the same with the other strings. You will end up with a symmetrical bundle that looks a little bit like a melon.

Use a pot into which the cabbage *just* fits so that you will not need too much liquid. The liquid should reach two-thirds of the way up the cabbage, and the cabbage will substantially shrink during cooking. Garnish the bottom of the pot with the rounds of onion and carrot, cut a good 1/2 centimeter (3/16 inch) thick. Put the cabbage on top, on its stem side. Thus prepared, the cabbage can stand for quite a long time until it is cooked.

Cooking the cabbage: Place the covered pot on very moderate heat. Sweat it for about 10 minutes and allow it to shrink as directed in *braising.* Then add the bouillon and the cooking fat and bring to a boil. *Or,* eliminate the sweating and the shrinking and immediately add the bouillon and the cooking fat.

Once it has begun to boil, place a round of greased parchment paper directly on top of the cabbage. Cover it with a cover that fits well. Put it in the oven. Allow from this point *3 1/2 hours* at a gentle and regular simmer. Make sure that it does not boil more strongly, because this will dry up the liquid and cause the cabbage to stick, particularly toward the end of cooking. Otherwise, there is nothing to touch in the pot.

To serve: Take the cabbage out of the pot. Put it in a strainer over a receptacle to drain well. Cut the strings. Keep it warm.

Strain the cooking juice through a fine strainer. Degrease it. Put it back into the rinsed pot so you do not have to use another one. Boil it strongly, uncovered, on strong heat to reduce the juice to about 2 deciliters (6 3/4 fluid ounces, generous 3/4 cup). Bind it with a little bit of arrowroot (SEE LIAISONS, PAGE 48).

Place the cabbage on a heated round plate. If the leaves on the top have colored a little bit too much under the bard, remove the brown parts. Baste it with the reduced juice. Serve on very hot plates.

Meatless Stuffed Cabbage, the Recipe of Our Friend Aristide *(Chou Farci Maigre, Recette de l'Ami Aristide).* This is an excellent method taken from a family notebook of good recipes. Even though it contains no meat, the cabbage is exquisite. The butter used can be clarified butter. If you like, you can replace this butter with good lard, if the meal does not have to be strictly meatless. And instead of basting the cabbage with butter before serving, you can use a light tomato sauce. Increase the number of eggs for a large cabbage (that is, to 4 eggs) as well as the amount of fat. *Time: 2 hours, 30 minutes. Serves 6.*

1 small white, firm cabbage weighing, once thoroughly clean, almost 675 grams (1 pound, 8 ounces).

To stuff it: 100 grams (3 1/2 ounces, 7 tablespoons) of butter; 2 eggs; 20 grams (2/3 ounce) of minced onions; 1/2 tablespoon of minced parsley; 7 grams (1/4 ounce) of salt; 2 grams (1/14 ounce) of pepper; 1 tablespoon of bread crumbs made with stale bread, grated when needed.

To serve: 60 grams (2 1/4 ounces, 4 1/2 tablespoons) of butter and 1 tablespoon of bread crumbs; or 2 good deciliters (6 3/4 fluid ounces, generous 3/4 cup) of tomato sauce.

PROCEDURE. Once the cabbage has been cleaned, the spoiled leaves and any leaves that are too green removed, and the stem cut at the level of the leaves, detach the first 5 large leaves surrounding the cabbage. They should be whole and perfect; if they are not too large, you can add a sixth leaf: these leaves are used to wrap the cabbage to return it to its original form. Set them aside.

Cut the cabbage into 4 pieces. Using a large kitchen knife, cut each quarter, placed on the cutting board, into extremely thin slices. Next, arrange these slices in little piles to cut them in the opposite direction, so that you obtain a hash that is as fine and regular as possible.

Use a *thick* pot. You can use the same pot that will be used for cooking the cabbage when it has been restored to its original shape, its size corresponding pretty closely to the original when it was not cooked.

Put the butter and the chopped cabbage into the pot. Do not cover it. On gentle heat, braise the cabbage, mixing it frequently with a wooden spoon. Gradually it softens, shrinks down, and takes on a beautiful uniform golden color. Allow *about a half hour* for this. Then add the onion and the minced parsley and let it gently simmer for

8–10 minutes: at the end of this time, everything will be thoroughly combined.

The mixture will have shrunk considerably in volume. It will be glistening and look like preserved cabbage, with a beautiful light brownish, even tint; the butter, on the other hand, will not have gone beyond the color of a nice olive oil. A gentle, steady braising, as directed, is the reason for this and, indeed, is the very principle of the preparation. If the cabbage stews too quickly, it will brown in the overheated fat without absorbing it, and so will remain dry. We therefore insist that you take the care and time needed for this part of the preparation. Turn off the heat. Allow the intense heat of the mixture to dissipate.

To stuff the cabbage: Grate the bread (SEE BREADING, PAGE 19). Mix the breading with the cabbage mixture. Add the eggs, previously beaten as for an omelet. Season with salt and pepper.

Use either a medium-sized terrine, a small soup tureen, or a small salad bowl that is not too deep. Line the interior with a supple napkin whose sides extend all around outside the receptacle. On this cloth, place the reserved leaves, with the outside rib placed against the side of the terrine and the stem toward the top. Place the leaves one on top of the other lengthwise, making sure their bottom ends are together too, so that they will completely enclose the chopped cabbage mixture.

Then place the mixture of cabbage in the hollow formed by the leaves. Pull the sides of the cloth up over them; bind them with a few turns of string right over the ribs of the cabbage leaves. This cabbage ball can be prepared in advance the evening before, if you like.

Cooking the cabbage: Put the package into a pot full of boiling water salted at the rate of 10 grams (1/3 ounce) per liter (4 1/4 cups) of water; there should be enough so that the cabbage is completely immersed in it. Bring it to a boil. Cover, then cook for *1 hour* at a regular, moderate boil. When it is half-cooked, turn the cabbage over so that the top part can be properly immersed; if necessary, add some liquid to compensate for the loss caused by evaporation.

To serve: Take the package out of the water. Untie the napkin. The cabbage should be beautiful and round, and also be firm since it will have lost almost none of its fat in the cooking water. Place it on a heated serving plate. Put the butter, divided into small pieces, onto a heated dish so that it only melts to a creamy state. Add a pinch of salt and pepper and the grated bread crumbs. Pour it on the cabbage or replace the butter with tomato sauce. Serve on burning hot plates.

Cabbage Stuffed with Chestnuts *(Chou Farci aux Marrons).* This is also one of those excellent family recipes: it comes from Lorraine and is intended for meat-free meals. The amount of butter that it requires might seem excessive, but you should not reduce it, since it is the only fat used in the recipe. And, as everyone knows, cabbage absorbs large amounts of fat; just think of how many bards, pork rinds, etc., you have to add when preparing it for a meat stuffing. *Time: 7 hours (2 good hours for preparing the cabbage, which can be done in advance the evening before; then 5 hours for cooking the cabbage). Serves 6.*

1 nice firm white cabbage, weighing 1 good kilogram (2 pounds, 3 ounces) after it has been trimmed; 3 medium-size onions (about 200 grams/7 ounces total); 350 grams (12 1/3 ounces) of nice fresh chestnuts; 175 grams (6 ounces, 3/4 cup) of butter; 2 deciliters (6 3/4 fluid ounces, generous 3/4 cup) of very good milk; 10 grams (1/3 ounce) of salt; a good pinch of ground pepper.

PROCEDURE. The stuffing. Shell the chestnuts as directed (SEE PAGE 522). Peel and cut the onions into thin rounds. To simplify things, use the same pot to make the stuffing and to cook the cabbage. The cabbage must just fit into it, because it will compact when cooking: use a deep pot in thick aluminum.

Add the rounds of onions with a piece of butter the size of a nice egg. On low heat, stir to mix and melt. Cover. Let the onions gently stew and soften without coloring: that is, for *15–20 minutes.* Then add the chestnuts and the rest of the butter *less* 50 grams (1 3/4 ounces), which is reserved for later.

Cover again. Simmer on very low heat for *a good half hour.* Mix it frequently with your wooden spoon, taking care that you do not squash the chestnuts into a mash. The chestnuts may break into pieces, but try to keep them as intact as possible, so that they cook gradually in the fat and take on the brownish tint of glazed chestnuts.

Season them with half of the salt and some pepper. Pour them into a plate with all of their fat.

The cabbage: Cut the stem at the level of the leaves; remove any that are spoiled or too green.

In a large pot filled with boiling water, immerse the cabbage with the stem side toward the bottom. The cabbage must be covered by the liquid. Cover. Bring it back to a boil. Let it boil very gently until the leaves have become rather softened so that they do not break when you handle them; that is, *15–20 minutes.*

Drain the cabbage. Refresh it in cold water. Squeeze it carefully between your hands to extract the water from it. Place it on a napkin that is spread out on the table. Unfold the leaves one by one without detaching them, bending them back onto the napkin, until you reach the small central leaves that you cannot open.

On top of this heart, place a little bit of stuffing. Then fold back a leaf. On this folded leaf, spread out 1 scant tablespoon of stuffing, then fold back the following leaf. And so on, spreading out the stuffing in the middle of the cabbage so that eventually you return it to its original shape.

Once all the leaves have been folded back, tie the cabbage with string in the shape of a cross, then tie a second time. Knot the 2 ends on the top of the cabbage, leaving some ends long enough so that, while it is cooking, you can lift it up in the pot. Prepared like this, it can stand, kept cool, until ready to be cooked.

Cooking the cabbage: Butter the bottom and sides of the pot with the reserved butter, spreading it out with your finger. Put the cabbage in it on its stem side. Sprinkle it with the rest of the salt and the pepper. Use no liquid for the moment. Cover, then place it on gentle heat.

Then allow for *5 hours of cooking.* The cabbage begins to "sweat" first, that is, to release its moisture and its juices, which will be enough with the butter to keep it from sticking to the bottom of the pot. About 3 times an hour, baste it with this cooking juice. To ensure that the cabbage does not stick despite these bastings, uncover it as little as possible: simply shake the covered pot so that the cabbage moves but does not turn over during the cooking.

Halfway through the cooking–that is, at the end of 2½ hours—add the milk, reserving 3–4 tablespoons to add to the cooking juice a few minutes before serving.

To serve: Place the cabbage on a heated round plate. With scissors, cut the strings. Pour the juice over and around it, having first completely dissolved the crust formed on the walls of the pot.

Red Cabbage *(Chou Rouge)*

The gross weight for a nice medium-size cabbage is 900 grams–1 kilogram (2 pounds–2 pounds, 3 ounces). After removing the wilted outside leaves and the large ribs and stem, this weight will fall to 800–850 grams (1 pound, 12 ounces–1 pound, 14 ounces), which will serve 6 people.

Flemish-Style Braised Cabbage *(Chou Rouge à l'Étuvée Façon Flamande).* The cabbage, cut into a julienne and *not* blanched, is put into a generously buttered utensil made from enameled steel or ovenproof glass. Add a chopped onion moistened with 3 tablespoons of vinegar and the same of water, seasoned with salt and pepper. Cover, then cook on very low heat for *2 good hours;* when it is half done, add 4 sour apples that have been peeled and minced, and 1 tablespoon of superfine sugar.

No liquid is used for cooking except the little bit of vinegar and water added at the beginning. When ready to serve, bind it with beurre manié.

Braised Red Cabbage with Red Wine *(Chou Rouge à l'Étuvée au Vin Rouge).* The cabbage, cut into a julienne and *not* blanched, and seasoned with salt and pepper, is gently braised in butter for a half hour (as when braising herbs for soup), then sprinkled with flour and moistened with red wine. Cover and cook gently for *2 hours.* The liquid must be almost completely reduced after cooking. Allow for a medium-size cabbage: 125 grams (4½ ounces, 9 tablespoons) of butter, 10 grams (⅓ ounce) of flour, and a glass (2 deciliters/generous ¾ cup) of red wine.

Brussels Sprouts *(Chou de Bruxelles)*

This type of cabbage is a valuable resource in winter, offering a fresh vegetable from November to the end of February. Choose them recently harvested, nice and firm, rather small, and as evenly sized as possible, so that they will cook equally.

Preparation of the sprouts: Peel them by eliminating any yellow leaves, although there should be very few if you chose well. Cut the stem or trunk about 1 millimeter from the beginning of the leaves; this should be enough to keep the leaves attached while cooking. Note that Brussels sprouts that have lost most of their leaves look very unpleasant.

Wash the Brussels sprouts in large amounts of cold water. Immerse them in a pot of fully boiling salted water: use 3 liters (12 3/4 cups) of water for 500 grams (1 pound, 2 ounces) of Brussels sprouts and 20 grams (2/3 ounce) of salt. This amount of water is needed because otherwise the sprouts will have a flavor that is a little too strong. Do not cover; rapidly bring it back to a boil and maintain it at a good level to preserve the sprouts' green color. Once boiling resumes, cook for *10–15 minutes,* depending on how tender the vegetables are. If you allow the sprouts to cook for too long, they will turn into a mush when they come out of the water. Make sure they are tender and properly done before draining them in a large strainer. Left in their cooking water, they will turn yellow, and refreshing them in cold water will not help.

The Brussels sprouts are then ready to be used for the following different recipes.

Sautéed Brussels Sprouts *(Choux de Bruxelles Sautés). Serves 6.*

750 grams–1 kilogram (1 pound, 10 ounces–2 pounds, 3 ounces) of Brussels sprouts, depending on how large the menu is.

PROCEDURE. For this recipe, it is essential to remove all the moisture from the Brussels sprouts, which they will retain despite the most meticulous draining, since they are cooked intact with all their leaves. So prepare it like all vegetables served à la maître d'hôtel, evaporating the moisture.

Instead of a sauté pan, use a skillet, which will heat up faster and more strongly; it should be large enough so that the Brussels sprouts are not too crowded. For 450 grams (1 pound) of sprouts, heat 20 grams (2/3 ounce, 1 heaping tablespoon) of butter in the pan, or, if you like, good lard. Add the drained Brussels sprouts. On very high heat, toss them in the pan almost continuously, to constantly move them about without touching them with a spoon or a fork, which would crush them. Allow *7–8 minutes,* so that the abundant steam given off will lessen and they will then begin to lightly color. Turn off the heat; add a pinch of pepper, a pinch of minced parsley, and 20 grams (2/3 ounce, 1 heaping tablespoon) of butter, divided into bits; shake the pan to mix everything well and pour it into a heated vegetable dish.

Brussels Sprouts with Chestnuts *(Chou de Bruxelles aux Marrons). Time: 1 hour. Serves 6.*

500 grams (1 pound, 2 ounces) of Brussels sprouts and 250 grams (8 7/8 ounces) of chestnuts.

PROCEDURE. For the chestnuts, use about half of the total volume of the Brussels sprouts. Cook the chestnuts in the bouillon as directed for purée of chestnuts (SEE PAGE 522), but *do not overcook them.* Mix them carefully with the Brussels sprouts sautéed as above in the pan. Serve in a vegetable dish.

Braised Brussels Sprouts *(Chou de Bruxelles à l'Étuvée). Time: 45 minutes.*

PROCEDURE. Cook the sprouts in boiling water, keeping them a little bit firm. Drain them thoroughly. Put them in a timbale or a utensil with, for 500 grams (1 pound, 2 ounces) of Brussels sprouts, 50 grams (1 3/4 ounces, 3 1/2 tablespoons) of butter divided into pieces. Cover tightly. Put it in a good medium oven for *about 20 minutes.* Serve in the same pan.

Brussels Sprouts Loaf *(Pain de Choux de Bruxelles).* A very fine family recipe, which is both simple and inexpensive. If you like, the loaf can be covered with a little bit of cream sauce or some jus that is lightly bound with starch. *Time: 1 hour, 30 minutes. Serves 6.*

1 kilogram (2 pounds, 3 ounces) gross weight of Brussels sprouts; 40 grams (1 3/8 ounces) of stale bread crumbs soaked in 1 deciliter (3 1/3 fluid ounces, scant

1/2 cup) of warm milk; 2 egg yolks, 100 grams (3 1/2 ounces, 7 tablespoons) of butter; salt, pepper, nutmeg.

2 deciliters (6 3/4 fluid ounces, generous 3/4 cup) of ordinary jus or the same amount of cream sauce (SEE CREAM SAUCE, PAGE 63).

PROCEDURE. Once the Brussels sprouts have been cooked and drained, squeeze them in small handfuls to extract all their water and pass them through a metallic drum sieve. Gather the purée in a pot; add the butter to it—except for a piece the size of a walnut, reserved to grease the mold—a good pinch of salt, a pinch of pepper, and as much grated nutmeg as can be held on the point of a knife. Put it on an extremely low flame to melt the butter, so you can thoroughly mix it with the Brussels sprouts without heating it too much, working the whole thing with a wooden spoon. Add the soaked bread, after passing it through a drum sieve, and the egg yolks. Taste it to check the seasoning.

Pour it into a carefully buttered charlotte mold with a capacity of about 1 1/4 liters (5 1/3 cups). Cook it for *1 hour* in the oven in the bain-marie (SEE PAGE 42). Unmold it on a round heated plate and pour the chosen sauce on it.

Brussels Sprouts Gratinée with Cheese *(Choux de Bruxelles Gratinés au Fromage).* Generously butter a shallow ovenproof bowl and sprinkle it with grated cheese. Arrange the drained Brussels sprouts in a slight dome, seasoned with a pinch of pepper and nutmeg. Cover it with grated cheese; place little pieces of butter on the surface or moisten it with melted butter. Brown it in a hot oven or on the shelf of the broiler for *7–8 minutes.*

Brussels Sprouts à la Crème *(Choux de Bruxelles à la Crème).* Drain the Brussels sprouts and chop them *coarsely.* Put them in a sauté pan with some butter and stir them on strong heat as directed for sautéed Brussels sprouts in order to evaporate the moisture, but without browning them. Sprinkle with flour (5–6 grams/ 1/5 ounce for 1 pound of Brussels sprouts), then mix and cook for 1 minute. Add 1 deciliter (3 1/3 fluid ounces, scant 1/2 cup) of thick cream. Season and gently simmer until the cream has been completely absorbed. Surround it with fried croutons to serve.

Brussels Sprouts au Gratin *(Choux de Bruxelles au Gratin).* Once the sprouts have been cooked and drained, dry them with butter in a sauté pan. Season them. Add a little bit of lean béchamel sauce to them to bind them (2–3 tablespoons for 500 grams/1 pound, 2 ounces of Brussels sprouts). Put them in an ovenproof plate and cover them with the same sauce, to which you have added some grated Gruyère to make a Mornay sauce. Sprinkle with grated cheese and brown, proceeding as for CAULIFLOWER AU GRATIN (PAGE 504).

Cauliflower *(Chou-Fleur)*

A perfectly white cauliflower is a primary condition of freshness and quality. So choose it when it is a beautiful pure white with tight florets that are firm to the touch and with short stems. Florets that are spread apart high on the stems are not the best.

Cauliflower, with its different preparations, is primarily a dish served at home for the family. This may be why its preparation often leaves much to be desired, particularly when it comes to peeling the vegetable. Many people are ignorant of the details, particularly the importance of removing the skin covering the stems. Hard and tough, the stems will not be cooked by the time the florets have turned to mush.

Preparing and cooking the cauliflower is the same for all the different recipes given below. For 6 people, allow 1 cauliflower weighing almost 1 kilogram (2 pounds, 3 ounces) gross weight, which will furnish, after peeling, about 650 grams (1 pound, 7 ounces).

Peeling and cooking cauliflower: Using a good small knife, cut off each floret one by one from the trunk or the large central stem. As you do so, trim some of the floret's stem, the part next to the trunk being quite tough; it will be enough to leave 1–2 centimeters (3/8–3/4 inch). Then, with the point of the knife, remove and scrape off the white skin covering the stems, going from the bottom right to the top. Once this skin is removed, the stems look a little translucent and are tinted green.

When you reach the center of the cauliflower,

the stems become thinner and more numerous. They are fragile, so do not now take them off one at a time, but detach them in bunches of the same size as before. As you go, put the bunches into a terrine of cool water. Add 2–3 tablespoons of vinegar if you are worried that there may still be some slugs lurking among the florets; it is mainly in the summer and during dry spells that you have to look out for them.

Cooking the cauliflower: Do this in boiling water, using enough to completely immerse the cauliflower. Thus, for 500 grams/1 pound, 2 ounces of peeled cauliflower, 2$^1/_2$ liters (10$^1/_2$ cups) of water salted at the rate of 10 grams ($^1/_3$ ounce) per liter (4$^1/_4$ cups). The type of utensil is not important as long as it can withstand sustained heat.

When the water has come to a rolling boil, immerse the cauliflower florets in it with the stem down. Bring it back to a boil, which must be kept *very strong* to keep the cauliflower white. Do not cover. Allow to cook for *about 15 minutes.* To be prudent, check before this time is up, because 1 minute too long will spoil everything, and the florets cook very quickly.

Immediately turn off the heat as soon as the stems are tender and supple under your finger. And since the cauliflower continues to cook even off the heat, immediately pour some *cold water* into the boiling water to stop the cooking. This will give you time to drain the bunches one by one; if you pour them all at once into the strainer, some will break. With a skimmer, lift out the bunches one by one, and either place them in a large strainer or in a large drum sieve or even on a folded towel, to drain them as much as possible.

While they are cooking and draining, prepare the rest of the ingredients for your chosen recipe.

Note the cooking water from the cauliflower can be used for meatless soups: for example, a peasant julienne soup, etc.; or used with herbs for a garnish of rice or semolina; or even for onion soup with or without the final addition of milk.

PRINCIPAL RECIPES

In addition to the recipes listed below, we would also like to cite:

Cauliflower Salad *(Chou-Fleur en Salade).* Simple or mixed: that is, cauliflower alone or with a jardinière. Be careful not to overcook them so that they do not break when you toss them in the salad.

Cauliflower with Mayonnaise Sauce *(Chou-Fleur à la Sauce Mayonnaise).* This is an entrée or an hors d'oeuvre for summer. The cauliflower is cooked and molded as for the recipe "au naturel" (which follows), then well chilled and served covered with the mayonnaise sauce. Enhance the appearance of this dish by surrounding the cauliflower with the alternating colors of a decoration of sliced tomatoes, without their water or their seeds, and a julienne of large green bell peppers.

Cauliflower Purée, Known as "Dubarry" *(Purée de Chou-Fleur, Dite "Dubarry").* As a garnish or as a vegetable. Passed through the drum sieve after cooking and bound with a little bit of rather thick potato purée (100 grams/3$^1/_2$ ounces for 400 grams/14$^1/_8$ ounces of cauliflower). Mix in 1–2 tablespoons of cream. Add, off the heat, 30 grams (1 ounce, 2 tablespoons) of butter.

Cauliflower Soufflé *(Soufflé de Chou-Fleur).* SEE SOUFFLÉS (PAGE 436). Cook the cauliflower, but do not overcook. Then mash it to a purée. Bind with a béchamel sauce: 2 deciliters (6$^3/_4$ fluid ounces, generous $^3/_4$ cup) for 250 grams (8$^7/_8$ ounces) of completely peeled cauliflower; 3 egg yolks. Add a piece of butter the size of a walnut and grated Parmesan and 4 egg whites whipped to a "snow." Sprinkle with grated Parmesan. Cook for *20–25 minutes.*

Cauliflower au Naturel *(Chou-Fleur au Naturel).* Use a large bowl or a small salad bowl or a small terrine the size of the original cauliflower—before it has been peeled and is still whole. This receptacle will be used as a mold.

In the bottom of the heated receptacle, carefully arrange the bunches of cauliflower, peeled and cooked as directed, *with the stem in the air,* so that you can, by working backwards, restore the cauliflower to its natural shape. Place the florets with the longest stems in the center, in the deepest part, so that all the stems will be nearly level: this is to ensure that it is stable when finally unmolded. Above all, proceed carefully given the cauliflower's fragility, and rather quickly so that the cauliflower does not have time to cool down too much. You can keep it warm by putting the receptable into a *bain-marie.*

Unmold on a plate covered with a napkin. Accompany it with your choice of sauce, served in a sauceboat: Hollandaise, mousseline, cream, white sauce, melted butter, etc. (In this case, make the white sauce with the cooking liquid used for the cauliflower.)

Cauliflower au Gratin *(Chou-Fleur au Gratin).* This is a classic recipe for cauliflower, the best known and also, most of the time, the worst prepared. *Time: 1 scant hour (including peeling). Serves 6.*

1 cauliflower weighing 1 kilogram (2 pounds, 3 ounces); 5 deciliters (generous 2 cups) of boiled milk; 30 grams (1 ounce) of flour and 30 grams (1 ounce, 2 tablespoons) of butter for a white roux; 40 grams (1 3/8 ounces, 3 tablespoons) of butter; 30 grams (1 ounce) of grated Gruyère; 30 grams (1 ounce) of grated Parmesan; 2 good tablespoons of white stale bread crumbs; salt, pepper, nutmeg.

PROCEDURE. Peel and cook the cauliflower as directed. While it is cooking and draining, prepare the sauce.

The sauce: In a small saucepan with a capacity of 3/4 liter (generous 3 cups), and with a *very thick* base because of the type of sauce, make a white roux. Dilute with the milk. Season with pepper and nutmeg, and salt cautiously, bearing in mind the amount of salt in the cheese. Keep it simmering while you prepare the rest of the dish.

The bread crumbs: Prepare as directed (SEE BREADING, PAGE 19). Keep them on a plate.

The cheeses: Grate them if you have not bought them already grated. Mix 2 good tablespoons of each kind with the bread crumbs. Reserve the rest, which will be added later to the sauce itself.

Dressing the cauliflower: Mold it as for the recipe au naturel.

Meanwhile, finish the sauce, adding the reserved cheeses to it. Work it with a whisk or wooden spoon on gentle heat to obtain a perfect mixture, the consistency of a nice, smooth, beautiful cream. Turn off the heat. Mix in the remaining butter *less* an amount about the size of a small walnut, keeping it in reserve with the bread crumbs. Check the seasoning and the salt.

With a metal spoon, pour some sauce gently between the stems of the cauliflower placed in the terrine, so that you fill all the spaces inside. This is infinitely better than garnishing the bottom of the plate with sauce, because the inside of the cauliflower will not receive any sauce.

Place over the terrine a round plate that is heatproof and that can also be served at the table. Turn everything over. The cauliflower should be quite round, in its original shape, and there should be no sauce left in the receptacle. Tablespoon by tablespoon, cover everything with the rest of the sauce, creating a creamy and thick layer to completely hide the cauliflower.

Sprinkle everything with the bread crumbs mixed with the reserved cheese. Divide the butter into small pieces and sprinkle them on the top of the cauliflower. This domed part will receive more heat than the rest, and the butter, melting, will prevent it from coloring too much.

To brown: As for all gratins, you should have very low heat underneath and a very strong heat on top. Allow *8–10 minutes* at most to obtain a nice golden crust. If the dish is left too long in the oven, the cauliflower will cook further and turn to mush, while the sauce will dry out or become oily. For these reasons, a good broiler is preferable.

If the cauliflower is browned in a oven, put the plate on a metal baking sheet and raise it up as much as you need to, either on some *cold* bricks, or on a pan filled with cold water. This is to guarantee that the sauce will not stick to the bottom of the plate.

To serve: Put the plate on a serving plate covered with a napkin.

Polish-Style Cauliflower *(Chou-Fleur à la Polonaise).* Peel and cook the cauliflower as directed. Mold it as for the recipe au naturel. Lightly press on the bunches with the back of a spoon, tipping the bowl to make every last remaining drop of cooking water run out.

Unmold it on a buttered plate. Sprinkle it with 60 grams ($2^1/4$ ounces, $4^1/2$ tablespoons) of noisette butter (SEE NOISETTE BUTTER, PAGE 80), in which you have colored 1 tablespoon of stale bread that has been freshly grated as for a breading. Serve immediately.

If you like, sprinkle the cauliflower with hard-boiled egg yolk mixed with minced parsley before you moisten it with the noisette butter.

Cauliflower Fritters *(Beignets de Chou-Fleur).* We would like to explain the following point, which does not have a very solid foundation: cauliflower, prepared as below, is known in haute cuisine as a *fritot,* only because it is accompanied by a tomato sauce. (In this case, for our quantities, allow at least 2 deciliters/$6^3/4$ ounces/generous $^3/4$ cup of sauce.)

Cauliflower fritters are usually prepared with leftovers. However, it would always be better to use cauliflower that has been cooked expressly for this purpose and intentionally kept a bit firm. *Time: 1 hour. Serves 6.*

1 small cauliflower weighing about 500 grams (1 pound, 2 ounces).

To marinate it: 3 scant tablespoons of oil; the juice of 1 small lemon; $^1/2$ tablespoon of minced parsley; salt and pepper.

For the frying batter: 75 grams ($2^2/3$ ounces) of flour; 20 grams ($^2/3$ ounce) of clarified butter; 1 scant deciliter ($3^1/3$ fluid ounces, scant $^1/2$ cup) of barely lukewarm water; an egg white whisked to "snow"; a pinch of salt and $^1/2$ pinch of pepper.

PROCEDURE. First prepare the frying batter according to the directions given (SEE FRYING BATTER, PAGE 666). When you are ready to use it, mix in the egg white.

Peel and cook the cauliflower if it is not already cooked. Thoroughly drain it. The florets must be divided into smaller sizes than when the cauliflower is served au naturel: about *half* the size or less. Spread out the florets on a large plate. Season them with salt and pepper; sprinkle them with minced parsley; moisten them with the oil and lemon juice. Marinate them for *20–25 minutes,* tossing them from time to time so that they are well soaked by the marinade.

Meanwhile, prepare the tomato sauce. Start to heat the frying fat so that when the cauliflower is ready, you simply have to turn up the flame to have the frying fat immediately at the correct degree of heat.

To fry the cauliflower: *Eight minutes before serving,* or a little more if you have to cook them in 2 batches, heat the frying fat until it is lightly smoking. This is the temperature required so that the envelope of batter is immediately sealed (SEE FRYING, PAGE 41).

Put the florets into the batter in groups of 4 or 5 at a time, tossing them around to coat them completely. Using a fork, take them out and drop them into the hot fat. Keep the heat under the frying basin high to compensate for the cold caused by adding the cauliflower. Gently shake the frying basin to move them around in the fat. When the batter is quite golden and dried out, take them out with the skimmer. Drain them on a spread-out napkin. Salt them very lightly.

To serve: Put them on a plate covered with a folded napkin.

Cucumber *(Concombre)*

This vegetable is prepared both cold as an hors d'oeuvre and hot for a vegetable plate or for a garnish. Particularly when cooking it, a white cucumber is best. Choose it at exactly the right point of maturity, when the seeds have not formed: if not, the seeds must always be removed.

To serve it with a sauce, cook it first in boiling water—that is, blanch it—for 24–25 or even 30 minutes, calculating from the moment the water has returned to a boil, and bearing in mind how fresh and tender the cucumber is. Use 10 grams ($^1/3$ ounce) of salt per liter ($4^1/4$ cups).

The quantity for 6 is 750 grams (1 pound, 10 ounces) of cucumber.

PRINCIPAL RECIPES

Cucumbers à la Crème *(Concombres à la Crème).* Cut the cucumber into pieces about 3 centimeters (1 1/4 inches) thick and then divide them into 4–8 pieces, depending on the size of the cucumber. Peel them, and shape them into a long, large olive. As you peel them, toss the pieces into a terrine of cold water. Cook them in boiling water. In a small sauté pan, for 750 grams (1 pound, 10 ounces) of cucumber, put at least 3 deciliters (1 1/4 cups) of sauce (SEE CREAM SAUCE, PAGE 63). Mix it with the well-drained cucumbers, tossing them lightly. Serve them in a heated vegetable dish.

Cucumbers à la Poulette *(Concombres à la Poulette).* The same preparations and quantities as above (SEE POULETTE SAUCE, PAGE 61).

Cucumbers à la Mornay *(Concombres à la Mornay).* The same preparation and quantities as above (SEE MORNAY SAUCE, PAGE 63).

Glazed Cucumbers *(Concombres Glacés).* Proceed as for carrots (SEE PAGE 484).

Stuffed Cucumbers *(Concombres Farcis).* Cut the cucumbers into pieces 5 centimeters (2 inches) long. Peel them and blanch them in plenty of boiling salted water: 5 minutes for a white cucumber, a few minutes more for the green ones. Cool them in plenty of cold water. With the handle of a small spoon, hollow out the interior to make little round containers. Fill them with a fine stuffing, prepared with lean veal meat and fatback bacon. So, for 12 containers, which will serve 6: use 150 grams (5 1/3 ounces) of veal and the same amount of fatback bacon; 2 small whole eggs; 45 grams (1 1/2 ounces) of white bread crumbs, which have been soaked in 3 tablespoons of milk; and 1 good tablespoon of minced parsley; salt, pepper, spices.

Arrange the cucumbers in a sauté pan that has been lined with a bard of bacon. Pour over veal jus, or, if you do not have it, bouillon, just to the top of the containers. Bring it to a boil. Cover it first with buttered parchment paper placed directly on top of it, and then the cover, and cook very gently in the oven for 1 scant hour. A fork must easily pierce the cucumber. Take them out and put them on the serving plate carefully, then keep warm.

Strain and degrease the cooking juice. Pour it into the rinsed-out pan. Boil it uncovered on strong heat until it reduces to 2 1/2–3 deciliters (1–1 1/4 cups). Bind it with arrowroot (SEE LIAISONS, PAGE 47). Off the heat, add 40 grams (1 3/8 ounce, 3 tablespoons) of butter. With a spoon, pour this bound juice onto the cucumbers after you have poured out the liquid that they might have released onto their plate while standing.

Cucumber Salad *(Concombres en Salade).* Peel the cucumbers. Cut them in half lengthwise to reduce the size of each slice and also because it is then easier to get rid of the seeds. Slice each half very fine. Sprinkle with fine salt and allow them to disgorge for a scant half hour. Drain them thoroughly and then put them on a napkin to drain further. Season them as for all salads, and sprinkle them with minced chervil.

Cold Stuffed Cucumbers *(Concombres Farcis Froids).* Use a long thin cucumber so that you can cut rounds with a diameter of 5–6 centimeters (2–2 1/4 inches) and avoid much waste. Remove the rounded ends. Cut the cucumber into slices or rounds 2 1/2 centimeters (1 inch) thick. Trace a circular incision no more than 1 centimeter (3/8 inch) from the edges. This layer will form the walls and bottom of the little cucumber shell; hollow it out gradually, following the line of this incision.

Blanch for about 10 minutes. Drain and wipe dry with a towel. Marinate for a scant half hour with lemon juice, a touch of vinegar and, if you like, some thin rounds of onion. Fill with your choice of ingredients: a vegetable salad, hard-boiled chopped eggs, smoked herring or salmon, etc.

Cucumbers Stuffed with Tuna *(Concombres Farcis au Thon).* For 6 rounds: 75 grams (2 2/3 ounces) of tuna packed in oil and 50 grams (1 3/4 ounces, 3 1/2 tablespoons) of fresh butter, mixed together and passed through the drum sieve to reduce them to a homogenous paste. Fill the rounds and cover the edges with the stuffing. Cover with a mustard-mayonnaise sauce, using for these quantities: 1 egg yolk; 1 1/2 deciliters (5 fluid ounces, 2/3 cup) of oil; 1 teaspoon of vinegar; 1 teaspoon of mustard. Cayenne pepper, as much as can be held on the point of a knife, is optional.

Chinese Artichokes *(Crosne)*

Originally from Japan, Chinese artichokes are now a common winter vegetable. Their rather fine taste is somewhere between an artichoke bottom and salsify.

Choose them large and white, which is an indication of their quality. Chinese artichokes that are grayish with brown spots come from poor soil; when you cook them, they take on a horrible, cinder-gray color and their taste is also very different. To guarantee both their flavor and their whiteness, and also to make it easier to clean them, Chinese artichokes must be fresh. Allow 500 grams (1 pound, 2 ounces) of Chinese artichokes for 6.

To clean: Wash the Chinese artichokes in several changes of cold water to completely remove any dirt. Drain them. With the tip of a small kitchen knife, remove the point at both their ends. Then lightly scrape them with the tip of the knife to remove the skin covering them. This takes a while, and the best way to do it is as follows: put the Chinese artichokes in a kitchen towel with a handful of sea salt. Close the towel and roll the artichokes back and forth inside it. The salt will rub against them and remove the skin. If the Chinese artichokes are not absolutely fresh, it will be necessary to soak them in a little bit of water, in advance, to soften this skin.

Then wash the Chinese artichokes in a substantial amount of water, rubbing them lightly between your hands. Drain them.

To cook: Chinese artichokes must always first be blanched in boiling water, the time depending upon the particular recipe.

Immerse them in a pot of salted boiling water. So, for 500 grams (1 pounds, 2 ounces) of Chinese artichokes, 1 1/2–2 liters of water (6 1/3–8 1/2 cups), and 15–20 grams (1/2–2/3 ounce) of sea salt. Bring it back rapidly to a boil on strong heat. Do not cover. For most recipes allow to boil for *10–12 minutes.* Chinese artichoke must always be left a little bit firm and crispy—it should snap easily in your fingers. Do not wait until it squashes between your fingers: if so, it will soften and be reduced to a watery mash as soon as it is taken out of the water; not only does this look most unpleasant, but, more important, the flavor is also distorted.

As soon as they have been properly cooked, drain the Chinese artichokes. Do this without haste and with great care because Chinese artichokes retain a lot of moisture. For recipes including a sauce, this will dilute the sauce and change its consistency.

PRINCIPAL RECIPES

Sautéed Chinese Artichokes *(Crosnes Sautés).* Blanch for 10–12 minutes. In a pan, strongly heat 50 grams (1 3/4 ounces, 3 1/2 tablespoons) of butter for 500 grams (1 pound, 2 ounces) of Chinese artichokes. Add the well-drained artichokes and sauté them on strong heat until they are very lightly browned. Sprinkle with salt and a little bit of minced parsley, then add a few drops of lemon juice and serve.

Chinese Artichokes à la Crème *(Crosnes à la Crème).* Blanch for only 5–6 minutes, because the artichokes must finish cooking in the cream. For 500 grams (1 pound, 2 ounces) of Chinese artichokes, just melt, without letting it heat, 40 grams (1 3/8 ounce, 3 tablespoons) of butter in a thick-bottomed pot. Add the well-drained Chinese artichokes, which should still be warm. Add 5–6 drops of lemon juice. Cover. Braise it on very low heat for *7–8 minutes.*

Then add 3 deciliters (1 1/4 cups) of light cream that has been previously boiled and is still boiling hot; a pinch of fine salt, a pinch of white pepper (2 grams/1/14 ounce); grated nutmeg (scarcely 1 gram). Shake the pot to mix everything well.

Keep the pot covered on moderate heat to maintain a rather strong boil for *a good 15 minutes* and thus reduce the cream by a good quarter.

To serve: Turn off the heat and add 3 tablespoons of *uncooked* cream right at the last moment, so that it heats without boiling and thus keeps its natural flavor.

Polish-Style Chinese Artichokes *(Crosnes à la Polonaise)*. *Blanched for 10–12 minutes,* then thoroughly drained. Put into a sauté pan without butter or anything else and sautéed on strong heat for a few instants to dry them out.

When all the moisture has evaporated as steam, season with fine salt and a pinch of pepper. Put them in a dome in a vegetable dish. Keep it warm on the open door of an oven. Spread over the chopped yolk of 3 hard-boiled eggs (for 500 grams/1 pound, 2 ounces of Chinese artichokes) and a nice pinch of minced parsley. In a small, very clean pan, heat 100 grams (3 1/2 ounces, 7 tablespoons) of butter as for noisette butter, to the point where it has taken on a blond color and gives off an odor of hazelnut. Cook in it about 30 grams (1 ounce) of good, stale bread crumbs that have been finely grated (SEE BREADING, PAGE 19). A few seconds will be enough for this.

Quickly moisten the Chinese artichokes with the butter and fried bread crumbs, and the juice of 1/4 lemon, then serve.

Chinese Artichoke Croquettes *(Croquettes de Crosnes)*. *Blanched for 10–12 minutes,* then drained and dried out on a napkin. Mixed with an Allemande sauce or a béchamel sauce bound with egg yolk. For the quantities of sauce and the preparation of the croquettes, refer to the directions given (SEE CROQUETTES, PAGE 438).

Chinese Artichoke Fritters *(Beignets de Crosnes)*. Prepare as for croquettes. Chill. Pick up a tablespoon at a time and dip into a light frying batter, then lift them out with a fork and immerse them in a large quantity of hot frying fat (SEE FRYING, PAGE 41).

Chinese Artichokes in Salad *(Crosnes en Salade)*. Served either alone or in a mixture of various ingredients. Seasoned as usual or bound with a light mayonnaise.

Zucchini *(Courgette)*

This vegetable, which was formally only known and cultivated in southern European countries, has spread everywhere. In general, the recipes for zucchini are the same as for eggplant. You can stuff them in various ways: like eggplants with tomato and rice; like stuffed tomatoes for a garnish, both home-style and Provençal style; and also like stuffed artichoke bottoms. First, the zucchini must be prepared as explained below. For stuffing, zucchini should be a medium size, about 10–12 centimeters (4–4 1/2 inches) long, not too thin, and with a more or less bulbous shape. Allow 1 zucchini per person.

Any smaller—that is, about the size of cornichons or small pickles—zucchini are prepared whole. Scrape them lightly, blanch for 2 minutes in boiling, salted water, then cook gently in fat, either butter or oil, until they have a soft and supple consistency. After this, put them in a gratin dish and cover with a good bound jus or a tomato sauce, or even a béchamel sauce. Sprinkle with fine bread crumbs and some grated cheese, according to preference, and with melted butter or oil, and then brown for *8–10 minutes* in the oven or preferably under a broiler.

To prepare the zucchini for stuffing: Scrape them with a small kitchen knife to remove the skin or peel them carefully. Cut them in half lengthwise. Hollow them out from one end to the other, leaving 1 centimeter (3/8 inch) of pulp on the edges and a little bit more on the bottom: they look like little boats. Do not hollow them out too much, because they will break during cooking. *Reserve the pulp to add to the stuffing.*

Immerse the zucchini in a large pot of salted water that is at full boil, using 7 grams (1/4 ounce) of salt per liter (4 1/4 cups). Let them boil gently *for 10–12 minutes,* depending on how tender the zucchini are; remember that they will finish cooking when browned. If you let them cook too much, they will break quite easily. Touch them from time to time to check that they are properly cooked; as soon as they give way underneath your finger, remove them carefully with a skimmer and put them side by side in a large drum sieve.

Once they have been well drained, arrange the zucchini on a well-oiled gratin dish. Garnish them with the chosen stuffing, either with the aid of a pastry bag (SEE STUFFED TOMATOES, PAGE 534) or picking up the stuffing in little packages with a metal spoon. With the blade of a knife, smooth out the stuffing, leaving a slight dome.

Belgian Endive *(Endive)*

You can prepare Belgian endive in several ways, with or without meat: either braised and served with its braising juice, which has been bound, or gently braised in butter and served just as it is, or under a cream sauce or Mornay sauce, or with an excellent jus that has been bound with starch. Braising is the most practical method, because it enables you to prepare enough for two meals at a time. Cooked this way, endive will keep for several days, without your having to do anything else. This reduces the time and trouble you need to take for cooking it.

Pick Belgian endives that have very tight white leaves, a sign of freshness. And choose them either small or medium. Large endives are generally reserved for salads. As much as possible, try to get them all the same size for even cooking. *Time: 1 hour, 30 minutes. Serves 6.*

About 750 grams (1 pound, 10 ounces) of Belgian endive, gross weight; 60 grams (2¼ ounces, 4½ tablespoons) of butter; the juice of half a lemon, medium size; 3 tablespoons of cold water; a good pinch of fine salt.

PROCEDURE. Remove a few of the limp or dying leaves that are found on the outside of the endive. Trim the stalk and lightly scrape the ends of the leaves.

Quickly wash the endives in large amounts of fresh water, making sure that the water reaches between the leaves to rid them of all the sand. There is a belief, which has for some time now been recognized as a mistake, that rinsing it in water makes the endive bitter. However, the cause of this bitterness does not come from washing, which is actually necessary to get rid of the sand, as well as to clean it. Drain the endives and shake them off well.

Use a sauté pan of thick aluminum, which is just large enough to arrange the endives in, one next to the other without crowding them too much. With the end of your finger, spread half of the butter around the bottom of the pan. Arrange the endives in it, head to tail. Salt them. Add the water, the lemon juice, and the rest of the butter, divided into small pieces.

Cover. Rapidly bring it to a boil. After this, place a round of generously buttered parchment paper directly on top of the endives. Cover, then place the pan in a medium oven so that it cooks gently, which is appropriate for this type of braising. If you do not have an oven, cook on very low heat, making sure that the endives do not stick to the bottom of the pan.

From the moment that you put the dish in the oven, allow 1 hour of cooking for small endives and 15 minutes more for medium-size ones; 1½ hours if they are cooking on the heat. Then take them out of their pan to thoroughly drain them before combining them with the chosen sauce. Press them lightly with the back of a spoon to extract all liquid, which would unfortunately dilute the sauce.

To preserve endives cooked in advance: Drain them and arrange them on a plate. Once they have cooled, cover them with buttered parchment paper and place them in the pantry (or the refrigerator).

When you are going to use them, you merely have to heat them up with a little bit of bouillon, or simply a little water and butter if they are to be served just as they are. Or, if serving with some sauce, reheat them in the sauce.

Belgian Endives with Mornay Sauce *(Endives à la Mornay).*

For 750 grams (1 pound, 10 ounces) of endives cooked as above, allow 3 scant deciliters (1¼ cups) of Mornay sauce. Thus: 20 grams (⅔ ounce, 1 heaping tablespoon) of butter and 50 grams (1¾ ounces) of flour for a white roux; 4 deciliters (1⅔ cups) of milk; bunch of parsley, etc.; 60 grams (2¼ ounces) of grated Gruyère *of which 20 grams (⅔ ounce) should be reserved for glazing*; 30 grams (1 ounce, 2 tablespoons) of butter to finish the sauce and 10 grams (⅓ ounce, 1 scant tablespoon) for glazing the plate.

PROCEDURE. Braise the endives as directed above. If they have been cooked in advance, be careful to heat them thoroughly in the manner described.

Meanwhile, prepare the Mornay sauce (SEE PAGE 63).

Use an ovenproof dish. Spread out a few tablespoons of the prepared sauce on the bottom of the dish. Arrange the endives there, *well drained.* Cover with the Mornay sauce. Sprinkle the surface with the reserved cheese. Spread 10 grams (1/3 ounce, 1 scant tablespoon) of butter, divided into small pieces, on top. Glaze (SEE GLAZING SAUCED DISHES, PAGE 15). Serve immediately.

Ardennes-Style Belgian Endives *(Endives à l'Ardennaise).* An excellent recipe, which was given us by M. Phil. Gilbert. Very simple to make, it allows you to present a much more substantial dish. *Time: 2 scant hours. Serves 6.*

750 grams (1 pound, 10 ounces) of medium-size Belgian endives, gross weight; 3 deciliters (1 1/4 cups) of bouillon; 100 grams (3 1/2 ounces) of lean bacon; 100 grams (3 1/2 ounces) of cooked or raw ham (raw when possible); 80 grams (2 3/4 ounces, 5 1/2 tablespoons) of butter; the juice of 1/4 lemon; pepper and nutmeg.

PROCEDURE. Trim and wash the endives as directed. Arrange them side by side in a sauté pan that has been buttered with 30 grams (1 ounce, 2 tablespoons) of butter. Sprinkle them with a pinch of pepper and grated nutmeg; cover with the bouillon. No salt is needed if the bouillon is properly salted. Add the lemon juice.

Bring it to a boil. Then place a round of buttered parchment paper directly on the endives and cover the pan tightly. Put it in the oven at a temperature that will maintain a gentle simmer and, *above all, a regular simmer,* which is essential.

Fatback bacon and ham: As soon as the endives are cooking, cut the fatback bacon, which has been previously trimmed of its rind, into small, 1-centimeter (3/8-inch) cubes. *Blanch* them. Keep them on a plate. Cut the ham the same way and add it to the bacon cubes.

Add the cubes to the endives *a good half hour* after the endives went into the oven, placing them among the vegetables. Recover it with the paper and the cover. Continue cooking it the same way *for 1 1/4 hours.*

To serve: Take the endives out with a fork, one at a time, draining them thoroughly over the pan. Arrange them in a vegetable dish or a hollow plate. Keep them warm. Put the uncovered pan on strong heat and boil the cooking juice strongly until it is reduced to *about 2 deciliters (7/8 cup).*

Just before serving, add the remaining butter, off the heat. Pour everything—the juice, the cubes of ham and bacon—onto the warm endives. Serve.

Flemish Endives *(Endives à la Façon Flamande).* This is the simplest and most economical method, which produces an extremely good result. The endives are excellent reheated the next day. *Serves 6–8.*

1 kilogram (2 pounds, 3 ounces) of Belgian endives, gross weight; 60 grams (2 1/4 ounces, 4 1/2 tablespoons) of butter.

PROCEDURE. Remove the spoiled leaves. Cut the endives into rounds 1 centimeter (3/8 inch) thick. Wash them quickly in large amounts of cold water. Drain them. Shake them in a towel so that not even one drop of water remains.

Butter the entire interior—the sides as well as the bottom—of a shallow sauté pan that is just large enough to hold the endives, heaped right up to the edge of the pot: during cooking they will noticeably compact. Right on top of the endives, place a round of generously buttered parchment paper: for this, use 10 grams (1/3 ounce, 1 scant tablespoon) of butter reserved from the total amount. On top of the paper, put a cover that *closes tightly:* this detail is of particular importance because the endives must cook from start to finish in their own moisture, without any additional liquid. If you do not have an appropriate cover, use a small, heavy baking sheet of thick metal, which extends all around the pan.

Put it in a gentle oven. Allow at least *2 hours* of very gentle and regular *cooking.*

To serve: To be properly done, the endives must have no traces of liquid and be heaped up and gathered together into a compact mass. If there is any liquid remaining, uncover the casserole and leave it in the oven for as long as is needed to evaporate the remaining moisture.

Then turn it over on a plate, as you would do

for a cake. They should look lightly golden and give off neither liquid nor fat. Sprinkle this surface with salt. Add some shine, if you like, by sprinkling a little bit of melted butter on top. Serve.

Spinach *(Épinards)*

Except during the very warm days of summer and the severe winter months, you can always get spinach; and even, thanks to successive sowings during spring and fall, young spinach. Older spinach that is about to go to seed or that has already gone to seed should be rejected.

Removing bad leaves means there is some waste, and the volume of spinach shrinks considerably when cooked, so bear this in mind when you purchase the spinach. You should assume that you will lose two-thirds of the gross weight of the spinach, and even more if the spinach is very young. For 6 people, you should therefore allow about 1½ kilograms (3 pounds, 5 ounces) of spinach, gross weight.

Blanching: Whatever the recipe, spinach must always be *blanched* in large amounts of boiling salted water. In fact, it is a less a question of *blanching* than of cooking the spinach, and here the term means a rapid boil in large amounts of water, the aim being to preserve the green color and at the same time to ensure its thorough cooking.

Allow for this preliminary cooking about 1¼ liters (5⅓ cups) for each 450 grams (1 pound) of spinach, gross weight, before washing, and an average 6–7 grams (¼ ounce) of sea salt for each liter (4¼ cups) of water.

To keep the spinach very green, you must blanch it at a rolling boil, without covering the pot. Use an enameled utensil or a large aluminum pot. Even untinned copper can be used, and with some advantage, because the untinned copper preserves the green color of the spinach while tin alters the coloring material in the vegetable.

Prepare the spinach carefully, leaf by leaf, pulling the stems back in reverse; and as you go, put them in a large receptacle of cool water. If the spinach is mature or nearly so, completely remove the stem, which is hard. If they are quite young, simply break off the stem at the level of the leaf.

Have the boiling water ready to go in your chosen pan.

Wash the spinach in 3 changes of water, and plenty of it each time, picking out the leaves with your hands to pass them to another receptacle, thus leaving the dirt at the bottom. Drain the spinach leaves in a drum sieve, shaking them well, then immerse in *boiling* water. Bring it back to a boil promptly on strong heat.

Once boiling has resumed, let it boil strongly and allow: *10 minutes of cooking* if the spinach is very young, *15 minutes* if it is a little bit older.

Then drain it on a drum sieve.

Cool it rapidly in a large amount of cool water. Rapid cooling prevents the leaves from turning yellow and from contracting a bad taste. Then lift them out in handfuls and strongly squeeze them between your hands, turning them over so that you extract as much water from them as possible. As these handfuls are squeezed, put them on a chopping board.

We do not suggest passing the spinach through a drum sieve. It is better to chop it, which gives a more natural look. You should use either a thin cleaver or a large knife, and chop finely until no whole pieces are left. Then put the spinach on a strong and clean kitchen towel. Fold the towel and twist it at both ends to extract any remaining water that you could not entirely remove by squeezing it in your hands.

The spinach is now ready to be included in your choice of dishes. It will gain a lot by not being left to wait for too long, a mistake that too many people make.

To dry out the spinach: This is a complement of the initial preparation. Indeed, before being prepared in any way, the spinach must be first dried out (SEE DRYING PURÉES, PAGE 14). For this you add only the amount of butter needed to prevent the spinach from sticking to the bottom of the pot during the few minutes it takes to dry out: thus, 25–30 grams (1 ounce, 1 scant tablespoon) of butter for 1½ kilograms (3 pounds, 5 ounces) gross weight of spinach.

Once the spinach has been dried out, it is ready to be used.

PRINCIPAL RECIPES

Creamed Spinach *(Épinards à la Crème).* The cream used here can be replaced by the same quantity of milk that has been reduced by half. *Time: 1 hour, 15 minutes. Serves 6.*

1½ kilograms (3 pounds, 5 ounces) of spinach (gross weight before cleaning); 75 grams (2⅔ ounces, ⅓ cup) of butter; 15 grams (½ ounce) of flour; 2 deciliters (⅞ cup) of cream (or 4 deciliters/1⅔ cup of milk reduced to 2 deciliters/6¾ fluid ounces/generous ¾ cup); salt, pepper, nutmeg, and a pinch of superfine sugar.

PROCEDURE. In a medium-size sauté pan, put 25 grams (1 ounce, 2 tablespoons) of butter; put in the spinach and dry the leaves out on strong heat, stirring for *4–5 minutes.*

Turn off the heat. Season with: a good pinch of salt, a small pinch of superfine sugar, and a bit of pepper and grated nutmeg. Sprinkle with the flour and mix it well, then stir it again on the heat for only 2 minutes.

Next, add the cream, little by little and *off the heat.* Then bring it to a boil, stirring constantly. Now turn the heat down very low. Cover and allow it to simmer for *20–30 minutes.* This supplementary cooking can also be done in a very low oven: in this case, place a round of buttered parchment paper on top of the spinach, underneath the cover.

Just a few seconds before serving, add the rest of the butter in little pieces to the spinach. From this point, *do not allow it to boil any more.* If the spinach must stand for a little while, it would be better to add this butter only when you are ready to serve. Otherwise, it will lose its creaminess.

To serve: *Spinach with croutons.* Prepare in advance about 15 small croutons shaped into triangles and fried in butter. Pour the spinach into a vegetable dish; smooth the surface with the back of a spoon and stick the croutons on top in a circle (SEE CROUTONS, PAGE 20).

Creamed spinach. Have 5–6 tablespoons of boiling cream ready, with a little bit of fine salt added. Once the spinach is dressed in the vegetable dish, sprinkle it with the cream and serve immediately.

Spinach with Meat Juice *(Épinards au Gras).* *Time: 1 hour, 15 minutes.*

The recipe is exactly the same, except that the cream or milk is replaced in the same quantities by very good bouillon or veal jus. This should be very carefully degreased: it goes without saying that this should be *without one atom of fat.* For this recipe, the fat must come from the butter only. We insist on this, because many cooks do not consider this to be important; and the result, both in terms of flavor and digestibility, is completely different.

Spinach for Garnish, or to Accompany Roasted or Braised Meats *(Épinards pour Garnitures, ou pour Accompagnement de Viandes Rôties ou Braisées).* Prepare the spinach au gras, as above. If you are not serving it on the same plate as the meat but are presenting it in a vegetable dish on the side as an accompaniment, leave out the croutons.

Spinach with a Simple Gratin *(Épinards au Gratin Simple).* These are best served at lunch. *Time: 1 hour, 15 minutes.*

In addition to the ingredients listed for Creamed Spinach, you need: 75 grams (2⅔ ounces) of very good, fresh Gruyère, grated; 1½ tablespoons of fine white bread crumbs; 20 grams (⅔ ounce, 1 heaping tablespoon) of melted butter.

PROCEDURE. Prepare the spinach à la crème or with reduced milk, as explained above. At the same time as the fine butter, add 45 grams (1½ ounces) of grated cheese.

The gratin: Generously butter the bottom and the sides of a round, heatproof, porcelain, shallow bowl. Put the spinach in; then, with the blade of a knife, smooth the surface into the form of a dome. Mix the bread crumbs and the remaining cheese on a plate. Sprinkle everything on the spinach and use a kitchen brush to moisten it with the melted butter.

Put everything into a good hot oven, being careful to make sure that the plate is raised on a shelf so that it is not in contact with the oven bottom, which will keep the spinach from boiling and ensure that the bread-crumb and cheese surface will receive the strongest heat. For this gratin, you will need *5–7 minutes,* depending on the temperature of the oven. If you do not have a good hot oven, slide the plate under the broiler.

Spinach à la Mornay ***(Épinards Gratinés, ou Glacés, à la Mornay).*** These can be served either at lunch or dinner. *Time: 1½ hours.*

You will need, in addition to the ingredients for creamed spinach: 2½ deciliters (1 cup) of Mornay sauce (SEE PAGE 63).

PROCEDURE. This is the same as for creamed spinach (PAGE 512). While the spinach is cooking, prepare the Mornay sauce.

The gratin or glazing: Use a porcelain dish, as above. Spread out 3–4 tablespoons of the sauce over the bottom of the dish and add the spinach. Smooth the top of it into a dome shape with the blade of a knife. Cover with the rest of the sauce, spreading it out tablespoon by tablespoon. Sprinkle the sauce with grated cheese (20 grams, ⅔ ounce) and then, using a brush, coat the cheese with melted butter.

Immediately put the dish in a very hot oven, taking the precautions explained above. If the oven is very hot, the glazing will be done in *3 minutes.* It is ready when the cheese combines with the butter, forming a golden layer on the sauce. Watch the oven constantly throughout this time, and serve immediately.

Spinach on the Stalk ***(Épinards en Branches).*** A simple and rapid method of preparing a small quantity of spinach for a garnish for braised meat or a small number of guests. *Time: 45 minutes.*

450 grams (1 pound) of young spinach; 80 grams (2¾ ounces, 5½ tablespoons) of butter; a pinch of salt and pepper; if you like, 1 tablespoon of heavy cream.

PROCEDURE. Remove the large stems from the leaves and wash the spinach leaves in a generous amount of cold water, then drain them without squeezing them in your hands as you would to dry a salad. Do not blanch them. With half of the butter, generously butter the bottom of a thick pot large enough so that the vegetables in it will not be piled up too high, and put in the spinach. Season with salt and pepper, then spread the rest of the butter, which has been divided into small pieces, on top of it. On strong heat, with the pot covered, let the spinach "melt." In 4–5 minutes, it will be wilted. Uncover the pot and finish cooking on very moderate heat for 30 minutes. Carefully turn the spinach over once or twice while cooking to bring up to the top those leaves that were at the bottom of the pot. Make sure that they do not color. All the liquid must evaporate. To serve, cover the spinach with the cream and reheat without boiling; or add, off the heat, a large walnut-sized piece of butter.

Spinach Soufflé ***(Soufflé aux Épinards).*** A simple and very good use of leftover spinach: either blanch it and chop it, then set aside for a soufflé for the next day; or use leftovers from spinach au jus or à la crème. In the latter case, you will not have to simmer them in the oven for as long as spinach that has only been only blanched in boiling water.

The ham listed is not essential, but it adds an agreeable note to the soufflé. The same is true for the Gruyère. By itself, the spinach lacks some flavor in this recipe. *Time: 1¼ hours for everything; if you are using leftovers, the time needed for cooking will be reduced. Serves 6.*

2–3 good tablespoons of spinach, blanched and chopped; 35 grams (1¼ ounces, generous 2 tablespoons) of butter; 10 grams (⅓ ounce) of flour; 1½ deciliters (5 fluid ounces, ⅔ cup) of light cream or reduced milk; 60 grams (2¼ ounces) of grated Gruyère (use the kind that is a little dry); 60 grams (2¼ ounces) of lean, cooked ham; 3 egg yolks; 4 egg whites whisked into snow; salt, pepper, nutmeg.

PROCEDURE. For details of all the steps, refer to the special article (SEE SOUFFLÉS, PAGE 436).

Once the spinach has been blanched, cooled, chopped, etc., as usual, put 15 grams (½ ounce, 1 tablespoon) of butter into a sauté pan. Melt it, then add the flour. Cook this little roux on gentle heat without allowing it to color. Add the spinach, salt, pepper, and nutmeg. Mix it over strong heat to evaporate the moisture from the spinach. Add the cream or the reduced milk. Cover. Simmer in the oven for *20–25 minutes.*

Take the pot out of the oven. Mix the spinach

over heat with a wooden spoon until it is properly thickened. Turn off the heat. Add the grated cheese; the ham cut into small cubes; the remaining butter. Check the seasoning. Proceed as directed for preparing vanilla soufflé (SEE PAGE 634) without, of course, the final sprinkling of superfine sugar.

Broad Beans *(Fèves)*

Whatever the recipe, the beans must always be absolutely fresh and shelled at the last moment. Unless they are very small and absolutely new vegetables, broad beans must be "skinned"—that is, their skins must be removed before cooking; as the season advances, the skin becomes increasingly thick and very indigestible, and it is absolutely essential to remove it. Assume that once this skin has been removed, the weight of the beans will have reduced by about one-quarter. That is, 500 grams (1 pound, 2 ounces) of shelled beans will yield, once the skin has been removed, 400 grams (14 ounces). Note, too, that 1 kilogram (2 pounds, 3 ounces) of beans in their shells furnishes 500 grams (1 pound, 2 ounces) of shelled beans.

Savory, which is used in the following recipes, is the condiment that is, so to speak, essential for broad beans. It is almost as common in gardens as thyme and tarragon, and you can also find it in stores in town.

Broad beans can be prepared as follows: à l'anglaise, à la maître d'hôtel, as directed in the preparation for English-style vegetables and à la maître d'hotel (SEE PAGE 470)—assume you will need *20–25 minutes* for cooking. *In a purée:* as for a purée of fresh, green peas; and, above all, as for a garnish for a braised meat—veal paupiettes, grenadines, etc., or warm ham. *À la poulette:* cooked as directed further on with cream and simmered in the same quantity of poulette sauce—that is, 4 deciliters (1 2/3 cups) of sauce once everything is complete.

The following two recipes are both simple but very different.

Broad Beans with Bacon *(Fèves au Lard).* *Time: 45 minutes (once the broad beans have been shelled and peeled). Serves 6.*

675 grams (1 pound, 8 ounces) of large, shelled broad beans; 125 grams (4 1/2 ounces) of lean bacon; 25 grams (1 ounce, 2 tablespoons) of butter; 15 grams (1/2 ounce) of flour; 3 deciliters (1 1/4 cups) of bouillon; 1 good teaspoon of minced savory; salt and pepper.

PROCEDURE. Cut the bacon into small cubes no bigger than 1 centimeter (3/8 inch) on each side. Blanch them (SEE BACON, PAGE 11). Drain them well. Remove the skin from the broad beans; cut them in two. Boil them in salted water for *8–10 minutes.*

Meanwhile, heat the butter in a medium-size pot. Lightly color the bacon in it. Then sprinkle it with the flour and mix until you have a golden blond color. Add the bouillon; stir until it boils. Turn the heat down very low. Thoroughly drain the broad beans. Put them into the pot with the sauce. Add the chopped savory and a pinch of pepper. Mix everything by shaking the pot, rather than using a spoon, so that you do not break the broad beans. Simmer it very gently for *a half hour.* From time to time, shake the pot to move the beans around. Serve on a vegetable plate or a shallow bowl.

Broad Beans à la Crème *(Fèves à la Crème).* *Time: 35 minutes. Serves 6.*

450 grams (1 pound) of shelled broad beans, 2 sprigs of savory.

***For the sauce:* 30 grams (1 ounce, 2 tablespoons) of butter and 25 grams (1 ounce) of flour for the roux; 4 deciliters (1 2/3 cups) of boiled milk; 1 1/2 good deciliters (5 fluid ounces, 2/3 cup) of heavy crème fraîche; a small bunch of parsley.**

PROCEDURE. **The sauce:** In a small saucepan, make a white roux. Dilute it with milk. Season with salt, white pepper, grated nutmeg. Bring it to a boil while stirring. Add the bunch of parsley. Let it cook gently.

The broad beans: Cook them in salted water (SEE COOKING FRESH VEGETABLES, PAGE 470), adding the savory to them. Allow *20–25 minutes*; as soon as they begin to yield to the touch, they are nearly done.

Then strain the sauce through a chinois into a sauté pan. Place it on strong heat and constantly stir the sauce with a large, wooden spoon, scraping over the bottom of the pan until the sauce has been reduced to no more than $2^1/_2$ deciliters (1 cup). Turn off the heat and add the cream in 2 or 3 batches. This returns the sauce to its normal quantity, and the cream is not boiled and therefore conserves its flavor.

Thoroughly drain the broad beans and remove the savory. Put them in the sauce and toss them in the pan to mix them well. Keep it warm without boiling until you are ready to dress them on a heated vegetable dish or timbale.

Chanterelles *(Girolles ou Chanterelles)*

Time: 35 minutes (including 25 minutes for preparation).

They may lack the savor and finesse of cèpes or morels, but chanterelles can be used as a garnish or make a very acceptable dish in a modest meal. For a garnish, choose the smallest ones, about the size of a small button; for all other recipes, you should use medium-size rather than large chanterelles, which do not have firm flesh once cooked and are rather like rubber. Before every recipe, cut the earthy stems off, then wash the chanterelles in cold water and thoroughly drain them on a clean towel, checking that pine needles or blades of moss are not attached to the gills of the mushroom.

For garnish: For 250 grams ($8^7/_8$ ounces) of chanterelles, heat 50 grams ($1^3/_4$ ounces, $3^1/_2$ tablespoons) of butter in a shallow pan, where the mushrooms are not piled too high; add the chanterelles, seasoned with salt and pepper and heated on strong heat, stirring with a wooden spoon until their own juices are completely reduced. Off the heat, add a dash of lemon juice.

Chanterelle Croûtes *(Croûtes aux Girolles).* (SEE MUSHROOM SHELLS, PAGE 492).

White Beans and Flageolet Beans *(Haricot Blanc et Flageolet)*

Recipes for white beans are equally good for flageolet beans, whether fresh or dried beans. To calculate the volume and the weight of dried beans, note that 1 deciliter (scant $^1/_2$ cup) weighs about 85 grams (3 ounces); and for the same recipes, $^1/_2$ liter (generous 2 cups) of dried beans corresponds to about 1 liter (4 cups) of fresh shelled beans, quantities that usually serve 6. For cooking dry beans, see the section on dry beans (PAGE 557), and, more particularly, the special procedures for cooking beans.

Fresh White Beans à la Maître d'Hôtel *(Haricots Blancs Frais à la Maître d'Hôtel).* Put the beans into a pot that contains, for 1 liter (4 cups) of shelled beans, $2^1/_2$ liters ($10^1/_2$ cups) of boiling water with 20 grams ($^2/_3$ ounce) of sea salt and a bunch of parsley added to it. Quickly bring it back to a boil. Allow *20–30 minutes* at a sustained boil, depending on the quality of the beans. For flageolets allow *30–40 minutes* and more. Before you drain them, check by touching them to see if they are tender and squash easily between your fingers. Then proceed as directed for vegetables à la maître d'hôtel (PAGE 470), allowing for this quantity of beans 75 grams of butter ($2^2/_3$ ounces, $^1/_3$ cup).

Fresh White Beans à la Ménagère *(Haricots Blancs Frais à la Ménagère).* Cook the beans as above; drain them either in a colander or by holding the cover on a tipped pot. Then add, for 1 liter (4 cups) of shelled beans, 40 grams ($1^3/_8$ ounces, 3 tablespoons) of butter worked into a paste with 10 grams ($^1/_3$ ounce) of flour (SEE BEURRE MANIÉ, PAGE 48) and then divided into little pieces; 3 tablespoons of the cooking water; 1 tablespoon of fresh, minced parsley; a pinch of salt and a pinch of pepper; and lemon juice. Heat while shaking the pot to combine the mixture and make the liaison. Pour into a heated vegetable dish.

Purée of Fresh White Beans *(Purée de Haricots Blancs Frais).* Cook the beans as above. Make them into a purée while they are still burning hot (SEE STRAINING PURÉES, PAGE 14). If the purée has been prepared in advance, spread some pieces of butter on the surface to stop it from drying out while it stands. Put to one side. A few moments before serving, moisten as directed (SEE PAGE 14). When it is time to dress the beans into a pyramid shape, add some cream to them or, if you do not have cream, some good reduced milk: 1 scant deciliter ($3^1/_3$ fluid ounces, scant $^1/_2$ cup) for

1 liter ($4^1/_4$ cups) of shelled beans. Add this gradually, stirring the purée vigorously to make it light; off the heat, add 40 grams ($1^3/_8$ ounces, 3 tablespoons) of butter divided into pieces. Mix well and serve.

The preparation is the same for dry beans. Note that they must be very thoroughly cooked.

Purée of White Beans with Tomatoes *(Purée de Haricots Blancs Tomatée).* A very good dish. To summarize: the beans are cooked, then simmered in a tomato sauce that has been well spiced, and finally everything is puréed. Depending on the season, you can use fresh beans or dry beans, and fresh tomato or conserve. *Time: 2 hours, 30 minutes (including cooking the dried beans). Serves 6.*

$^1/_2$ liter (generous 2 cups) of dry white beans.

***For the sauce:* 60 grams ($2^1/_4$ ounces) of minced onion; 25 grams (1 ounce, 2 tablespoons) of butter to color it; 10 grams ($^1/_3$ ounce) of flour; 2 deciliters ($6^3/_4$ fluid ounces, generous $^3/_4$ cup) of bouillon and $^1/_2$ deciliter ($1^2/_3$ ounces, scant $^1/_4$ cup) of white wine; 2 tablespoons of concentrated tomato purée; a bit of garlic the size of a pea.**

PROCEDURE. Cook the beans as directed. Meanwhile, prepare the sauce: lightly color the onion in the butter on gentle heat, then sprinkle with the flour; allow it to just slightly color. Add the wine, the bouillon, the tomato, the garlic. Allow it to boil for *15 minutes.* Next, add the beans, well drained, and simmer for *15 minutes.* Pass everything through a drum sieve. Put the purée into the rinsed-out pot. Season with pepper and grated nutmeg. Bring it to a boil, stirring with a wooden spoon. Let it boil for a few seconds. Turn off the heat: sprinkle the surface with pieces of butter, 20 grams ($^2/_3$ ounce) in total, mixing it in with a spoon just before serving.

White Beans in Salad *(Haricots Blancs en Salade).* Carefully drain the fresh or dried beans, then season while they are still warm so that better absorb the seasoning.

Beans with Tomato *(Haricots à la Tomate).* Mix the cooked fresh or dried beans together with a well-seasoned tomato sauce: 2 deciliters ($6^3/_4$ fluid ounces, generous $^3/_4$ cup) of sauce for 1 liter ($4^1/_4$ cups) of cooked beans.

Gratin of Puréed Beans *(Purée de Haricots Gratinés).* Take $^1/_2$ liter (generous 2 cups) of fresh, white beans or dry beans and cook as directed (SEE COOKING DRY VEGETABLES, PAGE 556). Once it has started to boil, add the bouquet garni; a little garlic clove, which is optional; and 2 large onions (weighing 200 grams/7 ounces in total), cut into rounds and previously colored with 25 grams (1 ounce, 2 tablespoons) of butter.

Once the beans have been thoroughly cooked, purée them with the onions. Reserve the cooking water. Return the purée to the rinsed pot; work it for a moment with the spoon to make it light and homogenous. Then add a pinch of pepper, 50 grams ($1^3/_4$ ounces, $3^1/_2$ tablespoons) of butter divided into small pieces, and 4–5 tablespoons of cooking water. Heat it, stirring it until the boiling is about to begin. Turn off the heat; if the purée has to stand for a while, sprinkle a few bits of butter on top.

About 15 minutes before serving, pour the purée into a heatproof, porcelain, shallow bowl that has been lightly buttered; smooth out the surface; sprinkle it with some fine bread crumbs (25–30 grams, about 1 ounce); moisten with 25 grams (1 ounce, 2 tablespoons) of melted butter. Brown it in a rather warm oven, allowing *8–12 minutes* depending on the oven temperature, or under a broiler. Serve with the heatproof plate set on a serving plate.

Bordeaux-Style Fresh White Beans *(Haricots Blancs Frais à la Mode de Bordeaux).* A very fine home-style recipe for July and August. Choose nice white beans that have been freshly shelled and are the same age: this ensures even cooking. Garlic is an essential condiment here, and furthermore its presence is not even suspected. If possible, use garlic from the Midi, which has a more subtle flavor. *Time: $1^1/_4$ hours. Serves 6.*

1 liter ($4^1/_4$ cups) of fresh white beans; $2^1/_2$ liters ($10^1/_2$ cups) of water; 10 grams ($^1/_3$ ounce) of sea salt; 1 nice tablespoon of good pork fat.

For the tomato sauce: **600 grams (1 pound, 5 ounces) of tomatoes (that is, 6 medium-size tomatoes); 1 good tablespoon of minced onion; 3 parsley sprigs; 1 sprig of thyme; 1/2 of a bay leaf; a clove; 1 teaspoon of fine salt; a pinch of ground pepper; grated nutmeg, as much as can be held on the point of a knife; 5 grams (1/6 ounce) of garlic; 1 tablespoon of good pork fat.**

1 teaspoon of freshly minced parsley to spread on the beans before serving.

PROCEDURE. Immerse the beans in strongly boiling water. Cover the pot by three-quarters. Gently boil it for *a half hour.* Then add the salt and the fat. Continue the cooking in the same manner for *another half hour.* Check at the end of cooking that the beans are not sticking together because the liquid has reduced.

While the beans are cooking, prepare the tomato sauce. Cut the tomatoes into 6 or 8 sections; remove the seeds. Heat the fat, preferably in a saucepan of thick aluminum. Put in the minced onion and color it lightly, mixing it with the wooden spoon. Then add the tomatoes and stir them on strong heat for *3–4 minutes* before adding the rest of the condiments. Cover and turn the heat down very low. Let it cook gently for *35–40 minutes,* stirring it from time to time.

Before straining the sauce, make sure that the tomatoes have lost all their moisture. If not, boil them strongly without the cover, stirring them for a few instants. Then pass it through a drum sieve to make a purée. You must obtain a nice, unctuous coulis; set it aside until ready to use.

To serve: Once the beans have been perfectly cooked, which you will know when a bean pressed between your fingers crushes easily, drain them thoroughly in a colander. The little bit of water remaining can be used in a soup.

Put the beans back into the pot. Add the tomato coulis. Place the pot on gentle heat for 2 minutes, tossing the beans from time to time to mix and heat all the ingredients. The tomato must just bind and coat the beans, but without becoming too heavy. However, if the beans must stand for a while, and if the tomato reduces too much during this time, dilute it with 1–2 tablespoons of the cooking water from the beans.

Pour it into a vegetable dish or heated plate. Sprinkle with the parsley and serve.

Green Beans *(Haricot Vert)*

Green beans would not be considered uninteresting vegetables most of the time if they were always prepared with the necessary care. It is essential that they are fresh, and the way they are cooked has a lot to do with how acceptable they are.

For many people, green beans are served only à la maître d'hotel or à l'anglaise: there are other excellent preparations, which we will describe below, many of which, along with a sauce, make for a more substantial dish. Whatever the accompaniment chosen, the preparation and initial cooking always remain the same. The cooking time is only slightly shortened when the beans are simmered in the sauce with which they are served. For all details, see cooking fresh vegetables (PAGE 470).

Peeling and cooking the beans: Break about 1/2 centimeter (3/16 inch) off at each end, removing the string that runs the entire length of the bean. If they are a little large, split the beans lengthwise. Wash them quickly in cool water. Immerse them in boiling, salted water, using 3 liters (12 cups) for 500 grams (1 pound, 2 ounces) of beans. Allow about *15 minutes* for cooking. The time is not exact because it depends on the quality of the beans. Note that green beans must always be a little bit firm and almost crunchy, though not excessively so.

Drain them immediately. Green beans do not have to be cooled, or rinsed, in cold water if they can be dressed as soon as they are cooked, and then served.

English-Style Green Beans *(Haricots Verts à l'Anglaise).* SEE VEGETABLES À L'ANGLAISE (PAGE 470). Use 1 kilogram (2 pounds, 3 ounces) of beans per person.

Green Beans à la Maître d'Hôtel *(Haricots Verts à la Maître d'Hôtel).* SEE VEGETABLES À LA MAÎTRE D'HÔTEL (PAGE 470). Allow 50 grams (1 3/4 ounces, 3 1/2 tablespoons) of butter for 450 grams (1 pound) of beans. The fine classic cooks suggested adding a pinch of superfine sugar, though this is optional.

Green Beans à la Crème *(Haricots Verts à la Crème).* Cook the beans only three-quarters of the way through in boiling water and carefully drain, then simmer the beans with a lean béchamel sauce in a sauté pan to finish their cooking; do not cover. Thus, for 450 grams (1 pound) of beans net weight: 3 deciliters ($1^1/_4$ cups) of béchamel sauce (SEE PAGE 52). The beans will be thoroughly cooked at the same time that the sauce is reduced. Restore the sauce to its correct consistency with 1 scant deciliter ($3^1/_3$ fluid ounces, scant $^1/_2$ cup) of good fresh cream. Heat without bringing to a boil, then serve.

Green Beans à la Poulette *(Haricots Verts à la Poulette).* Cook and drain as thoroughly as possible, because any excess liquid will dilute the sauce, then mix the beans with a poulette sauce prepared separately (SEE PAGE 61). Thus, for 450 grams (1 pound) of beans: a *roux blanc* made with 20 grams ($^2/_3$ ounce, 1 heaping tablespoon) of butter and 15 grams ($^1/_2$ ounce) of flour; 3 deciliters ($1^1/_4$ cups) of bouillon; 1 egg yolk; $^1/_2$ tablespoon of minced parsley; salt, pepper, a few drops of lemon juice. The bouillon can be replaced by the cooking water from the beans.

Sautéed Green Beans *(Haricots Verts Sautés).* Depending on the region and flavor, you can sauté them with butter or any product that will replace it, such as lard or oil. Allow 50 grams ($1^3/_4$ ounce, $3^1/_2$ tablespoons) of butter for 450 grams (1 pound) of beans. In simple home cooking, you can use a skillet instead of a sauté pan; heat the fat in it before adding the beans; sauté them on strong heat until they begin to color; sprinkle them with salt, and when they are dressed in their serving dish, with minced parsley.

In the Lyon style, color some finely minced onion in the fat and then add the beans. In the Provençal style, sauté the beans with olive oil and a little bit of garlic; and then add, off the heat, a bit of salted anchovy. You can also mix them with potatoes: cook them in boiling water and sauté in butter or fat. Depending on the season, you can use very small potatoes, left whole, or medium-size potatoes (long ones), cutting them into slices after cooking them.

Mixed Beans *(Haricots Panachés).* Mix with an equal quantity of flageolet beans and bind with butter as for a maître d'hôtel.

Green Bean Salad *(Haricots Verts en Salade).* If you are in a hurry, soak them in cool water to chill completely; drain them thoroughly. If not, they will take the seasoning badly. Then season them as an ordinary salad.

Home-Style Green Beans *(Haricots Verts à la Ménagère).* Cook the beans in boiling, salted water for only *10 minutes,* and finish cooking in a sauté pan with the sauce, prepared in advance. Thus, for 450 grams (1 pound) net weight of green beans: 30 grams (1 ounce) of finely minced onion, which has been gently softened without coloring in the same amount of butter or of good fat. Sprinkle with flour (10–12 grams/about $^1/_3$ ounce); mix for 1 minute without allowing it to color; dilute with at least 2 deciliters ($^7/_8$ cup) of the cooking water from the beans. Add a pinch of pepper and nutmeg and 1 tablespoon of minced parsley. Put the well-drained beans into the sauce. Cover and simmer *5–6 minutes,* until the beans are perfectly done. Just before serving, bind with a nice egg yolk (SEE LIAISONS, PAGE 47) and, off the heat, add 30 grams (1 ounce, 2 tablespoons) of butter.

Mangetout or Butter Beans *(Haricot Mange-Tout).* These come in many colors and types. The kind with a pale yellow color, a little bit bigger than large green beans, is the most well-known, at least in Paris, where it is mostly sold under the name of "butter beans." In fact, these are beans in the shell with seeds that are already formed, but the shell remains tender. At any rate, this is not a vegetable to serve to guests, but it is good for ordinary meals.

Always choose beans that have been harvested as recently as possible, and make sure you peel them carefully, particularly when they are older, because then the strings in them are very noticeable. Lightly break the two ends so that you can pull off the string all along the shell, leaving it attached to the end that has been broken off. Then break the beans into fragments about 2 centimeters ($^3/_4$ inch) long, which will also help you to completely remove the strings.

Their cooking and the principal recipes are the same as for green beans. For cooking in boiling water, we cannot give an exact time, because this depends on the age of the beans; for new beans, you can allow *20 good minutes at a boil.*

Beans Maître d'Hôtel *(Haricots à la Maître d'Hôtel).* Refer to the directions give for fresh sautéed vegetables or vegetables à la maître d'hôtel (PAGE 470).

Home-Style Beans *(Haricots à la Ménagère).* The same recipe as for green beans. For the sauce, the cooking water is replaced by milk, and the quantity is doubled, because the beans, having been cooked three-quarters of the way through, must simmer for 45 minutes in the sauce: the sauce is then reduced at the same time as the beans finish cooking.

Braised Beans *(Haricots à l'Étuvée).* This recipe deviates from the usual practice of first cooking the snow peas in boiling water, because all their cooking is done in a pot or terrine in the oven. But it is good only for young beans with seeds that have just formed, and with a shell that is quite tender.

Generously butter the bottom and sides of an ovenproof earthenware utensil (use 30 grams/1 ounce/2 tablespoons of butter). Add the beans (500 grams/1 pound, 2 ounces) with a nice medium onion that has been finely sliced into rounds, a nice heart of lettuce that has been cut into a fine julienne, a bunch of parsley, salt and pepper, a generous pinch of superfine sugar, and 6 tablespoons of water. On top of these ingredients, spread out 30 grams (1 ounce, 2 tablespoons) of butter divided into small pieces.

Cover and bring it to a boil directly on the heat; then place, directly on top of the beans, white parchment paper that has been buttered and that fits snugly in the pan. Put the cover back on, which must close and fit the pan as tightly as possible. Put it into a medium oven so that the beans cook in a very even and slow manner for *45 minutes.* After this, add $2^1/_2$ deciliters (1 cup) of cream. Continue cooking in the same conditions for *35–40 minutes.* To serve, remove the parsley and the paper. Send out the terrine, *covered,* on a serving plate.

Fennel *(Fenouil)*

Remove the wilted leaves, wash the stalks of fennel, shape them into a point, and, depending on their size, divide them into 2 pieces. Cook in boiling salted water until they are completely tender: *at least 1 hour.* Alternatively, treat them or braise them as for Belgian endive (SEE PAGE 509). Serve with a Mornay sauce, a cream sauce, a hollandaise sauce, tomato sauce, etc.

Lettuce *(Laitue)*

Served as a vegetable plate or as garnish for a cut of meat, the lettuce is braised. If you like, the lettuce can be blanched, then stuffed with a volume of veal stuffing about the size of a walnut, finely ground in a mortar.

If serving as a vegetable plate, you can add a garnish of glazed carrots with the lettuce arranged in a circle on the plate. Or you can dress it with slices of marrow that have been previously poached. To serve it à la crème, the best procedure is to add to its reduced cooking liquid some good heavy cream: thus, for the quantities given below, 1 deciliter ($3^1/_3$ fluid ounces, scant $^1/_2$ cup) of cream, all of which will give you a final quantity of 1 scant deciliter ($3^1/_3$ fluid ounces, scant $^1/_2$ cup).

Braised Lettuce *(Laitues Braisées).* For this kind of recipe, it's enough that each lettuce leaf is covered—that is, just glazed—by the juice, without any excess: each lettuce will have enough juice as guests help themselves.

The ingredients listed are those used for any braising. Pork rind thus plays an important role, because of the gelatin it adds to the juice, and it must never be omitted: use a nice fatty rind with at least $^1/_2$ centimeter ($^3/_{16}$ inch) of fat. The lettuce will absorb an unbelievable amount of fat, but if there is not enough, the lettuce will be soggy and bland, like a boiled herb. *Time: 2 hours. Serves 6.*

8 nice firm lettuces of medium size; 75 grams ($2^2/_3$ ounces) of onion; 75 grams ($2^2/_3$ ounces) of carrot; 80–100 grams ($2^3/_4$–$3^1/_2$ ounces) of fatty pork rind, fresh; a bouquet garni; 4 deciliters ($1^2/_3$ cups) of bouillon; 3 tablespoons of fresh cooking fat; salt and pepper; 30 grams (1 ounce, 2 tablespoons) of butter to finish.

Use bouillon that is very lightly salted: once it is reduced, there should be no more than 1 deciliter ($3^1/_3$ fluid ounces, scant $^1/_2$ cup), and the salt note will be much too strong if the bouillon is normally salted. So, before using it, dilute it by one-third.

NOTE. This is the classic method for braising lettuce. It can also be made by first preparing a mirepoix (SEE PAGE 21) with onion, carrot, and some bacon. The mirepoix is spread out over the pork rinds garnishing the bottom of the sauté pan; the amount of fat on the rinds can be slightly reduced in this case, because it is compensated for by the fat in the mirepoix. Arrange the blanched and tied-up lettuce on top. Cook as directed further down.

PROCEDURE. **Preparing the lettuce:** This can be done well in advance given the other preparations that will occupy your time. Once the lettuces are ready in their pan, they can stand, without spoiling, until they are put on the heat to braise.

Remove the wilted leaves on the outside. Cut the stem: not too close to the leaves. That way, the first leaves will not come away either now or when you are cutting them to a point. Put the lettuce in a terrine of fresh water with the head down, mixing them in a circular movement to rinse away the dirt. Make sure they do not contain any slugs.

Then immerse them, with the stem down, in a basin containing water at a rolling boil, salted at the rate of 10 grams ($^1/_3$ ounce) per liter. You can crowd them in there because the heat will instantly soften them. Quickly bring them back to a boil, then blanch for about *8 minutes.* The length of time is extremely important: too long, and the ends of the leaves will become mushy when you try to squeeze out the water; too short, and the time required for braising will not be enough to cook the lettuce.

Once blanched, remove the lettuce with a skimmer, so that you can immerse them in plenty of cold water. And, if you need to, change the water. Take them out once they have chilled and press them one by one between your hands to get rid of as much water as possible. As you do this, lay them out on a doubled kitchen towel. Season inside their hearts with salt and pepper. Then fold back the ends of the leaves by at least one-third, so that you make a small rectangular package (not a sausage), holding it in place with a few turns of string.

Putting them in a sauté pan: Use a sauté pan made of good aluminum, which can hold the lettuces side by side without their being too tightly crowded. As for any braising, do not use a pan that is too large, because more liquid would be needed to cover the lettuce, and they would then be boiled rather than braised. Put the pork rinds and vegetables into the sauté pan, following the method for basic braising (SEE PAGE 25). Arrange the lettuces on top, flattening them out a little. Put the bouquet garni between them.

The pan is now ready to be put on the heat when appropriate: that is, *about $1^1/_2$ hours before serving.*

Cooking the lettuce: On moderate heat and in a covered pan, "sweat" the lettuce for about 10 minutes; the juices are released with the effect of the heat and caramelize very lightly at the bottom of the pan. During this time, do not move anything: everything must remain the same from beginning to end of the cooking. From time to time, uncover the pan to smell the odor escaping from it. As soon as a *very light* odor of burning escapes and the steam turns from white to bluish, it is at a perfect stage of cooking, or, as the professional term describes it, *pincé* ("contracted"); if you heat it more, the lettuce will move from compacted and brown to burnt.

Then quickly add the bouillon, which should just cover the lettuce and the fat. Rapidly bring it to a boil. Then place a round of white buttered parchment paper directly on top of everything. Cover. Put it in the oven, if possible. From this point, cook for *$1^1/_2$ hours* at a very gentle and regular simmer, and during this time baste the lettuce with the cooking liquid, which will gradually reduce until it no longer covers them. Allow 15–20 minutes more if braising on the stove.

To serve: About 7–8 minutes before serving,

take out the lettuces, one by one, and place them in a large colander or drum sieve placed over a plate so that they are not crowded together. Gently press on them with the flat part of the skimmer to make the liquid run out; there will be a substantial amount, and this would dilute the reduced juice that is subsequently poured over the lettuces. With scissors, cut the string. With the back of the blade of a knife, gently scrape the darkened surface and trim the scraggly ends.

Dress them on a serving plate as they are trimmed. Keep them covered and warmed.

Strain the cooking juice through the chinois into a small sauté pan. Degrease it thoroughly. Reduce it to *1 scant deciliter (3¹/3 fluid ounces, scant ¹/2 cup)*. It should have the consistency of a light syrup, but if is too thick, lighten it with 1–2 tablespoons of bouillon. Off the heat, mix in the butter, divided into bits. Then baste the lettuce with the juice using a spoon. Serve.

Braised Lettuce *(Laitues à l'Étouffée).* A delicate but very simple recipe. Lettuce cooked this way has exactly the same flavor as lettuce cooked with green peas. *Time: 1 hour, 15 minutes. Serves 6.*

1¹/2 kilograms (3 pounds, 5 ounces) of small, new lettuces that have been completely trimmed; 6 small, young onions; a bouquet garni made with 1 sprig of parsley, 1 sprig of thyme, and 1 piece of bay leaf the size of a fingernail; 60 grams (2¹/4 ounces, 4¹/2 tablespoons) of good, fresh butter; 3 ordinary sugar cubes; a pinch of salt; 1 good tablespoon of flour.

PROCEDURE. Take off the wilted leaves and the end of the root; wash and drain the lettuce thoroughly. Place it on the table and cut it *crosswise* into a large julienne about a finger (2 centimeters, ³/4 inch) wide. Cut the heart, which is tender and delicate in new lettuce, into fine rounds. Peel the little onions without roughing them up too much so that they will not strip off.

Divide the butter into pieces the size of a hazelnut, reserving a piece about the amount of a small chestnut to use in the beurre manié for the final liaison.

Use a pot with a capacity of 2 liters (8¹/2 cups), made of aluminum, tinned steel, or even good earthenware, as long as it is not too thin. Put in about one-third of the chopped lettuce with one-third of the pieces of butter. Then press down with your hands to mix and pack it down as much as possible. Repeat twice with the remaining lettuce and pieces of butter. In the middle of this buttered lettuce, place the small onions, the bouquet garni, and the pieces of sugar. Sprinkle with salt. No liquid.

Thus prepared, the lettuce can stand in its pot until ready to be cooked. For me, there is nothing better than this dish.

Forty-five minutes before serving the small, young lettuce, put the *very well-covered* pot on an extremely moderate heat. It must cook evenly, in a small but pronounced simmer. Gradually, the lettuces release their own liquid. Once they are perfectly cooked, as well as the small onions, you should find at least 4 tablespoons of liquid. Do not reduce it: the dish would lose its character and flavor. Bind it with the reserved butter worked with the flour (SEE LIAISONS, PAGE 47). Remove the bouquet. Put the lettuce into a small vegetable plate. Serve with superfine sugar; if you like, you can add this at the table.

Chestnuts *(Marron)*

The kind of chestnut known in France as *marron de Lyon* ("chestnut from Lyon") is always preferable: this is a chestnut that is convex on its 2 principal faces. This point is even more important for a recipe that uses whole chestnuts. What is commonly known in France as a *châtaigne* ("chestnut") is flat on one side. Peeling it is long and bothersome because of its partitioned interior, and this produces a chestnut that is not attractive. Nice fresh chestnuts weigh in at 30–35 per 450 grams (1 pound).

All that said, even more important than the type is the quality of the chestnut used. Look for chestnuts with a tight, shiny shell and a nice brown color; the inside must be about as fresh as a newly cut potato. Chestnuts with a shriveled, blackish, and distended shell have a dried-out interior that cooking will not entirely fix; nor will they be good for purées, and they can only give you a bad result—no flavor and no cohesion because of the small clumps that can resist any drum sieve.

To shell the chestnuts: Whatever the procedure employed, *the chestnut shell must always be scored before heating;* otherwise, you risk a serious accident. There are several ways to remove the chestnut shell.

First method: Spread out the chestnuts on a baking sheet and put them in a very gentle oven for 7–8 minutes. If the oven is too hot, use a baking tray with sides, so that you can add a few tablespoons of cold water, which will vaporize and prevent the heat from coloring the chestnuts. As much as possible, these should not be allowed to color, not only because of appearance, but because this forms a barrier that prevents the chestnuts from absorbing liquid when cooked. Chestnuts are much more easily peeled when burning hot, so take them out of the oven only 3 or 4 at a time. You remove the shell and the skin underneath it at the same time.

For this method, use the point of a small knife to score along the most concave part of the chestnut, without cutting into the interior.

Second method: This possibly takes a little bit longer, but is preferable, since it is appropriate for all recipes using chestnuts, and helps keeps them intact, the scoring being done by another method.

With a small, sharp knife, remove a thin ribbon of shell around each chestnut, or you can make this incision in the shell itself without going into the skin underneath. This lets steam penetrate underneath the shell, which will then swell, making it easier to take off.

Put the chestnuts in a pot with enough *cold* water to cover well. Bring it to a boil. Let it boil for *only 1 minute.* Then turn off the heat and take out the chestnuts only by 2 or 3, so that you can shell them while they are burning hot. The 2 layers, shell and skin, should thus come off easily. If you let them cool even a little, the inside skin will dry out on the chestnut, making it quite difficult to remove.

(You can also use boiling water and put all the chestnuts in at one time. Let it cook for 5 minutes. The 2 layers of the chestnuts will come off the same.)

Third method: This procedure is slower and involves first removing the brown shell of the chestnuts before putting them in a pot of cold water. Bring it rapidly to a boil, then turn down to very low heat. As soon as the skin begins to come off, take them out 4 and 5 at a time so that you can skin them while they are burning hot.

Chestnut Purée *(Purée de Marrons).* Chestnut purée is mostly a garnish or an accompaniment for meat, fowl, or game. It can be entirely vegetarian or made using meat stock; in both cases the preparation is the same, differing only in the use of milk (diluted by half with water and to which butter is added) instead of bouillon; and the purée is then finished with milk instead of bouillon.

There is no point using choice large chestnuts for a purée: medium-size ones are good enough, but it is important that they are good and healthy and have a tightly stretched and shiny shell. *Time: 2 hours. Serves 6–8.*

750–800 grams (1 pound, 10 ounces–1 pound, 12 ounces) of chestnuts; 7 deciliters (3 cups) of bouillon; 15–20 grams (1/2–2/3 ounces) of the white part of celery; 30–35 grams (1–1 1/4 ounces, 2 tablespoons) of butter; a half sugar cube.

PROCEDURE. Remove the skins and the shells from the chestnuts as directed.

As soon as they have been shelled, put them in a pot of thick aluminum with high sides, just large enough so that when they are stacked in there they are covered by 6 deciliters (2 1/2 cups) of bouillon; if not, you may have to add a little bit more of bouillon or water, given that you need a reserve of 1 deciliter (3 1/3 fluid ounces, scant 1/2 cup) of bouillon to finish cooking the purée.

Add the finely minced celery to the chestnuts and the sugar. Bring it to a boil. Then turn the heat down very low. Cover it. Let it cook gently, very evenly, until you can crush a chestnut between your fingers easily, without any effort. For this, let it cook at a very gentle simmer for *about 1 hour:* some types of chestnuts require more time than others. Above all, do not allow it to boil fully; otherwise, the chestnut will be overcooked on the outside but the inside will be badly cooked, and you will get only a granular purée.

As soon as they are cooked, pass them through a metal drum sieve a few at a time, so that the chestnuts are all burning hot when you do so (SEE

STRAINING PURÉES, PAGE 14). Put the purée into a sauté pan. On strong heat and using a large wooden spoon, mix the purée to evaporate the moisture from it, so that it becomes quite thick (SEE DRYING PURÉES, PAGE 14). *Then turn off the heat.*

Add three-quarters of the butter in little bits, working the purée with the wooden spoon. Next, add the hot reserved bouillon, 1 tablespoon at a time, to bring the purée to the right consistency: that of a fine light purée of potatoes. On very gentle heat, heat the purée thoroughly *without allowing it to boil,* so that you do not spoil the flavor of the butter. Sprinkle the rest of the butter on the surface so that it does not brown. Keep warm. Just before serving, stir it with a spoon to mix in this butter.

Morels *(Morille)*

Depending on the weather at the time, the season for morels is variable, ranging from early April to the first days of May, but rarely longer than 15 days. As for all mushrooms, it is essential that they should be absolutely fresh.

Some people insist that morels should not be washed because some of their very subtle perfume is then lost in the water, but how else are you going to get rid of the soil or sand, which always remains lodged in their gills despite the most careful examination? It is certainly better to wash them; and given the precautions needed when washing morels, this can easily be described as the most complicated part of any recipe.

The average morel varies in size between that of a pigeon egg and a small chicken egg. Depending on their size and the recipe, you can use morels whole or divided into pieces.

Cleaning them: To do this properly, you need 2 containers of cold water.

Begin by eliminating the soil-stained tip of the stem. Then submerge the morels in a terrine. Let them soak for 5–6 minutes to moisten the sand that is lodged in the gills or cavities. Then take them out *with your hand, one by one,* to put them in a second container; as you do, open the gills so that if there is any remaining sand it can be removed by soaking the morel thoroughly in the water.

To be absolutely certain they are clean, rinse them in a third change of water, renewed in the first bowl.

After this, drain them in a strainer, always lifting them out with your hand: this procedure leaves behind in the bottom of the container any sand that has come out of the morels during the cleaning.

Put them in a towel and shake it to thoroughly drain them.

Morels à la Poulette *(Morilles à la Poulette).* This is one of the most common recipes. You can serve them like this in different ways: either simply in a timbale or a vegetable dish; or in a pastry shell or a vol-au-vent shell; in a pâte à foncer shell, as for a tart; or in little round pastry shells like those used to serve mushrooms. Whatever kind of shell you use, heat these shells first, putting them empty into the oven in advance so that they are as hot as possible when you garnish them with the morels. *Time: About 1 hour. Serves 6.*

500 grams (1 pound, 2 ounces) of morels.

To cook them: 25 grams (1 ounce, 2 tablespoons) of butter; 2 tablespoons of water; a pinch of salt and a pinch of pepper; juice of 1/2 lemon.

3 good deciliters (1 1/4 cups) of poulette sauce, which consists of a small white roux with 25 grams (1 ounce, 2 tablespoons) of butter and 20 grams (2/3 ounce) of flour; 3 1/2 deciliters (1 1/2 cups) of clear bouillon; 1 egg yolk; a small bunch of parsley; a good pinch of fresh minced parsley.

PROCEDURE. In a small saucepan, start the sauce as directed (SEE POULETTE SAUCE, PAGE 61). Let it cook gently for *15–20 minutes* while you prepare the morels. Wash and drain the morels. If they are small, leave them whole; if not, divide them into pieces. Put them into a sauté pan with the butter, water, salt, pepper, and the lemon. Quickly bring it to a boil, then cover it and turn the heat down very low so that it will simmer for *about 10 minutes.*

Pour out all the cooking juice by tilting the pan, holding the cover closed, above another sauté pan. Keep the morels warm in their casserole.

Then boil the juice of these morels, uncovered, to reduce it to *3–4 tablespoons.* Add the prepared poulette sauce, straining it through a chinois. Let it boil for 1 minute. Make the liaison with egg yolk. Then add the morels to the sauce and toss them in it.

Dress the morels how you want to serve them. Spread the minced parsley on their surface.

Sautéed Morels *(Morilles Sautées).* Wash and thoroughly dry the morels in a kitchen towel, then divide them into quarters if they are large, and season them with salt and pepper. Heat some butter in a nice, clean skillet and throw in the morels. Sauté them on strong heat so that they release their juices. Serve sprinkled with several drops of lemon juice and with minced parsley.

Morels à la Crème *(Morilles à la Crème).* Gently braise in butter, with 1 good tablespoon of minced onion for 500 grams (1 pound, 2 ounces) of morels. Then cover them with a cream sauce (3 good deciliters/1 1/4 cups) and let them simmer in it for 5–6 minutes before serving (SEE CREAM SAUCE, PAGE 63).

Stuffed Morels *(Morilles Farcies).* *Time: 1 hour. Serves 6.*

625 grams (1 pound, 6 ounces) of morels, each as large as possible.

For the stuffing: 150 grams (5 1/3 ounces) of fine sausage meat; 2 tablespoons of onion and 1 tablespoon of shallot, both very finely minced; 1 tablespoon of minced parsley; 1 piece of garlic the size of a pea; 50 grams (1 3/4 ounces) of white bread crumbs soaked in a few tablespoons of water or bouillon; 40–50 grams (1 3/8–1 3/4 ounces) of fatback bacon that has been finely minced.

For cooking: 100 grams (3 1/2 ounces, 7 tablespoons) of butter; 1 good tablespoon of fine brown bread crumbs; a pinch of minced parsley; a bit of lemon juice.

PROCEDURE. Clean the morels. Choose the 12 largest; cut their stems off at the level of the cap and set these caps aside to stuff them.

Coarsely chop the stems and add to the remaining mushrooms. In a small, very clean skillet, heat the minced fatback bacon. Add the onion, the shallot, and the minced mushrooms; stir it on strong heat for a few minutes to evaporate the juices released by the mushrooms. Spread everything out on a plate to chill.

Mix thoroughly in a terrine: the sausage meats; the white bread crumbs, thoroughly squeezed out; the chilled mushroom hash; the garlic, squashed with the blade of a knife; the minced parsley; salt, pepper, and spices.

With the point of a small knife, split the mushrooms on one side, then add 1 good teaspoon of the stuffing. Restore the mushrooms to their original shape. As you do this, arrange them on a round, heatproof plate that has been generously buttered. Sprinkle with the bread crumbs. On each morel, place a small piece of butter.

Put in a good, strong medium oven; allow *20 minutes* to cook and brown. When you take the plate out of the oven, spread the minced parsley over the top and moisten it with a few drops of lemon juice.

Turnip *(Navet)*

It is essential to know how to choose turnips, because there is a large number of species, many of which are no good. The best type of turnip to use for any recipe is easily recognizable: look for a slightly elongated shape with a fine yellow vegetable pulp. Every turnip that has a spongy, fibrous pulp when you open it should be rejected.

The different recipes for carrots are equally good for turnips when they are served as a vegetable dish. Also good is turnip purée: cooked as for glazed turnips and forced through a drum sieve, then mixed with potato purée and finished with cream instead of milk. Add just enough potato purée to make a good consistency.

Turnips au Jus *(Navets au Jus).* Made as directed for garnishes, the turnips are blanched for 5 minutes; once drained, they are colored in a skillet, then put into a sauté pan with some good jus; the pan should be large enough so that they are not too piled up.

Cook them gently, covered. Before serving them, and in the pan itself, bind them with the reduced juice and beurre manié.

Turnips for Garnish *(Navets pour Garnitures).* Cut the turnips into rounds 3–4 centimeters (1 1/4–1 1/2 inches) long. Divide each round into 4 or 6 parts depending on its size. Peel and skin them; that is, use a small knife to scrape off the corners of each quarter, shaping them into a large, elongated olive. Do not wash them because any moisture will prevent them from coloring. For this reason, wipe them one by one with a good towel to dry off all their natural moisture.

Late in the season, it is essential to blanch the turnips: this is to first reduce their strong odor and subsequently to begin their cooking. When cooking vegetables, this takes considerably longer in a sauce than in boiling water; and this is often limited by the time needed for the sauce that is part of the garnish.

To blanch the turnips: Shape them first, then put the turnips into a pot and cover with cold water. Bring to a boil, then boil *for about 10 minutes.* Cool them in a large amount of cold water. Dry them thoroughly in a towel.

To color the turnips: For turnips that look attractive, color them in very pure butter so that it does not form any dark residues that would stick to the vegetables. Before using the butter or fat, clarify it (SEE CLARIFIED BUTTER, PAGE 16).

In a small, very clean skillet, heat the clarified butter. Add the turnips. Sauté them on strong heat until they have taken on a light golden color. Then sprinkle them with a pinch of superfine sugar, which helps to color them. Continue to sauté them, watching over the skillet, until they turn a reddish-blond color.

Then put them in a strainer.

Let them drain for several minutes before using them for your chosen recipe.

Glazed Turnips *(Navets Glacés).* SEE CARROTS GLAZED AS A GARNISH (PAGE 484). Cook the turnips in exactly the same way.

Onion *(Oignon)*

Aside from its role as a flavoring, the onion features above all in French cuisine as a garnish. For a vegetarian dish, it can be stuffed; for this, choose medium-size onions, hollow them out, blanch them thoroughly in boiling salted water, and then garnish with the stuffings suggested for stuffed tomatoes. Brown them in the same way.

Small Onions for Garnish *(Petits Oignons pour Garnitures).* Onions should be cooked separately, not only to preserve their appearance, but above all to ensure that they retain their unique flavor. They should be moistened with the minimal amount of liquid required so that they cook in their own juices. They are infinitely more flavorsome made this way, and when added to a sauce, they retain an aroma that would have been lost if simply boiled. And the sauce will be all the better for it, the onions giving their aroma to the sauce.

Depending on the requirements of the dish, cook onions thoroughly or only three-quarters of the way through. In home kitchens, cooks often settle for coloring the onions rapidly, but this only begins to cook them. And this is not the authentic garnish of small onions.

Always use a small *heavy* pot, so that there is less chance of the onions sticking and the onions can more easily be kept warm until added to a dish for which they have been prepared.

A small onion should be the size of a large hazelnut. Look for onions of equal size, as much for appearance's sake as to ensure even cooking.

Peeling. To peel them easily, put the onions in a large strainer and immerse them in boiling water for only 1 minute. This loosens the peel and means that they can be stripped of their skins much more easily, without irritating your eyes.

With a small knife, trim the 2 ends, but not too much or the onions will fall apart. Then remove the yellow membrane and the first white layer, being careful not to strip the onion. With the point of the knife, cut a small cross in the root of the onion, so that, as Carême says, "the heart of the onion is anointed and the cooking accelerated."

Late in the season it is essential to blanch the onions: that is, to immerse them in boiling water for a more or less prolonged period. This gets rid of their sharpness and facilitates cooking, which will otherwise be imperfect. Depending on their degree of maturity, boil for at least 4 minutes and up to 7–8 minutes, then plunge into a large amount of cold water.

Categories for the preparation of onions is as follows: *au blanc,* for fricassees, blanquettes, etc.; *au brun,* for fish stews, meat stews, etc.; *glazed,* to accompany any dish. The term "glazed" can, in fact, include the first two preparations, as in the following recipes.

Small onions au blanc, for fricassées, blanquettes, etc.: Choose and peel the onions as above, and put them in a small pot just large enough to contain them.

For a dozen small onions, add: 20 grams (2/3 ounce, 1 heaping tablespoon) of butter; 3–4 tablespoons of water or, preferably, the cooking liquid from the dish the onions will accompany. This small quantity of liquid is enough, because the onions release their own liquid. Cover the pot. Put it on low heat.

Cook very gently, carefully stirring the onions occasionally. Continue until they are cooked. They must keep their shape intact, remaining white and brilliant, and be glazed by a light coating from their own juices, reduced to a spoonful at the very most.

For new onions, *35 minutes of cooking* will be enough. For more mature onions, allow *1 hour,* and increase the quantity of liquid to as much as double.

Watch carefully to make sure the onions do not color at all. After they have cooked, keep them covered and warm in their pot until using. If they are not used soon after they are cooked, add 2 or 3 spoonfuls of the sauce they are waiting to join.

Small onions au brun, for ragoûts, stews, fish stews, etc.: Peel them as directed. The best utensil is a sauté pan, large enough so that the onions can be easily moved about while they color. For a dozen small onions, gently heat 25 grams (1 ounce, 2 tablespoons) of butter. Add the onions. Do not cover.

On gentle heat, let the onions begin to take on a yellowish tint. When they begin to color, sprinkle a pinch of superfine sugar over them. Toss frequently, to move them around and help them color evenly. Allow for this *at least 20 minutes.* They should take on a beautiful golden tint, a little darker at both ends, stem and root.

Then add enough liquid so that they are almost covered: for this many onions, use about 2–3 deciliters (7/8–1 1/4 cups). Use a light jus or bouillon, *very lightly salted,* to which you might add some white wine, depending on the recipe. Cover and boil gently, proceeding as for onions au blanc. In the same way as for onions au blanc, they should finish cooking at the same time as the liquid reduces to a glaze. If, toward the end, the liquid is not reducing rapidly enough and the onions are almost fully cooked, remove the cover to speed up the reduction.

NOTE. In some recipes, when you do not want onions "glazed," cook small onions au brun without any liquid. That is, after blanching them for as long as needed given their age, sauté them with butter for *2 minutes* on strong heat. Then turn the heat down very low so that the onions cook and color simultaneously and gradually. Do not cover the pot, and toss the onions frequently.

The Onion Purée Known as "Soubise" ***(Purée d'Oignons Dite "Purée Soubise").*** Soubise purée makes an excellent garnish or accompaniment for numerous recipes. The procedures for preparing it vary according to the author and your resources; it follows the same principles as soubise sauce, which can be made as you like, either with or without meat, being careful to retain its white tint. In all cases, this requires the support of a liaison, generally a very thick béchamel; or it can be rice cooked with the onion.

An addition of crème fraîche is particularly recommended; we will indicate as much in the following recipe, one of the best for home cooking. If you do not have cream, add some butter to the purée to finish; and when there is no need to economize, you can even finish the creamed purée with butter. In that case, though, you need less butter. *Time: About 1 hour, 30 minutes. Serves 6.*

1 kilogram (2 pounds, 3 ounces) of onions; 100 grams (3 1/2 ounces, 7 tablespoons) of butter; 3 deciliters (1 1/4 cups) of clear bouillon or boiled milk.

For the béchamel: 30 grams (1 ounce, 2 tablespoons) of butter and 30 grams (1 ounce) of flour for the white roux; 4 scant deciliters (scant 1 2/3 cups) of boiled milk; a small bunch of parsley; salt, pepper, grated nutmeg.

To finish the purée: 1 deciliter (3 1/3 fluid ounces, scant 1/2 cup) of fresh, heavy cream; or, if you do not have it, 40–50 grams (1 3/8–1 3/4 ounces, 3–3 1/2 tablespoons) of fresh butter.

PROCEDURE. Peel the onions; cut them in 2 from top to bottom. Place the cut side on the table and cut them into very thin slices. Submerge them in a pot of boiling water to cover completely. Bring it back to a boil and maintain it at a lively rate for 5–10 minutes, depending on how old the onion is.

Then put the onion into a strainer to drain it thoroughly. In the same pot, just melt the butter; add the onion to it. Sauté it on strong heat for only 5 minutes to reduce its moisture, being careful not to allow anything to color. Then add the milk and the bouillon and a good pinch of salt if the bouillon is not already salted. Cover, and if possible put it in a very moderate oven where the liquid will be reduced at the same time as the onion finishes cooking: a result that you cannot easily obtain on the stove. Allow about *35–40 minutes* in the oven.

Meanwhile, prepare the liaison sauce in a small saucepan (SEE BÉCHAMEL SAUCE, PAGE 52). Do not cover, but allow it to simmer, mixing it very frequently; if not, it will stick as it reduces. When it is ready for use, there should be no more than 3 deciliters (1 1/4 cups), which means it will be very thick.

Once the onions are completely cooked, mix them with the sauce and take them off the heat. Force everything, gradually, through a drum sieve; nothing should be left on the mesh of the drum sieve. Put this purée into a sauté pan (SEE DRYING PURÉES, PAGE 14). Reduce it on strong heat until it has become thick enough so that adding the cream will have little effect on the consistency. Then add the cream, tablespoon by tablespoon. Keep it warm, without boiling, until you are ready to serve. If the purée is served as an accompaniment, serve it in a timbale or in a small heated vegetable dish.

Sorrel *(Oseille)*

It is best to choose "duck" sorrel, which is less acidic than "Belleville" sorrel, whose leaves are larger and their color darker. But whatever the variety chosen, the most important point is to pick young sorrel; that is, once the time has passed for the first sorrel of spring (the true new sorrel), you should use only sorrel that has been grown recently and is no more than 4–5 weeks old. This is because the older sorrel gets, the more oxalic acid it contains: this is why gardeners cut it as it grows, in order to force new growth.

Whether the sorrel is destined to be a garnish or served on the side as a vegetable, the purée is made in the same way. First softened—the term used by French professionals is "fondu" (melted)—rather than blanched, as chicory or spinach is, the sorrel is then gently braised. Its first liaison by a roux is then completed with a liaison of eggs, the characteristic of the most country-style preparation. You finish with cream, a fine butter, and a very concentrated veal jus (which explains the term "au jus" used for sorrel served on its own); the jus is generally supplied by the cooking juices from the braised meat, fricandeau, veal fillet, etc., for which the sorrel purée is the garnish. The treatment of sorrel in a good home kitchen is the same as in a professional kitchen; the only difference is the point when the sorrel is passed through a drum sieve: in a professional kitchen, this is done only after braising the sorrel; in a home kitchen, it is done before braising, to simplify the operations following the melting of the sorrel.

Let us also finally note the very simple preparation for sorrel in the country style. We list it further down because it can be used whenever you are in a hurry or when you do not have the ingredients needed for the other preparations. But it is mainly served with a garnish of eggs, preferably soft-boiled eggs with the yolk still runny.

Sorrel can also be prepared without meat, as we describe below, milk replacing the bouillon used for braising. Served separately as a vegetable plate, either with or without meat, the purée is garnished with quarters of hard-boiled eggs, allowing 1 egg per person.

Sorrel au Jus *(Oseille au Jus)*. *Time: 3 hours. Serves 6.*

1 1/4 kilograms (2 pounds, 12 ounces) of sorrel, gross weight; 50 grams of flour (1 3/4 ounces) and 20 grams (2/3 ounce, 1 heaping tablespoon) of butter for the

roux; 5 deciliters (generous 2 cups) of bouillon; 5 grams (1/6 ounce) of salt; a pinch of superfine sugar; 2 whole eggs and 1 egg yolk; 2 good tablespoons of heavy cream (or, if you do not have any, very good milk reduced); 4 tablespoons of very concentrated veal jus; 40 grams (1 3/8 ounces, 3 tablespoons) of butter to finish.

PROCEDURE. Check through the sorrel leaves to remove any foreign herbs, which are often found among them. There is no need to remove the stems—by bending them backwards—if the sorrel is young. Wash the sorrel in plenty of water, changing it once. Drain them in a drum sieve.

Use a medium-size deep pot with a thick bottom, because the sorrel diminishes considerably once heated. For this amount, put *only one-third* of the sorrel in with 1 or 2 glasses of water.

Put the pot on extremely low heat and allow it to "melt"—that is, to soften and reduce the sorrel gradually—very gently stirring it time to time with a wooden spoon so that it softens throughout. As it softens in the pot, add a good handful of the sorrel remaining in the drum sieve. Once everything has been placed in the pot and thoroughly melted, cover and let it boil for *5–6 minutes,* always on very gentle heat. (The need for heating it very gently is because of the tendency of sorrel to stick to the bottom of the pot, unless it is constantly mixed with a wooden spoon.)

Once the sorrel has been melted, pour it into a metallic drum sieve placed over a terrine. Allow it to drain for *about 20 minutes;* throw away the liquid that has run out of it. After this, turn it into a purée using a pestle or a wooden *champignon,* a special mushroom-shaped pestle.

While the sorrel is draining, prepare a blond roux in the rinsed and dried pot (SEE ROUX, PAGE 47). Then add to it: the sorrel purée, little by little, mixing it with a wooden spoon or whisk; the bouillon, in three or four stages; salt and sugar. If the bouillon has been salted, add rather less salt at this point; you can add more at the end if necessary. Bring it to a boil while stirring it. Turn down the heat. Place a round of buttered parchment paper right on top of the sorrel; cover the pot; put it in the oven if possible, at a heat sufficient to maintain a very gentle regular simmer for *2 hours.*

The liaison with egg: Beat the eggs, both whites and yolks, in a bowl as for an omelet. Add the cream or the milk to them. Pass it through a chinois into another bowl. (This is essential when using the whole egg, and not just the yolk, to eliminate the germ as well the unmixed parts of the whites, which will coagulate while cooking into white clots that look very unpleasant.)

Take the pot out of the oven. Proceed as for a liaison with egg (SEE LIAISONS, PAGE 49), first heating the eggs with a few tablespoons of sorrel. Pour everything into a pot and mix it with a whisk. Put the pot on gentle heat to simmer for *7–8 minutes* more. The egg liaison can boil without spoiling because of the flour in the roux.

Just before serving, add, *off the heat,* the final butter. Pour the sorrel in a vegetable plate or onto the serving plate if it is a garnish. Smooth the surface with the back of a spoon and moisten it with the veal jus. If the sorrel is being served as a vegetable, arrange the hard-boiled eggs all around the dish, the white part of the quarters leaning against the edge of the vegetable dish.

Creamed Sorrel *(Oseille à la Crème).* This is the description given on a menu for a dish that is strictly meat-free, when no fat other than butter can be used. Its preparation is exactly that of sorrel au jus except for the two following modifications: The bouillon is replaced by the same quantity of boiled milk; in place of the veal jus, sprinkle the surface of the sorrel with cream that has been boiled and very lightly salted.

Peasant-Style Sorrel *(Oseille Façon Paysanne).* This procedure is appropriate only for a small quantity of sorrel, given the conditions for softening it and the very abridged cooking time: thus, *scarcely 450 grams (1 pound) of sorrel, gross weight.*

Sort, wash, etc., the sorrel, as above. Assemble the leaves in small piles on the table to cut them into a julienne. Put them in a sauté pan with, for this amount, a piece of butter the size of a small egg (50 grams/1 3/4 ounces/3 1/2 tablespoons) or a little less of pork fat. Melt the sorrel on gentle heat, mixing frequently with a wooden spoon, which should be left in the sauté pan since sorrel, when softened like this, easily sticks. Allow *10–15 minutes* for it to be ready.

Bind it with the beaten egg white and yolk: use either 1 large egg or 2 small ones; then add 1 teaspoon of flour that has been worked thoroughly with a piece of butter the size of a chestnut. Salt. Mix it well. Cover the pan. Put it in a very medium oven for *about 20 minutes* to finish cooking the sorrel.

Green Peas *(Petits Pois)*

For peas, absolute freshness is a prerequisite. This is why it is always preferable, if you do not grow them yourself, to buy them in their shells. Choose them in shining and intact shells. Dull shells covered with little white marks contain hard and powdery peas.

If you can only buy them shelled, make sure that the peas retain their little stem, or germ, which attaches them to the shell; these come off when peas have been shelled for a long time and are therefore an indication that they are no longer fresh. Shell the peas only when you are going to cook them; if you must do this in advance. Keep them away from the air in a covered bowl or wrapped in a towel.

One liter (4¼ cups) of peas in their shells weighs 400 grams (14⅛ ounces) and supplies, if the shells are nice and full, about 2½ deciliters (1 cup) of green peas of all sizes; that is, large, medium, and small. You will then have to sort through them because one should not use peas of different sizes for the same dish, because some of them will not be sufficiently cooked while the others will turn to mush. So, for 1 liter (4¼ cups) of medium-size peas, you must allow about 5 liters (5¼ quarts) of peas in their shells, or a weight of 2 kilograms (4 pounds, 6 ounces).

Large peas are used in ragoûts, in meat sautés, in navarins, etc.; with bacon, with ham; in a purée as a garnish for braised meat; and in soups, particularly the Saint-Germain potage.

Medium-size peas are best for recipes in which they are braised, particularly à la française, to be served as a vegetable.

Very small peas do not cook well when braised because they crush. For this reason, Carême always suggested cooking them in rapidly boiling water and then adding the drained peas to the other ingredients for the dish. But cooking in boiling water does not give peas the same flavor as braising does, where all their juices are condensed.

Peas à la Française *(Petit Pois à la Française).*

This is the best way to prepare them. Even though it is extremely simple, there are, depending on taste and custom, several slight differences as regards the lettuce and onions, and their preparation, not to mention an optional liaison with beurre manié.

The *lettuce* is traditional and must never be omitted; but it is not to everyone's taste, so it's better to serve it separately from the peas. If the lettuce is very young and tender, cut it into 2 or even in 4; depending on its size, it should cook at the same time as the peas. Nonetheless, it is better to braise it alone in butter in advance and then add it to the peas.

Small onions are generally the rule, and like the lettuce, should be served separately from the peas so that guests can help themselves if they like them. That said, some recipes for peas à la française do not serve the onions used for cooking the peas. In this case, 2 young onions are enough for 1 liter (4 cups) of peas.

For the *bouquet garni,* use only some parsley sprigs, no thyme or bay. If possible, add a savory stem to the parsley.

The *liaison with beurre manié* is optional; do this before serving, using 10 grams (⅓ ounce) of flour worked with 20 grams (⅔ ounce, 1 heaping tablespoon) of butter per liter (4¼ cups) of peas; its disadvantage is that it always leaves a taste of flour and clumps the peas together in a compact mass. For these two reasons, reducing the liquid for the peas before serving is preferable. Using butter alone, without any flour, and adding it off the heat, produces a liaison effect that is not only sufficient but is actually even better.

At family meals in earlier times it was normal to use some *superfine sugar* with peas à la française. Add some if you like.

For cooking peas, we suggest using a covering system practiced, as in home cooking, because this is the best and most rational way to do it. So, use *a soup dish* that fits well on the pot, closing it tightly. In this soup dish, place ½ glass of *cold* water, replacing it when it has warmed up during the cooking process. As long as it fits snugly in the pot, a soup dish is better than any other cover and prevents any steam from escaping; and the steam, hitting the cold plate, condenses and is kept inside, helping to cook the peas. Home cooks also use this warm water if they need to add some water to the peas if the cooking liquid has reduced too much.

In suggesting using medium-size peas for the à la française preparation, we mean, of course, peas that are smaller rather than larger, and of an equal size. *Time: 40 minutes (once the peas have been shelled). Serves 6.*

1 liter (4¼ cups) of good, fresh medium-size peas; 125 grams (4½ ounces, 9 tablespoons) of fresh butter; the heart of a tender lettuce; 12 very small onions, no larger than hazelnuts; ½ glass of water (1 deciliter, 3⅓ fluid ounces, scant ½ cup); 3 sugar cubes (15–20 grams, ½–⅔ ounce); a bouquet made with 4 sprigs of parsley, and, if possible, a stem of savory.

PROCEDURE. Use a thick pot of aluminum or enameled steel (not cast iron, which would darken the peas, and not a thin-sided utensil, to which the peas might stick). It should have a capacity of about 2 liters (8½ cups), so that it is only two-thirds full when all the ingredients are added. First put in the peas, then add the cold water. Put the pot on rather strong heat. Cover it, as directed, with a soup plate, into which you pour some cold water. As soon as it has come to a boil, turn the heat down to moderate, but keep the peas cooking at a faster rather than slower rate. The peas should not reach a simmer, and most of all they must cook for only the necessary time, *30–35 minutes,* depending on their quality, because an excess of cooking would shrink them, spoiling their delicacy, and would also caramelize their sugar.

While cooking, you may need to stir the peas, but do not use a spoon, which would turn them into a mush; simply toss the pot to move them around. Make sure you change the water in the soup plate 2 or 3 times, each time it has warmed up. If you are not serving the peas immediately, turn the heat down very low to keep them warm without boiling.

At the end of the suggested cooking time, you should find scarcely a tablespoon of liquid left with the peas. In this case, it is not essential to use a liaison with beurre manié, the disadvantage of which we have already explained; it should be used only when the boiling has been irregular and there is too much liquid left when the peas are ready to serve. To avoid using flour, pour this excess liquid into a small sauté pan, strongly reduce it over high heat, and then add it to the peas *before* finishing them with the butter.

To dress the dish: Two minutes before serving, remove the bouquet. Quickly take off the strings from the lettuce; divide each half in 2 pieces lengthwise; put them on a plate. Arrange the small onions next to the lettuce.

Place the uncovered pot on the heat to reduce the remaining little bit of liquid, tossing the peas so that they do not stick. *Turn off the heat.* Add the rest of the butter to the peas (25 grams/1 ounce/2 tablespoons), divided into pieces, gently rolling and shaking the pot, which is enough to make the liaison.

Pour them into a timbale or a vegetable dish, arranging them in a slight dome. Arrange the 4 pieces of lettuce on top of the peas in the form of a cross. Surround it with the small onions. This method of dressing the dish makes serving easier, allowing the guests to choose whether or not to take the lettuce or onions.

Preserved peas: When they are preserved as they are (without extra salt and sugar), they can be prepared à la française with the lettuce and onions previously braised in butter and then added to the peas just before serving.

Canned peas must first be immersed in boiling water, nothing but a quick plunge, to remove their preserved taste. Drain them thoroughly. Dry them in a sauté pan over strong heat before adding the onions, the lettuce, and the liaison butter to them.

Peas à l'Anglaise *(Petit Pois à l'Anglaise).* Here again, medium-size peas are most often used. However, as we have said, you can use smaller peas.

To prepare the peas in the authentic English style, add fresh mint, using as much or as little as you like, depending on your preference, so that the flavor is more, or less, pronounced. English cooks often put a small bouquet of mint into the water used for cooking the peas, or you can add a few leaves to the garnish, which have been separately boiled if you like. *Time: 25–30 minutes for cooking. Serves 6.*

1 liter ($4^1/_4$ cups) of medium-size peas; 100 grams ($3^1/_2$ ounces, 7 tablespoons) of fresh butter; 1 level teaspoon of superfine sugar.

PROCEDURE. Cook the peas as directed for fresh vegetables à l'Anglaise (PAGE 470). Drain them and dry them as directed. Season them with a pinch of salt and a little superfine sugar. Serve them with the butter shaped into large shells, either separately or scattered on top.

Flemish-Style Peas *(Petit Pois à la Flamande).* This recipe, which is quite simple, includes carrots and should be made with medium-size peas. It can be summarized thusly: choose small carrots and cut them into finely peeled quarters, and then trim the corners to form elongated olives. To cook, just cover them with cold water, and add salt, pepper, and butter (SEE GLAZED CARROTS AS A GARNISH, PAGE 484). After 15 minutes at a lively boil, add the peas and the bouquet of parsley. Cover without completely closing the pot; cook for *25–30 minutes,* always on rather strong heat. The liquid should have completely reduced by the time the vegetables are cooked; if several tablespoons still remain, reduce by boiling it strongly with the cover off. Off the heat, add the butter, which acts as a liaison, and serve immediately. *Serves 6.*

7 good deciliters (3 cups) of peas; 150 grams ($5^1/_3$ ounces) of carrots already trimmed and cut; 80 grams (about $2^3/_4$ ounces, $5^1/_2$ tablespoons) of butter, using half for cooking the peas and carrots and the rest to finish.

You can also use canned peas, but do not add the carrots until they are completely cooked.

Green Peas with Bacon *(Pois au Lard).* This recipe is particularly good for large peas, but medium-size peas can also be used. *Time: 1 scant hour.*

For 6: 1 liter ($4^1/_4$ cups) of peas; 125 grams ($4^1/_2$ ounces) of lean bacon; about 10 very small onions; 25 grams (1 ounce, 2 tablespoons) of butter; 15 grams ($^1/_2$ ounce) of flour; 3 deciliters ($1^1/_4$ cups) of completely degreased bouillon; a bouquet of parsley.

PROCEDURE. Cut the bacon into dice 1 centimeter ($^3/_8$ inch) large. Blanch them (SEE BACON, PAGE 11). Drain. Heat the butter in a medium-sized pot. Gently color the bacon and small onions. Drain them on a plate.

In the fat of the pot, make a small blond roux with the flour (SEE ROUX, PAGE 47). Dilute with the bouillon. Bring to a boil. Put the peas into the sauce, along with the onions, the bacon, and the bouquet of parsley. Cover. Cook it gently for *a half hour* for medium-size peas, and a little longer for large peas. After this time, the sauce should be well bound, having reduced almost by half. Taste to check if it needs salt, then serve in a vegetable dish or a shallow bowl.

Purée of Fresh Peas *(Purée de Pois Frais).* An excellent summer garnish for braised meats. Use $1^1/_2$ liters ($6^1/_3$ cups) of large peas, shelled. Cook them as directed (COOKING FRESH VEGETABLES, PAGE 470), and once the cooking has begun, add a handful of green lettuce leaves cut into julienne, which will enhance the color of the peas and a bouquet of parsley. Once the peas crush easily, at the end of about *15 minutes,* drain them. (Keep the cooking water for a soup.) Remove the bouquet of parsley. While the peas are still burning hot, force them with the lettuce through a metal drum sieve. If you make this purée somewhat in advance, stir it for a moment with a wooden spoon, then spread a small piece of butter over the surface of the purée to keep it from browning. Keep it on the side.

Eight to ten minutes before serving, dry out the purée in a sauté pan (SEE DRYING PURÉES, PAGE 14) so that it can absorb the cream. Then put it on very low heat. Add to it, for these quantities, 1 deciliter ($3^1/_3$ fluid ounces, scant $^1/_2$ cup) of good fresh cream in 2 or 3 portions. Heat thoroughly as you add the cream, mixing it constantly. Taste to check if it needs salt. Add a good pinch of sugar. Just before serving, mix 30 grams (1 ounce, 2 tablespoons) of butter into the purée, *off the heat.*

Chinese Snow Peas or Mangetout *(Pois Mange-Tout).* These are also called "gourmand peas."

Before describing any recipes, let us first insist that their strings means you should peel them: lightly break the 2 ends so that you can pull off the string all along the shell, leaving the string attached to the end that you have broken off; then break the shell into 2 or 3 parts, which will enable you to check that the string has been completely removed.

All the recipes for peas in the grain are equally good for *mangetout*. When they are slightly older, they are generally prepared with bacon or ham.

Leeks *(Poireau)*

This vegetable is virtually only served in a casserole dish. You often see it alongside carrots and turnips as an accompaniment for boiled beef. It can, however, be appreciated in other ways; but whichever way you choose, only the white part of the leek is used.

Cook leeks either simply in salted water or, which is better, just covered with bouillon in a sauté pan with a bouquet garni. Place a round of parchment paper on top and then put the cover on. Cook in the oven. Drain thoroughly, then serve with a béchamel, Mornay, or other sauce, or served along on a plate, they can be accompanied with a sauce of your choice: white sauce, caper sauce, a vinaigrette, etc.

We should also like to mention the very savory recipe that features them in a tart (SEE LEEK FLAMICHE, PAGE 703).

Potatoes *(Pomme de Terre)*

Because of the large number of ways it can be prepared, this vegetable is the subject of a special section (SEE PAGE 539).

Pumpkin *(Potiron)*

Aside from soups and potages, pumpkin is rarely used in France; yet it's a versatile vegetable that has several uses: either in tarts, pies, etc., as the Americans and English like; or in purées, which is more suitable for French tastes, particularly prepared with eggs and Gruyère cheese, as described below.

When buying pumpkin, choose one that weighs at least one-quarter more than the weight indicated, to allow for waste from the seeds, the rind, etc.

Roast Pumpkin *(Potiron au Four).* *Time: About 1 hour. Serves 4–6.*

750 grams (1 pound, 10 ounces) of pumpkin, net weight; 30 grams (1 ounce) of flour; 60 grams (2 1/4 ounces) of grated Gruyère, fresh and rich; 10 grams (1/3 ounce, 1 scant tablespoon) of butter; 2 large eggs; 4 tablespoons of good milk, or cream if possible.

PROCEDURE. Peel and trim the pumpkin as directed (SEE PUMPKIN POTAGE, PAGE 103). Cook it quickly in salted water. Drain the water as thoroughly as possible, without reserving any. Crush the pumpkin pieces in the pot you are going to use. Put the pot over strong heat, and then reduce the excess moisture from it, mixing the purée continuously. Turn off the heat to allow the pumpkin to cool slightly.

Use a low metal receptacle, a heatproof porcelain dish, or a hollow bowl deep enough to hold the purée in a thick layer. Whatever receptacle you use, it should be able both to go in the oven and to be taken to the table afterwards, so that the purée can be served boiling hot. You want it to be just the correct size so that the purée comes right up to the rim. This purée will be rather runny when you pour it out; it does not rise like a soufflé. Butter the pan.

The liaison of the purée: In a bowl, dilute the flour with the milk or cream that has been boiled and chilled. Add the eggs; beat them until the mixture begins to foam. Season with salt, pepper, grated nutmeg. When adding salt, remember that you will also be adding cheese, which is already salty.

Now that the pumpkin has cooled slightly, pour in the liaison, mixing it with a wooden spoon. Add the cheese. Taste for salt, then pour it into the dish or timbale.

To cook: Put the pan in the lower part of the oven at a good, medium, constant heat. This is not to make a gratin, but rather to set the purée. Allow to cook for *20–25 minutes.* The purée is done when it can be lifted out on a fork. Present the pan on a napkin-covered plate.

Salsify *(Salsifis)*

Salsify is in season between November to the end of March. The best type is scorzonera, which has a black skin. Below, we give its principal preparations. Salsify can also be used as a garnish for ragout or a braised mutton, either the shoulder or the fillet.

Preparing salsify: Scrape the salsify with a knife, making sure you do not leave behind any fragment of skin. Remove the leaves; also cut off the point at the other end.

Divide the salsify into pieces of different lengths, depending on the recipe. For fried salsify: 7–8 centimeters (2³/4–3¹/4 inches) long. To accompany sautés or to be served in a sauce, the pieces should measure only 4–5 centimeters (1¹/2–2 inches). The size as well as the length are never the same in a bunch, so make sure you cut the large pieces into 2 lengthwise, and even into 4 if necessary, so that all the pieces are of about the same thickness.

As you go, put them into a terrine of vinegared water, using a tablespoon of vinegar per liter (4 cups) of water, so that they remain nice and white. Do not wait to put them there, because contact with the air will darken them.

Cooking salsify: Before being used in any recipe, the salsify must first be cooked in plenty of liquid. It is only when salsify is included in a home-style stew, or a sauce that has a long and extended cooking, that you can dispense with this initial cooking.

Many people are happy to cook salsify in boiling, salted water. However, it is better to do this in a *"blanc,"* which will help to keep the salsify white. This is essential for the dish (SEE BLANC, PAGE 12). This will always take a long time to cook; we can only give an approximate time, because salsify will sometimes cook more rapidly than at other times; this depends on the soil in which it was cultivated. *Allow, as an average, 1¹/2 hours of cooking,* from the moment when the boiling resumes after the salsify is put in the boiling liquid.

Fried Salsify *(Salsifis Frits).* This is the most popular recipe for salsify. *Time: 2 hours, 40 minutes (including 2 hours for the preparation and cooking and 40 minutes to marinate and fry). Serves 6.*

24–30 sticks about 7–8 centimeters (2³/4–3¹/4 inches) long; a small handful of nice green parsley.

Frying batter: 100 grams (3¹/2 ounces) of flour; a pinch of salt; 2 scant tablespoons of oil or melted butter; a scant 1¹/2 deciliters (²/3 cup) of lukewarm water; an egg white whisked into snow (SEE FRYING BATTER, PAGE 666).

PROCEDURE. Cook the salsify in a *"blanc."* Drain. Spread them out on a large plate; sprinkle them with fine salt, pepper, ¹/2 tablespoon of minced parsley, the juice of ¹/2 lemon. Let them marinate for *25 minutes,* moving them around from time to time. Eight minutes before serving, heat the oil for deep-frying until smoking (SEE FRYING, PAGE 37). Put the salsify into a frying batter 7 or 8 sticks at a time. Take them out with a fork to drop them into the frying fat. When they float to the surface and the batter is golden brown and nice and dry, take them out with a skimmer and place them on a towel that has been spread out. Sprinkle them with fine salt.

Fry the parsley. Dress the salsify in a heap on a round napkin-covered plate. Surround it with fried parsley (SEE PAGE 15).

Salsify au Gratin *(Salsifis au Gratin).* Cut and cook as directed, and combine them with a lean meatless béchamel sauce (SEE PAGE 52). For 6 people allow 40 sticks of salsify and 3 deciliters (1¹/4 cups) of sauce. Dress them in a low timbale or dish; sprinkle with fine bread crumbs and grated cheese; moisten with butter and gratin the dish (SEE MACARONI AU GRATIN, PAGE 566).

Sautéed Salsify *(Salsifis Sautés).* Heat some butter or some good pork or goose fat in a pan; throw in the salsify that has been trimmed and cooked. Sauté until it becomes a beautiful golden color. Season and dress on a vegetable plate. Sprinkle with minced parsley.

Salsify à la Crème *(Salsifis à la Crème).* Cut and cook the salsify, then simmer in a meat-free béchamel sauce (SEE PAGE 52) that is also light (5 grams/¹/6 ounce of flour for each deciliter/scant ¹/2 cup of milk). Let it reduce and then correct the consistency with crème fraîche: 5–6 tablespoons for the quantities listed for the au gratin.

Tomato *(Tomate)*

These can be found almost all year long in the markets of the larger cities, but their true season is from June to October.

Choose tomatoes that have a nice round shape like an apple. Any with bulging sides are inferior. Even if the tomatoes are crushed and turned into a sauce and not a single tomato left whole, nice, round tomatoes are preferable. Choose tomatoes that are perfectly ripe: they should be a beautiful red color without any green parts, with a smooth and tightly stretched skin over a pulp that is firm to the touch, which is a sign of their freshness.

Fresh Thick Tomato Purée for Several Uses *(Purée de Tomates Fraîches Très Épaisse, pour Divers Usages).* *Time: 45 minutes. Makes only 1 deciliter (3¹/₃ fluid ounces, scant ¹/₂ cup) of purée prepared immediately.*

750–800 grams (1 pound, 10 ounces–1 pound, 12 ounces) of nice, red, ripe, tomatoes; a small garlic clove, completely crushed; 2 sprigs of parsley broken into pieces; a small sprig of thyme and a bit of bay leaf the size of a fingernail; a small pinch of salt; a small pinch of pepper; 1¹/₂ cubes of sugar.

PROCEDURE. Cut the tomatoes in half. Squeeze each side to completely expel the water and the seeds. Slice them thinly. Put them in a thick aluminum pot with all the above ingredients. Tightly cover the pot and cook gently for a half hour.

Then pour the tomato into a drum sieve (preferably cloth, but at any rate, very fine) under which you have slid a plate. With a mushroom-shaped wooden pestle, quickly rub the mixture through the drum sieve. Put the purée into a medium-size sauté pan. Stir it on strong heat with a wooden spoon until the purée is reduced to 1 deciliter (3¹/₃ fluid ounces, scant ¹/₂ cups), which will consequently be very thick.

Tomato Fondue *(Fondue de Tomates).* This is something like a warm compote of tomatoes that concentrates their essential flavor. This fondue is used as a garnish for many preparations. It is better to make this dish when the tomatoes are fully mature. *Time: 1 scant hour. Serves 6.*

1 kilogram (2 pounds, 3 ounces) of tomatoes, gross weight; 30 grams (1 ounce, 2 tablespoons) of butter; 1 very small clove of garlic; a pinch of sea salt; a cube of ordinary sugar.

PROCEDURE. Squeeze the tomatoes to expel the water and the seeds. Put them in a colander with large holes, then plunge this into boiling water for 1 minute: this enables you to easily remove the skin using the point of a knife. Chop them coarsely. Put them back into the colander to drain as much of their own juices as possible.

Then put the tomatoes into a small sauté pan with butter, salt, sugar, and crushed garlic. Cover. Let it reduce very gently on very low heat. Toss the tomato from time to time so that it cooks evenly. (A sauté pan is absolutely essential for this type of cooking, so that the tomato is not heaped up in too thick a layer and can be evenly cooked by the gentle heat.) After about 1 hour, the fondue should be perfectly done.

Stuffed Tomatoes *(Les Tomates Farcies).* This could be considered the most important preparation for tomatoes; it includes innumerable variants, thus adapting to all tastes and to all circumstances: with a meat stuffing, a meat-free stuffing, served on the side as a vegetable, even as a small entrée, or as a garnish for a large main dish, either meat or game.

Both the regional and classic recipes add an infinite number of suggestions to prompt the cook's imagination, because this dish offers a way to use all kinds of leftovers. So, noodles, macaroni, rice cooked à l'Indienne (in the Indian style), or a risotto; fish, even in a sauce; trimmings from meat or fowl, stews, roasts, braises; pieces of hams; leftovers of pâté, terrine, etc.

For all the stuffing ingredients, note that if they are not already cooked—sausage meat, for example—they must first be part-cooked, because they will not properly complete cooking in the tomato.

Stuffed tomatoes served as vegetables are always presented on the same plate where they are cooked and browned. So put them in any type of gratin dish, whether metal, heatproof porcelain, or even rustic earthenware.

Preparation of tomatoes: Choose the same size of tomatoes, as much for symmetry as for even cooking. When using them for a garnish, do not use any tomatoes larger than medium size. When they are small or a medium size, you can leave them whole. When large, cut them in two across the thickest part.

With the point of a small knife, trace a circle around the stem the size of a two-franc piece; remove the part that has been scored and lightly press the tomatoes between your fingers without breaking them; turn them over to expel the water and the seeds from the inside, using the handle of a small spoon; absolutely nothing should be left apart from the pulp—that is, the flesh of the tomato. The seeds and water should also be expelled from tomatoes that have been divided in two.

Generously grease the chosen plate with butter or oil, depending on the recipe. Arrange the tomatoes there. Put a grain of salt and a hint of pepper into each one.

To garnish the tomatoes: This is generally done with a metal spoon. But in professional kitchens, and particularly when the quantity of tomatoes is considerable, and these tomatoes are small and have a narrow opening, it is often easier and more convenient to use a pastry bag.

Use a pastry bag made of cloth, fitted with a steel nozzle 8 millimeters (about 3/8 inch) in diameter, or a large cornet of strong paper whose end has been cut with a scissors to the right size. The tomatoes can then be stuffed more easily. Whichever way you stuff the tomatoes, make sure that the stuffing spills out over the edges of the tomato, making a small dome.

If the tomatoes are prepared in advance, cover them with a sheet of parchment paper and put them to one side. It is not necessary to keep them cool.

Stuffed Tomatoes for Garnishes and Vegetables *(Tomates Farcies pour Garniture et Légume).* This is the classic method: the stuffing here is duxelles (SEE PAGE 21) with an addition of bread crumbs, moistened with white wine and bouillon.

To serve them as vegetables, choose larger tomatoes and just before serving, simply surround with a few tablespoons of light tomato sauce. For vegetarian meals, you can replace the bouillon by a good vegetable bouillon. *Time: 1 hour (including 35–45 minutes to stuff the tomatoes and 15–20 minutes to cook them and to brown them). Serves 6.*

12 small tomatoes; 20 grams (2/3 ounce, 1 heaping tablespoon) of butter and 2 tablespoons of oil; 40 grams (1 3/8 ounces) of onion and 25 grams (1 ounce) of minced shallot; 150 grams (5 1/3 ounces) of minced mushrooms (you can use the stems and peelings); 1 tablespoon of concentrated tomato purée; 1 deciliter (3 1/3 fluid ounces, scant 1/2 cup) of white wine; 1 1/2 deciliters (2/3 cup) of bouillon; 3 grams (1/10 ounce) of garlic; 1 teaspoon of minced parsley; 8 grams (1/3 ounce, 1 scant tablespoon) of butter and 7 grams (1/4 ounce) of flour for a beurre manié (SEE PAGE 48); 30 grams (1 ounce) of finely grated white bread crumbs; 30 grams (1 ounce) of finely grated oven-dried bread crumbs; salt, pepper, and nutmeg.

PROCEDURE. **The stuffing:** In a small sauté pan, heat the butter and the oil. Add the onion and the minced shallot to it; mix it on the heat for a few minutes *without allowing it to color.* Add the chopped mushrooms and a pinch of salt, a bit of pepper, and a small pinch of grated nutmeg. Mix it over strong heat to rapidly evaporate the moisture from the mushrooms. After this, add the white wine. Reduce it completely, keeping the pan over strong heat. Then add: the bouillon, the purée of tomatoes, and the garlic, crushed. Then turn the heat down very low and allow it to simmer for *7–8 minutes.*

After this, add the beurre manié in little bits; mix it well. Then turn the heat up high under the pan, and, with your wooden spoon, stir until the mixture has become quite thick.

Prepare and garnish the tomatoes as directed. Before putting them in the oven, sprinkle the surface of the stuffing with bread crumbs. On each tomato, put a piece of butter the size of a pea; or a few drops of oil or melted butter. Allow *15–20 minutes* of cooking, depending on the strength of your oven.

When the tomatoes are cooked, they should be slightly soft and the surface of the stuffing should be covered with a thin crust. If using them for a garnish, take them out carefully, lifting them with a fork or a spatula and immediately putting them around the piece that they are to accompany.

Home-Style Stuffed Tomatoes with Meat *(Tomates Farcies au Gras à la Ménagère).* A simple and economical method for using meat leftovers. *Time: 45 minutes. Serves 6.*

6 nice tomatoes; 1 piece of good lard the size of a walnut, or 2 tablespoons of oil; 2 tablespoons of minced onion; the flesh of a nice tomato that has been coarsely chopped, without either skin or seeds; 60 grams (2 1/4 ounces) of white, stale bread, soaked in a little bit of bouillon; 60 grams (2 1/4 ounces) of cooked meat, finely minced; 1 scant tablespoon of minced parsley; 1 tablespoon of bouillon; 1 piece of garlic the size of a pea, crushed; salt, pepper, grated nutmeg; 1 egg yolk; 2 tablespoons of fine bread crumbs.

PROCEDURE. In a pot big enough to hold all the ingredients for the stuffing, gently color the onion in the fat or oil. Add the chopped tomato to it; allow it to simmer and reduce. After this, add: the bread (which has been squeezed dry and squashed with the back of a knife); meat, parsley, and the seasoning. Mix it all well, working it with the wooden spoon on the heat for 2–3 minutes. Finally, turn the heat very far down to incorporate the egg yolk. This stuffing should be moist and tender, but must also have a certain consistency to be stuffed into the tomatoes.

Garnish the tomatoes as directed, placing them in an oiled gratin dish. Sprinkle them with the bread crumbs and sprinkle them with a few drops of oil. Brown in the oven for *15–20 minutes.*

Provençal-Style Stuffed Tomatoes *(Tomates Farcies à Provençale).* In the Midi, people still refer to tomatoes by the very ancient name of "love apples"; and the stuffing includes salted anchovies, a very commonly used condiment in Provençal dishes. Naturally, olive oil is the fat used, even though the chef Durand, in a regional memoir, admits that butter is optional. As for the stuffing ingredients listed below, some people add capers and increase the quantity of minced parsley; others finish the stuffing with 2–3 tablespoons of braised beef jus. If you like, tomatoes stuffed like this can be served warm, as soon as they come out of the oven, or completely cold. *Time: 45 minutes. Serves 6.*

To stuff 6 nice tomatoes; 2 tablespoons of finely minced onions; the flesh, without the skin or the seeds, of 4 tomatoes, coarsely chopped; 1 piece of garlic the size of a pea; 1 teaspoon of minced parsley; 75 grams (2 2/3 ounces) of fresh bread crumbs soaked in a little bit of bouillon; 2 or 3 small *salted* anchovies; 2 tablespoons of finely grated bread crumbs (SEE BREADING, PAGE 19); 4 tablespoons of olive oil.

PROCEDURE. **The stuffing:** Heat 2 tablespoons of oil in a small saucepan and lightly color the minced onion; then add the flesh of 4 tomatoes, the minced parsley, the garlic (crushed under the blade of a knife), pepper and salt. Cook, covered, for *12–15 minutes.*

Detach and wash the anchovy fillets: pass them through a drum sieve with the bread that has been well squeezed out. Add this paste into the pan *off the heat,* then mix everything well and set it to one side.

The tomatoes: Cut them in 2 across the middle. Remove the seeds; season the inside with salt and pepper.

Strongly heat several tablespoons of oil in a medium-sized sauté pan; when it smokes, put in the tomatoes on their cut side, arranging them side by side without them touching: this is to ensure that the oil circulates completely around them. Turn them over with a fork at the end of *2 minutes,* when they are slightly wilting. Let them cook for *1 minute* only on the other side. This short cooking time lets you keep them whole while at the same time beginning to cook them. Depending on the number of tomatoes, do this in 2 or 3 batches.

Arrange the tomato halves on a shallow gratin plate. Lightly flatten their inside surfaces so that you can garnish each half with 1 tablespoon of stuffing. Sprinkle them with the breading; moisten the breaded surface with oil. Put them in a good, strong, constant medium oven, so that it finishes cooking at the same time as it browns and crisps. This should take *10–12 minutes.*

Jerusalem Artichokes *(Topinambour)*
An excellent vegetable at the end of winter, which should be used more often. It looks like a cross between a potato and celeriac, while its flavor is

similar to artichoke—that's why it is called a "Jerusalem Artichoke."

The different recipes that are good for Jerusalem artichokes are not those used for potatoes, as their appearance might suggest, but more those used for artichokes. You can prepare them as follows:

Braised: SEE ARTICHOKE (PAGE 476).

Fried: Peeled, cut into thick slices, cooked in butter or in a liquid of your choice; then dipped in a frying batter and fried in deep, hot fat. Served on a napkin with fried parsley.

In a purée: Peeled, thinly sliced, and cooked in butter or in milk or a bouillon of your choice. Passed through a drum sieve, but with potato purée added for the consistency.

For Jerusalem artichokes, use water, milk, or bouillon for the initial cooking. But braising them in butter, as we describe in the following recipe, is always the best way.

Jerusalem Artichokes à la Crème *(Topinambours à la Crème)*.

This is the most appreciated preparation. *Time: 50–55 minutes. Serves 6.*

600 grams (1 pound, 5 ounces) of Jerusalem artichokes, gross weight; 50 grams (1¾ ounces, 3½ tablespoons) of butter to cook them.

For the sauce: 3 deciliters (scant 1¼ cups) of excellent milk, reduced; 1½ deciliters (⅔ cup) of cream; 15 grams (½ ounce) of flour and 15 grams (½ ounce, 1 tablespoon) of butter for a white roux. Salt, pepper, nutmeg; 15 grams (½ ounce, 1 tablespoon) of butter to finish the sauce.

NOTE. There is another method for the initial cooking of the Jerusalem artichokes other than those already described: cook them first in salted water. Then simmer for about 10 minutes in a béchamel sauce, adding at the last moment a few tablespoons of cream and a little bit of butter, off the heat.

Alternatively, cook them in milk that has been lightly salted and previously boiled. Use this same milk to prepare the béchamel sauce, finishing it with cream and butter, as above. These two procedures are more economical, omitting the butter used for the braising, even though this can then be used for other dishes; but the taste and richness of the vegetables will then be lost.

PROCEDURE. **The Jerusalem artichokes:** Cut them in half; depending on the size of the vegetable, divide each half into 3 or 4 pieces, and each piece in 2 pieces lengthwise.

Peel and trim the pieces, shaping them into long, large olives, or the shape of potatoes served with fish. Do not wash the pieces, but wipe them and dry them with a good kitchen towel.

Cooking in butter: Heat the butter in a sauté pan. Add the pieces of Jerusalem artichoke. Sauté them on the heat for a few minutes.

Turn the heat down quite low. Or, if it is possible, put them in a very moderate oven, because they will cook more evenly there. One way or another, *cover it* and let it cook very gently for *20 minutes.* Frequently shake the pan so that the pieces do not stick to it. From time to time, toss them. They must not color, or only very slightly.

The sauce: Boil the milk with the cream. In a small saucepan, make a white roux (SEE PAGE 47); dilute it with the milk and the cream. Season it with salt, pepper, and nutmeg. Bring it to a boil. After this, completely drain the cooking butter from the Jerusalem artichokes by tipping the covered pan over a cup to pour out all the butter; it will serve for other uses.

Pour the sauce over the Jerusalem artichokes. Cover and keep the sauce at a gentle simmer for *20–25 minutes* to finish cooking. Just before serving, add, *off the heat,* the butter, divided into bits. Lightly shake the pan and toss the Jerusalem artichokes for a moment to be sure the butter is thoroughly mixed. Pour it into a heated vegetable dish. Serve immediately.

Truffles *(Truffe)*

The waste represented by the dirt is about one-fifth more than the weight given in the recipes, where the weights are a net amount. When you buy 450 grams (1 pound) of truffles, allow 100–110 grams (3½–3¾ ounces) of waste; this depends on the terrain where the truffles have been harvested. Do not wipe off the soil until you are ready to use them.

To clean the truffles: Soak them in lukewarm water for at least a half hour if they grew in clay soil, because this is rather difficult to remove. Once the soil covering the truffle has been well softened, rub the truffles first with your hands, and change their water at least twice.

Then, with a small brush that is made of horsehair and is not too hard, and that is *very clean* and *does not have the slightest odor* of any kind, brush them until there is not even the most miniscule piece of dirt left. Using a little piece of pointed wood, dislodge any dirt remaining in the furrows. Again, change the water in your receptacle while brushing.

As you clean the truffles, put them into a terrine of clear water. One by one, check them one more time before draining them and wiping them thoroughly with a towel.

Truffles with Madeira or Champagne on a Napkin *(Truffes au Madère, au Champagne, à la Serviette).* Apart from their perennial use as a condiment or garnish, truffles can also be served as a vegetable plate or an hors d'oeuvre. And don't make the mistake of believing that this is an imaginative use that is utterly modern; culinary recipe collections from the first half of the 18th century already mention the preparation of truffles "au Champagne" and "à la serviette," and they appear as well in today's luxury menus.

Even though dishes of this type have become, in modern times, an exceptional luxury, we shall nonetheless give a few directions and recipes here for them.

Today, references to "truffles in a napkin," "truffles in Champagne," and "in Madeira" all apply to a similar preparation, which can be summarized as follows: The truffles are cooked with a little mirepoix of onion, carrot, shallot, etc., then braised in butter and one of the above-mentioned wines. The cooking liquid is then strained and reduced, and an excellent veal jus or of a glaze of meat is added to make the sauce.

It is, above all, the way the truffles are served that determines the name under which they are presented. Serve the well-drained truffles slid into a napkin that has been folded, as for boiled eggs, and previously well heated, along with the plate on which it is placed. Strictly speaking, truffles served like this should be accompanied only by little shells of fresh, good-quality butter, offered in a butter dish. At least, this is what the classical authors intended; but these days, the truffles are served with the sauce on the side in a sauceboat. Or, in a very modern variation, the truffles are dressed in a shallow silver timbale and the sauce is poured on top of them. To justify the appellation "on a napkin," the timbale is placed in a napkin that has been folded on the plate, or even, as you will find in great restaurants, in a napkin used especially for that purpose.

"With Champagne" or "with Madeira," the truffles are dressed in a timbale and the sauce is poured over them. Or each truffle is placed in a little case of metal or a little dish of ribbed porcelain, on the bottom of which has been poured 1 tablespoon of sauce. Or each truffle is placed in a little paper container and the sauce is served on the side.

No matter which way they are served, you should choose for this kind of preparation some nice, large, round truffles with a medium gross weight of 80–90 grams (2 3/4 ounces–3 1/4 ounces); with the anticipated waste, this leaves you with truffles weighing about 70 grams (2 1/2 ounces). Truffles prepared like this are not peeled, which means that it is even more essential that they are meticulously cleaned. You should allow 1 truffle per person; if you cannot find medium-sized truffles, you will need 2 truffles for each guest.

The cooking time naturally varies with the size of the truffles: for large truffles, allow *about 20 minutes* at a gentle boil; for smaller truffles, *12–15 minutes* will be enough; it is better to cook for a few minutes more than less, but do not go to extremes. *Time: 15–20 minutes of boiling (depending on the size of the truffles). Serves 6.*

700 grams (1 pound, 9 ounces) of truffles, net weight; a little mirepoix with 30 grams (1 ounce) of carrot and the same of onion; 25 grams (1 ounce) of shallot; 1 fragment of bay and thyme; 2–3 parsley sprigs; 40 grams (1 3/8 ounces, 3 tablespoons) of butter.
4 deciliters (1 2/3 cups) of Madeira or Champagne; 25 grams (1 ounce) of meat glaze; a pinch of salt and a pinch of pepper.

PROCEDURE. In a small, deep pot just large enough to hold the truffles stacked up, gently color the mirepoix, which has been chopped thoroughly rather than cut so that it is as fine as possible (SEE PAGE 21). Then add the truffles, the wine, the salt, and the pepper. Cover with a napkin folded in quarters, and a cover that closes tightly. Let it cook very gently for the times given. Then carefully wipe of all pieces of mirepoix from the truffle.

Strain their cooking liquid through a fine chinois. Boil it to reduce it by half: in other words, to 2 good deciliters (generous 3/4 cup). Off the heat, dissolve the meat glaze in it. You can, just before serving, finish the sauce with fine butter: that is, 75 grams (2 2/3 ounces, 1/3 cup) for these quantities.

Serve in one of the various styles.

Grandmother's Truffles *(Truffes Grand-Mère).* *Time: 45–50 minutes of cooking.*

For 4: 4 truffles weighing 100–150 grams (3 1/2–5 1/3 ounces) each; 1 deciliter (3 1/3 fluid ounces, scant 1/2 cup) of very good Madeira; 4 extremely thin bards of fatback bacon; a pinch of salt and pepper; 4 tablespoons of white veal jus.

***For the dough:* 250 grams (8 7/8 ounces) of flour; 125 grams (4 1/2 ounces, 9 tablespoons) of butter; 1 egg; 1 deciliter (3 1/3 fluid ounces, scant 1/2 cup) of water; 7 grams (1/4 ounce) of salt; 1/2 egg beaten, to glaze the crust.**

PROCEDURE. Clean and peel the truffles (SEE PAGE 538). Put them in a bowl and sprinkle them with Madeira; cover them and allow them to soak for an hour, turning the truffles over two or three times in the liquid. Meanwhile, prepare the dough (SEE PÂTE À FONCER, PAGE 662). Once the dough has rested, roll it out to a thickness of 3 millimeters (1/8 inch) and cut 4 rounds about 20–21 centimeters (8–8 3/8 inches) in diameter. Using a pot cover of this size as a template will make things easier. On the dough round, make a cross out of 2 ribbons of fatback bacon long enough to cover the truffle. Put the truffle in the middle and season with salt and pepper, then sprinkle it with 1 scant tablespoon of the Madeira that the truffles have soaked in and 1 tablespoon of veal jus. Fold the dough on top of the truffle, paste the edges together so that they overlap, using a little bit of water; pinch the corners of the dough between your fingers so that they are thoroughly closed; brush it with the egg. From parchment paper or good kitchen paper, cut 4 rounds 3–4 centimeters (1 1/4–1 1/2 inches) larger than the rounds of dough. Butter them and place each truffle in its dough in the middle. Fold the paper all around the little package and tie it up.

Cook it in an oven on the middle shelf at a good medium heat, completely equal at the top and bottom, for *45–50 minutes.* The paper must not be scorched but should remain a dark brown. The dough inside will be golden. Serve the truffles on a plate, garnished with a napkin if you like, with their paper wrapping, or, if it has gotten too brown, take it out of the paper.

POTATOES
Pomme de Terre

Potatoes in Their Jackets *(Pommes de Terre en Robe de Chambre).* This describes potatoes that are cooked and then served in their skin, no matter which method is used: in water, steam, in the oven, in an earthenware utensil known as a "diable," which is placed under the cinders of a large fireplace, which can still be found in some places. We will concentrate here on the directions for the most current procedure—that is, in water. In all cases, choose potatoes that are rather large, have a nice, meaty, yellowish pulp, and are fully mature; and for even cooking, make sure that they are all the same size. Wash them in several changes of water and, if you need to, brush them with a scrubbing brush so they are absolutely clean.

Place the potatoes in a pot or a marmite just covered with cold water, bearing in mind that this water will have almost completely reduced by the time the potatoes have finished cooking. Add a little pinch of sea salt for 1 kilogram (2 pounds, 3 ounces) of potatoes. Cover and quickly bring it to a boil. Next, reduce the heat to maintain a *very gentle* boil; allow from this moment about a *half hour* for potatoes weighing 150–170 grams (5 1/3–6 ounces). At this point, they will be slightly cracked; their skin, if it is of good quality, will have burst; at the same time, a kitchen needle stuck into one of the potatoes will pierce it easily.

Immediately drain the rest of the water by tipping the pot, holding the cover on to keep the potatoes in it. Put the pot back, still covered, on very gentle heat or in the oven for a few minutes so that they dry out.

Serve them burning hot on a plate covered with a napkin; or you can, for smaller quantities, slide the potatoes into a folded-over napkin. At the same time, serve a very fine and fresh butter.

Potato Purée *(Purée de Pommes de Terre).* To be successful, this purée must have the finesse and lightness of a whipped cream, its flakes stacking up into a pyramid. This is possible only if the following rules are strictly observed:

First, use the appropriate type of potatoes: large Holland (somewhat elongated and of good quality) with a red or white skin, *but always with a yellowish pulp or flesh.*

Second, cook the potatoes for just long enough so that they are almost cooked. If this point is passed, the potato will absorb too much water and crumble, and the purée will then lack consistency, no matter how hard you then try to evaporate the moisture from them.

Third, immediately pass the potatoes through a *metallic drum sieve;* any other utensil, such as a strainer or a vegetable mill, will not give a satisfactory result: the potato will cool too much, and it will be impossible to get a good purée. If you do not have a drum sieve, crush the potatoes as below.

Fourth, work the purée with butter *before* adding any milk. Do this *rapidly and even excessively vigorously* to the point where, as a famous chef de cuisine once said, your arms go to sleep and do not wake up for an hour afterward.

Fifth, serve the purée *as soon as it is finished* (or not long after). Standing for a long time, which happens even in excellent restaurants, is the reason why potato purée served late is bad. It is essential, as the same chef suggested, never to prepare one large quantity of purée for the entire duration of all the meals offered, but to prepare it in batches: for each batch, cook the potatoes, pass them through a drum sieve, and work the purée with butter and milk.

NOTE. We have suggested cooking the potatoes as they are generally done. But they can also be cooked with steam and in the oven. In the latter case, do not peel the potatoes: simply brush them and wash them, then cook them in a hot oven; the length of cooking time depends on the degree of heat of the oven. *Time: 45 minutes.*

For 6: 1 kilogram (2 pounds, 3 ounces) of potatoes that yield, after peeling, 700–750 grams (1 pound, 9 ounces–1 pound, 10 ounces); 75 grams (2 2/3 ounces, 1/3 cup) of butter; 1 1/2–2 deciliters (2/3–7/8 cup), at the most, of good boiling milk; salt, white pepper, nutmeg.

PROCEDURE. Carefully peel the potatoes. Cut them into quarters. Put them in a deep pot with just enough water to cover them, and 12 grams (3/8 ounce) of salt per liter (4 1/4 cups) of water. Cover.

Boil them strongly so that they cook as quickly as possible. You can allow an average of about 20 minutes when cooking potatoes in water. But do not put all your faith in the clock; it is important to monitor the cooking so that you do not go beyond the desired degree: that is, the moment where the pulp, which yields to the touch, is sufficiently cooked that it can be passed through a drum sieve.

As soon as the potatoes are perfectly cooked, immediately drain off their water, keeping the cover on, so that you can then drain the water *right up to the last drop,* then leave the potatoes to keep warm in the pot. (When you are working on large quantities of potatoes, the next stage is to put the covered pot in the oven for a few minutes to completely dry out the potatoes.)

Rapidly pass them through a metallic drum sieve placed deep part down on a towel spread out on the table. Proceed as described, taking the care suggested and using the right movements (SEE STRAINING PURÉES, PAGE 14), taking the potatoes only by small quantities at a time so they will remain *burning hot.*

Scrape the bottom of the drum sieve and put everything in the pot where the potatoes were cooked. To repeat, *from the beginning until the end of this step, you should proceed with real haste to avoid allowing the potatoes to cool.* Quickly, using a large wooden spoon, vigorously stir and mix the purée in the pot, which should be kept on very low heat to keep the purée as warm as possible; this makes it easier to work with the spoon. Season with fine salt, white pepper, and a hint of grated nutmeg, and immediately add the butter to it, divided into 3 or 4 pieces so that it will mix in more rapidly. Work the purée, not by stirring, but by beating it, lifting it up to incorporate air, which will make it light. At the very last moment, when all traces of the butter that you have added to it have disappeared, add *3 generous tablespoons* of boiling milk. Beat it again to make it absorb this milk so that the purée will be become lighter and whiter by working it with the spoon.

In addition, add in two batches, 6 tablespoons—*that is, a total of 9 tablespoons, equivalent to 1½ deciliters (⅔ cup)*—still beating with all your strength between each addition of liquid. If necessary, add 1 or 2 tablespoons more; but note that it is not the milk itself that makes the purée light, but beating it with the spoon and the fact that the milk makes the spoon easier to work. Finally, and continually working it with the spoon, heat it well without letting it boil, which would spoil the effect of the butter.

If you are not serving it immediately, use the blade of a knife to lift off the purée from all around the edges of the pot and bring it to the center, then flatten it out and level it with a spoon. Pour 1 tablespoon of milk on top, which will spread out, thus preventing a crust from forming on the surface. Cover it and keep it warm, without allowing it to boil, until you are ready to serve the purée in a heated vegetable dish. One stir of the spoon will suffice to mix in this little bit of milk.

NOTE. You can add a pinch of superfine sugar to the seasoning of salt, pepper, and nutmeg. The effect is excellent: Carême noted it. When you have cream, it's a refinement to use it instead of milk; it must also be used boiling.

Simplified procedure: When you do not have a drum sieve, you can nonetheless make a very satisfactory purée as follows:

Cook the potatoes and pour out every last drop of water from the pot, then immediately add the butter, divided into several pieces. With a wooden spoon, vigorously work the potatoes to reduce them to a purée, and at the same time mix in and melt the butter. Do this on very low heat if possible, so the potatoes are kept quite warm. They will crush much more easily the hotter they are, and adding the butter at this time also greatly facilitates this operation. To do this, use the back of the spoon to crush the potatoes against the sides of the pot to reduce them to a batter without any clots. This is quickly done. Once all the potatoes have been completely squashed, begin to add the milk, a tablespoon at a time, beating the purée with the spoon, as already described, to give it the necessary lightness.

Gratinée Potato Purée *(Purée de Pommes de Terre Gratinée).* Once the purée has been prepared as above, spread it out in a buttered shallow pan, shaping it to a very slight dome. Sprinkle it with finely grated white bread crumbs (SEE BREADING, PAGE 19) mixed with some grated Gruyère. Sprinkle it with some melted butter and brown it quickly in a hot oven, or preferably underneath the broiler.

Duchess Potatoes *(Pommes de Terre Duchesse).* This is a dough made with potato and egg. It is currently used in the kitchen for croquettes made with cuts of meat, to edge plates that contain a stew, and for many other uses.

Long white potatoes are the only kind that should be used for this preparation: the others are not floury enough or lack consistency. Choose large potatoes, particularly if you can cook them in the oven, each with an average weight of 180–200 grams (6⅓–7 ounces) gross weight.

In most of the many uses for duchess potatoes, egg yolk is the only ingredient added. It is true that a whole egg is also added, but there is very little of this in comparison to the number of yolks: the egg white gives some lightness to the dough, but for some preparations—for edges and borders, for example—it might also increase the volume, thus compromising its firmness when cooked; for this reason, it is often left out. *Time: 45 minutes.*

An average of 5 egg yolks for 1 kilogram (2 pounds, 3 ounces) of potatoes, weighed once peeled, and 40–50 grams (1⅜–1¾ ounces, 3–3½ tablespoons) of butter.

PROCEDURE. Prepare and cook the potatoes, then pass them through a drum sieve, as described (SEE POTATO PURÉE, PAGE 540).

After passing it through the drum sieve, put the purée in a sauté pan; using a sauté pan is essential for working the dough. Season with salt, pepper, and grated nutmeg. Place it on strong heat. Add the butter. Using a large wooden spoon, continuously and vigorously mix the purée to dry it out until it is reduced to the state of a pâte à choux (PAGE 664)—a true batter that is nice and smooth, does not stick to the spoon, and is also firm enough to be picked up in one piece. The bottom of the pan can be slightly sandy as when making pâte à choux, but should nonetheless not color.

Turn off the heat. Wait 2 minutes before adding the yolks so that they are not seized by the dough's strong heat. Combine them in two stages, without first diluting them with water. Beat vigorously. Then turn up the heat for 1 or 2 minutes, *stirring uninterruptedly* while working the dough.

Pour the dough onto a buttered plate. Spread it out so that it cools more quickly, in a layer $1\frac{1}{2}$ centimeters ($\frac{5}{8}$ inch) thick. With a small piece of butter stuck on the end of a knife, dab the top to prevent the surface from hardening as it cools.

The dough is much more easily worked when it is cool or only lukewarm. Only if you are in a great hurry should you use it while it is still warm.

NOTE. Potatoes cooked in the oven produce a pulp that is not wet, and so there is no need to dry them out. Proceed as follows: the potatoes are put whole, not peeled, into the oven. Once they are cooked, split the skin; scrape the pulp into a warm terrine; season. Vigorously work the purée with a wooden spoon while it is burning hot. Add the butter, then the yolks, working as above.

Border of Duchess Potatoes *(Bordure de Pommes de Terre Duchesse).* *Time: 1 hour.*

Prepare the dough as described for DUCHESS POTATOES (PAGE 541). Lightly flour, the table. Sprinkle your hands with flour too, then work the dough for a few minutes until it has taken on some "body": that is, enough resistance and elasticity so that when you press your finger on the dough it does not retain the imprint.

Roll it into an even sausage shape. The length varies according to whether or not you want the border to be large or small, tall or short. Let us assume here a border that will serve 6, for a fish dish covered with a sauce and measuring about 12–13 centimeters ($4\frac{1}{2}$–5 inches) on the inside diameter. The quantities given for the dough above will be correct for this.

Roll the sausage shape dough to a length of 40–42 centimeters (16–$16\frac{1}{2}$ inches). Slide both of your hands under it to transfer it to a buttered serving plate, one that is heatproof; do not use a bowl. With your fingers, press together the 2 ends of the sausage-shape roll.

Then, with your fingers sprinkled with flour, press down lightly on this sausage-shaped circle to thin it out. Its height increases as its thickness diminishes. You will end up with a border 6–7 centimeters ($2\frac{1}{2}$–$2\frac{3}{4}$ inches) high, which will be wider at the bottom (about $3\frac{1}{2}$ centimeters/$1\frac{3}{8}$ inches) than at the top (about 1 centimeter/$\frac{3}{8}$ inch). The base can, depending on the case, sometimes be less thick: that is, only 2 good centimeters ($\frac{3}{4}$ inch).

If the diameter of the border is any larger, divide the sausage-shaped dough into 2 parts so you can transfer them to the plate without risking breaking it. Then press the 2 ends together.

If you like, decorate the border with patterns from the same dough: use little balls no larger than very small hazelnuts, which you can arrange on the crest of the border. With a brush dipped into beaten egg, both white and yolk (you will need only half an egg), brush the border on the outside only if it is cooked in the oven with the dish it is garnishing already placed in the center of the ring. If not, also brush the inside of the ring. If you like, use a fork to trace zigzags on the outside of the ring of dough.

With or without garnish, allow 8–10 minutes in a *very hot* oven, so that you can color the dough in the least possible amount of time, given that the ingredients from which it is made have already been cooked, as has the dish for which it serves as garnish.

Potato Croquettes *(Croquettes de Pommes de Terre).* This is an excellent garnish for roasted or braised meats, either prepared by the method used today, which is given first here, or prepared à la dauphine: that is, with the addition of pâte à choux (choux pastry) to the purée.

Generally, these croquettes are shaped into a large elongated cork, weighing about 50 grams/ 1 3/4 ounces (and about the same size as a small hen's egg), because this is the simplest shape. But there's nothing absolute about this, and, if you like, they can be shaped into little apricots, pears, pucks, etc. As for all croquettes, the essential thing is that their shape should be correct and regular.

Let us also suggest a pleasant variation, the addition of lean cooked ham or pickled tongue, cut into very small dice and incorporated in the purée at the same time as the egg yolks: thus, about 125 grams (4 1/2 ounces) for roughly 20 croquettes.

It is of paramount importance that potatoes that are to be used for a purée be cooked very attentively—they must not be overcooked. The croquettes can be prepared at least 1 hour in advance, so that you have nothing left to do but plunge them into the frying fat about 6–7 minutes before serving. *Time: 1 hour (plus 1 hour to chill the purée). Makes about 20 croquettes.*

900 grams (2 pounds) of large Holland (long, white) potatoes, weighed once peeled; 40 grams (1 3/8 ounces, 3 tablespoons) of butter; 5 egg yolks; salt, pepper, grated nutmeg.

***To bread the croquettes:* 400 grams (14 1/8 ounces) of bread crumbs weighed after they have been grated; 2 whole eggs beaten with 1/2 tablespoon of oil; salt and pepper. (SEE BREADING À L'ANGLAISE, PAGE 19).**

PROCEDURE. Cook the potatoes and prepare the dough exactly as directed for DUCHESS POTATOES (PAGE 541). While they are cooking, grate the bread.

Divide the dough into 2 parts. On a floured board, roll each part into a large sausage shape. Divide them in pieces and shape them with your hands, rolling them again on the floured board to give them the right shape. Line them up on the table. Coat them with bread crumbs as directed.

To fry the croquettes: Allow 6 minutes from the moment they are put into the lightly smoking frying fat (SEE DEEP-FRYING, PAGE 37). Do not put them all in at once, because they must float freely in the fat. Drain them on a towel once they are golden brown. Keep the first ones to come out of the frying fat warm. Sprinkle them lightly with fine salt.

Another way of preparing croquettes: This is more simple and rapid, because it does not use bread crumbs to coat the croquettes.

The dough is prepared in absolutely the same way. Once the dough has been rolled into a sausage shape, divide it into pieces weighing *only 25 grams (1 ounce) each,* then shape them into large balls in the palm of your hand. Dip them in whole egg beaten with salt and pepper. Spread out some flour on some paper and then immediately roll the croquettes in it. Roll them again on the floury table to adjust their shape. Keep them cool until you are ready to fry them, as above.

Potato Croquettes à la Dauphine *(Croquettes de Pommes de Terre à la Dauphine).* Also used for garnishes, these croquettes differ from ordinary croquettes, being more delicate and light, which is the result of using pâte à choux. *Time: 2 hours (including cooling the dough). Makes about 20 croquettes.*

800 grams (1 pound, 12 ounces) of large, long potatoes, peeled weight; 60 grams (2 1/4 ounces, 4 1/2 tablespoons) of butter; 4 egg yolks; salt, pepper, grated nutmeg.

***For the pâte à choux:* 1 deciliter (3 1/3 fluid ounces, scant 1/2 cup) of water; 3 grams (1/10 ounce) of salt; 40 grams (1 3/8 ounces, 3 tablespoons) of butter; 60 grams (2 1/4 ounces) of flour; 1 1/2 eggs.**

***To bread the croquettes:* See the previous recipe for how to coat croquettes à l'anglaise.**

PROCEDURE. Cook the potatoes just as for simple croquettes. Meanwhile, prepare the pâte à choux as directed (SEE PAGE 664). Then keep it on the side.

Pass the potatoes into a purée, dry them, etc. Turn off the heat. Add the butter and egg yolks, then the pâte à choux, tablespoon by tablespoon, continuously beating it with the spoon. Proceed exactly as directed for simple croquettes.

Potatoes with Bacon *(Pommes de Terre au Lard).* As we indicate below, this recipe scarcely varies, and it is the care brought to cooking the roux that above all makes the difference. If you like, the minced onion can be replaced by very small onions, which should be colored at the same time as the bacon.

Choose potatoes of an equal and medium size, so that they can be cut into equal quarters; otherwise, you will have to divide them up further. *Time: 1 hour. Serves 6.*

600 grams (1 pound, 5 ounces) of potatoes weighed after they have been peeled and trimmed; 125 grams (4 1/2 ounces) of lean bacon; 30 grams (1 ounce, 2 tablespoons) of butter or lard; 30 grams (1 ounce) of minced onions; 15 grams (1/2 ounce) of flour; 4 deciliters (1 2/3 cups) of degreased bouillon; 1 deciliter (3 1/3 fluid ounces, scant 1/2 cup) of white wine; a bouquet garni; 1 teaspoon of minced parsley; a pinch of pepper.

PROCEDURE. Once the potatoes have been peeled, divide them into quarters. With a small knife, trim (or pare) the corners; this is because any thin parts will cook more rapidly and then crumble while cooking, thickening the sauce and turning it to a mush. All these little trimmings are not wasted, because you can add them to a soup. Wash and drain the quarters.

Trim the rind of the bacon. Cut it into small cubes. Blanch it (SEE BACON, PAGE 11). Then dry it in a towel.

Heat the butter or the lard in a good cast-iron pot or any thick pot. On moderate heat, lightly color the lardons. Drain them on a plate and replace them with the minced onion. Let it soften and melt without coloring at all, stirring it with the wooden spoon for a few minutes. Sprinkle it with the flour and *turn the heat down very low* to cook the flour, until it gradually takes on a golden hue: thus, at least 4–5 minutes, during which time you should almost constantly stir this roux. (It is important for this type of preparation that the flour is cooked with prescribed care: otherwise, the onion will blacken or the flour will be insufficiently cooked and turn gluey.)

Dilute it with the bouillon and the white wine. Bring it to a boil on strong heat, stirring constantly. Add the pepper, bouquet garni, potatoes, and bacon. Once it has returned to a boil, cover the pot; turn the heat down very low and let it cook gently for *about 35–40 minutes.* As soon as the potatoes can be easily pierced by a fork, stop the cooking.

Using a small skimmer, take out the potatoes and the lardons to put them in a heated timbale, vegetable dish, or shallow bowl. If the sauce seems to be a little light and dilute, boil it strongly without the cover for 1 or 2 minutes. Note that, in any case, the sauce must be very lightly bound and condensed: 3 good deciliters (1 1/4 cups) will suffice. Pour it over the potatoes, sprinkle with parsley.

Potatoes Maître d'Hôtel *(Pommes de Terre à la Maître d'Hôtel).* These potatoes are not prepared the same way as other vegetable dishes served à la maître d'hotel, which are sautéed with butter and parsley. True maître d'hôtel potatoes are first boiled, then cut into slices, and then simmered in a good milk until it has completely reduced, and finally sprinkled with parsley to serve.

It is essential for this preparation to use a potato that is not too farinaceous, so that when it is cut into slices, the potatoes will remain unbroken during each step of the preparation. So choose potatoes that have a firm pulp and are not large but are instead long; these lend themselves better to being cut into slices.

The quality of the milk is another condition of major importance. If it is not good quality, the normal thing is to reduce it by half before using it: that is, for 3 good deciliters (1 1/4 cups), boil 6 deciliters (2 1/2 cups) of milk to reduce it to that quantity. *Time: 50 minutes. Serves 6.*

625 grams (1 pound, 6 ounces) of potatoes: that should be about 10 potatoes; 3 full deciliters (1 1/4 cups) of good milk; 60 grams (2 1/4 ounces, 4 1/2 tablespoons) of butter; 1 scant tablespoon of minced parsley; 7 grams (1/4 ounce) of fine salt; a pinch of grated nutmeg.

PROCEDURE. Wash the potatoes and put them in a pot with enough cold water to cover them completely; salt with sea salt using 12 grams (3/8 ounce) per liter (4 cups). Bring to a boil. Cover and cook it at a more or less gentle boil for *20 minutes.* Since the potatoes will finish cooking in the milk, they should be slightly firm rather than overcooked at this point. Nonetheless, check that they are sufficiently cooked by pressing a potato with your fingers.

The milk: Meanwhile, boil the milk in the same sauté pan where the slices of potatoes will then simmer. It should be large enough so that they fit into it easily. Thus, use a sauté pan about 22 centimeters (8½ inches) in diameter *with a thick bottom:* this is of major importance, otherwise the potatoes will stick. Once it has started to boil, boil it gently to reduce it if necessary, as previously explained. In any case, the slices must be put into *boiling* milk.

The potatoes: As soon as they are cooked, drain them and let them stand for 4–5 minutes so that they cool slightly and you are able to handle them. Then peel them and cut them into rounds that are not too thin: ¾ centimeter (5/16 inch) thick or so. Put them in the pan with the milk, salt, nutmeg, and half the butter. Using a fork, separate out the slices in the milk. Cover the pan, leaving an opening for the steam, and maintain it at a gentle simmer for *15 minutes,* at the end of which the milk should have completely reduced.

During this time, make sure that the potatoes do not stick, by gently shaking the pan to move them around, and if you need to, using a fork underneath them with great care so that you do not break them.

Just before serving, add the rest of the butter off the heat, divided into pieces, and mix it by shaking the pan. Pour it into a heated vegetable dish, and always do this very carefully so that you do not break the rounds, which should be kept as whole as possible. Sprinkle with the minced parsley.

Potatoes Maire *(Pommes de Terre Maire).* Or Potatoes à la Crème; the principle of their preparation is the same as for Potatoes Maître d'Hôtel, with which they are frequently confused. Professionals mark the difference by the obligatory use of cream and the omission of the minced parsley. *Time: 55 minutes. Serves 6.*

625 grams (1 pound, 6 ounces) of potatoes, cooked and cut as for Maître d'Hôtel potatoes; at least 3 deciliters (1¼ cups) of reduced milk; 30 grams (1 ounce, 2 tablespoons) of good butter; 2½ deciliters (1 cup) of good, fresh cream, not too thick; salt and grated nutmeg as for Maître d'Hôtel potatoes.

PROCEDURE. Proceed exactly as for POTATOES MAÎTRE D'HÔTEL. simmering in boiling milk with butter and seasoning. At the end of the cooking time, add the cream and shake the pan, so that this cream is fully distributed among the rounds. Allow it to boil gently for *5–6 minutes* and then pour everything into a heated vegetable dish.

Château Potatoes *(Pommes de Terre Château).* In modern restaurant terminology, this describes potatoes that accompany a châteaubriand fillet. Actually, this once referred to potatoes sautéed for a garnish: that is, in an oval shape, no longer than 5 centimeters (2 inches), and not wider than 3 centimeters (1¼ inches), cooked in butter, and uniformly fried golden and tender. *Time: 25–30 minutes of cooking.*

The methods of cooking château potatoes vary slightly, but their preparation always remains the same. Choose either small potatoes of the size mentioned above or large potatoes divided into 2 or 3 pieces about the size of the smaller potatoes. Apart from being shaped like a large olive, a château potato must have a smooth surface, without any knife marks left by peeling; that is why in haute cuisine, the potatoes are "turned." Not only does this give them a more authentic look, but it also means they can more easily be moved about in the pan, simply by shaking it gently.

Begin by dividing large potatoes into pieces the correct size. Peel them carefully. Then give them the desired oval shape, handling the knife as described in mushrooms for garnish (PAGE 490; the waste from these trimmings can be used in a soup.)

Do not wash the potatoes; simply wipe them with a towel.

The butter used to cook them must first be clarified; if not, it will burn and will leave tiny brown residues on the potatoes. This clarification is just as necessary for any substitute for the butter (SEE CLARIFYING BUTTER, PAGE 16). Allow 50–60 grams (1¾–2¼ ounces, 3½–4½ tablespoons) of butter for 450 grams (1 pound) of potatoes, weighed after they have been shaped.

Use a sauté pan big enough so that it can hold the potatoes side by side, without them being too crowded, which is extremely important in view of the way they are colored and cooked.

Cooking the potatoes: Just melt the clarified butter on a gentle heat. Put in the potatoes. Salt them lightly. Cook them very gently, tossing them every 2 or 3 minutes. This continual displacement is essential to stop brown spots forming on the side of the potato left for too long touching the bottom of the pan.

Allow *25–30 minutes* from start to finish at a gentle and regular cooking. To be perfectly done, the potato must yield to the touch. Serve them in a vegetable dish, taking them out with a skimmer so that you do not include the cooking butter; sprinkle lightly with salt and with nice freshly minced parsley.

Another procedure for cooking: Put the potatoes shaped as above into a deep pot. Cover them with cool water; salt it using 7 grams (1/4 ounce) per liter. Put it on strong heat and let it boil for only *5 minutes.*

Meanwhile, have the clarified butter already in the sauté pan. Heat it quickly on strong heat while you drain the potatoes; then quickly put them into the heated butter—let us repeat, *heated,* to the point where it can cook the potatoes without browning. It is of paramount importance that the butter is as hot as possible so that the moisture from the potatoes is, as it were, instantly dried out. At the same time as you put them in the pan, toss them so that all their surfaces are in contact with the hot butter. Salt them lightly. Immediately cover the sauté pan and put it in a very moderate oven. Allow *15 minutes* to cook, during which time you should toss them 3 or 4 times. Serve as directed above.

You can use the same procedure without an oven. That is, toss the potatoes first in the burning butter, then cook them on very gentle heat and in an uncovered pan, taking the same precautions as for the first method. For this, the cooking time is longer than in the oven, *about 30 minutes.*

NOTE. Whatever method used for cooking the potatoes, it is essential to avoid letting them color in the beginning, because any crust will stop both the heat and the butter from penetrating. They should color only gradually, and this should not be accelerated until the end.

Sautéed Potatoes *(Pommes de Terre Sautées).* Potatoes that are cooked entirely in butter are often confused with potatoes that are first cooked in water and then cut into slices to be sautéed in a pan. For the first method, you should refer to the recipe for CHÂTEAU POTATOES (PAGE 545), the term by which they are generally known today. Here, we describe the second method.

Use potatoes that are not very farinaceous, so that they do not break: choose potatoes that are a medium-size and also long, so that the slices, which do not have a very large surface area, are less likely to break. Cook them in water with their skin, as for potatoes in their jackets; avoid overcooking, which would make them less resistant. Peel them and cut them into equal slices 1 centimeter (3/8 inch) thick.

In a sauté pan, or more simply in a good thick skillet, heat some clarified butter (SEE PAGE 16); using clarified butter will avoid any black clumps, which might stick to the potatoes. Allow 50 grams (1 3/4 ounces, 3 1/2 tablespoons) of butter for 450 grams (1 pound), gross weight. Once the butter has been heated thoroughly, add the slices; toss them on strong heat until they have reached a beautiful golden color. Take them out with a skimmer and put them on a heated vegetable plate or other platter. Sprinkle with fine salt and minced parsley.

Potatoes to Accompany Fish *(Pommes de Terre pour Accompagnement de Poissons).* Choose small potatoes, and peel them, then shape them like olives 5 centimeters (2 inches) long. You should allow 1 potato per person; but bear in mind that some of the guests will take 2 and some of the potatoes will break while cooking.

Here, steam is the best method of cooking; so, if you do not have a special pan, proceed as follows: put the potatoes, covered with water, into a covered pot with 10 grams (1/3 ounce) of salt per liter (4 1/4 cups) of water. Bring it quickly to a boil and keep it boiling fast until a large pin can pierce a potato: that should be at the end of *15 minutes.* Drain the water, holding the cover on to contain the potatoes; then put the covered pot into a very moderate oven for 10 minutes to finish cooking in their own steam.

Note that because they need to be served boiling hot, the potatoes must be put on the heat just in time: that is, about *25 minutes* before serving the fish.

Potatoes Anna *(Pommes de Terre Anna).* A relatively modern recipe, and when it succeeds it is always a great hit. Potatoes Anna are a kind of loaf with a golden crust and a very moist interior. This loaf is molded from layers of thin rounds of potatoes, and cooked with butter only, in a special type of pan: a kind of thick sauté pan fitted with a cover so tight that it makes a perfect seal. If you do not have a pan for potatoes Anna, you can use an ordinary small sauté pan or a shallow charlotte mold with a diameter no larger than 15 centimeters (6 inches); either utensil should be quite thick. *Time: 1 scant hour.*

PROCEDURE. Peel the potatoes and shape them into large corks, which will enable you to then cut them into extremely thin rounds about 1/2 millimeter thick. Generously butter the bottom and sides of the utensil. Arrange the rounds inside, overlapping each other like the scales of a fish: make the first layer in a circle following the outline of the utensil; then a second layer next to that one, but change the direction in which they overlap. Make the third layer in the same direction as the first layer, and so on, changing the direction of the overlap in each round until the bottom of the mold is covered. Lightly season this first layer with salt, then spread a thin layer of butter on top, which has been previously worked in a dampened towel to soften it and to allow you to spread it without displacing the rounds. On this first buttered layer, arrange a second layer of potatoes, observing the same disposition; season, butter, and so on, until the utensil is almost filled. There should be a maximum of 6 layers. Cover with a final layer of butter; seal with a cover that closes as tightly as possible.

Put it in a *hot oven* and maintain it at the same temperature until the cooking has finished, for which you should allow *at least a good half hour.* You can tell it is done when you can stick a kitchen needle into it, or a knife, and feel no resistance.

To serve: Drain all the cooking butter before dressing the loaf on the serving plate; either pour the butter directly out of the pan, or unmold the loaf onto a flat plate, from which you can then slide it onto a serving plate.

Allow for about 500 grams (1 pound, 2 ounces) of potatoes, weighed after they have been shaped, 150 grams (5 1/3 ounces, 10 1/2 tablespoons) of butter. The amount of the butter may seem excessive, but remember that the potatoes must be completely bathed in the butter. And after you have cooked and drained the potatoes, the butter can be used in other preparations.

Lyon-Style Potatoes *(Pommes de Terre à la Lyonnaise).* This appellation always implies the use of onion, and its preparation is one of the simplest. The potatoes are cooked in their skins, as for POTATOES STUFFED IN THEIR JACKETS (PAGE 539), and they are then peeled and cut into thin slices. Meanwhile, cut some large onions into thin slices of equal thickness: this is extremely important to ensure even cooking. Gently color the onion in a pan with butter or good fat, tossing them often until they are very tender and are evenly golden; above all, do not allow them to brown. Take them off the heat, then drain them well and put them on a plate.

Put the slices of potatoes into a pan and sauté them until they have a nice golden color. Then add the onions to them and season with salt and pepper; sauté everything together for *2–3 minutes* to mix it well. Dress it on a vegetable plate and sprinkle it with a pinch of minced parsley.

Allow for 1 kilogram (2 pounds, 3 ounces) of potatoes, 200–250 grams (7–8 7/8 ounces) of onions and 100 grams (3 1/2 ounces) of butter or good fat.

Potatoes with Herring *(Pommes de Terre aux Harengs).* An excellent hot plate from Alsace, and a completely home-style recipe. *Time: 1 hour. Serves 5–6.*

1 kilogram (2 pounds, 3 ounces) of good potatoes, chosen medium-sized and rather long, so that you can cut them into regular slices with a small surface area; 2 nice sour herrings; 1 good deciliter (3 1/3 fluid ounces, 1/2 cup) of extremely fresh heavy cream; 40 grams (1 3/8 ounces, 3 tablespoons) of butter; 1/2 tablespoon of parsley and the same of shallots, very finely minced; salt and pepper.

PROCEDURE. Cook the potatoes as for POTATOES STUFFED IN THEIR JACKETS (PAGE 539).

Put the herring into a receptacle. Cover them with boiling water and let them soak for about 12 minutes. Drain them and remove the skin and bones, including the fine bones. Coarsely chop the meat and roe, if any.

Once the potatoes have been cooked, peel them and cut them into rounds about a good 1/2 centimeter (3/16 inch) thick.

Use an ovenproof plate. Generously butter the inside, then arrange a layer of potatoes on the bottom. Spread a layer of chopped herring on top. Sprinkle with parsley and shallot and a pinch of pepper. Over everything, spread out 2 tablespoons of cream. Cover with a layer of potatoes, always flat. Then put the herring, the parsley, the shallot, the cream, and so on on top. Finish with a layer of potatoes. Sprinkle lightly with salt and pepper. Spread the butter on top, divided into pieces.

Put it into a very moderate oven for *a half hour.* This is not to brown the dish but to ensure the potatoes absorb the cream. A regular and gentle simmer will guarantee this result; the top layer must color only very slowly, and must not go beyond a light golden tint. The inside should be absolutely moist but without excess liquid. Serve the dish good and hot on a serving plate covered with a napkin.

Potato Soufflé *(Soufflé de Pommes de Terre).*

For all details about cooking this, refer to see SOUFFLÉS (PAGE 436). *Time: 1 hour, 30 minutes (including 1 hour cooking in the oven). Serves 6.*

3–4 potatoes, depending on their size, which weigh a total of 500 grams (1 pound, 2 ounces) unpeeled; 40 grams (1 3/8 ounces, 3 tablespoons) of fresh butter; 1 1/2 deciliters (5 fluid ounces, 2/3 cup) of thick cream; 3 egg yolks; 5 egg whites whisked into snow; salt, pepper, nutmeg.

***Note:* If you do not have cream, replace it with reduced milk, but the flavor of the soufflé will not be so delicate. For absolute perfection, add a few tablespoons of cooked lean ham cut into very small dice; incorporate them at the same time as the egg yolks.**

PROCEDURE. Wash the potatoes. Put them in the oven to cook. In a very well-heated large oven, a scant half hour will suffice to cook them. But if the oven is just at that good medium heat that is appropriate for cooking a soufflé, you must allow double that time.

When you press the potatoes with a finger and the interior pulp yields to the touch, they are properly cooked. Take them out of the oven one by one. As you do, completely split the skin lengthwise and dump the pulp into a good-sized sauté pan, using the handle of a spoon. The pulp must be worked when *burning hot.* This is why you must take the potatoes out of the oven one at a time.

Add salt, pepper, and as much grated nutmeg as can be held on the point of a knife. Using a large, wooden spoon, work this pulp vigorously to reduce it to a very smooth purée. Add the butter; mix it in, stirring constantly. Heat it, stirring constantly and not stopping for a second, to dry out the purée: thickened thus to the state of a batter, it will better absorb the cream. Having evaporated any remaining moisture, add the cream tablespoon by tablespoon, stirring continuously.

Turn off the heat and add the egg yolks. Whisk the whites. First mix in one-quarter of the egg whites, and then the rest, taking the necessary precautions (SEE EGG WHITES, PAGE 10).

Use a round plate made of ovenproof porcelain, preferably a soufflé timbale; butter it generously. Add the potato mixture, 1 large tablespoon at a time, shaping it into a dome. Smooth the surface with the blade of a large knife and lightly paint the surface with melted butter. Make a few incisions in the dome. Put it into the oven for *25 minutes.* Serve immediately.

Stuffed Potatoes *(Pommes de Terre Farcies)*

These are made in two ways.

In the classic and essentially home-style method, the potatoes are peeled, hollowed out three-quarters of the way, and then stuffed with a meat stuffing and put in the oven to cook in the same dish in which they will be served. (Here, the oven is the substitute for yesterday's cover loaded with burning cinders).

In the modern method, the potato is first cooked in the oven with its skin. After this, empty out all the pulp, carefully handling the skin, which will have become a solid shell. Purée the pulp and add various ingredients, then put it back into the shell. Now put the potato, restored to its original shape, back in the oven for long enough that it can be served burning hot.

This second method offers more options in terms of the ingredients you use to refill the potato shell. The first method limits you to using meat, but the modern method allows for very diverse ingredients: leftovers of meat, fowl, game, fish, etc.; or simply, if you like, butter, egg yolks, milk or cream, or grated cheese. A potato cooked like this adapts to different circumstances. In this form, it can be served at a simple lunch for friends or at the beginning of a meal as a hot hors d'oeuvre, or toward the end as a vegetable.

Home-Style Stuffed Potatoes *(Pommes de Terre Farcies à la Ménagère).* *Time: 1 hour, 15 minutes.*

This method, which is almost a classic of its genre, comes from the master chef Colombié. You can use all kinds of leftover meat in this dish. If the meat does not have any fat in it, you should add a quarter of its volume of sausage meat.

If you use only sausage meat, add a whole raw egg to it, in the quantity of 1 egg for 500 grams (1 pound, 2 ounces) of sausage meat, and some stale bread crumbs, finely grated as for breading—about 1 good tablespoon for the above quantities. The egg and the bread give the stuffing some cohesion.

Allow for each potato an amount of stuffing about the size of a good egg. If you like, add a little bit of garlic to the stuffing, and a splash of white wine. In any case, add minced parsley and a good spicy seasoning with pepper, salt, and a spice mixture.

For this, choose potatoes that are as round as possible, about 8 centimeters (3¼ inches) in diameter, and all about the same size. Wash them; peel them. Shape each potato into a large disk about 5 centimeters (2 inches) thick, then hollow it out like a goblet. To hollow this out evenly, it is essential to use a Parisian scoop or a melon baller. Hollow out the potato, leaving a thickness of at least 1 centimeter (⅜ inch) for the bottom and the sides of the goblet (all the waste can be used for a soup). In terms of proportions, note that the goblet should be more wide than tall.

Once all the potatoes have been hollowed out, put them in a pot and cover them with cold water. Heat them very slowly; as soon as it boils, drain the potatoes and sponge them off well on a towel. Fill them with the stuffing, letting it spill over the sides, which will thus not be visible, and which gives it a dome shape.

Arrange the potatoes on an ovenproof plate that has been generously greased with butter or a good fat. Make sure they are rather close to one another. Put the plate for a moment directly on the heat to first brown the bottoms of the potatoes. Then put a little bit of bouillon in the plate, up to three-quarters the height of the potatoes, without reaching the stuffing. Put it in a good, strong, medium oven for about *30–40 minutes.* The complete cooking of the potatoes must coincide with the time that the stuffing turns golden and the liquid is absorbed or evaporated. The end result should be potatoes that have kept their shape but are meltingly soft.

Potatoes Stuffed in Their Jackets *(Les Pommes de Terre Farcies dans Leur Écorce)*

For this kind of preparation, you should choose nice, big, good-quality potatoes with *a yellow pulp,* because these are the most farinaceous. A large potato, unpeeled, weighs about 180–200 grams (6⅓–7 ounces) and the following recipes are based on this weight. Allow 1 large potato per person. Choose potatoes with a nice regular shape and an equal size.

When preparing these potatoes, it is essential that they are first cooked in the oven; the skin is used as a receptacle, and no other mode of cooking will make it solid enough. Moreover, potato pulp cooked in an oven is more farinaceous and dry than that of a potato cooked in water or steam, and so is better suited for this use.

Before being put in the oven, the potatoes must be carefully washed in cold water and then brushed if necessary, because their skin has to be perfectly clean.

The heat of the oven must be strong enough so that the shell or skin of the potatoes browns and becomes rather crisp without burning; otherwise, you will have to scrape off the burned part, which will spoil the look of the potato. With a very hot oven, like those in the kitchens of great restaurants, the preliminary cooking of the potatoes can be done in 20–25 minutes, even a little less. But in a good medium-heat oven, almost 1 hour is necessary to cook potatoes of this size. So it is impossible to be precise about the time needed.

Ardennes-Style Stuffed Potatoes *(Pommes de Terre Farcies à l'Ardennaise).* This is one of the simplest recipes: the pulp of the potatoes is worked into a purée, and minced ham, cheese, and egg yolks are added to it, then put back into the skins to crisp and brown in the oven. The essential thing is to serve them burning hot and not to have them wait too long once the gratin has formed; otherwise it will soften because of the steam escaping from inside. *Time: About 1 hour, 30 minutes. Serves 6.*

6 large potatoes; 3 egg yolks; 75 grams (2²/₃ ounces, 1/3 cup) of butter; 100 grams (3 1/2 ounces) of lean ham, finely minced; 75 grams (2 2/3 ounces) of grated Gruyère; 1 teaspoon of chervil and the same of minced parsley; 10 grams (1/3 ounce) of salt; a good pinch of pepper; a bit of grated nutmeg.

PROCEDURE. Cook the potatoes in the oven as directed (SEE ABOVE).

Cut them lengthwise in the middle to make 2 long halves. Using the handle of a fork, rapidly remove all the pulp from each side and put it in a *well-heated* utensil. It is essential to work the pulp while it is still burning hot. Work it vigorously, using a large wooden spoon, gradually adding three-quarters of the butter. Once the purée is white and smooth, add the salt, the pepper, the nutmeg, and the egg yolks, one by one, working it constantly. Finally, mix half of the grated cheese into it, then the ham, and the parsley and chervil, both minced.

Divide the purée among the shells, smoothing it over with the blade of a knife to make an even dome shape. As you do this, put the potatoes onto a baking sheet. Sprinkle the surface of the purée with the remaining cheese and sprinkle it with melted butter. Put it in a medium oven to crisp. Allow *about 20 minutes* so that the layer of gratin forms gradually until it is just nicely golden and not brown. Arrange them on a napkin-covered plate.

Stuffed Potatoes Marinette *(Pommes de Terre Farcies Marinette).* This is an excellent lunch plate for which you can use leftovers of roast or braised meat, beef or mutton, or even a simple boiled beef from a marmite. If you cannot find very large potatoes, use medium-sized ones weighing about 130 grams (4 1/2 ounces) each. Allow 2 per person. *Time: 1 hour, 30 minutes. Serves 6.*

6 large potatoes; 375 grams (13 ounces) of cooked meat, weighed completely trimmed; 70 grams (2 1/2 ounces, 5/8 stick) of butter; 1 nice onion (100 grams/3 1/2 ounces), minced; 15 grams (1/2 ounce) of flour; 2 deciliters (6 3/4 fluid ounces, generous 3/4 cup) of bouillon; 1/2 deciliter (1 2/3 fluid ounces, scant 1/4 cup) of white wine; 1 teaspoon of vinegar; 1/2 tablespoon of minced parsley.

PROCEDURE. Cook the potatoes in the oven as directed (SEE ABOVE).

In a small saucepan, place the onion with 25 grams (1 ounce, 1/4 stick) of butter and lightly color it. Then add the flour and make a small blond roux. Dilute it with the bouillon and the white wine. Season with the pepper and vinegar. Once it has begun to boil, maintain it in a small, nearly imperceptible simmering.

Remove the blotched parts of the meat. Cut them into slices 3 millimeters (1/8 inch) thick; then divide them further into small sticks of the same thickness, stacking them one on top of the other; then cut crosswise in the same way so that you have little dice 3 millimeters (1/8 inch) big.

Once the potatoes have been cooked, carefully score an oval on the top with the point of a small knife. Remove this part of the skin; it will later become the cover. Through the opening that you have made, completely take out the pulp or flesh of the potatoes, using the handle of a fork. Drop it onto a plate. Once all the potatoes have been emptied, quickly mash the pulp with a fork.

In a pan, heat the rest of the butter. Put the pulp into the warm butter; season it with salt and pepper; toss it until it is uniformly lightly brown. Turn off the heat; mix in the meat and the minced parsley; fill the shells with this mixture, a little bit above the edges, heaping it up carefully with a spoon. As they are garnished, arrange the potatoes on a baking sheet.

On strong heat, reduce the sauce for a moment. Pass it through a chinois into a bowl, squeezing it to force the onion through. With this sauce, *gradually* moisten the mixture in the potatoes, so that it has time to seep right through it. Make this easier by sticking a large kitchen needle into the potato. The amount of reduced sauce should supply at least 1 1/2 tablespoons for each large potato.

Once the sauce has been well absorbed, put the covers back onto the potatoes, so that you can restore them to their original shape.

Put them in the oven for *about 12–15 minutes,* depending on the degree of heat in the oven. Do not take them out until just before serving, because they must be eaten burning hot. If they have to stand for a short time, keep them in a very moderate oven. This will only slightly compact the mixture inside, which is nonetheless preferable to serving potatoes that are not hot enough.

Arrange the potatoes in a little heap on a napkin-covered plate and serve immediately.

Soufflé Potatoes in Their Jackets *(Pommes de Terre en Robe de Chambre Soufflées).* Even though the name is different, we list this recipe under stuffed potatoes (in their skins) because their preparation is the same.

For this, choose medium-weight potatoes (130–150 grams, 4 1/2–5 1/3 ounces) that are nice and round, if possible. *Time: 1 hour, 30 minutes. Serves 6.*

6 potatoes, total weight of 900 grams (2 pounds); 2 eggs; 50 grams (1 3/4 ounces, scant 1/2 stick) of fine butter; 3 tablespoons of cream, or if you do not have it, of very good milk that has been reduced; 5 grams (1/6 ounce) of salt; a pinch of pepper and a pinch of very finely grated nutmeg.

PROCEDURE. Cook the potatoes as has previously described. Remove a cover about 3 centimeters (1 1/4 inches) big from each one; it will not be used later on. Completely empty the potatoes into a *heated* receptacle, as directed for ARDENNES-STYLE STUFFED POTATOES (PAGE 550). Work the purée in the same way, adding the butter to it, then cream, egg yolks, and seasoning; finally take the usual precautions to add egg whites whisked into a snow (SEE MIXING IN EGG WHITES, PAGE 10).

Using an ordinary spoon, fill the shells of the potatoes, shaping the filling above the opening into a dome. Put them on a baking sheet and again put them into a hot oven for about *15 minutes.* The stuffing will rise like a soufflé and will expand on the surface, taking on a golden tint. Do not wait to serve them, because this stuffing will fall back down and lose its lightness.

NOTE. Some types of potatoes have a pulp that will make a larger volume of purée; and once you add the other ingredients, you might not be able to put it all back into the shells. If so, eliminate any excess before adding anything to the purée.

Potatoes Suzette *(Pommes de Terre Suzette).* A lunch plate that is very popular in the great restaurants. These are simply stuffed potatoes, but unlike the other preparations, it is the solidified pulp or flesh that acts as a shell, not the skin. The potato then looks like a large egg that is a beautiful golden color. So choose long, symmetrical potatoes, weighing about 180 grams (6 1/3 ounces). *Time: 1 hour, 15 minutes. Serves 6.*

6 potatoes; 60 grams (2 1/4 ounces, 4 1/2 tablespoons) of butter; 50 grams (1 3/4 ounces) of leftover chicken breast, either roasted or boiled; 50 grams (1 3/4 ounces) of pickled tongue or lean cooked ham; 3 or 4 small *cooked* mushrooms; if you like, a small truffle; 2 egg yolks; 1 deciliter (3 1/3 fluid ounces, scant 1/2 cup) of light cream or very good reduced milk; salt, pepper, and nutmeg.

PROCEDURE. Peel the potatoes. The method used is very important, because you must obtain a smooth surface like an egg shell. So do not peel the potatoes lengthwise, which is usually done, but rather crosswise, using a knife to peel all the way around, like "turning" a mushroom. In this way, the knife marks are invisible. When you do this, shape the potato into a *large egg with a pointed end.*

From the large end, cut off a very thin layer of the pulp, so that the potatoes can *stand up.* Without washing, dry them with a clean towel. On a lightly buttered baking sheet or dish, arrange the potatoes standing up; put them in a good hot oven, hot enough so that at the end of *30–35 minutes* they will have taken on a uniform golden yellow color; turn them from time to time.

Meanwhile, cut the chicken breast, the tongue, and the mushrooms into small dice of 1/2 centimeter (3/16 inch) on each side.

Once the potatoes have been cooked, turn the oven down very low so that you can empty them without their cooling off too much. Have a warm terrine ready. With the point of a small knife, score a line on the pointed end of a potato to make a little cover, then take it off; you will put it back very soon. Using the handle of a teaspoon, empty the potato, dropping the pulp into the terrine, being very careful not to damage the browned shell. Also empty out the cut off pointed end.

Once all the potatoes have been emptied, take out about one-quarter of the pulp from the terrine. Work the rest strongly with the wooden spoon; once this has reduced to a white and smooth purée, add salt, pepper, and nutmeg and 60 grams (2 1/4 ounces, 4 1/2 tablespoons) of butter. Mix it well. Then add the cream or the milk, the egg yolks, the chicken, tongue, etc.

Immediately fill the shells of the potatoes, shaping the top of the stuffing into a small dome. Put the lids back on each one. Return the potatoes to the baking sheet, still standing. Brush them with the rest of the melted butter.

Put them back in the oven to thoroughly heat the stuffing, which must be *burning hot.* Depending on the oven temperature, allow *7–10 minutes,* and a little more if necessary. Carefully watch them to avoid burning.

Take the potatoes out of the oven just before serving. Arrange them, still standing, on a round heated plate that has been covered with a napkin so that they do not slide around. Finally, brush them with a brush dipped in melted butter to give them a shine. Serve.

French Fried Potatoes *(Pommes de Terre Frites)*

The way in which these are served is variable, and depending on their shape, the way they are deep-fried also differs. However, the most important point to establish is the need for using a substantial quantity of hot fat in an appropriate cooking utensil. So refer to what has already been said on the subject—including the type of fat and the different degrees of heat (SEE DEEP-FRYING, PAGE 37).

A potato *with a very firm yellowish pulp* is the only one appropriate for frying.

Allow 1 potato, weighing about 150 grams (5 1/3 ounces) per person.

Potatoes Pont-Neuf *(Les Pommes de Terre Pont-Neuf).* The original pommes frites were cut into moon shapes and sold on street corners and on the bridges of old Paris. However, in fine restaurants, this name refers to potatoes cut into sticks, as we will show. This makes it easier to cut pieces of equal sizes. Choose potatoes of a medium size.

Peel the potatoes with a small knife. After this, square them off. To do this, place the potato on the table, and using a good, large kitchen knife, remove the domed part on 4 sides and the 2 ends. (The trims can be used in a soup or a purée.)

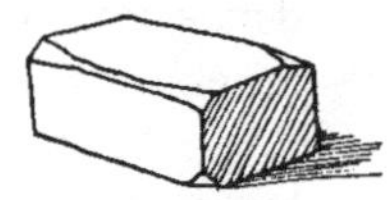

FIG. 65. THE SQUARED OFF POTATO.

Then divide it lengthwise into regular slices 1 centimeter (3/8 inch) thick. Pile these slices one on top of the other and cut them, still lengthwise, to get sticks 1 centimeter thick.

Wipe them well in a towel to rid them of their starch, which would make them stick to each other in the fat; if they have to stand for a while, leave them wrapped in their towel to avoid contact with air, which would darken them.

Make sure the frying fat is ready, *moderately hot,* about 10 minutes before serving. Add the potatoes, scattering them. Immediately turn up the heat to quickly bring the fat up to the temperature that it had before the cold potatoes were added, which has now immediately gone down by its contact with the cold potatoes.

Let them cook, carefully moving the utensil instead of using the skimmer. During this first phase, the natural moisture in the potatoes is evaporated. This is absolutely essential, and would actually be much more difficult if the potatoes were put into hotter fat, because the outside would be sealed, forming a barrier to the evaporation.

After 6–7 minutes, the cooking process is somewhat advanced: you can tell because the sticks float to the surface of the fat without causing any bubbles. To be sure, take a stick out. Press on it with your finger; the pulp should yield under the pressure. Now, turn the heat up very high to get the fat as hot as possible; in other words, *very hot.* This ensures that the potatoes take on a beautiful golden color and that their exterior will be nice and dry.

As soon as they are crusty and golden, take them out with the skimmer and put them on a towel to absorb the fat they have retained. Dust them with a fine salt, sprinkling from on high. Place them around the grilled meat they are accompanying or on a plate covered with a napkin if they are served on the side.

Straw Potatoes *(Pommes de Terre Paille).* Choose medium-size rather than large potatoes, weighing about 120–150 grams (4¼–5⅓ ounces). Peel them and square them off as directed for POTATOES PONT-NEUF (PAGE 552). Cut them lengthwise into even slices *2–3 millimeters (about ⅛ inch) thick.* Stack 4 or 5 of these pieces on top of each other; divide them lengthwise into matchsticks of the same thickness. This is a sort of julienne of potatoes—which, in effect, is what straw potatoes are.

Immerse this julienne into a terrine of cold water, mixing them around to dissolve the wet starch that forms around the sticks while you are cutting them, which would cause them to stick together in the frying oil. Dry the sticks in a towel by shaking them, just as when drying a salad. Then put them in a new dry towel to keep the air from them until you are ready to fry them.

Heat the frying mixture so that about 6–7 minutes before serving it will be *hot.* Scatter the sticks of potato in the frying basket. Immerse it into the deep fat, with the bottom of the basket lying directly on the receptacle itself. Move it carefully: this simple movement is enough to shift around the sticks in the fat. Take out the basket containing the straw potatoes at the end of *3 minutes.*

The potatoes are now cooked. A second immersion in frying fat, which should be even hotter, is necessary to color them and to dry them out. Do this only at the very last moment. While waiting, you can keep the sticks in the basket placed on a plate. They can stand, without spoiling, for quite some time if you have cooked them further in advance than suggested.

To serve: Again, heat the deep fat so that *1½ minutes* before serving the potatoes it is *very hot.* Put back the straw potatoes, but this time without the basket, placing them directly in the hot fat.

There is no point using a skimmer. Simply move the receptacle to stir the sticks. And in *7 or 8 seconds* (we did not say "minutes") they will have acquired their golden color and a desirable crunchiness. Take them out with the skimmer. Spread them out on a towel and proceed as for POTATOES PONT-NEUF (PAGE 552).

Potato Chips *(Pommes de Terre en Liard ou Pommes de Terre Chip).* Cut into extremely thin rounds, these fried potatoes are served like the others, as an accompaniment to grilled meats; according to modern tastes and the English style, they are also eaten cold as a snack, with tea or any other drink.

For this preparation, it is better to use potatoes of a medium size, and even small ones, considering that trimming would mean too much waste.

Peel the potatoes. Shape them into a long cork. To do this, first cut off each end; then take off as much pulp as necessary from along and around the potato to produce a log that is the same size from one end to the other. Place the log on the table to divide it into rounds of equal thickness: about *2–3 millimeters (about ⅛ inch).* Soak the rounds in cold water and then rinse in the same way as straw potatoes.

Make sure the frying mixture is *hot* about 7 minutes before serving. Spread the rounds in it. Turn the heat up under the hot fat frying mixture. Gently shake the utensil. When the potatoes come back up to the surface, stir them carefully, using the skimmer, until you see that they are nice and golden and good and dry—without, however, getting too dark.

Drain them as directed. The best way to serve them is on the side, on a plate covered with a napkin, even if they are accompanying a grilled meat.

Soufflé Potatoes *(Pommes de Terre Soufflées).* A soufflé potato looks like a tiny, very puffed-out cushion whose interior is almost empty, the pulp having stuck to the coating. The exterior is uniformly tinted golden and dry.

What makes the potato puff up is the steam from the water that it still retains, despite the degree of cooking that has already taken place in the deep-frying fat. To stop this steam from escaping, which is the only cause of the potato swelling up, it is essential to make the surface of the potato impermeable. This is achieved by plunging the potato, once it has already cooked and swelled, into a frying mixture at a very high temperature. This instantly creates a crust or skin that is resistant enough to prevent the steam escaping from the inside.

The essential conditions for success of soufflé potatoes can be summarized as follows:

First, the choice of potato. Always use the kind that has a yellowish, very firm pulp. Choose long and well-formed potatoes of a size a little larger than medium: that is, an average weight of 150–180 grams (5 1/3–6 1/3 ounces). In the largest ones, the pulp is not as compact. Any smaller, and the potato does not look very attractive, though they do swell up well. Choose them good and healthy: any blackened, spotted slices will not swell.

Second, cutting the potatoes evenly. A badly cut potato does not swell up. So do not be surprised at the level of detail given below for this step.

Third, a sufficient quantity of deep-frying fat. If you do not have enough fat, the temperature will be too greatly lowered by immersing the potatoes, and the cooking conditions will be altered.

Allow 2 kilograms of fat for 500 grams (1 pound, 2 ounces) of potatoes, net weight. The best frying fat to use is a mix of two-thirds beef kidney fat and one-third of good pork fat.

Fourth, the potatoes must be put into a frying mixture that is not too hot when they begin their cooking. Subsequently, the fat is gradually heated until it rises to a rather high temperature that will cause them to swell.

Fifth, the final immersion in frying fat that has been heated to its maximum degree to dry out the potatoes and make them impermeable.

PROCEDURE. The operation of swelling the potatoes is accelerated in professional kitchens by the simultaneous use of two deep-fat frying mixtures. In one, the first part of the cooking is done; the potatoes are swollen up in the other, using new fat so that they color less.

In home kitchens, this dual process is rarely possible: the same deep-fat mixture is used for both steps. First you cook the potatoes, encouraging them to begin swelling; then you take them out. The deep fat is subsequently heated to its extreme point for the final immersion. This is the procedure we use here.

To cut the potatoes: Peel and rinse the potatoes. Dry them and keep them in a towel until you are ready to cut them.

We have established that the principle reason for the potatoes swelling is the heat retained on the inside by the light exterior crust. But this skin will form only on an absolutely even surface. If the cut of the knife is not clean, a notch is left and, during cooking, this provides an opening for the grease to penetrate, which means the potato will not swell up. If they are cut on a bias, the thin side dries out and the thick side does not swell up because it is not cooked enough.

The slices must therefore be of a perfectly uniform thickness (5 millimeters/3/16 inch/1/2 centimeter) and so equal that they seem to have been cut by a machine. And actually, to obtain them thus, the person in charge of cutting the potatoes does turn himself into a sort of machine, all his movements must be accomplished with automatic precision.

So stand at an angle in front of a table that is solid and stable; take the three-quarters position (see *fig.* 66). Prolonging the line of your forearm ensures that the knife falls naturally in the right direction. Now, the position of the knife depends on the position of the arm, which itself depends on the position of the body; the person's weight should rest on the left leg—note this detail well. This is the position always used by professionals.

Begin by removing the rounded part of the potato on 3 of its sides only; the side that you leave domed provides a better grip when cutting the last slices. Then cut square each end of the potato. Squaring off the potatoes has nothing to do with promoting their swelling, but it gives them a firm balance on the table and makes it easier to handle the knife precisely when cutting the potatoes into slices. Also, these slices have a more original shape,

FIG. 66. THE POSITION TO TAKE IN FRONT OF TABLE WHEN CUTTING THE POTATO SECTIONS.

which is much more flattering to the eye than simple oblong slices.

Hold the potato with the domed side turned toward the inside of your hand. Shield your thumb behind your 4 fingers, the ends of which should be folded back over the potato so that you do not cut them.

Cut the slices 5 millimeters (3/16 inch) thick, as already mentioned. The cut of the knife should always be *from behind, pushing the knife in front of you* without stopping and without hesitating. If you misjudge and go back after having gone forward, pulling the knife back toward you, the slice will be no good. Get rid of it.

Do not grip the knife tightly in your fingers. This is an instinctive movement made by every beginner. On the contrary, you should hold it so lightly that someone could easily take it out of your hands without any effort. The typical size of a potato that

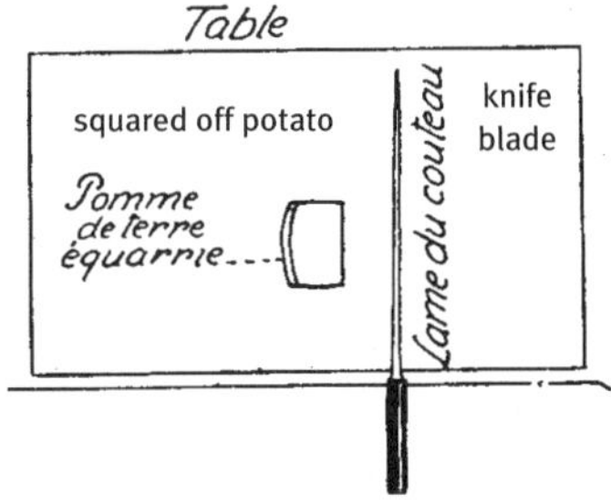

FIG. 67. THE TABLE, THE POTATO, AND THE KNIFE SEEN IN DIAGRAM.

will be souffléed is about 8 centimeters long (3 1/4 inches) and 5 centimeters (2 inches) wide.

To cook: Heat the frying fat to a *moderately hot* degree (SEE DEEP-FRYING, PAGE 37). Quickly distribute these slices in it *one by one* to separate them better: any that stick together will not swell up. Gently pass the skimmer under the potatoes to disperse them completely, being careful when you do this not to tear them: the slightest nick will prevent them from swelling.

Keep the frying basin on a rather strong, but not excessive, heat to gradually increase the temperature of the frying mixture. If the heat is carefully adjusted and the quantity of frying fat is right for the number of potatoes, they will float to the surface after 7–8 minutes, lying motionless as if on still water, which indicates that they are done: you can be sure of this when a slice yields under your finger.

At this point, turn up the heat, so that in *very few instants* the frying fat reaches its highest temperature. Gently shake the pan to move the potatoes around. Under the influence of this stroke of heat, as the potatoes swell and take on a golden tint, take them out with the skimmer, removing only a few at a time so that you do not damage them, and place them in the frying basket.

To finish: Once all the potatoes are in the basket, heat the frying mixture to a *very hot* degree—that is, until positively smoking.

Immerse the basket holding the potatoes, so that the bottom of the basket touches the bottom of the frying basin. The potatoes will detatch and disperse by themselves. Quickly raise the basket while also tilting it. With the skimmer, turn over the potatoes. *Immediately turn off the heat.* Allow the potatoes to dry out and color for *1 minute* in the hot frying fat.

Use the skimmer to lift a few of the potatoes up: if they sound like nuts when they bang up against each other, this indicates that their crust is correctly both firm and dry. Then lift out the rest with the skimmer, placing them in the basket and using it as a draining rack, or spread them out on a kitchen towel. Lightly sprinkle them with fine salt before dressing them on a napkin-covered plate, or surround the grilled meat with them.

NOTE. Sometimes, even if you cut the potatoes

properly, they do not end up swelling. This generally happens for two reasons: either the potatoes have been overcooked and have become tough, and it is then useless to try to make them swell; or they remain flat, a sign that they are not cooked *enough.* In this last case, you must put them back into a moderately hot deep fat for a few moments.

COOKING DRIED VEGETABLES
Cuisson des Légumes Secs

Beans, lentils, split peas, etc.: Be sure to use vegetables from the most recent harvest, which you will not know until you have tried them. Old vegetables have lost their quality; and no matter how long and with what care you cook them, they will burst and their starch will remain granular.

Soaking: The goal here is not to swell the vegetable or give back to it the moisture it has lost, because this would simply take too long. What's more, it is now recognized that prolonged soaking causes the starch to begin fermenting, which is as bad for health as it is for taste. So, it is not swelling that you want to achieve by soaking; slow and methodical cooking will ensure this better than any other method. The true goal of the soaking is to soften the skin of the vegetable and thus to facilitate the cooking, which is done by a gradual penetration of warm moisture into the starch: the swelling will result from this. In fact, soaking is useless unless it is late in the season.

For beans and vegetables that have not been shelled, it is enough to soak them until their skin begins to crinkle, a sign that it has softened up. Generally speaking, 2 hours will suffice for quality vegetables.

Warm water, but only just warm, is better than cold water. This cuts the soaking time in half.

First wash the vegetables, and in the case of lentils, they should always be first sorted to eliminate the little stones. Put them in a terrine; cover them completely with warm water. The water used for soaking the vegetables should not subsequently be used for cooking.

The cooking water: The question of water has real importance when cooking dried vegetables. Water loaded with calcium is very bad to use, because the calcium deposits envelop the skin and harden it, thereby preventing it from cooking correctly. The best water to use is filtered rainwater.

When your available water has a little bit of calcium in it—which you can tell by seeing if there's any deposit in your kettle—add a pinch of *baking soda (bicarbonate of soda)* or Vichy salts. The addition of the baking soda has a profound effect on the dried vegetables, so it should be used: and the cooking water in which it is dissolved is not wasted, but is excellent for other preparations: potages, purées, etc.

The amount of water needed for cooking them is, on average, about 3 deciliters (1¼ cups) for each 100 grams (3½ ounces) of dried vegetables. However, this amount of liquid varies depending on how the vegetables are used once they have been cooked: either they are left whole or puréed; or this purée forms the base of a potage, for which the cooking water is the only liquid used. The shorter the soaking time, the more liquid the dried vegetable requires for cooking, absorbing it as it swells: with a prolonged soaking, the vegetables have already absorbed this water.

For a purée served in place of a vegetable, be very exact about the amount of cooking liquid used; add it *boiling* as you go, using only as much as you need to ensure that the vegetables are still covered with water by the time the cooking is complete. This way, the vegetables are not waterlogged, nor will the purée have dried out for too long before you correct it with milk or water.

What you must add: A bouquet garni is essential to the proper cooking of the vegetables (SEE PAGE 22), to which should be added 1 celery branch. A hint of garlic goes very well here. As well as this bouquet, a medium onion stuck with a clove is generally added, along with some leek and carrot; this does, vary, though, depending on the final use. When the vegetable is intended for a purée, replace these different ingredients with a little bit of mirepoix (SEE PAGE 21).

Conduct of the cooking: Once the vegetables have been soaked, pick them up in handfuls to add to the pot: use an earthenware pot, a thick pot made of aluminum or enameled steel (no cast iron, which would darken the vegetables), or a tin-lined pan.

Cover the vegetables with the amount of cool water suggested. Salt with 7 grams (1/4 ounce) of sea salt per liter (4 1/4 cups). Put the pot on very gentle heat so that it heats only gradually. In this warm liquid, the starch swells little by little. Once this moisture has reached to the very core of the vegetables—in effect, restoring their natural water—you can bring the vegetables to a rolling boil. Allow *at least 45 minutes* to reach this point. Bringing it to a boil more quickly does not speed up the process—quite the contrary, in fact. The cooking time is not shortened, and the vegetable will not absorb enough moisture and will actually harden, so that even when puréed, it will remain grainy, no matter what you do.

With a metal spoon, remove the foam as soon as it rises to the surface, just when boiling is imminent. Once it begins to boil, add the bouquet garni to the vegetables and the fresh vegetables, which vary according to the recipe, or the mirepoix. Maintain the pot at a gentle, regular simmer from the beginning to the end of the cooking. *Cover the pot.*

If the simmering stops because the heat has diminished for one reason or another, make sure that you do not put the pot over very strong heat to bring it back to a boil: the flash of sudden heat would burst the skin of the vegetables. You must heat the liquid only very gradually to return it to the required simmer.

If, while cooking, the liquid reduces substantially, immediately add hot water, even boiling water, enough so that the vegetables are always well covered.

Cooking time: From the moment when the simmering is established:

Beans. 1 1/2–2 hours, depending on their type, quality, and use. They should remain whole, and not burst, but be tender to the point where they crush easily between your fingers into a smooth paste that has no lumps.

Lentils. 1 1/2–2 hours. They must be in the same condition as the beans.

Split peas. 2 1/4–2 1/2 hours, approximately. They must be already be half reduced into a purée in the bottom of the utensil, given that their starch has not been retained by a skin as for the vegetables above.

DRIED VEGETABLES
Légumes Secs

White Beans *(Haricot Blanc)*

A good procedure for cooking dry white beans is to blanch them before cooking. This is the current practice in the southern regions of France and is also recommended by qualified authors. Not only does this make the beans more tender but their cooking liquid can then be used again, since the preliminary blanching will have leached out the elements in the beans that leave a strong odor and unpleasant taste in the water. We strongly suggest that whenever you have the time to do it, use this procedure, as recommended by Urbain Dubois, among other celebrated chefs.

Once the beans have been soaked as directed, drain them and put them in a pot. Cover them amply with warm water (1 1/2 liters/6 1/3 cups for each 1/2 liter/generous 2 cups of beans). Place them on moderate heat. Watch for boiling to begin; as soon as this manifests, turn off the heat and allow the beans *to return to room temperature in their water; at the end of about 1 hour* they should have swollen considerably, and be about double their size, having regained the volume of fresh beans; at this point, they will have fallen to the bottom of the receptacle. Drain them. Throw away the water; its particularly strong odor should suffice to explain and justify this procedure.

Put the beans back into their receptacle. Add the necessary quantity of *boiling* water and the usual garnish of onion, salt, etc. Bring it back to a boil; cook it very gently as directed. *A good 1 1/2 hours of cooking* from this moment is generally sufficient.

Diverse preparations: The preparations for dried white beans are the same as those for fresh white beans, and you should refer to the section on fresh vegetables (SEE PAGE 470).

Red Beans *(Haricot Rouge)*

Creole-Style Red Beans *(Haricots Rouges à la Créole)*. An excellent home-style dish of exotic origin and easy preparation. *Time: 2 hours, 30 minutes (once the beans have been soaked). Serves 6.*

$2^1/_2$ deciliters (1 cup) of dry red beans; 1 onion weighing 25–30 grams (1 ounce); a small bouquet garni; 2 deciliters ($^7/_8$ cup) of Carolina or Indian rice (glazed rice); 125 grams ($4^1/_2$ ounces) of bacon; 125 grams ($4^1/_2$ ounces) of smoked ham; 2 sausages; 1 tablespoon of good lard; 4 deciliters ($1^2/_3$ cups) of cooking water from the beans.

PROCEDURE. Soak and cook the beans as directed (SEE COOKING DRIED VEGETABLES, PAGE 536). Allow approximately *$1^1/_2$ hours* of cooking: the beans must be tender and swollen but somewhat undercooked; they will finish cooking with the rice.

Cut the bacon and ham into large lardons 3–4 centimeters ($1^1/_4$–$1^1/_2$ inches) long and 2 centimeters ($^3/_4$ inch) thick or wide. In a pot large enough to contain all the ingredients listed above, heat the lard. Gently color the lardons and the sausages for about 10 minutes in it.

Then add the drained beans, the rice, which has been previously washed in several changes of water and rubbed between your hands to remove the starch that makes it gluey (SEE RICE, PAGE 561). Pour 4 deciliters ($1^2/_3$ cups) of the cooking water from the beans into the pot; add a pinch of pepper. Bring it to a boil; tightly cover the pot and turn the heat down very low to maintain a barely perceptible simmer for *35–40 minutes.* Do not stir the pot during this time, at the end of which the rice will have absorbed all the water, and its grains will be swollen and quite distinct; the beans will remain intact and everything should be fatty and unctuous without excess liquid. Then pour it into a dish or a timbale, shaping it into a slight dome, with everything mixed together as is.

Red Beans with Bacon *(Haricots Rouges au Lard).* A country-style dish that is always popular and that makes a succulent dish if you add a piece of salted pork in place of the small lardons. In this case, you should use salted pork taken from the less fatty pieces or very lean bacon: thus, for the quantities above, use 225 grams (8 ounces) of one or the other. If you want to use the garnish of little lardons, allow 125 grams ($4^1/_2$ ounces) of ordinary bacon.

The red wine, one of this recipe's characteristic ingredients, must never be omitted. Use it in the ratio of about one-quarter wine to three-quarters water. You should use a very good red wine. *Time: 2 hours, 30 minutes. Serves 6.*

$^1/_2$ liter/425 grams (generous 2 cups/15 ounces) of red beans; 60 grams ($2^1/_4$ ounces) of minced fresh salt pork; 1 large chopped onion; a bouquet garni; 1 piece of butter the size of a small egg (50 grams/$1^3/_4$ ounces/ $3^1/_2$ tablespoons); 1 level tablespoon of flour (10–12 grams); a good glass of red wine (2 deciliters, $^7/_8$ cup); salt and pepper.

PROCEDURE. Once the beans have been soaked as directed under COOKING DRIED VEGETABLES (PAGE 556), put them in their cooking utensil—an earthenware dish or deep pot, with a capacity of about 2 liters ($8^1/_2$ cups). Cover them with cold water about a good finger's height, 2 centimeters ($^3/_4$ inch), above their level. Add the wine and very little salt because of the bacon, which will increase the salty note. Bring it to a boil as directed.

Meanwhile, blanch the bacon without cutting it first (SEE BACON, PAGE 11). If you use salt pork, wash it and keep it in lukewarm water until you are ready to add it to the beans. Sauté the chopped onion in the pan with half of the butter: it should be a light golden blond only. Reserve it on a plate.

Once it has begun boiling, skim it; add the piece of bacon or pork, pushing it well down into the bottom of the beans; the minced bacon; the colored onion; and the bouquet garni. Cover. Cook as directed, adding as you go, if necessary, some *boiling* water, to compensate for the reduction by evaporation. Never leave the surface of the beans dry. Toward the end of the cooking time, stop adding water because when the dish is served there should be no more than *$2^1/_2$ deciliters (1 cup)* of liquid, which will be the sauce for the beans.

Allow *$1^1/_4$ hours at least of cooking* from the moment the boiling begins. If you have used bacon, you can assume *40–45 minutes for a big piece* to be completely done and a bit less for a little one. If a cooking needle pierces it easily, take it out and keep it warm. If you have used salt pork, you can leave it with the beans right until the end of cooking.

To serve: If serving with the garnish of small lardons, cut the bacon, cooked for this use with the beans, into small dice about 1 centimeter ($^3/_8$ inch) on each side. Sauté them in a pan to color them nicely with a piece of butter about the size of a walnut for the 125 grams (4½ ounces) of bacon indicated.

If, however, you have used salt pork, take it out and keep it warm. Remove the bouquet. With the flour and the remains of the butter, proceed as directed (SEE LIAISON WITH BEURRE MANIÉ, PAGE 48). Then add the colored lardons. Allow it to simmer for 2–3 minutes.

To serve, put it in a vegetable plate or in a shallow bowl. If, instead of the garnish of little lardons, you have used the salt pork or a large piece of bacon, quickly cut the meat into small slices and arrange these in a small circle on top of the beans.

Lentils *(Lentille)*

In all their various preparations, lentils are particularly associated with game: either puréed and served as an accompaniment for game, or whole; or they are cooked with bones and trimmings, particularly partridge, which communicates the flavor of game. Similarly, and particularly for purées, you can add the carcasses and bones of a goose, of roasted or braised duck, a ham bone, or the bone from a roast or leg of lamb. As for bacon, it is included here by long and justifiable tradition, the lentil by itself being somewhat dry. Carême, in his purées, cooked the lentil with a piece of lean ham and an old partridge, and seasoned the purée with a pinch of pepper and as much superfine sugar as could be held on the point of a knife blade.

For soaking, cooking, etc., see DRIED VEGETABLES (PAGE 556). We list here the principal recipes: they are all simple. A half-liter (generous 2 cups) of lentils weighs about 400 grams (14 ounces) and is sufficient to serve 6.

Lentils Maître d'Hôtel *(Lentilles à la Maître d'Hôtel).* Drain them thoroughly and proceed as directed (SEE VEGETABLES À LA MAÎTRE D'HÔTEL, PAGE 470). Allow 60 grams (2¼ ounces, 4½ tablespoons) of butter for ½ liter (generous 2 cups) of lentils measured uncooked.

Lentils with Bacon *(Lentilles au Lard).* Same procedure as for RED BEANS WITH BACON (PAGE 558), but omitting the wine. Or, even simpler, proceed as follows: for ½ liter (generous 2 cups) of lentils, add 175 grams (6 ounces) of bacon, cut into cubes of 1½ centimeters (⅝ inch.) Blanch these cubes (SEE BACON, PAGE 11) and lightly color them in 30 grams (1 ounce, 2 tablespoons) of butter. Put them into the well-drained lentils after you have cooked them; add 2 deciliters (⅞ cup) of jus, or, if you do not have it, good bouillon. Gently simmer for 15 minutes. Bind with a beurre manié made with 15 grams (½ ounce, 1 tablespoon) of butter and 10 grams (⅓ ounce) of flour (SEE LIAISONS, PAGE 47).

Lentils au Jus *(Lentilles au Jus).* For the same quantity of lentils, make a little blond roux with 15 grams (½ ounce, 1 tablespoon) of butter and 10 grams (⅓ ounce) of flour. Dilute with 2 deciliters (⅞ cup) of jus. Add the well-drained lentils. Simmer until one-quarter of the juice has been reduced. Here this has more the effect of a liaison than a sauce.

Meatless Lentils with Cream *(Lentilles à la Crème, en Maigre).* Same quantity of lentils; a little white roux with 15 grams (½ ounce, 1 tablespoon) of butter and 15 grams (½ ounce) of flour. Dilute with 2½ deciliters (1 cup) of light cream or very good milk that has been reduced; season with salt, pepper, and as much grated nutmeg as can be held on the point of a knife. Add the well-drained lentils. Simmer and reduce for 15 minutes. Finish with 30 grams (1 ounce, 2 tablespoons) of butter added off the heat.

Brittany-Style Lentils *(Lentilles à la Bretonne).* Same quantity of lentils; in 30 grams (1 ounce, 2 tablespoons) of butter, lightly color 1 good tablespoon of finely minced onion. Sprinkle with flour (10 grams/⅓ ounce); let it color slightly, until blond. Dilute with 2 deciliters (⅞ cup) of the cooking juice of the lentils. Add the drained lentils. Simmer until the liquid is almost completely reduced. Before serving, add 30 grams (1 ounce, 2 tablespoons) of butter off the heat.

Lentil Purée *(Lentilles en Purée).* Cook the lentils as directed with 1 medium-size onion stuck with a clove, 1 medium-size carrot cut into large rounds, a bouquet garni, 10 grams (⅓ ounce) of salt per liter (4¼ cups) of water. For this recipe, bacon is optional, but any bacon trimmings can be put to good use. For 4–5 deciliters (1²/₃–generous 2 cups) of lentils, allow 50–60 grams (1³/₄–2¹/₄ ounces) of bacon and blanch it first.

Stop cooking when the lentils yield to the touch. If they are overcooked, bits of skin will go through the drum sieve. Force the lentils through to purée (SEE STRAINING PURÉES, PAGE 14). Then put this purée back into the rinsed pot. Work it vigorously on the heat with a wooden spoon. Then add 3–4 tablespoons of bouillon to it, or simply the cooking water, to lighten it and dilute it a little. Once it has returned to a boil, which will manifest itself by showing bubbles, take it off the heat. Keep it hot. To serve, add 30–40 grams (1–1³/₈ ounces, 2–3 tablespoons) of butter, off the heat, and a pinch of pepper.

Lentil Salad *(Lentilles en Salade).* Once the lentils have been carefully drained, season them while still hot. If you like, add some beets cut into small cubes, anchovy fillets, etc. (SEE SALADS, PAGE 463).

Peas *(Pois)*

Split Pea Purée *(Purée de Pois Cassés).* This purée is as good for a garnish of braised meats, sausages, etc., as it is when served alone. In the latter case, it is completed with small croutons. Just as for a potage made from peas, you can add, if you like, a few leaves of spinach and some leek while cooking the peas to accentuate the color of the purée. The mirepoix suggested (SEE DRIED VEGETABLES, PAGE 557) is particularly recommended here: if the purée is to be strictly meatless, omit the bacon. *Time: Serves 6.*

6 deciliters (2¹/₂ cups) of split peas (about 560 grams/ 1 pound, 3³/₄ ounces); 1 good liter (4¹/₄ cups) of water; 10 grams (¹/₃ ounce) of salt; a mirepoix that contains: 20 grams (²/₃ ounce, 1 heaping tablespoon) of butter; 50 grams (1³/₄ ounces) of bacon; 50 grams (1³/₄ ounces) of carrot and the same of onion; a small bouquet garni. If you like, 6 spinach leaves and 20 grams (²/₃ ounce) of green leek leaves. Use 1 deciliter (3¹/₃ fluid ounces, scant ¹/₂ cup) of cream or good reduced milk; 50 grams (1³/₄ ounces, 3¹/₂ tablespoons) of butter to finish the purée. A dozen small fried croutons.

PROCEDURE. Soak and cook the peas (SEE COOKING DRIED VEGETABLES, PAGE 556). The amount of water suggested is fairly minimal; the peas have been husked and therefore absorb more water than other vegetables. As the water diminishes in the course of the cooking, add *boiling* water a few tablespoons at a time, just enough to cover the surface of the peas. Using such a small amount of water will shorten the time it takes to dry out the purée, stirring it on the heat to thicken it.

While it is coming to a boil, prepare the mirepoix (SEE PAGE 21). Add it to the peas. When the peas have begun to boil, also add the bouquet, the spinach, and the leek. Let it cook gently as directed for *at least 2 hours,* at the end of which the peas will, if they are of good quality, have already reduced to a purée.

Remove the bouquet; force the peas and the mirepoix, spinach, and leek through a fine metal drum sieve (SEE STRAINING PURÉES, PAGE 14). Then put the purée into a sauté pan. On strong heat, evaporate the moisture as directed (SEE DRYING PURÉES, PAGE 14). Turn off the heat, then add the butter in little pieces and the cream by tablespoons, mixing it as you go; season with pepper and add a pinch of superfine sugar. On very gentle heat, heat the purée without allowing it to boil, so you do not destroy the effect of the butter. If the purée is not served immediately, spread a few pieces of butter on the surface to prevent it from clouding over. Just before serving, stir it with a spoon to mix in the butter.

Serve the purée in a vegetable dish, smoothing it into a dome with the blade of a knife. Then place the fried croutons on top, arranged in a crown. Serve.

RICE AND PASTA

RICE
Riz

In French homes today, no one knows how to cook rice anymore; and it is a real shame because it is a good resource for daily meals.

People think the only thing they have to do is to cook the rice until it bursts; but a burst grain is a deformed grain, exhausted and flaccid, and it will turn to mush at the least touch. It's true that rice should be perfectly tender, but the grains should always be intact.

And rice that is "gluey" is considered repellent—and deservedly so! In fact, it is the reason that rice is loathed by so many people, who have never eaten rice the way it should be prepared. To appreciate the true value of rice—and let us repeat that it does have great value—it must be prepared by the methods used in its different countries of origin, where it is, if not the principal food, at least a common food. These methods vary according to the country and the type of rice harvested. But all are inspired by the same principle.

Remove the starch from the rice, which makes it gluey. Do not allow the rice while cooking to absorb anything more than the strict quantity of liquid necessary to thoroughly penetrate the grain.

The necessity of removing starch from rice is the first objective of the methods of preparation used in its countries of origin. Nonetheless, the method differs in different countries. In the Indian or Creole manner, the rice is cooked in a large quantity of liquid and served as is, the starch being released into the abundant water. In the Italian manner, the rice is cooked with minimal liquid, so the method for removing the starch is different: before any liquid is added to it, the rice is heated strongly in fat (SEE RISOTTO, PAGE 449). This sort of preliminary roasting completely modifies the effect of the starch.

In the Mongolian method, the rice is cooked with only the strict quantity of water necessary but is first washed repeatedly and meticulously—one example of where the storied infinite patience of the people of the Far East is exercised. For them, washing the rice is a step as important as the cooking itself. It is understood that these repeated washes are not, of course, for reasons of cleanliness; any more than "blanching" the rice, as practiced in French kitchens, is intended to start the cooking process. Washing and blanching have only the same goal—to remove the starch from the rice—and blanching is simply a more expeditious procedure than the numerous washings of the natives.

Note that cooking rice, by whatever method, is simply a matter of observation, because you cannot fix the duration of cooking time to the minute; it varies between 15 minutes and 25 minutes, the exact proper degree of cooking depending on both the type and and quality of the rice. One or two minutes too long or too short makes an important difference that you cannot understand until after personal experience. You can also avoid future mistakes by continuing to use the same kind of rice with which you have experimented. Rice keeps for a very long time, so having a large supply is not extravagant.

Diverse Principles

Weights and measures: 1 liter ($4^1/_4$ cups) of rice weighs 950 grams (2 pounds, 2 ounces); 1 kilogram (2 pounds, 3 ounces) measures 1.15 liters (scant 5 cups). You can thus allow about 100 grams ($3^1/_2$ ounces) for 1 good deciliter ($3^1/_3$ fluid ounces, scant $^1/_2$ cup) of rice, and about 90 grams ($3^1/_6$ ounces) for an exact measure. One large tablespoon, as full as it can be, weighs 25 grams (1 ounce).

Choice of rice: Long-grain glazed rice—that is, shiny rice—is either *Patna* rice imported from

India or *Carolina* rice, which comes from the United States. In general, these are appropriate for all recipes. Carolina rice, of the best quality, must always be chosen for desserts and when cooking in milk. It should also be chosen for Indian-style or Creole-style rice, both of which are cooked in a substantial quantity of water. Rice from *Piedmont,* short-grain rice that is a matte white color, is particularly appropriate for risotto and pilaf. For desserts, it does not give good results. It is also possible to buy "instant" rice, which cooks rapidly; this can be useful for people whose time is extremely limited.

That said, there are exceptions, and we will cite here the remark made personally to us by a qualified chef, who was talking about cooking rice à l'Indienne: "For my own part," he said, "I have used Carolina rice or Patna rice, which melted; while occasionally, through necessity and because there was no other type, I have cooked with Piedmont rice, and was surprised by the result, because the rice remained very firm and not at all pasty, which does not often happen."

Cooking long-grain Carolina rice requires more time and liquid than cooking short-grain rice. It is essential to remember this when you substitute one for the other.

Washing the rice: In its country of origin, people use a drum sieve or fine sieve for this. Handling it and draining it is much more effective and much easier than in a strainer, through which the grains will escape if the holes are big, and which will not let the water drain if they are small.

So put the rice in a drum sieve. Place the drum sieve in a receptacle full of cold water, which should be lightly warmed in winter, and which should completely bathe the rice without rising above the sides of the drum sieve. With your hands, pick up the rice in small quantities at a time. Keeping your hands in the water, rub the rice between your hands, gently and carefully, so that you do not break the grains. Change the water in the utensil as many times as you need to, so that no whitish or milky traces remain; after each change of water, continue to gently rub the rice between your hands. Often, you will need as many as 7 or 8 changes of water. The final water must be as clear as drinking water in a carafe.

Remove the drum sieve with the rice from the receptacle. Spread the rice out on the drum sieve to allow it to thoroughly drain. Thus washed, it can be put directly into the bouillon or *(jus)* for cooking it au gras, eliminating the need for a preliminary blanching.

The cooking liquid: *Except for cooking rice à l'Indienne,* which uses plenty of water, the cooking liquid must be carefully measured, proportional to the amount of rice. Depending on its quality, rice can, in some cases, absorb a little more liquid. But what is much more important to consider are the conditions for its cooking: whether the heat is more, or less, strong and the size of the utensil employed.

Indeed, if the rice is cooked in a utensil with a large bottom—such as a sauté pan or an enameled steel utensil—or in a deep pot with a smaller surface area, the amount of liquid needed will differ considerably for the same quantity of rice. This difference is even more marked depending on how strong the heat is, even if the same utensil is used.

For this reason, it is impossible to absolutely accurately predict the precise amount of liquid needed. You may need 2 times, 2 1/2 times, or even 3 times the volume of the rice, bearing in mind the loss due to evaporation. In a large receptacle and with moderate heat, you can assume the quantity of liquid to be 3 times the volume of rice: so, for 1 glass of rice you can allow 3 glasses of liquid. In a deep, narrow pot, and on low heat, 2 1/2 times the volume is amply sufficient because there will be less evaporation.

For cooking rice in milk, the proportions are different. SEE MILK RICE FOR DESSERTS (PAGE 588).

Note that it is always better to put in less liquid rather than too much at the beginning of the cooking. This is because it is easy to add some while it is cooking if the rice seems too dry to finish cooking. But an excess of liquid, once the rice is done, compromises the result.

The rice must finish cooking at the same time that all the liquid is absorbed. To put it another way, when the rice is ready, it must have "drunk up" all the liquid used for cooking it. Assume that cooking the rice should take about *15–25 minutes,* depending on the kind of rice and also depending on the kind of heat—that is, oven or stovetop.

It is always prudent to add additional liquid 1 tablespoon at a time. It is surprising just how little liquid is needed once the rice is already three-quarters done. Add this liquid without stirring the rice in any way: the liquid is poured on the surface and mixes in it all by itself.

Absolute rule: When cooking any rice—whether in fat, milk, a risotto, etc.—do not stir the rice once it has come to a boil. The smallest hole made in the mass of rice will displace the liquid, and the rice will stick to the bottom and burn.

The utensil: For cooking rice in a minimal amount of liquid—that is, in milk, fat, a risotto, pilaf, etc.—always choose a deep pot (in other words, one that is higher than wider) and with a capacity that is proportional to the volume of rice and liquid. This is to prevent too much liquid being lost to evaporation. Choose it with a *thick* bottom so that the rice does not stick.

PRINCIPAL RECIPES

Rice with Meat Bouillon *(Riz au Gras).* By "au gras," we mean rice cooked with a limited amount of meat bouillon. But the procedure remains the same if, instead of a meat bouillon, you use a bouillon of vegetables or fish.

Before cooking it in the bouillon, blanch the rice or rinse it in several changes of water, doing this very carefully, as described above.

PROCEDURE. First measure the rice to determine the amount of liquid necessary.

If you do not blanch the rice, wash it as directed previously (SEE WASHING THE RICE, PAGE 562), then immediately put it into the pot with the bouillon, as directed further down; cook it in the same way.

If you blanch the rice, put it into the pot in which you will cook it, choosing it according to the criteria outlined above (SEE THE UTENSIL, ABOVE), amply covered with *cold* water. Slowly bring it to a boil on moderate heat. Let it boil for *5 minutes,* and no more, counting from the moment it begins to boil. Pour the rice into a colander with medium-size holes; plunge this into a bowl of fresh water and shake the rice in it to wash it well there. Renew the cool water to get rid of the starch: the water must be limpid after the last wash. Thoroughly drain the rice.

Put it back into the pot with the bouillon, which should not have been completely degreased, and which can be either cold or warm. The amount needed is in proportion to that of the rice, depending on the instructions previously given (SEE PAGE 562): so, *about 2 1/2 times* the original volume of the rice. (If using bouillon that has been completely degreased, or if you are using a bouillon of vegetables or fish, add some butter, about the size of half an egg: the fat stops the rice from drying out at the end of cooking when all the liquid has been absorbed.)

Once the boiling has started, *cover the pot.* Put it into a moderate oven to maintain the liquid at a very small, slow, and regular simmer. The cooking time can vary a little bit depending on the kind of rice: so assume *15–25 minutes.*

If you do not have an oven, you can cook directly on the stovetop. No matter what type of heat is used, it must be extremely gentle and the simmering must be regulated as above. The time needed for cooking on the stove is a little bit longer because the utensil is not in an oven, surrounded by heat. The rice should be done at the same time as the liquid has been completely absorbed, and the grains should be tender and completely intact.

Once you have taken the rice out of the oven, use a fork to separate the grains carefully. It is then ready to serve. If it accompanies a dish that has been sauced, add a few tablespoons of that sauce to the rice.

Rice in Risotto *(Riz en Risotto).* SEE PAGE 449.

Milk Rice *(Riz au Lait).* SEE DESSERTS, PAGE 588.

Indian-Style Rice *(Riz à l'Indienne).* To accompany curries, fish, meat, or fowl.

For rice cooked like this, the true art is to keep the grains as white as snow, completely separated and absolutely tender: assume that they will triple in volume. Indian rice is generally served in a very high pyramid, and the grains must remain detached and so distinct that when they fall from the pyramid and roll around on the plate, they look like so many grains of wheat.

The kind of rice to use is either Carolina rice or Patna rice. The latter is preferable: and to ensure that the rice stays whole, it is essential to use rice from this year's harvest; otherwise, the grains will break. But this does not mean you cannot use Carolina rice.

We would like to make the point that Indian-style rice is better when prepared in relatively large quantities: that is, at least 225 grams (8 ounces). Drying it is much easier. Any left over is always usable, added to a potage just before serving, or mixing it into a stuffing for vegetables such as artichokes, zucchini, eggplant, etc.

The method of cooking used, both in India and the United States, is to boil it in plenty of water and then dry it out. The rice can be prepared in various ways, depending on region or convenience, but all are based on the same principle.

First: Use plenty of water, in which the rice releases its starch. The water should be kept at a rather lively boil, so that the grains of rice are continually moving in it, which helps to stop them from sticking together. Often in France, rice prepared like this is pasty and stuck together, because it has been cooked with too little water.

Second: Watch very carefully for the point when cooking is complete so that you can take it immediately off the heat. In France, people simply do not understand the fact that 1 or 2 minutes too much at the end of cooking makes a great deal of difference to the final result.

Third: Dry out the rice. The grains must swell a little more and at the same time become tender and light; in fact, this could almost be considered the second phase of cooking the rice.

250 grams (8 7/8 ounces) of Carolina rice; 3 liters (scant 12 3/4 cups) of *boiling* water; 30 grams (1 ounce) of salt; juice of 1 lemon (optional); in India, the lemon juice is used to accentuate the whiteness of the rice and help keep the grains intact.

PROCEDURE. **To cook:** Wash the rice in room temperature water, rubbing it between your hands. Renew the water. Dry it.

In a receptacle without a cover, boil salted water and the lemon juice, if using, on strong heat. When the water is *fully boiling,* pour in the rice in a shower of grains. Stir with the wooden spoon until it returns to a boil; after this, stop stirring. A rolling boil must be maintained from the beginning to the end of the cooking. That should take up to *17–18 minutes,* no longer.

Check the degree of cooking after *15 minutes* by taking out a grain of rice; it must be firm, not deformed; but when you squash it between your fingers, there should be no hard or crispy lumps. A minute more or less has such importance that if you are not yet experienced in this kind of cooking, you must try it again several times.

As soon as cooking is complete, rapidly drain the rice, because it will continue to cook if it is left in the hot water.

Drying out the rice: There are different ways to do this and we list below the most current.

First method. Once the rice has been cooked as directed, drain it in a colander; put it back in its pot, then cover it with cold water and stand it under a running faucet. Do not drain it again until it is completely cooled and the water is extremely clear. Spread it out on a large plate, sprinkling it lightly with fine salt, and then put it in a very moderate oven for *at least 20 minutes,* mixing it around and turning it over from time to time with a fork.

Some people rinse the rice in warm salted water; they dry it the same way.

Second method. As soon as the rice is cooked completely, drain the rice by tipping the pot, holding a cover over it, to pour out every last drop of water through the little opening left under the cover. Put the pot back in the oven without washing it first, so that the rice "sweats," as the old Creoles say, for the same time as above. Or, thoroughly drain the rice in a strainer and then, without washing it, spread it out on a plate to dry it out in the oven.

Third method. If you do not have an oven, drain the rice and cool it as soon as it is cooked and return it to its pot. You can then dry it out on the heat itself, tossing it frequently to move it around and to help the moisture evaporate, without directly touching the grains, which means that they do not break. But this is a risky method and is far less effective for "sweating" the rice than an oven, which provides an even, all-round heat in an enclosed space.

Whichever method you use, watch the rice carefully while drying it out so that you get the right result: grains that are separate, swollen, and tender. This is achieved by slowly and gradually evaporating the moisture they absorbed while cooking. And it is the reason why it is necessary, while drying them out, to maintain a very moderate heat; otherwise, the grains will harden and will be tough, like little pieces of rubber, when you bite into them.

Dressing the rice: To do this, use a large spatula or a light skimmer, or any other flat implement that you can slide under the rice so you do not break it or heap it up; pile it lightly into a pyramid on a well-heated plate, timbale, or vegetable dish.

You can also mold it into a border. For this, dry it out for only about 10 minutes, then season it with salt and pepper and pack it, without pressing down too hard, into a round mold that has been heavily buttered. Put it in a very moderate oven for *10 minutes.* Unmold it on a plate.

MACARONI
Macaroni

It is a false economy to buy cheap pasta, which is, by definition, of inferior quality. A good brand is the best guarantee. However, a good macaroni can be recognized by its yellowish tint, though this should not be too strong, which indicates artificial coloring; a a fine grain and even pieces; and it should also break clean and be as shiny as glass. Old, inferior macaroni has a grayish look and is powdery; it cracks and does not break clean.

Macaroni is sold in three different sizes: large, medium, and fine, each appropriate for different preparations. Also sold under the generic name of macaroni is "spaghetti," sticks of macaroni that do not have holes; and cannelloni, very large macaroni that is intended to be stuffed.

Below, we list the the principal methods for preparing macaroni. You should allow an average of 225–250 grams (8–8⁷/₈ ounces) of macaroni for 6 people.

If you want good results, always use an equal quantity of Parmesan and Gruyère. Choose Gruyère that is rather dry. Make sure that the Parmesan has a good flavor but is not too strong. If it tastes too strong, you would do better not to use it. If you leave out the Parmesan, increase the amount of Gruyere accordingly—that is, double it.

Cooking Macaroni

Whatever the recipe, the macaroni must always first be cooked in boiling water. The length of cooking time will vary with the size and the quality of the macaroni, and also according to the recipe for which it will subsequently be used. But in every case the conditions for cooking remain the same, and we will list first of all the two essential points, which are too often ignored or neglected: namely, *a large quantity of liquid* in which the pieces of macaroni must easily be immersed—Italian cooks say that "In order for there to be enough water, you must have too much of it"; and *moderate boiling.*

The macaroni must be cooked only when it is needed, and then immediately drained. Leaving it for too long in its water, or reheating it, will spoil the macaroni: in case of absolute necessity, you can cook the macaroni and drain it, then place the strainer over a pot in which you have put some of the boiling cooking water. Cover and keep everything warm until it is ready to prepare.

Sometimes you can add an onion stuck with a clove to the cooking water, and a bouquet garni, but this is not necessary and we do not suggest it here.

To cook the macaroni: In a deep pot, boil the water at the rate of at least 3 liters (scant 12¾ cups) for 250 grams (8⁷/₈ ounces) of macaroni, salted with 10 grams (⅓ ounce) of sea salt per liter (4¼ cups). When the water is *fully boiling,* add the macaroni, broken into shorter or longer pieces, depending on the recipe and your own preference; or you can even keep the sticks whole, plunging them gradually into the water to soften them and then arranging them in a circle in the pot. Without covering the pot, and on strong heat, quickly return it to a boil. As soon as it has done so, keep it boiling relatively strongly with the pot uncovered, so that the macaroni moves about in the water and does not stick together at the bottom of the pot. The exact length of cooking time depends on the recipe. Generally speaking, you can allow *10–20 minutes.* Do not wait for the last moment to take out a piece of macaroni and check to see if it is done: it must be swollen up, supple, and elastic, but still slightly firm. Avoid overcooking, which will diminish the flavor and make the macaroni break and fall apart.

Once the macaroni has been cooked sufficiently, pour it into a colander with large holes. Shake it well so that it retains absolutely no water, and then immediately use it in your chosen recipe.

PRINCIPAL RECIPES

Italian-Style Macaroni *(Macaroni à l'Italienne)*. This is the simplest way to prepare macaroni. It is very much enjoyed by people who like their macaroni "stringy." *Time: 25–30 minutes. Serves 6.*

250 grams (8 7/8 ounces) of large macaroni; 30 grams (1 ounce, 2 tablespoons) of butter; 40 grams (1 3/8 ounces) of grated Gruyère and the same of Parmesan; salt, pepper, grated nutmeg.

PROCEDURE. Cook the macaroni until it is properly done. Thoroughly drain it. Put it into a sauté pan that is large enough so that the macaroni is not too piled up. Sauté it on the heat to dry it out.

Then add salt, pepper, nutmeg, and the butter divided into pieces, and *only half* of the cheeses, mixed together. Sauté it to bind everything and heat it only long enough to ensure everything is well mixed and the cheese is melted. As soon as this is accomplished, add the remaining cheese. Again, shake the pan and heat it for an instant until everything is bound together.

Pour it into a heated metal timbale or into a vegetable dish.

NOTE. To "string," the cheese must not "cook." If the macaroni is heated too much after the cheese is added, the cheese will melt and will not string at all. That is why you add the cheese at the last moment, in two batches so that it mixes more easily, and after having heated the macaroni separately to dry it out.

Macaroni au Gratin *(Macaroni au Gratin)*. This name refers to two methods of cooking. At home, this tends to be macaroni prepared à l'Italienne, then placed in an ovenproof buttered plate and sprinkled with cheese mixed with bread crumbs, before being put into a very hot oven or under a broiler so that the surface very rapidly turns golden; if not, the macaroni will dry out.

The second method, more modern and also more succulent, includes adding a light béchamel sauce flavored with onion, parsley, thyme, and nutmeg. In particular, do not leave out the nutmeg, which is marvelous with macaroni and all recipes with cheese. If here, as elsewhere, in a situation where you cannot use Parmesan, double the quantity of Gruyère. You can add the béchamel sauce to the macaroni, prepared first with cheese as in macaroni à l'Italienne, and then pour everything into a heatproof plate to brown it. But the following method is simpler and seems to us more practical. *Time: 30 minutes. Serves 6.*

250 grams (8 7/8 ounces) of macaroni; 40 grams (1 3/8 ounces) of grated Gruyère; the same of Parmesan; 50 grams (1 3/4 ounces, 3 1/2 tablespoons) of butter for finishing the sauce, buttering the plate, etc.

For the béchamel sauce: **40 grams (1 3/8 ounces) of onion cut into fine rounds, braised with 20 grams (2/3 ounce, 1 heaping tablespoon) of butter; 5 deciliters (generous 2 cups) of good boiled milk; 1 sprig of parsley; 1 sprig of thyme; salt, pepper, grated nutmeg; 30 grams (1 ounce) of flour and 30 grams (1 ounce, 2 tablespoons) of butter for the white roux.**

PROCEDURE. The sauce. Prepare this following the second method described (SEE BÉCHAMEL SAUCE, PAGE 52). Braise the onion and infuse the milk that will be used to dilute the white roux: this procedure simplifies many things. Add very little salt, or none at all, bearing in mind the salt note of the cheese.

Meanwhile, cook the macaroni as directed.

Prepare the gratin plate: either a shallow bowl made of metal or ovenproof porcelain or a low timbale with a wide bottom. Butter it very lightly; any excess will rise to the surface as oil. Sprinkle it with the grated cheese, but not too much. Keep it ready.

Once the macaroni has been cooked completely, drain it. Add the cheese to the sauce, reserving *1 tablespoon for the gratin;* carefully mix it on the heat using a whisk. The sauce will not be stringy, because the cheese will have been well heated and cooked. Taste it to check the seasoning. Off the heat, add the butter after having reserved the amount of a small walnut to glaze the gratin.

To make the gratin: The most practical method is this: in the bottom of a buttered and cheesed plate, spread out a few tablespoons of sauce; spread out half of the macaroni in a very even layer. Cover with sauce. Then, on top, place the other half of the macaroni, leveling it *quite flat* in anticipation of the subsequent gratin. Cover it with the rest of the sauce. Sprinkle the surface of the macaroni with the reserved cheese. Bread crumbs are not needed here: the cheese will suffice.

Put the plate into a *hot* oven so that, as for every gratin, it is only the surface that receives the strong heat and not the bottom, which must not in any way crisp or color. This means that you must raise the plate on a cold support—a brick or a pot of cold water—to get it as close as possible to the heat source. A broiler is preferable.

Allow *7–8 minutes* to obtain a beautiful light golden tint. Before serving, "glaze" the gratin with a piece of butter the size of a small walnut; use a fork to spread this out and melt on the surface of the macaroni. Place the plate on a serving plate covered with a napkin. Serve quite hot.

Macaroni au Jus *(Macaroni au Jus).* Use large macaroni broken in pieces about 5–6 centimeters (2–2½ inches) long, which will need less time to cook. Carême suggests only 5 minutes of boiling—in effect, just blanching it—to keep the macaroni firm. Finish cooking it in a good jus, using enough so that it is almost completely absorbed at the same time as the macaroni is cooked: the macaroni must neither be bathed in it nor covered by it.

Use a sauté pan large enough so the macaroni is not too heaped up in it and can be moved around by shaking the sauté pan. Add a nice walnut-sized piece of butter. Cover. Simmer for *20–25 minutes* until the macaroni swelled by the jus becomes nice and tender.

Macaroni can be served thus at your choice, in a timbale or as a garnish of meat, just as it is, or with added cheese.

Neapolitan-Style Macaroni *(Macaroni à la Napolitaine).* A purée of tomatoes strengthened with a beef jus is characteristic of this preparation. In the most current method, the macaroni is cooked in boiling water and drained thoroughly, then put back into its pan with butter, tomato purée that has beef jus added to it, and grated Parmesan and Gruyère. Sauté everything vigorously for a few moments on low heat to melt the butter and the cheese. Below, we give a method that uses the same ingredients for an even better result. *Time: 1 hour, 15 minutes. Serves 6.*

300 grams (10½ ounces) of fine macaroni; 60 grams (2¼ ounces, 4½ tablespoons) of butter; 60 grams (2¼ ounces) of grated Parmesan and the same of Gruyère.

For the sauce: 2 deciliters (6¾ fluid ounces, ⅞ cup) of concentrated Neapolitan tomato purée; ½ deciliter (1⅔ fluid ounces, scant ¼ cup) of excellent beef jus, prepared by the simplified method (SEE JUS, PAGE 44); 1 deciliter (3⅓ fluid ounces, scant ½ cup) of white wine; a nice mirepoix with bacon, onion, carrot, etc. (SEE PAGE 21).

PROCEDURE. Color the mirepoix as directed. Then add the tomato, white wine, beef jus, bouquet garni, and a clove of garlic. Cook it gently for 45 minutes. Remove the bouquet garni and pass everything through the drum sieve, rubbing it through with the pestle. Put the sauce back into the rinsed pan and keep it warm and covered so that it will be ready when you need it.

Meanwhile, cook the macaroni as directed. Drain it thoroughly. Put it back in its pot and toss it on the heat for a few moments so that it will be *burning hot* when you add the butter to it, which you have divided into 10 little pieces. Turn off the heat, then shake the pot to melt and mix the butter; if the butter were to melt directly on the heat, it would become oily and lose its creamy and binding effect.

Spread 1 good tablespoon of sauce on the inside of a heated timbale or vegetable dish; this should have previously been thoroughly heated on the stove. Sprinkle it with the mixed cheeses. Put the macaroni in the timbale, alternating it in layers with the sauce and cheese, and finishing with a layer of sauce and cheese. Put the timbale in the oven for a minute. Serve boiling hot.

Macaroni Croquettes *(Croquettes de Macaroni).* SEE CROQUETTES (PAGE 438). Cook the macaroni in water, leaving the pieces whole. Line them up to cut them as directed for a *salpicon* (PAGE 439). Bind them either with a béchamel sauce, to which a little bit of tomato has been added, or with a tomato sauce that has been spiced up with a little bit of jus. For one or the other, add the grated Parmesan and Gruyère.

Milanaise style: As a small entrée: add a generous amount of ham and half the same again of mushrooms to the macaroni; bind it with the same sauce used for CROQUETTES OF FOWL (SEE PAGE 440) and add some grated cheese. Accompany with a light tomato sauce.

Macaroni Loaf *(Pain de Macaroni).* A simple and inexpensive recipe, this loaf can replace a small entrée of meat or fish in family meals in an agreeable and substantial manner. For a meatless meal, you can omit the ham. The tomato sauce accompanying the loaf is made, depending on the season, with fresh or canned tomatoes (SEE TOMATO SAUCE, PAGE 70). Use a charlotte mold with a 1-liter (4-cup) capacity, buttered with 15 grams (1/2 ounce, 1 tablespoon) of butter. *Time: 1 hour. Serves 6.*

175 grams (6 ounces) of medium-size macaroni; 80 grams (about 2 3/4 ounces) of nice, lean, cooked ham cut into small dice; 70 grams (2 1/2 ounces) of grated Gruyère; 2 eggs.

For the béchamel of the liaison: **30 grams (1 ounce) of onion cut into fine rounds, braised in 15 grams (1/2 ounce, 1 tablespoon) of butter; 3 1/2 deciliters (1 1/2 cups) of boiled milk; 1 sprig of parsley, 1 sprig of thyme, salt, pepper, and nutmeg; 18–20 grams (about 2/3 ounce) of flour and the same amount of butter for a white roux; 4 deciliters (1 2/3 cups) of tomato sauce.**

PROCEDURE. **The sauce:** Start cooking it, following the second procedure described (SEE BÉCHAMEL SAUCE, PAGE 52), which will simplify the steps (braising the onions and the preliminary infusion of the milk, which is used to dilute the white roux). Cover and allow it to simmer *very* gently while you prepare the next dishes. Just before draining the macaroni after cooking, add the grated cheese to the sauce.

The macaroni: Break it into as many small pieces as possible, which is essential if the loaf is to be solid. (For home cooking, it is more practical to do this before rather than after cooking the macaroni.) Cook it as directed in boiling salted water: *20 minutes* should suffice. Then drain it thoroughly; any remaining liquid will make the loaf less solid. Proceed quickly so that it does not cool down at all.

Put it back into the dried pot. *Off the heat,* first mix in the cheese sauce. Then gradually add the 2 eggs, previously beaten in a bowl (just as for an omelet, which means not too much, so that you do not make a foam). At the same time, add the diced ham. Taste it to check the salt note, which will depend on the cheeses and the ham you have used.

Pour it into the buttered mold. Poach it in an oven in a bain-marie (see page 42); allow *20 minutes of poaching.* The loaf must be firm enough to the touch when you press it lightly; it will gain very little volume while cooking. Take it out of its bain-marie. Put it in a very moderate oven, where it can be kept warm but without cooking further; leave it here for at least *15 minutes.* This rest is absolutely essential to give the loaf time to compact lightly and thus become completely solid; it will then unmold easily and neatly.

To serve: Unmold the loaf on a warmed round plate. Cover it or surround it with sauce, or you can serve the sauce in a sauceboat.

NOODLES
Nouilles

All the recipes for macaroni are applicable. Fresh noodles must be seasoned as soon as they have finished cooking, because they are much better this way. Note an Alsatian custom, which is to reserve a small quantity of *uncooked* noodles and brown them with a little bit of butter in a pan; when they are golden and crisp, spread them out, just before serving, on the prepared noodles.

Noodle Dough *(La Pâte à Nouilles)*

The quantity of eggs in noodle dough is extremely variable, as is the quantity of whites and yolks: the quality of noodles varies according to whether or not you use only yolks, or whole eggs and yolks, or only whole eggs. What remains the same regardless of the division of the eggs is the method of preparing the dough and cutting the noodles.

Noodle dough, like the *pâte à foncer* that is used for tarts, must have lost all its elasticity before it is cut. So whenever possible, prepare it several hours in advance, and even the evening before. If you are in a hurry, the shortest time it should be left for is 1 hour; but it is worth knowing that dough that has rested for a long time can subsequently be worked much better and procure particularly satisfying results. *Time: 3 hours. Serves 6.*

200 grams (7 ounces) of flour; 2 whole eggs and 1 yolk; 5 grams ($^1/_6$ ounce) of salt.

It is difficult to be exact about the ratio of egg to flour that should be used. Alsatian housewives first beat their eggs in a terrine, using 1 whole egg per person; then they add the flour a tablespoon at a time, stirring it and beating it "until it can no longer be stirred," as a family notebook of Alsatian recipes recommends. This indicates that the dough must be quite firm; and indeed, this is the principle followed by the most precise culinary authors. which explains the quantities they suggest. But this consistency is not achievable with the quantities suggested, because it depends as much on the size of the eggs as on the quality of the flour, which will absorb more or less egg or liquid. Indeed, 450 grams (1 pound) of very finely milled, good-quality wheat flour can absorb 1 deciliter ($3^1/_3$ fluid ounces/scant $^1/_2$ cup) of water more than 450 grams (1 pound) of ordinary flour. If the dough seems too moist, you can add a few pinches of flour, or, if it is too dry, a diluted egg yolk; or a whole beaten egg; or, if necessary, 1 tablespoon or more of water; add this liquid toward the end of the kneading, before all of the flour has been amalgamated, in the same way as for other doughs.

PROCEDURE. **The dough:** Sift the flour onto the table or the board. Make a well out of it. Add the salt with 1 tablespoon of water. With the ends of your fingers, mix and melt in this salt. Then break the eggs into the well. Begin by mixing the eggs with this little bit of liquid, always using just the ends of your fingers. Next, draw the flour into the well to incorporate it with the eggs, in the same way used for *pâte à foncer* (SEE PASTRY DOUGH, PAGE 662). Before you have finished mixing, check to see if more egg is needed—or, on the contrary, more flour. Once everything has been thoroughly mixed, knead the dough, by pushing it out (French *fraiser*) twice. Roll it into a ball. Wrap it in a kitchen towel and let it rest somewhere cool, for as long as possible, as we have already said.

The noodles: Divide the dough into 4 equal parts: this makes cutting the noodles easier. Then roll each part into a ball, but above all *without working it too much,* so that you do not give it any elasticity; using a rolling pin, roll out, that is, extend each ball into a sheet of dough as *thin* as possible. It should be as thin as paper, and these sheets should be completely even over the whole extent of the sheet of dough, with edges that are as straight as possible. While you are working the dough with the rolling pin, very lightly sprinkle the dough and the table with flour, using just the amount strictly necessary so that the dough does not stick to the table or to the rolling pin.

You can proceed immediately to cutting the noodles. That said, if you do have the time, it is a good idea to allow the sheets of dough to dry out for a good half hour so that they come to room temperature. You can either let them lie extended on the table; or, which is more convenient, hang them over a string, exactly as if drying out laundry.

To cut the noodles, roll each sheet on itself as if it were a sheet of paper. If the sheets have not been previously dried out, sprinkle the sheet with very, very little flour. With a kitchen knife that has a large and sharp blade, cut these rolls of dough crosswise into pieces 3–4 millimeters ($^1/_8$ inch) wide. If you want very fine noodles, these can be cut into strips only 2 millimeters ($^1/_{16}$ inch) wide.

Once this is done, use the tips of your fingers to pick up the pieces that you have cut so that you can unroll them. These thin ribbons of dough are the noodles. Spread them out on a baking sheet covered with parchment paper and let them dry for *1 hour.*

Cooking fresh noodles: Put them into a pot of boiling water salted at the rate of 7 grams ($^1/_4$ ounce) per liter, scattering them and stirring them with a fork to thoroughly separate them from each other. Make sure that they do not stick together while boiling. As soon as the boiling resumes, boil for *5 minutes,* no more. Drain thoroughly, then use immediately for your chosen recipe.

In Alsace, once the noodles have been cooked in boiling water, they are immediately put into a strainer and plunged into a terrine of warm water to rinse them. After this, they are drained and immediately prepared.

Noodles à la Crème *(Nouilles à la Crème).* Once the noodles have been drained, put them into a sauté pan. Season with salt, pepper, and nutmeg. Add, for the quantities above, 2 deciliters (6 3/4 fluid ounces, 7/8 cup) of thick crème fraîche. Boil it for only a few seconds while stirring. Off the heat, mix in 30 grams (1 ounce, 2 tablespoons) of butter divided into small pieces. Serve on a heated plate.

SPAGHETTI
Spaghetti

Cook and prepare in the same way as macaroni.

GNOCCHI
Gnocchis

This is good for meat-free meals and times when there are no fresh vegetables available. Gnocchi are a kind of dough dumpling, its ingredients and preparation being exactly the same as for a choux pastry dough *(pâte à choux)* with grated cheese added, and in which milk replaces the water. Use either Gruyère or Parmesan, depending on taste and availability.

You can serve gnocchi several ways. The simplest, once they are poached and drained, is to place them in layers on a buttered plate or in a shallow serving dish, and sprinkle with cheese and melted butter, then slowly color them in the oven for about 10 minutes.

Or, which is a much easier way, cover them with a lean béchamel sauce and gently brown in the oven. We describe this below. A variation is to use a shallow pastry shell as a receptacle. This is how you find gnocchi prepared in food stores.

In this case, make the shell in the same way as a strawberry tart (SEE PAGE 677). For the quantities of gnocchi given below, make a shell 22 centimeters (8 1/2 inches) in diameter and about 5 centimeters (2 inches) high. You can use a "génoise" mold or straight-sided cake pan to mold it. You can prepare the dough for this the evening before, and for even greater convenience, cook the shell in advance.

As for all pastry dough, the size of the eggs used for gnocchi determines the weight of flour used. To work out the number of eggs, assume you will use medium-size eggs that weigh about 50 grams (1 3/4 ounces) each. You should therefore allow 1 egg for each 30–40 grams (1–1 3/8 ounces) of flour. Gnocchi are naturally lighter and more tender and swell better when there is a substantial proportion of egg in the dough, that is, when you can allow a scant 100 grams (3 1/2 ounces) of flour for 3 eggs instead of 125 grams (4 1/2 ounces).

A particularly good recommendation: serve the gnocchi as soon as they come out of the oven and at the exact moment when they are properly cooked. If they stand for too long, they will dry out and flatten. *Time: 25–40 minutes. Serves 6.*

2 1/2 deciliters (1 cup) of boiled milk; 50 grams (1 3/4 ounces, 3 1/2 tablespoons) of butter; 125 grams (4 1/2 ounces) of flour; 3 eggs; 60 grams (2 1/4 ounces) of grated cheese; salt, pepper, nutmeg.

PROCEDURE. For details of how to prepare the dough, SEE PÂTE À CHOUX (PAGE 664). When it is finished, mix in the grated cheese, a pinch of pepper, and a pinch of grated nutmeg.

Meanwhile, put the water for cooking or poaching the gnocchi on the heat to boil. An appropriate utensil is a shallow pot or sauté pan: it is not the depth of the liquid that is important here, but rather its surface area, so that the gnocchi are not crammed up against one another. They cook better this way and their development is not impeded; you must expect them to double their volume with the action of the heat. Depending on the quantity of dough, you can poach them in 1 or 2 batches. Salt the water at a rate of 10 grams (1/3 ounce) per liter (4 1/4 cups).

To shape the gnocchis: You can proceed in one of three ways.

First method. Put the dough into a pastry bag with a $1^1/_2$-centimeter ($^5/_8$-inch) tip (SEE PASTRY BAG, PAGE 15). Hold it over the pan of boiling water and squeeze out a little piece 3 centimeters ($1^1/_4$ inches) long. Then, with a little knife, cut it off at the level of the nozzle to make it fall into the water. Continue until you have used up all the dough.

Second method. With a small spoon, scoop out the dough in pieces the size of a small chestnut; drop it into the water using a second small spoon to detach it from the first, dipping the spoon each time into water, or use the end of your finger.

Third method. Put the dough onto a pastry board that has been very lightly floured. Divide it, depending on the quantity, into 2 or 3 parts. Roll out each part under the palm of your floured hand, to make a long sausage that is about as thick as a finger; using a knife, which you should dip into water to avoid strings, divide the dough sausage into pieces 3 centimeters ($1^1/_4$ inches) long. Put them together on a plate or on an overturned pot cover, from which you will slide them all at once into the boiling water.

Poaching: Once all the gnocchi are in the water, bring it back to a boil. As soon as the boiling has resumed, turn the heat down very low so that you maintain a gentle simmer, as for all poaching. Cover the pan.

For poaching, allow *8–10 minutes.* This is enough to make them swell, and they will float back up to the surface. Take them out of the water with a skimmer and put them on a large drum sieve *one next to the other,* or on a clean kitchen towel that has been folded in half. While they drain, if you are working in batches, poach the rest of the gnocchi in the water, which has been brought back to boiling.

Once the gnocchi have been well drained, they are ready to be used for any recipe.

PRINCIPAL RECIPES

Gnocchi au Gratin *(Gnocchis au Gratin).* For the quantity above, allow about 4 deciliters ($1^2/_3$ cups) of sauce, and for this you should refer to béchamel sauce (SEE PAGE 52), following the second method. Thus: a small mirepoix braised in 20 grams ($^2/_3$ ounce, 1 heaping tablespoon) of butter; 4 deciliters ($1^2/_3$ cups) of boiled milk; 25 grams (1 ounce, 2 tablespoons) of butter and the same amount of flour for a white *roux;* plus 40 grams ($1^3/_8$ ounces) of grated Gruyère. In the bottom of a gratin dish, spread out a few tablespoons of sauce. On top of that, place a layer of well-drained gnocchi. Cover them with half of the sauce, a tablespoon at a time, and sprinkle this with half of the cheese. Then make a second layer of gnocchi, sauce, and cheese.

Put it in a moderate oven to first give the gnocchi time to swell again before the surface of the dish has colored. At the very last moment, bring the plate up to the top of the oven, or slide it underneath a broiler to color it. Allow *15 minutes* for the gnocchi to swell and color. Serve immediately, with the oven dish placed on a serving plate that has been covered with a napkin.

Semolina Gnocchi or Roman-Style Gnocchi *(Gnocchis de Semoule ou Gnocchis à la Romaine).* *Time: 1 hour, 30 minutes. Serves 6.*

100 grams ($3^1/_2$ ounces) of white semolina; 50 grams ($1^3/_4$ ounces) of Gruyère and the same of Parmesan, grated; 100 grams ($3^1/_2$ ounces, 7 tablespoons) of butter; 4 scant deciliters ($1^2/_3$ cups) of milk; 2 small raw egg yolks; a good pinch of salt, a pinch of white pepper, and a pinch of grated nutmeg.

PROCEDURE. In a saucepan with the milk, which has been seasoned with salt, pepper, and nutmeg and kept at a gentle simmer, pour in the semolina in a shower of grains. Mix for an instant; add a piece of butter the size of a walnut; cover the pan; put it into a moderate oven. Allow *10–15 minutes* at a gentle and uninterrupted boil, depending on the quality of the semolina. It should have absorbed all the milk and be perfectly swollen.

Take the pan out of the oven; break up the semolina with a fork. Mix in the egg yolks and 1 good tablespoon of grated cheese. Pour the semolina onto a baking sheet moistened with water and then spread it out into an even layer about 1 centimeter ($^3/_8$ inch) thick; smooth out this surface with the blade of a knife. *Allow it to completely cool;* if not, shaping the gnocchi will be impossible.

Turn over the baking sheet of semolina onto a towel spread out on the table. Cut the gnocchi into rounds with a pastry cutter, or divide the semolina block into strips with your knife, then divide these further into squares or rectangles 4–5 centimeters ($1^{1}/_{2}$–2 inches).

Arrange the gnocchi side by side on a gratin plate, which has been well buttered and sprinkled with grated cheese. They should not touch each other; this is so that they stay intact when they brown in the oven.

Sprinkle with grated cheese and moisten with the rest of the butter, which should first be melted. Put into a good, strong, moderate oven, so that you can both reheat the gnocchi and help form the gratin: *about 10 minutes.*

DESSERTS

Here we first provide all the information for preparing the different elements that can be used in desserts, as well as some details common to several recipes.

Almonds *(Amandes)*

To husk almonds: This consists in removing the skin or yellowish covering from the almonds.

Boil water in a saucepan. When the water is fully boiling, throw the almonds into it and *immediately* turn off the heat: the almonds must not boil. Mix them well in the water. Cover the saucepan and let them soak for *3–4 minutes* at the most. This should be enough time so that when you pick up an almond between your thumb and index finger, the almond easily slides out of its skin.

Pour them into a colander with large holes, then plunge them into cold water. Next, take them one by one between your thumb and index finger, with the index finger on the bottom, and place the almond on the table. Then press on the top with your thumb, at the same time pulling it back; this movement pushes the almond forward out of its skin. *For speed, professionals do this with both hands at the same time.*

Again, wash the almonds in fresh water. Drain them on a clean towel. Whatever they are going to be used for, they must always be well dried.

Sliced almonds: Once the almonds have been husked, wipe them off. Separate them into two halves. Place them on a table, with the inside part facing down. With a good knife, cut each half lengthwise into 7 or 8 slices.

Toasted almonds: Having been husked, spread whole almonds out on a clean baking sheet. Put it in a very mild oven to first dry them out. Then turn the oven up. Make sure that the almonds do not go beyond an even, light blond tint. Shake them frequently to move them around so that some parts do not color too much. When they are done, keep them dry until using.

Raisins *(Raisins Secs)*

Removing the stems: *Smyrna and Corinth.* Instead of removing the stems by taking off the raisins one by one, which takes forever, proceed as follows: sprinkle the corner of a kitchen towel with 1 tablespoon of flour; enclose the raisins in it by pulling the towel with your left hand into a pouch that is large enough so that you can, with your right hand, mix and rub this pouch, making the raisins in it move around under your fingers; the stems will thus come off all by themselves. Shake the raisins in a strainer with large holes and the stems will then fall out through them; if they are not all completely detached, simply rub the raisins for a few more moments between your hands with a little bit of flour. Then carefully examine them to see if there are any stems or small stones left, which are often mixed in with Corinth raisins. Finally, wash the raisins in lukewarm water. Drain them on a towel or leave them to swell, depending on how they will be used.

Málaga. Separate the berries; detach the stems with your fingers. Split the raisins with the point of a small knife to extract the seeds from them.

To swell them: Put the raisins into a small saucepan with water or wine and sugar. Gently simmer them in this syrup for *about 20 minutes,* tossing them from time to time.

Semolina Sugar (Superfine Sugar) *(Sucre Semoule)*

In professional language, and to differentiate it from glaze sugar, this sugar is commonly known and sold as superfine or caster sugar. Alternatively, you can obtain it by crushing loaf sugar, or if you do not have that, sugar cubes, crushing them on the table with a rolling pin. The resultant powder is then passed through a simple drum sieve.

Confectioners' or Powdered Sugar *(Sucre Glace ou Glace de Sucre)*

This is also powdered sugar, but its texture differs from superfine sugar. Superfine, or semolina, sugar looks like fine salt—that is, it comes in tiny grains, which explains its name—while glaze sugar looks like arrowroot powder or other starch. It is produced in a special sieve. You can find glaze sugar in all good food markets, because it is always used in pastry making and for making deserts.

Powdered Sugar Shaker or Confectioners' Sugar Shaker *(Glacière)*

This is a round container made out of metal with a cover pierced with holes. It is used to hold confectioner's sugar, which you sprinkle over fritters, crêpes, and a number of pastries. If you do not have this accessory, you can improvise with a small paper box, piercing holes in one of its sides. Note that you cannot cover foods with a light and even layer of sugar by using your fingers to sprinkle it. We would also like to make the point that *confectioners'* sugar should be used for this special powdering; ordinary crushed sugar, or superfine sugar, makes a poor substitute, particularly when glazing desserts and pastries in the oven.

Zest Sugar *(Sucre Zesté)*

Sugar with an orange or a lemon flavor—known in professional cooking as "zest sugar"—offers the capital advantage of communicating a flavor to the dish that you cannot get by cooking the peel in the preparation: it is a fact that boiling partly destroys the flavor of zest. Also, zest sugar is added at the last moment to the dish: as is done, for example, with liqueurs, where boiling would spoil the flavor.

Make zest sugar by using the sugar like a grater, rubbing the lemon or orange until the sugar has taken on a substantial yellowish color, which indicates that it has absorbed the zest's essence, while the fruit will be discolored where it was rubbed. Do not rub always in the same place; you do not want to completely expose the white interior skin, which is very bitter.

When you have sugar in big lumps, use a piece the size of a pigeon egg to rub on the peel. Once the sugar is well colored and humidified, use a little knife to scrape off the sugar that has been colored with the zest onto a plate. If you do not have loaf sugar, use ordinary sugar cubes, as large as possible, which will make the work easier.

Orange and Lemon Zest *(Zeste d'Orange et de Citron)*

Strictly speaking, the zest, or the exterior peel of the fruit, includes only the *colored* part of the rind: this holds the most flavor. On the other hand, the white skin that sticks to this colored part known as the zest must be carefully eliminated, because it communicates an unpleasant bitterness to any ingredient with which it comes into contact.

It is therefore essential, every time that the zest of either an orange or lemon is required, to remove the colored part in such a way that no fragment or bit of white skin remains. For this, you need to use a small knife with a very sharp blade, which cuts almost like a razor, so that you can remove the colored surface of the skin by, in effect, shaving it. Do not work in a spiral, but from one end to the other, so that you obtain ribbons about 7–8 centimeters (2¾–3¼ inches) long; their width will come from one stroke of the knife, applied evenly to the rounded surface without cutting into the interior. This is very simple, but it does require some care. Make sure you use oranges with a thick skin. Not only is the work made easier, but the zest is more highly perfumed.

Powdered Vanilla and Vanilla Sugar *(Vanille en Poudre et Sucre Vanillé)*

The following procedure is used by professionals, because they do not use products sold in little jars. It is very simple if you have a marble mortar.

For 1 vanilla bean, put 30 grams (1 ounce) of sugar *cubes* into the mortar. With good scissors, cut the vanilla bean into extremely small pieces, scarcely 1 millimeter thick, if possible. Do this right over the mortar itself, since the inside material escapes from the bean like grains of powder. Once all the pieces of bean interior and exterior have been mixed with the sugar, crush everything with a good wooden pestle. After about 10 minutes, pass the powder through a horsehair drum sieve onto a sheet of paper. Put the pieces remaining on the drum sieve back into the mortar; add the same quantity of sugar and begin the same work again.

You can begin again a third time, but passing it through the drum sieve will not be necessary, because the powder will be sufficiently fine. Keep it in a tightly closed container.

If you want vanilla sugar rather than vanilla powder, simply increase the amount of sugar: that is, 150 grams ($5^1/_3$ ounces) of sugar in cubes for 1 nice vanilla bean.

The Grain of Salt *(Le Grain de Sel)*

Salt is an obligatory ingredient in a number of sugared preparations, but in a very minimal quantity. It is to describe this minimal quantity that the term "grain of salt" was used by earlier professionals, as well as by modern ones. You can allow 2 grams ($^1/_{14}$ ounce) of fine salt for this quantity.

Cartridge Mold or Cylindrical Mold (Moule à Douille ou à Cylindre)

People unfamiliar with culinary terms do not know what this utensil is. It is a mold in circular or cylindrical form—hence the name—which is pierced in its center by a tube, such as is shown in the figure on PAGE 576.

Used for poaching in a *bain-marie,* the water penetrates the central cylinder; the composition in the mold is thus heated on all sides, and it sets more evenly, and also more rapidly, given that its thickness is less than in a full mold. The same effect is true if you are using this mold to set a cold composition, because the ice, or simply a cool ambient temperature, works more easily on the whole composition.

According to the uses for which they are destined, cylindrical molds are tall or short, fluted or plain—as the model in the drawing.

To mold a composition: After filling a mold, it is a good idea to strike the bottom of it on the table to help pack down the contents. First put a napkin, folded into quarters, on the table, to soften the shock. The mold must be struck very gently: you simply want to compress the contents a little bit, instead of pressing down on the top with a spoon, which would be detrimental to its lightness.

To unmold a dessert: The procedures vary with the nature of the composition. For a cream base, it is generally enough to detach the sides of the mold with the point of a small knife so that everything comes out of the mold.

In the situation where you must first dip the mold in warm water, proceed as follows: in a terrine large enough that the mold can be completely bathed in it, pour in some good hot water, just to the point where you can stick your hand in it without burning yourself. Holding the mold at a slight angle, plunge the mold completely into the water and then pull it out immediately; that is, you simply dip it, for no longer than the time needed for the "in and out" without haste.

In other cases, when a composition has been put in a closed mold to solidify in salted ice, first wash the mold in cool water and then proceed as directed in the chapter on frozen desserts (SEE PAGE 649).

To unmold, put a plate, with or without a napkin, on top of the mold. Hold both of them firmly in your two hands and then turn the mold and plate upside down.

To caramelize a mold: The first condition to note is that you must use a mold with a bottom that is sufficiently thick and perfectly flat, without any dents produced by impacts or otherwise. With a mold that has indentation, the sugar will burn in the indented parts, and stick without melting to the raised parts, which receive less heat. This way, the caramel turns granular and becomes an uneven and nasty color.

For a charlotte mold with a capacity of about 1 liter ($4^1/_4$ cups), allow 100 grams ($3^1/_2$ ounces) of superfine sugar. Make sure that the mold is perfectly clean; put in the sugar without any water. Place the mold on low heat. Have a towel ready so that you can handle the mold without burning yourself, and also a large receptacle containing cold water, in which you can, if necessary, put the mold.

Do not leave the mold for an instant. Watch over the melting sugar carefully; if it is happening on one side only, tip the mold to make the sugar slide over and thus reestablish the equilibrium. In this way, you ensure an even coloring on the dessert. The sugar must not go beyond a nice golden tint, and the cooking must not reach the point where bluish smoke comes off the sugar, which indicates that the caramel is burning; this gives it a very unpleasant, bitter taste. At the slightest sign of this, rapidly plunge the bottom of the mold into the cool water to stop the caramel cooking.

Once the sugar has reached its proper color, turn off the heat and tilt the mold, rolling it around between the fingers of your two hands to make the caramel on the bottom run onto the sides, right up to the top. Thus all the inside will appear to be covered with a layer of transparent enamel like a piece of enameled jewelry or vermeil. When cooling, numerous cracks will be produced. These are inevitable and unimportant.

Lining a Charlotte Mold with Ladyfingers

The mold: Whenever possible, use a mold with sides that are almost straight, because lining it with ladyfingers is much easier than when using a mold that is flared on the top. In a flared mold, the biscuits will not stick together perfectly, and you will have to slide little pieces of ladyfinger between the spaces to fill them in.

Charlotte molds or timbale molds made of tin-lined copper tend to be the right shape, while the earlier molds made of tin-lined steel, which were once used for rice cakes, are too flared on the top and too narrow at the bottom (see *fig.* 68, below).

Cut a circle of white parchment paper that exactly covers the bottom of the mold but that you can remove without difficulty. (Place the mold on a sheet of white parchment paper. Trace completely around it with a pencil; and cut it out with scissors.) Place it in the bottom of the mold just as it is, without buttering it or oiling it. Then cut a band of paper with straight sides the height of the sides of the mold, and long enough to go completely around it, then put it inside the mold. This lining of paper makes unmolding much easier.

FIG. 68. VARIETIES OF MOLDS FOR DESSERTS OR PASTRIES.

The ladyfingers: Use a kitchen knife of good medium size; a knife that is too small will ruin the ladyfingers.

Begin by lining the bottom with 3–4 ladyfingers. *Square them* first—that is, use your knife to slice off the edges on both sides so that you can push them close together, one against the other, without leaving any space between them: this is because ladyfingers are always more or less irregular on their edges. It is these thin edges that you should cut off with one slice of the knife.

Then align them, closely packed together, on their rounded side. Place the bottom of the mold on top of them and then, using the point of a knife held a little bit on the bias reaching underneath the bottom of the mold, cleanly cut off any part of the biscuits wider than the mold. Then line the inside of the mold with the biscuits you have cut, in the exact order you had them on the table, with the rounded side touching the side of the mold. Be sure to keep them tightly together.

For the ladyfingers used to line the sides of the mold, begin by trimming the round end of one of the biscuits. You will use it as a measure. Put it standing up in the mold, with the cut end at the bottom; then cut off the part that is higher than the edges, right at the level of the mold. Cut all the biscuits to the same length. After this, square them off, as explained, so that all the biscuits are completely straight and equal, like little sticks. Line them up one next to the other on the table to check that they fit tightly together exactly, without any space between them. Once this is done, stand them up in the mold, with the rounded side touching the parchment paper lining the side of the mold.

Put the trimmings of the ladyfingers aside: you might use them later, depending on the way you decorate the charlotte.

To Core Apples

It is impossible to cleanly core an apple using only the point of a small knife. A little tube of tinned steel, known as an "apple corer," is essential. Its diameter at the cutting opening is about 1 centimeter (3/8 inch), 12 millimeters (1/2 inch) at the most. *Do not peel the apples before coring them;* the skin supports the pulp and prevents it from bursting, which is a risk even when you are careful.

So, with great care, force the tube into the apple from the side of the stem, which should be right in the middle of the tube; hold the tube completely straight. Turn it lightly, which will help it move through the pulp, and stop when you get halfway through the apple. Take it out, pulling it out backward, and then force it into the opposite side so that it meets up with the place already pierced. Push the corer right through the apple, then pull it back; you will thus remove the entire interior of the apple contained by the tube.

By working on both sides of the apple, you are much less likely to break it than if you try to go through the entire apple in one motion.

The Ribbon

"Make the ribbon" is a professional term that indicates the degree of consistency of a batter or, indeed, any composition that has been thoroughly worked. To check this degree, raise a spoonful of batter above the receptacle: it must detach slowly from the spoon in an uninterrupted flow, thus forming a cord, or "ribbon," of batter. At the same time, batter containing egg yolks should have paled considerably and taken on a very light pale, straw yellow.

This result is reached only after working the batter vigorously and for quite some time. Unless worked thoroughly, the batter will be dense and heavy.

Cooking Sugar

Authors have not even so much as dreamed of agreeing to set uniform terms to define the successive phases, or degrees, of cooking sugar. We will thus use the terms that are most often in use today to determine these degrees.

Sugar in lumps, which have been mechanically sawed, must not be used for cooking because it tends to form grains or even decompose; this is because the mechanical saw is greased, and even an infinitesimal amount of grease causes the decomposition of the sugar. So instead of melting to a liquid at the beginning of cooking, it will coagulate into grainy opaque clumps like candy. In other words, you are taking a risk cooking with sugar that has had any contact with grease.

If you do not have a sugar loaf, which can be broken by hand but which is not sold much anymore in stores, use granulated sugar, as white as you can possibly obtain.

When first melting sugar for cooking, add just enough water to thoroughly wet it and thus ensure that it melts. If too much liquid is used, the cooking time will have to be prolonged so that the water can evaporate, and the syrup's degree of density will thus be compromised. Allow *approximately 1–2 deciliters (3 1/3–6 3/4 fluid ounces, 1/2–7/8 cup) of water per pound of sugar to be dissolved.*

For cooking sugar, use either a copper utensil that is not lined in tin or another pot, depending on availability. Do not use a utensil made of steel, tin, or cast iron, all of which are metals that should not come into contact with sugar while it is being cooked.

PROCEDURE. In your chosen utensil, put the sugar with the water. Let it melt on very gentle heat, taking care to mix the sugar from time to time with a silver spoon or a copper skimmer to ensure that it melts.

Once the sugar has completely melted, put the utensil on rather strong heat. Do not cover it. If you are working with an ordinary saucepan and on a gas flame, make sure that the flame does not go beyond the bottom of the saucepan and touch the sides: if you heat these sides too strongly, the sugar that splashes there in little drops from the boiling liquid will tint the syrup and give it a taste of caramel.

Boil without touching the sugar. As soon as the boiling is pronounced, remove the foam from the surface with a skimmer or silver spoon. Then, using a completely clean towel, which you moisten and rinse in cool water as you go, clean the inside surface of the utensil all around, to remove the scum that is left there by the foam, which would cause the decomposition of the sugar.

Small thread. Take a little bit of syrup between your thumb and index finger and then separate your two fingers a little bit. The sugar will form a small, viscous thread that lacks consistency.

Large thread. The threads formed between the fingers are very sticky and more resistant.

The soufflé. Dip the skimmer into the syrup, then immediately bring it up to your face and blow through the holes: on the other side, small, light bubbles will emerge like soap bubbles.

From this point on, always protect yourself by immersing your fingers in cold water before testing for the different stages, which will follow closer together. Have at hand a bowl of cold water: dip your index finger into it, then immediately dip it into the syrup, and immediately afterward dip it back again into the water.

Small ball. The syrup taken on the end of your finger forms a sort of glue, which you can roll into a soft ball.

Large ball. The ball is firmer. But if you bite into it, it sticks there like a soft glue and stretches like rubber.

Small crack. The syrup comes away from your finger when you dip it in water, like a skin; if you bite it, it will stick, but less so.

Large crack. Only a few seconds separate this from the previous stage. The skin formed by the syrup on the end of the finger is transparent but not colored; it is much more resistant and it will break under the tooth like caramel.

The syrup must immediately be taken off the heat, because it continues to cook even off the heat. You can keep it warm so that it maintains the same consistency while being used.

The Saccharometer

Its use is limited to syrups that do not have a high density. We will nonetheless suggest how to use it: pour the boiling liquid into a small container with a wide opening, deep enough so that the instrument can float there easily. Put it in there and leave it alone without holding it in any way. The number on the saccharometer right at the level of the liquid will indicate the degree of density. Remember that as the syrup cools, it will increase by one or two degrees of density for each ten-degree drop (on the Celsius scale).

CUSTARDS
Crèmes

Pots de Crème *(Crèmes en Petits Pots)*

These kind of creams can only, of course, be cooked in the same receptacles used to serve them, the consistency being completely different from crème anglaise (custard sauce). As well as using little pots, you can use small porcelain dishes. The same composition of cream can also be cooked and served in one large bowl.

1 liter (4¹/₄ cups) of milk; 7 egg yolks and 3 whole eggs (10 yolks total), 250–300 grams (8⁷/₈–10¹/₂ ounces) of sugar (depending on the cream's flavor, the quantity of sugar will vary). Thus *for each 1 deciliter (3¹/₃ fluid ounces, scant ¹/₂ cup) of milk:* 1 yolk, ¹/₃ of an egg white, and about 25 grams (1 ounce) of sugar.

Use these quantities to establish the amount of each ingredient needed for making all the custards. The difficulty is always when you want to prepare a pre-established number of pots and do not know how much cream will be required to fill them, but nonetheless have to mix together the milk, the eggs, and the sugar. So let us note that for *1 liter (4¹/₄ cups) of cream you will need:* 6¹/₄ deciliters (2²/₃ cups) of boiled milk; 150 grams (5¹/₃ ounces) of sugar; 4 yolks and 2 complete eggs (6 yolks and 2 egg whites).

To calculate the quantity of each ingredient, you should remember, particularly when making small quantities of cream, to always allow a little bit more because of the relatively significant waste that results from transferring ingredients from one terrine to another. Another thing: the size of the eggs should always be taken into considera tion, because the cream's ultimate success depends on using the correct proportion of eggs. You should also note the rule of putting "a grain of salt" into each cream: this is always suggested by Carême, and is similarly followed by all modern professionals.

The milk: If you do not have very good milk, you can enhance its quality by reducing it by a good third: That is, for the 5 deciliters (generous 2 cups) you will need, you should use 8 deciliters (3³/₈ cups). After having boiled it, let it reduce at a very gentle simmer until it is down to just the 5 deciliters (generous 2 cups) that you require.

The sugar: You can buy it in cubes, in powdered form known as as superfine (or caster) sugar, or granulated. The essential point is that it should be perfectly dissolved in the boiled milk before mixing into the eggs. One deciliter (3¹/₃ fluid ounces, scant ¹/₂ cup) of superfine sugar or granulated sugar weighs 90 grams (3¹/₆ ounces). This information allows you to replace quantities given in volume with quantities given in weight.

The flavor: There are two ways to flavor custards: by infusion or using liquid. Vanilla, lemon, orange, and almond, and even in some cases coffee, are flavors produced by infusion, adding the ingredients to the already reduced milk: that is, a half bean of vanilla for each ¹/₂ liter (generous 2 cups) of milk; or 2 ribbons of lemon or orange zest (SEE ORANGE AND LEMON ZEST, PAGE 574). Put the vanilla or the zest into *boiling milk.* Cover *tightly* and keep it hot but not boiling. Allow it to infuse for *a brief 15 minutes.*

Coffee, tea, caramel, and chocolate are the liquid flavors, and are not put into the boiling milk until it is mixed with the eggs.

Coffee: There are several ways of using it, and here are the two most popular.

First: Add some very dark, strong coffee to the boiled milk. Thus, 1 deciliter (3¹/₃ fluid ounces, scant ¹/₂ cup) of coffee for ¹/₂ liter (generous 2 cups) of flavored milk: that is, for 4 deciliters (1²/₃ cups) of boiled milk, you add 1 deciliter (3¹/₃ fluid ounces, scant ¹/₂ cup) of coffee. To make 1 deciliter (3¹/₃ fluid ounces, scant ¹/₂ cup) of coffee, use 25 grams (1 ounce) of freshly ground coffee and 1¹/₂ deciliters (5 fluid ounces, ²/₃ cup) of boiling water, allowing for the quantity of water that will absorbed by the ground coffee. If you want to darken the color a little bit, you can add some chicory: use a very small teaspoon for these quantities.

Second: Infuse *with whole coffee beans,* not ground, in boiling milk, as you would with vanilla or zest. The flavor is much finer, not marred by the particular bitterness of strong coffee; and all the strength of the milk is preserved, since it is not diluted by the water in the coffee. For these reasons, this method is preferable to the first; it is also recommended by the great chefs, both ancient and modern. But the weight of whole beans is higher than the weight of ground coffee beans. For *1/2 liter (generous 2 cups) of milk, you should allow 70 grams (2 1/2 ounces) of coffee beans,* roasting them until the beans begin to sweat. Then throw them into the *boiling* milk. Cover it and then let them infuse on very low heat but without any boiling for *half hour.* Pour it through a chinois or fine strainer.

If you have only coffee beans that have already been roasted, spread the beans out on a baking sheet to heat them in a moderate oven: a few minutes will be enough to start them sweating, and it is this oil that gives so much flavor to the infusion; infuse them in the same way. In both cases, coffee beans that have been infused no longer have any flavor, rather like an old crust of bread, and are not really good for anything except to throw away: they have released absolutely all their flavor.

The color of a cream made with coffee with the beans is paler than a cream made with liquid coffee. If you want to darken it, add a little bit of chicory, the taste being absolutely imperceptible: thus, scarcely 5 grams (1/6 ounce) of chicory for the quantities above. Or you could add little bit of very strong, dark liquid coffee: that is, 1–2 teaspoons prepared as an ordinary black coffee.

Chocolate: Always choose a very fine brand. *Allow 100 grams (3 1/2 ounces) for 1/2 liter (generous 2 cups) of milk.* Grate it or break it into small pieces. Put it into a saucepan with, for these quantities, *2–3 tablespoons* of water; gently melt it *without cooking it* or heating it too much, stirring it frequently with a spoon left in the pan. Once it has been well dissolved, it should form a thick and smooth paste. Dilute this gradually with a good glass of the hot milk, then pour it back into the pot with the remaining milk and mix it with the whisk. Then pour the chocolate milk on the eggs, proceeding as described below.

Caramel: Cook half of the sugar intended for the cream to a caramel; dilute it with a little bit of water and add it to the boiled and sugared milk.

Tea: Add an infusion of very strong tea to the boiled milk. That is, 1 deciliter (3 1/3 fluid ounces, scant 1/2 cup) of infusion added to 4 deciliters (1 2/3 cups) of milk to obtain 1/2 liter (generous 2 cups) of flavored milk.

PROCEDURE. *Time:* 1 scant hour for preparing the creams and then poaching, or cooking, them; 2 1/2 hours to chill the pots.

The cream: Boil the milk. Add the flavor as directed. Add the sugar to the flavored milk. Cover. Keep it warm without allowing it to boil, stirring it from time to time with a metal spoon until the sugar has completely dissolved.

Put the eggs and the yolks into a terrine or salad bowl. Mix everything with a small whisk or a wooden spoon that is very clean and has not been used for other things. Onto these beaten eggs, pour the flavored and sugared milk, adding small quantities at a time and stirring continuously with the whisk or the spoon so that they are well mixed with the liquid. That said, do not whisk it too vigorously, which will only provoke a foam that will then have to be removed; this is a waste that should be avoided.

Dip a fine towel in water and wring it out, then lay it over a strainer with large holes. Place this on top of another utensil: a terrine, or the saucepan used for boiling the milk, which has first been rinsed and dried. Strain the mixture of eggs and milk through it so that the germ from each egg is removed and is thus completely clean.

With a metal spoon, remove every last trace of foam from the surface of the mixture. This foam will not disappear when cooked if you let it remain; in fact, it will set solid on the surface of the cream, which is not very attractive.

To cook or poach: Use a sauté pan or any other utensil with a wide bottom and low sides, large enough to allow the pots to be put in it and not be too squeezed together, so that each one will be completely surrounded by the water. Place the still empty pots in the sauté pan: it is much better than filling them first and then transporting them into the utensil.

With a pointed spoon, fill the pots right up to the edge, because the creams will settle slightly when cooking. Then pour some *absolutely boiling* water into the sauté pan—you can use a funnel—so that it reaches to about two-thirds of the height of the pots.

Put the sauté pan in the oven and *immediately* cover it with a cover that is large enough so that it will be completely sealed. If the pots themselves have covers, do not use them. The cover of the sauté pan is good enough, and these little covers will prolong the cooking, or poaching, time.

It is absolutely essential to cover the sauté pan so that the surface of the cream is protected from a heat that is too strong. This excess heat would set the upper layer of cream too quickly, creating a carpet-like barrier that would stop the heat reaching equally to the bottom of the creams. Also, if the heat of the oven directly strikes the cream, it would create an unpleasant brown skin on the surface. The surface should remain *completely smooth, without any coloring.*

The heat of the oven must be strong enough so that the water is maintained at a degree very close to boiling—that is, as warm as possible, *but without ever boiling.*

This is of paramount importance: if the water begins to boil, the cream will be completely dimpled with little holes; or it will be tough and uneven, with some liquid rising to the surface, which people who have no experience mistakenly believe to be water that has spilled from the bain-marie into the pots, when it is really the result of bad cooking. It is therefore essential to check frequently and not allow the creams to boil. As soon as you notice the water simmering, which is a precursor to boiling, immediately take out a couple of tablespoons of this water and replace them immediately with the same quantity of cold water.

The length of time needed for poaching varies depending on the size of the pots or dishes. For pots with a capacity of *8–9 centiliters (2¾–3 fluid ounces, generous ⅓ cup), it takes 18–20 minutes.* For pots of *1 good deciliter (3⅓ fluid ounces), you can allow 23–25 minutes.* This time is appropriate for an oven with a rather strong heat so that throughout the cooking process the water is maintained *close to* boiling, as we have explained: in a less hot oven, a little more time will, of course, be needed.

Before taking out the sauté pan, check how well the creams are cooked by taking one pot and tipping it to establish how completely its contents have set: it should quiver slightly but remain solid.

Take the pan out of the oven. Leave the pots in it for only a few minutes. Then take them out of the water and let them completely chill, uncovered.

To serve: Thoroughly wipe the pots. Cover them with their little covers. Put them on a plate or on a serving plate, which you can cover with a small napkin to prevent the pots from sliding around while they are being served.

Peruvian Cream *(Crème Péruvienne).* A true family recipe, this is a delicious combination of chocolate, coffee, caramel, and vanilla, whose flavor is reminiscent of certain very fine chocolate bonbons.

Depending on the circumstances, the cream can be poached and served in small dishes, in small bowls, in cream pots, or in little round porcelain utensils. It can also be used as a dessert for lunch or dinner, accompanied by long thin biscuits, or as a delicate sweet at an informal party. *Time: 40 minutes (if prepared at least 4 hours in advance). Serves 6.*

6 deciliters (2½ cups) of milk; 65 grams (2¼ ounces) of whole roasted coffee beans; a quarter vanilla bean; 100 grams (3½ ounces) of chocolate; 90 grams (3⅙ ounces) of superfine or lump sugar; 5 egg yolks and 1 whole egg.

PROCEDURE. Infuse the coffee beans in the boiling milk as indicated on PAGE 579. Add the vanilla.

In a small saucepan, melt the sugar with 2 tablespoons of water. Then turn the heat down very low and cook it until it has reached a *very light* degree of brown caramel. If it browns too much, it will make the whole mixture unbearably bitter. You must then watch it carefully, and as soon as it begins to yellow, turn the heat down so that you do not risk going beyond the right point. As soon as this point is reached, plunge the bottom of the pan into a plate of cold water to stop the cooking. Then add 2–3 tablespoons of hot water; put it back on very gentle heat to dissolve the caramel into a nice smooth syrup, using a spoon. Set it aside.

Break the pieces of chocolate into 4–5 bits. Put them in a bowl just covered with a few tablespoons of the milk infused with coffee. Cover and place it on very gentle heat. When, at the end of a few minutes, the chocolate has softened, work it with the wooden spoon to reduce it to an even, smooth paste.

The cream: Pour the infused milk into a terrine through a strainer. Add the chocolate, lightened and diluted by the milk; then the caramel.

Then mix in the eggs and fill the pots, as described for POTS DE CRÈME (PAGE 580), and then cook in a bain-marie, again as described.

Caramel Custard *(Crème Renversée)*

A caramel custard is one of the most simple custards to make, as long as you are scrupulous about using the exact quantities given. This is more important than for any other kind of custard, because it must have a consistency solid enough to enable it to be unmolded. All the details of preparation, flavors, etc. are the same as for POTS DE CRÈME (SEE PAGE 579). The only difference is that the quantity of egg is greater. For this reason, caramel custards are not as delicate as the pots de crème: too much egg always robs a cream of its finesse, which means that it would be a mistake to try using more eggs than are necessary. *Time: 1 hour, 30 minutes (plus at least 2 hours for chilling the custard). Makes 1 liter (4¼ cups) of cream, enough for 6.*

For each 1 liter (4¼ cups) of milk, use 8 yolks and 4 whole eggs.

5½–5¾ deciliters (2⅓–scant 2½ cups) of boiled milk; 5 egg yolks; 2 very large eggs or 3 small ones; 150 grams (5⅓ ounces) of sugar.

Let us repeat that the size of the eggs is much more important here than for any other cream, because of the degree of solidity that a caramel custard requires.

The mold: It is best to use a cylindrical mold (SEE PAGE 575), which will help with poaching, or cooking, the custard.

We would like to remark again that a mold with a rather low shape would be better than a tall mold for this cream. This is because it must keep its shape after it is unmolded. If the mold is a little bit larger than is necessary for the quantity of custard—for example, a 1½-liter (6-cup) capacity for 1 liter (4¼ cups) of custard—this is unimportant.

If the mold is to be caramelized, choose an absolutely smooth mold with smooth sides (SEE TO CARAMELIZE A MOLD, PAGE 575). Otherwise, use a mold that is grooved.

When the mold is not caramelized, it must be greased inside with fresh butter. Spread the raw butter with the end of your finger, using an amount the size of a walnut for a mold of 1 liter (4¼ cups), and taking great care, particularly if the mold has grooves in its sides: If the sides are not completely buttered, the custard will break when it is unmolded, and even a very small part that is left without butter will produce this extremely unfortunate result.

Poaching: Once the custard has been prepared in the same way as for POTS DE CRÈME (SEE PAGE 579), pour it into the mold.

Put the mold into a sauté pan that is large enough so that there is a distance of 2 centimeters (¾ inch) between the sides of the mold and the pan. Pour in boiling water until it reaches 1 centimeter (⅜ inch) from the top of the mold, being very careful, of course, to avoid pouring any into the cream.

Put it into a rather hot oven. Cover the sauté pan with a large cover.

The conditions should be exactly the same as for poaching POTS DE CRÈME (SEE PAGE 580). *Allow 55–60 minutes of cooking* for the quantities of custard indicated. This time can vary by as much 10 minutes, depending on whether you have used a simple mold or a cylindrical mold.

In any case, before taking the mold out of the bain-marie, always check that the custard has set by touching it with the end of your finger.

Chilling and unmolding: When you take the custard out of the oven, allow the mold to remain in the water for another *good 15 minutes,* then take it out and leave it to stand in a place where the air can circulate freely. While it is cooling, the different ingredients set and bind together, and it is this that makes the custard solid enough to be unmolded.

Take it out of the mold only when you are ready to serve it. With the point of a knife, gently release the cream from the sides of the mold. Use a round plate covered with a little napkin; place it on the mold and turn everything over.

Crème Anglaise *(Crème Anglaise)*

This cream is always used with sugared desserts: either it is part of their composition or it is used as an accompanying sauce. The quantity of egg yolks varies depending on the different uses that can be made of this cream, but its preparation is always the same. *Time: 30 minutes.*

1–1 1/2 yolks for each deciliter (3 1/3 fluid ounces, scant 1/2 cup) of boiled milk, and 30 grams (1 ounce) of superfine sugar.

It is best to use a pot made of good aluminum, thick enough that it will not be sensitive to strong heat flashes. And choose one with a base that is relatively wide in proportion to the quantity of ingredients; a large surface area will mean that the yolks cook more evenly, and it is also easier to work with the spoon, which must be stirred continuously.

Cooking a crème anglaise requires attention and experience, because if it is even slightly overcooked, the cream decomposes (or "turns," the term often used); we will provide an explanation for this below. It is very easy to guard against all disasters by adding, *right at the very beginning,* 1 small teaspoon of arrowroot or starch for a cream using 1/2 liter (generous 2 cups) of milk; indeed, this is something that cannot be recommended too highly for beginners. Also it is good for those occasions when you have to watch several things at the same time. This small addition of starch is added not to give the cream a thicker consistency, but to prevent it from decomposing if it should start to boil. At the same time, this does ensure a more perfect mixture.

PROCEDURE. Boil the milk, and put in the zest or the vanilla to flavor the cream; be careful to split the vanilla bean lengthwise with the point of a small knife so that it releases all of its flavor. Keep it warm without boiling. Let it infuse for *15–20 minutes.* For cream flavored with coffee or chocolate, proceed as directed (SEE POTS DE CRÈME, PAGE 579).

In a small bowl, mix together the yolks and the superfine sugar *as well as the starch,* if using it. With a large wooden spoon, mix the sugar and the eggs, working them and beating them vigorously until the mixture makes the ribbon (SEE PAGE 577).

Gradually, dilute it with the warm infused milk, stirring constantly and vigorously during this time. Pour all the mixture into the pot, leaving the vanilla or the zest. Then put the pot on gentle heat and *do not stop stirring* on the bottom of the pot, stroking gently until the ingredients are completely combined.

This is obvious as soon as the light mousse covering the surface dissolves. When you lift out the spoon, you will see the back of it covered by the cream, which attaches to it like a light thin varnish, as if it were painted on. You must now turn off the heat immediately.

If you have not added starch, even a second of inattention at this point exposes you to the risk of seeing the cream turn. It will then appear dotted. It is the egg, too flashed by the heat, which has decomposed into little clumps. If this happens, very quickly plunge the bottom of the pot into cold water to diffuse the heat. Or even add to the cream 1 tablespoon of very cold water, vigorously beating it in for several moments.

Once the liaison has been obtained, pass the cream through a chinois into a terrine. Put a spoon back into it, and until this cream is well cooled, mix it every 3 or 4 minutes so that you prevent a skin from forming on the surface; this should certainly be avoided, because if it does form, you will have to reheat the cream and pass it through the chinois again.

Thickened Crème Anglaise *(Crème Anglaise Collée).* Crème anglaise is called this when some gelatin has been added, which is done when making cold desserts that need a certain solidity (SEE PAGE 18).

Add the gelatin, well dried off after soaking, to the cream after it is taken off the heat, 20–25 grams (3/4–1 ounce) for 1 liter (4 1/4 cups) of milk. Stir the cream off the heat until the gelatin has completely dissolved. Pass the cream through a chinois and proceed as above until it is almost cold. Avoid placing the cream on ice or on very cold water to hasten cooling it, because you will get very big lumps that will not dissolve when you heat the cream. And this will slow down the next stages, because the cream must be cold when you use it.

Buttercream *(Crème au Beurre)*

There are numerous uses for buttercream in pastry making and for desserts. Its base is a crème anglaise or custard cream, in which sugar syrup frequently replaces milk, and to which is added a certain amount of butter. Since this butter is not cooked in any way, it must be of the very best quality, the finest. The flavor varies according to taste and use.

Recipes for buttercream—or, as it is sometimes known, buttered cream—vary with the amount of ingredients. The two recipes below are the most current.

Buttercream with Syrup *(Crème Beurrée au Sirop).*

120 grams (4¹/₄ ounces) of sugar cubes and 1 deciliter (3¹/₃ fluid ounces, scant ¹/₂ cup) of water; 6 egg yolks; 200 grams (7 ounces, 14 tablespoons) of butter.

Depending on the flavor you are using, the work order will differ a little bit.

If you are flavoring it with *vanilla, lemon, orange, or praline,* add the vanilla bean or the zest or praline to infuse in the boiling syrup before you add the yolks.

If the flavor is *liquid*—an essence or some liqueur—do not add it until after the cream is cooked, adding it *at the same time as the butter.*

If you are flavoring it with *coffee,* replace the water used for the syrup with the same quantity of very strong black coffee.

If the cream is *chocolate,* moisten it first with water and heat it just to the point where it has softened and can be beaten with a small wooden spoon. Once worked into the consistency of a smooth, thick batter, incorporate it into the cream at the same time as the butter.

PROCEDURE. Put the sugar in a saucepan, preferably a little pot that has a pouring spout and is made of copper, and *not* tin-lined. Moisten the sugar with hot or cold water to activate the melting process. Once the sugar has been completely dissolved, place it on the heat. Remove the small foam that rises to the surface when it begins to boil. Let it boil to bring the syrup to the desired temperature: exactly *3 minutes. Turn off the heat.*

(If the flavor is produced by infusion—such as vanilla, zest, or praline—add the flavoring now to the boiling syrup. Cover. Keep warm for *20 minutes.*)

Put the yolks, which have had their germ very carefully removed, into a small saucepan. A sauté pan would be best. Whisk them a little bit first with a small whisk. Next, always off the heat, gently pour in the syrup, straining out the vanilla bean or the zest, and stir continuously as if you were pouring oil into mayonnaise.

Place it on extremely low heat. Replace the whisk with a wooden spoon, which is a better utensil to use for scraping the bottom of the saucepan continuously where the cream will heat most strongly; do this just until the spoon is uniformly covered with a light varnish-like layer. Immediately turn off the heat. If the cream has been overheated and is beginning to clump, proceed quickly, just as described for correcting crème anglaise (SEE PAGE 583). Working according to the rules, the cream should now be passed through a large muslin cloth twisted at both ends over a small terrine. You can also use a chinois or a very fine strainer.

Put the whisk into the cream, and from time to time stir to avoid a skin forming on its surface, letting it stand until it is no more than lightly or slightly lukewarm; if it chills completely, it will not be possible to add the butter. Once the cream is lukewarm, you can add the liquid flavor; you can also add the chocolate, reduced to a paste. If the butter is very firm, soften it first by squeezing it in the corner of a moistened towel. Divide it into pieces the size of a chestnut, then let it melt into the cream, mixing it continuously with the whisk.

The cream must be served immediately. Otherwise, particularly in winter, the butter will firm up again. If this happens, or if there is buttercream left over, restore it to the right consistency by gently softening it up in a bain-marie and working it with the whisk.

Milk Buttercream *(Crème Beurrée au Lait).*

125 grams (4¹/₂ ounces) of superfine sugar; 4 egg yolks; 2¹/₂ deciliters (1 cup) of good boiled milk; 200 grams (7 ounces, 14 tablespoons) of butter.

Milk buttercream is prepared in exactly the same way as crème anglaise (SEE PAGE 583). The butter, as for BUTTERCREAM WITH SYRUP (SEE AT LEFT), is added when the cream is just lukewarm.

If you are flavoring it with *vanilla, zest, or praline,* these ingredients are infused in the milk.

If you want a *coffee* flavor, you can either use very strong black coffee and reduce the amount of milk accordingly; or preferably you can infuse the milk with coffee beans.

For *chocolate,* proceed as for BUTTERCREAM WITH SYRUP (SEE OPPOSITE), adding it *at the same time as the butter.*

For the *liquid* flavors, you also add them at the same time as the butter.

Frangipane Cream *(Crème Frangipane)*

Used in pastry making and for decorating desserts, frangipane cream differs from pastry cream in two ways: first of all, because it uses a larger quantity of flour and butter (double that used for pastry cream); and second, because almond powder or crushed macaroons are added. The latter was once the characteristic ingredient of frangipane and gave it its flavor; at that time, it was finished with orange flower water. Depending on the dish in which the frangipane cream will be used, the flavor used can be vanilla, lemon, orange, etc.

The quantities below are an average established from different authors. *Time: 25 minutes.*

5 deciliters (generous 2 cups) of boiled milk; 100 grams (3½ ounces) of fine wheat flour; 100 grams (3½ ounces) of superfine sugar; 1 whole egg and 4 yolks; 50 grams (1¾ ounces, 3½ tablespoons) of fine butter; 15–20 grams (½–⅔ ounce) of crushed macaroons; a grain of salt (SEE PAGE 575). Flavored as you wish.

PROCEDURE. Bring the boiled milk back to a boil, then add the vanilla or the zest. Cover. Allow it to infuse in its heat for *12–15 minutes* without boiling.

Into a medium-size pot put the flour, sugar, salt, whole egg, and egg yolks. Mix and work everything with a wooden spoon for 2–3 minutes. Then dilute the mixture by pouring in the infused milk *little by little,* working it as you go with a wooden spoon, or preferably a small sauce whisk, to avoid lumps.

Then put the pot on low heat. Mix the cream gently *but without leaving it for a moment,* always scraping the spoon or the whisk on the bottom of the pot and in every direction so that the cream does not stick. When boiling begins, which is obvious from bubbles forming on the surface, continue to mix the cream for another 2 minutes. You do not have to worry about it decomposing here. It will not turn, because the flour in the mixture prevents this.

Then turn off the heat. Mix in the butter and the macaroons. If serving the frangipane warm, keep it in a bain-marie with a few pieces of butter on the surface.

If you are using it cold, pour it into a terrine. Lightly dot the surface with a piece of butter stuck on the end of a knife to avoid a skin forming.

Pastry Cream *(Crème Pâtissière)*

Just like frangipane, this is equally good for pastry making and some desserts. You can use it for cream puffs, profiteroles, éclairs, etc., and the flavor varies accordingly: vanilla, lemon, coffee, chocolate, etc.

The proportions of the ingredients differ according to the authors. Some do not use as many egg whites; this makes a finer cream. Others do not use any whites at all, and then the quantity of yolks is doubled: as you can imagine, this gives the cream a notable delicacy. Butter is included—at any rate, in a minimal amount—and many practitioners do not use it at all except for an infinitesimal quantity added to the surface to prevent a skin from forming. The recipe below offers a middle ground that is good for making pastry at home. It can, of course, be modified depending on circumstance.

The flour used must be the finest wheat flour, as beautiful and fine as possible. It would be a mistake to try to replace it with a starchlike rice flour, which has a sandiness that is utterly detrimental to the result you are looking for. *Time: 25 minutes.*

5 deciliters (generous 2 cups) of milk; 60 grams (2¼ ounces) of fine, sifted flour; 175 grams (6 ounces) of superfine sugar; 4 whole eggs; a grain of salt (SEE PAGE 575); 15 grams (½ ounce, 1 tablespoon) of fine butter.

PROCEDURE. Exactly the same as for FRANGIPANE CREAM (SEE AT LEFT). If the cream is made with coffee or chocolate, refer for the quantities, as well as for how to incorporate them, to POTS DE CRÈME (PAGE 579).

Whipped Cream
(Crème Fouettée Dite "Crème Chantilly")

Use cream that has been skimmed from the milk after 24 hours in very warm weather; 36 hours in cool weather in summer; and 48 hours in winter.

In the cities, notably in Paris, cream sellers sell either light cream, known as "cream for tea," or a very thick cream, known as "centrifuge." The light cream, which is skimmed off after 12 hours, foams up a lot but does not reach the right consistency. Centrifuge cream immediately turns into butter, and indeed it is whipped so that it does that: it must first be diluted with milk, using *a quarter of its volume of milk.* This makes it into a liquid that runs easily and only slightly sticks to the spoon. It is, of course, after the milk has been added that the cream is measured to furnish the given quantities.

The quantities given are always for cream that has not been whipped, calculating that *cream in a liquid state largely doubles in volume after it has been whipped.* Bear this in mind if you have to buy the cream already whipped from the dairyman. That is, $^1/_4$ liter (1 cup) of cream *to be whipped* represents $^1/_2$ liter (generous 2 cups) of whipped cream. Depending on the need, you can add superfine sugar, vanilla, or nothing at all, to the whipped cream.

To whip the cream: Put it in a salad bowl or a large terrine because the cream will double in volume when whipped. Put the receptacle on ice if possible, or a very cool place, *for at least 1 hour in advance.*

Using a supple wire whisk, whip the cream in the same way as when whisking egg whites (SEE EGG WHITES, PAGE 8), using small motions at first and without taking the whisk out of the cream with each turn. When it begins to form many bubbles, accelerate the movement of the whisk until the cream is firm enough that the branches of the whisk leave traces; a large piece falling from the whisk should also keep its shape. Stop now, because unlike egg whites, cream cannot be whipped for too long without spoiling: if the cream is whipped beyond the right point, *a few seconds too much will cause little clots of butter, and the damage is irreparable.*

Keep the whipped cream cool until you use it.

Milk Eggs *(Œufs au Lait)*

The difference between milk eggs and other creams is the equal proportion of yolks and whites used. The white helps to set the mixture firmly, and you can considerably reduce the quantity of egg in respect to the milk. But this is at the expense of the delicacy and flavor of the cream. Milk eggs should be served only as the simplest of home desserts. *Time: 45 minutes (2 plus hours for cooling). Serves 6.*

$^1/_2$ liter (generous 2 cups) of milk; 3 nice eggs; 125–150 grams ($4^1/_2$–$5^1/_3$ ounces) of sugar; 1 tablespoon of superfine sugar for glazing. Flavor according to preference.

The flavor is obtained in the same way as for the other creams—with vanilla, zest, almonds, or, in the classic tradition, orange flower water. You can flavor it with both lemon and orange flower water; but add the orange flower water only when you put the cream in the dish.

PROCEDURE. Boil the milk. As soon as it has boiled, add the sugar so that it will melt there, and the flavoring so that it will infuse in it without boiling. Cover. Turn off the heat.

Break the eggs, both whites and yolks, into a terrine or a salad bowl. Beat them with a fork as for an omelet, but do not foam them up too much. Pour the sugared and infused milk into the beaten eggs, making sure that the sugar is well dissolved. Mix with your whisk or wooden spoon without making too much foam, as explained in POTS DE CRÈME (SEE PAGE 580).

Pass the mixture through a fine strainer into a deep bowl or a metal or porcelain timbale that can be served at table. The bowl or timbale must be at least 5 centimeters (2 inches) deep so that the layer of cream is sufficiently thick.

The cooking should always be done in a bain-marie. Put the bowl or timbale into a large, shallow receptacle: a pot, sauté pan, or larger dish. Pour boiling water into the receptacle up to two-thirds of the height of the bowl or timbale.

Cover the receptacle with a large cover. Put it in the oven.

As for other creams, do not allow it to boil. *Assume 20–25 minutes* for cooking, or poaching. A cream that is properly set should just tremble in its bowl. Allow it to chill.

Glazing: Sprinkle the surface of the cream with superfine sugar. Heat a small, steel spatula until it is red, then run it over the cream as closely as possible without touching the sugar, which will melt and color to form a light layer of caramel.

Serve on a serving plate covered with a napkin.

Floating Islands *(Œufs à la Neige)*

This traditional home-style dessert should present no difficulty for the novice, either in terms of molding the egg whites consistently or indeed cooking them. You will manage this rather quickly with our directions. The poaching can be done in boiling water or, if you like, in the milk that is then used for the cream, in which case it is sugared in advance; it is this latter procedure that we will give here.

Flavor the cream according to taste with vanilla or lemon. You can also flavor it with coffee by infusing coffee bean, as directed (SEE POTS DE CRÈME, PAGE 579).

The quantity of yolks is a little less than is used for crème anglaise; but you must remember that this cream acts as a sauce in the dessert. The very small quantity of starch used helps when making the cream as directed. *Time: 1 hour, 15 minutes (plus the time needed to allow the cream to cool). Serves 6.*

6 eggs; 150 grams ($5^1/_3$ ounces) of superfine sugar; $^3/_4$ liter (generous 3 cups) of milk; 175 grams (6 ounces) of sugar, cubes or granulated; 1 teaspoon of starch; a ribbon of lemon zest.

PROCEDURE. **The milk:** Boil it in a sauté pan that is at least 20–22 centimeters (8–$8^1/_2$ inches) in diameter. A deep pot makes poaching the eggs difficult. Add the sugar cubes or granulated sugar, and the vanilla or the lemon. Cover and do not allow it to boil. Check to see that the sugar has completely dissolved.

The egg whites: First spread out the superfine sugar on a sheet of strong parchment paper, from which it will be much easier to sprinkle it onto the floating islands.

Whisk the whites (SEE PAGE 8). When they are in a firm "snow," sprinkle the sugar on them in a shower, and as you do so, mix it by cutting it and raising it with your spatula, as directed for mixing egg whites (SEE PAGE 10).

To mold and poach the egg whites: Turn on the heat under the pan with the milk in it. Bring it back to a boil. Then keep it at a very gentle simmer.

Pick up the firm egg whites with a large tablespoon or a large serving spoon. With the blade of an ordinary knife, smooth and shape rapidly the surface of the "snow," shaping it into a dome to give it an egg shape.

Strike the handle of the spoon on the edge of the pan to make the egg white fall into the boiling milk. Repeat to make 4 eggs—no more, because when they swell in the milk, they will poach badly if they do not have enough space. *After $1^1/_2$ minutes,* the part that has been submerged in the milk will have set, so turn the eggs over, using the handle of a spoon. Leave them in there for another *2 minutes.* Take them out with a slotted spoon. Drain them, lining them up on a spread-out towel or on a large strainer.

Proceed in the same way in series of four until you have used up all of the whites. With the quantities given, you should obtain at least about 15 eggs.

Make sure that you do not leave the eggs for too long in the milk, or heat the milk too much while poaching the eggs. If they are overcooked, they will be weakened, losing their shape, and they will no longer be edible. They should be cooked only enough to firm up the part immersed in the milk, just enough so that you are able to turn them over. So when you turn the eggs over, begin with the ones that were put first into the pan.

To help the egg come away from the spoon, you only have to dip the spoon in warm water before filling it with the "snow." You can also, when the spoon is full and the whites shaped into an egg, proceed as when molding large dumplings or quenelles: that is, hold the full spoon in your left hand, and then pass a second spoon, held in your right hand, under the egg-white egg to make it it come away and fall into the milk.

The cream: As soon as the eggs are poached, strain the milk through a fine chinois to get rid of all pieces of white.

Beat the egg yolk with starch in a saucepan. Dilute it gradually with the strained milk, which will still be warm. Combine them on the heat (SEE CRÈME ANGLAISE, PAGE 583), then allow it to chill.

RICE AND SEMOLINA DESSERTS
Entrements de Riz et de Semoule

Milk Rice for Desserts
(Riz au Lait pour Entrements)

It is essential here to use very fine rice, either Carolina or Patna, which are the only types that can withstand slow cooking without breaking up. The grains of these types of rice, while perfectly puffed up and tender, remain intact throughout the successive handlings required for making a dessert: mixing with eggs or cream, moldings, etc. This is impossible with rice of secondary quality, which will produce only a thick, pasty dessert.

For cooking rice in milk, you have a choice of two methods, each with its own advantages and its disadvantages. Cook the rice in the milk *with the sugar,* either in cubes or granulated, which you dissolve in the milk as soon as it is boiling; or cook the rice in the milk *without sugar,* and add it only at the end, which means using a superfine sugar so that you can mix it in.

The rice cooks a little less rapidly in milk that has been sugared in advance, because it is more difficult for it to absorb the sugared milk; a few more minutes are required. But once the cooking is done, there is nothing left for you to do. On the other hand, when the rice is cooked in the milk without sugar, you must mix in the sugar thoroughly afterward, taking great care that you do not break the grains. Furthermore, the melting sugar has a very unpleasant effect on rice that is served just as it is—to children or sick people, for example—without the addition of eggs or crème anglaise or a second cooking.

This is why, once all the advantages and disadvantages are considered, it is better to work *with the milk already sugared.*

For cooking rice in milk, allow for the milk *an average* of 4 times the volume of the rice: that is, for 1 glass of rice, add 4 glasses of milk.

This works out on average as *1 deciliter (3¹/₃ fluid ounces, scant ¹/₂ cup) of milk* for each 25 grams (1 ounce) of rice (very good rice, as has been explained above).

We say "on average" because depending on how the rice will next be prepared, a little more liquid might be necessary. And it is also essential to remember that in small quantities, the proportions are not so easily balanced as for large quantities, and you will need relatively more liquid to counter the evaporation. Nonetheless, do bear in mind that it is always better to have *too little than too much milk,* because if you need to you can always add a few tablespoonfuls in the course of the cooking *without mixing the rice,* but once the rice is perfectly cooked, any surplus liquid is absolutely prejudicial in all respects, so this should never be allowed to happen.

Measure the milk after it has been boiled; or measure it generously before putting it on to boil, because boiling will reduce the liquid.

The sugar is calculated at the rate of 12–15 grams (about ¹/₂ ounce) for each deciliter (3¹/₃ fluid ounces, ¹/₂ cup) of milk or for 25 grams (1 ounce) of rice. The exact quantity depends a little on how the rice will be used and your own particular preference. Add the butter in minimal quantities: 3–5 grams (about ¹/₁₀–¹/₆ ounce) for each deciliter (3¹/₃ fluid ounces, ¹/₂ cup) of milk.

Thus, to summarize the amounts:

125 grams (4¹/₂ ounces) of nice Carolina rice; ¹/₂ liter (generous 2 cups) of boiled milk; 60–75 grams (2¹/₄–2³/₄ ounces) of sugar, either in cubes or granulated; 15–20 grams (¹/₂–²/₃ ounce, 1–1 heaping tablespoon) of fine butter; a half vanilla bean or 2 ribbons of zest; and a grain of salt (SEE PAGE 575).

PROCEDURE. Rice cooked in milk must always be cooked *in the oven*; our quantities, cooking times, etc., assume this type of heat; if you do not have an oven, put the pot on *very gentle heat* after it has begun to boil, to maintain the liquid at the point described below. In this case, assume a longer cooking time.

To blanch the rice: Wash it in cold water. Put it in a pot, completely covered with cold water. Very slowly bring it to a boil on moderate heat. Then let it boil gently for *5 minutes.* Drain the rice in a strainer with medium-size holes; plunge it into a terrine of cool water and mix the rice there. Renew the water. Or leave the strainer under the faucet to chill it thoroughly—the professional term is "refresh." This washing rids it of its starch, and the cold water also has the effect of firming up the grains and keeping them intact while cooking in the milk.

While you blanch the rice, boil the milk in the pot that will then be used to cook the rice. It is essential to use a *thick* pot for this, because the rice will stick to a thin utensil. Note that the capacity of the pot should accord with the quantities of the rice and the milk: so, a capacity of 1¼–1½ liters (5⅓–6⅓ cups) for the quantities given above.

Once the milk has boiled, add the sugar and the flavoring as soon as possible: the vanilla or the lemon or orange peel. Turn off the heat; cover it tightly. Let it infuse off the heat, mixing it from time to time with a spoon to help the sugar dissolve.

Once the rice has been thoroughly refreshed in the water, drain it as completely as possible so that it does not retain any water, which would unfortunately dilute the milk. Put it in the pot with the milk, leaving the vanilla or the zest there; add the butter and the salt. Gently bring it to a boil. Then cover the pot and put it in a moderate oven. The boiling must be maintained at a very gentle level, scarcely visible: a simple *trembling* of the liquid, uninterrupted from the beginning to the end of cooking. You must never see any milk escape, spilling out from underneath the cover, which indicates that the boiling is much too strong.

At no point while cooking—that is, from the moment that boiling begins—*should the rice be moved* with a spoon or fork, because displacing the liquid will cause the rice to stick to the bottom of the pot.

Allow 35–40 minutes for cooking. But it is the state of the rice, above all, that regulates the length of cooking time. All of the liquid must have been absorbed, to the point that there is not even a small spoonful of it left, even when you tilt the pot considerably. The grains of rice must be whole and swollen at this time, but neither burst nor deformed, and perfectly tender and soft: it should crush between your fingers, or when you bite into it, without leaving a lump.

At this point, the rice is ready for the different uses for which it is intended. Turn off the heat. If it is for a hot preparation, use the very same pot to mix in the eggs. If the preparation is cool, transfer the rice immediately to a terrine and break it up carefully with a fork, then let it cool or, at least, come to room temperature before mixing it with the rest of the ingredients.

Rice Border for Warm Desserts *(Bordure de Riz pour Entremets Chauds)*

In the center of this border or ring of rice, you can place a compote, which varies with the fruits in season. In summer, this compote would be made with apricots, cherries, strawberries, raspberries, mirabelle plums, greengage plums, etc. In the fall, peaches, nectarines, pears, etc. and diverse fruits in a macédoine. In the winter: bananas, pears, apples, prunes, etc. The whole thus provides a dessert that adapts advantageously to the different seasons, which is always appreciated by most guests.

Whatever the compote chosen, the preparation of the border remains the same; the border and compote are served not burning hot but only lukewarm, which is the rule for desserts made from fruits: their flavor is thus enhanced.

The circle-shaped mold used is called a ring mold *(moule à bordure)*. The part of the mold holding the ingredients is always rather narrow, and is either smooth or worked—that is, made with ribs or grooves. The smooth bottom makes a right angle with the side: this is different from a savarin mold, whose bottom is rounded. This straight shape allows you to place either a decoration or the fruits themselves on top of the border, as for APRICOTS À LA CONDÉ (SEE PAGE 605). There are even molds that have a hollowed-out border: the bottom of these bulge inwards, and when you unmold it, a large circular channel is left, which holds the fruits more securely.

The drawings on PAGE 576 will give you an idea of the kinds of molds currently used. However, if you do not have one, you can also use a savarin mold.

Finally, let us say that it is possible to improvise when you do not have an appropriate mold handy: the rice can then be shaped into a border directly on the plate, and we will describe below how to do this. Clearly, such a border is not quite so impeccably neat, but with some skill, it is still quite presentable. *Time: 1 scant hour. Serves 6.*

125 grams (4 1/2 ounces) of rice; 5 deciliters (generous 2 cups) of milk; 65 grams (2 1/4 ounces) of sugar; 20 grams (2/3 ounce, 1 heaping tablespoon) of butter; a grain of salt (SEE PAGE 575); a quarter vanilla bean, or 1 zest of an orange or of a lemon; 3 nice egg yolks or 4 small ones. A round mold as indicated, with a capacity of about 1 liter (4 1/4 cups), measuring 18–20 centimeters (7–8 inches) in diameter.

PROCEDURE. Cook the rice as directed (SEE MILK RICE FOR DESSERTS, PAGE 588).

Butter the inside of the mold with a piece of butter the size of a walnut, spreading it with the end of your finger. Make sure you get it right into all the corners and all over, particularly if the mold is fluted.

Use the milk to dilute the egg yolks, from which their germ has been previously removed.

Once the rice has been cooked to the correct point, take the pot out of the oven. Leave the rice 2 or 3 minutes to cool slightly, so that it does not seize the egg yolks. Remove the vanilla bean or the zest. With a fork, break up the mass of rice in its pot, being careful not to damage the grains. Then add the egg yolk mixture gradually, mixing them well as you go, always using a fork.

With a large spoon, a pointed kitchen spoon, or similar, fill the mold with rice right up to the edge. Then lightly strike the mold on the table to settle the rice a little bit and put it immediately into a very moderate oven for 7–8 minutes, with the door left open if the oven is still very hot. All you are doing here is molding the rice and ensuring that it sets; very moderate heat is sufficient. Then simply keep it in a warm place before you unmold it for dressing it as a border.

To shape the rice into a border without a mold: Once the yolks have been incorporated into the rice, take it out a tablespoon at a time, arranging it in a circle on a round plate. With the back of the spoon dipped in warm water so that the rice does not stick to it, first roughly shape the border as if it had been molded; then smooth it all around and on the inside with the blade of a large knife. Keep it good and warm until you add the compote.

Rice Border for Cold Desserts *(Bordure de Riz pour Entremets Froids)*

Exactly as for a border of warm rice, you put in the center of this cold border a compote of fruits chosen according to the season—either a fresh fruit simply bound by an apricot syrup: pineapples, bananas, raspberries, strawberries, and others; or even a macédoine of fresh fruits. The dessert then takes the name of the fruit, and the whole dish is so fine and decorative that it can replace an ice cream, and is often even preferred.

The preparation of the rice is different from that used for the hot border: here the rice is bound with a thickened crème anglaise—that is, custard to which some gelatin has been added—then finished with whipped cream, which brings a great delicacy to the ensemble. The preparation is not at all complicated; it simply requires a lot of attention to detail, and it offers the great advantage of not requiring any ice: provided that everything is prepared sufficiently in advance, which itself is another benefit, given that this type of dessert must be served as cold as possible.

You have to allow *at least 3 hours* for the rice to set and cool completely. Nothing stands in the way of this border being prepared a lot earlier, as long as it is kept cool. Just before serving, and no sooner, dress the border with the decoration, separately prepared.

It is essential, and even fundamental to this recipe, to use a nice Carolina rice of the finest quality.

The kind of mold used is the same as that used for the border of warm rice. Refer to the relevant directions and drawings. *Time: 5 hours (1 good hour for preparing the rice; at least 3 hours to set the border without ice, 2 hours with ice). Serves 6.*

125 grams (4 1/2 ounces) of Carolina rice; 5 deciliters (generous 2 cups) of milk; 65 grams (2 1/2 ounces) of sugar; 20 grams (2/3 ounce, 1 heaping tablespoon) of butter; a grain of salt (SEE PAGE 575); one-third of a vanilla bean.

For the thickened crème anglaise: **70 grams (2 1/2 ounces) of superfine sugar; 3 egg yolks; 1 1/2 deciliters (5 fluid ounces, 2/3 cup) of milk; 2 sheets of gelatin.**

2 deciliters (6 3/4 fluid ounces, 7/8 cup) of whipped cream or 1 deciliter (3 1/3 fluid ounces, scant 1/2 cup) of thick cream to be whipped (SEE WHIPPED CREAM, PAGE 586).
A round mold with a 1-liter (4 1/4-cup) capacity.

PROCEDURE. Blanch and cook the rice as directed (SEE MILK RICE FOR DESSERTS, PAGE 588).

While the rice is cooking, prepare the thick crème anglaise as directed (SEE THICKENED CRÈME ANGLAISE, PAGE 583).

With a brush, oil the inside of the mold, preferably with sweet almond oil. Whip the cream.

Mixing the rice and molding it: Once the rice has been cooked to the correct point, pour it into a terrine. With a fork, mix it gently to thoroughly separate the grains without breaking them. Then first add the crème anglaise, *scarcely warm*, with the same precautions.

When everything is no more than lukewarm, mix in the whipped cream, proceeding exactly as you would for egg whites beaten to a snow (SEE PAGE 8). This is so that you preserve the cream's lightness. After this, fill the mold as directed for the border of warm rice.

Then put the mold in a very cool place to firm it up, covered with oiled parchment paper, which will keep it free of dust.

If you have ice: Break the ice into very small pieces; put them into a terrine or in a small bowl. Arrange the mold on top in such a way that the ice also fills the hollow center. Place a few pieces of medium-size ice on the oiled paper. Watch carefully for the next 2 hours so that as the ice melts, the water does not get into the mold. And if you have a refrigerator, you can place the mold on one of the shelves, covered by the oiled paper and already cooled, at least 2 hours before serving it.

To serve: If the utensil has been carefully oiled, it should be easy to unmold. It is wise to do this a little bit in advance. But only when you are ready to send it to the table should you arrange the fruit compote in the middle of the border.

Rice Pudding and Rice Cake *(Pudding au Riz et Gâteau de Riz)*

With modern usage we have come to call this very French rice cake, one of our typical home-style dishes, a "pudding." And it is precisely because, hot or cold, it is considered a dessert, that the term *pudding* is applied to it: young people object that the term *cake* refers to a kind of patisserie.

Rice pudding, as we have just said, is served as you like, either hot or cold. Served hot, or rather lukewarm, it is accompanied by an equally lukewarm sauce: a zabaglione or a crème anglaise with a flavor corresponding to the pudding's; perhaps an apple sauce or a fruit sauce of some kind, served in a sauce boat. Several tablespoons only can be poured around the pudding or on top of it, just to "mask it," depending on the consistency of the sauce.

Served cold, the cream that accompanies it can be replaced by a light purée of fruit cooked in syrup—apricots, peaches, pears, apples, etc.—or simply by a gelée or marmalade of fruits, especially apricots or red currants diluted with a little bit of water, then strained and perfumed with kirsch or rum.

If you like, you can add to the pudding raisins; preserved fruits, of one or several kinds, such as cherries, plums, bitter oranges, apricots, orange peel; almonds, crushed macaroons, etc. This is what differentiates it from an ordinary rice cake, to which nothing is added.

Raisins or fruits are incorporated into the rice *before* mixing in the whites, beaten to a snow. If using raisins, choose half Corinth and half Smyrna (SEE REMOVING THE STEMS, PAGE 573), a total weight of 125 grams (4 1/2 ounces) per 450 grams (1 pound) of *uncooked* rice. If using preserved fruit, cut it into small dice, in the quantity of 5–6 good tablespoons per 450 grams (1 pound) of rice.

The mold for the pudding or the cake is, depending on preference and circumstance, buttered and sprinkled with a fine white bread crumb, crushed macaroons, or chopped almonds or pistachios. Or even, in the classic manner, caramelized to a beautiful golden tint (SEE TO CARAMELIZE A MOLD, PAGE 575).

Whether cake or pudding, the preparation and quantities are exactly the same; the whites are always beaten to a "snow." Only the method of cooking can differ; normally a rice cake is put directly into the oven (in earlier days, what was generally used was a country oven or a cover loaded with hot coals). The pudding can also be cooked in the oven, but *always in a bain-marie:* the cooking takes longer, but it is done with greater regularity.

Rice Pudding ***(Pouding au Riz).*** *Time: 2 hours. Serves 6.*

125 grams (4$^1/_2$ ounces) of Carolina rice; 5 deciliters (generous 2 cups) of milk; a grain of salt (SEE PAGE 575); 50 grams (1$^3/_4$ ounces) of sugar; 20 grams ($^2/_3$ ounce, 1 heaping tablespoon) of butter; a small half vanilla bean or some lemon zest; 3 egg yolks; 3 egg whites beaten into a very firm snow. A 1-liter (4-cup) charlotte mold prepared as directed above, with either bread crumbs or caramel.

PROCEDURE. Prepare the rice as directed (SEE MILK RICE FOR DESSERTS, PAGE 588). Once the rice has been cooked, pour it into a terrine or salad bowl. Using a fork, separate the grains carefully so that you do not break them.

Take out the vanilla or the zest. Delicately mix in the egg yolks.

Beat the whites into a very firm snow (SEE EGG WHITES, PAGE 8) and mix them with the rice so that you can no longer see any sections of just white.

Pour the mixture into the mold, which must be filled to only 1$^1/_2$ centimeters ($^5/_8$ inch) from the edge. Immediately put it in a bain-marie in the oven (SEE THE DOUBLE BOILER, PAGE 42).

Allow *45 minutes of cooking,* from the moment you put it in the oven. After 35 minutes, take off the cover, so that the surface of the pudding dries out slightly. You can tell that the pudding is done by gently pressing your finger on it; it should be firmed up but also somewhat elastic. Then remove the mold from the bain-marie. Do not unmold the pudding immediately. First let it rest in a warm place for *a good 15 minutes* so that it settles down inside.

Chocolate Rice Cake ***(Gâteau de Riz au Chocolat).*** Cook as directed, using the same quantity of rice as above. Meanwhile melt 1$^1/_2$ squares (90–100 grams, 3$^1/_6$–3$^1/_2$ ounces) of grated chocolate in 2–3 generous tablespoons of warm water and then reduce it to a thick paste. Once the rice has been cooked, first mix in the chocolate and the same quantity as above of egg yolks and egg whites beaten into a snow. Pour it into a buttered mold sprinkled with white bread crumbs. Cook it in a medium oven for *35 minutes.* Serve a chocolate crème anglaise on the side in a sauceboat.

Home-Style Rice Cake ***(Gâteau de Riz Façon Ménagère).*** Here the quantity of eggs is diminished by almost half: that is, 2 nice eggs for 125 grams (4$^1/_2$ ounces) of rice, cooked as directed. And these eggs are simply beaten as for an omelet, and then added gradually to the rice when it has cooled slightly. A cake made like this is inevitably less light, and less tender than one with a larger quantity of eggs and in which the whites were beaten into a snow. Cook in the oven for *35 minutes.*

Milk Rice Gratinée ***(Riz au Lait Gratiné).*** A very simple home-style dish when you are serving only 2–3 people and do not want to go to the trouble of making a cake or pudding. Rice prepared like this can be served as you like, either warm or cold. Prepare the rice as directed (SEE MILK RICE FOR DESSERTS, PAGE 588). When it is cooked, take out the zest or the vanilla and mix in the egg, both the white and yolk, beaten very thoroughly: that is, use 2 eggs for each 100 grams (3$^1/_2$ ounces) of rice. Pour it into a shallow buttered bowl. Smooth out the surface. Sprinkle it with 2 tablespoons of superfine sugar. Put it into a hot oven on a high shelf so that the heat caramelizes the sugar; or, which is preferable, underneath the broiler.

Rice à l'Impératrice, a Cold Dessert *(Riz à l'Impératrice, Entremets Froid)*

There is nothing difficult in this preparation and it has the advantage that it can be made in advance. Rice à l'impératrice is one of France's best classic desserts: in classic cuisine, it was prepared using an Italian meringue made with kirsch gelée, without the need for an ice-cream maker. Modern cooking has simplified this recipe without taking away its merits.

The new recipe is as follows: some rice is cooked in milk by the ordinary method, and then you incorporate some preserved fruits, a marmalade of apricots, and a crème anglaise with a little bit of gelatin and some whipped cream. To sum it up, it is a kind of bavarois with rice and preserved fruits; the rice is used in a relatively small quantity and the proportions must be exactly calculated so that its flavor is quite strong and the whole thing holds together well, while remaining tender and light. It is also important to have a well-bound crème anglaise and cream whipped to be sufficiently firm.

To set the dessert, you do not necessarily need ice. Rice à l'impératrice should not be frozen like ordinary ice cream. It must only be chilled to the point where it has set and can be easily cut with a spoon, the rice remaining moist and soft.

(You can, if you like, make a decoration with the preserved fruit when you mold it. But this does not enhance the value or the flavor of the dessert, the quantity of fruits remaining the same whether they are mixed or applied along the outside. If the fruits have been mixed with the rice without removing any for the décor, you can demold it, then arrange a beautiful crown of preserved fruits around the base: either cherries and plums or greengage plums and apricots, etc. This decoration uses additional fruit beyond that listed among the ingredients.)

NOTE. The recipe given here includes cherries, plums, pineapple, and candied orange peel. You can, according to taste, equally use apricots, greengage plums, bitter oranges, angelica; however, apricot, which is already used in the form of a purée, is not a good idea. The essential point is to have a small variety of fruits, as much for flavor as for color: so, at least four different fruits.)

This dessert can be prepared the evening before. That said, it would be better to serve it the same day, because the whipped cream could turn slightly sour in 24 hours.

Rice à l'impératrice is served just as it is. But if it seems like a good idea to you, you can accompany it with a little bowl of very cold red currant syrup perfumed with kirsch. Another excellent accompaniment is apricot syrup made with a marmalade of apricots that has been diluted with a little bit of sugar syrup, then completed with 2–3 tablespoons of almond milk or orgeat syrup well perfumed with vanilla. *Time: 4–7 hours (2 scant hours for the preparation, cooking, chilling, mixing, etc.); to set the dish, 2 hours with ice, or 4 1/2–5 hours if you simply leave the mold in a cool place). Serves 10.*

100 grams (3 1/2 ounces) of Carolina rice; 4 deciliters (1 2/3 cups) of boiled milk; 60 grams (2 1/4 ounces) of sugar cubes; a half vanilla bean; 20 grams (2/3 ounce, 1 heaping tablespoon) of fine butter; a grain of salt (SEE PAGE 575).

***For the thickened crème anglaise:* 3 1/2 deciliters (1 1/2 cups) of boiled milk; 5 egg yolks; 150 grams (5 1/3 ounces) of superfine sugar; a half vanilla bean; 5 leaves of gelatin—that is, 10 grams (1/3 ounce).**

***For 125 grams (4 1/2 ounces) of preserved fruit:* 6–8 candied cherries; 4 mirabelle plums; 1 piece of pineapple; one-quarter of a preserved orange peel (see the note above on this subject); 4 tablespoons of good kirsch; 2 good tablespoons of apricot marmalade; 2 1/2 deciliters (1 cup) of thick cream for whipping, quite fresh, or 5 deciliters (generous 2 cups) of cream that has already been whipped; 1/2 tablespoon of sweet almond oil to oil the mold.**

PROCEDURE. Blanch and cook the rice as directed (SEE MILK RICE FOR DESSERTS, PAGE 588). Allow for cooking *at least 40 minutes.*

While the rice is cooking, prepare the *preserved fruits.* Cut each cherry into 4 pieces; cut the other fruits into cubes at least 1 centimeter (3/8 inch) on each side. Mix everything together in a bowl. Add 1 tablespoon of superfine sugar and the kirsch to it. Mix and let it macerate, tossing it from time to time until you are ready to add it to the recipe.

Soak the gelatin. Prepare the thickened crème anglaise (SEE PAGE 583) without neglecting to add the starch, which will prevent the cream from turning.

Pass the apricot marmalade through a horsehair strainer. Reserve it in a cup.

Once the rice has been cooked, pour it into a terrine that is large enough to then mix all of the ingredients in it. Take out the vanilla bean. With a fork, carefully separate the grains. Add the apricot purée and the preserved fruits with their kirsch. Mix with a fork.

When the crème anglaise is almost cold, add it to the rice, a little bit at a time. This cream must, of course, still be liquid, showing no traces of coagulation.

While allowing both the rice and the crème anglaise to cool, prepare the mold and whip the cream (SEE WHIPPED CREAM, PAGE 586).

The mold: If you have the choice, use a round mold with a hole in the center, 18 centimeters (7 inches) in diameter by 8–9 centimeters (3 1/4–3 1/2 inches) in height. If not, use an ordinary cylindrical mold, smooth or decorated, with a capacity of 1 1/2 liters (6 1/3 cups). Thoroughly oil the inside using a small brush, particularly in the hollowed-out parts of the design if there are any.

Mix the whipped cream with the rice, using the precautions and techniques recommended for egg whites beaten into snow (SEE INCORPORATING THE WHITES, PAGE 10).

Using a large spoon, fill the mold up to the edge and tap the bottom lightly on the table to settle the contents. Put a round of oiled parchment paper directly on top of the mixture. If you have ice, surround the mold with it in a terrine for 2 hours. If not, keep the mold in a place that is as cool as possible for 5–6 hours.

To serve: Lightly pass the blade of a small knife between the walls of the mold and the cream to loosen it, and turn the mold over on a round plate covered with a folded napkin or a kitchen towel.

Rice Croquettes, a Warm Dessert *(Croquettes de Riz, Entremets Chaud)*

A dessert that is popular in homes and that is made easy by the fact that rice croquettes are good in all seasons. Serve them alone or accompanied with a sauce, which lends a certain sophistication that allows you to serve them when the family dinner includes a few informal guests.

Depending on the season, this sauce can be made using a crème anglaise flavored with vanilla, chocolate, etc.; a red currant gelée simply melted and flavored with kirsch or rum; or even with a syrup prepared with a marmalade of apricots or mirabelle plums, passed through a drum sieve or diluted with a few tablespoons of warm water; or you could use an apple coulis (SEE PAGE 621).

Make the croquettes in whatever shape you like, either as large logs or as apples or pears; in the latter case, when they come out of the deep-frying mixture, add a sprig of angelica to be the fruit's stem. *Time: 2 hours, 30 minutes (including 1 hour to cool the rice). Serves 6.*

125 grams (4 1/2 ounces) of Carolina rice; 5 deciliters (generous 2 cups) of very good milk; 100 grams (3 1/2 ounces) of sugar, in cubes or granulated; 25 grams (1 ounce, 2 tablespoons) of good butter; 2 ribbons of lemon zest or a half vanilla bean; 3 egg yolks to bind the rice.

To bread the croquettes: 2 small eggs; 1 teaspoon of oil; about 225 grams (8 ounces) of white bread crumbs 3 days old from a loaf (or if you do not have it, the same amount of fine *white* bread crumbs from a baguette).

PROCEDURE. Blanch and cook the rice as directed (SEE MILK RICE FOR DESSERTS, PAGE 588). The rice should be nice and tender.

Take the pot out of the oven. Take out the zests of lemon or the vanilla. Let it rest for 5 minutes so that the heat does not seize the egg yolks. Then add the 3 diluted yolks, mixing them in delicately with a fork.

Then spread out the rice in an even layer about 2 1/2–3 centimeters (1–1 1/4 inches) thick on a plate that has been buttered. Spread a piece of butter stuck on the end of a knife over the rice to stop it browning, which would spoil it.

As for all croquettes, let them completely cool. That should take at least 1 hour.

To shape the croquettes: With a tablespoon, divide the rice *that has been well chilled* into pieces the size of a small egg, about 60 grams (2 1/4 ounces) in weight. As you do this, place them on a board sprinkled with flour.

Coat the end of the fingers of your right hand in flour so that the rice does not stick there. First roll these pieces of rice into balls so that you can then shape them into logs or apples or pears.

For logs. Roll them on the board to elongate them a little bit. Then compress each end.

For apples. Lightly flatten each ball. With a little piece of pointed wood (a toothpick, say), make a hole in the center where you would find the stem.

For pears. Roll the ball on one side only to elongate it so that it has a pointed shape at one end.

Dip the croquettes in the beaten egg, then the bread crumbs as directed (SEE HOW TO BREAD À L'ANGLAISE, PAGE 19).

Prepare the sprigs of angelica. Use little sticks, 4 centimeters (1½ inches) long and the thickness of a fruit stem, one for each croquette. Keep them on hand for when you dress them.

Now take care of the accompanying sauce, whichever one you have decided to use, so that everything is ready when the croquettes come out of the deep-fry mixture.

To fry the croquettes: Refer to the special section (SEE DEEP-FRYING, PAGES 37). *Eight minutes before serving,* put the croquettes into the deep fat frying mixture, which should be lightly smoking. Mix them from time to time. Once they have turned a nice golden brown, drain them on a kitchen towel.

With the point of a kitchen knife, make a small hole in each croquette: on the pointed end for the pears and in the little hollow for the apples. Stick the angelica into each one. Immediately arrange them in a circle or in a pyramid on a plate covered with a folded napkin, and serve them with the sauce or coulis in a sauceboat.

Semolina with Milk for Desserts *(Semoule au Lait pour Entremets)*

The perfect whiteness of the semolina is the most important point, even the only point, that must be observed here. Its size and origin are less important; a good semolina bought ready-made will do, as long as it is nice and white.

The quantities of milk for the cooking of the semolina are the same as for those of cooking rice with milk: that is, *1 good deciliter (3⅓ fluid ounces, ½ cup) of boiled milk for each 25 grams (1 ounce) of semolina.* The same is true for the grain of salt and for the sugar and the butter, except for slight variations depending on the use. These quantities will be given in the different recipes that include semolina cooked in milk.

Cooking it: Use a deep pot with a thick bottom. Boil the milk in it; off the heat, add the sugar, and mix it with a spoon until it is well dissolved. Bring it back to a boil, but not too lively. From a plate or bowl holding the semolina, pick up the grains, with your left hand, and rain them down from on high into the milk, mixing it at the same time with a wooden spoon held in your right hand. This is to stop the semolina from clumping. Let it boil for a few moments, *constantly stirring* the mixture, which immediately takes on a thick consistency. Then add the butter, a pinch of salt, and if the dish includes it, vanilla, zest, or another flavoring.

Cover the pot. Put it, if possible, into a very moderate oven, to maintain a *gentle,* steady boil. If you do not have an oven, keep the heat under the pot extremely low. In any case, avoid direct contact with the bottom of the gas—or other—no matter how gentle the degree of heat, because the lower layer of the semolina will be the only part to receive the heat, and it will stick, while the upper part will swell badly. This is why cooking in the oven is better than all other methods.

While it is cooking, do not touch the semolina in any way: you will make it stick to the bottom of the pot. Just be careful to maintain a completely even cooking from beginning to end; the boiling must be hardly noticeable and should only be manifested by some swelling or blisters on the semolina; splashes would be a sign that it is boiling too strongly, which must be avoided.

Allow 10–15 minutes for cooking, at the end of which the semolina should have absorbed all the milk. If this absorption is not complete, you must leave the semolina in the oven for 7–8 minutes longer.

Border of Semolina for Warm Desserts *(Bordure de Semoule pour Entremets Chaud)*

This is a dessert good for all seasons, like the RICE BORDER FOR WARM DESSERTS (PAGE 589). Refer to that recipe for details about the choice of accompaniments and the kind of mold you should use.

Here we will give the methods used for semolina puddings: That is, making the pudding with egg whites beaten into a snow and then poaching it in a bain marie. The semolina is thus much lighter than when using only egg yolks and when not using a double-boiler: That said, we will describe this simple procedure below, just in case of need.

As for all similar desserts, a semolina border does not have to be served burning hot: it is enough that it should be warm, just a little more than lukewarm. So, after it has been cooked in the bain-marie, it can stand in its mold for a rather long time before serving, which is always an advantage. *Time: 1 hour, 30 minutes. Serves 6.*

125 grams (4½ ounces) of large white semolina; 5 deciliters (generous 2 cups) of milk; 60 grams (2¼ ounces) of sugar, cubes or granulated; a grain of salt (SEE PAGE 575); at least a half bean of vanilla; 30 grams (1 ounce, 2 tablespoons) of butter.

3 egg yolks and 2 egg whites beaten into a snow.

50 grams (1¾ ounces) of raisins from Corinth and of Smyrna, half and half. (The raisins make a very pleasant addition; but it is by no means essential. You can therefore leave it out if necessary.)

A circular mold or a savarin mold of a 1-liter (4¼-cup) capacity.

PROCEDURE. Cook the semolina as directed. While it is cooking, prepare the raisins if you are going to use them (SEE RAISINS, PAGE 573). Butter the mold, greasing the inside with a piece of butter the size of a walnut and spreading it around with the tips of your fingers. Make sure that you spread the butter everywhere, particularly if the mold has ribs.

Once the semolina is cooked, take it out of the oven. Allow it to cool for 5–6 minutes. Then, with a fork, break up the mass. Take out the vanilla bean or the zest. Add the egg yolks and the raisins, carefully wiped dry. Mix everything well with the semolina.

Beat the egg whites into a very firm snow (SEE PAGE 8). Mix it in 2–3 batches into the semolina, doing this step thoroughly: that is, for this recipe, the egg white must be absolutely thoroughly mixed into the mass.

Fill the mold, using a spoon, until it is a little less than 1 centimeter (⅜ inch) from the edge. Strike it lightly on the table to settle its contents. Put it in the bain-marie in the oven (SEE THE DOUBLE BOILER, PAGE 42).

Allow about 35 minutes for poaching, or cooking, in the bain-marie—without boiling. The right degree of cooking has been reached when the surface of the semolina is both firm and elastic under the finger.

Remove the mold from the bain-marie. Let it rest for 7–8 minutes so that a little bit of settling takes place. The border can stand for rather a long time, as explained above.

To serve: Unmold the border on a round plate. Fill the inside space with the compote. Serve.

Simplified method. Once the semolina has been cooked and taken from the oven, add the egg yolks to it, using *only 4 yolks for 150 grams (5⅓ ounces) of semolina.* Fill the mold right up to the edge; the mold can have a smaller capacity than that used for the recipe with whipped egg whites mounted into snow, because the volume of the composition is reduced accordingly.

Put the mold into a very gentle oven. Otherwise, place it in the bain-marie and put it in an oven with the door open for *8–10 minutes.* Either method should guarantee that the egg yolks bind the semolina.

Finally, for an even briefer method, which is good if you do not have a mold of the right size, you can make a border that is perfectly acceptable, proceeding as directed (SEE TO SHAPE THE RICE INTO A BORDER WITHOUT A MOLD, PAGE 590).

Semolina Pudding, Cake, and Croquettes *(Pouding, Gâteau, et Croquettes de Semoule)*

The preparation of the pudding is exactly the same as for the semolina border, but you use a charlotte mold. You can also use a mold with an open center; note that the poaching time in this is shorter.

If you like, you can add the raisins, fruits, etc., that are suggested for RICE PUDDING (PAGE 591). The accompanying sauces are the same. The mold is breaded or caramelized the same way, or sprinkled with semolina, which replaces the bread crumbs.

Semolina Cake *(Gâteau de Semoule).* Proceed as directed for the rice cake (SEE PAGE 592).

Semolina Croquettes *(Croquettes de Semoule).* The same recipe as for rice croquettes. For details of how to first cook the semolina, see semolina with milk for desserts (PAGE 595).

If you like, you can add Corinth and Smyrna raisins that are first macerated in rum or cognac, mixing them with the semolina at the same time as the egg yolks.

As with the rice croquettes, you can also accompany them with a sauce; in season, a coulis of apples is particularly recommended.

VARIOUS DESSERTS
Entremets Divers

Mont-Blanc

The family dessert par excellence. The method of preparing the purée can vary in several ways: some people cook the chestnuts in a light syrup of water and sugar, which they subsequently reduce; others it milk; still others add the sugar after cooking. The recipe given here produces a very fine purée that preserves the taste of fresh chestnuts extremely well. We suggest forming the purée into large vermicelli to serve: this has always seemed to us better than the more common method of molding the purée in a circular mold, where, in our opinion, it compacts, becoming rather unpleasant.

If you like, cream can be whipped at home or bought already whipped at a good dairy shop. Either way, the whipped cream is lightly sugared and flavored with vanilla. *Time: 2 scant hours. (Can be prepared in advance.) Serves 6.*

350 grams (12 1/3 ounces) of good chestnuts; 2 deciliters (6 3/4 fluid ounces, 7/8 cup) of milk to cook them in; 100 grams (3 1/2 ounces) of superfine sugar (caster sugar); 50 grams (1 3/4 ounces, 3 1/2 tablespoons) of good butter; 1 small teaspoon of vanilla sugar or half that of vanilla powder (SEE PAGE 574); 2 deciliters (6 3/4 fluid ounces, 7/8 cup) of whipping cream.

PROCEDURE. **The chestnuts:** Boil them as directed (SEE PAGE 521) to shell them. As soon as they are peeled, throw them into a pot containing the boiling milk; the pot should be big enough so that when the chestnuts are stacked up in it, the boiling milk will cover them. Cover the pot. Keep it on gentle heat at a slow boil. Allow *40–45 minutes of cooking* for good fresh chestnuts. While they are cooking, make sure that the liquid does not reduce to the point of leaving the chestnuts high and dry, and add 1–2 tablespoons of milk if necessary. The chestnuts must be cooked to the point where they can be crushed without effort.

Force them quickly through a metallic drum sieve, taking 2 or 3 at a time and keeping the rest of them warm in the pot: the drum sieve must be placed directly over a clean and odor-free towel.

Rinse and quickly dry the pot. Put the fine semolina of chestnuts into it quickly, because the purée will harden if allowed to cool completely, then add the superfine sugar to it, the vanilla powder, and only half of the butter, divided into pieces. Using a large wooden spoon, mix everything while you heat it gently, for just long enough to mix it thoroughly. Then add, off the heat, the rest of the butter in pieces. Mix it well.

The vermicelli: If you want nice, long, and even vermicelli, choose the right strainer and use it sensibly. Use one with holes that are rather large—large enough to allow a hemp seed through. And stand it over a deep pot: this is the most appropriate receptacle.

Only put a little bit of purée at a time into the strainer. With the wooden champignon, lean on it *while sliding it.* As you go, transfer the vermicelli to the serving plate to stop them being crushed as they stack up underneath the strainer.

To dress them. With a fork, lightly arrange the vermicelli into a circle, exposing the bottom of the plate. Then, 1 tablespoon at a time, place large blobs of whipped cream inside the circle, dotting them here and there. Keep it cool while waiting to serve.

French Toast *(Pain Perdu)*

A very old recipe, still called "golden crusts" in some regions. It is simply slices of bread—whether milk bread, the bread known as brioche, or even a slice of white bread, if you must—soaked in beaten egg and then fried, not in deep fat, but in butter that has been previously clarified. The vanilla called for can be replaced with a zest of orange or lemon or by 1 tablespoon of orange flower water, added only after the sugared milk has cooled.

French toast is good for lunches and desserts. It is also good for snacks for infants. *Serves 6.*

6 slices of bread with a tender crust or 12 slices of milk bread cut 1 centimeter (3/8 inch) thick; a glass of milk boiled and chilled, into which you have infused 1 fragment of vanilla and dissolved 1 tablespoon of superfine sugar; 2 small whole eggs beaten in a shallow bowl with a pinch of fine salt and a pinch of powdered sugar; 100 grams (3 1/2 ounces, 7 tablespoons) of clarified butter; some confectioners' sugar, vanilla if possible, to finally powder the slices.

PROCEDURE. Clarify the butter as directed (SEE PAGE 16). Boil the sugared milk. Add the vanilla or zest to it.

Divide the small breads in two lengthwise, or cut the brioche into the thickness required. If you are using regular bread, use it when it is quite stale, remove all the crust, and always cut it 1 centimeter (3/8 inch) thick into rectangles about the size of playing cards, or into squares or even into rounds about 6 centimeters (2 1/2 inches) in diameter.

Arrange the little pieces of bread or slices on a plate. Moisten them with the chilled, flavored, and sugared milk. Turn them over so that they soak up an equal amount on the other side. Make sure that they are *just moistened* and not soaked, so that they do not break when you pick them up to dip them into the beaten egg.

To fry and serve the bread: Remove the slices from the plate. Arrange them on a napkin folded in half, so that they will drain for a few minutes.

In a good clean pan, heat the clarified butter until it smokes lightly. Then dip the slices of bread in the beaten egg so that they are completely covered by it everywhere. Pick them up on a fork and arrange them as you go in the pan.

Turn them over at the end of a few moments. Make sure that they do not color beyond a beautiful light gold.

Drain them again on a towel. Place them on a plate covered with a folded napkin. Sprinkle them generously with the confectioners' sugar.

Potato Croquettes *(Croquettes de Pommes de Terre)*

A family dessert, which is mainly served at lunch. These croquettes can be accompanied, if you like, with a hot, very liquid vanilla cream, or a cream sauce served in a sauceboat; a coulis of apples; apricot marmalade or red currant jelly diluted with a little bit of warm water, and with or without a liqueur added to it; etc.

These are prepared in the same way as CROQUETTE OF POTATOES FOR GARNISH (PAGE 542), following the style of duchess potatoes. You only add a bit of superfine sugar and vanilla sugar, in a quantity of 125 grams (4 1/2 ounces) of superfine sugar and 20 grams (2/3 ounce) of vanilla sugar for about 450 grams (1 pound) of potato purée; plus 4–5 tablespoons of cream or a very reduced milk. For a very popular flavoring, add to the dough a dozen hazelnuts that have been lightly roasted in the oven, had their skins removed, and then coarsely chopped.

PROCEDURE. Cook the potatoes, then force them through a drum sieve. Dry out the purée on strong heat before adding the sugar to it in one batch, and the cream bit by bit. Work it vigorously and finally add the egg yolks (4 for these quantities) and, if you like, the hazelnuts. To shape, bread, and fry the croquettes, proceed exactly as directed for CROQUETTES FOR GARNISHES (SEE PAGE 542). You can shape them into different forms, as with the rice croquettes, and if you want it to look like a piece of fruit, put a small sprig of angelica in it as the stem.

Clafouti *(Clafouti)*

This is a home-style recipe, even a rustic one, from the Limousin: it is a kind of flan or thick fruit crêpe. In principle, clafouti is made with black cherries; but you can also use other fruits: black plums, mirabelles, greengage plums, etc.

It is generally served warm, or rather lukewarm; but it is equally good cold. It is usually cooked in a tart pan made of thick metal and with serrated sides, which is one of the basic utensils of classic provincial kitchens. If you do not have a tart pan, you can use an ovenproof porcelain plate, in which the clafouti is served, cut into slices. *Time: 1 hour, 15 minutes. Serves 6.*

400 grams (14 1/8 ounces) of cherries or of any other fruit; 125 grams (4 1/2 ounces) of flour; 2 eggs; 100 grams (3 1/2 ounces) of superfine sugar; a pinch of salt; 2 deciliters (6 3/4 fluid ounces, 7/8 cup) of milk that has been boiled and cooled; 20 grams (2/3 ounce, 1 heaping tablespoon) of butter to grease the tart pan or dish. A tart pan about 24 centimeters (9 1/2 inches) in diameter and with sides at least 2 1/2 centimeters (1 inch) high.

Note that the quantities of the ingredients above can be modified depending on the size of the utensil used, because unlike other recipes, the details do not have to strictly observed. You must also increase the amount of sugar when you use acid cherries, and reduce it for the plums, depending on the type you use.

PROCEDURE. Into a small terrine or a salad bowl, sift the flour, then add the salt, only half the sugar, and the eggs. Mix it with a small wooden spoon, to make a batter. Then add the milk, 1 tablespoon at a time, always mixing with the wooden spoon. Always add the milk gradually, to avoid lumps forming in the batter.

Take out the pits from the fruit. If they are cherries, take the necessary precautions to avoid losing the juice. Put the pitted fruits on a plate.

Spread the butter in the tart pan with the tips of your fingers, making sure that every part of it is completely covered; if not, unmolding the clafouti will be difficult. If you use a baking dish, be sure to butter the sides as well as the bottom.

At the bottom of the utensil, pour a few tablespoons of batter, spreading it out with the back of the spoon to form a layer of batter 1/2 centimeter (3/16 inch) thick. Put it on the top shelf of the oven, leaving the door open, or in some other place that is warm enough so that the layer of batter will set in a few minutes. Then take out the utensil to rapidly arrange the fruits on the layer of dough or batter, as for a flan. Sprinkle them with the reserved sugar. Pour over the rest of the batter and spread it out with the back of a spoon to cover the fruits evenly.

Immediately put it in a good strong medium oven, placing the tart pan or the baking dish toward the bottom of the oven, as for all cakes. Allow *at least 40 minutes of cooking.* If the clafouti has been cooked in a tart pan, allow it to rest for about 10 minutes before unmolding it on a round plate.

Just before serving, sprinkle the surface with fine powdered sugar—that is, *glaze sugar or confectioners' sugar.*

Rum Soufflé Omelet
(Omelette Soufflée au Rhum)

This is one of those fine desserts that has become something of a classic in some families and that is always appreciated when it is well done.

An omelet cooked as a soufflé is entirely cooked in the oven. For all the details, it would be worth referring to soufflés (SEE PAGE 436) and, of course, to the section on whisking egg whites into a snow (PAGE 8). Let me take one more opportunity to say that using an entirely copper receptacle is essential here to obtain a very firm snow of whites. If not, you would be better not to attempt making the omelet. *Time: 25 minutes of cooking. Serves 6.*

4 egg yolks; 6 egg whites beaten into a very firm snow; 125 grams (4 1/2 ounces) of superfine sugar; 1 tablespoon of confectioners' sugar; 1 scant deciliter (3 1/3 fluid ounces, scant 1/2 cup) of very good rum.

PROCEDURE. Carefully separate the whites from the yolks, putting the yolks into a terrine or small salad bowl. Add the superfine sugar to the yolks; using a spatula or large wooden spoon, mix and work them together vigorously until the mixture makes a ribbon (SEE PAGE 577). Note that the lightness of the omelet depends on properly executing this stage.

In advance, prepare the dish where the omelet will be cooked and served, so that you will be able to put in the ingredients as soon as the whites have been mixed into the batter: it should be a long or oval dish made of silver or metal. With the end of your finger, spread out a piece of butter the size of a walnut over the bottom and on the sides. Sprinkle the bottom of the dish with confectioner's sugar, using a sugar shaker.

Beat the egg whites as directed (SEE PAGE 8).

Quickly mix *1 1/2 tablespoons* of rum into the egg yolk batter. Then *one-quarter* of the whipped whites; mix them thoroughly to dilute the batter and also to make it easier to add the rest of the whites, doing this as directed (SEE PAGE 10).

Use a spoon to put this mixture into the prepared dish, gently stacking the spoonfuls to make an oval heap about 12 centimeters (4 1/2 inches) high. With the back of the spoon, first smooth out the top of this little mountain; then use the large blade of a big knife to smooth over all the surface.

With the blade of the knife kept flat, make a large groove 3–4 centimeters (1 1/4–1 1/2 inches) deep lengthwise through the middle of the omelet. This groove will help the heat to reach the heart of the mixture, and will then serve as a reservoir to receive the rum. With the point of a knife, make a few incisions around the entire circumference of the omelet, again to help the heat to penetrate.

Immediately put it in the oven. It should be at a good medium heat; avoid using too hot an oven, which will cause a crust to form quickly, thus preventing the heat from reaching the heart of the omelet. On the other hand, if the heat is weak, the omelet will be too slow cooking and it will be syrupy inside.

First place the omelet dish on the stove over medium heat for 1 minute, as for soufflés, to thoroughly heat the bottom. Put it in the oven immediately. Allow to cook for *25 minutes.* After *20 minutes* in the oven, sprinkle the omelet with the confectioners' sugar. From that point on, do not leave the dish, but keep turning the plate to expose all the surfaces to the heat source of the oven until the sugar caramelizes into a light, brilliant layer. The omelet should also have doubled in volume, although it will not start to swell until *15 minutes* after you put it in the oven.

To serve: Once the omelet has been put in the oven, heat the rest of the rum in a very small saucepan with 1 tablespoon of superfine sugar.

As soon as the omelet is out of the oven, pour the rum into the groove made in the omelet. If the kitchen is close to the dining room, immediately light the rum. Otherwise, light it up only when you get into the dining room. When you do this, avoid using ordinary sulfured matches.

Omelet with Jam, Alsatian Method *(Omelette aux Confitures, Façon Alsacienne)*

A hot home-style dessert, which is as simple as it is rapid. Use either a red currant jelly or apricot marmalade, or any other jelly, according to your taste and means. The minced lemon can be replaced by a pinch of powdered vanilla. *Time: 25 minutes. Serves 4–5.*

3 eggs; 3 good tablespoons of confectioners' sugar (3 grams, 1/10 ounce); 1 almost level tablespoon of flour (15 grams, 1/2 ounce); a nice chunk of fresh butter (20 grams, 2/3 ounce, 1 heaping tablespoon); a good pinch of finely minced lemon peel; 1 good tablespoon of fruit preserves or jam to decorate the omelet.

PROCEDURE. Beat the sugar and the egg yolks together in a small salad bowl until the mixture makes a ribbon (SEE PAGE 577). Sprinkle in the flour little by little, beating continuously. Then the lemon peel, and a pinch of salt.

Whisk the whites into a snow (SEE WHISKING EGG WHITES, PAGE 8). Mix them into the batter of egg yolks, taking due care. Immediately melt the butter in a small pan measuring 20–22 centimeters (8–8 1/2 inches) in diameter for these quantities. Once the butter is warm, pour in the batter in one motion *off the heat.* It will even itself out.

Immediately put the pan into an oven that is *not too hot.* Let it cook *for 10–15 minutes,* depending on whether the oven is more, or less, hot. Less hot is better, because the batter must rise before coloring; it should reach almost double its original height. The omelet is done when you gently push your finger on top and it feels firm.

Without turning it over, slide it just as it is onto a long heated plate. Spread the jam on top of it. Fold the omelet in two. Sprinkle it with the confectioners' sugar. Serve immediately.

NOTE. We recommend sliding the omelet onto the plate without turning it over, because the part touching the bottom of the pan is more supple than the outside surface of the omelet, and is less in danger of cracking when you fold the omelet.

Zabaglione *(Sabayon)*

This word, an Italian word, indicates a warm, very foamy cream made with wine rather than milk, which is served as a sauce for warm desserts such as puddings or rice cakes, semolina, various croquettes, etc. In the Italian manner, zabaglione is served just like chocolate or coffee ice cream, in glasses or cups.

You use either a dry white wine flavored with, for example, vanilla sugar, orange-flavored sugar, lemon juice, or a little bit of liqueur—kirsch, rum, curaçao, etc.—or a fine wine—Marsala, Asti, Madeira, Sherry, etc. The flavoring depends on the dessert accompanying the zabaglione. You can also substitute water or milk for the wine and add a little glass of liqueur. But this combination, even though some people prefer it, is not a true zabaglione.

The classic composition of zabaglione includes only egg yolks. However, you can modify it to make it slightly more economical, by using some egg white: 1 white for 4 yolks. *Serves 6.*

3 egg yolks; 100 grams (3 1/2 ounces) of superfine sugar; 1 1/2 deciliters (5 fluid ounces, 2/3 cup) of white wine; juice of 1/2 lemon or 2 tablespoons of liqueur.

PROCEDURE. Use a small, very deep saucepan, one that is suitable for a bain-marie (SEE PAGE 42). Using a wooden spoon, mix the yolks and the sugar in the pan, working them vigorously until the mixture makes a ribbon (SEE PAGE 577). At this point, gradually dilute this batter with the white wine.

Then put the saucepan into another pot that is half full with *almost* boiling water. Using a small sauce whisk, which is essential here to make a foamy mixture, lightly beat it continuously until the cream is nice and foamy and has thickened; if you test it with your finger, it will feel nice and hot. The liqueur should be added only just before serving. If you have prepared the zabaglione in advance, keep it in the bain-marie, putting a few drops of wine or your chosen liqueur on its surface. Depending on the use, pour it on the dessert or serve it in a sauceboat.

Soufflé Fritters or Nuns' Farts *(Beignets Soufflés ou Pets de Nonne)*

First we would like to make the point that for success, a soufflé fritter should have almost tripled in volume in the deep-frying fat. Although covered with cracks, the overall shape should remain nice and round and the color should not have gone beyond a nice golden tint. A badly made fritter is deformed by lumps, and some fritters are no more than a combination of lumps stuck one to the other.

The batter ingredients and its preparation are exactly the same for soufflé fritters as for those of the choux batter. Only the proportions of the ingredients of the batter are different: notably for the eggs, whose enormous quantity causes the batter to swell excessively in the frying mixture. The sugar is always used in very scant measurements because of the way it colors when it is struck by the heat of the deep fat; it is better to leave it out of the batter, as we do here.

Soufflé fritters are fried in a large quantity of deep fat. The amount of fat must be large enough that they can circulate and develop easily. Thus, for a dozen fritters put in at the same time, allow at least 3 liters (12 3/4 cups) of liquid fat (SEE DEEP-FRYING, PAGE 37).

The quantities below make about 2 dozen fritters. *Serves 6.*

2 deciliters (6 3/4 fluid ounces, 7/8 cup) of cold water; 50 grams (1 3/4 ounces, 3 1/2 tablespoons) of butter; 125 grams (4 1/2 ounces) of flour; a pinch of salt; 3 nice eggs or 4 little ones (about 200 grams/7 ounces for the total weight). Flavor as you like: either 1 teaspoon of orange flower water or rum or grated orange or lemon zest.

PROCEDURE. **The batter:** Prepare it as directed (SEE CHOUX PASTRY, PAGE 664). The batter should be nice and smooth, thick enough that it does not run off the spoon when you lift it up and also so that it will fall off in one piece when you shake the spoon a bit.

The deep-frying fat: Heated to a *moderately hot* degree. Check this very carefully, because too little heat as well as too much will spoil the batter's development. To check it, use the following method: Throw a piece of batter the size of a walnut into the heated deep-frying fat. As soon as it has fallen to the bottom, the batter should rise to the surface. If it stays at the bottom and does not come back up almost immediately, the fat is not hot enough. In this case, the fritters will stay at the bottom of the fat and will flatten out instead of swelling up.

In addition, the batter should not color too fast, but only gradually, taking about 3 minutes: This will be the sign that the deep-frying fat is not too hot. During this time, the batter will have doubled its volume, almost without you noticing. As this indicates the fat is at the right temperature, turn down the heat. Immediately begin to distribute the batter into the fat.

The fritters: It is essential to work quickly when adding the batter to the deep-frying fat so that the fat does not drop too much in temperature while standing off the heat.

To shape the batter and to put it into the fat, you can follow different methods, depending on how much or how little experience you have.

First method. This is the usual one. Take a piece of dough (25–30 grams, about 1 ounce) on the end of a tablespoon, holding this in your right hand. Lift up the spoon, dragging it up the inside of the utensil containing the batter, rolling the portion of batter on the spoon to round it and smooth it out. Bring the spoon as close as possible to the deep-frying fat, and with the bent index finger of your left hand release the batter, pushing it or order to make it fall in a ball. With the same left-hand index finger, quickly clean the outside of the spoon. Repeat for each fritter.

The difficulty for novices and nervous cooks is to mold the batter into a good round shape on the spoon before releasing it with your finger. They could try other methods instead.

Second method. Divide the dough into little portions of the suggested weight to make so many fritters. On a table, *very lightly* sprinkled with flour and with your fingers also coated in flour, roll these portions into balls. Place them on a baking sheet without sides or on the overturned cover of a pot, from which you can slide them into the frying fat all at once.

Third method. This is highly recommended, and is also efficient. Arrange the portions of batter in small round heaps next to one another on a sheet of white parchment paper. Dip the loaded paper into the deep-frying fat, and the batter will immediately lift off.

Fourth method. Spread the batter out on a plate in a layer about 2 centimeters (3/4 inch) thick, the thickness of a finger. Dip the handle of a metal spoon into the deep-frying fat before breaking off a piece of dough the size of a walnut with the greased handle, and then drop this into the fat.

Whatever the method chosen, do not put into the deep-frying fat more fritters than can easily turn there as they develop. Bear in mind that the batter must almost triple in volume, and then estimate by eye the space needed in the frying utensil; work in 3 batches if necessary.

To fry the fritters: As soon as the utensil is loaded with the fritters, turn up the heat. As the fritters swell and color, gradually turn up the heat. If the operation takes too long, the fritters will deform and absorb the fat.

The batter swells in stages, bursting as it swells, then leveling off immediately as the pressure is released. Turn over any fritters in the frying fat that do not turn over by themselves, handling them very delicately with a steel wire skimmer.

Allow *about an average of 8 minutes* for the fritters to be perfectly cooked—that is, nice and firm and resistant to the touch.

Drain them on a napkin-covered baking sheet placed on the top shelf of a low oven so that they do not cool off while they are waiting.

Turn the heat off under the basin containing the fat to give the fat time to lose heat and to get back to the proper temperature before putting new batter into it.

To serve: It is always *confectioners' sugar* that should be used to cover the fritters. But instead of using a sugar shaker, which produces just a light dusting of sugar, it is much better to rapidly roll them in some sugar spread out on the bottom of a shallow bowl. Above all, do not use ordinary superfine sugar, which will not remain on the fritters.

Then arrange them in a pyramid on a plate covered with a napkin. Serve immediately.

Crêpes *(Crêpes)*

The recipes for crêpe batter are numerous because they vary from the simple homemade crêpe to the crêpes of haute cuisine. In the first instance, the main differences are due to region, family traditions, and customs.

A homemade crêpe is eaten just as it comes off the pan. In haute cuisine, on the other hand, the crêpe forms a base for culinary combinations, of which we will give two of the best known below.

But to whatever category they belong, a perfect crêpe is the result of a union of three elements that assure its digestibility: it must be light, perfectly cooked, and perfectly dry—that is, not greasy. The lightness comes from the batter; the cooking is a matter of care and experience; and dry crêpes are the result of measuring the fat more than carefully.

The pan must be thick, scrupulously clean, and greased with a purified fat, using *just exactly* what is required. Adding too much fat to the pan results in *a crêpe that is not dry and that has a sweaty, unpleasant look.* We insist on using a purified fat in order to avoid any residues forming, which would cause lumps and make the crêpe stick to the pan. This is why, if you do not have already have a supply of clarified butter, it is absolutely essential to first clarify the butter (SEE PAGE 16) used for greasing the pan. Equally, you can use oil.

To grease the pan: Many people use a piece of very fresh lard, a square of 4–5 centimeters (1 1/2–2 inches) stuck on the end of a fork, to rub the bottom of the pan: this procedure is good. Others use the same piece of lard as if it were a brush or swab, dipping it in the clarified butter, which is kept liquid, and then brushing the pan. You can also make a small pad of material rolled into a plug, then attach it to a stick. In professional kitchens, a brush is used. These different methods eliminate excess fat, which cannot be avoided if the fat—whether clarified butter, oil, or lard—is put directly into the pan.

The fire: Not a flame too full, nor a cinder too hot. On a coal stove, choose the plate nearest to the fire box; never place the pan directly on the glowing coals, whose heat is too brutal. Be careful that the bottom of the pan heats equally.

Jeanne-Marie's Crêpes *(Les Crêpes de Jeanne-Marie).* Here is the prototype of a family recipe: It was around 1830 that a woman from Brittany, Jeanne-Marie, from near Saint-Brieuc, brought it to "the masters" (as they used to say), whom she had served for almost half a century.

The merit of these crêpes is that they are dry and light, and thus very digestible. On the other hand, the batter does not need to stand, so the crêpe can be made instantly. And, something that is particular to this recipe, the pan here does not have to be first greased, as is usual for ordinary crêpes. *Time: 2 minutes of cooking for each crêpe. Makes about 12 crêpes.*

125 grams (4 1/2 ounces) of good flour; 3 whole eggs; 30 grams (1 ounce, 2 tablespoons) of butter; 2 1/2 deciliters (1 cup) of milk; 2 small teaspoons of orange flower water; 2 small teaspoons of rum; 5 grams (1/6 ounce) of fine salt.

PROCEDURE. **The batter:** The batter does not have to be made until 15 minutes before being used. Put the flour in a bowl and make a hole in the middle. Break in the eggs. Mix it well with a wooden spoon, combining the flour gradually with the eggs. Meanwhile, boil the milk in a small saucepan. Then, *off the heat,* put in the butter to melt.

Pour this milk carefully and gradually into the bowl of eggs and flour, mixing them with the wooden spoon to combine everything and avoid clumps. Add the salt, the orange flower water, and the rum, and mix it well: the batter is now ready.

Cooking it: Use a number 22 pan (that is, one with a 22-centimeter/8 1/2-inch diameter). *Put nothing into the pan: neither butter nor grease.*

Heat it, but not too much. Put in 1 tablespoon of batter, tilting the pan strongly in every direction so that the batter extends in a thin equal layer.

Make sure that your pan is on a sustained heat, placed in such a way that the entire bottom is equally struck by the heat. With the point of a small knife, loosen the edges of the crêpe all around, because, being thinner, they are more quickly cooked, and shake the pan a little bit without yet turning the crêpe over.

But here is the critical moment: With two hands, take the handle of the pan and take it off the heat. Give it a sharp toss in the air to toss the crêpe. Immediately put it back on the heat to cook the other side; the second side will, of course, be much more quickly cooked than the first. Then slide the crêpe onto a heated plate and keep warm.

Quickly pour a new tablespoon of batter into the pan just as it is, and in this case there will be no need to heat it first: the heat acquired during the cooking of the previous crêpe will suffice.

NOTE. If you do not have experience of tossing crêpes, you can limit yourself to turning them with a fork.

It may happen, if the pan is one that is not frequently used, that the two first crêpes will not be very successful; and this can also be put down to lack of practice on the cook's part. There is no reason to be surprised by this.

After having cooked 5–6 crêpes, you may notice that the last one tends to stick, which indicates that the pan is too hot. Be careful, before taking out some batter for a new crêpe, to lift it up with a spoon and let it fall back down into the bowl; otherwise, it will become too heavy at the end.

It is preferable not to sprinkle sugar over the crêpes as you pile them on the serving plate, given that the sugar will soften them when it melts. It would be much better to sugar them at the table itself using confectioners' sugar (SEE PAGE 574).

Crêpes Gil Blas *(Crêpes Gil Blas).* Served in our best restaurants for a long time, these are simply small, fine, light crêpes spread with hazelnut butter, and then folded in quarters and served on a napkin. They must be served burning hot, so when you have a lot of crêpes to make, you should use two pans at a time. *Makes about 12 crêpes.*

125 grams (4 1/2 ounces) of good flour; a grain of salt (SEE PAGE 575); 40 grams (1 3/8 ounces) of superfine sugar; 2 nice eggs or 3 small ones; 2 1/2 deciliters (1 cup) of excellent milk; 2 small teaspoons of cognac or fine champagne cognac and the same amount of orgeat syrup; 40 grams (1 3/8 ounces, 3 tablespoons) of clarified butter (SEE PAGE 16) for the pan.

For the hazelnut butter: 60 grams (2 1/4 ounces, 4 1/2 tablespoons) of good butter; 40 grams (1 3/8 ounces) of superfine sugar; 2 tablespoons of fine champagne cognac; 3–4 dry hazelnuts; 1/2 tablespoon of lemon-flavored sugar; 5–6 drops of lemon juice.

PROCEDURE. Mix the sugar with the flour and the salt, and sift everything together through the drum sieve into a small terrine or bowl. Make a hollow in the middle; put in 1 egg, the yolk and the white. Using a small wooden spoon, mix the egg, stirring it bit by bit into the flour; then add the other egg or eggs (one by one), working it the same way. Once everything has been mixed, add the milk gradually, which has been boiled and chilled, replacing the wooden spoon with a small sauce whisk to obtain a very smooth and runny batter. Let it rest for 1 hour, if possible, at a moderate temperature. Just before using, add the liqueur and the orgeat syrup to it.

The hazelnut butter: Shell the hazelnuts carefully to keep them intact; this is essential to help remove the skin: heat them on the top shelf of the oven, without roasting them, then rub the nice hot hazelnuts between your hands to get rid of the skin. Chop them with your knife. Reserve.

Flavor the sugar with lemon as directed (SEE ZEST SUGAR, PAGE 574). Put the pomade butter into a bowl (SEE SOFTENING BUTTER INTO A POMADE BUTTER, PAGE 16). Add the sugar to it; work everything for 1 minute with your wooden spoon at a moderate temperature so that the butter retains its creamy consistency. Then add the chopped hazelnuts, the lemon-flavored sugar, the fine champagne, and the lemon juice. Keep this butter at the same temperature until you use it to spread it on the crêpes.

The crêpes: Use a small pan with a diameter no larger than 22–24 centimeters (8 1/2–9 1/2 inches). Heat it, then spread the bottom with the clarified butter. Then, using a small ladle or a large spoon, pour in enough batter to cover the bottom of the pan, and tip it in all directions to spread it out in an equal thickness. When the batter touching the bottom of the pan has taken on a light color, turn over the crêpe, either by tossing it, or by simply turning it with the ends of your fingers, then allow the other side to color the same way. Slide it onto a heated plate and keep in a good warm place. And so on until you have finished the batter.

To spread the butter and dress the crêpes: On each crêpe, which you have kept nice and warm, spread 1 teaspoon of the prepared butter. Fold it in quarters as you go. Arrange the crêpes on a plate that has been strongly heated and that is covered with a little napkin, keeping them by fours and arranging them so that the four folded crêpes meet in the center of the plate, thus presenting a round shape. Quickly serve with burning hot plates.

Crêpes Suzette *(Crêpes Suzette).* The principle is the same as for Crêpes Gil Blas: the butter is flavored with curaçao and orange juice. Thus: 60 grams (2 1/4 ounces, 4 1/2 tablespoons) of butter made into a pomade with 40 grams ($1^3/_8$ ounces) of superfine sugar added to it, then some orange juice, 1 teaspoon of orange sugar or sugar made with orange zest, and 2 tablespoons of curaçao.

For the crêpe batter, use the same amount of ingredients listed for Crêpes Gil Blas, replacing the cognac and the orgeat syrup with the same quantities of curaçao and orange juice.

You can, if you like, follow the practice of good restaurants and arrange the crêpes folded in four on a serving plate made of silver or metal, without a napkin; sprinkle them with sugar, and just before serving, sprinkle them with curaçao that has been previously heated, which you can then set aflame. It is better in this case not to pile up too many crêpes, because those at the bottom will become too soft.

DIFFERENT PREPARATIONS OF FRUIT
Apprêts Divers de Fruits

Apricots *(Abricots)*

Apricots à la Condé, a Warm Dessert *(Abricots à la Condé, Entremets Chaud).* The characteristic of a preparation à la Condé, which is equally appropriate for bananas, peaches, pears, apples, etc., is rice, prepared just as it is for all desserts, and accompanied by fruit cooked into a compote. The sole difference between the various recipes concerns only the method of dressing the dish. Some suggest that the rice should be used as a base, others as a border, and others prepared as a croquette. Here we give the most practical and most decorative, which is to serve it as a border: the plate can then take an honorable place at a ceremonial dinner. *Time: 1 hour. Serves 6.*

8 nice apricots at the perfect point of maturity; 200 grams (7 ounces) of sugar cubes and 3 deciliters ($1^1/_4$ cups) of water; a half vanilla bean to cook them with in the syrup.

For the rice: SEE RICE BORDER FOR WARM DESSERTS (PAGE 589). The same ingredients and the same quantities.

To decorate the dish and finish it: 2 tablespoons of excellent kirsch; 6 nice candied cherries; 50 grams of angelica.

PROCEDURE. Prepare the rice as directed (SEE RICE BORDER FOR WARM DESSERTS, PAGE 589). A simple round mold is here preferable to any other because this makes it easier to dress the apricots on the border.

While you are cooking the rice, prepare the apricots, beginning by making the syrup for their poaching. Put the sugar and water in a medium-size pot; first allow the sugar to dissolve in the warm water before boiling it. Once you have boiled it, add the vanilla, then cover and continue cooking on very gentle heat, because the syrup must only "tremble."

Cut the apricots in half. Put them in the syrup with enough space around them so that they are not crowded. Proceed in several steps, and always maintain the syrup at the same point, a simple trembling of the liquid (the norm for poaching), which allows you to cook the fruit without deforming it.

Split a half-dozen of the pits to take the almonds out, then take off their skin and coarsely crush them. Put them in the syrup to give it the light flavor of bitter almond.

Watch the apricots closely to make sure that they are not overcooked, so that they maintain their shape and so that the skin left on them does not fold up over the weakened pulp. For this reason, they must always be kept *a little bit firm;* once they can be easily pierced with a large pin, take them out, sliding a fork underneath them to place them on a plate. Cover with a turned-over plate. Keep them warm.

Finally, select from your 16 apricot halves 4 of the least attractive, or any that seem to be a little overcooked. Put them back into the syrup to make the purée to bind this syrup.

The preserved fruit: Put the cherries in warm water to soften them. Wipe them off. Cut each one in half and keep them ready on a plate. Soak the angelica in warm water for 5 minutes to soften it and to get rid of its candied sugar. Cut it into ribbons at least $1^1/_2$ centimeters ($^5/_8$ inch) wide, and then cut these into regular rectangles 4–5 centimeters ($1^1/_2$–2 inches) long. Put them next to the cherries.

The syrup: Force the syrup and the apricot halves left in it through a fine chinois, rubbing it to make sure that everything passes through. Put everything back into the pot. Boil it strongly without a cover to reduce it to at least $1^1/_2$ deciliters (5 fluid ounces, $^2/_3$ cup). Keep it warm in the pot. Just before serving, add the kirsch to it.

Dressing the plate: *A good 15 minutes* before serving, unmold the rice border onto a round serving plate. Place the halves of apricots on the border, lightly leaning one against the other like fish scales. On each half, place a half cherry. All around the apricots make a circle with the rectangles of angelica, sticking them partly into the rice at a slight angle.

Keep it in a very moderate oven or at the open oven door until serving. At that moment, add the kirsch to the syrup, which must never boil or even be overheated. With a spoon, sprinkle it over the apricots and rice. Serve.

Apricots à la Bourdaloue *(Abricots à la Bourdaloue).* Divide the apricots in half and poach them in the syrup as for the preparation APRICOTS À LA CONDÉ (SEE PAGE 605). Then proceed exactly as directed for PEACHES À LA BOURDALOUE (SEE PAGE 608).

Apricot Fritters *(Beignets d'Abricots).* SEE FRUIT FRITTERS, PAGE 629.

Apricot Compote *(Compote d'Abricots).* SEE PAGE 624.

Bananas *(Bananes)*

Soufflé Bananas, a Warm Dessert *(Bananes Soufflées, Entremets Chaud).* An original method of serving a soufflé of bananas in containers, with the skins of the bananas serving as a receptacle. It is prepared in exactly the same way as a soufflé with fruit purée. For all the details of making it, refer to SOUFFLÉS (PAGE 436).

The bananas must be very carefully chosen: that is, very healthy and without spots, so that their empty skins will be firm enough—in this case, strong as thin cardboard. *Time: 35 minutes. Serves 6.*

12 medium-size bananas.

For the mash of the soufflé: 25 grams (1 ounce) of flour; 90 grams ($3^1/_6$ ounces) of superfine sugar; $2^1/_2$ deciliters (1 cup) of boiled milk; a small pinch of fine salt; 3 egg yolks; 20 grams ($^2/_3$ ounce, 1 heaping tablespoon) of fine butter; 5 egg whites beaten into a very firm snow; a small glass of very good kirsch.

PROCEDURE. First work out which side to place the bananas on so that they are stable and do not topple over after you have filled the skins: you can do this by placing the banana on the table before you open it. Then, opposite the side on which you will stand it, insert the point of a small knife and make a very clean double incision, so that you can remove a large ribbon of skin—a good quarter of the skin—without damaging the remainder. The ribbon is cut off square at each end.

Make two or three cuts of the knife in the pulp to cut it out and remove it in pieces with your fingers. Pass this pulp through a fine drum sieve.

Meanwhile, prepare the mash by diluting the flour and the sugar with the boiled milk in a sauté pan. Let it boil for 1 minute. Turn off the heat.

Off the heat, mix into this boiled mixture the egg yolks first, beating it strongly, then the purée of raw bananas, which preserve their flavor better when added at the end like this. Spread the butter, divided into little pieces, onto the surface, where it will melt and prevent the formation of a skin.

Whisk the whites into a very firm snow (SEE EGG WHITES, PAGE 8).

Add the kirsch to the mixture. Beat it a couple of times with the whisk to mix it well, along with the melted butter. Then thoroughly mix in one-third of the egg whites to make it easier to add the rest, taking the necessary precautions (SEE PAGE 10).

Now immediately fill the bananas. Take a skin in your left hand, and with a spoon fill it with the batter, making a dome that reaches rather far above the borders of the skin; more than double in height. Smooth the surface out a little bit with the back of the spoon. As you fill the bananas, arrange them on a round plate that can go into the oven and also be presented at the table; you can place them in the shape of a rosette. In this way, the bananas can be served as soon as they come out of the oven, which is essential for all soufflés. If the bananas were put into the oven on a baking sheet, the time and the trouble that you would then have to take to transfer them to the serving plate would cause a delay that would spoil the lightness of the soufflé.

Immediately after filling the skins, put the bananas into the oven, at a temperature a little warmer than is usually the rule for soufflés. It is very important here for the heat to penetrate into the batter quickly, and it should also, contrary to the norm, come rather more from the top than from the bottom. This is so that the surface of the batter dries and makes a light crust in *6–7 minutes,* which is a long enough cooking time; the inside of the batter will thus remain nice and moist.

After *3–4 minutes* in the oven, quickly sprinkle the bananas with confectioners' sugar. Serve them immediately when they come out of the oven.

Bananas à la Bourdaloue *(Bananes à la Bourdaloue).* Choose them rather small and not too ripe. Poach them gently in the syrup and proceed exactly as directed for PEACHES À LA BOURDALOUE (SEE PAGE 608).

Bananas à la Condé *(Bananes à la Condé).* The procedure is the same as the recipe for APRICOTS À LA CONDÉ (SEE PAGE 605).

Banana Fritters *(Beignets de Bananes).* SEE FRUIT FRITTERS (PAGE 629).

Cherries *(Cerises)*

Cherries Jubilee, a Warm Dessert *(Cerises Jubilé, Entremets Chaud).* An excellent recipe invented by Escoffier for the Jubilee of Queen Victoria of England. It is one of the most simple and quick recipes, taking only 20 minutes, and can be summarized thus: the cherries are rapidly cooked in a simple sugared syrup, and are then served with this reduced syrup, which is bound with arrowroot and then moistened with kirsch, which you set alight. Serve these cherries either in a silver timbale or in a porcelain dish. To be true to its origins, serve it in small silver dishes or in small, thin-sided porcelain containers.

The cherry to use is the large English cherry. As this is certainly not found everywhere, you can replace it with another type, as long as it is large, fleshy, and quite ripe. Choose the cherries one by one so that you buy them all intact and healthy: any that are blotted or spotted or overripe must be rejected. *Serves 6.*

625 grams (1 pound, 6 ounces) of cherries; 175 grams (6 ounces) of sugar cubes; 1 1/2 scant deciliters (5 fluid ounces, 2/3 cup) of water; 8–10 grams (1/3 ounce) of arrowroot; 3 good tablespoons of excellent kirsch.

PROCEDURE. In a medium-sized pot made of copper that has *not* been lined with tin, or if you do not have one, in an aluminum or enameled pot, put the water and the sugar. Heat it over medium heat, then boil it for only 2 minutes.

Remove the pits from the cherries as directed (SEE CHERRY COMPOTE, PAGE 625). Put the cherries in the syrup. Bring it back to a boil; let it boil briskly for *4 minutes.*

Then take out the cherries with a little copper skimmer, being careful to drain them thoroughly if using a spoon. Any contact with a tin-lined utensil will alter the fruit's red color.

Put them in a timbale or a dish, depending on what you have available. Or put them into 6 little dishes or ribbed porcelain dishes arranged on a round plate.

The syrup: While cooking, the cherries will have inevitably released their juices, which will have increased the quantity of syrup but will also have diminished its thickness. To bring the syrup back to the right consistency, boil it over strong heat to reduce to 2 deciliters (6 3/4 fluid ounces, 7/8 cup).

Dilute the arrowroot in a bowl with 2 small tablespoons of cold water. Pour it gradually into the boiling syrup, and mix using a stainless steel spoon. Once the arrowroot has been added to the syrup, maintain the syrup on very gentle heat for *7–8 seconds* only, making sure it barely simmers.

To serve: Strongly heat the kirsch in a small saucepan. If the cherries have been arranged in a timbale or a small dish, cover them with the syrup. Baste them with the *very hot* kirsch.

If they have been put into small porcelain dishes, pour into each one 2 tablespoons of syrup and 1 teaspoon of kirsch.

In both cases, do not set the kirsch alight until you are at the door of the dining room, and place the cherries on the table while the kirsch is still in flames.

Cherry Compote *(Compote de Cerises).* SEE PAGE 625.

Melon *(Melon)*

Macédoine of Melon *(Melon à la Macédoine).* An excellent cold dessert, which is even better when served iced. Its originality comes from the fact that the whole melon is used as the receptacle, holding not just its own flesh cut into pieces, but also a whole variety of seasonal raw fruit. Its preparation is one of the most simple and has the added advantage of being able to be made in advance.

Choose a good melon at its perfect point of maturity a medium-size rather than large, with a nice shape that does not have a side marked by contact with the sun, and if possible with its stem garnished with 2 or 3 leaves: this will act as a cover and the effect will be much more decorative. *Serves 6.*

1 medium-size melon; 375 grams (13¹/₄ ounces) of strawberries, large or small; 4 small ripe pears; 6 very ripe peaches; 50–60 grams (1³/₄–2¹/₄ ounces) of raspberries, rather a little firm than too ripe; about 30 carefully chosen grapes, white and red; 20 fresh almonds, peeled and split in two; 125 grams (4¹/₂ ounces) of confectioners' sugar or superfine sugar; 1¹/₂ deciliters (5 fluid ounces, ²/₃ cup) of kirsch and maraschino, or of kirsch alone depending on taste.

PROCEDURE. Cut the melon about two-thirds of the way up. The top part, hollowed out, will be used as the cover. The bottom part will be the receptacle.

Using a silver spoon or a silver-plated spoon, and no other utensil, begin by loosening the seeds and fibers. Empty them out by turning the melon over. With the cutting edge of the spoon, lightly pare the flesh and remove these trimmings. Having done this, detach the flesh, a spoonful at a time, putting each piece on a plate. Do not cut too close to the rind, and remove only the tender flesh that you would cut if the melon were served sliced.

The fruits for the macédoine: Have all the fresh fruits next to you.

If using large *strawberries,* cut them in half. The variety of strawberries known as Four Seasons is preferable.

Cut the *pears* into quarters; peel them and remove the core and the seeds. Slice them as thinly as you can. Put them into a shallow bowl. Cover them; contact with the air will darken them.

The *peaches* should be chosen quite ripe, so that they come away easily from the pit. Once you have peeled them, mince finely. Always using the cutting edge of the silver spoon, or with a knife that has a silver blade, cut the flesh of the *melon* into small pieces that are more or less regular.

To garnish the melon: Sprinkle the inside with sugar. Spread around 2–3 tablespoons of the pieces of melon on the bottom, also sprinkling these with sugar. On top of them, you can place some of all the prepared fruits, always handling them with a silver spoon, and not trying to arrange them symmetrically. Sprinkle these with sugar too. Continue to layer the melon, fruit, and sugar. After this, the final layer covering everything should be a thick one. Finally, baste with the kirsch alone or with the mixture of kirsch and maraschino. Then place the top of the melon back so that it looks just as it was before being cut. Fasten it with a small ribbon of cotton cloth passed crosswise underneath the melon.

To serve: Before serving the melon, keep it for *2 hours* in a very cool spot. If you have ice, wrap the melon in a kitchen towel, then put it in a terrine full of ice, keeping it raised in some way so that it is not inundated by the water produced by the melting ice.

Just before serving, remove the ribbon that holds the melon in place. Put the melon on a plate covered with nice green grape leaves, and serve with very cold plates. If you have ice, surround the melon with a few pieces of it.

Peaches *(Pêches)*

Peaches à la Bourdaloue, a Warm Dessert *(Pêches à la Bourdaloue, Entremets Chaud).* Equally good for apricots, bananas, pears, and apples, this is a classic preparation for fruit that can be made in many substantially different ways; but they all include the use of frangipane cream. This cream is characteristic of the preparation and can never be left out. You can leave out any of the other ingredients; in this case, poach the fruits in syrup, then simply dress them in a shallow dish between two layers of frangipane cream and brown lightly.

Below, we give the most practical recipe: a border of semolina (or rice, if you prefer), in the middle of which you pour a layer of frangipane cream. On the cream, place the fruit, first poached in syrup and glazed with an apricot glaze. You can, if you like, decorate it with candied cherries and almonds. The dressing can be done a few moments in advance and the plate then kept in a very moderate oven. This type of dessert must not be served burning hot, but only warm. *Time: 40 minutes. Serves 6.*

6 medium-sized peaches, perfectly ripe.

For the border: SEE BORDER OF SEMOLINA FOR WARM DESSERTS (PAGE 595) or RICE BORDER FOR WARM DESSERTS (PAGE 589). The same elements and the same quantities.

For the frangipane cream: 4 deciliters (1²/₃ cups) of milk; 80 grams (2³/₄ ounces) of flour; 80 grams (2³/₄ ounces) of superfine sugar; 2 egg yolks and 1 whole egg; 40 grams (1³/₈ ounces, 3 tablespoons) of fine butter; a small pinch of salt; 3 small crushed macaroons.

To poach the peaches: 200 grams (7 ounces) of sugar cubes; 2 deciliters (6³/₄ fluid ounces, ⁷/₈ cup) of water; a half vanilla bean.

For the syrup: 2 deciliters (6³/₄ fluid ounces, ⁷/₈ cup) of poaching syrup; 2 tablespoons of apricot marmalade, passed through a drum sieve to make a purée; 2 tablespoons of maraschino or kirsch.

To decorate it (if you like): 12 small candied cherries; about 18 husked almonds (SEE PAGE 573), cut in half.

PROCEDURE. Cook the semolina or the rice. At the same time, prepare the frangipane as directed (SEE PAGE 585). Once the cream is finished, sprinkle a few pieces of butter on the surface (taking it from the total amount listed) to prevent a skin forming. Put the pot of cream into a utensil containing boiling water so that it is kept warm while you are preparing the other ingredients.

Once the semolina or the rice has been cooked, add the yolks to them and mold a border as directed.

Then poach the peaches. Cut them in half. Pass these half peaches for a minute through boiling water to remove the skin if it does not easily detach.

Put sugar, water, and vanilla for the syrup into a sauté pan. Once the sugar has dissolved, boil gently for 2 minutes. In this syrup, place as many as you can of the half peaches, one next to the other, but above all without piling them up on one another. On very gentle heat, maintain the syrup at a simple simmer for *3–4 minutes* if the peaches are nice and ripe, and for *5–6 minutes* if they are a little bit firm. The point is not to cook them thoroughly, but only to soften them, *keeping them in their original shape, completely intact;* and the peach halves require less time than the whole fruit.

Then carefully drain these half peaches, lifting them out on a skimmer to transfer them to a bowl. Poach the rest of the peaches and put them with the first. Keep the required quantity of cooking syrup in the sauté pan, *2¹/₂ deciliters (1 cup).* Pour the surplus on the peaches in the bowl.

Rapidly boil the syrup remaining in the sauté pan on strong heat until it is reduced to *1 scant deciliter (3¹/₃ fluid ounces, scant ¹/₂ cup).* Next add the purée of apricot marmalade; and then, off the heat, the liqueur.

To dress the plate: Add the crushed macaroons to the frangipane cream. Mix it with a small whisk to combine the ingredients, as well as the butter melted on the surface. Unmold the border onto the serving plate. Pour the cream in the middle.

Take out the peaches one by one on a fork, draining them. Place them in a circle on top of the cream, reserving 3 or 4 halves to put in the center.

With a soft brush dipped in the liqueur-flavored syrup, spread a layer of syrup on the peaches; the surplus will spread out over the cream between the peaches. Then lightly pass the brush coated with syrup around the top of the border.

If you want to make a decoration, place the cherries on each peach half and the almonds on the border, either in a line, one after another, or stuck 2 by 2 like the wings of a wasp.

Peaches Cardinale, a Cold Dessert *(Pêches Cardinal, Entremets Froid).* This is one of the simplest cold fruit desserts to prepare. It is equally good for pears. The peaches, cooked without boiling in a light sugar syrup, should be dressed on a purée of uncooked strawberries onto which you spread fresh almonds. This is served very cold, and if possible on a mound of ice, either in a low silver timbale or in a jar of crystal or silver.

The strawberry purée, which is true to the original preparation, is today often replaced by a purée of raspberries, as for peach Melba. It is a matter of taste and means, and below we give both of them, so you can make your choice. Whatever the fruit used, make sure they are nice and healthy, ripe and quite red. If using strawberries, which produce a purée less vividly colored than the raspberries, you can strengthen its color by adding 4–5 drops of red vegetable coloring.

In a professional kitchen, particularly during the season for fresh fruits, sugar syrups are generally available, which have already been used for some preparation. However, the syrup in which the peaches are poached can be used immediately for the purée in place of the sugar listed.

At this point, it is worth reminding you that, when handling red fruits, the use of any tin-lined utensil must be avoided, since any contact with tin results in a purplish color. *Time: 30 minutes for the preparation (which must be done at least 2½ hours in advance). Serves 6.*

8–9 medium-size peaches, perfectly ripe.

For the cooking syrup: 250 grams (8⅞ ounces) of sugar cubes; 3½ deciliters (1½ cups) of water; 1 vanilla bean; 500 grams (1 pound, 2 ounces) of strawberries or the same weight of raspberries; 200 grams (7 ounces) of confectioners' sugar; 2 tablespoons of very good kirsch; about 30 fresh almonds; 2 kilograms (4 pounds, 6 ounces) of ice.

PROCEDURE. **The syrup:** For reasons of economy, we give here only the exact amount necessary to cook the peaches 3 or 4 at time, so that they can be completely immersed, which is an essential condition. However, the syrup must also be held in a pot narrow enough to rise to the correct height. So, use either a small, deep pot made of copper *not lined with tin,* or an enameled pot, or one made of aluminum. Add the sugar, water, and vanilla. Dissolve the sugar over medium heat, stirring it from time to time with a silver spoon to encourage it to melt.

Then gently bring it to a boil. Skim off the foam that rises to the surface. Let it boil for only *2 minutes.* Keep it warm.

The peaches: Remove their skin. To do this more easily and without having to scrape them, first plunge them for *scarcely 1 minute* into a pot of boiling water. The skin then detaches itself immediately.

Put the peaches in the syrup only four at a time, so that each is completely immersed. Control the heat under the pot so that the syrup trembles slightly, but without obviously boiling.

If the peaches are perfectly ripe, of a tender variety, and not too large, *7–9 minutes* will be enough to poach them—that is, to tenderize them—and *3–4 minutes* more will be required if they are a variety that is a little bit firm. For very lovely, larger peaches, you should assume *12–15 minutes* for poaching. Bear in mind that if they are overcooked, their pulp will be weakened: the peaches must not lose any of their shape. In any case, it would be better to keep them a little firm rather than to overcook them.

As they are poached, take them out with a pierced spoon or a skimmer. Drain them well and arrange them as you take them out in your chosen receptacle. Allow them to cool and keep them in a cool place.

The fruit purée: Peel and clean the strawberries or the raspberries as you put them on a drum sieve made out of horsehair or muslin, under which you have placed a plate. If the strawberries are of doubtful cleanliness, rinse them quickly in cool water and drain them well.

Using a wooden pestle, quickly turn the fruits to a purée, collecting it in a small terrine. To this purée, add the confectioners' sugar. Or, if you replace it with the syrup, boil it until reduced to no more than 1½ deciliters (5 fluid ounces, ⅔ cup). It is then quite thick. *Allow it to completely cool* before you mix it with the strawberry purée.

The almonds: Remove their skins. Cut them in half; cut each half into 4–5 small long pieces.

To serve: Put the peaches into your chosen serving dish. Add the kirsch to the fruit purée, then spread this purée over the peaches. On this purée, spread out the trimmed and cut almonds. Place the dish on a large round plate. Surround it with a little mound of crushed ice mounted as high as possible around the sides of the dish. Serve immediately.

Peach Melba, a Cold Dessert *(Pêches à la Melba, Entremets Froid.* This very famous cold dessert is generally known by this name. To summarize: beautiful peaches are cooked in syrup and chilled, then dressed on a layer of vanilla ice cream and covered with a strawberry purée.

You can prepare pears in the same manner. *Serves 6.*

6 beautiful tender peaches, perfectly ripe.

For the cooking syrup: SEE PEACHES CARDINALE (PAGE 609).

For the vanilla ice cream: 3 deciliters (1¼ cups) of good milk; 100 grams (3½ ounces) of superfine sugar; 3 nice egg yolks or 4 small ones; and a half vanilla bean.

For the fruit purée: 300 grams (10½ ounces) of nice red raspberries; 2 scant tablespoons of superfine sugar.

PROCEDURE. Prepare the cream for the vanilla ice cream sufficiently in advance that it is ready when you need to dress the dish (SEE VANILLA ICE CREAM, PAGE 651).

The syrup and the peaches: Proceed exactly as for peaches cardinale. The quantity of the syrup for the poaching can be increased, keeping the same relative proportions of sugar and water.

As the peaches are poached, place them in a bowl. Finally, pour their cooking syrup on top of them. Allow them to cool.

The raspberry purée: Once these have been picked and selected, quickly pass the raspberries through a horsehair drum sieve. Keep the purée in a bowl in a cool place. Fifteen minutes before serving, you should dissolve the superfine sugar in it. The purée differs slightly from that used for peach cardinale (SEE OPPOSITE PAGE); otherwise it would exaggerate the overall sugar note of the dish when added to the vanilla ice cream, which is itself already quite sweet.

Dressing the dish: Use a shallow crystal bowl placed on a silver dish, and spread out a finally chipped layer of ice on the bottom of the dish.

A few minutes before serving, thoroughly drain the peaches of their syrup and keep them ready on a plate. Give the ice-cream maker a few turns to smooth out the vanilla ice cream. For ready-made ice cream, work it a bit to smooth it out.

Scoop out the ice cream with a spoon and spread it out in an even layer at the bottom of the serving dish. Arrange the peaches on top of it, one next to the other. Cover them with the raspberry purée, adding it by spoonfuls. Serve immediately.

Peaches à la Coque *(Pêches à la Coque).* For infants and ill folks: the peaches are simply cooked in water like eggs, instead of being cooked in a boiling syrup. They are then served lukewarm or cold on a napkin-covered plate, accompanied with powdered sugar.

PROCEDURE. Do not peel the peaches. Plunge them into a pot of boiling water, where they must be completely submerged. Turn the heat down under the pot to keep the water just trembling. Allow to cook *12–15 minutes,* depending on the size, maturity, and quality of the fruit; a long pin should pierce them easily without effort, right up to the pit. Overcooking will spoil the flavor of the fruit and destroy its shape.

Drain the peaches on a kitchen towel. Remove the skin, which will come off very easily while leaving its color on the pulp. If you want to preserve this beautiful coloring, avoid touching the colored part of the peach, because this color is as fragile as that of the wings of a butterfly and will stick to your fingers and to the towel.

Peach Compote *(Compote de Pêches).* SEE PAGE 626.

Peach Fritters *(Beignets de Pêches).* SEE PAGE 630.

Peaches à la Condé *(Pêches à la Condé).* SEE APRICOTS À LA CONDÉ (PAGE 605)

Pears *(Poires)*

Pears à la Bourdaloue *(Poires à la Bourdaloue).* Depending on their size, they are divided in half or in quarters, and then cooked in a syrup (SEE PEAR COMPOTE, PAGE 626). For the rest, proceed exactly as directed for peaches à la bourdaloue (PAGE 608).

Pears à la Condé *(Poires à la Condé).* Divided into halves or quarters depending on their size, or left whole if they are very small; in this case peel them, "turning" them carefully like mushrooms. Cook them as for a compote, then proceed as directed (SEE APRICOTS À LA CONDÉ, PAGE 605).

Pears au Gratin *(Poires au Gratin)*. A rather easy dish that can be prepared well in advance, leaving you with nothing more to do than put it into the oven at the right time—that is, so that it cooks for about 20 minutes. Note that a warm dessert of this type should never be served burning hot, but only slightly more than lukewarm, so calculate when to put it in the oven, taking into account when you think you will serve it. *Serves 6.*

450 grams (1 pound) gross weight of pears of equal size; 40 grams (1 1/3 ounces, 2 1/2 tablespoons) of butter; 2 tablespoons of marmalade or preserves; 4 tablespoons of macaroon crumbs.

PROCEDURE. Cut the pears in half. Peel them. Remove the seeds and the tough parts of the core. Place the cut part on the table and slice the halves of pear into thin slices no more than 1/2 centimeter (3/16 inch) thick. Generously butter a gratin dish that can be served at the table. Arrange the slices of pears in it, in superimposed circles, without leaning the slices one on top of the other, but laying them out in opposite directions. This is to produce an even layer; and the small spaces produced between each layer will help the heat to penetrate.

In the opening formed by the circle, *put 2 good tablespoons of a marmalade or preserves of your choice:* apricots, plums, etc. Sprinkle everything with *4 tablespoons* of crumbs made from very well crushed and dried macaroons. Sprinkle little pieces of butter the size of a hazelnut on top (30 grams/1 ounce/2 tablespoons in total).

Put it in an oven hot enough to cook it rather quickly, so that the pears cook at the same time as the gratin forms. This gratin should be a beautiful gold without being brown, the pears perfectly moist, and the bottom of the plate just damp from their juices, released as a light syrup.

Pear Fritters *(Beignets de Poires)*. SEE FRUIT FRITTERS (PAGE 629).

Pear Compote *(Compote de Poires)*. SEE PAGE 626.

Apples *(Pommes)*

Baked Apples *(Pommes au Beurre)*. The professionals are in agreement that this dish should be prepared in the simplest manner: the apple is cored, peeled, filled with sugar, sprinkled with butter, and then cooked in the oven. But for family meals, baked apples seem only to be cooked on a slice of toast, which is particularly popular and adds a great deal to the dish. However, the toast makes adding any water to the apples impossible, no matter how little, because it would soak the bread. So it is essential to watch carefully throughout the cooking time, so that you do not allow anything to burn. If you prefer, cook the apples first, and then slide a slice of bread, fried separately in butter, underneath it; but in addition to the difficulty of managing this without breaking the apple, this fried bread is not as good as a slice cooked underneath the apple.

Because they are fragile, baked apples should be served in the same dish where they have been cooked: use a dish made of metal or heatproof porcelain, big enough to hold the apples next to one another, without touching.

The Rennet of Canada, with a golden smooth skin, is the best variety of apple; use medium-size fruits—that is, about 120 grams (4 1/4 ounces). These remain intact much better than large apples, which become more fragile with prolonged cooking. Allow 1 apple per person. Choose apples that are perfectly healthy without spots or bruises.

Ground cinnamon is most usually used for baked apples, but is often replaced with vanilla sugar.

Like most warm desserts of this type, apples do not have to be served as soon as they come out of the oven. Indeed, they are better when they are no longer burning hot. *Time: 20–25 minutes for cooking in a moderate oven.*

6 medium-size apples; 75 grams (2 2/3 ounces, 1/3 cup) of butter; 65 grams (2 1/4 ounces) of superfine sugar; a pinch of ground cinnamon or 1 tablespoon of vanilla sugar; 6 slices of stale bread with a tight grain, cut about 7 millimeters (1/4 inch) thick; half of a small lemon.

PROCEDURE. Core the apples as directed (SEE PAGE 577). Carefully peel them so that no knife marks can be seen, and so that the outside is absolutely smooth. To do this, work in the same way you handle the knife to "turn" mushrooms (PAGE 490).

As you go, put the apples into a terrine of fresh water acidulated with some lemon juice: this is to prevent them from browning from the air; immersed in the water, they can be left for some time without coloring. They can also be cored and peeled in advance, which is a stage of the work that takes a long time; to then prepare them for cooking should require only a few minutes.

With a cookie cutter—or, if you do not have one, a knife—cut slices of bread to have the same diameter as the apples that will stand on them. All the crusts should, of course, be removed.

Butter the bottom of the dish with 15 grams (1/2 ounce, 1 tablespoon) of butter, spreading it out with the end of your finger. Lay the slices of bread on the bottom of the dish and then put the well-drained apples on top of them. In a dish, mix the superfine sugar with the cinnamon or the vanilla sugar. Using a teaspoon, fill the inside of the cored apples with it.

Divide the butter into six parts—that is, 10 grams (1/3 ounce/1 scant tablespoon) each—and place one on each apple. Put the dish on the bottom of the oven.

Cooking them: A regular, medium heat is required. It is rather unusual for a home oven to be very hot at the bottom; but if it is, slide a baking sheet under the plate after 5–6 minutes.

Ten minutes after you have put them in the oven, sprinkle the apples with the butter that has run onto the dish, slightly tilting it to do this without taking it out of the oven. Baste again at *intervals of 4 minutes.*

Twenty minutes after you have put them in the oven, check whether the apples are done by sticking the point of a small knife into one them. Depending on whether it penetrates more or less easily, take the plate out of the oven or allow it another 2–5 minutes, depending on the heat of the oven. Keep them warm until serving; you can baste them one more time just before serving them, with the syrup formed in the dish by their cooking. Place the dish on a serving plate covered with a napkin.

Apples Bonne Femme *(Pommes Bonne Femme).* Also called concierge apples: the two names indicate just how simple the dish is. Apples prepared like this are excellent, and their look is completely original and pleasant. If you like, you can, for one person, cook only one apple in a small dish.

As for all the preparations known as bonne femme, its character is enhanced by using a simple, country-style serving dish. The apples are served in the same plate in which they have been cooked, and you should preferably use a plate of heavy brown earthenware, served on a napkin-covered serving plate.

Use Rennet apples—preferably the Rennet variety known as Canada, which has a shiny yellow skin. For even cooking as much as for the final appearance of the dish, choose apples of the same size and with an average weight of 120 grams (4 1/4 ounces), which should supply one apple per person. Do not use apples weighing any more than 130 grams (4 1/2 ounces). Large apples require a longer cooking time and thus reduce to a mush. *Time: 20–25 minutes. Serves 6.*

6 Rennet apples; 75 grams (2 2/3 ounces) of superfine sugar; 50 grams (1 3/4 ounces, 3 1/2 tablespoons) of butter; 3 tablespoons of water (if you are making one single apple in a small dish, use a little more water: about 1 more tablespoon).

PROCEDURE. **Preparing the apples:** Wipe the apples with a good cloth. *Do not peel them.* Core them as directed (SEE PAGE 577).

With the point of a small kitchen knife, make an incision around each apple 2 millimeters (1/16 inch) deep, cutting the apple exactly in the middle, as if you were making a box with two equal parts. Cut this deep through the skin all the way around: there is no need to cut deeper.

Use a dish that will hold the prepared apples with only a small space between them: the plate should be ovenproof, slightly concave, and made of metal, ovenproof porcelain, or clay; with your finger, spread out a walnut-size piece of butter on the bottom of the dish. Put in the apples. Fill the empty place in each apple with superfine sugar. Divide the butter into as many pieces as there are apples; put a piece into each apple, pressing it down lightly.

Once prepared, the dish can stand for a long time before being put into the oven. Do not add the water until the very last moment.

To cook: Pour the exactly measured amount of water into the bottom of the dish. Put it into an oven at a very even, moderate heat; avoid, in particular, too much heat coming from the top. Allow *20–25 minutes* for cooking, and baste the apples with their cooking juices about four times. Gradually, the apples will swell and the skin will rise like a cap, allowing you to see the white pulp. When basting them, be careful not to let the spoon touch this very delicate cap of skin, which will be deformed by the least contact.

Above all, prevent the apples from coloring too much, because they can quickly turn black; and if this happens, cover the apples with buttered parchment paper.

Perfectly cooked apples will still be intact, and naturally look like a mousse that has been molded into a bowl-shaped cap, half covered by a cap that forms a cover. At the bottom of the plate, the rather abundant juices will look like a clear syrup. Serve in the same dish, as suggested above.

Apple Charlotte *(Charlotte de Pommes).* The classic family dessert, which contains only simple ingredients and is easy to accomplish, assuming that you take due care. Its preparation never varies, apart from the marmalade, which can be made with either lemon peel or cinnamon, according to preference, as well as a little bit of white wine and, as we suggest, a final addition of apricot marmalade. Using this apricot marmalade is better than the suggestion of some authors, which is to brush the charlotte after you unmold it—particularly because the dish is generally accompanied by an apricot sauce, served in a sauceboat. But if, for reasons of economy, you leave out the apricot marmalade, add more sugar to compensate.

The type of bread used for the croutons is of great importance. If you do not have the special square bread that can be found in all bakeries in the towns, use the bread known as English bread, which has a very fine and tight grain; whatever you use, the bread must always be stale. When buying it, bear in mind the waste that results from removing the crust and the need to cut the croutons or toasts into a regular shape.

A true charlotte mold (see *fig.* 68, PAGE 576) is one in which the diameter of the opening is scarcely larger than the diameter of the bottom: in other words, the walls are almost straight up and down. The classic molds made of tin-lined copper can also be used, as well as some steel molds, which are also equipped with handles and were once used for rice cakes. But these are shorter and, more important, much more flared, and the toasts cannot be arranged in them the same way because the flared sides mean they are separated one from the other. It is essential that the toasts be closely packed together, right to the top, directly touching one another. *Time: 45 minutes (for cooking and the steps needed after unmolding, assuming that everything has been prepared in advance). Serves 6.*

1 charlotte mold with a capacity of at least 1 liter (4¼ cups), measuring 13 centimeters (5 inches) in diameter at the opening and 10 centimeters (4 inches) high.

For the toasts: **About 1 good liter (4¼ cups) of stale white bread crumbs; 100 grams (3½ ounces, 7 tablespoons) of butter.**

For the marmalade: **1 kilogram (2 pounds, 3 ounces) of apples, Canadian preferably; 30 grams (1 ounce, 2 tablespoons) of butter; 100 grams (3½ ounces) of superfine sugar; 2 small teaspoons of minced lemon peel; 2 tablespoons of apricot marmalade.**

For the apricot sauce: **2 deciliters (6¾ fluid ounces, ⅞ cup) of apricot marmalade; 1 deciliter (3⅓ fluid ounces, scant ½ cup) of water; 1 small glass of kirsch.**

PROCEDURE. **The croutons or toasts:** They should be as long as the mold is high: here, 10 centimeters (4 inches). Their width and thickness remain the same, whatever the size of the mold: that is, 4 centimeters (1½ inches) wide and 7–8 millimeters (5/16 inch) thick. Their size must be consistent; and to guarantee this, it is not efficient to cut them one by one, but rather you should follow the method used by professionals, which is described below.

To decorate the circumference of the mold of the size suggested, you will need about 15 toasts, bearing in mind that they could break while being handled. With a good large kitchen knife, first remove all the crusts from the bread. Then cut a rectangular block from the bread loaf, with one side 10 centimeters (4 inches) long—which is the length of the croutons—and the other side 8–12 centimeters (3 1/4–4 1/2 inches) long, depending on the size of the piece of bread: that is 2 or 3 times the width of a crouton. Meanwhile calculate, since you will get about 2 or 3 toasts from each slice of bread, the number of slices needed to get the right number of toasts: this will let you establish how thick your block of bread must be. If you can get 2 toasts from one slice, you will need 8 slices: so you need 8 times the thickness of the toast, which is *7–8 millimeters (about 5/16 inch)*. If you find that you can get 3 toasts from each slice, you will need only 5 slices. Once the block has been cut to the right thickness, first divide it lengthwise to obtain 2 or 3 pieces 10 centimeters (4 inches) long by 4 centimeters (1 1/2 inches) wide. You now only have to divide the pieces into slices 7–8 millimeters (about 5/16 inch) thick, and the croutons are ready.

You can decorate the bottom of the mold in several ways. The most decorative is to make a rosette of small crusts or toasts, cut into very elongated heart shapes, and closely packed side by side, like the toast walls above. *You will need a dozen of them.* To cut them, first square off a piece of bread as above, calculating that a heart-shaped crouton can be made from a triangle measuring 4 centimeters (1 1/2 inches) at its base and 5–6 centimeters (2–2 1/2 inches) high, and about 7–8 millimeters (5/16 inch). From a rectangle of bread 8 centimeters (3 1/4 inches) by 6 centimeters (2 1/2 inches), you will get three side-by-side triangles. You simply have to obliquely cut one side of two of the triangles—those on the outside of the bread—and then trim the two angles at the base a little bit, as well as the point of the triangles, so that they look like a heart.

Another method, which is certainly simpler, and is one we suggest for beginners, is to decorate the bottom of the mold with a round of bread. For this, cut a large slice of bread a good 1/2 centimeter (3/16 inch) thick. Place the bottom of the mold on top of it. Then trim all around with the point of a sharp knife, on the bias, underneath the mold, so that the round of bread is very slightly smaller than the mold. If you do not have a large enough slice, place 2 or 3 even pieces next to each other, then place the mold on top and cut in the same way. Alternatively, you can even cut 4 large toasts in heart shapes, which will not overlap each other, but will be placed flat, side by side, with a small round of bread in the center to complete the decoration.

If the mold is not immediately filled, wrap the croutons in a kitchen towel so that they do not dry out, and keep them in a cool place.

To line the mold: Butter it generously, using your finger to spread out the butter over the bottom and all over the sides.

Use a pot with a bottom large enough to be able to lay out a crouton in it. A small sauté pan would be best. Heat the butter *just enough to melt it* without boiling it. Dip the toasts in it one by one, those for the bottom of the mold first, on one of their sides only. Once they are dipped in the butter, put them in the mold with the buttered side down, as directed.

Once the bottom of the mold has been decorated, prepare the long croutons for lining the sides. In the same way, dip them in the butter and apply the buttered side to the mold, overlapping each toast by 1 good centimeter (3/8 inch). Arrange them very carefully, because if they are just slightly separate from each other, even in only one place, the stability of the entire piece will be compromised and it could collapse when you unmold it. As for those empty spaces that are normally produced between the toasts and the mold, you do not have to worry about it here. Everything is taken care of by the marmalade, which acts as a cement, evening out and compacting the entire piece.

Of course, the toasts surrounding the mold extend above the mold by the thickness of the toasts arranged on the bottom, on which they stand. The level must be completely even.

The marmalade: Prepare as directed (SEE MARMALADE OF APPLE FOR DESSERTS, PAGE 620). If you are using apples that have a very dense pulp—like, for example, the Rennet of Canada, at the end of the season—you should add 1 deciliter (3 1/3 fluid ounces, scant 1/2 cup) of water. Once the apples have been reduced to a marmalade—or rather, a rough purée—mix this purée over strong heat with a wooden spoon to reduce it until it has become quite thick and slightly gluey. When you stir with the spoon, the bottom of the pan should be visible. The consistency of the marmalade for a charlotte is of considerable importance: too light, and it will not offer enough resistance, but will also soften the toasts, so that everything will collapse when you unmold it. To finish, mix in the apricot marmalade.

Using a metal spoon, fill in the mold *so that the marmalade rises a little above the edge of the toasts a bit, thus forming a dome.* It will settle and reduce a little bit in volume while cooking; so, if it was lower than the croutons when you unmolded it, it would inevitably ooze into this empty space, causing a collapse. Finally, on top of everything place a round of bread that has been cut very thin and dipped into the melted butter. Put the charlotte into the oven immediately.

To cook: Put the mold onto the very bottom of the oven. If the temperature of the oven is very strong at the bottom, place the mold on a round metal sheet: this will allow you to turn it more easily if the mold does not have handles.

The oven should be at a good medium heat. Let the charlotte cook for *30–35 minutes.* It is no problem to leave it for 5–10 minutes longer if, by that time, the bread is not yet good and crusty and golden. It is not for the look, but for the stability of the charlotte that the coloring of the toast is necessary. When you take it out of the oven, place the serving plate on top of the mold and turn the whole thing over. *Do not remove the mold yet.* Let it stand for a few minutes to allow it to settle. Remove the mold *just before serving.*

Left in the mold, the charlotte can stand for a good 15 minutes; it only needs to be slightly more than lukewarm. This type of dessert does not have to be eaten burning hot—quite the contrary, in fact.

The apricot sauce: Dilute the apricot marmalade with lukewarm water. Pass it through a fine strainer into a small saucepan. Heat it until it boils. Keep it warm. Just before serving, add the kirsch to it and then pour it into a sauceboat.

Apples à la Bourdaloue *(Pommes à la Bourdaloue).* Divide the apples into quarters and cook as directed (SEE APPLE COMPOTE, PAGE 627) in a syrup flavored with vanilla. For all other details, see peaches à la bourdaloue (PAGE 608).

Apples à la Condé *(Pommes à la Condé).* Cut the apples into quarters and cook them as directed for apple compote (page 627) in a syrup flavored with vanilla. For all other details, see apricots à la condé (PAGE 605).

Apple Fritters *(Beignets de Pommes).* SEE PAGE 631.

Apples in Cream, a Warm Dessert *(Pommes à la Crème, Entremets Chaud).* This excellent dish is a classic, and is to be recommended in the fall: the apples, which are kept whole and half-cooked in a light syrup, are covered with a kind of pastry cream and put in the oven to finish cooking there. The apples and the cream can be prepared well in advance, so that you have nothing more to do except dress the plate before you put it into the oven: that is, about 45 minutes before serving. Note that, as with many warm desserts, this one does not have to be served burning hot, but only nice and warm.

Making this dish is ultimately quite simple: the only detail that requires special attention is cooking the apple in the syrup. You must not overcook it. We will provide some explanations on this subject.

Choose nice Rennet apples, good and firm, without spots and dents. They must be used whole, and the smallest spoiled part, which would have to be removed when cleaning the fruit, would cause a partial disintegration of the fruit. Allow for each person an apple of medium size, with a gross weight of 120 grams (4 1/4 ounces). *Time: 2 hours.*

6 apples.

For the syrup: 200 grams (7 ounces) of granulated sugar or lump sugar and 3 deciliters (1 1/4 cups) of water.

For the cream: **150 grams (5½ ounces) of superfine sugar; 40 grams (1⅜ ounces) of fine flour; 5 deciliters (generous 2 cups) of milk; 5 egg yolks; 40 grams (1⅜ ounces) of macaroons crushed into a fine powder; 1 scant teaspoon of lemon peel that has been finely minced.**

In addition: **6 good teaspoons of red currant jelly; an egg white whisked into a snow.**

PROCEDURE. Core the apples as directed (SEE PAGE 577). Peel them, and as you do so, put them in a terrine of cool water with a squeeze of lemon juice to keep them from browning.

Immediately prepare the syrup in a small, deep saucepan, where the quantities of sugar and water given will suffice to immerse an apple in it. If you want to cook several apples at a time, a much larger quantity of syrup will be required; it is essential that the apples are not only completely immersed in the syrup, but also that they are not in contact with one another. If you do not take these precautions, they will be crushed or badly cooked.

Melt the sugar in the water on the heat and allow it to boil for only 1 minute. This very light syrup is all that is required. Turn the heat down to *moderate* and put in an apple, one that has been well drained. Leave it in the syrup on the heat for *7–8 minutes,* maintaining the liquid at a simple simmer. After 4–5 minutes, turn the apple over; watch it carefully, because a rolling boil would make it burst: and at that point, you would have no alternative but to replace it with another one, because the apples for this recipe must remain whole and intact.

Essentially, the apple is being "poached," rather than boiled, and so an exact cooking time cannot be given, because it depends above all on the degree of ripeness and the quality of the fruit used. For this recipe, it is a matter of cooking the apple *halfway through.* It must retain a certain resistance, the outside being tenderized only to the point that it can be easily pierced by a metal spoon to a depth of about 1 millimeter.

Once this precise point has been reached, remove the apple from the syrup. Place it on a plate without keeping it in a warm spot. Boil up the syrup a little bit before putting the next apple in it. And so on, until all the apples have been successfully poached.

The cream: Prepare the cream as directed for frangipane cream (SEE PAGE 585). That is, work the sugar and flour with egg yolks, and dilute it with warm milk infused with lemon peel. Boil it for 2 minutes. Pour it into a terrine; add the crushed macaroons. Dot the surface of the cream with a little bit of butter and allow it to cool.

To dress the plate: Use a shallow dish or timbale or a medium-size bowl can go into the oven. Coat the bottom with a layer of cream 1 centimeter (⅜ inch) thick. Place the apples on top, with the widest opening at the top. Fill the inside of the apple with red currant jelly, making sure that it falls completely inside the apple and does not spread out over the apple.

Beat the egg whites into a snow and mix with the rest of the cream (SEE WHISKING EGG WHITES, PAGE 8). Immediately cover the apples with the cream in an even layer that hides them completely. Smooth the surface with the blade of a large knife. Put it into the oven immediately.

The oven temperature should be *very moderate.* If the heat is too strong, the cream will harden and then curdle, and the apples will dissolve into a purée. The dish thus loses all its character. It would be much better to have too little, rather than too much heat, because you can then get away with leaving the apples longer in the oven. Allow, at a good moderate heat, *a half hour for cooking.* When they are half cooked and when a light skin seems to be forming on the surface of the cream, use a sugar shaker to sprinkle them with a light layer of *confectioners' sugar,* which helps the apples to color.

To be perfectly cooked, the apples must remain perfectly whole, with their shape intact. The cream, golden on the outside, must be as smooth and unctuous as when you added the egg white.

Serve on a plate or in a dish presented on a serving plate that is covered with a napkin.

Apples with Orange Rice, a Warm Dessert *(Pommes au Riz à l'Orange, Entremets Chaud).* Easy to make, and with a decorative look, this dessert is both simple and excellent, and can be recommended as much for a sumptuous dinner as for a more modest meal.

It is prepared as follows: in the middle of an orange-flavored rice border are arranged some pieces of apples that have been cooked in syrup, then basted with this syrup that has been reduced, then bound with a purée of apricots and fortified with curaçao. The whole dish is completed with a julienne of orange peel and decorated with sprigs of angelica. *Time: 1 hour. Serves 6.*

6 medium-size apples, either Rennet or Calville; 375 grams (13¼ ounces) of lump sugar and ½ liter (generous 2 cups) of water for the syrup; 2 thick-skinned granular oranges that are nice and healthy (the peel or zest is the only part used); 3 tablespoons of apricot marmalade pressed into a purée; 40 grams (1⅜ ounces) of angelica; 4 tablespoons of curaçao; 1 good tablespoon of orange sugar.

A border of rice flavored with orange peel. For the quantities and the method, SEE RICE BORDER FOR WARM DESSERTS (SEE PAGE 589).

PROCEDURE. Prepare the rice border as directed. From one of the oranges, remove three ribbons of zest (SEE ORANGE AND LEMON ZEST, PAGE 574) so that you can use them to infuse the milk.

Cut and cook the apples by the method given for apple compote (SEE PAGE 627). Then subsequently reduce the syrup to at least 4 deciliters (1⅔ cups). Keep it in a sauté pan, warm and covered. Into this same pan will be put the apples, the apricot, etc., for serving the dish.

Prepare the orange sugar (SEE ZEST SUGAR, PAGE 574).

Completely remove the zest from the second orange. Divide the ribbons into pieces 3 centimeters (1¼ inches) long. Then stack them one on top of the other to cut them into a julienne that is as fine as wires, so to speak. Put all of it into a very small saucepan covered with cold water. Bring it to a boil and let it boil gently *for 8–10 minutes.* Drain thoroughly.

To finish and serve: Into the syrup pan, add the apricot marmalade (passed through a drum sieve), the orange sugar, and the julienne of zest; mix well. Then put in the apple quarters, along with the syrup that they have released while they have been waiting. Keep it warm *without boiling.*

If the angelica is dry, soak it first in lukewarm water for 15 minutes. Then split it through its thick part and trim it into about 10 long rectangles. Unmold the rice border onto a round plate. Using a fork, take the pieces of apple and place them in a pyramid in the middle of the border. Add the curaçao to the syrup. A tablespoon at a time, pour the syrup over the apples. Here and there scatter the sprigs of angelica, with their points in the air, sliding them in between the apple quarters. Serve.

Apple Mousse, a Warm or Cold Dessert *(Mousse de Pommes, Entremets Chaud ou Froid).* A dessert to be recommended because it combines so many good qualities: a beautiful appearance, a fine and pleasant taste, simple preparation, reasonable price, and finally the possibility of serving it either warm or cold, which means that it can be prepared in advance, an advantage that should often be considered.

The best accompaniment for a *cold* mousse is crème anglaise flavored with vanilla. If the mousse is served *warm,* the cream must be served at the same temperature, which is a little more than lukewarm, and might then seem a little bland. So replace it with an apricot sauce, simply an ordinary marmalade mixed with a little bit of water, then heated and passed through a fine strainer. You can add to it, off the heat, a few drops of kirsch; this is preferable to rum, which has a flavor that is too dominant. This same apricot sauce can also be used for the mousse when it is served cold. *Time: 2 hours, 30 minutes. Serves 6.*

700 grams (1 pound, 9 ounces) of nice Rennet apples from Canada, weighed completely peeled; 50 grams (1¾ ounces) of superfine sugar; 4 egg whites whisked into a snow with 20 grams (⅔ ounce) of superfine sugar; 80 grams (2¾ ounces) of superfine sugar to caramelize the mold.

PROCEDURE. **The apples:** Cut them into quarters. Carefully peel them. Remove the seeds and any spoiled parts. Then cut each quarter into very fine slices.

Put them in a thick aluminum *sauté pan.* The choice of pan is very important here; if the apples are piled up in a deep pot, it will take ten times longer to evaporate and reduce the moisture in them and thus get the right consistency for the purée. In addition, if apples are cooked a long time, the resulting purée will be extremely dark.

Do not add anything at all to the sauté pan with the apples. Just place a round of strong parchment paper on top of the apples, which should fit snugly into the pan. The inside of the pan should be generously buttered.

Put it into a moderate oven. Gradually the apples soften, forming a purée by themselves without getting any darker in color. Allow *45 minutes* so that they are completely cooked and no longer have any of their own moisture. Meanwhile, check them often. If you see them coloring under the paper, mix them with your wooden spoon. The important thing is that they cook uniformly, never stick, and scarcely color at all.

Then force them through a drum sieve, preferably one made of horsehair, on top of a plate: this will produce a homogenous and fine, relatively loose purée, leaving nothing on the drum sieve. Rinse the sauté pan. Put the purée back in it, making sure that you thoroughly scrape the bottom of the drum sieve. Add the sugar (50 grams, 1¾ ounces).

Dry the purée (SEE DRYING PURÉES, PAGE 14) until the point when you make a line on the bottom of the sauté pan with a spoon, the groove remains there, exposing the bottom of the pan from one end to the other of the line. Then pour the purée into a terrine big enough so that you can mix in the whites when the purée is no more than lukewarm.

The mold: Prepare it while you are cooking the apples. Use an ordinary charlotte mold with a capacity of about 1 liter (4 cups) for the quantities above. Caramelize it as directed (SEE PAGE 575).

The egg whites: We beg you to note that the conditions under which the whites are whisked and mixed with the purée are of capital importance (SEE EGG WHITES, PAGE 8). Once they have been mounted into a very firm snow, mix about a quarter of the purée into it to loosen it, then incorporate the rest with all due care (SEE PAGE 10).

Using a large spoon, immediately fill the caramelized mold. Strike it lightly on the table to settle it. Immediately put it in the oven in a bain-marie (SEE THE DOUBLE BOILER, PAGE 42). Contrary to normal practice, do not cover the pan if there is not enough space between the top of the mousse and the cover to let the mousse rise without touching the cover. You can replace the cover with a large piece of buttered parchment paper.

Cooking it: A relatively hot oven, but avoid any heat coming from the top, which would cause a skin to form rapidly, hindering the development of the mousse.

Once the surface of the mousse is lightly colored, cover it with buttered parchment paper. The mixture will swell gradually, rising and firming up.

Cook for *at least 1 hour.* When you touch the mousse, putting your finger right in the center, it will feel both solid and supple. Then take the mold out of the bain-marie. *Wait at least 15 minutes before unmolding,* given that some compression is essential whether the mousse is served hot or cold, and that this type of dessert must not be served burning hot.

To serve: Unmold it on a round plate. Surround it with just a few tablespoons of cream or apricot sauce to decorate the base of the mousse. The rest is served separately in a sauceboat.

The mousse unmolds quite easily, holds together perfectly well, and compresses very little. Its inside texture should be that of a light baba.

Apple Aspic *(Aspic de Pommes).* This cold dessert, which is a recipe that comes from a precious family notebook, is one of the most rapid and simple to make. It is extremely delicate and looks beautiful. The apples, mixed and decorated with candied fruit, are used in irregular fragments, set in their own gelée without any addition of gelatin; the light tint of the whole dish, completely different from the strong color of a normal marmalade, is barely stronger than a jelly. If you like, baste the aspic with a little syrup, made very simply from red currant jelly with a little bit of water and rum. Let us also note that any leftovers of aspic, if there are enough, can be used again, molded in a smaller mold to be served in the same way; but if you anticipate doing this, do not baste the aspic with syrup the first time you use it, because this would dilute it too much.

The aspic's success ultimately depends completely on how the apples are cooked, and the perception of when the apples are perfectly done is the unique difficulty of the process. So we will give some instructions on this subject, which in other cases might seem superfluous. Rennet apples from Canada are better than any others because of the density of their pulp. *Time: 30 minutes to make (plus 5–6 hours for the aspic to set). Serves 6–8.*

900 grams (2 pounds) of Rennet apples, net weight peeled; 400 grams (14 1/8 ounces) of sugar cubes; 2 deciliters (6 3/4 fluid ounces, 7/8 cup) of cold water and 1/2 teaspoon of lemon juice for cooking; 125 grams (4 1/2 ounces) of candied fruits: orange peels, cherries, angelica.

***For the syrup:* 2 tablespoons of red currant jelly; 2 tablespoons of water; 1 tablespoon of rum.**

PROCEDURE. Use a utensil with a large bottom, a sauté pan made of *thick* aluminum—which is essential here. Add the sugar, the water, and the lemon juice: the latter is not to flavor it, but to prevent the sugar from decomposing while cooking. Let it melt over medium heat.

Cut the apples into quarters; peel them and take out the core and the seeds. Then divide each quarter into slices 1/2 centimeter (3/16 inch) thick; use a medium-size knife for this, placing each quarter on the table. (If you have a large quantity of apples to prepare, throw them into a terrine of cold water as you cut them, so that they do not turn brown while they are waiting).

Once the sugar has completely dissolved, turn the heat up. As soon as it is boiling strongly, throw in the apples (after they have been well drained on a towel if they were put into cold water). After *2 minutes,* stir to move the apples on top to the bottom. Use a large wooden spoon or spatula to do this, so that you do not break the pieces.

Do not cover the sauté pan and *cook strongly for 20 minutes at the most.* If the apples cook over slow heat for a long time, they will disintegrate into a fine purée, color, and lose their fresh fruit flavor.

Stir from time to time with the spoon, as before. Toward the end of the cooking time, watch even more carefully: gradually the apples melt and become transparent, without coloring; the light foam produced at the beginning will disappear, as will any excess moisture. At the same time, the apple pieces, despite the care you have taken to mix them, will break into pieces, making a kind of thick sauce. At this point, you must be even more careful that they do not reduce into a purée.

The correct cooking point is this: no excess moisture is left on the surface of the apples. When you tip the sauté pan, the bottom must be studded with little transparent clumps, looking like cooked grains of tapioca. Then turn off the heat. If not, continue cooking until the correct point has been achieved.

The candied fruit: Cut them into little pieces and mix them together on a plate. Keep several whole cherries and a little bit of angelica, cut into rectangles, to decorate the bottom of the mold. About 3 minutes before taking the apples off the heat, delicately mix the candied fruit.

To mold: Use a charlotte mold of the appropriate capacity: here, 1 liter (1/4 cups). If it is too large for the quantity of apples, the aspic may disintegrate when it falls onto the plate when you unmold it. If you like, decorate the bottom with the candied fruit. Using a large spoon, place a thick layer of applesauce on the bottom. All around it, against the sides of the mold, make a pattern of candied fruit, then finish filling the mold. Strike it gently on the table to settle the contents.

Keep it in a cool place or in cold water for the time suggested.

To serve: Run a knife blade between the mold and the aspic. Place a plate or the serving dish on top. Turn everything over, and, if necessary, strike it with the back of a spoon. Do not baste it with syrup until you are ready to send it to the table.

If the aspic is not firm enough when you unmold it, this could be because there is too much moisture left in the apples, the result of badly conducted cooking.

Marmalade of Apples for Desserts *(Marmelade de Pommes pour Entremets).* Use apples of good quality, whatever the variety: otherwise, the resulting sauce will not be worth the work or the sugar used in its preparation. The Rennet apple, notably that known as Canadian, is better than any others because of its perfumed pulp, which is sweet and dense: it is this density that produces a good result. Always be careful to choose them perfectly ripe.

First cut the apples into quarters, because peeling them will be easier. Peel them carefully. Remove the middle part containing the seeds. If the apple marmalade is to be used as a purée—as for a mousse or soufflé, etc.—and first passed through a drum sieve, be very careful to remove all the woody parts of the core when you take out the seeds. After this, cut the quarters lengthwise into fine slices.

In a large, shallow pot, or sauté pan (in which the evaporation is easier), melt—and only *melt*—some butter: use an average of about 50 grams (1$^{3}/_{4}$ ounces, 3$^{1}/_{2}$ tablespoons) for each kilogram (2 pounds, 3 ounces) net weight of apples. Put the apples in it and baste them for this quantity with 1 deciliter (3$^{1}/_{3}$ fluid ounces, scant $^{1}/_{2}$ cup)—that is, $^{1}/_{2}$ glass—of good white wine, or if not, water. This liquid is, of course, only to be used for good apples that have a tight pulp, because for apples with a watery pulp no water is needed, although the wine should always be used because it adds flavor.

Sprinkle it with superfine sugar or granulated sugar. The quantity varies depending on the variety of apple used, and also depending on how the apple marmalade will be used. If no extra sugar will be added—as for a charlotte, say—and it will be served just as is, you will need to add more sugar. But this sugar can be added after cooking, once you have checked the flavor. For the moment, limit yourself to *50 grams (1$^{3}/_{4}$ ounces) of sugar.*

Finally, add the flavoring: either a vanilla bean or a ribbon of orange or lemon peel, being very careful not to include any bitter white part; also a little bit of cinnamon stick or powder.

If you have an oven, and an oven that is hot enough, put in the apples. Let them cook uncovered without them coloring or drying out too much. From time to time, move them around the bottom of the pan so that they cook evenly. Particularly toward the end of the cooking time, it is essential to mix them often. At this point, the juice of the apples combines with the sugar and begins to form a very light caramel, and you must carefully check that you do not allow it to color too much or to stick to the bottom of the pan.

When serving apple marmalade as a simple dessert, do not pass it through a drum sieve. But there are some preparations—such as a mousse, a soufflé, etc.—where a purée rather than a sauce, to describe it accurately, is required. If so, pass the apple marmalade through a horsehair drum sieve that is used only for sugared things; and then reduce it if it has to be quite thick.

Apple Coulis *(Coulis de Pommes).* To accompany warm desserts—rice, milk semolina, etc. *Time: 30 minutes. Serves 6.*

2 medium-size apples; 50 grams (1$^{3}/_{4}$ ounces) of sugar lumps; 2$^{1}/_{2}$ deciliters (1 cup) of water; a small glass of kirsch.

PROCEDURE. Cut into quarters, peel and seed, then finally slice the apples. Put them in a small saucepan with sugar and water. Cook them rapidly. Pass them through a metallic drum sieve and collect the coulis in the rinsed pan used for cooking the apples.

Some apples produce a very concentrated pulp, and if the coulis seems a little too thick, simply add 1–2 tablespoons of water to bring it to the consistency of a sauce.

And when you have an apricot marmalade or greengage plum marmalade, adding 1 tablespoon of this marmalade to the coulis is advised (after cooking the apples and before passing them through a drum sieve). Not only is the flavor enhanced, but the marmalade also acts as a light liaison.

Keep the coulis warm without allowing it to boil. Just before serving, add the kirsch or the rum, which must be heated up only a little.

Fruit Meringues *(Fruits Meringues)*

This is a hot dessert that is virtually a classic, and it is also very practical: the preparation can vary according to taste and the seasons, and can be adapted to ordinary family meals as well as those with guests. So instead of the rice base, you can equally well use semolina (SEE SEMOLINA WITH MILK FOR DESSERTS, PAGE 595), and in winter can include thick apple marmalade or orange rice or lemon rice mixed in equal parts with apple marmalade.

For this dessert, you can use apricots, pineapples, bananas, peaches, pears, apples, or plums. We use apricots here for a typical preparation. So for the other fruits, base the recipe on this one.

Bananas, like the other fruits, should be lightly

cooked in syrup. Leave them whole if small; if they are large, cook them in the syrup first and then cut into very thin slices. The *peaches* are poached whole or cut in half, depending on their size. The *pears,* depending on their size, can be cut in half or into quarters. The *apples* are cut into quarters and cooked as described (SEE APPLE COMPOTE, PAGE 627).

Fruits prepared like this must be perfectly ripe, very healthy, and without spots or blemishes, so that they remain perfectly intact after cooking in the syrup. In winter, this kind of dessert can also be made with preserved peaches and apricots; in this case, the fruits, having already been cooked, just need to be reheated before being served.

Even though this dessert takes rather a long time to prepare because of its different ingredients, its preparation is not difficult. It even offers the advantage that it can be made in advance, in terms of preparing the rice and the fruits, which you can then keep warm. There is then nothing more to do at the last moment than to make the meringue, cover the fruit and rice with it, and then put everything in an oven for about a half hour to dry out the meringue.

The dish used for this kind of preparation must be able to go into the oven and then be served at the table: use a round silver or metal plate, or an ovenproof porcelain plate. A silver dish can be used here without risking any damage, because the heat to which it will be exposed in the oven is very gentle, and no gratin will form on the bottom or sides of the dish.

Apricot Meringue *(Abricots Meringués).* *Time: 2 scant hours. Serves 6–8.*

12 medium-size apricots; 275 grams (9²/₃ ounces) of sugar, in cubes or granulated; 3¹/₂ deciliters (1¹/₂ cups) of water and a half vanilla bean for the syrup.

***For the meringue:* 5 egg whites whisked into a snow; 260 grams (9¹/₅ ounces) of superfine sugar; 30 grams (1 ounce) of confectioners' sugar.**

***For the rice:* 100 grams (3¹/₂ ounces) of Carolina rice; 4 deciliters (1²/₃ cups) of good boiled milk; 70 grams (2¹/₂ ounces) of sugar (in cubes or granulated); 25 grams (1 ounce, 2 tablespoons) of butter; a half vanilla bean; a grain of salt (SEE PAGE 575); 2 egg yolks.**

PROCEDURE. **The rice:** Prepare it as directed (SEE MILK RICE FOR DESSERTS, PAGE 588). When you take it out of the oven, allow it to cool for 4–5 minutes. Then remove the vanilla bean. Break up the mass of rice with a fork, mixing in the egg yolks, previously diluted with some water. Keep the rice warm.

The apricots: In a medium-size pot, melt the sugar and the water on low heat.

Cut the apricots in half without peeling them.

Once the sugar has melted, add the vanilla to it. Put the pot on strong heat and boil this syrup for *2 minutes* only. Turn the heat down very low.

Put into the syrup as many halves of apricots as it can hold without them being jammed together. Poach them—that is, cook them without boiling—for *about 7 minutes.* Do not forget that the apricot halves must remain perfectly whole, while also being quite soft, and you must watch carefully that they do not disintegrate into a purée. As soon as the apricots are perfectly done, take them out with a fork and put them on a large drum sieve turned upside down, or on a muslin cloth laid out over a large bowl.

Dressing the apricots: Pour the rice onto a plate and spread it out with the back of a spoon. Then, with the blade of a large knife, shape it into a round cake about 15 centimeters (6 inches) in diameter and 2¹/₂–3 centimeters (1–1¹/₄ inches) thick. On this cake, place the apricot halves in a dome. Cover with a large inverted bowl and keep it warm.

The meringue: Whip the egg whites as directed (SEE EGG WHITES, PAGE 8). Then add the *superfine* sugar, and whenever possible, get another person to help you. Gently drop a shower of sugar onto the whites while you cut and lightly raise the whites in the manner described for mixing (SEE PAGE 10). When you have no help, add the sugar in 2 or 3 batches, always by pouring it in a shower, so that you are able to make the movements suggested and take the necessary precautions.

Using a metal spoon, delicately place the meringue on top of the apricots. With the back of the spoon, shape it into a dome that covers the apricots and the rice. Smooth around the sides and the surface with the blade of a large knife. If you like, you can leave the meringue in a dome shape just as it is, or you can shape it in the following manner: either by making some large ribs like those of a melon, tracing a groove with the spoon and lightly pushing back the whites on each side; or tracing a double cross on it to make grooves that form a rosette. You must do all this quickly and with a light touch so that you do not squash the whites.

There are also, of course, the decorations or patterns that can be made by piping the meringue from a small pastry bag. Or, more simply, from a cornet of strong paper whose tip you have cut off. Or, pipe lines to form a design—a rose or another pattern—on the dome, or any other motif.

Finally, sprinkle all the meringue surface with the *confectioners' sugar,* using a container with a cover pierced with holes (SEE PAGE 574). Put it into the oven as soon as possible.

The cooking of the meringue: An extremely gentle heat. Truth to tell, the meringue is set not so much by cooking, but rather by drying out. It must set very gradually, and the very light golden color should not form on the surface of the meringue until after it has set. If the oven is too hot, the surface of the meringue hardens too quickly and makes a crust, which will then make it difficult for the heat to penetrate inside, where the moisture from the egg is trapped. Moreover, if the meringue colors too rapidly, you must take the plate out of the oven to stop it from turning brown; and all of this will result in a meringue that is badly cooked, flat, wrinkled, and sticky.

But a gentle and even heat produces a risen meringue, with a very dry surface that is crisp while the interior layer is tender; and you can cut it cleanly without it running or sticking to the spoon.

Allow *25–30 minutes* in the oven under such temperature conditions as we have just described. Once the layer of meringue is properly firm, the plate can be left in a very gentle oven without deteriorating.

Chilled Fruits *(Fruits Rafraîchis)*

The preparation is very simple: it is, to be brief, a kind of macédoine, which requires ice if it is be prepared successfully. If you do not have ice, you must find a way to serve this dish extremely cold.

The great variety of fruits used is characteristic of the dish; use them in proportions that are more or less equal. Even though, in the recipe given below, grapes are not included, you can always add a few red and white ones. What's more, you can use all the seasonal fruits; it is essential that they be perfectly ripe and also of good quality: so we recommend pulp fruits, such as apricots, peaches, pears, etc., choosing a very succulent variety.

The amount of sugar, whether larger or smaller, is determined by the type of fruits as well as the preference of the guests. So the quantity suggested below is an average.

The choice of the liqueur is optional: kirsch is always excellent, as is maraschino and also champagne. You can even mix one with the other. So, kirsch and maraschino, half and half, or maraschino and champagne; or cherry brandy and champagne—all depending on your taste and means.

For serving these fruits, use a shallow timbale or a silver dish or a crystal salad bowl. Choose one that is a little larger than you initially think you need: this will enable you to toss the fruits easily in it while they are macerating. *Time: 45 minutes (if you have ice). Serves 6.*

3 peaches; 3 apricots; 2 nice medium-size pears or 3 small ones; 3 tablespoons of small strawberries; 2 tablespoons of raspberries; 2 tablespoons of gooseberries and red currants; 24 small cherries; 12 fresh almonds; 2 tablespoons of superfine sugar; $1^1/_2$ deciliters (5 fluid ounces, $^2/_3$ cup) of the liqueur of your choice.

PROCEDURE. *The pears.* Cut them into quarters; peel them; remove their seeds; cut them into fine and equal slices. Put them in a small bowl covered with another plate, because contact with air will darken them.

The peaches. Peel them. If the skin is not coming off easily, plunge them into boiling water *for a few seconds.* Once you have peeled them, slice them as thinly as the pears.

The apricots. Generally, the skin is left on them. Cut them into thin slices.

The cherries. Remove the pits. If the cherries are a little sour, heat them for a few moments with 1 tablespoon of superfine sugar and 3–4 tablespoons of water. Afterward, spread them out on a plate to cool them off.

The strawberries and the raspberries. Remove their stems. If the strawberries need to be washed, do this quickly, and then drain them well.

The red currants. Remove their seeds with a silver fork.

The almonds. Remove their skins and cut them in half.

Mix together all the fruits and arrange them in a dish in layers that are equally thick, without making a dome in the middle, and then sprinkle each layer with a little bit of superfine sugar. *Note that each layer must contain a well-mixed assortment of fruits.* Baste with the chosen liqueur.

Place the receptacle in a terrine and surround it with little pieces of ice. Allow it to chill *for 20–30 minutes,* and toss the fruits every 5 minutes so that they are all impregnated with the syrup produced by the sugar melting in the liqueur and the juice released by the fruits. Do not take the receptacle out of the ice until just before serving.

Compotes *(Compotes)*

The principle for every preparation of compote is that the fruit is cooked in syrup, keeping its shape intact, and then served covered with its reduced or bound syrup. Consequently, the fruit used for a compote must be perfectly healthy and not overripe, so that they do not collapse in the syrup while cooking.

The syrup is made by poaching—that is, without boiling strongly—so that the fruit does not disintegrate. The quantity of syrup must be just enough to cover the fruit while cooking. For this syrup, you can use either granulated sugar or sugar cubes.

For red fruits, use a utensil made of red copper that has not been lined with tin, because *the tin alters the red color of the fruit;* or one made of aluminum, or even a good enameled pot. For other fruits, the best utensil to use is a small sauté pan, whose bottom is wider than that of deep pot and allows you to place the fruits in it without them stacking up. This ensures that the fruits poach more evenly. Always choose a utensil of the right size for the quantity of fruit, so that the syrup can cover them. If necessary, cook the fruit in two batches.

For handling any red fruits, never use a tinned metal spoon, which will turn the juice purplish. Always use a silver spoon or a stainless steel spoon.

Depending on circumstances, compotes can be served cold or warm; by "warm," we mean a temperature a little warmer than lukewarm, because the flavor of the fruits is much better than when compotes are served very hot. Served warm, compotes go especially well with a rice preparation or a semolina border or base; or in a pastry, such as a timbale or a pastry shell, etc. The combination makes an excellent dessert.

To intensify the natural flavor of any fruit that has a pit—such as cherries, apricots, plums, etc.—break up the pits with a hammer, put them in a small muslin or cheesecloth pouch, and add these to the fruit while it is cooking. (We will describe this procedure for the compote of pitted cherries.)

We would also like to suggest and recommend thickening the syrup for compotes with a starch, as we suggest for the cherry compote. As currently used by professional cooks, it compensates for the fact that some fruits do not produce a thick enough syrup, and enables you to avoid using too much sugar, which is often added to give the syrup more consistency. Even if we do not consider the cost of this, too much sugar in a compote ruins the flavor of the fruit. It is better to use arrowroot starch, which is even finer than potato starch and is needed in lesser quantities.

When a compote is served cold, it is better not to pour the syrup over the fruit until it has completely chilled, and also to do this only just before serving: the fruit will thus look more brilliant. When using a starch, this precaution is not necessary; the syrup can be poured on the fruit when it is warm and will remain like varnish.

Apricot Compote *(Compote d'Abricots).* This can, if you like, be prepared in the manner of mirabelle and greengage plums—that is, by pressing some of the less cooked fruits into a purée, which can be used to bind the reduced syrup; or you can make this mixture with an apricot marmalade, as we will describe below. *Serves 6.*

2 dozen apricots, perfectly ripe; 300 grams (10 1/2 ounces) of sugar and 3 deciliters (1 1/4 cups) of water; 1 tablespoon of apricot marmalade; 3 tablespoons of good kirsch.

PROCEDURE. Use a small sauté pan; put the sugar in it to dissolve in the water, which can be either warm or hot. Boil for *2 minutes;* cut the apricots in half, then remove the pits. Put as many apricots into the boiling syrup as can be placed there without stacking up. Then continue cooking on very gentle heat, maintaining the syrup at a very gentle simmer. The apricots should be nice and tender, but must also remain a little firm so that they do not collapse into a purée. When they have been perfectly cooked, take them out with a pierced spoon or with a fork. Depending on how you will use the compote, put them into a fruit bowl or another type of bowl.

Once all the apricots have been poached, add the apricot marmalade to the syrup. Boil it briskly until it reduces to 3 deciliters (1 1/4 cups). Off the heat, add the kirsch. Strain the syrup through a chinois onto the apricots. Carefully break six pits to take out the almonds in them. Remove the skin and cut them in half. Add them to the compote.

Cherry Compote *(Compote de Cerises).* Most appropriate here is the English cherry, or the Montmorency cherry: or at least similar a type of cherry. Black cherries, Bigarreau cherries, should not be used in compotes. *Serves 6.*

750 grams (1 pound, 10 ounces) of cherries; 150 grams (5 1/2 ounces) of sugar; 1 1/2 deciliters (5 fluid ounces, 2/3 cup) of white wine; 125 grams (4 1/2 ounces) of nice ripe red currants; 3 tablespoons of kirsch; 1/2 teaspoon of arrowroot.

PROCEDURE. Take the pits out of the cherries without breaking them, and, above all, without losing their juice. For this, you can use a little piece of pointed wood; or, which is better, the end of a piece of wire doubled over, its ends stuck into a cork for easy handling; a very fine hairpin stuck into a cork is just as good. As you go, put the pitted cherries into a bowl.

Smash a handful of pits and then put them into a cloth tied with a string; they will thus give the syrup used for cooking the cherries an agreeable taste of bitter almond.

Crush the red currants and place them in a towel to extract the juice from them; the quantity of red currants listed above should give you 3–4 tablespoons.

In a copper or aluminum pot, put the white wine, the red currant juice, and the sugar. Dissolve the sugar over the heat. Afterward, add the cherries and the pouch of smashed pits. Bring it to a boil. Maintain the cherries at a very gentle simmer for *7–8 minutes.*

Once the cherries have been cooked, cover the utensil. Keep it off the heat but warm for *10 minutes,* to allow the pits to infuse thoroughly into the syrup.

To dress the compote: Take out the pouch of crushed pits. Remove the cherries, taking them out with a silver spoon. Bring the syrup to a boil; it will have been diluted by the juice from the cherries. Allow it to boil for *2 minutes;* skim off the small foam that is produced. Pour the arrowroot into the boiling syrup, having diluted it first with a little bit of cold water in a cup. Allow it to boil for only another *2–3 seconds.* Off the heat, add the kirsch. Pour the syrup over the cherries.

Home-Style Cherry Compote *(Compote de Cerises Façon Ménagère).* The stems and pits are not removed; you simply shorten the stems. *Serves 6.*

750 grams (1 pound, 10 ounces) of Montmorency cherries; 3 deciliters (1 1/4 cups) of water; 150 grams (5 1/3 ounces) of granulated sugar; 1/2 teaspoon of arrowroot or potato starch.

PROCEDURE. Melt the sugar in the water in a utensil that is not *tin-lined,* as suggested previously. With scissors, cut the stems, leaving them only 2 centimeters (3/4 inch) long. Wash the cherries in cool water. Drain well.

Once the sugar has melted, place the pan on the heat; bring it to a boil. Then immediately put the cherries into the syrup and keep it on strong heat until the boiling has resumed. Then turn down the heat; cover the utensil. Keep it at a very gentle simmer *for about 10 minutes.*

Drain the cherries in a horsehair strainer, taking them out of the syrup with a silver spoon. Bring the syrup back to a boil. Remove the small foam, then make the liaison as directed in the previous recipe. Put the cherries into a fruit bowl or a serving dish and pour over the syrup; they will swell again in the warm syrup. Allow them to chill.

Strawberry Compote *(Compote de Fraises).* Use large, healthy strawberries that are not too ripe. For 675 grams (1 pound, 8 ounces) of strawberries, cook 200 grams (7 ounces) of sugar to the ball stage (SEE COOKING SUGAR, PAGE 577). Throw in the strawberries. Cover. Keep warm *without boiling* for *8–10 minutes.*

The syrup, which initially sets when it comes into contact with the strawberries, then liquefies and impregnates the strawberries. It must not be put back on the heat; the fruit is simply macerating here. Arrange them in a fruit bowl or a serving dish and cover them with syrup.

If you like, you can first reduce the syrup and add a glass of very good wine. Similarly, a light addition of red currant jelly, which you can dissolve before taking it off the heat, adds to both its flavor and its consistency at the same time.

Peach Compote *(Compote de Pêches).*

8 nice peaches; 175 grams (6 ounces) of sugar; 2 deciliters (6¾ fluid ounces, ⅞ cup) of water; a half vanilla bean.

PROCEDURE. Cut the peaches in half. Remove the skin, pulling it off with the blade of a small knife. If it does not come away easily, dip the skin side into boiling water for a few seconds only.

In a small sauté pan, put the sugar and the water. Once the sugar has been well dissolved, bring it to a boil. Let it boil for *2–3 minutes only.* Put the peach halves into the syrup, adding just enough so that they are not stacked up. Cover. Turn the heat down very low to keep the syrup at a *simple simmer for 5–6 minutes.* The peaches should be slightly firm rather than overcooked. Drain them immediately, and replace them with a new quantity of peaches, and so on.

Finally, pour the cooking syrup on top of them and allow them to cool.

Pear Compote *(Compote de Poires).* The exact type of pears, not to mention their size, cannot be specified here. If the pears are very small, leave them whole and with their stem. Any larger, and they should be cut in half or into quarters.

At any rate, they should be carefully peeled in the same way that you "turn" mushrooms, so that no knife marks can be seen, and so that they have a nice smooth surface. After this, if the pear has to be divided, cut it in half; hollow out the core and remove the seeds. As you do this, put the pears into a small terrine of cool, acidulated water; use lemon juice, or rub them all over with a piece of lemon, to stop them darkening before you put them into the syrup.

The syrup used for cooking the pear compote often includes wine, preferably red, and is flavored with lemon zest or cinnamon. When the syrup is based with water, flavor it with either vanilla or zest; your choice.

Simple Pear Compote *(Compote de Poires Simple).*

6 pears of medium size; 4 deciliters (1⅔ cups) of water and 275 grams (9⅔ ounces) of sugar; 1 vanilla bean.

PROCEDURE. In a small aluminum sauté pan, dissolve the sugar in warm water. Then boil for 2 minutes. Add the vanilla; cover; keep it off the heat while you prepare the pears.

Peel them. Cut them in two and proceed as directed above. Put only half the pears in the syrup, which should cover them completely. Then maintain the syrup at a very gentle simmer.

If the pears are a fine and succulent type, you will need very little time to poach them: *7–8 minutes.* As soon as the pulp yields to the touch or a pin pierces them without any resistance, take them out of the syrup.

Once all the pears have been cooked, rapidly boil the syrup to reduce it to 2 deciliters (6¾ fluid ounces, ⅞ cup). Bind it with arrowroot, then pass it through a chinois onto the pears.

Red Wine Pear Compote *(Compote de Poires au Vin Rouge).* An excellent home-style dish, which lets the fruits keep all their own flavor and adds no other flavoring. But the wine used, Burgundy or Bordeaux, must be very good, and the pears must also be a good type and of high quality if they are to be served as a dessert. Nice English pears that are just perfectly ripe, still a little firm and with an average weight of 100 grams (3 1/2 ounces), are the type of fruit to be chosen here.

10 pears; 100 grams (3 1/2 ounces) of sugar; 3 1/2 deciliters (1 1/2 cups) of water; 2 full deciliters (6 3/4 fluid ounces, 7/8 cup) of good red wine.

PROCEDURE. Use a good pot that is not lined with tin and that is big enough to hold all the pears when you stand them up, leaning them against one another. Put in the sugar to dissolve with the water and the wine.

With the point of a knife, remove the little button opposite the stem of the pears. Then peel them as directed. If the stems are very long, cut off a little piece with scissors.

Bring the syrup to a boil. Arrange the pears in the pot. Cover. Keep the syrup at a very gentle, regular simmer until the pears are nice and tender; *you need to allow 45 minutes.* From time to time, gently shake the pot to move the pears without touching them directly. When they are properly cooked, place them in a serving dish or a fruit bowl. Strongly boil their syrup, uncovered, to reduce it to 1 1/2 deciliters (5 fluid ounces, 2/3 cup). Baste the pears with it; if you like, garnish the stems with a little piece of curly paper. Serve warm or cold.

Apple Compote *(Compote de Pommes).* If you like, the syrup can be flavored with lemon or orange, by infusing some zest in it; alternatively, a better method, and the one we describe here, is to add to it, after cooking the apples, sugar flavored with lemon or orange peel; or vanilla flavor, either infused as a bean in the syrup or added in the form of vanilla sugar; you can also flavor the apples with cinnamon. Also, if you like, you can add to the reduced syrup some red currant jelly or even apricot marmalade, or Smyrna raisins, which you can put into the syrup to swell up (SEE RAISINS, PAGE 573).

But the most important consideration is to cook the apple quarters correctly; they must not be either deformed or mushy, and should look like raw fruit when they come out of the syrup, both in shape and color. That said, they should be tender enough so that they can be cut in two easily with a fork, and when they are put in the mouth, the pieces should melt there, but still keep the flavor of fresh fruit.

Choose very healthy apples without blotches or dents, which would leave brown spots on the pieces.

6 medium Calville or Rennet Apples; 375 grams (13 1/4 ounces) of sugar, either cubes or granulated, and 1/2 liter (generous 2 cups) of water; 1 good tablespoon of lemon-flavored sugar **(SEE ZEST SUGAR, PAGE 574)****.**

PROCEDURE. In a sauté pan, first dissolve the sugar in the water; keep it warm; bring it to a boil on strong heat, and then let it boil *very gently.* The syrup is now ready to receive the apples, which have been prepared separately in the following manner.

Divide each apple into two halves and then each half into three parts, which should give you nice, thick pieces. Peel these pieces carefully; remove the core and the seeds. As soon as they are peeled, immediately plunge the pieces into a terrine of cool water; if not, contact with the air will darken them almost instantaneously.

Once all the apples have been prepared, sliced and peeled, put *only one-third of them* into the syrup, after draining them thoroughly. This quantity allows them to be easily immersed in the syrup, enabling you to cook them properly.

Keep the pan on very gentle heat to maintain the syrup at *a simple simmer.* Any stronger boiling, and the thin parts of the pieces might break up, while the thick parts would not be sufficiently cooked. Do not cover the pan; watch carefully and continuously, because some types of apples, and the very best ones, are perfectly done *at the end of 5 minutes.*

They are properly cooked when a fine knitting needle easily pierces the pieces of apple.

As they are done, *use a fork* to remove the pieces that are properly cooked. These are the least thick pieces, of course, and you should watch them carefully as a result. Put them in a shallow bowl or in a salad bowl that has been prepared in advance.

Once the rest of the apples have been cooked with similar care, and all the pieces have been taken out of the syrup, put the pan on strong heat and boil the syrup vigorously to reduce it to a quantity of *4 deciliters (1$^{2}/_{3}$ cups)*. Off the heat, mix in the zest sugar. When the apples have cooled, put them into a little serving dish or fruit bowl, and pour the syrup on top.

Plum Compote, Mirabelles and Greengages *(Compote de Prunes, Mirabelles et Reines-Claude).* The preparation is the same for the two kinds of plums, with the only difference being that the greengage plums should first be cut in half. Even more carefully than for mirabelles, be careful not to let the syrup boil while the plums are in it. Being cut in half, they will disintegrate more rapidly than the whole fruit. Make a purée for thickening the syrup with any overcooked half plums. *Serves 6.*

600 grams (1 pound, 5 ounces) of mirabelle plums; 125 grams (4$^{1}/_{2}$ ounces) of sugar; 2$^{1}/_{2}$ deciliters (1 cup) of hot or lukewarm water; 3 tablespoons of kirsch.

PROCEDURE. In a small sauté pan, dissolve the sugar in the water. When it is completely melted, bring the syrup to a boil, then allow it to boil gently on very low heat.

Using the point of a small knife, take out the pits without breaking the plums. Given the small quantity of syrup, poach them in two batches; that is, cook half of them in the syrup at a *simple simmer;* they must be completely submerged. As soon as the plums are cooked, take them out with a pierced spoon and place them on a plate. Cook the other half.

From the total quantity of fruit, select 50–60 grams (1$^{3}/_{4}$–2$^{1}/_{4}$ ounces) of plums, choosing plums that are a little bit misshapen, which you will put back into the syrup and then cook rapidly for *5–6 minutes.* Then pour the syrup, with these plums, into a fine chinois and lightly rub them through with a wooden spoon. Only the skins must be left on the chinois.

If the compote is served warm, put the thickened syrup back into the pan; add the whole plums and keep it on one side until ready to serve; only at this point is the kirsch added.

To serve cold, the plums are immediately arranged in a receptacle and the thickened syrup flavored with the kirsch is poured over them.

Prune Compote *(Compote de Pruneaux).* *Time: 1 hour (once the prunes have been soaked).*

Soaking the prunes before cooking them is essential to soften their skin and allow the heat to penetrate. The time needed for soaking depends on the quality of the fruit: for beautiful choice prunes with a thin skin and a tender pulp, a little less than 1 hour will suffice, while prunes that are less good should be left overnight, or for the equivalent time. If you do not have time, and this initial soaking has to be shortened or even left out altogether, you will then have to take some very substantial precautions when cooking them, particularly if using very ordinary prunes. These are to heat the liquid so slowly and gradually that in effect the prunes are almost soaked: on the one hand, this will gain you some time, but on the other, you will lose a great deal of time having to watch over it. In brief, regardless of whether the prunes have been soaked, the liquid must not be allowed to boil until the fruit has softened and swollen so much that it almost seems fresh. Once this point has been reached, the boiling does not need to be prolonged to finish cooking the fruit; otherwise it will turn into a marmalade, the same as would happen for fresh fruit.

Choice prunes sold in little containers do not need to be washed before soaking them. But common prunes must be first rid of any dust by a quick rinse. Then put them in a small terrine, amply covered with *lukewarm* water, and keep them at a moderate temperature. Gradually they will swell as they absorb some of the water. The rest of the water will be used to cook them, particularly if they have been soaked for some time, which means that the water will have taken on a little bit of their flavor.

The cooking liquid: Use either water or water with wine added to it, preferably red, half-and-half; or a less known but very good alternative is to use a light infusion of tea, whose flavor is most reminiscent of lemon peel. Allow for 225 grams (8 ounces) of prunes a good $^{1}/_{2}$ liter (generous 2 cups) of liquid.

The sugar: Granulated or in cubes, and added at the rate of 40–75 grams (1$^{3}/_{8}$–2$^{2}/_{3}$ ounces) for 225 grams (8 ounces) of prunes, depending first on whether you like more or less sugar, and whether you want a juice that is more or less syrupy. But it is better to add the sugar only after cooking the prunes. They cook and swell better in a liquid that has not been sugared.

The flavor: Generally, this is furnished by lemon peel, orange peel, or a little bit of cinnamon: 2 grams (1/14 ounce) of cinnamon stick for 225 grams (8 ounces) of prunes.

To cook: Put the prunes in a deep pot, made of aluminum or enameled metal and big enough that the suggested amount of liquid covers them well. *It is essential that the prunes should be bathed in the liquid as they cook from beginning to end.* If the amount of liquid suggested is not enough, given the size of the utensil, or if the liquid reduces a little too much while cooking, add a few more tablespoons. This extra water will make no difference, because the liquid must be reduced after cooking. Add the flavoring. Bring it to a boil very slowly. Cover. Allow it to simmer very gently until the prunes are perfectly tender and well swollen, remaining whole, and not being at all burst.

The cooking time: This varies with the quality of the prunes and also the time needed for the preliminary soaking, as well as the point to which the soaking has softened and swelled the prunes already. You can allow *1 scant hour* for choice prunes, or for prunes that have been soaked overnight. This time is not counted from the moment boiling begins, but from the moment when the prunes have been put in to cook.

Once the prunes are *completely* cooked, tilt the pot (holding the fruit inside with the cover) to drain their juice into another, larger pot, where it will reduce more easily; to simplify things, you can put the prunes into a dish or a serving dish, then reduce the juice in the same pot used for cooking. Remove the zest or piece of cinnamon. Add the sugar. On strong heat, without a cover, boil it until the liquid is reduced by more than half, which should here be no more than 2 deciliters (6 3/4 fluid ounces, 7/8 cup), and until it has also taken on a lightly syrupy consistency. Pour it over the prunes and allow it to cool.

Fruit Fritters *(Beignets de Fruits)*

The good old, family dessert for all seasons. Whatever the fruit used, it should always be good quality and perfectly ripe; this last point is important, because if the fruit is overripe, it will be delicate to handle when macerated, and will then disintegrate in its coating of batter because of the strong heat of the deep-fat frying mixture.

Do not leave out first macerating the fruit with sugar and the appropriate liqueur, and allow it to macerate for long enough that it is thoroughly penetrated by the resulting syrup. This maceration, which is the equivalent of a marinade, does not require much trouble or expense, and will not delay making the fritters; there is plenty of time to accomplish it while the dough rests.

For all details of how to make the batter for frying, whatever the recipe, refer to the directions given on PAGE 666.

For cooking the fritters, we recommend that you follow precisely the directions given for all fruit fritters under deep-fat frying (PAGE 37). We will here summarize the principal points.

Deep fat should be smoking hot so that the dough will solidify instantly. Do not put any more fritters into the deep-fat frying mixture than it can easily contain, so that they can develop easily; and at the same time, do not add so many that the fat cools quickly and noticeably. So, if the size of the frying basin and the quantity of the fat are insufficient for the quantity of fritters, proceed in two batches. Put the fritters that are ready first in a very moderate oven to keep warm, if possible.

If you like, and depending on whether you have a hot oven or a broiler that heats well, the fritters can be served simply, sprinkled with sugar—known as glazed *à blanc*—or they can be glazed in the oven. At any rate, the use of confectioners' sugar and a sugar shaker (SEE PAGE 574) is essential.

To glaze *à blanc:* The fritters are drained on a towel as soon as they are taken out of the deep fat and then sprinkled with sugar. Arrange them in a pyramid on a round plate covered with a folded napkin or kitchen towel. Sprinkle them again with sugar and serve.

To glaze in the oven: A very hot oven is essential so that the glazing takes place *in a few seconds.* If not, it would be better not to try it.

Once the fritters have been drained, rapidly arrange them on a baking sheet. Sprinkle them generously with confectioners' sugar and put them immediately in the oven or under the broiler. *Do not leave them for even a moment,* because the sugar glaze melts almost instantaneously and will caramelize on the surface of the fritters in a shiny skin, which burns immediately if subject to too much heat.

Quickly arrange the fritters as above, but without sprinkling them again with sugar.

Banana Fritters *(Beignets de Bananes).* An adaptation of a very fine Creole recipe used in New Orleans in the South of the United States.

Choose nice bananas that are perfectly ripe. A little less ripe than overripe, because they will not have the necessary resistance: they will break when you first dip them into the frying batter, and will then melt under the heat of the deep-fat frying mixture. *Time: 1 hour, 15 minutes (at least 1 good hour in advance for preparing the frying batter and the bananas; 10–12 minutes to finish the batter and to fry the fritters). Serves 6.*

6 nice bananas; 3 tablespoons of rum and 2 tablespoons of superfine sugar in which to macerate them.

For the frying batter: 100 grams ($3^1/_2$ ounces) of fine flour; 1 egg yolk; 1 tablespoon of rum; 1 level teaspoon of fine salt; $1^1/_4$ deciliters ($4^1/_4$ fluid ounces, $^1/_2$ cup) of warm water; 30 grams (1 ounce, 2 tablespoons) of clarified butter; 1 egg white whisked into a snow; 3 good tablespoons of confectioners' sugar to sprinkle over the fritters.

PROCEDURE. **The frying batter:** Prepare as directed, notably for clarifying the butter (SEE FRYING BATTER, PAGE 666). Mix in the egg white beaten into a snow just before using the batter.

The bananas: Remove their skins. Cut them in two lengthwise with a silver-bladed knife. From each half, make two long slices of equal thickness. Sprinkle them with sugar and baste them with the rum. Put them in a cool place for at least a half hour. During this time, turn them over 2 or 3 times in the syrup formed by the sugar and the rum.

The fritters: Heat the frying fat in the frying basin so that you can bring it to the right temperature in a few minutes.

Spread a nice clean towel on the table. Place the slices of banana there and sponge them off with a towel. This is *essential,* because any moisture remaining on the fruit will prevent the batter from sticking to it. Note that the flavor of the rum will not be weakened by doing this.

Whisk the egg white and mix it into the batter. When you are ready to fry the fritters, the deep-fat frying mixture should be ready on the stove, *smoking.* Rapidly dip the slices of bananas one by one into the frying batter and plunge them into the deep-fat frying mixture, bearing in mind the advice already given about the number to add at one time.

Move the fritters around in the frying mixture, holding the frying basin by the handles and gently moving it from side to side.

As soon as the fritters are a nice *light* golden yellow, and without allowing them to brown, take them out with a wire skimmer and place them on a dry towel folded in two and spread out at the side of the stove, where their fat will drain off.

Glaze them *à blanc*—that is, sprinkle them with confectioners' sugar. Place them in a pyramid on a round plate covered with a folded napkin. Sprinkle them again with sugar and serve them boiling hot.

Peach Fritters *(Beignets de Pêches).* *Time: 1 hour, 15 minutes (1 hour for the preparation of the batter and the peaches; 12–15 minutes to finish the batter, fry, and if you like, glaze the fritters). Serves 6.*

9 medium-size peaches perfectly ripe; 2 good tablespoons of superfine sugar and 3 tablespoons of kirsch to macerate them.

For the frying batter: 150 grams ($5^1/_3$ ounces) of excellent flour; 2 small egg yolks; 1 tablespoon of cognac; a pinch of fine salt and a pinch of superfine sugar; a scant $1^1/_2$ deciliters (5 fluid ounces, $^2/_3$ cup) of lukewarm water; $1^1/_2$ tablespoons of butter, melted and decanted; $1^1/_2$ egg whites whisked into a firm snow. 3 good tablespoons of confectioners' sugar to sprinkle over or glaze the fritters.

PROCEDURE. Prepare the frying batter as directed (SEE PAGE 666). Just before using, mix in the whites beaten into a snow.

The peaches: Cut them in half. With a small

kitchen knife, remove their skins without cutting into the pulp. If the skin does not come off easily, plunge the peaches into boiling water *for a few seconds*—not minutes—and drain them on a towel. Then the skin will come off easily.

Arrange the peach halves on a large plate. Sprinkle them with sugar and baste them with the kirsch.

Put them in a cool place for *1 hour at least.* During this time, turn them rather often in the syrup formed by the sugar and the kirsch.

The fritters: Proceed as for *banana fritters.* Serve them either simply sprinkled with sugar or glazed in the oven.

Apple Fritters *(Beignets de Pommes).* Use beautiful, gray Rennet apples: better than all other varieties, these are the best to use for making fritters because of their firmer pulp.

There is nothing special, or even essential, about the frying batter suggested below. It is a batter that was used with great success by an old cook from the Poitou region, and it produced a light and crispy crust if the fritters were properly fried. You can, if you like, replace it with one of the batters used for bananas or peaches, or any other batter, depending on your taste or circumstance. *Time: 1 hour, 15 minutes (at least 1 hour for preparing the batter and letting it stand and the maceration of the apple slices; 12–15 minutes to finish the batter, fry, and, if you like, glaze the fritters). Serves 6.*

4 nice Rennet apples; 2 good tablespoons of superfine sugar and 3 tablespoons of cognac or rum to macerate them.

For the frying batter: 125 grams (4 1/2 ounces) of excellent flour; 3 grams (1/10 ounce) of salt; 1 nice egg yolk; 1 tablespoon of oil; 1 tablespoon of eau-de-vie. A scant 2 deciliters (6 3/4 fluid ounces, 7/8 cup) of lukewarm milk; 1 1/2 egg whites whisked into a snow.

PROCEDURE. Prepare the frying batter as directed (SEE PAGE 666).

Before peeling the apples, remove the core and seeds using a corer with a diameter of 1 1/2 centimeters (5/8 inch) (SEE TO CORE APPLES, PAGE 577). Then peel them. Cut them crosswise into equal rounds about 7–8 millimeters (5/16 inch) thick.

Put them on a plate, sprinkled on both sides with sugar. Baste them with the liqueur. Then allow them to macerate for at least a half hour, turning them from time to time very carefully so that you do not break them.

The fritters: Proceed as for banana fritters. Serve them either simply sprinkled with sugar or glazed in the oven.

Pineapple Fritters *(Beignets d'Ananas).* The canned pineapples used here are already divided into rounds, like the slices of apples for fritters. Macerate them with sugar and kirsch. Prepare the frying batter with 125 grams (4 1/2 ounces) of flour; 1 good tablespoon of olive oil; a grain of salt and a small pinch of sugar; 1 egg completely incorporated into the batter; 1 1/2 deciliters (5 fluid ounces, 2/3 cup) of water. When they come out of the frying batter, glaze the fritters in the oven.

Apricot Fritters *(Beignets d'Abricots).* Proceed as for peach fritters. Do not remove the skin from the apricots.

Fruit in Stale Bread Croûtes *(Croûtes aux Fruits)*

This is a kind of warm dessert that is generally welcome because, adapting to circumstances, it can be both simple and economical, and allows you to use things that otherwise might be wasted.

The variety of bread croûtes are infinite, and you can make them either with one fruit only, or with several. Whatever the filling used, the dessert is always made with a round croûte on which the filling is put.

Bread croûtes are generally cut from stale savarins or babas (rum cakes), or at least from those cooked the evening before and not basted; that is what works the best. If you do not have a savarin or baba, you can use a round of brioche, also stale. And if you have none of those, you can make the croûte with stale fine white bread. Or even, if you do not have this, make the croûtes from an ordinary bread loaf that is good and stale and does not have too many holes in it. In any case, the bread crusts are always removed. Whatever filling is used, the croûtes are always prepared in the same way, and given the same dimensions.

The preparation of the croûtes: *With a savarin or baba or brioche.* Divide the circular bread into slices, cutting on the bias (in the same way you would cut up a Lyon sausage) to obtain slices with a larger surface. They should thus be about 7 1/2 centimeters (3 inches) long and 4 centimeters (1 1/2 inches) wide. And they should all be the same thickness, about 6–7 millimeters (1/4 inch): that is, a little bit more than 1/2 centimeter (3/16 inch).

Trim them lightly all around to give them a more or less oval shape.

Arrange the croûtes on a baking sheet. Powder them with confectioners' sugar, or at least superfine sugar. Put them in the oven to glaze them—that is, to dry them and to caramelize the sugar. Watch them carefully, because the sugar will quickly go beyond a light golden color, particularly if the oven is hot, and the edges of the croûtes will burn and become too dry, which is absolutely to be avoided.

Take them out of the oven immediately. Keep them warm or let them cool a little bit, depending on whether or not the croûtes will be spread with something before they are filled.

With brioche. The croûtes, cut and trimmed as above, are glazed the same way.

With bread. Cut into ovals as above. Before glazing, the bread croûtes must be gently fried in butter. This will give the bread some flavor and also soften it, to make it more like the cake it is replacing. The butter should be previously clarified (SEE PAGE 16). If you do not do this, the impurities will stick to the croûtes as so many brown spots. Allow for about 15 croûtes—enough to serve about 6 or 8 people—75 grams (2 2/3 ounces, 1/3 cup) of butter. Fry the croûtes (SEE CROÛTES AND CROUTONS, PAGE 20).

Then dry them off on a towel to get rid of all the fat. Arrange them on a baking sheet and glaze them exactly as for the croûtes of savarin or baba.

Dressing the croûtes: Arrange them on a round plate and in a turban shape—that is, with the slices standing practically straight up, leaning against each other, as if being reshaped into a savarin. And if you are using bread, arrange the croûtes the same way. Supported by one another, they will stand very well when filled.

Lyon-Style Croûte *(Croûte à la Lyonnaise).* The name comes from the Lyon chestnuts that are used in its preparation. If you like, you can use leftover marrons glacés, or ordinary chestnuts prepared specifically for this dish. *Time: 30 minutes if the chestnuts are ready; 1 hour, 15 minutes if they have to be prepared. Serves 6.*

1 dozen croûtes prepared as directed above; 180–200 grams (6 1/4–7 ounces) of leftover marrons glacés, or 25 nice raw chestnuts; and to cook them, a syrup with 225 grams (8 ounces) of sugar, 4 scant deciliters (1 2/3 cups) of water, and a half vanilla bean.

30 grams (1 ounce) of raisins from Málaga, the same amount from Smyrna, and the same from Corinth;
4 tablespoons of apricot marmalade in a purée;
60 grams (2 1/4 ounces) of almonds; a wineglass of Málaga wine.

PROCEDURE. **The chestnuts:** *If they are glacéed.* Choose the largest pieces for the decoration. Combine the rest for a purée in a small saucepan with 1 tablespoon of water and 1/2 tablespoon of superfine sugar. Warm it for *7–8 minutes* simply to soften them. Pass them through a fine drum sieve, collecting the purée in a bowl. Set to one side.

If the chestnuts are prepared especially for this dish. Remove their shells and the skins and put them in a saucepan of cold water (SEE CHESTNUTS, PAGE 521).

At the same time, put the sugar and the water for the syrup in another saucepan. As soon as the sugar is melted, bring it to a boil. Add the vanilla, then maintain it at a very gentle simmer.

As the chestnuts are shelled and peeled, put them in the syrup. Let them simmer there for *20–25 minutes,* until they are easily pierced with a pin. Then drain them on a strainer. Spread them out in a drum sieve. Reserve a dozen of the best preserved. Then quickly pass the rest through the drum sieve while they are still boiling hot. Keep them in a bowl.

The raisins: Take care of these while the chestnuts are cooking. Take out their stems and clean them, then plump them up with a little bit of water and sugar as directed (SEE RAISINS, PAGE 573).

The almonds: Husked as directed (SEE PAGE 573) and then split in half: each half is cut into two lengthwise. Spread these pieces on a very clean baking sheet and roast them in a gentle oven until they take on a golden tint.

The croûtes: Cut as directed, which you can do in advance, keeping them wrapped in a towel; then glaze.

When they have chilled a bit, generously spread them on one side with the chestnut purée. Dip a brush into the apricot purée and spread it in a very fine layer on the chestnut purée, just to give it some shine. Arrange the croûtes on a baking sheet and spread the grilled almonds over them. Then press very lightly with the blade of a knife on the almonds to fix them in place.

To assemble the dish: Arrange the croûtes in a turban or circle. Keep the plate warm in a very gentle oven. Add the pieces of chestnuts that you have reserved to the drained raisins.

If there is any syrup left from the raisins, reduce it to a thick consistency. Add the apricot purée, then boil for at least 2 minutes. Turn off the heat to mix in the Málaga wine, and add the raisins and chestnuts. Pour it into the middle of the circle of crusts. Serve immediately.

NOTE. A turban of crusts that have been completely spread with apricot purée can be prepared 15 minutes in advance with no loss of quality and then kept warm *without its decoration.*

The same is true for a filling made in the same pan. But do not add the Málaga wine until just before serving, and only pour the filling inside the turban at the last moment so that you do not soak the croûtes.

Crusts with Madeira *(Croûte au Madère).* *Time: 30 minutes. Serves 6.*

1 dozen croûtes prepared as directed (PAGE 631).

For the garniture: 75 grams (2 2/3 ounces) of Málaga raisins, 75 grams (2 2/3 ounces) of Corinth raisins, and the same quantity of Smyrna raisins; 3 scant deciliters (1 1/4 cups) of Madeira wine, or, if you want to economize on the Madeira, 2 deciliters (6 3/4 fluid ounces, 7/8 cup) of white wine to cook the raisins and only 1 deciliter (3 1/3 fluid ounces, scant 1/2 cup) of Madeira to finish; 100 grams (3 1/2 ounces) of sugar; 6 tablespoons of apricot marmalade that has been strained through a drum sieve; about 2 dozen candied cherries and a few pieces of angelica.

PROCEDURE. **The raisins:** Clean them, rinse them, and plump them as directed (SEE RAISINS, PAGE 573), replacing the water with the 2 deciliters (6 3/4 fluid ounces, 7/8 cup) of white wine or the same quantity of Madeira into which the sugar has already been dissolved. Leave for *about 20 minutes,* during which time the wine will be transformed into a light syrup.

The croûtes: Prepare them as directed (SEE PAGE 631). Spread them lightly with the apricot purée. Arrange them in a turban shape.

To serve: Add the rest of the apricot marmalade to the raisins in their reduced syrup. Boil everything together for 1 minute. Add the deciliter (3 1/3 fluid ounces, scant 1/2 cup) of Madeira *without allowing it to boil.* Pour the raisins and their syrup into the interior of the turban. Quickly, because the syrup will soak the croûtes, arrange the cherries and the rectangles of angelica in a pattern, however you like, on the croûtes. Serve immediately.

Normandy-Style Croûte *(Croûte à la Normande).* This dessert, with very simple ingredients and easy to prepare, is made as follows: some of the apples are cooked into a marmalade and the rest in pieces in a syrup. The croûtes, spread with preserves, are arranged in a turban shape; in the middle, the marmalade contains the apple pieces; and everything is then, if you like, attractively decorated with candied cherries. Over this is poured the syrup, first thickened into a coulis with a little bit of marmalade.

If you have red vegetable coloring, you can color a part of the apple pieces pink, which makes the general effect of the croûte much more beautiful than with pieces that are all white. But just like the decoration of cherries, this is not essential. If you do not have an open jar of preserves, you can confine yourself to spreading the crust with a little bit of apple marmalade. The croûte can be dressed a little bit in advance as long as it is kept warm; it needs only to be lukewarm when served. Just before serving, and no sooner, baste it with the coulis. *Time: 45 minutes. Serves 6.*

1 dozen croûtes prepared as has been explained above; 8 medium apples; 12 candied cherries (optional); 2 tablespoons of apricot marmalade; 1 small glass of kirsch; sugar; lemon zest.

PROCEDURE. Prepare the croûtes as directed (SEE PAGE 631).

The apples: Put the two nicest aside for the pieces. Cook the six others to make a marmalade (SEE PAGE 620) with 75 grams (2 2/3 ounces) of sugar; 2 tablespoons of water; 1 tablespoon of chopped lemon zest; 25 grams (1 ounce, 2 tablespoons) of butter. The marmalade must be thick enough that it can be gathered into a little pile in the pot without spreading out there.

Meanwhile, cut the 2 reserved apples and cook them as directed for apple compote (SEE PAGE 627). Thus, a total of 16 thin pieces cooked with 75 grams (2 2/3 ounces) of sugar and 2 1/2 deciliters (1 cup) of water. Then drain them.

The coulis: Add 1 tablespoon of apple marmalade to the syrup used for cooking the apple. Allow it to simmer for 5 minutes. Pass it through a chinois, rubbing it to force everything through. Keep it warm until the moment that you add the kirsch. Depending on the type of apples you use, the coulis may seem a little thick, so you can dilute it with 2 tablespoons of warm water and add another tablespoon of superfine sugar to it.

Assembling the dish: Spread the glazed side of the croûtes with the preserves, or if you do not have them with a little bit of marmalade. Dress them as directed.

In the inside of the circle or turban, place the marmalade tablespoon by tablespoon, shaping it into a dome above the croûtes as high as possible. On the marmalade arrange, alternating, the white and pink apple pieces. Place the cherries here and there. Just before serving, add the kirsch to the warm coulis of apples and pour it 1 tablespoon at a time over the entire dish.

SOUFFLÉS
Soufflés

Before attempting to make the following soufflés, you should be aware of the principles on which their preparations are based (SEE SOUFFLÉS, PAGE 436). For all further details, refer to the typical recipe given below, for vanilla soufflé.

Vanilla Soufflé *(Soufflé à la Vanille)*

The simple but very delicate vanilla soufflé is a warm family dessert par excellence. It can be made and appreciated at all times, particularly when we begin to run out of fruit. *Time: 45 minutes. Serves 6.*

4 deciliters (1 2/3 cups) of very good milk; 100 grams (3 1/2 ounces) of sugar lumps; 40 grams (1 3/8 ounces) of rice starch or 30 grams (1 ounce) of sifted fine wheat flour; a nice half vanilla bean; 5 egg yolks; 6 egg whites whisked into a very firm snow; 30 grams (1 ounce, 2 tablespoons) of fine butter; 2 tablespoons of confectioners' sugar or superfine sugar. A timbale or a soufflé dish about 20 centimeters (8 inches) in diameter and 7 centimeters (2 3/4 inches) deep.

PROCEDURE. **The mash** ***(bouillie):*** *Reserve 3 tablespoons of cold milk,* that is, 1/2 deciliter (1 2/3 fluid ounces, scant 1/4 cup), to dilute the starch or flour.

Use a pot large enough that you can work in it easily when mixing in the egg whites beaten into snow; as much as possible, use a pot with low, flared sides—a sauté pan, in other words—one that is good and clean. Add the rest of the milk. Boil it; as soon as it rises, add the sugar and the vanilla and turn off the heat; cover the pot tightly. Let it infuse for *a scant 15 minutes,* being careful to mix it from time to time with a spoon to ensure the sugar completely dissolves.

Dilute the starch or flour in a bowl with the *cold milk* that you have reserved. At the beginning you must take great care not to make any lumps; add the cold milk only drop by drop, working it with a small wooden spoon. Pour this diluted flour or starch into the pot with the hot sugared milk, mixing with the spoon or with a small sauce whisk.

Place the pot on more or less gentle heat and bring it to a boil, stirring continuously with the whisk or spoon. When the bubbles appear on the surface of the *bouillie,* mix it on the heat for another *5–6 seconds* only. Then turn the heat down far enough so that it cannot either boil or heat too much. Divide the butter into very small pieces and spread these on top of the *bouillie.*

This *bouillie* must be completely ready *15–20 minutes* before you add the yolks and whites beaten into a snow; the butter melts and prevents a crust from forming.

NOTE. If you have some help to whisk the whites, you only have to add the butter and the yolks into the *bouillie* when it is taken off the heat, and to mix in the egg whites when it has cooled a bit. But we assume that in most cases there will be only one person, without help, to prepare the *bouillie* and then whisk the whites.

PREPARATIONS. So that you do not have to wait once the mixture is ready, make sure that before whisking the whites you prepare the utensil you are using for the soufflé. Butter the inside with a piece of butter the size of a walnut, spreading it out with the tips of your fingers. Using a sugar shaker, sprinkle this buttered interior with sugar. Keep the egg yolks ready in a bowl.

Whisk the egg whites into a snow (SEE WHISKING EGG WHITES, PAGE 8). As soon as they are well fluffed, mix them in.

The mixture: This must be done quite quickly, and the *bouillie* must be only *lukewarm.* If it were too warm, the whites would turn to liquid at the first touch of the spatula, and would thus lose their lightness. So make sure that neither the pot nor the *bouillie* has retained too much heat, because it is in the pot itself that you will mix the ingredients.

First add the yolks one by one to the *bouillie.* Stir with the wooden spoon to mix them and, at the same time, to mix in the butter that is spread on the surface. Take out the vanilla bean.

Take about *one-third* of the whites on the wires of a whisk so that you do not crush the rest with a spoon, and put them in the pot. Using a spatula or a wooden spoon with a large head, mix these whites *thoroughly* into the *bouillie:* that is, until the *bouillie* and the whites are completely combined. This helps to mix in the rest of the whites and also softens the *bouillie.*

Then add the rest of the whites, as directed for mixing them (SEE PAGE 10).

Finishing the soufflé: *As soon as you have finished adding the whites, the mixture must be cooked.*

Put it into the prepared utensil, either a timbale or a soufflé dish, taking it out with a large metal spoon. Place the spoonfuls one on top of the other to make a little mountain, but do not allow it to remain in this form. With the blade of a large knife, carefully smooth out the surface, shaping it to form a sort of pyramid raised in the middle of the utensil, if you are using a timbale or a porcelain soufflé dish. If using a bowl, smooth the top of the composition into a dome.

Then make 5 or 6 grooves all around the surface of the composition. Do this with the point of the knife to a depth of about $1^1/_2$ centimeters ($^5/_8$ inch), going *from the bottom to the top:* that is, from the side of the utensil toward the top of the soufflé. These grooves will allow the heat of the oven to penetrate the soufflé, which will cook more easily.

Put it into the oven immediately.

To cook: If the oven does not heat well from the bottom, make sure you proceed as explained in the article on soufflés (PAGE 436), first putting the soufflé on top of the stove.

If the heat of the oven is too strong, you must avoid seizing the surface of the soufflé by keeping it close to the opening of the oven for the first 10 minutes of cooking. The rising and swelling need time to happen before the surface forms a crust.

As soon as the soufflé is in the oven, close the door, even if it is a little too warm. *Allow to cook for 20 minutes* from the moment the soufflé is in the oven.

During this time, check the progress of the cooking from time to time by opening the oven door a little bit, but make sure you leave it open only for the shortest time possible, particularly if the stove is near an open window. Any introduction of cold air prevents the soufflé from rising properly.

If the soufflé colors too strongly on the side nearest the heat source, turn it so that it gradually colors on all sides. But when you do this, move it very carefully, because shaking it will cause the soufflé to fall.

After 18 minutes in the oven, sprinkle sugar on the surface of the soufflé with the sugar shaker. From this point on, do not let it out of your sight until the sugar melts evenly to form a light caramelized layer on the soufflé, or at least a shiny one. This is what is called "glazing."

This glazing requires *2–3 minutes,* and you should watch it carefully by looking into the oven, opening the door only slightly and closing it quickly.

To confirm whether the soufflé is perfectly cooked on the inside, stick a cooking needle into the middle of it. It should come out nice and clean. If, on the contrary, it comes out covered with the mixture in a state like that which you have put it in, or near it, cook for another 2–3 minutes.

As soon as you finish the glazing, take the soufflé from the oven and serve it immediately. It should rise above the sides by 6–7 centimeters (2½–2¾ inches)—that is, it should have doubled in height—and when you cut into it, it should be light and firm throughout, without obviously sagging.

Lemon and Orange Soufflé *(Soufflé au Citron, à l'Orange)*

For all details, refer to VANILLA SOUFFLÉ (SEE PAGE 634). Use the same quantities for the *bouillie,* replacing the vanilla with a peel that has been carefully rid of the white part; or better, zest the sugar (SEE PAGE 574). Melt the zested sugar into the boiled milk while it is hot *but without boiling it:* the flavor obtained is much stronger than by infusing the peel in the milk.

Optionally, you can add 30 grams (1 ounce) of candied orange peel or candied lemon peel cut into very small pieces. A little glass of curaçao added to the ingredients for the orange soufflé before mixing in the whites has an excellent effect.

Chocolate Soufflé *(Soufflé au Chocolat)*

Time: 50 minutes. Serves 6.

100 grams (3½ ounces) of chocolate in pieces; 4 deciliters (1⅔ cups) of very good milk; a half vanilla bean; 75 grams (2⅔ ounces) of sugar in cubes or granulated; 4 egg yolks; 6 whites whisked into a snow; 30 grams (1 ounce, 2 tablespoons) of fine butter; 3 tablespoons of confectioners' sugar; 30 grams (1 ounce) of starch, either rice (as for cream of rice) or potato, or 25 grams (about 1 ounce) of very fine flour.

PROCEDURE. First see the special section on soufflés (SEE PAGE 436) and for the details of preparing it, refer to VANILLA SOUFFLÉ (SEE PAGE 634).

Reserve *3 tablespoons of milk* to dilute the starch. Put the rest of the milk into a small saucepan. Bring it to a boil. Add the sugar and the vanilla. Cover. Keep it off the heat. Allow it to infuse for 15 minutes.

Grate the chocolate or break it into small pieces. Put it in a sauté pan large enough that you can then mix in the whites. Moisten it with *only 1 tablespoon* of lukewarm water. Gently melt it without cooking it on extremely low heat, stirring it often with a wooden spoon so that no lumps remain. Dilute it with the milk.

In a bowl, dilute the starch or the flour with the cold milk you have reserved, adding it gradually to avoid lumps. Then pour it into the pan with the chocolate.

Bring it to a boil on low heat, stirring it. Allow it to boil for a *few seconds.* Immediately turn off the heat. Spread the butter in little bits on the surface to prevent a crust. Keep it warm.

Whisk the whites and proceed exactly as for the vanilla soufflé.

Banana Soufflé *(Soufflé aux Bananes)*

Choose bananas that are rather firm but nonetheless perfectly ripe: Any that have large black spots and give way when you touch them should be rejected, because they will produce a purée that is too liquid. The number suggested below is appropriate for very nice, big bananas; if you use smaller bananas, you will need two more to obtain about 2 deciliters (6¾ fluid ounces, ⅞ cup) of purée, the amount needed for this recipe.

In professional cooking, soufflés made with fresh fruits like this one are also prepared with a very thick sugar syrup, cooked to the "crack" stage, but preparing this is much more complicated. The use of the *bouillie* as a base is the simplest current method, and procures a very good result. *Time: 45 minutes. Serves 6.*

6 nice bananas; 30 grams (1 ounce) of starch or cream of rice, or 25 grams (1 ounce) of excellent flour; 100 grams (3 1/2 ounces) of superfine sugar; 3 deciliters (1 1/4 cups) of milk that has been boiled and cooled; 4 egg yolks; 6 egg whites whisked to a very firm snow; 30 grams (1 ounce, 2 tablespoons) of fine butter; 2 teaspoons of lemon juice; 3 tablespoons of rum; 1 good tablespoon of confectioners' sugar.

PROCEDURE. First see the special article on soufflés (PAGE 436) and for the details of execution refer to VANILLA SOUFFLÉ (PAGE 634).

Prepare the mash, or *bouillie,* of the liaison using a small whisk, by diluting the starch or flour and 1 tablespoon of superfine sugar with the cooled milk in a sauté pan. Bring it to a boil, mixing it constantly; let it cook for *1 minute* and turn off the heat.

Immediately prepare the purée. Peel the bananas and pass them through a drum sieve, rubbing them with a wooden pestle. Mix this purée with the *bouillie* used for the base. Without putting it back on the heat, add the egg yolks and the remaining sugar, working the mixture with a whisk. Spread the butter, divided into pieces, on the surface of the mixture.

Prepare the soufflé dish. Whisk the whites. Add the rum to the mixture; beat it a couple of times with the whisk to mix it in. Then mix in the whites, proceeding as directed for the vanilla soufflé. Then follow all the directions for assembling the dish, and cooking and glazing the soufflé.

Fresh Apricot Soufflé *(Soufflé aux Abricots Frais)*

As for the banana soufflé, you should choose fruits that are perfectly ripe: this is important for their flavor and also because it is easier to make the purée. To get about 2 deciliters (6 3/4 fluid ounces, 7/8 cup) of purée, allow 18 small apricots.

The ingredients of the soufflé and their quantities are the same as for the banana soufflé. The rum is replaced by kirsch and the lemon juice is omitted.

The preparation is similar: the unpeeled apricots, cut in two and with their pits removed, are made into a purée by passing them through a drum sieve. The purée is then mixed with the *bouillie* used for the base, and you then continue in the same way as for the vanilla soufflé (SEE PAGE 634).

Apple Soufflé *(Soufflé aux Pommes)*

Time: 1 hour, 30 minutes. Serves 6.

1 kilogram (2 pounds, 3 ounces) of Rennet apples weighed before being peeled, to give after cooking 400 grams (14 1/8 ounces) of apple marmalade; 400 grams (14 1/8 ounces) of sugar cubes; 50 grams (1 3/4 ounces, 3 1/2 tablespoons) of butter; 1 vanilla bean or 1 stick of cinnamon; 1 deciliter (3 1/3 fluid ounces, scant 1/2 cup) of good white wine; 50 grams (1 3/4 ounces) of superfine sugar; 10 whisked egg whites.

PROCEDURE. First see the special section on soufflés (PAGE 436), and for details of how to prepare it, refer to VANILLA SOUFFLÉ (SEE PAGE 634).

Choose apples of irreproachable quality, good and ripe. Peel them; cut them into quarters; remove the seeds; slice them thinly. Spread them out in a sauté pan, on the bottom of which you will have melted the butter. Baste with the wine. Add the vanilla or the cinnamon. Then dust them with 50 grams (1 3/4 ounces) of superfine sugar.

Cook them in a rather hot oven, mixing them frequently to prevent them from coloring too much or sticking. When they are nice and golden, drain them, then force them through a horsehair drum sieve. Put the purée back into the rinsed pan.

Meanwhile make a syrup with the sugar and about 2 deciliters (6 3/4 fluid ounces, 7/8 cup) of water; cook it to the "crack" stage (SEE COOKING SUGAR, PAGE 577).

Pour the syrup into the marmalade. Put it back on the heat. Work it with a spatula, scraping on the bottom of the pan, until the marmalade has a consistency such that it can be piled onto a plate without spreading out. It must be gluey to the touch, a sign that all its moisture has evaporated.

Turn off the heat. Pour it into a shallow bowl large enough so that you can mix in the whites once it cools. Stir it often while it is cooling so that it does not form large lumps.

Whisk the whites. Lighten the marmalade by mixing in thoroughly 2–3 tablespoons of the whisked whites. Mix in the rest in four batches, taking due care (SEE PAGE 10). Put it into a timbale.

Put it into the oven. Twenty-five minutes, no more, should be enough. Sprinkle it with sugar when it comes out of the oven.

Small Cheese Soufflés *(Petits Soufflés au Fromage)*

Parmesan is the perfect cheese for this kind of recipe. You can, depending on preference and your occasion, replace it with an excellent Gruyère.

The recipe is good for small soufflés as well as for a soufflé made in a large timbale or in a shallow bowl. Small soufflés are almost always served at lunch as a warm hors d'oeuvre. If the cheese you are using is Parmesan, the soufflés are named accordingly. *Time: 35 minutes. Makes 12 little dishes, or serves 6.*

100 grams (3½ ounces) of sifted flour; 5 deciliters (generous 2 cups) of boiled milk; 100 grams (3½ ounces) of grated Parmesan cheese; 40 grams (1⅜ ounces, 3 tablespoons) of butter; 5 grams (⅙ ounce) of salt; a pinch of white pepper; a pinch of grated nutmeg; 5 egg yolks; 5 whites whisked to a very firm snow.

PROCEDURE. First see the special section on soufflés (PAGE 436), and for the details of how to make it, refer to VANILLA SOUFFLÉ (SEE PAGE 634).

Boil the milk enough in advance so that it is only barely lukewarm when you use it.

Put a piece of butter the size of a pea into each dish; spread it out with the end of your fingers. Arrange the dishes on a baking sheet.

In a sauté pan, carefully dilute the flour with the milk. Add salt, pepper, and nutmeg.

Bring it to a boil, stirring constantly. Then immediately turn the heat down. Add the grated cheese, *reserving about 1 tablespoon of it,* and stir it to mix it well.

Then *immediately* turn off the heat. Divide the butter into little bits and spread these out *on top of* the *bouillie.*

Add the yolks, then whisk and mix in the whites, as directed for the vanilla soufflé.

Fill the dishes by only two-thirds. On each little soufflé, spread a pinch of the reserved cheese. Place the baking sheet loaded with the soufflés on moderate heat. When it is burning hot, put it in the oven.

Once the soufflés are in the oven, cook for *12–14 minutes.*

Cheese Soufflé *(Soufflé au fromage)*

This is a recipe that can be recommended in all respects, because it uses only egg whites, to the exclusion of any yolks, and produces a particularly light soufflé. For all the details, refer to VANILLA SOUFFLÉ (SEE PAGE 634) and to the particular section on soufflés (PAGE 436). *Time: 35 minutes. Serves 6.*

6–7 egg whites, depending on the size of the eggs; 20–22 grams (about ⅔ ounce) of flour and 25 grams (1 ounce, 2 tablespoons) of butter for the white roux; 2 deciliters (6¾ fluid ounces, ⅞ cup) of light crème fraîche or excellent milk; 175 grams (6 ounces) of very good Gruyère, grating 125 grams (about 4½ ounces) and cutting 50 grams (about 1¾ ounces) into little dice ½ centimeter (3/16 inch) on each side; salt, pepper, nutmeg; and, if you like, as much cayenne pepper as can be held on the tip of a knife point.

PROCEDURE. Make a small white roux in a sauté pan (SEE PAGE 47). Dilute it with the cream or the milk: this milk should first have been boiled. Bring it to a boil; turn off the heat and incorporate the grated cheese and the dice of cheese; season. Spread a few pieces of butter on the surface of this *bouillie* and keep it on one side.

Butter the soufflé dish. Whisk the whites. Mix them with the *bouillie.* Dress the soufflé and continue as directed for a vanilla soufflé.

COLD AND WARM PUDDINGS
Poudings Froids et Chauds

Nesselrode Pudding *(Pouding à la Nesselrode)*

A chilled dessert dating from a good period for French cuisine, the middle of the nineteenth century. Created by the personal chef of the ambassador, the Count of Nesselrode, this high-style pudding had a place on the most extravagant menus, and still does. In fact, it is still popular not only for its exquisite delicacy, but also because even though it is a chilled dessert, its composition makes it much less cold than most iced desserts: a considerable advantage for many people.

It is accompanied by a sauce served on the side, made from crème anglaise flavored with maraschino. These days this accompaniment is usually omitted, because the pudding is enough on its own; for the same reason, we do not recommend the fantastic decorations that sometimes embellish it. The recipe given below is the authentic, original recipe.

Making this, even in a simple bourgeois kitchen, does not present any real difficulties, particularly if you have an ice-cream maker. One can do without this ice-cream maker by working the mixture in a terrine kept under ice; but the work, it goes without saying, takes much longer.

Do not try to make this without ice, simply firming up the pudding in a cold place. The ice is here *absolutely essential* to set the mixture, bringing it to the point where it can be unmolded: exactly like an ordinary ice cream.

Let us add too that marrons glacés cannot in any way be substituted for the chestnuts prepared as we describe here. This pudding, like all desserts with a chestnut base, can be made only with fresh chestnuts. *Time: 2 hours, 30 minutes plus 1 hour, 30 minutes to ice it. Serves 10.*

30 nice chestnuts; 50 grams (1 3/4 ounces) of sugar, cubes or granulated; 3 deciliters (1 1/4 cups) of water; a half vanilla bean, to cook them.

For the crème anglaise: 4 deciliters (1 2/3 cups) of milk; 150 grams (5 1/3 ounces) of superfine sugar; 6 egg yolks; a half vanilla bean.

75 grams (2 2/3 ounces) of Málaga raisins and 75 grams (2 2/3 ounces) of Corinth raisins; 2 1/2 deciliters (1 cup) of heavy cream for whipping; 3/4 deciliter (2 1/2 fluid ounces, scant 1/3 cup) of maraschino.

A charlotte mold with a capacity of 12–13 deciliters (5–5 1/2 cups), equipped with a cover that fits tightly.

To ice it: 8–10 kilograms (17 pounds, 10 ounces–22 pounds) of ice; 1 kilogram (2 pounds, 3 ounces) of gray sea salt.

PROCEDURE. To shell them, boil the chestnuts as directed (SEE PAGE 521). Then put them in a small saucepan with the water, the sugar, and the vanilla; cover. Cook them *very gently* for about *1 1/4–1 1/2 hours* until they can be perfectly reduced to a purée, once all the liquid has been absorbed. Pass them burning hot through a *fine* drum sieve, horsehair or similar, working with no more than 3 or 4 at a time. Collect the purée in a terrine. Beat it vigorously with a large wooden spoon to make it nice and smooth.

While the chestnuts are cooking, prepare the crème anglaise, as directed (SEE PAGE 583).

Also, clean the raisins, take out their seeds, wash them, and then soak them so that they swell up in 1 deciliter (3 1/3 fluid ounces, scant 1/2 cup) of water and 3 lumps of sugar (SEE RAISINS, PAGE 573).

Before mixing these different ingredients, prepare the metal container in which the mixture will be placed in the ice. Stand it in the ice for at least 10 minutes before the mixture is poured into it (SEE PREPARING THE SORBETIÈRE, PAGE 649).

The mixture: Add the crème anglaise to the purée in 4 or 5 batches so that you can mix it better, stirring it and working it vigorously with the wooden spoon; then add the well-drained raisins.

Pour the mixture into the metal container in which it will be iced. Proceed as directed (SEE TO FREEZING, PAGE 650) until it takes on the state of a light ice cream and is therefore rather consistent.

At this point, quickly whip the heavy cream (SEE PAGE 586). After you have worked the iced mixture one last time, add the whipped cream and the maraschino to it at the same time. The incorporation of whipped cream is extremely important, because the dish must be as light and frothy as possible. Do this spoonful by spoonful, taking great care not to crush or compact the cream: working incompetently and for too long when incorporating the cream will be extremely damaging.

To mold: In advance, line the inside of the mold with white parchment paper to make it easy to unmold without first having to pass it through hot water: use a round of parchment paper for the bottom and a band of paper for the sides. (The mold and the paper are neither buttered nor oiled.) Add the iced mixture with a large metal cooking spoon. Lightly tap the bottom of the mold once you have put it in, as directed (SEE PAGE 575). Fill the mold to 1/2 centimeter (3/16 inch) from the edge.

Cover the mixture with a round of white paper that has a diameter a little larger than that of the mold; seal with the cover. This cover, which may not always fit as tightly as an ice-cream container, must be sealed with a ribbon of butter the size of a small macaroni. This ribbon of butter, applied completely around the outside of the mold exactly at the place where it joins with the cover, hardens on contact with the ice and prevents the salted water from entering the mold.

Chill for *1½ hours.*

To serve: When you are ready to serve the pudding, remove the mold from the ice; dip it into a terrine of cold water to get rid of all traces of salt water and wipe it thoroughly. Remove the ribbon of butter with the point of a small knife and then the cover; unmold it on a round plate garnished with a napkin. Carefully remove the papers. Serve on its own or accompanied by a very cold crème anglaise flavored with maraschino.

Chestnut Pudding *(Pouding de Marrons)*

A cold dessert highly recommended for its fine flavor, its beautiful appearance, and the simplicity of its preparation. Briefly, it is a creamy purée of chestnuts alternating with layers of biscuits soaked in kirsch; and the whole is then covered and accompanied by a light vanilla-flavored crème anglaise.

You can use leftovers of marrons glacés, as long as they were fresh the night before or the same day, so that they can be even softer. This would, of course, be simpler, but it is not preferable in terms of the final results.

Ice is by no means essential to set this pudding, which is an advantage; but it is important to prepare it enough in advance that the different ingredients will be able to combine and amalgamate: the evening before, if possible. Above all, be careful not to place a weight on the pudding while it cools, as some amateurs suggest for any preparation containing biscuits. *Time: 2 hours (not including the time needed for icing); 7–8 hours to chill it without ice, or only 2 hours with ice or a refrigerator. Serves 7–8.*

For the chestnut purée: **500 grams (1 pound, 2 ounces) of nice chestnuts; 75 grams (2⅔ ounces) of sugar and 4 deciliters (1⅔ cups) of water; a half vanilla bean to cook them; 100 grams (3½ ounces, 7 tablespoons) of fine butter; 1 deciliter (3⅓ fluid ounces, scant ½ cup) of crème anglaise.**

125 grams (4½ ounces) of ladyfingers. For their syrup: 75 grams (2⅔ ounces) of sugar; 1½ deciliters (5 fluid ounces, ⅔ cup) of water; 1 deciliter (3⅓ fluid ounces, scant ½ cup) of kirsch.

For the crème anglaise: **½ liter (generous 2 cups) of milk; 135 grams (4¾ ounces) of superfine sugar; 5 egg yolks; a half vanilla bean.**

A 1-liter-capacity (4-cup) circular mold (SEE PAGE 576), or if you do not have that, a charlotte mold.

PROCEDURE. Prepare the chestnuts exactly as described for Nesselrode pudding.

While they are cooking, also prepare the crème anglaise (SEE PAGE 583). If you have time, you can also cut the ladyfingers and prepare the kirsch syrup.

Once the chestnut purée has been put into a terrine and vigorously worked for a moment, add the crème anglaise to it (1 deciliter/3⅓ fluid ounces/scant ½ cup) *lukewarm.* This dilutes the purée and makes incorporating the butter easier, which you then add by small pieces at a time, working everything with a spoon. If you were to add the butter to the chilled purée, it would first have to be made into a pomade (SEE PAGE 16).

The purée is now ready to use immediately. If not, keep it at a moderate temperature to avoid it chilling too much; otherwise, it would become too firm and make filling the mold more difficult.

The ladyfingers and the kirsch syrup: Cut the ladyfingers into three pieces. Slice lengthwise through each piece to halve the thickness and make thin slices. Keep them on a plate. Soak the kirsch into the pieces only when filling the mold.

In a small saucepan, melt the sugar in the water. Boil for 2 or 3 minutes. When it is nice and smooth and clear, put the syrup in a bowl. Add the kirsch to it.

To mold: Carefully oil the mold, particularly in the corners (SEE PAGE 18). Using a small wooden spatula or a teaspoon, and without pressing too much so that you do not make the purée more dense, spread a layer of purée 1 centimeter (⅜ inch) thick in the bottom of the mold.

With a brush dipped in the kirsch syrup, soak the slices of ladyfinger as you go, and place them one next to another on the purée in a nice, even layer. Above them spread out another layer of purée, thinner than the first. As you go, tap the bottom of the mold, as directed (SEE PAGE 575). And so on until you fill the mold. Make 7 layers of ladyfingers and 8 of purée.

Keep the mold in a cool place, as directed above.

To serve: Dip the mold in warm water. Unmold on a round plate. Pour several tablespoons of cream around the pudding. Serve the rest in a sauceboat.

Malakoff Pudding *(Pouding à la Malakoff)*

An excellent cold dessert that does not need ice, is easy to make, and can be prepared well in advance with ordinary ingredients. In short, a marmalade of apples and pears, Smyrna and Corinth raisins, candied orange peel, and slivered almonds alternating with layers of slices of ladyfingers soaked in liqueur and crème anglaise.

Apples and pears, according to the recipe given here, are cooked separately: you then add raisins to the apples and almonds to the pears; and, of course, each fruit alternates with the ladyfingers and the cream. If you must, and to simplify the preparation, you can cook the two fruits together: in this case, do not mix the raisins, orange peel, and almonds with them, but spread them on the marmalade when putting it in the mold. *Time: 1 scant hour to prepare the pudding; to have it set up, 3 hours without ice and 1 hour with ice or in a refrigerator. Serves 6–8.*

125 grams (4 1/2 ounces) of apples and 125 grams (4 1/2 ounces) of pears (weighed once completely peeled and without core or seeds); 2 tablespoons of superfine sugar to cook them. 25 grams (1 ounce) of Corinth raisins and the same quantity of Smyrna raisins; the same quantity of candied orange peel; 3 ordinary sugar cubes and 4–5 tablespoons of water to cook them.

Six ladyfingers (about 125 grams, 4 1/2 ounces); 8–10 almonds; 1 deciliter (3 1/3 fluid ounces, scant 1/2 cup) of kirsch or rum, whichever you prefer.

For the thickened crème anglaise: 6 good deciliters (2 1/2 cups) of boiled milk; 200 grams (7 ounces) of superfine sugar; 7 egg yolks; 1 teaspoon of starch (rice starch, or similar); a half vanilla bean or a ribbon of orange or lemon peel; 50 grams (1 3/4 ounces) of pieces of macaroons or ladyfingers; 8 sheets of excellent gelatin; 2 1/2 deciliters (1 cup) of rather thick cream that is very fresh.

A charlotte mold or a domed mold with a cover, with a capacity of 1 1/4 liters (5 1/3 cups).

PROCEDURE. Prepare the raisins as directed (SEE RAISINS, PAGE 573). Boil them gently for *5 minutes* with sugar and water. Then add the orange peel cut into small dice, and let it boil for another *5 minutes.* Turn off the heat. Allow it to cool.

Shell the almonds and cut them into slivers (SEE PAGE 573).

The marmalades: Prepare them in two separate saucepans so that you can alternate them in the mold. Put the fruits, peeled and finely sliced, into a small sauté pan with 1 tablespoon of superfine sugar and 2–3 tablespoons of water only.

Cook them gently (SEE PAGE 620) and reduce the mixture to a consistency of *very thick* marmalade. Then let it cool.

The crème anglaise: Prepare it as directed (SEE PAGE 583). When it is properly bound, put *2 good deciliters (6 3/4 fluid ounces, 7/8 cup) into a small saucepan for the sauce.* Keep this warm until just before serving, when the sauce is finished in its characteristically special way; pour a little bit of milk on the surface to prevent a skin from forming.

Add the gelatin to the rest of the crème; proceed as directed for thickened crème anglaise (SEE PAGE 583). When it is cooled, add 2 deciliters (6 3/4 fluid ounces, 7/8 cup) of unwhipped, raw cream to it, as well as the macaroons or other pieces of ladyfinger, crushed into a rough crumb. Note that this chilled cream must be still liquid when you put it into the mold, so that it sets evenly.

To mold it: Oil the inside of the mold (SEE PAGE 18). Thoroughly drain the raisins and the candied peel; mix them with the apple marmalade. Put the almonds into the pear marmalade.

Cut the ladyfingers in two lengthwise and then slice through them lengthwise across their thickness: that will produce four rectangular pieces for each ladyfinger. In a shallow bowl, pour 2–3 tablespoons of the chosen liqueur; add a pinch of superfine sugar to it.

Once the cream has been cooled *but is still completely liquid,* pour a layer 1 centimeter (3/8 inch) thick into the mold. On top of this layer of cream, place several pieces of ladyfingers, first dipping them lightly into the sugared liqueur. Over these ladyfingers, put a layer of apple marmalade with raisins. Then a layer of cream, then one of ladyfingers. Atop the ladyfingers, put the marmalade of pears with the almonds added to it. And so on, until you use up the ingredients. After adding each layer of cream, tap the mold on the table as directed (SEE PAGE 575). *Finish with a layer of cream,* which gives some stability to the pudding.

Immediately put it in a cool place, either in a terrine with ice (but do not add salt, which will have too powerful a cooling effect here). At the end of 15 minutes, once the cream has set, cover the mold with a round of white parchment paper to keep off the dust. Let it stand for the necessary time, as directed.

The sauce: Into the reserved cream, which has been kept warm in its little saucepan, mix only 1 tablespoon of egg white, which you simply beat in a dish to a nice foamy consistency, using a fork. At the same time, add the 1/2 deciliter (1 2/3 fluid ounces, scant 1/4 cup) of raw cream that you reserved.

Using a small whisk, whisk the mixture on very low heat until it becomes very foamy. Then add the liqueur. Keep it in a cool place. This sauce must be *quite cool* when you use it.

To serve: Run a knife blade around the circumference of the mold to loosen the cream. On top of the mold, put an upside-down round plate that is quite cold. Turn everything over. Hold the plate in your two hands with your thumbs leaning up against the mold. Shake it a little to detach the cream and to remove the mold.

Pour the cream evenly over the pudding. Serve.

Diplomat Pudding
(Pouding Diplomate)

A classic cold dessert that is always in favor, and will feature happily on a formal, ceremonial menu, even though the preparation is not very complicated. In brief, it is a Bavarian cream with a decoration of candied fruits, Smyrna and Corinth raisins, and ladyfingers soaked in kirsch. This differentiates diplomat pudding from diplomat cream. You can also add to the raisins a little bit of apricot marmalade, as for rice à l'impératrice.

Use a ring mold, one that is quite high; if you do not have one, use a savarin mold. A mold without an open center would not work: the mixture would not chill sufficiently to ensure the stability of the pudding. *Time: About 1 1/2 hours for preparing and chilling the cream; 3 hours for setting the pudding with ice or in the refrigerator. Serves 8–10.*

For the crème anglaise: **3 good deciliters (1 1/4 cups) of boiled milk; 175 grams (6 ounces) of superfine sugar; 5 egg yolks; a half vanilla bean; 1 small teaspoon of arrowroot; 4 sheets of gelatin; 3 deciliters (1 1/4 cups) of fresh heavy cream for whipping.**

125 grams (4 1/2 ounces) of Smyrna and Corinth raisins (half of each); 3 candied bitter oranges; 2 dozen candied cherries, known as "half sugared"; 6 ladyfingers (75 grams, 2 2/3 ounces); 1 deciliter (3 1/3 fluid ounces, scant 1/2 cup) of kirsch.

A 1 1/4-liter (5-cup) mold.

PROCEDURE. Prepare the raisins and let them swell for about 10 minutes, just covered with water containing 3 sugar cubes, as directed (SEE RAISINS, PAGE 573). Drain them well. Put them in a bowl; moisten them with 2–3 tablespoons of kirsch. Let them macerate for at least *20 minutes,* tossing them from time to time.

Prepare the crème anglaise, as directed (SEE THICKENED CRÈME ANGLAISE, PAGE 583). Let it cool to the point that it is *scarcely lukewarm.*

Lightly oil the mold with a brush. Place a decoration at the bottom of the mold with the candied fruits: the bitter oranges cut into slices or quarters, alternating with the cherries.

Cut the ladyfingers in three lengthwise and then slice them in half across their thickness to make 6 pieces per ladyfinger.

Pour the rest of the kirsch into a shallow bowl.

To mold: Whip the fresh cream (SEE PAGE 586). Mix the crème anglaise with it as directed (SEE CREAM AND FRESH FRUIT PUDDING, OPPOSITE PAGE).

As soon as you have mixed the two creams, pour a layer 2 centimeters (3/4 inch) thick over the fruit decoration, using a large kitchen spoon. Tap the mold on the table (SEE PAGE 575).

Place a layer of ladyfingers on the cream, dipping them in the kirsch as you go. On top of that, spread a layer of macerated raisins. Cover with a layer of cream, then ladyfingers, then raisins. And so on, making sure you tap the bottom of the mold on the table at each layer of cream, as directed. Finish with a layer of cream, which makes a solid base for the pudding.

Cover the mold with a round of oiled white parchment paper. Put it in a terrine surrounded with crushed ice, or place it directly in the refrigerator. Allow it to set for at least 3 hours. Unmold and serve like a Bavarian cream.

Cream and Fresh Fruit Pudding *(Pouding de Crème et de Fruits Frais)*

A very pleasant cold dessert, with the advantage that it uses all kinds of fruits, according to the season. The larger their variety, the better the effect. Their quantities are not at all precise, and can depend on the resources of the moment as well as taste. The only point to note is that the peaches must be perfectly ripe and of excellent quality, just as if they were to be served as a dessert themselves; avoid buying them overripe so that they do not end up as a mush. But though the proportion of fruits can be modified, the same is by no means true for the crème anglaise: nothing must be left out because you must always bear in mind that whipped cream will be added at the end, which will ultimately loosen up the ensemble.

The pudding is put on ice or in a refrigerator *3–4 hours* before being served, as much so that it can be served quite cold as to ensure that it sets. If it is impossible to procure ice, put an extra sheet of gelatin into the cream if the weather is warm. And a pudding that is prepared well in advance in the morning, to be served that evening for dinner, can be kept in extremely cold water as soon as it has been molded. *Time: At least 1 hour, 30 minutes, plus about 4 hours to chill it. Serves 6.*

For the crème anglaise: **2 1/2 deciliters (1 cup) of good milk; 4 egg yolks; 125 grams (4 1/2 ounces) of superfine sugar; 3 sheets of gelatin weighing a total of 6 grams (about 1/5 ounce); 1 small liqueur glass of kirsch; 2 1/2 deciliters (1 cup) of heavy cream for whipping; 2 scant tablespoons of superfine sugar; 60 grams (2 1/4 ounces) of ladyfingers.**

For the fruits: **2 medium-size peaches; 5 or 6 apricots, depending on their size, or the same volume of pears if you like, mixed with apples; 4 tablespoons of small strawberries, nice and healthy and cleaned; 2 small tablespoons of gooseberries; some good fresh grapes (Muscat if possible); if you like, 1 small liqueur glass of kirsch; superfine sugar.**

A high-sided angel food or cartridge mold (SEE PAGE 575) with a capacity of about 12 deciliters (5 cups).

PROCEDURE. **The fruits:** Peel the peaches and pears, then slice into thin slices. Slice the apricots too, but you do not have to peel them first. Mix everything together into a shallow bowl. Sprinkle them with 3–4 tablespoons of superfine sugar and then with 2 tablespoons of kirsch. Toss everything. Cover the plate. Keep it cool.

In another plate or in a bowl, toss the strawberries with 1 tablespoon of superfine sugar and 1 tablespoon of kirsch. Reject any that are slightly overripe, because they will turn into a mush. Add the raspberries and gooseberries and, if you have them, the grapes also: be careful when destemming the grapes not to pierce the skin so that their juice does not escape.

Kept apart thus, these most fragile fruits are more likely to remain intact, and it is also easier to arrange them in the pudding.

For everything, allow *1 good hour to macerate in a cool place.* In a warm temperature, the fruits risk liquefying in the sugar and the kirsch. If you have ice, put the receptacles holding the fruits on top of it. If not, put the receptacles in very cold water.

The cream: Prepare it while the fruits are macerating (SEE THICKENED CRÈME ANGLAISE, PAGE 583). Add the kirsch to it at the same time as the gelatin, off the heat. Let it cool until it is *scarcely lukewarm.*

Whip the heavy cream (SEE WHIPPED CREAM, PAGE 586).

Pour the little bit of kirsch used for macerating the fruit into the crème anglaise. Then mix the two creams as follows: with your left hand, hold the saucepan with the cream in it, and in your right hand hold a small sauce whisk. Pour the crème anglaise in a very thin stream *into the center* of the whipped cream, mixing it with the whisk that you turn gently in place, without either beating or whisking, which would make the cream collapse. From the beginning to the end, your movements should be both even and very slow.

Once it is mixed, immediately fill the mold; the mold should first have been carefully oiled, as directed (SEE OILING A MOLD, PAGE 18).

To mold: Cut the ladyfingers in thirds lengthwise and then slice through each piece in half across its thickness. At the bottom of the mold, make a layer of pieces of ladyfingers. Over them put a layer of fruits, arranged as you like. Using a kitchen spoon, pour a layer of cream about 2 centimeters (3/4 inch) thick over everything. Lightly tap the mold on the table (SEE PAGE 575). On the layer of cream, place a new layer of pieces of ladyfingers, then fruits. Cover with cream. And so on, finishing with the cream. After adding each layer of cream, gently tap the mold on the table. You should end up with four layers of each kind. The last layer must be cream; do not let it spill over the sides, but shape it more or less into a dome. This is to counter the settling that will happen as the pudding chills.

Cover everything with oiled parchment paper, putting the oiled part placed directly on the cream. If you have a refrigerator, place the mold on a shelf in the coldest part. If not, put the mold in a receptacle and surround it right to the top with crushed ice. But use *no salt,* which would lower the temperature too much. Do not bother to place lots of ice in the opening in the center of the mold: the cold from the ice on the bottom will be enough to firm up the cream. On top of the paper on the mold, put a good flat cover, even a baking sheet if you have nothing else. On top of this, place one large piece of ice. Let it stand for the time indicated.

To serve: Dip the mold in warm water as directed (SEE TO UNMOLD A DESSERT, PAGE 575), and unmold on a plate covered with a napkin. If the pudding does come out easily the first time, you only need to plunge it again into the warm water.

Mexico Pudding *(Pouding Mexico)*

A very fine, home-style cold dessert. Molded in a charlotte mold and cooked in a bain-marie, you can glaze it after chilling with chocolate or coffee (SEE ICING CAKES, PAGE 721) and accompany it with a crème anglaise. It can also be used as a cake for snacks and teas.

For the details of how to make the batter, refer to the directions given in the pastry chapter for chocolate cake (SEE PAGE 711). *Time: 30 minutes of preparation and 2 hours to chill the pudding. Serves 6.*

120 grams (4 1/4 ounces) of chocolate; 120 grams (4 1/4 ounces) of superfine sugar; 2 large eggs or 3 small ones; 120 grams (4 1/4 ounces, generous 1 stick) of fresh butter; 50 grams (1 3/4 ounces) of good flour.

A charlotte mold, with about a 1-liter (4-cup) capacity.

PROCEDURE. Soften the chocolate. Beat the yolks and the sugar in a terrine. Mix in the butter—make it into a pomade first (SEE PAGE 16)—and the chocolate, the flour, and the whites, whisked into a firm snow.

Pour it into a heavily buttered mold. Cook in the bain-marie in the oven as directed (SEE PAGE 42) for *45 minutes.* Remove the mold from the bain-marie and do not unmold it until the pudding has chilled.

Soufflé Pudding with Almonds *(Pouding Soufflé aux Amandes)*

A hot dessert that is particularly recommended for its lightness and the simplicity of its preparation as well as its ingredients. If you like, serve it covered with a little kirsch-flavored cream, rum-flavored cream, or a zabaglione, or very simply with a syrup made up of apricot marmalade or a red currant jelly diluted with a little bit of warm water, kirsch, or rum: this last accompaniment, quick and quite inexpensive, is excellent. *Time: 1 hour, 20 minutes. Serves 6.*

2 deciliters (6 3/4 fluid ounces, 7/8 cup) of milk; 80 grams (2 3/4 ounces, 5 1/2 tablespoons) of butter; 80 grams (2 3/4 ounces) of superfine sugar; 30 grams (1 ounce) of flour and 30 grams (1 ounce) of starch (rice flour); 35 grams (1 1/4 ounces) of almonds; 3 egg yolks; 3 whites whisked into a firm snow; a half vanilla bean. A cartridge mold (SEE PAGE 575), preferably not decorated, with a capacity of 1 liter (4 1/4 cups).

PROCEDURE. **The almonds:** Husk them. Slice about 10 of the most beautiful ones (SEE PAGE 573). Mince the rest as finely as possible.

Spread them out *without mixing them* on a very clean baking sheet. The chopped almonds are for the batter of the pudding: the sliced ones are for the mold. Place the baking sheet in a very gentle oven to first dry out the almonds. Then turn up the heat a little higher to toast them very lightly; watch them very carefully so that they do not go beyond a nice even blond tint. Keep them dry until you are ready to use them.

The batter: Boil the milk, put in the vanilla, take it off the heat, then cover and let it infuse warm for *20 minutes.* If the butter is hard in the winter, enclose it in a corner of a moistened towel and squeeze it to soften it. Then put *15 grams (1/2 ounce)* on the side for buttering the mold.

Use a saucepan with a capacity of 2 liters (8 1/2 cups) so that you can then add the whisked egg whites. Work the butter into a pomade as directed (SEE PAGE 16), then add the superfine sugar and mix it vigorously until the butter turns a lighter color.

Mix the flour and the starch, then add it in a shower. If you are using only flour, sift it through a drum sieve. Stir it with a spoon. Gradually mix it with the vanilla-flavored milk, using a small sauce whisk, which is better than a spoon for this.

Put it on a good heat, but not too strong. Bring it to a boil, constantly moving the spoon over the bottom of the saucepan, scraping everywhere. Once boiling has started, mix it for another 3–4 minutes to give the mixture a very thick consistency.

Turn off the heat. Wait a few minutes to allow it to cool slightly. Next add the egg yolks, mixing them rapidly so that they are not seized by the heat. Then mix in the *minced almonds.*

The mold: With a piece of butter that you have reserved, carefully butter the mold all over, particularly in its corners; otherwise, with this type of batter, the pudding may not easily unmold. Then sprinkle the slivered almonds inside the mold as evenly as possible; if you need to, fix them with the end of your finger to stick them into the butter.

Whisk the whites into a firm snow (SEE EGG WHITES, PAGE 8). Then add a quarter of the whites to the batter in two batches, mixing thoroughly and without the usual care taken for egg whites, so that you dilute the batter, which makes it easier to mix in the rest of the whites, working carefully (SEE PAGE 10).

As soon as the whites are incorporated, place the batter, a tablespoon at a time, in the prepared mold. Tap the mold lightly on a folded towel to settle it. Put everything immediately into the oven in a bain-marie, following the directions already given (SEE THE DOUBLE BOILER, PAGE 42). Allow *40 minutes to poach.*

The pudding rapidly begins to rise. After 10 minutes, it should reach the edges of the mold. If the saucepan of the bain-marie is not very deep, the batter will reach and even raise the cover. In this case, replace the cover with a large sheet of buttered parchment paper.

Once the pudding is cooked, remove it from the bain-marie and allow it to rest for *5–6 minutes* so that it settles slightly. Then unmold it on a round plate and cover it with cream, zabaglione, or syrup.

Brazilian-Style Pudding
(Pouding à la Brésilienne)

A warm dessert, in which tapioca is the only element of starch but does not reveal its presence in the pudding. To summarize, the ensemble looks like a savarin that is more or less light, depending on the proportions of the eggs relative to the tapioca. So for 125 grams (4 1/2 ounces) of tapioca, you can use only 3 yolks and 2 whites. Or, reducing the quantity of tapioca to 75 grams (2 2/3 ounces), use 4 yolks and 4 whites; this produces a pudding of great delicacy, rather like a soufflé. We give the recipe for this below.

If you like, you can use a cartridge mold, hollow in the middle, or a charlotte mold; this last is easier to caramelize. Poaching, or cooking, it in the bain-marie takes a little bit longer; assume *45–50 minutes* for cooking and 10 minutes less with a mold with an open center. You can omit the caramel and simply butter the mold, then sprinkle it with tapioca, almost like a layer of bread crumbs: strictly speaking, that makes it a tapioca pudding, because the name *Brazilian-style* applies only to the caramelized pudding.

If you like, accompany the pudding with a sauce made with red currant jelly or apricot marmalade diluted with warm water, and with a liqueur added to it, thus: 4 tablespoons of preserves, 1 deciliter (3 1/3 fluid ounces, scant 1/2 cup) of water, and 1 tablespoon of liqueur. *Time: 25 minutes for cooking. Serves 6.*

75 grams (2 2/3 ounces) of tapioca; 3 deciliters (1 1/4 cups) of milk; 60 grams (2 1/4 ounces) of sugar, in cubes or granulated; a grain of salt (SEE PAGE 575); 50 grams (1 3/4 ounces, 3 1/2 tablespoons) of butter; 3 ribbons of lemon peel; 4 egg yolks; 4 egg whites whisked into a snow.

A charlotte mold with a capacity of 1 1/2 liters (6 1/3 cups).

PROCEDURE. In a thick saucepan with a capacity of about 1 liter (4 cups), so that you can then mix in the egg yolks, heat the milk. Add the sugar and the lemon peel. Cover and let the sugar dissolve, stirring it from time to time.

When the sugar is well dissolved, bring the milk back to a boil. Add the tapioca in a shower, and add the butter and the salt. Stir with a spoon to mix everything. *Cover* and put the saucepan into a very gentle oven to cook for *25 minutes,* after which the swollen tapioca will have completely absorbed the milk.

While this is cooking, caramelize the mold as directed (SEE PAGE 575).

Once the tapioca has been cooked, gradually add the egg yolks to it (first beaten in a bowl), mixing them in with a wooden spoon and stirring vigorously. Then pour it into a terrine or a bowl so that you can mix in the whites.

Whisk the whites as directed (SEE PAGE 8). First mix one-quarter of them into the tapioca to loosen its consistency and to make it easier to mix in the rest, working with all due care (SEE PAGE 10).

Put the batter, a tablespoon at a time, into the prepared mold; it must only be three-quarters full. Tap it lightly on the table (SEE PAGE 575). Immediately put it in the oven in a bain-marie, following the directions given (SEE PAGE 42). The batter begins to rise after 6–7 minutes. It rises most in the latter stages of cooking. Then proceed as directed for SOUFFLÉ PUDDING WITH ALMONDS (PAGE 644). Unmold the pudding on a round plate and serve the sauce on the side.

Cabinet Pudding *(Pouding de Cabinet)*

A classic warm dessert, one that appears perhaps a little too often in pension hotels in its most simple form: that is, ladyfingers alternating with raisins, combined with a cream mixture. A more refined version of cabinet pudding includes candied fruits cut into small dice—orange peel, apricots, cherries, bitter oranges, etc.—using the same amount of these as raisins, the quantity of which is diminished accordingly. A special addition is to use some apricot marmalade. The cream, depending on whether economy is a concern, can be made with a varying number of eggs: either yolks only, or including some whites; or even only whole eggs. Serve with the accompaniment of your preference, a crème anglaise, a zabaglione, an apricot sauce, a red currant sauce, etc.

The following recipe is the simplest, without the candied fruit. And the cream is sufficiently delicate, because it contains fewer whole eggs than yolks. *Time: 40 minutes of cooking. Serves 6.*

125 grams (4 1/2 ounces) of ladyfingers; 60 grams (2 1/4 ounces) of Smyrna raisins and the same quantity of Corinth raisins; 120 grams (4 1/4 ounces) of sugar, cubes or granulated; 1/2 liter (generous 2 cups) of milk; 2 whole eggs and 3 egg yolks; flavor the cream as you like: with vanilla or with orange or lemon peel.

A timbale or charlotte mold with a capacity of 11–12 deciliters (4 1/2–5 cups).

PROCEDURE. Prepare the cream as for caramel custard (SEE PAGE 582) until the point when it is poured into the mold. Prepare the raisins (SEE PAGE 573). Butter the mold. Arrange the ladyfingers in successive layers, overlapping over each other, distributing some raisins on each layer. (If you add candied fruit, mix them with the raisins.) After you have arranged all the ingredients in the mold, there should be an empty space about a finger's width, 2 centimeters (3/4 inch), left above the biscuits. Little by little, pour in the cream mixture: it should be absorbed as you go by the ladyfingers, and there should be no surplus. Let it stand for *10–15 minutes* so that the ladyfingers absorb it thoroughly.

After this, put it in the oven in a bain-marie (SEE PAGE 42). The oven here must be relatively strong, so that during the *40 minutes of cooking* needed, the water in the bain-marie is maintained at a constant simmer. If the heat of the oven is too weak, the center of the pudding will not be cooked and will collapse into a crater, when the opposite effect, for it to rise, is required.

When it has developed and set at the same time, and has come away from the borders of the mold, take it out of the bain-marie. Wait about 10 minutes before unmolding it, so that the inside can settle. Also, this type of dessert should not be served burning hot.

Turn the mold over on a round plate. Sprinkle it with a few tablespoons of your chosen sauce, serving the rest in a sauceboat.

BAVARIAN CREAMS
Les Bavarois

Bavarian creams offer the very considerable advantage that they can be served instead of ice cream, if necessary, and they do not require any special equipment. They also are one of the most popular cold desserts of those that can be made at home. But two conditions are essential: you need excellent fresh cream, and you must pay attention to even the smallest details.

Derived from "Bavarian cheese," the present-day Bavarian cream in its most current form, which is the easiest to make in any season, is prepared as follows: gelatin is added to a crème anglaise, and next some whipped cream is incorporated; the Bavarian cream is then put on ice or in a refrigerator or even in a very cool place.

Bavarian creams are also made with fresh fruits: so, instead of the crème anglaise, use a fruit purée with sugar syrup added, as well as the essential gelatin, mixed with whipped cream; or add the fruit purée to the crème anglaise and the whipped cream.

The proportion of whipped cream and crème anglaise, or fruit purée, varies slightly among the experts. Generally, you can use equal quantities: that is, for 5 deciliters (generous 2 cups) of crème anglaise or fruit purée, add 5 deciliters (generous 2 cups) of whipped cream (note that for this quantity of whipped cream, you need only 2 1/2 deciliters/1 cup of heavy cream, because whipping it doubles the volume).

However, the amount of gelatin, which is reduced in today's Bavarian creams, varies slightly: the first point to consider is the quality of the gelatin, which will give a greater or lesser stability to the mixture. There is also the daily temperature to take into account. In a cold season, you need less gelatin. In the summer, from May onward, you will need more because you must bear in mind the heat of the dining room: the Bavarian creams, served quite firm, will melt by the time they reach the last guests. In any case, it is always better to add one more, not one less, sheet of gelatin, rather than risk the thing collapsing, and this extra gelatin will not alter the flavor of the dish. When flavoring with a liqueur, allow one sheet of gelatin more for each tablespoon of liqueur.

Of necessity, the mold used must be one with an open center (SEE PAGE 575). A full mold does not work, because the cream would not set evenly: the center would always be less firm and less cool than the surrounding parts. The mold can be plain or have grooved sides; it is better, if possible, to use one that is not too tall, because a Bavarian cream is not itself very high: this allows it to hold its shape while being served to the guests.

Bavarian cream is not accompanied by a syrup or a sauce, as are most cold puddings.

Vanilla Bavarian Cream
(Bavarois à la Vanille)

Time: 1 hour, 30 minutes for preparing the Bavarian cream; to set it, assume 1 hour, 30 minutes with ice and 2 hours in a refrigerator, or 5–6 hours without ice, depending on whether or not the place where you have left the Bavarian cream is more or less cool Serves 6–8.

For the crème anglaise: **1/2 liter (generous 2 cups) of good milk; 200 grams (7 ounces) of superfine sugar; 6 egg yolks; 1 teaspoon of arrowroot; 6–8 sheets of gelatin (about 12 grams/ 3/8 ounce); a half vanilla bean.**

3 deciliters (1 1/4 cups) of fresh thick cream for whipping.

An open-centered mold with a capacity of 12 deciliters (5 cups); 1/2 tablespoon of sweet almond oil, or any other oil that has no flavor, to oil the mold.

Optional: 2–3 kilograms (4 pounds, 6 ounces–6 pounds, 10 ounces) of ice, depending on the season.

PROCEDURE. Prepare the crème anglaise as directed (SEE THICKENED CRÈME ANGLAISE, PAGE 583).

Oil the mold (SEE PAGE 18). Whip the cream (SEE WHIPPED CREAM, PAGE 586).

The mixture: Do not wait for the crème anglaise to be absolutely cold before starting, because then it will be too firm for the effect of the gelatin and will be difficult to mix; on the other hand, if it is still warm it will make the whipped cream collapse. It should therefore be slightly cold and still have a lightly bound consistency, not yet fully set. Add the whipped cream with the same care taken for adding egg whites whisked into snow (SEE WHISKING EGG WHITES, PAGE 8) so that you preserve the cream's lightness.

To mold it: As soon as the two creams are combined, pour the mixture into a mold tablespoon by tablespoon, and right up to the edge, using a large kitchen spoon. When it is filled, take it between your two hands and tap it gently on the table to lightly settle its contents. Then, right on top of the cream, place a round of oiled parchment paper. If you have a refrigerator, put the mold on a shelf in the coldest part.

If you have ice, break it into very small pieces. Place it in a terrine or similar receptacle, big enough so that the mold is well surrounded.

If you do not have ice, keep the mold in the coolest place possible.

To serve: With the point of a small knife, lightly loosen the cream from the edges of the mold. Turn it over on a round plate garnished with a folded napkin or a kitchen towel; the Bavarian cream should thus unmold very easily, without having to be first dipped into warm water. But if the Bavarian cream has been standing in ice or a refrigerator, and the oil has congealed, dip the mold for a second into lukewarm water.

Coffee Bavarian Cream *(Bavarois au Café).* The same quantities and the same procedures as for VANILLA BAVARIAN CREAM (SEE PAGE 647), replacing the infusion of vanilla with an infusion of coffee. Thus, 75 grams (2 2/3 ounces) of coffee beans and 5 grams (1/6 ounce) of chicory, infused in boiling milk as directed (SEE POTS DE CRÈME, PAGE 579) for the *coffee flavor.*

Orange Bavarian Cream *(Bavarois à l'Orange).* The orange note here comes from the flavor of the fruit's peel. The juice is not used. And the flavoring should come in the form of "zest sugar"—that is, rubbed on the skin of the orange to obtain the flavor. The quantities are the same as those for VANILLA BAVARIAN CREAM (PAGE 647), replacing the infusion of vanilla with the orange-flavored sugar. The pink color characteristic of this flavor is acquired by using a few drops of vegetable coloring, added to the crème anglaise off the heat, before chilling the dish.

Thus: 4 oranges chosen preferably with a large crinkly skin, and 75 grams (2 2/3 ounces) of sugar cubes. Thoroughly wipe the oranges with a soft cloth. Rub the sugar, piece by piece, against the orange like a grater, until each piece is all colored orange, having taken up the orange skin, or zest. Once the milk has been boiled, add the zest sugar: cover and allow it to melt on very low heat. For all the rest, proceed as directed for VANILLA BAVARIAN CREAM (PAGE 647).

Chocolate Bavarian Cream *(Bavarois au Chocolat).* The same quantities and the same procedures as for VANILLA BAVARIAN CREAM (PAGE 647), preparing a thick crème anglaise with chocolate flavor, following the method given and using the quantity of chocolate suggested (SEE POTS DE CRÈME, PAGE 579).

ICED MOUSSES
Mousses Glacées

Whipped cream, or "Chantilly" cream (SEE PAGE 586), is the principal element, the base of every iced mousse. A simple charlotte mold with a tightly sealed cover is essential.

For mixing the whipped cream with the other ingredients for the mousse—fruit purée, or others—proceed as directed for mixing the egg whites that have been whisked into a snow (SEE PAGE 8).

To mold and to serve, refer to the directions given for NESSELRODE PUDDING (SEE PAGE 638).

Time needed to ice a mousse: 2 1/2 hours. Allow 4–5 kilograms (8 pounds, 13 ounces–11 pounds) of ice and 300 grams (10 1/2 ounces) of gray sea salt. (SEE PREPARING THE SORBETIÈRE, AT RIGHT).

Chocolate Mousse, Simple Method *(Mousse au Chocolat, Façon Simple).* Put 125 grams (4 1/2 ounces) of chocolate, broken into small pieces, into 1 1/2 deciliters (5 fluid ounces, 2/3 cup) of boiling water. Allow it to soften; dilute into a smooth paste. Dissolve 125 grams (4 1/2 ounces) of sugar in 1 deciliter (3 1/3 fluid ounces, scant 1/2 cup) of water; boil for 2 minutes; skim, mix with the chocolate; chill. Whip 1/2 liter (generous 2 cups) of cream; first add a quarter of it to the chocolate to make it easier to mix in the rest, taking due care (SEE PAGE 10). Mold, ice, etc. as directed.

Strawberry Mousse *(Mousse aux Fraises).* Boil 180 grams (6 1/4 ounces) of sugar already dissolved in 1 deciliter (3 1/3 fluid ounces, scant 1/2 cup) of water for 2 minutes; skim, chill. Press 375 grams (13 1/4 ounces) of small strawberries into a fine purée; add the juice of 1 orange and 1/2 lemon and the cold syrup. Whip 2 1/2 deciliters (1 cup) of fresh cream; mix it with the purée. If you like, add a few small whole strawberries. Mold, chill, etc.

Apricot Mousse *(Mousse aux Abricots).* If you like, it can be molded and chilled, or simply stacked into a dome shape and kept cool.

Press 650 grams (1 pound, 7 ounces) of small *uncooked* apricots into a purée. Dissolve 150 grams (5 1/3 ounces) of sugar in 3 tablespoons of water; boil for 2 minutes; *chill.* Mix 1 deciliter (3 1/3 fluid ounces, scant 1/2 cup) of good kirsch into the apricot purée. Whip 2 1/2 deciliters (1 cup) of fresh cream. Mix it with the purée. Serve the mousse surrounded by apricot halves cooked into a compote and chilled.

FROZEN DESSERTS
Les Glaces

A frozen dessert can be served either molded or in a stack, dressed tablespoon by tablespoon on top of each other; it can also be served in little ice cream dishes. In the latter case, it melts more rapidly than a frozen dessert that has been molded because it soon becomes less cold. But on the other hand, this relatively moderate temperature is appreciated by most of the guests.

Molding is a step that is absolutely distinct from freezing, which comes next, and it takes much longer.

Frozen desserts include two kinds of compositions: ices made with cream, using a crème anglaise that is flavored as you wish; and ices made with syrup, mostly used for fresh fruits, whose juices or pulp are added to the syrup.

Preparing the Sorbetière (Ice-Cream Maker)

First of all, let us make the point that a "sorbetière" does not—despite the way the term is commonly used today—refer to the entire equipment used for preparing ices: a sorbetière is the metal receptacle in which you put the mixture that you want to freeze, and this is then placed in a wooden pail filled with crushed ice.

To prepare it, surround the receptacle with crushed ice, putting the mixture that you want to freeze in either the sorbetière or a mold.

To this crushed ice, add gray sea salt, which lowers the temperature of the ice, thus increasing its cooling power: the ice alone will not suffice to freeze the mixture to the right consistency. The amount of salt needed is about 250 grams (8 7/8 ounces) for each kilogram (2 pounds, 3 ounces) of ice, if you are not also using saltpeter. (We do not suggest using it because you cannot get it as easily as sea salt.)

The *amount of ice* required varies depending on the capacity of the equipment. It is important to note that in every case, the crushed ice must go at least 6 centimeters (2 1/4 inches) above the height of the mixture inside the metal ice-cream container. The quantity also varies depending on how long the mixture will stand once it has been frozen; and in particular, on whether it will be molded; because, for the initial preparation of the mold, you will naturally need more ice. The average amount is 4–5 kilograms (8 pounds, 13 ounces–11 pounds) of ice for 1 liter (4 1/4 cups) of mixture to be served in scoops or served in little dishes. That said, if you do not want to run the risk of last-minute problems, it is a good idea to make sure you have a large supply of ice and do not limit yourself to the quantity that is strictly necessary.

When buying the ice substantially in advance, make sure you wrap the block of ice with a cloth cover folded into quarters to avoid any contact with the air, which would make it melt. Also keep it in as cool a place as possible.

Crush the ice only when you are ready to use it. If you have a large mortar, break up the block of ice in it, using a hammer to make *pieces the size of small walnuts.* You could also do this in a wooden box with low sides; the pieces will not then be able to escape, as they would if doing this in a stone sink or on the floor of the kitchen, for example.

Let us also remark that the smaller the pieces of ice, the more rapidly the mixture will cool. If the mixture, once it has been frozen, must stand for a rather long time in the sorbetière before being served, and if a second batch of ice is needed to replace the ice that has melted, use ice pieces the size of an egg. Too low a temperature would freeze the mixture too much, and should be avoided. The mixture will harden, making it extremely difficult to serve, in scoops or otherwise; and, what's more, the flavor of a mixture that is too cold is substantially weakened.

PROCEDURE. *The metal sorbetière must be prepared 15 minutes before putting in the mixture that you want to freeze.* This is so that the cold can be concentrated inside the utensil and seize the mixture as soon as it is poured into the metal ice cream dish.

With a very clean, odor-free towel, first wipe the inside of the metal sorbetière. Cut a round of white parchment paper and put it over the top. The edges of the paper must fold over the metal ice cream container, which makes the cover fit more tightly. You can even double it if one sheet does not seal it tightly enough. This seal is very important, particularly because of the salt. You must be very careful about this before beginning to surround the sorbetière with ice and salt.

Place the post of the metal sorbetière in the socket at the bottom of the wooden pail. After this, surround the metal ice-cream container with layers of crushed ice; sprinkle them with salt. As you go, mix the ice with the handle of a long wooden spoon, making sure at the same time that the metal sorbetière turns effortlessly.

Freezing: About a half hour before serving the ice cream, either as it is or put into a mold, and when the sorbetière has already been on ice for 15 minutes, open the sorbetière carefully, remembering that there is always a risk that a grain of salt will fall into it. Pour in the mixture, *never filling it by more than two-thirds:* it is essential to leave sufficient space to allow for the continual movement of the mixture during the freezing process.

Close it up with a round of paper under the cover, as before. *Immediately begin to turn the handle.* Letting the mixture stand without moving would provoke the formation of ice crystals in the mixture, and these could not then be dissolved. Turn the handle without stopping, but not too quickly at the beginning, until the mixture is completely frozen. During this process, there is no need to uncover the metal ice-cream container. *Allow 15–20 minutes until you reach the freezing point,* and here let us note that there is a difference between freezing a mixture made with syrup and one with cream.

A composition made with a syrup (a "lean cream," or sorbet) *will take*—that is, will freeze—more rapidly and more easily than a composition made with cream (a "fat cream"). The cream composition must be worked much more vigorously, particularly when it reaches its setting point.

If the cream must stand, proceed as directed below, *but leave it longer in the freezer* (SEE OPPOSITE PAGE).

How to Mold a Frozen Dessert

First you need a special mold with a cover that closes tightly, like the cover of a metal sorbetière. You also need extra ice. You also need another wooden pail smaller than the first, and shorter than the pail for the sorbetière; or if not, a similar receptacle and preferably one made of wood, because the ice melts in it less quickly.

The *empty* mold, exactly like the metal sorbetière, must be chilled in advance so that its temperature is the same as the mixture, which has already been frozen. Otherwise, the frozen mixture will melt in the mold and subsequently freeze into little crystals.

Put a small piece of ice, not crushed, into the bottom of the receptacle. Place the mold on top of it, empty and closed. Surround it with ice crushed to pieces a little larger than the ice used for freezing, plus salt, almost right up to the height of the top of the mold.

Once the mixture has been properly frozen, place the pail holding the sorbetière next to the receptacle holding the mold. Have at hand a bowl of water that is just *lukewarm,* and a large silver or silver-plated spoon.

Uncover the metal sorbetière; uncover the mold and be careful that no salt falls into it. Dip the spoon into the lukewarm water. Take a spoonful of the mixture. Quickly place it in the mold; it should easily come away from the warmed spoon. Dip the spoon into the water before each new spoonful, and so on.

As you put the mixture into the mold, stir it so that you do not have any empty spaces. Fill the mold *as completely as possible,* until the mixture is almost at the point of spilling over. Directly on top of the mixture, put a supple round of white parchment paper that has a diameter a little larger than the top of the mold: this is so that you can fold it down all around the mold underneath the cover. Then put on the cover. It should take a little bit of force to fit it on, because of the paper. A tight seal is thus assured, just as for the metal sorbetière. Put the ice *around and on top of* the mold, with salt, using 180–200 grams (6 1/3–7 ounces) per kilogram (2 pounds, 3 ounces) of ice. Cover everything with a damp kitchen towel. Keep the receptacle in a very cool place *for about 1 1/2 hours.*

When you must leave it longer in the freezer: Add some fresh ice and salt, and pour out some of the salted water from the first icing. Note that the quantity of salt for freezing a molded mixture varies depending on whether it has to stand for more or less time in the ice. That is, the freezing power of the ice is increased by the salt, and the longer the mixture must stand, the less salt should be used: otherwise, the mixture would become hard and brittle.

To unmold: Use a rather deep receptacle, large enough that you can completely immerse the mold easily by simply plunging it in.

Fill this receptacle with warm water. Dip your hand in and you should be able to feel a good heat, as for a rather hot bath: about 35° Centigrade (95° Fahrenheit).

First, rinse off the mold in cold water. Then plunge it into the receptacle of warm water, either standing up or lengthwise, but so that it is completely covered by the water: just dip it in and take it out, without stopping and without letting go of the mold.

Carefully wipe the mold. Remove the cover and the paper. Pass the blade of a knife around the frozen dessert, following the inside wall of the mold. Place a napkin folded into quarters on top of the frozen dessert, or a small round towel. With a plate on top, turn everything over. Remove the mold straight up to free it.

Ice Creams *(Glaces à la Crème)*

The quantities of egg yolk and sugar for frozen desserts with a base of crème anglaise are extremely variable; those given here represent a good average: in other words, use 10 yolks and at least 300 grams (10 1/2 ounces) of sugar per liter (4 1/4 cups) of milk. Reducing the number of yolks results in a drier dessert; the number of yolks suggested is based on the assumption that you will use yolks from good, medium-size eggs weighing about 60 grams (2 1/4 ounces). Note the quantity of sugar, which is larger than that used for an ordinary cream.

Light cream is preferable to milk whenever possible—which indicates the importance of using good-quality milk. Hence the recommendation to enhance it by first reducing the milk by at least one-quarter: that is, to obtain 7 1/2 deciliters (generous 3 cups), boil and reduce 1 liter (4 1/4 cups) of good milk to this quantity.

A little bit of whipped heavy cream added to the frozen mixture a few instants before taking it out of the metal sorbetière lends a wonderful richness to the iced cream: that is, 3–4 tablespoons for about 1 liter (4 1/4 cups) of crème anglaise.

As for the quantity of iced cream, allow for 6–8 people at least 1 liter (4 1/4 cups) of cream, prepared as directed (SEE CRÈME ANGLAISE, PAGE 583).

Vanilla Ice Cream *(Glace à la Vanille).* 7 1/2 deciliters (generous 3 cups) of good boiled milk; 8 egg yolks; 225 grams (8 ounces) of superfine sugar; a vanilla bean.

Boil the milk and infuse the vanilla for 20 minutes. Make the crème anglaise as directed. Chill. Freeze.

Chocolate Ice Cream *(Glace au Chocolat).* 6 1/2 deciliters (2 3/4 cups) of boiled milk; 4 nice egg yolks or 5 small ones, the quantity of egg yolks in this cream being a little bit less; 125 grams (4 1/2 ounces) of good chocolate, *vanilla-flavored.* If not, put a half vanilla bean in the milk; 125 grams (4 1/2 ounces) of superfine sugar, given that the chocolate is already sugared.

Soften the chocolate, broken into pieces in a cup, with 1–2 tablespoons of water, heating it gently, and then proceed as directed (SEE POTS DE CRÈME, PAGE 579). Chill. Freeze.

Praline Ice Cream *(Glace Pralinée).* 125 grams (4 1/2 ounces) of praline (SEE PAGE 707), or of very good natural pralines (not candied pralines) that have been pounded in a mortar and sifted, then added to 1 liter (4 1/4 cups) of strained vanilla crème anglaise. Freeze.

Coffee Ice Cream *(Glace au Café).* The best procedure, as far as the subtlety of the flavor goes, is to infuse whole beans of coffee in the milk, as directed (SEE POTS DE CRÈME, PAGE 579). Thus: 60 grams (2 1/4 ounces) of good coffee beans infused into 7 1/2 deciliters (generous 3 cups) of very good milk; 9 egg yolks; 225 grams (8 ounces) of superfine or granulated sugar. Make the crème anglaise. Cool. Freeze.

Candied Fruit Ice Cream *(Glace Plombières)*

Here we will give the most simple modern recipe: a vanilla cream to which whipped cream, candied fruits, and apricot marmalade are added. Formerly, candied fruit ice cream also included almond paste, and it is easy to imagine that this remarkably improved the flavor. Today, the ice cream is molded in a bombe, but in the classic method it was simply served in a mound. Also, the apricot marmalade, instead of being applied in alternating layers in the mound, was often just poured over the whole. Here we give the necessary directions for both serving methods. *Time: To serve in a mound, 40 minutes, once the vanilla cream has been prepared and chilled. A good 1 1/2 hours more to mold the ice cream into the bombe. Serves 6–8.*

The vanilla cream first requires: 1/2 liter (generous 2 cups) of light cream or at least 2.8 liters (3 quarts) of ordinary milk boiled and reduced to 1/2 liter (generous 2 cups); 200 grams (7 ounces) of superfine sugar; 8 egg yolks; a half vanilla bean.

You will then need: 2 deciliters (6 3/4 fluid ounces, 7/8 cup) of very fresh thick cream; 4 soupspoons of apricot marmalade; 8 candied cherries; 1 small bitter orange; 1 slice of candied pineapple (about 180 grams, 6 1/3 ounces); 2 small glasses of kirsch.

(The fruits suggested here are by no means the only ones that can be included. You can equally use mirabelle plums, greengage plums, candied orange peel, and some little dice of angelica depending on your tastes and means.)

PROCEDURE. Prepare the vanilla cream for the basic frozen dessert as directed (SEE CRÈME ANGLAISE, PAGE 583). Allow it to completely chill, stirring it often to prevent a skin from forming. Whip the thick cream (SEE PAGE 586).

The candied fruits: Cut them into small dice of a good 1/2 centimeter (3/16 inch) big. Put into a bowl, then moisten them with the kirsch and let them macerate in a cool place until you add them to the cream.

To freeze the cream: Prepare the ice-filled pail for the sorbetière *40 minutes* before serving. Pour in the cream and freeze it as directed. After *20 minutes,* when the cream is well iced and rather firm, add the macerated fruits with their liqueur. Then mix in the whipped cream, adding it a tablespoon at a time. Reseal the metal ice cream container. Turn it again in the ice-filled bucket for *7–8 minutes* to reestablish the consistency that the fruits and the creams have diminished.

To serve in a mound: Prepare your serving plate, covering it with a napkin folded into a rectangle or a lacy round doily.

Scoop out the ice cream with a soupspoon; arrange it 1 tablespoon at a time, placing each scoop next to the other, to make the first layer of ice cream. On this layer, place here and there in little piles *7–8 teaspoons* of apricot marmalade.

Cover these with another layer of ice cream, always arranging it 1 tablespoon at a time. Then place the apricot marmalade on top, as before.

And so on, without attempting any symmetry, placing the tablespoons of cream on top of one another to make a bumpy pyramid.

To mold the ice cream into a bombe (SEE HOW TO MOLD A FROZEN DESSERT, PAGE 650): Use a simple unembossed mold with a capacity of 1 liter (4 1/4 cups). Cover the bottom with 1 good tablespoon of ice cream. Mix it well so that when the ice cream is unmolded, the surface will be nice and smooth. On this layer of ice cream, lay out a bed of apricot marmalade. Continue to fill the mold with the marmalade between each layer of ice cream. *Make sure that this apricot marmalade is very well enclosed between the layers of ice cream without touching the walls of the mold:* this would make it difficult to unmold the ice cream.

Close the mold and proceed for all the rest as directed, including the unmolding. *Allow 1 1/2 hours* for its time in the ice.

Orange Ice Cream with Crème Fraîche *(Glace à l'Orange, à la Crème Fraîche).* It is a raw cream that we are dealing with here; the preparation is one of the simplest, giving the cream a particular subtlety and unctuousness. *Serves 6–8.*

6 nice oranges yielding 1/2 liter (generous 2 cups) of juice; 1 lemon; 1/2 liter (generous 2 cups) of heavy fresh cream; 250 grams (8 7/8 ounces) of sugar cubes; a few drops of red vegetable coloring.

PROCEDURE. Zest two oranges and the lemon (SEE ZEST SUGAR, PAGE 574) with about 15 of the sugar cubes. Squeeze all the juice from the oranges and the lemon, then strain it. Add the sugar to the juice, including the zest sugar; very gently heat it to ensure the sugar dissolves. Mix the heavy cream with the juice. Dissolve a few drops of red vegetable coloring in 1–2 tablespoons of the mixture and add them to the whole, which would otherwise be a grayish color. Freeze and mold it in a mold a little bit larger than a 1-liter (4-cup) capacity.

Mixed or Two-Flavor Ice Cream *(Glace Panaché ou Deux Parfums).* The most current combination includes an ice cream, generally vanilla, and an ice of fruits in syrup—strawberries, raspberries, orange, etc.

In a house that has only one metal sorbetière, you must prepare it in advance, because the two mixtures for the frozen dessert must be separately frozen there.

Begin by freezing the mixture that is the most resistant to freezing and molding: the mixture with cream. Prepare and pre-ice the mold. Cut a piece of heavy paper or cardboard to the inside shape of the mold, of exactly the correct dimensions, so that it can stand firm and upright in the middle of the mold, thus dividing it in two from the top to the bottom.

Fill half of the mold with the frozen cream, tapping it down and compressing it as you go. Cover it.

Quickly clean out the sorbetière, scraping the interior with a spoon or a supple piece of cardboard. Drain the water from the pail. Prepare the pail with ice, as before. Pour the other mixture into the sorbetière, the one made with a syrup. Freeze it as before.

Fill the other half of the mold with the second mixture, always compacting it. Once the two halves are filled, remove the cardboard. If this is difficult, it is because it is sticking to the cream mixture. You need only to run the blade of a large knife dipped into warm water along this side, and the ice cream will come away from the cardboard. Tap it down again. Cover with parchment paper and the cover, proceeding as directed (SEE HOW TO MOLD A FROZEN DESSERT, PAGE 650).

Fresh Fruit Ices, Syrup Ices *(Glaces aux Fruits Frais, Glaces au Syrop)*

Depending on the type of fruit, these are made using either the pulp, which is strained to make a purée, or the juice—both of them always uncooked—with a sugar syrup added. The mixing is done cold.

Purées are made with apricots, pineapples, bananas, strawberries, raspberries, melons, peaches, pears, etc. and with all fruit that has a more or less firm pulp. For a mixture using a purée of fruit, include an equal quantity of syrup. Thus for 1/2 liter (generous 2 cups) of purée, 1/2 liter (generous 2 cups) of syrup, reaching 30° Baumé, added cold.

The fruit juices used include cherry, lemon, red currant, orange, etc. The proportion of syrup varies here with the fruit: depending on how much juice a fruit, such as red currant, provides to make up most of the preparation. For lemon or orange, it is the sugar syrup that makes up most of the ice mixture; the fruit's flavor comes only from the infusion of its peel and a minimal quantity of its juice.

The fruit purées are enhanced by lemon juice, added in a proportion relative to their nature and to their own acidity; you can also add, if you like, a little bit of kirsch, rum, curaçao, or orange flower water, depending on the type of fruit.

The use of a saccharometer (SEE PAGE 578) must be considered essential, to check the density of the composition—that is, the mixture of the purée or fruit juice with the sugar syrup: even professionals do not do without it. The degree of the composition varies, depending on the nature of the fruit, between 18° and 22° Baumé. This last measurement is a maximum. If the saccharometer indicates a higher degree, add some water to the composition, tablespoon by tablespoon. If, on the other hand, the density is below 18° Baumé, add a little bit of syrup or superfine sugar that has been thoroughly dissolved. Do this until you have obtained the necessary degree.

The syrup: To make syrup of the correct density—that is, 30° Baumé—assume 100 grams (3 1/2 ounces) of sugar per deciliter (3 1/3 fluid ounces, scant 1/2 cup) of water and a boiling time of 20 minutes. Any longer will cause the liquid to evaporate, and the consistency of the syrup will thus be affected. At the degree suggested, the syrup is very fluid. You can prepare it cold by dissolving the sugar in cold water a long time in advance. Sugar prepared like this preserves the integrity of the fruit's flavor better. But, generally speaking, people use cooked syrup, which is quicker to prepare.

As a general rule of thumb, 100 grams (3 1/2 ounces) of dissolved sugar produces 7 centiliters (generous 1/4 cup) of liquid. Remember this when calculating how much syrup is required; that is, to obtain 5 deciliters (generous 2 cups) of syrup, you must dissolve 300 grams (10 1/2 ounces) of sugar cubes in 3 deciliters (1 1/4 cups) of water.

Cooking the syrup: In a copper pan that is not lined with tin, or in an ordinary, very clean saucepan, put the sugar lumps and the water. With very low heat under the utensil, make sure that the sugar has thoroughly dissolved; stir it from time to time with a silver spoon.

Then turn the heat up so that the mixture comes to a boil. Let it boil for *2 minutes.* Remove the light foam that forms on top. If the preparation includes an infusion of zest, put this zest into the boiling syrup, then pour the syrup into a terrine. Cover it and allow it to cool. If necessary, you can hasten the cooling by putting the terrine in cold water.

PASTRIES

ESSENTIAL KNOWLEDGE

The oven: In pastry making, even more than for any other food preparation, baking is supremely important: if done badly, the harm is irreparable. The same dough cooked under different conditions can produce cakes that are either perfect or spoiled, even if their preparation has, in both cases, been irreproachable.

For cooking any pastry, whether in an oven fueled by coal, gas, or electricity, you must be mindful of the following points:

First, the oven must be heated *sufficiently in advance* that it will have reached the right temperature when the cakes are put into it; the temperature must be kept constant, without any spikes in the heat or lapses, throughout the cooking time.

The rule of heating the oven in advance applies strictly to all cakes, because a pastry will be damaged if put into an oven at a temperature that is not correct for the type of cake.

This rule is even more important when it is a matter of a yeast-risen dough—a baba, a brioche, etc.—because although a puff pastry dough or a pie crust or lining dough can stand for a while until the oven comes to the right temperature, a risen dough must be put into the oven as soon as it has arrived at its proper point of fermentation. And since the timing for this fermentation cannot be estimated exactly, because it depends on how quickly the yeast ferments as well as on the temperature and other conditions, the oven must be ready by the time you think you will need it; for these preparations, the oven must be waiting for the dough.

Second, in home ovens you must never try to attempt to cook *cakes that are too large.* Their heat is distributed too unevenly, and you cannot extend the cooking time for a large piece of pastry without the exterior of the cake burning before the interior is done: this will happen no matter how much care you take.

Third, *the middle shelf* that divides the oven into two parts *is generally removed;* the cakes are therefore placed on the lower part of the oven—in professional terms, on the hearth. Let us add, however, that, given the differences in the way that ovens are built, experience alone can determine if the cakes should be placed directly on the hearth or, on the contrary, slightly above it.

Fourth, *an even oven temperature* is of prime importance for cooking pastries. It is often difficult to achieve with home ovens, a fact that obliges you to take certain precautions. Often the heat at the top of the oven is too strong as well as that of the hearth or, in stoves fired by coal, of the foyer; in this case, you can place, between the cake and the source of too strong heat, a metal sheet or even a large earthenware plate or simply some bricks placed standing up.

There are gas and electric ovens specially constructed for pastry making, which give excellent results; independent from the stove, placed on a counter at the right height, they make it much easier to watch over the pastry. We would also like to note the increasingly common use of ovens with thermostats, which gives greater control over the baking.

Fifth, *the heat of the oven can be checked* using a sheet of white paper placed on the hearth underneath the cake.

If, after a few minutes, the paper remains exactly as you have put it there, the oven is *almost cold.*

If, after a few moments, the paper turns a light yellow, the oven is at *a good medium heat.*

If, as soon as you put it in the oven, the paper burns and crisps, the oven is *very hot.*

Sixth, a home oven requires *much more attention,* much more frequently than a pastry oven or a restaurant oven. You will therefore have to open the door frequently: this should not be done except by opening the door just a crack, and for only the time needed to glance inside without fresh air hitting the cake, interrupting its rising.

Moistened paper: If the heat at the top of the oven is too strong and causes the surface of the cake to color too rapidly, you can protect the batter using a piece of moistened paper. Paper that is only buttered is not appropriate for cooking pastry.

Use a sheet of *very clean* white paper, never something printed. Crumple it lightly and dip it in cool water, then shake it off before putting it on the cake. You should repeat this from time to time; whenever the cake looks as if it is browning too much, soak the same paper again and again.

To recognize when the cake is perfectly cooked: Use a cooking needle or a large knitting needle made of metal. Stick it into the very center of the cake; leave it there for only 1 or 2 *seconds*. Withdraw it quickly and then, to judge the heat, bring it close to your lip, without actually touching it, or you may burn yourself. Actually, this is the same procedure used by someone doing the ironing, and bringing a hot iron close to her cheek to check the temperature. A better method is to take out the needle and quickly touch it against the back of your left hand.

Depending on how much the needle burns, you can judge the heat accumulated inside the cake, and consequently its degree of cooking: for some pastries, it is not enough that the needle comes out dry, without any dough sticking to it, for the cooking to be complete.

The Cooking Equipment and Its Maintenance

The marble or the board: Both serve as the workbench—that is, the surface on which you work the dough. Marble is popular not only because of its natural coolness, which makes the work easier, but also because of its smooth finished surface: this has particular importance when rolling out and extending the dough, particularly for puff pastry. This marble is a simple sheet a little bit thicker than the marble of an ordinary sink: it should measure about 70 centimeters (28 inches) long and 50 centimeters (20 inches) wide.

In home kitchens, the marble is generally replaced by a wooden patisserie board of the same size, thick, perfectly smooth, and with a well-planed surface. When washing it, work very quickly and dry it carefully immediately afterward, because moisture can make the wood swell.

The rolling pin: This tool is supremely important, so it should be chosen carefully and well cared for. Choose one made of wood, about 50 centimeters (20 inches) long with a diameter of about 4–5 centimeters (1½–2 inches): it should also be *straight*, without handles at its ends. As with the board, do not wash the rolling pin except superficially, and do not allow it to remain in water.

The scraper: This small steel accessory is a good replacement for an old knife, allowing you to scrape the table and even your fingers without risk of cutting yourself (*fig.* 69).

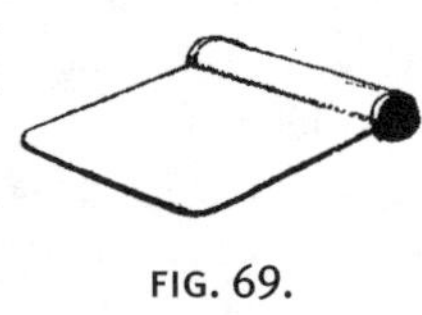

FIG. 69. THE SCRAPER.

The corne, or pastry scraper: An accessory that is extremely useful, for putting dough into terrines, and whisked egg whites into a bowl. It is an oval sheet made of horn—hence its French name—that measures about 12–14 centimeters (4½–5½ inches) long and 8–9 centimeters (3¼–3½ inches) wide.

Its flexibility as well as its shape are the reasons for its usefulness.

Before using it, soak it in warm water for 5 minutes to soften it. If you do not have one—and they cannot be found everywhere—you can use a flexible rubber disk or a rectangle of celluloid in about the same shape as the corne, to fulfill the same function.

Baking sheets: These are made of thick black steel in a rectangular or round shape. Round sheets are known as *tourtières* by professionals: these generally have a tiny border. Clean them by wiping them down carefully, rubbing them as soon as possible after use, either with paper or with cloth. If you do not use them every day, oil them to avoid even the smallest spot of rust.

The mold: The appropriate mold to use will be explained in the recipes for which they are used, and the drawings of the principal ones can be found on PAGE 576. Make sure you keep them meticulously clean and in a place that is perfectly dry.

Various Elements of Doughs and Batters

The flour: The quality is particularly important: always use the finest white flour. Make sure that it is good and dry. Always pass it through a horsehair drum sieve just before using it. This sifts out the little lumps and gives the flour the necessary lightness and uniformity.

The eggs: Do not fail to check for freshness, smelling them as you break them and before putting them into the batter: one bad egg is enough to spoil everything. It is even easier to break them one by one into a saucer: carefully smell them, then slide the egg into the "well" or into a terrine, and do this for all the eggs. Professionals always work in this manner.

The butter: Though it should have a relatively firm consistency, the butter must also be malleable so that it can be incorporated into the flour, for pastry or pie crust dough, or into puff pastry. To reach this perfect stage, firm the butter up well: in the summer, keep it on ice, or at least put it a long time ahead in a very cool place and in quite cold water.

Having thus hardened up the butter, put it into the corner of a towel, *moistened* so that the butter does not stick to the fabric. Then fold the two sides of the towel over, pressing down strongly. Do this two or three times to give a certain suppleness to the butter. At the same time, any traces of whey will be absorbed by the towel.

In any case, when you are making puff pastry *(pâte feuilletée)*, or pie or lining dough *(pâte à foncer)*, the butter must not be made malleable by any method other than this *hand* work, which should be done on very firm butter.

The yeast: For *leavened* doughs—such as brioche, baba, etc., which increase in volume by fermentation before they are put into the oven—*the following recipes always assume that the yeast used comes in dry cakes.*

The action of this yeast in cakes is much more rapid and consistent than liquid beer yeast, which is used in Alsace and certain regions of the north. Its use is now quite widespread, and you can find it at all the bakeries.

Its freshness is essential: if not, the dough will not rise effectively. You can recognize fresh yeast by its gray color, which makes it look like a piece of putty. As it grows old or is exposed to the air, it turns brown. You should therefore remove any brown pieces. For this reason, get a little bit more from the baker than you need, because a few bits will probably be wasted.

Baking powders: From England or elsewhere, these leavening agents can never replace yeast cakes or beer yeasts for raised doughs, because the action of these powders is produced only during cooking, and under the effect of strong heat. Use them only for doughs of the plum cake variety.

Principles and Standard Terms of Pastry Making

Before beginning a pastry dough, all the ingredients must be weighed, measured, and assembled in position on the table, as well as the accessory tools. Have the salt in a saucer, as well as the superfine sugar, etc.

Mixture of the flour and the water *(la détrempe)*: The French term is a professional term for the blend of the flour and the liquid plus all the other ingredients that are incorporated into the flour right at the beginning.

The well: This is a basin made in the mound of flour, allowing you to introduce the water, the eggs, and so on, without letting them run onto the board. When working the dough on a plank, a marble slab, or in a terrine, making a well in the flour is essential and the first step to every operation.

To make the well, proceed as follows: sift the flour onto the pastry board. Using the ends of the fingers of your right hand as a spatula, make a hole in the middle of the mound of flour, moving the flour aside with a circular movement to form an even and regular border. In the middle of the circle, the wood of the board or the marble will be exposed, forming the "well."

Rolled-out pastry: This is a sheet of pastry that has been rolled out by the rolling pin.

To roll out: To spread out the pastry with a rolling pin to bring it to the required thickness.

To knead *(fraiser)*: That is, to squash the dough under the palm of your hand, pushing it out in front of you, little by little (SEE PASTRY DOUGH OR LINING DOUGH, PAGE 662). The aim of this is to combine the various elements of the dough, making it smooth.

To butter and flour molds: You can directly heat and melt the butter in the mold and then tip it to spread the butter everywhere; you can dry off the excess when it is almost cool, but it is better to work with a brush dipped in melted butter, not too warm, so that you spread it equally all over: the dough will stick to any place without butter, and where there is too much butter, it will have a pockmarked appearance.

Once the butter has cooled, sprinkle it with flour, then turn the mold over and gently shake it to shake off the excess. If too much flour is left, a thick skin will form, which will come away after cooking, and give the cake an unpleasant appearance.

WORKING THE DOUGH

Puff Pastry *(La Pâte Feuilletée)*

Working the dough is done in four stages, each equally important, the success of the puff pastry depending on the competent completion of all four operations:

First, the mixing, or *détrempe,* which is the combining of flour and water to make the dough in which the butter is then enclosed. This must be done rapidly, or the dough will warm up, particularly if the person making the dough does not have very cool hands. Mixing 225 grams (8 ounces) of flour must take no longer than 5 minutes. Any longer will produce an elastic dough, which is disastrous, because this will enclose the butter badly and shrink while cooking.

Second, the buttering—that is, the incorporation of butter into the dough mixture. The strict rule here is that in all seasons, no matter what the temperature, the butter and the mixed dough must have the same consistency, so that they can be easily combined and unified. If the butter is firmer than the dough, it will escape by making holes in the dough under the pressure of the rolling pin. On the other hand, if it is softer, it will slide around and will also escape by running out.

Third, the turning, which equally distributes the butter in the dough by spreading it out with the rolling pin. Spreading the butter out evenly is the reason that the dough raises in multiple sheets when baked, but to achieve this, the turning must be accomplished with geometrical precision and meticulous care.

Fourth, the cooking of the puff pastry, which must be done in a very warm oven that heats primarily from the bottom. The cooking time varies, of course, with the size of the puff pastry and is given for the individual recipes.

NOTE. When you work puff pastry dough, note the following points:

First, use *flour of excellent quality*—that is, first-rate white wheat. Ordinary flour does not swell enough.

Second, as regards the fat used, we would like to declare here the opposite of what many people believe, who have never tried it: namely, that a very good margarine can easily *replace butter* when preparing a puff pastry. On the advice of an emeritus professional, Chef Reboul, we have personally had experience of it, with a very satisfying result. The substitution passes unnoticed. The quantity and handling remain the same.

Third, *keep the dough cool,* particularly in the summer. While the dough is resting, keep it in a very cool, even cold, place. If you have ice, never put it into direct contact with the dough, because only the butter will become stiff, which will prevent it from mixing with the dough, the consistency of the dough remaining the same when it is cool. Do not forget to cover the dough with a towel while it is resting, because the air will dry it out; it will then split when you work it again, allowing an opening for the butter to escape.

Fourth, as soon as the dough has been turned six times, it is best *not to wait too long* to trim and cut the puff pastry. If the dough is prepared in advance, leave the two last turns until about 10 minutes before using it.

Fifth, once the pastry dough has been cut, glazed, etc., it must be *put into the oven without delay.*

Note that however you use puff pastry, it must always be *very cleanly cut.* Any irregularity or frayed edges will create an obstacle to its rising evenly.

Preparation of the Puff Pastry. The normal proportion of this dough is an equal weight of flour and water. So, for 500 grams (1 pound, 2 ounces) of flour, 500 grams (1 pound, 2 ounces) of butter, 2½–3 deciliters (1–1¼ cups) of water, and 10 grams (⅓ ounce) of salt.

The mixture: Sift the flour onto the marble or the board. Make a well. Put in the salt and water. First stir the salt with your fingers to make it dissolve before putting in the flour.

The left hand does not touch the flour. To make this mixture, use only the *end of the fingers* of the right hand, gradually bringing the flour into the well to mix it with the water. Even though you are doing this gradually, to avoid lumps, you must also do it rapidly for the reasons already given. The dough must be soft enough to stick easily to the hands and the board; a moist mixture produces a puff pastry that is lighter and much easier to work than a firm mixture. Do not forget that its consistency must be rigorously similar to the butter that will soon be enveloped in it.

It is impossible to be exact about the amount of water required because of the differences between flours, which absorb more or less liquid, and because you may need to add some water while mixing; this should, of course, be a minimal quantity. If you have to add some, it will only be because all the measured water in the well has been absorbed and there is some dry flour left, while the dough that is already mixed has the right consistency. At this point, if the dough that has already been mixed is perfect, you know that adding the remaining flour will make it firmer: this is why, anticipating this firmer consistency, and to counter it, you must immediately add some water, very carefully, and drop by drop as it were, letting it drip *from the fingertips* with which you are working the dough, so that it does not spill out.

Once the mixture has been finished, very lightly knead the dough, still using the right hand only. The dough should look like an unformed mass, as if it were made out of plaster, and working it should give it some cohesion and make it smoother. *One or two minutes at the most* should be enough to achieve this, bearing in mind that the dough should not become too elastic.

Scrape your fingers off above the pile of dough. Very lightly sprinkle flour on the table in the same place where the mound of flour stood: this part must be shielded while you are working the mixture. Scrape the board, pushing the dough onto the part of the board that is floured, then assemble it in a half ball. Give it a few cuts with a knife or with the dough scraper to slash it: the air penetrating these openings will cause the dough to lose its elasticity. Let it rest in a cool spot for *20–25 minutes.*

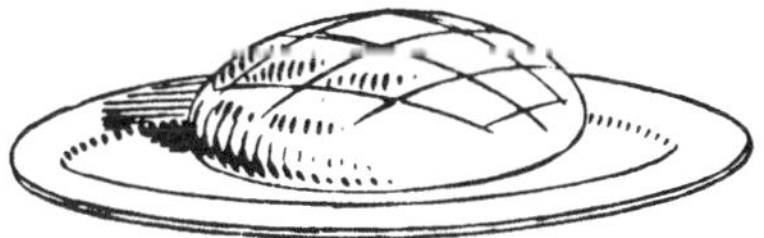

FIG. 70. SLASHING THE DOUGH.

To be good for use, the dough, once rested, must easily retain the imprint of a finger stuck into it quite forcefully. If this mark immediately fills out, the dough bouncing back like rubber, you know the mixture is bad. In this case, it is better to sacrifice the flour you have used and to begin again with new flour, working more rapidly this time.

Buttering and mixing: To have the butter at the right consistency, proceed as directed (SEE PAGE 657), first firming it up thoroughly and then softening it when you incorporate it into the dough.

Once the dough has rested and lost all of its elasticity, thoroughly scrape the board: it must be absolutely clean. Sprinkle it with a light dusting of flour. Place the ball of dough in front of you. With the palm of your hand, flatten it out into a round form or in a square to a very even thickness of 2–3 centimeters (¾–1¼ inches).

After working the butter well, flatten it out into a smaller cake, but one that is about as thick as the dough, and the same shape: round if the dough is round, square if the dough is square.

Place the cake of butter on the dough. Just like an envelope for a letter, fold the four sides of the dough over the top of the butter so that the edges meet perfectly, and so that they completely hide the butter and join, sticking to each other without covering each other, because then the dough would be too thick there. Whether the shape is round or square, fold the dough in the same way, like a closed envelope. When square, this is quite straightforward. If round, very gently pull on the edges of the dough to thin it, so that when you pull it over the butter its thickness is reduced by half, which means that the two edges of dough will be as thick as the rest of the dough when applied on top of the other. Each time you fold the dough, strike it lightly with the rolling pin to even it out.

These details and observations are to make you understand just how important it is that the whole layer of dough enveloping the butter be as evenly thick as possible: if you do not do this perfectly, the butter will not spread out the same way, and the layering of the dough will be defective.

Allow it to rest for *10 minutes* before beginning the "turning".

Turning: First, let us define what we mean by "turn": *to turn the dough is first to spread it out like a ribbon with the rolling pin and then to fold it.* The number of times the dough is rolled out and then folded is the number of turns that are made.

A. Make a well of flour. add the salt and the water.

B. Lightly knead the dough mixture with the ends of your fingers of your right hand until it is the consistency of a soft butter.

C. Allow the mixture to rest, then flatten it with the palm of your hand.

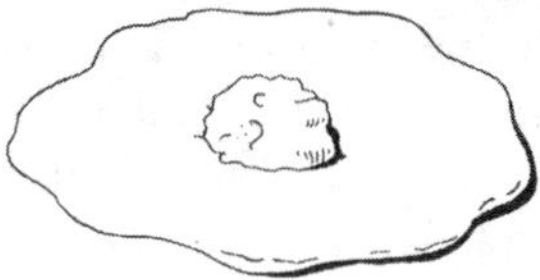

D. Place the worked butter in the center of the dough and flatten it into a cake.

E. Like an envelope, fold over the four sides of the dough on top of the butter.

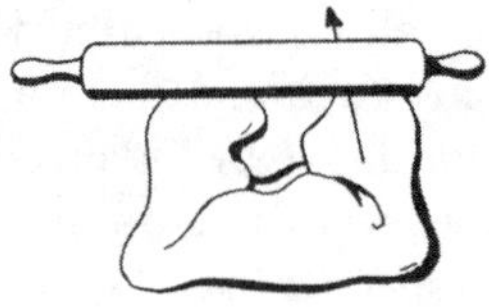

F. Lightly flatten with your rolling pin, pushing it forward in front of you.

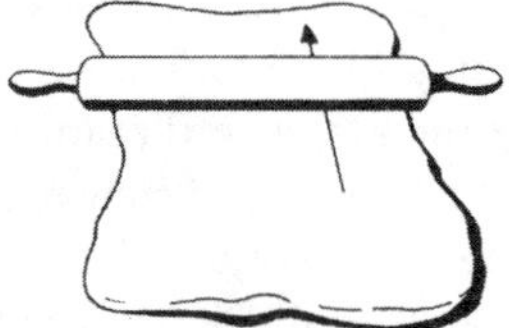

G. Roll out to obtain a ribbon of $1^1/_2$ centimeters ($^5/_8$ inch) thick.

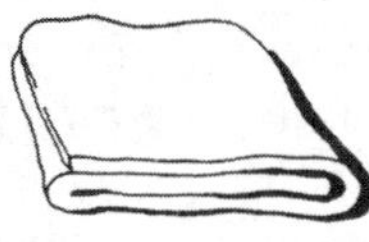

H. Fold the ribbon into three.

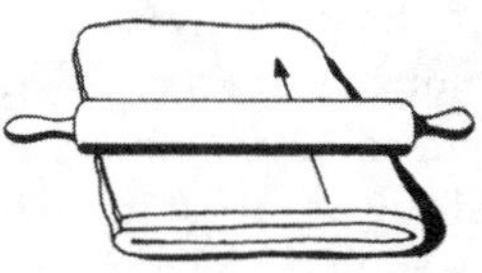

I. Place the rolling pin perpendicular to the fold and roll out the dough again. these last three operations are known as "turning."

FIG. 71. WORKING PUFF PASTRY.

A. Make a well of flour. add the salt, the very cold water, the butter, and the egg.

B. Gradually drag the flour into the well to mix it with the ingredients there. if the dough is too wet, add a little bit of flour.

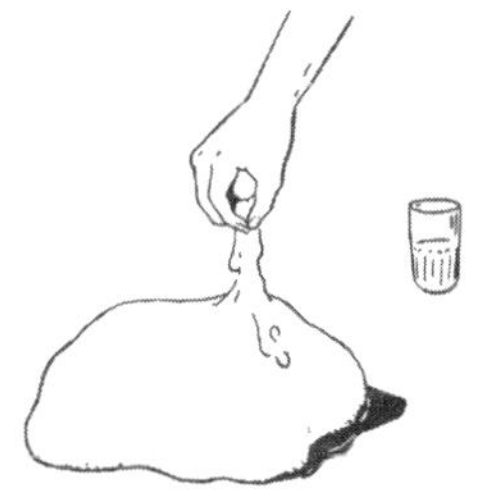
C. When all the flour has been incorporated, the dough must be soft enough that it comes away from your fingers and stands in one mass.

D. With the palm of your hand, push out the dough bit by bit; this is called kneading.

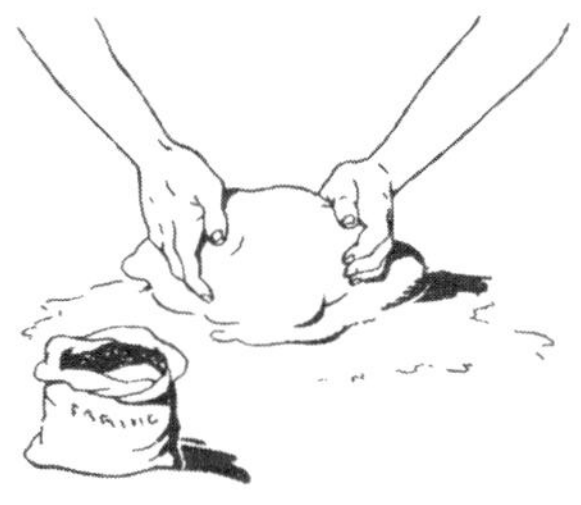
E. Roll the dough into a ball.

F. Wrap it in a towel and let it rest for at least 2 hours before shaping it.

FIG. 72. WORKING PASTRY CRUST DOUGH.

Very lightly sprinkle the board and the dough with flour. Then use the rolling pin to tap out your square of dough: this is simply to extend it a little farther in both directions; but make sure you do not mark any grooves in it. Your dough is now ready to be turned.

Place the square of dough in front of you, putting the rolling pin right in the middle of the square, and then pushing it away from you very evenly, to extend the dough into a ribbon of *very even* thickness, about 1$^{1}/_{2}$ centimeters ($^{5}/_{8}$ inch). Handle the rolling pin with both hands placed *flat* on top, leaning lightly on it.

It is very important that the dough be evenly thick throughout. (This is why the rolling pin must be handled very evenly and also carefully, to avoid forcing out the butter, which is more likely to escape during the first turn. If this happens, lightly dust both the rolling pin and the dough with flour.)

Once the dough has been thus rolled out halfway, move it to bring closest to you the end of the part that has already been rolled out. Then place the rolling pin at its point of departure and roll out the second part of the dough in the same way you have just done for the first. This procedure is better than trying to roll out the dough by rolling the pin toward you, without moving the dough; always moving forward makes handling the rolling pin easier. At any rate, and no matter the direction in which you roll, you must never roll backward, even with a small motion, over dough where the rolling pin has already passed. But if the dough is too thick after the first roll, there is no disadvantage in passing the rolling pin over it again to thin it out, in the same direction—that is, always pushing it away from yourself.

Once rolled out, dough made with the quantities suggested should make a completely straight ribbon

60 centimeters (24 inches) long and 20 centimeters (8 inches) wide by 1 1/2–2 centimeters (5/8–3/4 inch) thick. The size of this band varies, of course, with the quantity of dough, given that the thickness of the dough must always be the same, finally about 2 centimeters (3/4 inch).

If working with smaller quantities than those suggested here—say, half—you must assume that the length of the ribbon will be about half or less: approximately 35 centimeters (14 inches) long with a width of 12 centimeters (4 1/2 inches). The width is one-third of the length: this means that the dough, once folded in thirds, will always form a square. This geometrical precision is of great importance not just for spreading the butter inside the dough, but also for formation of the expanding layers that are the result from it.

Once the dough has been rolled out, and flattened according to the rules, fold the ribbon in three. Sprinkle it very lightly with flour and press on it with the rolling pin, just as you would lightly touch the iron to your handkerchief, to solder these three parts together. *The first turn is now done.*

Immediately do the second. Move the square of dough so that it looks to you like a book with its spine on the right. Then roll out the dough with the rolling pin, in exactly the same way as the first time, and fold it in three.

Now the second turn is done. To avoid any confusion about the number of turns, mark these two turns by by gently hitting the dough in two places with the rolling pin. Cover with a towel. Allow it to rest *in a cool place* for 10 minutes.

(Note that at each new turn of the dough, it is rolled out and then folded in the direction perpendicular to the previous turn. The width of the ribbon becomes its length; this length is then is rolled out into the width, and so on.)

After 10 minutes of rest, make two more turns in the same way. Make four small marks with the end of the rolling pin. Let it rest a second time for 10 minutes. Finally, make two last turns. Thus you have made the six required turns. Make a little X-shaped cross on the dough to indicate that the turns are complete. Let it rest one last time for 10 minutes. The dough is now ready to be used.

Half (or Rough) Puff Pastry *(Demi-Feuilletage).* This is a dough that contains a lesser proportion of butter—that is, *half*—compared to the flour, and for which only *four turns* are made.

Rough or half puff pastry is made in exactly the same way as full puff pastry, and not by mixing butter and flour in the same way as for a pancake, as many people wrongly believe. Unless you have great skill and make the necessary turns, dough prepared in such a manner will be rather heavy for the various uses to which half puff pastry is put.

Pastry Dough or Lining Dough *(La Pâte à Foncer)*

These days, this name is used by professionals for what was previously named *pâte brisée,* or "short pastry."

Depending on how this dough is used, the ingredients vary as well as their quantities. So, mixed into the flour, there might be only water, salt, and butter, the last in smaller or greater quantities, and for which lard is frequently substituted when making crusts for pâtés; or eggs, either whole or as yolks, can be added to these ingredients as a base; or superfine sugar; or a flavored liquid like orange flower water.

These different ingredients and their quantities are given in the recipes for each dough. Here, for reference, we will explain how to work the dough, which is always done in the same way.

We will use for our demonstration simple pastry dough, which is made with only flour, salt, water, and butter: these are in the proportion of half the weight of flour, that is, 250 grams (8 7/8 ounces) of butter per 450 grams (1 pound) of flour. Use 10 grams (1/3 ounce) of salt and about 2 deciliters (6 3/4 fluid ounces, 7/8 cup) of water per 450 grams (1 pound) of flour.

The butter: In warm weather, put the butter in a cool place long enough in advance to firm it up. Otherwise, the butter, softened by the heat, will absorb almost all the flour; and if you add the normal quantity of water, the dough will be excessively soft. However, if you are using less water than the normal quantity, the dough disintegrates—or is "burned," according to the professional term—and is more difficult to work than if it is too soft. This double inconvenience can be avoided by having the butter at the right consistency, previously firmed up and then worked as directed (SEE PAGE 657). It is also a good idea to let the dough rest in a cool place for a longer time before using it.

Preparation of Pastry Dough. Mixing it: Sift the flour onto the table or the pastry board. Make the well. Add the salt; the water, *very cold*; the butter, well softened, particularly in winter; when using a large quantity of butter, divide it into large pieces. *If the dough includes egg,* add it to the well at the same time.

With the end of the fingers of your right hand, first dissolve the salt into the liquid; this is very important so that you do not find it later spread unevenly around in the dough.

When the dough includes sugar, the same precaution must be observed, dissolving the sugar in the liquid at the same time.

After this, and always using your fingers, work the butter with the liquid without yet touching the flour; do not do so for long, to avoid melting it with the heat of your hand.

Then begin to add the flour little by little into the well to combine it with the ingredients there, always using the end of your fingers, and taking it equally from every side so that you maintain a wall that prevents the liquid from running out.

With the dough scraper, clean the butter from your fingers that is stuck on them and put it back into the dough. Continue to incorporate the flour, squeezing it more forcefully with your fingers. It is at this point, before all the flour is added, that you must judge the consistency of the dough; because if you need to add a little more water than the normal amount, it must never be added once all the flour has been incorporated, since the water will not mix with the dough. On the other hand, if the dough is too soft, you can always add a little bit of flour.

The quantity of the water in the dough in the mixture cannot be absolutely fixed to within 1 tablespoon: it depends not only on the consistency of the butter, as we have explained above, but also on the flour used: some flours, notably the finest and the best flours, absorb, or "drink," more than others. So always add the water while mixing the flour, and always pour it into the moistest part of the dough: you are therefore working it in with your fingers, and, so to speak, a drop at a time.

Once the mixing is finished, and when all the flour is incorporated, the dough will be rather soft and should come away easily from your fingers. Scrape it to get it off. Also scrape it off the board. Gather the dough in a heap in front of you to work it.

Working the dough: The point of this is to thoroughly unify all the elements of the dough to make it fine and smooth. *Fraiser,* or "to work," is the term used by professionals, equivalent to *briser,* or "to break," which was used by the classic authors, a term that makes sense once you understand the process.

Gather the heap of dough in front of you at the edge of the board. With the palm of your right hand—that is, the part between the thumb and the wrist—pull out the dough in little parts the size of a chestnut and slide them in front of you, crushing them vigorously on the wood, and pushing them toward the other end of the board, where gradually you will form another heap of dough. During this process, the rather soft dough will stick a little bit to the wood.

When all the dough has been squashed on the board bit by bit, it has been worked *once.* Gather the dough that has been worked in front of you at the edge of the board and begin exactly the same process again. Working the dough *twice* is generally considered appropriate.

Sprinkle the board with a light dusting of flour, and then with both hands roll the dough into a ball. Wrap it in a towel and put it in a cool place to let it rest for at least *2 hours.*

Resting the dough: This has the goal of making the dough lose the elasticity that has been created by this lengthy working, which is often done with warm hands.

Unlike doughs that include a leavening agent, pastry dough must not have any elasticity. When you use it, it must preserve the impression left by sticking your finger into it, without contracting even slightly. If the dough has "body"—that is, elasticity—it will retract once it has been rolled out, and you will have no control over it and it will not keep the dimensions that you need. When it cooks, it will also behave badly, and give you a tough result.

Rest is the only way it will lose the elasticity that makes it inappropriate for any use. The longer the rest, the easier and more satisfactory will be its use. Assume 2 hours as a minimum. This delay can be shortened, if absolutely necessary, by professionals who are very skillful, able to handle it adroitly and rapidly; that said, whenever professionals have the time, they prepare their dough well in advance, and even suggest making it the evening before, if possible. Not only is a rested dough easier to shape, but it takes on a much more beautiful color when it is cooked.

Rapid procedure for home cooking: The quantities of flour, butter, and salt are the same as above, but you proceed as follows: make a well in the sifted flour on the board or on the marble, and in the center put the butter, firmed and then softened to its proper consistency as directed (SEE PAGE 657), the salt, the sugar, and the egg yolk, if using them, *but no water.* With the end of the fingers on your right hand, work the butter and the salt, the sugar and the egg, if the dough has any, to mix them well; then, still using the ends of your fingers, mix in the flour gradually, taking it from the circumference of the well, and combine it with the butter until the flour is used up and everything is reduced to large lumps gathered in the center of the board, and not scattered around all over the surface; this part of the job can be done slowly. At this moment, with your left hand, take a receptacle containing about 1 deciliter (3 1/3 fluid ounces, scant 1/2 cup) of quite cold water for 250 grams (8 7/8 ounces) of flour, and pour the water in a thin line down the fingers of your right hand, which you will use *rapidly and lightly* to blend and combine the pieces of flour and butter; make sure you do not squeeze strongly with your whole hand. As soon as you have made a smooth, supple ball of dough that does not stick to the board and is not too soft (the ball must not lose its shape), do not add any more water and do not work the dough any longer. If you have worked with the necessary skill, the dough will not have any elasticity, and it will keep the impression of a finger stuck into it. Five minutes will be enough to make a dough with 225 grams (8 ounces) of flour. *Do not work it with your palm, and let it rest for 20 minutes,* or 1 hour if the dough includes egg.

Let us add that if the dough does not contain egg, it is particularly fragile and crusty, but on the other hand, it will soften more easily on contact with any liquid. Fruit tarts made with a dough that does not include egg are excellent eaten as soon as they have been completely chilled or when they are lukewarm, but they soften too much if they have to stand for a long time, because the fruit juice penetrates the crust.

A good trick, which will be a benefit to people who have warm and sweaty hands and who therefore do not make dough successfully, is to make this pastry dough with the flat of the blade of a large knife with a rounded point, without touching the dough with the fingers.

Choux Pastry or Cream Puff Pastry *(La Pâte à Choux)*

This dough is used for many varieties of choux: éclairs, profiteroles, ramequins, gougères, gnocchi, soufflé fritters, etc. Its preparation is rapid and one of the most simple.

The principal ingredients are always the same: water or milk, butter, flour, whole eggs. Only their proportions vary, depending on their use; thus the amount of butter is increased when water replaces milk. We give the appropriate quantities for each recipe involving the use of choux pastry. The quantities given directly below can be used as the typical pastry recipe for choux, à la crème or other, éclairs, etc. *Time: 30 minutes.*

2 1/2 deciliters (1 cup) of cold water; 100 grams (3 1/2 ounces, 7 tablespoons) of butter; 125 grams (4 1/2 ounces) of sifted flour; 3 grams (1/10 ounce) of fine salt; 8 grams (1/3 ounce) of superfine sugar; 4 medium-size eggs.

PROCEDURE. Now matter how fine and clean the flour is, first sift it over a sheet of paper. This is an essential precaution to take for all pastry, particularly here, to give the flour the lightness needed for perfect mixing. If you do not do this, you will have little lumps in your dough.

Use a deep saucepan, just large enough to be able to work the dough in it: so, about a 2-liter (8-cup) capacity for our quantities. Add the cold water; the butter, divided into small pieces so that it will melt more rapidly, which is important here;

the salt; and the sugar, which is included in the dough as much for flavor as for the color it produces while cooking.

Put the saucepan on rather strong heat, but not too strong, so that the butter has time to melt before the milk begins to boil; otherwise, the flour will not be thoroughly mixed in. *Do not cover the saucepan.*

Have everything ready at hand: the flour and a large wooden spoon. Carefully watch the saucepan. As soon as the liquid boils and bubbles up like milk, turn off the heat and immediately add the flour *all at once.* Quickly grab a wooden spoon and mix everything vigorously, working the dough until it is nice and smooth; this takes a moment.

Then turn the heat on under the saucepan to *dry out* the dough—that is, to evaporate as much moisture from it as possible; during this time, do not stop working and moving the dough with the wooden spoon. When you have experience, you can do this on strong heat. Inexperienced people should use more moderate heat.

To dry out the dough, spread it out thoroughly on the bottom of the saucepan with a wooden spoon, then turn it *immediately* and spread it out again. You can more effectively evaporate the humidity this way, successively exposing sides of the dough to the heated bottom of the saucepan. You can tell that the dough is sufficiently dried out when it comes away easily from the saucepan without any bit sticking to the sides or the spoon. The fat must lightly sweat from it; and the bottom of the saucepan, without coloring in any way, must be a little bit sandy, feeling gritty underneath your spoon.

The purpose of drying out the dough is to give it a consistency that will allow it to absorb a larger quantity of eggs. It is the eggs that give the dough more lightness, while an excess of the liquid that has served in its preparation will leave it heavy and limp after cooking. It would therefore be better to dry it out thoroughly, and as long as the bottom of the saucepan does not color, there will be no disadvantage in prolonging the duration of this work.

Then turn off the heat: you are done with it. Put the saucepan on the table. Add the eggs to the dough as follows: break a whole egg into a saucer or into a bowl to check its freshness, and then put it into the dough. Vigorously work it with the spoon to mix it well before adding another one. Incorporate them all like this, working vigorously between each new addition of egg.

For smaller quantities of dough, as those of the quantities above, it is better to beat the eggs lightly in a bowl first and then to add them to the dough half an egg at a time: this makes mixing easier, and also enables you to add the right amount of egg. When, on the other hand, you are working with larger quantities, the eggs can be added two at a time. Either way, do not add more egg until the previous addition has been perfectly mixed, beating it and raising the dough to make it lighter in cooking.

The dough is ready when it reaches a consistency that allows it to keep its form when you let it drop a tablespoon at a time, and that will, at the same, time be fluid enough to flow like a ribbon when you lift up its entire mass (SEE THE RIBBON, PAGE 577).

Note that there is no way to remedy a dough that is too soft, while it is always easy to add egg to remedy a dough that is too firm. Thus, do not add the final amount of egg until you are completely sure that it is necessary. This explains why it is so important to calculate the weight of eggs in the quantities.

The last stage in the process is to add the chosen flavor, either 1/2 tablespoon of orange flower water or lemon peel that has been minced as finely as possible (both the flavor and the sugar are, of course, left out of dough that is used for preparations such as gnocchi, ramequins, gougères, potato croquettes à la dauphine, cheese soufflé fritters, or ham fritters, etc.).

The dough rises and swells better when it is used as soon as you have finished making it; so it is normal practice to prepare it only at the moment when it is needed. If necessary, it can stand for 20–30 minutes in a warm place, with the saucepan covered to avoid browning.

Brioche Dough, Savarin Dough, Cookie Dough, etc. *(La Pâte à Brioche, la Pâte à Savarin, la Pâte à Biscuit, etc.)*

For details of how to prepare these, refer to the recipes in which the doughs are used (SEE DIVERSE PASTRIES, PAGE 675).

Frying Batter *(La Pâte à Frire)*

A frying batter must, above all else, fulfill the following conditions:

It must stick well to objects that are dipped in it; produce a smooth crust, without lumps, to avoid a bumpy appearance; and be at the same time crisp on the outside and tender on the inside.

The recipes are numerous; they vary according to the nature of the food to be fried and also depending on the era, the geographical location, the means available, and the ideas of each person. For their choice and for the quantity of ingredients, you can refer to all our recipes that use frying batter: various meat, vegetables, fish, etc., fritters. These provide not only the directions most appropriate to the case, but also the quantities of dough needed for the amount of food to be fried. We limit ourselves below to the proportions for the most up-to-date recipes.

Preparation of Frying Batter. The preparation is almost always the point at which a frying batter fails, much more so than the choice of the recipe. Everything is important in the preparation, beginning with an understanding of the action of the various ingredients that can make up a batter.

Ingredients that can be included in a frying batter: *Beer.* Intended to give lightness to the batter, by acting as a sort of leavening. For this action to be produced, the batter must be left for long enough to allow the beer to begin to ferment. Beer has no effect in a batter prepared just before using it.

Wine. This figures sometimes in certain recipes. It acts on both the flavor and the fermentation of the dough, and again this requires time to rest. This kind of batter is mostly used for fruit fritters; and it is a refinement to choose the wine to suit the fruit, following the excellent practice of the old Creoles of Louisiana, a method certainly imported from the ancient French provinces.

Oil. This makes the batter crisp. More and more, it is used as a substitute for butter because it does not have a strong taste; be careful, for example, not to use walnut oil. Olive oil is the best to use.

Butter. This is mostly used in regions that use clarified butter, which is free of all the whey and other materials that burn in the batter, unless you are using a butter of fine quality. When its use is indicated, it is a good idea to take the precautions we suggest, in order to purify it.

Egg yolk. This adds to both the substance and the density of the batter, which begins to approach a cake batter. It therefore introduces a certain heaviness.

Egg white. This is included in all recipes for frying batter because it adds lightness. It is rarely used without being whisked, and the procedure is by no means modern, because the oldest recipes call for the whites to be beaten into a snow.

Cognac, rum, kirsch, or other liqueurs are used primarily for their flavor; but this note of alcohol has a good effect on the batter.

Sugar. This must be superfine sugar, and not confectioners' sugar.

NOTES. When there is time, it is always better to prepare a frying batter *at least 2 hours in advance:* first, because once it has rested, it sticks better to the foods dipped in it; and also because it just begins to ferment, making the dough lighter.

The *preliminary sifting of the flour,* which is obligatory for all doughs, is even more essential for frying batter: it gets rid of the little clumps of flour that so often make the batter lumpy. Do this sifting through any kind of drum sieve or strainer over a sheet of paper.

For preparing the batter, choose *a utensil*—a clay pot or salad bowl—*of the right capacity,* so that the batter is still quite deep when the last pieces are dipped in it.

Use very slightly lukewarm water, because the heat helps the batter to ferment. We say very slightly because if it is any warmer, it will dilute the flour badly. For this reason, mix the batter in the beginning with cold water and finish with warm water when there is no more risk of forming lumps. When wine or beer are used, do this in the same way: add warm water at the end.

If the *butter* is not *already clarified,* it must be sufficiently heated to rid it of its whey and casein. Put it in a cup and put the cup in very warm water, and then leave it there until it becomes clear like oil. Do not pour it into the flour when it is warm, but only when it is lukewarm, being very careful not to allow the deposit at the bottom to fall into the batter.

To dilute the batter. The method for diluting the batter is extremely important, particularly when preparing it just before using, which means that the batter does not have time to rest and lose its elasticity. An elastic batter shrinks, slides over the food, and does not coat it, except imperfectly; the crust that it forms is tough.

Put the flour into a terrine or a salad bowl. With the ends of your fingers or a small wooden spoon, make a large well to expose the bottom of the terrine. Add the salt, the oil or the melted butter, and when the recipe includes it, egg yolk or whole egg, cognac or other liqueur, superfine sugar, etc. In short, add all the ingredients for the batter except the white beaten into a snow and all of the liquid.

Next, if you are not using either egg yolks or whole eggs, pour into the well where you have already put the salt, oil or butter, a little bit of water or beer, which replaces the liquid supplied by the egg. First mix the different ingredients in the well, gently turning the wooden spoon without touching the flour at all. If the batter includes egg yolk, it must first be well stirred *alone*—that is, before mixing it at all with any other ingredient.

Then begin to pull into the well *very little* flour at a time, turning the wooden spoon in any direction but always not too rapidly.

When, after a moment, the mixture becomes more consistent, drop *several drops* of liquid into the middle, stirring the spoon all the time to mix it in.

Continue to pour in the liquid, in a very thin stream and always into the middle of the batter, where you stir with the spoon. And at the same time continue to bring in the flour, little by little, taking it evenly from all around the receptacle. *From beginning to the end, stir the spoon in a circular movement.* You can stir in any direction and change the direction several times, *but you must never beat or raise the batter with the spoon:* a batter worked in this way will stick badly to any foods dipped in it.

The batter must be perfectly smooth, without any lumps, looking like a liquid cream or a nice starch, which is liquid enough to run off the spoon easily, while still perfectly covering the spoon. If the batter is too light, the crust will not be thick enough; if it is too thick, the crust will be heavy and pasty.

Carefully check the batter to see if more liquid is needed, given that the quantities suggested are an average and some flours absorb more than others: so, for example, 1–2 tablespoons of liquid for each 150 grams (5 1/3 ounces) of flour used.

When the batter is properly finished, cover it. Let it stand somewhere that has an average temperature of about 20° Centigrade (68° Fahrenheit) to encourage its fermentation.

Just before you are going to use the batter, and if it includes egg whites, beat them into a snow that is firm enough so that when you blow on them, they do not give. Mix them in by stirring in the same way that you mixed the batter, and so that you can no longer see even a small amount of white.

NOTE. While you are dipping all the objects to be fried into the batter, do not put the terrine on the stove; even a slightly warm stove would thicken the batter. So be sure to place the terrine on a mat, or similar object, to isolate it from the heat.

Everyday Frying Batter *(Pâte à Frire d'Emploi Courant).*

125 grams (4 1/2 ounces) of flour; 3 grams (1/10 ounce) of salt; 1 soupspoon of oil or melted butter; about 2 deciliters (6 3/4 fluid ounces, 7/8 cup) of lukewarm water; 1 egg white beaten into a firm snow.

Frying Batter for Fruit Fritters *(Pâte à Frire pour Beignets de Fruits).*

125 grams (4 1/2 ounces) of flour; 1 soupspoon of oil or melted butter; a pinch of salt and a pinch of sugar; 1 deciliter (3 1/3 fluid ounces, scant 1/2 cup) of beer; 1 soupspoon of cognac; 1 whole egg; about 1/2 deciliter (1 2/3 fluid ounces, scant 1/4 cup) of lukewarm water. Let the batter rest in a warm place for 3–4 hours before using.

Frying Batter for Vegetable Fritters and Diverse Meat Fritters *(Pâte à Frire pour Beignets de Légumes et Fritots Divers).*

125 grams (4 1/2 ounces) of flour; 3 grams (1/10 ounce) of salt; 1 soupspoon of oil; 1 egg yolk; 2 scant deciliters (6 3/4 fluid ounces, 7/8 cup) of boiled milk; 2 egg whites whisked into a snow.

Frying Batter for Fish *(Pâte à Frire pour Poissons).*

100 grams (3 1/2 ounces) of flour; 2 soupspoons of oil; 2 whole eggs; 2 deciliters (6 3/4 fluid ounces, 7/8 cup) of beer; a pinch of salt. Beat the whole eggs with salt and oil and 4 tablespoons of the beer; mix in the flour and finish diluting it with the rest of the beer. It should be a very runny batter. (If you do not have beer, use the same quantity of lukewarm water, but beer is preferable.)

SHELLS FOR VOL-AU-VENT, ETC.
Croûtes pour Vol-au-Vent, Etc.

Shell for Vol-au-Vent *(Croûte de Vol-au-Vent)*

There are different ways of proceeding: not for the dough, which is invariably a puff pastry, made with equal quantities of butter and flour and turned six times, but for cutting or trimming the dough. The vol-au-vent can be made from one large piece of dough or from two pieces or even three. Here we give the method that uses one piece only, which is the quickest, and the method that uses two pieces, which makes a lighter vol-au-vent.

For anyone with a little experience of working puff pastry, preparing a vol-au-vent offers no difficulty. But there is the matter of the oven; this is of such importance that it is better not to risk making this dish if the oven heats irregularly, having little or no heat coming from the bottom, and offering no way to moderate the heat toward the end of the baking. Baking a vol-au-vent begins in a very hot oven to make the dough rise, but must be finished with moderate heat; if not, the shell will burn on the outside while the inside will not be sufficiently cooked (SEE THE OVEN, PAGE 655). Moreover, you must follow to the letter the directions for baking the vol-au-vent, which we explain precisely below.

Let us remember that a good margarine can very well replace butter in the dough for a vol-au-vent, the quantities remaining the same.

The necessary accessories: These are a *tourtière,* or a baking sheet made of thick black steel, round, with a slight edge, on which the dough is placed. A small kitchen knife with a very sharp blade. A kitchen brush to brush on the egg. A tart circle about 18 centimeters (7 inches) in diameter, as a template to cut the dough; or if not, use a plate, a cover, or any round object of this size. Plus a smaller circle, a cookie cutter or similar, about 12 centimeters (4 1/2 inches) in diameter to mark the position of the cover (otherwise, use a round object of the same diameter).

Vol-au-Vent in One Piece *(Vol-au-Vent en Une Pièce).* *Time: 1 hour, 45 minutes. Makes 1 crust, or serves 6.*

250 grams (8 7/8 ounces) of excellent white flour; 250 grams (8 7/8 ounces) of butter; 5 grams (1/6 ounce) of salt; 1 1/2 deciliters (5 fluid ounces, 2/3 cup) of water. A little bit of egg yolk diluted with 1–2 tablespoons of water to glaze the vol-au-vent.

PROCEDURE. Prepare the dough as directed (SEE PUFF PASTRY, PAGE 658), observing the recommendation not to make the last two turns until just 10 minutes before cutting them into a vol-au-vent.

Roll out the dough with your rolling pin to a square of about 22 centimeters (8 1/2 inches) on each side and with a completely even thickness of 2 centimeters (3/4 inch). On top of this dough, place the circle you are using as a pattern. *Very cleanly* cut the dough that sticks out all around the circle, directing the point of a small knife *obliquely toward the outside.* This means the thickness of the dough is therefore cut a little bit on the bias.

With the brush dipped in water, moisten only the center of the baking sheet. Lightly roll the dough round onto the rolling pin to transfer it to the baking sheet, placing it so that the side that was up now faces *down;* this means that, given the oblique manner in which the dough has been cut, the most flared part, the largest, is on top. Press down on the middle to completely fix the dough to the sheet and to prevent it shrinking while cooking.

When you handle the dough this way, be very careful not to touch the edges of the dough; they must remain as sharp as the knife blade left them, otherwise it will rise badly in the cooking. Then indent the dough: in other words, with the *back* of the blade of the small knife, you lightly slash the circumference of the dough right through, *from bottom to top.* These cuts help the heat to penetrate, and when cooked transform into ridges.

With the brush dipped in the beaten egg, brush the surface of the dough, being very careful not to allow anything to spill over the edges; that is, over the outer edge of the dough. The egg will set there while cooking and would impede the dough from rising.

Lightly push a cookie cutter with a 12-centimeter (4½-inch) diameter onto the dough to mark the cover; with the point of the knife stuck 2–3 millimeters (about ⅛ inch) into the dough, accentuate the mark that you have made. Then trace a light grid on the cover, like the one you find on a galette. Put the dough in the oven.

To cook: A hot oven. Allow *about 30 minutes for cooking.* Place the *tourtière* or baking sheet at the bottom of the oven with the shelf removed. After 4–5 minutes, the layers begin to develop, and after 5 minutes the dough has almost risen to the height the vol-au-vent will reach, and will begin to color. This is the moment to cover it with a sheet of paper to avoid too deep a color; at the same time, if the oven heats strongly from the bottom, slide another sheet underneath the *tourtière* or baking sheet. Do this very carefully, because *any shock will make the pastry fall.* For the same reason, avoid opening the oven door too often, or, at least, open it only for a very short time.

The dough is perfectly done when it feels firm and resistant when you press your finger lightly on it; meanwhile, its color should be nice and golden. Only at this point should you take off the cover; if the baking is not complete, the vol-au-vent will fall slightly.

Then put the baking sheet on the open door of the oven to keep the vol-au-vent as hot as possible. Now, for all the following steps, you must work skillfully and quite rapidly; if not, the dough will weaken.

With the point of a small knife, follow the line that you have already traced, and take off the cover. (Be careful not to burn yourself on the puff of steam escaping from the interior.) Quickly remove the layer of badly cooked dough from the interior, which will have collapsed when you opened the crust. To do this, put the handle of the knife into this layer of dough; bring the knife toward you, picking up in one movement the weakened dough, grabbing it between your thumb and index finger to take it out. Remove it from the baking sheet.

Immediately put the emptied vol-au-vent back in the oven to dry out the interior. Place the cover next to it, with the interior facing up. A few moments will be enough to dry it out. *Watch it very closely, because this weakened crust will burn in the blink of an eye. Then slide the crust onto a rack; left on the sheet, it will take on a burned flavor. Keep it at a very gentle heat if does not have long to wait to be used. This is better than having to reheat it later on.*

Vol-au-Vent in Two Pieces *(Vol-au-Vent en Deux Pièces).* The quantities of the dough suggested for a vol-au-vent made in one piece will be enough here: but if you are not used to cutting the dough, it would be better to increase them slightly. The surplus will consist in trimmings of puff pastry, which are useful for a number of cakes, rissoles, etc. Thus: 375 grams (13¼ ounces) of flour and the same of butter; 7–8 grams (¼–⅓ ounce) of salt; 2¼ deciliters (scant 1 cup) of water.

PROCEDURE. Roll out the dough, not into a square, but into a rectangle from which you can cut two squares, one next to another: that is, about 45 centimeters (18 inches) long and 22 centimeters (8½ inches) wide and of a very even thickness, about 1½ centimeters (⅝ inch). With your knife, cut this rectangle into two squares. Roll one of these squares onto the rolling pin to transfer it to a moistened baking sheet. Place the tart circle on top of it. Cut the dough that sticks out *completely straight,* perpendicularly, and not at all on a bias, but very neatly. Remove the trimmings, which are not used here.

Cut the second square of dough on the board in exactly the same way. With a cookie cutter exactly 12 centimeters (4½ inches) in diameter, remove the center of this second round of dough to make a ring that is 3 centimeters (1¼ inches) wide and has an exterior diameter of 18 centimeters (7 inches), like the first round.

With the brush, moisten only the outside of the round of dough on the baking sheet, to make the ring that you are going to place there stick better. Fold the ring in half over itself, then in four. Take it with the ends of your fingers, being careful not to press on the outside border, which would subsequently rise badly; put the entire folded piece on one of the edges of the round of dough; then unfold it to arrange it there properly. After this, slash the dough, as explained in VOL-AU-VENT IN ONE PIECE (PAGE 668).

Dip the brush in the beaten egg and paint the inside of the vol-au-vent, as well as the surface of the circle, being careful not to allow any to run onto the inside or outside edges.

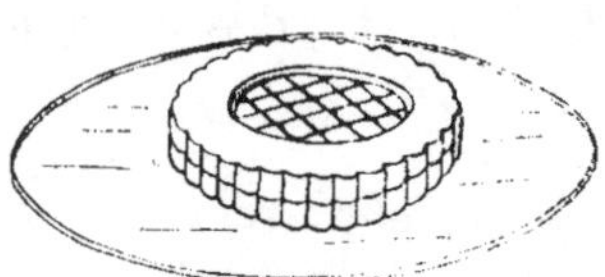

FIG. 73. THE CUT AND GRIDDED DOUGH.

With the point of a knife, and following the interior circumference of the ring, mark on this lower part of dough where the cover will be, once baking has made it rise to the level of the ring. Mark a grid (*fig.* 73). Then score the surface of the ring diagonally, stopping about 2 millimeters (less than 1/8 inch) from the interior and exterior edges, not for decoration, but to prevent the dough shrinking when it is cooked.

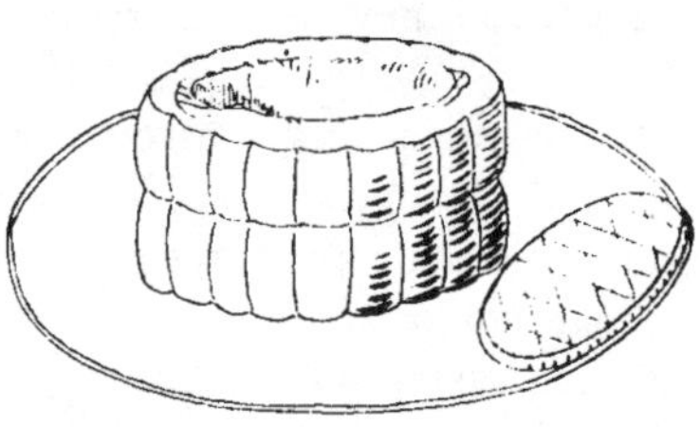

FIG. 74. CRUST OF THE VOL-AU-VENT IN TWO PIECES, READY TO BE GARNISHED.

Put it in the oven. For the cooking, follow all the directions given for the first method. But the time here is shorter; assume about *25–30 minutes.* You will know it has been properly cooked in the same way; the dough rises and levels out, and you no longer can see an open space in the center. Proceed the same way for removing the cover and drying out the interior of the crust (*fig.* 74).

Crusts for Bouchées *(Croûtes pour Bouchées).* These are cut like a vol-au-vent into a puff pastry that has been turned six times, using a cookie cutter or a ribbed pastry cutter (*fig.* 75). The current size of cutter used for bouchées served as hors d'oeuvres is 7–9 centimeters (2 3/4–3 1/2 inches) in diameter, depending on whether you want it larger or smaller. And you must always be aware of the slight shrinkage that happens when the dough is cooked. *Time: 1 hour, 30 minutes. Makes about 20 bouchées.*

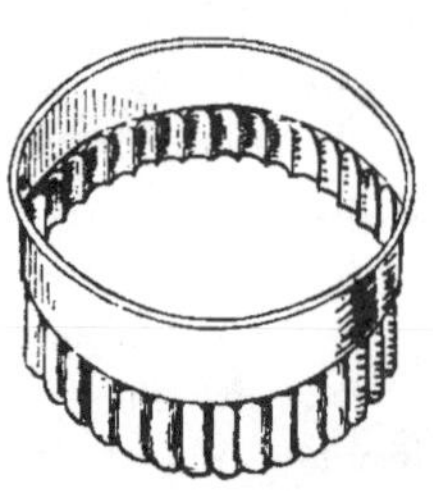

FIG. 75. RIBBED PASTRY CUTTER.

250 grams (8 7/8 ounces) of flour; 250 grams (8 7/8 ounces) of butter; 5 grams (1/6 ounce) of salt; 1 1/2 deciliters (5 fluid ounces, 2/3 cup) of water; 1 egg beaten with 1 tablespoon of water to glaze them.

PROCEDURE. Prepare the dough as directed (SEE PUFF PASTRY, PAGE 658). Once the sixth turn has been completed, and after the dough has rested for 10 minutes, roll it out into a square with an even thickness of 1 scant centimeter (3/8 inch)—that is, it would be better here to be 9 millimeters than 11 millimeters.

Lightly dampen the *tourtière* or baking sheet with water where you will place the bouchées. Put the cookie cutter on top of the dough. With the palm of your hand, strongly press down, so that with one cut the dough is cleanly sliced: let us repeat, just one bruise on the puff pastry will prevent the dough from rising. Put this round of dough on the baking sheet, *turning it over.* Proceed in the same manner for the rest of the dough, leaving a space of 1 centimeter (3/8 inch) between each round of dough.

With a small brush dipped into beaten egg, lightly coat the surface of the bouchées, keeping any of it from spilling onto the edges: the egg, which will immediately set in the heat of the oven, would make it difficult for the dough to rise.

Using a small *ungrooved* cookie cutter 3 centimeters (1 1/4 inches) in diameter, previously dipped in warm water so that it penetrates more cleanly, mark the cover on each round. Do not push it in by more than 1 millimeter. (If you do not have a small cookie cutter, make this incision with the point of a small knife.) After this, make three or four diamond-shaped cuts, keeping the blade almost flat.

Put them in a rather hot oven. The dough starts developing instantly, and as it expands into individual sheets, it has a tendency to lean. With your thumb, correct any bouchées that pop their caps. Watch carefully and turn the baking sheet so that they all receive an equal heat. If they color too quickly, cover them with a lightly moistened sheet of parchment paper.

Assume *15 minutes* for cooking. The bouchées should have risen by about 5 centimeters (2 inches).

As soon as they are taken out of the oven, flip open the little covers with the point of a knife and put them aside. With the handle of a small spoon, take out the dough from inside the bouchée, to make room for the filling that will be put into the bouchée: you need enough room for a good soupspoon of some filling, which should not be added until just before serving.

If the crusts are prepared somewhat in advance, put them to one side. You can pass them through the oven for a few moments before putting in the filling.

Shells for Timbales and for Molded Patés *(Croûtes de Timbales et de Pâtés Moulés)*

The dough used here is pastry dough *(pâte à foncer);* the proportions and the ingredients can vary a little bit depending on the recipe, but the procedure remains the same. The lining of a timbale mold or a pâté mold is completely different from that for a tart or a flan. The dough must first be made into a kind of cap, which is then laid in the mold. Professionals prepare this cap in a simple and rapid fashion, which is quite easy to follow if the method is demonstrated; but the written explanation is not as easy to understand. We will explain it, but will also give another method, which is not easier to do but is much easier to understand without an actual demonstration. *Time: 30 minutes (not including the time needed for the dough to rest). Serves 10, for which you should use a timbale or a charlotte mold measuring 13–14 centimeters (5–5$\frac{1}{2}$ inches) in diameter at the top and 11 centimeters (4$\frac{1}{4}$ inches) high.*

300 grams (10$\frac{1}{2}$ ounces) of flour; 175 grams (6 ounces) of butter; 1 egg; 1 good deciliter (3$\frac{1}{3}$ fluid ounces, $\frac{1}{2}$ cup) of water; 7 grams ($\frac{1}{4}$ ounce) of salt.

PROCEDURE. **Professional procedure:** Once the dough has been rolled into a ball to rest, flatten it into a nice round pancake 22 centimeters (8$\frac{1}{2}$ inches) in diameter, with a thickness of 2 centimeters ($\frac{3}{4}$ inch). Turn it over so that the seam of the gathering of the ball is on top. Lightly sprinkle it with flour; fold it in two, with the two adjacent edges toward you, and the seam where the ball came together now on the inside of the fold (see *fig.* 76, PAGE 672).

Without moving this large folded pancake, and with your hands on each side, gradually bring the two ends in toward the middle of the edges until it looks like the drawing on PAGE 672. The work involves gradually and gently, with the ends of your fingers, making folds in the dough, and then removing them as you go by thinning out the dough, finally passing the rolling pin over it very lightly, just as you would use a clothes iron. Push the rolling pin directly in front of you, squeezing the dough toward the bottom of the cap to make it deeper. Do this very lightly so that you do not stick the two thicknesses of the fold together, even though they are somewhat protected by the powdering of flour inside. Turn the cap over rather often (always with the opening in front of you) because the dough underneath will not be as stretched out as the dough on top, where the rolling pin passes over it directly. Finally, pass the rolling pin over the cap to give the dough a completely even thickness of *8 millimeters (less than $\frac{3}{8}$ inch)*. This means, of course, the thickness of the doubled dough.

Then open the cap by sliding in your fist. Carefully transfer it to the mold, previously thoroughly smeared with butter, where it should fit as snugly as a lining.

Then, with your fingers, press on the dough in all directions evenly, to perfectly fill and fit the angle in the bottom, and push the dough so that you make the excess rise toward the edge of the mold. With a small knife, trim the dough sticking out over 6the edges of the mold, *being careful to leave 1$\frac{1}{2}$ centimeters ($\frac{5}{8}$ inch) sticking out. The*

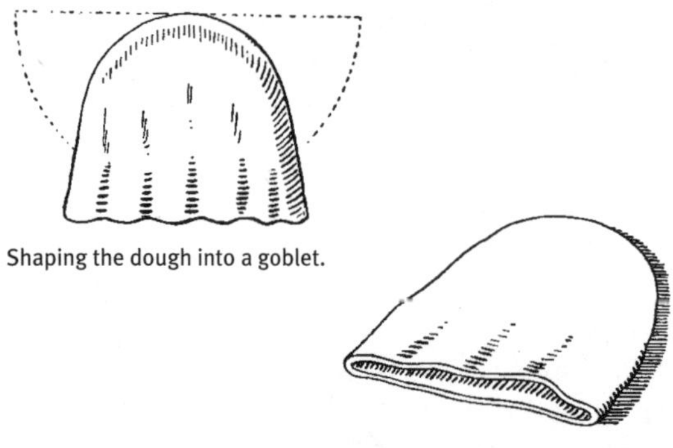

Shaping the dough into a goblet.

The finished cap of dough.

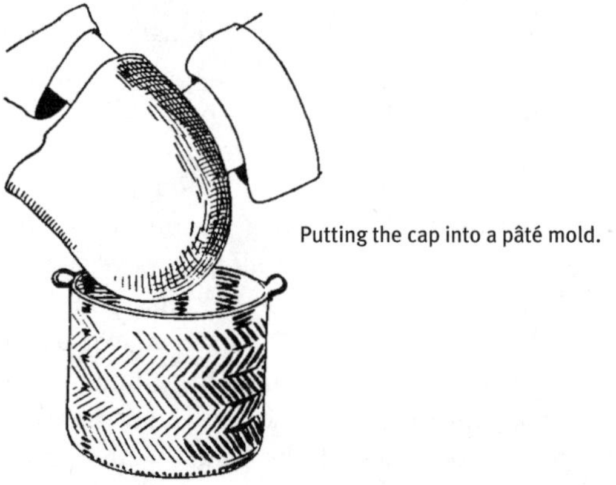

Putting the cap into a pâté mold.

FIG. 76. MAKING A CAP OF DOUGH.

part of the dough going beyond the edges of the mold is called the "crest."

Simplified procedure: Place the charlotte mold or timbale, with the bottom up, on the table. Roll out the dough and sprinkle it with flour exactly as above; the same sizes.

Place the flattened dough, with the floured side down, on the bottom of the turned-over mold. Lightly press down on the dough with both hands in all directions, so that it takes on the shape of the mold, and also diminishes in thickness. If you have a proper timbale mold, this is easy and the dough can thus be molded up to the very edge of the mold. However, with a mold with handles on it, you can only mold it three-quarters of the way.

With great care, remove it so that it keeps its shape. Then place it folded in two on the board, with the opening in front of you. Open it up a little bit without moving it around, to lightly powder the inside with flour. Shorten the width of the cap a little bit by carefully gathering the two sides toward the middle with both hands. Then roll the rolling pin lightly over the still folded cap, pushing the dough toward the bottom.

Again, bring the sides toward the middle and pass the rolling pin over it, the triangular overlays produced by bringing together the dough will be removed as the rolling pin passes over, just like under a clothes iron. Without this frequent and repeated gathering, the cap would open out into a bowl instead of taking the deep form of the timbale. This done, turn the cap over two or three times, always with the opening in front of you. While you do this, the rolling pin must be particularly worked lengthwise, to increase the cap's depth. Ultimately, this gives the same result as is achieved with the "professional" technique. Make sure the dough is as thick as required and then line the mold, as directed in the previous instructions: "Then open the cap by sliding in your fist, etc."

The cover: If the cover is decorated with patterns of dough, you will need at least another quarter of the quantity of dough suggested for the crust for a pâté or timbale shell. If the crust is only a simple layer of dough, as for timbales in the classic style, in which the bottoms become the tops after cooking, the trimmings left from the dough after you have lined the mold will suffice. Either way, the dough should be 1/2 centimeter (3/16 inch) thick.

The decorated cover. We here will take as an example the cover of rabbit pâté en croûte, one of our recipes. Roll a piece of dough the size of an egg into a ball to flatten it out into a pancake the same size as the opening of the mold, more or less. You should have an excess of 1 good centimeter (3/8 inch) to fuse with the dough lining the sides of the mold.

With a brush, lightly moisten the inside of the crest of dough in the mold. Put the cover piece right onto the mold. Join the edges of the cover to the crest, squeezing the dough strongly between your thumb, placed inside, and your index finger, on the outside. Do this in such a way that the dough of the lining and the dough of the cover are very well joined, one to the other, to a width of 2 centimeters (3/4 inch). With a small knife, even out the crest by trimming it, leaving 1 centimeter (3/8 inch) of crest above the mold. Crimp or pinch this crest both inside and outside with the special pasty crimper used for this function.

With the rolling pin, roll out that the remaining dough to a thickness of 3–4 millimeters (1/8 inch) only. Using a ribbed cookie cutter 5 centimeters (2 inches) in diameter, cut 10–12 rounds. With the same cookie cutter, applied twice in opposite directions in the middle of the round, divide each round into two ovals. On each oval, with the back of the blade of a small knife, mark the veins of the leaves. Lightly moisten the cover of the pâté. Place the leaves on top of them in a circle, lightly leaning on each other.

Cut some new rounds and some new ovals with a smaller cookie cutter (4 centimeters/1 1/2 inches in diameter). Make a new line of leaves, their ends falling on the first. Finally, gather all the trimmings of the dough to spread them out with the rolling pin to a thickness of 1/2 centimeter (3/16 inch). With cookie cutters of 9, 7, and 5 centimeters (3 1/2, 2 3/4, and 2 inches) in diameter, cut three graduated rounds. Glue these rounds one on top of the other by moistening them lightly; place them above the second row of leaves. Then make a hole in the middle of the cover with an unribbed cookie cutter 1 centimeter (3/8 inch) in diameter, going right through the dough to the filling. This is so the steam can escape while it is cooking. Into this opening, place a small piece of cardboard rolled into a tube, its end resting directly on the filling, to form a chimney tube for the steam to escape.

Then lightly and evenly glaze the dough with a brush dipped into a thoroughly beaten egg.

The simple cover. Gather the trimmings of the dough cut from around the mold after you shaped it into a ball: a crest of 1 centimeter (3/8 inch) is sufficient here. Allow it to rest for 3–4 minutes. Roll out this dough with the rolling pin until it is flat as above, and join it in exactly the same way. Then trim any excess dough from around the mold. Proceed as above to let the steam escape and for the egg glaze.

To decorate the crust of a timbale: This involves repeated designs in dough used to decorate the sides of the timbale. The dough used is a noodle dough. The proportions of this dough for the timbale are: 60 grams (2 1/4 ounces) of flour; 2 egg yolks; 2 grams (1/14 ounce) of salt and 3 grams (1/10 ounce) of superfine sugar; a few drops of cold water. The sugar is used here more for coloring the dough when it cooks, and to make the decoration of the timbale stand out.

Mix the dough with your fingers. If you need to add a little bit of water, do this very carefully and drop by drop, because the dough must remain rather firm (SEE NOODLE DOUGH, PAGE 568). Push it out with the palm of your hand twice; wrap it in a towel until you are ready to use it.

Roll it out under the rolling pin to a thickness of *2 millimeters (about 1/12 inch).* Cut decorations in it following your own taste and imagination: rectangles or rounds cut with a cookie cutter, either smooth-edged or scalloped, and then cut into crescents. With rectangles, you can make four rosettes, tied together by two garlands of crescents, one across the top and one across the walls of the mold.

Once the mold has been very generously buttered, apply the little dough decorations by pushing them down firmly to stick them to the butter in the mold. Dampen them with a brush. Then put the pocket or cap of the lining dough into the mold. Press firmly on it with your fingers so that the decorations are well secured; this is why you moistened them first. Then proceed as above to line the mold as usual.

Timbale shell cooked empty: In professional terms, this is called cooking *à blanc*—that is, without a filling, which is not added until the shell is cooked. A shell cooked like this is perfectly edible, given that the ingredients for the dough are the same, but it is mainly used as a receptacle.

Decorate the buttered mold, if you like, and then line it with the cap of dough, exactly as described. After this, line the inside of the dough-lined timbale with parchment paper and fill as described with cherry pits, lentils, split peas, etc. for the TART SHELL COOKED À BLANC (SEE PAGE 678). Next, place a sheet of paper on top to form a dome, and place on top of that the decorated cover of dough. Make an opening in the cover for the steam to escape. Glaze. Cook in a good hot oven.

After cooking, remove the cover. Completely empty the filling and remove the paper. Glaze the inside of the timbale and dry it uncovered for a few minutes at the opening of the oven.

Croûte à la Crème for a Timbale *(Croûte à la Crème pour Timbale)*

Taken from a family journal from Alsace, this recipe produces an exquisite crust with a dough reminiscent of a mousseline brioche. This is the method used in Alsace for working the dough, and it produces a unique, characteristic lightness without the use of any leavening agent. If you like, you can put a fricassee of chicken or mushrooms or a compote of fruits into this shell. It is good for all uses. *Time: 1 hour, 45 minutes. Serves 6.*

100 grams (3½ ounces, 7 tablespoons) of fresh butter; 5 tablespoons of light cream; also 5 tablespoons of very fine light dry flour (100 grams/3½ ounces total); 6 medium-size fresh eggs; a pinch of salt; 1 tablespoon of fine white bread crumbs.

A charlotte mold with a capacity of about 1¼ liters (5⅓ cups). If not, use a small pot of the same size instead. The mold has to be filled only three-quarters full, because the dough rises while cooking.

PROCEDURE. Sift the flour. Butter the mold and sprinkle the inside with flour. Use an earthenware bowl of a medium size so that you can easily mix the dough in it. Using a large wooden spoon, first work the butter (SEE SOFTENING BUTTER INTO A POMADE, PAGE 16). When it is perfectly smooth, add only *1 tablespoon* of cream. Work it only until it is completely mixed with the butter; this first tablespoon takes the longest to dissolve. Add the salt. Then add *1 egg yolk.* Beat it to mix it well. After this, add *1 tablespoon* of flour. Mix it in while beating the dough.

Then begin again, following the same order: the tablespoon of cream, egg yolk, and the tablespoon of flour. Each ingredient must be perfectly mixed before you add the next one. The mixture is also affected by vigorously working the spoon, lifting up the dough reasonably high: this makes the dough absorb air and become lighter.

Then beat the whites into a firm snow (SEE EGG WHITES, PAGE 8) and incorporate them into the dough with due care (SEE PAGE 10). In one movement, pour the dough into the mold. Lightly tap the bottom of the mold on the table to compact the dough. Put everything in the oven, directly on the bottom.

Cooking it: Use an oven of good medium heat, coming mostly from the bottom, to encourage the dough to rise. If the heat coming from the top is stronger, the surface of the dough will immediately form a crust and the interior will compact into a sort of damp mass, nothing even vaguely approaching this type of croute. To stop this crust forming too rapidly, cover the mold at the end of about 10 minutes with moistened or buttered parchment paper. For the rest, observe all the usual care required for pastry making.

Allow 1¼ hours for cooking. The dough must rise substantially. You can tell that the cooking is complete when the cake has stopped rising and looks like and has the consistency of a well-cooked brioche. The outside circumference must have a golden-brown color and be firm all over, which you can confirm by sliding the blade of a knife between the croute and the mold.

It is better to make the croûte in the timbale before you unmold it: the mold provides support. Do this as soon as you take it out of the oven. With the point of a small kitchen knife, trace a circle on the surface of the croute at least 3 centimeters (1¼ inches) from the edge. This will allow you to raise the top crust as a cover. Then, using the handle of a small wooden spoon, dig out the inside carefully, leaving at the bottom and all around a thickness of dough about 3 centimeters (1⅛ inches). (The dough removed from the inside, which will resemble brioche dough, can be carefully dried in the oven; made into bread crumbs, it is very good in a potage.)

Then unmold the croûte. Keep it in a warm place or in a low oven, along with its cover, turned upside down, so that it is still warm when you pour in the fricassee or the compote, just before serving.

To serve: Put the croûte on a plate and cover it with its cover. You can, for easy serving, cut it into pieces immediately, the top part of the croute and its cover; cut the rest and the bottom part when offering seconds.

DIVERSE PASTRIES
Pâtisseries Diverses

Fruit Tarts or Flans *(Tartes ou Flans de Fruits)*

In the pastry section of professional kitchens, puff pastry trimmings are used for the shells of tarts. But in home kitchens, and when there are no trimmings, you replace them with a fine pastry dough *(pâte à foncer),* made with ingredients that can vary a bit but are always prepared the same way.

In home pastry making, cooks often prepare a dough that is called—incorrectly, I might add—"half (or rough) puff pastry" *(demi-feuilletage),* because it is turned a few times with the rolling pin. This dough is actually a galette dough, the recipe for which you will find under TWELFTH NIGHT CAKE (PAGE 679).

As a typical fruit tart or fruit flan recipe, where the cooking is done in the shell itself, we will give a recipe for cherry tart. It is also good for other fruits.

We will also give the method of cooking a tart crust *à blanc,* a professional term that means cooking it alone, without any filling, which is not added until afterward. You cook the crusts this way for strawberry tarts and tarts that are filled with compotes of preserves, etc. The same procedure is good for small tarts.

Cherry Tart *(Tarte aux Cerises).* *Time: 50 minutes to line, fill, and cook the tart; the dough should be prepared at least 2 hours in advance. Makes a tart for 6.*

150 grams (5 1/3 ounces) of flour; 90 grams (3 1/6 ounces, 6 1/3 tablespoons) of butter; 1 egg; 3–4 tablespoons of cold water; 7–8 grams (about 1/4 ounce) of superfine sugar; 3 grams (1/10 ounce) of salt.

1 kilogram (2 pounds, 3 ounces) of nice cherries; 1 1/2 tablespoons of superfine sugar.

PROCEDURE. **The dough:** SEE PASTRY DOUGH OR LINING DOUGH PAGE 662. Make the well in the sifted flour. Add: salt, sugar, *very cold* water, the egg, and the butter. Mix it as directed. Force the dough across the board under the palm of your hand *(fraiser)* two times. Reassemble it into a ball. Allow it to rest in a cool place for *at least 2 hours.*

To mold the dough: People in some households, particularly in the country, frequently and wrongly use molds made of light metal with a wavy border. Lining them—that is, applying the dough—is easier, but unmolding them is difficult, because there is the risk of the shell breaking. Furthermore, in this type of mold, the dough has a very good chance of sticking or not cooking correctly because the bottom generally does not offer a perfectly flat surface, and the shape of the utensil does not allow you to lift up the tart while it is cooking to check how much the crust has colored.

The mold to use is a large ring mold, called a tart ring or a flan ring. These rings, whatever their diameter, are about 2 1/2 centimeters (1 inch) high. They are made from rather strong white metal that has a very small lip on the outside, enabling you to lift them during the cooking process *(fig. 77).* To use the ring, *you also need a tourtière,* which is a round plate of *thick* dark metal with a slightly raised border that allows you to hold it and turn it easily in the oven.

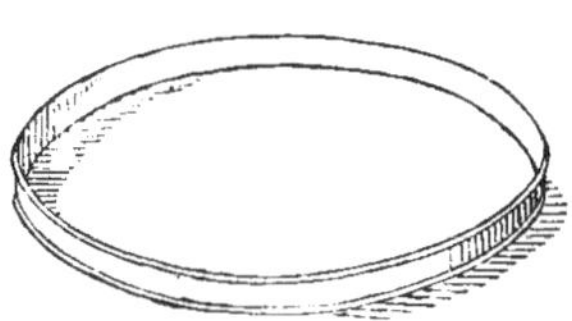

FIG. 77. FLAN RING OR TART RING.

To line the tart ring: Thoroughly grease the inside of a tart ring 24–25 centimeters (9 1/2–10 inches) in diameter with a piece of unmelted butter the size of a nice bean, spreading it out with the end of your fingers, while turning the ring with your other hand.

Have the *tourtière* ready and scrupulously clean, but not buttered (because the butter would burn on it) and not floured (because the flour would also burn).

Dust the pastry board with a sprinkling of flour. Put the dough on it and roll it on the board to give it a round form, nice and even, which will make it easier to subsequently work it with the rolling pin.

First tap a little bit on the ball with the rolling pin to flatten it out into the shape of a nice round thick pancake. Then roll—that is, extend the dough with the rolling pin—*into a round as even as possible, with a completely even thickness of 6 millimeters—that is, a good 1/2 centimeter (about 3/16 inch)—and with a circumference that is 3 centimeters*

(1 1/8 inches) larger than the circumference of the ring used. This surplus is the amount needed to extend the dough to the top edge of the ring.

To achieve this result, you must proceed methodically, and not carelessly, because this work is one that must succeed at the first attempt. Once the dough has been rolled out one time, it will lose much of its quality if you attempt to rectify your mistake, and do better, by gathering the dough again into a ball and rolling it out a second time to give it a better shape.

Always work the rolling pin from the center toward the edges. Roll out the pin in all directions, replacing it back in the middle after each roll, without going back down the road already traveled. This makes it easier to maintain the round shape and to keep the thickness of dough as even as possible.

Place the buttered ring next to you on the table, which should be lightly dusted with flour, then raise the sheet of dough by sliding your two hands under it, and lay it over the top of the ring. Allow a little bit of the dough to fall into the ring's interior. With your thumb against the inside wall, press on the dough to mark the bottom angle; but without pressing so hard that you thin the dough there, which will become fragile when it is cooked. The easy way to do this is to slightly raise the ring and turn it toward you.

Then fold out the dough that extends over the edges of the ring. Pass the rolling pin over it, pressing down on it to cut away the excess dough. The edge of dough thus forms a sort of pad. Lightly squeeze this pad of dough lining the edge of the ring between your fingers to make the dough rise a little bit above the edge of the ring, without making it extend over the edge of the ring, which would make unmolding the tart complicated. This part, the dough that sticks out, is called the "crest" of a tart or a flan.

With a pastry crimper, crimp the entire circumference of this crest *vertically* to give it a better appearance.

Pick up both the ring and the dough in your hands, with your thumbs inside the ring. Raise this very slowly and place it on the *tourtière.* If the dough does not contain eggs, it will be much more fragile, so the sensible thing to do is to mold it right in the ring already placed on the round *tourtière.* Roll the dough around the rolling pin, place it on the ring, and then unfold the dough, pressing it from the center toward the edges to get rid of any air from between the *tourtière* and the dough, which would cause the dough to blister. Form the edges as explained. You can also dust the dough with flour and fold it into quarters, thus forming a quarter circle; the flour will stop the folded layers of dough from sticking. Put the dough on the *tourtière* with the point of the quarter circle in the center, and then unfold it, pressing it onto the bottom.

With the point of a small knife, make 4–5 nicks in the bottom of the tart to avoid air bubbles. Just little nicks, and not cuts, which would allow the juice of the fruits to escape when cooking. This juice would burn on the plate and make the dough stick to it.

To fill the tart: Sprinkle the bottom of the tart with 1 tablespoon of superfine sugar. Remove the pits from the cherries without breaking them, using steel wire folded in two or a new hairpin stuck into a cork. Arrange the cherries, with the split side down, in lines close together, running from edge to edge.

Cooking it: *Put the tart into the oven as soon as it is filled;* the juice from the fruits would soak into the dough if it were to stand for too long.

Put the tart at the bottom of the oven. The oven should have a good medium heat coming mostly from the bottom. Fifteen minutes after putting the tart in the oven, check whether the oven heat is too strong from the bottom. In that case, slide another plate under the *tourtière* to protect the bottom of the tart.

Cook for about 35 minutes. However, before taking the tart out of the oven, make sure that the dough on the sides and also on the bottom is nice and dry and perfectly colored.

Once the tart has been taken from the oven, remove the ring. Slide the tart onto a rack. Sprinkle the fruits with a very fine sugar or confectioners' sugar, using a sugar shaker. Or paint the cherries with a little bit of red currant jelly diluted in 1 tablespoon of water to make a medium-weight syrup, glazing the fruits without softening the crusts. Allow it to chill, either completely or nearly, depending on your preference.

Apricot Tart *(Tarte aux Abricots).* *Time: 40 minutes (once the dough has rested).* Cut the apricots in half and arrange them in a circle on the tart, first sprinkling the bottom with sugar as for the cherry tart; place the apricots round side up, slightly overlapping each other. After cooking, you can also sprinkle them with confectioners' sugar or apply a syrup of apricot preserves diluted with a little bit of water.

Apple Tart *(Tarte aux Pommes).* *Time: 40 minutes (once the dough has rested).* Cut peeled and seeded apple quarters into even slices 2 millimeters (1/16 inch) thick. Arrange them in a circle, starting on the outside and overlapping the slices; arrange the slices for each row in an opposite direction until you reach the center of the tart. After cooking, sprinkle with confectioners' sugar or cover with a little bit of a jelly made with the peels and trimmings from the apples, sugar, and water, and with a little bit of apricot marmalade added.

Lemon Tart *(Tarte au Citron).* *Time: 1 hour, 45 minutes. Serves 6.*

1 flan ring 24–25 centimeters (9 1/2–10 inches) in diameter.

For the dough: 150 grams (5 1/3 ounces) of flour; 75 grams (2 2/3 ounces, 1/3 cup) of butter; a pinch of salt; about 1 deciliter (3 1/3 fluid ounces, scant 1/2 cup) of water. Prepare the dough by the method given for half puff pastry (SEE PAGE 662).

To fill the tart: 4 egg yolks; 150 grams (5 1/3 ounces) of superfine sugar; 2 large Rennet apples from Canada with a dense pulp, weighing a total of 400–500 grams (14 1/8 ounces–1 pound, 2 ounces); 1 1/2 lemons.

PROCEDURE. Prepare the dough; while it is resting, make the filling. With a large wooden spoon, beat the egg yolks and the sugar in a terrine until the mixture turns white and makes the ribbon (SEE PAGE 577). Then add the lemon zest, finely grated, without any of the bitter white part of the skin; the juice of 1 lemon strained in a fine strainer; and the 2 peeled apples, removing their seeds and grating them only just before mixing them in so that the pulp does not turn brown. Mix everything thoroughly and pour it into a flan ring lined with the dough (SEE TO LINE THE TART, PAGE 675).

Immediately put it into a medium-heat oven and cook for *35–40 minutes.* The surface of the tart must be uniformly golden and the interior set like a milk flan. When you take it out of the oven, unmold it onto a pastry rack and then serve it either lukewarm or cold, depending on your preference.

Plum Tart *(Tarte aux Prunes).* Depending on their size, simply pit the plums (particularly if they are mirabelles), or cut them in half like the apricots.

Strawberry Tart *(Tarte aux Fraises).* This differs from other fresh fruit tarts in that the shell is cooked *à blanc*—separately, in other words—and only then is it filled with the strawberries, which are always used *uncooked.* Next, cover the strawberries with a red currant syrup, either a simple one or made with red wine or flavored with kirsch, as suggested below.

Small wild strawberries or ever-bearing strawberries are best. However, you can also use Héricart strawberries or any other of a medium size. If they are too large, cut them in half.

The shell can be cooked several hours in advance and even filled in advance, as long as the strawberries are left whole; but do not add the syrup until the last moment, or at least a short time in advance. The syrup must be cold or barely at room temperature when it is poured over the strawberries. *Time: 1 hour, 30 minutes (the dough having been prepared in advance). Serves 6.*

For the dough: 150 grams (5 1/3 ounces) of flour; 75 grams (2 2/3 ounces, 1/3 cup) of butter; 1 egg, using only half, reserving the rest to glaze the shell; 3 grams (about 1/10 ounce) of salt; 6 grams (1/5 ounce) of superfine sugar; 3–4 tablespoons of cold water.

For the filling: 300 grams (10 1/2 ounces) of strawberries; 4 tablespoons of red currant jelly; 50 grams (1 3/4 ounces) of superfine sugar or sugar cubes; the quantities of wine and kirsch are given below and are subject to the choice of syrup.

PROCEDURE. The proportions of the dough given here are the same as for the cherry tart; these also assume the use a flan ring or tart ring 24–25 centimeters (9 1/2–10 inches) in diameter. Prepare the dough and line the ring in the same way; afterward, cook as is directed for the TART SHELL COOKED À BLANC (AT RIGHT). Let the crust cool.

To fill the tart: To correctly place the strawberries in the crust, pierce them with a fine kitchen needle and place them side by side and close together, but not so that you crush them.

To pour the syrup: Once the shell is filled with strawberries, cover them with a barely lukewarm syrup, pouring it over them with a spoon. Then, using a small brush, thoroughly spread this syrup everywhere, using enough so that it oozes down between the strawberries.

To prepare the syrup: *Simple syrup.* Put the red currant jelly in a small saucepan with the superfine sugar and 3 tablespoons of water. Cook gently, stirring it from time to time with a small spoon. It is ready when it is thick and gummy.

Kirsch syrup. Once the simple syrup has been prepared as above and is almost cold, add 2 tablespoons of very good kirsch.

Wine syrup. Into a small copper pan that has not been lined with tin, put 2 1/2 deciliters (1 cup) of red wine (Bordeaux or Burgundy) with the sugar, either superfine or in cubes. (Tin makes the wine purple.) Boil it rapidly without a cover to reduce the wine by two-thirds. Then add the red currant jelly. Cook gently until the syrup is thick and gummy, as above.

Tarts with Preserved Fruits *(Les Tartes avec Compotes de Conserve):* These are a great alternative when the season for fresh fruit has passed. You can also garnish the tarts with pieces of apple cooked in a syrup or with a marmalade.

Drain the fruits well, then lay them out symmetrically in the cooked shell without crowding them too closely together, so that the syrup can spread across the bottom of the crust. Add the sugar to the liquid or the juice used for the preserves and then reduce it to the consistency of a thick syrup. Depending on the type of fruit, you can also add to the syrup a little bit of apricot marmalade that has been puréed, or some red currant jelly that has been diluted, etc. Baste the fruits with the syrup, which here should still be warm.

Tart Shell Cooked *à Blanc (Croûte de Tarte Cuite "à Blanc").* Line the ring with the dough, proceeding exactly as directed for the CHERRY TART (PAGE 675). Place it on the tart plate. Make 7 or 8 nicks in the bottom of the dough with the point of a small knife to avoid blistering when it is cooked.

The tart must be given a temporary filling; it is surely easy to understand that when put into the oven just as it is—that is, empty—the dough of the borders is unsupported and will therefore weaken, while the dough on the bottom will swell. To avoid this, professional pastry makers use cherry pits, kept from one year to the next; you can replace them with lentils, split peas, or grains of rice, none of which are wasted, because they can be used again and again for this purpose.

First cover the bottom of the tart dough with a round of fine white buttered parchment paper, with the buttered side down. Then place all around the inside edges a ribbon of buttered paper. Fill the tart right to the top with lentils, peas, or rice, depending on what you have. If you do not put parchment paper between the dough and the dried vegetables or grains, they will become encrusted in the dough, particularly if the dough is slightly soft, and you will then have to remove them, and risk breaking the shell.

To cook: When the tart is filled, immediately put it in the oven. The oven temperature must be medium and well sustained, coming primarily from the bottom. As the point is not to color the shell, you do not need the heat to come from the top.

At the end of 25 minutes, make sure that the dough on the border is good and dry and slightly colored; if it is not sufficiently dry and colored, wait 5–6 minutes; then take the *tourtière* out of the oven.

Remove the ring and take out whatever you put into the tart shell, including the parchment paper. With a small brush dipped in beaten egg, paint the inside and outside. Then put the shell back in the oven to dry it out, which requires *7–8 minutes.*

Now slide it off the tourtière onto a rack or a small grill and let it *cool completely.* If, when you take out the filling, you see that a bubble has formed in the bottom of the tart, pierce it here and there with the point of a knife, *but on the bias* to avoid letting any syrup or juice escape through this opening.

Twelfth Night Cake *(Galette des Rois)*

"This is made in several ways," says a fine old cookbook from the time of Louis XV: "knead 2 liters of nice flour with three-quarters of a pound of fresh butter and a sufficient quantity of water and salt, etc. If you want your galette to be flaky, flatten the dough with the rolling pin, fold it over and flatten it again, then fold it again the same way, etc."

Now this same method, more than two centuries old, and still currently used by French housewives, is the classic formula that can be found in the most up-to-date professional cookbooks, and is the one we give here. It produces what folks like to call a "rough puff pastry," this name describing both the look of the dough as well as the way it is worked with the rolling pin. However, the term *rough puff pastry* is not used by professionals for this dough (SEE PAGE 675); they call it simply "galette dough." This is another reason to affirm the authenticity of this recipe. *Time: 1 1/2 hours to roll out the dough and turn it and to make and cook the cake (once the dough has been prepared and rested for at least a good half hour). Makes a cake for 6.*

250 grams (8 7/8 ounces) of flour; 190 grams (6 2/3 ounces, 3/4 cup plus 1 heaping tablespoon) of butter; 5 grams (1/6 ounce) of salt; 7 grams (1/4 ounce) of superfine sugar; 75 centiliters (generous 3 cups) of cold water; a little bit of egg yolk diluted in 2 tablespoons of water to glaze the cake.

PROCEDURE. Make the well. Add the salt and the sugar with 1 tablespoon of water and stir everything with your fingers to dissolve it well. Add the butter, which should have previously been well softened as directed (SEE PAGE 657), and the rest of the water. Mix it in the same way as for PASTRY OR LINING DOUGH (SEE PAGE 662), adding a little bit of water if necessary. The dough must be more firm than soft. *Do not push it out with the palm of your hand across the board.* Simply gather it into a ball. Place it on a plate sprinkled with flour, and cover with a towel. *Allow it to rest for at least a half hour,* and even longer if possible.

It is not until after the dough has rested that it can be turned. Sprinkle the board with flour. Place the ball of dough there and also sprinkle it with flour. Tap it with the rolling pin to flatten it out a little bit, first into an oval, to make the work that follows easier. Roll it out with the rolling pin into a ribbon of even thickness, about 60 centimeters (24 inches) long and 22 centimeters (8 1/2 inches) wide. Fold it in three, thus making the turn (SEE PUFF PASTRY, PAGE 658). Turn the dough a total of three times, with rests of 8–10 minutes in-between each turn.

Once it has been turned three times, fold in the four corners of the square of dough toward the center (*fig.* 78), and then fold in the edges of the dough between the corners to give the whole a round shape. Sprinkle the board with flour. With the rolling pin, which you should always handle starting from the center and moving out toward the edges, roll out this dough to a very equal thickness of 1 1/2–2 centimeters (5/8–3/4 inch), attempting as you go to give it as round a shape as possible. This is because, just as for true puff pastry, you cannot, if there are any imperfections, roll the dough back into a ball and start all over: this work would involve extra turns, thereby affecting the quality of the dough.

If the circumference is uneven, as happens frequently to people who have no experience in this particular task, you can restore the cake's roundness by pushing the excess pieces back into the mass of the dough using the back of a knife, a process called "nibbling." For the traditional hidden charm, delicately slide the point of a knife into the edge of the dough; into this small opening, slide the bean or charm, then squeeze the opening back together, which will close easily. Or if you want it to be obvious where the charm has been placed, push it inside the cake through the bottom and make a mark.

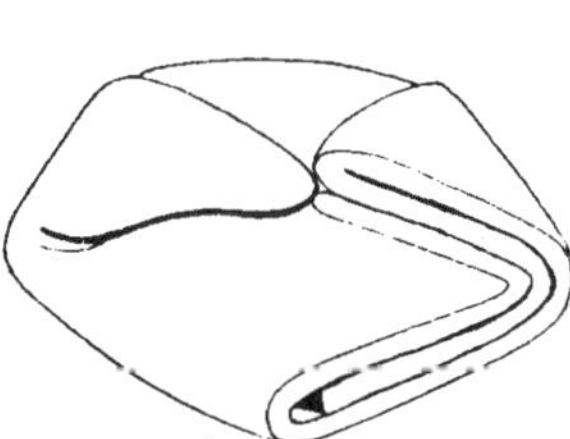

FIG. 78. FOLDING IN THE CORNERS OF THE DOUGH.

Place the round of dough on a thick, very clean baking sheet that has been neither oiled nor floured. Using a small brush or a feather, paint the top of the cake with the egg yolk *without allowing any of it to run over the edge;* because, as for puff pastry, the egg will set in the heat and make it difficult for this part of the cake to rise. Score it in a grid or other pattern with a fork. Pierce it here and there in four or five places to avoid blistering. Put it in the oven.

Cooking it: SEE THE OVEN, PAGE 655. An oven with a good strong medium heat, so that after 5 minutes the dough will have already changed and begun to rise: if the dough languishes in a cooler oven, it will rise badly. Assume *30–35 minutes* for cooking; any longer will harden the dough and cause too thick a crust to form. If the bottom of the cake is pale after cooking, which should not happen if your oven is at the proper temperature, turn the cake upside down and put it back in the oven for a few minutes to color. Then place the cake on a cake grill to allow it to cool. It should only be served lukewarm, so it is to this point, and no warmer, that you should reheat it if necessary.

Brioche *(Brioche)*

The method given here is utterly modern and does not include the preparation of a leavening agent, which was normal practice until just a few years ago. This makes working the dough much easier, and even the most untrained novice can try making brioche, and succeed; always on the condition that very fine white flour is used, and the cake yeast is nice and fresh (SEE PAGE 657).

First make sure you are thoroughly familiar with all the directions about the oven, the flour, the yeast, etc. that are applicable to pastry making (SEE PAGES 655–658). First we will give the recipe for mousseline brioche because it is the one most likely to succeed in home ovens; then the crown brioche.

As for the head brioche, you will do better not to even try to make it. It must bake in the oven for a long time, and the more sugary dough would color too strongly in a home oven. We give the same advice for small head brioches; these require an oven at an extreme temperature, where they should be left for only 5 minutes. In a home oven, this time is too short to color them. And if they are left there for more than 10–12 minutes to color them better, they will simply dry out. We therefore suggest that you do not attempt them.

Mousseline Brioche *(Brioche Mousseline).* *Time: About 7 hours (assuming that the dough has been made the day before in the evening, allow about 6 hours so that it rises 2 more times, and 40 minutes to cook the brioche). Makes a brioche weighing a little more than 450 grams (1 pound).*

250 grams (8 7/8 ounces) of fine white flour; 190 grams (6 2/3 ounces, 3/4 cup plus 1 heaping tablespoon) of good butter; 7–8 grams (1/4 ounce) of yeast in cake form; 5 grams (1/6 ounce) of salt; 10 grams (1/3 ounce) of superfine sugar; 3 medium eggs; 1/2 deciliter (1 2/3 fluid ounces, scant 1/4 cup) of water that is slightly tepid.

PROCEDURE. **Summary:** Make the well and add the water; dissolve the yeast in the water. Add butter, eggs, sugar, salt, and then rapidly mix everything. Gather the dough in a wooden bowl; allow it to rise to double its volume. Knead the dough; allow it to rise for a second time. Put it in a high-sided mold; allow it to rise for a third time. Brush it with egg, then cut a cross on top of the dough. Cook in a moderate oven.

Do not use more than the quantities suggested here if you want a very good result; and rather than increasing them to make a larger brioche, it would definitely be better to use two sets of ingredients and make two similar pastries. This way, you can make a simple crown brioche and a mousseline brioche.

It is essential that the butter should be firm. Firm it and then soften it as directed (SEE PAGE 657).

In summertime, when it is very warm and you are making the dough the evening before, 10 grams (1/3 ounce) of yeast per 450 grams (1 pound) of flour will be enough. If you want to make the dough in the morning for that very same day, you can increase the amount of yeast to 12 grams (3/8 ounce) and even 15 grams (1/2 ounce) when you are in a hurry.

In wintertime, it is better to prepare the dough with 15 grams (1/2 ounce) of yeast for each 450 grams (1 pound) of flour, even if the dough is made the evening before. When you are making quite a large quantity of brioche dough, as in professional kitchens or bakeries, just 10 grams (1/3 ounce) per 450 grams (1 pound) is sufficient, because the action of the yeast is facilitated by rather high quantities; but when you are working with only 225 grams (8 ounces) and even 450 grams (1 pound), such an amount of yeast is very small: even a little bit less would result in such an imbalance that it would be better, as we suggest, to always assume 15 grams (1/2 ounce) per 450 grams (1 pound).

Preparations: Sift the flour onto the pastry board; form it into a well.

Weigh the yeast and place it directly in the well as soon as you take it off the scale so that you do not lose any of it, which would have some impact on such small quantities.

Put the salt and the sugar together in a saucer.

Break the eggs into a small terrine.

Heat a little bit of water to a lukewarm temperature; then measure the amount required, and keep it at hand in the deciliter measure or a glass. The water must be no more than lukewarm, having just lost its chill: any warmer, and it would burn the yeast, preventing it from having an effect. You should not use water that you have already boiled, because the boiling makes it lose certain properties that encourage the dough to ferment.

Having assembled all these ingredients, also have at hand some flour, so that you can powder your hands if necessary. Also have the dough scraper, or if you do not have one, the blade of an old knife that is no longer sharp, to scrape either your fingers or the board without cutting anything.

The dough: Pour the water into the well where you have already placed the yeast. With the end of your fingers of your right hand, completely dissolve the yeast in this water without touching the flour at all. Then place in the well the piece of butter, rendered just malleable, as already explained.

Finally add: the salt, the sugar, the eggs.

With *the end of your fingers,* mix and work the butter, eggs, liquid, etc. for only a moment, without yet touching the flour. This is simply to first dissolve the salt and the sugar and to mix the yolks and the whites, given that the butter will not combine with the liquid without the flour.

Next, *little by little,* bring the flour into the well to mix it there; do this by turning your right hand in a circular movement with your fingers elongated, always bringing the flour toward the middle and taking it equally from everywhere; the circle should remain as regular as possible, at least until all the liquid has been absorbed.

As the flour is brought into the well, mix it there *lightly* between the ends of your fingers, but without kneading it and without closing your fist, so that it runs out between your fingers. You are simply stirring with the ends of your fingers held together, using your thumb to crush the butter into the dough as you go and as you bring in the flour: that is all the work required here.

In 2 or 3 minutes for these quantities, all the flour should be mixed. At this point, you will have a shapeless mass with bits and pieces that have come loose. First scrape off your fingers; dip them in the extra flour to clean them better and drop all these scrapings into the dough. Also scrape the board, gathering all these scrapings into the dough.

Lightly sprinkle the board with flour. Dip your hands in the extra flour and gather the dough into a block or a ball, *always without kneading it.* This is to simply make it easier to pick up, because it will still stick to your hands and to the table, being rather soft. Do this for just 1 or 2 minutes. Do not worry about the state of the dough, which may be unequal: all this will disappear when the dough rises because of the fermentation.

Gather the dough with the dough scraper and then, lifting it in both hands, put it into an unfloured wooden bowl. Scrape up the little bit remaining on the board and then drop it onto the dough; it will even out by itself.

Cover the bowl, or even wrap it with a small covering. Put it in a place that is sheltered from any air currents, at a temperature of 18–20° Centigrade (64–68° Fahrenheit): you can check this by putting a thermometer there.

NOTE. In the winter, if the bowl has been kept in a cold place, it is a good idea to first heat the bowl slightly before putting in the dough. And in all seasons you must protect it with a covering, which will protect the dough from strong heat in the summer and from the cold in the winter. (A large wooden bowl with a rounded bottom helps the dough to rise; and the temperature is kept more constant in a wooden bowl than in a clay one, the dough rising best under these conditions).

Extreme temperatures are equally bad for brioche dough: the cold considerably retards the action of the yeast; it even prevents it. So bakeries always have a supply of brioche dough ready by keeping it on ice. And in the summertime, high temperatures make the butter sweat out, and then separate from the dough. For the first rising in particular it is essential to avoid excess heat.

Leavening the dough: *First rising. The dough must double in volume,* which will require about *4 hours of time* with the quantity of yeast indicated. Since these are small quantities here, the flared shape of the bowl will make it difficult to be sure how much the dough has increased in volume, something that would be easier if the dough were in a receptacle with straight sides. You will therefore have to estimate the acquired volume. If the dough has been prepared the day before in the evening, it will have risen as much as it can, and there will be no need to make a guess. When the dough is fully risen, the surface will be smooth and even and all the dips and tears will have disappeared; it will be a light, even-looking mass.

After this first rising, *punch down the dough:* make the dough return to its original volume. For this, *do not take it out of the bowl,* but simply put your hands all around the dough to pull it away from the walls of the bowl without turning it over, and push it right to the bottom. That's all. Immediately the dough will collapse as if deflated, leaving pleats on its surface; all this will disappear when it rises a second time. Again, cover the bowl and allow it to rise a second time.

Second rising. The dough must again reach double its original volume; in other words, rise as completely as it did the first time. But the rising will be more rapid this time around, and it may rise even more if you can let it stand at a temperature a little above 20° Centigrade (68° Fahrenheit). *Assume about 2 hours.* At the end of this second rising, turn your attention to the mold.

The mold: Molds known as "mousseline brioche" molds are much higher than they are wide. A mold appropriate for these quantities is made of tinned steel and measures 13 centimeters high (5 inches) and 11 centimeters ($4^1/_4$ inches) in diameter at the opening. It is a completely straight mold without handles.

But you can equally use a timbale mold or a charlotte mold if you add parchment paper to increase the height of the walls. *Always use a mold with straight sides,* preferably one made of tin-lined copper. Molds made of beaten steel, the old models, are too low and too flared: do not use them.

When you use a mousseline brioche or charlotte mold, it must always be lined with parchment paper inside to make unmolding the brioche easier. If you use a charlotte mold, the paper must, of course, extend beyond the edges of the mold, because the paper must make up for the fact that its sides are not tall enough. The parchment paper must be rather strong, since it will be the only support for the dough as it rises and cooks (for a true brioche mold, simple paper will suffice).

Let us assume that you use a small charlotte mold *made of tin-lined copper,* which in most cases is what you are likely to have instead of a mousseline brioche mold, which is pictured in our drawing (PAGE 576). For these quantities, it should be about 12 centimeters ($4^1/_2$ inches) in diameter and 8 centimeters ($3^1/_4$ inches) high.

First cut a band of parchment paper 20 centimeters (8 inches) high to go all around the sides. With scissors, cut a fringe all along one of the edges of the band.

Now place a piece of parchment paper on the bottom of the mold, and with the point of a knife trace the circumference of the bottom on it. Then, with your scissors, cut a perfectly round piece—cutting it smaller rather than larger—so that when you put it inside the mold it sits there easily and can easily be taken out.

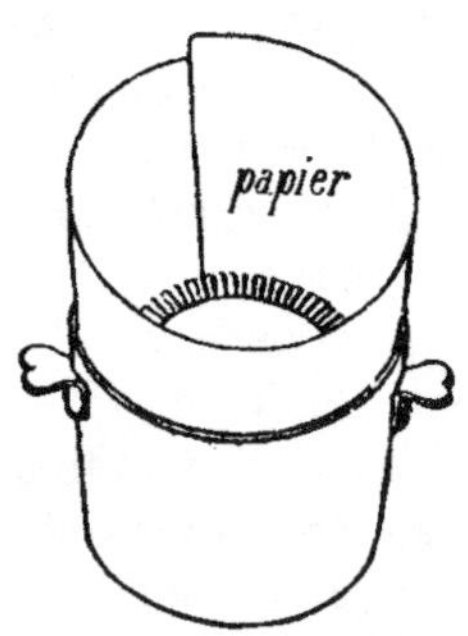

FIG. 79. LINING THE MOLD WITH PAPER.

Soak a large brush in butter by dipping it in unmelted butter, and then butter the band and the round of paper.

Place the fringed band in the mold, putting the side without butter against the mold (*fig.* 79). The fringed part should thus be touching the bottom of the mold. If one band is not large enough to make the entire round, you can add another piece that is also fringed, overlapping the other band on each side for more stability.

Once the band has been installed, place the round of paper at the bottom of the mold, as usual putting the side without butter against the mold.

To mold the brioche: The dough, once it has doubled in volume for a second time, is ready to be put in the mold to undergo a *third rising,* which is characteristic of a mousseline brioche.

But before molding it, you must work it gently. This work is done on a pastry board sprinkled with flour, or even on a large cloth that has also been floured, which is easier for handling this wet dough. A kitchen towel, which is rather strong and firm and can be stretched out on a table, is a lot easier than any other surface, on the condition that it does not have even the slightest odor; this is what professionals use today.

Sprinkle the towel with flour. Coat your hands with flour. Pour the dough from the bowl on the towel, using a dough scraper to help you. Work the dough for only a few moments in the following way *and without kneading it at all.* Always work with your fingers flat, like a spatula; that is the way to do it. First of all, with your fingers together and extended, tap lightly, making just a few small blows on the dough to flatten it out a bit, into a thick cake. Do this almost without pressing on it at all; since the dough is wet, it spreads out immediately. Then gather it into a ball—as well as you can given its consistency—always keeping your hands extended and the fingers together like spatulas. Tap it into place all around, not rolling the dough at all, but giving it little taps here and there, making the same movements that you would use, for example, to fluff up a piece of fabric on a store counter: this comparison gives an exact idea of the movements that must be made.

Tap for barely 2 or 3 minutes, and once the dough has been compacted and gathered together, immediately transfer it to the mold by sliding your hands under it. It is not important that the top is not smooth: the third rising will fix everything.

Lightly tap the mold on the table, not so much to even out the surface of the dough, because the rising will take care of that, but so the dough will be firmly lodged on the bottom of the mold and all around the sides.

Place the mold in a very well sheltered place with a temperature of at least 20° Centigrade (68° Fahrenheit).

The dough must again double in volume before being placed in the oven. It is extremely easy to check this in the mold; it is enough to compare the height to which the dough has risen against where it stood when it was placed in the mold.

Allow about 2 hours for this, but wait to put it in the oven until the dough has risen to the right point.

The more the dough rises in the mold, the more the brioche will be light and fine; the dough will subsequently rise less while cooking, but will then do so more evenly. It is therefore essential to wait for this last third rising to be *complete* before putting the mold in the oven.

Meanwhile, turn your attention to the oven, as directed (SEE THE OVEN, PAGE 655).

To glaze and put it in the oven: The temperature of the oven at the moment you put the mold into it must be such that after 5 minutes a sheet of white paper will have taken on a very light yellowish tinge: no more.

When the dough has risen *for the third time*—this time in the mold—glaze it before putting it in the oven. Place the mold on the table. Do not shake it too much because any movement will make the dough fall.

Dip a brush in beaten egg, both white and yolk. Brush it lightly over the dough without pressing, which would make the dough collapse, and do not add too much glaze there, because the brioche would brown too much while cooking.

Immediately afterward, take a large pair of scissors and dip it in hot water, then wipe it dry and make two large cuts in the shape of a cross: sink the blade of the scissors rather deeply, turning it in the dough before cutting, so that you enlarge the opening. Act rather quickly and carefully, because the dough will collapse if you take too long for this movement.

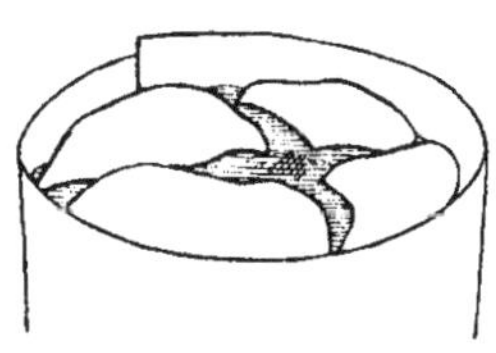

FIG. 80. CUTS IN THE DOUGH.

This double cutting helps the heat reach from the top down into the middle of the dough (*fig.* 80). Let us repeat here that you must do this very quickly and just before putting it in the oven.

Then quickly put the mold in the oven, placing it either on a round *tourtière* or baking sheet in heavy steel. This plate also protects the bottom of the mold from the strong heat coming from the bottom, and enables you easily to turn the mold while cooking without any sharp movements.

To cook: For a brioche of this size, assume *40 minutes.*

Constantly check the brioche by opening the oven door a little bit, taking just the amount of time needed to glance in without cooling the oven. About *4–5 minutes* after putting the mold in the oven, check to see what has happened to the dough: it should have swollen a little bit more, or, at any rate, it should have regained its height, which is likely to have fallen due to the incision. If it is already colored a little bit, this is because the oven is too hot on top. In this case, it would be sensible to place a paper on top of the mold, not buttered but *moistened* (SEE PAGE 656).

Toward the end of the cooking, let the heat diminish a little; otherwise, the brioche will be too darkly colored before it finishes cooking. Before taking out the brioche, pierce it with a kitchen needle, leaving it there for *7–8 seconds.* Immediately afterward, apply the point of this needle to the back of your left hand; if the needle burns you, the brioche is cooked. If not, leave it for a few more moments in the oven.

In general, it is a bad idea to leave the brioche in the oven any longer than is necessary: the dough will dry out and all the moisture that makes it tender will evaporate.

So, as soon as it is cooked, take the mold out of the oven. Immediately unmold the brioche and remove its paper, then place it on a rack or a little basket so that the air circulates under it.

It may be that the circumference of the brioche is not colored enough, an unfortunate result that is due, in particular, to an oven in which the heat is unequally dispersed. In this case, unmold the brioche and remove its paper, then lay it down on a rack and put it back in the oven: the heat, which is always stronger on the top in this type of oven, will then strike the pale part. Make sure you turn the brioche gradually, watching as it colors, and never leaving it beyond a few minutes, because you must always avoid drying out the interior.

Crown Brioche *(Brioche en Couronne).* The quantity of dough required for a mousseline brioche can easily be increased for a crown brioche. We have said that in home ovens you must never try to cook too large a piece of pastry, because the heat there is not sufficiently even. But the crown brioche, large as it is, is the exception. You can increase the diameter, but the thickness of the crown should always be about the same. It follows that a crown brioche made with 450 grams (1 pound) or with 225 grams (8 ounces) of flour will require no more time for the first than for the second, because it is only the thickness of the cake is that is critical, and not its larger diameter. *Cooking a crown brioche requires a very hot oven.*

PROCEDURE. **The dough:** This should be prepared exactly as directed for the mousseline brioche with this small, unique modification: to make it less moist, it is a good idea to slightly reduce the quantity of liquid; handling the dough after this, to shape it into a crown, will be much easier as a result. For example, for the quantity given for the mousseline brioche, you should assume 3/4 deciliter (2 1/2 fluid ounces, scant 1/3 cup) of water *per 450 grams (1 pound)* of flour to make a crown brioche instead of the full deciliter (3 1/3 fluid ounces, 1/2 cup). Here will use the same quantity of dough as for the MOUSSELINE BRIOCHE (PAGE 680).

The dough should have risen twice in the wooden bowl; and completely risen—that is, it should have doubled in volume, as explained for a mousseline brioche. So we will pick it up here, just when it has risen a second time and is now being lightly worked on the table. At this point, *rather than transfer it into a mold, you make it into a crown.*

To clarify, let us pick up our dough just at the last directions, which say "Tap for barely 2 or 3 minutes, and once the dough has been compacted. . . ." Now instead, fashion it into a ball, rolling it lightly between your two floured hands. Do not hesitate to flour the board or the towel several times, particularly in the summer.

The baking sheet should be prepared as before.

The sheet: Made of thick black steel, rounded and with a very small border. The size is not important. If you like, you can put two small crowns on one large sheet, as long as it can go into the oven, and above all *be able to turn there easily.* Whatever sheet you use, it must be completely *smooth* (SEE BAKING SHEETS, PAGE 656).

Grease it lightly with butter. Keep it ready on the table. It must be *absolutely cold,* because even if it is only slightly warm, the dough will run.

To form the crown or circle: Once your dough has been gathered into a ball, thoroughly scrape the board or the towel and sprinkle them with flour. Dip the middle finger and the index finger of your right hand into the flour. Stick them right into the middle of the ball to make a hole right down through to the bottom. Enlarge this hole by simply moving your two fingers inside the hole while turning the dough on the board. It is essential that the board or the towel be always lightly coated with flour while doing this, so that the dough does not stick.

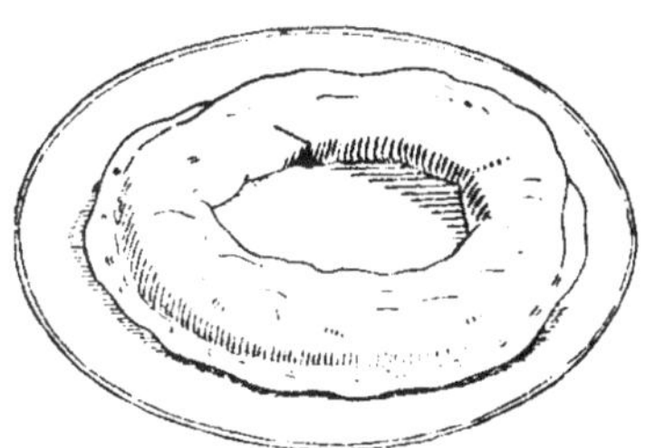

FIG. 81. THE RING OF DOUGH.

Once the hole has been properly formed in the ball, let the dough rest for only 2 or 3 minutes. Then, with your hands dipped in flour, gradually enlarge the hole to make a crown or ring of an even thickness and with the diameter of a sausage. Before transferring it to a baking sheet, the crown must more or less be the right size, because once it is on the sheet it is too late to correct it.

Lift the dough ring with both hands and transfer it to the sheet. Correct the shape with the tips of your fingers; the inside diameter, for this quantity of dough, should be about 14 centimeters (5 1/2 inches). Always using the ends of your fingers, lightly press on the *outer* edge of the ring to thin it out on the sheet, thus forming a small flat strip in which the imprint of your fingers leaves a kind of design (*fig.* 81).

After this, leave the sheet and the dough in a place sheltered from air currents, at a temperature of 20° Centigrade (68° Fahrenheit) for *30–40 minutes.* During this time, the dough will begin to rise, but the effect is not considerable; you only notice it because the surface of the dough bubbles and roughs up a little bit.

To glaze: Just before putting it in the oven, glaze with a large, flat brush dipped in beaten egg (both the white and the yolk), diluted with a little bit of water. Brush it lightly on the dough.

Take a large pair of scissors. Dip it in warm water, because when it is warm it will not stick to the dough; dry it off and make some cuts in the ring halfway up the height of the dough (*fig.* 82).

These slashes are meant to ensure that the heat penetrates rapidly into the dough, and also to decorate the brioche. For this second reason, do not limit yourself to cutting straight in front of you; this will produce blisters in the shape of unattractive slots. Make the slashes or cuts in the shape of a crescent, and to get them proceed as follows: stick one blade of the scissors into the dough just above the little decorated strip. Using *only* this blade, and while keeping the scissors completely open, cut halfway through the dough, making the outline of a crescent; do not close the scissors to cut the dough until the first blade, which is the only one you have used so far, has reached the inside edge of the circle. This will produce the right cut.

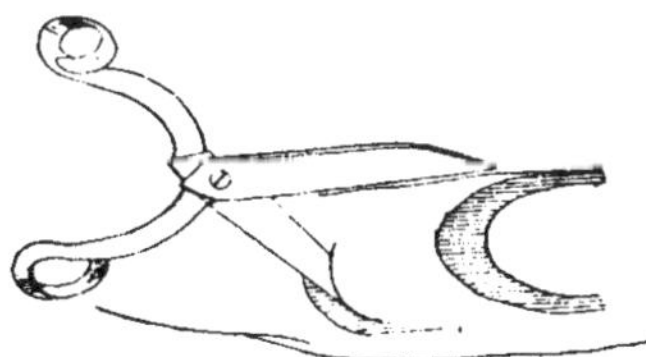

FIG. 82. CUTTING THE DOUGH.

Immediately put the baking sheet and the brioche into the oven.

Cooking it: The temperature of the oven must be much higher for a crown or ring brioche than for a mousseline brioche. A white paper put into the oven should be noticeably brown after *only 1 minute.*

A *very hot* oven is essential to seize the crown so that it keeps its shape. Later, you lower the temperature so that the color is not too strong.

If the oven is not hot enough, the dough will spread out and the brioche will lose its shape and thickness; then you will have to leave the brioche for longer in the oven; and the moisture of the dough will evaporate, and the brioche will no longer be tender.

Depending on the strength of your oven, place the baking sheet either on the steel shelf dividing the oven in two, which will bring the dough closer to the heat at the top of the oven, or directly on the bottom of the oven. In the latter case, remove the steel shelf, which would prevent the strong heat from reaching the top of the dough.

If the brioche seems to be coloring too much, protect it with moistened parchment paper.

Monitor the brioche by opening the oven door a little bit after a minute to glance inside. Turn the baking sheet quite often if the oven does not heat evenly on all sides.

To be successful, a brioche made with the quantities suggested here must not bake for more than *a good 15 minutes.* At this point, test it with a kitchen needle; it should be properly cooked and the color should be dark enough.

Remove it from the sheet and place it on a cake rack when you take it out of the oven. If the oven heats too strongly from the bottom, the bottom of the brioche will undoubtedly be a little bit too brown; what's more, the odor of burning should have alerted you during the final minutes of cooking. So, while the dough is still burning hot, use the blade of a large knife to rapidly scrape the bottom of the ring to remove this darkened layer. Then with a soft, very clean brush or a very dry kitchen brush, brush away any burned parts that might have fallen into the ring's crevices when scraped.

Kugelhopf *(Kugelhopf)*

In Alsace, this excellent cake maintains an important place in home pastry cooking, and it is now very popular in other places, under the name of "Cougloff." Depending on the region in Alsace, the recipes vary in terms of the quantities and procedures, but the ingredients remain the same, always producing a leavened dough, like a brioche, which is cooked in an earthenware mold of the same special shape, as sold by all pottery merchants.

The quantities given below are appropriate for a mold with a capacity of 2 liters (8½ cups)—known as a number 3—measuring 20 centimeters (8 inches) at the opening, not including the border. If the cake is to be served alone, this is a good size for 6–8 people. Do you think you will be serving other cakes and tarts as well? In that case, this will serve double that number of people. *Time: 3 hours. Serves 6–8.*

370 grams (13 ounces) of the best flour; 170 grams (6 ounces, ¾ cup) of butter; 40 grams (1⅜ ounces) of superfine sugar; 10–25 grams (⅓–1 ounce) of cake yeast (assume 30 grams/1 full ounce per 450 grams/ 1 pound of flour); 5 grams (⅙ ounce) of salt; 4 nice eggs; 1½ deciliters (5 fluid ounces, ⅔ cup) of milk, just lukewarm; 100 grams (3½ ounces) of Málaga raisins (optional); about 30 dry sweet almonds.

Kirsch is used in some recipes: 1 good tablespoon for the quantities indicated.

NOTE. In Alsace, they use liquid beer yeast. Since this is difficult to get except in the east and north, it is replaced by yeast in dry cakes, whose action is also quite rapid.

PROCEDURE. **The mold:** This is quite special, so we provide an illustration (see *fig.* 68, PAGE 576). *Made of ovenproof earthenware,* with a central cylinder known as an interior chimney, this mold lets the heat of the oven act simultaneously on all the parts of the dough and cook the inside of the cake in a short time, which would otherwise take longer in another type of mold. If you must, you could use a metal mold; but a mold made of ovenproof earthenware, which is always used in Alsace, is much better: the dough rises more effectively there, and also cooks better, because the thickness of the earthenware mold favors an even cooking temperature.

Another advantage: when cooked in an earthenware mold, the cake takes on a beautiful, special tint, with a thin and smooth crust as if it were lacquered, which a metal mold cannot provide. These earthenware molds for Kugelhopf are sold by all the kitchenware merchants who also sell large pieces of glassware. Let us also point out that a new earthenware mold sometimes has a flaw: it may not unmold well, and some parts of the crust will stick to the mold, which you will then have to remove in order to stick them more, or less, successfully onto the cake. Also, home kitchens often have molds that have been used for a long time and are likely to be marked inside with many small cracks.

If you need to use a new mold, first boil it for a good half hour in water that has either baking soda or potash dissolved in it. Next, rinse the mold and soak it in warm water. Dry it thoroughly, then generously coat the inside with butter or any *odorless fat.* After this, put it in the oven for 10 minutes, and if you like, for another 10 minutes again before using it.

PROCEDURE. Mixing the dough is done in the same way as for brioche, with the difference that it is done in a terrine or, which is preferable, in a wooden pastry bowl.

So that the fermentation begins as soon as the dough is finished, have all the ingredients at a *lukewarm* temperature, including the terrine used for mixing the dough. In the middle of summer, this will be room temperature; in other seasons, you will have to take some precautions, which are extremely important.

In cool weather or in winter, warm the terrine in advance by standing it for a moment in hot water, and then very carefully wipe it dry. You can also warm the *mold* in the same way, avoiding getting it wet on the inside. The *eggs,* if they come straight from the pantry, must also be warmed in advance: it takes longer to warm the inside, so immerse them in water just warm enough to take the chill off, leaving them there for 7–8 minutes. If the flour is stored in a cool place, spread it out on a piece of paper that has been slightly warmed, or store it somewhere in the kitchen where it is warmer. Bring the butter to the same lukewarm temperature before you use it, cut into pieces.

The almonds: Husk them. Cut them in half, and then divide them into three or four strips lengthwise. Spread them out on a tart pan to dry them out in the oven *without coloring* (SEE ALMONDS, PAGE 573).

The mold: With a kitchen brush or simply a feather dipped into half-melted butter, thoroughly paint inside the mold so that the sides are coated with a good layer. This butter should have been clarified to remove its whey, and if you are not certain that it is pure, melt it in a cup and allow it sit to eliminate the casein; otherwise, the whey could make the dough stick to the walls.

Once this butter has been decanted, allow it to cool partly before buttering the mold. If it were warm, only a thin layer would stick to the walls; the almonds, which you are going to apply, would not stay in place, and ultimately the cake itself might stick there.

Scatter the almond strips against these thoroughly buttered walls. To decorate the cake and make it more attractive, you can also place some almond halves all around the bottom of the mold.

The Málaga raisins: Remove their stems. Cut the largest ones in half or thirds, depending on their size. Carefully take out the seeds with the point of a small kitchen knife.

The dough: Sift the flour into the terrine. Make the well, then put in the salt and sugar. Dilute the yeast in a small cup with 1–2 tablespoons of milk that is just *lukewarm:* any warmer, and it would burn the yeast; pour everything into the well. Add the eggs to it, as well as the butter, previously softened (SEE PAGE 657). Mix it exactly as directed for the brioche. Finally, mix in the raisins.

As soon as the dough is finished, put it into the mold. The best thing is to put it directly in there by tipping it out of the terrine and into the mold; the dough will run out of it easily, and so that you lose nothing you can push it out with a pastry scraper or with a spoon. While doing this, make sure that you avoid blocking up the small central hole of the chimney. The dough must fill the mold by a little more than half, but not by as much as two-thirds: it is going to rise *before* cooking, and in the oven it will rise even more.

Then put the mold in a warm place, either on a shelf above the stove or in some other place, as long as the temperature is *at least 25° Centigrade (77° Fahrenheit)* and there are no problems with air currents. If the temperature reaches as high as 30° Centigrade (86° Fahrenheit), so much the better. However, you do not want it any warmer than that, which would be a double disadvantage: the dough would break down and fail to rise, and the butter would run down the walls of the mold. In the summer, the temperature of the kitchen should be enough to make all this trouble unnecessary; even so, make sure you always leave the mold sheltered from air currents. You can also protect it with a piece of cloth or a large kitchen towel folded in half.

You can tell when the dough has risen to its proper point because once it has inflated into a dome, the surface will begin to *chap and crack.* At this point, it should have reached the top of the mold—assuming you are using an earthenware mold of the size suggested—and be level with the edge. At this point of fermentation you must put it in the oven; left any longer, the dough would liquefy. Instead of rising, it would spread out, and while cooking it would bubble and spill out over the mold. Place the mold on a round sheet, either a *tourtière* or any heavy metal sheet, which will protect the bottom of the mold from direct heat when you stand it on the bottom of the oven; this will also allow you to move the mold more easily without shaking it up too much: you turn the sheet without touching the mold.

The *oven temperature* must be a good medium heat. A piece of white parchment paper should have taken on a very light yellow tint after 10 minutes.

To cook: After you have put it in the oven, the dough will rise more. If, after a moment, you notice that it is rising more on one side than another, turn the cake 180°. On the other hand, if the heat is too strong from above and causes the surface of the dough to color too rapidly, place a piece of parchment paper on top, moistened and, if necessary, remoistened. Above all, it is important that the dough does not brown, because this crust would thicken, making it difficult for the heat to reach inside: the cake would be heavy as a result. Do not open the oven too often, and do it quickly. Toward the end of cooking—that is, at the end of 45 minutes—reduce the heat a little bit. For the quantities given, assume *a good hour for cooking.*

The cake is perfectly done when it is firm to the touch and comes away easily from the mold. Ensure that nothing sticks around the circumference and turn the mold over on the table, then slide the blade of a knife into the opening of the chimney of the mold to remove any dough stuck there, which would make it difficult to release the cake from the mold. Then place the kugelhopf on a rack or drum sieve to allow it to cool. If you like, you could sprinkle it with confectioners' sugar.

Savarin *(Savarin)*

The savarin is valued both as a cake and as a base for numerous desserts, where it is used as a border. It is not "syruped"—that is, basted with its own characteristic syrup—until the moment that it is served or sold. It is normal practice today in all bakeries and professional kitchens to cook it well in advance, the evening before or even two evenings before. If you do this, you must first put it in a moderate oven for a moment to soften it before basting it with the lukewarm syrup.

The procedure we give below for making it is, like that for brioche, quite modern, and greatly simplifies working the dough, while still producing a perfect result. *Time: About 3 hours for preparing the dough, letting it ferment and rise, and then cooking it. Makes a mold 26 centimeters (10 1/2 inches) in diameter.*

250 grams (8 7/8 ounces) of fine wheat flour; 10 grams (1/3 ounce) of yeast in cake form; 1 deciliter (3 1/3 fluid ounces, scant 1/2 cup) of *not boiled* milk, just lukewarm; 3 good-size eggs, or 4 little ones; 75 grams (2 2/3 ounces, 1/3 cup) of butter; 15 grams (1/2 ounce) of superfine sugar; 5 grams (1/6 ounce) of salt; a half-dozen husked and chopped almonds.

***For the syrup:* 150 grams (5 1/3 ounces) of sugar cubes; 2 1/2 deciliters (1 cup) of water; 1 scant deciliter (3 1/3 fluid ounces, scant 1/2 cup) of kirsch; the same amount of orgeat syrup.**

PROCEDURE. Sift the flour into a wooden bowl (SEE BRIOCHE, NOTE, PAGE 681) or if you do not have one, a warmed terrine. Make the well. Put in the yeast; dilute it with 1/2 deciliter (1 2/3 fluid ounces, scant 1/4 cup) of milk, using only the index finger of your right hand. Then in the same way, bring in the flour gradually, just enough to obtain a light mush. With your hand, *lightly* fold the flour into this batter. Leave the bowl uncovered on the table.

After 5–7 minutes, examine the flour mixture. It should be chapped or cracked like a moleskin because of the action of the yeast. When it has reached this state, add the eggs all at one time, after having first broken them into a bowl.

First, mix everything with the end of your fingers, then add a little bit of lukewarm milk: 1–2 tablespoons. Then work the dough, taking it in handfuls for 2 minutes. Again pour in 1 tablespoon of milk; again, work it with your hand. In all, work it for no more than *5–6 minutes.*

Using a pastry scraper or a card, scrape off your fingers and carefully loosen everything from the sides of the bowl, mixing everything back with the rest of the dough—that is, mix in all the fragments of dough that have been left on the sides of the bowl while you were doing this work. Otherwise, the dough would dry there, and then form lumps in the mass.

Cover the bowl. Put it somewhere completely sheltered from any air currents, in a place where the temperature reaches 25–30° Centigrade (77–86° Fahrenheit). Under these conditions, the dough will rise in *30–35 minutes.* The dough should have more or less doubled in volume. This is the moment to finish it with butter, salt, and sugar.

The butter: Melt it into a liquid, heating it in a little saucepan. Do not bother decanting it from the whey on the bottom. Pour it *lukewarm* into the middle of the dough at the same time that you add the sugar and the salt. Toss everything together three or four times; then, using your hand as a shovel, turn over the dough to mix it, while using your other hand to turn the bowl, always moving the dough from the edges toward the center, toward you. Incorporating the butter requires a little less than 5 minutes. The dough should take on a thick consistency; when it no longer sticks to the bowl and can be raised in one piece, the work is done. It is time to mold it.

To mold it: Use a classic unadorned ring mold (see *fig.* 68, PAGE 576). Butter it in advance with melted butter, spreading it out with a brush. Sprinkle the chopped almonds on the bottom.

Pick up the dough one piece at a time, breaking it with your fingers, and transfer it to the mold, evening out its thickness. Fill it halfway to allow room for the dough to rise due to the fermentation. Pastry bakers generally only fill the mold by one-third, leaving two-thirds empty for the dough to rise.

Again, stand the mold at a temperature of 25–30° Centigrade (77–86° Fahrenheit), sheltered from all air currents. The dough must reach the top edge of the mold. Depending on the temperature, the strength and freshness of the yeast, etc., the time for rising can vary from a half hour to 1 hour, and even longer. As soon as it has reached the top edge of the mold, the savarin must be put into the oven. The dough has a tendency to expand toward the center, so it is sensible at this time to put a chimney made of a simple white piece of rolled-up parchment paper inside the mold.

Cooking it: The oven must be at a medium heat, as for a mousseline brioche, and the heat must come mainly from the bottom.

After 5 minutes, the dough should rise. If it is already colored and a crust has formed, which means that the temperature of the oven is a little too strong, immediately cover the cake with a sheet of moistened paper. Remove the paper chimney as soon as the dough has firmed up, which would be after about 10 minutes.

Allow about 35–40 minutes for cooking.

Unmold the savarin immediately on a rack placed over a *shallow bowl,* bearing in mind that it will be basted only when it is lukewarm.

The syrup: Put the sugar with the lukewarm water in a small saucepan. Boil for *1 minute.* When this syrup is no more than *lukewarm,* add the kirsch and the orgeat. Using a small ladle, generously baste the savarin, which should be only lukewarm, as explained. The savarin must absorb as much of the syrup as possible.

If you prepare the syrup in advance, preserve the flavor of the liqueurs by adding them to the syrup only just before using it, after you have brought it to lukewarm temperature.

Baba *(Baba).* What distinguishes this cake from a savarin, which uses the same dough, is the addition of Corinth and Smyrna raisins. Thus, for the quantities of savarin dough, add 75 grams (2 2/3 ounces) of raisins to the dough before molding it. Some authors also suggest using candied fruits, chopped or minced into very small pieces, but that is the exception.

The mold to use is an angel food mold (or circular mold) that has a hollow center and is tall with decorated sides. The flavor of rum is characteristic of the baba; for the basting syrup, use the same quantities of sugar and liquid as for the savarin: that is, 3 deciliters (1 1/4 cups) of water and 1 deciliter (3 1/3 fluid ounces, scant 1/2 cup) of rum.

Prepare the dough in exactly of the same way as for a savarin. Place it in the same buttered mold, only half-filling it; let it rise until it reaches the top of the mold; put a paper chimney inside the mold. Cook the baba and baste it with syrup, as directed for the savarin.

Northern Cake *(Gâteau du Nord)*

It is from the region of the Artois, and our Flemish regions, that this kind of cake reaches us. Today it is frequently sold in the major pastry and bakery shops in Paris, and it is very popular for breakfast and for snacks. It is excellent hot, straight out of the oven, with tea and chocolate. It keeps very well and is even good when several days old. These factors, together with the fact that it is very simple and sells at a very reasonable price, means that it stands in the first rank of recipes for home pastry-making.

If you like, make the cake as a large ball and put it directly into the oven like this; or it can be cooked in a rectangular mold in the shape of a baguette, which is particularly recommended because it allows the cake to be divided into nice regular slices. If you do not have a rectangular mold with hinges and pins and no bottom, like those used by pastry bakers, you can use a simple steel loaf pan of the same size: that is, for the quantities given below, about 10 centimeters (4 inches) high, 10 centimeters (4 inches) wide, and 25 centimeters (10 inches) long. The small interior ridge of the loaf pan will make it impossible to unmold the cake, so either flatten it with a few blows of a hammer or cover it with a thin band of paper, sticking it down with a little bit of butter. *Time: About 4 hours for preparing the dough and letting it rise, and then cooking the cake. Makes 1 kilogram (2 pounds, 4 ounces) of cake.*

500 grams (1 pound, 2 ounces) of flour; 180–200 grams (6 1/3–7 ounces, 3/4 cup–14 tablespoons) of butter; 12 grams (3/8 ounce) of salt; 25 grams (1 ounce) of superfine sugar; 1 deciliter (3 1/3 fluid ounces, scant 1/2 cup) of milk; 20 grams (2/3 ounce) of yeast in cake form; 3 nice eggs; 150 grams (5 1/3 fluid ounces) of Smyrna raisins.

PROCEDURE. Heat the milk; put 2 tablespoons in a little cup that you will use to dilute the yeast, but only when this milk is no more than *scarcely lukewarm.*

Pour the rest of the warm milk into a bowl; immediately add the butter, divided into small pieces, to melt in it.

In a wooden mixing bowl (SEE BRIOCHE, NOTE, PAGE 681) or, if you do not have one, in a warm earthenware terrine, place the flour; make a well. Add the salt and the sugar and the eggs. With the ends of the fingers of your right hand, break the eggs and mix them first with a little bit of flour; next, and while you continue to mix rapidly, pour the melted butter in *very gently,* pouring it in a thin stream over your fingers that are working the dough. Finally, add the well-diluted yeast. Forcefully knead the dough by squeezing it between your fingers. Use only your right hand, until it no longer sticks to the terrine or to your fingers, and can be picked up in one single piece.

Remove the mass of dough from the terrine and place it on the board, where it must be worked *just like bread,* by forcefully throwing the ball of dough onto to the board several times, or onto a table covered with a towel; or by rolling the dough into a large sausage, one end of which you grab and beat strongly against the table or the board. The reason for this is to get the dough to absorb air and become lighter; whichever way you decide to work the dough, lift it up quite high each time in one piece and then throw it down strongly onto the table. Only when you have done this should you add the raisins to the dough, because otherwise they would be forced out of it.

To let the dough rise: Put the dough back into the wooden bowl or heated terrine, which should first have been lightly sprinkled with flour. Cover it completely with a cloth. Keep it at a temperature of about 25° Centigrade (77° Fahrenheit). The dough must double in volume: allow at least *2 hours for this, and do not wait for cracks or crevices to appear on the surface,* but immediately remove the dough from the terrine and place it on the board or the table; twist it and stretch it with your hands, which will stop the fermentation and instantly return the dough to its original volume. Then mold it in the following way.

To mold the dough: Place the dough in one large block to the mold, where it will spread out by itself. It must not fill the mold by more than *one-third.* On the mold, mark the maximum height to which it should rise, and allow *about 1 hour for this.* Cover the mold and keep it at the same temperature as before.

If the cake is not molded: with both hands, roll the dough into a ball and place it on the steel baking sheet that will go in the oven. Cover it with a light cloth and keep it at the same temperature as for the first rising. Like the molded cake, let it rise by only one-third this time.

Cooking it: As soon as it has risen, put it in a good medium oven, with a heat that comes mainly from below. If you like, you can first glaze the cake with a little bit of milk or egg white.

As soon as the surface of the dough begins to form a crust, cover it with parchment paper. Allow *1 hour of cooking* for a molded cake; 15 minutes less for an unmolded one. In the oven, the dough rises more strongly during the second part of the cooking than the first. The cake is correctly cooked when it comes away from the mold and feels firm to the touch. Do not unmold it until 10 minutes after taking it out of the oven, to allow it to settle a little bit, which will ensure its stability. Finally, place it on a rack or a drum sieve, which will help the steam to evaporate.

Plum Cake *(Plum-Cake)*

This cake probably has the largest number of recipes, both in England and in France. Its ingredients are always the same, but the quantities are extremely variable, if economy is an issue. And the procedures for mixing these same ingredients can also be different.

True English plum cake never rises very high. Whatever the size of the cake—that is, whatever its weight—a true English plum cake is scarcely more than 7 centimeters (2³/₄ inches) high. If you do not have an appropriate mold, and if you use a simple charlotte mold, you must be careful not to put in too thick a layer of dough; this would affect the lightness of the cake.

The great pitfall of this kind of cake is that the raisins may not rise evenly while baking. For this, there are many reasons: too much heat from below, which causes the butter to melt and the dough to liquefy, so that the raisins fall to the bottom and form a layer, from which they never rise again. Also, too little heat: the dough slackens, and after cooking the butter sets to wax.

The following recipe is based on an equal quantity of flour and butter; it is therefore not an economical recipe. For 450 grams (1 pound), it includes 12 eggs, a good average, because even the richest plum cakes do not use more than 16 eggs. This recipe is one of the most used in the best bakeries today. The cake lasts perfectly for more than a week. *Time: 1 hour–1 hour, 15 minutes for cooking. Makes a plum cake of about 600 grams (1 pound, 5 ounces).*

125 grams (4¹/₂ ounces) of excellent wheat flour; 125 grams (4¹/₂ ounces, 9 tablespoons) of good fresh butter; 125 grams (4¹/₂ ounces) of superfine sugar; 125 grams (4¹/₂ ounces) of Smyrna and Corinth raisins, half and half; 25 grams (1 ounce) of candied orange peel; 3 nice eggs; 3 grams (¹/₁₀ ounce) of baking powder; 2 tablespoons of rum.

PROCEDURE. Before doing anything else, attend to the oven (SEE PAGE 655). When you put the cake in, it must be at a good medium heat, and completely even throughout.

Clean the raisins (SEE PAGE 573). Put them in a bowl with the orange peel cut into small dice not larger than the smallest Corinth raisins; baste with the rum. Toss them from time to time. *Leave them to macerate this way for as long as possible; the more they have swollen, the better they will spread out and be supported by the dough.* For this reason, we insist on the necessity of macerating the fruit for a very long time.

Prepare the *mold.* Tin-lined copper is always preferable to ensure the cake cooks evenly. If you do not have anything available except a charlotte mold, make sure it is large enough so that this quantity of dough will spread out wide over the bottom. So, for the quantities given above, use a charlotte mold with a capacity of 1¹/₂ liters (6¹/₃ cups). What is also important is that the walls be good and straight, because it is difficult to line the interior with paper in a mold that is slightly flared.

Using good, heavy uncoated paper, cut a round that is wider than the bottom of the mold by at least 1 centimeter (3/8 inch). Also cut a band that can go all around the circumference of the mold, to the right height. *Lightly* heat the mold. With the end of your finger or with a brush, rub a little walnut-size piece of butter all over the interior; the butter should maintain the consistency of a pomade so that it makes the paper adhere. Carefully butter the angle at the bottom. Then apply the round, folding up the surplus. Press down on the middle and chase out the bubbles of air to the edges that form under the paper, which would swell up under the dough while cooking. Apply the band around the mold. It need not go higher than the top edge if you are using a charlotte mold of the size we have suggested for these quantities.

Lay out a large piece of parchment paper on the table. Place the drum sieve over it. Pour in the *flour.* To mix it better, add the baking powder. Strain everything by tapping the drum sieve. Leave it on the paper.

The dough: Use an earthenware terrine, or a large salad bowl, in which you can easily work the dough with a large wooden spoon. Add the *butter* in a pomade, as directed (SEE PAGE 16). Then mix in the *sugar,* turning the spoon in any direction. The mixture whitens, but it will not harden. Allow *7–8 minutes* of this work for these quantities.

Then add the *eggs.* In the winter, take them out in advance to warm in the kitchen, because very cold eggs will harden the butter, making the work more difficult. Or you can easily return them to the right temperature by immersing them for several minutes in some water that is a little more than lukewarm.

Add them *one by one,* the white and yolk at the same time, at intervals of 3 minutes. Beat the dough vigorously throughout, lifting it up rather high with a spoon so that it can absorb air and become lighter. (In the winter, after you have added the eggs, the dough may clump and fall apart from the cold; simply reheat the terrine in water that is slightly more than lukewarm, continuing all the while to work the dough, which will gradually regain its homogeneous consistency.)

Immediately afterward, mix in the *raisins* and their little bit of liquid without working the dough.

Finally, add the *flour,* pouring it in a shower *gradually,* by shaking the parchment paper above the terrine. For this, it is better to have the help of another person, if possible. Otherwise, if you have to work the mixture by yourself, you should do it as follows: Use a large wooden spatula, or if you do not have one, a piece of rather firm card; as the flour falls, split the dough with the spatula or the card, as if it were the blade of a knife, placing it right in the center of the terrine. Go all the way to the bottom; then turn over the spatula to raise as much of the dough possible, and throw this dough back down on the flour. During this time, with your left hand, slowly turn the terrine, and immediately put the card or spatula back into the center of the dough, using the same movement. In effect, this is exactly the movement used for mixing egg whites into a snow (SEE PAGE 8), until the flour has been completely absorbed in the mixture. This gives you rather a compact mass.

Immediately pour it into the prepared mold. To distribute the dough evenly, strike it very gently on the table (covered with a kitchen towel folded into four, which softens the shock). The irregularities on the surface from the bits scraped off the sides of the terrine are not important and will disappear in cooking. Put it in the oven immediately, after removing the metal shelf that divides the oven in half.

To cook: At the beginning, avoid *too strong a heat from the bottom.* Place the cake as high as possible in the oven; you should be able to touch the shelf with the end of your fingers without burning yourself. Otherwise, you must put the mold on a thick metal *tourtière* that is *cold.*

After *7–8 minutes,* the dough should have evenly risen. The inequalities will have leveled out, any small bumps simply indicating where the raisins are. Then cover the mold with parchment paper folded into quarters, soaked in water and then shaken. The dough will continue to rise evenly. After *about 20 minutes,* when it has finished rising, you no longer need to worry about the heat from the bottom affecting the raisins. You can now increase the heat of the oven a little.

Remove the moistened paper after the first crust has formed, which is usually produced toward the middle of the baking, so that the part that has risen can brown like the rest of the cake.

Allow a total of 1–1¼ hours of cooking for these quantities. During the last 20 minutes, reduce the heat a little. The cake is perfectly cooked when it is firm to the touch. A kitchen needle stuck into the center of the cake must come out of it burning hot.

Let the cake cool almost completely in the mold. Be careful not to detach the paper from it while it is still warm, because the paper helps prevent the dough from shrinking; with scissors, cut the edges of it into pointed teeth, and do not remove it until you serve the cake, *after it has completely cooled.*

Another Recipe for Plum Cake *(Autre Formule de Plum-Cake).* *This is also highly recommended:* the dough of this one is more dense, containing less egg than in the previous recipe. Its preparation is simple, and it has the advantage of distributing the raisins equally in the cake while it is cooking. *Time: 15 minutes to prepare the dough; 2 hours of rest; 1 hour of cooking.*

> **150 grams (5⅓ ounces) of fine wheat flour; 100 grams (3½ ounces, 7 tablespoons) of butter; 125 grams (4½ ounces) of Corinth raisins and 125 grams (4½ ounces) of Smyrna raisins; 20 grams (⅔ ounce) of superfine sugar; 5 grams (⅙ ounce) of baking powder; 2 whole eggs; 3 tablespoons of milk and ½ tablespoon of rum; if you like, add 1 tablespoon of candied orange peel and the same of citron, cut into very small pieces.**

PROCEDURE. Sift the flour and the baking powder into a terrine. Combine the butter with it, previously softened (SEE PAGE 657). Vigorously knead everything with the ends of the fingers of your right hand until the butter has been completely absorbed into the flour.

Into this sandy dough, add immediately: the raisins, cleaned as directed (SEE PAGE 573); orange and citron; sugar and baking powder, previously combined in a saucer by mixing with the ends of your fingers. Thoroughly mix all the ingredients. After this, gradually pour the beaten eggs into the dough with the rum and the milk, mixing it all together as you go with a large wooden spoon. Vigorously beat the dough, lifting the spoon high, until it has the well-bound consistency of a thick mayonnaise.

Then *allow the dough to rest at a moderate temperature for 2 hours.* This resting is of fundamental importance, because it allows the raisins to gradually absorb moisture from the dough, which results in their equal distribution in the cake when cooking. You can let this dough rest for longer, but you must not try to shorten the time.

Then pour the dough into the mold, prepared as directed for the previous recipe, and with the same capacity. Proceed exactly the same way for cooking.

Savoy Cake or Sponge Cake *(Biscuit de Savoie)*

This batter is the type that professionals call "biscuit batter." The proportion of the ingredients of sponge cake does not vary: all the authors fix it at 375 grams (13¼ ounces) of a mixture of flour and starch, and 14 eggs for 500 grams (1 pound, 2 ounces) of superfine sugar. But it is essential to note the size of the eggs used, which determines their number: the quantity given assumes eggs of a medium size, weighing at least 50–55 grams (1¾–2 ounces). If the eggs are smaller, increase their number proportionally.

The flour must be particularly dry for this recipe; if not, it mixes badly. You must, before sifting it, spread it out on a sheet of paper and dry it in a very moderate oven—without coloring, of course.

The starch to use is rice starch, sold in small packages as "cream of rice," or you can use potato starch.

The sugar to use is superfine sugar, the finest possible.

The kind of molds to use are the special Savoy sponge cake molds. They are shaped like a dome, rather elevated compared to the base, and decorated with fluting that is more or less ornate. But you can also use any mold with a similar shape. Whatever the shape, it must be filled to only two-thirds of its height; this is essential given that the dough rises quickly and immediately, without actually setting. If the mold were too small, the dough would reach the top while still in a fluid state and would bubble out over it like a mousse.

A sponge cake of the size given here is better the next day than it is on the day it is made. *Time: 1 hour, 30 minutes for working the dough and cooking the cake.*

250 grams (8⁷/₈ ounces) of powdered sugar; ¹/₂ soupspoon of vanilla sugar (SEE PAGE 574); 7 medium eggs; 200 grams (7 ounces) of flour and starch, mixed in equal parts—that is, 100 grams (3¹/₂ ounces) of each—reserving 1 level tablespoon of this mixture to flour the mold and rectify the quantities of dough; 15 grams (¹/₂ ounce, 1 tablespoon) of butter to butter the mold.

A mold with a capacity of about 1¹/₂ liters (6¹/₃ cups).

PROCEDURE. Here we suggest that the egg yolks should be added gradually. If you are using larger quantities, mix them into the sugar two yolks at a time.

Once the flour has been well dried out, mix it with the starch. Pass the mixture through the drum sieve onto a sheet of paper. Take out the amount needed to prepare the mold (SEE TO BUTTER AND FLOUR MOLDS, PAGE 658).

Put the sugar into a terrine, reserving one or two soupspoons for the egg whites. Add the vanilla sugar. Make a well or hole in the middle of the sugar. Separate the eggs, reserving the egg whites, making sure that you do not include any bit of yolk, which would prevent you from whisking the egg whites successfully. Using a spatula or large wooden spoon, mix the yolk with very little sugar and begin working it vigorously until the yellow has paled considerably. Right to the end of this process, the sugar must only be mixed in with the yolks gradually, which are added one by one; this means that it will have time to liquefy. If you try to add too much sugar at one time, you will get the opposite result. The yolk will clump into hard parts, which are difficult to dissolve.

Then add a second yolk and mix it immediately into the part that has already been worked. After this, begin again to incorporate the sugar, little by little, always beating the batter produced with the same vigor, until this mixture has whitened and taken on a light, foamy consistency. And so on and so forth until the last yolk. You must allow 2–3 minutes at least of vigorous work before adding each yolk. The batter is ready when it has taken on a *creamy white* tint, and makes the ribbon (SEE PAGE 577).

Then whisk the whites into a good firm snow, as directed (SEE PAGE 8). Immediately mix in 1 good tablespoon of the whites into the batter, using a spatula, to lighten the batter and make it easier to add the rest. *At the same time* that you add this small quantity of egg whites, add a little bit of the flour and the starch that you have prepared. After this, mix in *half* of the egg whites as directed (SEE INCORPORATING THE WHITES, PAGE 10) at the same time as half of the flour, letting it shower down little by little into the terrine.

Once this first mixture of whites and flour has been completed, add the second half in exactly the same manner.

Immediately fill the mold to only *two-thirds* for the reasons already given. Place it on a round baking sheet or *tourtière,* which will allow you to turn it more easily. Put it into a *very moderate* oven. Maintain this temperature for three-quarters of the cooking time, which will be a total of *45–50 minutes* for a cake of this size. So after about 35 minutes, reduce the temperature a little.

When the dough has risen to the edges of the mold and risks coloring too much, cover the mold with moistened paper. If you need to turn the cake, make sure you don't jolt it, which could make the dough fall.

Ensure that it is perfectly done by sticking a kitchen needle into the center of the cake. Pull it out after *5–6 seconds;* it should be burning hot and dry from one end to the other. If not, prolong the cooking a little. Then unmold it on a rack and allow it to cool.

Ladyfingers *(Biscuits à la Cuiller)*

So called because a spoon *(cuiller)* was once used to handle the dough, rather than the pastry bag that is used now. These ladyfingers keep very well; that said, they are better and more tender when freshly made. That is why it is better to make them more frequently, and in small quantities at a time.

Just like the batter for a Savoy cake, the quantities and ingredients for the dough used for ladyfingers are always the same. They vary only according to the size of the eggs used. Here we suggest the quantity currently used of 16 eggs for every 450 grams (1 pound) of sugar. Make sure they are absolutely fresh; many ladyfingers, particularly those that you buy, have a doubtful taste, caused by using eggs that are old and badly preserved.

The flavoring can vary: vanilla sugar; lemon or orange peel; or orange flower water, which is almost classic, and is the most generally used.

Shape the ladyfingers before cooking on sheets of very clean, strong, white parchment paper that has no odor. This procedure, frequently used, is in fact better than cooking them directly on an oiled baking sheet, because it leaves the cookies much more tender on their bottom side. *Time: 1 hour. Makes about 40 ladyfingers.*

125 grams (4½ ounces) of *superfine* sugar; 90–95 grams (3⅙–3⅓ ounces) of very dry flour, sifted; 4 medium eggs; flavor as you wish. Some *confectioners' sugar* in a sugar shaker (SEE PAGE 574) to sprinkle over the cookies before cooking. If you do not have a sugar shaker, you can use a fine strainer or a sugar spoon.

PROCEDURE. Have the sheets of paper ready, as well as some extremely clean baking sheets, without any trace of grease and well wiped down. Also prepare the pastry bag: it should have a nozzle with a diameter of at least 1 centimeter (⅜ inch) (SEE USING A PASTRY BAG, PAGE 15).

Make the dough exactly as for SAVOY CAKE (SEE PAGE 693). As soon as it is ready, fill the pastry bag by three-quarters, using a pastry scraper or a piece of stiff paper. Form the ladyfingers on the sheets of paper, using the nozzle and piping them out as for ÉCLAIRS (SEE PAGE 698). Form little sticks about 11–12 centimeters (4¼–4½ inches) long, leaving a space between them of at least 6 centimeters (2½ inches) because they will expand a great deal when they cook.

Once all the ladyfingers have been formed, sprinkle them *lightly* with confectioners' sugar. After 3–4 minutes, sprinkle them again, but more generously, so that you almost completely cover the surface of the ladyfingers with sugar, without worrying about any that falls on the paper, which will be removed later.

Let them sit for a few moments, just long enough for the sugar to melt partly while still clinging to the surface: this sugar forms pearls on the ladyfingers when it is cooked. If, on the other hand, the ladyfingers were put in the oven as soon as they had been sprinkled with sugar, the sugar would caramelize and would come off the ladyfingers after cooking. That said, do not wait too long, because if the sugar melts too much, it will sink into the dough and soften it, weakening the ladyfingers.

Before putting them in the oven, get rid of any excess sugar, including the sugar that fell between the biscuits onto the sheet of paper; do this by shaking the sheet of paper. The dough should be both stable and light, so that it will not be deformed or come away when you do this. Take a corner of the sheet of paper in each hand, at the end nearest to you. Raise it, giving it a few small sharp shakes to move the sugar down to the front of the sheet. Raise the sheet a little more to incline it and to make the sugar spill off onto the table.

Then place the sheets of paper on the baking sheets and put them into a moderate oven: neither the ladyfingers nor the paper should color during the *20–25 minutes of cooking.* With an oven that is not hot enough, this time must be prolonged and the ladyfingers will be dried out inside; but this is better than too much heat, which would caramelize the sugar and color the ladyfingers.

During the first stage of cooking, avoid opening the oven—or at least open it rapidly, taking all due care—because otherwise the ladyfingers will collapse.

If the oven is not large enough to cook all the ladyfingers at once, it is still better to prepare the rest of the dough, rather than letting it stand in the mixing bowl while cooking the first ovenload.

Genoise *(Génoise)*

This kind of batter is a variation of the dough for ladyfingers, and is very often used in pastry making: in large cakes, whether iced or not; decorated with candied fruits; or baked in special pans to be divided into small pieces that you glaze with fondant to make petits fours of different colors and flavors. But no matter the use, or even the proportions of its ingredients, the method of working the batter remains the same.

We will use this recipe to make a dessert cake, a sweet or a snack, which you can coat with either apricot preserves or icing. A genoise offers the advantage that it will keep very well for several days. *Time: 1 hour. These quantities are for a mold known as a* manqué *(see fig.* 68, PAGE 576*), a round cake pan 22 centimeters (8 1/2 inches) in diameter and 4 centimeters (1 1/2 inches) high.*

125 grams (4 1/2 ounces) of sifted flour; 125 grams (4 1/2 ounces) of sifted superfine sugar; 60 grams (2 1/4 ounces, 4 1/2 tablespoons) of butter; 4 medium-sized eggs. 1 teaspoon of vanilla sugar or lemon peel or 1 scant tablespoon of liqueur.

***To coat with apricot marmalade and glaze the genoise:* 2–3 soupspoons of apricot marmalade; 1 tablespoon of rum; 1 tablespoon of water; 5–6 tablespoons of confectioners' sugar.**

PROCEDURE. Butter and flour the mold as directed (SEE PAGE 657) so that everything is ready. If the dough must wait, it will not have the same lightness.

It is essential to mix the eggs with the sugar in a utensil that is slightly heated. The bowl that is used in professional pastry making and that is better than any other is a copper egg white bowl, which should be kept in a warm place while working. If you do not have one, use a warm terrine and stand it in a saucepan containing warm water, then put it on very gentle heat to maintain it at the same temperature without boiling. However, you must not raise the heat to the point of "seizing" the eggs, when the whites would coagulate. In winter, you can first bathe the eggs in *lukewarm* water to take off their chill, and you should work in a room where the temperature is not too cool.

Before beginning to mix the eggs with the sugar, put the butter in a very small saucepan to melt, either on extremely low heat or in a receptacle containing boiling water. It must not be too warm when it is used, or it will turn into oil and mix badly. It must be just melted, liquid and lukewarm.

Put the eggs, both the yolk and white, into the egg basin with the sugar. Mix it well, using an egg-white whisk, and whisk it continuously, *raising* the batter with the whisk to make it absorb the air, which will make it white. To be at the right point, the batter, when picked up with the whisk, must fall, making a ribbon (SEE PAGE 577). At this point, take it off the heat and continue to whisk until the batter has cooled.

Then add the flavor that you are using. Whisk it to mix it: with a pastry scraper or a card, scrape off the batter stuck to the walls of the utensil and mix it with the rest. Then mix in *the flour,* which you drop in a light and continuous shower from the paper into the dough, proceeding as for whisked egg whites (SEE PAGE 8). Work quickly; otherwise, the batter will become heavy.

Next, gently pour in the decanted and melted *butter* without working the batter too much, which would reduce its lightness. The butter has a tendency to fall to the bottom: you should then mix it, lifting up the batter again for a completely equal mixture.

As soon as the mixing is finished, pour the batter into the mold, which you must fill only by two-thirds. Immediately put it into a moderate oven. Assume here a baking time of about *1/2 hour.* The batter must rise by only one-third. You can tell that the cooking is done when you press a finger in the middle of the cake, and the cake is firm and does not retain the imprint of your finger.

Unmold onto a rack. Ice the cake (SEE ICING CAKES, PAGE 721). For this recipe, what was the top of the cake becomes the bottom when served.

Genoa Cake *(Pain de Gênes)*

The proportions of the ingredients of this cake can vary slightly according to the different recipes, particularly in terms of the starch or eggs. The recipe provided here makes an excellent cake with a very moist batter, exactly as can be found at a fine pastry shop. Making a Genoa cake does not present any complications, but it does require some care and also some trouble to crush and grind the almonds, which calls for some strength, and for which the use of a mortar with its large wooden pestle is absolutely essential. *Time: About 1 hour, 30 minutes. Makes a cake of 18–20 centimeters (7–8 inches) in diameter.*

250 grams (8 7/8 ounces) of almonds; weighed *shelled;* 25 grams (1 ounce) of superfine sugar; 125 grams (4 1/2 ounces, 9 tablespoons) of fine butter; 75 grams (2 2/3 ounces) of rice starch (known as cream of rice); 4 whole medium-size eggs; 2 tablespoons of kirsch.

A round, tin-lined steel *manqué* mold (cake pan), number 20. That is, measuring 20 centimeters (8 inches) at

its largest diameter, 4 centimeters ($1^1/_2$ inches) high and with precisely a 1–liter (4-cup) capacity (see *fig.* 68, PAGE 576).

PROCEDURE. The almonds. Husk the almonds as directed (SEE PAGE 573). If you have a little machine to grate the almonds, pass them through the machine. Then put them into the mortar. (Using the machine does not enable you to dispense with the mortar, because only using the mortar will result in a pastry that is delicate enough).

If you do not have a mechanical grater, put the shelled almonds, just as they are, into the mortar with a whole egg and 50 grams ($1^3/_4$ ounces) of sugar. (The sugar and eggs prevent the almonds from turning into oil under the pestle). First, tap lightly to break the almonds. After this, drag the pestle in a circular path over the entire surface of the mortar; if you continue to tap in the same place, the almonds will turn to oil.

If the almonds have previously been put through the machine—in effect, completing the first stage of the work—you will not have to tap them first to break them, and can immediately begin to grind them by dragging the pestle.

As the almonds are reduced to a paste, and as this paste thickens, add an egg, which will lighten and facilitate the work, which is rather tedious. When the last egg is added, the worked paste should be delicate enough that you cannot see any actual pieces of almond in it, or at least very few, and if you can, they should be no larger than a grain of tapioca. In this state, the paste can stand for several hours without spoiling, until you are ready to finish it, which means that you can take a rest.

The mold: Prepare it in advance, because the almond paste must not stand once the butter and sugar are added to it. Coat the inside with butter that is scarcely melted. On the bottom, apply a round of tissue paper, or even the yellowish, *very light* paper that is used by bakers to wrap their bread, a little undercut so that it does not go beyond the sides at all.

While you do this, press on the paper with your fingers, going from the center to the edges to expel the air, which would otherwise make the surface of the cake uneven while cooking. Note that, for this cake, the bottom becomes the top when it is unmolded.

The almond paste: Mix the rest of the sugar into the almond paste remaining in the mortar, handling the pestle as before.

Break the butter into small pieces. Put it into a large bowl that has previously been dipped in boiling water and then thoroughly wiped dry. Using a wooden spoon, work it to make it *more runny* than butter that is softened to a pomade (SEE PAGE 16), but not so much that it becomes oil. If the butter is very firm, place the bowl in a terrine of warm water to make this work easier and to keep the butter in a runny state.

Pour it, or if possible get a second person to pour it, in a small stream into the mortar while you vigorously turn the pestle, then add the kirsch. After several moments, the paste will have become notably paler and taken on the smooth and foamy consistency of whipped cream, so move it into the center of the mortar with the special pastry scraper or with a piece of cardboard.

Put the starch on a sheet of paper to drop it in a shower onto the paste, which is now a batter—again, with the help of another person, if possible—while you turn the batter to mix it, using a spatula or a card with the same movements used for mixing egg whites (SEE PAGE 10). As soon as this mixture is done, pour the batter into the mold by tipping the mortar over it. It should fill the mold by three-quarters. Strike it several times lightly on the table to compact the batter. *Put it in the oven immediately.* If the batter stands, it may separate and the cake will be very heavy. For the same reason, we also recommend that you mix in the butter and the starch rather quickly.

To bake: Do this in a moderately hot oven—one that is rather more than less hot and maintains an even heat throughout.

The cake should rise very evenly, without making a dome, and it should not begin to color until after 15 minutes. If it colors earlier, cover the cake with parchment paper that has been generously buttered. *Allow 30–35 minutes for baking;* it is done when the cake comes away from the side of the mold, and when it feels firm if you press down quite strongly with your finger. The cake, once it has risen, will settle in the last stage of cooking; it will take on a beautiful golden tint, which is not too dark.

Then take it from the oven and immediately unmold it onto a rack or a drum sieve. While it cools, the cake will settle and shrink a little bit more, returning to about the height it had when first put into the oven. Do not remove the paper until it has completely cooled.

Cream Puffs and Eclairs *(Choux à la Crème et Éclairs)*

For details of how to prepare the dough, see CHOUX PASTRY (PAGE 664). Formerly, a spoon was used to shape the dough to form the puffs, or it was lightly rolled on a floured table and then cut into small pieces. These days, using a pastry bag to form the puffs has become the norm. To work evenly and quickly, this is infinitely more practical than any other method, so we describe it here first. Use a pastry bag furnished with a nozzle with a diameter of 1 centimeter (3/8 inch) (SEE USING A PASTRY BAG, PAGE 15). Meanwhile, have ready two small steel baking sheets that are quite clean. Do not oil them. *Time: 45 minutes. Makes about 20 cream puffs.*

Use the same quantities as those for choux pastry (SEE PAGE 664).

To form the puffs: Put the dough into the pastry bag—all or part of it, depending on how much you have. Form the puffs as directed for using a pastry bag.

Make little piles in the shape of macaroons, the dimensions varying according to the kind of puffs. Leave a space of 2–3 centimeters (3/4–1 1/4 inches) between each pile so that they do not join together when they are cooked. *The weight of dough for a medium-size puff is 25–30 grams (about 1 ounce).*

If you do not have a pastry bag: Using an ordinary metal spoon, place little piles of dough on the baking sheet, leaving an interval between them as recommended above. Run your left index finger down the spoon to make sure all the dough comes away from it. Lightly rectify the shape of the pile of dough with the spoon; in baking, the inequalities will disappear and the surface will become uniform.

To form éclairs: Here a pastry bag is essential. The nozzle must have a diameter of 1 1/2 centimeters (5/8 inch), the diameter regulating both the width and the height of the pastry. Proceed to form the éclairs as explained for using a pastry bag (SEE PAGE 15).

To glaze the puffs: Pass a small brush dipped in beaten egg over the surface of the puffs, making sure that none falls on the baking sheet, because when it cooks the egg will stick to the baking sheet and the puffs will not swell any more. Put them in the oven immediately.

To bake: An oven with a *medium* temperature, maintained at the same degree throughout the cooking time. In a hotter oven, the crust will form too quickly, and the dough inside will not rise well. It is better to have an oven that is slightly less hot than too hot. The baking time will be longer and the color paler, but the cakes will not suffer as a result.

Put the sheets with the puffs on them on the bottom of the oven, after first removing the shelf that divides the oven in two.

To check how well the puffs are cooking, do not crack open the oven door except for the time needed to have a quick glance. This is particularly important during the middle stage of baking: this is the moment when the dough has risen and then sets; if it collapses at this point, it will not rise again.

The cooking time varies slightly according to the size of the puffs and, of course, the temperature of the oven. *Allow 25 minutes to a good 1/2 hour* and even more.

Once the puffs have doubled in volume and taken on a beautiful golden tint, they must not be taken out of the oven until they are *perfectly firm to the touch and dry on all of their surfaces.* Note this point carefully; otherwise, you will see the puffs gradually collapse, and take on the unfortunate appearance of flat pancakes, bumpy and with a badly cooked interior—and there is no remedy. Carefully check them before taking them out of the oven, and cook then for as long as necessary.

When you take them out of the oven, arrange them on a rack or a large drum sieve so that, when surrounded by the colder air, they will not weaken or soften in their own steam. They must be completely cooled before being filled.

To fill cream puffs and éclairs: Once the puffs have cooled completely, use either the point of a knife or a small pointed stick like a pencil to make a small hole in the side, just big enough to introduce a small nozzle or the end of a large paper cone containing the cream for the filling. Or, with very clean kitchen scissors, cut around the top of the puff to make a sort of candy dish, leaving the cover attached to the bottom part, with the uncut part forming a hinge. Fill the puff using a spoon or a pastry bag.

For *éclairs,* you cut the entire length of the cake with scissors with just one snip, and on both ends, like a kind of snuffbox. Fill it with pastry cream (SEE PAGE 585) using a spoon. Glaze them by whatever method you prefer (SEE ICING CAKES, PAGE 721).

The principal methods for cream puffs: *A first method.* The puffs, having been baked and filled with whipped cream or pastry cream, are simply sprinkled with confectioners' sugar.

Another method. Place the puffs on the baking sheet, and after glazing them, sprinkle them with minced almonds, and then with a very small pinch of superfine sugar. Put them in the oven to bake.

Or even. The puffs are cooked, chilled, and filled, then dipped in sugar cooked almost to the point of caramel. *Or:* they are *glazed,* either with fondant or with a cooked or uncooked icing.

For the puffs known as *pains de la Mecque,* or Mecca bread: Lay out the puffs in an oblong shape on the baking sheet, then sprinkle them with superfine sugar and split them in the middle with the blade of a knife to resemble a large bread in miniature. The oven should be milder because of the sugar, which adds to the color.

Gougère *(Gougère)*

An excellent pastry for lunch, made with choux dough and cheese, which looks like a crown brioche. *Time: 20 minutes to make the dough; 35–40 minutes of cooking. Serves 6.*

125 grams (4½ ounces) of flour; 60 grams (2¼ ounces, 4½ tablespoons) of butter; 2 grams (1/14 ounce) of salt; 2½ deciliters (1 cup) of boiled milk, *chilled;* 4 medium eggs; 75 grams (2⅔ ounces) of fresh Gruyère cheese, net weight without the crust.

PROCEDURE. Cut the cheese into very small cubes of 3–4 millimeters (about ⅛ inch) on each side; keep them to one side. Prepare the dough as directed (SEE CHOUX PASTRY, PAGE 664). From the quantity of eggs indicated, you can remove one-third of the beaten egg to glaze the cake. Once the dough is finished, mix in only *two-thirds* of the small cheese dice.

Butter a round baking sheet made of thick black steel, the type known as a *tourtière.* With an ordinary wooden spoon, take out the dough in pieces the size of an egg; place them one by one on the *tourtière,* side by side, to form a ring or crown, lightly pushing on the dough with your finger to make it come away from the spoon.

Having placed the first 2 or 3 tablespoons on the sheet, calculate how much dough you have and figure out what size to make the ring. For the quantities above, you can assume you will have about 14 tablespoons, to make a ring with a diameter slightly more than 20 centimeters (8 inches) on the outside and at least 10 centimeters on the inside of the ring. After cooking, the outside diameter of the ring will increase by 5–6 centimeters (2–2½ inches); the inside diameter will remain about the same. With the back of a spoon applied lightly, correct the outline of the ring of dough to make an even circumference.

Add 1 scant tablespoon of milk or water to the rest of the beaten egg. Using a flat brush or a feather, spread the egg thinly on the surface of the ring of dough, then scatter the small cubes of cheese over the ring.

Put it in a medium oven, which must not be too hot. As for all choux dough, you should not use a hot oven, because the crust forms too quickly, which means that the inside of the dough will not rise well. The cake must swell considerably before it takes on any color. *Assume 35–40 minutes for cooking.*

For both cooking it and knowing when it has been properly cooked, refer to the special article on CREAM PUFFS (PAGE 698). Note that a gougère may have risen sufficiently and taken on a color that makes it look as if it has been perfectly cooked, but the inside may still not be properly cooked. In such a case, the cake will collapse when it comes out of the oven. For this reason, it is a good idea, if you are not familiar with this kind of dough, to leave the cake for a few minutes more in the oven so that the dough dries out further and sets.

Ramequins *(Ramequins).* In a relatively modern style, these are simply puffs with cheese and are derived from the gougère, to which you should refer for preparing the dough. For dressing and baking, follow the directions given for CREAM PUFFS (PAGE 698). Allow about 40 grams (1 3/8 ounces) of dough for each ramequin. You can serve them as hot hors d'oeuvres on a plate covered with a napkin, piling them up in a little heap. Or you can, if you like, fill each ramequin when it comes out of the oven with 1 tablespoon of Mornay sauce (SEE PAGE 63) that has a good deal of cheese added to it and should be a little thick.

Talmouses *(Talmouses).* In the eighteenth century, talmouses, already popular even then, were a kind of small, triangular-shaped tart that was filled with a very rich white cheese, butter, flour, eggs, a little bit of milk, and pepper, and then cooked.

Since then, recipes for talmouses have proliferated. The simplest is this: a round of dough approximately 10 centimeters (4 inches) in diameter, cut out of rough puff pastry or lining or pastry dough; turn up the edges on three sides to form a triangle, then arrange on it a puff made with either ramequin or gougère dough. Glaze the puff; place a few small cheese cubes on top of it and bake it in the oven like a ramequin or other puff.

To a choux dough made with Gruyère, add some good white cheese: either Marolles, Gervais, or some other white cheese mixed with fines herbes, etc. Serve this excellent hot hors d'oeuvre burning hot, piled into a pyramid on a napkin.

Apple Turnover *(Chausson aux Pommes).*

One of the classic popular cakes; its name varies with the region. It is simply a layer of round dough, relatively large and with raw apples piled onto one of its halves; the other half is folded over the apples, and the edges are pinched together to enclose the apples. Patisserie bakers mainly use leftovers or trimmings of puff pastry; in many places, if you do not want to go to the the trouble of making the turnover dough at home, it is easy to buy trimmings of puff pastry from the bakery.

This pastry is eaten cold and keeps very well, for 2 days at least, in a cool place. *Time: 1 scant hour (the dough having been made in advance). Makes two medium-size turnovers, each one large enough to serve 6 people, or one large one to serve 12.*

***For the dough:* 250 grams (8 7/8 ounces) of flour; 125 grams (4 1/2 ounces, 9 tablespoons) of butter; 2 eggs, half of one being reserved for the glazing; 6 grams (1/5 ounce, 9 tablespoons) of salt; 6 grams (1/5 ounce) of sugar; 1 scant deciliter (3 1/3 fluid ounces, scant 1/2 cup) of water. Or 600 grams (1 pound, 5 ounces) of puff pastry trimmings.**

***For the filling:* 1 kilogram (2 pounds, 3 ounces) of apples, weighed completely peeled (that would be about 1.15 kilograms/2 pounds, 8 ounces gross weight); 100 grams (3 1/2 ounces) of superfine sugar.**

PROCEDURE. **The dough:** Prepare it enough in advance so that it has time to rest for *at least 2 hours.* Mix it as directed (SEE PASTRY DOUGH OR LINING DOUGH, PAGE 662), adding the salt, sugar, and butter to the water in the well, together with the eggs, first beaten in a cup as for an omelet, and from which you reserve half an egg for glazing.

Knead *(fraiser)* the dough twice. Gather it together into a ball. Keep it in a cool place, wrapped in a towel, until you are ready to use it.

The apples: Fifteen minutes before making the turnover, cut the apples into quarters. Take out the core and the seeds. Peel them and cut them into slices. Put them into a terrine with the sugar. Toss them to spread the sugar around, and do this another two or three times before you put them into the dough.

Making the turnover: If you are making two turnovers, divide both the dough and the apples into two equal parts.

All the following directions apply to either one large turnover or, of course, to two smaller ones, which you can work on at the same time.

Roll the dough into a ball. Very lightly dust the board with flour. First tap the dough with the rolling pin to flatten it out a little bit into a thick pancake. Next, handle the rolling pin from the middle toward the edges, without going back over the road already traveled—in other words, each time you lift up the rolling pin, put it back down in the middle of the rolled-out dough. This will produce a sheet of dough 5–6 millimeters (1/8–3/16 inch) thick; nice and round, which means that you will not have to cut it; and about 28–30 centimeters (11–12 inches) in diameter.

Lift up the sheet of dough in both hands; place it on a baking sheet or *tourtière* made of heavy steel. On half of the rolled-out dough, place the apples, leaving *a border of 1½ centimeters (⅝ inch)* at the edges. Also put fewer apples toward the edges than in the middle of the dough.

With a small brush, lightly moisten the border, then pull the other half of the dough over the apples. The edges will stick together where the dough was moistened. Squeeze them lightly to seal.

Once this is done, lift up the dough borders that are joined together, pinching them as you go to fold them over. This produces a kind of strip, which prevents the apples from escaping. With the reserved egg, glaze only the top of the turnover. Then use a fork to score a grid on the glazed side. Using a small knife, make seven or eight deep punctures in the dough for the steam to escape while baking. Put it in the oven immediately.

The oven: A good medium heat, sustained and regular, and coming mostly from the bottom. Strong heat should be avoided. The baking will not take place any faster—in fact, the reverse will be true—and the inside of the turnover will remain pasty.

Allow 35–40 minutes for cooking.

Take the turnover out and put it on a rack until it is nearly completely cooled.

Milk Flan *(Flan au Lait)*

A classic pastry for holidays in our rural regions, this flan or tart is eaten cold and must therefore be prepared several hours in advance. In the rural style, it is made in tart pans with serrated edges, which help the cooking; but if even a little of the cream mixture runs over the edge, it cannot be unmolded without breaking the crust; for this reason, a pastry ring placed on top of a baking sheet is preferable. For all details of how to prepare this, refer to FRUIT TARTS OR FLANS (SEE PAGE 675).

In the country, they use the milk from the most recent milking for its cream; this is not boiled and some fresh cream is added, to make up a third of the total volume. In town, of course, this is impossible. Excellent milk is required; and having boiled it to reduce it, and thus improve it, you should use it chilled. If you have fresh cream, it can only be an advantage to add some of it in the quantity suggested above.

Instead of the orange flower water, the characteristic flavor of a country-style flan, you can, if you like, substitute vanilla-flavored sugar or lemon peel sugar; or even a few macaroons that have been thoroughly finely crushed. *Time: 1 hour (once the dough has rested). Makes a flan 23 centimeters (9 inches) in diameter serving 6–8.*

For the dough: **125 grams (4½ ounces) of flour; 60 grams (2¼ ounces, 4½ tablespoons) of butter; 1 small egg; 3 tablespoons of water; 5 grams (⅙ ounce) of sugar and 4 grams (about ⅐ ounce) of salt.**

For the custard: **4 deciliters (1⅔ cups) of excellent milk; 2 whole eggs and 2 yolks; 125 grams (4½ ounces) of superfine sugar; 40 grams (1⅜ ounces) of sifted flour; 30 grams (1 ounce) of clarified butter; 1 tablespoon of orange flower water; a small pinch of salt.**

PROCEDURE. Prepare the dough (SEE PASTRY DOUGH OR LINING DOUGH, PAGE 662), kneading it *(fraiser)* twice. Line the ring as directed (SEE FRUIT TARTS OR FLANS, PAGE 675), so that you have a crest that reaches over the top edge by 1 scant centimeter (⅜ inch). Make sure you do not pierce the bottom, because here this would let the custard escape.

The custard: First work the sugar and the whole eggs in a terrine with a wooden spoon for a few minutes. Add the yolks. Mix in the flour, raising the whole mass with the wooden spoon; then dilute everything with the milk gradually, using a small sauce whisk. Finally, add the orange flower water, the little bit of salt, and the butter that is just melted without being warm.

In order not to spill the custard when you move the flan, place the baking sheet with the empty crust on the oven door. Pour the custard in there until it is about ½ centimeter (³⁄₁₆ inch) from the edge of the crest. Then gently place the filled flan in the oven; a strong heat, rather than a moderate one, coming as much as possible from the bottom.

If at the end of some time, bubbles begin to appear in the bottom of the dough, pierce them with a kitchen needle to chase out the air. The custard, which has set by this point, will no longer be in danger of running out.

If the surface of the custard colors too much at the end of 15 minutes, cover the flan with moistened parchment paper. Allow *35–40 minutes* for baking; but bake for 5 minutes more rather than 5 minutes less.

After you take it out of the oven, wait 10 minutes before taking off the ring; if it does not come of easily, it will be enough to slide the point of a small knife between the ring and the crust. Then slide the flan onto a small rack and allow it to cool completely. To serve, powder with confectioners' sugar.

Quiche Lorraine *(Quiche Lorraine)*

This is a milk flan in which fresh cream replaces the milk: the use of fresh cream is characteristic of quiche. The recipes vary a little bit: the oldest use some bread dough, and the bacon used here was often not included.

The quiche is molded in a tart pan made of thick steel with a fluted edge and is served in the cooking utensil itself. This is due to the difficulty of unmolding the quiche without breaking the crust unless you have a large spatula with a shortened handle, which is used in some regions in the east, that you slide under the tarts to take them out of the mold. Even so, as far as a quiche is concerned, this is often useless, because the custard spills out a little and makes the crust stick to the serrated borders of the tart pan. When you do not have a serrated tart pan, you can make the quiche in a flan circle (SEE FRUIT TARTS OR FLANS, PAGE 675). As for all preparations of this type, a quiche is served quite hot. *Time: 1 hour, 45 minutes (including time for resting the dough). Serves 8.*

For the dough: **200 grams (7 ounces) of flour; 100 grams (3½ ounces, 7 tablespoons) of butter; ¾ deciliter (2½ fluid ounces, scant ⅓ cup) of water; a pinch of salt.**

For the filling: **about 200 grams (7 ounces) of lean bacon; 50 grams (1¾ ounces, 3½ tablespoons) of butter; a good ½ liter (generous 2 cups) of ordinary cream, *completely fresh*; 5 medium eggs; 2 nice pinches of salt.**

A tart pan with fluted sides about 25 centimeters (10 inches) in diameter.

PROCEDURE. Prepare the dough as directed (SEE PASTRY DOUGH OR LINING DOUGH, PAGE 662), kneading it twice. Let it rest for 1 hour.

Meanwhile, trim the bacon of its rind, then cut into it small slices ½ centimeter (3/16 inch) thick. Blanch them (SEE PAGE 15) and drain them.

With the rolling pin, roll out the dough as for a tart into a nice round pancake that has an even thickness of at least ½ centimeter (3/16 inch) and a diameter of 25–26 centimeters (10–10½ inches). Slide your two hands under the dough to transfer it to a tart pan that has been generously buttered; with the ends of your fingers, press the dough into the bottom and particularly onto the fluted sides. Then fold the dough over the sides and pass the rolling pin over it to cut off this excess.

Beat the eggs as for an omelet and salt them, then gradually mix the cream into them. Divide the butter into thin slices and spread them out over the bottom of the quiche. Place the bacon on top, pressing lightly on it so that the pieces stick to the bottom and will not float to the surface when the custard is poured into it. Then cover everything with the custard, without allowing any to spill onto the sides of the dough. Carefully slide the tart pan into the oven; a good medium heat coming *mostly from the bottom. Allow 30–35 minutes* for cooking.

Gruyère Cheese Quiche *(Salée Vaudoise). Time: 45 minutes (plus 1 hour for resting the dough).*

The mold used in the Vaud region is also a black steel tart pan, but one with sides that are unfluted and also flared, which allows you to unmold it without risk. If you do not have this utensil, use a flan circle, as already explained above. The ingredients and quantities for the dough are the same as for the quiche. Note that, if you like, some lard can be used; for example, for 100 grams (3½ ounces) of fat you can use 50 grams (1¾ ounces) of lard and 50 grams (1¾ ounces, 3½ tablespoons) of butter. The dough is worked in the same way.

For the filling: **125 grams (4½ ounces) of very good real Gruyère cheese, lean rather than fat; 3 medium eggs; 2½ deciliters (1 cup) of fresh cream.**

The quiche is served burning hot, with the custard completely puffed up when it comes out of the oven. It is delicious that way; but cold it is also very good.

PROCEDURE. Make the dough exactly as for the quiche; line the well-buttered tart pan the same way. Here the shell, before being filled with custard, is half cooked "à blanc" (SEE PAGE 678)—that is, put in the oven for *about 10 minutes,* in the usual way, to thoroughly dry the dough.

Meanwhile, beat the eggs with the cream and the cheese, adding it gradually, with a good pinch of pepper; there is no need for salt because the cheese is salted. Once the crust has been in the oven for the time required, remove the contents that you used to prevent it from blistering, and then pour in the prepared custard. Put it back in the oven for *20 minutes* with a heat that comes more from the bottom than the top. The heat coming from the bottom should be rather strong to ensure that the custard colors, taking on a lovely golden color as the custard swells and rises mostly in the middle of the tart.

Onion Tart *(Tarte aux Oignons).* Made in Alsace and in the east, this savory preparation is derived from quiche and is also similar to the leek tart, or *flamiche.* Here the leeks are replaced with onion, and like a quiche, eggs are added to give it the consistency of a milk-based flan.

If you like, and depending on what is available, mold the tart in a steel tart pan with a straight edge, as for the Gruyère quiche, or in a flan ring.

The quantities for the dough and how it is worked are the same as for the quiche, with the sole modification that half the butter is replaced with good lard: that is, 50 grams (1 3/4 ounces) of lard and 50 grams (1 3/4 ounces, 3 1/2 tablespoons) of butter. *Time: 2 hours.*

For the filling: 250 grams (8 7/8 ounces) of onion; 750 grams (1 pound, 10 ounces) of *smoked* bacon, net weight without the rind; 50 grams (1 3/4 ounces, 3 1/2 tablespoons) of butter; 3 1/2 deciliters (1 1/2 cups) of milk, boiled and cooled; 4 whole eggs; 1 tablespoon of fines herbes, minced finely; a good pinch of ground pepper; a pinch of salt.

PROCEDURE. Make the dough as directed for the quiche. While it is resting, prepare the onions; if possible, choose large onions, which are easier to cut into rounds that are as fine as possible. Put these rounds into a saucepan of boiling water (1 liter/4 1/4 cups). Boil strongly for *6–7 minutes.* Pour them into a strainer and plunge this into a large quantity of cold water.

Meanwhile, cut the bacon into little cubes about 1 centimeter (3/8 inch) on each side; blanch them (SEE PAGE 15). Drain them and dry them on a towel.

Melt the butter in a medium-size saucepan. Put in the lardons to color them lightly. Then add the onions; on low heat, let them shrink and soften, *without coloring whatsoever, for 20 minutes.* Just a few moments before you take them off the heat, add the fines herbes.

Line the tart pan or the flan ring. With the point of a small knife, pierce the dough on the bias in five or six places here and there.

About 45 minutes before serving, beat the eggs, as for an omelet, in a small terrine; add the milk to them. Mix in the onions and the bacon. Add the pepper and check if you need to add any more salt. Pour this mixture into the mold lined with dough. Put it into the oven immediately.

Bake for *35–40 minutes,* following the previous directions. About halfway through this time, the mixture develops: it swells and its color gradually takes on a beautiful golden tint. Onion tart is served good and hot.

Leek Flamiche *(Flamiche aux Poireaux)*

A flamiche is a kind of flan whose original recipe is authentically rustic and varies according to the region. The recipe that we give here is truly savory; in short, it is a tart or flan garnished with leeks cooked in a milk sauce, with small lardons added; if you like, you can leave them out for a meat-free dish. Note that the leek used should be taken only from the entirely white part of the vegetable. *Time: 1 hour (once the dough has been made and rested). Serves 6.*

For the dough: 200 grams (7 ounces) of flour; 100 grams (3 1/2 ounces, 7 tablespoons) of butter; a pinch of salt; half a beaten egg, both white and yolk; 1/2 deciliter (1 2/3 fluid ounces, scant 1/4 cup) of water.

For the filling: 300 grams (10 1/2 ounces) of leek, the white part only; 60 grams (2 1/4 ounces, 4 1/2 tablespoons) of butter; 30 grams (1 ounce) of flour;

4 deciliters (1 2/3 cups) of boiled milk; 75 grams (2 2/3 ounces) of lean bacon; salt, pepper, nutmeg.

PROCEDURE. Make the dough as directed (SEE PASTRY DOUGH OR LINING DOUGH PAGE 662) kneading it *(fraiser)* twice. Let it rest for *1 hour* or more.

Cut the white part of the leeks into fine rounds. Cut the bacon, its rind removed, into small cubes about 1 centimeter (3/8 inch) on each side. Blanch them as directed (SEE PAGE 15).

Melt half of the butter (30 grams/1 ounce/ 2 tablespoons) in a medium-size saucepan. Put in the bacon and color lightly. Then add the leeks *on very gentle heat* and soften them for *a scant 15 minutes,* stirring them from time to time with a wooden spoon and *without allowing them to color whatsoever.*

Add the flour and mix in. Allow it to cook, always without coloring, for a few minutes. Gradually dilute it with the milk, adding it cold or warm. Season with pepper, salt, and grated nutmeg. Bring it to a boil on stronger heat, stirring continuously with the spoon. Then turn the heat down very low to maintain a very gentle simmer *for about 25 minutes.*

To make and cook the flamiche: Roll the dough into a rather tight ball. With the rolling pin, flatten it into a nice round pancake about 1/2 centimeter (3/16 inch) thick and about 28 centimeters (11 inches) in diameter. Slide both your hands under the dough to transfer it to a large *tourtière* (that is, a round plate of heavy steel, like one used to place tart circles on; this is not a mold).

Meanwhile, divide the rest of the butter into pieces the size of beans, and keep them ready at hand.

Then with your fingers raise the edges of the dough all around, making a large strip to prevent the sauce from spilling onto the *tourtière.* With the point of a small knife, lightly pierce the bottom of the dough to avoid blistering. Allow just enough time before serving, evenly spread out the leeks. Quickly spread over them the pieces of butter you prepared in advance. *Immediately put it in the oven so that you do not give the leek filling time to soften the dough.*

A hot oven, with the heat coming from the bottom, to seize the bottom of the dough underneath. Heat from above is needed only to glaze the surface, because the filling is already cooked. Cook for *about 20 minutes.*

If the flamiche has to stand, keep it in a very gentle oven with the door open. To serve, slide it on a round plate and send it out *burning hot.*

Pound Cake *(Quatre-quarts ou Tôt-fait)*

Known by one or other of both these French names, this is a homemade cake that is extremely simple to make, earning it the name *tôt-fait* (soon made), while the name *quatre-quarts* (four-quarters) is a reference to the proportion of its ingredients. Some recipes have variations to try to give some lightness to the dough, since the original formula is rather heavy and dense. However, since this is the recipe for a true pound cake, achievable by even the most unschooled pastry novices, we give it first. The next recipe produces a dough that is actually lighter, but this is not characteristic of a true pound cake, which is simple and quickly prepared.

You normally make this cake in a large mold with rather low sides; for the quantities given below, use a mold about 22 centimeters (8 1/2 inches) in diameter. *Time: 35–40 minutes.*

125 grams (4 1/2 ounces) of superfine sugar; 125 grams (4 1/2 ounces) of sifted flour; 125 grams (4 1/2 ounces, 9 tablespoons) of butter; 2 rather large eggs weighing a total of 125 grams (4 1/2 ounces); the grated zest of a lemon.

PROCEDURE. **The mold:** Butter it and flour it (SEE PAGE 658).

The dough: Sift the flour onto a sheet of paper.

Melt the butter in a small saucepan; keep it scarcely lukewarm during the summertime, a little warmer in winter. This is because butter, when it is too warm in summer, tends to fall to the bottom of the batter, while in winter, if it is not warm enough, it will firm up too rapidly when it mixes with the cold batter. In both cases, it will be impossible to incorporate the butter effectively without taking these precautions.

Use a terrine large enough to be able to combine and work easily all the ingredients of the batter. First put in the sugar, the grated lemon zest, and the eggs, both the whites and the yolks. With a wooden spoon, beat everything together for only 2 minutes, to mix everything thoroughly without trying to make the batter light.

Next, pour in the butter in a thin stream, gently stirring with the spoon to mix it in. Then add the flour by dropping it gradually onto the batter in a shower, using a spatula or a firm card to mix it in the same way as for beaten egg whites (SEE PAGE 10).

Once the batter is smooth and homogenous, pour it into the mold; it should be filled only three-quarters of the way, because the batter will increase by a quarter its volume while cooking. Place the mold on a steel baking sheet and put it into the oven immediately.

Cooking it: An oven of good but moderate heat to give the batter, which is a little heavy, the time to cook easily. If the batter colors too quickly, cover the cake with buttered parchment paper: the buttered side against the cake. If the oven does not heat evenly, turn the cake from time to time so that each of its surfaces is exposed to the strongest heat.

Cook for *25–30 minutes.* Unmold onto a rack or a drum sieve to allow the steam inside to evaporate.

Recipe for a lighter pound cake. The proportions are the same as in the preceding recipe for the sugar, butter, flour, lemon zest, and eggs; plus: 1 yolk; 75 grams (2 2/3 ounces) of Corinth raisins macerated in a very small glass of rum (SEE RAISINS, PAGE 573).

PROCEDURE. Put the egg yolks in a terrine with the sugar and the lemon peel. Using a wooden spoon, beat the mixture until it makes the ribbon (SEE PAGE 577). Then add the raisins.

Whisk the whites into a firm snow. Add them to the terrine, alternating with the flour: that is, a small part of egg white and a little bit of flour in a shower, and so on. Finally, pour the melted butter into the batter, stirring very delicately with the spoon so that the dough retains the lightness given to it by the egg whites. Immediately pour it into the buttered and floured mold. Cook as above.

Champigny Cake *(Gâteau Champigny)*

A specialty of a fine Parisian pastry bakery, which has been very famous for a long time. To sum it up, this is a cake made of a square of puff pastry, which is stuffed with apricot marmalade. It is essential that this marmalade be free of whole pieces of fruit and that it be very thick. If you do not have any of this in your pantry, homemade, go to a fine food store and buy almost double the quantity given below so that you can then reduce it to the right consistency, which is this: when you dip two fingers into the marmalade and then separate them, it should form a strong glue. Dropped onto a plate, it should spread out very little. While the marmalade is reducing on the heat, mix it continuously, gently drawing the spoon across the bottom of the pot. *Time: 1 hour, 15 minutes total.*

***For the puff pastry:* 250 grams (8 7/8 ounces) of flour; 1 1/2 deciliters (5 fluid ounces, 2/3 cup) of water; 5 grams (1/6 ounce) of salt; 250 grams (8 7/8 ounces, 1 cup plus 2 tablespoons) of butter.**

250 grams (8 7/8 ounces) of very reduced apricot marmalade; 50 grams (1 3/4 ounces) of confectioners' sugar flavored with vanilla, to sprinkle over the cake.

PROCEDURE. Prepare the puff pastry, making six turns as directed (SEE PUFF PASTRY, PAGE 658). Roll it out to a thickness of scarcely 5–6 millimeters (about 3/16 inch), into an exact rectangle 30–32 centimeters (12–12 3/4 inches) long and 15–16 centimeters (6–6 1/4 inches) wide: so that when it is divided in two crosswise, the rectangle of dough will provide two squares of dough that are perfectly equal.

With a large knife, cut these squares cleanly, cutting off 2–3 millimeters (1/16–1/8 inch) at the edges to give them a perfectly straight line. Place one of these squares on a baking sheet that has been lightly moistened with a brush dipped in water. On the dough, spread out the apricot marmalade in a layer at least 1 centimeter (3/8 inch) thick. On all four sides, leave a border about 2 centimeters (3/4 inch) wide that is not coated with apricot. Use a brush to moisten the edge *lightly* with water. Roll the second square of dough on the rolling pin to pick it up and then, holding the rolling pin a few centimeters above the square covered with marmalade, unroll the dough over it, exactly lining up the edges of the two squares. Press on the edges *not* coated with marmalade to thoroughly seal the edges.

Put it in a good strong medium oven. Allow *15–20 minutes* for baking. But if the oven is good, *after 12–15 minutes* the cake must be very close to being perfectly done—in other words, a beautiful reddish color, with the dough firm enough that it does not yield to the touch.

When the cake has partially cooled, coat it generously with confectioners' sugar.

Success Cake *(Gâteau Dit "Le Succès")*

An exquisite cake, a kind of pastry-shop cake, that is nonetheless quite simple to make. Its name differs according to the choice of decoration, and also according to the bakeries, but its filling always remains the same: three rounds of almond paste (marzipan) superimposed, covering a thick layer of praline cream. The whole piece, both in shape and size, resembles a tambourine. The surface is decorated quite simply: either glazed with white fondant or with coffee fondant; or covered with a light layer of cream when it is filled, and sprinkled with chopped almonds. We suggest using the latter decoration because it is the easiest and quickest to make and has an excellent taste. As for the shape, this seems to date from the origin of the cake. One can always ice it with fondant, depending on taste and abilities. In any case, the sides of the cake are always covered with cream and almonds no matter which decoration is used on top.

The rounds of dough can be made well in advance because they do not contain butter, and can be kept somewhere quite dry, like macaroons. The same is also true for the praline, which can be kept in reserve. Equally for the almonds, which are husked, dried, and then crushed in a grinder. So, when you are preparing the cake, you need only to make the cream and allow it to cool before putting the rounds of almond paste on top.

Dress the cake well in advance, preferably the evening before. The dough thus becomes more tender and moist because of the cream; and the whole piece has more cohesion and stability, which means that the cake can be cut more neatly. *Time: About 4 hours (2 scant hours for the rounds of almond paste; 1 hour for the praline; 1 hour for making and chilling the cream; 15 minutes to dress the cake). Makes a large cake about 25 centimeters (10 inches) in diameter, enough to serve 12–15 people.*

For the almond paste: 300 grams (10 1/2 ounces) of crushed almonds; 300 grams (10 1/2 ounces) of superfine sugar; 7 egg whites beaten very firm.

For the praline cream: 3 1/2 deciliters (1 1/2 cups) of milk; a half vanilla bean; 200 grams (7 ounces) of superfine sugar; 7 egg yolks; 200 grams (7 ounces) of praline; 300 grams (10 1/2 ounces, 1 1/3 cups) of very good butter.

For the decoration: 60 grams (2 1/4 ounces) of toasted chopped almonds; 2 tablespoons of fondant to glaze it if you like.

PROCEDURE. **The rounds or layers of almond paste:** *The baking sheets.* Whether these are made of black steel, round or square, is unimportant. But given the size of the cake, a sheet for each round is necessary. If you do not have three sheets, you should cook the rounds one after the other on the same sheet, being careful in this case *to completely chill it before placing a new round of dough there.*

Once the baking sheets are scrupulously clean, heat them lightly before buttering them with a brush: just as if oiling them. Do not use too much butter on the sheet, because the dough will run and spread out while baking. Place the buttered sheets on the table.

The almonds. Husk them as directed (SEE PAGE 573). Dry them in an extremely gentle oven *without roasting them at all.* Then pass them through a mechanical grater, using a cylinder fine enough to make a powder rather than just pieces. Put this powder on a paper spread out on a table and mix it with the superfine sugar.

The egg whites: Whisk them into a snow as directed (SEE PAGE 8).

The marzipan: Drop the sugared almond powder in a shower onto the whipped whites, and as you do so, mix the whites as directed (SEE PAGE 10).

Next, powder the baking sheets that you have already buttered with a light dusting of flour. Put a pastry or flan ring of the right diameter onto each sheet, using this to mark the size of the round, so that you can trace a regular, even circumference line.

With a pastry scraper or a large card, take out the marzipan dough and divide it among the three sheets. Using the blade of a large kitchen knife, flatten the dough into a pancake, leveling the surface to give it the same thickness at the edges as in the center. Immediately put it in the oven.

Baking it: An oven with an extremely moderate heat, to give the dough time to cook without coloring too rapidly. So watch it carefully.

Cook for *1/2 hour:* by then, the rounds will have notably collapsed and taken on a blond tint, a light café au lait. Take them out of the oven at this moment and let them cool on the sheets before sliding the blade of a knife under them. They are extremely fragile when still hot. Turn them over, then put them into the oven for a few moments to thoroughly dry and to color the part that was in contact with the sheet, which will often not be colored in a home oven. Then allow them to completely cool.

If you do not have a sufficient number of sheets, you must shape and cook the rounds one after the other, being careful to keep the rest of the dough in a cool place; then, before dressing a new layer, be careful to grease and powder the sheet again, and to cool the *bottom side* under the water tap so that the sheet is no longer hot.

The praline: If you do not have any in reserve, prepare it as indicated at right.

The praline cream: This is actually a buttercream. First, prepare a crème anglaise with milk infused with vanilla, sugar, and egg yolk, as directed (SEE CRÈME ANGLAISE, PAGE 582). Let it almost cool, stirring it rather often during this time with a wooden spoon to keep it smooth and well combined.

Meanwhile, crush the praline again; this has already been reduced to a powder, but an *absolutely fine* powder is essential. In winter, soften the butter as directed (SEE PAGE 657). On a board, mix the softened butter and the praline together, using the large blade of a big knife to produce a perfectly mixed and homogeneous batter or paste. Use your knife to transfer this paste into the barely lukewarm crème, from which the vanilla bean has been removed. Mix it thoroughly. The praline cream is ready to fill the cake.

Assembling the cake: Once the rounds have been absolutely cooled, place the ring on top of them, one after the other, and use a large knife to cut off everything that goes beyond the circle.

Place the first round on a rack, and with the knife transfer a little less than half of the cream there. Level it out perfectly with the knife and cover it with the second round. Then transfer the same quantity of cream there, reserving only a very small part to spread over the sides of the cake and its surface if you do not glaze it with fondant.

Level the cream on the second round, and finally cover it with the third, placing it so that the *bottom* of the round is on top, given that the side that stood on the plate while cooking is smoother. With a knife, spread all the sides of the cake with the reserved cream; you can easily do this by using your left hand to lift up the grille or rack on which the cake stands, while you coat the cake, turning it. Also, spread this cream over the surface of the top if you are not covering the cake with fondant.

Then coat the sides and the top surface with not too finely chopped almonds, picking up a handful in your right hand to sprinkle them all over: hold the rack with the cake in your left hand over a plate, which is where the excess almonds will fall.

The finished cake must be kept for at least 2 hours in a very cool place.

Praline *(Le Pralin).* Currently employed in pastry making for all kinds of uses, praline, a mixture of almonds and sugar cooked to a caramel, is a nougat that is finely crushed. Preserved in a metal container, it will keep indefinitely, and it is therefore to your advantage to prepare a certain quantity of it in advance, particularly given that the work is neither longer nor more complicated when making, say, 450 grams (1 pound) of praline than a lesser quantity.

The proportions are an equal weight of superfine sugar and almonds (ready for use). The almonds are first husked (SEE ALMONDS, PAGE 573), then dried in the oven. For this, spread them out on a baking sheet and put them in a very gentle oven. Watch them carefully and move them often; they must take on a very light blond, uniform tint, without any brown spots, which would give a burned taste to the praline. They are now ready to be used.

Use a copper saucepan that is not lined with tin, or if you do not have that, a good strong saucepan in aluminum. Tin would melt and mix with the sugar when cooking. Put only the superfine sugar in the saucepan: *no water at all,* just a few drops of lemon juice.

Melt the sugar gradually on low heat, and use a very clean wooden spoon to mix the unmelted sugar into the sugar that has already liquefied. Be patient; don't be too hasty. Otherwise, you may see the sugar burn on the bottom or become grainy and turn into dull insoluble crystals. Make sure you use a wooden spoon that has never been used in any greasy dish, because any trace of fat is harmful to the cooking of the sugar.

What you are doing is cooking the sugar to a caramel. Once the sugar has gradually and fully taken on a beautiful *dark blond* tint, and as soon as you see it smoke, immediately turn off the heat; immediately throw in the almonds, which you must have on hand. Using a wooden spoon, mix and combine everything together, quickly and while the sugar is still liquid: it sets very rapidly.

Then pour the mixture onto the corner of a marble slab that has been very lightly oiled with sweet almond oil: or if you do not have one, onto the tinned, oiled back of a large saucepan cover.

Let it cool well before crushing this nougat. Then pass it through a metallic drum sieve that is not too fine, or a medium-size strainer, above a sheet of paper. Then crush it and roll it under a rolling pin to make a kind of fine and even crumb. Keep it dry.

Mocha Cake *(Gâteau Moka)*

Even though this cake looks the same as other cakes, the way it is made differs. In principle, it is a sponge cake cooked in a low mold, then divided into disks, and filled and covered with a mocha cream. But the sponge cake batter can be made in several ways; it can even be a genoise batter. Furthermore, the cream—the type known as buttercream—can be made with syrup, or with what is known in professional pastry making as an "Italian meringue." Below, we give the recipe most suitable to modern preparations. The sponge cake must be prepared enough in advance so that it is completely cooled when the cream is ready: hot or lukewarm it cuts very badly. Finally, the cream must be used when it is still a little bit lukewarm; If not, it will take on a consistency that makes handling it difficult. *Time: 1 hour for the preparation and cooking; 2 hours to cool it. Makes a cake 20 centimeters (8 inches) in diameter.*

For the batter: **4 whole eggs; 125 grams (4 1/2 ounces) of superfine sugar; 110 grams (3 7/8 ounces) of good wheat flour, carefully sifted through a drum sieve onto a sheet of paper.**

For the buttercream: **150 grams (5 1/3 ounces) of sugar, in cubes or crystallized; 1 deciliter (3 1/3 ounces, scant 1/2 cup) of water; 4 egg yolks; 40 grams (1 3/8 ounces) of ground coffee; 150 grams (5 1/3 ounces, 10 1/2 tablespoons) of fine butter.**

PROCEDURE. Warm up a terrine or a salad bowl by passing some boiling water through it; wipe it dry; break in the eggs, both the whites and the yolks; add the superfine sugar. Using a whisk a little larger than a sauce whisk, work the eggs and the sugar until this mixture has obviously paled in color and makes the ribbon (SEE PAGE 577).

Then, with your left hand, lift up the sheet of paper covered with flour, and drop this in a shower onto the batter, while using your right hand to stir with a spatula or a stiff card, as you would do for whisked egg whites beaten into a snow (SEE PAGE 8).

The mold: Choose the mold known as *à manqué,* also called a *round cake pan* (see *fig.* 68, PAGE 576). For these quantities, it should be 20 centimeters (8 inches) in diameter. Butter the inside of it with unmelted butter, spreading it with the tip of your finger. Pour in the batter, which should fill it by only three-quarters. Strike it lightly on the table to level out the batter. Put it in the oven, always in the lower part.

To cook: *Very moderate oven.* If the heat is too strong, the dough rises a great deal, but then falls. At the right temperature, cook it for *30–35 minutes.* The dough will rise by about one-third; when it has done so, cover it with a sheet of paper to stop it from coloring excessively.

When you take the cake out of the oven, unmold it immediately onto a rack or drum sieve, so that the air can circulate completely around it and prevent it from softening. Allow it to completely cool.

The buttercream: Prepare it as directed (SEE BUTTERCREAM, PAGE 584).

Using a long, large-bladed knife, divide the sponge cake crosswise into three disks of equal thickness.

(Note that what was the top of the sponge cake while cooking is going to become the bottom: This is because the cake pan is slightly flared, so when the sponge cake is turned over, it provides a larger base; and also because while cooking, the top of the cake receives direct heat and therefore forms more of a crust than the batter on the bottom of the pan. For this reason, it is better to use this part as the base.)

On this slice or disk that will serve as the bottom layer, spread out a rather thick layer of buttercream on the cut side. Place the middle slice on top and spread out another layer of buttercream. Cover with the third slice. Using a knife blade, cover everything uniformly with a layer of buttercream.

Put the rest of the buttercream into a cone of strong paper, cutting the end with scissors. Then, using it as a pastry bag, decorate the cake as you like. Put it on a plate that is covered with a tea napkin, one that is large enough across the bottom so that the cake can be placed on it completely *good and flat*, so that you do not leave any ripples on the surface. Keep it in a cool place so that it firms up nicely before being served.

We have not suggested using crystal sugar for the decoration, as can be seen at some pastry shops, because although preparing this sugar is not difficult, it takes quite a long time. It can be summarized thus: use the rolling pin to crush some sugar cubes. Pass the fragments through a strainer with holes the size of the grain you want to obtain; then roll these grains over a screen to turn them into round grains by rubbing them.

Minute Cake *(Gâteau à la Minute)*

This is a kind of light pound cake with raisins, very popular at tea; actually, it is a type of plum cake, and given the slight thickness of the cake, it needs only 25–30 minutes to bake. Use a low mold, a cake pan (see *fig.* 68, page 576), or a simple tart ring placed on a baking sheet or tart pan. *Time: 35–40 minutes total. Makes a cake measuring 24 centimeters (9 1/2 inches) in diameter and 2 1/2 centimeters (1 inch) in height.*

125 grams (4 1/2 ounces) of flour; 125 grams (4 1/2 ounces, 9 tablespoons) of butter; 125 grams (4 1/2 ounces) of superfine sugar; 75 grams (2 2/3 ounces) of Corinth raisins; 4 grams (1/6 ounce) of baking powder; 2 eggs; 1 tablespoon of rum; 1 additional tablespoon of superfine sugar.

PROCEDURE. Prepare the raisins as directed for *plum cake* (SEE PAGE 691). The initial maceration is just as important.

Cut a round of white parchment paper 3 fingers larger than the edges of the cake pan or of the ring. Lightly oil the pan or the sheet and the inside of the tart ring just enough so that the paper sticks to it. Apply the round of paper to the bottom, pushing it down to mark the angle clearly: push it up along the sides, fixing it as you go with a few vertical pleats.

Work the butter into a pomade in a terrine (SEE PAGE 16). Add: the sugar, the eggs, the raisins, and the flour. Work the dough and the mixture absolutely as directed for plum cake (SEE PAGE 691). Observe to the letter all the directions about making sure the different ingredients are all lukewarm.

Pour the batter into the pan or ring. Strike it lightly on the table to even out the batter. Sprinkle over the reserved sugar. Put it immediately into a steady and medium oven.

Cooking it: Because of the raisins, note the same precautions for plum cake about the heat coming from the bottom. The batter must at least double in height. It may rise more while cooking, but it will subsequently settle. Avoid leaving the oven door open for a long time. If the surface colors too quickly, cover the cake with a buttered paper.

You know it is properly cooked when you can press it lightly with your finger and feel it firm, but supple and elastic. If you were to wait for it to become firmer, it would dry out. For this cake, it is not a matter of waiting until it comes away from the paper the way other cakes come away from the pan; the paper is used here to prevent the cake from shrinking after cooking.

If the cake does not seem cooked enough, it will not spoil if left in the oven for another 5–10 minutes—or even more, depending on the temperature of the oven. Remove it from the pan. Place it on a rack on the paper side.

Do not take off the paper until it has cooled completely.

Orange Cake *(Gâteau à l'Orange)*

Very fine and very delicate, this cake is as good accompanied by a cream for a dessert as it is when served alone as a snack. Actually, it is a ladyfinger batter with crushed almonds added to it. It keeps very well and stays fresh for two or three days. *Time: 45 minutes of preparation; 30–35 minutes for cooking. Makes a cake about 20 centimeters (8 inches) in diameter.*

125 grams (4 1/2 ounces) of superfine sugar; 125 grams (4 1/2 ounces) of almonds, crushed or grated; 60 grams (2 1/4 ounces) of rice starch (cream of rice); 3 whole eggs; 1 orange; 1 small walnut-sized piece of butter.

PROCEDURE. The mold to use for this cake is the mold known as *à manqué* or a cake pan (see *fig.* 68, PAGE 576), 20 centimeters (8 inches) in diameter at the bottom and 22 centimeters (8 1/2 inches) at the opening. Cut a round of light, white parchment paper exactly the size of the mold so that it does not come up the sides at all. Butter it on both sides, along with the sides of the pan. Apply the round of paper to the bottom, pushing it down well with your fingers so that it sticks perfectly, avoiding any bubbles, which would make hollow places in the batter when it is baked.

Husk the almonds as directed (SEE PAGE 573). When completely dried, pass them through a mechanical grater; or if you do not have this accessory, crush them in the mortar. With a very clean small grater, grate all the zest or colored skin of the orange, being careful not to include any of the white skin, which is quite bitter. Set to one side.

Squeeze all the juice from the orange into a cup through a fine strainer or a cloth strainer.

Using a wooden spoon, beat the egg yolks with the sugar in a terrine until the mixture, now a light mousse, has obviously lightened in color.

Add the starch, dropping it down in a shower while you continue to beat it, then add the orange peel and the almonds, either crushed or grated. These will substantially thicken the batter. Add the orange juice at the same time, and continue to beat the batter until thoroughly mixed.

Whisk the egg whites into a firm snow and mix them into the batter, taking due care (SEE PAGE 10). Immediately pour the batter into the pan, which it should fill by only about half. Lightly strike the mold on a towel folded in four on a table, to completely level out the batter.

Baking it: Immediately put it in a good medium oven; and, of course, it should go at the very bottom of the oven, so that the batter receives more heat from the bottom than from the top.

Allow a good 1/2 hour for cooking. The batter rises gradually and evenly, without bulging. It doubles in height while rising, then returns almost to its original height as baking finishes. The baking is complete when the cake comes away from all around the sides of the mold and is quite firm, while still remaining supple to the touch.

Unmold it onto a drum sieve or a rack with the paper side facing *up.* Do not remove the paper until the cake has completely cooled, because it stops the cake from shrinking.

Queen of Sheba Cake *(Gâteau Reine de Saba)*

A chocolate cake of particular finesse, from a recipe that was once transcribed from a family collection of recipes. This entirely fanciful name has spread since then, along with the recipe, which is offered unchanged here, although more methodically outlined.

What distinguishes this cake, and what makes it very popular, is an interior that is soft and smooth, giving the impression of a chocolate bonbon. So make sure, above all, to avoid overcooking, which would work against that effect. Even if it is solid enough that it can be cut into slices, the cake should remain very tender. This is why we recommend a square cake pan, if you have one, because cutting the cake is much easier in this shape.

It can be prepared one or two days in advance; at any rate, do not frost it until the day you serve it. In fact, it can easily be kept for up to a week if you are careful to wrap it in aluminum foil; if you like, you can also prepare the batter for several cakes at a time. *Time: 1 hour for preparation; 35 minutes for cooking. Serves 6–8.*

**125 grams ($4^1/_2$ ounces) of almonds, net weight;
125 grams ($4^1/_2$ ounces) of very good chocolate;
125 grams ($4^1/_2$ ounces, 9 tablespoons) of good fresh butter; 125 grams ($4^1/_2$ ounces) of superfine sugar;
3 egg yolks; 4 whites whisked into a firm snow;
50 grams ($1^3/_4$ ounces) of excellent white flour;
12 grams ($^3/_8$ ounce) of vanilla sugar (SEE PAGE 574).**

To frost the cake: **30 grams (1 ounce) of chocolate;
125 grams ($4^1/_2$ ounces) of confectioners' sugar.
A square cake pan 20 centimeters (8 inches) on each side and 4 centimeters ($1^1/_2$ inches) high or a round pan of the same height about 22 centimeters ($8^1/_2$ inches) in diameter (see *fig.* 68, PAGE 576).**

PROCEDURE. Husk the almonds as directed (SEE ALMONDS, PAGE 573). If you have a special grinder for this use, pass them through the machine using *the finest blade.* If not, do the work in the mortar, working the pestle as directed for GENOA CAKE (SEE PAGE 696); in this case, to keep the almonds from turning oily, add some superfine sugar (taken from the total quantity) and 2–3 tablespoons of water. This will make a true almond paste.

Break the chocolate into very small pieces. Put it in a bowl with a scant 3 tablespoons of hot water. Keep it warm to soften it, and then work it with a small wooden spoon to bring it to the state of a perfectly smooth paste.

Into an earthenware terrine containing all the ingredients for the batter, put the butter that has been worked into a pomade (SEE PAGE 16). Using a wooden spoon, mix in the prepared chocolate. Add the egg yolks *one by one,* always vigorously working the batter; then the superfine sugar, little by little; the almond paste, constantly turning and beating the mixture in any direction at all; and finally the flour, previously sifted onto a sheet of paper and in which the vanilla sugar has been mixed; drop it in a shower on the paper from a low height and mix it as you go.

To mold it: Butter the inside and particularly the corners of the pan with a kitchen brush dipped in half-melted butter. Then sprinkle flour over it (SEE PAGE 658).

Whisk the whites into a very firm snow (SEE EGG WHITES, PAGE 8). First mix in one-third of the whites thoroughly, and then the rest (SEE PAGE 10). Pour it into the pan. Lightly tap the pan on a folded towel to slightly compact the batter.

Put it immediately into a good medium oven, one with more heat coming from the bottom than the top, so that the surface of the cake does not form a crust too rapidly, which will keep the batter from rising. It rises a good deal, and will reach its complete development in the middle of cooking. Allow *30–35 minutes for cooking.* Before taking out the cake, test it with a cooking needle: it must come out very clean, only shiny and *burning hot.*

Unmold the cake when it comes out of the oven, turning it over onto a rack. After cooking, the top of the cake becomes the bottom, so there is no problem about marks from the wires of the rack.

Allow the cake to completely cool before frosting it with an uncooked chocolate icing (SEE PAGE 723).

Chocolate Cake *(Gâteau au Chocolat)*

This is a contemporary, very simple recipe, and not terribly expensive, the chocolate and butter featuring in modest quantities. The cake hardly collapses at all after cooking and remains tender inside.

Use either a cake pan (see *fig.* 68, PAGE 576) or an ordinary tart ring, according to availability. *Time: 45 minutes of preparation; 30 minutes of cooking. Serves 6.*

100 grams ($3^1/_2$ ounces) of chocolate; 3 eggs; 100 grams ($3^1/_2$ ounces) of superfine sugar; 50 grams ($1^3/_4$ ounces, $3^1/_2$ tablespoons) of fresh butter; 50 grams ($1^3/_4$ ounces) of fine sifted flour; 1 teaspoon of powdered vanilla (SEE PAGE 574).

PROCEDURE. Put the chocolate squares into a very mild oven to soften them.

In a terrine, beat the egg yolks with the sugar, using a wooden spoon, until the mixture has taken on a whitish tint and makes the ribbon (SEE PAGE 577). Add the butter to it, after making it into a pomade in a bowl (SEE PAGE 16). In the same bowl, now emptied, work the chocolate into a paste; add it to the mixture.

Add the flour, dropping it in gradually in a shower. Keep everything at a lukewarm temperature while you whisk the whites.

Whisk the whites into a very firm snow (SEE PAGE 8). Mix one-third of them into the mixture thoroughly to soften the batter. Add the rest as directed (SEE PAGE 10). Fill the pan, generously buttered and floured (SEE PAGE 658).

Put it immediately into an oven with a good heat coming from the bottom. Allow about *25 minutes for cooking.* The batter, which shrinks from all around the sides of the mold, will have a firm surface, be supple to the touch, and remain soft and moist inside, giving the false impression that it is not properly cooked.

Immediately unmold it on a rack and allow it to cool. If you like, you can serve the cake just as it is, or frosted (SEE ICING CAKES, PAGE 721).

Chestnut Cake *(Gâteau de Marrons)*

This recipe comes from a precious family notebook, where it is described as "perfect." It deserves to be because this cake, even though it is one of the simplest to make, gives the impression of coming from a very fine patisserie. It can be served two ways: as a cold dessert, covered with whipped cream, or as a cake, a snack, or for tea; and in this case, iced with an uncooked coffee or chocolate icing. This cake keeps for several days. *Time: 2 hours. Serves 8–10.*

50 nice chestnuts; 250 grams (8 7/8 ounces) of superfine sugar; 200 grams (7 ounces) of good fresh butter; 5 eggs; a good pinch of powedered vanilla (SEE PAGE 574).

PROCEDURE. Boil the chestnuts to shell them (SEE CHESTNUTS, PAGE 521); as they are peeled, put them into a saucepan containing, for the quantities above, 1/2 liter (generous 2 cups) of boiling water. Bring it back to a boil. Cover and cook gently; *25–30 minutes* should be enough for them to be properly done: the pulp should be transparent when you open a chestnut. Prolonging the cooking time will allow them to absorb too much liquid for this recipe.

While they are still burning hot, force them through the drum sieve, 4–5 at a time. Collect the purée in a terrine. Mix it with a wooden spoon. Add the superfine sugar to it, which will melt and dilute the puree; then the egg yolks, one by one, beating the purée vigorously as you go; and the vanilla powder. Finally add the butter, after making it into a pomade (SEE PAGE 16).

Butter a charlotte mold that measures, for the quantities above, 18–20 centimeters (7–8 inches) in diameter by 10 centimeters (4 inches) high.

Whisk the egg whites into a firm snow (SEE WHISKING EGG WHITES, PAGE 8). First mix in a quarter of them thoroughly, then the rest as directed (SEE PAGE 10). Pour the batter into the mold. Lightly strike it on a folded towel on the table to compact it. Put it into a very moderate oven immediately.

Allow *a good 1/2 hour* for cooking, noting that the cake will lose its tenderness if it is baked for too long. You must bake it for only long enough to set the batter so that it can be unmolded. But it must be absolutely smooth like the inside of a fine bonbon, though dense enough that it can be cut into thin slices without crumbling.

The dough rises very little. As soon as the batter comes away from the mold, it is done.

Let it just about cool to ensure that the cake settles before you unmold it. Frost it with uncooked chocolate or coffee icing (SEE ICING CAKES, PAGE 721).

Meringues *(Meringues)*

The composition of meringues includes only egg whites and superfine sugar, whose proportions can vary slightly.

But the success of meringues depends on three conditions that never change: First, the way in which the whites are whisked into a snow, and for which the use of an egg white basin made of copper is preferable (if you do not have this, beat the eggs in a small copper basin for cooking sugar); second, the methodical and carefully planned method of shaping the batter; third, the very gentle heat of the oven. *Time: 1 hour, 45 minutes.*

50 grams (1 3/4 ounces) of *superfine* sugar for each egg white used; 4 egg whites make 2 dozen meringues, each meringue being made up of two parts. These parts are, depending on the filling, simply stuck together by some marmalade, or hollowed out in the form of a cup and filled with a cream, then joined together.

PROCEDURE. **The preparations:** Before doing anything else, adjust the oven temperature. Strictly speaking, it is not so much a question of cooking here: rather, a matter of drying out the batter without letting it color. A plate warmer that heats up well, found in many home ranges, is here preferable to the oven itself.

Meanwhile, gather together on the table all the ingredients so that you have everything ready at hand while you work. Thus: the *egg white basin,* placed on top of a towel rolled into a ring, and a whisk; *a pastry pouch* (SEE USING A PASTRY BAG, PAGE 15), with a nozzle that has a diameter of 14 millimeters (1/2 inch) and fitted with a cork stuck into the opening of the nozzle as a kind of valve or faucet; *1 or 2 baking sheets made of thick steel* for pastry, scrupulously clean, lightly but extremely evenly buttered and dusted with flour; *a silver tablespoon; a wooden spatula* or a very large wooden spoon that is used only for creams and pastry; the superfine *sugar,* weighed; the *egg whites,* carefully examined.

The batter: Whisk the whites into a firm snow (SEE WHISKING EGG WHITES, PAGE 8). When they have reached the correct point, add 1 tablespoon of sugar to them; whisk to mix. This light addition of sugar helps the whites to solidify; a few turns of the whisk will suffice, and the consistency will be substantially firmer. After this, mix in all the sugar, pouring it in a shower onto the egg whites, proceeding as directed (SEE INCORPORATING THE WHITES, PAGE 10). Once the mixing is done, it will produce a batter that, when raised on the spatula, will fall off in thick and smooth ribbons.

To shape the batter: If possible, have another person hold the pastry bag all the way open. With a spatula, fill it as directed (SEE PAGE 15). (The quantities of the dough above supply enough to fill an ordinary pouch twice.) Make little piles the look and size of a half egg.

Once the baking sheet has been covered, generously sprinkle the meringues with *confectioners' sugar.* Allow everything to rest for *about 10 minutes,* so that the inside of the meringues will be impregnated with the sugar, which will form little pearls on the surface when cooking. After this, hold the sheet vertically over a sheet of paper to shake off all the excess sugar; the meringues will not budge. Put it in the oven.

To bake: Leave the meringues in the oven for *at least 45 minutes to 1 hour.* At the end of this time, they should have taken on only a milky tint, different from the snow-white of the raw batter. The small pearls of sugar, spread irregularly around the surface, will be colored only slightly more than the rest: nothing more.

This is the moment to make them into shells, without allowing them to cool. Pick them up one after the other in the palm of your left hand, flat side up. With the two fingers of your right hand, gently press on the meringue, also pushing down the thin crust, which will collapse, following the round outside shape of the meringue.

Put them back in the oven, with the hollowed-out side up, to dry the inside: 5–6 minutes will be enough.

After the meringues have cooled, keep them dry until you fill them. Put them in a metal box and they will keep almost indefinitely.

Macaroons *(Macarons)*

This recipe is one that produces macaroons with a tender inside, and has become a sort of classic; this is one of the oldest and most popular recipes. A mortar is essential for working the almonds; you can, if you like, add a few bitter almonds to accentuate the characteristic flavor of the macaroon. *Time: 1 hour, 15 minutes. Makes 2 dozen macaroons.*

250 grams (8 7/8 ounces) of almonds, weighed without their husks; 4–5 bitter almonds (optional); 250 grams (8 7/8 ounces) of sugar *in cubes*; and 250 grams (8 7/8 ounces) of very fine powdered sugar, known as *confectioners' or icing sugar;* 7 egg whites.

PROCEDURE. Husk the almonds (SEE PAGE 573). Then spread them out on a large drum sieve to dry in a plate warmer, or at a warm room temper ature, but not in an oven. For this recipe, it is a matter of drying them out well *without roasting them.* They are ready when they break easily when you bend them.

Put them into the mortar with *one-third of the sugar cubes.* With the pestle, first crush them; then, moving the pestle all around the walls of the mortar, reduce everything to powder; then pass it through a metallic drum sieve placed over a large paper.

Put any almond pieces remaining on the drum

sieve back into the mortar. Add to them *the second third of sugar cubes* and pound them more. Pass them a second time through the drum sieve.

Put the little bit of residue remaining on the drum sieve into the mortar, adding to it *the rest of the sugar cubes.* Work it some more, then finally add all the powder that has passed through the drum sieve to it at the same time as the confectioners' sugar, *reserving 50 grams (1¾ ounces) of the sugar.*

Put everything back into the mortar and then incorporate into the powder, *one after the other,* 4 egg whites in their natural state—that is, just as they are once they have been separated from the yolk. Vigorously work the mixture for 2 minutes between each new addition of egg white. You need to get a very firm and smooth paste or batter from this.

Whisk the 3 other egg whites into a firm snow (SEE WHISKING EGG WHITES, PAGE 8). Then add to them the rest of the confectioners' sugar, which should prevent them from separating. Mix them in, tablespoon by tablespoon, with the batter still in the mortar, taking due care and with the movements suggested (SEE PAGE 10).

Put the dough into a pastry pouch with a nozzle that has a diameter of 1½ centimeters (⅝ inch) (SEE USING A PASTRY BAG, PAGE 15). Shape the macaroons: either directly on the baking sheets, which have been lightly buttered and floured; or on sheets of strong parchment paper laid out on unbuttered baking sheets. Using paper will mean that the inside surface of the macaroon will be slightly tacky, so you will be able to stick the macaroons together two at a time when they come out of the oven. So, on a baking sheet or on parchment paper, lay down the macaroons—that is, shape them—at a distance of 4 centimeters (1½ inches) from each other, because the batter will spread out while baking. Press on the pouch to make the batter into a round shape 4 centimeters (1½ inches) in diameter, which will expand to about 5 centimeters (2 inches) after baking.

Put them into a rather moderate oven with the heat coming *mostly from the top;* it is the top and not the bottom of the macaroons that must dry out to form a light crust. Avoid any air drafts when you open the oven door to check the macaroons. Allow *15–18 minutes for cooking.*

If the macaroons have been shaped on the paper, take them off as soon as you take them out of the oven.

Madeleines *(Madeleines)*

Here we are dealing with those very well known cakes that are molded in the shape of an elongated shell. The recipes for the batter vary, not in terms of the ingredients, which are always the same, or their size, but in terms of how the batter is prepared. We give here the simplest procedure: it produces very delicate cakes. *Time: 1 hour. Makes a dozen medium-size madeleines.*

125 grams (4½ ounces) of flour; 125 grams (4½ ounces) of superfine sugar; 125 grams (4½ ounces, 9 tablespoons) of butter; 4 eggs; 1 teaspoon of concentrated orange flower water; 40–50 grams (1⅜–1¾ ounces) of clarified butter to butter the mold.

PROCEDURE. Clarify the butter as directed (SEE PAGE 16). With a brush, generously butter the molds; as you do, place them upside down on a baking sheet to drain the excess butter.

In a small saucepan, gently heat the butter for the batter without letting it boil. It must be just melted so that, when left to stand, the casein element will fall to the bottom of the saucepan, forming a whitish deposit.

Sift the flour onto a sheet of paper.

In a small terrine, work the eggs with the sugar, using a wooden spoon or a small whisk until the mixture makes the ribbon (SEE PAGE 577). Add the orange flower water, then the flour, dropping it in a shower as you mix it, just as you would for whisked egg whites beaten into a snow (SEE PAGE 8). Finally, pour the melted butter in a small stream into the center of the batter, turning it gently with the wooden spoon to mix. Make sure you do not allow the deposit at the bottom of the saucepan to run into the dough.

Fill the molds by only two-thirds, and as you do so, place them on a baking sheet. Put them immediately into a good medium oven, not too strong.

Cook for *25 minutes.* If the oven is a little hot, cover the madeleines with paper at the end of about 10 minutes.

Unmold them as soon as they come out of the oven, and arrange them on a rack or frame so that they can be surrounded by air as they cool.

Fritters *(Merveilles)*

Depending on the region and with a few variants in the preparation, these are known as oreillettes, roussettes, nœuds-d'amour, bugnes, etc. But a characteristic they all share is that they are deep-fried: and in the Midi, it is, of course, oil that is the cooking fat.

The good, authentic recipe given here has been used for more than a century by an old family from the Charente, where, traditionally, it cannot be a holiday unless there is a large platter of merveilles. We are publishing it here exactly as it has always been made, as much in terms of the ingredients, where rough brown sugar is used instead of white sugar, as in the way the batter is worked: the greater part of the work is done in a terrine in a completely home-style fashion. The frying fat used is good lard.

Merveilles prepared like this make a sandy fritter with an outside that has a beautiful golden tint. The outside crust is about 3 millimeters (1/8 inch) thick. Perfectly crunchy, they do not have any greasy trace. You eat them cold. They will last for a week, kept in a tin or metal box. *Time: 45 minutes of preparation (but 15 hours to allow the batter to stand); 30 minutes of cooking.*

1 1/2 kilograms (3 pounds, 5 ounces) of flour; 750 grams (1 pound, 10 ounces) of rough brown sugar; 8 whole eggs; 250 grams (8 7/8 ounces, 1 cup plus 2 tablespoons) of good butter; 5 grams (1/6 ounce) of good salt; 4 hefty tablespoons of rum; as much of cognac; 3 good tablespoons of orange flower water; the zest of a lemon, finely minced; a vanilla bean.

PROCEDURE. Use a large earthenware terrine big enough to be able easily to work all the ingredients listed above. Put in the flour with the brown sugar. Mix them by rubbing them together between your hands to reduce the small lumps of brown sugar to a powder. Pick out any lumps that do not break up, then crush them and pulverize them using a pestle. Again, mix to make a perfectly fine and homogeneous powder from the flour and brown sugar. Then mix in the minced lemon zest, only the colored part of the skin.

Make the well, heaping up the powder against the walls of the terrine all around to expose the bottom of the receptacle. Break in the eggs. Add the salt, liqueurs, orange flower water, the inside of a vanilla bean, previously split, and the butter. Divide the butter into pieces the size of chestnuts, working it in a towel first to soften it, if necessary.

Now, with the ends of the fingers of your right hand, mix the butter, eggs, and liqueurs, turning them gently to avoid breaking the wall of flour; then mix that in, proceeding as for all other doughs. The mixture will gradually increase in volume and take on a firmer consistency, and you can then work it with your two hands.

Once all the flour has been mixed in, turn the dough out onto the table or a board. Gather it together in a heap: work it by squeezing it and pushing it under the palm of your hands, kneading just as you would proceed for bread. Assume it will take *20 minutes* of vigorous work to finish. The dough must then have the consistency of a sort of putty, lending itself to all kinds of handling, without keeping any marks where it has been joined together.

Gather it into a ball in the terrine. Cover it and let it rest for *at least 15 hours* in a very temperate environment.

To shape the fritters: Divide the dough into pieces with an average weight of 60 grams (2 1/4 ounces). Roll them vigorously between your hands into the form of a ball on a lightly floured table. Using a rolling pin, roll out each ball into a very thin sheet of dough, about 25 centimeters (10 inches) long and 16 centimeters (6 1/4 inches) wide.

With a special pastry roller or using the blade of a knife, make three parallel cuts lengthwise on each sheet, 4 centimeters (1 1/2 inches) apart, beginning and stopping about 4–5 centimeters (1 1/2–2 inches) from each end. Each sheet now will be 4 strips that are joined together at each end by a ribbon of the same width. Interlace these ribbons two by two, passing each pair of strips over the other one time only, simply to give the whole thing a feeling of undulation. Note that these cakes are in the frying mixture for only a very short time, so you must prepare a substantial quantity of dough in advance, all ready to be placed in the frying basin.

To fry: Heat up to the temperature appropriate for hot deep-frying (SEE DEEP-FRYING, PAGE 41). Given the extreme thinness of the dough and the loss of temperature caused by immersing the fritters, this is the proper amount of heat to use here.

Keep the frying basin on sustained heat. Put in the fritters 2 or 3 at a time, adding a new sheet of dough as you take one out to maintain the equilibrium of the temperature. The dough swells as soon as it is immersed in the hot fat. Turn the merveilles over, using a skimmer, and lift them out onto a large plate as soon as they are golden on both sides. That would be after *2–3 minutes* at the most. They will dry by themselves on the plate and become crunchy almost instantly.

If you like, sprinkle them with vanilla sugar (SEE PAGE 574) to serve them.

Anchovy Sticks *(Allumettes aux Anchois)*

In the towns of the Midi in Provence, these anchovy sticks have been a fashionable culinary delight for a long time; their preparation nonetheless differs according to circumstance. Buy this from the pastry shop, and it is a puff pastry wrapped around the anchovy, with a stuffing of fresh fish. For locals, in their old family kitchens, it is a kind of lining dough (pâte à foncer), which was once known as *pâte brisée;* only anchovy is used for these, and the anchovy sticks are cooked like fritters, in a large quantity of fat.

There is also a variant that is not at all southern, coming instead from Switzerland, but it is worth mentioning: grated Gruyère is added to the dough for the sticks. (The anchovies used here are, or course, salted anchovies, which come in a barrel, and not anchovies packed in oil.)

Home-Style Anchovy Sticks *(Allumettes aux Anchois, Façon Ménagère).* *Time: 2 hours (including time for resting the dough). Makes 20 sticks.*

500 grams (1 pound, 2 ounces) of flour; 300 grams (10 1/2 ounces, 1 1/3 cups) of butter; 2 deciliters (6 3/4 fluid ounces, 7/8 cup) of water; 10 grams (1/3 ounce) of salt; 1 dozen salted anchovies.

PROCEDURE. Prepare the dough as directed for lining dough (SEE PAGE 662). Knead it *(fraiser) two* times. Let it rest for 1 good hour. Then, using your rolling pin, give it three turns, as for puff pastry, leaving it to rest for 8–10 minutes between each turn.

Meanwhile, soak the anchovies in a generous amount of fresh water to desalinate them. Drain them and dry them on a towel. Scrape off the skin. With a small knife, separate the fillets and remove the backbone: each anchovy will therefore provide two fillets. Remove the minuscule bones and trim the edges, scraping with a knife any remaining barbs or scraps.

Once the dough has been turned for a third time, let it rest for only a few minutes. Then divide it into two equal parts. Spread it out with the rolling pin into two long strips of precisely the same size—that is, 2–3 millimeters (about 1/8 inch) thick at the most, with a length of about 12 centimeters (4 1/2 inches). The length of the strip is not so important because it varies according to the amount of dough used. The only thing that must be considered is the thickness of the dough and the width of the strip: the width of the strip will be the length of the sticks, which must be cut crosswise from the strip.

On one of the strips, place the fillets of anchovies crosswise at a distance of 3 centimeters (1 1/4 inches) from each other. Using a brush dipped in fresh water, moisten the dough between each fillet. Over this first strip holding the anchovies, place the second strip: to do this, fold the second one in two, then pick it up and place it on one end of the first strip, and then unfold it, carefully and evenly to extend it. Join the two strips together by pressing down with your fingers all around the anchovy fillets.

With a rolling pastry cutter or a good large knife, divide the dough between the fillets, to get pieces about 11–12 centimeters (4 1/4–4 1/2 inches) long by 3 centimeters (1 1/4 inches) wide.

To fry them, refer to the directions given (SEE FRITTERS, PAGE 715).

Anchovy Sticks with Puff Pastry *(Allumettes aux Anchois avec Pâté Feuilletée).* Prepare the dough with an equal weight of butter and flour, exactly as directed (SEE PAGE 658). Cut the strips and arrange the anchovies on the dough in the same manner and with the same size as above, but note that you must make *the two strips thicker: that is, 3–5 millimeters (1/8–3/16 inch).* If you are going add some fish stuffing to the anchovy fillets (SEE FISH DUMPLINGS, PAGE 461), add a little bit of crushed anchovies to it.

Cut the sticks very cleanly, because any frayed edges will prevent the dough from rising. Place them on a baking sheet moistened with water, glaze them with beaten egg, and put them immediately into a rather hot oven. Bake for *10–13 minutes.*

Cheese Sticks *(Allumettes au Fromage).* Very popular at the tea table; they keep for several days in a metal box; reheat them in a moderate oven. If you like, you can put a little bit of English mustard into the dough: that is, 2 grams (1/14 ounce), which you dilute along with the salt in the water of the well. According to preference, you can also add as much cayenne pepper as can be balanced on the point of a knife. *Time: 1 hour, 30 minutes.*

200 grams (7 ounces) of flour; 125 grams (4 1/2 ounces, 9 tablespoons) of butter; 70 grams (2 1/2 ounces) of *very dry* grated Gruyère; 5 grams (1/6 ounce) of fine salt; 1 deciliter (3 1/3 fluid ounces, scant 1/2 cup) of water.

PROCEDURE. Rapidly mix the dough in the manner indicated for lining dough (SEE PAGE 662). Do not knead it. Let it rest for 15 minutes. Lightly sprinkle the board with grated cheese and a dusting of flour. Roll out the dough with the rolling pin into a strip about 45 centimeters (17 3/4 inches) long by 20–23 centimeters (8–9 inches) wide, sprinkling it as you go with grated cheese. Fold over one-third of the strip as for puff pastry; sprinkle with cheese and embed it with a light pass of the rolling pin. Fold over the opposite third; sprinkle with cheese and pass over the rolling pin. After this first turn, turn the dough three times without resting it in between, sprinkling it as you go with cheese: that makes 4 turns total (SEE PUFF PASTRY, PAGE 658).

Divide the square of dough into two. On the board sprinkled with the rest of the cheese, roll out each part successively into a strip 12 centimeters (4 1/2 inches) wide (this will be the length of the sticks) and at least 1 good millimeter thick.

Paint the dough with a brush dipped in cold milk; with the blade of a large knife, cut the strips crosswise into smaller strips *1 centimeter (3/8 inch) wide.* As you go, place them on a thick, steel baking sheet, with barely no space between them, because the dough will shrink in cooking. Put them into a very moderate oven. Bake for *12–15 minutes.* Do not allow it to color beyond a golden blond: the cheese will give an acrid taste to the dough if it burns. The dough will swell and almost triple in height and the width of the sticks will reduce, while the length will remain the same.

Cats' Tongues, or Finger-Biscuits *(Langues-de-Chat Fines)*

The dough for this kind of cookie varies, but they are always cooked in the same way; it requires the use of thick black steel baking sheets: the cats' tongues will color too much on a thin baking sheet. If possible, it is a good idea to have two baking sheets, so that you can shape the dough on the second while the first is in the oven. Also, you need a pastry bag fitted with a nozzle 1/2 centimeter (3/16 inch) in diameter (SEE USING PASTRY BAG, PAGE 15). If you do not have one, you can use a large cone of heavy paper, cutting the end to the right diameter. You have to prepare as many cones of paper as the number of times you would need to refill the pastry bag, because these paper cones can be used only once. *Time: 1 hour for the preparation. Makes 5 dozen.*

125 grams (4 1/2 ounces, 9 tablespoons) of fine butter; 160 grams (5 2/3 ounces) of good sifted wheat flour; 140 grams (5 ounces) of *confectioners' sugar;* 1/2 teaspoon of vanilla powder (SEE PAGE 574); 2 egg whites beaten into a snow.

PROCEDURE. Once the flour has been strained through a drum sieve or sifted, mix in the confectioners' sugar and the vanilla powder, then sift everything a second time through the drum sieve onto a stiff sheet of paper. Leave it on the table. Have ready the baking sheets, lightly buttered, as well as the pastry bag or the paper cones.

In a terrine large enough to be able to mix the whites, work the mixture as directed (SEE SOFTENING BUTTER INTO A POMADE, PAGE 16).

Then whisk the egg whites into a snow (SEE PAGE 8).

Add the prepared flour and sugar to the butter made into a pomade by lightly shaking the sheet of paper above the terrine while mixing with the wooden spoon, without working the dough too much.

Finally, incorporate the egg whites beaten into a snow with the movement and care required for this mixture (SEE PAGE 10). Immediately afterward, fill the pouch or the paper cone. Pipe the dough onto the baking sheet in little sticks about half the length of a pencil. Leave about 3 centimeters (1 1/8 inches) of space between each little stick, because the dough will spread out a great deal when baking.

Then immediately put them into an oven at a good medium heat for *7–8 minutes,* until only the edge of the cookies has taken on a lightly brown golden tint. Take the baking sheet out of the oven and loosen the cookies from it by passing the flexible blade of a large knife under them.

Hazelnut Tile Cookies *(Tuiles aux Noisette)*

Simple to make, these cookies keep for a relatively long time because the dough contains no butter. Just protect them from moisture in a metal box so that they remain firm and crunchy. *Time: 45 minutes. Makes 20 cookies.*

100 grams (3 1/2 ounces) of superfine sugar; 100 grams (3 1/2 ounces) of hazelnuts, weighed without shells and skinned; 90 grams (3 1/6 ounces) of fine wheat flour that is good and dry; 1 whole egg; 1 fresh egg white; 1 tablespoon of orange flower water.

PROCEDURE. **The hazelnuts:** Remove the shells using a nutcracker, but make sure you do not break the nut; spread them out on a baking sheet; put them in a nice warm oven. Watch carefully so that you can take them out, because as soon as they are well heated *they will begin to turn yellow:* scratch the skin of a hazelnut to see this. Take the baking sheet out of the oven. Once the hazelnuts have cooled, rub them between your hands to get rid of the skin.

Chop them finely. If you do not have a small mechanical grater, proceed as follows for the right homogeneity: with a large knife, first roughly chop the hazelnuts; then pass them through a medium-size strainer; put back on the table any pieces left behind, and chop them again to pass them through the strainer again. Repeat until everything has passed through: this way, you will get pieces of an equal size.

The batter: Sift the flour into a terrine; add the sugar and the chopped hazelnuts. With a wooden spoon, first stir everything. After this, *one by one* add the whole egg and *the fresh white*—that is, not beaten—and then the orange flower water. Mix as you go, turning the wooden spoon vigorously. Once the sugar has been completely dissolved, do not beat the dough to the point of producing a foam: it just needs to be light and well mixed.

To shape and cook: It is absolutely essential here that the baking sheets made of black steel be perfectly clean and without dents. Paint them with the melted butter; then wipe them carefully with a piece of supple paper to even out the layer of butter, which should be extremely thin. Sprinkle with flour; turn over the baking sheet, tapping it lightly to make the excess flour fall away. On the powdered baking sheet, distribute the dough, 1 tablespoon at a time, dropping it in little ovals 7–8 centimeters (2 3/4–3 1/4 inches) long and 5 centimeters (2 inches) wide, and 3–4 millimeters (scant 3/8 inch) thick at most. Leave 2–3 centimeters (3/4–1 1/8 inches) of space between the ovals, because the dough will spread out while cooking. When you have filled the baking sheet, lift it up in both hands and strike it against the table with 3 or 4 light taps. This is to spread out the dough a little before putting it in the oven, where the heat will finish spreading it out. If you leave out this *very important* detail, the dough will be seized by the heat and will swell slightly like a meringue instead of spreading out.

Put them in a good hot oven. Given that the dough is so thin, *baking for 4–5 minutes should be enough in a properly heated oven.* Watch carefully so that you can quickly turn the baking sheet if the biscuits color too much on one side. At the same time as you put the biscuits in the oven, you should have ready, at hand, the *rolling pin,* upon which the hazelnut tiles are shaped, and *a large kitchen knife* with a wide blade to detach them from the baking sheet. Warm the blade of this knife.

Once the dough rounds have taken on a uniform golden color, put the baking sheet on the open door of the oven. For this you must work quickly, while the dough is still warm and therefore supple; when cooled, it will break. Slide the blade of the knife, *quite flat,* underneath a dough round and immediately put this hot round onto the rolling pin, pressing down on it with the palm of your hand. Instantly, the dough will take the form of a tile. Continue in the same way, applying the rounds to the rolling pin side by side. Once the rolling pin is completely full, slide the tiles onto the table; they will now be cool enough that they will not lose their shape. And continue to remove and curve all the remaining dough rounds in the same way.

Note that when you put the rounds, which are in reality ovals, onto the rolling pin, arrange them in the right direction to make a tile: that is, put them on lengthwise.

Do not cook too many cookies at once, because the dough will cool while it waits. If you do not have several baking sheets, allowing you to arrange the dough in advance and then put them in the oven one after the other, cool the baking sheet that you are using before buttering it and flouring it again.

Palets de Dames *(Palets de Dames)*

Dry petits-fours like cats' tongues, tile cookies, etc., which are served on the same occasions, these cookies are small rounds of very thin dough stippled with Corinth raisins. They are very simple to make: you do not even need a pastry bag; just place the dough on the baking sheet with a spoon. *Time: 30 minutes (once the raisins have been macerated in the rum). Serves about 4 dozen.*

125 grams (4½ ounces, 9 tablespoons) of fine butter; 125 grams (4½ ounces) of superfine sugar; 125 grams (4½ ounces) of wheat flour; 2 eggs; 125 grams (4½ ounces) of Corinth raisins; 3 good tablespoons of rum.

PROCEDURE. Begin by cleaning the raisins (SEE PAGE 573). Wash them in rather warm water; drain them. Put them in a cup with the rum to macerate. Toss them from time to time so they all absorb it and swell. As is true whenever dry raisins are used, these benefit from being macerated well in advance, because they swell and thus keep their place better in the dough.

In a terrine, work the butter as directed (SEE SOFTENING BUTTER TO A POMADE, PAGE 16), then add the sugar and work everything vigorously until the mixture becomes a light, homogeneous cream. Then add the eggs one by one, always working them vigorously. If the weather is cold, the eggs should first have been put into some nice warm water for a few moments so that adding them does not make the butter clot; this does not spoil the batter, but it does call for more vigorous, prolonged work.

Then mix in the flour, dropping it gradually from the sheet of paper on which it was sifted. Finally, add the raisins.

On a *thick* baking sheet of dark steel, lightly buttered, place little heaps of dough the size of a walnut, spaced at least 3 centimeters (1⅛ inches) apart, because the dough spreads out when baking. Put it in a good medium-hot oven; *6–7 minutes of baking* will be enough, because only the edges of the cakes should become colored. Lift them off the plate by sliding a large blade of a knife under them, and allow them to cool on a rack or on a drum sieve.

Shortbread *(Petits Sablés)*

Simple as this dough is to prepare, it nonetheless has one essential requirement: that it be worked rapidly with a rather cool hand. If the work takes a long time, the dough loses its sandy character; and there is quite a lot of butter, so if your hand is warm, it will melt as you work and mix badly with the flour.

It is best to work in a cool place, particularly in summer. When the temperature is warm, firm up the butter; conversely, in a cool season, keep it in a temperate place; work it slightly in advance in the corner of a wet towel to make it more malleable.

You cut this kind of small cookie with a special pastry cutter to make each piece into the shape of a quarter of a small pancake, which is characteristic of shortbread. This is a round cutter, fluted, and divided inside by two strips of crossed metal. But a simple round cutter can equally be used. You cut the dough before putting it in the oven. It is only a little more work; and even if you do not require having shortbread with the proper shape and appearance, the dough is cut into a round shape; but then you use a pastry cutter with a smaller diameter. *Time: 1 scant hour (5–6 minutes for preparing the dough; at least 1/2 hour for resting; 15 minutes of baking).*

125 grams (4 1/2 ounces) of flour; 100 grams (3 1/2 ounces, 7 tablespoons) of butter; 60 grams (2 1/4 ounces) of superfine sugar; 1 egg yolk; 1 tablespoon of cool water; a good pinch of vanilla powder (SEE PAGE 574).

PROCEDURE. Mixing the flour and sugar, sift them onto the pastry board. Make the well. Put in the egg yolk and the water, and use the tips of your fingers to dilute this yolk with the water. Add the butter, broken into little pieces. Always using the tips of your fingers, combine the butter and the yolk, working it strongly. Then, little by little, bring in the flour to combine with the butter, pressing everything between the fingers of your closed hand and allowing the dough to escape between them as you go. Continue like this until you have exhausted all the flour. For these quantities, *5–6 minutes* should be enough: the important thing is not to make the butter melt by working it for a long time.

Scrape the dough stuck to your fingers and to the board. Dry your hand by rubbing it with a little flour, and gather the dough into a ball. Cover it with a towel; let it rest in a cool place, as directed. Worked by an experienced person with a cool hand, the dough can be cut almost immediately, but this is rather exceptional.

When you use it, the dough must retain the imprint of your finger when you press it into it. Any elasticity will make it impossible to use the rolling pin to roll out the dough. Note, too, that an overworked dough will flake and break underneath the rolling pin.

Sprinkle the board with a *very light* dusting of flour. Place the ball of dough on it. With two or three passes of the rolling pin, flatten it slightly. Then, going from the center toward the edges of the dough, roll it out to an even thickness of 5–6 millimeters (3/16–1/4 inch).

Then press down the pastry cutter, as explained above. Be sure, doing this, not to leave any space between the divisions, because the trimmings of dough cannot then be used without the dough losing its characteristic sandiness. As you cut them, slide these pieces of dough onto a baking sheet that has been lightly greased. A space of 1/2 centimeter (3/16 inch) between the cakes will suffice.

Put it into a medium oven. An oven that is too hot will make the dough color too early, which prevents the inside from cooking.

Bake for 15 minutes. This time is determined by the thickness of the dough and remains the same, regardless of the size of the shortbread. After 5 minutes, the dough will not have taken on any color whatsoever, and will have already swollen noticeably. Do not allow it to color to more than a nice golden tint.

When you take it out of the oven, slide the cookies onto a rack or onto a large metallic drum sieve to allow them to cool there; work with caution, because the warm dough is very fragile.

Waffles *(Gaufres Simples)*

The mold used here is a small, flat waffle iron, oval-shaped and with an interior that is square with diamond shapes. If it has not been used in a long time, or if you do not have experience, expect that the first two or three waffles will not be successful. Do not be discouraged, because the knack is rapidly acquired.

300 grams (10 1/2 ounces) of sifted flour; 200 grams (7 ounces, generous 3/4 cup) of butter; 200 grams (7 ounces) of rough brown sugar *(cassonade);* 2 eggs; 1 teaspoon of cinnamon powder; a pinch of salt; grated lemon zest or vanilla powder, per your choice.

PROCEDURE. **The batter:** Work the butter into a pomade in a terrine (SEE PAGE 16). Add the brown sugar, which has first been reduced to an homogeneous powder and passed through a drum sieve. Mix it with your wooden spoon or your whisk and add, constantly whisking or stirring: cinnamon, zest or vanilla, salt, the eggs. In cold weather, the eggs should first have been warmed for 3 minutes in warm water: if you do not do this, it will be more difficult to mix them in and will take a long time.

Add the flour all at once. Without working the dough too much, mix it, turning it with a spatula or a large wooden spoon. Using a pastry scraper or stiff cardboard, gather the dough from the sides of the terrine to even out the surface of the mass. Put it in a cool place to firm up the dough as much as possible. It can thus be prepared well in advance in order to give it a firmer consistency.

The waffles: Lightly sprinkle the board with flour. Take out the dough in large pieces; roll them under the palm of your hand and form some nice long sausages. Divide them with a knife into pieces about 20 grams ($^2/_3$ ounce) each; then lightly roll them to make them into little dumplings.

Heat the waffle iron on strong heat. Lightly butter it. Place a little dumpling of dough in it. Close it, squeezing it tightly. Heat for 30 seconds. Open it to see if it has colored sufficiently. Close it again and turn it over to cook the other side. Scrape the spillings from the outside with a knife. Figure *$1^1/_2$ minutes* for each waffle. Do not grease the waffle iron, except for the first and second waffles.

ICING CAKES
Glaçage des Gâteaux

You frost in various ways depending on the type of cake and the means at your disposal: fondant; royal icing; cooked icing; or uncooked icing, known in France as minute icing. Below, we describe these different methods.

In all cases, a cake must not be iced until after it has almost completely cooled, because the heat will melt the icing, which will thin out and therefore become too fragile.

In many cases, a cake cannot be iced until it has first been coated with preserves, preferably apricot: the culinary term is *abricoter.* Apart from the resulting flavor, this produces a smoother surface and a more durable sheen. If you do not have apricot purée prepared specifically for this special use, dilute some apricot marmalade with a little bit of warm water; pass it through a drum sieve and heat it lightly. This sort of gelée must have a thick consistency, like glue; otherwise, it will be absorbed by the cake. Using a brush, spread it out in a thin layer on the surface of the cake while it is still warm. Allow it to dry for a few moments, then apply the icing as directed in the different recipes.

Fondant *(Fondant)*

This is the method of icing that produces the most beautiful shine. Also, fondant is the icing most often used by the professionals, who always have a store of it in reserve. Kept in a dry place, it lasts for a very long time and it is quick to use. It has a number of applications: icing éclairs, petit-fours, dessert cookies, bonbons, etc.

PROCEDURE. If you do not have sugar that has been broken by hand, use good crystallized sugar for the reasons already given (SEE PAGE 577).

Put the sugar in a copper saucepan that is *not tin-lined*—or, lacking that, one made of good thick aluminum. Moisten it with *$^1/_2$ liter (generous 2 cups) of cold water for 1 kilogram (2 pounds, 3 ounces) of sugar*; once it has been thoroughly dissolved, cook it as directed (SEE COOKING SUGAR, PAGE 577) to bring it to the "large thread" stage: a drop of syrup taken between the thumb and index finger must, when you separate your fingers, form a very gluey, resistant thread; at this point, immediately turn off the heat. Immediately pour the syrup onto a very clean marble slate, one that is not at all oily.

Then use a wooden spatula, because a wooden spoon, even a large one, does not offer a large enough flat surface. With the spatula, work this sugar in a back-and-forth movement, going from front to back and from back to front, moving it with the regularity of a machine. Gradually, you will see the sugar whiten and finally form into something like a solid body, while remaining soft and smooth.

The fondant is now finished. Put it in an earthenware pot if you do not need it immediately and keep it well covered with paper in a dry place, just as you would a pot of preserves.

To use fondant, take the quantity required and put it in a small saucepan. Add the liqueur that will provide your chosen flavor—kirsch, rum, anisette, curaçao, etc.—a few drops at a time, mixing it and working it vigorously with a small wooden spoon. If you are using a coffee flavor, the infusion must be a real essence. Then heat up the fondant to room temperature in a bain-marie or on very low heat, ready for you to ice the cakes. If it is a large cake, put the cake on a pastry rack, thus separating it from the marble. Then pour the fondant over it directly from the saucepan; rapidly smooth it out with the blade of a large knife. Put the excess back into the saucepan for another time. If icing small cakes, hold them in your fingertips, and dip them in the fondant and then place on the rack to drain.

Royal Icing *(Glace Royale)*

This icing is used for a number of small cakes, for cookies, genoises, etc. It forms a thin white opaque layer on the cakes. The same mixture is used to decorate the cakes with a pastry bag—that is, to trace designs, letters, and names on them, in a thin string, such as you see at the pastry shops and on spice cakes.

A mixture of unbeaten egg whites and *confectioners' sugar* (SEE PAGE 574), royal icing is one of the simplest to make: the essential condition is that it should be worked vigorously and for a long time. If you do not take enough time or use enough force, the icing will not be the right consistency.

You should allow *approximately 1–1½ egg whites for 100 grams (3½ ounces) of confectioners' sugar.* The egg white is too variable in its volume to be precise about the proportion to use; you can easily evaluate this by eye while working, adding the sugar gradually until it has the right consistency for the use you will make of the icing.

The consistency differs depending on whether you want to ice a cake or to decorate it with a paper cone or pastry bag. For icing cakes, the icing must be rather light, to make a layer only 1 millimeter thick. When using it in a cone, the icing must be more dense so that it does not spread out when leaving the nozzle.

PROCEDURE. Pass the confectioners' sugar through a horsehair or silk drum sieve to reduce it to a perfectly homogeneous powder. Almost always, there will be some lumps; these will not come apart, nor will they dissolve during the work. This means that sifting it first through a drum sieve is necessary.

Put the egg white into a large bowl. Take a small wooden spatula or a very small wooden spoon that has never had contact with any fatty material whatever—bouillon or similar. With the spoon, pick up the sugar and work it with the egg white, gradually adding as much sugar as the egg white can absorb; it is just at that point, as explained above, that the mixture takes on the right consistency while remaining perfectly smooth and flowing.

To ice: Depending on the type of cake, you can either apply royal icing directly, or first lightly coat the cake with apricot marmalade. When it is a large cake, put it on a rack placed on a piece of very clean marble. Pour the royal icing directly onto the cake, allowing it to run from the bowl in an equal layer. Dry it in open air. The excess will spill all around it, so scrape it up and put it back in the bowl. You can keep it for other uses, covered with a dampened towel folded in quarters.

To decorate with the cone: Make a paper cone.

Do not lighten the icing with liqueur; add only a few drops of lemon juice, which will thicken it. Fill the cone three-quarters full. Then fold it on the top to completely enclose the icing.

With scissors, cut the pointed end *very slightly* to allow a passage for the icing. Hold the top of the cone between the three fingers of your right hand. Lightly squeeze on the top, pushing down with your thumb while you direct the point of the cone over the cake, in the same way that you would hold a pencil to write.

Cooked Chocolate Icing *(Glace Cuite au Chocolat)*

This can be prepared in many ways: the best is to in cook a sugar syrup to the right degree, and then incorporate the chocolate into it, previously melted. In this way the chocolate is not subject to strong boiling: this, we know, will spoil its flavor.

For the quantity of ingredients, we will give below the amount needed for icing a cake with a surface of about 25 centimeters (10 inches) in diameter.

PROCEDURE. Put 150 grams (5⅓ ounces) of chocolate into a large bowl or into a small terrine, divided into very small pieces, with 3 soupspoons of *lukewarm water.* Keep this in a warm place to soften the chocolate until it can be worked with a small wooden spoon to make a perfectly smooth paste.

Meanwhile, in a small copper saucepan that is not tin-lined—or if you do not have that, one made of good thick aluminum—melt the sugar (150 grams, 5⅓ ounces) with 1 deciliter (3⅓ fluid ounces, scant ½ cup) of water. Cook it to the "large thread" degree, as for fondant.

Turn off the heat. Drop by drop, pour the syrup into the chocolate paste, working the mixture forcefully just as you would make a mayonnaise. This gives you an icing that sticks to the spoon in a smooth and shining layer. It must be slightly more than lukewarm when used so that it will spread out on the cake more easily. But not too warm, because then it would slide off the cake without covering it sufficiently.

To ice the cake: If you like, spread apricot marmalade onto the *cooled* cake and place it on a small rack. Ice it immediately. Place the cake on the open oven door: if you were to actually put it into the oven, this would have to be at an extremely low temperature, barely on. Under the influence of this very gentle heat, the icing sets into a brilliant skin. At this point, avoid any air currents, which would dull the brilliance of the icing.

Scrape off the remaining icing in the bowl and collect it together at the bottom. Pour a little bit of water on it to prevent it from forming a crust. You simply heat it up to lukewarm to use it next time.

Ordinary Icing or Uncooked Icing *(Glace Ordinaire ou Glace Crue)*

This icing is also called *minute icing.* This is the simplest icing to prepare, and the best that is within everyone's reach. The sugar, always *confectioners'* sugar, simply has water or liqueur added to it, and is then vigorously worked cold. Depending on the case, you can use this icing just as it is or very slightly warmed. Cold, it has a more durable shine. Warm, it dries more rapidly but does not preserve its shine as well.

You can flavor this icing with chocolate, coffee, kirsch, curaçao, etc.—all the appropriate liqueurs.

Liqueur Icing *(Glace à la Liqueur).* Pass the confectioners' sugar through a horsehair or silk drum sieve to break up any lumps and to reduce it to a perfectly fine powder. For 100 grams (3 1/2 ounces) of sugar, add a soupspoon of the chosen liqueur and the same quantity of cold water.

Work everything vigorously with a small wooden spoon for *7–8 minutes* until it takes on the consistency of a very smooth paste, thick enough to pour out slowly in a large thread when you lift it up on the spoon. Too dilute, and it will be absorbed by the cake; too thick, and it will not have enough shine.

Uncooked Chocolate Icing *(Glace Crue au Chocolat).* Put 25 grams (1 ounce) of chocolate, cut into very small pieces, into a small saucepan with only 1/2 tablespoon of water. Put the saucepan in a warm place to soften the chocolate without cooking it at all, until the point where, using a wooden spoon, you can stir it into a smooth paste that does not have even the slightest lump.

Meanwhile, put 100 grams (3 1/2 ounces) of confectioners' sugar, previously passed through a drum sieve, in a bowl with 2 tablespoons of water, and work the mixture as explained above. Worked to the necessary point, add the sugar to the chocolate paste. Work everything very vigorously with the wooden spoon.

Then put the saucepan into some receptacle that is half filled with boiling water, but *off the heat,* just to bring the icing to a lukewarm point, so that it is runny and has a beautiful shine. If you need to, you can add a few drops of lukewarm water (no more).

To ice: If it is a large cake, pour the icing directly on it, which spreads out over the surface. If they are small cakes, cream puffs, profiteroles, éclairs, etc., dip the surface of the cake into it, then place it on a rack. Dry as directed for the cooked chocolate icing.

Uncooked Coffee Icing *(Glace Crue au Café).* Dilute the confectioners' sugar with very strong coffee essence; 2 soupspoons of essence for 100 grams (3 1/2 ounces) of sifted confectioners' sugar. Work it as directed above.

To ice cold: With the tip of a small kitchen knife or table knife, pick up the icing and spread it out in an even layer on the cake, as if you were spreading a piece of toast with preserves. Dry it as directed.

To ice warm: In a small saucepan, dissolve the sugar as above with the coffee essence, using a little bit more of it: that is, 1/2 tablespoon more. Lightly warm the icing in the bain-marie or on very low heat. Pour it on the large cake; or, if these are small cakes, dip the surface of one side in it. Dry as directed.

PRESERVES

GENERAL PRINCIPLES

Just the word *preserves* evokes family life: because, when making them, the skill of homemakers, who rely on instinct and tradition, seems sometimes to surpass the more scientific and more theoretical talents of the professionals. Also, we will always prefer a simple pot of "homemade" preserves to industrial products, no matter how renowned: homemade preserves, despite everything, inspire a more complete confidence.

By "preserves," we mean all the preparations where fruit is involved, either whole or in a marmalade, or in the form of a jelly.

Before summarizing the principles and the best recipes for all of them, we would first like to establish the fundamental rules of all preserves: nowadays, these are too often ignored, or, which is sometimes worse, misunderstood.

The Materials

The best utensil, and preferable to any other, remains the traditional red copper basin that is not lined with tin (*fig.* 83): passed down from one generation to another, this is the foundation of well-cooked preserves; it is one of those things that you lend to one another, and if necessary, you can rent it from the coppersmith in your quarter or neighborhood. For a number of years, however, this classic utensil has been replaced by an aluminum basin, which has the advantage that it does not require so much care. You can leave the preserves in it until the next day without any drawback: for certain fruit preparations, where the fruit must macerate in the syrup, this eliminates the obligatory change to another utensil when the first basin is copper. For you must get this thoroughly into your head: without any excuses, *the preserves must not remain in the copper basin once they begin to perceptibly cool.*

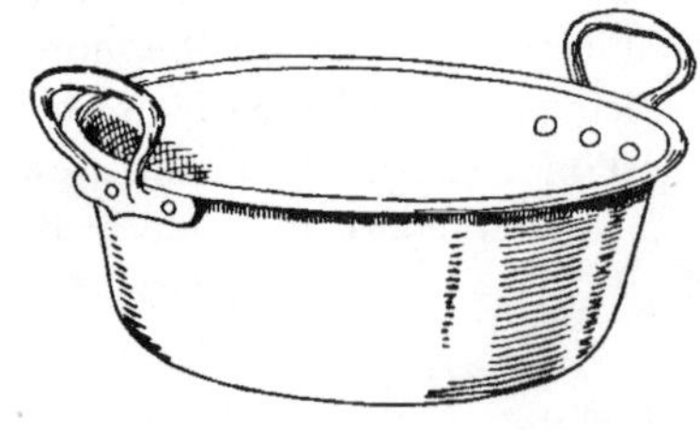

FIG. 83. COPPER BASIN FOR PRESERVES.

Another prohibition: *never use tin-lined utensils.* These alter the color of the fruits; red fruits particularly, which when in contact with the tin, take on a purplish red or burgundy tint, which is unappetizing, to say the least. For this reason, scrupulously abstain, while working, from using tinned spoons. Or, indeed, iron and steel utensils.

Whether it is made of copper or aluminum, the basin must have a large bottom surface for heating. This must be thick, flat, and without dents. The basin must be large enough, in regard to the contents, that the foam produced by the lively boiling does not threaten to spill over. You can assume, as an average for the capacity of the utensil, that this should be double the volume of the preserves that you are going to cook in it.

A copper basin is, of course, always kept perfectly clean; the only maintenance it needs is to scour it with a very fine scouring powder. You should not use products—pastes or similar—that are designed to make the metal shine. The drawback of these products, because of the fatty materials they contain in greater or lesser quantities, is that they break down the sugar, or make it "turn." Be careful when cleaning the inside of the basin to dig with a large pin around the nails or rivets affixing the handles; these are generally encircled with a little bit of verdigris, which happens from one season to the next in even the best-kept kitchens.

As essential as the basin is a *skimmer* (*fig.* 84), also made of red copper in a square shape, slightly

FIG. 84. SKIMMER FOR PRESERVES.

rounded at the corners. Follow the same procedures for maintaining it: clean out the holes one by one with a large needle. Then wash it in very warm water so that the metal dries rapidly. If possible, after drying them off, put the utensils on the stove or in a very gentle oven to finish drying them out.

The other equipment that you need is *a large horsehair drum sieve.* If it is tin-lined, a metallic drum sieve must not be used. However, you can use a drum sieve made of stainless steel.

To deseed the fruits, use a *silver* fork or a fork of stainless steel. The ladle used for transferring the preserves to put in jars must also be either silver or stainless.

An accessory that is often useful is *a large wooden spatula* or *a large wooden spoon,* squared at the ends and with a long handle, which is better than the skimmer at certain points for mixing the preserves. It must be used only for similar preparations, and it must never make contact with any fatty food whatsoever, whether bouillon or milk: this is because the grease, with which the wood can become impregnated, might turn the sugar.

To collect the fruit juices, some *terrines* are necessary, terrines made of fired white earthenware and at least as big as the copper basin.

The Sugar

This plays a premier role in all preserves. Apart from counteracting the acidity of the fruit—whether that is more or less pronounced—the sugar is a preservative: even though not quite as important as the preservative effect caused by cooking, it is significant nonetheless. What frequently goes wrong is the part played by the sugar in the coagulation of certain preserves.

As has been said by a well-known scientific popularizer—and practitioners and experienced homemakers all agree—sugar is no good for setting red currant, apple, or quince preserves. That is achieved by a particular element contained by these fruits in large amounts: pectin, which is transformed by heat into a kind of gelatin, itself a type of preservative.

Thus it is essential to recognize two categories of fruits: those that include a substantial quantity of pectin, such as the fruits just cited; and those in which the pectin is absent, or that have only a very small quantity: apricots, strawberries, raspberries, cherries, etc. All the sugar you can add to them will not convert them into a jelly; you would get only a more or less thick syrup, but that's all.

The quantity of sugar is therefore not fixed, and absolutely immutable for all fruits, as we will see in the recipes that follow. It is always essential to understand that using too much sugar, just like using too little, is not without its disadvantages: too much sugar considerably weakens the particular flavor of the fruit, and the preserves will also crystallize; everything becomes a candied fruit. On the other hand, not using enough sugar will cause fermentation, if the fruit has not been cooked for long enough. But overcooking also destroys the flavor of the fruit.

What kind of sugar must one use? Preferably, this should be loaf sugar, broken by hand with a very clean instrument. Regular sugar cubes, having been sawed with a machine, may granulate—that is, break down—while cooking, turning into sugar candy; this effect is caused by the oil with which the mechanical saws are coated. This kind of sugar must therefore not be used.

If you cannot get loaf sugar broken by hand, particularly if economy is a factor, you can use crystallized sugar; but the jellies will not have the same clarity as when made with loaf sugar. Make sure you get it as white as possible, and skim it even more carefully.

Cooking

The faster a preserve is cooked, the better the flavor of the fruit is preserved in it. It is always necessary to distinguish depending on the nature of the preserve.

For marmalades and preserves, where the fruit is a certain size and has a rather dense pulp—apricots, for example—the boiling must not be too lively. First of all, because the syrup will be cooked before the fruit has been sufficiently penetrated by the sugar, and there will be a risk of fermentation;

and second, because despite careful watching, this preserve will easily stick to the bottom of the basin if set over too strong a heat.

For preserves made only with fruit juice—as for jellies—or with fruit of only a small size—strawberries, say—the boiling must be maintained very strongly on strong heat. The color of the fruit is also clearer as a result.

Do not cook large quantities at a time, because unless you have an enormous flame or a gigantic basin, the cooking conditions will not be favorable. You will crush the fruit when you mix it, if there is too much, all jammed up together; the cooking will be slowed down if the mass of fruits to be heated is too large; skimming becomes difficult and the foam will threaten to boil over, so you will then have to turn down the heat. Thus, when you have large quantities of fruit to cook, it is better to resort to working in batches.

An absolute rule: *do not step away from the stove from the moment when the basin is placed on the heat until the moment that it is taken off,* because preserves burn with an unexpected rapidity, especially during the second phase of cooking.

In effect, the cooking for every preserve takes place in two stages; *the first* is to evaporate the natural water from the fruit, whether you are cooking the fruit itself, or the juice, as for jellies; the *second,* which follows immediately, is the real stage of cooking, when there is nothing left other than the pulp or the pure juice. As the ingredients pass from one stage to the other, you will see that the steam, which is given off from the basin during the first phase of cooking, has disappeared; this is the beginning of the second period: the boiling is restricted, and despite the heat it will stay at the same level in the basin.

This second period, much shorter than the first, requires attentive surveillance so that you do not go beyond the right point of cooking. For marmalades and whole fruits, it is essential to stir the preserves almost continuously, which risk sticking to the bottom of the basin. *Toward the end, diminish the heat,* so that you do not risk going beyond the correct degree of cooking.

Working on the principle that the more rapidly a preserve is cooked, the more the fruit keeps its color and flavor, you can leave out the water added for melting the sugar, proceeding as directed for apricot preserves (SEE OPPOSITE): that is, by putting the fruit, cleaned and ready for cooking, into an earthenware terrine with the sugar in alternate layers, and then letting them macerate for at least 12 hours, covered and sheltered from dust and flies. But it is not just to assure the evaporation of the water, which prolongs the cooking. This method also offers the advantage of allowing you to proceed in two stages if you do not have the necessary time the same day to prepare the fruit, cook it, and then put it in jars.

The perfect point of cooking: *It is not by watching the clock that you can fix the point at which a preserve is properly cooked.* Though it is possible to determine more or less the time needed for such-and-such an interval or point of cooking, it is absolutely impossible to establish that after so many minutes of cooking, a preserve is ready to be put into jars. The length of the cooking time depends on conditions that are essentially variable: the strength of the heat, which itself depends on the type of stove and how the heat is produced; the quantity and quality of the fruit that you are dealing with; etc. In short, there are as many differences in cooking time as there are variables. The clock therefore has absolutely nothing to regulate here.

When cooking all preserves, *the only trustworthy indication is to recognize the degree of cooking called "à la nappe."* This is true for all preserves and jellies, whatever the nature of the fruit.

The expression *à la nappe,* which is unique to cooking preserves, means a degree that corresponds to the stage in sugar cooking that is called "small thread": 32–33° on the saccharometer.

The test is made during the second stage of cooking, when, as we have said, the boiling manifests as small tight bubbles.

At the beginning, when you dip the skimmer into the preserves and lift it above the basin, then tip it, you will see the syrup drip off it rapidly in tight drops. Repeat this every minute, and you will notice, as the cooking progresses, that the syrup does not detach any more from the skimmer, except in large drops, spaced apart. The perfect point is reached at the instant when you can hold the skimmer perfectly horizontally above the basin—as you would hold a knife to cut—and the syrup descends and slowly gathers together toward the middle of the edge: 2 or 3 drops joining together to form one large, flat one.

This point can also be established by touching, by picking up a little bit of preserve on the end of your index finger. Put your thumb underneath, then separate the two fingers by 1–2 centimeters (3/8–3/4 inch): the preserves become very gluey, stretching out between the fingers in a rather resistant thread. Finally, you can test by dripping the preserve onto a cold plate: the drops must not spread out, but remain in a dome shape with a light skin rapidly setting on the surface.

To fill and cover the jars: Once the basin has been taken off the heat and placed on the table, gently stir the preserves with a silver ladle to thoroughly mix the fruits and their syrup.

Set out on the table all the jars, which will first have been washed in hot water and dried with a *perfectly dry* towel: the jars must be absolutely clean to guarantee that their contents are preserved.

Fill one jar, then rapidly clean the edge with a clean moist towel and *immediately* cover it with the special transparent or cellulose paper that you can find these days at grocers. Moisten these with some water to soften the side that will be on the outside of the jar; stretch it out completely so that it does not stick anywhere on the preserve, and then tie it or secure it with the elastic that is generally contained in the packets of preserved paper.

If you do not have this special paper, cover with parchment paper. But always do this when the preserves are still boiling, which guarantees a kind of sterilization that helps with the preservation. If you are working with a large quantity of fruits, you will find that once you have filled a few pots, you will have to put the basin back on the heat so that the preserves are boiling hot, but be certain not to recook them. Earthenware jars, which are not likely to burst, can be filled without precautions. For glass jars, first put 1 tablespoon of preserves in them to reheat the jar, then after a moment continue filling. Avoid any drafts while doing this, because a rapid change of temperature can make the glass burst. Whatever the receptacle, either earthenware or glass, fill them to the edge, because all preserves settle when they cool.

Another method to cover the jars. Long ago, we abandoned the technique of dipping the rounds of paper in cognac before applying them directly to the preserve, to act as an insulation: the effect of the alcohol does not last long enough. Cognac has now been replaced by purified glycerin, whose preservative action lasts a great deal longer; you can find this glycerin at all pharmacies. Using a small brush, coat one side only of the rounds of paper, and place the coated side directly on the preserves. Then cover the pots with a round of rather strong paper: this should either be solidly attached with two turns of string to keep out the air, or glued to the sides of the jar with egg white. This second method eliminates the need for string: the seal is perfect and looks neat and attractive. Proceed as follows: cut some white paper into squares larger than the edge of the jars by 1 centimeter (3/8 inch) at the most. Dip one side of this paper in egg white beaten in a saucer, and place this dipped side on the jars. On top of these, lined up by their height, place a long plank to press down lightly on top of these papers and prevent them from buckling. When everything is dry, cut the paper even with the edges of the jars. *[Translator's note: It is now the preferred technique to purchase special canning (or freezing) jars, with accompanying screw-on bands and dome lids that self-seal with the heat of the sterilized jar.]*

PRESERVES AND MARMALADES
Confitures et Marmelades

Apricot Preserves *(Confiture d'Abricots)*

Apricots from an espalier are not, of course, used for this purpose, but rather, the fruits from trees that are growing in the open and have clearly reached maturity. The sugar used here is generally calculated at three-quarters of the net weight of the fruit. It is rather unusual to use an equal weight here.

The recipes for apricot preserves have several differences.

Current method: This is the one used for marmalade. So: dissolve the sugar with a little bit of water (2 deciliters/6 3/4 fluid ounces/generous 3/4 cup per kilogram/2 pounds, 3 ounces). Bring it to a boil, then skim. Add the fruits, cut in half. Cook gently until reaching the point *à la nappe.* Take it off the heat and mix in the kernels, extracted from the pits and previously blanched. *[Translator's note: The blanching of the kernels is important since it detoxifies the cyanogens in the almond-shaped inner pit.]* Put them in jars.

Another method: This attempts to preserve the fruit intact. Once a general boiling is well established across the entire surface of the basin, turn the heat down very low to maintain the syrup at a simple simmer for about 10 minutes. Next, pour the mixture into a terrine, or leave it until the next day. During this time, the fruit is infused with the sugar. Then put the mixture back on the heat and again bring it to a gentle simmer until the syrup has reached the *nappe* point. The kernels are added as above, before putting it in the jars.

Below, we give a cross between these two recipes, in which the fruit is not reduced too much to a marmalade: a notable amount of the fruit, if it is not too ripe, will remain whole. This method is also very practical, and gives an excellent result. *Makes enough for about 15 ordinary jars.*

4 kilograms (8 pounds, 13 ounces) of apricots, gross weight; 375 grams (13 1/4 ounces) of sugar for each 450 grams (1 pound) of fruit, weighed without pits.

PROCEDURE. Using a knife, preferably with a silver blade, split the apricots in two. Reserve the pits. Remove the little ends of stem still attached to the apricot. Then with your knife, remove every spot, blemish, or spoiled part from the fruit.

In a terrine that is made of white earthenware and perfectly clean, place the apricots and the sugar in alternate layers, beginning with the apricots: the fruits should be laid quite flat, each layer being one fruit thick. Finish with a thick layer of sugar that covers everything completely. Allow it to macerate like this in a temperate place for *24 hours.* (If the quantity of fruits requires that the preserves be cooked in two or three batches, divide the apricots into that same number of terrines with the appropriate quantity of sugar. If not, the division of the sugar will never be equal. For this reason, weigh the sugar for each portion of fruit and add it separately.)

The kernels: Break the pits open. Choose the most attractive intact kernels. Throw them into a small saucepan of boiling water. Boil for 1 or 2 minutes, and allow them to remain for several moments in the water with the heat turned off. Remove their skins; cut them in half. Set aside between two plates, to add them to the finished preserve.

Cooking it: After 24 hours, the apricots will be sitting in a large amount of syrup, produced from their juice and the melted sugar. Pour everything into the basin, and be careful to pour out the sugar that you will find deposited on the bottom of the terrine, half melted.

Place the basin on the heat. With the skimmer or a large wooden spoon, gently stir right to the bottom of the basin to encourage the sugar to melt. Once the boiling has started, cook rather slowly, so that the pulp of the apricot is well penetrated by sugar. If, among all the fruits, you come across some less ripe ones, crush them against the sides of the basin using the skimmer. If they were to remain whole, they would not reach the same point of cooking as the others, and there would subsequently be a risk of fermentation.

As the foam rises, remove it with the skimmer and place it on a horsehair or stainless steel drum sieve placed over a terrine; there will be a lot of it. Meanwhile, very gently run the skimmer or the large spoon across the bottom of the basin to keep anything from sticking there. (The usefulness of this maneuver is confirmed by the small mass that you'll find, hardened and colored, stuck to the end of the skimmer.)

Once all the foam has been produced, pour the clear juice back into the basin that has run down through the drum sieve into the terrine.

Allow the mixture to cook, mixing constantly until it has reached the degree known as the *nappe.* It is a good idea to check it as soon as you see that the apricots have become translucent, or when you lift the syrup out of the basin on the skimmer and the sugar sticks while still being slightly granular, instead of being smooth and runny. If the preserves taken between your thumb and index finger form a resistant thread, and if several drops poured on a plate keep their domed shape, immediately turn off the heat. Mix in the kernels and put the preserves into jars immediately.

Plum Preserves *(Confiture de Prunes)*

The same procedure as for apricot preserves. That said, it is advisable, particularly when using greengage plums, to cook small quantities at a time, and to cook them rapidly. This is to preserve the nice green color of the fruit. For a similar result, shorten the initial maceration of the fruit considerably if you want to follow the first recipe for apricot preserves. That one is particularly recommended for mirabelle plums.

Furthermore, for greengage plums and for red plums, especially purple plums, it is the recipe to follow. It offers the great advantage of eliminating the fruit skins, which are often very hard.

PROCEDURE. Split the plums and take out the pits. Put them in a basin with 1/2 liter (generous 2 cups) of water for each kilogram (2 pounds, 3 ounces) of fruit. Soften the fruit on *low heat,* stirring to prevent it from sticking. It should take *15–20 minutes* for the fruit to be cooked enough that they can be passed through a drum sieve to make a purée.

Pour everything gradually onto a horsehair or stainless steel drum sieve placed over a shallow bowl. With the wooden pestle, scrape *without pushing too hard,* so that the skins, which come off as you go, are left behind.

Measure the purée obtained. Pour it into the rinsed basin. Add 750 grams (1 pound, 10 ounces) of sugar per liter (4 1/4 cups) or kilogram (2 pounds, 3 ounces) of puree. (The sugar should be either superfine sugar or a fine white granulated sugar.)

Bring it to a boil on *very moderate* heat, stirring the marmalade gently but *continuously* with a large wooden spoon, drawing it across the bottom of the basin. Cook it until the *nappe* is reached. Put it into jars.

Cherry Preserves *(Confitures de Cerises)*

Cherries, like all red fruits in general, spoil when they are cooked for too long. To cook them with the necessary speed, you must work only on small quantities, thus allowing the boiling point to be reached promptly, and to be maintained at the same level. This is why cherries cooked in large quantities are shriveled, hardened, and a kind of a dark brown-garnet color, as is their syrup; while cherries prepared under the right conditions remain plump and pulpy, and their color, like their syrup, is a beautiful light red-garnet.

The kind of cherries to choose for preserves is the English cherry, the Montmorency cherry, a nice light red with a short stem. Allow for the weight loss caused by removing the pits, assuming that it will be a little bit more than one-quarter of the gross weight.

The quantity of sugar used varies according to the type of fruit. For good cherries, it is about three-quarters of the net weight of the fruit, and can even be reduced to half if the cherries are very sweet and sugary. On the other hand, if the cherries are quite acid, you can allow an equal weight of sugar and fruit.

An excellent practice that we would like to suggest, and that is currently very widespread, is to add some red currant juice to the cherry preserves. Not only does the red currant offer a very happy combination of flavors, but it also supplies a gelatinous consistency to the preserves that the cherries themselves cannot provide, because they do not have the necessary pectin. And adding the red currants, which give consistency, allows you to abbreviate the cooking time a little, preserving the beautiful light color of the fruit.

Cherry preserves are prepared in different ways. The most current involves first dissolving the sugar in the basin just moistened with water, and bringing it to a boil, then plunging in the pitted cherries, adding the red currant juice if you are using it. It is then cooked on strong heat until it reaches the degree known as *à la nappe.*

Here, we give another recipe that is excellent: the cherries are cooked in two stages, thus being infused between stages with the sugar, which constitutes the preservative element of the preparation. They also require a shorter cooking time, especially if you add some red currant juice to them, which, as we have explained, plays a double role.

Per kilogram (2 pounds, 3 ounces) of cherries *weighed without pits:* 1/2 liter (generous 2 cups), that is, 500 grams (1 pound, 2 ounces) of red currant juice; an equal weight of sugar; that is, 1 1/2 kilograms

(3 pounds, 5 ounces) of sugar. If the cherries are very sugary, then three-quarters of the total weight (that is, 1.125 kilograms/2 pounds, 8 ounces) will suffice.

PROCEDURE. Put the sugar in the basin. Moisten it with 2 1/2 deciliters (1 cup) of water per kilogram (2 pounds, 3 ounces). Allow it to melt on very gentle heat.

While the sugar is melting, pit the cherries. First carefully remove the stems so that you do not damage the fruit. As you do, take out the pit, using a little piece of wood stuck into the cherries, pushing the pit out on the other side; work carefully to keep the cherry completely whole without any splits, except the one made through the fruit at both ends.

Or you can use a steel wire that is sufficiently flexible, about 10 centimeters (4 inches) long. First, fold it into a loop like a hairpin; then twist the two wires together at their middle and insert the two ends in a cork. Stick the arch, now transformed into an elongated loop, into the cherries from the side where the stem has been lifted, so that you can grab the pit from above and drag it out through the single opening that you have made: you must do this without crushing the cherry or without deforming it too much.

Once the sugar has melted, add the pitted cherries. Place the basin on strong heat. With the skimmer, gently stir the cherries to mix them with the sugar without tearing the fruit. Once a general boiling manifests, allow it to boil rapidly for only *7–8 minutes.* Remove the foam amassed on the surface of the basin, and then pour all the contents into a terrine of glazed earthenware. Allow it to rest there until the next day. In this state, the cherries are not fully cooked and will become completely infused with sugar, thus releasing a certain amount of extra juice.

The next day, put the preserves back into the basin, which should first have been well rinsed and dried. Add the red currant juice to it, prepared as directed for the jelly (SEE PAGE 735). Bring it to a boil on very strong heat. Once the boiling is thoroughly established across the entire surface of the basin, let it boil strongly for *2–3 minutes only.* Then remove the cherries with the skimmer to put them back into the terrine.

Boil the syrup, always very strongly, until it has reached the point of the *nappe.* Then pour back the cherries. Boil for another *3–4 minutes.* Skim a last time. Put it in jars.

Strawberry Preserves *(Confiture de Fraises)*

Preparing this is always a particularly delicate matter, no matter which method you follow. Much more so than for other preserves, it is important that the strawberries be handled in only small quantities at a time, because of their essentially fragile nature; otherwise, you risk turning the fruit into a marmalade, when actually each strawberry must remain whole in the thickened syrup.

The method most generally used, and the one we give here to obtain the best result, can be summarized as follows: cook the strawberries in a very thick sugar syrup; drain them and bring the syrup to the *nappe* point; add the strawberries to the reduced syrup and put it in jars.

The preferred variety is the Héricart strawberry. Whichever kind you choose, use only strawberries that are completely fresh and healthy and a little bit firm: that is, not overripe. Clean them meticulously and reject any that are too ripe or crushed, which will have therefore begun to ferment; to have "turned." As you clean the strawberries, avoid piling them up, because they will crush one another more easily that way. Do not wash them except when absolutely necessary, if they have some sand or dirt that you cannot get off any other way. You must then rinse them rapidly in small quantities at a time in cool water *before* taking off the stems, to avoid the water penetrating the strawberries; then spread them out on a clean odorless towel to dry them before putting them in the syrup. The water and their own moisture would slow down the cooking, which should be conducted as rapidly as possible.

Use sugar in pieces, preferably broken by hand as directed (SEE PAGE 725). *Makes enough for about 7 jars of medium size.*

2 1/2 kilograms (5 pounds, 8 ounces) of strawberries, weighed without their stems; same weight of sugar.

PROCEDURE. Break up the sugar. Put it in the basin, moisten it with water (about 2 deciliters/ 6 3/4 fluid ounces/generous 3/4 cup *per 450 grams/*

1 pound of sugar). When it has melted, cook it as directed (SEE COOKING SUGAR, PAGE 577) to bring it to the degree known as "soft ball," which should register as 38–40° on the saccharometer.

Quickly put the strawberries into the syrup; their introduction will cause a kind of a momentary crystallization. Carefully move the strawberries from the bottom to the top without breaking them, using only two or three movements of the skimmer. Maintain a very strong heat underneath the basin. Watch for the moment when boiling starts again. When it has started to boil again on the entire surface of the basin in a layer of boiling foam from the middle to the edges, let it boil strongly until the point when the strawberries have taken on *the shiny aspect of candied fruits and have acquired a uniform color that is the same as the syrup.* Picked up on the skimmer, they will be whole, and perfectly distinct in their shape though substantially weakened since they are no longer bathing in the syrup. As we have already said, it is not possible to mathematically fix the cooking time required. With the quantities given and with fruit of good quality, you can always allow approximately *5–8 minutes.*

Then take the basin off the heat to stop cooking. Promptly remove the strawberries with the skimmer and put them on a horsehair or stainless steel drum sieve placed over a terrine, where they will not be too crowded. Allow them to drain for a few moments and pour the juice that runs out from underneath the drum sieve into the basin. All of this must be done quickly so that you do not allow the syrup to cool.

Put the basin on strong heat. Bring it back to a boil; sustain it to reduce the syrup that the natural water from the strawberries has diluted. The consistency of the syrup must be the same as it first had; you will have to make several successive tests. A drop of syrup dropped onto a cold plate must firm up there and keep a good round and domed shape. The saccharometer would give you a reading of 32–33°.

Then turn off the heat to stop the cooking. With the skimmer, remove the foam covering the syrup. Pour the strawberries into the basin and carefully mix them into the syrup. Put them immediately into jars.

The strawberries have a tendency to float to the surface; before consuming, it is enough to mix them gently to distribute them equally in the syrup.

Variation: This very simple procedure gives an excellent result. However, make it only if you have Héricart strawberries, known as strawberries of Lyon, which should be perfectly ripe, nice and dry; and handle them in only small quantities at a time—that is, never more than 2 kilograms (4 pounds, 6 ounces).

Pick through the strawberries and reject any that are not healthy; if necessary, wash them rapidly in cold water and dry them on a towel or brush them with a soft brush to thoroughly clean any that have some dirt on them. Remove the stems, and in an earthenware terrine lay out, in alternate layers, the strawberries and their weight in superfine sugar (the strawberries having been weighed after they have been selected and their stems removed). Let them rest for at least 12 hours and up to 24 hours in a cool place, covered.

Pour the fruit and the sugar carefully into a copper cooking basin. On low heat, allow the sugar to melt without touching the fruits, moving the basin from time to time to ensure that nothing sticks. Once the sugar has melted, bring it to a boil on strong heat. Cook for 10 minutes. Then carefully remove all the foam. Turn off the heat. If the basin is aluminum, you can leave the preserves in it. If not, you must immediately transfer them, always carefully, into the rinsed and dried terrine where the fruits have macerated. Let them rest again for 24 hours, and cover once they have completely cooled. Cook again, this time with the sugar in the form of a syrup: let it cook at a lively boil for *10 minutes,* skimming if necessary. The syrup will not cook long enough to reduce significantly, and the strawberries, moistened or full of their own water, will naturally produce large quantities of juice. Put them in jars immediately and cover.

Orange Preserves *(Confiture d'Oranges)*

There are probably an infinite number of recipes originating in households, each family possessing its own, which differs in some respect from the others. Moreover, these recipes relate to different preparations: fruit in marmalade, fruit in quarters, or jelly, and that's without even considering the matter of the peel. Therefore we provide several recipes, each of which has a different advantage, so you can make your own choice.

Note that for marmalades and preserves, where the peel of the fruit is part of the preserve, it is important to choose oranges with large, thick skins that are well colored. Only these thick skins, which are more porous and therefore more easily penetrated by cooking, are tender enough; thin skins, on the other hand, harden and become like leather.

Orange Preserves in Quarters with Peels *(Confiture d'Oranges en Quartiers, avec Écorces).* Allow for each 450 grams (1 pound) of oranges, gross weight, 675 grams (1 pounds, 8 ounces) of sugar: this large amount of sugar has the effect of conserving the fruit and almost avoids the need for cooking it. Use superfine sugar or granulated sugar. *Makes nearly 3 jars.*

PROCEDURE. With a small knife, divide the skin of each orange into quarters, without cutting into the pulp. Remove the peels without breaking them. Let them soak for *24 hours* in a substantial amount of cool water, salted at the rate of 20 grams (2/3 ounce) per liter (4 1/4 cups) of water.

Remove all the rest of the white skin from the oranges. Separate the quarters. Peel them very carefully and extract the seeds, taking great care so that you do not rip the skin. In a large terrine, put them to macerate with the sugar in alternate layers for 24 hours. If you use granulated sugar, lightly moisten each layer with water to encourage it to dissolve.

The peels: Drain them. Cook them in a large quantity of unsalted boiling water *for about 2 hours:* a regular boil, not violent but sustained. Cover. Strain. The peels are cooked when they have become translucent, quite soft, and tender to the bite. Drain them. With a good knife, and by laying the peel flat on the table, cut them lengthwise into a very fine julienne.

To cook: Arrange a layer of sugared oranges on the bottom of the basin; above them, a layer of skins, and so on.

Put this on a low heat that spreads out completely over the bottom of the basin, so that the heat is perfectly equal. Let the sugar gradually melt without stirring. Just remember to give the basin a light movement from time to time to circulate the contents and thus prevent them from sticking. The cooking, from beginning to end, must be done over low heat.

The sugar liquefies gradually as the orange tenderizes. As soon as it comes to a boil, you must watch carefully so that it does not go beyond the proper point of cooking. In this case, it is a little bit more than *à la nappe:* it would register as 34° on the saccharometer. At this point, the quarters, which are swollen and practically intact, will be bathed in an abundant amber syrup, and the transparent skins will be perfectly tender. As soon as you have reached this point, stop the cooking: any longer, and the pulp of the quarters will fall apart and the peels will harden. Put them into jars immediately.

Orange Marmalade *(Marmelade d'Oranges).* Plunge the oranges into a basin of fully boiling water so that they are completely covered. Cover and maintain a rather lively boiling until the head of an ordinary pin easily pierces the peel. As soon as they pass this test, put the oranges one by one into a terrine of cold water: let them soak there for 2 days.

Divide the oranges into quarters. Remove the cottony part in the center with scissors. Remove the seeds. Cut the quarters crosswise, including the skin, into slices as thin as possible.

Meanwhile, put some granulated sugar of a weight equal to that of the oranges into the basin. Moisten it with 2 glasses—that is, 4 deciliters (1 2/3 cups) of water per kilogram (2 pounds, 3 ounces) of sugar. Once this has melted, place it on the heat and bring it to a boil; skim. Put the oranges into the syrup. Reduce the heat to maintain a very gentle boil for about *1 hour,* to give the orange peel time to be completely infused with syrup; it must be quite tender and translucent. Cook the marmalade until the *nappe* point is reached. Put it into jars.

Marmalade of Bitter Oranges *(Marmelade d'Oranges Amères).* Marmalade of bitter oranges, which has a rather special taste, is the essential accompaniment for morning toast and tea in Anglo-Saxon countries; it is something that people have become accustomed to in France, and despite the large amount of sugar required for making it, it is attractive because the whole fruit is used. The quantities given below make about 14 jars, each weighing 450 grams (1 pound). A bitter orange currently cultivated in the Midi is perfectly ripe in February. A darker color than the sweet orange, it is smaller and has a rough skin.

For 1 kilogram (2 pounds, 3 ounces) of oranges: 2 lemons; 4 kilograms (8 pounds, 13 ounces) of super-fine sugar or crystallized sugar; 3½ liters (14¾ cups) of water.

PROCEDURE. Wash the fruits, both the oranges and the lemons. With a sharp kitchen knife, cut them into quarters, take out the seeds, and let them soak in a small bowl in 4 deciliters (1⅔ cups) of cold water. Cut the quarters, skin and pulp, into a *very fine* julienne. Put this julienne into a glazed earthenware basin; add cold water; cover and allow it to soak at least 24 hours; a few hours more is fine. After macerating, put the fruits into a copper marmalade basin and add the seeds, collected together in a bag made of muslin, along with the gluey liquid that has formed. Bring it to a boil and cook it on low heat, covered, for 1 hour; take off the cover, then add the sugar and mix to encourage it to melt, and cook while stirring for another 45 minutes. It is perfect when the skimmer is covered with a thin layer of jelly like a varnish. The marmalade must not go beyond an amber tint. Put it into jars and cover.

This preserve rises very little while cooking, so the basin can be filled more than is usual.

Tomato Preserves *(Confiture de Tomates)*

Strictly speaking, this is a preserve that is rather liquid. The two recipes given below do not include anything other than sugar and the flavoring provided by vanilla. Neither ingredient can be left out: you must therefore assume an equal weight of sugar and tomato pulp, and 1 vanilla bean for each kilogram (2 pounds, 3 ounces) of pulp.

Choose tomatoes that are round, without ribs; nice and red, perfectly healthy, ripe, but not too ripe.

PROCEDURE. Cut the tomatoes in half to extract the seeds and juice from them, pressing them over a terrine; keep this juice. Then remove their skin: to do this, put the tomatoes on a skimmer 2 or 3 at a time with the skin side down, and hold them right on the surface of a saucepan of boiling water for *a few seconds*. Then place them on a plate, and with the point of a knife lift up the skin, which comes away easily. This procedure is much better than immersing the tomatoes before you cut them, because it will then be difficult to comfortably extract the seeds.

Depending on their size, cut each tomato into four or six pieces. Weigh them.

Put an equal weight of sugar into the basin. Moisten it with the juice you have reserved from the tomatoes, passed through a cloth to eliminate the seeds, which would give a bitter flavor to the preserves. Add a little bit of water to this liquid; ½ glass for every 450 grams (1 pound) of sugar. Allow it to dissolve completely over extremely gentle heat, stirring it from time to time.

After this, bring it to a boil; allow it to boil for *2–3 minutes* only; skim; put the vanilla and the tomatoes into this syrup; let it cook at a gentle simmer over moderate heat for *12–15 minutes*, no longer. Then pour everything into a large terrine. Let it rest there for at least *24 hours*.

Then put the preserves back into the basin on the fire. Bring it to a boil, stirring the bottom with a spatula. Skim. Turn the fire down to give the hard parts time to cook perfectly. Let it cook until it reaches the correct degree—that is, *à la nappe*.

Take out the vanilla and put the preserves in jars.

Other procedure: Cut the tomatoes in two. Pass them through a fine drum sieve so that nothing remains on the sieve except the skin and the seeds.

Put some sugar in the basin in a weight equal to that of the tomato purée. Pour this over the sugar and allow it to melt on very gentle heat. Then turn up the heat. Add the vanilla. Cook the preserves, stirring constantly with the spatula until it has reached the right point. Take out the vanilla and put the preserves in jars.

Carrot Preserves *(Confitures de Carottes)*

This is like an orange preserve. And it is more economical than the latter for anyone with a kitchen garden.

Carrots of the best quality, nice and red in the center and not too mature. An equal weight of sugar and peeled carrots; 2 lemons, 2 glasses of water *per 450 grams (1 pound)* of carrots.

PROCEDURE. Cut the peeled carrots into pieces. Cook them in a copper basin with the first glass of water until they are nice and tender. Pass them through a drum sieve to make a purée. Reserve. Remove the zest or colored part of the lemon. Cut it into ribbons about 1 centimeter (3/8 inch) long and 2 millimeters (1/16 inch) wide.

In the rinsed basin, dissolve the sugar with the second glass of water. Then add the lemon peel. Cook it to the *nappe* point. Then add the carrot purée and the lemon juice to the syrup. Let it boil for just a few moments. Put it into jars.

Chestnut Preserves *(Confitures de Marrons)*

Rather than the term *preserves,* used in families, we would use the term *purée,* which better defines this. This purée's particular advantage is that it is good for improvising sugared desserts. It does not keep for more than 1 year at the most, because it whitens and becomes chalky like marrons glacés, of which it also tastes. *Makes enough for about 5 jars with a capacity of 3 deciliters (1 1/4 cups) each.*

Equal weight of sugar and cooked chestnuts; 2 deciliters (6 3/4 fluid ounces, generous 3/4 cup) of water for each kilogram (2 pounds, 3 ounces) of sugar used; 2 kilograms (4 pounds, 6 ounces) of chestnuts, gross weight; a half vanilla bean pounded into a powder for 2 kilograms (4 pounds, 6 ounces) of chestnuts.

PROCEDURE. Remove the first shell of the chestnuts. Plunge them into a receptacle of unsalted boiling water in which they will be completely submerged; boil them until they are completely cooked. Remove their skins, taking them out of the water only one at a time, so that they are still burning hot when they are squashed into a paste in the mortar, five or six at a time. As you go, empty out the mortar, transferring the paste to a plate.

Finally pass the paste through a drum sieve to eliminate the bits of skin left after peeling.

Put some sugar into the copper preserve basin, moisten it with water, and let it dissolve over very low heat. Mix the chestnut paste with the sugar underneath it. On very moderate heat, cook it, stirring with a wooden spoon, until the water has completely evaporated from the syrup. That said, the purée should be a little bit runny: the spoon should not leave a groove that exposes the bottom of the basin.

Off the heat, add and mix in the powdered vanilla. Immediately pour the burning-hot paste into the jars: if not, it will settle badly.

Grape Preserves *(Raisiné)*

This kind of preserve is made only with the juice, or "must," of the grape—a simple grape preserve. Or, various fruits can be added to the must, chosen according to region or circumstance: pears, quince, apples, slices of melon, squash, or even carrots instead of pears.

Generally the recipe for grape preserves, whether simple or with fruits, does not include sugar, assuming that you are going to use only grapes that are naturally sugared as would be for example those of the Midi.

To counteract the possible acidity of another type of grape, you add sugar in the quantity of 300–500 grams (10 1/2 ounces–1 pound, 2 ounces) per liter (4 1/4 cups) of must.

Assume that the waste from the residue of the grapes after pressing will account for about one-quarter of the weight of fresh grapes—so about 12 kilograms (26 pounds, 7 ounces) of grapes will produce about 9 liters (9 1/2 quarts) of juice. At the same time, to reach the right cooking point—which for preserves is the *nappe* or "thread" stage—the juice must be reduced by two-thirds: in other words, 9 liters (9 1/2 quarts) of must or juice supplies 3 liters (3 3/16 quarts, 12 3/4 cups) of grape preserves. If you add some sugar to it, this will, of course, increase the volume by that quantity.

The particular grape used is red, although you can also add some white grapes. Choose grapes that are good and ripe, of a good quality and a sweet type; leave out any moldy or spoiled grape.

Simple Grape Preserves *(Raisiné Simple).* Seed the grapes and crush them, pressing them on a drum sieve to extract the juice from them. Measure the must. Pour it into the copper cooking basin. If you are adding sugar to the must, mix it in at this point.

Bring it to a boil on strong heat. Skim carefully and allow it to reduce, turning down the heat toward the end to reach the right point of cooking and produce the quantities given above. Put it into jars.

Grape Preserves with Fruits *(Raisiné aux Fruits).* Classically, the primary fruit to use is pears, chosen from a sweet and sugared kind: either Messire Jean, Doyenné, Martin Sec, etc.; and quinces, in a quantity equal to that of the pears. Thus, in total, about 300 grams (10½ ounces) of fruit, weighed completely peeled, for each liter (4¼ cups) of must. Pears and quince are cut into quarters proportional to the size of the fruits, then peeled, and their seeds and granular parts in the center are carefully removed.

Cook the must alone, as for simple grape preserves, until reduced by only *half.* Then put in the prepared fruits and lower the heat a little. From this moment, do not stop gently stirring the mixture, using a large wooden spatula and scraping directly on the bottom of the basin where the preserves have a tendency to stick. Be particularly vigilant toward the end of the cooking, and proceed carefully, so that you do not break the pieces of fruit, which should remain whole while infused by the syrup. In this final period, slow down the boiling a little more, until the moment when the syrup has reached the right point. Put it in jars, dividing the pieces equally among them.

Burgundy Grape Preserves *(Raisiné Dit "de Bourgogne").* As above, this includes pears and quince, adding the same amount of apples as pears, but reducing the amount of quince. If you like, add some melon and any fruit available, but do not worry about preserving the fruit intact because this is a kind of marmalade, in which everything is mixed. So, once the fruits have been peeled and had their seeds removed, cut them into fine slices.

Prepare the must as directed; add sugar to it, if necessary; cook and reduce by half; then add the fruits. This done, proceed exactly as above until the marmalade has taken on a thick consistency, so that when you take it between your thumb and index finger and then separate the two fingers, it forms a gluey string. A tablespoon put on a plate must not obviously lose its shape. Put it into pots.

NOTE. It is not possible to be precise about the cooking time for grape preserves, no matter which type of preparation it is. For the quantities above and with very good heat, you will need at least 2 hours; but in some cases, you should expect to need up to 4 hours.

JELLIES
Gelées

Red Currant Jelly *(Gelée de Groseille)*

The most popular of all preserves to spread on toast for children. That's why it requires so few steps, its preparation varying according to taste and means, and regulated by only a few rules.

There is first of all the question of the fruit itself. It is essential here that it be good and ripe because of its natural acidity. You can use only red currants: but whenever you can, it is always better to add a third of white currants to the total quantity of fruit. The jelly is thus sweeter and less dark.

The addition of raspberries into the red currant jelly is not essential, even though the practice has become almost universal. The quantity is not fixed, varying between a fifth and a sixth of the weight of the red currants.

The yield of the fruit can be established thus: 1 kilogram (2 pounds, 4 ounces) of red currants, unseeded, provides 600–650 grams (1 pound, 5 ounces–1 pound, 7 ounces) of juice—that is, 6–6½ deciliters (2½–2¾ cups). In other words, you must assume that the waste will account for a little less than two-fifths of the gross weight.

Generally, the amount of sugar is fixed at a weight equal to the juice.

Red Currant Juice *(Le Jus de Groseilles).* How do you obtain this? Methods differ: you can proceed either by pressing the fruit or by melting it.

By pressing: Even though this procedure is nowadays used less and less in home preserve making, we will nonetheless give some directions on this subject. Do not seed the red currants: simply sort through the bunches to remove any debris. Wash them in substantial fresh water and drain them on a drum sieve. Break them up into a terrine with your hands. Strain them in small batches at a time through a towel made of a strong cloth: 2 people, each holding one end of the towel, twist it strongly over another terrine. When everything has been strained, put the dregs (skins and pulp) back into its terrine and moisten it with a few tablespoons of water, added very parsimoniously, because this water then has to be evaporated, which would prolong the cooking. One more time, strain the dregs so that you thereby obtain all the juice you can extract from it. (When you add raspberries, they are mixed with the red currants from the beginning.)

There are fruit presses available that are simple to use and that produce a much larger quantity of juice than you can obtain by other means, but this juice is not absolutely clear, and the jelly produced from it will not be *transparent.*

By melting: This is the procedure currently used today because it is simpler, does not require the help of a second person, and produces exactly the same result as the other. Once the fruits have been washed, *seed them.* Put them in a basin with very little water: 4–5 tablespoons per kilogram (2 pounds, 3 ounces). Bring them to a boil on very low heat. Watch and stir from time to time, because the berries have a tendency to stick to the bottom of the utensil. Once they have come to a boil, reduce the heat a little so that the boiling is manifested only as a simmer. If possible, cover the basin. Let the berries melt—or rather, collapse—thus releasing their juice, for *10–12 minutes.* Then pour everything onto a horsehair or stainless steel drum sieve placed over a terrine. Allow it to drain for *about 20 minutes,* making sure that from time to time you clear away the seeds obstructing the mesh of the drum sieve. You can press lightly on the berries with the back of a silver fork or a skimmer.

The Different Methods of Cooking. To appreciate their advantages or recognize the drawbacks, you must first remember this principle: *the faster a jelly is cooked, the better it conserves the flavor of the fruit* and—in the case of red fruits—its beautiful color. So the perfectionist methods tend to shorten the cooking time.

First method: This one is quite simple: the juice, whether obtained by pressing or by melting, is measured, then put into the basin, off the heat, with the sugar. Allow the sugar to completely dissolve first—this will take *10–12 minutes.* Then place it on strong heat. Very carefully, remove the foam that begins to develop from this point on. Boil strongly throughout, until the *nappe* has been reached, then put it immediately into jars.

Second method: This is a perfectionist method, which attempts to shorten the cooking time by virtue of the principle explained above. It leaves out the first part of cooking the juice with the sugar, which is the longest stage.

As a result, the sugar is *first* cooked to an elevated degree, the "ball." When it has reached this point, you can add the red currant juice to it. On strong heat, bring it back to a boil and cook vigorously until the *nappe* is reached. Put it immediately into jars.

Third method: The red currant berries are put directly into the syrup to burst there and release their juice. This procedure, which cuts out the need for squeezing or first melting the fruit, is even more expedient. At the same time, thanks to the residue or the sugared dregs, it produces a kind of marmalade that, when put into pots, is very popular with small children, and thus provides an extra staple for them. This method is no more extravagant than the others—though one might object that the quantity of sugar is equal not to the juice, but to the red currants in their raw gross state. It has enough advantages that, we will suggest, it is preferable to the other methods.

This recipe produces a jelly with a very fine taste. The quantity of raspberries—115 grams/4 ounces for every 450 grams (1 pound) of red currants—thus represents in total one-fifth of the weight. This is an average, which one should not reduce, if possible. As far as the sugar goes, the recipe is based on the amount given here. It is possible that the fruit preserves will take longer to reach the right point if the syrup is used in a lesser quantity. *Makes enough for a dozen ordinary jars.*

3 kilograms (6 pounds, 10 ounces) of red currants, of which one-third are white, weighed when seeded; 750 grams (1 pound, 10 ounces) of raspberries, weighed cleaned; 3 3/4 kilograms (8 pounds, 4 ounces) of sugar.

PROCEDURE. Seed the red currants using a silver or silver-plated fork, clean the raspberries, and prepare the sugar syrup as directed (SEE COOKING SUGAR, PAGE 577). Cook it to the soft-ball stage.

Then add the currants and raspberries together. Stir and mix with the skimmer. The heat must be strong enough that it returns to a boil rapidly. When it has done so, and is threatening to boil over, turn off the heat for *7–8 minutes.* This gives the fruit time to burst and to release its juice before cooking.

Turn the heat back on high and boil it strongly. Carefully skim it. Turn off the heat again when all the boiling mass has risen. Allow it to rest for another *3–4 minutes.*

One last time, turn the heat back on and boil it strongly. Once again, skim very carefully and watch it closely, making several tests with a drop of syrup poured onto a plate, so that you can stop the cooking as soon as the *nappe* is reached.

Have ready a large horsehair or stainless steel drum sieve placed over an earthenware terrine. Pour the contents of the basin into it and allow the juice to pass through. Without waiting for everything to cool, gently stir the fruits using a wooden spoon or a silver spoon, without leaning or pressing on it: this is simply to move things around and to help the juice to run out. Immediately put the jelly into jars.

Red Currant Jelly, Another Method *(Gelée de Groseilles, Autre Façon).* This procedure leaves the jelly with a delicious taste of fresh fruit; the consistency of this jelly is less firm than jellies that are cooked until the *nappe* is reached, but this does not affect its preservation, which will still be perfect at the end of a year—as we have found out by experience. *Superfine* sugar is indicated here and should not be replaced by granulated sugar, which will not melt nearly rapidly enough; it is essential to do the work very quickly. You should allow an equal weight of sugar and currants, and it is preferable that half of these be white currants.

When making this jelly, absolutely do not go beyond a weight of 6 kilograms (13 pounds, 4 ounces) in total—that is, the quantity of both fruit and sugar.

PROCEDURE. Seed the fruit. Put a glass of water into the basin for the quantities given above. In alternate layers, add the currants and the sugar, *without crushing* the currants and finishing with a layer of sugar. Place the basin on a *very sustained, very strong heat, which heats the whole surface of the bottom of the utensil.* This is very important, so that you reach a general boil very quickly: expect this boiling to manifest after *10–12 minutes* for the quantities above. Until then, touch nothing in the basin.

The foam is first produced all around, coming up from the sides toward the center and spreading out over the layer of sugar. As soon as the surface of the basin has been covered by a boiling foam—known by the French as making a *bouillon* ("bubbling")—turn the heat off immediately to stop the boiling and make the foam fall back. Then turn the heat back on to produce a second *bouillon* in the same way. Proceed as follows a third time: three *bouillons,* in other words. If the currants are not very sweet, make a fourth *bouillon,* but no more.

There is no need to remove the foam, which gradually condenses and dissipates. Make sure you rotate the basin from time to time to move its contents without using the skimmer.

Pour the entire contents of the basin onto a large horsehair or stainless steel drum sieve *without pressing on it.* In several minutes all the juice, very clear, is released; pressing on the berries would barely provide any more and the clarity of the juice would be compromised.

Put it immediately into jars and cover.

Red Currant Jelly Made Cold *(Gelée de Groseilles à Froid).* Even better than the previous method, red currant jelly prepared as we shall describe retains all the flavor of fresh fruit, because it does not undergo any form of cooking at any time. Prepared carefully and kept in a very dry place, this jelly will keep for at least a year.

Only red currants are used in it. You must choose them perfectly ripe. The sugar used is known as *confectioners' sugar* (SEE PAGE 574) in a quantity of 1 kilogram (2 pounds, 3 ounces) for each liter (4$^{1}/_{4}$ cups) of juice, which works out as equal weight.

PROCEDURE. Squeeze the red currants in a cloth, as directed for red currant juice obtained by pressing, but without adding any water to the dregs, because in this case the water will not be evaporated by boiling and might cause fermentation.

To this juice, first measured and collected in a terrine, add the sugar, poured in slowly and gradually, turning the mixture in all directions using a silver spoon, just as you would proceed for a mayonnaise. Stir the mixture again for about 10 minutes to ensure the sugar completely dissolves.

Pour it into the very small chosen jars and keep them uncovered in a very dry place for 2–3 days. The jelly should then have taken on a thick consistency. Cover the pots as usual, and, if possible, stand them in the sun for 2 days.

Apple Jelly *(Gelée de Pomme)*

Everyone knows that the variety of apples is extremely numerous; but not all of them can be used for jelly. Some have no flavor; others lack gelatinous elements or pectin, which is essential for any fruit jelly. When it is not a question of using a particular variety, the Rennet apple should certainly be chosen, preferably the Rennet of Canada. On this, there is a general consensus. Use good healthy fruit, not too ripe: the pulp of a fruit that is overripe will disintegrate while cooking, and the juice will be cloudy.

Should apples for jelly be peeled or not? On this point, opinion is divided. All agree, however, that the skin of the apple has a very agreeable flavor and that the seeds have a mucilaginous element that is very good. From this, one can certainly conclude that it is not necessary to peel the apples except when they are spotted or have some blemish: the spots give the juice a taste of musk, or overripeness. Also, once the apples have released their juices for the jelly—whether for a marmalade or for apple butter—it is not essential that they should first have been peeled, because for the second use they are passed through the drum sieve. It is thus not worth the trouble, as certain recipes suggest, to peel the apples and to then enclose the peels and the seeds in muslin so that you can take them out of the fruit easily after cooking.

The quantity of water for cooking the apples has no real importance apart from this: the water must be enough to thoroughly submerge the fruit throughout its cooking. If there is too much, the cooking time of the jelly will naturally be prolonged accordingly—that is, by the time necessary for the proportions to be reestablished by evaporating the excess water. For a general calculation, use this measure: *1 good half liter (generous 2 cups) of water per 450 grams (1 pound) of fruit.*

The *quantity of sugar* is, depending on whether you prefer it more or less sweet, about 750 grams (1 pound, 10 ounces), 900 grams (2 pounds), or 1 kilogram (2 pounds, 3 ounces) per liter (4¹/4 cups) of juice. In terms of the jelly's consistency, the quantity of sugar here is unimportant because the pectin contained in the apple is the main element that solidifies the juice.

If you like, you can add to the finished jelly some lemon peel, cut into very small slices that have previously been blanched in boiling water. This flavored water is added to the apple juice.

Much more than for any other jelly, apple jelly must be perfectly clear, pure and transparent as crystal. On this subject, we give extensive recommendations in the recipe below. And it is for this reason that we suggest something that is not always done, *straining the jelly through cloth* before putting it in jars: because, no matter how much care you take, some bits of solidified foam will remain in the jelly. Straining it first means that you will obtain a jelly that is absolutely limpid.

Also, as we have already said for all preserves and jellies, we advise you not to work with too large quantities. You should therefore stop at a maximum weight of *3.1–3.6 kilograms (7–8 pounds)* of apples at a time.

PROCEDURE. **The apples:** Depending on where they come from, make sure you wipe them carefully with a soft cloth to get rid of all powder and impurities; if you think you must wash them, do this rapidly and dry them immediately.

Cut them into thin pieces: 6 or 8 pieces, depending on the size of the apple. *Do not peel them.* As you do so, put them in a terrine of cool water so that the pulp does not brown.

Put all the pieces of apples into the basin. Pour

the water on top of them—which, let us not forget, should thoroughly immerse them. Put them on a good, sustained heat that spreads out as evenly as possible across the surface of the basin. Otherwise, the apples at the center of the basin will receive more heat than those around them, and will reduce to a marmalade before the others are cooked: you will then have to mix everything to reestablish the equilibrium, which will compromise the clarity of the juice. And this leads me to make a recommendation that must be scrupulously followed: *do not touch the apples while cooking,* so that you do not disintegrate the pulp. Carefully watch for the moment when the boiling begins. Then cover the basin, using a cover, if possible, or by stretching a cloth over it. *Turn down the fire considerably.* If they cook too strongly, the apples will burst and reduce to a purée. You must let them cook like this right to the point where, when you press on the pieces with your finger, you feel that they are nice and soft and yield under the pressure. About *12–15 minutes* from the moment boiling begins should be enough to bring them to this point. Except for a few pieces that will have reduced to a marmalade, most should have preserved their shape.

Use a large horsehair or stainless steel drum sieve placed over a terrine of white fired earthenware. Very carefully take out the apples, using a skimmer to place them on the drum sieve in equal layers. Then pour the liquid over the top. Do not compact them or press them directly, because any pressure will release pulp into the juice. At the most, after about 10 minutes, you can tap the side of the drum sieve lightly, inclining it a little bit to encourage the juices to run off.

To thoroughly drain 3–4 kilograms (6 pounds, 10 ounces–8 pounds, 13 ounces) of fruit, allow *about a half hour.* Let it rest, still without mixing the juice, for about the same time again. Then measure the juice to determine the quantity of sugar to add to it: either with a liter measure (or cup), or by weighing it in some utensil (whose weight you have first established), bearing in mind that 1 liter (4¼ cups) of juice weighs about 1 kilogram (2 pounds, 3 ounces). Do this gently, tilting the terrine over the utensil to avoid mixing the small deposit in the bottom with the juice.

Rinse the basin in warm water and wipe it dry. Pour in the juice. Add the determined quantity of sugar to it. Place the basin on very low heat and first ensure that the sugar has completely dissolved by stirring it from time to time with the skimmer.

The jelly: Then place the basin on very strong heat. As soon as the foam begins to appear, remove it with the skimmer as often as necessary: this is the only way to obtain a completely transparent jelly. Nor should you allow the foam to accumulate on the walls of the basin in the form of a gray scum; this is principally caused by the sugar, which might break down if you allow it to stay there. This is why each time you remove the foam, you must be careful to wash the utensil that you have used—either a copper skimmer or a silver spoon—with warm water. You can also wipe all around the circumference of the basin with a dampened cloth.

Cook it until it has reached the point known as *à la nappe* (SEE PAGE 726).

Have a terrine ready in advance with a fine cloth or muslin stretched over the top. As soon as the jelly is ready, pour it into the terrine placed on the ground: this lets you work more easily, because this burning jelly requires prudence in your movements. Lightly twist the cloth. Once all the jelly has been strained, fill the jars. Be careful while you are filling them to stir the jelly in the terrine from time to time with the ladle to prevent it from partially coagulating.

Quince Jelly *(Gelée de Coings)*

Its preparation is exactly the same as for apple jelly, to which you should refer for all details.

Choose large quince, preferably the variety known as *Portugal,* perfectly ripe without, however, being overripe: a nice accented yellow color without any brown spots, which indicate that they are spoiling.

Just like apples, they are not peeled. Simply wipe them with a rather rough towel to remove the cottony down covering the skin.

Depending on their size, divide the quince into 6–8 pieces. Remove their seeds, the hardest part of the core, and the stem; and as you go, put the pieces into cool water.

Then proceed as for cooking apples, except that

here more water is used because of the longer cooking time: quince takes much longer to cook than apple, so you must anticipate how much liquid will evaporate. You should thus measure *1 liter (4¼ cups) of water for every 450 grams (1 pound) of peeled quince.*

The length of time needed for cooking the quince is impossible to estimate precisely, because certain species of quince cook more quickly than others. It can vary from 45 minutes to 1½ hours and even more. In any case, the boiling must be extremely gentle so that the pulp of the fruit does not disintegrate. And you should cover the basin to avoid too much evaporation.

You can tell that the quinces are cooked when, like apples, they give under the pressure of your finger. The end of a match should pierce right through without any difficulty.

The quantity of sugar for quince jelly can be established at an average of 800 grams (1 pounds, 12 ounces) of sugar for each liter (4¼ cups) of juice, that is a little more than three quarters weight of sugar per pound of fruit.

Orange Jelly *(Gelée d'Orange)*

An excellent procedure adapted from home-style preserves, which was given to us by the old master Colombié. Allow here for 1 liter (4¼ cups) of juice, about one-third of apple juice, for setting the jelly: that would be 7 deciliters (3 cups) of orange juice and 3 deciliters (1¼ cups) of apple juice; and 800 grams (1 pound, 12 ounces) of granulated sugar per liter (4¼ cups) of the mixture of juices.

PROCEDURE. To get 3 deciliters (1¼ cups) of apple juice, use 500 grams (1 pound, 2 ounces) of Rennet apples that have a firm pulp and are perfectly healthy (SEE APPLE JELLY, PAGE 738). For 7 deciliters (3 cups) of orange juice, you need about 10–12 oranges, each weighing an average of 150 grams (5½ ounces). Using a small kitchen knife, remove from one-third of the oranges some large ribbons of zest—the colored part only, without lifting off any of the white part. Make a little packet with these peels.

Cut the oranges crosswise and press them in a glass juicer; or forcefully by hand, into a terrine. Strain the juice through a chinois (SEE PAGE 33).

Combine the apple and orange juice and the sugar in the basin; place it on strong heat. When it begins to boil, skim, then moderate the heat to maintain the liquid at the same point without it boiling over.

With a moistened towel, carefully wipe the inside of the basin each time that the foam rises; this is because the sugar will caramelize there, and the color and flavor of the juice will be somewhat modified by it.

Cook it until the *nappe* is reached. Toward the end of the cooking, add the small packet of zests to the jelly, which must boil for *5–6 minutes.* Take it out and then put the jelly in jars.

Black Currant Jelly *(Gelée de Cassis)*

This is prepared in exactly the same way as red currant jelly, using the method where the juice is obtained by first melting the fruit in the basin and then pouring it into a sugar syrup that has been cooked to the soft-ball stage.

The amount of sugar used can be less than for red currants, since the black currant is less acidic; however, if it is good and ripe, as it must be to have all its juices, you can make the jelly with 800 grams (1 pound, 12 ounces) of sugar per kilogram (2 pounds, 3 ounces) or liter (4¼ cups) of juice.

You can add some white currants to the black currants to reduce the black color of this fruit at the same time as they substantially accentuate the flavor. The quantities are rather variable for this: according to taste, it can be one-sixth, a quarter, or even a half of the total quantity of juice.

PROCEDURE. Wash, drain, then seed the black currants and red currants. Leave them to burst in the basin with 1 deciliter (3⅓ fluid ounces, scant ½ cup) of water for each kilogram (2 pounds, 3 ounces) of fruit. Drain them on the drum sieve.

Cook the sugar in the basin to the soft-ball stage (SEE PAGE 578). Then pour the juice into the sugar, which will immediately stop the cooking. Turn off the heat under the basin for a few minutes so that the sugar completely dissolves into the juice. Then bring it back to a boil. As soon as it begins to boil, skim it again very carefully.

Cook it to the *nappe.* It is appropriate here not to go beyond that, since black currant jelly does not have to be quite as cooked as the other jellies. Put it into jars.

Wild Blackberry Jelly
(Gelée de Mûres Sauvages)

You can prepare this like red currant jelly with three-quarters of sugar for every 450 grams (1 pound) of juice. Or in the following way:

Use an equal weight of granulated sugar. Macerate the fruit with the sugar for a few hours. Put everything in the basin on strong heat. As soon as everything rises, boiling across the entire surface of the basin, turn off the heat. Wait a few moments to allow the boiling to fall back completely. Turn on the heat and again boil it strongly. Do this again. Do it again a third time. In summary, give it three boilings.

Pour it over a large horsehair or stainless steel drum sieve. Let the jelly strain through. Put it in jars.

DRINKS

Hot Chocolate *(Chocolat)*

The first rule to establish when making this, either with water or with milk, is that the chocolate must never boil. And since this rule is based on the principle for manufacturing chocolate, which is always followed by the industrial manufacturers who are particularly authorized to formulate it, this must also apply to the preparation of chocolate drinks. Thus it is a mistaken belief that the hot chocolate is enhanced by prolonged simmering: what has given credibility to this idea is that in homes one tends, for reasons of economy, to reduce the quantity of chocolate in relation to that of the milk, and then to boil the milk for some time, thus reducing the liquid and so the chocolate is restored to its normal proportion, which is less diluted and obviously better.

Allow 20 grams (2/3 ounce) of chocolate for each deciliter (3 1/3 fluid ounces, scant 1/2 cup) of liquid. A coffee cup generally measures 2 deciliters (6 3/4 fluid ounces, generous 3/4 cup) when not too full; this corresponds to the use of 1 square of chocolate *extracted from a packet* of 12 squares weighing 450 grams (1 pound). If the cup is more generously filled—that is to 2 1/2 deciliters (1 cup)—you must use 1 1/4 tablets.

PROCEDURE. Break the squares in half. Put them in the saucepan where you will work the mixture of *hot* liquid—water or milk; use one of such a size that the liquid will just cover the chocolate. Cover the saucepan. Put it on very, very low heat; 2 minutes will be enough to soften the chocolate.

Using a small whisk—or if you do not have that, a wooden spoon—work the chocolate off the heat until it is reduced to a homogeneous and smooth paste. Then pour in the necessary quantity of *boiling* liquid, beginning with several tablespoons in order to better dilute the paste. Add the rest of the still-boiling liquid. Then pour it into a chocolate pitcher that has previously been rinsed in boiling water. Make it foam with the special accessory called a "foamer," turning its handle by rubbing it flat between your hands, or with a small whisk worked in the same way. During this time, keep the chocolate pitcher in a warm place.

If the hot chocolate must stand, keep it in a bain-marie.

Do not let any skin form in the milk used. If the milk is boiled just before using, the cream will not have had the time to clump; if not, the milk must be carefully strained before mixing it with the chocolate.

To make the hot chocolate foamier, add some egg yolks, proceeding as directed in the very old kitchen recipes. This is to be recommended not only for the effect obtained, but also and most of all for the particular smoothness it gives the chocolate. Follow the usual method for thickening with egg yolk to dilute the eggs with the chocolate (SEE PAGE 49). You can allow 3 nice yolks for 1 liter (4 1/4 cups) of liquid.

Black Coffee *(Café Noir)*

There are an infinite number of apparatus for making black coffee at the table, whose inventors or manufacturers have the responsibility for explaining the techniques and boasting their merits. Here we will confine ourselves to directions for the use of the classic filter coffee maker, the Dubelloy, *in earthenware or in stoneware;* tin-lined steel must not be used: the tin is too thin and the steel that is soon exposed will spoil the coffee. Never allow the grounds to remain in the filter. Wash it in perfectly clean hot or warm water and then dry it thoroughly.

You can allow a maximum of 10–12 grams (1/3–3/8 ounce) of coffee for a current size of smaller coffee cup, which has a capacity of 1 deciliter (3 1/3 fluid ounces, scant 1/2 cup) at most; 12 grams (3/8 ounce) provides enough coffee to satisfy lovers of strong coffee, particularly when the preparation is enough for 3–4 cups of coffee at a time. To simplify the weighing, establish a rough figure and then add a little extra: for example, for 4 cups of strong coffee, you can assume 50 grams (1³/₄ ounces) of roasted coffee.

The amount of water corresponding to the coffee used for each cup of coffee—that is, 10–12 grams/¹/₃–³/₈ ounce—is 1 deciliter (3¹/₃ fluid ounces, scant ¹/₂ cup).

But you must be careful, because this quantity does not include the amount of water needed to soak the coffee, which will remain in the grounds. This quantity is difficult to establish exactly, given that in relative terms there will be more water left in the grounds when preparing only 1 cup of coffee than when preparing 6 or even 10 cups at the same time.

For a cup of coffee prepared alone, you should allow 1¹/₂ deciliters (5 fluid ounces, ²/₃ cup) of boiling water.

For 6 cups of coffee, allow no more than 7 deciliters (3 cups) of water.

For 10 cups of coffee, that would be scarcely 12 deciliters (5 cups) of water.

Coffee must always be prepared carefully. Everything must be ready, and you must assume *15 minutes* for the operation; and it is essential that the receptacle—that is, the coffeemaker into which the coffee runs—should be kept warm throughout. For this, place the coffeemaker in a saucepan of very warm water, like a bain-marie.

In advance, the coffee must be very finely ground. Pour it into the filter. Cover it with the disk with the holes in it and the cover. Stop the spout of the coffeemaker with a little cork of new cloth or a little plug of absorbent cotton, which you renew frequently.

Meanwhile, generously measure the necessary amount of water—cold filtered water—into a small covered kettle.

The operation: Anticipating the moment when you will serve the coffee, rapidly heat the water on strong heat. As soon as it starts to boil, sprinkle the coffee with as many tablespoons of this boiling water as there are cups. Cover. Allow it to swell for *5 good minutes.* The effect of this first basting is to swell the coffee so that it then effectively retains the water, which, if it were poured on all at once, would pass too quickly through the coffee without absorbing the aroma from it.

Once the water in the kettle has been put back on the heat, keep it at a simple simmer: boiling it too strongly or for too long would spoil it for coffee. After 5 minutes, pour *about one-quarter of it* over the coffee. Re-cover both the filter and the kettle. Let it infuse for *3 minutes*; then pour the rest of the water in equal intervals *every 2–3 minutes* in small quantities. Each time, cover the filter and the kettle.

Keep the coffeemaker in the bain-marie until you are ready to serve.

To serve: At home, you can bring the coffee to the table in the coffeemaker itself, where it has been brewed, protected by its cover. If you want to serve it in a silver coffeepot, or similar, make sure that you heat this utensil with fully boiling water before pouring in the coffee.

Café au Lait *(Café au Lait).* The coffee for this is prepared in advance and in sufficient quantities so that it can be consumed over several days: keep it in a well-corked bottle. You can serve it cold, heating it in its cup when it is mixed with boiling milk; or, if you like, pour the necessary quantity into a small pot and reheat it in a bain-marie.

Although adding even a hint of chicory is not recommended for coffee served after a meal, the same is not true for café au lait: a certain amount of chicory, say about a fifth, is always essential. *Makes ¹/₂ liter (generous 2 cups).*

60 grams (2¹/₄ ounces) of roasted coffee; 15 grams (¹/₂ ounce) of chicory; 6 deciliters (2¹/₂ cups) of water.

PROCEDURE. Put the chicory into the bottom of the filter and the finely ground coffee on top. Heat the water. As soon as it begins to boil, pour 3 tablespoons of water into the filter. Cover and allow the grounds to swell *for 5 good minutes.* Then boil the water again, which must not continue to boil between times, because prolonged boiling will spoil it for coffee. Then pour this water onto the coffee, now swollen like a sponge, in 3 or 4 additions, at intervals of *2–3 minutes.* Make sure you re-cover the filter each time.

Once the water has been completely strained

through the coffee, remove the filter containing the grounds. Place it in a receptacle; in the saucepan used for heating the water if necessary. With one movement, pour over the grounds all the coffee that has already been filtered once, and then replace the filter on the coffeemaker. This double filtering produces a coffee that is infinitely stronger in terms of color and taste; the grounds are no longer good for anything except to throw away, the coffee powder having released all the flavor it can.

Once the liquid has completely ceased draining, pour the coffee while still quite hot into a very clean bottle. Cork it immediately, using a new cork so that you do not spoil the coffee with a strange taste.

Iced Coffee *(Café Glacé).* This is an iced drink and not an ice. Its consistency is also quite special: it does not have the firmness of a sorbet, but only that of a newly melted snow; note this point carefully.

As for the quantities of the ingredients used, these vary according to taste and means. To sum it up, iced coffee is café au lait that you bring to a certain point of coagulation. To obtain it very creamy, replace the milk entirely by cream, or use cream and reduced good milk in equal quantities, or almost equal. It is this latter procedure that we will describe below.

When using cream, a subtle note of vanilla does best. We therefore suggest it; but it can be left out, particularly if the iced coffee is made only with milk.

Iced coffee is served in coffee cups with a capacity of about 1 deciliter (3 1/3 fluid ounces). Stand them on their saucers first, and fill as you go with a small silver spoon. You can allow 2 liters (2 1/8 quarts, 8 1/2 cups) of iced coffee for about 15 people. *Makes 2 liters (2 1/8 quarts, 8 1/2 cups).*

200 grams (7 ounces) of freshly ground coffee; 6 deciliters (2 1/2 cups) of water; 1 liter (4 1/2 cups) of milk; 1/2 liter (generous 2 cups) of perfectly fresh cream; 450 grams (1 pound) of sugar cubes.

***To ice it:* 8 kilograms (17 pounds, 10 ounces) of ice; 1 1/2 kilograms (3 pounds, 5 ounces) of sea salt.**

PROCEDURE. Boil the milk. When it has risen, keep it at a very slight simmer to allow it to reduce to 3/4 liter (generous 3 cups). Then turn off the heat. Add the vanilla; cover the saucepan. Let it infuse off the heat.

Make the coffee as directed (SEE BLACK COFFEE, PAGE 742), using water that is good and boiling, poured over in at least four turns, and a well-covered coffeepot. The quantity of liquid coffee that you must finally obtain is *5 deciliters (generous 2 cups).*

Pour the coffee into a glazed terrine. If the filter is not very fine, pass the coffee through fine muslin when you pour it into the terrine. Add the sugar, mixing it from time to time with a silver spoon until it dissolves completely. Then add the milk, having first removed the vanilla bean; if some black grains of vanilla appear in the milk, you can also strain that through the muslin.

Allow it to chill completely. After this, mix the cream into the café au lait. About 1 hour before serving the iced coffee, ice it in the ice cream maker (SEE PAGE 649). We assume here that you will be using an ice cream maker with a capacity of 3 liters (3 1/4 quarts).

Then ice it as directed, remembering always to observe this unique peculiarity: from time to time, uncover the ice cream maker to allow air in, which is warmer and will therefore prevent the café au lait from setting too firmly. It must, we repeat, have the consistency of melting snow. It is therefore not necessary to put more ice around the ice cream maker if the mixture has to stand before being served. The iced water and the remaining ice will be enough to maintain the consistency of the coffee. If, just before serving, the mixture seems a little firm, add a soupspoon of coffee with a few drops of milk, and that will be enough to make it perfect.

Tea *(Thé)*

Whatever their origin, the varieties of tea, Ceylon or China, are innumerable, and here we will offer no advice about which to choose. But aside from all such considerations, two things are equally essential to obtain excellent tea.

First, the good state of the tea maker, which must be used only for tea, and not for herbal tea or any other type of drink. If the teapot is made of porcelain or metal, the inside of it must never be washed in soapy water or in caustic soda. The tea leaves must never be allowed to stand in the pot once you are finished; empty the tea pot immediately, rinse it in either hot or cold water, then put it in the cupboard, where you leave it without its cover, and even upside down if possible, so that the air can get in, but no dust. This means that there will be no need to wipe the inside of the teapot, something that you must only do, if necessary, with a completely clean cloth: if not, you will be left with an unpleasant taste of towel.

Second, the water used: in fact, its importance may be even greater. We are not going to consider its type or quality here, or discuss what is more, or indeed less, suitable for making good tea: you take the water that you have. But what we would like to draw attention to is this: that you use fresh water taken expressly for this purpose from the tap, just at the moment that you put it on to boil to make the tea, put it in a saucepan or a kettle reserved for this use; water that has remained for a long time on the heat in any receptacle gives a bad taste to the tea.

As for preparing the tea itself, the procedure does not vary, whether you do this in the kitchen or at the tea table. Begin by heating the teapot and pouring boiling water in there to almost a third. Empty this water. Then replace it with the tea. On average, you need 1 teaspoon of tea per person, plus 1 teaspoon "for the pot." So, for 4 people use 5 teaspoons. Note carefully that for more than 5–6 people, this quantity should not be used, because it becomes too large; you can then figure 1 teaspoon for 2 people.

Pour the boiling water on the tea, just enough to thoroughly wet it. Immediately close the cover of the teapot; wait *5 minutes*. When the tea leaves have completely opened and have uncoiled completely, fill the teapot with water that is still fully boiling. The tea is now ready to be poured into the cups.

Serve the tea with *uncooked* milk. Cooked milk denatures the flavor of the tea, and also dilutes badly, floating in the cups in white threads, which is unattractive. Light cream taken from the surface of fresh milk is infinitely preferable to milk. Lemon cut into thin rounds is very popular with some people.

Lemonade *(Citronnade)*

The quantities of sugar given here anticipate the addition of seltzer water or some pieces of ice in the lemonade. Otherwise, and particularly if you do not like very sugared drinks, you can reduce the quantity of sugar a little. *Time: Prepare it 6 hours in advance. Makes about 2 1/2–2 3/4 liters (2 5/8–3 quarts).*

2 liters (2 1/8 quarts, 8 1/2 cups) of cold filtered water; 500 grams (1 pound, 2 ounces) of sugar lumps; 4 nice big lemons that are good and juicy.

PROCEDURE. Use a terrine made of white earthenware, which is meticulously clean and without any cracks, because these can retain the odor of whatever the receptacle previously held. Dissolve the sugar there *cold* in the water.

Remove the peel of the lemons, as directed (SEE ORANGE AND LEMON ZEST, PAGE 574). Put the ribbons of zest in the terrine with the melted sugar. Cut the lemons in half. Squeeze all the juice, using a lemon press made out of glass, or if you do not have one by squeezing them in your hand. Do not allow the seeds to fall into the terrine. Cover. Let it infuse for 4–5 hours. Pass it through a fine chinois. Cool it until ready to serve.

Orangeade *(Orangeade)*

You can prepare it in different ways, all of which, including the most ancient, are based on the use of a cold liquid—sugared water or syrup—in order to preserve the taste of fresh fruit in the juice. Here we give the best contemporary recipes.

The Easiest Method. Proceed exactly as for lemonade, using the same quantity of oranges in place of the lemons. Thus, for 2 liters (2 1/8 quarts, 8 1/2 cups) of filtered water: 500 grams (1 pound, 2 ounces) of sugar, 4 very nice oranges.

Made with a Cooked Sugar Syrup. The quantity of fruit used here is larger, and the drink is obviously much the better for it. Thus: for 1 1/2 liters (about 1 1/2 quarts, 6 1/3 cups) of filtered water; 500 grams (1 pound, 2 ounces) of sugar; 9–10 nice oranges; 2–3 lemons, depending on their size and according to how acid or sweet the oranges are; the zest of an orange.

PROCEDURE. In a copper saucepan that is not lined with tin—or if you do not have one, a thick aluminum saucepan—put the sugar to dissolve. Then place the pot on very strong heat; once it has started to boil, skim the syrup, then pour it into a terrine and allow it to cool completely.

Remove the zest from only one orange (SEE PAGE 574). Put it to one side.

Squeeze the oranges as already indicated. You can also proceed as follows: hold half an orange in your left hand, then stick a wooden spoon right into the middle of it, perfectly clean and without odor, turning this spoon so that you break the pulp to loosen it completely from the skin; but it is essential after this to press the pulp in a cloth, using two people to twist the cloth. This method extracts the most juice.

Also extract the juice of the lemons.

Combine, in a nice earthenware receptacle or in a stoneware receptacle, the orange juice, the lemon juice and the zest, and the completely cool syrup. Let it macerate in a cool place for *2–3 hours.* Strain it through a cloth. Set it aside to cool.

Orangeade with Sugared Zest *(Orangeade avec Sucre Zesté).* This is a method used by certain large ice cream manufacturers, which provides a very perfumed drink.

2 liters (2 1/8 quarts, 8 1/2 cups) of filtered water; 250 grams (8 7/8 ounces) of sugar lumps; 8 oranges and 4 lemons.

PROCEDURE. Zest the sugar as directed (SEE ZESTED SUGAR, PAGE 574). Melt the sugar cold in water. Squeeze the oranges and lemons. Add their juice to the sugared water. Strain through a fine cloth. Cool, if possible, on ice or in a refrigerator.

Strawberry Water *(Eau de Fraises)*

An exquisite summer drink. A refinement is to add to the glasses, according to taste, a little bit of champagne or a very small quantity of red Bordeaux wine, or even a few drops of kirsch.

500 grams (1 pound, 2 ounces) of Héricart or Morère strawberries, perfectly ripe and chosen perfectly healthy; 375 grams (13 1/4 ounces) of granulated sugar; 1 1/2 liters (about 1 1/2 quarts, 6 1/3 cups) of water.

PROCEDURE. Into a copper pan or an aluminum saucepan—in any case, not in a tin-lined utensil, because the tin gives a purplish tint to red fruits—put the sugar and the water. Let it dissolve in a warm place. Clean the strawberries, and if you find some of them partly spoiled or spotted, remove the bad part with the blade of a silver knife: the least blemish will give a bad taste to the infusion. Wash them rapidly in clean water. Place the pot, with the sugar on the bottom, on strong heat. As soon as the liquid boils, turn off the heat and immediately add the strawberries. Cover. Let it infuse for 1 good hour. Spread a fine cloth, previously moistened and twisted out, over a small horsehair or stainless steel drum sieve. Pour in the strawberries and the liquid. Let them drain without pressure. Then subsequently cool the mixture on ice or in a refrigerator. Serve either in carafes or in champagne glasses.

Sweet Punch *(Punch Doux)*

A family recipe that gives a very slightly alcoholic punch. *Makes enough for about 15 glasses.*

200 grams (7 ounces) of sugar cubes; 1 lemon; 1 orange; 1 1/2 deciliters (5 fluid ounces, 2/3 cup) of rum and the same of eau-de-vie; 1 liter (32 fluid ounces, 4 1/4 cups) of light tea (15–20 grams/1/2–2/3 ounce of tea).

PROCEDURE. Rub orange and lemon on the sugar (SEE ZEST SUGAR, PAGE 574). Squeeze the juice out of these fruits and strain it through a cloth. Infuse the tea. Pour it quite hot onto the sugar in the pot; mix it to ensure the sugar dissolves; add the rum and the eau-de-vie. Heat the mixture *without boiling.* If you like, you can pour it directly into the glasses or into an appropriate container.

MENUS

LUNCH FOR RECEPTIONS

Serves 50–60 guests.

300 sandwiches and various canapés.

150 brioche breads with foie gras

500 grams (1 pound, 2 ounces) of small brioches (about 50 pieces)

Two kilograms (4 pounds, 6 ounces) of cakes for lunches.

1 kilogram (2 pounds, 3 ounces) of assorted baked genoises (about 80 pieces).

1 kilogram (2 pounds, 3 ounces) of small fruit tarts and cream puffs (about 100 pieces).

1 kilogram (2 pounds, 3 ounces) of iced petits fours (about 70 pieces).

1 kilogram (2 pounds, 3 ounces) of dressed fruits.

3 large cakes (or a mounted piece and two cakes) which can be divided into 20 or 24 parts: iced genoise, mocha cake, queen of Sheba . . .

One English plate per person including: jellied ham, a slice of roast beef. A galantine of fowl and a garnish of Russian salad or a macédoine of vegetables in pastry shells.

About 4–5 liters ($4^1/_4$–$5^1/_4$ quarts) of iced coffee.

12–15 bottles of champagne or sparkling wine.

10 liters ($10^1/_2$ quarts) of orangeade and lemonade.

Three liters (about $3^1/_4$ quarts) of fruit juice (in summer) or 2 liters ($2^1/_8$ quarts, $8^1/_2$ cups) of warm consommé (in winter).

To make 150 sandwiches, you will need: 2 kilograms (4 pounds, 6 ounces) of white bread from the day before; 450 grams (1 pound, 4 sticks) of butter; 250 grams ($8^7/_8$ ounces) of purée of foie gras; 200 grams (7 ounces) of ham; 200 grams (7 ounces) of potted meat; 200 grams (7 ounces) of smoked salmon; 100 grams ($3^1/_2$ ounces) of smoked tongue and 100 grams ($3^1/_2$ ounces) of caviar (which is served as a canapé on buttered black bread or buttered toast, and which must not be squashed between two slices of bread).

How to Prepare the Sandwiches. The tools: A knife with a very fine and long blade to cut the bread; a cutting board; a wooden spatula to soften the butter; a round-ended knife to butter the sandwiches and the canapés; a sharp and pointed knife.

PROCEDURE. Thoroughly knead the butter to soften it. It must have the consistency of a custard (if necessary, you can work it in a dish that has first been warmed in warm water, which will allow you to spread it more easily). Place the bread on the cutting board, and using the round knife spread the butter without excess. With a large knife, cut a slice as thin as possible. Again, butter the bread and slice the second slice. Garnish the first with foie gras, ham, etc. Cover it with the second slice, pressing the buttered side down on the filling. With a very sharp knife, cut off the crusts and the excess of the spread. Cut the sandwich into a triangle or a rectangle and place it on the serving plate. Once the plates are filled, cover them with a white napkin that that has been lightly moistened to keep the bread from drying out. The canapés are made with only one slice of bread, which is covered with the garnish, and the garnish is visible. Canapés are therefore more decorative than sandwiches. They are minuscule (four pieces are cut from one slice of white bread) so that they can be eaten in one mouthful. White bread is often replaced by rye bread, which is firmer.

It is always essential to have sandwiches, canapés, petit fours, etc. in reserve, so that you can refill the plates of the buffet as they are consumed. For cocktail receptions, reduce the quantity of sugared foods and increase the number and variety of sandwiches and canapés.

COCKTAILS, SURPRISE PARTIES, RECEPTIONS

From 6 o'clock on. As the number of guests increases, the number of pieces you anticipate serving per person diminishes accordingly: for a reception of 20 people, you need 5 sandwiches per head; for one of 100 people, 3 sandwiches per head will be enough. But in this case, you must increase the variety of food offered.

For this kind of reception, you never exactly know the number of guests nor the time of their arrival, and the amount consumed is very variable, depending on the ambiance. Have some reserves at hand: a preserved foie gras, sausage that has not yet been cut, bottles yet uncorked, which will not be used except when necessary. If you want to avoid waste and thievery, have a competent person to refill the plates and the buffet as they are needed: food presented at the beginning will not be fresh by the end of the evening, and late arrivals cannot be properly served. Whatever the season, you must anticipate a substantial reserve of ice to cool things, and various drinks: cocktails, sparkling wine or champagne, aperitifs, orangeade, lemonade, fruit juices.

For a group of 10 people, you must anticipate:
50–60 varied canapés (canapés are more decorative than sandwiches). Thus, 450 grams (1 pound) of white bread giving 30–40 little sandwiches cut in half, or 60–80 triangular canapés, with a garnish of butter and ham, rounds of tomatoes, hard-boiled eggs; anchovies, tomato, and olives; watercress, mayonnaise, tomato; white cheese, paprika, minced nuts; mousse of foie gras or potted meats; dry sausage; mustard and slices of Gruyère; sardines in oil with butter and lemon; anchovies; etc. Also 250 grams (8⅞ ounces) of dry petit fours or biscuits, 250 grams (8⅞ ounces) of fresh petit fours, a large coffee cake (a tart for simple receptions); olives, roasted peanuts, sugared almonds, cheese squares.

Drinks: Champagne or sparkling wine (2 bottles); lemonade and orangeade (2 liters/2⅛ quarts/8½ cups); aperitif (1 bottle); iced coffee (⅔ liter/2¾ cups); cocktails (15 glasses for 10 people); tomato juice, flavored with catsup if you like (1 or 2 cans depending on their size).

LUNCH MENUS FOR SPRING

Radishes with Butter, Broad Bean Salad
Grilled Cod
Boiled Potatoes
Flemish-Style Peas
Fruits

✣

Artichokes Vinaigrette
Lamb Stew
Spring Vegetables
Cherries à la Condé

✣

Baked Eggs with Cream
Risotto Milanese
Green Bean Salad
Cheeses and Fruits

✣

Cauliflower au Gratin
Roast Wild Duck
Château Potatoes
Lettuce Salad
Strawberry Tart

✣

Sautéed Morels
Tournedos à la Paysanne
Sautéed Potatoes
Cheeses
Raspberry Ice

✣

Skate Fritters
Veal Blanquette
Broad Beans with Bacon
Wild Strawberries, Fresh Cream

✣

Crab à la Diable
Macaroni Loaf
Asparagus with Butter Sauce
Cheeses and Fruits

✣

Anchovy Sticks
Boiled Beef à la Crème
Sautéed Green Beans
Cherries Jubilee

✣

Salt Cod with Fines Herbes
Carrots à la Crème
Cheeses
Cherry Tart

DINNER MENUS FOR SPRING

Watercress Soup
Beef à la mode
Potato Purée
Beet and Mâche Lettuce Salad
Clafouti

✣

Potage Parmentier
Mushroom Shells
Braised Lettuce
Semolina Cake with Raspberry Purée

✣

Herb Soup
Fish Soufflé
Asparagus with White Sauce
Cherry Tart

✣

Potage Julienne
Roast Veal
Sautéed Potatoes
Green Bean Salad
Fresh Apricot Soufflé

✣

Split Pea Soup
Mussel Pilaf
Carrots à la Crème
Strawberry Tart

✣

Fresh Puréed Broad Bean Soup
Salted Beef
Fresh Noodles with Tomato Sauce
Champigny Cake

✣

Cream of Leek Soup
Roast Leg of Lamb
Braised Chicory
Fruit Meringue

✣

Purslane and Fresh Pea Soup
Cod à la Valencia
Asparagus Hollandaise
Orange Soufflé

✣

Sorrel Soup
Home-Style Ham Hors d'Oeuvres
Carrots à la Crème
Apricot Tart

LUNCH MENUS FOR SUMMER

Raw Vegetable Hors d'Oeuvres
Ham Omelet
Lamb Chops
Potatoes Pont-Neuf
Fruits

⁂

Cauliflower with Mayonnaise
Veal and Ham Pâté
Madras Salad
Cheeses and Fruits

⁂

Chilled Melon
Sole à la Bonne Femme
Peas à la Française
Apricot Fritters

⁂

Eggs in Aspic
Roast Leg of Mutton
Fresh White Beans, Tomato Sauce
Cream Cheese
Fruits

⁂

Stuffed Artichoke Bottoms
Potato Soufflé
Carrots à la Vichy
Apricot Compote

⁂

Eggs Lorraine
Veal Cutlets à la Gendarme
Green Beans à la Maître d'Hôtel
Basket of Fruits

⁂

Grapefruit
Fish in Cream Sauce au Gratin
Old-Style Stuffed Artichokes
Cheeses and Fruits

⁂

Eggs à la Maintenon
Neapolitan-Style Macaroni
Green Bean Salad
Apricot Mousse

⁂

Tomatoes Stuffed with Tuna
Shoulder of Mutton with Turnips
Cheeses and Fruits

DINNER MENUS FOR SUMMER

Potage à la Portugaise
Whiting à la Hôtelière
Soufflé Potatoes in Their Jackets
Plum Compote

⁂

Consommé
Bordeaux-Style Cèpes
Chicory Loaf à la Crème
Pears Cardinale

⁂

Rustic Vegetable Soup
Coquilles au Gratin à la Ménagère
Potatoes Anna
Peach Tart

⁂

Cauliflower Soup
Cheese Soufflé
Veal Flank with Tarragon
Macédoine of Melon

⁂

Sorrel Soup
Squab with Green Peas
Celery au Jus
Pears au Gratin

⁂

Stuffed Tomatoes
Classic Chicken Fricassée
Lemon Cream

⁂

Celeriac Soup with Gruyère
Eggs à la Bourguignonne
Spinach à la Mornay
Peach Compote

⁂

Deep-Fried Cheese Soufflé Fritters
Beef à la Mode
Potato Purée
Normandy Cake

⁂

Traditional Carrot Soup
Rabbit Marengo
Braised Chicory
Peach Fritters

LUNCH MENUS FOR AUTUMN

Alsatian Salad
Red Mullet Gratin with Tomatoes, Garlic, and Wine
Brussels Sprout Loaf
Fruits

⁂

Artichoke Bottom Hors d'Oeuvres
Guinea Fowl in Cream Sauce
Château Potatoes
Cheeses
Normandy-Style Croûte

⁂

Cèpes à la Provençale
Mutton Pilaf
Hard-Boiled Egg and Lettuce Salad
Cheeses and Fruits

⁂

Eggs with Tripe
Roast Saddle of Hare
Chestnut Purée
Chicory and Tomato Salad
Cheeses and Fruits

⁂

Salade Niçoise
Partridge with Cabbage
Potatoes à la Maître d'Hotel
Cheeses and Fruits

⁂

Poached Hake, Mussel Sauce
Neapolitan-Style Eggplant
Peach Tart *or* Fresh Fruits

⁂

Stuffed Bell Peppers
Duck with Turnips
Cheeses
Pear Fritters

DINNER MENUS FOR AUTUMN

Potage Brunoise
Navarin or Mutton Stew
Stuffed Tomatoes
Apples in Crème

⁂

Vegetable Pot-au-Feu
Deep Fried Skate
Potatoes Suzette
Pineapple Cake

⁂

Soupe de la Mère Onèsime
Flemish Endive
Rice Pudding

⁂

Cream of Cauliflower Soup
Rabbit Stewed in Wine
Potato Purée
Jeanne-Marie's Crêpes

⁂

Purée of Lentil Soup
Roast Pheasant
Potatoes Pont-Neuf
Celeriac Salad
Flan

⁂

Garbure Soup in the Peasant Style
Sautéed Brains
Carrots à la Bourgeois
Apple Marmalade and Meringue

⁂

Petite Marmite
Fish Gratin with Noodles
Braised Jerusalem Artichokes
Lemon Tart

LUNCH MENUS FOR WINTER

Scrambled Eggs with Mushrooms
Stuffed Veal Scallops
Spinach with Bacon
Cheeses and Fruits

⁂

Frog's Legs
Calf's Liver Grilled à la Bercy
Cream Puffs

⁂

Cheese Soufflé
Sauerkraut with Ham Hocks and Sausage
Fruits

⁂

Leek Flamiche
Rib Steak à la Maître d'Hotel
French Fried Potatoes
Endive Salad
Meringues with Whipped Cream

⁂

Mussels à la Marinière
Gougère
Carrots à la Crème
Pear Compote *or* Fresh Fruits

⁂

Fish Soup
Navarin
Cheeses
Apples Bonne Femme

⁂

Shrimp and Red Cabbage Salad
Leeks Vinaigrette
Sausage from Tours
Chicken with Rice
Apple Fritters

⁂

Roast Pumpkin
Pork Cutlets à la Charcutière
Potato Purée
Fresh and Dried Fruits

⁂

Mussels à la Bordelaise
Cabbage Stuffed with Chestnuts
Soufflé Fritters *or* Fruits

⁂

Ardennes-Style Stuffed Potatoes
Blanquette of Veal
Carrots à la Vichy
Cheeses and Fruits

DINNER MENUS FOR WINTER

Pumpkin Potage
Salsify Fritters
Gnocchi au Gratin
Crusts with Madeira

⁂

Purée of Lentil Soup
Shoulder of Mutton à la Boulangère
Coffee Creams in Little Pots *or* Coffee Pots de Crème

⁂

Potato Soup
Onion Tart
Mexico Pudding

⁂

Cream of Rice Soup
Boiled Leg of Mutton, Caper Sauce
Steamed Potatoes
Apple Charlotte

⁂

Potage à la Condé
Brains in a Vol-au-Vent
Roast Pumpkin
Dessert Omelet

⁂

Cabbage Soup
Meat Rissoles
Vanilla Soufflé

⁂

Jerusalem Artichoke Potage
Fillet of Pork, Cream Pepper Sauce
Braised Endive
Apple Turnover

⁂

Rustic Vegetable Soup
Salsify au Gratin
Mont-Blanc

⁂

Potage Saint-Germain
Veal Casserole
Braised Fennel
Rice Cake, Apricot Sauce

⁂

Onion Soup
Potatoes Maire
Rum Soufflé Omelet

FORMAL LUNCHES

Fillet of Sole Marguery
Ham à la Financière
Garnish of Mushrooms and Green Peas
Terrine of Domestic Rabbit
Lettuce Salad
Cheeses
Fresh Pineapple

⁂

Warm Hors d'Oeuvres
Archduke Sautéed Chicken
Tournedos with Garnish of Seasonal Vegetables
Madras Salad
Cheeses
Chilled Fruit Cup

⁂

Coquilles Saint-Jacques
Lamb Chops on Soubise Purée
Braised Lettuce
Cheeses and Fruits

⁂

Lobster à la Newburg
Beef Fillet Saint-Florentin
Ham Cornets
Green Bean Salad
Cheeses
Raspberry Ice Mousse

⁂

Braised Calf's Sweetbreads with Financière Garnish
Stuffed Duck in the Limousin Style
Endive Salad
Cheeses
Banana Soufflé

⁂

Sheep's Kidneys Turbigo
Fricandeau (or Braised Veal)
Carrots and Onions Garnish
Asparagus Hollandaise
Cheeses
Macédoine of Melon

FORMAL DINNERS

Consommé
Turbot, Mousseline Sauce
Roast Saddle of Venison, Pepper Sauce
Chestnut Purée
Mousse of Foie Gras
Russian Salad
Cheese Plate
Orange Bavarian Cream

⁂

Chicken and Rice Soup
Salmon with Mussel Sauce
Duck à l'Orange
Straw Potatoes
Mixed Salad
Cheeses
Peach Melba

⁂

Potage Solferino
Sea Bass with Shrimp Sauce
Fillet of Beef with Onions and Carrots
Stuffed Artichoke Bottoms
Galantine of Fowl
Celery Root Salad
Cheeses
Diplomat Pudding

⁂

Oxtail Soup
Brill
Saddle of Lamb, Madeira Sauce
Garnish of Vegetables and Mushrooms
Stuffed Chicken
Lettuce Salad
Cheeses
Apple Aspic

GENERAL INDEX

D

N

O

T

V

INDEX OF FRENCH RECIPE TITLES

D

E